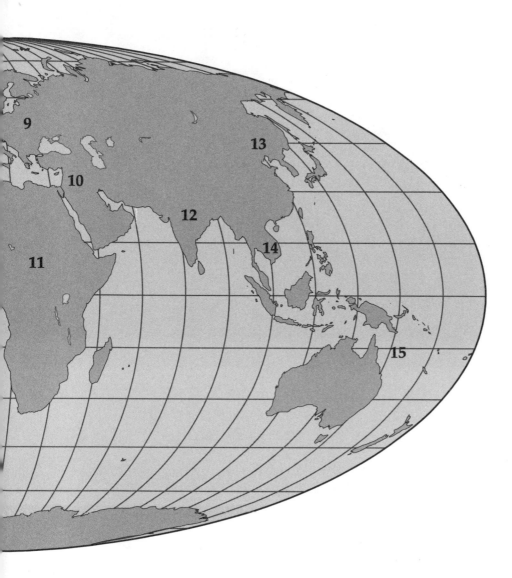

Chapters

GLOBAL VOICES, GLOBAL VISIONS

GLOBAL
VOICES

GLOBAL
VISIONS™

A Core Collection
of Multicultural Books

LYN MILLER-LACHMANN

R. R. BOWKER®

A Reed Reference Publishing Company

New Providence, New Jersey

Published by R. R. Bowker, a Reed Reference Publishing Company
Copyright © 1995 by Reed Elsevier Inc.
All rights reserved
Printed and bound in the United States of America

Library of Congress Cataloging-in-Publication Data

Miller-Lachmann, Lyn, 1956–
Global voices, global visions : a core collection of multicultural
books /Lyn Miller-Lachmann.
p.   cm.
ISBN 0-8352-3291-3
1. Culture—Bibliography.   2. Multiculturalism—Bibliography.
3. Civilization, Modern—Bibliography.   I. Title.
Z5579.6.M56   1995
[HM101]
016.306—dc20   95-36829
                                                                    CIP

ISBN 0 - 8352 - 3291 - 3

9 780835 232913

To my parents

CONTENTS

LIST OF CONTRIBUTORS

Mohammed Bamyeh. Assistant Professor of Sociology, University of Massachusetts, Lowell. (Chapter 10. The Middle East)

Ruby Bell-Gam. Librarian, University of California, Los Angeles. (Chapter 11. Africa)

Heather Caines. Librarian, New York Public Library. (Chapter 6. Latin America and the Caribbean)

Robert Cummings. Chair and professor, Department of African Studies and Research Center, Howard University. (Chapter 11. Africa)

Arlen Feldwick. Ph.D. candidate, University of Arizona, Tucson. (Chapter 15. Australia, New Zealand, and the Pacific)

Jaswinder Gundara. Manager, Languages and Literature Department, Metro Toronto Reference Library. (Chapter 5. Canada)

Elaine Goley. Instructor, Northwest College, Houston Community College System. (Chapter 4. United States: Native Americans)

Cecil Hixon. Office of Adult Services, New York Public Library. (Chapter 1. United States: African Americans)

Edward Ifkovic. Professor of Literature, Tunxis Community Technical College, Farmington, Connecticut (Chapter 9. Eastern Europe)

Anju Kapur. Research Associate, South Asian Studies Center, University of Pennsylvania. (Chapter 7. Britain and Ireland)

Babs Kruse. Librarian, Riverton (Wyoming) Public Library. (Chapter 4. United States: Native Americans)

Richard Lachmann. Associate Professor of Sociology, State University of New York at Albany. (Chapter 1. United States: African Americans)

Ginny Lee. Free-lance writer, Fairfield, California. (Chapter 13. East Asia; Chapter 14. Southeast Asia)

Suzanne Lo. Librarian, Asian Branch, Oakland Public Library. (Chapter 13. East Asia; Chapter 14. Southeast Asia)

Susan Ma. Librarian, San Jose Public Library. (Chapter 13. East Asia; Chapter 14. Southeast Asia)

Christine McDonald. Director, Crandall Library, Glens Falls, New York (Chapter 6. Latin America and the Caribbean)

Diana Morales. Director, Walter Branch, Houston Public Library. (Chapter 3. United States: Latinos)

Paul Murray. Professor of Sociology, Siena College, Loudonville, New York. (Chapter 1. United States: African Americans)

Carlos Najera. Librarian, Northwest College, Houston Community System. (Chapter 3. United States: Latinos)

Razia Nanji. Assistant University Librarian, University of Florida, Gainesville. (Chapter 11. Africa)

Shobhan Parthasarathy. Librarian, Saratoga Springs Public Library. (Chapter 12. South and Central Asia)

Brenda Randolph. Director, Africa Access, Silver Springs, Maryland. (Chapter 11. Africa)

Patricia Rubio. Professor of Spanish, Skidmore College, Saratoga Springs, New York. (Chapter 6. Latin America and the Caribbean)

Maureen Haley Terada. Outreach Coordinator, South Asian Studies Center, University of Washington, Seattle. (Chapter 12. South and Central Asia)

Barbara Walden. Subject Bibliographer, University of Minnesota Library (Chapter 8. Western Europe)

Albert J. Williams-Meyers. Professor of History and Black Studies, State University of New York, College at New Paltz. (Chapter 1. United States: African Americans)

Jennifer Wu. Librarian, North Seattle Community College. (Chapter 2. United States: Asian Americans)

ACKNOWLEDGMENTS

I would like to express my appreciation to all those who helped me in the massive undertaking that has resulted in this book. It grew out of discussions with my esteemed former editor at Bowker, Marion Sader, as we worked on *Our Family, Our Friends, Our World: An Annotated Guide to Significant Multicultural Books for Children and Teenagers*. During that project, we came to realize that educators and others who work with young people needed more background. My current editors at Bowker, Catherine Barr and Larry Chilnick, took over the project and shepherded it to the end. I am grateful to them for their unflagging support. Were I to spend the rest of this page describing the outstanding—one might say, miraculous—work Ron Schaumburg did in pulling the manuscript into shape, he would still remain underappreciated. His faith, effort, and persistence went well beyond the call of duty.

I would like to thank my colleagues at the Siena College Library for their help and support. Finally, I thank my dear husband, Richard Lachmann, for his infinite patience and understanding, and my children, Derrick and Madeleine, just for being there.

INTRODUCTION

by Lyn Miller-Lachmann

I. A MULTICULTURAL SEASON

When I began my career as a high school social studies teacher in the New York City Public Schools in 1980, I taught in two inner-city schools located within a mile of each other. One was a neighborhood school where most of the students were Puerto Rican and a fourth of them were African American. Refugees from Central America also were just beginning to arrive. The second school was an academic-specialized school. Students had to take a test for admission, and the school attracted the top students from all over the city. These students came from all ethnic groups, including recent immigrants from dozens of countries around the world.

I wanted to learn more about the backgrounds and cultures of my students. Many of them asked me to help them find books, written at an adult level, that would help them to understand their own heritage. Unfortunately, very few such books existed at that time. Most of the fiction in the school library consisted of either the classics of European and American literature or the mainstream fiction published at the time—novels and short stories written by white, middle-class authors, many of them graduates of university writing workshops. One of my few encounters with ethnic and world literature at the high school where I taught was Salman Rushdie's *Midnight's Children*. Reading it in the teacher's lounge, I felt as if the world had opened to me. An author of great talent had transported me out of the bounds of my own culture and experience.

Today, my students and I would confront the opposite problem: how to choose among the vast number of books on multicultural subjects published in the last fifteen years. Which ones portray the culture honestly and authentically, without resorting to stereotypes? Which ones are accessible to readers with varying levels of background and sophistication? Which ones are well written? Which ones offer the particular perspectives of women, or men, or members of religious minorities, within a given culture?

Influenced by the increasing diversity of the population of the United States and the instant availability of information from around the world, readers, booksellers, teachers, librarians, and publishers are seeking books that represent authentically the experiences of groups once ignored, excluded, or misrepresented. Those groups include the so-called visible minorities within the United States: African Americans, Asian Americans, Latinos, and Native Americans—new immigrants as well as long-time residents who historically had been excluded from the mainstream, prevented by discriminatory laws and practices from melting into the melting pot. Though the works of Jewish-American, Irish-American, and other ethnic authors have for a century asserted cultural traditions apart from the melting pot, attention has only begun to focus upon writers of color. Written in their own voices, from their unique perspectives, their literature and personal narratives have challenged stereotypes and opened readers' eyes to the vitality of traditions and communities that have flourished under the cruelest of circumstances. Works of nonfiction—histories, sociological studies, ethnographies, essays, and manifestos—present another side of the story, forcing mainstream scholars to take into account the darker aspects of the American reality. From penetrating studies of the African-American underclass to reassessments of Columbus's voyage from the point of view of the people who were here before he came, new multicultural voices have challenged what we believe to be both true and morally just.

Broadly defined, the term *multicultural* embraces every inhabited region of the world. Just as the works of African Americans, Asian Americans, Latinos, and Native Americans have broadened awareness of the culture and history of the United States, the writings of authors in other countries have offered a deeper understanding of the world that lies beyond this country's borders. Multicultural works of literature, nonfiction, and biography also reveal what happens when cultures meet and clash, or when people from one culture try to survive within another. In such books, history is told from the point of view of the colonized struggling for self-rule, of the victims of oppression overcoming their victimization through the written word, of the ignored or unknown asserting their right to be heard. As rapid changes occur throughout the world—the breakup of the Soviet Empire and the rise of nationalism in Eastern Europe being just two examples—new books are published to help us understand these new realities.

The rise of interest in multicultural publishing is a product of changing times. Demographic shifts in the United States, increasing global interdependence, and the collapse of colonial systems and empires are among the principal factors contributing to the emergence of new voices and their success in the publishing world. There is growing recognition that our society must educate itself about this complex and changing reality if Americans of various backgrounds and traditions are to live together and thrive in the coming years. As literary critic and essayist Henry Louis Gates, Jr. eloquently writes:

> Ours is a late-twentieth-century world profoundly fissured by nationality, ethnicity, race, class, and gender. And the only way to transcend those divisions—to forge, for once, a civic culture that respects both differences and commonalities—is through education that seeks to comprehend the diversity of human culture. Beyond the hype and the high-flown rhetoric is a pretty homely truth: There is no tolerance without respect—and no respect without knowledge. Any human being sufficiently curious and motivated can fully possess another culture, no matter how "alien" it may appear to be. (*Loose Canons: Notes on the Culture Wars.* New York: Oxford University Press, 1992. p. xv)

Changing Realities

Demographic Changes

North America has always been home to immigrant peoples, beginning with the prehistoric humans who wandered here over the Bering Strait some 30,000 years ago and continuing with the Europeans who began arriving in search of freedom and opportunity in the 1600s. Latino and Asian-American communities have also existed in the United States for many generations. Recent advances in travel, the effects of wars and other social upheavals, and other factors make immigration an increasingly important aspect of life in this country.

Those arriving from Latin America, Asia, the West Indies, and elsewhere have settled in cities and towns in all regions of the country. Between 1980 and 1990, the number of Americans of Hispanic origin increased by 56 percent, while the Asian-American population more than doubled, with an increase of 107.8 percent. Today, African Americans comprise approximately 12 percent of the population of the United States, with Latinos 9 percent and Asian Americans 3 percent.

It would be a mistake, however, to assume that members of immigrant communities are completely homogeneous. In this book, terms that identify ethnic groups are used quite broadly to incorporate a number of cultures that are in fact distinct and often historically antagonistic. Even within a given culture, members often recognize distinctions among subgroups, such as those whose families have lived here for a generation or more and those who are more recent arrivals. Among the African-American population, for example, are the descendants of "Free Persons of Color"—people of African origin who for two centuries have been members of the Northern urban middle class—as well as recent immigrants from Africa, Haiti, Jamaica, and other countries in the West Indies. The term "Asian Americans" includes a number of cultural groups: Japanese Americans, many of whom are now fourth- or fifth-generation residents; Hawaiians, whose islands became U.S. territory in 1898; at least four waves of immigrants from China or Taiwan; refugees from Southeast Asia who fled after the end of the Vietnam War in 1975; Filipinos; Koreans; Asian Indians; Pakistanis; and other groups, many of whom arrived after the liberalization of immigration quotas from Asia after 1965. The term "Latino" includes descendants of those who lived in the southwestern United States when it was part of Mexico; successive waves of Mexican and Cuban immigrants; political refugees from Central and South America; professionals seeking expanded opportunities; and migrants from Puerto Rico, whose legal status as residents of a U.S. commonwealth has set them apart from other immigrants. Among the American Indian Nations are hundreds of separate cultural and language groups, including the Alaskan Inuit.

[Editor's note: Generally, throughout this book, the use of the terms "African Americans," "Asian Americans," and "Latino" reflects the author's best understanding about the acceptance of such designations by members of the groups themselves. Hyphens are omitted, except when the term is used in its adjective form. The terms "Native Americans" and "American Indians" are used interchangeably. Some members of individual Indian nations have expressed a preference for the latter term, but at present many others continue to refer to themselves as Native Americans, as do the writers of many of the publications cited in the bibliography. Outside the United States, other terms, such as "indigenous" or "aboriginal" peoples, may be more widely accepted. Some people object to the masculine connotations of the word "Latino." Still, this term has largely superseded "Hispanic" as the term of choice. When referring to women in the group and their literature, the feminine "Latina" has been used. In some instances—such as when discussing census data or older works—terms used in the source material, such as "Black," "Asian," or "Hispanic" have been maintained for the sake of clarity.]

The increase in immigration over the last three decades has coincided with the civil rights movement and other efforts by various groups to assert their cultural identity. From the activism of the 1960s grew such movements as Black Power, the demand for bilingual education, and campaigns by various American Indian nations to gain control over their natural and economic resources.

The demographic shifts that have changed the face of American society have contributed in several ways to the rise of multicultural publishing. The human drama and impact of the story has inspired novelists, poets, historians, and social scientists. An increase in the African-American, Asian-American, Latino, and Native American population means a rise in the number of writers from those groups and a larger potential readership within them. As more members of minority groups attend college, the audience grows for books geared to the educated adult reader—literary fiction, history, social sciences, essays, biography, and autobiography. The demand for multicultural literature is also on the rise among readers from mainstream cultures, as more and more recognize that the continued strength of our democracy and our society as a whole depends upon our learning about each other and overcoming the prejudices that threaten to drive us apart.

Global Interdependence

As the United States becomes a more diverse society, its relationship with the rest of the world likewise becomes more complex. Technological advancements and the instant availability of information from virtually everywhere on the planet mean that Americans immediately feel the impact of international political, social, and economic events. For example, if today an earthquake destroys ports in Asia, or if unrest strikes the oil-producing nations, or if floods wipe out crops in South America, then tomorrow computer parts will be unavailable, or gas prices will increase, or supermarket produce shelves will be empty.

Naturally, much of what gets published here concerning other nations and regions of the world tends to address topics that are of direct and immediate importance to Americans. Some books are rushed into print to exploit public interest in a current event. Examples include the paperback biographies that demonized Saddam Hussein during the Gulf War of 1991. Other books are written by Western writers from a Western point of view, hoping to interpret events and cultures for a Western audience or to further a particular position in the debate on contemporary policies or issues. However, every major news event—the Gulf War included—has had its share of well-reasoned and insightful analyses. Usually, these explorations have taken the form of nonfiction, but often works of fiction or personal narratives, written by those from the culture itself, have best conveyed the full meaning of what has happened.

Today's global "hot spots"—and to a great extent, the most active areas of publishing—cover a number of issues and regions of the world. One of the most dramatic and far-reaching events of the past decade has been the collapse of the Soviet Empire. The vacuum left by Communism's collapse has led to resurgent nationalism and bloody clashes among ethnic groups, not just in Eastern Europe but in other nations that depended upon support from Moscow. Contemporary accounts written by observers from those nations can shed light on the upheaval. But so, too, can documents from the Holocaust and other works, both fiction and nonfiction, that explore the rise and impact of regional ethnic hatreds over the centuries.

The emergence of the Pacific Rim as an economic power is a topic of vast interest in the United States today. A number of books are available by Western writers examining how and why Japan and other East Asian nations have achieved economic success. Readers will not find such books discussed in the bibliography. Instead, the titles included here are those that explore the many Asian cultures in greater depth. Thoughtful readers of such works will not necessarily learn how to emulate the secrets of Asian business success but rather how these societies' unique traditions have contributed to their development and what problems or contradictions remain to be resolved. Through literature and a broad selection of nonfiction we can learn enough about our trading partners around the world to meet their needs, work together, and attain mutual prosperity.

As the world's economic systems become increasingly interdependent, so do its sensitive ecological systems. Scientists have found that human activity—the destruction of the rain forests, the depletion of the ozone layer, and the release of pollutants in the atmosphere—is responsible for many climatological disasters, from drought and famine in Africa to destructive hurricanes in the Caribbean. These "natural" events in turn contribute to other economic, political, and social problems, which demand greater understanding but defy simple solutions. Today, also, indigenous peoples throughout the world are demanding greater control over the natural resources found in their territories. As concern about the global environment rises, the media—including the publishing industry—are finally listening to the indigenous voices that for centuries have warned of the earth's destruction and have offered alternative ways of living in harmony with nature.

The United States is not the only country to have experienced an increase in immigration over the past decades. Improved transportation combined with massive political and economic crises have contributed to a global migration of peoples. The demographic makeup of Canada, Great Britain, Western Europe, and Australia has changed markedly as a result of immigration from Asia, the Caribbean, Africa, the Middle East, Europe, and elsewhere. Some countries—most notably, Canada—have embraced cultural pluralism and the works of immigrant writers. In other countries, however, immigrant writers have remained all but invisible, their works published by alternative presses or abroad. Nonetheless, these writers have eloquently documented the experiences of cultural dislocation, hostility, and discrimination they have faced in their new home.

The Emergence of New Voices

Individual writers of distinction have contributed greatly to the development of multicultural literature and its acceptance among mainstream critics.

Those writers have in turn influenced and smoothed the way for others. Trailblazing multicultural authors have forced critics to reassess the "canon"—the list of great books that any educated person presumably knows—which had for centuries been dominated by white male authors of Western origin. Writing in *The Chronicle of Higher Education* (June 26, 1991), Peter Erickson observes:

> It is useful to understand why the word "multicultural" should emerge now. During the last three decades, substantial bodies of work by minority writers have emerged. The power of this work resides not only in the strength of individual achievements but also in the cumulative, collective force that comes from the subtle interrelations among authors' works within each minority tradition. The overall result is a substantial, though by no means total, shift of literary power toward the emerging minority literatures. It is this shift, more than anything else, that has prompted the current reassessment of the canon.

For the most part, the works cited in *Global Voices, Global Visions* as alternatives to the established canon are works of literature—fiction, drama, and poetry. But "minority" writers are producing a growing body of distinguished contributions to the fields of history, the social sciences, and biography. Important books today include works from U.S. writers outside the mainstream, as well as from the colonized peoples of Africa and Asia, the oppressed of Latin America, and the dispossessed aboriginal groups of Australia, New Zealand, and Canada.

To many observers, decolonization was the key event in the rise of multicultural writing around the world. Until the peoples of Africa and Asia won their independence, the colonizers largely controlled the telling of history. Those subjugated to their rule seemed silent, their experiences—often of harsh, dehumanizing oppression—were not heard. Occasionally, though, writers in the colonies attacked the culture and politics of imperialism while helping to forge the identity of a new nation. Raja Rao's novel *Kanthapura* (1938) and the writings of Rabindranath Tagore explore the colonial experience in India, presenting the process of independence from the perspective, not of the colonizers, but of the colonized. These works in turn profoundly influenced Salman Rushdie's acclaimed historical novel of India's independence struggle, *Midnight's Children*. The autobiographies of independence leaders such as Mahatma Gandhi and Kwame Nkrumah and the poetry and essays of Leopold Senghor, in addition to telling the stories of these major figures in world history, have inspired succeeding generations of postcolonial writers of all genres. Algerian sociologist Franz Fanon's *The Wretched of the Earth* is a firsthand analysis of the conditions of life for the poor under the colonial system; his work has changed the way many people look at the economic and social systems of the so-called Third World. Following Fanon, new generations of historians and social scientists are challenging traditional versions of the origins of civilization itself.

Within the United States, leaders and thinkers from outside the mainstream have critiqued this country's failings and sought to strengthen the foundations of democracy not just by claiming their own place within it but by expressing a vision of what democracy should be and ways of achieving it. African Americans such as Frederick Douglass, W.E.B. Du Bois, and Martin Luther King, Jr. have contributed enormously to the social debate as they brought new perspectives to the American conception of democracy and formulated strategies for community building and political action. Similarly, Native American leaders such as Chief Seattle, Chief Joseph, and the framers of the Iroquois Confederacy have produced works drawing upon the values of their cultures, offering thoughtful readers insights that may hold the key to survival in the future.

Works of literature from different cultures and ethnic traditions are emerging as some of the most vital in the world today. In the first half of the century, significant authors of color included Langston Hughes, Paul Laurence Dunbar, Jean Toomer, Ralph Ellison, and Zora Neale Hurston. Since 1969, with the awarding of the Pulitzer Prize in fiction to N. Scott Momaday's *House Made of Dawn*, more than a dozen Pulitzer Prizes, National Book Awards, and National Book Critics' Circle Prizes have gone to more than a dozen works by minority authors, including Alice Walker's *The Color Purple*, August Wilson's *Fences* and *The Piano Lesson*, Gloria Naylor's *The Women of Brewster Place*, Oscar Hijuelos's *The Mambo Kings Play Songs of Love*, Toni Morrison's *Beloved*, and Louise Erdrich's *Love Medicine*. In 1993 Toni Morrison became the first African-American writer to win the Nobel Prize for literature; she was also the first U.S.-born author to win the prize since 1976 and only the second woman from the United States to win. Other authors—John Edgar Wideman, Rodolfo Anaya, Sandra Cisneros, Amy Tan, and Michael Dorris, to name a few—have won significant literary prizes and are developing worldwide reputations

On the international stage, significant individual works and bodies of literature have come out of regions once considered marginal or insignificant. In 1993, the awarders of the Booker Prize—the British equivalent of the three top American literary awards—gave a "Booker of Bookers" to the best novel coming out of Britain and the Commonwealth in the award's twenty-five-year history. The winner was *Midnight's Children*. Perhaps the best known body of literature to emerge from the developing world is the Latin American "boom" of the past three decades. Among the authors of the boom were four Nobel Prize winners—Miguel Angel Asturias, Pablo Neruda, Gabriel García Márquez, Octavio Paz—and numerous others whose works have had worldwide impact and influence. Africa, too, boasts significant authors and a growing body of literature. In the past decade alone, three African novelists—Wole Soyinka, Naguib Mahfouz, and Nadine Gordimer—have won Nobel Prizes. Very different in terms of their backgrounds, styles, and themes, the three laureates point to the continent's enormous cultural diversity and richness. Another recent Nobel Prize winner is the Afro-Caribbean poet and dramatist Derek Walcott.

The increasing frequency with which the Nobel Prize Committee has honored writers from Africa, Asia, and Latin America is both evidence of and a contributing factor to the rise in multicultural literatures. In his moving 1971 Nobel Prize acceptance speech, Pablo Neruda marveled at how a poet from a poor, isolated country such as Chile could win the world's most important literary prize. Today, small, poor, or newly independent countries regularly contribute prizewinners. The international acclaim they receive draws increasing attention to other works emanating from that country and region.

The "shift in literary power" from the privileged to the dispossessed, from the colonizers to the colonized, from the culturally dominant groups to the less powerful but no less eloquent minorities says much about the nature of literature in the modern world. Ironically, many of the world's most important writers live in countries where a large percentage of the population cannot read, much less afford to buy books. Yet in giving voice to the powerless and exploring their relationship to those in power, writers from the Third World, as well as their descendants in the United States and Europe, touch upon basic human issues. Their experiences—tragedies, triumphs, conflicts, and insights—are real and significant. Today's new voices show humans enduring the extremes of power and oppression. They tell of cowardice and nobility, of defeat and humiliation, and of the fundamental struggle for dignity. People who long have been considered mere *objects* of others' history are making themselves *subjects* of history. In the process, they are creating dynamic literatures and causing that profound shift in the balance of literary power. Writing about his own troubled continent, the essayist Eduardo Galeano captures the spirit of these new voices:

> In Latin America a literature is taking shape and acquiring strength, a literature that does not lull its readers to sleep, but rather awakens them; that does not propose to bury our dead, but to immortalize them; that refuses to stir the ashes but rather attempts to light the fire. This literature perpetuates and enriches a powerful tradition of combative words. If, as we believe, hope is preferable to nostalgia, perhaps that nascent literature may come to deserve the beauty of the social forces which, sooner or later, by hook or by crook, will radically alter the course of our history. And perhaps it may help to preserve for the generations to come—in the words of the poet—"the true nature of all things." ("In Defense of the Word: Leaving Buenos Aires, 1976." In *The Graywolf Annual Five: Multicultural Literacy*. Ed. by Rick Simonson and Scott Walker. St. Paul, Minn.: Graywolf Press, 1988. p. 125.)

Changes in the College Curriculum

Demographic changes, increased global interdependence, and the growing prominence of multicultural writing have led college administrators and faculty to reassess their curriculum. As in most cases of immigration, a disproportionate number of the immigrants are young—single men and women and families with children. Because of this influx, schools and adult education programs are reporting greater cultural diversity among enrollees. In 1991, the University of California at Berkeley—the state system's premier campus—had an incoming freshman class that contained more Asian Americans than whites; overall, 45 percent of that campus's students were non-Hispanic whites. According to the National Center for Education Statistics, the combined percentage of African Americans, Asian Americans, Latinos, and Native Americans attending two- and four-year colleges increased from 15.4 percent in 1976 to 20.6 percent in 1991. That percentage is expected to increase even more as the percentage of college-age individuals from those groups rises; experts estimate that by the end of the century, more than 40 percent of all Americans between the ages of 18 and 24 will be members of minority and recent-immigrant groups.

Following the social protest movements of the late 1960s, there was an upsurge of interest in ethnic studies. The level of interest declines in the mid-1970s. By that point, in fact, an undergraduate in an American Studies Program at an Ivy League university could complete four years of education without having read a single book—literature or nonfiction—by an African-American, Asian-American, Latino, or Native American author. Today, that would be impossible. At the University of California at Berkeley, students are now required to take an ethnic studies course that compares at least three ethnic groups and their experiences in the United States. Survey results reported in *Change* (January/February 1992) found that 34 percent of 196 representative universities and two- and four-year colleges, especially those located on either coast, now require some sort of multicultural education. Most of the courses offered to fulfill that requirement focus on diversity both within the United States and around the world. One-third offer more-advanced courses in ethnic and women's studies, and 54 percent have broadened their courses in literature, history, and the social sciences to include multicultural perspectives.

Schools generally take one of three basic approaches to incorporating multiculturalism into the curriculum. According to the 1992 survey, the most common approach involves adding multicultural authors to courses already in existence. A second approach is to develop new courses; this is a method often used by schools that implement a diversity requirement, such as the University of California at Berkeley. A third approach goes even further in establishing interdisciplinary programs in ethnic studies (e.g., Afro-American Studies or Chicano/Latino Studies) or area studies (e.g., Latin American Studies or East Asian Studies) or some combination of the two (e.g., African/African-American or Black Studies). When such programs were initially established in the 1960s and 1970s, they tended to appeal principally to students from the same ethnic background as the one under study. Today, class enrollment is more diverse. In recent years, a second generation of scholars has joined the initial pioneers, the number of majors has increased, and academic societies and associations have been established to offer support to researchers.

Efforts to create a more inclusive curriculum are not without controversy. Some scholars vehemently defend the traditional Western-oriented curriculum against attempts to add to or change it (see, for example, *Illiberal Education* by Dinesh D'Souza, New York: Free Press, 1991). At the opposite extreme are radicals who have used ethnic studies programs as platforms to attack other groups and advance their own agendas without engaging in the rigorous scholarship needed to support their assertions. Still, many thoughtful, capable academicians—among the best known, perhaps, are Henry Louis Gates, Jr. and Cornel West—are trying to develop a middle position, one that builds bridges between groups and balances awareness of the full range of cultures and heritages that make up the American demographic landscape. In support of that effort, according to Carol G. Schneider in *Liberal Education* (May/June 1991), the Association of American Colleges provides grants to colleges for the creation of "general-education courses that see diversity—in both culture and perspective—as an integral dimension of any intellectually rigorous encounter with either 'Western' or 'world' civilizations."

The Commercial Success of Multicultural Books

Beyond the campus, multicultural books have found an audience among general readers. Publishers once assumed that readers would not pick up a book set in a distant and unfamiliar country or about any group not part of the U.S. mainstream. Today, of course, many such books earn not just critical acclaim but a spot on national bestseller lists. *The Color Purple*, *The Women of Brewster Place*, *The Joy Luck Club*, and Terry McMillan's *Waiting to Exhale* are among the multicultural novels that have spent the better part of a year on the *New York Times* bestseller list. Literary works with multicultural themes often reach broader audiences (and enjoy additional sales) when they are adapted for the stage or the screen. Examples include *The Color Purple*, *The Joy Luck Club*, *The Autobiography of Malcolm X*, *The Mambo Kings Play Songs of Love*, Nicholas Gage's biographical work *Eleni*, Georgio Bassani's classic novel of Jews in World War II Italy, *The Garden of the Finzi-Continis*, Manuel Puig's *Kiss of the Spider Woman*, and a number of works by the African-American playwright August Wilson. Ariel Dorfman's harrowing play *Death and the Maiden*, about a Latin American woman's encounter with her torturer, had successful runs in the United States and abroad before being adapted for film.

The major publishers have made a long-term commitment to publishing multicultural books because they realize financial success comes from producing works that appeal to an increasingly diverse readership. Playing a major role in the marketing of multicultural books is a new type of independent bookstore serving culturally diverse communities. Virtually every major city in the United States now has at least one bookstore specializing in books by African and African-American authors. Bookstores with an Asian-American, Latino, and Native American focus are alive and thriving, as are independent bookstores, such as feminist bookstores, that have embraced multiculturalism as part of a broader political and social commitment. Distributors such as the Multicultural Publishers' Exchange have emerged to supply the specialized bookstores as well as libraries and schools in need of multicultural materials. Even the large bookstore chains have recognized the need to include and promote multicultural books. Most have special sections for ethnic studies and international books, but they also include multicultural works in their general sections for literature, history, and the social sciences. Bookstores of all kinds, in all areas of the country, run special displays to promote Black History Month and other events.

The Publishing of Multicultural Books

When the "melting pot" ideology dominated, and immigrants were pressured to give up their separate cultural identities in favor of a mainstream American culture, few in publishing discussed the issue of multiculturalism. Nonetheless, a vibrant literature emerged that reflected the experiences of Jewish immigrants from Eastern Europe and other newcomers from Ireland, Italy, Scandinavia, and elsewhere. Often written in the immigrants' original language, these novels and personal narratives were published by specialized ethnic presses. In rare cases some were later translated and published by major houses. A few of the most prominent ethnic writers in this country—Saul Bellow, James T. Farrell, Bernard Malamud, John O'Hara, and Isaac Bashevis Singer—achieved fame in their lifetime. Some, such as Anzia Yezeirska, only received mainstream publication and attention years after their death. Others still await discovery by readers outside their own cultural groups.

In the "melting pot" scheme, those who could not blend because of their race—African Americans arriving in bondage and suffering legal discrimination long after their emancipation, Chinese Americans denied their full rights as citizens, and American Indians dispossessed of their land and heritage—were generally ignored by mainstream publishers, their experiences often represented by less-than-sympathetic outsiders. Among the rare exceptions were a handful of books by former African slaves, whose narratives were promoted by antislavery crusaders in the years prior to the Civil War. Generally, though, readers in the last century and the first half of this one formed their impressions of ethnic peoples through the stereotypes depicted in works produced by white writers. Tales about the Western frontier, for example, typically fostered negative perceptions about Indians. Even a well-meaning work such as *Uncle Tom's Cabin*—written by Harriet Beecher Stowe, a white woman who favored abolition, and told, in part, from the point of view of a slave family—reinforced white notions of what was considered a "good" slave. The term "Uncle Tom" soon became a derogatory term for a black person who caters to whites.

After World War II, the number of publishers and books rose dramatically. A few African-American writers made it into the mainstream, though not without a great deal of struggle. Among these were Gwendolyn Brooks, Richard Wright, and Ralph Ellison. Reflecting the social trends of the 1960s, publishers brought out the writings of Martin Luther King, Jr., Coretta Scott King, Malcolm X, Stokeley Carmichael, Eldridge Cleaver, and other influential black leaders. In the early 1970s the writings of American Indian historian Vine Deloria, Jr. were released by major houses. Generally, though, activism declined in the early 1970s and with it the commitment on the part of colleges to their ethnic studies programs. Consequently, mainstream editors became more reluctant to publish works by minority authors. After 1975, however, the interest in multicultural literature returned. In *Loose Canons*, Henry Louis Gates, Jr. identifies three factors contributing to this revival. One was the continued strength of women's studies programs and the support they offered to black women writers. A second was the individual contribution of Toni Morrison, herself a writer of distinction but also at the time an editor at Random House, who brought into print the works of many other African, African-American, and Caribbean authors. The third factor was the arrival of a new generation of talented minority scholars who produced exciting work that offered new perspectives and insights. Women have played a major role in each of these factors, so it is not surprising that women authors are disproportionately represented in the recent explosion in African-American literature.

Today, more and more Asian-American, Latino, and Native American authors are also finding homes with the major publishing houses. It is still true, however, that small and alternative presses are more likely to produce the types of books neglected by their larger commercial counterparts—poetry, drama, alternative political commentary, and the writings of those considered to lack a mainstream or "crossover" audience.

Just as older ethnic presses published the works of Jewish and other immigrant writers, presses specializing in Latino or Native American writing have emerged. The largest publisher of Latino materials in the United States, Arte Público Press, currently has a list of more than 200 titles of literature (including juvenile literature), history, social sciences, biography, and reference. By some estimates, Arte Público has published more books for adult readers by Latinos or about the Latino experience than all the major publishing houses in the United States combined. What's more, the publisher has embarked on a project to bring back into print every work of Latino writing ever published in this country. Several presses today specialize in different aspects of the writing of Native Americans. One of the largest, Greenfield Literary Review Press, focuses on literature, folklore, and the writings of the Indian nations of the

Northeast. Clear Light Press offers political commentary as well as fiction and poetry. Other publishers focus on writing from individual Indian nations or of the native peoples of certain regions.

In addition to the ethnic presses, feminist, gay, environmental, political, and literary presses also produce works by minority or recent-immigrant authors. The feminist publisher Firebrand Books has offered works by African-American, Asian-American, Latina, and Native American women, while the Nature Company has published Native American writings on the environment. Curbstone Press, which began by publishing the poetry and essays of Latin American revolutionaries, now includes on its list fiction and nonfiction by Latino authors. One of Curbstone's most successful books to date has been the autobiography of a former gang member in Los Angeles, Luis J. Rodriguez's *Always Running: La Vida Loca—Gang Days in L.A.* Other literary presses have published highly acclaimed books by culturally diverse authors, including Frank Chin's *Donald Duk* (Coffee House Press) and Julia Alvarez's *How the García Girls Lost Their Accents* (Algonquin Books of Chapel Hill). Because the literary presses are traditionally receptive to works that are unique in content and style, they are natural allies of multicultural literature. Successful books published by small presses are sometimes reissued by mainstream presses, usually in tandem with other works by the same author. Many culturally diverse authors began with small presses and later found a home with the major houses. Others continued to publish with both.

Among the alternative political and literary presses are those with an exclusively international focus. Since the mid-1970s Three Continents Press has concentrated on literature and criticism about regions of the world often neglected by the mainstream presses, particularly works from the Middle East and Africa written in either Arabic or Persian. Readers International was formed in the early 1980s to publish books, mostly fiction, by authors whose works had been banned in their own countries. The countries from which the works originate span the globe; the authors' styles range from conventional to highly experimental.

Once dedicated to the publishing of scholarly works, university presses now play a major role in the publication of multicultural materials, producing diverse works of literature and nonfiction for a general adult readership. As is true of the small literary presses, once in a while books from university publishers "cross over" into the mainstream market due to the relevance of their subject matter and the quality of their writing. As Catharine R. Stimpson noted in the *New York Times Book Review* (September 22, 1991), the increasing interest in multicultural issues, both on campus and in the wider society, has influenced the publishing programs of many university presses:

> For some presses, these changes only accentuated their longstanding interests in specific disciplines. For other houses, it meant charting a new course. For university publishing generally, it meant a renewal of the attitude that university presses are, according to Bruce Wilcox of the University of Massachusetts Press, "barometers of important ideas," however controversial.

The University of Oklahoma Press began publishing works about American Indians in 1932 and today is one of the most prolific publishers of books of this type. The University of New Mexico Press and the University of Nebraska Press also specialize in books about Native American peoples; the latter is especially strong in works about the indigenous people of Canada, including the Métis (of mixed Indian and European descent). In addition to works of nonfiction, biography, and autobiography, these houses produce many literary titles, including several excellent anthologies widely used as college texts.

University presses have also emerged as a primary publisher of works by and about Asian Americans, especially general nonfiction, personal narratives, drama, and short stories. Foremost among these houses are the University of Washington Press, the University of Hawaii Press, and the University of California Press.

A final source for multicultural books, particularly those originating from outside the United States, is the international publishing house. In recent years, several publishers from other countries have expanded their operations to the United States. Kodansha International, based in Japan, publishes works not just about Asia but about different areas of the world; among its recent titles is the autobiography of the late Czech reform leader Alexander Dubček. Since the mid-1960s the British publisher Heinemann has undertaken an ambitious multicultural publishing project, releasing more than a hundred literary works and personal narratives in its African Writers series and the works of more than four dozen West Indian writers in its Caribbean Writers series. Like Kodansha, Heinemann has expanded its editorial and distribution operations, opening offices in the United States and publishing minority voices in this country as well. The recent trend toward mergers of American, European, and Australian publishing houses will likely result in more books from abroad being made available to readers in the United States.

II. THE CORE COLLECTION

The Scope and Organization of this Book

The goal of *Global Voices, Global Visions* is to offer a selection of significant and recommended works of multicultural literature, nonfiction, and biography, written by authors from the United States and throughout the world. Virtually all of the books have been published in English in the twentieth century and are available in the United States, though some worthy out-of-print titles have been included because many are still available in libraries and it is hoped that they will soon come back into print. The books described are intended for general adult readers who are interested in learning more about a particular group or culture, whether or not they themselves are members of the particular group or culture. Each of the listings includes a detailed annotation that describes the book's content and how the work fits into the larger cultural context. In many cases the listing includes a brief discussion of other books by the same author or similar books on related subjects.

By necessity, these listings are selective; some readers will no doubt disagree with certain choices or wonder why other titles have been omitted. This bibliography is not intended to serve as an exhaustive guide to every work about every culture and population group in the world. Instead, the purpose is to identify what a panel of experts considers to be the most significant works, authors, themes, and issues related to diverse cultures. *Global Voices, Global Visions* is written to serve as a starting point from which readers can access key works on a range of topics to develop a broader foundation for finding other materials and evaluating newer publications.

The book is organized in fifteen chapters. The first four chapters present works by and about African Americans, Asian Americans, Latinos, and Native Americans. No doubt, the choice to emphasize only these four groups will stir controversy. Where, some will ask, are books about Jewish Americans, Italian Americans, or Irish Americans? In preparing this volume, the author and contributors chose to focus on writings from the most neglected segments in American society, those whose voices are only now beginning to be heard. To be sure, throughout their history in this country, many ethnic groups have faced obstacles in publishing, as in other fields, because of their religious or ethnic backgrounds. Nonetheless, as a rule, writers from those groups have been successfully published for many decades. Since World War II, in fact, many of these writers have become part of the American literary mainstream. Today, much of the literature from those groups reflects their increasing assimilation.

At the same time, the editors of this book recognize that many ethnic Americans of European descent are seeking information about their roots. The intense concern of Irish Americans about the fate of Northern Ireland is one example; another is the devotion American Jews feel toward Israel and their desire to understand the scars left by the Holocaust. Surprisingly, researchers recently discovered that, compared to other groups, European-American college students actually know the *least* about their international roots. When these young people learn about their own cultural heritage, including ways their ancestors suffered at the hands of others, they are better able to empathize with people from different backgrounds. Readers interested in understanding ethnic cultures not specifically identified in the first part of the book are directed to subsequent chapters, where they will find descriptions of many works about the history, culture, and politics of Ireland, Italy, Greece, the countries of Eastern Europe, and other lands that many American families once called home. Those looking for materials about the evolution of Judaism and the Holocaust will find a number of relevant titles in the chapters on Western and Eastern Europe; in addition, the chapter on the Middle East offers titles on a variety of subjects, including modern Hebrew verse, the rise of the Zionist movement, and the situation in Israel today.

After the first four American chapters, books about the rest of the world are covered in eleven chapters organized by region. In most cases, the regional divisions are fairly straightforward and widely recognized by literary critics, political analysts, and area studies experts. Perhaps the most controversial chapter division is the one made between the Middle East and Africa. Politically, religiously, and culturally, the nations of the Middle East—Syria, Iraq, Saudi Arabia, and so on—have much in common with the countries of North Africa, such as Morocco, Algeria, Tunisia, Libya, and Egypt. Both areas are predominantly Muslim and Arabic-speaking, though with significant Christian minorities. In recent decades, the two regions have also been allied politically in their opposition to Israel and in their failed attempts to establish a united Arab government. Since antiquity, Egypt has served as a conduit between the civilizations of Africa and those of southern Europe. The Arabic-speaking areas of North Africa have always engaged in trade with the African nations to the south. Like their northern counterparts, many of the ethnic groups of sub-Saharan Africa also practice Islam and speak Arabic as a second language. Generally, writers and scholars from North Africa consider themselves to be African writers and are published as such by the principal publishers of literature from this region. The chapter division in this book thus reflects this growing awareness.

Another area of potential controversy concerns the placement of countries that until 1990 were part of the Soviet Union. In these now-independent regions are a number of diverse ethnic and religious groups that are just beginning to exert their autonomy. To be sure, at this time very little fiction or nonfiction is available from or about these nations. For the sake of simplicity, however, this bibliography groups the former Soviet Republics within the region to which they are most closely linked. For example, Latvia, Lithuania, and Estonia are covered in Chapter 9, Eastern Europe; Georgia, Armenia, and Azerbaijan in Chapter 10, the Middle East; and Kazakhstan in Chapter 12, Southern and Central Asia, but their location in this bibliography is certain to be a much larger issue in the future, when more is published.

The Audience for This Book

Global Voices, Global Visions may be used by a wide-ranging audience in a number of ways. For librarians, it serves many purposes. As a purchasing tool, it offers more-extensive descriptive annotations and suggestions for ways of using various titles than the typical list of recommended books. Many of the annotations, for example, point out whether a book is better suited for a general reader or for one with some background in the subject. Librarians who serve a given readership are best able to decide whether a particular title is a good choice for their library. Readers planning to travel to another country may want more in-depth information about that country's history, culture, and current situation than what is available in the popular travel guides. Other readers may be looking for novels by authors who share their cultural heritage, while yet others may be researching a culture or the life of an ethnic leader. With a subject index and chapters organized by group or region, with subdivisions for literature, nonfiction, and biography, this bibliography is a handy source for librarians handling a wide variety of requests for reader's guidance.

Some titles—for instance, anthologies—will appeal especially to college and high school teachers looking for materials to incorporate into their courses. The experts who contributed the annotations—area specialists in their fields, and, in many cases, themselves college professors—describe books that can be used as required or supplemental readings in literature, history, social science, or introductory ethnic studies courses.

This book can also be used directly by individual adult and older teenage readers. Written in an accessible, nontechnical manner, the chapter introductions and annotations serve as short book reviews to help readers identify the books they would like to find in libraries and bookstores. This bibliography includes—in addition to recent publications—classic titles and works of nonfiction that provide background about current events. For instance, a reader who enjoyed Terry McMillan's *Waiting to Exhale* can consult this bibliography to find other works in print by McMillan or books on the same theme by other African-American authors. Those who are following the turmoil in the former Yugoslavia may want to look at a number of works of nonfiction that address this topic, or they may be drawn to read Ivo Andric's *The Bridge on the Drina*, a novel published in 1945 that reveals much about the deep-rooted historic animosities among peoples in this region. Through this list, members of specific ethnic groups, including those seeking information about their European origins, will find works that broaden and deepen their awareness of their own culture as well as help them to become more aware of the heritage of their friends, neighbors, and colleagues.

Book discussion groups will also benefit from using the bibliography. Many such groups are sponsored by churches, synagogues, adult education programs, or ethnic clubs that have a special interest in the types of multicultural books listed here. Other, less formal book discussion groups that have a more general focus might find ideas for meeting topics and title selections by browsing through the chapters.

Criteria for Selection

The experts who chose the books and prepared the annotations in this volume include public librarians, college and university librarians, professors, professional reviewers, and writers with a particular interest and expertise in the area. Most of the contributors are themselves from one of the cultures featured in the chapter; most have completed years of study in the area. Several write regularly for *Multicultural Review*. In many cases they have assembled previous recommended lists for their own libraries or have authored other reference works on aspects of multicultural literature and ethnic history. These contributors have used a variety of criteria to select books for the list. Specific criteria are discussed in the various chapter introductions, with additional rationale sometimes appearing in the entry itself. The general criteria used, however, are as follows: accessibility; balance in terms of the list as a whole; representation of the culture or country; depth, accuracy, and quality of the treatment and the writing; significance of the topic and its presentation; currency, and presentation of new or seldom-seen perspectives. In some cases, the book's in-print status has also been taken into account. Each of the criteria is discussed below in more detail.

Although the contributors recommend each book that appears as a main entry, the works discussed may not appeal to everyone. The text indicates whether a book may confuse those with absolutely no background in the subject or whether it may bore or seem superficial to those who do have some knowledge. Often the annotations refer to other books that were written by the same author or that address related subjects. In some cases, the contributor mentions in passing similar books that might be well known but that, for one reason or another, are not recommended. Books that are missing from the list but that some readers might consider worthy may not have been listed here for any of several reasons. They may have been, in the contributor's estimation, less worthy of attention and thus cut for lack of space, or they may have come out too late for inclusion in this edition.

Accessibility

Because this bibliography is intended for use by general adult readers, introductory college students, advanced high school students, educators, and librarians, the accessibility of a work—that is, its overall ease of understanding—is a principal criterion for selection. A variety of forms, genres, and styles of literature are represented; still, the works chosen tend to be mainstream rather than experimental in style. For example, a contributor may recommend one volume of poetry over another because the edition contains explanatory material that makes the poems easier to grasp. Given this criterion, "popular" poets such as Pablo Neruda and Yevgeny Yevtu-shenko are usually recommended over their more "literary" counterparts.

Similarly, in the case of fiction or essays, the degree of accessibility often determines which of a prolific author's works receives the main entry and which are recommended in the entry for further reading. The histories included here offer broad discussions of eras and regions rather than focusing upon obscure events, theories, or archival sources. By the same token, recommended works in criticism and the social sciences are not narrow and technical but rather general in their scope and appeal, with writing that is lively and often personal. Some academic specialists might dismiss works such as Stephen Kinzer's *Blood of Brothers: Life and War in Nicaragua*, Amos Oz's *In the Land of Israel*, and Ross Terrill's *The Australians* as "journalism" rather than serious scholarship. Admittedly, the interviews or personal narratives in such works may lack the rigor of statistical analyses demanded by professional social scientists. Yet these works nonetheless convey the vigor of a country, region, or culture. Thus, for purposes of this bibliography, such titles are excellent overviews for readers who have little previous exposure to the topic. Many of the books cited also include lists of references and other sources, thus providing good jumping-off points for those who want to explore a subject further.

All of the books included in this bibliography are published in English. Some, especially literary works, have been published in bilingual editions, primarily English-Spanish. Bilingual editions that the contributors consider equal in quality to the English versions are given preference in the listings. In this way the contributors hope to enhance the reader's access to and appreciation of literary works in their original language of publication.

Balance

Most of the chapters cover a large number of countries within a region or a number of cultures within a country. The contributors have attempted to achieve a balance by selecting works representing a variety of experiences—those of the elite, the middle class, and the poor; of men and women; of religious and ethnic minorities; of political leaders and dissidents. In areas where there is significant controversy, such as the Middle East, the contributors have attempted to represent all political views, from the extreme right to the extreme left and the various points in between.

In some cases, achieving such a balance was difficult. As noted above, it is hard to discuss new nations, such as those of the former Soviet Union, about which there is little published material, either fiction or nonfiction. Often, works that do exist cannot be recommended because they are poorly written or out of date. For these reasons, there is virtually nothing in this bibliography on Macedonia, Albania, or most of the former Soviet Republics.

A different challenge arises when there is a preponderance of materials from one country or one minority group. For instance, virtually all of the literary and nonfiction works discussed in Chapter 12, Southern and Central Asia, are from or about India. This, perhaps, is not surprising, given the size of India's population and the fact that English is one of its two official languages (the other is Hindi). Another country represented by a relatively large list of entries is Chile. For a number of reasons, Chilean novelists, poets, and dramatists have outpaced their colleagues from more populous Latin American nations in getting translated and published in the United States. What's more, many Chilean writers in exile have been able to get their works into print by means of alternative presses. Thus, the disproportionate numbers of titles from certain countries is a product not of bias on the part of the contributor but of that country's higher literary output or its writers' greater ability to get published in English.

Representation of the Culture

To obtain a complete picture, readers will want to examine a number of books, both fiction and nonfiction, that are written from a variety of perspectives. Contributors have chosen books that they feel authentically represent different countries, regions, or cultures. This task is challenging, because no one book can encompass every facet of a complex culture. An effort was made in preparing this bibliography not to recommend books that present only single aspects of a culture or that reinforce stereotypes, such as novels that portray all Arabs as terrorists and short story collections that depict India merely as an exotic land filled with beautiful princesses and ruthless rajahs. In some cases, the contributor spells out in the chapter introduction the specific reasons why a given book has not been included.

At the same time, many of the works in this bibliography honestly and unflinchingly examine the problems and realities within a culture, realities that may contribute to prevailing stereotypes, but they present a more complex view. For instance, one of the main characters in Michael Dorris's *A Yellow Raft in Blue Water* is an alcoholic American Indian, but her alcoholism is not the focus of the story. Instead, the author explores the rich and complex personalities of three generations of American Indian women who, through their interactions, ultimately find strength in each other and in their shared traditions.

Many of the literary works included in the bibliography deal with universal themes or issues, but the stories could not have been set just anywhere. Events and characters are directly affected by the specific locales in which the stories take place, and the author offers the reader the sense of a distinct time and place.

Many of the authors write from first-hand knowledge of their own cultures. Others are immigrants writing about the process of immigration and adjusting to a different culture. To be sure, this does not guarantee the writer's portrayal will be authentic. Writers are people too, and they have their own blindnesses and biases. Class, gender, or other factors may affect their interpretations. They may write to advance personal or political agendas; some may be tempted to sensationalize their work, hoping to draw more notice or increase their chances for commercial success. In general, however, authors who write about their own culture have an advantage. Their background and familiarity with the nuances makes it easier for them to offer an insider's view, one with a certain level of insight and depth. Their works are from the perspective of the culture, looking at people, things, and events from that point of view and giving the reader a sense of the culture's complexity.

Other authors choose to write, not about their culture of origin, but about other cultures from their perspective as observers. Ruth Prawer Jhabvala, for example, was born in Czechoslovakia but is married to an Indian and has lived in both India and England for years. Her novels and screenplays reveal penetrating insight into her adopted worlds. Certain authors base their works not on their personal experiences of a culture but on those of parents, grandparents, or earlier generations. In some cases, authors of extraordinary talent can draw upon their experiences and imagination to write convincingly and compassionately about cultures other than their own. For example, the Australian novelist Thomas Keneally wrote about the genocide of the Australian Aborigines in *The Chant of Jimmie Blacksmith*. He then went on to write *Schindler's List*, the fictionalized account of a German industrialist who saved over a thousand Jews from Nazi genocide during World War II. Another author, Brian Moore, has written authentic historical novels about his own troubled Northern Ireland and about the conflicts in Haiti.

In the areas of nonfiction and biography, most of the authors are not from the culture itself. Contributors have generally preferred entries that provide a perspective arising from within the culture. Books that are concerned more with U.S. foreign policy than with the country or region itself have been left out. For example, Kinzer's study of Sandinista Nicaragua has been recommended because the author focuses on the Nicaraguans themselves, not on the policies of the Reagan administration. Kinzer describes his own views and experiences in Nicaragua, but for the most part he lets the Nicaraguans—of all viewpoints and backgrounds—speak for themselves. Not found in this bibliography are works written by authors from outside a culture that, in the contributors' eyes, tell us more about the author than about the culture purportedly under study.

Quality of the Treatment

Another major criterion for selection is the quality of the writing and the presentation. Different genres call for different standards. For literature, the paramount concerns are style, depth of characterization, plot development, and the exploration and integration of theme. In nonfiction and biography, weight is given to the accuracy of the facts and the credibility of the total presentation, as reflected in authors' sources and documentation of research. For analyses of controversial social and political issues, contributors chose works that offer even-handed, balanced treatment. Many of the books described here do take sides. However, the authors of such books clearly state their positions and do not claim to be neutral or objective. These books also consider opposing arguments and marshal credible evidence to challenge them. In addition, partisan works of nonfiction or biography are included if they make a compelling case for their side, based on the author's thorough understanding of the culture.

Essays and autobiographies by definition take sides because they reflect the point of view of an individual. Works included here have been judged on the strength of the writing, the clarity of the argument, and the power of the author's story. By that standard, the most valuable and highly recommended books are ones that convey the impact of culture in shaping the author's mind and soul and, in the process, help the reader to understand other works from the same culture. An outstanding example of such works is Eduardo Galeano's trilogy of essays on Latin America, *Memory of Fire*.

The contributors also took into account the stylistic elements and literary traditions of the cultures that produced the works. The myths prominent in Native American literature, the magical realism that suffuses much Latin

American literature, or the vast numbers of characters in novels from Eastern Europe may seem strange to readers accustomed to a more realistic tradition or to stories populated by only a few main characters. Nonetheless, such elements are essential for conveying the flavor of the cultures that produced the works. The contributors have chosen books that respect those traditions (entries frequently cite awards that books have won in their country of origin), while keeping in mind the importance of clarity to readers in this country.

Significance of the Work

In recent years, many worthwhile multicultural books have been published, more than this bibliography can accommodate, more than libraries can afford to purchase, and more than readers can find time to read. For this reason, the contributors have selected a mix representing the most significant authors as well as emerging voices and new perspectives. The relative importance of a work has been determined in a number of ways, based upon the type of work and the overall focus of the chapter.

In certain cases the contributors consulted works of criticism to help them gauge which of an author's several works are the most significant. Other guidelines include the author's position or reputation within his or her own society and the influence that person has had upon other writers; the impact of the work; and its reception within the culture that produced it (not the response by critics in the United States or the United Kingdom); prizes received; and the existence of feature films or other adaptations based upon the work. In some cases literary works by historically significant authors have not been included because the works themselves are less well written or less accessible than the same author's essays or autobiographical writings. For example, as a playwright, Václav Havel produced works that are not considered to be particularly important in the context of Eastern European literature, as opposed to the politics of the region. Yet in the years leading up to the 1989 Velvet Revolution and his ascension to the presidency of Czechoslovakia, Havel produced a book of essays, *Open Letters*, which is included in this bibliography because it illuminates for Western audiences both the culture of and the profound political changes in that part of the world. Some of Havel's best-known plays are mentioned in passing in that entry.

For general nonfiction and essays, significance is a product of such factors as the importance of the subject, the scope of coverage, awards the book has received, its influence upon other works of nonfiction, and the book's or the author's influence upon events. Under those guidelines, many controversial books and debatable arguments have been included in this bibliography, among them polemical works by Israeli and Palestinian authors, Afrocentric works about the origins of civilization, and revisionist histories of Columbus's voyage to the Americas. Most of these books have been ignored or omitted in other bibliographies because of their controversial or one-sided viewpoints. Nevertheless, they merit mention here because they have had a profound influence upon both political events and subsequent scholarship. The contributors believe that such works can profitably be read by anyone seeking the most thorough understanding possible of a culture or region and its history.

In the case of biographical works, significance is less easy to define. As a rule, traditional subjects of biographies—particularly mainstream European political or literary figures—are not represented here. Instead, the contributors identify works that tell about the lives of people from minority cultures or those that historically have been oppressed. Thus, Chapter 8, Western Europe, contains no biographies of Adolf Hitler. Instead, it offers the stories of an early German-Jewish feminist, an Algerian-French rock musician, Communist and anticommunist political martyrs in Greece, fighters in the Spanish Civil War, and a number of Jewish figures during the Holocaust, ranging from the eminent Leo Baeck to the otherwise unknown Etty Hillesum. Half of the biographical works in Chapter 5, Canada, are written or told by indigenous people; the rest focus upon other ethnic and minority groups. Missing are the life stories of prime ministers Pierre Trudeau and Brian Mulroney.

Currency

Virtually all of the works included in the bibliography were written in the twentieth century. The exceptions are works that have only recently been "discovered" or reprinted; new translations or interpretations of classic works, such as the *Bhagavad-Gita*; and older pieces included in anthologies. To provide a broader context, influential historical works not fully annotated here are often mentioned in passing in the chapter introduction. Although the contributors have made an effort to identify new or emerging authors and their works, some notable books on multicultural themes published in 1994 or later have not been included; more time needs to pass before it will be possible to evaluate the lasting impact of these titles.

In the realm of nonfiction, the contributors sought to identify the most current works about fast-changing areas of the world, although publication deadlines made it difficult to review titles that appeared much after the first part of 1994. In some cases, though, the contributors recommend an older title if in their opinion a more recent book failed to meet the criteria outlined above. Contributors have also included certain older nonfiction titles because such works provide valuable background to current issues, offer eyewitness accounts of important historical events, or introduce themes and approaches later adopted by others. For the same reason, listed here are certain autobiographies and personal narratives, such as those by significant African Americans and Native Americans, that were written before the twentieth century.

Representation of Previously Ignored Perspectives

Global Voices, Global Visions seeks to introduce perspectives that have previously been overlooked on recommended lists. In their introductions, the contributors of individual chapters expand on what this means in terms of their own selections. However, some points need to be made here.

In recent years, the Afrocentric interpretation of history has stirred enormous excitement—and controversy. The writings of African and African-American scholars such as Cheikh Anta Diop, Ivan van Sertima, and Molefi Kete Asante have challenged traditional views about the origins of civilization. African, African-American, and Caribbean social scientists such as Franz Fanon and Walter Rodney have critically examined Europe's role in the underdevelopment of Africa. The contributors to Chapter 11 have chosen to devote their limited space in the annotations to less well-known works that largely reflect this African sensibility. In their introduction the contributors also identify titles that in their view, although written by European and European-American scholars, present a more complex and thoughtful view of African history. A few of the most important of those, such as the works of Basil Davidson, are annotated. No doubt, some readers will argue that this Afrocentric emphasis presents a one-sided picture. A counterargument is that, for decades, traditional European scholarship regarding Africa also offered only one side, a perspective that many experts increasingly realize has misrepresented and demeaned African peoples.

Immigration, coupled with rising political activism by indigenous groups, is changing the demographic and cultural landscape, not just in the United States but in Canada, Great Britain, Western Europe, and Australia and New Zealand. As a multicultural bibliography, *Global Voices, Global Visions* emphasizes works by and about the immigrants, minorities, and indigenous peoples in each of these societies. For Canada, this means that the literary works of outstanding mainstream authors such as Margaret Atwood and Robertson Davies are not included, while those of immigrant, Native Canadian, and Québecois (French Canadian) writers are. Half of the entries in the chapter on Great Britain and Ireland are about Ireland—its historical struggle against British domination, the years of the Irish Republic, and the current turmoil in Northern Ireland. Almost all of the rest focus upon the experience of immigrants to England from the West Indies and Asia. The clash of cultures and ideologies in Western Europe is a principal theme of that chapter; special attention is given to Jews, recent immigrants from Africa and the Middle East, Eastern European refugees and migrants, Gypsies, Basques, and the indigenous Sami Lapps. Finally, in Chapter 15, covering Australia, New Zealand, and the Pacific, writers such as Patrick White, Thomas Keneally, and Janet Frame appear alongside an emerging group of Aborigine, Maori, and South Pacific authors whose names are unfamiliar to most readers but whose excellent writings explore ancient, long-ignored cultures.

Availability

Most of the works recommended in these pages are currently in print and available in English in the United States, either through a U.S. publisher or through a distributor of books from abroad. However, many important, even groundbreaking, books on multicultural themes are currently out of print. Some out-of-print works of particular value are described here if they are still widely available in libraries. It is hoped that this bibliography will encourage publishers to reprint those classics.

Methods of Selection

In assembling their lists, contributors consulted a variety of sources. Principal sources for general reviews include *Booklist*, *Choice*, *Library Journal*, the *New York Review of Books*, the *New York Times Book Review*, *New Yorker*, and multiculturally oriented publications such as *Multicultural Review*. Scholarly review sources include journals in academic specialties as well as ethnic and area studies journals. Lists of awards for recently published books have also been examined.

Over the years the critical assessment of books can change; some fall out of favor while others may not find their audience until years after their original publication. To develop a long-term perspective, the contributors also surveyed other bibliographies and recommended lists; literature reviews in various fields; historiographical works; works of literary criticism; and reference works in literature, history, the social sciences, and biography. Contributors sometimes used "best books" lists published by the American Library Association or individual public library systems, which often generate lists of books of particular interest to their users.

Ultimately, however, the contributors relied upon their own knowledge, expertise, and preferences. Each chapter thus reflects the unique and valuable contribution of its author or authors.

Organization

Each chapter in *Global Voices, Global Visions* includes a map that identifies the country or region under discussion. The introduction then provides an overview of the major cultural groups, events, and issues of that region, pointing out exemplary works that address those topics. This allows libraries with limited budgets and readers with limited time to spot the books that are most important. Many of the introductions also mention in passing other titles that do not appear as full annotated entries for one reason or another—perhaps they fall outside the bibliography's scope, they have not yet been translated into English, or they may have flaws that prevent an enthusiastic recommendation.

The annotations themselves are divided into three sections—literature, nonfiction, and biography. Literature includes works of fiction, drama, and poetry. Nonfiction includes general histories, works of social science, and literary and cultural criticism, as well as essays, lectures, atlases, and travel writings. Biography includes individual and collective biographies, autobiographies, and personal narratives. In some cases, works might easily fit into more than one classification. For anthologies that contain both literary and nonfiction selections, the majority of the content determines its placement. Readers in search of eyewitness accounts are encouraged to check both nonfiction and biography listings.

The annotations, each approximately 150 words long, describe the content of the book, its (and its author's) contribution, and possible uses and audiences. Many annotations mention other works by the same author or related works on the same subject. The annotations will help the reader to understand what makes a book successful, where it fits into the cultural picture, and how to evaluate books published on related themes that will be published in the future.

Because many books cut across cultural and regional lines, there are a number of cross-references between chapters. Cross-referenced entries are not numbered or indexed; rather, they include the number of the main entry. The book concludes with indexes, organized by author, title, and subject.

Many of the chapters reflect the input of more than one contributor. Where all contributors produced a more or less equal share, the multiple contributors are listed alphabetically. Otherwise, the contributors are listed according to the amount of their input. Where two or more contributors have contributed annotations to a chapter, each annotation is followed by the initials of its contributor. In some chapters, a small number of annotations were written by contributors of other chapters. Each of those entries is followed by the initials of its contributor.

A final note: Every effort has been made to ensure that the information in this bibliography is as accurate and current as possible. In some cases certain editions of works may have gone out of print or other editions may have become available since publication of this volume. Also, the prices given are subject to change by publishers.

1

UNITED STATES:
AFRICAN AMERICANS

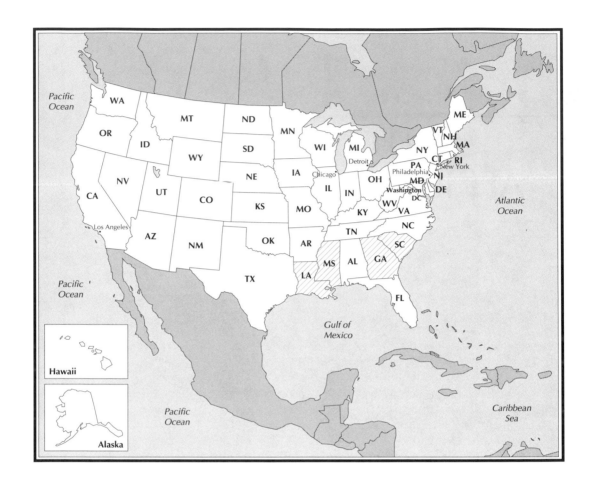

STATES WITH HIGHEST CONCENTRATION OF AFRICAN AMERICANS

1. Washington, D.C. - 65.6%
2. Mississippi - 35.6%
3. Louisiana - 30.8%
4. South Carolina - 29.8%
5. Georgia - 27.0%

CITIES WITH LARGEST AFRICAN-AMERICAN POPULATION

1. New York - 2,102,512
2. Chicago - 1,087,711
3. Detroit - 777,916
4. Philadelphia - 631,936
5. Los Angeles - 487,674

Source: 1990 U.S. Census

1

UNITED STATES: AFRICAN AMERICANS

by Cecil Hixon, Richard Lachmann, Paul T. Murray,
and A. J. Williams-Meyers

The history of African Americans has been a long and complex one, characterized by tragedies and triumphs, promises made and hopes unfulfilled. While other immigrants came to this country voluntarily, most of those who came from Africa did not. They did not flee their homeland because of religious or psychological persecution; they were not seeking economic opportunities and a better life. Instead, they were removed forcibly from the lives they knew, separated from their families, stripped of their dignity and heritage, and shipped here, in chains, as cargo on slave ships. Even those who later came to the United States from the West Indies to seek economic opportunity or freedom from political oppression can trace their family histories to those who survived this dreaded voyage, known as the "middle passage." Long after slavery was outlawed, the association of black skin with inferiority and servitude persists in the minds of many.

It is no wonder, then, that African-American novelists, poets, dramatists, historians, and social scientists are obsessed with history. In contrast to those who live in the much older nations of Europe or even the nations of Latin America, it is said that people in the United States have little understanding of or appreciation for their history. Those in the majority culture tend to look forward rather than backward, to believe in the idea of perpetual improvement and progress. For African-American writers, however, history is a means of recovering a past stolen in the journey from Africa to America and a past denied in the course of defending slavery, segregation, and the inferiority of a people based upon their race. African-American writers call on all Americans, black and white, to look to the past in order to confront their sins and to overcome them. They also urge us to see the nobility and successful struggles of African Americans in the past that may serve as an inspiration and a role model for the future.

African-American writers have found much to criticize in the mainstream view of history, which tends to portray the United States as a model civilization, the savior of the world. To convey such an image, however, it is necessary to downplay the less palatable aspects of our evolution. For example, schoolchildren learn that, during the Colonial era, people banded together to cast off the yoke of oppression. Through revolution, they severed political ties with the mother country and founded a union of democratic states, dedicated to the principles of liberty, freedom, justice, and equality—for some. In reality, the foundling nation depended on slavery as the basis of its economy. Although such bondage was an embarrassment, the direct opposite of the noble ideals embodied in the Declaration of Independence and the Constitution, commentators at the time defended it as a "necessary evil" for the country's development. So long as it was confined to the South, slavery was tolerated as "peculiar."

In the mid-1860s the Civil War erupted. Lincoln's goal was to preserve the Union; to do so he ended slavery and devised Constitutional protections for the former slaves. Largely, however, Reconstruction failed; the white power elite replaced slavery with the "Jim Crow" policies of segregation in the South that continued to tarnish the American ideal of justice for all.

Rapid industrialization and economic growth throughout the nineteenth and into the twentieth century enabled the United States to emerge as a world power. For African Americans, however, the racial problem continued to fester, compounded by the lingering legacy of slavery. An excellent contemporary account of the situation can be found in Gunnar Myrdahl's classic 1944 work, *An American Dilemma*, which explores the issue of race in the context of our basic assumptions about freedom, justice, democracy, and the "melting pot."

In 1954, the Supreme Court outlawed school segregation in the landmark *Brown* v. *Board of Education of Topeka* decision, seen by many as a sign that the United States was at last beginning an earnest effort to settle its debt with African Americans. Racism, many believed, was in retreat.

A New Look at History

This chapter lists books by and about African Americans that challenge the mainstream version of history at virtually every point. Most of the works described here present historical issues from an African-American perspective. Seeing things from a new point of view can be eye-opening. In some cases, these works confront the dominant version directly by presenting new information or new interpretations of events. In other cases the works make the picture more complete by telling the stories of individuals and events that previously were overlooked.

For example, two autobiographical works by Frederick Douglass (*The Life and Times of Frederick Douglass: An American Slave* and *Narrative of the Life of Frederick Douglass*) describe the brutality experienced during a childhood spent in bondage. His work sharply challenges the apologists of his day who attempted to justify slavery by trumpeting its "benevolence." Books such as *The Life of Benjamin Banneker* by Sylvio A. Bedini and *The Real McCoy* by Portia James reveal the contributions, too often ignored, of African-American intellectuals of the past. Carter G. Woodson's classic *The Education of the Negro* describes how African Americans in the antebellum South overcame obstacles to obtain an education. Similarly, James Anderson's *The Education of Blacks in the South, 1860–1930* discusses how African Americans established their own schools after the Civil War to provide education on their own terms. Both of these works challenge the image of slaves and newly freed African Americans as ignorant, uneducated, and intellectually inferior; on the contrary, they underscore how, throughout their history, African Americans have valued education.

Much of the power of African-American writing derives from its focus on history, a fact reflected in the major prizes awarded to many black writers. In 1993, for example, Toni Morrison became the first American author in almost two decades to win the Nobel Prize in literature. Her works of fiction, which draw upon historical events and settings, have also received the Pulitzer Prize and the National Book Critics Circle Award. Charles Johnson's *The Middle Passage*, a compelling novel depicting the agonies experienced by the African people on board a slave ship, received the National Book Award. Playwright August Wilson, each of whose plays represents a separate decade in the twentieth century, has won the National Drama Critics Circle Award, the Pulitzer Prize, and the Tony Award for Best Play. Charles Fuller's *A Soldier's Play*, a historical drama of African-American soldiers during World War II, was also a Pulitzer Prize winner for drama. John Edgar Wideman's *Brothers and Keepers*, an exploration of his family's past, earned him a Pulitzer Prize for nonfiction.

Like their African-American counterparts, some prominent white historians have challenged the mainstream versions and brought African-American history to the forefront of historical inquiry. Among the more important of these historians are Eugene Genovese, author of *Roll, Jordan, Roll*, and Herbert Gutman, author of *The Black Family in Slavery and Freedom*.

Henry Louis Gates, Jr. has noted that African-American literature began with slave narratives, such as those of Frederick Douglass. Most of the slave narratives, however, went unpublished or were largely unnoticed by the reading public of the time. The first novel by an African American to examine the experience of slavery, William Welles Brown's *Clotel, or the President's Daughter*, was published in 1857—not in the United States but in England. A more recent work, Barbara Chase-Riboud's *Sally Hemings*, draws on extensive research to reconstruct the slave experience and incorporates many of the themes and personages that appeared in *Clotel*, including Thomas Jefferson. Harold Courlander's *The African*, Frank Yerby's *The Dahomean*, and Alex Haley's 1976 bestseller, *Roots*, all focus on the lives of people captured into slavery; the stories begin in Africa and trace the families and traditions these people create in the New World. Other novels depict slavery as the archetypal experience, which, decades after Abolition, continues to mold the African-American psyche and define relations between whites and blacks. Examples of such works include Ralph Ellison's classic *Invisible Man*, which many consider to be the greatest American novel of the twentieth century, and Barry Beckham's *Runner Mack*. The protagonist in *The Chaneysville Incident* by David Bradley is unable to understand himself or his relationship to his family and his people's past until he learns about the slaves who preferred to die rather than live in bondage. In *Mumbo Jumbo*, Ishmael Reed argues compellingly that African Americans will find political direction and cultural integrity by exploring the hidden truths of their history.

Often, mainstream accounts of slavery downplay the extent of slave resistance and rebellion. The absence of such events leads some observers to conclude that slavery must have been a benign institution because so few victims of it chose to resist or flee. Many of the books described in this chapter, both fiction and nonfiction, challenge that notion. Toni Morrison's *Beloved*, for example, is based on the true story of a defiant fugitive slave who slits her young daughter's throat rather than have the child grow up in slavery. *William Styron's Nat Turner: Ten Black Writers Respond*, edited by John Henrik Clarke (1968), appeared in reaction to Styron's controversial novel *The Confessions of Nat Turner*, based on the true-life memoirs of a slave who led a revolt in Virginia in the 1830s. The contributors to Clarke's book debate whether a white writer can effectively portray a black character, especially a historical one. More important, perhaps, the book uses scholarship to discuss the larger issues of slave resistance and the importance of incorporating African-American perspectives on American history. Other valuable works on slave resistance described on the following pages include Herbert Aptheker's *American Negro Slave Revolts*; John W. Blassingame's *The Slave Community*; and *Denmark Vesey: The Slave Conspiracy of 1822*, edited by Robert S. Starobin. Daniel Littlefield, Jr.'s *Africans and Seminoles: From Revolt to Emancipation* explores a little-known aspect of slave history: His book focuses on the black Seminoles—slaves who escaped to Florida and joined forces with the Seminole Indians, who themselves were fighting against relocation by the U.S. government.

Many African-American fiction writers of the post–Civil War decades produced highly realistic portraits of the lives of freed slaves in the rural South. These works were intended mainly for a white readership and were didactic in purpose. James Weldon Johnson's *Autobiography of an Ex-Colored Man* presents a panorama of life experiences in the South, culminating in a move up North to Harlem. Charles Chesnutt's books about Southern black culture, such as *The Conjure Woman*, initially were well received, but publishers refused to print his later works because they addressed the issue of miscegenation. Paul Laurence Dunbar, the first African American to win acclaim as a poet, was popular in large part for his use of dialect. Since then, many African-American novelists have reassessed the post–Civil War period, emphasizing the betrayal of the promise of Reconstruction (*Do Lord Remember Me* by Julius Lester; *Jubilee* by Margaret Walker), the coming to terms with the wounds of slavery (*Beloved*, by Toni Morrison; *Family* by J. California Cooper), and the struggles of close-knit families forced to defend their land, their freedom, and even their lives (*The Autobiography of Miss Jane Pittman* by Ernest Gaines; *Youngblood* by John Oliver Killens).

In the years after the Civil War, a new generation of African-American political leaders emerged, the best known of whom are Booker T. Washington and W.E.B. Du Bois. While Washington advocated "self-improvement" and a more gradual approach to integration, Du Bois demanded racial justice and immediate social change. The classic biography of Washington is Louis R. Harlan's *Booker T. Washington: The Making of a Black Leader*. More recently, David L. Lewis has written a comprehensive two-volume biography of Du Bois, *W.E.B. Du Bois: Biography of a Race*. Another noted leader in the first half of this century was the Jamaican-born Marcus Garvey, who emerged as a spokesman for many African Americans, especially those in the urban North, with his call for unity among all African peoples in the struggle for liberation and a return to the black ancestral land of Africa. His life is the subject of David Cronon's *Black Moses*.

Around the turn of the twentieth century, a growing number of African Americans realized that both their economic opportunities and civil rights would be limited if they remained in the rural South. In a matter of a few years, the Great Migration to the urban North produced thriving African-American communities in the Harlem neighborhood of New York City, on

Chicago's South Side, and in many other cities. Widespread discrimination in housing forced African Americans to settle in all-black neighborhoods. The process of residential segregation and class integration is described in Allen Spear's *Black Chicago* and in Nicholas Lemann's *The Promised Land*.

The Harlem Renaissance

Harlem, in particular, became the setting for the flowering of African-American culture known as the Harlem Renaissance. Writers nurtured by this movement include Zora Neale Hurston and Claude McKay, whose works blended African, Caribbean, and American themes with European literary forms to create a distinctive and thoroughly modern style that reflected the growing diversity of black experience and expanded the definition of authentic African-American identity. In such novels as *Ollie Miss*, George Wylie Henderson describes how the integrity of Southern black rural communities serves as a defense against the unrelieved brutality of white racism. Marita Bonner, in her short stories and dramas, uses modernist allegories to make similar points. Rudolph Fisher's detective novel, *The Conjure Man Dies*, celebrates the vitality of Harlem society at its zenith. Among the other prominent writers of the Harlem Renaissance are Jean Toomer, whose experimental work *Cane* was rediscovered decades after its 1923 publication; the poet Countee Cullen; and Langston Hughes, widely recognized as the greatest African-American poet.

Some authors of the Harlem Renaissance tackled such thorny issues as the rigidity of black social relations and discrimination on the part of light-skinned African Americans toward their darker-skinned fellows. Jessie Fauset's *The Chinaberry Tree* was the first work of this sort. Wallace Thurman's *The Blacker the Berry* and Dorothy West's *The Living Is Easy*, both written after the heyday of the Harlem Renaissance, address the narrowing of opportunities for Northern blacks during the Depression. Indeed, the Depression made it harder for black authors to find financial sponsors or to get published. Even so, the authors active during this era have had a permanent influence on African-American literature.

The Harlem Renaissance also witnessed the emergence of other art forms, including painting and dance. But the art form most closely identified with this period is jazz, a uniquely American form of music that combines influences from African and classical sounds as well as from jazz's immediate predecessor in popular music, ragtime. An accessible book about the origins and history of this genre is Nat Hentoff's *Jazz Is*. Also recommended is *Beyond Category*, John Edward Hasse's biography of the seminal composer Duke Ellington, and Martin Duberman's classic biography of singer Paul Robeson. While the sounds of jazz filled the clubs in the North, African Americans in the South pioneered another essentially American musical form, blues, which in turn gave birth to rock 'n' roll. The story of the early bluesmen and their lives is the subject of Alan Lomax's *The Land Where the Blues Began*.

Struggle Against Segregation

Many of the books in this chapter, both fiction and nonfiction, explore African-American life just before and during the civil rights movement. In the South especially, this era was marked by segregation policies called "Jim Crow" laws (named after the stereotyped black slave caricatured in minstrel shows), which tested the limits of American justice, liberty, and democracy.

Like the blacks living under apartheid in South Africa, African Americans in the South encountered legal restrictions, brutal violence, alienation, and other abuses of their fundamental human rights. During this time a number of African Americans were executed; sometimes these deaths were carried out officially through the legal process (although often on trumped-up charges), but sometimes they occurred as lynchings, without any pretense of legality, at the hands of white mobs. These events are the basis of Ernest Gaines's novel *A Lesson Before Dying*, Albert French's novel *Billy*, James Goodman's compelling study *Stories of Scottsboro*, and Howard Smead's *Blood Justice: The Lynching of Mack Charles Parker*. The notorious 1955 lynching of Emmett Till in Mississippi is the subject of a novel, Bebe Moore Campbell's *Your Blues Ain't Like Mine*, and a work of nonfiction, Stephen Whitfield's *A Death in the Delta*. James Baldwin's classic novel *If Beale Street Could Talk* addresses unequal justice as meted out to African Americans living in the urban North.

Many novelists portray Southern communities on the eve of the civil rights struggle. Among them are Thulani Davis, whose novel *1959* highlights divisions between the older and the younger generation over issues of political activism. Ernest Gaines's classic *The Autobiography of Miss Jane Pittman* tells the story of an ex-slave who lives to witness the triumph of the civil rights movement and its impact upon her community.

Among the notable nonfiction works on the civil rights movement are the biographies of Dr. Martin Luther King, Jr. by David Garrow and David L. Lewis, as well as the memoirs penned by Dr. King's widow, Coretta Scott King. Other important biographies are Kay Mills's *This Little Light of Mine*, about the life of Fannie Lou Hamer, a grass-roots civil rights fighter from Mississippi, and Carl Rowan's recent biography of Supreme Court Justice Thurgood Marshall. Many of the participants in the movement, including Ralph D. Abernathy, James Farmer, Charlayne Hunter-Gault, and Anne Moody, have published their memoirs. Recommended general histories of the civil rights movement include *Parting the Waters: America in the King Years*, by Taylor Branch; *My Soul Is Rested: The Story of the Civil Rights Movement in the Deep South*, by Howell Raines; and *Eyes on the Prize: America's Civil Rights Years*, by Juan Williams.

By the late 1960s the focus of the movement had shifted from the Deep South, where it began, to the urban ghettoes of the North and West. Martin Luther King, Jr. worked to expand on legal and political gains by seeking basic economic reforms. At the time of his assassination, King's crusade for civil rights was being transformed into a Poor People's Campaign. Malcolm X's uncompromising message of racial pride and self-determination, expressed in his *Autobiography* and elsewhere, appealed to ghetto residents and continues to inspire young people. James Cone's *Martin and Malcolm and America* compares the philosophies of these two leaders and argues that their ideas were beginning to converge at the time of their deaths. Several of Malcolm's heirs in the Black Nationalist movement, among them Eldridge Cleaver, Angela Davis, and James Forman, have autobiographies featured in this list. Black Nationalism also emerges as a theme in the poetry and plays of Amiri Baraka; the concept merges with feminist consciousness in the works of Nikki Giovanni, Gwendolyn Brooks, Audre Lorde, and others.

Themes and Counterthemes

Today, African-American creative writers and sociologists continue to draw upon the past to understand the present. Their works today explore such important issues as religion, family life, and relationships between men and women. Education remains a crucial and constant concern, because many African Americans see education as an important avenue for escaping poverty and oppression. James Comer, best known for his pioneering work in helping schools, parents, and children work together in the inner city, describes his mother's commitment to her children's education in *Maggie's American Dream*. Sara Lawrence Lightfoot's *Balm in Gilead* tells the story of her mother's struggle to become one of the first African-American women to receive an M.D. and work as a physician. In *Black Boy*, novelist Richard Wright, author of the classic *Native Son*, describes his rage at being denied an equal education in the South at the beginning of the twentieth century and his journey North in search of knowledge. More than half a century later, journalist Brent Staples details his quest for a Ph.D. in philosophy and the obstacles he had to overcome in *Parallel Time*. Many works of nonfiction, most notably Jonathan Kozol's *Savage Inequalities*, focus on the challenges facing African-American children, who—four decades after the Supreme Court order on desegregation—must still struggle to achieve equal educational opportunities.

A number of sociologists—mostly white conservatives, but even a few African Americans—claim that the poverty, crime, and violence prevalent among some black communities stems from the stereotyped dysfunctional structure of the African-American family: absent father, single mother, and illegitimate children. In his book *The Truly Disadvantaged*, African-American sociologist William Julius Wilson acknowledges that this stereotype may have some basis in fact. But he takes the argument a logical step further by adopting a broader and more historical view. He traces the deeper roots of economic and social problems to the devastating legacy of slavery and discrimination, which contributed to the bleak employment prospects of men who could support families, and he presents the thesis that when middle-class African Americans abandoned the inner cities, the result was a loss of the strong moral values needed to sustain a community. The long-term impact of slavery is further explored in Herbert Gutman's *The Black Family in Slavery and Freedom, 1750–1925*. In *Climbing Jacob's Ladder*, Andrew Billingsley dismantles stereotypes by exploring the wide diversity of family structures within African-American communities.

The family as a source of strength across generations is a theme of novels by Paule Marshall, who offers images of working-class and middle-class Caribbean families settling into a new life in the United States. Lorraine Hansberry's acclaimed play *A Raisin in the Sun* features a traditional middle-class family confronting housing discrimination and white hostility. The role of traditional families in nurturing community values is explored in Jessie Fauset's *The Chinaberry Tree*, Ann Petry's *The Street*, and Connie Porter's *All-Bright Court*. Melvin Dixon's *Vanishing Rooms* examines gay relationships, while novels by Octavia Butler and Nella Larsen deal with interracial relationships. Alice Walker's widely read *The Color Purple* and Maya Angelou's autobiographical novel *I Know Why the Caged Bird Sings* portray strong young women who break away from their troubled environments to create unique kinds of family for themselves. Finally, John Edgar Wideman (*Sent for You Yesterday)* and Brent Staples (*Parallel Time*) plumb their own family histories to understand why they became successful writers while younger brothers turned to lives of crime and violence.

A major theme in African-American writing, indeed in all literature, is the relationship between men and women. Since the 1970s, African-American women authors gained prominence with books that take a largely critical view of African-American men. Novels by Alice Walker, Gloria Naylor, Ntozake Shange, Toni Cade Bambara, Gayle Jones, and Terry McMillan depict the vital role that women play in sustaining communities in which men often are absent, whether because of forced separation by slaveholders, the demands of their employers, or the devastating effects of poverty. For their part, some male authors have grown resentful of the frequent depictions of black men as brutes and rapists with no regard for their families. In response, they have written stories in which men are strong and responsible father figures; some of these works also show women as cold and manipulative. One work that turns things on their heads is *Platitudes*, Trey Ellis's parody of black women novelists.

Many black writers regard religion and folkways, which have survived through slavery, as the essential core of African-American identity and community. To some, Christianity is an alien ideology that prevents people from discovering the value of true African beliefs and practices. James Baldwin often expounds this view, as does Arthenia Millican in *Deity Nodded*. But other writers, such as Leon Forrest (*Two Wings to Veil My Face*) see Christianity as a positive force, and even Baldwin, in his presentation of love as the basis for racial reconciliation, finds virtues in Christianity. A number of African-American authors embrace the form of Islam developed in the United States by Elijah Muhammad and later adapted by Malcolm X, while such works as *Invisible Man* and *Mumbo Jumbo* regard the Nation of Islam as a dangerous and malignant force—or at least a worthy target of satire. Noteworthy nonfiction treatments of the role of religion in African-American life include James Baldwin's essays in *The Fire Next Time* and Samuel G. Freedman's *Upon This Rock: The Miracles of a Black Church*.

The journey through African-American history finds us in a present in which some problems have been overcome, but many others remain. After the heroic successes of the civil rights era, many people today feel a sense of disillusionment and confusion. Even successful African Americans continue to experience firsthand the continual sting of racial prejudice and intolerance. Personal narratives and works of fiction published in recent years by Brent Staples, Jill Nelson, Lorene Cary, Darryl Pinckney, Brent Wade, Denis Williams, and others portray the modern African American as both blessed and vulnerable.

About This Chapter

This bibliography of works by and about African Americans is large, but it is by no means exhaustive. The books in this chapter are recommended for at least one of several reasons. Many of them stand among the masterpieces, not just of American writing, but of world literature in the twentieth century. Others possess unusual historical interest; works from the nineteenth century shed light on the African-American experience under slavery and in the first decades after Emancipation, or they help us understand the origins of important literary trends and movements. Some works were chosen for the glimpses they provide into the lives of people as they leave their rural communities and adapt to the harshness of modern urban life.

A significant percentage of literary titles in this chapter were published in the early 1990s. Although they possess substantial merit, inclusion here is not meant to imply that each work is inevitably destined to stand the test of time.

In seeking to be inclusive, the editors recommend certain works primarily because they reflect the range of styles and themes found in contemporary African-American writing.

In selecting works of nonfiction, a principal goal has been to include key works covering the major historical periods and aspects of life in both the South and the North. Along with focusing upon the principal social, economic, and political issues, the nonfiction titles also provide a far-ranging survey of African-American culture and artistic achievements. There are works about African-American folklore, humor, and music. Sports are represented by Arthur Ashe's landmark three-volume work *A Hard Road to Glory*. Works are included by major African-American historians and social scientists such as W.E.B. Du Bois, Carter Woodson, and William Julius Wilson. So, too, are books by prominent historians and social scientists who are not African American but who, in the opinion of the editors, have succeeded in presenting the African-American experience without condescension or stereotype.

Each of the entries is signed with the initials of its contributor. For nonfiction, most of the works about African-American history before 1954 were selected and annotated by A. J. Williams-Meyers. Works about events taking place after 1954, along with general works of political science and sociology, were selected and annotated by Paul T. Murray. Cecil Hixon developed the first draft of the list for fiction, drama, and poetry; Richard Lachmann then revised the list. Williams-Meyers, Murray, and Lachmann contributed sections to this introduction, which was then rewritten by the book's editor-in-chief, Lyn Miller-Lachmann, who also wrote some of the annotations.

The contributors would like to thank Phyllis Meredith and Joyce Bickerstaff for their comments and suggestions.

LITERATURE

1   Andrews, Raymond. *Baby Sweet's*. Illus. by Benny Andrews. Univ. of Georgia Pr. 1988, $10.95 (0-8203-1069-7). 232pp. Fiction.

This novel takes place on Independence Day, 1966, in fictional Muskhogean County, Georgia. John Morgan, Sr., the wealthiest and most prominent white citizen of the county, is celebrating his fortieth wedding anniversary. But all is not as it seems. A series of flashbacks reveals that the life of Morgan's son, John Jr., is far from what had been planned for him. The junior Morgan is an artist who paints portraits of black nudes. He has abandoned his family's home and businesses to befriend blacks and romance "white trash" women. The blacks of Muskhogean County also have given up traditional ways. They have given up their narrow social life, which had centered on the barbecue joint owned by Appalachee Red, the mixed-race illegitimate son of John Jr. Now they concentrate instead on finding decent factory jobs.

The novel climaxes when various prodigal sons and daughters return to the county. In the process they force the older blacks and whites who never left home, most notably John Morgan, Sr., to confront the consequences of their philandering and their hypocrisies. The characters speak in vivid language and the author maintains a light tone in this portrayal of relations between the races in the rural South in transition.   RL

2   Angelou, Maya. *I Know Why the Caged Bird Sings*. Random 1970, $23.00 (0-394-42986-9); Bantam $5.50 (0-553-27937-8). 256pp. Fiction.

The first, and the most acclaimed, of the author's five autobiographical novels, this compelling and beautifully written volume covers the heroine's life up to age sixteen. As a girl, Angelou divided her time between the home of her religious grandmother in rural, segregated Arkansas and the more cosmopolitan environment of St. Louis, where her mother lived. The novel also takes place in both settings, presenting the life of black females as a series of assaults and psychological degradation by men, black as well as white. The transforming moment in this work comes when the heroine, only eight years old, is raped by her mother's boyfriend. The girl becomes mute for five years. As the story ends, the protagonist regains both her voice and her self-esteem. She is last seen as a mother caring for her newborn son.

Angelou's story continues in *Gather Together in My Name* (Random, 1974), *Singin' and Swingin' and Gettin' Merry Like Christmas* (Random, 1976), and *The Heart of a Woman* (Random, 1981). Her poetry is found in a number of collections exist. Her two most recent works are "On the Pulse of Morning," the poem she read at the 1993 Inaugural of President Bill Clinton, and the best-selling essay collection, *Wouldn't Take Nothing for My Journey Now* (Random, 1993).   RL

3   Ansa, Tina M. *Baby of the Family*. Harcourt 1989, $18.95 (0-15-110431-X); $8.95 (0-15-610150-5). 265pp. Fiction.

This, the author's first novel, takes us into the world of eccentric characters, local customs, and domestic life in small-town Georgia during the 1950s. The main character, Lena McPherson, is born with a caul (a thin veil-like membrane) covering her face. According to folklore, the caul indicates she will grow up to possess magic powers, such as seeing into the past and future. As Lena grows older, she is increasingly plagued by these powers. She has bouts of sleepwalking and is troubled by visions of ghosts. As the novel ends, Lena has learned to accept her family's love and to make her own uncertain way in life.   CH

4   Austin, Doris Jean. *After the Garden*. NAL 1988, $11.00 (0-452-26079-5). 336pp. Fiction.

Set in the North in the decade just before the beginning of the civil rights movement, *After the Garden* is a coming-of-age novel. The protagonist, Elzina Tompkins, lives with her grandmother, Rosalie, on the most fashionable street in the black section of town. Elzina matures when she falls in love with handsome Jesse James. Although Rosalie scorns Jesse because he hales from impoverished Kearny Avenue, she nevertheless allows the young couple to live with her after they marry. The marriage is strong, even though Jesse spends much of his time with friends rather than his wife.

The author ably conveys the differences between two distinct, yet intertwined, black worlds through her vivid descriptions, her sharp ear for different styles of black speech, and her accurate rendering of human emotions. Perhaps the greatest strength of this novel, however, lies in the richness of the characters. Readers will especially be absorbed watching Elzina mature.

RL

5 Baldwin, James. ***Go Tell It on the Mountain***. Dell 1985, $5.99 (0-440-33007-6). 224pp. Fiction.

This semiautobiographical novel tells the story of Johnny Grimes, a sensitive Harlem youth, and his conflict with his brutal stepfather, Gabriel, a fundamentalist preacher. On one level, Gabriel's abuse of Johnny symbolizes his rejection of blackness. On a deeper level, it reflects Baldwin's feeling that Christianity, too, rejects blackness. Another theme, and a major source of tension between stepfather and son, is Johnny's difficulty in coming to terms with his homosexuality. At the end of the novel, Johnny discovers he has a great gift for sermonizing and becomes a preacher, as did Baldwin himself.

Later, though, Baldwin went on to reject the church and to openly celebrate his homosexuality. In 1948 he left the United States, and while he spent most of the rest of his life in France, his writing continued to deal mainly with the life of blacks in the United States. Among Baldwin's most acclaimed works are the novels *Giovanni's Room* (orig. pub. 1956; Dell, 1985) and *Another Country* (orig. pub. 1962; Dell, 1985); the play *Blues for Mister Charlie* (o.p., 1964); and the essays collected in *Nobody Knows My Name* (orig. pub. 1961; Random, 1992). RL

6 Baldwin, James. ***If Beale Street Could Talk***. Dell 1986, $5.99 (0-440-34060-8). 197pp. Fiction.

This beautifully written novel tells the love story of Tish and Fonny. Tish, nineteen years old, is pregnant with Fonny's child. Fonny, a sculptor, is in jail, awaiting trial for a rape he did not commit. All the members of both families rally around the couple, helping Tish prepare for the birth of the child and fighting for Fonny's acquittal. Tish's deeply religious mother journeys to Puerto Rico to meet with Fonny's accuser; there she tries, unsuccessfully, to convince the woman to admit that Fonny was not her rapist.

Baldwin expresses both families' rage and helplessness at Fonny's imprisonment by whites who are certain that any accused black must be guilty of the crime. At the conclusion of the novel Tish gives birth to a son, but she wonders whether the boy will ever get to see his father. RL

7 Bambara, Toni Cade. ***Gorilla, My Love***. Random 1992, $9.00 (0-679-73898-3). 177pp. Fiction.

Toni Cade Bambara is a novelist, essayist, and short story writer as well as an active organizer of African-American artists who traveled to Cuba and Vietnam in the 1970s. *Gorilla, My Love*, her most famous volume, collects short stories she wrote between 1959 and 1970. The stories, set mainly in New York City, often explore young people's experiences growing up black in a harsh urban setting. "The Lesson," for example, features poor children who travel downtown to visit an expensive toy store; the story records their shock at seeing toys that cost more than their families' food budgets. "The Survivor" portrays a woman who escapes a bad relationship with an abusive man and finds solidarity with other black women. Bambara's novel *The Salt Eaters* (Random, 1981) is set in rural Georgia and describes the politicization of black women in the 1960s and 1970s. RL

8   Baraka, Amiri. ***Dutchman***. o.p. Drama.

This play, which generated intense interest and provoked much controversy when it was first staged, is set on a New York City subway car. Lula, a young, sexually provocative white woman, dominates the first act. She taunts Clay, a quiet black intellectual, for not being assertive enough and for being untrue to his blackness. In the second act Clay finally musters a response, saying he is repressed "to keep myself from cutting all your throats." Despite his anger toward Lula, he refuses to resort to violence; nevertheless, the play ends when Lula fatally stabs Clay as the other white passengers look on approvingly.

This powerful drama presents a vision of how white Americans have suppressed blacks and then mocked them for their restraint and lack of self-confidence.   RL

9   Baraka, Amiri, and William Harris, eds. ***LeRoi Jones–Amiri Baraka Reader***. Thunder's Mouth 1991, $14.95 (1-56025-007-0). 540pp. Poetry.

Amiri Baraka, who initially wrote under the name LeRoi Jones, is generally viewed as the founder of Black Nationalist poetry and is an inspiration and spiritual leader for younger African-American poets. His experiences with racism in the Army, and then his rejection of what he described as "the Negro sickness" while a student at Howard University in the 1950s, led him to travel to Cuba. There he found parallels between the anticolonial struggles of the Third World and those of blacks in the United States. By the mid-1970s, he had embraced Marxism as his political model. Baraka's poetry comprises the full range of language with which African Americans express themselves. Using a wide range of styles and idioms to express the experiences of being black in the United States, the writer presents his vision of political and personal transformation.   RL

10   Beckham, Barry. ***Runner Mack***. Howard Univ. Pr. 1984, $9.95 (0-88258-116-3). 213pp. Fiction.

Henry Adams, the protagonist of this powerfully symbolic work, moves North to find opportunity and to pursue his dream of becoming a professional baseball player. Baseball, in this novel, connotes the American way of life; Adams's inability to win a place on a team represents the rejection of blacks by American white society. In fact, Adams's experiences recapitulate the entire history of African Americans in this country. His job interview, for example, is portrayed as a slave auction.

Adams becomes radicalized by his experiences with racism, first in a Northern slum, then as a draftee in the Army in Alaska. He joins with a revolutionary named Runner Mack in a plot to blow up the White House. However, when a planned rally draws few supporters, Runner Mack hangs himself and Adams steps in front of a speeding truck. This rich novel, complexly structured with numerous flashbacks, has a sharply satiric tone.   RL

11   Bonner, Marita, Joyce Flynn, and Joyce Stricklin, eds. ***Frye Street and Environs: The Collected Works of Marita Bonner***. Beacon 1987, $13.00 (0-8070-6309-6). 287pp. Fiction/Drama.

This volume brings together Marita Bonner's best essays, plays, and short stories. The stories, written in the 1920s and 1930s, portray black urban life in Chicago. A principal backdrop for the tales is Frye Street, a racially integrated neighborhood where blacks are destined to remain poor while many whites improve themselves and move on. The Depression deepens the endemic and severe poverty. Daily suffering grows into horrible disaster as people without resources are staggered by seemingly minor and random events.

Also contained within this volume is Bonner's allegorical play *The Purple Flower*, first published in 1928 and now her most famous work. In it, a series of black characters—known as "Us"—attempt to approach a purple flower, symbol of the American dream. Their leader, a figure much like Booker T. Washington, counsels patience and hard work. But one of the white "Devils"— "artful little things with soft wide eyes, such as you would expect to find in an angel"—attempts to rape a sweet young Us. As the play ends, the black characters wait to see if one of their young men will confront and kill the rapist.   RL

12   Bradley, David. ***The Chaneysville Incident***. Borgo 1991, $30.00 (0-8095-9096-4); HarperCollins $13.00 (0-06-091681-8). 432pp. Fiction.

The narrator of this novel is John Washington, who, like the author, is a college professor. Washington is called to the deathbed of his childhood mentor, Jack Crowley, who proceeds to tell him stories about his father, Moses, and about an event in Chaneysville, Pennsylvania a century earlier. In that (true) incident, thirteen runaway slaves chose to be killed by their captors rather than return to bondage. The story inspires Washington to conduct his own research into the incident and into the life of his father. As he does, he becomes less the detached professor and more the committed historian of his race. He also rejects Christianity, which he blames for killing blacks by taking away the spirits that in Africa had given them an afterlife. The novel climaxes with revelations about Moses, the Chaneysville incident, and the essential truth of being an African American. This book won the PEN/Faulkner Award in 1982.   RL

13   Brooks, Gwendolyn. ***Annie Allen***. o.p. Poetry.

This book won the Pulitzer Prize for poetry in 1950—the first time the Prize was awarded to an African American writer. The volume traces the youth and maturation of Annie Allen, who is in part modeled after Brooks herself. Brooks grew up in the Bronzeville section of Chicago, where much of her poetry is set. Thematically, Brooks's work addresses the problems of growing up in a world of poverty and discrimination. Stylistically, her poetry uses formal language, which makes references to classical and modern European poetry and to European and African art, mixed with colloquial expressions of the day. In the late 1960s, Brooks shifted her focus to the political issues of her day; subsequently, her poetry reflected a dramatic change in tone and content.   RL

14   Brown, Cecil. ***The Life and Loves of Mr. Jive Ass Nigger***. Ecco 1991, $9.95 (0-88001-309-5). 213pp. Fiction.

George Washington, the protagonist of this irreverent, humorous, and pointed novel, is stranded in Europe without money. An American diplomat offers the college-educated Washington a job as a window washer. Instead, he becomes a gigolo in Copenhagen. Although sexually adept, he loses his money at a bar where he holds forth on literature, contending that classical European works really are about African Americans. Ultimately, he is badly beaten in a bar fight and resolves to return to the United States. In the author's world, whites never see blacks as whole people, only as stereotypes: the servile janitor, the sexual athlete, the rapist.

Brown studied writing under LeRoi Jones (Amiri Baraka) but was excluded by Saul Bellow from his writing classes at the University of Chicago. Brown later became a script writer for Richard Pryor. His autobiography, *Coming Up Down Home: Memoir of a Sharecropper's Son*, was published by Ecco in 1992.

RL

15   Brown, Wesley. *Tragic Magic*. o.p. Fiction.

We meet the narrator, Melvin Ellington (The Mouth), on his first day home after being paroled from prison, where he served two years for refusing to enter the military during the Vietnam War. Melvin—in love with the sound of his own voice and his command of the English language—compares his fluency with words to Duke Ellington's (no relation) with music. Through flashbacks, Melvin tells of his childhood in Queens and of his time in prison. Melvin's pacifism is dramatized through his refusal to go to Vietnam and again, at the end of the novel, when he witnesses a man being stabbed to death in a senseless fight. This novel, a celebration of language, makes a powerful statement of the need for nonviolence on both a political and a personal level.   RL

16   Brown, William Welles. *Clotel, or the President's Daughter.* Repr. of 1853 ed. Ayer 1969, $21.00 (0-405-01853-3); Carol Publg. $7.95 (0-8216-0180-6). 245pp. Fiction.

First published in England in 1853, this was the first novel by an African American to appear in print. It opens with a narrative of Brown's own childhood in slavery and his escape to the North and then to Britain, where he became active as a writer in the abolitionist movement. The novel then tells the story of Currer, a mulatto woman who becomes the concubine of Thomas Jefferson. Later, she is the mistress of a hypocritical pro-slavery minister. Her daughters, Clotel and Althesa, separated from their mother when she is sold to a new master, also become concubines, prized for their light skin. When Clotel grows up, she, too, is separated from her daughter by her slave masters. Eventually, Clotel escapes. About to be recaptured by slave hunters, she jumps off a bridge to her death in the Potomac River. Like the better-known *Uncle Tom's Cabin*, this novel portrayed for Northern and European readers the horrible realities of slavery.   RL

17   Butler, Octavia E. *Kindred.* 2nd ed. Intro. by Robert Crossley. Beacon 1988, $11.95 (0-8070-8305-4). 288pp. Fiction.

Science fiction author Butler has woven a surrealistic tale of violence, rape, and slavery. Dana, an African-American writer at the beginning of her career, is married to Kevin, a fellow writer who is white. As the two move into their new home, Dana is suddenly transported from Los Angeles in 1976 to a Southern plantation in the early nineteenth century. There, Dana saves Rufus, a white boy, from drowning in a river; Rufus's father "rewards" her by threatening to kill her with a shotgun. Throughout the novel Dana is repeatedly transported to this nightmarish plantation. Over time Rufus grows into a cruel youth. Ultimately, he rapes Dana, who becomes pregnant and thus, paradoxically, begins her family's lineage.

Through Dana and her journeys through time and space, Butler explores disturbing aspects of African-American history: the love-hate relationship between the slaves and their masters; the sexual exploitation of black women by whites; the biracial heritage of African Americans born of these unions; the legacy of slavery seared into the African-American consciousness. Dana's twentieth-century relationship with a white man is seen in a new light when explored in the historical context of violation and oppression. This is an accessible and gripping book, with appeal not just to fans of science fiction but to a broad segment of readers. LML

18 Campbell, Bebe Moore. *Your Blues Ain't Like Mine*. Putnam 1992, $22.95 (0-399-13746-7); Ballantine $12.00 (0-345-38395-8). 352pp. Fiction.

Racism in this country is often regarded as a problem only for its victims. But Bebe Moore Campbell's remarkable second novel adds another dimension. The book begins with a fictionalized account of the murder of Emmett Till, the fourteen-year-old black boy who was lynched in 1955 for speaking to a white woman in a rural Mississippi town. As in real life, the murderer is acquitted by an all-white jury. But in Campbell's retelling of the story, over the next thirty years the murderer's family, unable to adapt to the new world resulting from the civil rights movement, falls into poverty. Members of Till's family seek a new life in the North; ultimately, however, they fall prey to the evils of the inner city. In clean, elegant prose, Campbell offers a powerful reminder that racism is a crime for which everyone pays. CH

19 Cartier, Xam W. *Be-Bop, Re-Bop*. Ballantine 1990, $4.95 (0-345-36764-2). 147pp. Fiction.

This novel opens at a wake. Double was an aficionado of jazz who had taught his daughter—the unnamed narrator of the book—that jazz was both a route to personal salvation and the link to the whole history of Africans in the United States. Jazz music calms the narrator's mother, Vole, when she becomes angry at some of the guests at the wake. Vole and the narrator dance to jazz as they remember Double. In flashbacks, the reader compares the narrator's childhood in 1950s St. Louis and Double's youth before World War II in the same city. At the conclusion of the novel, the narrator, now a single mother on welfare, turns to jazz and her memories of her father's love for music, to gain the strength she needs to cope with poverty and the rigors of city life. This stylish and engagingly written first novel by an African-American woman is an ode to jazz and the place it has in the lives of many African Americans.

Cartier is also the author of *Muse-Echo Blues* (Ballantine, 1992). RL

20 Chase-Riboud, Barbara. *Sally Hemings*. Buccaneer 1992, $21.95 (0-89966-915-8); Ballantine $12.00 (0-345-38971-9). 300pp. Fiction.

Sally Hemings was a light-skinned slave and half-sister of Thomas Jefferson's wife. Some historians and many African Americans believe Hemings was also Jefferson's mistress. In the novel, Sally is sent to Paris with one of Jefferson's daughters. Although French law would have allowed her to stay in Europe as a free woman, she returns to Virginia, where she becomes Jefferson's lover. The story unfolds through the eyes of a white lawyer, Nathan Langdon, who interviews Hemings, Jefferson, and others who knew her. This novel explores the ambiguities of the sexual and romantic relationship between a master and his slave. The Jefferson of this novel is self-serving even as he espouses principled opposition to the institution of slavery.

Chase-Riboud is the author of *From Memphis and Peking* (o.p., 1974), a collection of poems about her travels in Africa and China in the 1960s, as well as other novels, including *Echo of Lions* (o.p.), about the Amistad slave rebellion. RL

21 Chesnutt, Charles W. *The Conjure Woman*. Intro. by Robert Farnsworth. Univ. of Michigan Pr. 1969, $13.95 (0-472-06156-9). Fiction.

Charles Chesnutt was the first commercially successful African-American author. His books, written mainly for white audiences, sought to show the richness and diversity of the black experience after slavery and to portray the abilities and achievements of emancipated Negroes. *The Conjure Woman*, a collection of short stories, is his most impressive work. The main character in the stories is Uncle Julius, who, in the eyes of the narrator, a white Northerner, is a stereotypical Negro. However, Chesnutt wants the reader to see what the narrator cannot, that Julius is clever and sensible. Julius gets his way with whites by tricking and outthinking them. The stories, which draw on images from folktales and African trickster legends, are often ironic and descriptive of Southern life at the end of the nineteenth century.

Chesnutt's later works deal with issues of mixed-race relations, themes so troubling to white readers and editors that Chesnutt found it impossible to get his last novels published. RL

22 Colter, Cyrus. *A Chocolate Soldier*. o.p. Fiction.

The narrator of the novel, Meshach Coriolanus Barry, is a successful preacher. At one time Barry had sexually abused his daughter, Carol. As a way of explaining his own life and thereby apologizing to Carol, he now tells her the story of Cager Lee, his classmate at the all-black Gladstone College in Tennessee during the 1920s. Lee becomes a radical who sees little point to his studies and drops out of school. A sympathetic professor gets Cager a job as servant to the elderly, rich racist Mary Dabney. Cager gets Dabney to reconsider her racism, but his own growing militancy leads him to murder her. He, in turn, is lynched by a white mob. The novel ends on a note of despair; Barry loses his faith in God, while Cager, despite his commitment to ideals, is seen as misguided and counterproductive.

Colter is also known for his collection of short stories, *The Beach Umbrella* (o.p.). His novel *Night Studies* (o.p.) explores the intertwined histories of blacks and whites and addresses the difficulties they face in forging personal and racial identities. RL

23 Cooper, J. California. *Family*. Doubleday 1991, $18.95 (0-385-41171-5); $9.00 (0-385-41172-3). 231pp. Fiction.

J. California Cooper is the author of three collections of short stories and seventeen plays. *Family*, her first novel, is the story of a slave family as told by its matriarch. After the death of two children born into the cruelty of slavery, the matriarch gives birth to a daughter. She names the child Always, because she knows she will always love her. Always is sold to another owner. After enduring years of hardship, she grows determined to survive and vows to destroy those who tormented her and her mother. This compelling novel explores the legacy of slavery, the process of recovery undertaken by those who experienced it, and their inspiring struggle for survival.   CH

24   Courlander, Harold. ***The African.*** Henry Holt 1993, $14.95 (0-8050-3000-X). 320pp. Fiction.

This novel, first published in 1967, is the story of Hwesuhunu, a young Dahomean captured and sold into slavery in the early nineteenth century. The ship transporting him is wrecked off of St. Lucia, but Hwesuhunu is recaptured. Renamed Wes Hunu, he becomes the property of a series of masters in Georgia. Through Wes Hunu's eyes, the reader sees the harshness of slavery and the struggle of slaves to retain their dignity and their African identities. Eventually, Wes Hunu escapes to the wilderness, where he meets up with Indians and other escaped slaves. At the end of the novel, he steals a horse and plans to ride to safety in Ohio. A powerful and convincing character, Wes Hunu is a precursor of Kunta Kinte, the main character of Alex Haley's *Roots (see main entry).*

Courlander also is the author of several collections of folktales, including *The Cow-Tail Switch and Other West African Stories* (Henry Holt, 1987) and *The Drum and the Hoe: Life and Lore of the Haitian People* (Univ. of California Pr., 1973).   RL

25   Cullen, Countee. ***Color.*** Repr. of 1925 ed. Ayer 1970, $14.00 (0-405-01919-X). 108pp. Poetry.

This volume of poems, first published in 1925, established Countee Cullen as a major figure in the Harlem Renaissance. The works in this collection are mainly written in traditional European forms, such as the sonnet, the quatrain, and the epigram. In this volume are love sonnets on the beauty of brown-skinned people, observations on the pain of death, and poems that confront the cruelty of racism.

Cullen also is the author of *The Ballad of the Brown Girl: An Old Ballad Retold* (o.p., 1927), which retells a Southern black folktale in formal English quatrains. His novel *One Way to Heaven* (o.p., 1932), set in Harlem, explores class divisions among blacks and the tensions between Christian and pagan beliefs. The outstanding poems of his tragically short career appear in the posthumous collection *On These I Stand: An Anthology of the Best Poems of Countee Cullen* (o.p., 1947).   RL

26   Davis, Thulani. ***Nineteen Fifty-Nine.*** Grove 1992, $18.95 (0-8021-1230-7); HarperCollins $10.00 (0-06-097529-6). 295pp. Fiction.

Willie Tarrant is a twelve-year-old girl living in the small segregated town of Turner, Virginia. One day in 1959, a group of black students from a nearby college arrive to demand their right to sit at a lunch counter reserved for whites. Willie's coming of age parallels the political awakening among her formerly complacent neighbors. The event becomes a flashpoint, transforming the town, affecting relationships among the black residents as well as with the privileged whites. Elderly Negroes discover their solidarity with the students as they express pride in their history. Young people like Willie realize that they can make a future for themselves by escaping from their modest homes and challenging segregation and inequality.

The author ably conveys the tone of small-town life. The characters all know each other and feel both comfortable and constricted in their home town. This inspiring novel documents an important moment in the civil rights era and explores a young girl's coming of age in a rural Southern community.

RL

27   Delany, Samuel R. ***Dhalgren***. Bantam 1983, $4.95 (0-553-25391-3). 879pp. Fiction.

Winner of both the Hugo and Nebula awards, Samuel Delany is one of the leading science fiction writers of the current generation. *Dhalgren* is set in the near future in a city that has been destroyed by an unidentified catastrophe and that now is plagued by random violence and gang terrorism. The heroes of the novel are African Americans trying, with little success, to restore order and a sense of community: Kid, a young poet; Amy Taylor, a dynamic minister; and George Harrison, a mythic hero. Delany's novels, which enjoy wide readership among science fiction fans, are noted for their experimental style and for the preponderance of African, African-American, and Asian protagonists. Among his other noted works are *Babel-17* (o.p., 1966) and *Stars in My Pocket Like Grains of Sand* (Bantam, 1984). RL

28   Demby, William, and Nathan A. Scott, Jr. ***The Catacombs.*** Repr. of 1965 ed. Northeastern Univ. Pr. 1991, $12.95 (1-55553-099-0). 256pp. Fiction.

This novel, set in Rome, has a highly unusual structure. William Demby himself appears as the narrator, recounting news events from the years 1962 to 1964. At the same time he tells a love story about two fictional characters, Doris and the Count. As the novel evolves, the imaginary characters become less important. Doris becomes pregnant on Christmas Day and soon disappears from the story; readers never see her child born. Demby comes to realize he no longer needs to escape into the fantasy world of Doris and the Count. Eventually he comes to take charge of his own life and learns to comment more forcefully on contemporary reality.

Demby's earlier novel, *Beetlecreek* (o.p., 1950), portrays blacks and whites trapped in a small town. The novel climaxes with the young black protagonist's murder of a white recluse who tried to bring white and black youth together. In *Love Story Black* (o.p., 1978) a middle-aged professor is attracted to an aging entertainer when he is commissioned to write a magazine article about her. RL

29   Dixon, Melvin. ***Vanishing Rooms***. NAL 1992, $9.00 (0-452-26761-7). 224pp. Fiction.

This novel, set in New York City in the 1970s, is told from the points of view of three interconnected characters. Jesse—a gay black professional dancer and aspiring choreographer—mourns the murder of his white lover, Metro, who was killed by a gang of teenagers. Flashbacks reveal how Metro was unfaithful to Jesse and how he reduced Jesse's blackness to a mere sexual fetish. After the murder Jesse moves in with a woman, Ruella, another member of their dance company. Their brief romance ends when Jesse reasserts his gay identity and begins a relationship with another black dancer. Ruella, the novel's second narrator, is devoted to her brother Phillip, who is languishing in jail. Through her relationship with a Muslim named Abdul, she finds both an anchor for her life and a stronger way to assert her heritage. The third narrator, Lonny, is half Italian and half black. A participant in Metro's murder, Lonny avoids confronting his racial heritage and his sexuality by becoming a male prostitute. The novel concludes with the performance of a dance Jesse has choreographed in memory of Metro. The dance embodies the novel's conclusion that Jesse can reconcile his gay and black identities. RL

30 Dove, Rita. **_Thomas and Beulah_**. Carnegie-Mellon Univ. Pr. 1985, $9.95 (0-88748-046-2). 79pp. Poetry.

Rita Dove won the 1987 Pulitzer Prize for this collection of poetry, which takes its name from her maternal grandparents. The poems tell of their move from rural Georgia, their courtship and marriage in Ohio, and the family they raised, including Rita herself. Thomas and Beulah are the anchors of the family. Through their love for each other and for their offspring, they help to armor the family against setbacks and the pain of racism. Dove's poetry draws upon many influences, among them Langston Hughes, Gwendolyn Brooks, and Amiri Baraka. But her rhetorical style also has much in common with that of Robert Frost, and her phrasing, imagery, and meter convey an almost biblical tone. The poems reflect themes of African-American history, especially slavery and the civil rights movement, as well as the personal experiences of Dove and her family.

In 1993 Rita Dove was named Poet Laureate of the United States. In addition to her poetry, Dove has published a collection of short stories, _Fifth Sunday_ (Univ. Pr. of Virginia, 1985), and a novel, _Through the Ivory Gate_ (Pantheon, 1992). RL

31 Dumas, Henry. **_Goodbye, Sweetwater: New and Selected Stories_**. Thunder's Mouth 1988, $10.95 (0-938410-58-X). 356pp. Fiction.

In 1968, at age thirty-four, Dumas was killed by a white police officer in New York City. This volume brings together two previous posthumous collections of Dumas's short stories, _Ark of Bones and Other Stories_ (o.p., 1970) and _Rope of Wind and Other Stories_ (o.p., 1979). Dumas's allegorical stories, influenced by the modern parables of Franz Kafka, echo with allusions to biblical and African myths. In "Ark of Bones," a character named Fish-head, who is stable and conventional, follows a man called Head-eye—ugly and weird, though smart and insightful—to an ark rising up from the Mississippi River. The ark contains the spirits of enslaved Africans. Fish-head comes to identify more with these dead souls than with his living African-American brethren. In "Will the Circle Be Unbroken?" a white jazz fan tries to enter a club to hear his black friend play the African horn. Although warned off by the doorman, the white man enters anyway. When his friend blows his horn, the white man and all the other white spectators die—destroyed, like the walls of Jericho, when Joshua's priests blew their trumpets and the army raised a mighty shout. These spare but powerful stories reflect black history in symbolic terms and reflect what the author sees as lack of order and community among African Americans.   RL

32   Dunbar, Paul Laurence. ***The Complete Poems of Paul Laurence Dunbar***. Intro. by W. D. Howells. Hakim's 1993, $10.95 (0-317-05269-1). 289pp. Poetry.

Paul Laurence Dunbar, regarded as the first major African-American poet, is best known for poems written in Negro dialect. Often humorous, and at times ironic, those poems present, in idealized form, the language, folkways, and beliefs of rural blacks in the late nineteenth century. Dunbar also wrote many poems in standard English, some of which addressed the plight of blacks more directly.

Dunbar is the author of several novels, the best of which is *The Sport of Gods* (o.p., 1902). Its black protagonist, Berry Hamilton, is framed for a theft and sentenced to ten years in prison. His wife and children flee to New York, where they become involved in vice. A deathbed confession by Hamilton's white accuser results in his release from prison. He comes North to be reunited with and save his family. This work is Dunbar's most direct commentary on the damage racism inflicts on the lives of blacks.   RL

33   Edwards, Junius. ***If We Must Die***. Howard Univ. Pr. 1984, $9.95 (0-88258-117-1). 124pp. Fiction.

Will Harris, the protagonist of *If We Must Die*, is a Korean War veteran. He tries to register to vote but is prevented from doing so. Fired from his job and blacklisted, he is set upon by a white mob that almost kills him. At the end of the novel he is semiconscious and perhaps dying. This novel is a searing indictment of Southern racism and brutality.

Edwards also is known for his short stories, such as "Duel with the Clock" (1967), which explores the plight of soldiers addicted to drugs. His most famous story is "Mother Dear and Daddy" (1966), in which five recently orphaned siblings listen to their relatives argue over who will take which children. All the relatives want the three light-skinned girls, but none want the two darker-skinned boys.   RL

34   Edwards-Yearwood, Grace. ***In the Shadow of the Peacock***. Ivy 1989, $3.95 (0-8041-0419-0). 304pp. Fiction.

This novel, which follows events from the 1940s through the 1960s, opens as Noel and Frieda leave the racism of the South for the promise of good jobs in Northern defense industries. Soon after they arrive in Harlem, though, a riot breaks out and Noel is killed trying to save an old woman from a burning building. That night Frieda gives birth to their daughter, Celia. As Celia grows, Frieda strives to keep her safe from racism and, later, from the temptations of the Peacock Bar. At first Celia creates an identity for herself through her sexual relationships with men, but eventually she comes to see them as self-centered and vain—another sort of peacock. Celia deals with overt and subtle racism, first as a college student and then as a token black employee at a publishing house. This beautifully written first novel, set against a sweeping backdrop of much recent history, captivates readers with its strongly drawn, compelling characters.   RL

35   Ellis, Trey. *Platitudes*. Random 1988, $9.00 (0-394-75439-5). 160pp. Fiction.

Dewayne Wellington struggles to write a novel about sixteen-year-old Earle Tyner and his efforts to win the love of beautiful Dorothy, a student at a fancy Catholic school in New York City. Unable to complete the book, Wellington advertises for a collaborator. Answering the ad is Isshee Ayam, the award-winning author of *Hog Jowl Junction* and *My Big Ol' Feets Gon' Stomp Dat Evil Down*. Soon, though, she expresses contempt for Wellington's "misogynistic" writing. In composing her part of Wellington's story, Ayam relocates Earle to the rural South, where he is guided and inspired by strong women of color who teach him pride in his heritage. This comic novel is really two books in one. In the chapters purportedly written by Wellington, it offers a jaundiced view of teen life and fantasies in contemporary urban America. In the chapters by Ayam, Ellis creates a wicked parody of the themes and styles of Alice Walker and Gloria Naylor. Ellis raises important questions about the way African-American authors address race and gender. Some may be offended by Ellis's crude humor and satire, but others will enjoy this work of masterly parody by a promising new author.   RL

36   Ellison, Ralph. *Invisible Man*. Random 1992, $17.50 (0-679-60015-9); $10.00 (0-679-72313-7). 568pp. Fiction.

The unnamed protagonist of this novel aspires to become the next Booker T. Washington. But his true fate is foreshadowed early in the novel when his white benefactors amuse themselves by blindfolding him and making him fight other young black men. He is expelled from college for showing a white trustee the poverty of the nearby black town. Looking for a job, he carries a briefcase containing what he thinks is a letter of recommendation from the president of his college; in fact, the letter recommends that he be kept on the run. In New York City, he is used and then rejected by the white radical Brotherhood in its rivalry with the Black Nationalist Ras. At the conclusion of the novel, the protagonist falls into a hole. He finally reads the contents of the letter in his briefcase, realizes he has been betrayed, and decides to write the book we have just read: a chronicle of African-American invisibility.

Critics often cite *Invisible Man* as the best American novel since 1945. At his death in 1994, Ellison was at work on a long-awaited second novel. He also published two books of literary and political essays, *Shadow and Act* (orig. pub. 1964; Random, 1972) and *Going to the Territory* (Random, 1986), which advocate the integrationist and humanistic point of view of his great novel.   RL

37   Fair, Ronald L. *World of Nothing: Two Novellas*. Ultramarine 1970, $25.00 (0-89366-096-5); Chatham $11.95 (0-911860-44-4). 133pp. Fiction.

The title character of "Jerome," the first novella in this volume, is the son of a black woman named Lula and a white priest. While everyone who encounters Jerome sees him as a religious figure, Lula sees him as a devil and murders him. At the end of the story, Jerome is placed in the position of crucifixion, becoming a black Christ. "World of Nothing" describes the lives of an activist named Red Top, the wealthy Joanne, and Frenchy Coolbreeze, a white jazz musician who befriends and follows Red Top.

Fair's first novel, *Many Thousands Gone* (o.p., 1965), is set in the fictional town of Jacobsville, Mississippi, where whites use brutal violence and psychological intimidation to keep blacks in slavery until 1938—more than seventy years after Emancipation. *We Can't Breathe* (o.p.), winner of the ALA Best Book Award for 1972, is about five boys who, like Fair himself, grew up in Chicago during the 1930s. Fair's work combines vivid descriptions of social realism with carefully structured religious allusions in his plots and imagery.

RL

38   Fauset, Jessie R. ***The Chinaberry Tree and Selected Writings.*** Repr. of 1931 ed. Frwd. by Marcy Knopf. Northeastern Univ. Pr. 1994, $13.95 (1-55553-207-1). 384pp. Fiction.

The Chinaberry Tree, originally published in 1931, is the third novel by noted Harlem Renaissance writer Jessie Fauset. It tells the story of narrow-mindedness among residents of the town of Red Hook, New Jersey. The title refers to the huge chinaberry tree that Colonel Halloway, a white man, brought from the South for his lifelong lover, Aunt Sal, a black woman who had been his mother's maid. Though he cannot marry her because of her color, Halloway does everything possible for Aunt Sal and the beautiful daughter he has by her, Laurentine. Aunt Sal is content with her life, even though she suffers enormously, not only from white prejudice but from the reproaches of her fellow blacks. The novel underscores the importance to the black townspeople of maintaining a strict moral code, but it also conveys the harsh impact of that code on the innocent girl Laurentine.   CH

39   Fisher, Rudolph. ***The Conjure-Man Dies: A Mystery Tale of Dark Harlem***. Univ. of Michigan Pr. 1992, $34.50 (0-472-09492-0); $13.95 (0-472-06492-4). 300pp. Fiction.

Rudolph Fisher, graduate of Brown University and a physician who practiced in Harlem, was also a central figure in the Harlem Renaissance because of his novels and short stories. *The Conjure Man Dies*, an elaborately plotted novel, is considered a groundbreaking work of its genre because its heroes are two accomplished black New York City police detectives. They set out to solve the murder of a Harvard-educated African king, who had settled in Harlem to become a spiritual advisor. This work and Fisher's first novel, *The Walls of Jericho* (orig. pub. 1928; Ayer, 1969), depict Harlem in its pre-Depression heyday. Fisher is especially attentive to the linguistic and lifestyle differences among blacks and readily mocks the pretensions of the new black middle class, especially its desire for integration with, and respect from, whites.

RL

40   Flowers, Arthur. ***Another Good Loving Blues***. Viking 1993, $20.00 (0-670-84821-2); Ballantine $10.00 (0-345-38103-3). 224pp. Fiction.

Blues pianist Lucas Bodeen is in love with conjure woman Melvina Dupree in Sweetwater, Arkansas in 1918. Melvina accompanies Lucas to Memphis, where he plays the blues, inspired by his love for her. Eventually, though, Lucas becomes incapacitated by whiskey. Melvina is encouraged by Hootowl, an old conjure man, to go to Mississippi to search for her mother, Effie, who is also a conjure woman and who had deserted her when she was just a baby. Hootowl also gets Lucas to stop drinking and accompany Melvina on her search.

Flowers has written an absorbing love story. His style is inspired in part by the African griot (storyteller) tradition; indeed the narrator of the novel is a griot. Blues music also sets the tone for the novel and allows the narrator to express the depth of the love between Lucas and Melvina. Flowers paints a glowing portrait of the lives and culture that many African Americans created for themselves in the first part of the twentieth century.   RL

41   Forrest, Leon. *Two Wings to Veil My Face*. Pref. by Toni Morrison. Another Chicago Pr. 1988, $8.95 (0-9614644-4-5). 320pp. Fiction.

Leon Forrest began his career as a reporter for various community newspapers on Chicago's South Side. He went on to edit *Muhammad Speaks* (o.p.). Since the publication of his first novel, *There Is a Tree More Ancient Than Eden* (orig. pub. 1973; Another Chicago Pr., 1988), Forrest has devoted himself to teaching and to literary endeavors. His first two novels, this one and *The Bloodworth Orphans* (orig. pub. 1977; Another Chicago Pr., 1987), share many of the same vividly drawn characters. Reflecting the fact that slavery shattered many families, Forrest's protagonists have been abandoned by their parents. By portraying their search for personal identity, Forrest presents the spiritual and political choices open to African Americans. The most vital decision is whether to escape the violence and sexuality of street life through the pursuit of religion and whether to accept the teachings of Catholicism, fundamentalist Protestantism, or Islam. Forrest's complex and elaborate plots are enlivened by a style that uses the language and imagery of spirituals, oral storytelling, and popular songs to convey the characters' emotions and actions.   RL

42   French, Albert. *Billy*. Viking 1993, $20.00 (0-670-85013-6). 224pp. Fiction.

This grimly realistic novel, the author's first, is set in Banes, Mississippi in 1937. Slow-witted and immature Billy Lee Turner, ten years old, lives in the Patch, the poor black section of town, with his loving mother, Cinder. One day he and a friend are attacked by two teenage white girls. Struggling to free himself, Billy stabs one of the girls with his penknife and kills her. In a gripping scene, the boy and his mother flee through the woods, tracked by Sheriff Tom and Deputy Hill. Billy is caught and tried, and although the killing was clearly unintentional and Billy is incapable of understanding what he did, he is convicted of first-degree murder. Although sentenced to death, Billy at first is unhappy simply because he is separated from his mother. Only when another prisoner is electrocuted does Billy begin to realize the true horror of the fate that awaits him. The racism of Mississippi officials and the gruesomeness of capital punishment are searingly conveyed in the conclusion of this powerful and affecting work.   RL

43   Fuller, Charles. *A Soldier's Play*. o.p. Drama.

Winner of the 1982 Pulitzer Prize for drama and the basis for a major motion picture (released under the title *A Soldier's Story*), this play examines the circumstances surrounding the murder of an oppressive black sergeant during World War II. The sergeant, Vernon Waters, commands a company of black troops. Despite his long record of bravery, he suffers ridicule by a group of racist white officers. At the same time he adopts many of their attitudes toward blacks. His dictatorial methods and contempt for his soldiers leads to the suicide of a young soldier. When Waters himself is murdered, suspicion falls on the white racists. However, a black officer sent to investigate the case discovers that the guilty person is a man from Waters's own company who wanted revenge for the sergeant's harsh treatment of his fellow blacks. This highly regarded work explores the deadly consequences of racism.   LML

44   Gaines, Ernest J. *The Autobiography of Miss Jane Pittman*. Bantam 1982, $4.99 (0-553-26357-9). 256pp. Fiction.

In this novel, a woman who is over one hundred years old looks back on her life, which began when she was born into slavery before the Civil War. After Emancipation, the young free woman exchanges her slave name, Ticey, for the more distinguished name Jane. Unable to bear children, Jane becomes the foster mother of Ned, who opens a school for freed blacks. Soon, though, Ned is run out of town by the Ku Klux Klan. When he returns to Louisiana to preach black civil rights, he is killed by a vigilante. As Jane nears the end of her life, she is shaken by news of the murder of Jimmy Aaron, a young civil rights worker. Jane joins the protests against his death by drinking from a whites-only water fountain.

Gaines's moving and panoramic historical novel found a broad audience as a television film starring Cicely Tyson. His 1978 novel, *In My Father's House* (Random, 1992), depicts the tension between Phillip Martin, a civil rights leader, and his illegitimate son, Robert X.   RL

45   Gaines, Ernest J. *A Lesson Before Dying*. Knopf 1993, $21.00 (0-679-41477-0); Random $11.00 (0-679-74166-6). 236pp. Fiction.

This novel, set in Louisiana in 1948, is about Jefferson, a semiliterate twenty-one-year-old black man who is tried for his role as a bystander in the murder of a white. His attorney attempts to defend him by arguing that he is as ignorant as a hog, but Jefferson is convicted and sentenced to death. Jefferson's godmother, Miss Emma, asks a local teacher, Grant, to teach the young man a lesson in his own humanity so he can die with dignity. Grant's efforts are nearly undermined, not only by his own cynicism but by Reverend Ambrose, who is more concerned about saving Jefferson's soul than about his search for dignity. Through small actions and expressions of love and concern, Jefferson learns to recognize his essential humanity. The courage with which he faces execution teaches Grant a transforming lesson.

Throughout the work Gaines focuses on his central theme: the meaning of manhood. His powerful writing prevents the story from turning melodramatic. The interactions between the black protagonists and the white characters effectively convey the tension prevalent in the South of that era.   RL

46 Giovanni, Nikki. ***Black Feeling, Black Talk, Black Judgement***. Morrow 1971, $7.45 (0-688-25294-X). Poetry.

The publication of the works in this omnibus edition marked Nikki Giovanni as a powerful new voice among African-American writers. Her poetic style, influenced by the blues tradition, emphasizes rhythmic meter. Her work is both political and personal. Politically, Giovanni's poems express her view that blacks must "kill the nigger" in themselves and embrace the Third World revolutionary movements with which they should be linked. She is critical of American black soldiers who killed nonwhite (Asian) people during the Vietnam War. On the personal level, many of her poems deal with issues of love, sex, and her growing awareness of the meaning of black womanhood. Her extended autobiographical essay, *Gemini* (Viking, 1976), deals with similar themes.   RL

47 Golden, Marita. ***Long Distance Life***. Doubleday 1989, $18.95 (0-385-19455-2); Ballantine $10.00 (0-345-37616-1). 336pp. Fiction.

Filled with the drama and upheaval of a modern American family, this novel, the story of three generations in an urban setting, introduces us to the Johnson family. Naomi is the strong-willed daughter of sharecroppers who goes North and, through hard work, is able to purchase several attractive houses and become a landlord. Naomi's husband, her one true love, is Rayford Johnson, an educated, proud man and a follower of Black Nationalist leader Marcus Garvey. Their daughter Esther gives birth out of wedlock to a son fathered by her married lover. Although herself the product of loving parents, Esther is incapable of giving her son the love he deserves because she hasn't yet learned to love herself. After a nervous breakdown, she realizes she has something to offer and joins the civil rights organization in Birmingham. When she returns five years later, she resumes her relationship with her now divorced lover, becomes pregnant again, and gives this new child all the love she now possesses. The story has a tragic ending, yet the readers are enriched for having shared this family's experience.   CH

48 Gomez, Jewelle. ***The Gilda Stories***. Firebrand 1991, $20.95 (0-932379-95-8); $9.95 (0-932379-94-X). 256pp. Fiction.

When the reader first meets Gilda and her companion, Bird, they are presented through the eyes of a young girl, an escaped slave who during her flight killed a man who tried to rape her. In the course of the novel Gilda lives a number of lives. In her first incarnation, she is the mistress of a Louisiana brothel in 1850. Gilda and the young girl are able to read each other's thoughts; indeed, Gilda and the girl seem to merge by the end of the first chapter. Gilda later appears in California in 1890; as a widow in rural Missouri in 1921; a beautician in South End, Boston, in 1955; an off-Broadway actress in 1971; and a singer-songwriter in New York in 1981. Like the slave girl, Gilda murders several men who attempt to force themselves upon her sexually. The final two chapters take place in the future: Gilda is a reclusive romance writer in New Hampshire in 2020, and later she lives in Machu Pichu, an ancient Incan fortress in Peru. There, no longer needing to flee, Gilda is reunited with all the companions of her many lives. Although she had been intimate with several women, she feels closest to Bird, who follows Gilda through time and space. Throughout the novel Gilda's identity is malleable and ambiguous, yet she always retains the power to read the minds of others. This supernatural fantasy evokes the unity among women of color and draws connections across significant moments of struggle in African-American history over the past two centuries. RL

49 Guy, Rosa. *A Measure of Time*. Bantam 1986, $4.50 (0-553-25611-4). 368pp. Fiction.

This panoramic novel traces the life of Dorine Davis, beginning in the 1920s when she is eight years old in Montgomery, Alabama, and continuing until she becomes, at age forty, "the original self-made millionaire" in Harlem. The characters Dorine encounters over the years reflect the range of personalities found within the black community, including those who, like Dorine, sometimes turn to illegal business activities to make their way in life. The author, who was born in Trinidad and lives in Manhattan, addresses gender and racial conflict and explores the relations between African Americans and Afro-Caribbeans.

Guy is best known for her young adult novels, including *The Friends* (Henry Holt, 1973), *Ruby* (orig. pub. 1976; Dell, 1992), and a series of mystery novels that feature Imamu Jones. RL

50 Haley, Alex. *Roots*. Doubleday 1976, $25.00 (0-385-03787-2); Dell $6.99 (0-440-17464-3). 736pp. Fiction.

This famous and immensely popular novel opens in 1767, when Kunta Kinte, a Mandinka warrior from an old and respected family, is kidnapped from Gambia by white slave traders and sold into slavery in the American colonies. Kinte, the most vivid character in this novel, possesses an unquenchable desire for freedom. His attempts to escape cease only when his owner amputates his foot. Kinte passes on his knowledge of, and pride in, his African heritage to his daughter Kizzy, who in turn raises her half-white son, George. With 200 years of American history as his backdrop, Haley traces his family's emergence into freedom after the Civil War and their struggle with segregation and racism throughout the ensuing decades. The story ends with Haley's return to Africa to discover his roots. In 1977 this book won both a special Pulitzer Prize and the National Book Award and was later made into two spectacularly successful television miniseries. RL

51 Hansberry, Lorraine. *A Raisin in the Sun*. Random 1994, $4.99 (0-679-75533-0). 130pp. Drama.

This play is based on an incident in Hansberry's own life. As the first African-American family to move into a formerly all-white Chicago neighborhood, the Hansberrys turned to the NAACP for legal help in overturning an ordinance restricting home sales there to whites only. In the play, a young man, Walter Lee Younger, wants to use the proceeds from his father's life insurance policy to buy a liquor store. Instead, his mother, Lena, uses the money to buy a house in a white neighborhood. When the whites offer to buy the house back, Walter Lee learns to place his racial identity ahead of his personal ambition and refuses to sell. This character embodies not just the rage and harshness found in many American black men, but also their strength and their desire for dignity. The play won the New York Drama Critics Circle Award and in 1961 was made into a film starring Sidney Poitier. Hansberry died in 1965 at the age of thirty-four.   RL

52   Harper, Michael, and Anthony Walton, eds. ***Every Shut Eye Ain't Asleep: An Anthology of Poetry by African Americans Since 1945***. Little, Brown 1994, $12.95 (0-316-34710-8). 327pp. Poetry.

This anthology includes major poems by thirty-five African-American writers active since 1945. Most of the poets are well known and have published numerous volumes of their own work. By bringing these authors together in one book, it is possible to see the common themes and issues they explore: racism and political commitment; childhood and families; the experience of exile; and the contributions of African-American cultural figures past and present. Jazz and the blues receive a great deal of attention, and many of the poems take on the rhythm of those uniquely African-American musical forms. For each author, the editors provide a brief biography, a commentary, and a selected bibliography. Overall, the poems are well chosen to give the reader a sense of the rich variety of contemporary African-American verse.   LML

53   Henderson, George Wylie. ***Ollie Miss***. Repr. of 1935 ed. Intro. by Blyden Jackson. Univ. of Alabama Pr. 1988, $12.50 (0-8173-0388-X). 304pp. Fiction.

This novel, first published in 1935, is set in the Deep South in the early part of this century. The protagonist, an eighteen-year-old girl named Ollie, mysteriously arrives on Uncle Alex's farm to work as a hired hand. Neither the reader nor the other characters in the novel ever learn of her origins. The author conveys the rigor and bleakness of life on a farm in the South. It is essentially an all-black world; the only white character in the novel makes a brief appearance but never speaks. Ollie is abandoned by her only love, Jule. He offers to come back to her when he learns she is carrying his child, but she rejects him. Ollie is an unsentimental, independent, and engaging character who attempts to live equally with men by working as hard as they do.

Henderson's second novel, *Jule* (Univ. of Alabama Pr., 1989), first published in 1946, is a sequel to *Ollie Miss*. Its main character is young Jule, the illegitimate son of Ollie and old Jule. Some of the whites the boy meets in rural Alabama are friendly, but others are racist. Jule is forced to flee when he fights off a white rival for his black girlfriend's attention. In New York City he encounters the brutalities of urban ghetto life, but eventually, with help from a white friend, he becomes a union printer. The novel ends when Jule returns to the South to attend his mother's funeral and to marry his old sweetheart.   RL

54   Himes, Chester. ***A Rage in Harlem***. Random 1989, $8.00 (0-679-72040-5). 159pp. Fiction.

Chester Himes is best known for his detective novels, which are set in Harlem and which feature the exploits of two black detectives, Coffin Ed Johnson and Grave Digger Jones. Himes wrote these works, which are influenced by Raymond Chandler, after he moved to Europe in 1954. Although Himes wrote in English, most of his books were first published in French and later issued in the United States.

A Rage in Harlem is a slight revision of the author's earlier *For Love of Imabelle* (o.p., 1957). The protagonist, Jackson, lives with Imabelle, who swindles him. Jackson is shaken down twice, first by the police and then by his crooked brother Goldy, whose main scam is selling tickets to heaven to innocent Harlemites. Detectives Johnson and Jones are violent avengers who brutally beat and sometimes kill the crooks, even when such punishment is of no help to the victims of crime. *A Rage in Harlem* was made into a film starring Danny Glover and Gregory Hines in 1991.

Himes's first novel, *If He Hollers Let Him Go* (orig. pub. 1945; Buccaneer, 1994), is set in Los Angeles during World War II and chronicles the humiliation of a serious black factory worker falsely accused of rape by a white woman. —RL

55   Hughes, Langston. *The Langston Hughes Reader*. Braziller 1981, $17.50 (0-8076-0057-1). 502pp. Poetry.

Langston Hughes is the most famous African-American poet of this century. His early poems, collected in *The Weary Blues* (o.p., 1926), depart from the sometimes precious and elitist poetic style of the Harlem Renaissance. In his blank verse, Hughes makes use of contemporary black vernacular and the rhythms of folk and blues music. During the Depression, his poetry became more explicitly radical as Hughes became attracted to the antiracist and egalitarian ideals of the Communist Party. *Montage of a Dream Deferred* offers a verse portrait of postwar Harlem. This volume contains "Harlem," his most famous and widely quoted poem, which asks, "What happens to a dream deferred?" The dominant theme in Hughes's poetry is the everyday life of American blacks living with racism, poverty, and limited opportunities.   RL

56   Hughes, Langston. *The Ways of the White Folks*. Random 1990, $9.00 (0-679-72817-1). 256pp. Fiction.

The connecting theme in these stories is the insincerity and racism of whites. In "Little Dog," for example, a white spinster, Clara Briggs, meets the black janitor of her apartment building when she adopts a little white dog. Realizing she is sexually attracted to the janitor, she moves to another building rather than confront her unacceptable desires. "Father and Son" tells the story of Bert Lewis, the illegitimate son of a white man, Colonel Thomas Norwood, and a black woman. Norwood pays for Bert's college education in Atlanta but refuses to acknowledge Bert when he visits home. Furious, Bert strangles him. A white mob lynches both Bert and his docile brother Willie. Hughes's other prose works include the semiautobiographical novel *Not Without Laughter* (orig. pub. 1930; Macmillan, 1995) and several volumes of "Simple Stories," in which Harlem street philosopher Jesse B. Semple uses his college-educated sidekick as a foil for his humor and cynicism.   RL

57   Hunter, Kristin. *God Bless the Child*. Repr. of 1964 ed. Intro. by Phil Petrie. Howard Univ. Pr. 1987, $8.95 (0-88258-154-6). 336pp. Fiction.

Rosie Fleming, the heroine of this novel, lives with her grandmother, a maid who serves a rich white family. Granny has adopted the haughty airs of her employers and shares their prejudices even after they fire her. Rosie's mother,

Queenie, is earthy and promiscuous. As ambitious as Granny, Rosie works a respectable day job, waits on tables in a sleazy bar at night, and makes money on the side as a numbers runner. Eventually, Rosie saves enough money to buy the home once owned by Granny's former employers, but the house turns out to be infested with roaches. Rosie suffers a nervous breakdown and dies. Despite its many subplots and characters, this novel presents a clear view of black urban life in the North and the ways in which blacks are often betrayed by whites.

Hunter's 1966 novel *The Landlord* (o.p.) was made into a feature film. Her children's books, including *The Soul Brothers and Sister Lou* (o.p., 1968) and *Boss Cat* (o.p., 1971), present positive black role models who avoid such traps as teenage pregnancy and religious escapism and who instead work hard to escape the ghetto.   RL

58   Hurston, Zora Neale. ***Their Eyes Were Watching God.*** Frwd. by Ruby Dee; Intro. by Sherley Williams; Illus. by Jerry Pinkney. Univ. of Illinois Pr. 1991, $24.95 (0-252-01778-1); HarperCollins $13.00 (0-06-091650-8). 288pp. Fiction.

Zora Neale Hurston—writer, folklorist, anthropologist, winner of a Guggenheim Fellowship—is probably the most famous woman artist to emerge from the Harlem Renaissance. Many critics cite this novel as one of the most important works of this century. Although the protagonist, Janie Crawford, is very beautiful, she has never known what it feels like to be loved. She works hard but receives few rewards until Teacake, a man many years her junior, comes into her life. Amidst a great deal of gossip, they leave the town together. Through the adventure they share, Janie comes to realize the true meaning of love.

The narrative structure of the book has Janie recounting the story of her "marriage" to Teacake through conversations with a friend. Many African-American writers use this device; it is common, for example, in J. California Cooper's early short stories. Like the visiting friend, the reader is taken on a magical journey through the recollections of the speaker.

Alice Walker, herself an accomplished author, is credited with reintroducing Zora Neale Hurston's work to the reading public. In the late 1970s, while doing research for a short story about voodoo practices, Walker stumbled across *Mules and Men* (Borgo, 1990), Hurston's book of folklore, and from that point she dedicated herself to restoring Hurston's work to print.   CH

59   Johnson, Charles. ***Middle Passage.*** Macmillan 1990, $17.95 (0-689-11968-2); NAL $9.00 (0-452-26638-6). 160pp. Fiction.

Johnson's acclaimed novel features Rutherford Calhoun, a black man and ne'er-do-well who stows away on a ship to escape the twin terrors of debt and marriage. The ship, however, is bound for Africa to collect its cargo: slaves.

Middle Passage reflects Johnson's meticulous research in the literature of the sea and the horrific facts of slavery: the hideous conditions on board, the rampant disease, the human suffering. Typical of the author's attention to detail is his description of the captain, who enjoys his reputation as a "tight packer" of slaves. Johnson explains how the packing was done and vividly portrays its deadly consequences. By conveying the sights, sounds, and smells of the voyage, Johnson gives his readers not only an engaging piece of literature but also a compelling lesson in history. This novel won the National Book Award in 1990; Johnson was the first African-American male writer to earn that prize since Ralph Ellison won for *Invisible Man* in 1953.   CH

60   Johnson, James Weldon. ***The Autobiography of an Ex-Colored Man.*** Viking 1990, $6.95 (0-14-018402-3). 240pp. Fiction.

This fictionalized autobiography recounts the life of an unnamed protagonist, the son of a white man and a black woman, beginning with his idealized childhood in rural Georgia. When the father deserts the family, the boy and his mother move to Connecticut, where they encounter racism for the first time. His best friends are Shiny, an intelligent and proud black kid, and Red, a dumb white boy. Later, on his way to Atlanta University, he is robbed of his college tuition money. Forced to work, he becomes a cigar roller in Florida, a gambler in New York City, and a ragtime piano player who is befriended by a wealthy white man and taken on tour in Europe. Returning to the United States, he visits with wealthy urban blacks in the North and in Atlanta and then witnesses a lynching in the countryside. Terrified by the violence, the narrator decides to pass as a white man. He returns to New York City and marries a white woman. When he meets his old friend Shiny he feels remorse for abandoning his black heritage and for missing out on the opportunity to contribute to the history of his people.

First published in 1912, this book became for many whites the definitive account of black life in the United States, presenting a view of white racism, miscegenation, and class and color differences among blacks. Johnson is also the author of *God's Trombones* (orig. pub. 1927; Viking, 1990).   RL

61   Jones, Edward P. ***Lost in the City.*** Morrow 1992, $19.00 (0-688-11526-8); HarperCollins $10.00 (0-06-097557-1). 256pp. Fiction.

The fourteen stories in this powerful and beautifully written first book are all set in Washington, D.C. Although the characters are oppressed by the brutality of the city and suffer from poverty and racism, they never lose their pride nor do they express self-pity. In "The Night Rhonda Ferguson Was Killed," the protagonist, Cassandra, hears that her friend Rhonda is about to sign a recording contract. Encouraged by her friend's success, Cassandra breaks with her family and friends and makes plans for a new life, only to learn that Rhonda has been killed by her boyfriend. In "Marie," an eighty-six-year-old woman tells her life story to a student conducting a project in oral history. By recounting the indignities she suffers during her endless efforts to prove to the Social Security office that she still qualifies for benefits, Marie expresses her sense of self-worth and teaches the student a valuable lesson. Jones's ability to create memorable characters and convey their emotions is shown again in "A New Man," the story of Woodrow L. Cunningham, who wanders the city in search of the teenage daughter he had chased away in a moment of anger.   RL

62   Jones, Gayl. ***Corregidora.*** Repr. of 1975 ed. Beacon 1986, $12.00 (0-8070-6315-0). 185pp. Fiction.

Ursa Corregidora, heroine of this novel, learns how her grandmother suffered at the hands of Simon Corregidora, a Portuguese slaver in Brazil. Ursa's grandmother and her mother, Simon's child, urge her to "make generations" of black children so that they can remember those indignities and live beyond them. But when Ursa's drunken, violent husband Mutt throws her down a flight of stairs, she miscarries and has to undergo a hysterectomy. Ursa's relationships with men parallel her grandmother's abuse as Simon's slave. Ultimately Ursa finds solace as a blues singer. Her inner strength allows her to overcome male brutality and live as an independent woman.

Jones also is the author of a second novel, *Eva's Man* (Beacon, 1987), and of short stories and poetry.   RL

63   Jones, Nettie. *Mischief Makers*. McKay 1991, $9.00 (0-679-72785-X). 163pp. Fiction.

In the 1920s, Raphael de Baptiste, young and beautiful, with only a "chocolate drop" of Negro blood in her veins, leaves her Detroit home and her black lover to become a nurse—a white nurse—farther north. There, in the beautiful wilderness of Leelanau County, she meets Mishe Masaube, a Chippewa Indian, the man she will marry and by whom she will bear three daughters. The daughters are all beautiful, with looks that defy all racial labels.

This highly erotic historical tale is also a novel of race and racism in America—a sometimes cautionary fable of those brave or foolish souls who cross the boundaries and taboos set by our society. Haunting and magical, *Mischief Makers* is a visionary novel of color and class in America, and it confirms Nettie Jones's reputation as an exciting new author.   CH

64   Kelley, William M. *Different Drummer*. Doubleday 1990, $8.95 (0-385-41390-4). 223pp. Fiction.

This novel takes place in 1957 in Sutton, a fictional small Southern town near the Gulf Coast. The protagonist, Tucker Caliban, decides there is no hope of finding racial justice in the South. He salts his farmland, shoots his livestock, burns down his house, and, accompanied by his wife and young child, walks north. Inspired by his example, other blacks follow him. The whites in the town—especially the Willson family, the county's main landowners—bemoan the loss of their workers, the backbone of the local economy. They also resent the fact that the targets of their racial animosity have left. In a flashback, readers learn that the patriarch of the Willson family, a Confederate general, was a slaveholder whose property included Caliban's great-great-grandfather. The Reverend Bennett Bradshaw comes to Sutton to organize the black activism sparked by Caliban's action. But the poor and ignorant whites, who ordinarily pass their days milling around the general store, erupt in fury and lynch Bradshaw.

This novel of the early civil rights era weaves elements of fantasy into an essentially realistic situation. In doing so, the book captures some of the surrealism of life in the South at the end of the Jim Crow era.   RL

65   Kenan, Randall. *Let the Dead Bury Their Dead*. Harcourt 1992, $19.95 (0-15-149886-5); $10.95 (0-15-650515-0). 334pp. Fiction.

This collection of twelve short stories is set in the imaginary town of Tims Creek, North Carolina, which also serves as the setting of Kenan's novel *A*

Visitation of Spirits (Doubleday, 1990). The isolated town was founded by an escaped slave as a haven for his fellow refugees. The stories and folklore of the community are written down by a scholar, Reginald Kain. The supernatural and the place of eroticism in people's lives are central themes in these stories. In "Clarence and the Dead," a toddler capable of speaking in full sentences conveys romantic messages to Ellsworth Botts from his dead lover. In "Ragnarok! The Day the Gods Die," the Reverend Hezekiah Borden gives a funeral sermon over the casket of a woman who was his secret mistress. As he tries to recite passages from the Bible, however, his words are mysteriously transformed into lurid stories of their sexual escapades. In "Tell Me, Tell Me," the spirit of a small black child, who decades before was murdered by a judge, appears and confronts the judge's widow. These powerful stories portray believable and sympathetic characters who inhabit a world both mundane and magical.   RL

66   Killens, John Oliver. ***Youngblood.*** Repr. of 1953 ed. Frwd. by Addison Gayle. Univ. of Georgia Pr. 1982, $14.95 (0-8203-0602-9). 512pp. Fiction.

Set in fictional Crossroads, Georgia at the height of Jim Crow segregation in the early twentieth century, this novel tells the story of the Youngblood family. Joe and his son, Robby, struggle to maintain their dignity in the face of white racism while reaching out to the few whites willing to treat them with friendship and fairness. In a powerful scene, Robby fights with white boys to defend his sister, Jennie Lee. Robby is arrested; to secure his release from jail, his mother, Laurie Lee, is forced to whip the boy while the white police look on. Joe is severely beaten while demonstrating for his civil rights; as he is dying, a decent white man offers his blood for a transfusion. At the conclusion of the novel, Robby becomes a union organizer.

John Killen is a prolific author of novels, plays, short stories, essays, and children's books and an active mentor of younger writers through the Harlem Writers Guild. His novel *And Then We Heard the Thunder* (orig. pub. 1963; Howard Univ. Pr., 1984) depicts an all-black Army unit during World War II.

RL

67   Larsen, Nella. ***Quicksand.*** Repr. of 1928 ed. Greenwood 1970, $39.75 (0-8371-1127-7). 246pp. Fiction.

Like the author herself, the heroine of this novel is the daughter of a West Indian man and a Danish woman. Helga Crane seeks both a racial identity and sexual fulfillment. She decides not to marry the president of a black college because she finds him sexually inhibited. After traveling to Chicago, New York, and Copenhagen, she has a religious awakening, marries the Reverend Pleasant Green, and ends up the mother of four children, living in poverty in the South and regretting the choices she has made.

Larsen's second novel, *Passing* (orig. pub. 1929; Ayer, 1970), is about a mulatto who passes for white and has a white husband. But attracted to the black world of Harlem, she reveals her racial heritage.

The author's career was a short one. She endured a bitter divorce and, even more traumatic, was falsely accused of plagiarizing her short story "Sanctuary." She gave up writing and worked as a nurse in New York City.   RL

68   Lester, Julius. ***Do Lord Remember Me***. o.p. Fiction.

35

UNITED STATES:
AFRICAN AMERICANS

The protagonist of this novel, the eighty-three-year-old Reverend Joshua Smith, realizes that he will soon die and looks back upon his life. Born in 1900, Smith still recalls the stories his father told him about their ancestor, a slave named Tremble. Tremble won his own freedom by betraying fellow slaves who were planning a rebellion. Tremble feared the uprising would end in a massacre of the slaves. Throughout his own life, Smith, like Tremble, has been an accommodationist. To prevent a violent confrontation, for example, Smith once made his son Josh apologize to a white man for a wrong he did not commit. Although Smith is a prominent evangelist and has been financially successful, his other son, a civil rights activist, regards his father with contempt. Lester presents Joshua Smith's compromises with compassion and understanding, ultimately portraying the Reverend as a victim of the racism he did not have the strength to confront.

Lester is best known for his books for children and young adults and his collections of African-American folktales. He also is the author of *Lovensong: Becoming a Jew* (o.p., 1991).   RL

69   Lorde, Audre. ***The Black Unicorn***. Norton 1995, $9.00 (0-393-31237-2). 136pp. Poetry.

Audre Lorde's poetry gives honest and eloquent expression to her experiences as an African American, a lesbian, a feminist, and a poet. The poems in this work draw on African symbolism and folktales to express racial pride, explore the dimensions of spirituality, and celebrate the role of mothers in preserving black life and culture. Her love poems are unusual for the frankness with which they acknowledge her lovers and her erotic feelings. Lorde's poems express her bond with the victims of prejudice in the United States, South Africa, and Latin America and reveal the parallels that exist between racial oppression and sexual oppression.

The author of other volumes of poetry, including *From a Land Where Other People Live* (Broadside, 1973), Lorde is also known for her memoirs. *The Cancer Journals* (Aunt Lute, 1980) discusses her mastectomy and fear of death. *A Burst of Light* (Firebrand, 1988) describes the recurrence and spread of her cancer and her coming to terms with death.   RL

70   Major, Clarence. ***Such Was the Season***. o.p. Fiction.

The main character of this novel is Annie Eliza, matriarch of a black middle-class family in the new South who sees her children as they really are and loves them in spite of themselves. After many years in the North, her nephew comes back to Georgia. Annie Eliza teaches him important truths about his past and helps him discover what his future could become. With its memorable characters and its themes of greed, deception, and passion, this novel will stay in the reader's consciousness for years.   CH

71   Marshall, Paule. ***Daughters***. NAL 1992, $11.00 (0-452-26912-1). 416pp. Fiction.

This novel, set in New York City and the West Indian island of Triunion, follows the protagonists from the 1940s to the 1980s. Ursa Beatrice Mackenzie—a middle-class American black woman, selfish and dedicated to her career—has a shallow and unsatisfying relationship with Lowell Carruthers. In her work as a political researcher, she documents how the poor blacks of Midland City, New Jersey, have been betrayed by their black mayor, who is subservient to white business interests. Ursa's story parallels that of her American mother, Estelle, and her West Indian father, Primus Mackenzie. Primus, once a political idealist, is about to sell out the people of his island to American investors who plan to build a resort on the island. Meanwhile, Estelle also succumbs to cynicism as she bemoans the waning energy of the civil rights movement and the dwindling hopes of American blacks.

This powerful plea for principled action and dedication to causes wider than oneself is the central theme in Marshall's work. Her first novel, *Brown Girl, Brownstones* (orig. pub. 1959; Feminist Pr., 1981) describes how the protagonist's strong parents and her Afro-Caribbean heritage help protect her against the racism and materialism of American culture.   RL

72   Marshall, Paule. ***Praisesong for the Widow***. NAL 1984, $9.00 (0-452-26711-0). 256pp. Fiction.

Avey Johnson, sixty-two-years old, is in mourning for her dead husband, Jerome. At the urging of her daughters, Avey takes a Caribbean cruise. While at sea she has two important dreams. In the first, her Aunt Cuney drags her to Ibo Landing, which tradition holds was the spot from which slaves walked on water back to Africa. That dream reminds her of how she has lost her Afro-Caribbean heritage. In the second dream she remembers how her husband stopped loving her and became distant as he worked day and night to make enough money to move the family from the ghetto to the suburbs. Her dreams, combined with the prodding of an old man she meets, convince her to go on an excursion to rediscover her identity as an African. She sells her house in North White Plains and moves to the sea islands off South Carolina, rejecting materialism and vowing to pass on her true culture to her daughters and grandchildren. This memorable novel explores the choices of identity and lifestyle that confront many middle-class African Americans.   RL

73   Mayfield, Julian. ***The Hit and The Long Night.*** Repr. of 1958 ed. Northeastern Univ. Pr. 1989, $14.95 (1-55553-065-6). 310pp. Fiction.

Julian Mayfield was an actor, a writing teacher at Howard University, and an advisor to Kwame Nkrumah of Ghana and Forbes Burnham of Guyana. He is best known for his first two novels, *The Hit* (1957) and *The Long Night* (1958), which are brought together in this volume. Both novels are set in Harlem in the 1950s. *The Hit* tells the story of Hubert Coley, a former store owner who is reduced to being a janitor. He spends the family's income on the numbers, hoping to "hit" but never doing so. He abuses his wife, Gertrude. Their son, James Lee, is so repelled by his parents' lives that he is afraid to marry. The protagonist of *The Long Night*, ten-year-old Steely, is sent by his mother to collect her $27 winnings on the numbers. But Steely's friends rob him. In a series of comic episodes the boy attempts to collect the money through work and theft. Finally he rolls a drunk who turns out to be his father. Both novels present gritty and convincing portraits of bleak lives in the Harlem of the 1950s.   RL

74   McClellan, George M. ***Old Greenbottom Inn and Other Stories*** Repr. of 1906 ed. A M S 1974, $17.45 (0-404-00199-8). Fiction.

This collection of five short stories contains the best work of this early black author. The title story is about a mixed-race woman who falls in love with a white man. The man overcomes racism and other social stigmas to return her love. She becomes pregnant, but the man is murdered by a jealous black who, in turn, is lynched by a white mob. In "The Death of Hanover," the writer uses the death of a racehorse as an opportunity to celebrate the naturalism and emotional expressiveness of his black characters. All the stories are set in Tennessee, where McClellan grew up and where he worked as a school-teacher and principal.

Many of McClellan's sentimental poems appear in *The Path of Dreams* (Ayer, 1916). One poem is an ode to his son, Theodore, who died of tuberculosis after he was denied treatment because of his race. His story "Gabe Yowl," like "Old Green Bottom Inn" and other works, relates the horror of Southern justice as it was applied to blacks.   RL

75   McClusky, John. ***Look What They Done to My Song***. o.p. Fiction.

Mack, the hero of this novel, is a horn player who wants to use music to teach blacks as well as whites about Malcolm X's message of mutual understanding and respect. Mack travels cross-country in search of an audience. In Columbus, Ohio, he falls in love with the materialistic Sassie Mae. On Cape Cod, he learns respect for his black heritage from the elderly Sledges; their sense of pride contrasts with the self-hatred of Mack's lover, Michelle, who is ashamed of being black. He befriends Ubange, a hustler, whose failed schemes force them both to escape to Boston. There he meets Novella, who understands his music and is sympathetic to his political hopes. He also meets Reverend Fuller, who shows Mack that the church is the proper place for his music and his message.

McClusky's second novel, *Mr. America's Last Season Blues* (Louisiana State Univ. Pr., 1983), tells the story of Roscoe Americus, Jr., an injured football player, as he struggles in vain to return to professional sports. In the process, Roscoe comes to realize his true place in the black community.   RL

76   McKay, Claude. ***Banana Bottom***. Repr. of 1970 ed. Harcourt 1974, $7.95 (0-15 610650-7). 317pp. Fiction.

Claude McKay, a Jamaican who settled in New York, was a central figure in the Harlem Renaissance. This novel, first published in 1933 and set in Jamaica, is his most famous. The heroine, Bita Plant, is seduced at age twelve by a white landowner. She is later adopted by Malcolm and Priscilla Craig, Calvinist ministers who give her an English education in an effort to obliterate all traces of her Afro-Caribbean heritage. The Craigs arrange for Bita to marry Herald Newton Day, a divinity student who rejects his blackness. But their plans are foiled when Day is caught committing an act of bestiality. Bita decides to marry Hopping Dick, a handsome and adventurous man, who at the last moment rejects Bita and turns to Christianity. Eventually Bita marries Jubban, a black laborer from her hometown of Banana Bottom. In a happy ending, Bita inherits property from Squire Gensir, a white admirer, and settles down to raise her son Jordan, teaching him the best of both Afro-Caribbean and European culture. McKay's earlier novels, *Home to Harlem* (orig. pub. 1928; Northeastern Univ. Pr., 1987) and *Banjo* (orig. pub. 1929; Harcourt, 1970), feature Caribbean men who live in exile in New York City and Marseilles. RL

77 McKnight, Reginald. ***The Kind of Light That Shines on Texas***. Little, Brown 1992, $18.95 (0-316-56056-1); $9.95 (0-316-56059-6). 194pp. Fiction.

The stories in this collection, largely autobiographical, are humorous and thought-provoking. The title story is a prime example of the author's talent. In a junior high school class there are only three black students: Reginald, Marvin, and Ah-So. Reginald is the only one of the three ever to speak in class. Marvin, two grades behind, does nothing but sleep in class; Ah-So, a black female, just sits and stares. One day in gym class, Reginald accidentally hits the school bully, a white boy, with a ball. The two have a confrontation, but Marvin steps in and beats up the bully. In doing so Marvin seems to be lashing out at all the racial oppression he and his black classmates have suffered. Reginald develops a new-found respect, not only for Marvin, but for his own blackness. CH

78 McMillan, Terry. ***Mama***. Pocket Books 1994, $5.99 (0-671-88448-4). 260pp. Fiction.

Mildred Peacock, the heroine of this novel, divorces her husband because he abuses her. To support their five daughters, Mildred takes a job in a factory, but eventually she is forced to work as a prostitute and to collect welfare. Her daughters do well, moving to California and attending college. The eldest daughter, Freda, becomes active in the radical black feminist movement. She becomes involved with Delbert, who drives her to drink. At the end of the novel, Freda joins AA, and Mildred returns to Michigan to attend community college, having found that she can both be a good mother and attend to her own needs and desires.

McMillan's focus on African-American women and their struggle for independence from men is also a theme of her 1992 bestseller, *Waiting to Exhale* (Viking). Her 1989 novel *Disappearing Acts* (Viking) earned praise for its depiction of an unlikely young African-American couple. RL

79 McPherson, James Alan. ***Elbow Room: Short Stories***. Macmillan 1987, $10.00 (0-684-18822-8). 241pp. Fiction.

In the introduction to *Hue and Cry* (Fawcett, 1979), his first volume of short stories, James Alan McPherson stated that he wanted his stories to be "about people, all kinds of people." Indeed, his work addresses racial conflict while portraying white as well as black characters fully and with compassion. *Elbow Room*, another collection of stories, earned the author the Pulitzer Prize for fiction in 1978.

"A Loaf of Bread" begins with a boycott of a white-owned grocery store and ends with a reconciliation between the black organizer and the Jewish store owner. "Elbow Room" explores the marriage of a black woman and a white man and sympathetically portrays their efforts to raise their biracial child to be comfortable in both worlds.

In some of his stories, McPherson—who attended Harvard Law School—uses crimes and trials to examine the obstacles facing blacks in their quest for equal justice. His spare and powerfully written tales reveal the universal themes in the drama of racial conflict and the desire for mutual understanding.   RL

80   Meriwether, Louise. *Daddy Was a Number Runner*. Feminist Pr. 1986, $10.95 (0-935312-57-9). 240pp. Fiction.

Francie Coffin, twelve years old, narrates this novel, which is set in Harlem during the Depression years of 1934 and 1935. The poverty and harshness of Francie's life is symbolized by the bedbugs that climb the walls and bite her at night. Francie loves to read, but the school she attends is continually disrupted by gangs of girl students. Her father, James, takes odd jobs but also works as a number runner in a futile effort to keep his family off welfare. Her two older brothers work for a pimp. For moral guidance, Francie turns to her mother, who is devoutly religious. Her eldest brother is arrested for a murder he didn't commit. Though he is cleared eventually, the injustice traumatizes the family and drains them financially. Meanwhile, Francie must constantly fight off sexual advances, propositions, and fondling by strangers. She finally asserts herself by kneeing one of her tormentors in the groin. At the end of the novel, Francie, who maintains her strength and dignity despite the disasters around her, is becoming an adult, sure of her identity and her goals in life.

RL

81   Millican, Arthenia. *The Deity Nodded*. o.p. Fiction.

This novel paints a vivid and often troubling picture of what it meant to grow up in South Carolina during the final decades of segregation. The heroine, Tisha Dees, born out of wedlock and in poverty, is put up for adoption. As a young woman, she becomes pregnant and is forced into marriage. Later she moves north. But troubled by the hypocrisy of both the well-off whites and the blacks she meets, she returns to her roots among the poor but down-to-earth black Southerners. Eventually, to the horror of her family, she rejects Christianity and joins the Nation of Islam because it seems to offer hope in this world, rather than in the next. Tisha realizes that by traveling and by overcoming difficulties she has learned to feel confident about herself and her place in the world.

Millican also is known for *Seeds Beneath the Snow* (o.p., 1969), a collection of twelve slice-of-life stories set in real and fictional South Carolina locations. The stories focus on young people, some of whom persevere in a harsh world, and some of whom fail or harm others, either through their lack of maturity or because they possess deep character flaws.   RL

82   Morrison, Toni. *Beloved*. Knopf 1987, $27.50 (0-394-53597-9); NAL $10.00 (0-452-26446-4). 288pp. Fiction.

Sethe, a young, pregnant slave woman, attempts to flee with Beloved, her two-year-old daughter. Cornered and facing recapture, Sethe kills the girl rather than see her suffer life as a slave. Sethe soon gives birth to another girl, whom she names Denver. Eighteen years later, in 1873, Sethe and Denver are free, but the ghost of Beloved still haunts them. One day a young woman comes to their house. She is twenty years old and calls herself Beloved; she has the voice of a child and seems not to know where she comes from. She becomes attached to Sethe; Sethe in turn believes Beloved is her daughter, back "from the other side." Sethe becomes increasingly attached to Beloved, who gains more and more power over her as the rest of the family watches and waits in horror.

A haunting book with great poetic power, *Beloved* portrays a hidden aspect of a people's historical memory: the relationship between the living and the dead. Another theme is the choices black women are forced to make in a world of social oppression. This book displays slavery, an institution so cruel that freedom could never heal the wounds it inflicted. Sethe is a woman who is both hard to understand and hard to forget. *Beloved* won the Pulitzer Prize for fiction in 1988. Its author, the recipient of the Nobel Prize in literature in 1993, is also the author of *The Bluest Eye* (orig. pub. 1969; NAL, 1994), *Sula* (orig. pub. 1973; NAL, 1987), *Song of Solomon* (Knopf, 1977), *Tar Baby* (Knopf, 1981), and *Jazz* (Knopf, 1992). LML

83   Morrison, Toni. *Jazz*. Knopf 1992, $21.00 (0-685-53430-8); NAL $10.00 (0-452-26965-2). 229pp. Fiction.

While Morrison's earlier works are set in rural areas or small towns, this novel takes place in Harlem in the early part of the twentieth century. Joe and Violet Trace are an older couple for whom the fires of passion have died. Joe has an affair with the teenage girl Dorcas, but when he learns that Dorcas is having a relationship with a boy her own age, he shoots her. Violet becomes obsessed with the dead girl. She disrupts Dorcas's funeral, visits the aunt who raised her, and keeps a picture of her in the apartment. Intertwined with the story are flashbacks to Joe and Violet's early life in the South and their journey North as part of the Great Migration, as well as stunning descriptions of Harlem in the 1920s. More than simply a story about a love triangle, *Jazz* is the tale of a social and cultural movement and a vibrant community.

Shortly after the novel's publication, Morrison became the first African-American to win the Nobel Prize in literature. LML

84   Morrison, Toni. ***Song of Solomon***. Knopf 1977, $24.00 (0-394-49784-8); NAL $4.50 (0-451-15261-1). 320pp. Fiction.

Young Macon Dead—nicknamed Milkman because he nursed at his mother's breast long into childhood—lives with his parents, Macon and Ruth, and his two older sisters, Lena and First Corinthians, in a silent, loveless mansion filled with terrible family secrets. As an adolescent, Milkman visits his shunned and impoverished aunt, Pilate, her daughter, Reba, and Reba's unfortunate, unhappy child, Hagar, with whom Milkman has a sexual relationship. Through the three women, Milkman learns of his father's past. He undertakes a frightening journey from his Michigan home through Pennsylvania and Virginia to uncover the secrets his father has hidden from him for so many years. His search also leads him into a religious confrontation with his best friend, Guitar Bains. Bains evolves from a hedonistic youth into an angry adult, poised to take revenge against the whites for every act of violence they perpetrated against blacks.

Song of Solomon is a complex, challenging, and thought-provoking work that reveals its mysteries only gradually, through multiple flashbacks, references to biblical and classical literature, and an ambiguous ending. Milkman is an unforgettable character who struggles to escape his troubled family and achieve manhood on his own terms.   LML

85   Mosley, Walter. ***Devil in a Blue Dress***. Norton 1990, $18.95 (0-393-02854-2); Pocket Books $5.99 (0-671-51142-4). 224pp. Fiction.

Ezekiel "Easy" Rawlins, a young, tough black veteran living in 1948 Los Angeles, wants only two things: respect and enough money to pay his mortgage. When he is fired from his factory job, he falls in with a white mobster, who hires him to track down a missing woman, a light-haired, blue-eyed beauty. As Easy plumbs his usual hangouts for clues, he relays information to the mobster, runs afoul of the police, meets the mysterious woman, discovers a murder—of which he is suspected and which, to clear himself, he investigates. Mr. Mosley writes in a talking-blues style that is its own kind of music. By telling stories of a black man in a white man's world, he gives his hero a special edge in the gray world of private detectives.   CH

86   Naylor, Gloria R. ***The Women of Brewster Place***. Viking 1988, $4.50 (0-318-37688-1). 192pp. Fiction.

Gloria Naylor's first novel—really more a cycle of interwoven short stories—recounts how seven women come to live, and how their lives intertwine, on the inner-city street called Brewster Place. Mattie Michael, the matriarchal figure of the community, moved here years before, forced to leave home because she was pregnant. Other characters include an unwed mother of six, a displaced middle-class college student, a lesbian couple, an abused woman, and a middle-aged woman who wants to find a husband but who fears it may be too late. The circumstances that lead each of the characters to Brewster Place are unique, but together the women discover bonds of unity as they tear down the walls that have kept them from attaining their dreams.

   This novel received the National Book Award in 1983. Naylor's other acclaimed works of fiction include *Mama Day* (Random, 1989) and *Bailey's Cafe* (Harcourt, 1992).   CH

87   Neely, Barbara. ***Blanche on the Lam***. Viking 1993, $4.95 (0-14-017439-7). 192pp. Fiction.

Blanche White has moved with her two children from New York back to the relative safety of her small hometown in North Carolina. She is convicted of passing bad checks, but to avoid serving time in jail, she leaves her children with her mother and skips town. Blanche lands a job as a servant to a wealthy but bizarre white family: an amiable but slightly retarded son, a neurotic daughter, and her lazy husband, all of whom depend on the alcoholic and cantankerous mother for cash. Blanche witnesses various misdeeds and becomes an amateur detective, solving the murders of a white sheriff and a black gardener. Although otherwise a fairly standard mystery story, Neely's novel is notable because it features a black female protagonist.   RL

88   Nelson, Alice Dunbar. *The Goodness of St. Rocque and Other Stories.* Repr. of 1899 ed. Ayer 1977, $19.25 (0-8369-8817-5). 224pp. Fiction.

This collection, first published in 1899, illuminates the New Orleans Creole world in which the author grew up. Many of Nelson's stories are romances or sentimental tales in which young lovers die. She uses flowers as symbols of romance and writes beautiful descriptions of nature. These stories are valuable for the way they present the rich blend of black Creole life: the melding of Catholicism and black magic; of French, Spanish, African, and American cultures; of dialect and standard English.

Nelson, a prolific essayist and critic, was married for a few years to the noted poet Paul Lawrence Dunbar. Her diary, which covers her political and literary activities from 1921 until her death in 1935, was edited by Gloria Hull and published in 1984 as *Give Us Each Day: The Diary of Alice Dunbar-Nelson.*

RL

89   Perry, Richard. *Changes.* Macmillan 1974, $6.95 (0-672-51850-3). 175pp. Fiction.

Bill Taylor, the protagonist of this novel, is a black writer and university professor. He wants to help his people but is indecisive about which path to take. Personal problems also stand in the way: His marriage is falling apart, and meanwhile the campus is agitated by the murder of a townsperson by an African exchange student. What's more, Taylor's time and emotional energy are consumed by the demands of Bukay, an inmate in a nearby insane asylum whom the well-meaning Taylor has sought to help. Echoing Black Muslim teachings, Bukay tells Taylor that he is 6,000 years old and that he is the "inventor" of the white race, an act that Bukay has now decided was a mistake. Bukay creates a highly contagious virus that is supposed to turn everyone black again. When Taylor protests the plot, Bukay hypnotizes him. Although the ending contrives to weave all the disparate plot elements together, this novel is a gripping portrayal of the dilemmas of a well-meaning and progressive black man who shuns radical solutions.

RL

90   Petry, Ann. *The Street.* Houghton 1992, $9.70 (0-395-57380-7). 448pp. Fiction.

This vivid novel about urban black life in America in the 1940s tells a spiritually moving and emotionally powerful story. In the days of segregation, blacks of all social classes and walks of life found themselves living in the same neighborhood. The street thus becomes a metaphor for the entire black community. In the book, a young woman growing up encounters a range of characters—doctors, lawyers, ministers, businesspeople, maids, artists, factory workers, and the unemployed. From these contacts she learns the values of her culture and makes the choices that will govern the rest of her life.

Combining documentary detail with intimate and perceptive observation, Petry portrays her black characters without condescension, pleading, or distortion. A gripping tale peopled with utterly believable American archetypes, *The Street* overflows with the classic pity and terror found in the best imaginative writing.

CH

91   Pinckney, Darryl. ***High Cotton***. Farrar 1992, $21.00 (0-374-16998-5); Viking $11.00 (0-14-017503-2). 320pp. Fiction.

Like the author, the unnamed narrator of this novel grew up in a middle-class black family in Indiana and attended Columbia University. The narrator is awkward around whites, in whose preconceived notions all blacks are militants who come from impoverished backgrounds. But his comfortable background and intellectual interests also make it hard for him to "act black" around his fellow African Americans. Despite his estrangement, the narrator is enchanted with his relatives and their stories of life in the South, which he refers to as the "Old Country." But the narrator's efforts to create an identity for himself produce little but confusion. For a time he adopts the pose of an artist; later he becomes Minister of Information for a radical group called the Heirs of Malcolm. The book's absorbing plot and clear narrative allows the reader to sympathize with the narrator and his struggle to define himself as an African American.   RL

92   Porter, Connie. ***All-Bright Court***. Houghton 1991, $19.45 (0-395-53271-X); HarperCollins $10.00 (0-06-097498-2). 256pp. Fiction.

All-Bright Court is a steeltown housing project in the heart of the Rust Belt, near the dying Great Lakes. Although located just outside the big city of Buffalo, New York, the inhabitants rarely venture there. The lives of the people in All-Bright Court are dominated by the Capital Steel Company, which sometimes employs the residents but more often lays them off. The novel centers on the Taylor family—Samuel, Mary Kate, and their five children, including Porter, an emerging young writer. Although the residents look upon the projects as a way station to a better life, many will be trapped there forever; yet they still impart to their children the hope for a better life.

This novel offers a compelling portrait of a working-class family and the strength of a community in the years of the Rust Belt's decline.   CH

93   Reed, Ishmael. ***Mumbo Jumbo***. Macmillan 1989, $11.00 (0-689-70730-4). 256pp. Fiction.

In 1920s New Orleans, white city officials seek to suppress the spreading popularity of the "Jes Grew" movement—an African-based religious movement that some blacks see as an alternative to the repressiveness of Christianity. PaPa LaBas, a black detective and the novel's protagonist, searches for The Work—the sacred text written by Jes Grew himself. He is impeded in his efforts by Hinckle Von Vampton, a white thief who belongs to the Wallflower Order, a secret society, and to its military wing, the Knights Templar. Eventually, LaBas learns that The Work has been destroyed by Abdul Hamid, a Black Muslim editor, who considers it obscene. In an epilogue, an elderly PaPa LaBas addresses a college audience of the 1970s as the Les Grew movement shows signs of reviving. Through its use of parody and elaborate literary allusions, *Mumbo Jumbo* celebrates African and African-American cultures as a vital antidote to Christianity.

Another major work by this author is *Flight to Canada* (Macmillan, 1976). This book tells the story of Uncle Robin, a slave who inherits a Virginia estate when he rewrites his owner's will. Harriet Beecher Stowe (the real-life author of *Uncle Tom's Cabin*) tries to buy the rights to his story. Instead, Uncle Robin commissions Raven Quickskill, who had escaped to Canada, to write this fictional narrative.   RL

94   Shaik, Fatima. *The Mayor of New Orleans: Just Talking Jazz*. Creative Arts
         1989, $13.95 (0-88739-050-1); $9.95 (0-88739-071-4). 160pp. Fiction.

This volume is a collection of three short novellas, all set in New Orleans. The title work, "The Mayor of New Orleans," tells of an elderly black jazz trumpeter and raconteur who once served as mayor. He finds that, despite good intentions, he can do little to solve the city's problems. Instead, he gives away the furniture from city offices to the poor and to nuns and ends up in jail. "Monkey Hill" is set in the 1960s as desegregation comes to New Orleans. A young girl, Levia, listens to adults as they talk of racial tensions. She removes the bullets from her father's gun, teaching her family and neighbors a lesson about how to live together. The third novella, "Before Echo," tells about a woman named Joan who as a child was sent to live in New Orleans. Now a young adult, Joan decides to return to her mother and to her former home in the swamp country. In telling the stories of three engaging and endearing characters, Shaik shows readers the rigid lines of race and class that few in New Orleans are able to cross despite that city's image of liberalism and libertinism.   RL

95   Shange, Ntozake. *For Colored Girls Who Have Considered Suicide When the
         Rainbow Is Enuf*. Macmillan 1989, $5.95 (0-02-024891-1). 80pp. Drama.

This highly acclaimed and popular play was produced on Broadway in 1976. Seven nameless black women characters act out a series of twenty poems about the lives of black women in the United States. The women express the agonies of their relations with unfeeling and brutal black men, who themselves are victims of racism and poverty. Yet the women rise above bleak reality with humor, especially in a poem where they verbally skewer the men who have abandoned them and in the joy with which they dance. In another poem, an eight-year-old girl tells of her admiration for Toussaint L'Ouverture, a liberator of slaves and a Haitian hero. At the end of the play, the women come together, realizing their essential unity and finding the god within them, through the experience of sharing their pain. With its invented spellings and use of the vernacular, Shange's poetry celebrates black English, and her sense of the dramatic makes for an absorbing and memorable theatrical experience.   RL

96   Shange, Ntozake. *Sassafras, Cypress and Indigo*. St. Martin 1983, $9.95 (0-
         312-69972-7). 224pp. Fiction.

This novel tells the story of three sisters from Charleston, South Carolina. Sassafras, the eldest, is a weaver who wants to become a writer. She lives with Mitch, a drug addict who abuses her. Cypress, the middle sister, is Sassafras's opposite; she refuses to become involved emotionally or sexually with any man. Shange presents both women and Mitch as products of environments marked by deprivation and discrimination. The youngest sister, Indigo, hears her dolls speak and finds magic in everyday life. She is most in touch with the black folk culture of the South.

Shange expresses her characters' emotions through music and dance and by alternating poetic passages with much choppier prose. The experimental style, with its varied forms and meters, reflects Shange's origins as a poet. Her two best-known volumes of poetry are *Nappy Edges* (orig. pub. 1978; St. Martin, 1991) and *A Daughter's Geography* (orig. pub. 1983; St. Martin, 1991). Her other well-known novel is *Betsey Brown* (St. Martin, 1985), the story of a spunky, determined teenager who becomes a pioneer in the integration struggle in St. Louis in 1959. **RL**

97 Sherman, Charlotte W. *One Dark Body: A Novel.* HarperCollins 1993, $20.00 (0-06-016924-9); $10.00 (0-06-092466-7). 224pp. Fiction.

This novel is set in the fictional Deep South town of Pearl. Its coal mines are exhausted, and many blacks have left for the North. Nola Barnett, age fifteen, gives birth to a daughter named Septeema. Nola's lover, El, has committed suicide, and in mourning, Nola abandons her daughter and heads for Chicago. Twelve years later, Septeema, nicknamed Raisin, is living with Miss Marius and Nathan, who take care of several other abandoned children. Raisin, who narrates much of the book, loves the sociability of Pearl and the whispers of the spirits she hears in the woods. Nola's return to Pearl, the reconciliation between daughter and mother, and the maturing of Raisin are key events in this well-written novel. A subplot, one that parallels the way Raisin comes to understand the qualities of womanhood, is the story of a boy named Sin-Sin and a man named Blue, who years ago had witnessed his father's lynching and his mother's rape by whites. Without a father to guide him, Sin-Sin turns to Blue for lessons in what it means to be a man. Raisin, Sin-Sin, and Blue are powerfully drawn characters who sustain the reader's interest in this novel. **RL**

98 Shockley, Ann Allen. *Loving Her.* Repr. of 1974 ed. Naiad 1987, $7.95 (0-930044-97-5). 192pp. Fiction.

Loving Her is one of the first novels to feature a black lesbian character. Renee, a young black married woman with a small daughter, works as a singer in a nightclub, where she meets Terry, a rich older white lesbian. Renee's marriage is not a good one, and she is under constant pressure from her hectic life. Terry, immediately attracted to Renee, pursues a relationship with her. The story has a tragic ending, but readers are introduced to two memorable characters. **CH**

99 Southerland, Ellease. *Let the Lion Eat Straw.* o.p. Fiction.

Survival and love are the themes in this, the author's first novel, originally published in 1979. The protagonist, Abeba Williams, was born in the rural South but was reared in a Northern ghetto. She discovers the separate worlds of her grandmother in the South and her mother in the North. The novel explores the need for courage and honesty despite the odds and speaks movingly of black family love, sacrifice, and commitment.

Like her characters, the author also understands the pain of separation from the culture of her childhood. Southerland was born in Jamaica and now lives in the United States. This theme of separation also informs much of Southerland's poetry, several volumes of which have been published.   CH

100   Thurman, Wallace. ***The Blacker the Berry.*** Repr. of 1929 ed. Ayer 1969, $21.95 (0-405-01897-5); Macmillan $7.00 (0-02-054750-1). 262pp. Fiction.

This novel, first published in 1929, offers a searing critique of discrimination by lighter-skin "colored" African Americans against darker-skinned Negroes during the 1920s. The protagonist is Emma Lou Morgan, the dark-skinned child of light-skinned Jane Lightfoot Morgan. Jane chases away her darker husband and humiliates her daughter throughout her childhood growing up in Boise, Idaho. While attending the University of Southern California, Emma is denied acceptance by a Negro sorority because she is "too dark." She leaves college and encounters similar discrimination in New York at the hands of mulatto employers and landlords. She is exploited financially by her boy-friend, Alva, a part-Filipino mulatto. At the end of the novel, Emma accepts the counsel of light-skinned Gwendolyn Johnson. Gwendolyn, who cele-brates her color and her African heritage, advises Emma to leave Alva and take pride in herself.

Through her sharp, satiric tone, the author argues that African Americans must overcome self-hate and abandon intraracial prejudice if they wish to confront white racism fully.   RL

101   Toomer, Jean. ***Cane.*** Random 1994, $12.50 (0-685-70623-0). 116pp. Fiction.

Jean Toomer is unusual among writers of the Harlem Renaissance for his interest in experimenting with literary forms. This work, first published in 1923, is a series of short stories and vignettes, intercut with poems and con-cluding with a play. The first group of stories, set in the South, address the reality and the consequences of miscegenation. One vignette features Becky, a white woman who has borne two interracial babies. Because she lives in a remote cabin, both whites and blacks can avoid confronting their discomfort-ing feelings her existence triggers in them. At the end she is burned alive in her house. In "Blood-Burning Moon" Louisa has two lovers. The black one murders his white rival and is himself burned by a white mob. The middle section of the book depicts the repression and anonymity of blacks living in the North. The concluding play, "Kabnis," is about a man who returns to Georgia from New York hoping to educate and uplift his fellow blacks but who falls into despair.

Toomer also is the author of an epic poem, *Blue Meridian*, which was written in the 1920s but which was only published in full in 1980. Like *Cane*, it is a contribution to the development of modernist European literature and reflects Toomer's hopes for unity between the black and white communities in the United States.   RL

102   Van Dyke, Henry. ***Ladies of the Rachmaninoff Eyes*** Repr. of 1965 ed. Chatham 1975, $15.00 (0-911860-49-5). 214pp. Fiction.

This novel is narrated by Oliver Eugene Gibbs, a seventeen-year-old black boy who observes the relationship between his Aunt Harriet Gibbs and her white,

Jewish employer, Etta Klein. The two women have been together for years; although they argue often, they have a deep and abiding affection for each other. Oliver's observations provide grist for his own reflections on how to live in an integrated—though often racist—society. At the end of the novel Oliver leaves home to enroll at Cornell University. His efforts to enter the literary world are told in a sequel, *Blood of Strawberries* (o.p., 1968).

Van Dyke also is the author of *Dead Piano* (o.p., 1971). In that novel, a black family—Dr. Finley Blake, his wife, Olga, and their daughter, Sophie—receives threatening letters from "the Committee." Soon their home is invaded by a couple of hired black thugs. In a series of flashbacks, readers learn how the Blakes achieved success and grew apart from each other and from their community. **RL**

103 Wade, Brent. *Company Man*. Algonquin 1992, $18.95 (0-945575-73-4); Doubleday $9.50 (0-385-42563-5). 240pp. Fiction.

Bill Covington, a rising executive in a big computer company, has a beautiful wife and a red Jaguar XJ6. When Bill was a child, his grandmother told him to get rid of his "niggerishness." As a consequence, in adulthood he has no identity at all, keeping himself distant from both his white colleagues and the mostly low-level black employees in his office. Despite his material success, he suffers from impotence and anxiety attacks and his sleep is interrupted by nightmares. His carefully constructed life is threatened when his patron, the head of the company, announces plans to shift operations to Mexico, a move that would cost most of the black workers their jobs. The workers and Bill's father-in-law, an old civil rights leader, urge him to oppose the move. Covington's problems are compounded when a white secretary falsely accuses him of sexual harassment.

The author, himself a corporate executive, has written a gripping and convincing portrait of the pressures under which seemingly privileged black executives operate and the costs of success in a white-dominated society. **RL**

104 Walker, Alice. *The Color Purple*. 10th anniv. ed. Harcourt 1992, $19.95 (0-685-57146-7); Pocket Books $5.99 (0-671-72779-6). 252pp. Fiction.

Although Alice Walker had written several previous novels and was a contributing editor to *Ms.* magazine, she found enormous commercial success with this novel. *The Color Purple* is the story of the love between two sisters and the struggles experienced by an oppressed gender. Young Celie, the principal character, is raped by her stepfather; before the age of fifteen she has borne two children by him. She is forced to marry a cruel widower with five children. The one person who truly loves Celie is her beautiful older sister, Nettie. Celie's husband attempts to rape Nettie, and when she fights off his advances, he bars her from his home and intercepts all of Nettie's letters to Celie. The sisters are separated by miles when Nettie becomes a missionary family's nanny; she later marries the missionary when his wife dies. The missionary has adopted two children—they turn out to be Celie's—and Nettie raises them as her own. After a life full of misery and oppression Celie finds happiness with her husband's mistress, Shug. Shug helps Celie to discover the hidden strength she possesses. With the help of Shug, Celie finds the letters her sister had written over the years. The novel ends as Celie's husband makes amends for his actions and Celie and her family are reunited.

CH

105 Walker, Margaret. *Jubilee.* Bantam 1984, $5.95 (0-553-27383-3). 432pp. Fiction.

The heroine of this novel, set in the years before and after the Civil War, is Vyry Ware Brown, a slave whose father is her white master, Dutton, and whose mother is Setta, a slave who dies when Vyry is two years old. Vyry works as a servant to Dutton's wife, Salina, who hates this girl, the product and proof of her husband's adultery. As a young woman, Vyry falls in love with Fandall Ware, a freed black man. When she tries to escape slavery to live with him, she is caught and whipped in front of Dutton. She later marries Innis Brown. After the Civil War they are chased off the land and forced to travel the South in search of work. At the end of the novel, Vyry again meets Ware, who has become rich in Reconstruction. She gives her son to him to raise under better conditions. This novel offers a panorama of black history in the middle of the nineteenth century, told through the lives of characters, all of whom, black and white, are sympathetically drawn. Walker is also known for her poetry, which has been collected in *This Is My Century: New and Collected Poems* (Univ. of Georgia Pr., 1989).

RL

106 West, Dorothy. *The Living Is Easy.* Repr. of 1948 ed. Ayer 1970, $23.50 (0-405-01942-4); Feminist Pr. $13.95 (0-912670-97-5). 376pp. Fiction.

This novel, first published in 1948 and rediscovered in the 1970s, is set in Boston in the period just before World War I. Light-skinned Cleo has come north from South Carolina to search for the prosperity she lacked growing up. As a child, always starved for affection, she pulled a number of outrageous and dangerous stunts to win adults' attention. In Boston she meets and marries Bart Judson, an honorable and hardworking banana wholesaler who is much older than Cleo but quite wealthy. Cleo invites her three sisters to live with her but then proceeds to destroy their marriages. She mocks her dark-skinned husband as "Mr. Nigger" and pushes him to bring in ever more money to support her ostentatious lifestyle. He tries to please her, even though she has stopped sleeping with him. Eventually, Bart Judson plunges into bankruptcy, and the sisters are forced to take menial jobs. *The Living Is Easy* is a pointed critique of social striving among middle-class Northern blacks. The racism that drives the plot arises from color differences among blacks. West, daughter of a former slave, has also written short stories. In 1995 she published her second novel, *The Wedding* (Doubleday), which also addresses conflicts between dark- and light-skinned blacks.

RL

107 Wideman, John Edgar. *Sent for You Yesterday.* Random 1988, $11.00 (0-679-72029-4). 208pp. Fiction.

This novel is the third volume of Wideman's Homewood Trilogy, which also includes *Damballah* (Random, 1981), a collection of short stories, and *Hiding Place* (Random, 1981), a novel. All three works are set in Homewood, a black neighborhood in Pittsburgh where Wideman himself grew up. The two narrators of this novel, Doot and John, leave Pittsburgh for the calm of rural Wyoming, but they now return to Homewood to learn the history of their families and community. The central character of their story is Brother Tate, whose son Junebug died in a fire. Tate is silent for the next sixteen years until his own mysterious death. Doot and John learn about Tate and others from the stories told by Tate's friend Carl French. Themes of life and death, exile and return are further explored in the story of Albert Wilkes, who disappears for seven years after murdering a policeman, only to be gunned down by the police on his return to Homewood. This novel won the PEN/Faulkner Award for fiction in 1983. It is eloquent in its creation of varied characters and its melding of those characters' lives in a multilayered narrative.   RL

108   Williams, Denis. *Crossover.* o.p. Fiction.

This, the author's first novel, tells the story of Richard (Ike) Isaac, a freshman at an Ivy League college. Raised by a strong-willed mother in middle-class surroundings, Ike has little racial consciousness. He is interested mainly in his white girlfriend, Cheryl, and in the promise of success that will come with a degree from a prestigious school. However, Ike increasingly is drawn in by the demands of his militant black friends for racial solidarity. Set in 1969, the novel offers a fictionalized account of the armed takeover by black students of a campus building at Cornell University, where Williams is on the faculty. The confrontation in *Crossover*, like the historical one at Cornell, is resolved peacefully. Isaac gains a sense of his solidarity with and obligations toward his race, as well as a greater degree of personal maturity.   RL

109   Williams, John A. *The Man Who Cried I Am.* Repr. of 1967 ed. Thunder's Mouth 1985, $11.95 (0-938410-24-5). 400pp. Fiction.

As this novel opens in 1963, Max Reddick, a noted black novelist and former speech writer to a liberal U.S. President, is in Amsterdam dying of cancer. His friend Harry Ames, an even more famous black American novelist, has died under mysterious circumstances. Reading through Ames's papers, Reddick learns that the President has authorized a plan to detain blacks in concentration camps at the first sign of unrest and that the U.S. government is party to an effort by an alliance of white nations to prevent African unity. Reddick leaks the information to the radical Minister Q, even though it costs him his life. As Reddick finds the courage to confront both his own cancer and the cancer of racism in America, he discovers his inner voice, to which he gives the name Saminone and who speaks in the vernacular of American blacks.

   !Click Song (Thunder's Mouth, 1987) is a bitter novel about black novelist William Cato Douglass, whose fortunes decline as he writes increasingly better novels, while his white friend, Paul Cummings, becomes rich and famous through his mediocre books.   RL

110   Williams, Sherley Ann. *Dessa Rose.* Berkley 1987, $5.50 (0-425-10337-4). 236pp. Fiction.

A historical novel with racial and sexual repression at its heart, *Dessa Rose* uses irony and humor to create a richly textured picture of the South. This work builds upon the tradition of the slave narrative. Dessa liberates herself by articulating her own experience, much as the authors of those historical works did. Furthermore, she attempts to liberate her descendants by spinning out a narrative in which she represents their history. Williams, who is also an acclaimed poet, makes personal and communal knowledge of history fundamental to her novel, emphasizing the need for the conscious and imaginative rewriting of history.   CH

111   Wilson, August. ***Fences***. NAL 1986, $6.95 (0-452-26048-5). 120pp. Drama. ·

This play, which won both the Pulitzer Prize for drama and a Tony Award for best play in 1987, established August Wilson as the leading African-American dramatist of the contemporary era. The protagonist, Troy Maxson, is a embittered garbage collector. In the days before Jackie Robinson, Troy was denied the opportunity to play professional baseball because of his race. His son Cory now dreams of playing football, but Troy belittles his ambition, convinced that blacks will forever be the victims of discrimination. Troy also humiliates his wife, Rose, by bringing home his illegitimate baby daughter for Rose to raise after his mistress died in childbirth. Set in Pittsburgh in the 1950s, *Fences* explores the limits of opportunity for blacks just before the civil rights era. Wilson creates absorbing drama out of the conflicts and disappointments of his unforgettably powerful characters.   RL

112   Wilson, August. ***The Piano Lesson***. NAL 1990, $7.00 (0-452-26534-7). 112pp. Drama.

August Wilson won his second Pulitzer Prize for this 1990 play, which takes place during the Depression of the 1930s. Boy Willie Charles arrives from the South at the Pittsburgh home of his sister Berniece and his uncle Doaker Charles. Boy Willie wants to sell the family piano and use the money to buy a farm from the white family whose ancestors had held his family in slavery. Berniece refuses to sell the piano because a slave ancestor of hers had carved images of his relatives onto the piano legs. The battle between Boy Willie and Berniece symbolizes the conflict between Southern blacks, confident of their cultural heritage and eager for economic advancement, and blacks who gave up their communities in a largely unsuccessful search for monetary gain in the North. Wilson's vivid characters and sharp dialogue make for an engaging and realistic drama.   RL

113   Wilson, August. ***Two Trains Running***. NAL 1993, $18.00 (0-525-93565-7); $8.00 (0-452-26929-6). 128pp. Drama.

This play, which takes place in 1969, is set in Memphis Lee's coffee shop, a neighborhood gathering place about to be torn down as part of an urban renewal project. Memphis and his friend Holloway are contemptuous of Black Nationalists and other political activists. They mock Sterling—a newcomer to town, who has just been released from prison—because he plans to attend a memorial rally for Malcolm X. Memphis and Holloway are more absorbed by the preparations for the funeral of Prophet Samuel, a local religious leader they admired for his wealth. The political issues of that time are addressed, for the most part indirectly through the characters' personalities and dreams.

This play won the New York Drama Critics Circle Award for the best play of 1991–1992. It continues August Wilson's project of writing a play set in each decade of the twentieth century and addressing contemporary events in African-American history. Other works include *Joe Turner's Come and Gone*, set in 1911; his first play, *Ma Rainey's Black Bottom*, set in the 1920s; *The Piano Lesson* (the 1930s) *(see main entry)*; *Seven Guitars* (1940s); and *Fences* (the 1950s) *(see main entry)*. RL

114 Wright, Richard. *Native Son.* Repr. of 1940 ed. HarperCollins 1969, $24.95 (0-06-014762-8); HarperCollins $6.50 (0-06-081249-4). 544pp. Fiction.

This novel, first published in 1940, is one of the classics of American fiction. Its grim portrayal of the protagonist, Bigger Thomas, has influenced subsequent generations of writers who seek to express the dehumanizing effects of racism. Bigger Thomas is a petty criminal, living in poverty in Chicago during the Depression. He finds work as a chauffeur for Mr. Dalton, who also is the landlord of the tenement where the Bigger family lives. Thomas is made uncomfortable by the friendliness of Mr. Dalton's daughter, Mary, and her Communist boyfriend. After driving a drunken Mary home from a nightclub, Thomas carries her to her bed. Hearing Mary's mother call to her, Thomas fears being discovered in a white woman's bedroom. He accidentally suffocates her to death with a pillow, and then decapitates the body and burns it in a furnace. Later, Thomas murders his alcoholic girlfriend, Bessie Mears, because he is afraid she will betray him. Thomas is arrested and charged with murder. The police unsuccessfully attempt to get Thomas to confess to rape as well. Thomas gains a sense of confidence and worthiness only by assuming the identity of a vicious murderer. This stark and haunting novel shows the depths of fear and rage to which blacks can be pushed by white prejudice and abuse. Wright also is well known for his semiautobiographical *Black Boy: A Record of Childhood and Youth* (1945) *(see main entry)*. RL/CH

115 Yerby, Frank. *The Dahomean: An Historical Novel.* o.p. Fiction.

The protagonist of this novel is Nyasanu, the son of Gbenu, a tribal chief. When Gbenu is killed in a war with the neighboring Maxi, Nyasanu is promoted to chief ahead of his older brother because of his bravery in battle. The King gives one of his daughters, Princess Yekpewa, to Nyasanu in marriage and names him a governor. On their wedding night Nyasanu learns that Yekpewa is not a virgin; she had committed incest with her half brother. The Princess betrays her husband, arranging for bandits to kidnap him and sell him into slavery. The novel concludes with Nyasanu's arrival in the United States. His life in slavery is depicted in a sequel, *A Darkness at Ingraham's Coast* (o.p., 1979). *The Dahomean*, which shows the complexity and sophistication of African society before its European colonization, succeeds because of the depth and appeal of Nyasanu as a character. The work is unlike Yerby's many other novels, which are generally undistinguished (but popular) romances and adventure stories. RL/CH

116 Young, Al. *Snakes.* o.p. Fiction.

This novel is set in Detroit in the late 1950s and early 1960s. The protagonist, MC Moore, is an orphan who lives with his strict grandmother Claudette in a poor neighborhood. MC learned to play the piano while living with his Uncle Donald in Mississippi. At his Detroit high school he is encouraged to become a musician by his friends. One of these, Champ, is on his way to becoming a drug addict and introduces MC to marijuana and to prostitutes. Another friend is Shakes Harris, whose strict parents prohibit him from becoming a musician. MC joins with Jimmy Monday and blind Billy Sanchez in a group that records MC's song "Snakes," which wins a prize. At the end of the novel, MC moves to New York City, with his grandmother's blessing, to become a professional musician.

Young also is known for his novels, *Who Is Angelina?* (o.p., 1975), about a twenty-six-year-old woman's struggle to achieve a sense of self separate from the men in her life, and *Ask Me Now* (1980), which tells how a family is reconciled after the faked kidnapping of the protagonist's fifteen-year-old daughter. RL

NONFICTION

117 Abrahams, Roger D. ***Deep Down in the Jungle: Negro Narrative Folklore from the Streets of Philadelphia***. Aldine 1970, $24.95 (0-202-01092-9). 278pp. Nonfiction.

For two years during the late 1950s, Roger Abrahams, a student of folklore, collected the stories, toasts, and jokes told by African-American men in the Philadelphia ghetto. In the first part of this book he discusses the significance of these distinctive cultural practices in the context of the urban black experience. He explains, for example, how success in verbal contests helps a black man establish his status and achieve a positive masculine identity for himself and his group in a basically hostile environment. Abrahams examines classic folk heroes in the stories he gathered, from tricksters such as "the Signifying Monkey" to bad men such as "Stackolee." He finds that, while storytellers in this community prize the guile and cunning of the trickster, they favor even more the "hard-man" style of coping with their world. The second half of this book includes the full texts of many of the toasts and jokes that Abrahams collected. PTM

118 Anderson, Elijah. ***A Place on the Corner: Identity and Rank Among Black Streetcorner Men***. Univ. of Chicago Pr. 1981, $10.95 (0-226-01954-3). 237pp. Nonfiction.

For three years Anderson observed the men who frequented Jelly's bar and liquor store located in a run-down building on the South Side of Chicago. This anthropological study examines the social relationships and informal status system created by the black men who are regulars at the bar. The author describes how members of this "extended primary group" implicitly create standards of conduct. Then, during their interactions, they demonstrate to each other how they live up to those standards. For example, two primary values of the group are having a visible means of support and possessing "decency." Anderson discusses several other values that are used to confer status on group members. Although Anderson occasionally lapses into sociological jargon, this work offers a vivid portrait of the social world of African-American men in the inner city. PTM

119 Anderson, Elijah. *Streetwise: Race, Class, and Change in an Urban Community*. Univ. of Chicago Pr. 1990, $19.95 (0-226-01815-6); $11.95 (0-226-01816-4). 316pp. Nonfiction.

Anderson reports on his extended observations of two adjoining neighborhoods in Philadelphia: one racially mixed and middle- to upper-class; and the other largely black and low-income. Focusing on the nature of street life and public culture in these communities, Anderson describes how the apparent civility of the middle-class residents masks a growing concern about the dangers that they see emanating from the black ghetto nearby. He also examines the social and economic changes occurring within the low-income black community, noting that manufacturing jobs are disappearing, only to be replaced by drug dealing as the main source of income. Intriguingly, Anderson finds that residents of both neighborhoods employ street wisdom as a means of negotiating everyday interactions at minimum risk and maximum mutual respect in a world full of uncertainty and danger. PTM

120 Anderson, James D. *The Education of Blacks in the South, 1860–1935*. Univ. of North Carolina Pr. 1988, $37.50 (0-8078-1793-7); $13.95 (0-8078-4221-4). 366pp. Nonfiction.

This seminal historical study traces the development of separate and unequal educational institutions for African Americans in the southern United States from the time of Emancipation until the start of the New Deal. At the end of the Civil War, African-American intellectuals and many ex-slaves understood that mass education was vital if they were to achieve political or economic parity with whites. However, hopes for universal education were dashed with the end of Reconstruction and the rise of "Jim Crow" segregation policies in the South. Much of this book explores the ideological struggles—not just between whites and blacks, but among southern blacks as well—over the limited educational institutions that southern states were willing to permit and to fund for African Americans. Anderson concludes that whites limited black education to keep African Americans in servile positions and to retard the development of a black intellectual elite. Still, throughout this bleak era, African Americans struggled to expand educational opportunities, taking advantage of any openings to deepen their schooling as individuals and as a people. PTM

121 Aptheker, Herbert. *American Negro Slave Revolts.* 5th ed.; 50th anniversary ed. Frwd. by John H. Bracey. International Publishers 1993, $9.95 (0-7178-0605-7). 428pp. Nonfiction.

A view commonly held among historians is that, compared to other countries where slavery existed, few slave revolts took place in North America. This book dispels that myth by documenting over 200 incidents of slave resistance in the American territory before the Civil War. The author notes that "discontent and rebelliousness were not only exceedingly common, but, indeed, characteristic of American Negro slaves." To support that view, this well-written and influential early study cites several conspiracies among enslaved Africans in New York, such as the "Negro Revolt" of 1712; the 1720 uprising in

Stono, South Carolina; the Virginia conspiracies of Gabriel Prosser and Nat Turner; and the involvement of Africans in the series of Seminole wars in Florida against federal troops.   AJWM

Asante, Molefi Kete. *Afrocentricity.*
See entry 1277.

122   Ashe, Arthur R., Jr. *A Hard Road to Glory.* 3 vol. set; Rev. ed. Illus. Amistad 1993, $89.95 (1-56743-009-0). 240+542+624pp. Nonfiction.

In this comprehensive history, the late tennis champion Arthur Ashe has compiled a detailed record of the accomplishments of African-American athletes and the discriminatory barriers they had to overcome. Each volume chronicles a major period of athletic competition (1619–1918; 1919–1945; and 1946–1986), and each contains chapters on the major sports: baseball, basketball, boxing, football, and track and field. Other chapters on horse racing, cycling, wrestling, tennis, and golf are included for the periods in which these sports involved many black athletes. Each volume contains a lengthy appendix listing the records of and honors awarded to prominent African-American athletes, coaches, and teams. An abridged edition and individual paperback editions are also available from the same publisher.   PTM

123   Baldwin, James. *The Fire Next Time.* Random 1992, $8.00 (0-679-74472-X). 120pp. Essays.

This collection of essays addresses the state of race relations in the United States in the early 1960s. Written when the civil rights movement was still a rising force in American politics, Baldwin's essays advocate a goal of integration between the races. He condemns Christianity because it is the ideological source for white racism as well as black self-hatred. In Baldwin's view, Christianity's promise of everlasting life denies the tragedy of death, and in so doing it prevents people from finding meaning in this life through courageous acts and noble deeds of love toward others. But he also recounts his chilling meeting with Nation of Islam founder Elijah Muhammad and concludes that this movement propagates a doctrine of black racial superiority that is merely a mirror image of white racism. Baldwin's view of the United States is bleak, relieved only by a vision of a new secular practice of love between the races.

For more about this writer, see *James Baldwin* (Knopf, 1994) by David Leeming, who worked for a time as Baldwin's personal secretary and who was permitted unprecedented access to the writer's papers, family members, and friends.   RL

124   Bell, Derrick. *And We Are Not Saved: The Elusive Quest for Racial Justice.* Basic Books 1987, $19.95 (0-465-00328-1); $13.00 (0-465-00329-X). 336pp. Essays.

Bell's analysis of the legal status of African Americans takes the form of ten "chronicles" narrated by Geneva Crenshaw, a fictional civil rights attorney. In these parables Crenshaw/Bell covers a variety of contemporary issues, including affirmative action and school segregation, reparations for slavery, and tensions between black men and black women. The author argues that neither the American legal system nor traditional civil rights strategies are sufficient for dealing with the persistent problems of African Americans. Instead he advocates a strategy called the "third way," which would use existing legal structures to achieve a more democratic and just society for all Americans. Bell's creative and unorthodox approach to these difficult issues is not what most readers might expect from a distinguished legal scholar, but he skillfully presents complex questions in a way that will stimulate a thoughtful response.

RL

125 Berry, Mary Frances. ***Military Necessity and Civil Rights Policy: Black Citizenship and the Constitution, 1861–1868.*** o.p. Nonfiction.

The book argues that African Americans were emancipated and given rights of citizenship during the Civil War because the army needed black men to fight as soldiers for the Union cause. According to the author, the Reconstruction Amendments (13th, 14th, and 15th, ratified 1865, 1868, and 1870, respectively) were concessions by American whites designed specifically to enhance the legal status of blacks and make them eligible for military service. Berry's book offers a unique perspective on the Emancipation Proclamation and the various Constitutional Amendments. It is also provides a useful background for understanding African Americans' subsequent participation in U.S. military conflicts.

AJWM

126 Billingsley, Andrew. ***Climbing Jacob's Ladder: The Enduring Legacy of African-American Families.*** Simon & Schuster 1993, $27.50 (0-671-67708-X); $14.00 (0-671-67709-8). 444pp. Nonfiction.

Billingsley examines patterns of contemporary African-American family life in their broad historical, societal, and cultural context. He argues that black families "are both weak and strong, but their strengths are by far more powerful and contain the seeds of their survival and rejuvenation." Billingsley also notes the wide variety of family types in the African-American community, which include Caribbean, working-class and middle-class families, and interracial marriages. He emphasizes that many of the recent problems of African-American families are largely the result of changes in industrial technology and the decline of the black working class. Billingsley sees the solutions to these problems arising from traditional black family values, including educational attainment, spirituality, service to others, and economic independence. Rather than waiting for assistance from the government or the larger society, Billingsley argues, African-American individuals and institutions, especially the black church, hold the key to the future of the African-American family.

PTM

Blackett, R. J. ***Building an Antislavery Wall: Black Americans in the Atlantic Abolitionist Movement, 1830–1860.***
See entry 820.

127 Blassingame, John W. ***Black New Orleans, 1960–1880.*** o.p. Nonfiction.

Rather than focusing on the political aspects of Reconstruction, this well-documented study explores its sociological impact on the lives of blacks in

New Orleans. Blassingame examines such aspects as black education, religion, family life and structure, economic activities, and social interactions. He concludes that—compared to other major cities, such as Charleston, Washington, D.C., and Baltimore—the New Orleans black community was far more diverse, dynamic, and cosmopolitan.   AJWM

128   Blassingame, John W. *The Slave Community: Plantation Life in the Ante-Bellum South.* 2nd rev. & enl. ed. Illus. Oxford Univ. Pr. 1979, $15.95 (0-19-502563-6). 432pp. Nonfiction.

Blassingame offers a detailed and intimate study of plantation life in the South prior to the American Civil War. He argues convincingly that, although slavery enchained the bodies of blacks, it could not suppress their souls. As brutal and inhuman as the institution of slavery was, it did not succeed in its goal of fostering the "Sambo" personality—the infantile, submissive "darkie." Nor did it crush African culture. Instead the African spirit thrived, engendering the likes of Nat Turner and other rebellious blacks who rose up to escape—or to murder their masters. *The Slave Community* reveals how the lives of both the enslaved and the enslavers were ultimately shackled together in a love-hate relationship that defined the way of life on the plantation and the economic development of the South.   AJWM

129   Branch, Taylor. *Parting the Waters: America in the King Years, 1954–1963.* Simon & Schuster 1989, $16.00 (0-671-68742-5). 1,064pp. Nonfiction.

Branch has written a comprehensive history of the civil rights movement from 1954 to 1963. He skillfully shows how grassroots protests against Southern segregation worked to change subsequent federal policies. The author offers many revealing glimpses of Martin Luther King, Jr.'s early years and his achievements, but also describes the achievements of many lesser-known workers whose efforts made a difference. Among the individuals portrayed are Ella Baker, the dynamic organizer of the Southern Christian Leadership Conference; Robert Moses, who led youthful volunteers into Mississippi for the Student Nonviolent Coordinating Committee; John Doar, an idealistic young attorney in the Civil Rights Division of the Justice Department; and Rev. Vernon Johns, who preceded King as pastor of the Dexter Avenue Baptist Church in Montgomery, Alabama. Despite its thousand-page length, *Parting the Waters* is well written and never dull. Branch is now working on a second volume, covering the period from 1964 to 1968.   PTM

Bunche, Ralph J. *An African-American in South Africa: The Travel Notes of Ralph J. Bunche, September 28, 1937–January 1, 1938.*
See entry 1283.

130   Carson, Clayborne. *In Struggle: SNCC and the Black Awakening of the Nineteen Sixties.* Illus. Harvard Univ. Pr. 1981, $28.00 (0-674-44725-5); $12.95 (0-674-44726-3). 384pp. Nonfiction.

Carson chronicles the brief and turbulent history of the Student Nonviolent Coordinating Committee (SNCC) from its origins in the student sit-in movement of 1960 to its disintegration during the repression of the Black Power movement in 1969. During this span SNCC was the most militant and uncompromising organization lobbying for civil rights in the South. Carson describes how SNCC members led sit-ins in cities such as Nashville and Atlanta; continued the Freedom Rides when CORE withdrew; and launched voter registration campaigns in rural counties of the Deep South where other civil rights organizations feared to tread. Despite SNCC's many heroic accomplishments, Carson concludes that the organization began to fall apart as early as the Mississippi Summer Project of 1964, increasingly torn by internal conflicts and a shift to a more nationalistic stance. Readers may also want to consult James Forman's *The Making of Black Revolutionaries (see main entry)*, which traces many of the same events through the eyes of one of SNCC's key leaders.   PTM

131   Carson, Clayborne, ed. ***Malcolm X: The FBI File***. Intro. by Spike Lee. Carroll & Graf 1991, $23.95 (0-88184-751-8); $12.95 (0-88184-758-5). 512pp. Nonfiction.

Malcolm X left few written records to document his life's work. Ironically, the most complete files on his life and death were the ones compiled by the Federal Bureau of Investigation. Carson used the Freedom of Information Act to obtain these files, which begin in 1953, shortly after Malcolm X was released from prison, and continue through the investigation of his assassination. These records are valuable, not only for the light they shed on Malcolm's activities with the Nation of Islam but for documenting the extent to which the FBI engaged in surveillance of this militant black leader. The book includes a detailed thirty-page chronology of Malcolm's life.   PTM

132   Carter, Stephen L. ***Reflections of an Affirmative Action Baby***. Basic Books 1991, $23.00 (0-465-06871-5); $12.00 (0-465-06869-3). 286pp. Nonfiction.

Carter, a professor at Yale University Law School, explores the philosophy and impact of affirmative action—policies that give preferential treatment to minorities in an effort to redress the effects of segregation and racism. He describes the deepening divisions within the black community over the issue and the increasing isolation of black dissenters who have taken positions at odds with those of the civil rights establishment. Carter's own feelings can best be described as ambivalent. On the one hand, he knows he speaks as a black professional who has benefited directly from racial preference in law school admission policies. On the other hand, he resents the implication that his professional status is the result of his race rather than his personal abilities. Carter does not entirely reject the idea of affirmative action, but he says that racial considerations should not play a major role in college and professional school admissions. The author advocates what he terms "a reconciled solidarity" in which people of color work together to solve their common problems regardless of their political ideologies.   PTM

133   Chafe, William H. ***Civilities and Civil Rights: Greensboro, North Carolina, and the Black Struggle for Freedom***. Illus. Oxford Univ. Pr. 1980, $9.95 (0-19-502919-4). 436pp. Nonfiction.

Historian Chafe chronicles the evolution of the civil rights movement in Greensboro, site of the first student sit-in on February 1, 1960. Chafe advances the thesis that North Carolina was interested in maintaining an outward image of racial moderation, thus creating conditions where such protest could emerge. This "civility," however, masked an underlying resistance to fundamental social change, which he cites as the cause of growing black frustration during the 1960s. Only after a violent confrontation on the campus of North Carolina A&T [Agricultural and Technical] State University in 1971 did Greensboro's white leaders begin seriously to address the needs of the black community. Chafe documents the conflict between a unified black community that pressed for change and a white power structure that sought to "contain and diffuse the many stages of black insurgency." PTM

Cham, Mbye, and Claire Andrade-Watkins. *Blackframes: Critical Perspectives on Black Independent Cinema*.
See entry 1286.

Clarke, John Henrik, ed. *Marcus Garvey and the Vision of Africa*.
See entry 1290.

134 Clarke, John Henrik, ed. *William Styron's Nat Turner: Ten Black Writers Respond.* Repr. of 1968 ed. Greenwood 1987, $49.75 (0-313-25957-7). 128pp. Essays.

This book brings together essays by noted black writers and thinkers reacting to *The Confessions of Nat Turner*, a novel by a white author written from the first-person perspective of a historical figure: the revolutionary slave Nat Turner. Published in 1969, William Styron's psychological novel attempted to get into Turner's mind and analyze his thoughts about slavery, slave society, and his place in "the world the slaveholders made." In his book, Styron appears to have adopted the view that slavery was a "nurturing" institution, a view held by early twentieth-century progressives such as historian U. B. Phillips and now largely discredited. Angered by the novel, writers such as Lerone Bennett, Jr., Vincent Harding, John A. Williams, John Henrik Clarke (the editor), and others argue that Styron has reduced Turner and his 1831 Virginia rebellion to a historical position of "impotence." Among the issues raised is the controversy over whether a writer outside the culture can write convincingly about the culture. Although many of the commentators included here take an extreme position, their concerns merit consideration. AJWM

135 Comer, James P., and Alvin F. Poussaint. *Raising Black Children: Questions and Answers for Parents and Teachers*. NAL 1992, $12.00 (0-452-26839-7). 400pp. Nonfiction.

Comer and Poussaint, two leading black psychiatrists, have prepared this practical guide for black parents and others involved in raising African-American children. They address the special problems of race that black children will face growing up in a racist society. The book is divided into six sections, each one dealing with a different stage of childhood from infancy to adolescence. Each chapter poses a series of questions and offers concise responses. The topics range from general issues all parents face (for example, "At what age should we allow our son or daughter to date?") to topics of specific concern to African-American families (for example, "My daughter has bought skin-bleaching cream. Should I say anything?"). This book will not only be helpful to black parents but to white teachers, social workers, and others who are involved with the development of black children. **PTM**

136 Cose, Ellis. *The Rage of a Privileged Class: Why Do Prosperous Blacks Still Have the Blues?* HarperCollins 1994, $20.00 (0-06-018239-3). 176pp. Nonfiction.

Journalist Cose explores the dilemmas facing middle-class African Americans who, despite their status and their accomplishments, continue to suffer prejudice at the hands of a white-dominated society. Many would see these successful individuals as "privileged," but virtually all have endured subtle racial slights and often outright hostility. Cose's book is filled with vivid examples. He himself was thrown out of a restaurant because a waiter mistook him for a troublemaker. Others report that store clerks follow them around suspiciously or that cab drivers refuse to pick them up. Prejudice is no less insidious in school or the workplace; in those settings many African Americans must constantly justify their existence and defend their achievements.

Cose lists the "dozen demons" that plague successful African Americans and the destructive effects they have on the psyche. Among these demons are outright exclusion from jobs and clubs, assignments to community service positions, low performance expectations, and the assumption that any African American reaching a top position did so merely because of affirmative action. In describing the range of responses to these problems, Cose acknowledges the strength and adaptability of African Americans who have dealt with racism for centuries. Ways of coping with the problem include outright rage, but the author notes that humor remains one of the most important—and most effective—strategies. This is a powerful and thought-provoking book, one that has much to say to Americans of all races. **LML**

137 Cruse, Harold. *The Crisis of the Negro Intellectual: A Historical Analysis of the Failure of Black Leadership.* Rev. ed. Morrow 1984, $14.00 (0-688-03886-7). 696pp. Nonfiction.

This book is a polemical dissertation on the cultural ethos of the black intelligentsia over the fifty-year period from the 1920s to the 1970s. The author laments the fact that black thinkers have yet to break out of their "cultural, creative, and ideological antecedents" to create an effective strategy for political and economic liberation and help lead the United States out of its racial morass. Originally published almost thirty years ago and subsequently revised, the book has much to offer today's black intellectuals struggling to find an appropriate ideology and a way to convert thought into effective action. Enlightening in its exploration of the race question, this book is a useful companion to contemporary memoirs of African-American intellectuals, such as Brent Staples's *Parallel Time* and Jill Nelson's *Volunteer Slavery (see main entries).* **AJWM**

138 Davis, Angela Y. *Women, Race and Class.* Random 1983, $10.00 (0-394-71351-6). 288pp. Nonfiction.

The book explores how sex, ethnicity, and money have affected the way women, black as well as white, perceive themselves and value themselves in a society dominated by white men. Citing evidence that racism existed in the feminist movement from its beginnings in the nineteenth century, Davis sheds light on persistent racism among feminists today. Other sections of the book address a range of women's issues, including rape, reproductive rights, and the changing role of women in the workplace. Davis is also author of *Angela Davis: An Autobiography (see main entry)*.   AJWM

139   Dillard, J. L. ***Black English: Its History and Usage in the United States***. Random 1973, $11.00 (0-394-71872-0). 361pp. Nonfiction.

Black speech is often derided as "bad English," "nonstandard English," and the "language of the ghetto." To counter that perception, the author has written a book whose thesis is that Black English is a bona fide language. What's more, the grammar of this speech is anchored securely in a historical foundation of African and African-American cultural traditions. This is a useful book for educators and for general readers interested in the origin, structure, and variety of language.   AJWM

Drake, St. Claire. ***Black Folk Here and There***.
See entry 1297.

140   Du Bois, W.E.B. ***Black Reconstruction in America: An Essay Toward a History of the Part Which Black Folk Played in the Attempt to Reconstruct Democracy in America, 1860–1880.*** 2nd ed.; Repr. of 1969 ed. Frwd. by David L. Lewis. Macmillan 1992, $18.00 (0-689-70820-3). 768pp. Nonfiction.

This book, first published in 1934, is an engaging revisionist approach to the Reconstruction period in American history. Traditionally, historians have tended to portray Reconstruction as the nadir of the democratic process. But in Du Bois's interpretation, it reflected democracy its best, a time when blacks and whites together, bolstered by the most progressive state constitutions ever formulated, created wide-sweeping social legislation. In this way, Americans hurried to reconstruct a war-torn South in hopes of forestalling political betrayal by—and violence at the hands of—the Southern Redemptionists, who longed for the day when the South would "rise again."   AJWM

141   Du Bois, W.E.B. ***The Souls of Black Folk***. Buccaneer Books 1986, $22.95 (0-89966-535-7); Viking $8.99 (0-517-10169-6). 280pp. Essays.

This is vintage Du Bois writing on racism in the United States during the late Postreconstruction period. The book—a powerful series of essays on the socioeconomic plight of African Americans in the face of an all-pervasive ideology of white supremacy—explores Du Bois's now-famous thesis: "The problem of the twentieth century is the problem of the color-line." When it was first published, the book had a powerful impact on African Americans, whom Du Bois identified as a potential force in the organization of society. It stands today as one of the classic works in the history and sociology of the African-American people.   AJWM

Du Bois, W.E.B. *The World and Africa: An Inquiry into the Part Which Africa Has Played in World History.*
See entry 1298.

142   Edelman, Marian Wright. *The Measure of Our Success: A Letter to My Children and Yours.* Beacon 1992, $15.00 (0-8070-3102-X); HarperCollins $9.00 (0-06-097546-6). 128pp. Essays.

Edelman, head of the Children's Defense Fund, has written a short book of advice specifically for her three sons but also for all parents and children. In it she describes the legacy of service and concern for the underprivileged that she received from her parents and teachers. The heart of her book consists of twenty-five "lessons for life." These include such direct admonitions as "be honest" and "never give up." Emphasizing the importance of family relationships and responsibilities as well as the need to be of service to others, the author reinforces the old-fashioned virtues of hard work and personal integrity. Her straightforward advice is a welcome alternative to the selfish materialism that dominates much of our popular culture.   PTM

143   Fager, Charles. *Selma 1965: The March That Changed the South.* o.p. Nonfiction.

Fager describes how the 1965 civil rights campaign in Selma, Alabama resulted in the historic Selma-to-Montgomery March and, ultimately, the passage of the Voting Rights Act. His vivid account relates the events leading up to the fateful confrontation on the Edmund Pettus Bridge, where peaceful marchers were assaulted by Sheriff Jim Clark and his posse of mounted deputies. Fager chronicles the efforts of civil rights activists to confront the forces of white supremacy and to overcome the determined resistance of the activists' segregationist opponents. The book vividly conveys the tension between Clark, a fervent segregationist, and Selma's Chief of Police Wilson Baker, who believed that a more moderate response would more effectively contain the demonstrators.   PTM

144   Franklin, John Hope, and Alfred A. Moss, Jr. *From Slavery to Freedom: A History of African Americans.* 7th ed. Knopf 1994, $45.00 (0-679-43087-3). 579pp. Nonfiction.

Using history, interpretation, and analysis, this important work describes the struggles of an African people to etch its image into the American character. It can be read as a companion volume to Nathan Huggin's *Black Odyssey (see main entry)*, a more impressionistic and personal treatment of similar material. The book first examines the lives of blacks in their African homeland, with a look at the many cultures and social structures that existed before the days of the slave trade, and progresses through the Colonial, Revolutionary, Civil War, and Reconstruction periods. After describing the African American's arduous trek across time, the book analyzes issues of concern to the black community today.   AJWM

145 Fredrickson, George W. ***White Supremacy: A Comparative Study in American and South African History***. Oxford Univ. Pr. 1981, $12.95 (0-19-503042-7). 356pp. Nonfiction.

The author demonstrates both the parallels and the differences that exist between racism in America and the system of apartheid as it was practiced in South Africa. Although blacks constitute a minority in the United States, they far outnumber whites in South Africa. In both countries, however, conflict arose from whites' belief in their racial superiority, a belief that was institutionalized through both the political and legal systems. The book analyzes how these social systems reinforced concepts of white supremacy and what impact the policies had on the black people forced to live under them.   AJWM

146 Freedman, Samuel G. ***Upon This Rock: The Miracles of a Black Church***. HarperCollins 1993, $22.50 (0-06-016610-X); $12.00 (0-06-092459-4). 384pp. Nonfiction.

Freedman has written a compelling portrait of St. Paul Community Baptist Church in the East New York section of Brooklyn and its dynamic pastor, the Rev. Johnny Ray Youngblood. The book traces Youngblood's growth from his days as a college student in New Orleans to his present urban ministry. By 1980, six years after Youngblood came to the small struggling church, he was able to purchase a much larger building to house his growing flock. Youngblood works intimately with this large and diverse congregation, providing spiritual direction but also helping them deal with personal problems. St. Paul's is one of the few positive forces in its community—fighting against drugs and crime and promoting business ownership, family stability, and academic achievement. Freedman's work pays tribute to the resilience and vitality of the black church, one of the strongest institutions of the African-American community and a crucial force in tackling the challenges of the contemporary urban ghetto.

PTM

147 Garrow, David J. ***The FBI and Martin Luther King, Jr.*** Viking 1983, $11.00 (0-14-006486-9). 320pp. Nonfiction.

Garrow's careful study of FBI files reveals the shocking story of J. Edgar Hoover's crusade to discredit and destroy Martin Luther King, Jr. The FBI began closely monitoring King's activities in early 1962, after the Bureau learned that Stanley Levinson, a suspected Communist, had been acting as King's financial and literary advisor. When King refused to stop working with Levinson, Attorney General Robert Kennedy authorized wiretaps on his office and home telephones. In late 1964, Hoover's aide, William Sullivan, launched a campaign to discredit King, moving the Bureau's activities beyond surveillance to active harassment. FBI agents leaked transcripts of King's conversations to conservative newspaper editors and to members of Congress and mailed an anonymous threatening letter to King. The Bureau's campaign against King ended only with his assassination in 1968. The author provides disturbing proof that Presidents Kennedy and Johnson knew of—and authorized—the FBI's activities.

PTM

148 Genovese, Eugene D. *Roll, Jordan, Roll: The World the Slaves Made*. Random 1976, $17.00 (0-394-71652-3). 823pp. Nonfiction.

This thorough and evocative cross-disciplinary study of "the peculiar institution" (slavery) gives the reader a detailed look at life in bondage. Challenging the ideas expressed by writers during the progressive era, who attempted to portray slavery as a "civilizing" experience for Africans, Genovese portrays it as a system devoted to stripping its victims of their humanity. Even so, Genovese explains, slaves and their masters were so mutually dependent that the system of slavery inevitably allowed Africans to find ways to define and express their spirituality, culture, and individual dignity. These strengths sustained them through generations of bondage.   AJWM

149 Giddings, Paula. *When and Where I Enter: The Impact of Black Women on Race and Sex in America*. Morrow 1984, $22.95 (0-688-01943-9); Bantam $11.95 (0-553-34561-3). 403pp. Nonfiction.

In this analytical history, the author underscores the close relationship between racism and sexism and shows how awareness of the link has led many black women to become not just civil rights advocates but feminists as well—the critical link between the black liberation and women's rights movements. Giddings describes the efforts of noted courageous black women such as Ida B. Wells and Mary McLeod Bethune and less well-known individuals such as Frances Ellen Harper, Nannie Helen Burroughs, and Anna Julia Cooper. The book honors the contributions of black women to the struggle against the twin evils of racism and sexism.   PTM

150 Goodman, James. *Stories of Scottsboro*. Pantheon 1994, $27.50 (0-679-40779-0). 465pp. Nonfiction.

The Scottsboro case became a symbol of the injustices African Americans suffered at the hands of the Southern legal system. In 1931 two white women charged nine young black men with rape. Even though later court testimony proved that the women were prostitutes, the nine blacks were convicted and sentenced to death. The NAACP, at that time virtually the sole source of legal assistance for Southern blacks, ignored their plight, but the American Communist Party championed their cause, winning widespread admiration among African-American communities for its principled stand. The convictions were overturned twice by the Supreme Court, first because the nine men had lacked adequate legal representation and then after a second trial—which again resulted in death sentences—because blacks had been systematically excluded from the juries.

    This book ably conveys the horrors endured by African Americans caught in the clutches of racist jails and courts and underscores the deeply troubling issues raised when the charge involves the rape of white women by black men. The author explains how the Scottsboro case made white Americans aware of the extent to which African Americans were deprived of their rights in the South. What's more, the case served to embolden the NAACP to become more active, not just in asserting African Americans' legal rights but in displacing the Communist Party as the primary champion of racial equality.

RL

151   Goss, Linda, and Marian E. Barnes, eds. *Talk That Talk: An Anthology of African-American Storytelling.* Intro. by Henry Louis Gates, Jr. Simon & Schuster 1989, $12.95 (0-685-28304-6). 521pp. Nonfiction.

This volume offers nearly one hundred stories from the African-American oral tradition. The stories are divided into types, among which are animal stories, ghost stories, humorous tales, didactic tales and sermons, historical narratives, and family stories. Although some of the stories come from Africa and the Caribbean, most of them originated in the continental United States but draw upon African motifs. The authors collect their stories from a variety of sources. Some of the storytellers—Langston Hughes, Zora Neale Hurston, and Maya Angelou—are professional writers; others are political leaders, such as Dr. Martin Luther King, Jr.; King's daughter Yolanda; and Dick Gregory. An introduction by Henry Louis Gates, Jr., professor of African-American Studies at Harvard, offers a scholarly but accessible overview of the major themes, storytelling styles, and works contained in the book.

This volume has a broad audience, from general readers to folklore specialists to teachers looking for materials for classroom use. An index guides the reader to stories appropriate for particular age groups, and there is an extensive bibliography for further reading.   LML

152   Graham, Hugh D. *The Civil Rights Era: Origins and Development of National Policy, 1960–1972.* Oxford Univ. Pr. 1990, $40.00 (0-19-504531-9). 590pp. Nonfiction.

Much has been written about the civil rights policies of the federal government, but Graham's account is perhaps the most comprehensive and detailed. He describes the way civil rights legislation was formulated under the Kennedy, Johnson, and Nixon administrations, tracks the resulting congressional maneuvering and debates, and details how federal agencies and courts implemented the laws. Prior to 1965—a period Graham identifies as Phase I—the emphasis in the civil rights movement was on legislation against discrimination. During Phase II, after 1965, the goal shifted from equal treatment to equal results. Through meticulous scholarship, the author analyzes the impact of protests and demonstrations by African Americans on the government's efforts to devise a fair and effective civil rights policy. An abridged edition is available in both hardcover and paperback.   PTM

153   Greene, Melissa Fay. *Praying for Sheetrock.* Addison Wesley 1991, $21.95 (0-201-55048-2); Fawcett $10.00 (0-449-90753-8). 352pp. Nonfiction.

The civil rights movement came relatively late to rural McIntosh County, Georgia, but it produced momentous social and political changes. For one thing, it led to the dismantling of a corrupt political machine that had been in power for several decades. The main focus of the book is Thurnell Alston, who emerged as a spokesman for McIntosh County's black community and who persevered against long odds to win election to the county commission in 1978. Following this triumph, however, civil rights militancy soon ebbed and Alston gradually lost his crusading zeal. His political career came to a tragic end ten years later when he was arrested and convicted on drug charges.   PTM

154   Gutman, Herbert G. *The Black Family in Slavery and Freedom, 1750–1925*.
Random 1977, $20.00 (0-394-72451-8). 664pp. Nonfiction.

According to some critics, the African-American family is "a tangle of pathology," a "sick institution" that can only produce "sick" offspring. This book responds to that charge. To counter much of what he views as unsound science, the author uses the techniques of the sociologist and the historian to muster solid evidence that reveals the long-term impact of oppressive and degenerative slavery. His goal is to show scientifically that, between 1750 and 1925, the black family was a vitally adaptive institution, capable of supporting its members and serving as a source of strength. Gutman's work is continuing and stands as a powerful counterstatement to the conventional wisdom about the black family.   AJWM

155   Hacker, Andrew. *Two Nations: Black and White, Separate, Hostile, Unequal*.
Illus. Macmillan 1992, $24.95 (0-684-19148-2); Ballantine $10.00 (0-345-38096-7). 320pp. Nonfiction.

In the first section of this book the author presents his observations on racial definitions and divisions in the United States—what it is like to be an African-American and why white Americans react as they do to blacks. In the second part, Hacker examines the various ways race affects living conditions and the quality of life . Particularly valuable are his many statistical comparisons of the social and economic conditions of blacks and whites in a number of categories, including family organization, employment, income, education, crime, and politics. In each of these areas Hacker identifies how much of the observed difference can be attributed to race and how much is due to other factors, such as social class. Hacker sees a huge chasm between blacks and whites and detects disturbingly few signs that the chasm will be bridged during the coming century.   LML

156   Hampton, Henry, and Steve Fayer. *Voices of Freedom: An Oral History of the Civil Rights Movement from the 1950s Through the 1980s*. Bantam 1991, $16.95 (0-553-35232-6). 720pp. Nonfiction.

This book, based on interviews conducted for the PBS documentary television series *Eyes on the Prize*, is organized into thirty-one chapters, each one a significant episode in the history of African Americans. This story of the struggle for civil rights begins with the lynching of Emmett Till in Mississippi in 1955. Subsequent chapters are devoted to such events as the Montgomery bus boycott, the Little Rock crisis, the Freedom Rides, the Birmingham demonstrations, the March on Washington, the Mississippi Freedom Summer, and the Selma-to-Montgomery March. Also included are chapters on Muhammad Ali, the 1967 election of Carl Stokes as mayor of Cleveland, and the Attica prisoners' revolt of 1971. The final chapter addresses the Boston school busing controversy of 1974. Each episode is told through the words of key participants and eyewitnesses.   PTM

Harris, Joseph. *Global Dimensions of the African Diaspora*.
See entry 1303.

157 Hentoff, Nat. *Jazz Is*. Illus. Limelight 1984, $17.95 (0-87910-003-6). 288pp.
Nonfiction.

This volume offers a collection of lyrical portraits of leading jazz artists, intercut with Hentoff's personal recollections of moments when his life was touched by encounters with great jazz compositions and their creators. Hentoff ably conveys the power of such great performers as fabled trumpet player Louis Armstrong, singer Billie Holiday, and pianist Cecil Taylor. He also analyzes the ways in which dynamic innovators contributed to the evolution of jazz: Teddy Wilson, the epitome of swing; Gerry Mulligan, the organizer of experimental jam sessions; and Miles Davis, the primary inventor of "cool jazz." Hentoff presents a frank discussion of how racism has prevented Duke Ellington from being recognized as the greatest American composer of the century and how it has blinded Americans to the universal importance of other jazz greats.

Readers who want a comprehensive history of jazz should consult Gunther Schuller's *Early Jazz* (Oxford Univ. Pr., 1968) and *The Swing Era* (Oxford University Pr., 1989). RL

158 Herskovits, Melville J. *The Myth of the Negro Past*. Repr. of 1941 ed. Intro. by Sidney W. Mintz. Beacon 1990, $16.00 (0-8070-0905-9). 416pp. Nonfiction.

Some ethnologists have argued that, over the centuries, the system of slavery stripped North American blacks of their essential "Africanness" to the extent that they could no longer identify themselves as people of African origin. In this book, first published in 1941, the author disputes that claim. Citing sociological and ethnological research, Herskovits finds that, indeed, African peoples in the Americas retained many of their African traditions. Often, as a way of enhancing their ability to survive and thrive in their adopted land, Africans blended their own traditions with Amerindian and European cultural currents. In the preface to the 1958 edition, Herskovits wrote: "Afro-American groups [throughout the Americas] integrated old beliefs with new, reinterpreting both to fit a pattern of sanction and value that functions effectively in meeting the political needs of life." AJWM

159 Higginbotham, A. Leon, Jr. *In the Matter of Color, Race, and the American Legal Process: The Colonial Period*. Illus. Oxford Univ. Pr. 1978, $40.00 (0-19-502387-0); $14.95 (0-19-502745-0). 512pp. Nonfiction.

In this book, Judge Higginbotham, an expert in the law, analyzes how "the matter of color" shaped the legal process during the Colonial era and resulted in an unjust society for people of African descent. White perceptions about blacks and their place in society were codified in the founding nation's laws to ensure that the boundaries separating "brahmin and untouchable" remained inviolable. Higginbotham identifies the "nexus between the brutal centuries of Colonial slavery and the racial polarization and anxieties of today." The author laments the fact that, despite the demise of slavery, African Americans remain pariahs in their own country. AJWM

160 Holloway, Joseph E., ed. *Africanisms in American Culture*. Illus. Indiana Univ. Pr. 1990, $29.95 (0-253-32839-X); $9.95 (0-253-20686-3). 272pp. Nonfiction.

Much was lost when enslaved Africans were brought forcibly to the Americas: family ties, ethnic identification, a sense of place. Still, recent research increasingly demonstrates that many aspects of African culture—what the author calls Africanisms—managed to survive the transition. Four essays concern the enduring African religious heritage, and others identify Africanisms in language, art, music, folkways, etiquette, and European-American culture. This volume complements and extends the work of such authors as Carter G. Woodson, Lorenzo Turner, and Melville Herskovits, to whom this book is dedicated.   BR

161 Huggins, Nathan I. *Black Odyssey: The Afro-American Ordeal in Slavery*. Random 1990, $12.00 (0-679-72814-7). 250pp. Nonfiction.

This clearly written and accessible book presents an evocative narrative that conveys the misery of enslavement from the Colonial period through the Civil War. This is a particularly good choice for introductory readers because of its tight organization and lively, vivid storytelling. As a historical narrative, the book complements *From Slavery to Freedom* by John H. Franklin and Albert Moss *(see main entry)*.   AJWM

Jacobs, Sylvia M., ed. *Black Americans and the Missionary Movement in Africa*.
See entry 1310.

162 James, Portia. *The Real McCoy: African-American Invention and Innovation, 1619–1930*. Illus. Smithsonian Inst. 1990, $17.50 (0-87474-557-8). 100pp. Nonfiction.

This book surveys the artistic creativity, imagination, and mechanical innovation of black inventors. For example, the reader learns that, although Thomas Edison is credited with the invention of the lightbulb, the filament that actually produces the light was invented by a black man, Lewis H. Latimer. Another black inventor, Garrett Morgan, produced the first practical electric traffic light, while Jan Matzeliger created devices that made possible the mass production of shoes. The author makes the point that many inventions that have enhanced the American industrial system, increased workplace productivity, and made our lives more comfortable were the product of black genius.   AJWM

163 Jones, Howard. *Mutiny on the Amistad: The Saga of a Slave Revolt and Its Impact on American Abolition, Law and Diplomacy*. Illus. Oxford Univ. Pr. 1987, $25.00 (0-19-503828-2); $11.95 (0-19-503829-0). 288pp. Nonfiction.

This book analyzes a dramatic historical incident: the first documented case in which Africans used the court system to challenge the legal foundation of slavery. In 1839 some African men who had been sold into slavery in Africa and who were being transported on the Spanish vessel the *Amistad* mutinied. They killed some of the crew, seized control of the vessel, and demanded that the ship return to Africa. When the *Amistad* reached American waters it was subsequently captured by a U.S. warship and the slaves held as pirates. The American president, Martin Van Buren, wanted to turn the men over to the Spanish government, but in 1841 the Supreme Court, citing international laws that prohibited the slave trade, declared them free. The Africans were helped in their case by John Quincy Adams, formerly president of the United States but at that time a representative from Massachusetts and an ardent campaigner against slavery. Funds raised through a charity drive enabled the Africans to buy passage back to their homeland. AJWM

164 Jones, James H. ***Bad Blood: The Tuskegee Syphilis Experiment.*** Expanded ed. Free Press 1993, $22.95 (0-02-916675-6); $14.95 (0-02-916676-4). 300pp. Nonfiction.

Jones tells the story of a secret forty-year study, conducted by the United States Public Health Service (PHS), to analyze the serious complications that arise in the final phase of untreated syphilis. The study, which eventually involved 399 black men from Macon County, Georgia, was not concerned with treatment. Despite the fact that syphilis is often fatal, the men received no drugs—even after 1943, when penicillin was found to be an effective treatment for the disease. The author examined archival materials from PHS files and conducted interviews with participants in the study to reconstruct both the manner in which the project was carried out and the rationale for its continuation. He also describes the role of Peter Buxton, a courageous social worker, who learned of the study while working for the PHS and who revealed its existence to the press in 1972. Jones's research documents a sordid chapter in the history of American medicine. PTM

165 Jordan, Winthrop D. ***White over Black: American Attitudes Toward the Negro, 1550–1812.*** Univ. of North Carolina Pr. 1968, $50.00 (0-8078-1055-X); Norton $15.95 (0-393-00841-X). 651pp. Nonfiction.

This book traces the historical evolution of attitudes, beliefs, and myths that many whites hold about Africans, Africa, and "blackness." According to the author, attitudes entrenched in Europe (mainly England) during the 1700s form the basis for many of these distorted views. The book argues that, in the early Colonial period, the system of forced labor conscripted people largely without regard to their race. In later years, however, white men—motivated by what the author calls a psychological need to control people and events—changed the system so that slavery became a racial system that involved only black laborers. Today, the legacy of that profound change can still be seen manifested in such ideologies as white supremacy and racism. AJWM

Kapur, Sudarshan. ***Raising Up a Prophet: The African-American Encounter with Gandhi.***
See entry 1411.

166 Katz, William L. ***Black Indians: A Hidden Heritage.*** Illus. Macmillan 1986, $16.95 (0-689-31196-6). 208pp. Nonfiction.

By providing gripping insights into the historical relationships between American Indians and Africans in the Americas, this book is a testament to the indomitable spirits of two peoples who, since the arrival of Columbus, bonded together in communities of mutual respect and intermarriage. For many years, these Afro-Amerindian communities helped strengthen the people's will to resist total white domination. Their tale is one worth reading, not only because it involves people often relegated to the margins of history but because it underscores the inherent interrelatedness of the American family.

AJWM

167 Katz, William L. *The Black West.* Rev. ed., Repr. of 1971 ed. Illus. Open Hand 1987, $29.95 (0-940880-17-2); $15.95 (0-940880-18-0). 352pp. Nonfiction.

With this book, William Loren Katz assumes the mantle of historical truth from such little-known writers of black history as Delilah Beasley (*Negro Trailblazers of California*, 1919) Richard R. Wright, Jr. (*Negro Companions of the Spanish Explorers*, 1902), and Jack Conroy with Arna Bontemps (*They Seek a City*, 1945). The author challenges one of the key tenets of the "mainscript"—that is, the mainstream version of history—which describes only a very marginal role for blacks in the settlement of the American West. However, in the words of the author: "For black youngsters to truly feel a part of the United States and for white youngsters to see them as part of the nation, the black frontiersmen, settlers, cowboys, and cavalrymen must ride across the pages of textbooks just as they rode across the Western plains." His book is an excellent choice for introductory readers, while those seeking more specialized information may want to consult the older studies named above and the other primary sources upon which Katz has based his research.

AJWM

Keto, C. Tsehloane. *Africa Centered Perspective of History.*
See entry 1317.

168 King, Martin Luther, Jr., and James M. Washington, ed. *A Testament of Hope: The Essential Speeches and Writings of Martin Luther King, Jr.* HarperCollins 1986, $24.95 (0-06-250931-4); Harper SF $18.00 (0-06-064691-8). 676pp. Essays.

Editor James M. Washington has collected Martin Luther King, Jr.'s most important writings and public statements. Included are thirty-five essays on nonviolence, the civil rights movement, and black power; the texts of well-known sermons and speeches; transcripts of four interviews; and the full texts of his five books. Especially notable are the "Letter from the Birmingham Jail," the "I Have a Dream" speech from the March on Washington, and King's first book on the Montgomery bus boycott, *Stride Toward Freedom* (orig. pub. 1958; Harper SF, 1987). This work is a basic source for anyone studying the life and work of Martin Luther King, Jr.

PTM

169 Kluger, Richard. *Simple Justice: The History of Brown v. Board of Education and Black America's Struggle for Equality.* Random 1977, $25.00 (0-394-72255-8). 823pp. Nonfiction.

Kluger provides a detailed and comprehensive account of the Supreme Court's historic 1954 *Brown* v. *Board of Education of Topeka* decision. He tells the story of each of the five separate school desegregation cases from Kansas, Virginia, South Carolina, Delaware, and the District of Columbia that were consolidated into the *Brown* suit. Kluger offers vivid portraits of all of the key actors in this suit: the black parents and children who were plaintiffs; the lawyers for the NAACP, who perfected a winning legal strategy; the lawyers for the defendants, who fought to preserve segregation; and the nine justices of Supreme Court, who labored to reach a unanimous decision. The author's extensive personal interviews with the participants enable him to reconstruct the behind-the-scenes debates and decision making within the NAACP Legal Defense Fund and among the justices. This is a lengthy book, as befits its important subject, but it is uniformly well written and rich in human drama.

PTM

170 Kotlowitz, Alex. ***There Are No Children Here: The Story of Two Boys Growing Up in the Other America***. Doubleday 1991, $21.95 (0-385-26526-3); $12.95 (0-385-26556-5). 335pp. Nonfiction.

Kotlowitz describes the struggles of Lafayette and Pharaoh Rivers—age twelve and nine, respectively—who live in the Henry Horner Homes public housing complex in Chicago. Following the boys over a two-year period from 1987 to 1989, Kotlowitz relates details of their day-to-day existence and the obstacles they encounter growing up in poverty in an urban ghetto. During the time covered by the book, the boys wrestle with school, attempt to resist the lure of the gangs, and mourn the death of friends, all while searching for some inner peace. Without pretending to journalistic objectivity, Kotlowitz shows great affection for his subjects. His compelling personal portraits of the two boys put a human face on the abstract problems of poverty, urban decay, and family instability.

PTM

171 Kozol, Jonathan. ***Savage Inequalities: Children in America's Schools***. Crown 1991, $20.00 (0-517-58221-X); HarperCollins $12.00 (0-06-097499-0). 288pp. Nonfiction.

Following an extensive series of visits to public schools in cities such as East St. Louis, Illinois; Washington, D.C.; New York; Chicago; San Antonio; and Camden, New Jersey; Kozol reports on the education of children from poor families. The picture he paints is hardly encouraging: Buildings are crumbling, classrooms are crowded and lack adequate equipment and textbooks, teachers believe their students cannot learn, children are overwhelmed by the problems in their homes and communities, and there is insufficient funding to meet educational needs. In every community he visits, Kozol finds that, although decades have passed since the Supreme Court's 1954 *Brown* v. *Board of Education of Topeka* ruling, minority children are still isolated. Racial segregation is reinforced by discrimination based on social class, with children from poor families receiving consistently inferior educational opportunities. Kozol eloquently argues that the United States must redirect school funding so that the students with the greatest needs will obtain their fair share of financial resources.

PTM

172 Lawson, Steven F. ***Running for Freedom: Civil Rights and Black Politics in America, 1941–1988***. Illus. Temple Univ. Pr. 0-87722-792-6, $39.95 (1990). 320pp. Nonfiction.

Lawson describes the struggle of African Americans to regain the right to vote and to exercise political power in the period from 1941 to 1988. He shows how the tactics of protest and confrontation were used by the civil rights movement to win access to the voting booths for Southern blacks. The most notable achievement of this movement was the passage of the 1965 Voting Rights Act, which struck down most of the barriers to black enfranchisement. Lawson maintains that the growing electoral power of black voters at both the local and national levels has been accompanied by increased reliance on the process of bargaining and compromise associated with professional politics. Despite these gains, Lawson questions whether conventional electoral politics will be able to address the fundamental economic problems experienced by African Americans.   PTM

173   Lemann, Nicholas. *The Promised Land: The Great Black Migration and How It Changed America.* Knopf 1991, $24.95 (0-394-56004-3); Random $13.00 (0-685-57357-5). 410pp. Nonfiction.

Lemann does not attempt to write the complete history of the migration of African Americans from the rural South to the cities of the North and West. Instead, he selects one significant migratory stream—the exodus from the Mississippi Delta to the south side of Chicago—and uses it illustrate the transformation of American race relations. Lemann skillfully alternates between personal portraits and social and political analysis. He traces the life of Ruby Lee Haynes who moved from Clarksdale, Mississippi to Chicago and raised her children in the notorious Robert Taylor Homes. At the end of the book she has moved back to Mississippi seeking to escape the violence and miserable living conditions she found in the North. Her story is interspersed with Lemann's critical examination of the efforts of politicians and federal officials to grapple with the urban problems caused by this migration.
                                                                         PTM

Levine, Barry, ed. *The Caribbean Exodus.*
See entry 753.

174   Littlefield, Daniel F., Jr. *Africans and Seminoles: From Removal to Emancipation.* Greenwood 1977, $49.95 (0-8371-9529-2). 278pp. Nonfiction.

Littlefield's work is an interesting study of the significant roles (slave, freeman, warrior, spouse) that Africans assumed among the Seminole Indians of Florida up to the Civil War. In these communities, argues the author, "the union of Red and Black was based in great measure on political and military expediency." The Seminoles warred against the federal government to prevent forced removal from their ancestral lands, while escaped slaves resisted recapture by their former owners. During these wars much of the "tribal" leadership and many of the fighters were Africans. In fact, one report that field commanders sent back to Washington stated there were more blacks than Indians in the line of battle. The relationship of Black and Red took a turn for the worse when both groups were removed beyond the Mississippi River. There, according to the author, the Seminoles—influenced by Indians from local tribes—developed racial prejudice against blacks. This book, like *Black Indians* by William Loren Katz *(see main entry),* explores a "hidden history" of the union between two oppressed groups.   AJWM

175   Litwack, Leon F. *North of Slavery: The Negro in the Free States, 1790–1860.* Univ. of Chicago Pr. 1965, $13.95 (0-226-48586-2). 318pp. Nonfiction.

In the mid-1800s, the French traveler Alexis de Tocqueville commented on the white resentment toward blacks that he detected among residents in the states of the American Northwest, where slavery never existed. Another author, C. Vann Woodward, observed that after the Civil War the North introduced segregation to the South. The thoughts of both these men speak to the essence of Litwack's all-encompassing study of racial hatred against African Americans during that seventy-year period from 1790 to 1860. This book reveals the pervasive nature of racism in the North, and it refutes the myth that racial harmony existed in regions unsullied by a history of slavery.

AJWM

176   Lomax, Alan. *The Land Where the Blues Began.* Illus. Pantheon 1993, $25.00 (0-679-40424-4). 544pp. Nonfiction.

Noted folklorist and blues expert Alan Lomax traveled through the Mississippi Delta region over a period of decades to study the blues and the people who performed it. Blues, according to Lomax, began around 1900 as a means of African-American self-expression in the face of economic and political oppression. Blacks had few outlets to describe their struggle and their sadness; they had to be careful about speaking out in the society of Jim Crow, lest they meet a violent death at the hands of white racists. Based upon African and African-American motifs transmitted through the generations, the blues evolved into a fully developed musical genre. In addition to offering an analysis of blues songs, Lomax describes the men and women, young and old, who wrote and performed this music. He explores their lifestyles, economic and social conditions, and the role of the church. His book concludes with portraits of the great bluesmen of the Delta region. A bibliography, discography, filmography, and song appendix round out this well-researched, thoughtfully presented, and useful book. *The Land Where the Blues Began* will appeal mainly to blues fans but is lively enough in its presentation to attract the introductory reader as well.

LML

177   Lukas, J. Anthony. *Common Ground: A Turbulent Decade in the Lives of Three American Families.* Knopf 1985, $19.95 (0-394-41150-1); Random $15.00 (0-394-74616-3). 672pp. Nonfiction.

Lukas traces the controversy surrounding the desegregation of Boston's public schools in the 1970s by telling the stories of three families who were affected by these events. The Drivers are upper-middle-class white liberals who chose to live in an integrated neighborhood and who sent their sons to the local public school. The Twymons are a black family living in the Roxbury ghetto, whose children are bused to schools in the all-white Charleston section as part of the court-ordered desegregation plan. The McGoffs are a white working-class family living in Charleston who withdrew their children from school to protest the desegregation plan. As Lukas describes their efforts to cope with the racial conflict in their community, the reader is introduced to other significant figures in this case, including Federal Judge W. Arthur Garrity, school committee chair Louise Day Hicks, and Mayor Kevin White. Lukas's reporting combines an understanding of the larger issue of segregation in education with an appreciation of the human costs involved, both in maintaining the status quo and in bringing about social change.

PTM

178 McAdam, Douglas. ***Political Process and the Development of Black Insurgency, 1930 to 1970***. Illus. Univ. of Chicago Pr. 1985, $12.95 (0-226-55552-6). 304pp. Nonfiction.

McAdam offers a political interpretation of the rise of the civil rights movement. The key event was the migration of Southern blacks to the North and the resulting growth of their political strength within the Democratic Party. McAdam maintains that because they depended on black voting blocs in key Northern cities, Democratic candidates could no longer continue ignoring the way blacks' constitutional rights had been suppressed in the South. He argues that social insurgency is best understood as the result of changes in the structure of political opportunities. Although his discussion of sociological theory may be too technical for most readers, McAdam presents a valuable analysis of the growth and decline of black insurgency during the 1950s and 1960s. PTM

179 McMillen, Neil R. ***Dark Journey: Black Mississippians in the Age of Jim Crow***. Illus. Univ. of Illinois Pr. 1990, $14.95 (0-252-06156-X). 464pp. Nonfiction.

McMillen has written a carefully researched history of racial segregation in Mississippi, considered by many to have been the most brutal state of the Deep South. Focusing on the period from 1890 to 1940—after the end of Reconstruction and before the first stirrings of the civil rights movement—the author documents the exclusion of African Americans from state politics, their miserable schools, the struggles of black workers and sharecroppers, and their migration to the North. The most chilling section of this book describes how the courts deprived blacks of the most basic legal rights and how the extralegal terrorism of lynching discouraged blacks from protesting or otherwise attempting to improve their lives. PTM

180 McPherson, James M. ***The Negro's Civil War: How American Blacks Felt and Acted During the War for the Union***. Ballantine 1991, $12.00 (0-345-37120-8). 358pp. Nonfiction.

The book dispels the notion that during the Civil War blacks were passive, that they did not understand the value of freedom and the struggle necessary to obtain it. The author proves his thesis—that blacks actively participated in the American Civil War—through the extensive use of contemporary documents. The result is an intimate look at the war through the eyes of those whose very presence in the country triggered the conflagration. AJWM

181 Morris, Aldon D. ***The Origins of the Civil Rights Movement: Black Communities Organizing for Change***. Illus. Free Press 1984, $24.95 (0-02-922120-X); $14.95 (0-02-922130-7). 368pp. Nonfiction.

Morris presents a sociological analysis of the origins and development of the civil rights movement during the 1950s and early 1960s. He notes that the urbanization of Southern blacks during the first half of the twentieth century "created the conditions that generated the resources needed to support a sustained movement against racial domination." Foremost among these resources is the black church, which not only contributed charismatic leadership, but also provided membership, an organizational framework, a common culture, and financial backing for the movement. Morris further credits black colleges, universities, and protest organizations such as the NAACP and the Southern Christian Leadership Conference (SCLC) for helping advance the crusade against segregation. By arguing that the civil rights movement was fostered by organizations and institutions firmly rooted in the African-American community, Morris takes issue with other scholars who trace the origins of the movement to the actions of agencies outside of the black community.   PTM

182   Moses, Wilson J. *The Golden Age of Black Nationalism, 1850–1925*. Illus. Oxford Univ. Pr. 1988, $11.95 (0-19-520639-8). 348pp. Nonfiction.

The author states that his purpose in writing this book is "to provoke controversy and to provide a new thesis concerning the Golden Age of Black Nationalism." Moses's argument is that Black Nationalism was more conservative than radical, more rightist than leftist. Drawing on the thoughts and writings of leaders such as Sutton Griggs, Martin Delaney, Frederick Douglass, Alexander Crummell, W.E.B. Du Bois, Marcus Garvey, and Mary Church Terrell (of the National Association of Colored Women), the book identifies four main conservative forces that fed the early Nationalism movement: African civilization, messianic self-conception (Ethiopian mysticism), authoritarian collectivism, and black separatism. The book complements Sterling Stuckey's *Slave Culture*, E. David Cronon's *Black Moses*, and Dorothy Sterling's *Black Foremothers (see main entries)*.   AJWM

183   Norrell, Robert J. *Reaping the Whirlwind: The Civil Rights Movement in Tuskegee*. Illus. Knopf 1985, $19.95 (0-394-53688-6); Random $10.36 (0-394-74407-1). 272pp. Nonfiction.

According to this book, a number of factors present in Tuskegee, Alabama, during the mid-1950s combined to spark the civil rights movement there. For example, the presence of Tuskegee Institute and a large Veterans Administration attracted many well-educated black professionals to the area. One of them, sociology professor Charles Gomillion, became a leading figure in the struggle for civil rights when he founded the Tuskegee Civic Association, whose mission was to press for black voting rights. The 1964 Supreme Court decision *Gomillion* v. *Lightfoot* overturned Tuskegee's practice of gerrymandering city limits to exclude potential black voters and paved the way for the election of blacks to the city government. Through meticulous research, Norrell traces the evolution of "civic democracy" in Macon County and describes the effects of growing strength among black voters on both black and white residents of Tuskegee.   PTM

184   O'Reilly, Kenneth. *Racial Matters: The FBI's Secret File on Black America, 1960–1972*. Free Press 1989, $29.95 (0-02-923681-9); $14.95 (0-02-923682-7). 400pp. Nonfiction.

In this carefully documented study, O'Reilly describes how the Federal Bureau of Investigation attempted to undermine and destroy the black freedom movement during the 1960s and early 1970s. He reveals how in 1961 the FBI informed police in Birmingham, Alabama that the civil rights demonstrators known as the Freedom Riders would be arriving. The FBI then refused to intervene when the police allowed Klansmen to organize a brutal attack on the demonstrators. O'Reilly also describes how J. Edgar Hoover launched a systematic effort to harass and discredit Martin Luther King, Jr., a subject covered in greater detail in David J. Garrow's *The FBI and Martin Luther King, Jr. (see main entry)*. Two final chapters are devoted to the COINTELPRO program of the late 1960s in which the FBI targeted militant black organizations for police intimidation and provocation. O'Reilly accuses the FBI of inciting police violence against black activists, which ultimately resulted in the destruction of the Black Panther party. PTM

185 Pemberton, Gayle. *The Hottest Water in Chicago.* Faber 1992, $19.95 (0-571-12936-6); Doubleday $10.95 (0-385-46842-3). 286pp. Essays.

This collection of personal essays ranges over a variety of topics, but most deal with family, education, or some aspect of popular culture. Readers will learn about the author's middle-class family—her father, a "race man" with the Chicago Urban League; her grandfather, an architect in Minnesota; her outspoken grandmother; and the sister with whom she shared youthful adventures. Pemberton recounts personal experiences from her youth, recalls her education and teaching career, and offers observations on such literary and cultural figures as Andrew Wyeth, Bigger Thomas, and the opera *Porgy and Bess*. All of the essays are infused with Pemberton's humor and consciousness of her racial identity. PTM

186 Powledge, Fred. *Free At Last? The Civil Rights Movement and the People Who Made It.* Repr. of 1991 ed. HarperCollins 1992, $15.00 (0-06-097463-X). 720pp. Nonfiction.

Powledge covered the Southern civil rights movement for the *Atlanta Journal* and the *New York Times*. This book is a comprehensive history of the movement from the 1955 Montgomery bus boycott to the 1965 Selma-to-Montgomery March by a reporter who sympathized with its objectives. He describes each of the major phases of the movement, including the student sit-ins; the Freedom Rides; the integration of the University of Mississippi; the demonstrations in Georgia, Alabama, and Washington, D.C.; and the Mississippi Freedom Summer. What distinguishes Powledge's book from other accounts is his emphasis on the people who made up the movement. Each chapter is sprinkled with excerpts from interviews with civil rights activists, lawyers, and government officials who reflect on the significance of the events in which they participated. PTM

187 Quarles, Benjamin. *The Negro in the American Revolution.* Univ. of North Carolina Pr. 1961, $29.95 (0-8078-0833-4); Norton $9.95 (0-393-00674-3). 231pp. Nonfiction.

This is a seminal study of the important part blacks played in Colonial America's struggle for independence from England between 1776 and 1783. In making the point that blacks learned the strategies of combat from their experiences during the French and Indian War and earlier struggles, Quarles presents to his readers an image of the African warrior quite unlike the stereotype of the "dancing, happy darkies" so prevalent at the time. The nearly 5,000 African revolutionaries were courageous, determined, and dependable soldiers, without whom the struggle for independence would have taken longer, if indeed it succeeded at all. Quarles is also the author of *Black Abolitionists* (orig. pub. 1969; Da Capo, 1991). AJWM

188 Raines, Howell. *My Soul Is Rested: Movement Days in the Deep South Remembered.* Viking 1983, $11.00 (0-14-006753-1). 472pp. Nonfiction.

Raines conducted nearly one hundred interviews with key participants in and observers of the civil rights movement during the late 1950s and early 1960s. Major sections of this book are devoted to the Montgomery bus boycott, the student sit-ins, the Freedom Rides, the demonstrations in Birmingham and Selma, and voter registration efforts by the Student Nonviolent Coordinating Committee (SNCC) in Mississippi. In addition to interviewing such well-known figures as Martin Luther King, Jr., John Lewis, Julian Bond, and Rosa Parks, Raines also interviewed such little-known activists as Mississippi farmer Hartman Turnbow and Selma school girl Sheyann Webb. Other subjects included leading segregationists, law officers, lawyers, and reporters who covered the movement. This is not a comprehensive work, however. Such key events as the demonstrations in Albany, Georgia, and the organization of the Mississippi Freedom Democratic Party are not mentioned. Also missing are interviews with James Forman, Stokely Carmichael, and other Black Power advocates. PTM

189 Rivlin, Gary. *Fire on the Prairie: Chicago's Harold Washington and the Politics of Race.* Illus. Henry Holt 1991, $24.95 (0-8050-1468-3); $14.95 (0-8050-2698-3). 320pp. Nonfiction.

Rivlin reports on Harold Washington's successful 1983 campaign to become the first black mayor of Chicago, his stormy four years in office, and his untimely death in 1987. The first half of the book describes how Washington built a coalition of blacks, Latinos, and liberal whites to challenge the entrenched political machine that had so long dominated the Chicago scene. Much of the second half of the book analyzes the struggles between Washington and his white opponents on the city council, who were led by Alderman Ed Vrdolyak. Because they retained control of the council, the machine politicians frustrated many of Washington's reform efforts. Rivlin conveys his strong admiration for Washington's skills as a politician and his dedication to populist principles. PTM

Scott, William R. *The Sons of Sheba's Race: African Americans and the Italo-Ethiopian War, 1935–1941.*
See entry 1332.

Skinner, Elliott. *African Americans and U.S. Policy Toward Africa, 1850–1924: In Defense of Black Nationality, 1850–1924.*
See entry 1334.

190 Smead, Howard. *Blood Justice: The Lynching of Mack Charles Parker.* Illus. Oxford Univ. Pr. 1986, $25.00 (0-19-504121-6); $9.95 (0-19-505429-6). 304pp. Nonfiction.

On the evening of April 24, 1959, a vigilante mob of eight men entered the jail at Poplarville, Mississippi, and seized Mack Charles Parker from his cell. Parker was accused of raping a white woman two months earlier, but he had never been convicted of the crime. The mob drove to a bridge over the Pearl River, shot Parker, and threw his body into the water. When it became clear that there would be no state prosecution against any members of the mob, the Justice Department tried—without success—to obtain indictments on federal kidnapping charges. Local whites protected the mob by refusing to cooperate with federal authorities, and once again Southern justice had allowed a white mob to get away with murder. In chilling detail, Smead recounts the events surrounding Parker's lynching and the subsequent investigation and legal actions. He bases his account on extensive interviews with Parker's associates and residents of Poplarville, including two members of the mob. He concludes that the Parker case was one of the last lynchings in the South because it provoked national outrage. Southern leaders got the message that vigilante-style justice was no longer acceptable and had to look for other ways to maintain white supremacy.

PTM/AJWM

191 Spear, Allan H. ***Black Chicago: The Making of a Negro Ghetto, 1890–1920.*** Repr. of 1967 ed. Univ. of Chicago Pr. 1969, $12.95 (0-226-76857-0). 248pp. Nonfiction.

Spear's acclaimed work is a thoroughly researched study of the rise of black Chicago as a typical ghetto set apart from white Chicago: separate, unequal, and highly underdeveloped, though diverse in terms of social class and occupation. The book assesses how the forces of late nineteenth- and early twentieth-century American racism limited the ability of African-American migrants to Chicago to realize the American Dream. During the time span covered by this book, race relations in the United States did not undergo any significant transition for the better; instead, the era was noted more for the continuation of the violent past. The tense and explosive nature of Chicago society over the issue of race mirrored similar situations in cities across the country. Competition over jobs, housing, and other resources affected all the migrants, regardless of education and income. Just before the end of the second decade, in the summer of 1919, Chicago was simply one of many major cities caught in the grip of racial violence known as "the Red Summer."

AJWM

192 Starobin, Robert S., ed. ***Denmark Vesey: The Slave Conspiracy of 1822.*** o.p. Nonfiction.

This short but well-researched collection of documents concerning the 1822 Charleston, South Carolina slave conspiracy is a monument to the fortitude of African resistance. Underscoring the point that discontent and rebelliousness were more characteristic of slaves than is often believed to be the case, the documents in this volume reveal the high level of political and cultural consciousness that characterized the conspirators and their leader, the freedman Denmark Vesey. The degree to which whites feared slave uprisings such as this one, and their panicked response to the discovery of the plot, provide a vivid contemporary picture of racial tensions in the pre–Civil War South.

AJWM

Steady, Filomena C., ed. *The Black Woman Cross-Culturally*.
See entry 1337.

193   Steele, Shelby. *The Content of Our Character: A New Vision of Race in America*. Repr. of 1990 ed. HarperCollins 1991, $11.00 (0-06-097415-X). 192pp. Nonfiction.

In this provocative and controversial volume, Steele raises a number of serious questions about race relations in the United States and strategies for gaining racial equality. He writes from the perspective of a successful black professional who has been assimilated into the middle-class lifestyle of mainstream America. He reminds the reader that the African-American population is not homogeneous but includes people who hold a variety of political views and who live in a range of social situations. Steele's most controversial position is his reservations about the value of affirmative action and preferential quotas for members of minority groups. He argues that such policies arouse the resentment of the nonminority population. More than that, they also raise unfair doubts about whether African Americans who attain positions of responsibility are qualified or whether they have simply been promoted because of the color of their skin. Steele urges blacks to shift focus from white racism and black victimization to begin building a more positive identity by taking advantage of opportunities for constructive growth and development. This volume has generated both lavish praise and vitriolic criticism; few people can read it and remain neutral. Another book on a similar theme is *The Rage of a Privileged Class* by Ellis Cose *(see main entry)*.   PTM

194   Stuckey, Sterling. *Slave Culture: Nationalist Theory and the Foundations of Black America*. Oxford Univ. Pr. 1988, $32.50 (0-19-504265-4); $13.95 (0-19-505664-7). 416pp. Nonfiction.

Tracing the roots of African cultural tradition (known as Africanisms) that the slaves preserved when brought to the United States, Stuckey argues that during the nineteenth century a single African-American people emerged. Despite the fact that the Africans came from diverse cultures and backgrounds, and despite the oppressive and divisive nature of slavery, an African nationalism, forged by a pan-African impulse, contained "values that bound slaves together and sustained them under brutal conditions of oppression." This emotional and cultural oneness of the people fostered a sense of African nationalism, which became the wellspring for Black Nationalism in the nineteenth and twentieth centuries. The author discusses the impact of slave culture on the intellectual and nationalist development of such leading black figures as David Walker, Henry Highland Garnet, W.E.B. Du Bois, and Paul Robeson.   AJWM

195   Terkel, Studs. *Race: How Blacks and Whites Think and Feel about the American Obsession*. New Pr. 1992, $24.95 (1-56584-000-3); Doubleday $12.95 (0-385-46889-X). 416pp. Nonfiction.

A gifted interviewer, Studs Terkel has a great talent for listening to people as they discuss the issues (in this case, race) that are most important in their lives. Some of the interviews in this book involve experts with national reputations, such as Lerone Bennett and Dr. Kenneth Clark. Most, however, reflect the thoughts of everyday working people—steelworkers, police officers, students, and lawyers. Although many of the interviewees are from Chicago, they reflect a wide variety of backgrounds and perspectives: single mothers, interracial couples, civil rights activists, black nationalists, and white bigots. Their comments are so far-ranging that it is difficult to generalize about the state of race relations today, except to say that the topic arouses strong feelings in nearly everyone.   PTM

196   Terry, Wallace. ***Bloods: An Oral History of the Vietnam War by Black Veterans***. Ballantine 1985, $5.95 (0-345-31197-3). 320pp. Nonfiction.

As a reporter for *Time* covering the Vietnam War from 1967 to 1969, Wallace interviewed many African-American servicemen. *Bloods* contains first-person accounts by a representative cross-section of twenty black combat veterans, including enlisted men, noncommissioned officers, and officers from all branches of the armed forces. They come from a variety of backgrounds and express widely differing reactions to their time in Vietnam. By calling attention to the unique experiences of black servicemen, Terry's work is a valuable addition to the growing body of literature on the Vietnam War.   PTM

197   Thompson, Vincent B. ***The Making of the African Diaspora in the Americas, 1441–1900***. Illus. Longman 1988, $27.95 (0-582-64238-8). 465pp. Nonfiction.

This is an important book for readers wishing to understand how African peoples have been dispersed throughout the Americas, especially during the era of slavery. The book compares and contrasts events in both hemispheres, exploring how new communities of Africans and people of mixed descent were established in the New World. By examining the events that have occurred within these groups across the generations, the book portrays a historical continuum of African settlements and outlines the lives of African peoples within, and their contributions to, the many cultures found in the Americas.   AJWM

198   Van Deburg, William L. ***New Day in Babylon: The Black Power Movement and American Culture, 1965–1975***. Univ. of Chicago Pr. 1992, $29.95 (0-226-84714-4); $13.95 (0-226-84715-2). 378pp. Nonfiction.

This book analyzes the Black Power movement, which flourished during the late 1960s and early 1970s. According to the author, the movement arose because of frustration with the lack of racial progress made by more traditional liberal programs. At the same time, and perhaps more importantly, African Americans were developing a liberating sense of pride. Van Deburg identifies two principal themes of Black Power: pluralism and nationalism. The pluralists were those who worked to gain control over the economic, educational, and political institutions of their communities. The nationalists were a diverse group who saw no prospect of gaining power within white institutions and who therefore advocated long-term sociocultural autonomy for African Americans. Van Deburg traces the development of Black Power on college campuses, in sports, in labor unions, in the armed forces, and in prisons. The most original part of his analysis examines the impact of the movement on African-American folk culture, literature, and the performing arts.   PTM

199   Van Sertima, Ivan. ***They Came Before Columbus: The African Presence in Ancient America***. Random 1976, $23.00 (0-394-40245-6). 288pp. Nonfiction.

The author challenges the notion that the only people European explorers of the New World encountered were the American Indians. Van Sertima compiles an exhaustive array of material from various disciplines to prove that there was a pronounced pre-Columbian African presence in the Americas. Oceanographic evidence suggests that Africans used equatorial and Gulf Stream currents and knew how to harness the prevailing winds to voyage west across the Atlantic. What's more, diaries, letters, and journals of Europeans contain many references to Africans in the Americas, and Van Sertima identifies numerous cultural and linguistic similarities, such as agricultural and architectural techniques, that suggest a strong African influence, especially on the Mayan and Aztec civilizations. Both scholar and novelist, Ivan Van Sertima describes some of the most dramatic scenes in history, including the launching in 1310 of two hundred master ships and another two hundred supply boats from the coast of Mali and a sea expedition led by the Mandingo king himself in 1311.   AJWM

200   Watkins, Mel. ***On the Real Side***. Simon & Schuster 1995, $27.50 (0-671-68982-7); $15.00 (0-671-51103-3). 652pp. Nonfiction.

African-American humor has a long history, beginning with African proverbs and lore. During the period of slavery, humor became a highly sophisticated means of both survival and escape, and this pattern continued under the segregation policies of the Jim Crow era. More recently, African-American humor has become very much part of mainstream American culture through such well-known performers as Bill Cosby, Richard Pryor, and Eddie Murphy.

Watkins's detailed but highly readable survey pulls together three centuries of African-American humor and places it within a larger social and political context. Although today's mainstream black comedians are known for their political edge, directed at white society, political commentary has always been part of both the content and style. The author also notes that characters such as Stepin Fetchit and Amos 'n' Andy were created by blacks for presentation to black audiences. Soon, though, white writers and performers appropriated these characters and used them to stereotype and humiliate African Americans. Watkins's study restores the original meaning and integrity to these efforts. He also discusses some of the less famous comedians whose performances reflected a powerful and incisive critique of a racist society.

LML

201   Weisbrot, Robert. ***Freedom Bound: A History of America's Civil Rights Movement***. Illus. Norton 1989, $21.95 (0-393-02704-X); NAL $11.00 (0-452-26553-3). 368pp. Nonfiction.

Weisbrot has written a brief general history of the civil rights movement from 1960 to 1970. He traces the origins of the student sit-in movement and its impact on the 1960 presidential election. In addition to describing the major campaigns of the movement in the South, Weisbrot also examines the growing militancy among blacks in the ghettoes of the North. Other chapters review the development of Black Nationalism and the subsequent white reaction to civil rights protests. Weisbrot concludes that the coalition of moderate blacks and liberal whites "wrought a self-limiting revolution that abolished formal barriers to equality" while doing little to address the basic economic problems of most African Americans.   PTM

202   West, Cornel. ***Race Matters.*** Beacon 1993, $15.00 (0-8070-0918-0); Random $9.00 (0-679-74986-1). 112pp. Essays.

In this collection of eight previously published essays, West discusses a variety of issues facing African Americans in the early 1990s. His topics include the confirmation of Supreme Court Justice Clarence Thomas, black conservatism, affirmative action, Malcolm X, black-Jewish relations, and black sexuality. He brings a fresh philosophical perspective to his analysis of political, social, and cultural problems. A recurrent theme in his writing is the failure of contemporary black leadership. He argues that the proper role for a black leader of the 1990s "is to be a race-transcending prophet who critiques the powers that be and who puts forward a vision of moral regeneration and political insurgency for the purpose of fundamental social change for all who suffer from socially induced misery."   PTM

203   White, Deborah G. ***Ar'n't I a Woman? Female Slaves in the Plantation South.*** Repr. of 1985 ed. Norton 1987, $7.95 (0-393-30406-X). 216pp. Nonfiction.

Many books about slavery tend to tell the story from the male perspective. In this work, however, Deborah White takes a different approach by examining the lives of slave women. She argues that it is a historical distortion to portray slave women as merely passive and concerned only with domestic issues. Writers who express that view include Stanley Elkins (*Slavery, A Problem in American Institutional Life*, 1968), John Blassingame (*The Slave Community*, 1977) (*see main entry*), and Robert Fogel and W. Stanley Engerman (*Time on the Cross: The Economics of American Slavery*, 1974). Such works create a sense of feminine powerlessness and invisibility, which does not reflect the reality. Instead, White's thesis is that slave women in America were not submissive, subordinate, or prudish—nor were they expected to be so.   AJWM

204   Whitfield, Stephen J. ***A Death in the Delta: The Story of Emmett Till.*** Illus. Free Press 1988, $29.95 (0-02-935121-9); Johns Hopkins Univ. Pr. $12.95 (0-8018-4326-X). 224pp. Nonfiction.

The facts in the 1955 murder of Emmett Till differ little from hundreds of other Mississippi lynchings. A young black man makes a fresh remark to a white woman; he is abducted from his uncle's home in the middle of the night and savagely beaten; his lifeless body is dumped into a local river. But this story has one critical difference from other incidents: Two of Till's killers were arrested and charged with murder. Still, after a perfunctory trial, both were acquitted by an all-white jury. What makes the Emmett Till lynching a memorable case in African-American history, this author maintains, is the outraged national reaction to his death. Though Till's murder would not be the last Mississippi lynching, Whitfield argues that the case effectively ended the state's isolation from the rest of the United States and paved the way for the civil rights movement to arrive a few years later.   PTM

205   Williams, Eric. ***Capitalism and Slavery.*** Repr. of 1944 ed. Univ. of North Carolina Pr. 1994, $34.95 (0-8078-2175-6); $14.95 (0-8078-4488-8). 310pp. Nonfiction.

Williams offers a fascinating account of the historical relationship between the enslavement of Africans and the rise of Western capitalism. The book shows how the profits from the purchase and sale of Africans fueled the Industrial Revolution. The book also documents the economic exploitation of white landowners by growing monopoly capital, the replacement of white indentured labor with enslaved labor, and the rise of an ideology of white supremacy. Eric Williams destroys the myth that whites needed black laborers because they themselves were unable to work the fields under the hot tropical sun. Whites could and did work in the fields. But the use of enslaved African labor proved more efficient, more practical, and cheaper. In defining racism as a consequence of the economic system of slavery, Williams departs from the thinking of Winthrop Jordan, whose book *White over Black (see main entry)* ascribes racism to intellectual or political perceptions.   AJWM

206   Williams, Juan. ***Eyes on the Prize: America's Civil Rights Years, 1954–1965.*** Viking 1988, $11.95 (0-14-009653-1). 320pp. Nonfiction.

Williams has written a comprehensive history of the civil rights movement for the general reader. The organization of the text closely follows the award-winning PBS documentary *Eyes on the Prize.* Williams describes eight major campaigns of the movement, including the Montgomery bus boycott, the Little Rock crisis, the sit-ins, the Birmingham protests, the Mississippi Freedom Summer, and the Selma-to-Montgomery March. The narrative is interspersed with interviews of civil rights activists and profiles of organizations involved in the movement. Especially compelling are the numerous photographs that capture the action and emotions of the movement. A useful epilogue profiles the lives of key figures in the book, and an excellent bibliography directs readers to other sources of information.   PTM

207   Williamson, Joel. ***The Crucible of Race: Black-White Relations in the American South Since Emancipation.*** Oxford Univ. Pr. 1984, $35.00 (0-19-503382-5). 561pp. Nonfiction.

Williamson's book is a masterpiece of historical analysis that traces the historical roots of Southern racism, a process that has defined the nature of race relations throughout the entire nation down to the present day. The author shows how perceptions of race are created and nurtured by a society. Perceptions of blacks, Williamson writes, have "seared the white soul, marking the character of the Southern mind radically and leaving it crippled and hobbled in matters of race long after the mark itself was lost from sight. . . ."

                    AJWM

208 Wilson, William Julius. ***The Declining Significance of Race: Blacks and Changing American Institutions.*** 2nd ed. Univ. of Chicago Pr. 1980, $10.95 (0-226-90129-7). 204pp. Nonfiction.

In this sociological analysis, Wilson examines the relationship of race and class in contemporary American society. He advances the controversial hypothesis that in recent years racial discrimination has become less important than economic class in determining the social position of African Americans. He reviews the history of race relations in the United States to show how changes in the nature of economic production have altered the dynamics of racial domination. Modern industrial society, he argues, has produced a black class structure similar to the class structure among whites. Wilson does not claim that racism has vanished or that class is the sole cause of all black problems. Rather, he maintains that "a preoccupation with race and racial conflict obscures fundamental problems that derive from the intersection of class with race." PTM

209 Wilson, William Julius. ***The Truly Disadvantaged: The Inner City, the Underclass, and Public Policy.*** Univ. of Chicago Pr. 1990, $13.95 (0-226-90131-9). 266pp. Nonfiction.

This book concerns the social and economic problems of the black underclass. Although his data and examples are drawn largely from Chicago, his analysis applies generally to America's older industrial cities. He first documents the social problems of the inner city, especially crime, unemployment, poverty, and the challenges faced by single-parent families, particularly those headed by women. The cause of these problems, he maintains, is not so much racism as it is broader changes in the American economy, specifically the decline in industrial employment opportunities for unskilled black males. These problems are then aggravated when middle-class blacks migrate from the inner city. Wilson argues that race-specific public policies are not enough to solve these problems. To gain the support of white politicians and voters, antipoverty programs must be universal and not aimed at specific minority groups. He suggests that policies focusing on economic growth and new-job creation have the best chance of solving the multiple problems of the ghetto underclass. Although his writing sometimes suffers from overuse of academic jargon, Wilson raises important policy issues affecting the future of African-American communities. PTM

210 Wood, Peter H. ***Black Majority: Negroes in Colonial South Carolina from 1670 Through the Stono Rebellion.*** Norton 1975, $9.95 (0-393-00777-4). 384pp. Nonfiction.

This book argues that the South was not a single cultural entity, as typified by the colony of Virginia. On the contrary, several "Souths" may have existed even before the middle of the eighteenth century, each with a distinct history and culture. Peter Wood reconstructs a rich and dynamic picture to illustrate that, for a considerable length of time, blacks in South Carolina outnumbered whites. That in turn had a profound impact on the social and economic development of the state. The book demonstrates, for example, that Africans brought to the colony many new and vital skills, thus challenging the conventional wisdom that Africans arrived with nothing other than "their color and temperament." What's more, Wood states, South Carolina became a major rice producer thanks to African expertise in cultivating the grain, which had been farmed for centuries in West Africa. The book also discusses the Stono Rebellion, a slave revolt that preceded the more notorious Denmark Vesey conspiracy in Charleston by a century. AJWM

211 Woodson, Carter G. *The Education of the Negro Prior to 1861.* Repr. of 1919 ed. Ayer 1968, $28.50 (0-405-01846-0). 454pp. Nonfiction.

This groundbreaking work, first published in 1919, identifies two key periods in the history of Negro education under slavery. From the beginnings of slavery in North America until around 1835, a majority of whites, both Northern and Southern, supported limited education for slaves. Many owners believed that slaves would be more efficient if they could read at least a little, while missionaries and reformers saw education as a way of uplifting slaves morally and socially. However, by the mid-1830s, the Industrial Revolution was transforming slavery from a patriarchal (and comparatively benign) institution into a harsher and more purely economic one. Southern states, worried that educated blacks would only foment insurrections, began to prohibit their education. In the North, meanwhile, a few dedicated reformers fought to preserve educational opportunities, anticipating the need for schools and colleges once the slaves were freed. In this book, Woodson, who was Dean of Liberal Arts at Howard University, describes the heartbreaking struggle of blacks, both slave and free, to obtain an education despite the many obstacles. He is thus one of many early-twentieth-century African-American historians to challenge the mainstream notion that enslaved blacks accepted their fate passively. This classic work of history has profoundly influenced more recent works by both African-American and white scholars. RL

BIOGRAPHY

212 Abernathy, Ralph D. *And the Walls Came Tumbling Down.* Illus. HarperCollins 1989, $25.00 (0-06-016192-2); $12.95 (0-06-091986-8). 640pp. Autobiography.

For twelve years Ralph Abernathy was Martin Luther King, Jr.'s most trusted lieutenant. The two young ministers worked closely together to organize the Montgomery bus boycotts in 1955 and 1956. In 1957 they founded the Southern Christian Leadership Conference (SCLC) to carry on the fight for civil rights in the South. Abernathy was deeply involved in nearly all of the major civil rights campaigns of the 1960s, including the Birmingham protests, the March on Washington, and the Selma-to-Montgomery March. When King was assassinated in 1968 Abernathy took over as head of SCLC. In this autobiography Abernathy describes in detail his work with King in the civil rights movement. In addition, he tells of his youth in rural Marengo County, Alabama, his experiences in the segregated army during World War II, and his efforts to lead the civil rights movement in the years following King's death. PTM

213 Anson, Robert Sam. *Best Intentions: The Education and Killing of Edmund Perry.* Random 1988, $10.00 (0-394-75707-6). 288pp. Biography.

Anson relates the tragic story of Edmund Perry, a young black man from Harlem who was an honors graduate of Phillips Exeter Academy and who had earned a scholarship for Stanford University. On the night of June 12, 1985, just ten days after his graduation, Perry was shot and killed while trying to mug a New York City plainclothes police officer. Anson examines the disparate worlds that Perry inhabited and tries to explain why a young man with so many opportunities should meet such a tragic end. Through extensive interviews with Perry's family, teachers, classmates, and friends, the author learned that Perry had grown up in a stable family with a strong mother who was a local community school board member. At the end of eighth grade he was selected to attend Exeter on the basis of his outstanding academic record. Perry continued to do well in his studies and was respected by students and teachers alike. But during his senior year he had become increasingly preoccupied with the subject of race and had used and dealt drugs on a regular basis. Anson concludes that Perry died because he was unable to balance the conflicting demands of developing his black identity while achieving success in a white environment.   PTM

214   Ashe, Arthur, and Arnold Rampersad. *Days of Grace: A Memoir*. Knopf 1993, $24.00 (0-679-42396-6); Ballantine $5.99 (0-345-38681-7). 304pp. Autobiography.

Completed shortly before Ashe's death from AIDS in 1993, this work is not an autobiography, but a series of reflections on topics of importance in his life: his experiences as captain of the U.S. Davis Cup team; his involvement in the antiapartheid movement; sex and sports; academic standards for collegiate athletes; differences between male and female athletes; and problems of black leadership. A major portion of the book is devoted to a discussion of AIDS, his efforts to deal with his illness, and the ethics of the media, which forced him to make his condition public. He also discusses "the burden of race" and concludes that dealing with the effects of racism has been more difficult than confronting AIDS. The book ends with a moving letter by Ashe to his five-year-old daughter in which he urges her to be proud of her family and her African-American heritage. This memoir shows Ashe as a man of substance and sensitivity with interests that ranged far beyond the world of professional athletics.   PTM

215   Bedini, Silvio A. *The Life of Benjamin Banneker*. Repr. of 1972 ed. Landmark 1984, $25.00 (0-910845-20-4). 434pp. Biography.

Bedini has written a biography of the self-taught African-American mathematician and astronomer from Tidewater, Maryland, who was born the son of a freed slave in 1731 and who was living proof, the author says, "that the color black was [a result] of nature and not a sign of inferiority." Although Banneker's path to social and economic success was hampered by national policies, he was nonetheless able to cultivate his intellect. His almanac, *The Pennsylvania, Delaware, Maryland, and Virginia Almanac and Ephemeris*, published annually from 1792 to 1802, challenged the reputation of Benjamin Franklin's *Poor Richard's Almanac*. His mathematical acumen rivaled that of Thomas Jefferson; George Washington appointed him to the commission that surveyed the site for the nation's capitol. The biography is well researched and depicts Banneker as one of the "early American mathematical practitioners who applied the sciences in the developing new republic." The book complements *The Real McCoy* by Portia P. James *(see main entry)*.   AJWM

216   Brown, Claude. ***Manchild in the Promised Land***. Macmillan 1990, $55.00 (0-02-517325-1); NAL $4.95 (0-451-15741-9). 416pp. Autobiography.

Brown's autobiography is the powerful story of a young boy growing up on the streets of Harlem during the late 1940s and early 1950s, where he was exposed to crime, gang wars, and the drug trade. Because of his reckless lifestyle, he was shot at the age of thirteen, arrested, and sent to reform school on two occasions. Most of his boyhood friends became victims of violence or drug addiction. In this book adults are presented in an unfavorable light, with the exception of Mr. Papenek, a teacher at Wiltwyck school who encouraged Brown to continue his education. Managing to survive the dangers of life on the streets, Brown attended night school and earned his high school diploma. His story ends as he leaves Harlem to attend college. Brown's vivid narrative gives the reader a view of life on Harlem's mean streets. Although the events he relates happened more than forty years ago, many of the conditions he describes have changed little since then.   PTM

217   Brown, Elaine. ***A Taste of Power: A Black Woman's Story***. Illus. Pantheon 1992, $25.00 (0-679-41944-6); Doubleday $14.95 (0-385-47107-6). 464pp. Autobiography.

In August of 1974, Elaine Brown assumed the chair of the Black Panther Party. At that juncture the party was in disarray; following years of harassment by the FBI and local police agencies, the party's founder, Huey Newton, had fled to Cuba. Brown describes her childhood in North Philadelphia and a brief period as the mistress of a wealthy Hollywood writer. In 1968 she joined the Black Panther Party and for the next seven years was a key member. Much of this autobiography describes violent confrontations between the Panthers and the police, other Black Nationalist groups, and various factions within the party. She provides intimate portraits of Panther leaders, including Newton, Bobby Seale, Eldridge Cleaver, Ericka Huggins, and Jonathan Jackson. Brown helped to refashion the party's image from a band of gun-toting revolutionaries to a legitimate community organization running an innovative school in Oakland and supporting successful political candidates. Her account, written from a feminist perspective, criticizes the male chauvinism within the party and details her problems as a woman leader in a largely male organization.   PTM

218   Buckler, Helen. ***Daniel Hale Williams: Negro Surgeon***. o.p. Biography.

Buckler offers a lively and gripping biography of Williams, a black American surgeon who in 1893 performed the world's first open-heart operation. The book is a saga of a man in pursuit of the American dream, one who, because of his race, had to struggle harder and longer for his reward. Through perseverance and devotion to academic excellence, Williams sought to prove to white America that blacks could be educated. His drive brought him to the medical profession, where he earned impeccable credentials. Helen Buckler paints for her readers a portrait of a complex and gifted man, one who dedicated his life to uplifting other black Americans.   AJWM

219 Cary, Lorene. ***Black Ice***. Knopf 1991, $24.00 (0-394-57465-6); McKay $10.00 (0-679-73745-6). 238pp. Autobiography.

Lorene Cary was one of the first African Americans to attend the prestigious St. Peter's preparatory school, which had only recently begun to admit women. Outwardly, Cary's years there were a success: At the end of her junior year she was elected vice president of the student council. Two Ivy League universities accepted her; and at her high school graduation ceremony in 1974, she received a major school award. Even so, Cary says, she did not enjoy her time at St. Peter's, where she felt pressured to work twice as hard to justify her existence there. Although her friends came from diverse backgrounds, she never felt that she really "belonged." Nonetheless, Cary went on to teach for many years at St. Peter's and to serve on the school's board of trustees. This memoir is her means of coming to terms with her past, with the culture shock that she felt, and with the feeling that, as an African American, she was not truly part of the mainstream. Her insights shed light upon the lingering effects of slavery and racism, as manifested in a lack of trust and a continued sense of isolation from those who are different. This book, while appealing to general readers, will be of special interest to adolescents for its honest discussions of issues close to young people.   LML

220 Chestnut, J. L., Jr., and Julia Cass. ***Black in Selma: The Uncommon Life of J. L. Chestnut, Jr.*** Farrar 1990, $22.95 (0-374-11404-8); Doubleday $13.00 (0-385-41938-4). 432pp. Autobiography.

Chestnut was born and raised in Selma, Alabama. After graduating from Howard University Law School in 1958 he returned to Selma, where he became one of nine black lawyers in the state and the only one in Dallas County. At this time the city and the county were under the firm control of the White Citizens Council and Sheriff Jim Clark. Chestnut worked closely with the civil rights organizations that were seeking to break the segregationists' hold. Then Martin Luther King, Jr. targeted Selma for a voter registration campaign. The brutal confrontation between Clark's posse and civil rights demonstrators on the Edmund Pettus Bridge finally brought change for Selma's black citizens. By describing conditions in Selma both before and after "Bloody Sunday," Chestnut provides an insider's perspective on the changes in race relations in one Deep South community.   PTM

221 Cleaver, Eldridge. ***Soul on Ice***. Dell 1970, $5.99 (0-440-21128-X). 210pp. Autobiography.

In this series of autobiographical essays, Cleaver expresses the anger and the search for identity that characterized life for many African Americans in the late 1960s. The first section of the book contains reflections on his experiences in prison and the story of his religious quest that led to his becoming a follower of Malcolm X. In the second section he comments on a variety of topics, including white youth, the works of James Baldwin, boxing, and the Vietnam War. The third section includes three love letters exchanged between Cleaver and Beverly Axelrod, the white lawyer who represented him. The final, and most controversial, section discusses the relationships that black men have with women, black as well as white.   PTM

222 Comer, James P. *Maggie's American Dream: The Life and Times of a Black Family*. Intro. by Charlayne Hunter-Gault. Illus. NAL 1988, $18.95 (0-453-00588-8); $10.00 (0-452-26318-2). 352pp. Biography.

Comer, a noted child psychiatrist and educator, recounts the story of his parents and their efforts to raise and educate their four children. Hugh and Maggie Comer were uneducated migrants from the rural South who settled in East Chicago, Indiana, during the 1920s. Hugh found work in the steel mills, while Maggie worked as a domestic for white families. The Comers embraced middle-class American values: hard work, thrift, home ownership, religion, and, above all else, education. Maggie insisted that her children excel in their academic work and encouraged them to set high goals for themselves. After her husband's death she put all four children through college. The first half of the book is Maggie Comer's first-person narrative of her life as dictated to her son. In the second section, James Comer describes his own experiences growing up in this tightly knit family and then going to college at Indiana University and medical school at Howard University. In the final chapters he explains how his mother's teachings influenced him to dedicate his career to improving the education of black children attending inner-city schools.   PTM

223 Cone, James H. *Martin and Malcolm and America: A Dream or a Nightmare*. Orbis 1991, $22.95 (0-88344-721-5); $14.95 (0-88344-824-6). 358pp. Biography.

Cone compares the lives and teachings of the two most influential black leaders of the recent era, Martin Luther King, Jr. and Malcolm X. Tracing the formative influences on each man and the evolution of their ideas, Cone underscores their differences: While King regarded America as an unfulfilled dream, Malcolm X saw it as a nightmare for the black man. Cone goes beyond this simple dichotomy, however, to point out how their teachings complemented and corrected each other. He argues that as the two men grew and changed, they came to appreciate each other's views and their positions began to converge. Cone sees Martin and Malcolm as representing the two sides of the African-American identity, "the 'yin' and the 'yang' deep in the soul of black America." Not everyone will agree with this thesis, but his well-researched argument is sure to stimulate thoughtful reflection.   PTM

224 Cronon, E. David. *Black Moses: The Story of Marcus Garvey and the Universal Negro Improvement Association*. 2nd ed. Illus. Univ. of Wisconsin Pr. 1960, $12.95 (0-299-01214-X). 302pp. Biography.

An immigrant to the United States from Jamaica, Marcus Garvey (1887–1940) fought white oppression with the fiery racial pride that he inherited from his ancestors, maroons (fugitive slaves) who resisted British military forces that sought to reenslave them. This book reveals that Garvey—often called the Black Moses—had strengths, weaknesses, and enormous charisma. He founded the Universal Negro Improvement Association (UNIA) and launched a newspaper, the *Negro World*. His unstinting efforts to liberate black people propelled him to the forefront of Black Nationalism in the United States, where, as a powerful orator, he urged blacks to return to Africa, their ancestral home. The impact of his teachings and the strength of his support made Garvey one of the greatest threats to the ideology of white supremacy.

AJWM

225 Davis, Angela Y. *Angela Davis: An Autobiography.* Repr. of 1974 ed. International Publishers 1988, $9.95 (0-7178-0667-7). 408pp. Autobiography.

Angela Davis was raised in Birmingham, Alabama and educated at Brandeis University. She achieved national notoriety when she was dismissed as a philosophy instructor at UCLA because of her membership in the Communist Party. In this autobiography she describes her radicalization as a college student and her growing involvement with the black community in Los Angeles. A major portion of the book describes her flight, capture, imprisonment, trial, and subsequent acquittal on charges of conspiracy in connection with the 1970 shootout at the Marin County Courthouse, which ended in the deaths of Jonathan Jackson, three San Quentin prisoners, and the judge who was trying them.

PTM

226 Delany, Sarah L., and A. Elizabeth Delany. *Having Our Say: The Delany Sisters' First 100 Years.* Ed. by Amy H. Hearth. Kodansha 1993, $20.00 (1-56836-010-X). 210pp. Autobiography.

Sadie and Bessie Delany were born in Raleigh, North Carolina, where their father was a teacher and vice-principal at St. Augustine's School. As young women the Delanys moved to Harlem, where they attended Columbia University. Sadie became a teacher of home economics in the New York City public schools, and Bessie became the second black woman dentist in New York State.

This book is based on interviews conducted Amy Hill Hearth when the Delanys were both over 101 years old. The sisters take turns telling the story of their remarkable family and their lives together. They describe their father, born in slavery, who became the first black bishop of the Episcopal church. They also tell of their mother, who could have passed for white but who refused to do so. They recount stories from their childhood, including the introduction of Jim Crow drinking fountains and streetcars in turn-of-the-century North Carolina and recall Harlem during the 1920s, when they associated with famous blacks, including band leader Cab Calloway and writer James Weldon Johnson.

Readers will be charmed by the sisters' distinctive personalities—the feisty Bessie, who was nearly lynched for talking back to a drunken white man, and the sweet Sadie, who pretended to ignore the racial insults she encountered. They also will be enriched by the sisters' description of life among middle-class African Americans and by their outspoken reflections on their first hundred years.

PTM

227 Douglass, Frederick. *The Life and Times of Frederick Douglass: An American Slave.* Repr. of 1881 ed. Carol Publg. 1984, $20.00 (0-8065-0873-6); $8.95 (0-8065-0865-5). 514pp. Autobiography.

The great black abolitionist Frederick Douglass wrote two classic autobiographies, each geared to a different audience. Secondary students and other introductory-level readers will appreciate the briefer and more accessible *Narrative*, much of which is devoted to a discussion of his days as a young child living with his grandmother and later with various relatives of his owner/father. It tells of his life on the streets of Baltimore, Maryland, in pursuit of knowledge, his defiance of a white overseer, his escape from slavery, and his role as an abolitionist. *Life and Times* is a more interpretive and perceptive treatment, which examines in detail Douglass's adult life after the Civil War. It is a moving account of the many accolades, federal appointments, and honors bestowed on a black man despite the limits society placed on African Americans. More important, however, Douglass explores his personal beliefs and feelings about a country that was founded on democratic principles but that was unable to guarantee democracy for all its citizens because of their color.

AJWM

228   Duberman, Martin B. *Paul Robeson*. Knopf 1989, $24.95 (0-394-52780-1). 784pp. Biography.

Duberman traces the remarkable accomplishments and tragic downfall of Paul Robeson, one of the most talented and controversial African Americans of the twentieth century. Robeson first came to public attention as an all-American football player at Rutgers University, where he also was valedictorian of his class. After graduating from Columbia University Law School, Robeson embarked on a career as a singer and actor on the stage and screen. During the 1930s, he articulated leftist political views, praising the Soviet Union for its lack of racial prejudice and supporting the Loyalist cause in the Spanish Civil War. During the anticommunist hysteria of the Cold War, Robeson refused to abandon his political beliefs. Duberman documents the U.S. government's efforts to persecute Robeson because of his procommunist sympathies. Because of this harassment, Robeson's physical and mental health began to deteriorate and he never regained the prominence he had once enjoyed. Duberman describes Robeson's personal and public life, drawing upon the Robeson family archives and supplemented by more than one hundred personal interviews with his friends and associates.   PTM/AJWM

229   Du Bois, W.E.B. *John Brown.* Repr. of 1909 ed. Kraus 1969, $25.00 (0-527-25285-9); International Publishers $4.95 (0-7178-0375-9). 414pp. Biography.

This book adds a vital new perspective to our understanding of one of the most intriguing and complicated personalities in American history. While earlier historians often depicted John Brown as a fanatic, fiend, or traitor, Du Bois challenges that depiction with an image of a white American who dedicated his life to the love and understanding of African Americans and to their freedom from bondage. In this book John Brown emerges as an unusual leader with a deeply religious outlook and with a fervent devotion to the cause of freedom.   AJWM

230   Farmer, James. *Lay Bare the Heart: The Autobiography of the Civil Rights Movement*. NAL 1986, $9.95 (0-452-25803-0). 370pp. Autobiography.

Farmer spent nearly all of his adult life deeply involved in the civil rights movement. In 1942 he was one of a small group of Chicago pacifists who formed the Congress of Racial Equality (CORE) to protest racial segregation and discrimination using the principles of nonviolent resistance that Gandhi practiced. CORE remained a relatively small and unknown organization until 1961, when Farmer, as executive secretary, launched the Freedom Rides. He recruited an interracial team of civil rights activists to travel from Washington, D.C., into the South to test the integration of bus stations. When the riders reached Birmingham, Alabama, they were attacked by a band of white toughs. The resulting publicity created a national incident that forced the federal government to take action to protect civil rights workers and guarantee desegregation of transportation facilities. In his autobiography, Farmer recounts this and other tales from his days in the civil rights struggle. PTM

231 Forman, James. ***The Making of Black Revolutionaries.*** 2nd ed.; Repr. of 1972 ed. Open Hand 1985, $16.95 (0-940880-10-5). 592pp. Autobiography.

As executive secretary for the Student Nonviolent Coordinating Committee (SNCC) from 1962 to 1966, Forman was a key participant in many of the critical struggles of the civil rights movement. In this autobiography he describes the growing radicalism he and other freedom fighters developed while working in communities across the Deep South, including Fayette County, Tennessee; Monroe, North Carolina; McComb, Mississippi; Albany, Georgia; Danville, Virginia; and Selma, Alabama. Forman describes his personal evolution from a militant integrationist to a revolutionary nationalist. He explains why he rejected nonviolence and helped to develop the Black Power philosophy. According to Forman, the version of Black Nationalism that emerged in the late 1960s was the natural consequence of the civil rights struggles earlier that decade. This book is the powerful personal testament of one of the more radical leaders of the black liberation movement. PTM

232 Garrow, David J. ***Bearing the Cross: Martin Luther King, Jr., and the Southern Christian Leadership Conference, 1955–1968.*** Morrow 1986, $22.95 (0-688-04794-7); Random $18.00 (0-394-75623-1). 696pp. Biography.

Garrow's exhaustive study of Martin Luther King, Jr.'s role in the civil rights movement covers the period from the Montgomery bus boycott of 1955 to his assassination in Memphis in 1968. Garrow describes in great detail King's major campaigns, including demonstrations against segregation in Albany, Georgia (1962), Birmingham, Alabama (1963), and St. Augustine, Florida (1964); the protest marches in Washington (1963), Selma (1965), and Mississippi (1966); and later demonstrations in Chicago (1966) and Memphis (1968); as well as the plans for the Poor People's Campaign. In addition to chronicling King's activities and the workings of his organization, Garrow documents his dealings with Presidents Kennedy and Johnson and the FBI's surveillance of his personal life. This is only a partial biography, however, because it tells the reader nothing about King's life prior to the Montgomery bus boycott. Though his scholarship cannot be faulted, Garrow's dense, academic prose makes *Bearing the Cross* very slow reading, which will be more appealing to those with a special interest in King's life.

233   Harlan, Louis R. ***Booker T. Washington: Vol. 1: The Making of a Black Leader, 1856–1901; Vol. 2: The Wizard of Tuskegee, 1901–1915.*** 2 vols. Illus. Oxford Univ. Pr. 1972; 1986, $15.95 (0-19-501915-6; 0-19-504229-8). 300+562pp. Biography.

Harlan offers an exhaustive two-volume study of the nineteenth-century charismatic black leader who rose from slavery to the heights of black power. In that position, Booker T. Washington commanded audiences with some of the country's most influential whites, but his complex personality shrouded his true character. History remembers him as the "Great Accommodationist" who catered to the whims of white America. From his base at Tuskegee Institute in Alabama, Washington's "Tuskegee Machine" held sway over the lives and professions of many blacks around the country through his own patronage system, which served as a conduit for federal and other appointments. Those who were Washington's enemies found they had difficulty advancing their careers. Yet beneath the image of an "accommodationist" was a man who worked aggressively pushing the country to guarantee the rights of all Americans.   AJWM

234   Hasse, John Edward. ***Beyond Category: The Life and Genius of Duke Ellington.*** Simon & Schuster 1993, $25.00 (0-671-70387-0). 448pp. Biography.

Edward Kennedy "Duke" Ellington was born in 1899 to a middle-class black family in Washington, D.C. He developed an early interest in music, and from the time of his arrival in New York City in the early 1920s until his death in 1974, he was the leader of America's most popular big band. Many of the century's greatest jazz musicians played with the Ellington orchestra. This engaging and comprehensive biography presents the many sides of the man. He was an African American who suffered racist slights even as he became famous and wealthy. He was also a musician whose creations earned him worldwide recognition as America's greatest composer, whose pieces and performances enjoyed tremendous responses in the United States and in Europe. The author dissects Ellington's most important works, clearly explaining their place in the development of classical and popular music in language understandable even to readers who have no musical background.

Ellington himself is the author of a memoir, *Music Is My Mistress* (Da Capo, 1976). His son Mercer is the author, with Stanley Dance, of a book of candid and insightful recollections, *Duke Ellington in Person: An Intimate Memoir* (Da Capo, 1979).   RL

235   Haygood, Wil. ***King of the Cats: The Life and Times of Adam Clayton Powell, Jr.*** Illus. Houghton 1993, $24.95 (0-395-44094-7); $12.95 (0-395-70068-X). 496pp. Biography.

During the 1960s Adam Clayton Powell, Jr. was the most powerful black politician in the United States. He also was the most colorful and controversial. The congressman from Harlem became chairman of the Education and Labor Committee and played an important role in the passage of the liberal social programs of the 1960s. Powell's power was curtailed, however, when the House voted to strip him of his chairmanship and then to expel him from his seat. Haygood chronicles Powell's rise and fall, from his privileged youth as the son of the pastor of the largest Baptist congregation in the United States to his last days in self-imposed exile on the Caribbean isle of Bimini. He describes how Powell's outspoken leadership of protests in Harlem during the Depression established his credentials as an uncompromising advocate of racial equality and formed the basis for his subsequent rise to power. He also devotes much attention to Powell's flamboyant personal life—his three marriages and numerous affairs, his love of liquor and fast cars, his extensive travel to Europe and the Caribbean. Haygood offers a detailed portrait of Powell's political career and his contributions to the struggle for black liberation. PTM

236 Hunter-Gault, Charlayne. *In My Place*. Farrar 1992, $19.00 (0-374-17563-2); Random $11.00 (0-679-74818-0). 257pp. Autobiography.

On January 9, 1961, Charlayne Hunter and Hamilton Holmes became the first African-American students to enroll at the University of Georgia. Hunter planned to study journalism, and Holmes would enter the premedical curriculum. Shortly after Hunter's arrival on campus, white students surrounded her dormitory, breaking windows and shouting racist slogans. University officials suspended Hunter and Holmes "for their own safety" but were soon forced to readmit them. Eventually, the hostility subsided; both young people graduated and went on to distinguished careers. Twenty-five years later, Hunter-Gault was invited back to the Athens campus to deliver the commencement address.

In this autobiography she describes the youthful experiences that prepared her for this assault on segregated education. Born in South Carolina, she was raised in Covington, Georgia and then moved to Atlanta. Her father, a military chaplain, was usually stationed away from his family, except for one year when they joined him in Alaska. There his daughter learned to survive in a largely white environment. When she returned to Atlanta, she immersed herself in extracurricular activities and compiled an outstanding academic record. Following high school graduation, she and Holmes applied to the University of Georgia. It took eighteen months of legal maneuvering by NAACP lawyers to gain their admission. Her memoir reveals the personal side of this critical battle of the civil rights era. PTM

237 Jones, James Earl, and Penelope Niven. *Voices and Silences*. Illus. Macmillan 1993, $24.00 (0-684-19513-5). 368pp. Autobiography.

Born in rural Mississippi and raised by his grandparents, James Earl Jones emerged in the 1960s as one of the country's premier actors. Here he tells his story, beginning with his earliest memories of his parents' departure. He recounts his efforts to overcome a stutter and how, while in college, he decided to study acting. Ironically, his career choice brought him back in touch with his father, a political organizer and actor who had encountered great hardship and only modest success. Jones's relationship with his father, his thoughts on race and racism, and his version of the controversy surrounding his performances as Paul Robeson in 1977–1978 are among the most memorable moments of a well-written and compelling account of this actor's life and work. The book includes photographs from Jones's life and from his major performances, a series of journal entries, a list of his performances, and an index. LML

238 King, Coretta Scott. *My Life with Martin Luther King, Jr.* Rev. ed. Henry Holt 1993, $17.95 (0-8050-2445-X); Puffin $4.99 (0-14-036805-1). 368pp. Autobiography.

Coretta Scott, from Marion, Alabama, was a vocal music student at the New England Conservatory of Music when she met Martin Luther King, Jr. in 1952. The following year they married. When he completed his graduate studies at Boston University, the young couple moved to Montgomery, where he began his ministerial career as pastor of the Dexter Avenue Baptist Church. During the next fourteen years King would become the internationally acclaimed leader of the African-American civil rights movement, while his wife made a home for their family and raised their four children. Coretta King's account of their life together shows the domestic side of the civil rights leader as a husband, son, father, and family man.   PTM

239 Lewis, David L. *King: A Biography.* 2nd ed. Univ. of Illinois Pr. 1978, $12.95 (0-252-00680-1). 481pp. Biography.

Biographies of Martin Luther King, Jr. are numerous and written from a variety of perspectives. Most, however, tend toward hagiography—idealizing his virtues and accomplishments while overlooking his strategic and personal shortcomings. What sets Lewis's biography apart is his objectivity and willingness to consider King's life from a critical perspective. Lewis follows King's career from his youth in a prominent black Atlanta family; his education at Morehouse, Crozier Theological Seminary, and Boston University; his years as a pastor and protest leader in Montgomery, Alabama; and his subsequent career as a national civil rights leader. Lewis is especially good at tracing the intellectual roots of King's nonviolent philosophy. While praising his success in the Birmingham demonstration and his efforts in obtaining passage of the Voting Rights Act, Lewis faults King's leadership of the Albany, Georgia movement and his ill-fated campaign in Chicago. Lewis reminds the reader that not all segments of the black community supported King's strategies nor shared his nonviolent philosophy. Though Lewis's biography is not the final word on the life of Martin Luther King, Jr., it is nonetheless a valuable contribution to our understanding of the man.   PTM

240 Lewis, David L. *W.E.B. Du Bois: Biography of a Race.* 2 vols. Henry Holt 1993; 1995, $35.00 (0-8050-2621-5; 0-8050-2534-0). 735pp. Biography.

In 1903 W.E.B. Du Bois wrote, "The Negro ever feels his two-ness—an American, a Negro: two souls, two thoughts, two unreconciled strivings." Thus, in one sentence Du Bois eloquently summarized the existential dilemma of African Americans. No leader, before or since, has had a greater influence on black intellectual development than the aristocratic Du Bois.

The first volume of this biography covers the years from Du Bois's boyhood in western Massachusetts to the end World War I. Author Lewis traces Du Bois's educational quest from Fisk University to Harvard and then to the University of Berlin and tracks his academic career as a young sociologist at Wilberforce University, as a researcher at the University of Pennsylvania, and as a professor at Atlanta University.

Far more interesting, however, is the story of Du Bois's political evolution. He emerged as a national figure in the early 1900s when he questioned Booker

T. Washington's willingness to accept black disenfranchisement and his emphasis on vocational education. Du Bois championed full civil rights for African Americans and liberal arts education for "the talented tenth."

Soon his scholarly and literary accomplishments were overshadowed by political activism. Du Bois almost single-handedly organized a forum for militant black protest. First he created the Niagara Movement and then joined with white activists to found the National Association for the Advancement of Colored People. Lewis chronicles Du Bois's dual role in the NAACP as its only black officer and as editor of *The Crisis*. Because Du Bois was involved in virtually every major issue facing African Americans, this book is much more than a biography of a single man; it is a carefully documented account of this pivotal era in black history. A second volume, covering the period up to Du Bois's death in 1963, was scheduled for publication in 1995.   PTM

241   Lightfoot, Sara Lawrence. ***Balm in Gilead: Journey of a Healer***. Addison Wesley 1989, $13.41 (0-201-51807-4). 320pp. Biography.

Lightfoot tells the story of her mother, Margaret Lawrence, a pioneering black psychoanalyst. The daughter of an Episcopal minister, Lawrence was born into the black middle class. At the age of fourteen, she left Mississippi for New York, where she attended an elite classical high school, then Cornell University and Columbia University Medical School. She married Charles Lawrence, a sociologist from a family of teachers. Lightfoot recounts her mother's education and medical training, her courtship, the birth of her children, and her teaching at Meharry Medical College in Nashville. Her narrative breaks off in 1947 when the family returned to New York and Lawrence began her training in psychiatry. In addition to being the biography of a remarkable woman, this book provides revealing insights into the life of the black middle class, which valued ties and skin color, education and achievement, and which demonstrated a strong sense of obligation to help their less fortunate brothers and sisters.   PTM

242   Malcolm X, and Alex Haley, ed. ***The Autobiography of Malcolm X***. Ballantine 1992, $20.00 (0-345-37975-6); $12.00 (0-345-37671-4). 464pp. Autobiography.

Malcolm X's autobiography stands as one of the classic works of African-American literature. In it he describes a series of remarkable transformations that shaped his life. The first of these changes occurred at the age of fourteen, when he moved from Michigan to live with his sister in Boston. There he gravitated to the fast life on the streets and soon became a small-time hoodlum known as "Detroit Red." By the age of twenty he had been arrested for burglary and sentenced to prison for ten years. In prison he read widely and was introduced to the teachings of Elijah Muhammad. Upon his release from prison in 1953 he joined Muhammad's Nation of Islam and soon became minister of his mosque in Harlem. As the leading spokesman for the Black Muslims, Malcolm was widely known for his militant Black Nationalist ideology and his criticism of the nonviolent civil rights movement. Malcolm's final transformation took place after his split with the Nation of Islam and his pilgrimage to Mecca in 1964. Adopting the name El-Hajj Malik El-Shabazz, he returned to the United States and founded the Organization of African-

American Unity and the Muslim Mosque Inc. to continue his political and religious mission. Malcolm's fierce, uncompromising honesty and his ability to radically change the direction of his life makes his story one of the most memorable and inspirational American biographies.   PTM

243   Mills, Kay. *This Little Light of Mine: The Life of Fannie Lou Hamer*. Illus. NAL 1993, $24.00 (0-525-93501-0); $12.95 (0-452-27052-9). 400pp. Biography.

Mills tells the life story of Fannie Lou Hamer, the legendary Mississippi civil rights leader. She describes Hamer's first contact with civil rights workers in the summer of 1962. When she attempted to register to vote at the Sunflower County court house, she was fired from her job as a plantation timekeeper and evicted from her rented home. Rather than being intimidated, Hamer went to work as a full-time organizer for the Student Nonviolent Coordinating Committee. Whether she was leading the singing at a mass meeting, organizing the Mississippi Freedom Democratic Party, testifying before the 1964 Democratic convention, or running for Congress, Hamer was the most dynamic and inspirational grassroots leader to emerge from the Mississippi movement. The author interviewed more than one hundred of Hamer's fellow civil rights workers and examined numerous published works and manuscript collections in preparing this work. What emerges is not just the biography of a courageous and determined African-American woman, but the story of a grassroots movement and how it was able to overthrow the system of white supremacy that had long dominated Mississippi politics.   PTM

244   Moody, Anne. *Coming of Age in Mississippi*. Dell 1992, $5.99 (0-440-31488-7). 384pp. Autobiography.

Moody describes her girlhood in small-town Mississippi during the 1950s and how she learned the brutal realities of black oppression while working as a maid and baby-sitter for a white family. When she left home to attend college in Jackson she became involved with the civil rights movement. Eventually, she dropped out of school to become a full-time organizer for CORE in rural Madison County. She relates her firsthand experiences on the front lines of the movement from 1963 to 1966. Moody vividly portrays the routine heroism of civil rights workers, who faced the prospect of death each day. She also describes the ever-present fear for her life that eventually forced her to leave Mississippi.   PTM

245   Nelson, Jill. *Volunteer Slavery: My Authentic Negro Experience*. Noble 1993, $21.95 (1-879360-24-1); Viking $9.95 (0-14-023716-X). 243pp. Autobiography.

In 1988 Jill Nelson was hired as a staff writer for the *Washington Post Magazine*. After working for several years as a freelance magazine writer in New York City, she moved to Washington, D.C., lured by the prospect of financial security and the challenge of working for one of America's most influential newspapers. This book is Nelson's chronicle of her two unhappy years at the *Post*, her conflicts with her editors and coworkers, her struggles as a union leader, and her inability to "fit in" with the paper's corporate culture. Nelson was frustrated by constant disagreements with her editors over how to report on African-American issues. When a white male reporter was selected to write the lead story on the verdict in the trial of Marion Barry, mayor of Washington, D.C., she realized that resigning from the *Post* was the only way she could regain her personal happiness.

Nelson's account is not limited to a discussion of office politics at the *Post*. Instead it ranges widely over her personal life and history. She shares memories of her unhappy youth, her sister's mental illness, her brother's drug addiction and recovery, her strained relations with her demanding father, and summers with her mother on Martha's Vineyard. She speaks openly of her lovers and the difficulties she has encountered raising her teenage daughter. This is an intensely personal account of one African-American woman's struggle to find her place in corporate America.   PTM

246 Robinson, Jo Anne, and David J. Garrow, ed. ***The Montgomery Bus Boycott and the Women Who Started It***. Illus. Univ. of Tennessee Pr. 1987, $32.50 (0-87049-524-0); $14.95 (0-87049-527-5). 208pp. Autobiography.

Robinson was a professor of English at Alabama State University in Montgomery when Rosa Parks was arrested on December 1, 1955. More important, however, she was also president of the Women's Political Council (WPC). For more than a year, members of the council had been protesting their treatment on the city's bus line. When they learned of Parks's arrest they immediately organized a one-day boycott. Robinson describes how the WPC helped launch this historic protest against segregated transportation. This memoir reminds the reader that Martin Luther King, Jr. did not create the bus boycott; rather, he joined a movement that was already well under way.   PTM

247 Rosengarten, Theodore. ***All God's Dangers: The Life of Nate Shaw***. Random 1989, $14.00 (0-679-72761-2). 608pp. Biography.

Rosengarten relates the life story of Nate Shaw, an illiterate but eloquent Alabama tenant farmer. Shaw's struggles to support his family in the rural "Black Belt" were no different from those of thousands of other African Americans in the early decades of this century. But in 1931 he took the radical step of joining the Sharecroppers Union, a fledgling group of poor black farmers organized by the Communist Party. Members and organizers of the union were subjected to constant police intimidation and violence. In December 1932, Shaw and other union members faced a posse of deputy sheriffs who tried to confiscate a neighbor's livestock. In the ensuing shootout the deputies were forced to retreat; but when they returned in greater force, Shaw was arrested, convicted, and sent to prison for twenty years. By recording Shaw's life story, Rosengarten captures a vivid first-person account of life in the rural South in the early years of this century, but, more important, he preserves the memory of a courageous African American who fought for his freedom against overwhelming odds.   PTM

248 Rowan, Carl T. ***Dream Makers, Dream Breakers: The World of Justice Thurgood Marshall***. Little, Brown 1993, $24.95 (0-316-75918-X). 496pp. Biography.

Rowan provides an intimate portrait of his good friend Thurgood Marshall, the first African-American justice on the U.S. Supreme Court. Although the book is not a comprehensive biography, Rowan relates many colorful incidents from Marshall's life. He describes Marshall's first civil rights case as a young lawyer, in which he successfully represented a black man applying to the University of Maryland Law School—the same school that had rejected Marshall. Soon he went to work full time for the NAACP, fighting for the rights of black defendants, often at considerable risk to his own safety. A major segment of Rowan's narrative is devoted to Marshall's role in the historic *Brown* v. *Board of Education of Topeka* decision. (For more about that case, see the entry for Richard Kluger's *Simple Justice*.) He also traces Marshall's subsequent career as a federal judge, as Solicitor General under President Johnson, and finally his service on the U.S. Supreme Court from 1967 to 1991. Rowan includes not only his glowing evaluation of Marshall as an advocate and a jurist, but also Marshall's uncensored opinions about politics and politicians. He gives the reader an intimate portrait of Thurgood Marshall, the man.   PTM

249   Staples, Brent. ***Parallel Time.*** Pantheon 1994, $23.00 (0-679-42154-8). 288pp. Autobiography.

This memoir opens with the murder of Blake Staples, the author's younger brother, who had been a drug dealer in Roanoke, Virginia. At the time, Brent Staples was a graduate student at the University of Chicago, completing his Ph.D. and on his way to a career in journalism. Currently he is a member of the editorial board at the *New York Times*. Staples recounts the chance events that gave him the opportunity to become the only member of his family to attend college and achieve success. Repeatedly, Staples encountered a subtle form of racism, which discounted his abilities and led many whites to regard him as an object of charity. Others regarded him as a symbol of the possibilities open to hard-working blacks in this country. Staples tells of his resistance to such stereotypes, as a student at Chicago trying to confront Saul Bellow, the Nobel Prize–winning novelist whom Staples regarded as racist, and later as a journalist at mostly white newspapers. This moving work coveys the difficulty of living in two worlds, still largely separate: one black and one white.   PTM

250   Sterling, Dorothy. ***Black Foremothers: Three Lives.*** 2nd ed. Frwd. by Margaret Walker; Intro. by Barbara Christian. Illus. Feminist Pr. 1988, $11.95 (0-935312-89-7). 224pp. Biography.

This book, written in the form of three short biographies, provides exciting insights into the lives of black women whose careers, taken together, span the nineteenth and twentieth centuries. The three are Ellen Craft, who was born a slave in Georgia but who successfully escaped her bondage; Ida B. Wells, a Mississippian who started teaching at the age of sixteen; and Mary Church Terrell, born in Tennessee and the daughter of the South's first black millionaire. Their stories move these women from the margins of history to its forefront through the literary skills of the author. The book's title is appropriate, because the reader encounters three equally indomitable and courageous fighters for human decency and freedom who have profoundly influenced succeeding generations of African-American women.   AJWM

251   Urquhart, Brian. ***Ralph Bunche: An American Life***. Norton 1993, $27.50 (0-393-03527-1). 480pp. Biography.

Ralph Bunche was the only African-American member of the United States delegation to the 1945 conference in San Francisco, which drafted the Charter of the United Nations. Later, as an Undersecretary General of the UN, Bunche developed the organization's mediation and peacekeeping roles. Bunche's fearlessness and untiring efforts to bring warring parties together led him to negotiate truces between Israel and her neighbors following the 1948 war. For that effort, Bunche received the Nobel Peace Prize in 1950, becoming the first African American to win a Nobel Prize.

Urquhart, who was Bunche's successor at the UN, chronicles Bunche's youth in nonsegregated, albeit racist, California and his precocious academic career, which culminated in his collaboration with Gunnar Myrdal in researching *An American Dilemma*. This book also describes Bunche's continuing involvement in the civil rights movement, even as he continued his activities as a UN peacemaker in the Middle East, Cyprus, Kashmir, and the Congo. Bunche emerges as an extraordinarily innovative and effective diplomat, a man concerned with the plight of African Americans even as he rose above and traveled beyond the limited opportunities typically available to blacks of his generation.   RL

252   Wideman, John Edgar. ***Brothers and Keepers***. Peter Smith 1992, $21.00 (0-8446-6603-3); Viking $9.00 (0-14-008267-0). 256pp. Autobiography.

Wideman is a college professor of literature and a highly acclaimed novelist. His younger brother, Robby, is currently serving a life sentence for murder. Both grew up in Pittsburgh's Homewood ghetto, but one attended college on an athletic scholarship and became a Rhodes scholar, while the other lived on the streets dealing drugs and engaging in petty crime. Wideman visited his brother in prison and attempted to bridge the gap between them by exploring how their lives turned out so differently. The result is this book, written in two voices—John's, which is cool and analytical, and Robby's, which is passionate and impulsive. As he reestablishes his relationship with his brother, John Wideman helps the reader understand Robby's rage against a society that he feels never allowed him to develop his considerable talents in a positive direction.   PTM

253   Wright, Richard. ***Black Boy***. Repr. of 1945 ed. HarperCollins 1969, $19.95 (0-06-014761-X); $6.50 (0-06-081250-8). 544pp. Autobiography.

In this classic autobiography, Wright relates the story of his childhood in the South during the early 1900s. To a large extent his is a tale of brutality—the physical brutality of frequent beatings administered to a rebellious youth by his family and teachers and the brutal oppression of the segregated society that would not allow him to develop his own personality. He describes the difficult lessons he learned while trying to get an education and earn a living within the limited roles available to black men in the South. Wright's youth was a constant struggle against the confines of his segregated world and the restrictions his family sought to impose on him. Despite the odds against him, Wright was convinced that he was destined for something better than life in the segregated South. This book documents his efforts to escape his captivity. The narrative ends when Wright, at the age of nineteen, decides to head North so that he "might learn who I was, what I might be."   PTM

2

UNITED STATES: ASIAN PACIFIC AMERICANS

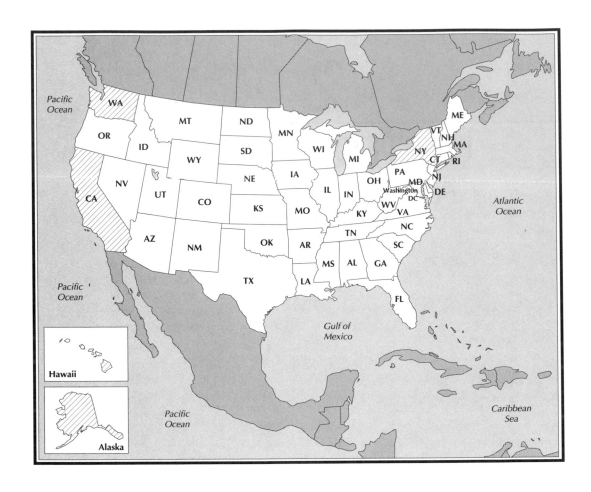

STATES WITH HIGHEST
CONCENTRATION OF
ASIAN PACIFIC AMERICANS

1. Hawaii - 61.8%
2. California - 9.6%
3. Washington - 4.3%
4. New York - 3.9%
5. Alaska - 3.6%

Source: 1990 U.S. Census

COUNTRIES OF ORIGIN
OF ASIAN PACIFIC AMERICANS
BY PERCENTAGE

1. China - 22.6%
2. Philippines - 19.3%
3. Japan - 11.7%
4. India - 11.2%
5. Korea - 11.0%
6. Vietnam - 8.4%
7. Hawaii - 2.9%
8. Samoa - 0.9%
9. Guam - 0.7%

2

UNITED STATES: ASIAN PACIFIC AMERICANS

By Jennifer L. Wu

The term "Asian Americans" was coined in the late 1960s by a group of college students predominantly of Chinese, Japanese, or Filipino descent. Their goal was to promote the emerging collective identity and the growing political solidarity among people of Asian descent in the United States. The term gained wide acceptance when government bureaucracies began to organize diverse ethnic subgroups into umbrella categories to assist in the allocation of economic and political resources.

The Asian Pacific American population in the United States has doubled each decade since 1970. According to the 1990 census, it is the fastest growing population group in the country. Included in the group are people from China, Japan, the Philippines, Korea, Vietnam, Cambodia, Laos, Thailand, and India. The Hmong, people from the mountainous region of Southeast Asia, are included, as are those from such Pacific Islands as Hawaii, Samoa, and Guam. In recent years the term "Asian Pacific Americans" has been used to reflect the increased presence and cultural uniqueness of persons from the Pacific Islands.

A Brief History

The first Asian immigrants to settle in the mainland United States were Filipinos, who lived along the bayous of southeastern Louisiana as early as 1763. Known as "Manilamen," they were descendants of sailors on trade ships that sailed between Mexico and the Philippines. In the mid-nineteenth century large numbers of Chinese and Japanese laborers arrived in Hawaii to work on sugar plantations. Others came to California to mine gold, build the transcontinental railroad, or work on farms. They were a valiant and vital part of the frontier scene of the American West.

But beginning in the late nineteenth century, a series of discriminatory exclusion laws were enacted to limit the numbers of Asians entering the country and to restrict the activities of those already here. Such laws set up barriers to their entry, made it difficult for them to start families, and barred them from participating in democratic citizenship.

Bigotry and violence haunted the Asians. A small number of Korean and

Asian Indian immigrants and a larger number of Filipino laborers started to arrive in the early part of the twentieth century. Then the 1924 Immigration Act halted the entry of virtually all Asian immigrants, except some special classes: students, professionals, merchants, and diplomats.

In the spring of 1942, a few months after the attack on Pearl Harbor, President Franklin Roosevelt issued Executive Order 9066. As a result, over 110,000 West Coast Japanese Americans were herded into the Southwestern deserts and placed in internment camps. The resulting disruption of families and livelihood, the physical hardship of relocation, and the unwarranted suspicion that fell on those who had adopted the United States as their home make this tragic event the central part in Japanese-American history.

Decades after the end of World War II, in 1965, the abolition of the discriminatory quota system for immigration led to a new influx of middle-class, highly skilled professionals from Asia. The end of the Vietnam War ten years later brought a wave of refugees from Southeast Asia. Since the 1980s, new wealth from the Pacific Rim is making an impact on the immigration scene.

Because of their distinct physical characteristics, Asian Americans, like other ethnic groups of color—Native Americans, African Americans, and Latinos—often encounter discrimination. Although Asian Americans have made considerable progress in the past two decades because of their increased numbers and the growing economic and political importance of the Pacific Rim, hate crimes and economic injustice are still among their major concerns.

Since the establishment of university ethnic studies programs in the 1970s, Asian-American historians have been digging into the buried past to write about American history from the Asian-American perspective. For example, Yuji Ichioka explores the life of first-generation immigrants in *Issei*, Sucheng Chan focuses on different groups in a series of books including *Entry Denied: Exclusion and the Chinese-American Community in America, 1882–1943* and *Hmong Means Free: Life in Laos and America*, and Michi Weglyn reveals what she calls the "untold story of America's concentration camps" in her pioneering study *Years of Infamy*. Weglyn's work helped to spark the movement in which Americans of Japanese descent demanded redress for the wrongs they suffered during World War II. As a result, Congress in 1988 passed the Civil Liberties Act to authorize compensatory payments to surviving Japanese Americans interned during the war.

History books such as *Strangers from a Different Shore* by Ronald Takaki help explain the stories behind the derogatory terms "chink," "Jap," and "coolie" and dispel the many myths about the Asians, from "Yellow Peril" to "Model Minority."

Stereotypes and Invisibility

Early portrayals of Asians in American literature and pop culture by white writers were frequently patronizing, dehumanizing, and stereotypical. These novels and stories were populated with characters that were evil (Fu Manchu), inscrutable (Charlie Chan), exotic (Lotus Blossom), dutiful (cooks and servants), or treacherous ("dragon ladies"). A detailed discussion of early images of Asians in American literature appears in William F. Wu's *Yellow Peril: Chinese Americans in American Fiction 1850–1940* and Elaine H. Kim's *Asian American Literature: An Introduction to the Writings and Their Social Context*. Edith Eaton, a Eurasian who wrote at the turn of the century under the pseudonym Sui Sin Far, was the first fiction writer in America who cast

Chinese-American characters in a positive and humane light. Three of her stories appear in the anthology *The Big Aiiieeeee!!!* edited by Jeffrey Paul Chan and others.

Meanwhile, first-generation Chinese and Japanese immigrants in the United States wrote poems, short stories, and diaries in their own language, some of which were published in ethnic-language newspapers or magazines. Even though many second-generation writers wrote in English, they found it difficult to get their works published. For example, John Okada did not live to see the publication of his novel *No-No Boy*. Okada's widow burned the manuscript of his second novel after a Japanese-American archive refused to accept his papers because the curators did not recognize his name. Since its publication, however, *No-No Boy* has become a classic in Japanese-American literature.

First published in 1974, *Aiiieeeee! An Anthology of Asian-American Writers* ushered in a new era of Asian-American literary consciousness. The book was edited by a group of fervent and angry young Asian-American writers, Frank Chin, Jeffrey Paul Chan, Lawson Fusao Inada, and Shawn Wong. Rejected by some publishers as "too ethnic" or even "irresponsible," *Aiiieeeee!* was accepted by Howard University Press, predominantly a publisher of African-American titles, which published the landmark anthology on its first list of publications. Editors Chin and Wong subsequently wrote an essay, published in the *Yardbird Reader* (1974), in which they acknowledged the support of the African Americans who "were quicker to understand and appreciate the value of Asian-American writing than whites. . . . The blacks were the first to take us seriously and sustained the spirit of many Asian-American writers. . . ." A second anthology, *The Big Aiiieeeee!*, was published by NAL in 1991.

Breaking Silence

Many Asian Americans celebrated in 1976 when Maxine Hong Kingston's *The Woman Warrior* was published by Knopf and won the National Book Critics Circle Award that year. Her subsequent book, *China Men*, won the National Book Award in 1981. Though Kingston's literary fame and commercial success were unprecedented, she cautioned her readers not to expect her to be the representative of her race. In an interview published in *Women Writers of the West Coast Speaking of Their Lives and Careers*, edited by Marilyn Yalom (Capra Press, 1983), Kingston said:

> I don't like to hear non-Chinese people say to a Chinese person, "Well now I know about you because I have read Maxine Hong Kingston's books.". . . The problem of how representative one is will only be solved when we have many more Chinese-American writers. Then readers will see how diverse we people are.

When Kim Ronyoung's *Clay Walls* was published by the Permanent Press in 1986, it was hailed as "the first novel in fifty years [since Young Karg's *East Goes West*, 1937] to examine what it means to be Korean in America." Explaining her purpose in writing the book, Kim stated: "A whole generation of Korean immigrants and their American-born children could have lived and died in the United States without anyone knowing they had been here. I could not let that happen." She finished the book a year before she died.

Indo-American author Bharati Mukherjee, angered at Canada's open racism toward South Asian immigrants, left Canada in 1980 and resettled in the United States. In an interview, she elaborated on what it means to be an

American: "Mine is a clear-eyed but definite love of America. I'm aware of the brutalities, the violences here, but . . . I feel there are people born to be Americans. By American I mean an intensity of spirit and a quality of desire. I feel American in a very fundamental way, whether Americans see me that way or not." She won the 1988 National Book Critics Circle Award in fiction for *The Middleman and Other Stories*.

In challenging the patriarchal tradition, Asian-American women created their own anthologies of writings by and about themselves. Early examples include *The Forbidden Stitch* and *Making Waves*. *Home to Stay* is a collection of fiction writings by Asian-American women, whose cross-cultural perspectives illustrate the increasingly pluralistic American experience.

Moving the Image

Independent Asian-Pacific-American media arts emerged from the civil rights and ethnic studies movements of the late 1960s. Asian-American writers are making headway into American literature and popular culture. Meanwhile, Asian-American artists are using film, video, radio, and other media to create alternatives to the stereotypical portrayals in Hollywood movies and other forms of mass entertainment. Russell Leong, in *Moving the Image*, documents their efforts to change the way Asians are portrayed and perceived.

Writings by Issei (first-generation Japanese immigrants) and Nisei (second-generation) are often preoccupied with the harsh experiences of the internment camps. More recently, younger Sansei (third-generation) writers are exploring new themes. David Mura's *Turning Japanese* and Lydia Minatoya's *Talking to High Monks in the Snow* describe the authors' journeys to their ancestral Japan, searching for a reconciliation of their split cultural identity.

Refugees from Southeast Asia, after their initial struggle for survival and adjustment, are beginning to tell their life stories in books such as James Freeman's *Hearts of Sorrow* and John Tenhula's *Voices from Southeast Asia*. It is refreshing to learn about Paul Thai, a refugee from Cambodia who becomes the first Asian-born member of the Dallas police force, in Sharon Fiffer's *Imagining America* (o.p., 1991). Le Ly Hayslip chronicles her life in the United States in her memoir *Child of War, Woman of Peace*, which continues the story she began in *When Heaven and Earth Changed Places*.

In 1980, writer Amy Ling searched in vain for an entry under "Chinese-American authors" in the Library of Congress Subject Headings. The staff at the Library of Congress told her that no book had been published on the subject, and so as far as the list was concerned, the subject did not exist. The incident prompted Ling to write *Between Worlds: Women Writers of Chinese Ancestry* so she could "put these writers on the scholarly map, to give them a heading in the Library of Congress Subject Catalog to validate their existence and their work, to retrieve them from oblivion."

In the 1980s and 1990s, there has been a growing recognition of Asian-American literature by the mainstream culture. The University of Washington Press has published an entire line of recovered or out-of-print works by important Asian-American writers, including Carlos Bulosan, John Okada, Monica Sone, Louis Chu, and Bienvenido N. Santos. Asian-American books are now published by ethnic, feminist, and academic presses as well as major publishing houses. There has been a surge of literary activity in the past few years. Among the first-time Asian-American fiction writers, Fae Myenne Ng, Gish Jen, Cynthia Kadohata, Peter Bacho, and David Wong Louie are well received.

David Henry Hwang won a Tony Award in 1988 for his play *M. Butterfly*. Amy Tan's *The Joy Luck Club* and *The Kitchen God's Wife* were enormous bestsellers.

Looking Ahead

Sorrow, pain, anger, suffering, loss, separation, loneliness, concentration camps, marginalization, exclusion, exploitation, struggle, violence, prejudice, discrimination. . . .

These words appear often in books by and about Asian Americans. They represent much of the collective experience of Asian Americans over the past century and a half. Yet the Asian-American experience is multifaceted and multidimensional. There are some happy stories that Asian Americans can celebrate. There is also a need for inspiring and well-written biographies about famous Asian-Pacific-American men and women, pathbreakers in such fields as science, art, music, sports, business, and politics. Readers seeking to understand the depth and complexity of the culture need to hear from different Asian Americans who have settled in different regions of the country. They also need to hear more from writers of Cambodian, Laotian, Thai, Indian, Pakistan, Bangladeshi, and Samoan descent. Garrett Hongo, in the introduction to *The Open Boat: Poems from Asian America*, points out that the Asian-American experience need not be seen as "monolithic" or "conventional." He invites his fellow Asian-American writers to integrate and diversify.

Through the years, many talented but stifled Asian-American writers have died by the roadside. Some are still hanging on by the edge of the cliff. At its worst, the limited degree of Asian-American book publishing to date reflects what might be called a form of institutional racism in the information distribution system of this country. At best, it is a cycle of omission. Few books by Asian-American authors were published by mainstream publishing houses. Those that did see print often were not reviewed by major critics and therefore did not appear on the shelves of bookstores or libraries. Perhaps the picture is changing. If so, an important segment of the population will no longer be denied its legitimate collective memories and their individual voices will no longer be stilled. When other populations have the opportunity to learn about their Asian-Pacific neighbors, they can replace ignorance and misinformation with insight and understanding. The books described in this chapter represent a ray of hope that literature about these diverse and vital people will help secure their place in the evolving multicultural community.

LITERATURE

254 Asian Women United of California, ed. ***Making Waves: An Anthology of Writings By and About Asian-American Women***. Illus. with photos. Beacon 1989, $18.00 (0-8070-5905-6). 480pp. Anthology.

This is an anthology of autobiographical writings, short stories, poetry, essays, and photographs by and about Asian-American women since the early 1970s. Represented in this collection are established and emerging women writers from the older immigrant groups, such as Japanese and Chinese. Here, too, are writings by recent arrivals from countries such as India, Pakistan, Vietnam, Cambodia, and Thailand.

Sucheta Mazudar begins the anthology with a concise chronological overview of the Asian-American experience from the woman's perspective. The selected works are divided into seven sections, organized thematically around issues relevant to Asian-American women. Each section carries a title drawing on water imagery, such as "Crashing Waves: War," "Moving Currents: Work," and "Making Waves: Activism" and begins with an introduction of its theme. The essays, some serious and some hilarious, cover topics such as mail-order brides, the exploited unskilled workers in the silicon industry, and the stereotyped media images of Asian-American women. Some of the essays overlap. A nine-page chronology of Asian-American history by Judy Yung provides a historical backdrop. *Making Waves* is a fine companion to *The Forbidden Stitch* (*see main entry*).

255   Bacho, Peter. *Cebu*. Univ. of Washington Pr. 1991, $25.00 (0-295-97113-4); $12.95 (0-295-97132-0). 212pp. Fiction.

This darkly comic novel opens as Ben Lucerco, a young second-generation Filipino-American priest, escorts his mother's casket in a plane from Seattle to her hometown, the Philippine city of Cebu. This is Ben's first trip to his ancestral land. A series of scenes involving sin, sex, violence, and self-crucifixion begins in Cebu and continues with Ben's return to his Seattle parish, where sex and gang violence are part of the alienated world. Throughout the book, Ben wrestles with the classic conflicting urges of the spirit and of lust and must confront the differences between Filipino and American culture. This is also the story of Aunt Clara, a patron to Ben's family and a shrewd manipulator of the corrupt world of money and power in the Philippines after World War II. Bacho's debut novel won the 1992 Before Columbus Foundation American Book Award.

256   Berson, Misha, ed. *Between Worlds: Contemporary Asian-American Plays*. Theatre Communications Group 1989, $13.95 (1-55936-004-6). 272pp. Drama.

The six playwrights represented in this anthology, the first of its kind, are Americans with ancestry in China, Japan, and the Philippines. Ping Chong, Philip Kan Gotanda, Jessica Hagedorn, David Henry Hwang, Wakako Yamauchi, and Laurence Yep are recognized names in Asian-American theater and literary circles. Each playwright's section includes an autobiographical remark, biographical information, and a short note about each play. The plays, which range widely in style and theme, reflect the tremendous diversity of Asian-American culture. Editor Misha Berson explains in her introduction that most of the characters in these plays are suspended "between worlds": between two cultures, between marriage and divorce, between life and death, between war and peace.

Tony Award winner David Henry Hwang, author of *M. Butterfly*, emphasizes the importance of exploring racism and stereotypes among various ethnic groups as the United States becomes increasingly multiethnic. He predicts, "In the long run, if the ethnic theaters do their jobs properly, they should phase out their own existence. . . . The future is . . . in multicultural theaters that will do a black play, an Asian play, a white play, whatever."

257 Bruchac, Joseph, ed. ***Breaking Silence: An Anthology of Contemporary Asian-American Poets***. Greenfield 1984, $9.95 (0-912678-59-3). 300pp. Poetry.

This is a collection of works by fifty recognized and emerging poets in the United States and Canada, selected on the basis of variety and appeal to the general reader. Organized alphabetically by author, the selections are accompanied by brief biographical information and a photograph of each writer. Most of the poets represented, including Mei-mei Berssenbrugger, Marilyn Chin, David Mura, Joy Kogawa, and Cathy Song, have ancestry in China, Japan, the Philippines, and India. Some of the writers had published or have since published their own volumes of poems. Bruchac introduces the poets as Asian-American writers who "are adding to the literature and life of their nations and the world, breaking both silence and stereotypes with the affirmation of new songs." The title poem, "Breaking Silence" by Janice Mirikitani, is a powerful piece about her mother's testimony before the U.S. Congress on behalf of Japanese Americans who sought redress for being interned in camps during World War II.

258 Chan, Jeffrey P., and others, eds. ***Aiiieeeee! An Anthology of Asian-American Writers***. NAL 1991, $5.99 (0-451-62836-5). 304pp. Anthology.

Originally published in 1974, this landmark revolutionary anthology heralded a liberated Asian-American literary sensibility. The editors, a group of outspoken, angry young Asian-American writers, say of their work, "Asian America, so long ignored and forcibly excluded from creative participation in American culture, is wounded, sad, angry, swearing and wondering, this is our AIIIEEEEE! It is more than a whine, shout or scream. It is fifty years of our whole voice."

The introduction documents in strong words the history of racism in American culture and its effects on Asian-American literature and manhood. The fourteen pieces culled from various sources include short stories, excerpts from novels, and plays by American writers of Chinese, Japanese, and Filipino descent, some of them long neglected by the literary mainstream. They articulate the "elegant, angry, and bitter life" of Asian Americans from the pre–World War II period to the early 1970s. For this edition, the editors have added a new preface that continues and expands their spirited discussion of the Asian-American literary tradition.

259 Chan, Jeffrey P., and others, eds. ***The Big Aiiieeeee! An Anthology of Chinese-American and Japanese-American Literature***. NAL 1991, $15.00 (0-452-01076-4). 650pp. Anthology.

The Big Aiiieeeee! is a sequel and companion volume to *Aiiieeeee! (see separate entry)*. This comprehensive collection includes poetry, prose, short stories, and excerpts from fiction, drama, and the social sciences, Although some popular, well-known writers are excluded, the book features twenty-seven established and emerging Chinese-American and Japanese-American writers, from the earliest years of Asian-American writing to contemporary pieces.

The book begins with a controversial essay by Frank Chin, "Come All Ye Asian-American Writers of the Real and the Fake," in which he outlines his narrow definition of an "authentic" Asian-American literary tradition. Selections include the revealing *An English-Chinese Phrase Book*, compiled in 1875 by

Sam Wong and his assistants. This book was widely used by first-generation Chinese immigrants as a survival tool in a hostile and violent land. Here, too, are bilingual Cantonese poems from *Songs of Gold Mountain*, compiled and translated by Marlon K. Hom. The collection contains three short stories by Sui Sin Far, a Eurasian woman who wrote about Chinese people from her own experiences at the turn of the century. It also includes a dramatic picture book by Taro Yashima, a famed Japanese-American artist.

As in their previous collection, the editors present a vital anthology of Chinese-American and Japanese-American literature.

260 Chin, Frank. *The Chickencoop Chinaman and The Year of the Dragon: Two Plays*. Intro. by Dorothy Ritsuko McDonald. Univ. of Washington Pr. 1981, $14.95 (0-295-95833-2). 172pp. Drama

The searing and bitter dialogue in these two plays reveals how Chinese-American history, culture, and the legacy of Chinese-American manhood has been destroyed by a racist society. *The Chickencoop Chinaman* (1972), about a new generation of restive young Asian Americans, was the first Asian-American drama produced by an off-Broadway theater in New York. *The Year of the Dragon* (1974) was the first Asian-American play produced on national television. Set in San Francisco, the play depicts the disintegration of a Chinatown family and the oldest son's desperate struggle for identity. In her valuable introduction, Dorothy Ritsuko McDonald discusses Chin's biographical background, his historical perspective, and his deliberately unconventional language.

Frank Chin is one of the first Asian-American playwrights whose plays defy stereotypes. A fifth-generation Chinese American, Chin is also a writer, critic, and editor. But he is more renowned for his harsh literary criticism. The stories in his collection *The Chinaman Pacific & Frisco R. R. Co.* (Coffee House, 1988) share the haunting central theme of the devastating impact that distorted history and forced cultural assimilation have had on Chinese Americans. The book won the American Book Award from the Before Columbus Foundation in 1989.

261 Chin, Frank. *Donald Duk*. Coffee House 1991, $11.95 (0-918273-83-8). 173pp. Fiction.

Donald Duk is a twelve-year-old Chinese-American boy who goes to a private school and whose father owns a Chinese restaurant in San Francisco's Chinatown. He is embarrassed by his name and seems to be ashamed of everything Chinese. He is particularly embarrassed when his history teacher reads to the class that the Chinese were passive, nonassertive, timid, and introverted.

In his dreams, Donald is transported back to the Sierras in 1869. He witnesses how the strong and heroic Chinese crew building the transcontinental railroad worked bravely against the harsh, impenetrable granite mountains, how they cleverly executed a labor strike, and how they won a track-laying competition against other workers. He also discovers that not one Chinese was allowed to take part in the picture-taking ceremony. Donald comes through the dream lessons with a newfound ethnic pride. He takes to heart his father's lesson: "You gotta keep the history yourself or lose it forever."

Frank Chin is a playwright, writer, editor, and critic. This is his first novel; he is also author of two plays, *The Chickencoop Chinaman* and *The Year of the Dragon (see main entry)* and is coeditor of two anthologies of Asian-American literature, *Aiiieeeee!* and *The Big Aiiieeeee! (see main entries)*

262   Chu, Louis. *Eat a Bowl of Tea*. Carol Publg. 1986, $5.95 (0-8184-0395-0). 250pp. Fiction.

Originally published in 1961, this novel paints a genuine portrait of New York's Chinatown in the late 1940s from the perspective of its inhabitants. It is in part a satire on the manners, mores, and sufferings of an enclave of aging men forced by exclusionary American laws to live out their days without the comfort of their wives and families. The book is also a tale of adultery and retribution—a study of how a young Chinatown couple reconcile their dreams with grim realities. Although in some instances the actions and reactions of the characters do not ring true, Chu writes earthy and authentic Chinatown dialogue that reveals the interrelationships within the community.

In an introduction to the 1979 edition, Jeffrey Chan, coeditor of the Asian-American anthology *The Big Aiiieeeee!*, comments: "The vision of a Chinatown community in transition, from a bachelor to a family society, that Chu describes in his pioneer work acknowledges the path of social and historical development that community traveled." The book was adapted into a popular film by the same name.

263   Geok-Lin Lim, Shirley, and Mayumi Tsutakawa, eds. *The Forbidden Stitch: An Asian-American Women's Anthology*. Calyx 1989, $32.00 (0-934971-10-2); $16.95 (0-934971-04-8). 290pp. Anthology.

This book, one of the first general anthologies of works by Asian-American women, evocatively represents the diverse lives and distinctive thoughts of women whose ancestors are from different parts of Asia, among them India, Hong Kong, Japan, Malaysia, Vietnam, and Pakistan. Coeditor Shirley Geok-Lin Lim writes in her introduction, "If we form a thread, the thread is a multicolored, many layered, complexly knotted stitch."

Because the purpose of the book is to showcase new voices, many better-known Asian-American writers are not represented. Included are poems, short stories, and photographs of artworks. Reviews of books by women writers are grouped at the end. The book covers some themes seldom addressed in works by Asian-American women, such as self-destruction, sexual abuse, and domestic violence. Other works deal with the themes of self-definition, image, family, and work.

The publication of this work and a similar anthology, *Making Waves (see main entry)*, in the same year indicates that Asian-American women have become increasingly aware of the ambiguity and complexity of their identity and are ready to sew the "forbidden stitch."

González, N.V.M. *The Bamboo Dancers*.
See entry 1595.

264 Hagedorn, Jessica, ed. ***Charlie Chan Is Dead: An Anthology of Contemporary Asian-American Fiction***. Viking 1993, $14.00 (0-14-023111-0). 640pp. Fiction.

Charlie Chan, the "most famous fake 'Asian' pop icon," is known for his asexual, obsequious mannerisms and his "fortune-cookie" broken English. As the writings in this groundbreaking anthology show, that image is indeed dead. This collection, the first of its kind from a major commercial publisher, is a mixed bag of stories by forty-eight Asian-American writers. Some are well known, such as Carlos Bulosan, Toshio Mori, Maxine Hong Kingston, Bharati Mukherjee, and Amy Tan, but about half are new and emerging voices. Many of the stories are complete in themselves, while others are excerpts from longer works. The selections reflect a wide range of literary styles, from traditional to moderately experimental. Among the themes addressed are contemporary life, ambiguity, aging, love, and death.

Hagedorn, Jessica. ***Dogeaters***.
See entry 1596.

265 Hongo, Garrett, ed. ***The Open Boat: Poems from Asian America***. Doubleday 1993, $12.00 (0-385-42338-1). 335pp. Poetry.

In his introduction to this outstanding anthology of contemporary Asian-American poetry, Hongo, himself a poet, challenges the notion held by some critics and scholars that Asian-American literary culture is monolithic. He makes a passionate call to a new generation of writers to come forward "to encourage diversity, intellectual passion, and an appreciation of verbal beauty." The introduction also provides a capsule history of Asian-American immigration and the evolution of Asian-American literature. The thirty-one Asian-American poets included in the anthology represent a wide range of perspectives, themes, and styles. The book includes some familiar names—such as Maxine Hong Kingston, David Mura, and Jessica Hagedorn—as well as many new voices.

Hongo, a fourth-generation (Yonsei) Japanese American from Hawaii, has written two volumes of poetry: *Yellow Light* (Univ. Pr. of New England, 1982) and *The River of Heaven* (Knopf, 1988), which was the 1989 Lamont Poetry Selection and a finalist for the 1989 Pulitzer Prize in poetry.

266 Hwang, David H. ***FOB and Other Plays***. o.p. Drama.

Playwright Hwang states that the six plays in this collection represent his "attempt to explore human issues without denying the color of my skin." *FOB*, which won an Obie Award as best play of the 1980–1981 off-Broadway season, deals with the stigma and dilemma of new immigrants labeled as FOB ("fresh off the boat"). *The Dance and the Railroad* is a historical play based on the Chinese railroad workers' strike of 1867. In writing the play, Hwang says, his purpose was to refute the stereotypes of Chinese laborers as passive and subservient and to show them instead as strong, hardy, and rebellious men. *Family Devotions* is a caustic autobiographical play about an affluent suburban Chinese-American family and their born-again Christian faith. Hwang refers to these three plays as his Chinese-American trilogy.

In 1989, Hwang became the first Asian-American playwright to win the

Tony Award with his intriguing Broadway hit *M. Butterfly*, based on the true story of a twenty-year love affair between a French diplomat and a Beijing Opera star, a male Chinese spy masquerading as a woman.

267   Jen, Gish. ***Typical American***. NAL 1992, $10.00 (0-452-26774-9). 304pp. Fiction.

"It's an American story: Before he was a thinker, or a doer, or an engineer, much less an imagineer . . . Ralph Chang was just a small boy in China, struggling to grow up his father's son. " So begins Gish Jen's story. In 1947, Ralph—whose Chinese name is Yifeng—leaves his elite family in Shanghai to study engineering in New York. After the Chinese Communist takeover in 1949, Ralph loses touch with his family. Stranded and penniless, he is thankful when he is miraculously reunited with his older sister, the know-it-all Teresa, in the United States. Ralph marries Helen, Teresa's young and beautiful friend from China, then pursues his Ph.D. and becomes a lackluster tenured professor. Teresa studies medicine, and Helen becomes the mother of two girls.

Ralph buys a new suburban home and invests in a fast-food restaurant. In the process he becomes a true believer in "typical American" mottoes, such as "What you can conceive, you can achieve," and is an avid reader of self-help books, such as *Ninety Days to Power and Success*. The rest of the story is packed with seduction, adultery, and tragedy. Jen's first novel about one immigrant family's pursuit of the American dream is fast-moving, humorous, and full of ironies.

268   Kadohata, Cynthia. ***The Floating World***. Ballantine 1993, $10.00 (0-345-38162-9). 208pp. Fiction.

In this novel, Olivia, a precocious adolescent, recounts her travels with her family during the 1950s. Life is hard for Japanese Americans during that time. Good work is not easy to come by. Olivia's family—mother, stepfather, three younger brothers, and grandmother—drifts from town to town through Oregon, California, and Arkansas, lured by prospects for a better job for her stepfather. "We were traveling then in what [my grandmother] called *ukiyo*, the floating world. The floating world was the gas station attendants, restaurants, and jobs we depended on, the motel towns floating in the middle of fields and mountains. . . . [I]t also referred to change and the pleasures and loneliness change brings. . . . *We* were stable, traveling through an unstable world. . . ." Although she finds her grandmother obnoxious, it is through her that Olivia establishes a link with her Japanese past.

In this lyrical first novel, Olivia's unconventional Japanese-American family and their encounters subtly illustrate the multifaceted characters of the people. Kadohata's second novel, *In the Heart of the Valley of Love* (Viking, 1992), is a futuristic tale set in 2050 with a loose plot about life in a chaotic Los Angeles.

269   Kanazawa, Tooru J. ***Sushi and Sourdough: A Novel***. Univ. of Washington Pr. 1991, $12.95 (0-295-97083-9). 256pp. Fiction.

This well-researched historical novel is a saga of one of the first few Japanese settlers in Alaska during the gold rush days at the turn of the century.

Kanazawa, a retired journalist, bases much of his book on his own childhood in the frontier town of Juneau and his father's experiences in Alaska.

In the opening pages, Matajiro Fuse, a Japanese barber lured by dreams of gold and adventure, leaves San Francisco and finds his way to Alaska in 1897. He stays in the Alaska interior as a prospector for five years before he returns to the Northwest. Fourteen years later he comes back to Juneau with his wife and four American-born children and opens a barber shop. The second half of the narrative focuses on Fuse's younger son, Thor, his boyhood, his friendly Scandinavian neighbors, and his summer work at a cannery.

The close-knit Issei (first-generation Japanese-American) community, the exploited life of Alaskan natives, and the excitements of frontier life are realistically portrayed with convincing details. *Sushi and Sourdough* fills in some blank pages about the social and economic history of Japanese immigrants during the Alaskan gold rush era.

270 Kim, Elaine. *Asian-American Literature: An Introduction to the Writings and Their Social Context.* Temple Univ. Pr. 1984, $19.95 (0-87722-352-1). 248pp. Anthology.

This collection traces the experience of Asian Americans through their writings from the late nineteenth century to the 1970s. The editor selected these works because, she says, they reflect "the evolution of Asian American consciousness and self-image as expressed in the literature." Chapters are organized thematically and address a range of topics, including images of Asians in Anglo-American literature, early Asian immigrant writers, second-generation self-portraits, and "Chinatown cowboys" and "warrior women."

An excellent scholarly work for serious readers interested in gaining an in-depth understanding of Asian-American literature in its larger social context, the book includes extensive reference notes, a bibliography, and an index.

271 Kim, Ronyoung. *Clay Walls.* Permanent Press 1986, $22.00 (0-932966-66-7); Univ. of Washington Pr. $14.95 (0-295-96927-X). 304pp. Fiction.

After the publication in 1937 of Younghill Kang's *East Goes West*, fifty years elapsed before another major novel appeared that examines what it means to be Korean America. Whereas Kang's novel looks at life on the East Coast, *Clay Walls* sensitively portrays the struggle for survival and identity of an immigrant family on the West Coast. It captures the history and culture of the Korean community in Los Angeles from the mid-1920s to the mid-1940s. The story is skillfully told in three sections from the different perspectives of the mother, Haesu, the father, Chun, and the American-born daughter, Faye.

Haesu and Chun come from different backgrounds. Within the "clay walls" of their home, the couple battles over money, sex, children, and Korean politics. Chun builds up a promising wholesale produce business, but he loses the family fortune in one high-stakes gamble. Chun disappears, and Haesu takes over the responsibility for the family. She perseveres, maintaining her dignity and pride through it all. The book ends on a positive note as the next generation grows up and, after the end of World War II, takes its place in a more receptive United States.

The story in this, Kingston's first work of fiction, is set in San Francisco in the
1960s and centers on Whittman Ah Sing, a fifth-generation Chinese American
and a Berkeley graduate in English literature. Whittman is a dreamer, a disillusioned playwright, and an unstoppable talker, fervent about "yellow power"
and scornful of conventional mores. He drifts from one odd job to another,
smokes pot, takes a wife so as to dodge the draft, and hunts for a lost grandmother in Reno. Like the Monkey King of Chinese legend, whose religious
name means "Awareness-of-Emptiness," Whittman is egocentric, mischievous, scintillating, and at the same time vulnerable and empty. In the legend,
the Monkey King is completely at the mercy of his controlling goddess despite
his magical prowess. Similarly, the author tosses Whittman between mockery
and compassion. At the end of the book, she says, "Dear American monkey,
don't be afraid. Here, let us tweak your ear, and kiss your other ear."

Though some readers may be challenged by the book's many allusions to
both Western and Chinese classics and lore, *Tripmaster Monkey* is a witty,
rollicking tale told by a gifted and award-winning storyteller.

273   Lai, Him Mark, Genny Lim, and Judy Yung, eds. ***Island: Poetry and History of
Chinese Immigrants on Angel Island***. Bilingual (Chinese-English) ed. Illus.
Univ. of Washington Pr. 1991, $16.95 (0-295-97109-6). 174pp. Poetry.

This volume contains 135 poems that were carved by Chinese immigrants into
the wooden walls of the barracks at Angel Island in San Francisco Bay between 1910 and 1940. Community efforts saved the barracks from demolition
and turned them into a historical site in the early 1970s.

An introduction to this bilingual education documents the history of Angel
Island. The poems are augmented with explanatory footnotes, photos, and
interviews of former detainees, visitors, and workers. Written in the classical
Chinese poetic style, the poems express the immigrants' despair and rage at the
humiliating treatment they received on the island. In their original language,
the poems are uneven in literary quality. Their very existence, however, dis-
proves the commonly held view that Chinese immigrants were illiterate and
uneducated. The skillful translations capture not just the meanings and the
feelings of the original poems, but their raw energy as well. Conveying a vivid
image of a bitter part of Chinese-American history, *Island* is a unique collection
of great historical importance.

274   Lee, Gus. ***China Boy***. NAL 1991, $19.95 (0-525-24994-X); $10.95 (0-452-
27158-4). 320pp. Fiction.

Kai Ting is born to a once-wealthy family who flees China in the 1940s and
resettles in a poor, predominantly black neighborhood in San Francisco. The
youngest of the four children and the only son, Kai Ting enjoys a happy,
pampered childhood until his doting mother dies when he is six years old.
The father remarries a non-Chinese woman who sets out to eradicate from the
household every vestige of Chinese culture, including family heirlooms, the
mother's pictures, even the Chinese food the family adores. Banished to the
streets by his mean-spirited stepmother, Kai encounters a parade of kind

souls: a Chinese scholar, a tough Italian fatherless boy, a Hispanic auto mechanic, and a group of big-hearted former-boxer coaches at the YMCA who teach him to fight back and survive in life.

This endearing autobiographical tale of a boy's coming of age is both hilarious and heartbreaking. The author calls the book "a multiethnic novel." The sequel, *Honor and Duty* (Knopf 1993), follows Kai's life through his years at the U.S. Military Academy at West Point.

275 Ling-chi Wang, L., and Henry Yiheng Zhao, eds. *Chinese-American Poetry: An Anthology*. Univ. of Washington Pr. 1992, $19.95 (0-295-97154-1). 272pp. Poetry.

This anthology of English-language works by American poets of Chinese ancestry is the first of its kind. According to its editors, the book is a "documentation of the continuity as well as far-reaching changes in the Chinese poetic tradition and simultaneously a contribution to a much-neglected aspect of contemporary American poetry." The bilingual poets represented here respond in different ways to the strong influence of Chinese culture; some embrace it, while others react with ambivalence or rebel against it, especially the patriarchal tradition. Some writers highlight aspects of American life, and others make social criticism an essential element in their poems. Included are some of the most prominent Chinese-American authors, including Mei-mei Berssenbrugger, Diana Chang, Alan Chong Lau, Russell Leong, Shirley Lim, Amy Ling, Nellie Wong, and John Yao.

The editors originally planned to compile a bilingual volume, but no publishers seemed interested. Instead they published a Chinese translation in Shanghai in 1990. This English version appeared in the United States in 1992.

276 Lo, Steven C. *The Incorporation of Eric Chung*. Algonquin 1989, $14.95 (0-945575-18-1). 220pp. Fiction.

This is a first-person narrative of Eric Chung, who comes to Texas from Taiwan in 1972. He starts his career in a small town as a computer operator during the night shift. Within a few years he moves his way up the corporate ladder until he becomes division president of a large electronics enterprise in Dallas. His assignment is to open up the China trade for the company. He and his predecessors soon learn that in doing business with China, "the rocks were hard and the earth was thick; those who couldn't hang on for the long haul, those Westerners, would, one by one, fall away."

Eric is "a quick study" and a wry observer of American business practices. He notes, for example, the naiveté with which executives venture into China's uncharted waters. He also gives a hilarious insider's look at the college life of a group of Taiwanese graduate students. The story shifts back and forth between the two different worlds. This is a first novel by Lo, who was born in Taiwan and who is an international business consultant.

277 Louie, David Wong. *Pangs of Love*. Knopf 1991, $18.50 (0-394-58957-2); NAL $9.00 (0-452-26888-5). 240pp. Fiction.

This is a collection of eleven short stories, some of which have previously appeared in literary magazines and one of which, "Displacement," was chosen for *The Best American Short Stories 1989*. The title story tells of the gulf between a widowed mother who speaks minimal English and her son who speaks very little Chinese. The son wants to tell his questioning mother that his Chinese-speaking Caucasian girlfriend, the mother's favorite, has left him, and that his brother has settled into an openly gay lifestyle, but he can't find the language to do so.

Most of the stories in this collection, Louie's first book, have Chinese-American characters, but the themes of the stories are about universal feelings of love, loss, healing, alienation, and generational conflicts. Though the stories are uneven in quality, Louie's writing has a certain coolness and a compelling satirical undertone. He is considered among the country's promising young writers.

278   McCunn, Ruthanne Lum. ***Thousand Pieces of Gold: A Biographical Novel.*** Illus. with photos. Beacon 1989, $9.95 (0-8070-8317-8). 312pp. Fiction.

This biographical novel recounts the true story of a Chinese-American pioneer woman named Lalu Nathoy, later known as Polly Bemis (1853–1933). Born in a poor village in northern China, Lalu was snatched from her starving family by bandits and sold to a Chinese saloonkeeper in a gold-mining camp in Idaho. Having gained her freedom through a poker game, she set up a boarding house. Eventually, she married her long-time companion, Charlie Bemis, and settled on an Idaho homestead.

At a time when anti-Chinese sentiments were high in the West, Lalu made enduring friendships in her community and became a respected figure in Idaho lore. Some of her personal effects are kept in an Idaho museum, and Polly Creek was named after her. In the book, Lalu is portrayed as a strong-spirited woman who took charge of her own life. This novel, illustrated with old photographs, provides a glimpse into the lives of Chinese pioneer women in the frontier West

279   Mirikitani, Janice, ed. ***Ayumi: A Japanese American Anthology***. Illus. o.p. Anthology.

This first bilingual anthology represents the community efforts of contemporary Japanese Americans to document and preserve the creative process of four generations of Japanese-American writers and artists in this country. Especially valuable are the works of the first-generation immigrants, whose voices have seldom been recorded. Some of the pieces contained in this volume are translated into English for the first time.

The anthology includes personal journals, short stories, poetry, and art work. The writings are divided into sections: first-generation immigrants (Issei); second-generation (Nisei); and third- and fourth-generation (Sansei and Yonsei). Both established writers and emerging new voices are represented. Their unique perspectives, coupled with the color plates included in the volume, provide rare insights into Japanese-American experiences. Short biographies of the contributors are provided.

280   Mirikitani, Janice. ***Shedding Silence***. Celestial Arts 1987, $14.95 (0-89087-496-4); $8.95 (0-89087-493-X). 176pp. Poetry.

Janice Mirikitani is a Sansei (third-generation Japanese-American) writer and a community activist. This collection of poetry and prose is a lyrical expression of raging social and political protest. The pieces, some with graphically violent images, feature women who rebel against the exploitation and oppression of sexism, racism, and war. Mirikitani's deep commitment and compassion come through clearly in her writing. "When There Is Talk of War," a brief prose piece inspired by the true story of a Japanese-American victim of the atomic bomb, is a deeply touching and powerful message against the horrors of war. The title piece is a drama in which a Sansei daughter challenges the passive attitudes of her family.

Mirikitani's first volume of poetry was *Awake in the River* (o.p., 1978). She is also the editor of *Ayumi (see main entry)*, a collection of literary and visual art by four generations of Japanese Americans, and is coeditor of *Making Waves* (edited by Asian Women United of California, *see main entry*), an anthology of writings by Asian-American women.

281   Mori, Toshio. *Woman from Hiroshima*. o.p. Fiction.

In this, the author's first novel, the protagonist, an Issei (first-generation Japanese immigrant) woman, tells her grandchildren about her life from the time she left Japan as a young woman to join her husband in San Francisco to becoming a serene grandmother at the end of World War II. During that time she helps her husband run a bathhouse and a flower nursery, lives in a concentration camp, and sees her sons go off to war. She advises her grandchildren "to face the hardships and triumphs of life without giving up hope. . . . You don't have to die in order to become brave. You are brave when you try to live." The story is based on the life of Mori's mother, to whom the author dedicates the book.

282   Mori, Toshio. *Yokohama, California.* Repr. of 1949 ed. Univ. of Washington Pr. 1985, $12.95 (0-295-96167-8). 176pp. Fiction.

Toshio Mori is a prolific and talented writer whose works reflect warmth, subtle humor, and cosmic wisdom. He has produced hundreds of short stories, many essays, and several novels, often writing at night after a long day's work in the fields of botanical nurseries.

Originally published in 1949, *Yokohama, California* is a pioneering work, the first collection of short stories by a Japanese American. Set in the fictional semirural community of Yokohama, California, it is alive with the people, gossip, humor, and legends of Japanese America in the late 1930s and early 1940s. The author records the voices, sensibilities, and tranquillity of the Issei (first-generation immigrant) community before the era of World War II internment camps.

Among Asian-American literary circles, Mori is a beloved and admired master. In his introduction to the original edition, William Saroyan called Mori "the first real Japanese-American writer." Lawson Fusao Inada, author of the introduction to this new edition, noted that from Mori's perspective, these stories are not "minority" but "majority" stories. He praises Mori as "a true folk artist in the finest sense of the term—one who conveys our very soul." Mori's second collection, *The Chauvinist and Other Stories* (Univ. of California Asian-American Studies Center, 1979), chronicles in a quiet and compassionate way the Japanese-American experience from the early 1930s through the war years.

283 Mukherjee, Bharati. *Jasmine*. Fawcett 1990, $5.99 (0-449-21923-2). 244pp. Fiction.

This novel shows how a Hindu woman, suspended between two cultures, defies fate. The first-person narrative is fast-paced; the heroine is pretty, intelligent, romantic, and adventurous. When Jyoti is a little girl in rural India, an astrologer foretells a life of widowhood and exile for her. Jyoti marries a technical college student. To separate her from her past, he gives her a new name, Jasmine. After her husband falls victim to a terrorist bomb, Jasmine finds her way to Florida. She kills a man who rapes her and flees to an Indian enclave in New York. She changes her name again, this time to Jass, and works in Manhattan as a nanny for a professor and his wife. After moving to Iowa, she marries a small-town banker and takes on a new identity as Jane Ripplemeyer. The banker is paralyzed after being shot by a bankrupt farmer. Jane then heads for California with the Manhattan professor. As Jane puts it, "I am not choosing between men. I am caught between the promise of America and old-world dutifulness." She decides to choose adventure, risk, and transformation. She proclaims: "Watch me re-position the stars" as she scrambles ahead, "greedy with wants and reckless from hope."

Mukherjee is an Indian-born award-winning writer who immigrated to Canada in the 1970s. Angered by Canada's treatment of South Asians, she resettled in the United States in 1980.

284 Mukherjee, Bharati. *The Middleman and Other Stories*. Fawcett 1989, $4.99 (0-449-21718-3). 206pp. Fiction.

With this book, Bharati Mukherjee became the first naturalized American citizen to earn the National Book Critics Circle Award for best fiction, which she won in 1988. Mukherjee once said that her characters are "conquerors" who with "eagerness and enthusiasm and confidence . . . chase the American dream." In this collection of eleven short stories, she recounts with tenderness and humor the tales of culture clashes that affect newcomers from the Third World: the wife of a Bombay business man alone in New York; an aristocratic Filipino woman in Atlanta; an Italian-American girl visiting her Afghan boyfriend's family at Thanksgiving.

Darkness (Fawcett, 1992), Mukherjee's first collection, contains stories that are bitter and nostalgic, reflecting her pronounced anger at the treatment she and other South Asian immigrants received in Canada. In contrast, *The Middleman and Other Stories* reflects her growing optimism in her adopted country, the United States.

285 Murayama, Milton. *All I Asking for Is My Body*. Repr. of 1975 ed. Intro. by Franklin Odo. Univ. of Hawaii Pr. 1988, $5.95 (0-8248-1172-0). 120pp. Fiction.

Originally published in 1959, this was the first literary work to reveal the human situation of the Japanese-Americans' life on Hawaiian plantations, which began with the arrival of the first Japanese contract laborers in 1885. Murayama notes that there was a hierarchy and a separation of races, deliberate moves by the plantation owners to destroy any sense of cohesion among the laborers. Set in the 1930s, this story of the Oyama family is told through the eyes of the younger of the two sons. Bound by the traditional filial obligation, the oldest son gives his body and soul to hard plantation labor in order to pay off a huge family debt. His hopeless situation is saved only by his younger brother, who wins a big sum at gambling before joining the army to escape the plantation life. This novel is a powerful criticism of both the feudalistic plantation system and the authoritarian Japanese family system from the perspective of second-generation immigrants to American territory.

286 Ng, Fae Myenne. **Bone**. HarperCollins 1994, $11.00 (0-06-097592-X). 193pp. Fiction.

"We were a family of three girls. By Chinese standards, that wasn't lucky. . . . Leon [the father] told us not to care about what people said . . . [that] 'Five sons don't make one good daughter.' " This contemporary family story, as told by the oldest daughter, Leila, is set in San Francisco's Chinatown. Mah, the mother, is a seamstress, Leon is a merchant seaman, and middle daughter Nina escapes from Chinatown to work as a flight attendant in New York. To put an end to her conflicted life, youngest daughter Ona jumps to her death. Leila also recounts the family tales about Grandpa Leong's lost bones and other family secrets.

Bone is about how one family deals with grief and loss. It is also about the younger generation in Chinatown trying to move on to the world outside and their ambivalence about their dowdy parents, who endure many hardships to give the next generation a better chance in life. In this much-acclaimed debut novel, Ng conveys the hopes, griefs, and unadorned facts of the lives of two generations of Chinese Americans with strikingly simple and unsentimental language.

287 Okada, John. **No-No Boy.** Repr. of 1957 ed. Univ. of Washington Pr. 1980, $12.95 (0-295-95525-2). 176pp. Fiction.

The story's protagonist, Ichiro Yamada, is one of the few Japanese-American men who refused the draft during World War II. Thus branded a "no-no boy," he is sent to prison for two years. He returns home to Seattle to a strong-willed mother who is fanatically loyal to Japan; his father, a broken man and a drunk; and his younger brother, who is ashamed of him. Many of his old friends who fought in the war shun and despise him. Plagued by a deep sense of self-doubt and bitterness, he tries desperately to find his identity and a place in society. In one of his many internal monologues, he imagines a conversation with his mother: "I wish with all my heart that I were Japanese or that I were American. I am neither and I blame you and I blame myself and I blame the world which is made up of many countries which fight with each other and kill and hate and destroy again and again and again."

With its biting rhetoric, *No-No Boy* is a poignant and gripping novel about the fragmented Japanese-American community in the aftermath of the war. Sadly, even today, the issue of the "no-no boys"—the second-generation Japanese-Americans who refused to fight in the war while their citizenship rights and loyalty were questioned and their families were unjustifiably detained in concentration camps—is not entirely resolved within the community. Originally published in 1957, this novel, the first to speak out against the placid image of the interned Japanese Americans, has become a classic of Japanese-American literature.

Rachlin, Nahid. *Veils: Short Stories*.
See entry 1142.

Santos, Bienvenido N. *The Praying Man*.
See entry 1602.

288   Santos, Bienvenido N. *Scent of Apples: A Collection of Stories*. Intro. by
Leonard Casper. Univ. of Washington Pr. 1979, $14.95 (0-295-95695-X).
250pp. Fiction.

Philippines-born Bienvenido N. Santos was stranded in the United States
during World War II. Since then, he has divided his time between the two
countries, writing about himself and his countrymen. "I belong to the literature of two great countries: the Philippines, land of my birth; and the United
States, sanctuary, a second home."

This American Book Award–winning collection of sixteen short stories is
Santos's first work to appear in the United States. Most of the stories are from
You Lovely People, which Santos published in the Philippines in 1955. The first-
person narrator provides a thread through these stories. Santos writes with
humor and humanity about the Filipino "marginal men" in American society.
In his introduction, Leonard Casper writes, "[T]he recurring theme in Santo's
work is how hard it always is, yet how important, to be 'Filipino' at heart,
with all that that implies about human decency, good humor, and honor,
consideration beyond courtesy, and putting both hands to a common burden;
while at the same time trying to make a life out of being overseas Filipinos,
Philippine Americans." The preface by Santos sketches his personal history in
America.

289   Santos, Bienvenido N. *What the Hell for You Left Your Heart in San Francisco*. Cellar Book Shop 1987, $12.50 (971-10-0319-8). 192pp. Fiction.

This is a novel about a young Filipino journalist in San Francisco. He is
searching not only for ideas about starting a new magazine aimed at Filipino-
American readers but also for his long-lost father from the Philippines. The
magazine never materializes, and his father is never found. But during his
meandering, he discovers many human-interest stories, mostly about his own
countrymen.

With a self-effacing style and a light sense of humor, Bienvenido Santos
writes about the new breed of middle-class Filipino immigrants in America—
rich doctors, well-connected businessmen, and rebellious college students.
But his heart always returns to the "old timers"—the poor, laboring exiles
who struggle to survive. Santos wrote this novel while he was stranded in the
United States during a period of martial law in the Philippines. He wanted the
book to be funny, he said, "because these were sad times."

290   Tan, Amy. *The Joy Luck Club*. Putnam 1989, $18.95 (0-399-13420-4); Ivy
$5.95 (0-8041-0630-4). 288pp. Fiction.

Since 1949, four Chinese women in San Francisco have been meeting to play
mahjong, invest in stocks, eat dim sum, and exchange stories. They call their
gathering the Joy Luck Club. Each mother-and-daughter pair takes a turn

telling their stories in the first person; the eight narratives parallel two complete rounds of a game of mahjong. The mothers recount tragic tales of their past in China, while the American-born daughters tell tales of their contemporary lives. Their stories interweave into an enchanting novel.

Tan deftly centers the stories on the bittersweet relationships between the mothers, who hold fast to old traditions and unrealistic aspirations for their daughters, and the daughters, who fight fiercely for success and independence. As one of the mothers says, "I wanted my children to have the best combination: American circumstances and Chinese character. How could I know these two things do not mix?" This best-selling first novel is artfully told, full of drama and lighthearted humor. It was a finalist for the National Book Award and the National Book Critics Circle Award. The film version, with a screenplay cowritten by Ron Bass and Amy Tan and directed by Wayne Wang, received outstanding reviews when it was released in 1993.

291 Tan, Amy. ***The Kitchen God's Wife***. Random 1993, $12.00 (0-579-74808-3). 415pp. Fiction.

Set in contemporary San Francisco, like the author's *The Joy Luck Club (see main entry)*, this novel tells of the relationship between a Chinese-born mother, who runs a dingy flower shop in Chinatown, and her American-born married daughter, who is a school speech specialist and married to an American. Each woman keeps a secret from the other for many years.

The book begins as the daughter introduces her dowdy, nagging mother. The story comes to life when the mother tells the dark secrets of her past in China. Then, amidst tears and laughter, the daughter shares her secret: she has multiple sclerosis. The book ends as the mother presents to her daughter a little porcelain statue, "Lady Sorrowfree," which represents the kind, estranged wife of the despotic Kitchen God. She tells her daughter, "[W]hen you are afraid, you can talk to her. She will listen. She will wash away everything sad with her tears. She will use her stick to chase away everything bad." The daughter understands that Lady Sorrowfree represents her mother.

292 Watanabe, Sylvia, and Carol Bruchac, eds. ***Home to Stay: Asian-American Fiction by Women***. Greenfield 1990, $12.95 (0-912678-76-3). 300pp. Anthology.

In recent years there has been a burgeoning of literary activity by Asian-American writers, especially women. This collection of Asian-American women's fiction features such prominent writers as Maxine Hong Kingston, Amy Tan, Bharati Mukherjee, and Hisaye Yamamoto, as well as some emerging writers. They represent a diverse range of Asian cultural heritage from China, Japan, India, the Philippines, Indonesia, Malaysia, and Hawaii, but writers from Korea and Vietnam, Laos, and Thailand are not represented. Included are excerpts from novels and short stories, some of which are appearing in print for the first time. The stories are arranged in order of the age of their narrators—girls, young women, and old women. The arrangement of these well-chosen pieces provides the reader with a sense of the sweep of life; the book ends with stories of death and celebration. Each piece is preceded by a photograph of the writer and a brief biographical note that comments on the writer's views and experiences. Editor Sylvia Watanabe introduces the stories as having "arisen smack-dab out of the mainstream of American tradition. Their cross-cultural perspectives address what is increasingly becoming common American experience."

293   Wong, Shawn. ***Homebase: A Novel.*** NAL 1991, $8.00 (0-452-26529-0). 144pp. Fiction.

This is a poetic novella told in the first-person voice of a Chinese-American young man whose engineer father died when he was seven and whose mother died when he was fifteen. "When they died, I needed more than my fifteen years to carry me through. There is more violence in forgetting at fifteen. . . . I wanted to forget my love, not their memory." He tries to hold on to the memories of his parents and the stories of his ancestors to stave off the loneliness of his life. "You are more alone at fifteen than any other age. No lovers. Without a father, mother, brother, sister, there is nothing except your own energy that keeps loneliness and pity at arm's length. . . . I never let up a single day." Movingly and evocatively, the author writes from his heart about love, loss, and his search for identity. This award-winning book has also been translated into German.

294   Yamamoto, Hisaye. ***Seventeen Syllables and Other Stories.*** Intro. by King-kok Cheung. Kitchen Table 1988, $21.95 (0-913175-15-3); $9.95 (0-318-42007-4). 170pp. Fiction.

Hisaye Yamamoto is a distinguished writer of short stories, a poet, and a respected critic of Asian-American literature. She received the 1986 American Book Award for lifetime achievement from the Before Columbus Foundation. Born in 1921, she was interned at a desert camp in Arizona during World War II. This first American collection of her short stories spans forty years of her career. Her stories are peopled with stifled, enduring Issei (first-generation immigrant) mothers and often irrational Issei fathers, frustrated because they have been unable to achieve their ambitions in the United States. Her writing captures with compassion and deep understanding the rural Japanese-American community before World War II, the pain of internment, the uneasy relationships between husbands and wives, and the generational conflicts among immigrant parents and their American-born children. Yamamoto has great empathy for other people of color, often delivering subtle satires on white and Asian prejudice.

295   Yamauchi, Wakako. ***Songs My Mother Taught Me: Stories, Plays, and Memoir.*** Feminist Pr. 1994, $35.00 (1-55861-085-5); $14.95 (1-55861-086-3). 350pp. Anthology.

At long last, a much-awaited collection of short stories, plays, and a brief memoir by Wakako Yamauchi, a Japanese-American short story writer who has been highly regarded in the Asian-American literary circle. For over forty years, Yamauchi has written about the common lives of two generations of Japanese in America, in particular the highly circumscribed lives of Japanese-American women. Her writings provide an emotional connection to the harsh lives of rural immigrants of the early twentieth century, the shattering experiences of the mass wartime relocation, and the postwar migration to urban centers. Her spare, lyrical prose is emotionally intense, yet full of grace and dignity. Yamauchi is an insightful, warm, and intimate storyteller who captures the sensitivity and strength of her often-vulnerable characters.

Yamauchi's work was first introduced in *Aiiieeeee! An Anthology of Asian American Writers* in 1974. Since then, her short stories have been widely anthologized and several of her plays have been produced. She was perhaps best known for her play "And the Soul Shall Dance," developed out of an original short story.

In the sixteen-page introduction, Garrett Hongo briefly covers Yamauchi's personal life and literary style and the eighteen well-selected pieces. The selections are organized into broad categories such as country stories, plays, and recollections. Valerie Miner's Afterword reflects on Yamauchi's writings.

NONFICTION

296   Agarwal, Priya. ***Passage from India: Post-1965 Indian Immigrants and Their Children***. Illus. with photos. Yuvati 1991, $18.95 (0-9630579-0-1). 102pp. Nonfiction.

This book explores the generational and cultural chasm between Indian immigrants after 1965 and their American-educated children. Indians who work in professional occupations constitute a relatively small population in the United States, but they enjoy considerable success. However, as a group, their impact on the social, civic, and political life in mainstream American society is disproportionately small. The author suggests that more participation from women and second-generation Indians will help the Indian-American community gain political influence.

This brief study, based primarily on interviews and participant observations, does not examine the descendants of the earlier Indian immigrants, who were largely farm laborers and members of the merchant class. The journalistic style of writing makes it accessible to the general reader. There is very little information available today about Asian Indians, either in popular or academic sources. This work helps fill that void. Included are some photos and a limited bibliography.

> Ashabranner, Brent. ***An Ancient Heritage: The Arab-American Minority***. See entry 1154.

297   Chan, Sucheng. ***The Asian Americans: An Interpretive History***. Macmillan 1991, $24.95 (0-8057-8426-8); $11.95 (0-8057-8437-3). 240pp. Nonfiction.

In this well-written and meticulously researched analysis, Sucheng Chan presents "a quick overview of important aspects of Asian-American history within a framework that emphasizes the commonalities in the experiences" of various subgroups. She focuses on Asian Americans as shapers of their lives, who actively fight against discrimination and who contribute to the making of America. She also capably demonstrates both the commonalities and differences among the several Asian-American ethnic subgroups. Chan highlights the critical role of women immigrants. Each chapter focuses on a different theme and covers such topics as the international context of Asian emigration, resistance to oppression, women and families, and the second-generation dilemma. The excellent film list, chronology, and extensive notes and references all add to the book's research value. Sucheng Chan's conscientious research and interpretation shed new light on the Asian-American experience.

298 Chan, Sucheng, ed. ***Entry Denied: Exclusion and the Chinese Community in America, 1882–1943***. Temple Univ. Pr. 1991, $49.95 (0-87722-798-5); $22.95 (0-56639-201-1). 320pp. Nonfiction.

This collection of eight essays deals with the period from 1882 to 1943, during which all Chinese (except for a few "exempted classes"—merchants, students, diplomats, and travelers) were prevented from entering the United States. Exploring the legal aspects of exclusion, the first half of the book documents that, despite common perception, the Chinese were more than mere passive victims of immigration policies; instead they have persistently challenged the discriminatory laws in courts. Other chapters focus on the organization and structure of the "Chinatowns" in many larger U.S. cities, noting that these enclaves evolved in response to the exclusion era. The last chapter analyzes *Songs of Gold Mountain*, a two-volume collection of poems portraying life under exclusion.

In view of the dearth of English-language materials on these six decades, which comprise the "dark ages" of Chinese-American history, general readers may find that this scholarly yet accessible work contains illuminating and useful information. Appended is a English-Chinese glossary. This book is part of the publisher's Asian-American History and Culture series.

299 Chan, Sucheng, ed. ***Hmong Means Free: Life in Laos and America***. Illus. Temple Univ. Pr. 1994, $44.95 (1-56639-162-8); $16.95 (1-55639-163-3). 288pp. Nonfiction.

The Hmong are a group of ethnic Laotians. The 1990 census counted some 100,000 Hmong in the United States. Over 40,000 live in California, and there are other large enclaves in Minnesota and Wisconsin. Sucheng Chan, a noted scholar and general editor of Temple University's Asian-American History and Culture series, collaborated with four of her Hmong students at the University of California, Santa Barbara (UCSB) to produce this first collection of the Hmong experiences as told from their own perspectives. The students collected oral histories from members of their own families and wrote autobiographies to chronicle stories of survival and adaptation by three generations of immigrants.

The narratives document the Hmong's experiences as slash-and-burn mountain farmers in Laos. They tell of life during war and revolution, in the refugee camps of Thailand, and as immigrants to the United States. The introduction by Chan offers a fresh perspective of the war in Southeast Asia and provides a historical and social framework for the personal stories that follow. There are also an extensive bibliography and an index.

The accounts in this book are edited from tape transcripts to enhance readability. However, the original voices of the speakers are preserved on cassette tapes available through the library at UCSB. This anthology provides much-needed coverage of the little-known Hmong people.

300 Conrat, Maisie, and Richard Conrat. ***Executive Order 9066: The Internment of 110,000 Japanese Americans.*** Illus. with photos by Dorothea Lange. o.p. Nonfiction.

Under Executive Order 9066, signed by President Roosevelt on February 19, 1942, over 110,000 Japanese Americans were removed from California, Oregon, and Washington and placed in interment camps in the interior of the country. Some of them stayed there for four harsh years, losing their personal property and, more important, their dignity. This book contains black-and-white photographs from a museum exhibition that documented this tragic experience and that are accompanied by quotations from books, newspapers, and the *Congressional Record*. The picture images and words are evocative and haunting.

The book was originally published in 1972 and reissued twenty years later, on the fiftieth anniversary of the executive order, but it is now out of print. When the exhibit and the book first appeared, they caused considerable controversy. In the decade that followed, Japanese-American communities across the nation broke the self-imposed silence about the internment and mounted a vigorous campaign to press for redress. On August 10, 1988, President Reagan issued a formal national apology and signed the Civil Liberties Act of 1988, which provided compensation to the survivors.

301 Cordova, Fred. ***Filipinos: Forgotten Asian Americans.*** o.p. Nonfiction.

Through a collection of 250 photographs, documents, essays, excerpts from oral histories, and journals, this pictorial essay presents a sweeping look of Filipino life in the United States from 1763, when Filipinos first settled in Louisiana, to 1963.

The material is organized into chapters focusing on such topics as the Louisiana "Manilamen" of the eighteenth century; the journey to America; the Filipinos as a labor force in agriculture, the Alaskan canneries, and the U.S. Navy; anti-Filipino movements; Filipino women, families, and students; the second generation; church and community activities; and the impact of World War II. Funny anecdotes, colorful vignettes, and captioned photographs are scattered throughout the book. *Forgotten Filipinos*, which originated as a community project, sensitively chronicles the Filipino-American spirit and collective voice.

302 Daniels, Roger. ***Asian America: Chinese and Japanese in the United States since 1850.*** Rev. ed. Univ. of Washington Pr. 1990, $17.50 (0-295-97018-9). 402pp. Nonfiction.

Roger Daniels, a recognized scholar in the field of Asian-American history, has written a thoughtful overview of Chinese and Japanese Americans, the subgroups of Asian Americans who have been in this country the longest. By examining the period from the mid-nineteenth century to the mid-1980s, he describes and interprets the political and socioeconomic aspects of these two subgroups and concludes that their experience has been "integral to the American mosaic."

The book is organized topically and chronologically, with each group discussed separately. Although a discussion that compared and integrated the two groups would have been illuminating, Daniels has provided a fresh historical perspective on these important segments of Asian-American experience. This objective and well-researched work includes an index and a valuable selected bibliography listing archival manuscripts and other source materials.

303   Daniels, Roger. ***Concentration Camps: North American Japanese in the United States and Canada During World War II.*** Reissue. Krieger 1993, $17.50 (0-89874-819-5). 262pp. Nonfiction.

In the spring of 1942, over 110,000 men, women, and children—Americans of Japanese descent—were uprooted from the three Pacific Coast states and shipped off to ten concentration camps isolated in the wastelands of the nation's interior. This book, originally published in 1971, is the first study that tries to examine and explain why the relocation occurred.

Historian Roger Daniels points out that the event cannot simply be written off as a "mistake." He demonstrates that the internment, which he calls a "legal atrocity," was the tragic if logical consequence of over three centuries of American racism. He builds his argument on a careful, multifaceted analysis of various factors: the anti-Japanese movement prior to the war, the behind-the-scenes political and legal battles, and the impact of mass incarceration. He also examines resistance and protest by the evacuees, an aspect often over-looked by other commentators. The 1981 edition of the book adds a new chapter on the Japanese-Canadian experience for comparison. Notes on sources and selected documents are included.

304   Daniels, Roger, Sandra C. Taylor, and Harry H. Kitano, eds. ***Japanese Americans: From Relocation to Redress.*** Rev. ed. Univ. of Washington Pr. 1992, $22.95 (0-295-97117-7). 264pp. Nonfiction.

This collection of essays focuses on the experiences of Japanese Americans, from their evacuation and internment during World War II to the first redress payments made in 1990. Essay topics include the political and cultural back-ground of the issue; the turmoil of being uprooted; life in the camps (including the little-known internment camps for "enemy aliens"); public reactions to the camps; the evacuation experience of Japanese groups in Hawaii, Canada, and Peru; the emotional and economic impact; the redress movement; and the opposition of former military officials to redress. For this edition, a new section has been added that recounts the process by which redress became law in 1988.

This valuable collection is a mixture of moving personal reminiscences, scholarly research, and position papers. It deftly demonstrates the severe psychic and economic toll of incarceration on Japanese Americans. Appended are relevant legal documents, a supplementary bibliography listing books on the topic published since the first edition, and an index. Daniels is also the author of *Prisoners Without Trial: Japanese Americans in World War II* (Hill & Wang, 1993). This book, part of the publisher's Critical Issue series, offers a concisely written overview of the internment for introductory-level students.

305   Espiritu, Yen Le. ***Asian-American Panethnicity: Bridging Institutions and Identities.*** Temple Univ. Pr. 1992, $39.95 (0-87722-955-4); $18.95 (1-56639-096-6). 240pp. Nonfiction.

"Panethnicity" is a new term describing solidarity among racially, culturally, and linguistically diverse ethnic subgroups. Espiritu studies the continuing interaction between internal and external factors that form and transform Asian-American panethnicity, which first emerged in the late 1960s. Among the external factors she cites are government bureaucracies, electoral politics, social service funding, affirmative action programs, and census classification. These forces tended to lump diverse ethnic subgroups into umbrella categories to facilitate distribution of economic and political resources. Individuals and organizations competing for those resources thus feel pressured to realign their ethnic identities to meet the standards of the broader designation. In the process, the needs and concerns of certain ethnic communities may be overlooked. The book explores the question of who stands to benefit most in promoting pan-Asian consciousness—and at whose expense.

Despite the author's use of social science jargon, this well-researched work on a rarely studied topic is accessible to interested readers. Illustrated with statistical tables and figures, the book includes an excellent bibliography, a list of interviews, and an index.

Fathi, Asghar, ed. *Iranian Refugees and Exiles since Khomeini.* See entry 1169.

306   Freeman, James M. *Hearts of Sorrow: Vietnamese-American Lives.* Stanford Univ. Pr. 1989, $49.50 (0-8047-1585-8); $15.95 (0-8047-1890-3). 446pp. Nonfiction.

Hearts of Sorrow is about "the end of an era, a world lost, a way of life that exists only in memory." It is also about survival in a new land. Fourteen Vietnamese refugees, ranging in age from sixteen to eighty and representing a wide variety of backgrounds, tell their life stories in their own words. Freeman, an anthropologist, points out the distinction between immigrants and refugees: Immigrants, he says, *choose* to come to a new life, whereas refugees are *forced* to flee, often for their lives. He wrote the book hoping to gain new insights about the Vietnam War from the different perspectives of the refugees, while the Vietnamese Americans cooperated in hopes that their accounts of their history, cultural values, and heartbreaking experiences will set the record straight.

Segments of the narratives are organized thematically and chronologically into five sections: childhood and character, war, liberation, flight to freedom, and heartache beneath success in the United States. Two introductory chapters and a concluding interpretive chapter discuss the history of the Vietnamese refugee experience and implications of the research. This is an outstanding work of the oral history genre.

307   Fugita, Stephen S., and David J. O'Brien. *Japanese-American Ethnicity: The Persistence of Community.* Univ. of Washington Pr. 1994, $17.50 (0-295-97376-5). 218pp. Nonfiction.

This study argues that traditional Japanese culture structures social relationships in such a way that contemporary Japanese Americans assimilate into mainstream American life while remaining highly involved in their own ethnic communities. After presenting the theoretical framework, the authors analyze the findings of their survey of second- and third-generation Japanese Americans in three California communities during 1979 and 1980.

Although Japanese-American women are recognized as the backbone of their communities, an increasing percentage (approaching sixty percent) of them marry non-Japanese men. This phenomenon will continue to impact the communities. Thus, the authors' findings are weakened by the fact that the survey samples did not include women and was conducted more than a decade and a half ago. Nonetheless, this empirical study contributes to an in-depth understanding of an important aspect of the Japanese-American experience for serious readers. An extensive list of references and an index are provided. This is a companion volume to the authors' *The Japanese-American Experience (see main entry)*.

308 Gesensway, Deborah, and Mindy Roseman. ***Beyond Words: Images from America's Concentration Camps***. Illus. Cornell Univ. Pr. 1987, $39.95 (0-8014-1919-0); $21.95 (0-8014-9522-9). 192pp. Nonfiction.

In 1980 a trove of art was discovered containing 130 watercolors depicting Poston, a World War II Japanese-American internment camp in Arizona. The authors of this book tracked down the artist, Gene Sogioka. They also located and interviewed some two dozen other painters who had been in the camp. Although during the incarceration the artists had been allowed to express themselves through their paintings and drawings, many of them had never reproduced or shown their art publicly. In *Beyond Words*, paintings and drawings are interspersed with excerpts from interviews, newspapers, and other sources to document graphically the mass incarceration. The book's twelve chapters, organized by theme, include four complete interviews and three political-historical background narratives. Short biographical sketches of the artists and reference notes are included at the end of the book.

The images, ranging from landscapes to caricatures, are a visual record of camp life as seen through the artists' eyes. Such pictures speak more eloquently and vividly than the text.

309 Gillenkirk, Jeff, and James Motlow. ***Bitter Melon: Inside America's Last Rural Chinese Town.*** Rev. ed. Illus. Borgo 1993, $46.00 (0-8095-4978-6); Heyday $19.95 (0-930588-58-4). 144pp. Nonfiction.

Locke, located in the Sacramento Delta in California, was built in 1915 by Chinese agricultural laborers seeking refuge from white violence. It is the last surviving town of this kind. This book's title refers to a cucumberlike Chinese vegetable that yields a bitter taste for the first few bites. Indeed, life in America was like a bitter melon to these Chinese, who encountered segregation and discrimination in the hostile land. However, they persevered through this hard time and transmitted their hope to the second generation. An introduction by Sucheng Chan examines the significance of Locke in Chinese-American history. The fifty-eight photographs are supplemented by thirteen interviews of the remaining town residents and other historical essays. *Bitter Melon* is a window through which readers can glimpse the character and history of California's Chinese pioneers.

310 Hendricks, Glenn L., Bruce T. Dowling, and Amos S. Deinard, eds. ***The Hmong in Transition.*** Center for Migration Studies 1986, $19.50 (0-913256-94-3). 475pp. Nonfiction.

This collection of articles, based on a Hmong Research Conference held at the University of Minnesota in 1983, is still a rather valuable resource on the little-known Hmong people of Southeast Asia who have resettled in all parts of the United States. This volume explores how Hmong society and culture have changed during the years of wartime migration and resettlement. It also includes studies on the situations of Hmong in Southeast Asia and Australia. A broad spectrum of resettlement issues are discussed, including cultural adaptation, Hmong youth, language, health care, social services, and mental health. The sometimes esoteric academic language has been edited to make the materials accessible to the general reader.

311   Hune, Shirley, and others, eds. ***Asian Americans: Comparative and Global Perspectives***. Washington State Univ. Pr. 1991, $30.00 (0-87422-071-8). 290pp. Nonfiction.

Asian-American studies has made considerable inroads during the past decade. Demographic shifts and the growing ecopolitical importance of the Pacific Rim have brought academic legitimacy to the field. This anthology of essays offers comparative and global perspectives on the Asian-American experience. As the third volume in the Association for Asian-American Studies anthology series, the book provides an overview and assessment of the topic, raises questions and issues, and offers fresh insights into the Asian-American community's new sense of identity. Other titles in the series are *Reflections on Shattered Windows* and *Frontiers of Asian-American Studies: Writing, Research, and Commentary*.

312   Ichioka, Yuji. ***Issei: The World of the First-Generation Japanese Immigrants, 1885–1924***. Illus. Free Press 1988, $32.95 (0-02-915370-0); $14.95 (0-02-932435-1). 380pp. Nonfiction.

Drawing on Japanese- as well as English-language sources, including government archives, documents, immigrant newspapers, and periodicals, Ichioka reconstructs the life of the Issei (first-generation Japanese immigrants) from 1885 to the passage of the 1924 Immigration Act. The author demonstrates that the early Japanese immigrants were faced with three obstacles. American anti-Japanese exclusionary laws classified the Japanese as "aliens ineligible to citizenship." Deprived of their naturalization rights, Japanese immigrants were powerless in the American political arena. Also, because Japanese immigrant laborers were exploited by their own Japanese labor contractors and barred by the powerful American Federation of Labor from union membership, they were relegated to undesirable, low-paid seasonal farm jobs. The final obstacle came from the Japanese government itself, which regularly sacrificed the immigrants' interests in the name of diplomatic expediency.

This is a landmark scholarly study of early Japanese immigration, a history marked by bitterness and resentment. Drawing on Japanese sources, Ichioka reveals an untold side of American immigrant history. Included are extensive notes, a well-selected list of primary and secondary Japanese and English source materials, and a useful index.

313   Jensen, Joan M. ***Passage from India: Asian Indian Immigrants in North America***. Yale Univ. Pr. 1988, $42.00 (0-300-03846-1). 352pp. Nonfiction.

Several thousand Indian workers and political refugees migrated to North America between 1830 and 1930. As this book shows, the experiences of these people reveal the clash of interests among immigrant workers, employers, political parties, trade unions, and ethnic groups. Jensen analyzes the causes of the Indian emigration and traces their movement to Canada and the United States. She studies the complex interplay of various groups that led to the implementation of exclusionary public policies in both countries. Jensen also examines the role of Indian Americans in the 1914 uprising against British rule in India.

Exclusion policies were reversed in the United States in 1946. Since 1962, Indians have immigrated in large numbers to form a growing presence in the United States. This scholarly work provides a comprehensive historical background on the Asian-Indian immigration. Extensive notes and a selected bibliography are provided.

314   Kitano, Harry H., and Roger Daniels. *Asian Americans: The Emerging Minority.* 2nd ed. Prentice 1995, $21.00 (0-13-315185-9). 224pp. Nonfiction.

This concise overview covers all major Asian-American groups in one single volume. It provides an interdisciplinary account, connecting historical and social-psychological perspectives. The book examines immigration legislation and explains how different groups adapted to their new country in different ways. One chapter addresses a "hidden" minority: the Pacific Islanders, a distinct group that includes the Samoans, the Guamanians, and native Hawaiians. The authors, both noted historians, also present census data on each group, describe their accomplishments, and offer a model for studying Asian-American adaptation to America.

315   Knaefler, Tomi Kaizawa. *Our House Divided: Seven Japanese-American Families in World War II.* Frwd. by A. A. Smyser. Illus. Univ. of Hawaii Pr. 1991, $19.95 (0-8248-1045-7). 144pp. Nonfiction.

Our House Divided tells the stories of seven Japanese-American families in Hawaii who were divided geographically and emotionally by the war between Japan and the United States. Many of these Japanese immigrants to Hawaii— at that time a territory of the United States—were originally from Hiroshima Prefecture, site of the atomic bombing in 1945. Their personal accounts illuminate a poignant and little-known aspect of the war: that families were divided and brothers sometimes found themselves fighting on opposite sides. Their often painful recollections also reveal the dilemma of the Issei (first-generation Japanese Americans), who were caught in the middle of a bitter battle between the two nations to which they were so strongly attached, and the dilemma of the Nisei (second-generation Japanese Americans), who maintained their patriotism during harsh trials and who proved their loyalty through their celebrated combat achievements.

The stories, based primarily on interviews, are told with graceful simplicity by Knaefler, a Japanese-American journalist whose own family was divided by the war. The text appeared originally as a series in the *Honolulu Star Bulletin* in 1966. Book publishers initially rejected the manuscript, deeming it too sensitive for publication. It was finally published in 1991 to commemorate the fiftieth anniversary of Pearl Harbor.

316   Kwong, Peter. *The New Chinatown*. Farrar 1988, $9.95 (0-374-52121-2). 198pp. Nonfiction.

This study examines the complex character and internal dynamics of New York City's Chinatown, emphasizing the post-1965 era. The past three decades have seen many changes, the result of the sudden influx of new immigrant labor and overseas Chinese capital. According to Kwong, there are two distinct subgroups of Chinese Americans in New York: the Uptown Chinese, who are educated, well off, and professionally trained; and the Downtown Chinese, who reside in the ethnic enclave of Chinatown and provide a pool of cheap labor, easily exploited by the garment industry and restaurant business.

He discusses the political intricacies among traditional feudalistic Chinese tongs, social service agencies, grassroots organizations, labor unions, and American political party structure in Chinatown. Perhaps the most important chapter is on labor movements in Chinatown, a topic rarely covered in other studies. He argues that, if they hope to improve their status, Chinatown workers must build their own grassroots organizations and form alliances with labor and political groups that share similar interests. Kwong, who draws on English- and Chinese-language sources for this book, bases his analysis on his experiences as a long-time resident and activist in New York's Chinatown.

317   Lee, Joann F. *Asian-American Experiences in the United States: Oral Histories of First- to Fourth-Generation Americans from China, the Philippines, Japan, India, the Pacific Islands, Vietnam, and Cambodia*. Illus. McFarland 1991, $24.95 (0-89950-585-6). 240pp. Nonfiction.

Lee interviewed a variety of first- to fourth-generation Asian Americans to explore the impact of their cultural past and their American present on their lifestyles and attitudes. The interviewees, including people of Indian, Vietnamese, and Cambodian ancestry, comment on such issues as immigration, resettlement, language, education, and discrimination. The first-person narratives are divided into three general categories. Living in America features individual profiles; Aspects of Americanization covers specific topics and events; and Reflections on Interracial Marriage examines this controversial issue. The anecdotal, personal reminiscences are easy to read and revealing in their diverse perspectives.

318   Leong, Russell, ed. *Moving the Image: Independent Asian Pacific American Media Arts 1970–1990*. Pref. by Linda Mabalot. Illus. Univ. of California, Los Angeles, Asian-American Studies Center 1992, $19.95 (0-934052-13-1). 312pp. Nonfiction.

This book examines what it means to be a film and media artist with an Asian-Pacific heritage. Since the late 1960s, these artists have produced a body of film, video, and radio work, providing alternatives to the stereotypical portrayals of Asian Americans in Hollywood films and mass media. This is the first volume to document and examine the historical development and theoretical statements of Asian/Pacific American media arts from 1970 to 1990. The volume features essays, reminiscences, interviews, anecdotes, and calls for action. Included are interviews with filmmaker Wayne Wang and famed cinematographer James Wong Howe. Well edited, artistically designed, and generously illustrated with film stills and archival photos from the early 1900s to the 1990s, this innovative work documents the accomplishments of a diversified group of Asian- and Pacific-American media artists and provides a much-needed forum for their creative and divergent perspectives. An annotated resources list includes some of the media producers and consultants.

319   Ling, Amy. *Between Worlds: Women Writers of Chinese Ancestry*. Elsevier 1990, $37.50 (0-08-037464-6); $16.95 (0-08-037463-8). 292pp. Nonfiction.

In her preface, Amy Ling laments that throughout her education in the United States, from first grade through a Ph.D. in comparative literature, she never read any works by Chinese-American authors. Nor did she encounter any Chinese characters, except stereotypical "Heathen Chinee" characters that caused her deep humiliation. Enlightened by African-American and feminist scholars in the 1960s and 1970s, she began to uncover the literary history of Chinese-American women. She concluded from her research that in the field of Chinese-American literature "the women not only outnumber the men but the women's books are more authentic, more numerous, quite simply—better."

This volume includes full-length narratives, autobiographies, memoirs, fictionalized memoirs, and novels, written in English and published in the United States by women of Chinese or partial Chinese ancestry. The material is generally arranged in chronological and thematic order. The major unifying theme is how each author has responded to the political and social circumstances that position her "between worlds." Extensive notes, an annotated bibliography, and an index are provided.

320   Nakano, Mei T. *Japanese-American Women: Three Generations, 1890–1990*. Mina Press 1990, $21.95 (0-942610-05-9); $11.95 (0-942610-06-7). 256pp. Nonfiction.

This is the history of three generations of Japanese-American women, told from a woman's perspective. Nakano believes that Japanese-American women have been "largely invisible," and she attempts to examine who these women are, how they spend their time, and the kinds of cultural expectations and imperatives they bear. The book is divided into three segments: the Issei (first generation), the Nisei (second generation), and the Sansei (third generation). "Okaasan" (mother), a separate essay by Grace Shibata, is a deeply felt portrait of the writer's mother, whose life exemplifies the bravery, resourcefulness, and endurance of the Issei women. It adds a human texture to the historical account.

The book is based largely on secondary sources and would have benefited from better editing. Nonetheless, a woman-centered historical text on three generations of Japanese-American women is long overdue.

321   Nee, Victor G., and Brett De Bary Nee. *Longtime Californ': A Documentary Study of an American Chinatown*. Repr. of 1972 ed. Stanford Univ. Pr. 1986, $45.00 (0-8047-1335-9); $14.95 (0-8047-1336-7). 438pp. Nonfiction.

Originally published in 1972, this noted study traces the historical development of San Francisco's Chinatown, beginning in the late nineteenth century. The authors use oral history and historical primary sources to trace Chinatown's origin as a response to racism against Chinese in the United States. Among the people interviewed are representatives of various segments of the community, including aging bachelors, new arrivals, "the establishment," workers, women, and youth. Many excerpts from the interviews are reproduced verbatim, capturing the voices and feelings of people who have never spoken out before.

The interviews are generally arranged in chronological order. The study explores the following broad questions: What forces created Chinatown, and which ones continue to perpetuate its existence? What has been the source of its exceptional cohesiveness and resilience as an American ethnic community? What is the consciousness of its people? Appended are profiles of social classes in Chinatown and some pertinent immigration laws.

322 O'Brien, David J., and Stephen S. Fugita. *The Japanese-American Experience*. Indiana Univ. Pr. 1991, $29.95 (0-253-34164-7); $12.95 (0-253-20656-1). 188pp. Nonfiction.

Social scientists O'Brien and Fujita identify two main themes in the Japanese-American experience. The first is what they call "structural constraints," the discriminatory actions that limited the options open to the first-generation of Japanese Americans. The second is the response of the people to those constraints. The authors observe that Japanese culture, both in Japan and among Japanese Americans, tends to value the group above the individual. This trait facilitates assimilation into mainstream American life while preserving the individual's important ties to the ethnic community. Assimilation, note the authors, is likely to continue among younger Japanese Americans, who will become increasingly concerned with the "symbolic" aspects of ethnicity but who will continue to be highly involved with their ethnic community.

This brief and clearly written general history is organized chronologically, emphasizing the period from World War II to the modern day and projecting trends into the future. Photos and a useful bibliographic essay are included. Fujita and O'Brien are authors of a more scholarly work, *Japanese-American Ethnicity (see main entry)*.

Rouchdy, Aleya, ed. *The Arabic Language in America*.
See entry 1201.

323 Rutledge, Paul J. *The Vietnamese Experience in America*. Illus. Indiana Univ. Pr. 1992, $29.95 (0-253-34997-4); $10.95 (0-253-20711-8). 192pp. Nonfiction.

This brief analysis of the experiences of Vietnamese refugees in the United States begins with the fall of Saigon in 1975. It describes the refugees' flight to countries offering asylum, first in Asia and then in the United States. Based on interviews and other sources, the book describes how the Vietnamese continue their struggle to survive, resettle, and adapt to their new environment. The book concludes with a portrayal of contemporary Vietnamese-American society. Rutledge highlights the achievements of the Vietnamese people in the United States, but he does not look deeply at other persisting problems, such as youth who drop out of the public school system and who resort to crime and violence. This book is part of the Minorities in Modern America series.

324   Takaki, Ronald. ***Strangers from a Different Shore: A History of Asian Americans***. Viking 1990, $13.00 (0-14-013885-4). 584pp. Nonfiction.

According to the author, his intent in this book is to "re-vision" American history so that it includes Asians in a broad and comparative way. The book presents Asian Americans as active "makers" of history rather than merely its passive victims. Takaki draws from existing research and a variety of other sources: oral histories, songs, diaries, letters, posters, court petitions, newspapers, autobiographies, poems, and novels. He incorporates these voices generously into his lively narrative.

Takaki explores a number of important questions: Why did Asian immigrants come to the United States? How are the experiences of the various Asian groups similar to and different from one another? How do the experiences of Asian Americans differ in different geographical regions? How do the two waves of Asian immigration (from 1849 to 1924 and from 1965 to 1985) compare? His analysis of the patterns and conditions of the Asian immigrants in Hawaii and California is especially illuminating.

Takaki, a historian and a talented storyteller, has succeeded in putting together a highly interesting overview of Asian-American history for the general public. The work covers many people and events often omitted from standard histories and helps to dispel myths and stereotypes about Asian Americans. This volume was honored as both an American Library Association and a *New York Times Book Review* notable book of 1989. More recently, Takaki has written a general history of American immigration and cultural diversity titled *A Different Mirror: A History of Multicultural America* (Little, Brown, 1993).

325   Tateishi, John. ***And Justice for All: An Oral History of the Japanese-American Internment Camps***. Random 1984, $18.95 (0-394-52955-3). 288pp. Nonfiction.

During the years of World War II, more than 110,000 Japanese-American civilians who lived on the West Coast were sent to concentration camps in remote wastelands in the country's interior. None of these people was ever charged with any crime; their offense was being of Japanese descent at a time of war with Japan. Tateishi, who was incarcerated at age three, served as director of the Japanese-American Citizens League Committee for Redress. In this book he assembles interviews of thirty former internees to convey the camp experience in human and personal terms.

Painful memories had kept Japanese Americans in self-imposed silence for forty years. The moving accounts collected here reveal the trauma of unjustified imprisonment. There are both shared experiences and unique stories; as the author writes in the preface, there are "some of pain and hardship, some bittersweet, some with touches of humor, many with an extraordinary dedication to American ideals. But underlying all of the accounts is a sense of personal tragedy for having experienced a nation's betrayal of a people's loyalty and faith."

326   Tenhula, John. *Voices from Southeast Asia: The Refugee Experience in the United States*. Frwd. by Liv Ullmann. Illus. Holmes & Meier 1991, $32.50 (0-8419-1110-X). 247pp. Nonfiction.

Over a ten-year period, Tenhula interviewed 130 refugees from Vietnam, Cambodia, and Laos who have settled in the United States since 1975. In this book, he lets them "tell their stories from their own perspectives and in their own voices." The result is a compelling, moving, and often poignant oral history of people caught in a war that most of them did not understand. Their stories and poems reveal the terror and horror of war atrocities, the traumatic experience of exodus, and the challenges of starting over in a new country where they encounter both hospitality and hostility. There are a few success stories. Members of the emerging younger generation who manage to adjust seem to offer the greatest hope; they are fast becoming part of the American landscape.

The powerful book provides a better understanding of the Southeast Asian refugees and examines how they are transforming—and are being transformed by—Western society. This is the first book in the Ellis Island series.

327   Tsai, Shih-shan Henry. *The Chinese Experience in America*. o.p. Nonfiction.

Covering the years from the nineteenth century to the 1980s, this study discusses the differing experiences of three groups of Chinese in America—sojourners, American-born Chinese, and student-immigrants. The successes and failures of each group are placed in a historical context and analyzed through theories of assimilation. Although the study describes the Chinese experience in the United States, it also attempts "to examine an American national character that is filled with paradoxes: narrowness and magnanimity, benevolence and exasperation, sympathy and hostility, Christian love and racial hatred."

Though this is not a comprehensive work, the book contains some useful information on Chinese-American history. The details and statistical analysis in some chapters may hinder reading.

328   U.S. Commission on Civil Rights. *Civil Rights Issues Facing Asians in the 1990s: A Report of the United States Commission on Civil Rights*. William S. Hein 1993, $55.00 (0-89941-216-5). 233pp. Nonfiction.

The United States Commission on Civil Rights conducted a study on the civil rights issues facing Asian Americans in the 1990s and issued this report on its findings and recommendations. The report compiles evidence showing that, contrary to widely held belief, Asian Americans still face wide-ranging prejudice, discrimination, and barriers to equal opportunity.

Beginning with a concise historical review, the report demonstrates America's long history of anti-Asian policies and incidents. Other chapters present the commission's research and field investigations into such problems as anti-Asian violence, relations between the police and the community, access to education, employment discrimination, access to public services, political representation, battered women, and media coverage. This report serves to heighten public awareness of the difficulties Asian Americans confront. Although it is a government document, the text is very readable.

329   Vallangca, Caridad C. *The Second Wave: Pinay and Pinoy*. Illus. by Tomas Concepcion. Strawberry Hill 1987, $9.95 (0-89407-043-6). 280pp. Nonfiction.

This is a collection of more than forty oral histories telling the story of Filipino immigration to the United States between 1945 and 1960. It continues where Roberto Vallangca's *Pinoy: The First Wave (see main entry)* left off. Unlike the "old-timers" of the first wave, the women (Pinay) and the men (Pinoy) of the second wave are mostly professionals: bankers, lawyers, doctors, nurses, teachers, and journalists. They left their war-torn country and settled throughout the United States.

This book explores many aspects of the Second Wave migration. What sort of immigration laws did these people face? How did their heritage affect their lives in the United States? How did materialism affect their lifestyles? How did Pinays adjust their career paths? Through the personal accounts and Vallangca's introductory essays, *The Second Wave* tells the story of the continuous immigration of Filipinos of the post–World War II era. A list of immigration laws and a resource list are appended.

330   Vallangca, Roberto V. *Pinoy: The First Wave (1898–1941)*. Illus. by the author. Strawberry Hill 1977, $6.95 (0-89407-000-2). Nonfiction.

Pinoy is a collection of seventeen oral histories of Filipino immigrants who came to the United States between 1898 and 1941. "Pinoy" is the name the early male Filipino pioneers, now referred to as "old-timers," called themselves. Two of the stories are from Pinays, Filipino women, who came during the same period. Eight short essays cover such topics as history, marriage, religion and magic, prejudice, dance halls, and gambling. One essay is a plea for tolerance called "Not All Pinoys Look Alike." In these personal accounts, the old-timers tell about their lives as domestics, farm hands, cannery workers, and plantation laborers. They speak of their pain at being treated as the lowest of all "Orientals." The text is written in very plain language. The thirteen illustrations of Pinoy life are by the author, a doctor in chiropractic medicine, who painted murals on barroom walls to finance his education. Another book, *The Second Wave (see main entry)*, continues the story of Filipino immigration up to 1960.

331   Weglyn, Michi. *Years of Infamy: The Untold Story of America's Concentration Camps*. Illus. Morrow 1978, $15.45 (0-688-07996-2). 351pp. Nonfiction.

During World War II, more than 110,000 West Coast Japanese Americans were driven from their homes and their communities and banished to desert concentration camps. In this book Weglyn meticulously examines previously unpublished documents relating to the mass incarceration. Her research leads her to challenge the official policy that stated the evacuation order was "militarily necessary." She argues compellingly that the real reasons behind the decision were economic exploitation, explicit racism, and a plan to use the internees for reprisals against Japan's government. Documentary evidence, extensive notes, a personality list, and an excellent bibliography that includes audiovisual resources and oral history collections are featured. Weglyn's brilliantly researched exposé is considered one of the influential factors that inspired the redress movement. (For more on that movement, see main entry for John Tateishi's *And Justice for All*.)

332   Yung, Judy. ***Chinese Women of America: A Pictorial History***. Illus. Univ. of Washington Pr. 1986, $16.95 (0-295-96358-1). 128pp. Nonfiction.

This is the first book to document the experiences of Chinese women in America from 1834 to 1985. Based on the work of the Chinese Women of America Research Project, Judy Yung creates a visual record of the "buried past" of those women by piecing together scraps of archival documents, oral histories, census data, and 135 carefully selected visual images from the project.

Part I, which studies the little-recorded early period, is of special value because it illuminates the harsh and exploited lives of the pioneering women in remote rural camps, urban cities, and on Hawaiian plantations. Part II covers the social awakening and the struggle of the second generation. Part III examines the growing social consciousness of, and new opportunities for, contemporary Chinese-American women. The images are supplemented with concise and critical annotations that put the personalities and historical background in perspective. Appended are statistical charts based on historical census data.

BIOGRAPHY

333   Alexander, Meena. ***Fault Lines: A Memoir***. Feminist Pr. 1993, $35.00 (1-55861-058-8); $12.95 (1-55861-059-6). 240pp. Autobiography.

Meena Alexander is an Indian-born poet who now resides in Manhattan. The author has traveled widely, savoring cultures in India, Sudan, England, and the United States. She describes herself as "a woman cracked by multiple migrations. Uprooted so many times she can connect nothing with nothing." She explains, "My two worlds, present and past, were torn apart, and I was the fault line, the crack that marked the dislocation."

In *Fault Lines* Alexander describes members of her family, including her maternal grandmother, a busy political activist, and her mother, who grew up in a stern Presbyterian boarding school where mirrors were forbidden. She traces her growth as a poet, wife, and mother in an evocative prose narrative sprinkled with her previously published poems and poetic fragments of thoughts on issues of race, gender, and self-identity.

334   Bulosan, Carlos. ***America Is in the Heart: A Personal History***. Repr. of 1946 ed. Intro. by Carey McWilliams. Univ. of Washington Pr. 1973, $13.95 (0-295-95289-X). 352pp. Autobiography.

Carlos Bulosan was an internationally known Filipino writer. In *America Is in the Heart* he traces his childhood as the son of a poor peasant. When he migrated to the United States in 1931, he was stunned by the degradation, misery, and violent racism that greeted the laborers in the new land. "Where would I begin the pilgrimage," he asks, "this search for a door into America?"

When it was first published, the book was presented as "personal history." In his introduction to this edition, however, Carey McWilliams argues that Bulosan probably did not experience first-hand all the brutalities and indignities described in his account. Rather, his book should be read as a composite of many personal histories, and as such, it reflects the collective life of thousands of Filipino immigrants in California and elsewhere in the 1930s.

Eventually, Bulosan realized that he might never be fully accepted in his adopted homeland. He wrote: "You did not give America to me, and never will. America is in the hearts of the people that live in it. But it is worth the coming, the sacrifice, the idealism." Earthy yet eloquent, revolutionary, and powerful, *America Is in the Heart* has been translated and widely read in many parts of the world. Readers wanting to read the author's poems, essays, and short stories should see *If You Want to Know What We Are: A Carlos Bulosan Reader*, edited by E. San Juan, Jr. (West End, 1983).

335   Fiffer, Sharon S. *Imagining America: Paul Thai's Journey from the Killing Fields of Cambodia to Freedom*. o.p. Biography.

This is the true story of a Cambodian refugee who became the first Asian-born member of the Dallas police force. Paul Thai was eleven years old in 1975 when the communist Khmer Rouge took over Cambodia. From the labor camps and the killing fields, he escaped with his family over the border to Thailand. In 1981, Paul Thai, his parents, and eight siblings flew to Dallas. Just like other refugees, they tried to "live" again. "We Cambodians are refugees, . . . not immigrants. . . . We came here to find life, period. Cambodia is death. Here is life."

Much toThai's disappointment, he discovered that, at age eighteen, he was too old to attend school, but he got a job as a school janitor. Through self-study, night classes, and his undaunted commitment to help his people, Thai eventually joined the Dallas police force. Some may find the author's long commentary on Cambodia's history and American values distracting. However, throughThai's keen observing eyes and candid remarks, we get a refreshing look at the images of the United States and the refugee immigrants.

336   Hayslip, Le Ly, and James Hayslip. *Child of War, Woman of Peace*. Doubleday 1993, $22.50 (0-385-42111-7); $12.95 (0-385-42117). 374pp. Autobiography.

In this sequel to the much-acclaimed autobiography *When Heaven and Earth Changed Places* (1993), Le Ly Hayslip continues her saga as a young Asian bride from "hell"—the war-torn Vietnam—to "heaven"—the United States. This book opens as Le Ly arrives in San Diego in 1970 and concludes in 1992, when she is a twice-widowed woman with three grown sons. She tells of life in the "land of the 'enemy'—a Vietnamese woman struggling to survive among the 'cat-eyed' Westerners . . . of searching for two halves that make a perfect whole. . . . It is about coming to terms with the past while reaching out for a better future. I have been told it is America's story, written with a bamboo pen."

In the beginning, Le Ly found herself lost and lonely in a world "without ancestors—without cause and effect—where I had no yesterday and no tomorrow." At the end of the book, she is an independent woman, a crusader of hope, and the founder of East Meets West, a nonprofit world peace organization dedicated to establishing humanities programs in Vietnam. This sequel continues an epic memoir that carries a healing message. A film adaptation of both of Hayslip's books, titled *Heaven and Earth*, and directed by Oliver Stone, was released in 1994.

337   Houston, Jeanne Wakatsuki, and James D. Houston. *Farewell to Manzanar*. Bantam 1983, $3.99 (0-553-27258-6). 160pp. Autobiography.

Jeanne Wakatsuki was seven years old in 1942 when her family was uprooted and sent to the detention camp at Manzanar, California, along with 10,000 other Japanese Americans. This book begins by describing her family life before the war. Her father was a proud, successful fisherman directing operations aboard his own boat. During three and a half years of internment, however, the family disintegrated. The father turned into a despondent alcoholic. Afterwards, the father continued to drift through life while Jeanne, now an adolescent, responded to her sense of shame and unworthiness by striving desperately for acceptance in white America.

Twenty-five years after Manzanar, Jeanne Houston started recalling her camp experiences by using a tape recorder and an old high school yearbook. As the photos brought the camp memories back, she dredged up feelings that had been submerged for many years. From recollections and other research writings, Jeanne and her husband pieced together a personal story about how one family tries to survive the impact of evacuation.

338   Hyun, Peter. *Man Sei!: The Making of a Korean American*. Univ. of Hawaii Pr. 1986, $17.50 (0-8248-1041-4). 186pp. Autobiography.

In 1976, Peter Hyun brought the ashes of his parents from Hawaii back to Seoul for burial. He then journeyed through Korea, the homeland he had left more than fifty years ago. He wrote this book to document his family history and his childhood memories.

The story begins on March 1, 1919 as Peter, then a boy of twelve, witnesses the historic uprising against the Japanese colonial rule. Throngs of Koreans poured onto the streets, chanting *"Man Sei!"* (a phrase that literally means "ten thousand years," or "Long live Korea!") On the third day after the protesters declared independence, Japanese soldiers crushed the peaceful demonstration with a bloody onslaught. A year later, Peter's mother fled with her eight young children to Shanghai to join their father, who had been one of the key leaders in the independence movement. In 1924 Peter's family moved to Hawaii. Hyun's account gives a glimpse of the oppressive and impoverished conditions in Korea and China between 1919 and 1924. The subtitle is somewhat misleading because the memoir ends before Peter started his new life in the United States, but the book offers insight into the cultural roots and experiences of Korean Americans before immigration.

339   Ishikawa, Yoshimi. *Strawberry Road: A Japanese Immigrant Discovers America*. Trans. from Japanese by Eve Zimmerman. Kodansha 1991, $19.95 (4-770-01551-8). 256pp. Autobiography.

Eighteen-year-old Yoshimi Ishikawa leaves the tiny island of Oshima in Japan in 1965 to join his brother who had emigrated to work as a contract laborer on a strawberry farm near Pomona, California. He enrolls in the local high school and also helps out on the farm. From his small niche in the world, Ishikawa makes perceptive—and at times disturbing—observations about American society in the turbulent 1960s. He comments on the exploitation of illegal Mexican migrant workers, the struggles of Japanese Americans to establish their roots in their new country, labor strikes and boycotts, and antiwar demonstrations. He also describes his young lust, his coming of age, and his search for the meaning of the American dream.

Experiences during his stay led Ishikawa to write: "We immigrants have no past. Although we can reinvent a present and a future faster in this country than anywhere else, . . . [w]hen we come to America, we have to discard our past—and we give up a great deal." Since writing this book, Ishikawa has returned to his native Japan. *Strawberry Road*, originally written in Japanese, won the Ohya Nonfiction Award and was a bestseller in Japan.

340 Kikumura, Akemi. ***Through Harsh Winters: The Life of a Japanese Immigrant Woman***. Intro. by Hiroshi Wagatsuma. Chandler & Sharp 1981, $11.95 (0-88316-543-0). 176pp. Biography.

Akemi Kikumura taped the life history and reflections of her mother, Michiko Tanaka, in Japanese and translated her story into a moving and vivid first-person narrative in English. Michiko came with her husband to California in 1923. The young couple's innocent dreams about the United States were soon shattered by the harsh realities of life in a hostile land. Her husband's compulsive gambling caused great strain on the family. Michiko worked long hours on a farm, tended to household chores, and took care of their thirteen children. Life was so hard that internment in a camp in Arkansas during World War II was a rest for her, because it was the only time she did not need to worry about food or shelter for the family.

Kikumura, an anthropologist, also interviewed relatives in Japan and in the United States to gather background material. In an epilogue, she provides an analysis of her family from an anthropological perspective. The detailed research notes, extensive bibliography, and appendices on the Japanese-American family and the author's methodology add research value to the book, which celebrates and validates the strength and spirit of a humble but courageous Issei (first-generation immigrant) woman.

341 Kingsbury, Martha. ***George Tsutakawa***. Illus. Univ. of Washington Pr. 1990, $24.95 (0-295-97021-9). 176pp. Biography.

George Tsutakawa—painter, sculptor, teacher, and internationally renowned designer of fountains—has achieved a rare synthesis between the artistic traditions of the United States, where he was born in 1910, and those of Japan, his parents' native land, where he went to school for ten years.

In six chronologically arranged sections, Kingsbury discusses Tsutakawa's life and his artistic development. She identifies two distinct periods in his life. In the first, Tsutakawa studies with diverse masters and enjoys the exhilarating company of the artists who come to be known as the "Northwest School." During this time Tsutakawa considers himself a modern artist in the Western tradition. The mid-1950s mark the transition to the second key phase in his development. Having achieved success as an artist, Tsutakawa returns to Japan, where he rediscovers a deep appreciation for his Japanese heritage—in particular, the Asian view of nature. He is also intrigued by the ritually stacked shapes of the Tibetan rock mounds called "obos" and begins to use these forms in his designs for fountains. This book, sensitively written by an art history professor and strikingly illustrated with examples of Tsutakawa's artworks, was published in connection with a retrospective exhibition honoring Tsutakawa in his eightieth year. Appended are a chronology and a selected bibliography including books, catalogues, and films.

342   Kingston, Maxine Hong. ***China Men***. Random 1989, $10.00 (0-679-72328-5).
Collective biography.

This book, a companion volume to *The Woman Warrior (see main entry)*, is a fictional rendition of the lives of the men in Kingston's family. These men, the "grandfathers" and "fathers," were the strong, resilient, and rebellious plantation workers in Hawaii and the railroad construction workers in the Sierra Nevada whose backbreaking labor helped build the nation. *China Men* is Kingston's effort "to claim America" for her silent ancestors.

The book opens with a parable in which the emasculation of Asian men in North America is equated with the enslavement of women in old China. Kingston has been told very little about her male ancestors, so she addresses her father in the beginning of the book: "I'll tell you what I suppose from your silences and few words, and you can tell me that I'm mistaken. You'll just have to speak up with the real stories if I've got you wrong." Kingston uses her brilliant imagination and dazzling narrative skills to blend family history, historical facts, "talk-story," and reconstructed legends and myths to spin fiery tales of her family's past. Her stories are rich in graphic imagery that burns into the reader's memory. In this book, as in *The Woman Warrior*, the lines between reality and fantasy are not always clear. Though both books are classified by the publisher and library cataloguers as nonfiction, many critics consider them to be fiction in the best and deepest sense of the word. *China Men* received the National Book Award for best nonfiction in 1981.

343   Kingston, Maxine Hong. ***The Woman Warrior: Memoirs of a Girlhood Among Ghosts***. Knopf 1976, $24.95 (0-394-40067-4); Random 1989, $10.00 (0-679-72188-6). Autobiography.

Kingston begins her tale with a warning from her mother: "You must not tell anyone . . . what I am about to tell you." She then proceeds to retell her mother's account of a family secret about a "No Name aunt." Written as an autobiography, the narrative alternates between the real world of a struggling daughter whose family runs a laundry in Stockton, California during the 1940s and 1950s and the "talk story" Old Country world created by her mother.

Evoking the Chinese legendary woman warrior Fa Mu Lan, who disguised her female identity and led an army to victory, Kingston sees herself as a woman warrior, using words as her swords to rage against subordination by men and to combat racism. She breaks taboo and speaks the unspeakable. The "ghosts" in the subtitle refer to the shadowy figures from the past as well as the threatening white people who spell trouble and evil for Chinese immigrants.

In this book, Kingston creates a new style of writing, one in which family history, talk story, reconstructed legends, fantasy, and meditation are freely mixed. Her prose is dramatic, poetic, and fiercely emotional. This much-discussed best-selling literary work won the National Book Critics Circle Award for nonfiction in 1976. It has been translated into Chinese. A later book by Kingston, *China Men (see main entry)*, is a fictionalized retelling of the lives of the men in her family.

344 Lee, Mary Paik. ***Quiet Odyssey: A Pioneer Korean Woman in America***. Edited, with an essay by Sucheng Chan. Univ. of Washington Pr. 1990, $14.95 (0-295-96969-5). 264pp. Autobiography.

The book is made up of two parts. The first is an autobiography written by Mary Paik Lee in 1984, when she was eighty-four years old. Lee is one of the last survivors among the several thousand Korean pioneers who traveled to Hawaii at the turn of the century. Lee's family resettled in California a year later to seek farm work. In later years, the family sold produce and managed apartment buildings. Her memoir spans eighty years of her life. With straight-forward simplicity, Lee reveals how her family struggled to survive in a hostile environment. She also remembers the sympathetic relationships among the African-American, Mexican, and Korean migrant workers at the time. Lee's autobiography is significant because there were few Korean women immigrants in early twentieth-century America and very little is known of their lives.

The rest of the book is by historian Sucheng Chan, who verified the historical details of Lee's account, edited the text, and contributed a detailed introduction, three appendices, and a bibliographic essay on Korea and Koreans in the United States. Her scholarly work turns a simple life story of an immigrant woman into a valuable historical document.

345 McCunn, Ruthanne Lum. ***Chinese-American Portraits: Personal Histories 1828–1988***. Illus. Chronicle Books 1988, $29.95 (0-87701-580-5); $16.95 (0-87701-491-4). 174pp. Collective Biography.

Puzzled by the idiomatic expression addressed to her, "a Chinaman's chance"—which in fact means "no chance at all"—author Ruthanne Lum McCunn felt compelled to spend the next ten years researching the Chinese-American experience. She combed through documents, newspapers, memoirs, books, personal papers, and pictures. She also conducted numerous interviews. The resulting volume, *Chinese-American Portraits*, reveals the lives of "women and men who have fought against the odds. They have not always won. . . . But they refused to give up the struggle—and they have endured."

The book is divided into three sections: Pioneers, Generations, and Contemporaries. From a Chinese graduate of Yale in 1854 to a recent filmmaker who emigrated from Hong Kong, the seventeen biographical essays are deftly illustrated with 150 photographs featuring the broad range of the Chinese immigrants' experience. The last chapter describes some of the major discriminatory laws that have affected the Chinese in the United States. This book of social history with its well-annotated photos is a pleasure to browse through like a family album. McCunn is also the author of the biographical novel *Thousand Pieces of Gold (see main entry)*.

346 Minatoya, Lydia. ***Talking to High Monks in the Snow: An Asian-American Odyssey***. HarperCollins 1992, $20.00 (0-06-016809-9); $11.00 (0-06-092372-5). 288pp. Autobiography.

This is a memoir by a Sansei, a third-generation Japanese American who grew up in New York in the 1950s. As children, Minatoya and her sister loved to listen to their mother's old family tales and Japanese lore. Later, when Minatoya lost her university teaching job, she felt "in-between." She fled to Japan to live among the "ancient souls" of her ancestors. She took a teaching job and visited her mother's clan, proud descendants of samurai. The experience left her both enthralled and humbled. On parting, the revered patriarch of the family enjoined Minatoya to remember her Japanese heritage and to "be proud." Minatoya went on to teach in China and also traveled in Nepal.

Minatoya declares that she is "a woman caught between standards of East and West." Blessed with natural curiosity and professional training as a clinical psychologist, she is able to observe what others easily miss. Her personal odyssey is told with a mellow voice and natural humor. Her prose is lyrical, with a touch of dreamy quality. This delightful book won the PEN/Jerard Award in 1991.

347   Mura, David. ***Turning Japanese***. Doubleday 1992, $12.00 (0-385-42344-6). 376pp. Autobiography.

This memoir by a Sansei (third-generation Japanese American) tells of a year the author spent in his ancestral homeland. Poet David Mura won a writing fellowship to Japan in 1984. Growing up in a largely Jewish suburb of Chicago, he knew more French and Yiddish than Japanese. He notes: "[M]uch of my life I had insisted on my Americaness, had shunned most connections with Japan and felt proud I knew no Japanese." But somehow he created poems about his Japanese grandfather, the Japanese atomic bomb victims, and the Nisei (second-generation Japanese Americans). "[M]y imagination had been traveling there for years, unconsciously swimming the Pacific, against . . . my parents' desire, after the internment camps, to forget the past." Accompanied by his Caucasian wife, Susie, he landed at the Tokyo airport, "[a]stonished that all the faces at customs looked like mine."

Travel in Japan allowed Mura to confront his ambivalence, his desire to belong, and his long-repressed rage over the feeling that he never completely belonged in the United States. Mura embarked on a search for answers about identity, race, sexuality, and his emotional struggle with his father. This is a candid, enlightening, and poetic memoir. Mura's anthology *After We Lost Our Way* (1989) won the National Poetry Series Contest.

348   Okubo, Mine. ***Citizen 13660***. Illus. Univ. of Washington Pr. 1983, $14.95 (0-295-95989-4). 226pp. Autobiography.

In this illustrated memoir, artist Mine Okubo chronicles the intimate details of her life in the Tanforan Assembly Center and the internment camp at Topaz, Utah during World War II. Through stark drawings and terse narrative, Okubo unsentimentally delivers a vivid eyewitness account of both the humor and the pathos of this poignant episode in American history. Half-page drawings are accompanied by a continuous descriptive text. The title refers to the family number assigned to Okubo and her brother by the evacuation authority. Okubo was a young student in Europe on an art fellowship when the war in Europe broke out in 1939. She returned to San Francisco and worked on the Federal Arts Project until the mass evacuation order sent her away to camp. Originally published in 1946, the book is the first personal account of the mass incarceration. This new paperback edition has a recent preface by the author.

349   Pai, Margaret K. *The Dreams of Two Yi-min*. Illus. Univ. of Hawaii Pr. 1989,
$22.95 (0-8248-1179-8). 216pp. Biography.

This book is one of the few personal accounts about early Korean immigrants
(*yi-min*) in Hawaii. In telling the story of her parents, Do In Kwon and Hee
Kyung Lee, Margaret Pai uses as her backdrops the Korean Independence
Movement and the vibrant Korean immigrant community in Hawaii in the
first half of this century. Pai's mother emigrated from Korea as a "picture
bride" in 1912 but returned in 1919 to support the massive demonstration
against Japanese colonial rule. She was twice imprisoned for her involvement
with the movement before she managed to return to Hawaii three years later.
Her father immigrated to Hawaii as a young contract sugar plantation worker.
In time, he became a moderately successful owner of a furniture upholstery
factory who held patents on several of his designs. Pei spent most of her
childhood growing up with her family in the factory, which was located in an
old dilapidated building in Honolulu.

350   Scharlin, Craig, and Lilia V. Villanueva. *Philip Vera Cruz: A Personal History
of Filipino Immigrants and the Farm Workers Movement*. o.p. Biography.

Philip Vera Cruz gained national prominence during the 1960s, when he led a
historic grape strike by Filipino farm workers in California. The strikers joined
with Mexican migrant laborers to form the well-known United Farm Workers
Union under the leadership of Cesar Chavez. Born in 1904 in the Philippines,
Vera Cruz came to the United States in 1926 and spent the next half century as
a laborer and union organizer. Eventually he became vice president of the
UFW. In 1987 he returned to the Philippines for the first time in sixty years to
receive the Ninoy Aquino Award for lifelong service to the Filipino community in America.

Philip Vera Cruz depicts the declining community of the aging Filipino farm
workers, whose contributions to the labor movement have been largely overlooked in published materials. It is a valuable companion to Carlos Buloson's
America Is in the Heart (see main entry), which portrays the growing Filipino
labor community in the United States during an earlier era. Although portions
of the book, such as Vera Cruz's criticism of UFW leadership, seem controversial, this book represents Vera Cruz's call for compassion, interethnic unity,
and justice.

351   Sone, Monica. *Nisei Daughter.* Repr. of 1952 ed. Univ. of Washington Pr.
1979, $12.95 (0-295-95688-7). 238pp. Autobiography.

Originally published in 1952, *Nisei Daughter* is an autobiography by a young
Nisei (second-generation Japanese American) woman. The book primarily
centers on Sone's happy childhood in the Seattle hotel owned by her father
and tells the story of her family's trip to Japan before World War II. As an
adolescent, Sone expressed outrage at the prejudice and injustices she encountered in the United States, but she reckoned that "in the end, we had swallowed our pride and learned to endure." The wartime order to evacuate the
West Coast, imposed on people of Japanese descent, sent her family to the
Minidoka Camp in Idaho. After a short stay, Sone was released. She moved to
Chicago, then attended Wendell College in Idaho on a scholarship. The book
ends on a hopeful but subdued note as Sone dutifully declares, "I had discov-

ered a deeper, stronger pulse in the American scene, . . . for now I felt more like a whole person instead of a sadly split personality. The Japanese and the American parts of me were now blended into one."

Although written with humor and good cheer, the book subtly describes the psychological bruises incurred by the Nisei after the internment camp experience, when they shed their Japanese cultural identity hoping to find acceptance in mainstream America.

352   Uchida, Yoshiko. ***Desert Exile: The Uprooting of a Japanese-American Family***. Illus. Univ. of Washington Pr. 1982, $14.95 (0-295-96190-2). 160pp. Autobiography.

This book offers a moving personal account of the uprooting and incarceration of one Japanese American family during World War II. Both of Uchida's parents were university graduates who emigrated from Japan. Her father was a businessman in a large Japanese company. Uchida describes her happy childhood growing up in a middle-class neighborhood. She was a senior at the University of California, Berkeley when the war began. The family's tranquil lives were abruptly ended when the FBI seized her father. Later the family was reunited at a camp in Topaz, Utah.

Uchida describes the harrowing evacuation, the bleak camp existence (they lived in horse stalls at the Tanforan Assembly Center), and the hardships of life at Topaz. Uchida explains that she wrote this book with the hope that knowledge of the past will prevent such a desert exile from ever happening again. Throughout the book, Uchida also conscientiously pays tribute to her parents and to the hard-working, self-denying first generation of Japanese immigrants. Uchida is an award-winning author of over twenty books for young people.

353   Wang, An, and Eugene Linden. ***Lessons: An Autobiography***. Addison Wesley 1988, $17.26 (0-201-09400-2); $9.57 (0-201-07408-7). 288pp. Autobiography.

Wang arrived in the United States from China in 1945. He earned a Ph.D. in applied physics from Harvard and invented an important element of computer memory. With $600 in savings and no business experience, he opened a one-man shop in Boston in 1951 to market his innovations in digital electronics. Thirty-five years later, Wang Laboratories had evolved into a worldwide multibillion-dollar high-tech company that employs over thirty thousand people. A brilliant entrepreneur and a dedicated humanitarian, Wang received the Medal of Liberty in 1986. Though Wang Laboratories suffered a setback after its founder retired and died in 1990, *Lessons* makes inspiring reading about a fascinating man who was willing to make decisions and take risks.

354   Wiseman, Carter. ***I. M. Pei: A Profile in American Architecture***. Illus. Abrams 1990, $60.00 (0-8109-3709-3). 320pp. Biography.

I. M. Pei, probably the most famous architect of his time, has designed some of the twentieth century's most distinguished buildings, including the Kennedy Library in Boston, the East Building of the National Gallery in Washington, D.C., the glass pyramid for the Louvre in Paris, and the seventy-one-story tower for the Bank of China in Hong Kong.

Born to a prominent banking family in pre-Communist China, Pei came to the United States as a student in 1935. He received a bachelor's degree in engineering from MIT and a master's degree in architecture from Harvard. By combining these two disciplines, Pei created bold forms and daring geometrical layouts in his works. He has received every important honor in his field. Often described as charismatic, diplomatic, and self-assured, Pei moves with charm and ease among the rich and famous. This book, which provides in-depth analyses of eight of Pei's most important buildings, contains many revealing anecdotes and is profusely illustrated with stunning color photos.

355   Wong, Jade Snow. ***Fifth Chinese Daughter***. Univ. of Washington Pr. 1989, $12.95 (0-295-96826-5). 256pp. Autobiography.

Originally published in 1945, *Fifth Chinese Daughter* is the first autobiography by an American-born Chinese-American woman. Jade Snow, an artist in ceramics, writes about her life as the fifth daughter of an owner of a small clothing factory in Chinatown. As she gradually ventures into the white American culture, she begins to challenge the conventional expectations and limitations of a female in a patriarchal Chinese society. She supports herself through college; and after several years of lackluster secretarial jobs, she decides to open her own ceramic shop, which becomes an instant success.

Although the third-person writing style is polite and somewhat stilted, the book provides good social observations of family life in Chinatown during the 1930s. There are images of hardworking parents, obedient children, Chinese cooking, Old World virtues, and colorful rituals. Jade Snow includes portrayals of other representative Chinatown characters as well. In her sequel, *No Chinese Strangers* (1975), Jade Snow tells of her new roles as wife and mother and describes her visit to China, which gives her a new sense of identity.

356   Yoneda, Karl G. ***Ganbatte: Sixty-Year Struggle of a Kibei Worker***. Ed. and intro. by Yuji Ichioka. Univ. of California, Los Angeles, Asian-American Studies Center 1983, $8.95 (0-934052-07-7). 240pp. Autobiography.

Born in Los Angeles in 1906, Karl Goso Yoneda is a *Kibei*—a person born in the United States but educated in Japan. During his early years in Japan, he avidly read books by such great thinkers as Tolstoy, Voltaire, Rousseau, and Marx, after whom he chose his English name Karl. On returning to the United States from Japan in 1926, he became a labor activist and a dedicated member of the Communist Party. He worked as a restaurant helper, editor, union organizer, chicken rancher, and longshoreman. During World War II he served in the U. S. Army as a propagandist in Asia, while his family was incarcerated in the Manzanar, California, internment camp. His wife, Elaine Black, is an ardent Russian-Jewish-American labor organizer.

The title of this book, *Ganbatte*, means "stick to it." Although Yoneda describes himself simply as an "ordinary working stiff," his life represents sixty years of struggle for the cause of working people. Yoneda has written several books in the Japanese language. This volume reveals a little-known aspect of Asian-American labor history.

3

UNITED STATES:
LATINOS

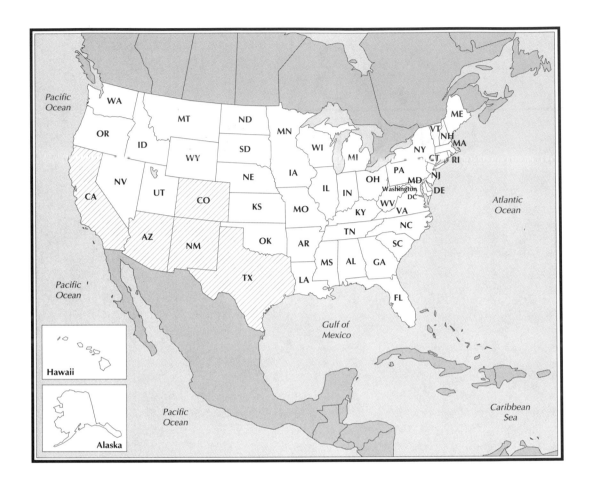

STATES WITH HIGHEST
CONCENTRATION OF
LATINOS

1. New Mexico - 38.2%
2. California - 25.8%
3. Texas - 25.5%
4. Arizona - 18.8%
5. Colorado - 12.9%

PLACES OF ORIGIN
OF LATINOS BY
PERCENTAGE

1. Mexico - 60.4%
2. Puerto Rico - 12.2%
3. Cuba - 4.7%
4. Other - 22.7%

Source: 1990 U.S. Census

3

UNITED STATES: LATINOS

by Lyn Miller-Lachmann, Diana Morales, and Carlos Nájera

The Latino population of the United States is a diverse group made up of people with ancestries from many different Spanish- and Portuguese-speaking countries and cultures. The terms used to describe the various groups—Latino (and the feminine form, Latina), Hispanic, Mexican American, Chicano—reflect this diversity. For the purposes of this chapter, the more recently adopted term Latino/Latina is preferred over the term Hispanic. Also, the more general and less politically charged term Mexican American will refer to the largest of the Latino groups; as a rule, the term Chicano refers specifically to the literary and political movements that arose during the 1960s and 1970s.

The majority of Latinos are of Mexican origin and reside in the Southwest. Some trace their family roots to the original Indian residents of the region, including the Aztecs. Others are descended from the Spanish who settled the region from the sixteenth to the nineteenth centuries. These residents, like the Mexican emigrants who arrived in the United States after the 1848 Treaty of Guadalupe Hidalgo, are often of mixed European and indigenous descent. Their bloodlines may be further complicated by intermarriage with Anglo-Americans, American Indians, or other groups. Although migrant farm work has traditionally (and stereotypically) been associated with Mexican Americans, the vast majority of Latinos today live in the cities of the West and Southwest and engage in a variety of occupations. In the works of fiction and personal narrative described in this chapter, lawyers and teachers appear as prominently as agricultural workers, factory workers, and labor organizers. Criminals and gang members are also represented, as are those who overcame or rejected those temptations. Among the works by Mexican Americans are books that describe the immigrant experience as well as books featuring second-, third-, fourth-, and fifth-generation Americans.

The next two largest Latino groups, Puerto Ricans and Cuban Americans, have a shorter history in the United States. Both islands became colonies of the United States following the Spanish-American War in 1898. Although Cuba gained its independence in 1934, Puerto Rico remains a commonwealth, and its people are U.S. citizens. Despite their close ties to the United States, relatively few residents of these islands migrated to the U.S. mainland until the 1940s and

1950s, when air travel became widely available. Puerto Ricans began to arrive in significant numbers in New York City in the 1940s. Today the majority still live in the New York metropolitan area; the term "Nuyorican" refers to this largely assimilated group. In contrast to the Cuban-American exiles, Puerto Ricans often maintain close ties to the island and may visit frequently. Judith Ortiz Cofer's *Silent Dancing: A Partial Remembrance of a Puerto Rican Childhood* illustrates the connections between the island and the mainland.

A small number of Cubans also arrived in the 1940s; this initial migration forms the background for Oscar Hijuelos's novels *Our House in the Last World* and *The Mambo Kings Play Songs of Love*. Most Cubans, however, arrived after Fidel Castro's leftist revolution in 1959. They made Miami their base, because the city shares Cuba's climate and offers proximity to their homeland and the relatives who stayed behind. Cuban migration to the United States occurred in waves. First to come during the early years of Castro's rule were the prosperous professionals. The next wave, in the late 1960s and the 1970s, brought the shopkeepers. Finally, the poorer classes—many of whom happen to be darker-skinned—arrived on the 1980 Mariel boatlift and, in the early 1990s, on makeshift rafts. Today, the majority of Cuban Americans live in Miami, though Cuban-American communities exist as well in New Jersey, Los Angeles, and other cities.

The Latino population in the United States also includes many people from the Dominican Republic, most of whom live in New York City, and an undetermined number from the nations of Central and South America. (These immigrants have been classified together as "other Hispanic" by the U.S. Census, which has also grossly underestimated the number of undocumented refugees from El Salvador and Guatemala.) The story of one Dominican-American family, forced to come to the United States because of the political activities of the father, a doctor, is the subject of Julia Alvarez's humorous novel *How the García Girls Lost Their Accents*. Though a few Central and South Americans have lived in the United States for generations, most of the migrants (particularly from the strife-torn nations of Central America) have arrived within the past two decades. Among the Central and South Americans are political exiles, war refugees, and those seeking economic opportunities; they include both unskilled workers and highly educated professionals. Many, like the Chilean exiles featured in the anthology *Paradise Lost or Gained*, are uncomfortable with the term Latino, which does not distinguish between their culture and that of the vastly larger group of Mexican immigrants. Despite fleeing a rightist, rather than a leftist, dictatorship, many Chileans found they had more in common with the first waves of Cuban exiles.

The diverse ways Latinos from different cultures lived in their native lands and the different ways they experienced immigration are reflected in the books included in this chapter. Readers seeking a general introduction to the subject should begin with Earl Shorris's well-written nonfiction work *Latinos: A Biography of the People*. In the past decade, a number of anthologies of fiction, drama, poetry, and essays by Latino writers have been published that also offer the reader a general overview. Although there is some overlap among the contents of these anthologies, most are organized by genre (such as short fiction or drama), theme (such as feminist writing or the literature of exile), or national origin of the contributors. *Cuentos Chicanos*, edited by Rudolfo A. Anaya and Antonio Márquez, presents the work of the first generation of Mexican-American (Chicano) writers, while writers of the second generation have their say in *Mirrors Beneath the Earth*, edited by Ray González. The perspective of woman writers of various Latino traditions is the focus of *Woman of Her Word*, edited by Evangelina Vigil. Two collections contain drama by Latino playwrights: John Antush's *Recent Puerto Rican Theater* and Jorge A. Huerta's *Necessary Theater: Six Plays about the Chicano Experience*. *Growing Up Latino*, edited by Harold Augenbraum and Ilan Stavans, offers memoirs and stories centered on the themes of childhood, adolescence, family life, and the search for identity; Tiffany López's *Growing Up Chicana/o* is more narrowly focused on the experiences of young people of Mexican descent. Nicolas Kanellos's anthology *Short Fiction by Hispanic Writers of the United States* is a well-balanced collection that features an excellent introduction.

Most works of Latino literature and autobiography discussed in this chapter are relatively recent: Almost all were written after 1960. Americo Paredes's *George Washington Gómez* was written during the 1930s, but it was not published until 1990. In addition, there are few works of general nonfiction. The choice of books for inclusion reflects the comparatively short history of most Latino groups in the United States, but it also reflects the status of Latino people and culture, many of whom have long been regarded as "second-class citizens" at best. Like the Indian peoples with whom they shared many aspects of their culture, the Mexicans who overnight became U.S. citizens in 1848 often lost their land and their civil rights. Denied a place in the history books, they instead tell of their heritage and experiences in novels such as *George Washington Gómez*, in Aristeo Brito's *The Devil in Texas*, in the short stories of Sabine R. Ulibarrí, and in autobiographies such as Floyd Salas's *Buffalo Nickel* and Lydia Mendoza's *Lydia Mendoza: A Family Autobiography*. Family history figures prominently in these and many other works by Mexican-American writers; for them, writing is a way to recover a story that has largely been left out of mainstream accounts of the Southwest and its settlement.

Having spent the longest time in the United States, Mexican Americans have produced at least two distinct generations of writers. In the nineteenth century and first half of the twentieth century, popular music, theater, and poetry appeared from time to time, often published in Mexico (if published at all) and generally in Spanish. Nicolas Kanellos's *A History of Hispanic Theatre in the United States: Origins to 1940* (University of Texas Press, 1990) examines this early history as it relates to works of drama. Critics generally consider José Antonio Villarreal's *Pocho*, which appeared in 1959, as the first major work of Chicano literature written in English. That novel, which tells of an immigrant family caught between two cultures and the assimilation of the teenage protagonist, was followed by John Rechy's *City of Night* in 1963 and Floyd Salas's *Tattoo the Wicked Cross* in 1967. Interestingly, neither of these two novels focuses on the protagonists' Mexican-American heritage, at least in the traditional sense. For example, *City of Night* explores the world of big-city male hustlers, and Aaron D'Aragon, the protagonist of *Tattoo the Wicked Cross*, is of "pure Spanish" lineage and therefore feels superior to the part-Indian "Mexicans." In Raymond Barrio's *The Plum Plum Pickers*, published in 1969, the reader sees the emergence of a Chicano political and cultural consciousness. Barrio's novel focuses on the conditions facing migrant workers in California and their first steps toward organized resistance. Tomás Rivera's classic *. . . Y No Se lo Tragó la Tierra/And the Earth Did Not Devour Him* explores the lives, culture, and folk traditions of migrant workers, as does Sabine R. Ulibarrí's collection of short stories, *Tierra Amarilla*. Both these works were written originally in Spanish, as were Brito's *The Devil in Texas* and many of the novels of Rolando Hinojosa. Emerging as one of the most significant Mexican-American writers at this time was Rudolfo A. Anaya, whose award-winning *Bless Me, Ultima*, published in 1972, explores traditional Indian spirituality as a source of strength for a family under pressure from the outside world. Anaya's second novel, *Heart of Aztlán*, deals with political and social issues in the context of the Aztec myth of Aztlán. Other novelists in the first generation include Miguel Méndez, Alejandro Morales, Victor Villaseñor, Estela Portillo-Trambley, and Ron Arias. Portillo-Trambley was one of the first Mexican-American woman writers to gain prominence; her short story collection *Rain of Scorpions* explores social realities from the perspective of women—wives, mothers, and daughters. Another unique perspective from this first generation is that of Ron Arias, in whose novel *The Road to Tamazunchale* the protagonist embraces U.S. popular culture as a source of inspiration and fantasy.

In addition to writing novels and short stories, the first generation of Mexican-American authors produced several noted works of drama and personal narrative. Chief among them is Luís Valdez's play *Zoot Suit*, the story of a group of Mexican-American teenagers unjustly imprisoned for a murder in 1943. Significant autobiographical works of this era are Ernesto Galarza's *Barrio Boy* and Oscar Z. Acosta's *Autobiography of a Brown Buffalo*.

In the 1980s a second generation of Mexican-American writers emerged. One feature that distinguished this new generation was the significant presence of woman writers, including Sandra Cisneros, author of *The House on Mango Street* and *Woman Hollering Creek*; Denise Chavez, author of the short story collection *The Last of the Menu Girls*; and Mary Helen Ponce, author of the humorous novel *The Wedding* and the short story collection *Taking Control*. Each of these works of fiction presents working-class Latinas (usually Mexican-American women, but sometimes immigrants from Central America) struggling against the limitations placed upon them by families and society. Ana Castillo's acclaimed novel *So Far from God* explores women's relationships with each other and with the supernatural; like Anaya and other authors of the first generation, Castillo emphasizes spiritual themes, notably the clash between traditional Indian religions and Catholicism. In addition to these and other woman writers of fiction, the new generation has witnessed the success of woman poets and essayists, such as Pat Mora and Gloria Anzaldúa. These two writers have articulated feminist perspectives within the context of their culture; Anzaldúa also has examined issues related to sexual orientation.

The male writers to emerge in the second generation have distinguished themselves less through fiction than through drama, essay, and autobiography. Their styles and points of view are quite diverse, ranging from the political activism of playwright Carlos Morton and poet/essayist Luís J. Rodríguez to the apolitical reminiscences of Gary Soto and the socially conservative perspective of Richard Rodríguez, an advocate of assimilation and outspoken opponent of bilingual education.

For Puerto Ricans, Cuban Americans, and other recent arrivals to the mainland United States, history is still unfolding. Works of fiction, drama, and poetry examine cultural roots and the shock of new surroundings. Puerto Rican writers such as Nicholasa Mohr, Judith Ortiz Cofer, and the poet Tato Laviera have focused on New York City and its physical and cultural distance from the island. Because of the lack of general nonfiction, the literary testimonies of these and other Puerto Rican authors—Piri Thomas, Ed Vega, Abraham Rodríguez, Jr., Miguel Piñero, Edward Gallardo, and the playwrights included in John Antush's anthology—are the principal points of access to the Puerto Rican experience on the mainland. Like their Mexican-American counterparts, many Puerto Rican writers have focused on the harsh realities of urban life. Women writers such as Mohr and Cofer have examined women's roles within the family. Even more of an issue for the Puerto Rican authors, however, is the question of race. While Mexican Americans' lineage may be Indian or European or both, Latinos from the Caribbean region (encompassing Puerto Rico, Cuba, and the Dominican Republic) often trace part of their heritage to Africa. Dark-skinned Puerto Ricans and others are often mistaken for African-Americans, as Piri Thomas, with his Anglicized surname, discovered. Much of his autobiography, *Down These Mean Streets*, describes his search for identity in a society that considered him a black man. Race—and the stigma of being black in the United States—is also a major theme in Richard V. Irizarry's *Ariano*, one of the plays in Antush's anthology. For poet Tato Laviera, on the other hand, African heritage is a source of pride and a point of solidarity with other multicultural Americans, as he writes in his collection *AmeRican*. Laviera's poetry bears the influence of Cuban poet Nicolas Guillén, one of the major figures in the worldwide artistic movement of African and African-descended peoples known as Negritude.

The dominant themes of Cuban-American writers and of the nonfiction about Cuban Americans have been the Cuban Revolution, life under Castro's regime, and the experiences of exile. Notable exceptions to this rule include the works of Oscar Hijuelos, who has portrayed the Cuban community in Harlem that existed for almost two decades before Castro's rise to power, and José Barreiro, whose novel *The Indian Chronicles* presents the indigenous view of Columbus's voyages. Despite the unity of theme, however, works of fiction by Cuban-American authors are quite diverse, especially in terms of style. While Cristina García and Virgil Suárez have written realistic, linear works, many other writers use elements of fantasy, magical realism, and discontinuous chronologies in ways similar to the more experimental Latin American and European authors. The story-within-a-story, told by an enigmatic narrator, is a device employed by both Omar Torres in *Fallen Angels Sing* and Elias Miguel Muñoz in *The Greatest Performance*. Roberto Fernández's *Raining Backwards* uses imaginary newspaper clippings, dream sequences, communications from the dead, and futuristic speculations to narrate a bizarre tale of an exile family coming apart.

Readers seeking to appreciate the diversity of the Latino experience through fiction, drama, poetry, nonfiction, and autobiography will not have to look hard, so long as they are willing to peruse the catalogues of publishers outside the mainstream. The majority of books described in this chapter have not been published by large presses, or if they have, they have gone out of print. From the late 1960s to the present, small presses—particularly those specializing in works by Latino authors—have played a critical role in developing and maintaining Latino literature, publishing new authors and bringing older works back into print. The pioneering small press was Quinto Sol, which published Chicano literature almost exclusively. Today, its work has been taken over by Bilingual Press/Editorial Bilingue and by Arte Público Press, which has reached out to writers from other Latino traditions as well. Other small presses that have played a role include the politically oriented Curbstone Press, publisher of the anthology *Mirrors Beneath the Earth* and Luís J. Rodríguez's *Always Running*; the feminist publisher Aunt Lute Books, which brought out Gloria Anzaldúa's poetry/essay collection *Borderlands/La Frontera*;

and the literary revival house Second Chance Press, publisher of Floyd Salas's *Tattoo the Wicked Cross*. Many of the nonfiction works, essay collections, and even some classic works of fiction have been published by academic presses, such as the University of New Mexico Press.

Latino authors often feel compelled to write in English to reach a larger mainstream audience. But the success of Latino presses has made it possible for many of them to express themselves in their own language and vernacular. For this reason many of the anthologies contain prose and poetry printed in the language in which it was written, whether Spanish or English, without translations. Collections by individual poets such as Tato Laviera and Gloria Anzaldúa contain poems in one or the other or both languages. Several books on the list, including . . . *Y No Se lo Tragó la Tierra*, are available in bilingual editions. A number of the Mexican-American authors use an urban slang known as *calo*, which uses Spanish words or combines the two languages to create new words altogether. One also finds the Puerto Rican equivalent of *calo*, known as "Nuyorican" slang, in Laviera's poetry and in much of the fiction and drama as well. Even without a knowledge of Spanish, the reader will find a great deal to enjoy, to appreciate, and to learn from in the enormously creative and varied output of these Latino authors.

LITERATURE

357 Alegría, Fernando, and Jorge Ruffinelli, eds. *Paradise Lost or Gained: The Literature of Hispanic Exile*. Arte Público 1991, $11.00 (1-55885-037-6). 240pp. Fiction/Poetry.

Two noted Latin American writers—a Chilean and a Cuban—have edited this collection of works by Latin American exiles living in the United States. Among the works included are short stories, poems, and essays; many are in Spanish and have not been translated into English. Also included are reproductions of artworks.

Although the essays are quite specialized and may be of little interest to the general reader, the short stories and poems offer glimpses into the experiences of groups who have received little attention in other publications. For the Chileans, Cubans, and others who came to the United States to escape political repression in their own countries, their new land promised new opportunities as well as the temptation of assimilation. The title character of Guillermo A. Reyes's "Patroklos," for instance, finds fulfillment through his work with an alternative theater group. Ironically, although democracy returns to Chile, he decides to apply for U.S. citizenship because he realizes he cannot live openly as a gay man in Chile. Characters in other works grope for a sense of identity in a country where the overwhelming majority of Latinos are from cultures very different from their own. Alegría has also edited *Chilean Writers in Exile* (o.p., 1982), a collection of works by Chilean authors who settled in Europe, the United States, and Canada.   LML

358 Alvarez, Julia. *How the García Girls Lost Their Accents*. Algonquin 1991, $16.95 (0-945575-57-2); NAL $10.00 (0-452-26806-0). 308pp. Fiction.

Fleeing a failed coup attempt that he helped to plan, Dr. Carlos García arrives in New York from the Dominican Republic with his wife, Laura, and their four daughters. The daughters—sensible Carla, beautiful Sandra, artistic Yolanda, and rebellious Sofia—must adapt not just to a more Spartan lifestyle but to the language and culture of a new country as well. Although the Garcías never attain the wealth and position they once enjoyed, they eventually have a comfortable existence and adjust, though imperfectly, to their adopted country. The four girls lose much of their Spanish and speak mostly English, even at home. Their wild, defiant, and often promiscuous behavior outrages their elders. Remaining close, they conspire and engage in humorous intrigues against parents, boyfriends, and each other. The story begins in the present, and each story deals with events set farther in the past; the end of the book describes the Garcías' flight from Dominican authorities. Through this unusual structure, the novel explores the cycle of the family members' rebellion, accommodation, and change. The lively, humorous narrative engages readers as it portrays the complexity within one family's experience of immigration. In her second novel, *In the Time of Butterflies* (Algonquin, 1994), Alvarez turns her attention to the Dominican Republic, the land of her birth. Three sisters who have joined the opposition to Trujillo's dictatorship are killed in a suspicious road accident, leaving the surviving sister to remember their lives and the chain of events that led to their deaths. LML

359 Anaya, Rudolfo A. ***Bless Me, Ultima***. Warner 1994, $19.95 (0-446-51783-6); $5.50 (0-446-60025-3). 272pp. Fiction.

The Marez family lives on the Llano Estacado in 1940s New Mexico. In addition to the difficulties they face in their everyday struggle for survival, the Marezes hope that their three sons, who are away at war, will return safely. Ultima, an aged healing woman, comes to live with the Marezes. Observing their problems, she attempts to stabilize and restore the harmony the family once enjoyed. Antonio, age seven, is the youngest family member. The love he has for his parents and siblings is unquestionable, but it creates a conflict. From the day of his birth, his mother has hoped that he will become a learned man and a priest, but his father dreams that Antonio will become a "Marez man"—a plainsman. In his own quest for identity, Antonio explores Indian, Mexican, and Anglo cultural values and is influenced by the loving wisdom and spirit of Ultima, who fosters in him the ability to draw strength from life's experiences.

Anaya has written several other works that portray the Latino experience in New Mexico in the twentieth century. Among them are the novel *Alburquerque* (Univ. of New Mexico Pr., 1992), the story of a boxer in search of his dual Mexican-Anglo roots who falls in love with a Latina running for mayor, and the epic poem *The Adventures of Juan Chicasparas* (Arte Público, 1984), which weaves together Mexican and Southwestern mythology and the lives of young *pachucos* ("street kids"). DM

360 Anaya, Rudolfo A., and Antonio Márquez, eds. ***Cuentos Chicanos: A Short Story Anthology***. Univ. of New Mexico Pr. 1984, $12.95 (0-8263-0772-8). 194pp. Fiction.

This anthology presents the short fiction of twenty-one Chicano authors, many of whom gained prominence in the 1960s, 1970s, and early 1980s. Among the writers included are Rudolfo Anaya, Nash Candelaria, Ana Castillo, Denise Chavez, and Alberto Alvaro Ríos. A few of the stories are offered in Spanish, without translation, but most are in English. Many of the stories have family relationships as their principal theme, while others touch upon issues of education, discrimination, the Vietnam War, the migrant experience, and the experiences of an emerging generation of Chicano intellectuals. The works in this collection reflect a wide variety of forms and styles, from the experimental style of Ana Castillo's "Ghost Talk" to the gritty realism of Mario Suárez's "The Migrant" to Ron Arias's "Lupe," which begins with a grotesque supernatural event. In addition to being a good introduction to the diversity of the Chicano experience and to the works of a number of established and emerging writers, this anthology is one of the first of its kind, a model for collections that have followed.   LML

361   Anaya, Rudolfo A. ***Heart of Aztlán***. Univ. of New Mexico Pr. 1988, $13.95 (0-8263-1054-0). 214pp. Fiction.

Set in New Mexico in the 1940s, Anaya's novel presents Clemente Chavez, a ranch worker who loses his job and moves his family to Albuquerque in search of work. Continued unemployment, alcohol, and despair take their toll upon him and his entire family. In desperation, Clemente turns to the barrio wise man, Crispin, who urges him not only to seek the source of his plight in the injustice experienced by Mexican Americans but also to lead his people in overcoming that injustice. Ultimately, Clemente becomes that leader, a mission in which he attains personal and community salvation.

Based loosely upon the myth of Aztlán, the secret Aztec holy place believed to be somewhere near present-day New Mexico, Anaya's second novel is rich in traditional Aztec symbolism, which he juxtaposes with the details of mid-twentieth-century urban life in the United States. Although most critics consider *Heart of Aztlán* to be less polished than Anaya's first novel, *Bless Me, Ultima (see main entry)*, it both expands his range and stands as one of the major works in the politically conscious strain of Chicano literature.   LML

362   Antush, John, ed. ***Recent Puerto Rican Theater: Five Plays from New York***. Arte Público 1991, $11.00 (1-55885-019-8). 180pp. Drama.

After emerging in New York City in the late 1960s and the 1970s, Puerto Rican theater enjoyed a successful decade in the 1980s. With the support of the New York Shakespeare Festival and other arts organizations, a number of plays were produced for the first time and enjoyed successful runs off-Broadway. Antush has chosen four such plays—*Bodega*, by Federico Fraguada; *First Class*, by Cándido Tirado; *Midnight Blues*, by Juan Shamsul Alam; and *Ariano*, by Richard V. Irizarry—along with Ivette M. Ramírez's *Family Scenes*, which has yet to be produced. A lengthy introduction places the plays within the context of "Nuyorican" theater and helps the reader to understand their major themes. The plays represent a variety of experiences, from the small business owners of *Bodega* to the drifters of *First Class* and the middle-class family in *Ariano*. One of the most poignant plays, *Ariano* reveals the distinctions of skin color that Puerto Ricans must adapt to on the mainland; the father, Ariano, pays a blonde woman to have a child for him when his son, Serafin, is discriminated against in school because of his dark skin. Family conflicts also appear in different forms in the other plays. The brothers of *First Class*—one of them adopted—argue over who was the favorite of their recently deceased prostitute mother. This is a well-balanced collection that shows the range of styles and themes in Puerto Rican drama in the 1980s. **LML**

363 Anzaldúa, Gloria. ***Borderlands—La Frontera: The New Mestiza.*** Aunt Lute 1987, $19.95 (1-879960-13-3); $9.95 (1-879960-12-5). 203pp. Poetry/Essays.

Anzaldúa is a *tejana*, a descendant of the original Indian and Mexican inhabitants of the Southwest who lost their land and autonomy when Texas and the other Southwestern states became part of the United States in the 1840s. She grew up in the Rio Grande Valley of Texas and describes herself as standing at the "crossroads" of cultures and identities—Mexican, Indian, and Anglo, female, a lesbian, a professor, and a writer. Through poems and essays, she explores the meaning of her multiple identities. She details both the history of the border region and its present situation, and she analyzes the mythology and symbolism of the ancient Aztecs who have inspired her creative work. She explores the place of women within her own culture and within Anglo society, discussing in particular what it means to be both Chicana and lesbian. Finally, she examines her family history, her experience as the first member of her family to leave the border area (she has lived in California and the Northeast), and her development as a writer. She writes her essays and poems in English and Spanish; several are printed in both languages. Through them, the reader understands how language itself is also part of Anzaldúa's identity. This is a varied, well-written, and thought-provoking collection that reveals both a talented woman and the rich cultures that have played a role in her development. **LML**

364 Arias, Ron. ***The Road to Tamazunchale.*** Doubleday 1992, $8.00 (0-385-42012-9). 192pp. Fiction.

Arias, a journalist and feature writer, has written the tale of Fausto, a dying old man who spends his final days in a reverie of history and the supernatural. Fausto imagines that with Carmela, the niece who takes care of him, he travels to Cuzco to warn the Indians of an attack on the garrison there. Later he meets a young guide, Mario, and a shepherd, Marcelino Huanca, who has strayed, along with his alpacas, from his Peruvian coca field. In another dream, Fausto fantasizes that he, Mario, and Marcelino shepherd a group of Mexicans across the border and on to Los Angeles, all the while telling them they have no future in the United States and might as well be dead.

Arias's brief novel is filled with humor, irony, and symbolism drawn from Indian lore, Latin American history, and contemporary U.S. culture. It offers an unusual perspective on death and the process of dying. For Arias and for his protagonist, Fausto, the moments before death are not mournful moments but creative ones in which a person's individual and collective histories come together in bizarre and revealing ways. **LML**

365 Augenbraum, Harold, and Ilan Stavans, eds. ***Growing Up Latino: Memoirs and Stories.*** Houghton 1993, $22.45 (0-395-62231-X); $12.70 (0-395-66124-2). 416pp. Anthology.

The selections in this volume—some fictional, many autobiographical—focus on coming of age and the diversity of the Hispanic experience in the United States. Dominican, Chicano, Cuban, and Puerto Rican authors are spotlighted.

The first of the book's three divisions, called "Imagining the Family," depicts family relationships and their effects on children. Included in this section are Julia Alvarez's "Daughter of Invention," an excerpt from *How the García Girls Lost Their Accents (see main entry)*; Judith Ortiz Cofer's "Silent Dancing," from the book of the same name; and Ed Vega's short story "An Apology to the Moon Furies," from *Casualty Report*. Another division, "Gringolandia," looks at Latinos who live and survive in an environment that is totally foreign to them. Among the eight selections are a chapter from *Down These Mean Streets* by Piri Thomas *(see main entry)*, a chapter from *Autobiography of a Brown Buffalo* by Oscar "Zeta" Acosta *(see main entry)*, and Nicholasa Mohr's "Mr. Mendelsohn," from *El Bronx Remembered*. The final division, "Songs of Self-Discovery," includes stories with the theme of cultivating and learning inner strength. Two of the inclusions are Gloria Anzaldúa's "People Should Not Die in June in South Texas" and "Aria," the first chapter in Richard Rodríguez's autobiography, *The Hunger of Memory*.

In their introduction, the editors provide a good framework for the materials selected. They also include an excellent bibliography of suggested readings. DM

366 Barreiro, José. *The Indian Chronicles*. Arte Público 1993, $19.95 (1-55885-067-8). 300pp. Fiction.

When Christopher Columbus and his Spanish fleet made landfall on Hispaniola in 1492, they were not attacked by the native Taíno Indians. However, resistance developed swiftly when the Indians saw that these newcomers were greedy and lacking in respect for Taíno culture. Barreiro's novel tells the story of Diego Colón, the adopted Taíno son of Christopher Columbus and an eyewitness to the clash of cultures between the European explorers and his native people. At the age of twelve Diego learned to speak Spanish quickly and became an interpreter, developing a friendship with Father Bartolomé de las Casas. At the friar's request many years later, Diego began writing his memoirs. Spanning more than half a century, from the arrival of the explorers to the signing of a viable peace treaty with the last Taíno insurgents, this novel presents a native perspective on history, one based on real people and primary-source documents. Diego's narrative is not vehemently critical of Columbus, but neither is it very kind. The explorer is portrayed, not as the larger-than-life heroic figure of tradition, but as a human being with irreparable faults.

The Indian Chronicles, the first novel by its Cuban-born author, is a strong complement to the many nonfiction accounts of Columbus's voyage and offers a perspective that is different from, but as critical as, Argentine writer Abel Posse's *The Dogs of Paradise (see main entry)*. DM

367 Barrio, Raymond. *The Plum Plum Pickers.* 2nd ed. Bilingual Press/Editorial Bilingue 1984, $14.00 (0-916950-51-4). 232pp. Fiction.

This classic work of Chicano literature is set in the 1960s in the farmlands of the Santa Clara Valley of California, during the early years of the unionization struggle. The story is told mainly through the eyes of Manuel Gutiérrez, a hard-working migrant farm worker, and his wife, Guadalupe, who is constantly worried and dreamy. They struggle to raise their three children in unsanitary conditions in a one-room shack, hoping they can give their children the education that will liberate them from the migrant life. Manuel's friend Pepe Delgado has become a foreman. Pepe is able to send his teenage children to school, although two of the children rebel against their father's discipline and against the discrimination they face in high school. Pepe's success has also come at some cost. He has allied himself with the cruel manager, Morton J. Quill, whose life is being threatened by an unknown radical who calls himself J. Murrieta, after the Mexican revolutionary Joaquin Murrieta. Manuel's activist nephew, Ramiro Sánchez, is an admirer of Cesar Chavez and has become the lover of Pepe's second daughter, Margarita. Other characters include the labor recruiter Alberto Morales, whom Manuel ultimately defies; the farm owner Turner; and the gentle owner of the nursery, Schroeder, who helps Manuel and his family. The very memorable characters of this novel—decent, hardworking, intelligent, articulate, and fed up with the way things are—give the reader a vivid sense of migrant life in a community on the verge of change.   LML

368   Brito, Aristeo. ***The Devil in Texas***. Trans. from Spanish by David W. Foster. Bilingual Press/Editorial Bilingue 1990, $22.00 (0-927534-05-3); Doubleday $8.00 (0-385-42015-3). 224pp. Fiction.

The town of Presidio—its name means "prison" in Spanish—and the Ojinaga Valley in south Texas are the settings for this tale, which spans one hundred years and five generations in a family's history. Throughout the story, the devil haunts the family and the community, leading to dispossessions, betrayals, and violent deaths.

   The principal focus is the family of Francisco Uranga, an activist lawyer who tries in vain in the late nineteenth century to gain back the land taken from Hispanic Texans by Anglo invaders. Francisco wants to document the conditions under which the dispossessed—now mostly migrant farm workers—lived. One of his sons is murdered, and his frail grandson, Chente, the child of his surviving son, dies of a lung disease at the age of twelve. These two spirits haunt Vicke, Chente's sister and the mother of Marcela. Fifty years later, Marcela is pregnant with her first child. As her husband, José, goes off to work in the fields, Marcela has a horrifying vision. Later the river floods. José returns in time to rescue Marcela and Vicke, but Marcela dies in childbirth. The unnamed son then becomes the narrator of the story. At the funeral of his father the son recalls José's life. He also relates his vision of a time in which Presidio will no longer be a place of exploitation, suffering, and tragedy for its Mexican people.
                                                                              LML

369   Castillo, Ana. ***So Far from God***. Norton 1993, $19.95 (0-393-03490-9); NAL $9.95 (0-452-27209-2). 256pp. Fiction.

One night, Sofia's three-year-old daughter—forever to be known as La Loca—has a seizure and dies. At her funeral she returns to life, escaping her coffin and flying up to the church roof. This is only the beginning of the strange things that happen to La Loca and her three sisters—rebellious Esperanza, conservative Fe, and sensuous Caridad. All four of the daughters die in their twenties, but not before making an impact upon the small town of Tome, New Mexico and its Mexican-American residents. Esperanza, the eldest, becomes a reporter for the Albuquerque television station, then takes a job in a Washington, D.C., station. She disappears while covering a Mideast war. Jilted once, Fe finally marries but then dies after a year of working in (and ultimately blowing the whistle on) a toxic chemical factory. One day Caridad, who develops clairvoyant powers, jumps from a mesa with a young woman with whom she has fallen in love. Even La Loca returns to the grave from which she was resurrected. They leave Sofia, who has learned much from her daughters, as the newly elected progressive mayor of Tome and the founder of an organization of mothers of martyred and saintly daughters.

Castillo's novel is both poetical and political, reveling in the mixed Spanish and English of the region and revealing the poverty, dignity, and humor of the residents. The most accessible of Castillo's works, it moves rapidly from scene to scene, but it fills the reader's mind with vividly drawn characters and situations. LML

370 Chavez, Denise. *The Last of the Menu Girls*. Arte Público 1991, $9.50 (0-934770-46-8). 160pp. Fiction.

From her summer job as a hospital aide who distributes and collects menus for patients to an unsatisfying turn at teaching drama to children, Rocío Esquibel is the common thread that weaves together the seven stories presented in this volume. An array of characters from Rocío's family and neighborhood in New Mexico influence her development and ultimately her decision to become a writer. Women—mother, sisters, friends, neighbors, extended family—and their roles in society figure prominently in the narrative. In their dialogue they reveal their expectations and disappointments. Rocío also observes and learns from them as her own identity evolves.

From the beginning, when Rocío proclaims that she never wanted to be a nurse, and throughout the selections that follow, she rebels against the preset roles expected of women. Her mother becomes an enthusiastic supporter, suggesting that the people of Rocío's old neighborhood are an untapped source of material for her stories.

Chavez is also the author of the comic novel *Face of an Angel* (Farrar, 1984), which features a small-town waitress who is writing a book on "service." DM

371 Cisneros, Sandra. *The House on Mango Street*. Random 1991, $9.00 (0-679-73477-5). 128pp. Fiction.

Awarded the Before Columbus Foundation American Book Award for 1985, this is Cisneros's first work of fiction. The selection of vignettes that make up the novel are the thoughts of a young girl—the author's alter ego—as she comes of age in the barrios of Chicago. In the first selection, "The House on Mango Street," Esperanza speaks of arriving at the family's new house and describes her disappointments concerning what a house should be and look like. Other selections in the novel introduce the reader to other residents of Mango Street—Lucy, the Texas girl who smells like corn, and Rachel and Sally, who are good friends. In observing life in the neighborhood, Esperanza witnesses poverty, racism, and relationships shattered by abuse. The strength she gathers from positive family relationships allows her to overcome the negative impact of her environment and use it to her advantage in her writing. In "Mango Says Goodbye Sometimes," the last story in the book,

Esperanza explains how using her imagination to tell stories takes her away from the neighborhood. Recognizing that she is too strong to be held there much longer, she acknowledges that her writing will be her way of remembering to come back for those who cannot leave Mango Street. DM

372 Cisneros, Sandra. ***Woman Hollering Creek and Other Stories***. Random 1991, $20.50 (0-394-57654-3); $10.00 (0-679-73856-8). 165pp. Fiction.

This collection of vignettes and short stories introduces the reader to women of various ages and tells about their lives in the border region of Texas and Mexico. The book is divided into three parts. In the first, the stories are told through the voices of very young girls. Esperanza, the narrator of the author's first novel, *The House on Mango Street (see main entry)*, reminisces about the warm feelings of childhood friendship in "My Lucy Friend Who Smells Like Corn." In "Eleven," Rachel wishes she were old enough to dispute ownership of an ugly red sweater. "Barbie-Q" is a bittersweet selection about two girls who dream of possessing expensive toys like the ones advertised on television, but they must settle for dolls bought only "slightly" damaged at a fire sale.

In the second and third parts of the book, the women are older. Seduced by the first man she falls in love with, the young woman in "One Holy Night" must confront the truth about his deception. In "Woman Hollering Creek," Cleofilas arrives in Texas as a new bride. Her expectations concerning love and marriage—all based on the soap operas she watches faithfully—are challenged as she is confronted by the realities of life in a male-dominated society. The stories in this volume portray the hopes and expectations of Chicana women in Texas, but they could be about Hispanic women anywhere. The *New York Times* selected this work as a Noteworthy Book for 1991. DM

373 Corpi, Lucha. ***Eulogy for a Brown Angel***. Arte Público 1992, $17.95 (1-55885-050-3). 190pp. Fiction.

On August 29, 1970, during the disturbances following the National Chicano Moratorium, Gloria Damasco, Chicana activist, and her friend Luísa discover the body of a murdered child: Michael Cisneros, a member of a wealthy and powerful California family. Matthew Kenton, the detective assigned to the case, is highly suspicious of the only witness to come forth: Mando, a young Chicano gang member. Mando supplies Gloria with a crumpled newspaper article found at the scene of the crime, but he becomes the second person to fall victim to the murderer. When evidence shows Michael's death cannot be gang-related, the police shift the focus of their investigation to Joel Galeanos, a freelance journalist who lives near the crime scene. Developing a close relationship with the Cisneros family and using deductive as well as clairvoyant abilities, Gloria is a tenacious sleuth, discovering the perpetrator and the motive for the crime. Corpi effectively uses the streets of the East Los Angeles barrio and the activism of Chicano Movement of the 1970s as backdrops for this novel. Her use of the Mexican legend "La Llorona" in characterizing those involved in the novel's conclusion is an interesting technique in this feminist mystery. DM

374 Fernández, Roberta. ***Intaglio: A Novel in Six Stories***. Arte Público 1990, $9.50 (1-55885-016-3). 160pp. Fiction.

Thirteen-year-old Nenita keeps an album of her family's history and through it tells the story of six women living in the Rio Grande Valley of Texas in the early part of the twentieth century. These women—Nenita's ancestors and friends—journey across the river, from Mexico to the United States and back again, telling of what they see and experience. Through stories told by Zulema, young Nenita hears of the exciting events of the Mexican Revolution. The sisters Amanda and Leonor are steeped in spirituality. Leonor reads fortune-telling cards, and Amanda uses herbs and other potions to communicate with the dead. Andrea, the ballerina, sends postcards from every place she performs, and Nenita uses the postcards to tell the story of Andrea's life. The other characters include Filomena, who migrated to the United States in search of work and never returned, and Nenita's young friend Esmeralda. This charming first novel explores a South Texas community from a teenager's point of view and in the process presents a group of remarkable and memorable Latina women.   LML

375 Fernández, Roberto. ***Raining Backwards***. Intro. by David Kirby. Arte Público 1988, $9.50 (0-934770-79-4). 224pp. Fiction.

Cuban-born author Fernández offers a series of vignettes concerning a large Cuban exile family living in Miami in the 1970s. As the introduction by David Kirby points out, this "is not a set of interrelated stories but a novel that develops in cycles." At the center is the Rodríguez family, María de los Angeles (known as "Mima"); her husband, Jacinto; their eldest son, Keith, who is arrested for dealing cocaine and trafficking in stolen property and is suspected of being a pro-Castro revolutionary; their younger son, Joaquin, known as Quinn; and their daughter, Connie, who is in love with the American boy Bill Cloonan. Keith escapes from jail and allegedly leads a guerrilla movement in the Everglades. Connie dies in a freak accident and then sends letters from the hereafter. Quinn, his mother's favorite, becomes Pope, and Mima leaves her business to join him in Rome. Interspersed with the Rodríguez family saga are tales involving other Cuban exiles—for example, an older woman who seduces her delivery boy and then accuses him of rape—and excerpts from newspaper stories and radio broadcasts. The result is a fascinating postmodernist work. Though it will not appeal to everyone, *Raining Backwards* is the work of a unique voice in Cuban-American literature.   LML

376 Gallardo, Edward. ***Simpson Street and Other Plays***. Intro. by John Antush. Arte Público 1990, $11.00 (1-55885-004-X). 225pp. Drama.

The work of Puerto Rican playwright Edward Gallardo is well represented in this collection of three plays, each exploring family relationships among Puerto Ricans and other Latinos in New York.

The title play is about Lucy Rodríguez; her daughter, Angela; her various women friends; and her son, Michael, who has just been released from a mental institution. Angela has left her husband. As Lucy, Angela, and the friends prepare for a celebration, they argue and hurt each other; Michael—the former mental patient—is clearly the voice of sanity. Even more pessimistic in its view of the family in the United States is *Waltz on a Merry-Go-Round*, which is set in upstate New York and which portrays the reunion of five

Puerto Rican sisters on the anniversary of the death of one sister's husband, who was an Anglo. The play also explores the relationship between a middle-class Puerto Rican family and the poor whites who work for them. The final play, *Women Without Men*, is set in New York City during World War II; most of the characters have husbands who were or are in the military. The focus of the play is the love-hate relationship between Orquidea Juventud and her daughter, Soledad, who longs to break the cycle of abuse that defined her childhood. A useful introduction by John Antush rounds out this volume.　　LML

377　García, Cristina. ***Dreaming in Cuban***. Knopf 1992, $19.50 (0-679-40883-5); Ballantine $10.00 (0-345-38143-2). 256pp. Fiction.

The 1959 triumph of Fidel Castro divides the middle-class del Pino family. Until the day she commits suicide, Celia remains loyal to the revolution, to the point of becoming a neighborhood magistrate. Her husband, Jorge, supports the revolution at first but quickly becomes disillusioned, although he does not leave the country until his cancer gets worse and he must seek medical treatment in New York. Lourdes, his eldest child, leaves Cuba with her husband, Rufino, shortly after she is raped by a revolutionary soldier. She eventually becomes a successful small businesswoman and has a stormy relationship with her rebellious daughter, Pilar. Celia and Jorge's second daughter, Felicia, struggles against madness. Their only son, Javier, takes a job in Czechoslovakia, returning to Cuba only when he, too, is dying. Throughout the novel, the ghost of Jorge appears to the del Pino women and becomes a source of strength, especially for Lourdes. In the climax, Lourdes and Pilar return to Cuba and experience the chaos of the Mariel boatlift, an event that ultimately leads Lourdes to betray her mother.

García's first novel offers a number of memorable female characters who bring to life the conflicts, contributions, and tragedies of the Cuban Revolution. Also well-portrayed are the intergenerational conflicts between the Cuban exiles in the United States and their children, who have embraced the values and culture of their new land.　　LML

378　García, Lionel. ***Leaving Home***. Arte Público 1985. o.p. Fiction.

Adolfo Arguelles was once a baseball player in Mexico. Although he still fancies himself a notorious ladies' man, he now lives in poverty in southern California, dependent on the generosity of others. Through him, García tells the story of several families. For two years Adolfo has lived with the widow María and her family—her eldest daughter, Young María (who moved away and married an Anglo), her sons Arnoldo and Adam, and her youngest daughter, the pretty and sweet Carmen. Leaving María in search of his old mistress, who is the mother of his son, Adolfo boards briefly with Antonia, who cheats him, and then moves into a broken-down shack with Manuel García, an alcoholic professor who once taught school in Mexico. During this time, the teenage Carmen also moves out. Working in a movie theater, she contracts tuberculosis; she is sent to a state sanitarium, where she recovers and matures into a woman who is strong because she has faced death. When World War II breaks out, Arnoldo, María's son, goes off to fight, but he is killed, as is Young María's husband, Eddie. After years of drifting, Adolfo returns to comfort María, and she takes him in.

Leaving Home, now out of print, is García's first novel. Perhaps his best work is the gritty and compelling *Hardscrub* (Arte Público, 1989), about a poor white family in Texas. The family is falling apart because of the father's drinking, but the youngest son struggles to make a better life for himself.   LML

379   Goldman, Francisco. ***The Long Night of White Chickens***. Grove 1992, $21.95 (0-87113-509-4); $12.00 (0-87113-541-8). 450pp. Fiction.

When five-year-old Roger Graetz contracts tuberculosis while staying with his mother's family in Guatemala City, Abuela sends an orphan to the United States to serve as the family maid. Roger's father—a Jew born in the United States who has settled with his upper-class Guatemalan wife and son in a lower middle class suburb in Boston—unofficially adopts the thirteen-year-old girl, Flor de Mayo Puac, and sends her to school. She eventually graduates from Wellesley and returns to Guatemala to work with orphans. There she is murdered under suspicious circumstances. When the Guatemalan newspapers allege that she was part of a baby-selling scheme, Roger, now twenty-five years old, returns to Guatemala to find the truth. He is assisted by an old friend, Luís Moya, a Guatemalan journalist who has recently run afoul of the military regime. Together, they remember Flor's often secret life (and Moya's brief affair with her) and try to understand the country that gave birth to her and killed her.

Goldman's first novel portrays a protagonist growing up in a bicultural family, in a community where no one except his beloved "sister" comes close to sharing his heritage and experiences. The attempt to return to one's country of origin to make sense of it, as well as the dangers of doing so, are important themes of this work.   LML

380   González, Genaro. ***Rainbow's End***. Arte Público 1988, $9.50 (0-934770-81-6). 200pp. Fiction.

Heraclio Cavazos is forced to leave Mexico after unsuccessfully attempting to organize laborers in his village. Daring the raging floodwaters of the Rio Bravo, he enters the United States illegally. Fatigued by the difficult journey, he envisions the International Bridge spanning the Mexican-U.S. border as a pastel-colored rainbow that leads to a better way of life.

This novel traces the lives of Heraclio and two generations of his family as they migrate through the fields of the Rio Grande Valley and assume roles as drug dealers and pushers in pursuit of their piece of the American pie. The family's evolution reflects life in the border region, portraying the plight of newly arrived immigrants, laborers toiling for miserly wages, brushes with a *curandera* (a folk healer or sorceress), family relationships, and love. Throughout the novel, Don Heraclio witnesses their struggle and adds biting commentary to the plight. His dreams and their outcome are ultimately not much different from those of his offspring.

Genaro González is also the author of *Only Sons* (Arte Público, 1991), a novel depicting the relationships and differences between generations of males within a Hispanic family.   DM

381   González, Ray, ed. ***Mirrors Beneath the Earth: Short Fiction by Chicano Writers***. Curbstone 1992, $13.95 (1-880684-02-0). 336pp. Fiction.

Thirty-one Chicano writers offer their short fiction in this anthology. Most of the writers whose works are contained in *Cuentos Chicanos (see main entry)* also appear here, but there are a number of young writers who have emerged since the mid-1980s, among them Sandra Cisneros, Leroy V. Quintana, Luís J. Rodríguez, Lucha Corpi, Benjamin Alire Sáenz, and Luís Alberto Urrea.

Some new themes are introduced as well. Sáenz's story "Alligator Park," for instance, presents the violence in El Salvador through the eyes of a Mexican-American lawyer who tries to prevent the deportation of a fifteen-year-old Salvadoran refugee boy caught between the government and the guerrillas. Rodríguez's story "Sometimes You Dance with a Watermelon" is one of several that portray the urban immigrant experience. Death and the supernatural are dominant elements in many of the stories; among the most harrowing is Corpi's "Insidious Disease," which describes the narrator's discovery of a dead child in the aftermath of a riot. Other stories are humorous: Mary Helen Ponce's "The Marijuana Party" describes three middle-aged women getting high on a joint left behind by a teenage visitor. This collection is highly recommended not only for the variety of experiences and styles contained within but also for the rich quality of so many of the contributions.

LML

382 Hijuelos, Oscar. ***The Mambo Kings Play Songs of Love***. Farrar 1989, $18.95 (0-374-20125-0); HarperCollins $12.00 (0-06-097327-7). 384pp. Fiction.

Winner of the Pulitzer Prize, this novel introduces the brothers Cesar and Nestor Castillo, who come to New York City from Cuba's Oriente Province in 1949 to make their career as musicians. Nestor, the sensitive younger brother, has just escaped a disastrous love affair. He will rewrite the song of his lost love twenty-two times, and it will become a hit that the brothers play on the *I Love Lucy* show, the high point of their career. Along with triumph comes great sadness, as Nestor dies shortly thereafter in an auto accident, leaving a widow and two young children. Without his talented younger brother, Cesar struggles to rebuild his band, the Mambo Kings, but womanizing, alcoholism, and several failed business ventures leave him alone and penniless, drinking himself to death in a Harlem hotel room as he recalls his past glory. Nephew Eugenio emerges to tell the story of his father's tragic gift, his uncle's love, and five decades of Cuban Americans who have made New York their home.

Hijuelos is also the author of *The Fourteen Sisters of Emilio Montez O'Brien* (Farrar, 1993), the story of a large family of Cuban-Irish heritage living in rural Pennsylvania, the progression of the generations, and the ways in which each member comes to terms with multiple cultures and experiences. LML

383 Hijuelos, Oscar. ***Our House in the Last World***. Repr. of 1983 ed. Persea Books 1991, $18.95 (0-89255-069-4); $7.95 (0-89255-165-8). 236pp. Fiction.

In his first novel, Hijuelos focuses on the Santinio family. In 1943 Alejo and Mercedes leave their rural village near Holguín, Cuba, to escape limited opportunities and to reunite with Alejo's older sister. Moving to the United States brings pain as well as possibilities. Their sons Horacio and Hector are born in their parents' adopted land. Alejo squanders his money as fast as he can earn it, and Mercedes quarrels with another of Alejo's sisters. Mercedes and the boys return to Cuba, but Hector, two years old, falls deathly ill from a "Cuban illness." He spends a year recovering in a Connecticut hospital, where he forgets his Spanish. Hijuelos chronicles the two boys' maturation and their father's decline, as overeating and alcohol abuse take their toll. Family strife and love are intertwined in the lives of these unique and vividly drawn characters. The author gives readers a vivid sense of a life in the Cuban-American community before Castro's rise and the interactions between Cuban-Americans and Puerto Ricans who made their home in Harlem in the 1950s.

LML

384   Hinojosa, Rolando. *Dear Rafe*. Arte Público 1985, $8.50 (0-934770-38-7). 136pp. Fiction.

Part of Hinojosa's Klail City Death Trip series, this book is in two parts. The first is a series of letters from Jehu Malacara to his cousin (and Hinojosa's alterego) Rafe Buenrostro. The letters reveal the intrigues of Jehu, a banker in the fictional Klail City in the lower Rio Grande Valley of Texas. The novel is rich with the humor that colors the lives of the local inhabitants. Even the surnames of the cousins are humorous; *Malacara* in Spanish means "bad face," and *Buenrostro* means "good face." The second part of the book, narrated by P. Galindo, is a series of interviews with local residents who are investigating Jehu's unexplained departure from his job at the Klail City Savings and Loan. The local residents are more than ready to share their gossip and opinions, particularly in discussing the Jehu's deeds and misdeeds.

Hinojosa is a prolific novelist who sets most of his works in Klail City and who uses the same recurring group of characters. The series began with *Klail City* (Arte Público, 1986), originally published in Spanish in 1976. Other works in the series are *Claros Varones de Belken—Fair Gentlemen of Belken County* (Bilingual Press/Editorial Bilingue, 1986), *Partners in Crime* (Arte Público, 1985), and *Becky and Her Friends* (Arte Público, 1993). Hinojosa has also written an English-language version of Tomás Rivera's classic . . . *Y No Se lo Tragó la Tierra*, titled *This Migrant Earth* (Arte Público, 1986). He explores relations between wealthy ranchers and their Mexican-American workers in *Rites and Witnesses* (Arte Público, 1989).

DM

385   Huerta, Jorge A., ed. *Necessary Theater: Six Plays about the Chicano Experience*. Arte Público 1989, $17.00 (0-934770-95-6). 368pp. Drama.

This book features six notable plays written in the 1960s, 1970s, and 1980s that focus upon the experiences of Mexican Americans. All are written by Latino playwrights, though not necessarily by Mexican Americans. The earliest work in the volume is Luís Valdez's first major play, *The Shrunken Head of Pancho Villa*. Combining real and surreal elements, this play explores the role of Mexican history and culture in the development of a Chicano identity. Mexican traditions, both indigenous and Catholic, are also at the heart of *Guadalupe*, written by the Teatro de la Esperanza, a group influenced by Valdez and his Teatro Campesino. The same theater group has also contributed the play *La Victima* to this volume. Judith and Severo Perez's *Soldierboy* focuses on a Mexican-American family adjusting to the return of a son from World War II and that son's efforts to come to terms with the war and with the death of his best friend on the battlefield. *Latina*, by Milcha Sanchez-Scott and Jeremy Blahnik, examines the lives and humiliations faced by undocumented women working as maids in southern California. Arthur Giron's *Money* looks at the politics involved in grants from foundations; Giron explores how Chicano and other arts activists have been co-opted by the system.

Huerta's collection is strengthened by a general introduction. There is also a useful introduction to each play and a biographical sketch of each playwright.   LML

386 Kanellos, Nicolás, ed. *Short Fiction by Hispanic Writers of the United States*. Arte Público 1993, $15.00 (1-55885-044-9). 256pp. Fiction.

Kanellos, noted author and director of Arte Público Press, has assembled a collection of short fiction representative of the Hispanic experience in the United States. The introduction explains that the prevalence of short fiction in Hispanic literature is in large part a result of the oral traditions maintained and handed down across the generations. Works by twenty-one celebrated Mexican-American, Cuban-American, and Puerto Rican authors present varied and revealing perspectives on life and culture. All of the material in this anthology has appeared in books published by Arte Público Press.

Among the works included are "Too Much His Father's Son," a chapter from Genaro González's *Only Sons*, about the intergenerational relationships of men in a family; Judith Ortiz Cofer's "Silent Dancing," about the author's bicultural childhood; and a chapter from *Rain of Gold (see main entry)*, Victor Villaseñor's personal family narrative. Other contributors include Lucha Corpi, Rolando Hinojosa, Max Martínez, Margarita Mondrus Engle, Alejandro Morales, Elías Miguel Muñoz, Virgil Suárez, Sabine Ulibarrí, and Helena María Viramontes. All selections are prefaced by brief sketches of the authors and of their major works. The quality of authors in this anthology make it suitable for any Hispanic literary collection.   DM

387 Laviera, Tato. *AmeRican*. Intro. by Wolfgang Binder. Arte Público 1984, $7.00 (0-934770-31-X). 80pp. Poetry.

Puerto Rican poet Laviera offers a volume of interconnected poems that explore America's ethnic heritage. In a style reminiscent of the Afro-Cuban poet Nicolás Guillén, he describes the various groups that have made the Americas (particularly the United States) their home and focuses more directly upon the experiences of his fellow Puerto Ricans. The triple heritage of Puerto Rico—Indian, African, and Spanish—figures prominently, as does the politics of *independencia*. Laviera, who has lived much of his life in New York City, captures the essence of the Nuyorican experience, primarily through his use of language. Some of the poems are entirely in English and others entirely in Spanish; many of them combine the two languages to create multiple meanings and new ways of experiencing language itself. Several of the poems are single sentences—polysyllabic statements, each line a discrete, staccato syllable. An introduction by German literary critic Wolfgang Binder serves as a useful guidepost to Laviera's work, placing it in the context of both Caribbean and Nuyorican literature.

Other poetic works by Laviera include *La Carreta Made a U-turn* (Arte Público, 1992), which is organized around the themes of urban life and Puerto Rican music and culture; *Enclave* (Arte Público, 1985), which explores Nuyorican identity; and *Mainstream Ethics* (Arte Público, 1988), which, like *AmeRican*, addresses the place of Latino peoples within U.S. society.   LML

388 López, Tiffany A., ed. *Growing Up Chicana/o: An Anthology*. Frwd. by Rudolfo Anaya. Morrow 1993, $20.00 (0-688-11467-9); Avon $11.00 (0-380-72419-7). 272pp. Fiction.

In his introduction to this anthology, Rudolfo Anaya defines *Chicano* as a word created by Mexican-American activists in the 1960s to add new meaning and strength to their identity and to distinguish themselves culturally, not only from Anglos, but also from other groups traditionally identified as Latino. The twenty Chicana and Chicano authors represented in this book bring their unique perspective to these stories, which deal primarily with the coming of age.

Boundaries created in childhood by culture, religion, gender, and family form the historical context for the stories in the first of four divisions, "La Historia: Journeys in the Borderlands." The section titled "From the Veins of Los Abuelos" presents writings that emphasize the importance of elders and family relationships in Chicano culture. Learning experiences are the theme of the selections in the third part, "La Tierra y la Escuela: From Where We Learn." "Passages: We Who Are Not as Others" includes stories whose focus is the rites of passage.

Introductory sketches give glimpses into each author's literary philosophy. Among the authors represented are Alicia Gaspar de Alba, Ron Arias, Olivia Castellano, Louie the Foot González, Gerald Haslam, Mary Helen Ponce, Thelma Reyna, Alberto Alvaro Ríos, Orlando Romero, Marta Salinas, Helena María Viramontes, and Rosa Elena Yzquierdo.   DM

389 Martínez, Max. *The Adventures of the Chicano Kid and Other Stories*. Arte Público 1989, $9.50 (0-934770-08-5). 200pp. Fiction.

In his first collection of short stories, Martínez reveals his gift for social satire. The title story gives a new spin to the traditional hero of the American West. The Chicano Kid, paragon of virtue and a "Macho's Macho," rides into the village of Santo Gringo to defend his sister's honor after she is raped by his despicable, Anglo arch-enemy, Alf Brisket. The humor thinly disguises Martínez's bitterness over the strained relationship between Anglos and Hispanics in the Southwest. Other selections present various versions of life in Texas, from small towns to the barrios of San Antonio and Houston. The author's themes concern the problems of racial and cultural conflict. Other works by Martínez include *Schoolland (see main entry)*, a novel about rural family life in the 1950s, and *A Red Bikini Dream*, a collection of short fiction portraying contemporary life and relationships.   DM

390 Martínez, Max. *Schoolland*. Arte Público 1988, $9.50 (0-934770-87-5). 250pp. Fiction.

This novel, by the author of the short story collection *Adventures of the Chicano Kid (see main entry)*, is told from the point of view of a boy on the verge of adolescence, the seventh of nine children in a close-knit Mexican-American family. The unnamed narrator is emotionally attached to his Grandpa, who moves in with the family after his wife dies. The parents own a small ranch in South Texas. Although they are poor, they are far from the poorest in their rural area; even lower down, economically, are the farm hands and the migrant workers whose children can only attend school for part of the year. In the eventful year covered by the novel, the boy helps his Grandpa to dig a well on their property. There is a drought that almost costs the family its ranch. The narrator loses his old girlfriend and befriends an Anglo girl. One sister gets a divorce, and another marries an enterprising immigrant from Mexico who works for the family. An older brother has to flee to San Antonio with his girlfriend, whom he has made pregnant, to avoid dishonoring the girl's family and initiating a feud. Paulie, the narrator's next-older brother, is an ill-tempered youth who quits school to work, but both he and the narrator mature as the year ends. Their beloved grandfather is declining in health at the same time. This leads to the bittersweet ending of this poetic novel that vividly portrays a family, a place, and a way of life.   LML

391 Martínez-Serros, Hugo. ***The Last Laugh and Other Stories.*** Arte Público 1988, $9.50 (0-934770-89-1). 120pp. Fiction.

In this collection of eleven mostly interrelated stories, Martínez-Serros explores life among the Mexican-American residents of South Chicago in the years between the Great Depression and the 1950s. The title story concerns the Rivera family's struggle to make ends meet. The two youngest sons, Jaime and Lazaro, work stoking the furnace in exchange for a low-rent apartment. Jaime and Lazaro appear in other stories as well, several of which deal with education and the young Mexican-American children's struggle to maintain their dignity and desire to learn despite their teachers' prejudice and low expectations. Another character who figures prominently is the rigid priest, Father Tortas, who earns the enmity of Jaime and Lazaro's father, José María Rivera. The longest and in many ways the most compelling story is "Victor and David," based on the biblical tale of Cain and Abel. The two brothers are close as children, but they begin to drift apart when David, the younger, becomes an honor student and a baseball standout. David begins speaking correct English and hanging out with rich Anglo girls from the North Shore. When Victor loans David the car he bought with his wages from working at a grocery story, David drives by and pretends not to see his brother. In an impulsive act, Victor kills David by striking him with a fast pitch as the two are practicing for David's big game.   LML

392 Méndez, Miguel. ***Pilgrims in Aztlán.*** Trans. from Spanish by David W. Foster. Bilingual Press/Editorial Bilingue 1992, $24.00 (0-927534-22-3); $14.00 (0-927534-23-1). 184pp. Fiction.

Through the eyes of an old man, Loreto Maldonado, who lives in a town on the Mexico-U.S. border, the reader sees a procession of Mexicans traveling North in search of an alternative to the grinding poverty at home. With few exceptions, the pilgrims to Aztlán—the ancient Aztec city purported to be in the southwestern United States—do not find wealth. Instead they find continued poverty, exploitation, and death.

Méndez's characters symbolize the different fates of people in the border region. Lencho, a veteran of the Revolution, watches his son die in a Mexican village, unable to afford a doctor; later he is put in jail for speaking out against the government he once supported. Other characters die of heatstroke in the Arizona fields. The parents of Frankie Perez pin their hopes for success on their assimilated son, who dies on a battlefield during World War II. Even the successful suffer in the United States. An immigrant businessman prospers by exploiting his fellow Mexicans but dies in a street crime. An Anglo couple accumulates great wealth, only to have their son become a hippie and a vagabond in Mexico. Méndez's novel, originally published in Spanish, has become a classic of Chicano literature and is a success in Mexico as well.

LML

393   Mohr, Nicholasa. *In Nueva York*. Arte Público 1988, $9.50 (0-934770-78-6). 196pp. Fiction.

Rudi's Luncheonette on the Lower East Side of New York City is the setting for these eight interrelated stories about a Puerto Rican community. Among the protagonists is Old Mary, who eagerly anticipates the arrival of William, the child she left behind in Puerto Rico forty years earlier. She imagines him to be tall and blond, like his biological father; in fact, he is a dwarf, not even four feet tall. William, however, becomes a well-liked member of the community; in "The English Lesson," he helps Rudi's shy wife from Puerto Rico adjust to life in New York. He also shows his courage in "The Robbery," a story that features Rudi and the bereaved mother of a fifteen-year-old boy whom Rudi shoots after the boy robs the luncheonette. Characters featured in other stories include Rudi's wife, Lali, who has an affair with William's brother, and a homeless old man, a former sailor who befriends a seven-year-old girl.

Mohr is best known for her novels for children and young adults. *In Nueva York* is a good choice for teens as well as adult readers; another short story anthology, *Rituals of Survival: A Woman's Portfolio* (Arte Público, 1985), is intended for a more adult audience. Her coming-of-age novel, *Nilda*, set in New York City and originally published in 1973, was reprinted by Arte Público Press in 1985. She is also the author of the noted memoir *El Bronx Remembered* (Arte Público, 1986).

LML

394   Mora, Pat. *Borders.* 2nd ed. Arte Público 1993, $7.00 (0-685-64977-6). 88pp. Poetry.

Of this writer's volumes of poetry, *Borders* is perhaps the most accessible to the broadest audience. It is recommended for high school classes because of its focus on the Latino's mixed heritage and upon Mora's observations about her own children, growing up in a bicultural middle-class family in the Midwest. The thin volume is divided into four parts. The first explores Mexican and Latino symbols and heritage; among the most moving of the poems is a tribute to Mexican-American migrant worker, scholar, and writer Tomás Rivera: "the boy from Crystal City, Texas/not a legend to be shelved/ but a man whose *abrazos* [embraces] still warm/us yet say, 'Now you.' " In the second part, Mora describes her families—the one that raised her in El Paso, Texas and the one she is raising—and reflects upon the ten years she devoted exclusively to home and family. In the third part, she explores what it means to be a woman within both the Latino and the Anglo cultures—vulnerable to cultural constraints and often abandoned in the end anyway. In the fourth part, she writes as a woman journeying out into the world to discover her own strength and the strength of other women.

Mora's other works of poetry, *Chants* (Arte Público, 1984) and *Communion* (Arte Público, 1991), are also recommended. They explore the roots, myths, and symbols of the Mexican American's triple heritage—Indian, Spanish, and Anglo—as well as the Southwestern desert landscape.   **LML**

395   Morales, Alejandro. ***The Brick People.*** 2nd ed. Arte Público 1992, $9.50 (0-934770-91-3). 320pp. Fiction.

At the turn of the nineteenth century, Mexicans fleeing the turmoil and oppression of their country's economic distress provided a readily available force of inexpensive labor for the Simons Brick Factory of Pasadena, California. This book is a fictional account based on the history of that company and its exclusive dependence on Mexican workers. Beginning in the mid-nineteenth century and spanning approximately a hundred years, the narrative traces the contributions of Mexican immigrants to the expansion and growth of California. It follows the lives of two families as they struggle to survive and provide for future generations. A critical point in the story involves the laborers' attempts to improve the conditions at the factory by organizing a union.

Morales's account of this period in California history is accurate and illuminating, showing how actual events affected the families in different ways.   **DM**

396   Morales, Alejandro. ***The Rag Doll Plagues.*** Arte Público 1992, $17.95 (1-55885-036-8); $9.50 (1-55885-104-6). 200pp. Fiction.

In 1788, a plague decimates the inhabitants of the New World's most populous colony, Mexico City. Don Gregorio, Royal Physician, arrives from Spain to use his skills and knowledge to put an end to the fatal illness. His presence in Book I of the novel initiates a cycle of struggle against unknown forces that will be repeated by his descendants. Book II is set in the present-day barrio of Santa Ana, California. There a young Chicano physician, Dr. Gregorio, tries to understand and ease the suffering of his patients. He watches helplessly as the woman he loves dies from AIDS. Book III, set in the future, has as its backdrop the technocracy called Lamex, a confederation of the Southwestern United States and Mexico. In that very structured society, the grandson of Dr. Gregorio discovers that the blood of Mexican natives has adapted to the virulently polluted atmosphere and can be used to inoculate people against the many plagues that are laying waste to civilization.

Throughout the novel, all three physicians must balance their professional goals with their personal desires. Ultimately they realize that their most significant sacrifice is love.   **DM**

397   Morton, Carlos. ***The Many Deaths of Danny Rosales, and Other Plays.*** Arte Público 1983, $11.00 (0-934770-16-6). 160pp. Drama.

One of the principal works of Chicano theater in the 1970s and early 1980s, *The Many Deaths of Danny Rosales* describes the injustices faced by Chicanos in Texas. Shifting between the present and the past, the play presents the trial of Sheriff Fred Hall, accused of the cold-blooded murder of twenty-six-year-old Rosales. Flashbacks show Rosales's arrest late at night, his beating by police in front of his wife, his premeditated murder by Hall and Hall's future son-in-law, the complicity of Hall's wife in driving the body hundreds of miles away for burial, and the struggle of Hall's daughter, Debbie, as she wrestles with her conscience and eventually reveals the crime and confesses to her own role in disposing of the body. Despite Debbie's testimony, the all-white jury convicts Hall only on minor charges. The playwright shows how Danny Rosales died five times: he was born poor, deprived of an education, murdered by officers of the law, buried five hundred miles away, and finally denied justice in the Texas courts.

The other plays in the collection are shorter and less well developed, but *The Many Deaths of Danny Rosales* is a poignant, tautly written portrayal of injustice.   LML

398   Muñoz, Ellás Miguel. ***The Greatest Performance***. Arte Público 1991, $9.50 (1-55885-038-4). 152pp. Fiction.

Rosa Rodríguez is the older of two children, the only daughter of a well-to-do Cuban family. When the Revolution comes, the parents send her and her brother to Spain to keep her brother from being conscripted into Castro's army. In the cold, unhappy months she spends there (where she must fight off the advances of the "uncle" who serves as her guardian), she remembers her classmates in Cuba—Maritza, the dedicated Communist girl upon whom Rosa has a crush, and the shy boy Marito, already identified as a *pájaro*, a homosexual. Soon afterward, her parents leave Cuba for the United States, and the family is reunited; Rosa eventually goes to college and graduate school and becomes a professor of Spanish. She hides her lesbianism from her parents, who fret over her advancing age and the fact that she has not married. Marito, too, ends up in the United States with his family, but not before his father is arrested and he is "deflowered" by a man who exploits effeminate boys. When his father discovers his homosexuality, Marito is expelled from the house; his mother ends up in an insane asylum. Marito becomes a successful artist and experiences sexual liberation in New York and San Francisco, where he and Rosa reunite. Their joy is cut short, however, by the AIDS epidemic. Muñoz's novel is a compelling portrait of two characters—outlaws in their native country and tragically deprived of fulfillment in their adopted land of freedom.   LML

399   Olivares, Julian, ed. ***Decade II: A Twentieth Anniversary Anthology***. Arte Público 1993, $12.00 (1-55885-062-7). 256pp. Fiction.

The 1973 inaugural issue of *Revista Chicano Riqueña* began a history of excellence in Hispanic literature. To reflect more accurately the increasing cultural diversity of its contributors, the publication changed its name to *The Americas Review* in 1986. Today, it remains the most acclaimed Hispanic literary publication in the United States. Fourteen writers whose works appeared in the first-anniversary edition, *A Decade of Hispanic Literature: An Anniversary Anthology*, are also featured in this collection of prose and poetry: Jimmy Santiago Baca, Nash Candelaria, Lorna Dee Cervantes, Lucha Corpi, Sandra María Esteves, Roberta Fernández, Angela de Hoyos, Tato Laviera, Leo Romero, Luís Omar Salinas, Ricardo Sánchez, Rosaura Sánchez, Ed Vega, and Evangelina Vigil-Piñón. The newer artists in the balance of the collection are represented by Elías Miguel Muñoz, Pat Mora, Alberto Ríos, and twenty-one others. Considering the caliber of authors included and the *Review*'s ability to identify emerging talent, this is an important acquisition for any Hispanic literature collection.   DM

400   Paredes, Americo. *George Washington Gómez*. Arte Público 1990, $9.50 (1-55885-012-0). 302pp. Fiction.

In 1848, after the defeat of Mexico in its war with the United States, hundreds of thousands of Mexicans living north of the Rio Grande became reluctant U.S. citizens. Many Mexican farmers and ranchers lost their lands and faced discrimination at the hands of a growing number of Anglo settlers, for whom they were obliged to work as laborers in order to survive. Others of these new citizens sought to fit into their new social and cultural environment.

Originally written in the 1930s, Paredes's classic novel features a young boy given the name George Washington by his parents—who seek accommodation with the new system—but who is called Gualinto by his beloved grandmother, who longs for the way things were. In school also, the boy is caught between two cultures because the teachers prohibit him from speaking Spanish and tell him that the Anglo way of life is superior to his own Mexican culture. At the same time, his parents struggle to keep their land and their independence in the face of widespread dispossession; ultimately, their efforts lead to threats against the entire family. Told in the child's voice, this is a gripping historical novel that will appeal to a wide audience.

Paredes is perhaps best known for his works on music and folklore, including *With a Pistol in His Hand: A Border Ballad and Its Hero* (Univ. of Texas Pr., 1958).   LML

401   Piñero, Miguel. *Short Eyes*. Intro. by Marvin F. Camillo. Farrar 1975, $10.00 (0-374-52147-6). 128pp. Drama.

This is the most famous play by Piñero, a Puerto Rican poet and playwright who began writing while incarcerated in New York's notorious Sing Sing prison in the 1970s. After its performance at the New York Shakespeare Festival in 1974, it won a number of awards, and Piñero went on to publish other poems and plays about prison life, the Nuyorican experience, and Puerto Rican identity.

Short Eyes features seven men—three Puerto Ricans, three African Americans, and the Irish-American Longshoe—who share a cell block at the House of Detention. Into their group comes Clark Davis, a nervous, middle-class white man who has been accused of child molestation. Child molesters—"short eyes" in prison slang—are held in special contempt by prisoners and guards as well; in fact, as Clark arrives, a guard says he hopes the prisoners kill him. In graphic detail, Clark confesses his sins to Juan, the oldest prisoner of the group; Juan in turn tries to persuade Ice, an African American, to treat Clark with humanity despite his heinous crime. Instinctively, however, like the animals they have become in the prison environment, the other prisoners—notably Longshoe, a substance abuser who acts tougher than all the others—stalk Clark, harass him, and kill him, then cover up the murder. This is a well-written, powerful work that considers race relations and the conditions that brutalize people in or out of prison.   LML

402   Poey, Delia, and Virgil Suárez, eds. *Iguana Dreams: New Latino Fiction*. Pref. by Oscar Hijuelos. HarperCollins 1992, $12.00 (0-06-096917-2). 376pp. Fiction.

The wife-and-husband team of Poey and Suárez have put together a sizable anthology of recent writings by Latinos. Most of the twenty-nine authors represented here have published novels or short stories, and some of the contributions are excerpts from these. This collection covers the major Latino groups—Mexican Americans, Puerto Ricans, Cuban Americans, Dominican Americans, and others. The brief introduction highlights many of the themes touched on in the stories—language and bilingualism, the attempt to develop and preserve a bicultural identity, differences among Latino cultures, the experience of political exile, religion, and family life. Although most of the stories are short, they offer glimpses of many different literary styles and can help the reader select longer, more developed works by these authors. This sampler is also a good choice for high school and introductory college and university courses.   LML

403   Ponce, Mary Helen. **Taking Control**. Arte Público 1987, $9.50 (0-934770-70-0). 128pp. Fiction.

Ponce's first published collection of short stories uses humor and irony to explore the situations of a variety of Mexican-American women. Most of the families featured are middle class. The members of the comfortable, assimilated family in "The Campout" are made aware of their distance from both Mexican and U.S. culture during their summer vacation in Mexico. In "El Marxista," the department head asks a Latina college professor to host a self-centered and surprisingly prosperous Marxist from an unnamed Latin American nation. "La Josie" features a single mother who is trying to raise her child but whose sleep is disturbed by the couple next door because of their violent arguments, which often end when the wife, Josie, leaves in the middle of the night. But when the mother calls the police, Josie and her husband accuse her of fighting with her boyfriend. Eventually, the mother moves out and marries a middle-class man, but, in an ironic twist, the man leaves her. Later, she sees Josie one day in the supermarket—still with the same man.

   Ponce portrays many types of women—young and old, poor and middle-class. Her stories help the reader understand how women—although their lives are constricted by custom or by their relationships with insensitive, abusive men—can break through expectations to liberate themselves.

                                                                           LML

404   Ponce, Mary Helen. **The Wedding**. Arte Público 1989, $9.50 (0-934770-97-2). 199pp. Fiction.

Everyone knows a wedding horror story—where everything goes wrong or the couple shouldn't have gotten married in the first place. Such a horror story lies at the heart of this humorous, bittersweet novel. Young Blanca, an eighth-grade dropout who works at a turkey-processing factory and dreams of true romance, is attracted to Sammy-the-Cricket, the toughest fighter in Los Tacones. Cricket is mean, crude, and disrespectful; the minute Blanca commits to him, he treats her like dirt. Her friends want to talk her out of marrying Cricket, but they, too, are caught up in the enthusiasm leading up to the wedding—choosing the dresses, going to showers, planning the reception. Blanca wants the biggest wedding in town, though she and Cricket, a trash collector with an eighth-grade education, can scarcely afford it. Cricket complains about the expense and tries to avoid spending money on anything but his own entertainment. On the wedding day, he is terribly hung over, and a rival gang has threatened to crash the evening dance. Other disasters include a junior bridesmaid who throws up during the service, a badly behaved ringbearer, and the bride's stomach upset that turns into something more serious. With pointed wit, Ponce captures the life and language of working-class Mexican-American teenagers who must soon face adult problems and responsibilities. LML

405 Portillo-Trambley, Estela. *Rain of Scorpions and Other Stories.* Rev. ed. Bilingual Press/Editorial Bilingue 1993, $24.00 (0-927534-28-2); $14.00 (0-927534-29-0). 208pp. Fiction.

This book, originally published in 1975 and revised for this edition, contains eight short stories and a novella, "Rain of Scorpions." This piece is set in Smeltertown, a small polluted town owned by an Anglo conglomerate, ASARCO. When the company decides to avoid lawsuits by relocating all of the residents, a character named Fito urges citizens to leave on their own to increase pressure on the Anglo bosses and embarrass them into providing better conditions. Although not much changes, the characters grow and are better able to understand that they have the capacity to create the perfect place within themselves.

Four of the other stories have a feminist motif. "Pay the Criers" is the story of proud and hard-working Refugio, who has died and left her savings to her daughter, Juana. Chucho, the shiftless son-in-law, squanders the money intended for Juana's grand funeral. "The Paris Gown" features Clotilde, who refuses to accept the dictates of the patriarchal society that has arranged her marriage to a much older man. Appearing in the nude at her engagement dinner, Clo convinces her father that she is crazy and that she must be allowed to live in Paris. In "If It Weren't for the Honeysuckle . . . ," Beatriz is caught up in the turmoil of an abusive relationship. By deciding to murder her husband, she achieves liberation and restores the harmony she once enjoyed. "The Burning" is about the conflicted relationship between Leila, a *cuandera* (folk healer), and the women of the nearby village.

The remaining stories are all new to this edition. "Leaves," "Looking for God," and "Village" involve disillusionment, life's cruelties, and the perseverance of the human spirit. "La Yonfatayn" is a light-hearted glimpse into the romantic intrigues of a young widow who identifies with the movie actress Joan Fontaine. DM

406 Portillo-Trambley, Estela. *Trini.* Bilingual Press/Editorial Bilingue 1986, $22.00 (0-916950-61-1); $14.00 (0-916950-62-X). 248pp. Fiction.

Trini, a thirteen-year-old Tarahumara Indian girl living in northern Mexico, witnesses the death of her mother in childbirth. Her widowed father, a miner, hires the Indian Sabochi, and later a young man named Tonio, to help him take care of the house and the children. Later, Tia Pancha comes, and the family makes a dangerous journey across the mountains, the river, and Indian country in search of work. Throughout these ordeals, young Trini maintains her love for Sabochi. Her love for Tonio grows as well, especially after he leaves to make his own life. Trini endures great tragedies—the illness of her father, her violent rape by a pimp, the death of the baby that was born of the rape, and a rocky marriage to Tonio—but she is also blessed with great determination and, ultimately, good fortune. Crossing into the United States to give birth to her second child (fathered by Sabochi when they were trapped in a freak snowstorm), she befriends a dying hermit who gives her a parcel of land—her life's dream—in exchange for her friendship and for her promise to carry out his cremation. This gripping novel is filled with memorable and well-drawn characters. Portillo-Trambley explores aspects of Tarahumara spirituality and its relation to Catholic beliefs and values, both of which help Trini to survive in a harsh world. LML

407 Rechy, John. *City of Night.* Grove 1988, $10.95 (0-8021-3083-6). 400pp. Fiction.

Though it does not deal with ethnic issues as such, Rechy's book is considered one of the classics of Chicano literature. The son of a Scottish father and a Mexican mother, Rechy has written several works about the urban underlife, including *Bodies and Souls* (Carroll & Graf, 1983). In *City of Night*, the unnamed narrator grows up in poverty in El Paso, remembering how his father—a talented Mexican musician who caved in to alcohol and despair in the United States—fondled him as a child and encouraged his drinking buddies to do so as well. After his father dies, and following his stint in the Army, the "youngman" travels to New York City, Los Angeles, San Francisco, Chicago, and New Orleans, working as a male hustler and meeting a variety of characters who, in some way or another, seem to presage his own fate. In this gripping novel, Rechy describes the life cycle of the male hustler: Until the age of thirty, he is attractive and pursued; if he plays it right, he can command large sums of money from old, burned-out men who have no other way of finding love. There are the unlucky ones, like Skipper, an alcoholic whose lover, a Hollywood director, has replaced him with younger, more attractive men; Skipper now tells of his humiliation and turns tricks for drinks and a few dollars. Other characters are equally memorable in this early work that has inspired other explorations of the gay urban milieu. LML

408 Rivera, Tomás. **...** ***Y No Se lo Tragó la Tierra—And the Earth Did Not Devour Him.*** 2nd ed.; Bilingual ed. Trans. from Spanish by Evangelina Vigil-Piñón. Arte Público 1991, $10.00 (0-934770-72-7). 206pp. Fiction.

This novel is one of the best-known works of Chicano fiction. Told in a series of twelve vignettes with anecdotes between them, it is the story of a year in the life of an anonymous migrant boy. Using the boy's voice and the conversations he overhears, the author depicts the plight of 1940s migrant farmworkers. Two men ponder the downfall of a "boss" responsible for the death of a child in "Los Niños No Se Aguantaron." "Es Que Duele" reveals a young man's thoughts as he transcends the disappointment of being unfairly expelled from school and worries about how his father will receive the news. Victimized by an unscrupulous Chicano couple trusted by his parents, the boy in "La Mano en la Bolsa" witnesses a murder. In the title story, a young man is angry at God for not alleviating the illness and backbreaking work that are the realities of the migrant way of life. His mother cautions him that because he lacks respect he will be swallowed by a crack in the earth. The boy, however, discovers that cursing God only makes him feel stronger. Through the remaining stories, the reader is introduced to other aspects of the migrant experience.

Originally published in Spanish, Evangelina Vigil-Piñón's excellent translation of this work is titled *. . . And the Earth Did Not Devour Him* and is available in a bilingual edition. Rolando Hinojosa has also published his rendition of this award-winning classic under the title *This Migrant Earth*.   DM

409   Rodríguez, Abraham, Jr. ***The Boy Without a Flag: Tales of the South Bronx.*** Illus. by R. W. Scholes. Milkweed 1992, $11.00 (0-915943-74-3). 115pp. Fiction.

Rodríguez's literary debut features seven short stories that describe the lives of Puerto Rican youngsters in the South Bronx. The title story portrays an intellectually gifted eleven-year-old whose militant father has told him about how the United States exploits Puerto Rico. Hoping to gain his father's admiration, the boy refuses to salute the flag at school and is sent to the principal's office. When his father is called in, the boy is disillusioned to see his father humbled by the school's authority. Several stories describe teenage girls' coming of age and the perils of early pregnancy. In "The Lotto," two best friends agonize together when both miss their periods and begin to feel sick. Dalia's mother buys her a home pregnancy test kit; her more urbane friend Elba has an appointment at the clinic. Dalia's test is negative, but Elba's is positive; the news drives the friends apart.

Despite their realistic subject matter, these are sweet tales, filled with the innocence of youth soon to be lost. While they are of interest to general readers, their subject matter and characters make them an especially good choice for high school students. Rodríguez is also the author of *Spidertown* (Viking, 1993), a novel about a teenage drug dealer in the South Bronx who attempts to call it quits.   LML

410   Romero, Leo. ***Celso.*** Arte Público 1984, $7.00 (0-934770-36-0). 80pp. Poetry.

This volume of interconnected poems features Celso, a Mexican-American Everyman who experiences, observes, and comments on life. Romero begins the volume with Celso's youth and includes a poem about his mother, who died shortly after giving birth, and about his father, whom he never met and whose disappearance led Celso to distrust the adult world. Frustrated in love, Celso becomes an alcoholic and wanders drunkenly through life, experiencing both the joys of nature's beauty and the horror of approaching death. Religious symbolism figures prominently in his story, as he imagines himself a biblical martyr or stumbles into a church, where he disrupts Mass and is rejected by those from whom he seeks help. He spends most of his life alone, despite the occasional romantic liaison or visits from drinking buddies who pass out and litter the floor of his tiny house. Nonetheless, as he feels death approaching, Celso is emotionally touched by Doña Carmela, who takes him to her house and listens to his story. Romero's poems are moving and accessible, and this coherently organized volume is a good choice for introductory literature classes on the high school and college levels.   LML

411   Salas, Floyd. ***Tattoo the Wicked Cross.*** Second Chance 1982, $22.00 (0-933256-26-4); $16.00 (0-933256-27-2). 352pp. Fiction.

In a story that takes place just after the end of World War II, fifteen-year-old Aaron D'Aragon and his best friend, Barneyway, are sent to a California reform school for fighting. The boys, who are of pure Spanish descent, find themselves at odds with several other prisoners, including the black youth Buzzer and his "Mexican" (mixed Spanish and Indian descent) pal, Rattler, who sports a tattoo of a cross on his forehead. Barneyway, who arrives first, is beaten and raped by Buzzer and his friends. When Aaron arrives, he is disgusted by his friend's passivity. Despite his small stature, Aaron struggles to survive in an environment in which the prisoners, encouraged by their guards, beat and violate one another. He knows that if he complains to prison authorities or informs on his fellow inmates, he risks being killed. Aaron allies with two white youths, Dominic and Jenson, but when Dominic is released and Jenson escapes, Aaron is left on his own to face Barneyway's tormentors—Buzzer, Rattler, and the guard Big Stoop. Hampered by his size and the fact that Barneyway will no longer fight, Aaron considers ever more deadly means to stop the attacks.

Salas, born in Colorado and descended from the original Spanish settlers of the Southwest, spent time in juvenile detention and in California reform schools. His brutally realistic novel offers a compelling portrait of a teenager caught in desperate circumstances from which there is no escape.   LML

412   Suárez, Virgil. *Latin Jazz*. Arte Público 1989, $18.95 (0-688-08475-3). 290pp. Fiction.

Hugo, a political prisoner in Castro's Cuba, and his relatives in exile in the United States tell the story of Hugo's bold escape and their reunification during the Mariel boatlift of 1980. Hugo is also searching for Lucinda, a fellow guerrilla who, like him, was imprisoned after Castro came to power and who turned against many of his former allies. Hugo's escape brings his father Esteban and his nephew Diego from Los Angeles to Miami. There Diego, a musician, confronts his former wife about her affair with the keyboard player in Diego's band. Esteban joins Diego's boss in piloting a ship to Mariel to pick up refugees. On the ship he has a brief but exciting fling with a reporter from Houston. Back home, Hugo's sister and her husband take advantage of a business opportunity as they await Hugo's arrival.

Suárez's novel is filled with suspense, humor, and joy. It is a celebration of Cuban exiles and the life they have made in the United States. Suárez, who was born in Cuba in 1962 but who left with his family four years later, is also the author of *The Cutter* (o.p., 1991), which describes the efforts of a young dissident to flee Cuba after his parents' departure five years earlier.   LML

413   Suárez, Virgil. *Welcome to the Oasis and Other Stories*. Arte Público 1992, $9.50 (1-55885-043-0). 124pp. Fiction.

This slender volume contains six stories that feature young Cuban Americans—immigrants during the 1980 Mariel boatlift or young adults who came to the United States with their parents. The title story features a *Marielito* painter hired to fix up a Los Angeles apartment building called the Oasis; he is given free rent as long as he keeps an eye on the building owner's mistress, who is having an affair with a neighbor. "A Perfect Hotspot" highlights the relationship between a man who owns an ice cream truck and his teenage son, an accomplished swimmer who would rather spend his summer working as a lifeguard. In "Full House," a son watches his father run up gambling debts, drive his older son away, and eventually get shot by a fellow gambler. The final story, "Headshots," portrays a Cuban-American college student—an athlete and the pride of his family—who takes LSD and wanders through the French Quarter of New Orleans with three friends; when his younger brother is later arrested for possession of crack cocaine, he remembers his own wild day. The stories—varied in style and situation—explore different experiences of Cuban-American youth in the late 1980s. LML

414 Torres, Omar. *Fallen Angels Sing*. Arte Público 1991, $9.50 (1-55885-024-4). 200pp. Fiction.

The protagonist of this gripping, stylistically complex novel is Miguel Saavedra, a young Cuban-American poet and musician who flees Miami when his affair with a married woman is discovered by her husband. Miguel arrives in New York and finds a job exporting washing machines to Honduras. In the process he makes contact with members of an anti-Castro terrorist organization in New Jersey. After reading a poem at an anti-Castro rally, Miguel is also approached by supporters of Castro, who invite him to Cuba to read at a rally before the leader himself. His anti-Castro colleagues urge him to go so that he can assassinate Castro. Before his departure he meets with shadowy conspirators in transvestite bars and in basements where *santería* (a mixture of Cuban and African religions) is practiced. In a possible premonition of his own fate, one of Miguel's anti-Castro contacts is shot dead. The author vividly portrays the feelings of the exile upon his return to Havana, as the taut plot moves toward its violent conclusion.

Torres, who emigrated to the United States as a child, has written several novels in Spanish. This is the first to be translated into English. LML

415 Ulibarrí, Sabine R. *Tierra Amarilla: Stories of New Mexico*. Trans. from Spanish by Thelma C. Nason; Intro. by Erlinda G. Berry. Illus. by Kercheville. Univ. of New Mexico Pr. 1993, $12.95 (0-8263-1438-4). 167pp. Fiction.

A direct descendant of the original Spanish colonizers of the territory, Sabine R. Ulibarrí was born in New Mexico and has spent much of his life there. The tales in *Tierra Amarilla* depict life in a small New Mexico town. Reminiscences of the author's youth, they affirm that the unique magic and quality of life and culture there still exist.

In one story, the narrator marvels at the grace and dignity of a wild stallion's quest for freedom. In another, the citizens enjoy attending Mass when it is celebrated by a priest who innocently—and to their delight—mangles the Spanish language. Other tales tell about a young boy who is charmed (and a bit frightened) by an old man's claim that he is the son of honeybees and about a young boy who bears his father's name and who wonders how that fact will shape his own identity.

Other books by this author continue Ulibarrí's journey into the lives and customs of Tierra Amarilla. *Mi Abuela Fumaba Puros y Otros Cuentos de Tierra Amarilla—My Grandma Smoked Cigars and Other Stories of Tierra Amarilla* (TQS, 1977) tells of witches casting spells and cursing (in the more contemporary sense of the verb); of an encounter with La Llorona, the weeping woman of legend; of pranks and mischief unleashed against nuns at a Catholic school; and of respect for a sect of religious zealots known as Penitentes. The title story of this collection is about the author's grandmother, whose custom was to smoke cigars in honor of the memory of her late husband. In his third collection, *El Condor and Other Stories* (Arte Público, 1988), Ulibarrí portrays the conflicts between Hispanic and Anglo residents of New Mexico.

The author's characters are vivid and endearing, and his stories preserve the rich folklore and traditions of Tierra Amarilla. All three bilingual publications retain the baroque flavor of the Colonial Spanish spoken in the region.

DM

416   Valdez, Luís, and El Teatro Campesino. *Luís Valdez—Early Works: Actos, Bernabé, and Pensamiento Serpentino*. Arte Público 1990, $10.00 (1-55885-003-1). 200pp. Drama.

The theater group El Teatro Campesino was formed during the 1965 Delano, California grape strike by the United Farmworkers Union. The nine *actos* (one-act plays) contained in this volume grew out of the early improvisations by the group; later plays evolved to incorporate the concerns of more-urban Chicanos. In "Las Dos Caras del Patroncito," the boss trades places with a farmworker and experiences firsthand what it is like to be in the other's position. The tables are also turned on the prospective buyer in "Los Vendidos," in which it is revealed that Honest Sancho's "used Mexican" lot is a clever setup and that Sancho is a mindless puppet. "No Saco Nada de la Escuela" is a call for Chicanos to learn about their culture and share their knowledge with each other. "Soldado Razo" explores the general dissatisfaction with the war in Vietnam through the eyes of a young Chicano and his family.

"Bernabé" is a play in seven scenes. Valdez has called the work a *mito*, or myth. It brings together realistic barrio characters and indigenous deities to tell the story of a young *campesino* (peasant) who would give up his life for his love: the Earth. "Pensamiento Serpentino" is a poetic essay that expresses Valdez's artistic vision for Teatro Campesino and that implores Chicanos to look to their ancient Indian heritage for artistic inspiration. Valdez is also the author of *Zoot Suit (see main entry).*

DM

417   Valdez, Luís. *Zoot Suit and Other Plays*. Arte Público 1992, $13.00 (1-55885-048-1). 214pp. Drama.

The most famous of Valdez's plays, *Zoot Suit* is based on the 1943 "Sleepy Lagoon Murder" trial in Los Angeles, California, which arose out of a clash between two rival Hispanic gangs. Documented as a blatant example of racial injustice, twenty-five young men, mostly Mexican-Americans, were accused, tried, and sentenced to life in prison. The first act of the play focuses on the party and feud that led to the murder, arrest, and subsequent trial of the accused. The second act finds the men serving time in prison. It explores the thoughts and feelings of Henry Reyna, the central character, who contemplates his romantic relationship with Alice Bloomfield, the young attorney from the defense committee. Although all the men are eventually released from prison, their lives will never be the same. At play's end, those who know Henry give differing stories of what eventually happened to him, leaving the audience to develop its own conclusions.

The most recognizable character to emerge from this work is Pachuco, Reyna's alter ego, dressed in a flashy zoot suit. Throughout the play Pachuco (the word means, roughly, "street kid") toys with the audience, prodding and delivering barbs in *Calo*, the pachuco patois, offering perceptive commentary as well as comic and emotional relief.   **DM**

418   Vega, Ed. ***Mendoza's Dreams.*** Arte Público 1987, $9.50 (0-934770-56-5). 200pp. Fiction.

Vega presents this series of interrelated stories told by a loquacious observer of life in the barrio, Ernesto Mendoza, creator of dreams. The wildly comic tales have one common theme: the protagonists always triumph over adversity.

The story lines are unforgettable. A nun coerces a deformed circus clown to take her virginity; a Vietnam veteran, coming home to find his fiancée grossly overweight, helps her achieve a remarkable weight loss by conducting "search and seizure" maneuvers in Central Park; a drunk is saved by a Puerto Rican angel who accompanies him on a shopping excursion on Christmas Eve; and an enterprising grocer attempts to increase profits by raising a goat in the basement of his building. Even the Three Stooges make cameo appearances in the introductory selection.

Puerto Rico–born Vega spins his fiction from his observations of life in New York City's Spanish Harlem. He is noted for his short stories and for two novels, *The Comeback* (Arte Público, 1987) and *Casualty Report* (Arte Público, 1991).   **DM**

419   Vigil, Evangelina, ed. ***Woman of Her Word: Hispanic Women Write.*** 2nd ed. Arte Público 1987, $13.00 (0-934770-27-1). 180pp. Fiction/Poetry.

This anthology presents the work of twenty-nine women writers and artists from the 1970s and 1980s. Included are works of poetry and fiction, essays, literary criticism, and art reproductions. The women represent a number of national origins and literary traditions. Prominent Mexican-American writers include Sandra Cisneros, Ana Castillo, Roberta Fernández, Helena María Viramontes, and Pat Mora. Also featured are Puerto Rican authors Judith Ortiz Cofer, Nicholasa Mohr, Sandra María Esteves, and Luz María Umpierre and other authors who trace their roots to the Dominican Republic (Esteves, who is of dual heritage), Cuba (Achy Abejas and Iliana Rivero), Costa Rica (Rima de Vallbona), and Chile (Marjorie Agosín). Several of the poems and prose works are offered in Spanish, without translation. While a few of the works present explicitly feminist themes, others describe childhood experiences and memories, indigenous symbols and traditions, or the clash of cultures in the United States. The artworks included in the anthology, representing both the Mexican-American and the Caribbean traditions, add a visual dimension to the themes expressed in the poetry and the prose, showing the diversity of images and styles that exist within Hispanic culture.   **LML**

420   Villarreal, José Antonio. ***Pocho.*** Doubleday 1994, $8.95 (0-385-06118-8). 187pp. Fiction.

Originally published in 1959, *Pocho* is considered the first major work of Mexican-American literature. The novel is set in Santa Clara, California during the Depression and features Richard Rubio, a teenager who must come to terms with the fact that as a Mexican-American he is different from many of his high school peers. He is also different from his parents, who emigrated from Mexico during the Revolution and who are struggling to survive both economically and psychologically in a new society while maintaining their traditional ways. His father dreams of his days as a colonel who rode with Pancho Villa; he feels he is entitled to have affairs while his dutiful wife stays at home. As Richard makes decisions about religion and relationships (including a romance with a married woman), his own parents' marriage is breaking up. Choosing assimilation (thereby becoming a "pocho") rather than claiming his Hispanic identity, Richard enlists in the military to fight in World War II.

Villarreal's coming-of-age novel vividly evokes the Depression-era California community, a mixture of many cultures. He also conveys the experiences both of immigrants who cling to their original culture and of their children who eagerly embrace the new country. Later novels by Villarreal include *The Fifth Horseman* (Bilingual Press/Editorial Bilingue, 1984), which is set in Mexico, and *Clemente Chacon* (Bilingual Press/Editorial Bilingue, 1984), which portrays a Chicano businessman coming to terms with his past.   LML

421   Villaseñor, Victor. *Macho!* Repr. of 1973 ed. Arte Público 1991, $9.50 (1-55885-027-9). 236pp. Fiction.

During the late 1950s and early 1960s the U.S. government, responding to the cry of agribusiness for cheap labor, increased the number of Mexican immigrants allowed to enter the country under the Bracero Program. Roberto García, a Tarascan Indian from the mountain region of Michoacan, Mexico, is influenced by the *Norteños* (residents of northern Mexico) and their tales of opportunities across the border in the United States. Befriended by Juan Aguilar, an experienced *bracero* (migrant agricultural worker), Roberto journeys north to seek wealth in the produce fields of California. Unable to secure legal entry, both decide to cross the border *a la brava*—the brave way. Enduring many hardships, including capture by federal immigration agents, accidental poisoning, and being abandoned by *coyotes* (smugglers), the men succeed in finding employment. Efforts by the United Farmworkers Union to gain better working conditions, salaries, and living quarters for migrant workers serves as a background for the novel.

Victor Villaseñor is also the author of *Rain of Gold (see main entry)*, an autobiographical bestseller that chronicles his family's migration from Mexico to California.   DM

422   Viramontes, Helena María. *The Moths and Other Stories*. Arte Público 1990, $9.00 (0-934770-40-9). 120pp. Fiction.

Society's roles and its expectations of Latina women are examined in this collection of eight short stories. Most of the characters struggle to cope with the rigid standards imposed upon them by their culture and by the male authority figures in their lives, usually fathers or husbands. In several stories, the Catholic church is a factor in the oppression of women. The young woman in "The Moths" is beaten by her father because she is disrespectful and rebellious. In "Growing," Naomi struggles to understand why her adolescence has changed her place in society, while in "Birthday" Alice agonizes over the decision to abort a pregnancy. The women in "The Broken Web," "The Long Reconciliation," and "Snapshots" face the cultural demands placed on them by marriage. The protagonists are mostly Chicanas, although one selection, "Caribboo Cafe," portrays a Salvadoran woman who has lost a child to the political turmoil in Central America. The characters intuitively know that something is wrong in their lives, yet they struggle to identify the problem. The women in Viramontes's stories are persistent in attempting to find solutions to their dilemmas, however high the cost of their attempts at independence.   DM

NONFICTION

423   Bean, Frank D., and Marta Tienda. ***The Hispanic Population of the United States***. Illus. Russell Sage Foundation 1988, $49.95 (0-87154-104-1); $18.95 (0-87154-105-X). 480pp. Nonfiction.

Sociologists Bean and Tienda use the 1980 U.S. Census and other publicly available demographic data to provide an overview of the state of the Hispanic population. Among the topics covered are vital statistics, marriage and the family, education, labor force participation, income, and wealth. The authors offer useful information on distinct Hispanic groups—Mexican Americans, Puerto Ricans, Cuban Americans, and residents who trace their origins to other places in the Caribbean and Central and South America. They also discuss the differences between U.S.-born Hispanics and those born outside the mainland United States, thus providing the reader with an analysis of general issues related to immigration and assimilation. The text is clearly written, and the study benefits from a variety of useful and easy-to-read maps, graphs, and charts. Although much has changed since the mid-1980s and the book is in need of updating, it is a solid introduction to the issues themselves and to the three largest Hispanic groups in the United States.   LML

424   Bruce-Novoa, Juan D. ***Chicano Authors: Inquiry by Interview***. Books on Demand 1980, $79.10 (0-685-23398-7). 304pp. Essays.

In the late 1970s, professor of Chicano literature Juan D. Bruce-Novoa embarked upon a project to interview by mail and telephone all of the major authors in the first generation of twentieth-century Chicano writing. Although some authors are missing due to death or unwillingness to participate, this book contains revealing interviews with fourteen well-known authors, including Rudolfo Anaya, Rolando Hinojosa, Tomás Rivera, Tino Villanueva, Estela Portillo, and Ron Arias. These writers discuss their backgrounds and the personal experiences that led them to write, their encounters with the publishing world, major themes in their writing, their perceived role as writers within the Chicano community, and the place of Chicano literature within the larger body of American literature. Some of the authors reflect upon the place of the Spanish language in their work, and many discuss their writing in political terms. Even though the questions and the organization of the interviews are the same throughout the book, the authors express diverse opinions that reflect the diversity of their works. Tying the interviews together are Bruce-Novoa's useful and accessible introductory materials, which include a detailed timeline of publications in fiction, poetry, drama, and anthologies.

                                                              LML

425   Bruce-Novoa, Juan D. *RetroSpace: Collected Essays on Chicano Literature*. Arte Público 1990, $11.00 (1-55885-013-9). 190pp. Essays.

Noted literary critic Bruce-Novoa offers fourteen essays on the history and current state of Chicano literature. He begins with an exploration of ethnic literature in general and a history of Hispanic literature in particular, drawing distinctions and parallels between Chicano (Mexican-American) and Riqueño (Puerto Rican) literature. Other essays discuss the role of the Spanish language in the literature, views of Mexico, and portrayals of Chicanos in Mexican literature. Publishers of Chicano literature and the publishing experience also receive attention. Although there are no essays on individual authors, Bruce-Novoa has his own favorites and is frank in his opinions about issues of controversy. For instance, he calls upon other critics of Chicano literature not to ignore well-written works such as Ron Arias's *The Road to Tamazunchale* and John Rechy's *City of Night (see main entries)* simply because they do not deal directly with Chicano identity. He also champions the self-critical and ideologically troublesome writing of Oscar Z. Acosta. Bruce-Novoa's essays are written in a personal and accessible manner and thus would be of interest to the general reader with an interest in the subject as well as to the specialist in literature.   LML

426   Cockcroft, James D. *Outlaws in the Promised Land: Mexican Immigrant Workers and America's Future*. Grove 1986, $14.95 (0-8021-1206-4). 304pp. Nonfiction.

Cockcroft examines the history and politics of migrant agricultural labor in the southwestern United States, beginning with the dispossession of the former Mexican citizens in the 1840s and ending with the debate over the Simpson-Mazzoli Bill, which was later incorporated into the 1988 Immigration Reform and Control Act. Cockcroft looks at factors that have led millions of Mexicans to cross the border in search of work and that have motivated employers in the United States to hire them for jobs few U.S. citizens would take. He also describes the evolution of U.S.-Mexico relations with respect to migrant labor. Opposed both to the unrestricted flow of immigrant workers from Mexico and to draconian measures to prevent it, Cockcroft calls upon strengthened unions in the United States and in Mexico to protect the rights of workers, to ensure fair wages, and to improve the lives of desperate people so they would not have to migrate in search of a better life. Although the book's description of the current situation is dated, the historical information is solid; the basic problems and factors leading to the migration have changed little since the book was written a decade ago.   LML

427   Gann, L. H., and Peter Duignan. *The Hispanics in the United States*. Westview 1986. o.p. Nonfiction.

Gann and Duignan provide a solid overview of the history and current situation (as of the mid-1980s) of Hispanics in the United States, beginning with the first Mexican settlers who involuntarily became part of the United States after the annexation of Texas and the 1948 war with Mexico. The authors examine successive waves of migration from Mexico as well as the arrival of Hispanic Americans from Puerto Rico, Cuba, the Dominican Republic, and Central and South America. Most of the book, however, focuses on Mexican

Americans, by far the largest group numerically. Present-day issues covered include culture and the arts, Hispanic politics (in all their ideological diversity), education, religion, and the social problems of crime and addiction. With respect to such controversial issues as bilingual education, illegal immigration, and political refugees, the authors present both sides of the arguments and offer their own opinions. For the most part, they take a moderately conservative position politically, although one that is less extreme and strident than that taken by Linda Chavez in her hotly debated work, *Out of the Barrio* (Basic Books, 1991).   LML.

Levine, Barry B., ed. *The Caribbean Exodus*.
See entry 753.

428   McWilliams, Carey. *North from Mexico: The Spanish-Speaking People of the United States*. Matt S. Meier, ed. Greenwood 1990, $55.00 (0-313-26631-X); $12.95 (0-275-93224-9). 376pp. Nonfiction.

Originally published in 1948, this work has become a classic. It presents the history of the Mexican Americans from their own perspective and often in their own words. McWilliams explores the early Spanish settlement of the present-day southwestern United States and describes the complex relations between the settlers and the Indians—the region's earliest inhabitants. The intermarriage of Indians and Spaniards created a *mestizo* (mixed-race) population and brought about the color and class distinctions between light-skinned "Spaniards" and mixed-race "Mexicans," a distinction that has persisted across centuries. McWilliams also exposes the prejudice and violence against Spanish-speaking people that occurred when they became part of the United States after the 1848 Mexican Cession. The book explores the culture of the borderlands—an area of continued migration between the United States and Mexico—and the cultural differences among the Hispanic people of New Mexico, California, and Texas.

McWilliams died in 1990. Matt S. Meier updated McWilliams's work, adding chapters about Chicano political organizations, the evolution of Mexican-American culture in the latter part of the twentieth century, and recent U.S. efforts to control immigration from Mexico.   LML

429   Mora, Pat. *Nepantla: Essays from the Land in the Middle*. Univ. of New Mexico Pr. 1993, $19.95 (0-8263-1454-6). 208pp. Essays.

In this volume, poet Mora (*Chants*, Arte Público, 1984; *Communion*, Arte Público, 1991; and *Borders (see main entry)*) offers twenty essays on Latina identity, life, and art. Education is a major concern for this college professor; she laments the alienation and low achievement of Latino students and calls for a more culturally sensitive curriculum that goes beyond simple discussions of food, holidays, crafts, and costumes. Among her essays are descriptions of her own family, growing up in El Paso, and her attempts to give her three children a sense of their dual Latino/Anglo heritage in Cincinnati, Ohio, where very few Spanish-speaking people live. She explores what it is like to be a woman of dual heritage: Latino, with its values of machismo, female submission, and large, close-knit families; and American, where women are pressured to conform to media images of beauty and sexuality. Several of the essays describe trips Mora took to Pakistan, the Dominican Republic, Cuba, Guatemala, and her family's land of origin, Mexico. She reveals her unique (and often awkward) position as a well-to-do U.S. tourist in lands in which she has cultural roots. Mora's essays have much in common with those of fellow Latina writer Gloria Anzaldúa, author of *Borderlands—La Frontera* (*see main entry*). However, while Anzaldúa's work deals with indigenous symbols, sexual orientation, and the nature of creativity, Mora's is more concerned with cultural and political issues in the present. LML

430 Morin, Raul. *Among the Valiant*. Frwd. by Lyndon Baines Johnson. Borden 1963. o.p. Nonfiction.

Originally published in 1963, this book offers historical and biographical information about the Mexican-American soldiers who fought in World War II and in the Korean War. Morin's account is organized around interviews with the soldiers, who talk about their backgrounds, their service in the armed forces, and the reaction to their contributions within their own community and within the larger society. While emphasizing the patriotism of the soldiers, the book also points out that Latino servicemen, like those from other minority groups, have not received their due in textbooks and other mainstream accounts of the wars. The foreword to this edition was written by Lyndon Johnson during his tenure as vice president under John F. Kennedy. DM/LML

431 Portes, Alejandro, and Alex Stepick. *City on the Edge: The Transformation of Miami*. Univ. of California Pr. 1993, $25.00 (0-520-08217-6). 281pp. Nonfiction.

Few cities have undergone such rapid change in the past four decades as Miami. Once a sleepy resort town in southern Florida, it has now become an international city in which Spanish may be heard as often as English. Portes and Stepick analyze the changes in Miami that began with Fidel Castro's triumph in Cuba in 1959, an event that caused hundreds of thousands of Cubans to flee to the United States in distinct waves. The authors examine all aspects of the Cuban migration, beginning with the prosperous (and primarily lighter-skinned) first migrants and continuing through 1980 with the Mariel boatlift; the refugees who arrived in that wave, known as *Marielitos*, were poor and black. Also receiving a great deal of attention is the relationship between the relatively successful Cuban immigrants and Miami's African-American residents, who saw their own mobility stymied and whose dissatisfaction erupted in the 1979 Liberty City riots. Portes and Stepick consider other migrations as well—particularly those of the Haitians and the Nicaraguans—which they contrast with the Cuban experience. This is a valuable study not only of Latino immigration but also of the evolution of one American city in the context of national and global events.

Along with Robert L. Bach, Portes is the author of *Latin Journey: Cuban and Mexican Immigrants in the United States* (Univ. of California Pr., 1985). He wrote *Immigrant America: A Portrait* (Univ. of California Pr., 1990) in collaboration with Rubén G. Rumbaut. LML

432 Rieff, David. *The Exile: Cuba in the Heart of Miami*. Simon & Schuster 1993, $21.00 (0-671-77604-5); $11.00 (0-671-88627-4). 240pp. Nonfiction.

Author of *Going to Miami: Exiles, Tourists, and Refugees in the New America* (Viking, 1988), Rieff has returned to the city for a new look at the Cuban exile community after the fall of Communism in the former Soviet Union and Eastern Europe. He finds many of the Cuban exiles awaiting their triumphant moment of return to their native land, only to have their hopes dashed with Castro's persistence in power well into the 1990s. Rieff delineates the various generations of exiles and U.S.-born Cuban Americans and their attitudes toward the United States, Cuba, and the possibility of return. He also finds a great deal of ambivalence, even among older Cuban Americans. These exiles have romanticized their childhoods in Cuba, and many are aware that the reality may be far from the ideal, especially after years of Communist rule and austerity and deprivation as a result of the U.S. blockade. In addition, Rieff explores the internal divisions within the Cuban-American community and the economic and social situation of community members, many of whom have achieved extraordinary material success in their adopted land. The most compelling moments of Rieff's well-written and accessible study come when he describes an individual family—Raul and Niñón Rodríguez and their U.S.-born son, Ruly—who serve as a microcosm of the achievements and dilemmas facing Cuban Americans in that most Cuban of cities, Miami.   LML

433 Shorris, Earl. *Latinos: A Biography of the People*. Norton 1992, $25.00 (0-393-03360-0); Avon $12.50 (0-380-72190-2). 640pp. Nonfiction.

Shorris offers a fascinating documentary portrait of the Latino past and present, focusing on individual and family experiences. He covers a wide variety of topics, beginning with Latino roots in the cultures of Mexico, Puerto Rico, Cuba, the Dominican Republic, and the nations of Central and South America. Other topics include the assimilation process, education (especially bilingual education), political action, entrepreneurship, the world of work, urban gangs, and refugees. Although Shorris offers a brief background narrative for each chapter, most of the chapters feature biographies of Latino figures or descriptions of everyday life and people. Schoolchildren and their teachers figure prominently; Shorris spent a great deal of time observing classes and visiting families in a New York City neighborhood that has drawn migrants from throughout the Americas. Other chapters offer slices of life in Los Angeles and Miami. At the end of the book are two *testimonios*, one from a Mexican-American family and one from a Cuban-American family. Family members describe their experiences of immigration and growing up in the urban barrios of the United States.

Shorris's approach allows the reader to get to know the individuals—with their varied cultural, national, economic, and social backgrounds—that make up the Latino population today. The reader sees that Latinos are not one monolithic group, nor have their experiences in the United States been identical.   LML

Urrea, Luis A. *Across the Wire: Life and Hard Times on the Mexican Border*. See entry 782.

BIOGRAPHY

434   Acosta, Oscar Z. ***The Autobiography of a Brown Buffalo***. Random 1989,
$10.00 (0-679-72213-0). 199pp. Autobiography.

Disenchanted with his life as an attorney in urban California, Acosta undertakes a pilgrimage to discover his true cultural identity. *Autobiography of a
Brown Buffalo* is the novelized version of this endeavor. Traveling from California to Texas via Idaho and Colorado, and engaged in a frenzy of uninhibited
drug use and countless sexual encounters, he remains as lost as ever. Ad-
venturing in Juárez, Mexico, Acosta realizes that his cultural identity derives
from proud Mexican-Indian origins. Visualizing himself as a beautiful brown
buffalo, he "thunders" toward his next destination, Los Angeles, where he
intends to join other brown buffaloes in their quest for equality.

In his followup book, *The Revolt of the Cockroach People* (Random, 1989), the
transformation of Acosta is completed. No longer the complacent, culturally
orphaned attorney, Acosta becomes an activist in the Chicano civil rights
movement. He participates wholeheartedly in protest marches and demonstrations. Utilizing his skills as an attorney for the cause, he defends other
soldiers in the revolution against trumped-up charges and false accusations.
Considering himself a revolutionary, Acosta envisions Emiliano Zapata and
Pancho Villa, the heroes of the Mexican Revolution, as his contemporaries.
The word "cockroach" in the title refers to the Mexicans who marched in
support of Zapata and Villa, singing the common man's revolutionary an-
them, "La Cucaracha" ("The Cockroach").

On vacation in Mazatlán, Mexico, in 1974, Acosta mysteriously disappeared. Although stories surfaced suggesting that he was involved with the
CIA or that he was murdered because of his political activism, he was never
heard from again.   DM

435   Cofer, Judith Ortiz. ***Silent Dancing: A Partial Remembrance of a Puerto Rican
Childhood.*** 2nd ed. Arte Público 1991, $9.50 (1-55885-015-5). 120pp. Autobi-
ography.

Silent Dancing is a collection of essays and poetry written about events the
author remembers from her childhood. The daughter of a career Navy man,
Cofer was born in Puerto Rico. When her father was on assignment in the
United States, the family lived in Paterson, New Jersey. During his long ab-
sences overseas, Cofer, her brother, and her mother lived with his family in
Puerto Rico. As a young woman, she was aware of the cultural differences
between Puerto Rican and American society and how feminine roles and
expectations differed in each. Cofer also understood the significance placed
by her parents and their families on preserving their cultural identity. These
biographical essays represent what many contemporary immigrant families
experience. The family attempted to be part of the dominant culture while
maintaining the values they brought with them from Puerto Rico.

Cofer has also written several works of fiction about life in Puerto Rico,
including the novel *The Line of the Sun* (Univ. of Georgia Pr., 1991) and *The
Latin Deli: Prose and Poetry* (Univ. of Georgia Pr., 1993), which focuses on
Puerto Ricans in New York and New Jersey.   DM

436 Galarza, Ernesto. **_Barrio Boy_**. Univ. of Notre Dame Pr. 1971, $8.95 (0-268-00441-2). 250pp. Autobiography.

Chicano writer and labor organizer Galarza describes his childhood in rural Mexico and his emigration to the United States during the years of the Mexican Revolution. Raised by his divorced mother and his two uncles, Gustavo and José, "Little Ernie" moved from Jalcocotan, an Indian village in southern Mexico, to Tepic, Mazatlán, and finally to a multicultural neighborhood in Sacramento, California, as his uncles' employment by the Southern Pacific Railroad took them farther north. Galarza's working-class family valued education and refused to let the boy work, except after school and during vacations; nonetheless, he had a number of experiences that convinced him of the workers' need to organize for better conditions. Along with the closeness and joyous celebrations, there was also fear, particularly of becoming involved in the violence of the revolution, and tragedy, as the 1918 influenza epidemic claimed the life of Galarza's mother and his beloved uncle Gustavo. This classic memoir, published in 1971, offers a window into a turbulent period in Mexican history and an immigrant experience in the early twentieth century.   LML

437 Mendoza, Lydia. **_Lydia Mendoza: A Family Autobiography_**. Ed. by Chris Strachwitz and James Nicolopolus. Arte Público 1993, $32.95 (1-55885-065-1); $17.95 (1-55885-066-X). 400pp. Autobiography.

Along with her parents and siblings, Lydia Mendoza was a major performer of Mexican and Mexican-American music, not only in the Southwest, but wherever Mexican Americans lived in the United States. Her career spanned more than five decades and led her, in 1978, to perform before President Jimmy Carter at the Kennedy Center in Washington, D.C. She was the first female performer of Mexican-American popular music to attain stardom, which she did after years of hardship and poverty. In this volume, she, her family members, and her friends and associates tell her inspiring story. The reader sees a musical career evolve over the decades as the young musicians themselves matured and had families of their own. Lydia Mendoza speaks of her affection for her audience and her love of the traditional musical forms, which she describes. She also discusses the emerging recording industry that brought her works to a wider audience.

Compilers Strachwitz and Nicolopolus, who have written on various American folk music traditions, have brought to life an inspiring and appealing story. They also provide a useful section of notes, a comprehensive discography, and a bibliography of other works on the Mendoza family and on Mexican and "Tex-Mex" music.   LML

438 Rodríguez, Luís J. **_Always Running: La Vida Loca: Gang Days in L.A._** Curbstone 1993, $19.95 (1-880684-06-3); Simon & Schuster $10.00 (0-671-88231-7). 260pp. Autobiography.

Rodríguez wrote this book as an attempt to reach his teenage son, who had become attracted to a Chicago street gang. Rodríguez himself had been a gang member, drug user, and petty criminal in Los Angeles during his adolescent years, before he joined the struggle for Chicano political rights. Rodríguez describes his immigrant parents and his school experiences, where he and his older brother were labeled as retarded and disruptive. Eventually, his brother's abilities were discovered and encouraged by a sympathetic teacher, but Luís drifted toward gang life and was expelled from several schools for fighting. As a boy, he was keenly aware of the ethnic and class differences separating the Chicano students from the Anglos. He knew that Chicanos, regardless of their ability, were steered onto a vocational track that would lead only to low-status, low-paying employment. Through the efforts of his father, Rodríguez discovered the library and began to read the works of Malcolm X, Claude Brown, and Piri Thomas, whose lives a generation earlier seemed to parallel his own. He also met a political activist who ran a local community center. The activist helped him negotiate his return to high school and to become a spokesman for the Chicano students. At that time, he also began to write poetry and won both a national competition and a college scholarship. This book, dedicated to more than a dozen friends whose lives the street claimed, is a compelling autobiography of a gifted writer and leader, whose struggle has much to say to young people today.   LML

439   Rodríguez, Richard. *Hunger of Memory: The Education of Richard Rodríguez.* Bantam 1983, $5.99 (0-553-27293-4). 208pp. Autobiography.

When Richard Rodríguez started school in Sacramento, California, he could not speak English. Spanish was the language used at home by his working-class Mexican-born parents. This autobiographical work portrays the author's experience in the American education system and how he achieved academic success by suppressing the Mexican part of his cultural heritage. The sense of loss that comes from suppressing this memory is the hunger alluded to in the title. That hunger, according to the author, must be endured as the cost of assimilation. Rodríguez argues that it is important to overcome the private nature and comfort of the Spanish language in order to achieve a public identity that allows complete immersion and that yields better success in American society. Rodríguez's assimilationist stance and opposition to bilingual education drew heavy criticism from the Chicano intelligentsia, but 1980s conservatives lauded the book as sensitive and insightful.

Rodríguez's exploration of his life and its social and political implications continues in *Days of Obligation* (Viking, 1992). In this work, he reflects upon Mexican history and contemporary California and describes his immigrant father, his religious development, and his homosexuality in the age of AIDS.
DM

440   Salas, Floyd. *Buffalo Nickel.* Arte Público 1992, $19.95 (1-55885-049-X). 347pp. Autobiography.

Floyd Salas was born in Colorado during the Depression to working-class Mexican-American parents. He was the third of four children, and much of his life was influenced by two older brothers. Eddy, the eldest, was a genius who encouraged young Floyd to set and achieve goals; Al was a petty thief and heroin addict who attempted to pull Floyd into his world.

Boxing was an activity at which Al, when still a "clean" youth, excelled. Introduced to the sport at a very young age, Floyd continued practicing the discipline that boxing required into adulthood. At various times he relied on that discipline to help Al overcome addiction to heroin.

Married and a father while still a teenager, Floyd entered the world of petty criminals, with Al as his mentor. Salas served time in a youth detention center, charged with assault of a police officer. This and other factors induced him to end his criminal career very soon after it began. His successful return to school to pursue a college education and his decision to become a writer were marred by tragedy when Eddie, despondent that he had disappointed his father, committed suicide. Four of Al's nine children also die, victims of either homicide or suicide.

Salas is also the author of *What Now My Love* (Arte Público, 1994) and *Tattoo the Wicked Cross* (*see main entry*), novels that reveal other aspects of his varied background.   DM

441 Soto, Gary. *Lesser Evils: Ten Quartets*. Arte Público 1988, $9.50 (0-934770-77-8). 160pp. Autobiography.

Best known as a poet and an author of juvenile fiction, Soto offers the reader forty brief autobiographical sketches, grouped into ten loosely related "quartets." Many of the themes are both personal and universal. As an adult, Soto worries about growing old and fantasizes about having an affair. Other essays explore his childhood in a multiethnic working-class neighborhood in Fresno, California. Soto describes his father's tragic death in a work-related accident and the impact it had upon the family, both psychologically and economically. He also relates how the coworker responsible for the death subsequently avoided the Soto family, even though he had been a family friend for years. Soto's Mexican-American heritage comes through most clearly when he describes festivals and rites of passage, but the reader receives the impression of a sensitive and observant child growing up amidst a variety of cultures and drawing something from each in his journey to adulthood.

Soto's works of poetry include *The Tale of Sunlight* (o.p., 1978), *Who Will Know Us?* (o.p., 1990), and *A Fire in My Hands* (Scholastic, 1991). Among his other autobiographical prose works about his childhood in California are *Living Up the Street* (Dell, 1992), *Small Faces* (Dell, 1993) and *A Summer Life* (Univ. Pr. of New England, 1990).   LML

442 Thomas, Piri. *Down These Mean Streets*. Random 1990, $11.00 (0-679-73238-1). 352pp. Autobiography.

Published in 1967, Thomas's autobiography has become one of the most influential narrative works written during this period, of the stature of *The Autobiography of Malcolm X* and Claude Brown's *Manchild in the Promised Land* (*see main entries*). Though Thomas's life shares much in common with the lives of these African-American writers—including frequent moves, alienation from his family, a descent into heroin addiction and petty crime, and imprisonment—he also deals with issues specific to the Puerto Rican experience. The eldest child in a large two-parent family, Piri rebelled against his conservative parents, who urged their children to assimilate. He was the darkest-skinned of the Thomas children, and many who saw him thought he was black rather than Puerto Rican. After his family moved to Babylon, Long Island, he left home at the age of sixteen to hustle on the streets of Harlem, where he had spent much of his childhood. With a black friend, he joined a ship's crew and journeyed to the South to discover who he was; there, as elsewhere, he encountered a double dose of racism. Upon his return he became addicted to heroin and turned to increasingly violent crimes. He participated in the shooting of a policeman and landed in prison, where he served six years. The autobiography ends with Thomas's growing self-awareness in prison and his release; in the final chapter he returns to Harlem, only to observe his old friends self-destructing on the street, victims of the racism they had internalized.   LML

443   Villaseñor, Victor. ***Rain of Gold***. Arte Público 1991, $19.95 (1-55885-030-9); Dell $12.00 (0-440-50512-7). 551pp. Autobiography.

Rain of Gold has been called the "Hispanic-American *Roots*." It is the author's personal history, tracing the origins of his family to California. Beginning at the Lluvia de Oro mine in central Mexico, the narrative follows three generations of the Gómez and Villaseñor families as they migrate north to the United States. It illustrates their common tenacity and will to overcome incredible obstacles, including the Mexican Revolution of 1910, the Depression of the 1930s, and extreme poverty and racism. The women of the family are characterized as strong, keeping the family unit together at all costs. The drama of the narrative is lightened by the romance between the author's parents, the beautiful and shy Lupe Gómez and the daring bootlegger Salvador Villaseñor.

Using a rich oral tradition preserved by generations of relatives, Villaseñor has written a history of one family's immigrant experience that reads like a novel.   DM

4

UNITED STATES:
NATIVE AMERICANS

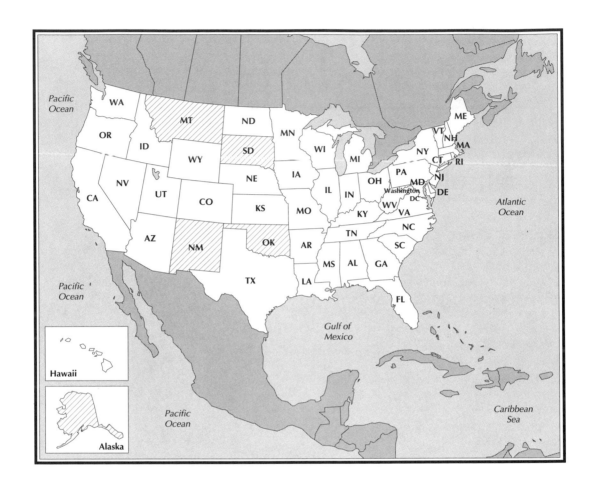

STATES WITH HIGHEST CONCENTRATION OF NATIVE AMERICANS

1. Alaska - 15.6 %
2. New Mexico - 8.9 %
3. Oklahoma - 8.0 %
4. South Dakota - 7.3 %
5. Montana - 6.0 %

LARGEST TRIBES OF NATIVE AMERICANS

1. Cherokee - 369,035
2. Navajo - 225,298
3. Sioux - 107,321
4. Chippewa - 105,988
5. Choctaw - 86,231

Source: 1990 U.S. Census

4

UNITED STATES: NATIVE AMERICANS

by Babs Kruse and Elaine Goley

When asked which books she would most like to have non-Indians read in order to better understand and appreciate Native Americans, Genia paused and asked, "You mean, on the *subject* of Native Americans? . . . Well, I *am* one, so I don't really feel any need to read about it. I'd rather read about other things." Her reaction was hardly surprising, given the tendency of many readers to prefer books and articles outside their immediate range of daily experiences—to expand their awareness, rather than confirm it. Fortunately for this chapter of the bibliography, however, others (especially the older people) had definite favorites. Some titles were expected and were on almost everybody's lists; a few were unfamiliar or downright obscure and came as total surprises. Regardless of the publication status of the recommended titles, these personal offerings were given special consideration in the final selection.

After talking with people, we then scanned mail-order catalogues from several Indian presses and bookstores to find other titles and to confirm titles already tentatively included. A few non-Indians were also asked to submit lists, and current book reviews provided a score of the newest releases. Many titles, both old and new, appeared repeatedly. Whether the authorship was Indian or non-Indian, male or female, did not seem to be a factor, either in the catalogues or in the personal recommendations. Even potential problems with unfortunate wordings in titles did not seem to perturb many. The number of times a given title was recommended was considered a good indicator of its value. Final determination on inclusion or deletion was made only after we read the book.

With rare exceptions, the recommended lists contained only nonfiction and biographies. Although an effort has been made to find and include a few samples of the better fiction available, the composition of the collected annotations still reflects that original preference. To an old favorite by Frank Waters and a Pulitzer Prize winner by N. Scott Momaday have been added more-recent favorites by Michael Dorris, Louise Erdrich, Leslie Marmon Silko, and James Welch and stunning new fiction by such gifted storytellers as Joseph Bruchac and Sherman Alexie.

197

All books, regardless of how they were nominated, had to meet certain criteria in order to appear in the final bibliography. First, works of both fiction and nonfiction had to be accurate in their depictions of Native American culture. This meant that they were not only accurate in stated or implied customs, values, attitudes, and so on, but also in freedom from generalization. A statement that may be true about Kickapoo religious beliefs, for example, becomes inaccurate when generalized into a statement about "Indian religion." Furthermore, any assumptions made by a writer had to be clearly identified as such, not stated as categorical truths. Conflicting theories and alternative interpretations of historical evidence had to be included in nonfiction treatments, and at some point in most fiction as well.

Second, the books had to be informative. Some books on the initial list made excellent reading and were quite accurate, but the Native American characters and cultures in them were only incidental and the information they contained was minimal. Given the large number of titles available in this subject area, such books were eliminated to make room for equally good but, to our minds, more useful works.

Third, preference was given to books that offered well-rounded portrayals of Native America. From the multitude of political and military histories that have been (and continue to be) written, only a few of the groundbreaking classics and the most eloquent contemporary treatments were chosen. Most of the information is already rather widely known, and for the works contained in this chapter we preferred to emphasize daily life and culture—the everyday activities and concerns of many past and present Native Americans.

The criteria demanded that the books be well written, able to stand alone on their merits as literature, and that the language they contain be accessible to a wide range of seriously interested readers. Books with racial or sexist stereotyping were avoided, even if they had other merits. A few of the older books on the final list contain "emotion-laden" words that did not have the same connotation when they were written as they do now; advance warnings are included in the individual annotations.

Although we attempted to include materials representing general cultural areas across the entire continental United States, specific tribal histories were usually eliminated, including a number of important works by such authors as Angie Debo, Henry F. Dobyns, Alfred L. Kroeber, and Ruth Underhill. A few exceptions were made for particularly interesting books about lesser-known tribes, such as the Eastern Shoshone, and for a few outstanding books that met the first five criteria so well that they deserved inclusion. Examples include *Cheyenne Autumn* by Mari Sandoz and *The Death and Rebirth of the Seneca* by Anthony F. C. Wallace. Many of the nonfiction works, such as *Trail of Tears* by John Ehle and *Let Me Be Free: The Nez Perce Tragedy* by David Lavender, examine key events and turning points in the confrontation between specific Indian Nations and the United States government.

Two extensive nonfiction series should be mentioned here, both highly recommended for overall accuracy, thoroughness, and readability. The Civilization of the American Indian series, published by the University of Oklahoma Press, currently consists of more than 200 entries. Case Studies in Cultural Anthropology, a series published by Holt, Rinehart, and Winston, contains ethnographies from around the world; some titles are currently available as reprints by HBJ College Publications. These are scholarly works and their format may be at times unappealing, but they are not difficult to read.

Most individual titles had to be eliminated from this list for space consider-
ations, but readers are encouraged to seek them out. A new series edited by
A. LaVonne Brown Ruoff is American Indian Lives, from the University of
Nebraska Press; two titles in that series are discussed in this chapter.

There are numerous excellent anthologies of Native American literature
available today, but only a few samples are listed here. Anthologies are useful
for high school and college courses in literature, history, or political science,
but they are seldom read outside the classroom. Some of the high-quality
anthologies considered were eliminated in favor of recommending full works
by the authors and poets whose works appear in the collections. Short-story
collections were kept to a minimum for similar reasons. Sun Tracks is an
American Indian literature series sponsored by the American Indian Studies
Program and the Department of English, University of Arizona; six of its
publications are annotated here. A recent series to watch for is American
Indian Literature and Critical Studies, which the University of Oklahoma
Press started publishing in 1992; recommended for academic libraries, the
series is edited by Gerald Vizenor.

Many older books are hostile, romanticized, or insidiously condescending
in their attitudes toward Native Americans. Fortunately, newer, better books
have come along to replace them. Some of the true classics, however, will
probably never be improved upon. As books that have survived decades of
upheaval in societal attitudes, political and cultural awareness, and writing
styles, they are timeless treasures that have been repeatedly judged among
the most valuable, most insightful, best written, and most appealing to a wide
spectrum of thoughtful readers. They still have much to say to those who care
to listen. Among these are the works of Theodora Kroeber (*Ishi, Last of His
Tribe* and *Almost Ancestors*) and Mari Sandoz.

We have tried to present a collection that balances classics with the best of
the new, past lives with present and future lives, and everyday concerns with
political and artistic ones. The definition of present-day concerns, of course,
varies from region to region, Nation to Nation, generation to generation, and
individual to individual. The militant factions are the most vocal and they
speak for those whose primary concerns are legal and political; sovereignty
and treaty rights are critical issues, and some of the best writings on these
topics are included here. Examples include *Custer Died for Your Sins* by Vine
Deloria, Jr. and the recent collection of essays by a group of noted Indian
scholars and activists titled *Exiled in the Land of the Free*. For other groups,
especially in the West, energy development and water rights are the main
issue, as described in such works as *Breaking the Iron Bonds* by Marjane Ambler. Another concern is the desire to improve the popular perception of local
tribal histories, general Native American history, and individual Native Americans as ordinary human beings. Perhaps the two most common issues, however, are the pressing need for improved economic conditions and the education of children. Economics, employment, and education are connected to
legal issues, concerns about development and control of natural resources,
and the growth of understanding. Clearly, all of these causes and effects are
interrelated, and when one element is explored, solutions to others may
become apparent. Unfortunately there are few books available that address
these themes. Among the notable exceptions annotated here are *Song of the
Earth Spirit*, a photo essay by Susanne Anderson; *Teepee Neighbors* by Grace
Coolidge; *Light of the Feather* by Mick Fedullo; *The Aboriginal Sin*, a collection of

autobiographical poems by Tim Giago; *American Indian Sports Heritage* by Joseph Oxendine; and *Teaching American Indian Students*, edited by Jon Reyhner. Coolidge's book, written in the early 1900s by the wife of a missionary, is particularly unusual. She and her husband, a Native American, were both highly critical of the poor quality of education found in mission and government Indian schools. But her views and those of her husband apparently diverged at that point. As a mother and a neighbor, Grace Coolidge was outraged at the fact that Indian children were separated from their families, even when they attended boarding schools on the reservation. In her opinion that approach resulted in nothing but pain and failure. Her husband, on the other hand, was upset that the separation did not last long enough to ensure that assimilation would be permanent. The other books mentioned above shed much light on the new directions, special problems, and exciting possibilities of modern Indian education.

A special effort has been made to include humor in the collection. Joking and teasing are integral to the traditions of many North American Indian tribes, and although many of the culturally defined "joking relationships" may have faded, the humor has not. Laughter, now as then, leavens the harsh realities of everyday life. *The Powwow Highway*, a popular novel by David Seals, and *The Lone Ranger and Tonto Fistfight in Heaven* by Sherman Alexie are examples of humorous fiction; humor also surfaces frequently in the nonfiction.

Many works of fiction and art on this list have roots in the folklore and mythology of American Indians. Novels such as *House Made of Dawn* by N. Scott Momaday, *Ceremony* by Leslie Silko, and *Fools Crow* by James Welch contain myths and folktales as stories within the main story. Though other novels and short stories are not drawn so directly from individual tales, most do contain traditional symbols, elements, and themes, such as the triplestrand braids that appear throughout Michael Dorris's *A Yellow Raft in Blue Water*. An appreciation of these works, as well as the poetry of Simon Ortiz and the art of Howard Terpning, Beatien Yazz, and others, would be incomplete without an understanding of their basis in oral tradition and of the belief that the oral tradition is the source of creativity, imagination, and renewal for Native peoples.

For the introductory reader and students at the high school level, an excellent choice for discovering American Indian folklore is John Bierhorst's *The Mythology of North America*, which contains extensive explanatory material as well as examples from the major types of tales from various cultures. The most exhaustive source, however, is Joseph Campbell's *The Way of the Seeded Earth*, part of his massive *Historical Atlas of World Mythology*. Volumes 2 and 3 of *The Way of the Seeded Earth* focus upon North American Indian groups. Other collections explore individual regions or types of tales. Teresa Pijoan's *White Wolf Woman*, for instance, presents transformation tales, mostly derived from the Plains Indians. Susan Feldman's *The Storytelling Stone*, drawing on the resources of the Bush Collection of Religion and Culture at Columbia University, offers a wide selection of creation myths and didactic tales. D. M. Dooling and Paul Jordan-Smith's collection *I Become Part of It* explores the relationship between folklore and American Indian spirituality. *American Indian Myths and Legends*, edited by Russell Erdoes and Alfonso Ortiz, combines classic legends with more-recent tales; about a third of the tales are adapted by the editors themselves, while the others are presented in more or less original form. Christopher Vecsey's *Imagine Ourselves Richly* explores the connection between the oral tradition and ways in which various Indian Nations governed themselves and confronted white encroachment. Finally, *Keepers of the Animals* and its companion volume *Keepers of the Earth* by Michael Caduto and Joseph Bruchac are unique books that help adults who work with children understand the American Indian oral tradition as it relates to specific natural and environmental themes; included are lessons in storytelling and activities that increase both children's and adults' awareness of traditional American Indian value systems.

In assembling this bibliography, the editors hope to offer enough interesting, accurate, informative, thought-provoking, entertaining, and stimulating books that even Genia will be able to find something here she'd rather read!

LITERATURE

444 Alexie, Sherman. *The Lone Ranger and Tonto Fistfight in Heaven*. Grove 1993, $21.00 (0-87113-548-5); HarperCollins $12.00 (0-06-097624-1). 223pp. Fiction.

Sherman Alexie is an exceptional writer, and his stories of modern life on the Spokane Indian Reservation convey to the reader a vivid sense of time and place.

Told from the viewpoint of several different speakers, the episodes in this book encompass a variety of people and situations, captured with uncanny realism and abundant humor. In many of these stories the author shows what happens when a people's collective will to survive encounters the destructive power of the collective feeling of resignation—when raw despair threatens to extinguish flickers of hope. Other stories follow the rhythm of daily life and death—and convey the comfort of good food, good loving, and good jokes.

Some of Alexie's insights take the breath away. His lyrical prose is so skillful that readers may not even be aware they are reading. The author's vivid metaphors and his use of many narrators may be confusing at first, but the rapid flow and the uniqueness of his characters pull the reader along. Alexie's stunning use of language and many shades of humor make an otherwise painfully honest book a joy to read.   BK

445 Allen, Paula Gunn, ed. *Spider Woman's Granddaughters: Traditional Tales and Contemporary Writing by Native American Women*. Fawcett 1990, $12.50 (0-449-90508-X). 256pp. Fiction.

This varied collection of stories by and about Native American women is well chosen, well written, and an instructive pleasure to read. Some are beautiful retellings from the oral traditions of various tribes, a few are autobiographical, and the rest are short stories and excerpts from novels set in historic and modern times. They weave a rich tapestry, because the women in these stories are warriors, each in her own way, fighting for loved ones, for dignity, against isolation from communality— fighting to live beautifully day by day.

Allen prefaces each selection with an explanation, placing it in the appropriate ritual and literary context. Her thoughtful introduction explains the aesthetic processes of both the oral and Western/European traditions, and the "serious dislocation" that results from using one to judge the other. She also points out the flaws in purist rigidity and maintains that such "intellectual apartheid" subtly helps create and reinforce apartheid in social, political, and practical affairs. These stories shatter stereotypes and serve as testaments to continuance, the power of spirituality, and the miraculous strength of hope. Along with the stories are notes, brief biographies of the authors, a glossary, and a short bibliography of recommended reading.   BK

446   Brant, Beth, ed. ***A Gathering of Spirit: A Collection by North American Women***. Firebrand 1984, $22.95 (0-932379-55-9); $10.95 (0-932379-56-7). 242pp. Fiction.

This anthology offers the poetry and prose works of approximately three dozen Native American women writers from the United States and Canada. Among the themes identified by Brant, who is herself a Bay of Quinte Mohawk, are the physical reality of being a woman and a Native American, spiritual concerns, and the rituals of production and creation. Most of the contributors have not yet become well known, and they represent more than two dozen Nations in the United States and Canada. Some live on reservations, but most live in cities and towns far from their childhood homes. Several of the contributors are inmates in prison. Half of the contributions are poetry; the others are short stories and essays; all are written from a feminist perspective. Many of the contributors connect the destruction of Native American civilizations to the destruction of the environment and the oppression of women. Along with the personal and community tragedies are expressions of strength—in tribal traditions, in mothers, in grandmothers, in other women, and in the struggle for justice and human rights.   LML

447   Bruchac, Joseph. ***Dawn Land***. Fulcrum Publishing 1993, $19.95 (1-55591-134-X). 336pp. Fiction.

This novel tells of Bruchac's Abenaki Indian ancestors, who populated the northeastern United States over 10,000 years ago. The protagonist, Young Hunter, is sent to an unknown land north and west in pursuit of a cruel, inhuman giant known as One-Eye. His three loyal dogs accompany him; several times they save his life. Young Hunter comes into contact with and befriends another people, the People of the Long Houses, and together they defeat the giant.

By describing the values and ways of living of Native Americans before the coming of the whites, this gripping novel involves us in their vision and love of the Earth. These people lived in harmony with their surroundings and maintained an ecological balance with the environment. The reader observes how different cultures lived—agricultural civilizations as well as hunters—and how each respected and depended upon other living creatures. Bruchac is a great storyteller in the oral tradition of his ancestors. He has woven much of Abenaki culture, folklore, and mythology into his work. *Dawn Land* is the saga of a valiant people who must commune with the spirits of the Earth to survive.   EG

448 Bruchac, Joseph, ed. ***New Voices from the Longhouse: An Anthology of Modern Iroquois Literature***. Greenfield 1988, $12.95 (0-912678-68-2). 292pp. Fiction.

This collection includes short stories and poems written by modern Native American authors from the Nations of the northeastern United States and Canada—the Mohawk, Seneca, Onondaga, Iroquois, and Abenaki, among others. The authors, most of whom are not widely known, delve into the traditions of the Northeastern Nations and discuss their history of marginalization and oppression after the arrival of white settlers. Bruchac's introductions offer additional insights into the unique ways of life of these groups. For example, he discusses the importance of the longhouse, the large dwelling that served as a gathering place for members of extended families. The poetry and prose reflect the perspectives of people who feel caught between two cultures, but who seek to strengthen and reclaim their Native American heritage. Many of the writers are women, and their works combine a modern feminist perspective with their Indian roots.   EG

449 Bruchac, Joseph, ed. ***Singing of Earth: A Native American Anthology***. Illus. by Frank Le Pena. Nature Company 1993. o.p. Poetry/Fiction.

This book presents the environmentally friendly message of Native American cosmology and mythology. The book offers poetry and prose from traditional Native American folklore, as well as from contemporary writers such as N. Scott Momaday. There are five parts, each devoted to one aspect of man's interaction with nature.

The book makes the point that European philosophy tends to view man as separate from nature. In fact, "man against nature" has been one of the principal themes of European and white American literature. In contrast, Amerindian cultures see man as a *part* of nature—a part of the whole, coexisting with the rest of the natural world.

Lavishly bound in red cloth, the book includes captivating prints in rich earth tones by Native American artist Frank Le Pena. The art is naive, but it retains all the complexities of Native American cosmology and folklore. Charming in its simplicity and style, the book carries a complex message about preserving nature, leaving it unspoiled for future generations. This is a highly recommended addition to any book collection.   EG

450 Bruchac, Joseph, ed. ***Songs from This Earth on Turtle's Back: An Anthology of Poetry by American Indian Writers***. Greenfield 1983, $10.95 (0-912678-58-5). 300pp. Poetry.

This volume includes modern Native American Indian writers, such as Peter Blue Cloud (Mohawk), N. Scott Momaday (Kiowa), Simon J. Ortiz (Acoma Pueblo), Gladys Cardiff (Cherokee), Nia Francisco (Navajo), and other important Indian writers. Chapters include short biographies of the authors and several of their poems. Fifty-two poets are included, allowing the reader to appreciate a broad sampling of poems and themes from a variety of traditions. In its own way, each piece in this collection connects Indian cultural beliefs that originated thousands of years ago with messages commonly expressed in modern Indian art, such as survival, unity with nature, and unique cultural identity.   EG

451   Craven, Margaret. *I Heard the Owl Call My Name.* Repr. of 1973 ed. Buccaneer 1991, $21.95 (0-89966-854-2); Dell $4.99 (0-440-34369-0). 250pp. Fiction.

Doctors give Mark, a young minister, three years to live. Hoping Mark may
learn enough of the meaning of life to be ready when he learns of his
imminent death, the wise old bishop assigns him to an isolated parish
among the Kwakiutl Indians of the Pacific seacoast. Kingcome Village is a
small community three miles upriver from a long ocean inlet, surrounded
by steep mountains and the cedar rain forest. There Mark and his parishio-
ners approach each other watchfully, both sides polite and careful but un-
sure. The minister's natural humanity, respect, sense of humor, and compassion gradually involve him more and more deeply with the villagers,
their sufferings, small pleasures, cultural traditions, seasonal activities, and
special joys, until he becomes as much a part of their lives as they become
of his.

When the owl calls his name one night almost two years later, an old
grandmother confirms his sudden realization that he is about to die. As he
struggles with the knowledge, the villagers quietly enfold him in a gift of
peace that means more to him than life itself.

Told with honesty and quiet restraint, this gentle, deeply moving novel
unfolds patiently and with humor. Descriptions are brief yet vivid; the reader
feels drawn into the embrace of the mountains, living in the shadow of tall
cedars, accustomed to the rains and to the sight of canoes on the timeless
river. Comparatively short for a novel of such evocative power, this book is
not about words or doctrines; it is about spirit, life and death, and the search
for meaning—the search, as one character says, for "the only place I know
myself."   BK

452   Day, A. Grove, ed. *The Sky Clears: Poetry of the American Indians.* Repr. of
1951 ed. Greenwood 1983, $55.00 (0-8032-5047-9). 204pp. Poetry.

The editor has compiled over 200 translated poems and lyrics from about forty
North American tribes, chosen as the finest examples of the only truly native
New World poetry. The informative foreword and first chapter contain a number of important cautions. Editor Day notes that the book was intended for
pleasure and appreciation, and so he judged the translations on their literary
merits, not necessarily for their literal proximity to the original words. His
choices were also restricted by the fact that there are relatively few surviving
remnants of the vast oral tradition of poetic literature that flourished among
the 2,000 independent tribes living on the continent in 1492.

For the native peoples, poetry and ritual were composed for specific purposes and often in lyric shorthand, which can make it difficult to understand
these works outside of their cultural contexts. Frequently repetitive, and often
accompanied by ritual actions, the rhythmic verses were full of symbolism,
figurative language, and allusions to commonplaces of everyday life that
would puzzle most modern readers. Still, these poems evoke a complex world
of shared emotions and events among the close-knit audience. By providing
clear explanations and backgrounds for the works, Day places the selections
in their context, thus adding to the reader's enjoyment and appreciation. The
book includes a bibliography of 211 poetry sources and an index.   BK

453 Deloria, Ella Cara. ***Waterlily***. Contrib. by Agnes Picotte; Aftwd. by Raymond J. DeMallie. Univ. of Nebraska Pr. 1988, $30.00 (0-8032-4739-7); $9.95 (0-8032-6579-4). 244pp. Fiction.

Written in the 1940s, but not published until 1988, *Waterlily* is a warm and satisfying novel of the lives of a Teton Sioux woman and her daughter in the early 1800s. Reflecting the author's extensive knowledge and deep feeling, the story illustrates the dynamics of the Dakota kinship system, the most significant aspect of life for people of the tribe. The goal of functioning honorably within the rules and responsibilities of this highly developed system made a person human and civilized. The kinship system was rigid and demanding, but at the same time flexible and humane. The characters in this book honor the system in their own individual ways, discovering that within the restrictions lie a deeper freedom, a sense of belonging, room for creativity, and the opportunity for fulfillment and great happiness.

A Yankton Sioux who was also a prolific ethnologist, linguist, teacher, writer, and lecturer, Ella Cara Deloria successfully transforms a great deal of information into a good story. At the same time she dispels the notion that traditional Indian women were little more than dutiful drudges leading dull, unrewarding lives. Agnes Picotte's biographical sketch of the author, the publisher's foreword, and Raymond J. DeMallie's afterword all contribute to the interest and value of the book.   BK

454 Dorris, Michael. ***A Yellow Raft in Blue Water***. Henry Holt 1987, $16.95 (0-8050-0045-3); Warner Books $10.00 (0-446-38787-8). 356pp. Fiction.

Three generations of women in a Native American family struggle with their identity and their family's secrets in this moving novel. Fifteen-year-old Rayona—half Indian and half African American—is abruptly taken by her mother, Christine, from their home in Seattle to the reservation in Montana where Christine grew up. Rayona tells of running away from the reservation and returning to find her own place in the community. Christine then tells her story: her love-hate relationship with her brother, Lee, their mother's favorite child who died in Vietnam; her own struggle against alcoholism and liver disease; and the man on the reservation, Lee's best friend, who gave her another chance at love. The novel ends with the testimony of Christine's "mother," Aunt Ida, who describes Christine's illegitimate birth and her own struggle to accept her duty to raise the child as her own. Rich in symbolism and poetic in style, his novel portrays three strong women who must confront a painful past and make peace with themselves and each other in order to find a better future.

Dorris is also the author of a short story collection, *Working Men* (Henry Holt, 1993), and the autobiography *The Broken Cord (see main entry)*.   EG

455 Erdrich, Louise. ***Love Medicine***. New & expanded ver. Henry Holt 1993, $24.00 (0-8050-2798-X); HarperCollins $12.00 (0-06-097554-7). 352pp. Fiction.

The story begins in spring 1981, with June Kashpaw's death in a freak snowstorm. Members of her extended family and friends gather in mourning on the North Dakota reservation. The gathering provides the opportunity for them to reflect upon their lives and to make plans for the future. A key figure is "Grandpa," Nector Kashpaw, June's father-in-law, who was educated in government schools and enjoyed success as an actor but is now senile and confused about his identity. His brother, Eli, who was hidden from the government and never attended boarding school, is still in control of his faculties. Other characters include June's niece Albertine, her son King, and King's half-brother Lipsha Morrissey, who mixes a love potion for his grandparents that accidentally kills Grandpa.

In this novel, Erdrich mixes equal doses of poignancy and humor to offer a portrait of contemporary life on the Chippewa reservation, examining issues such as family bonds, assimilation, alcohol abuse, and spirituality. Several of her other novels focus upon the same community and many of the same characters. Chronologically the earliest (although published later) is *Tracks* (Henry Holt, 1988), which begins with the epidemic that decimated the Chippewa community, *The Beet Queen* (Bantam, 1989), and, most recently, *The Bingo Palace* (HarperCollins, 1993), which continues the story of Lipsha Morrissey.   LML

456   Giago, Tim A., Jr. *The Aboriginal Sin: Reflections on the Holy Rosary Indian Mission School*. Indian Historian Pr. 1978. o.p. Poetry.

Although perhaps not exceptional as a collection of free verse, this autobiographical work is nevertheless a small gem that provides a rare look at the mission boarding schools, an experience common to many Native Americans who grew up between the 1890s and 1950s. To fulfill their task of transforming young "heathen savages" into "civilized Christians," the mission schools typically used a four-pronged approach: forcibly separate the children from their families at least six days a week; strictly forbid the use of native languages and discussion or observance of any Indian customs or beliefs; maintain absolute control with harsh military-style discipline, Spartan dormitories, and meager rations; and teach "modern living" skills with long hours of backbreaking practice. Emphasis on academics varied with the school.

The schools were rigid, yet the author/poet manages to show the human side. He describes schoolboy antics, pining after the girls (who were educated separately), constant hunger, pain and fear, pride, loneliness, and the irrepressible flashes of humor. He allows us a small, personal glimpse of history as experienced by one Oglala schoolboy.   BK

457   Hillerman, Tony. *The Blessing Way: A Joe Leaphorn Mystery.* Repr. of 1970 ed. Armchair Detective Library 1990, $18.95 (0-922890-09-9); HarperCollins $5.99 (0-06-100001-9). 224pp. Fiction.

The first, and still among the best, of Hillerman's mysteries, *The Blessing Way* pits Lt. Joe Leaphorn, Navajo detective, against the cunning of a murderous Wolf-Witch. Only through Leaphorn's patient observation and his knowledge of ancient and contemporary Navajo ways is his shadowy adversary unmasked.

The canyon, mesa, and desert country through which Leaphorn and the other well-drawn characters move is briefly yet vividly painted. The author immeasurably enriches his swift and suspenseful story by embedding it within Navajo daily life and tradition. Although not of Indian heritage,

Hillerman has been formally honored by the Navajo for his depiction of the people, their beliefs, and customs.

Dance Hall of the Dead (orig. pub. 1973; HarperCollins, 1990) earned him the coveted Edgar Award from the Mystery Writers of America. Also recommended are such titles as *A Thief of Time* (HarperCollins, 1988) and *Coyote Waits* (HarperCollins, 1990), in which Joe Leaphorn joins forces with Sgt. Jim Chee of the Tribal Police. Although the two men differ in their view of their shared heritage, they pool their talents to solve crimes. **BK**

458 Kinsella, W. P. ***The Moccasin Telegraph: And Other Tales****. Godine 1993, $12.95 (0-87923-981-6). 192pp. Fiction.

Like its predecessors *Dance Me Outside* (Godine, 1978), *Scars* (o.p., 1978), and *Born Indian* (o.p., 1981), this collection of stories bursts with life. The narrator is Silas Ermineskin, a young Cree and a budding author living on a fictionalized reservation in Alberta, Canada. The observant Silas and his motley assortment of friends are still "hanging out," high school graduates and dropouts who have not yet established the future patterns of their lives. In the meantime, no one on or off the reservation gets any respect (except for old people and Mad Etta, the shrewd medicine lady) unless they've earned it the hard way. The characters include Indians and whites of all ages, circumstances, beliefs, and stations in life, and the book describes what happens when the lives of such people intersect and diverge.

The stories are by turns tender, tragic, buoyant, mischievous, fatalistic, or bemused. But they share a unifying thread of humor in its many varieties—sometimes gentle, often wryly understated, occasionally outrageous, and always wickedly funny. The hardest part, for the reader, is remembering that these people and their lives are fictional. **BK**

459 Lesley, Craig. ***River Song****. Dell 1990, $8.95 (0-317-99666-5). 307pp. Fiction.

A sequel to Lesley's acclaimed first novel, *Winterkill* (orig. pub. 1984; Dell, 1990), *River Song* follows Danny Kachiah as he tries to establish connections with his teenage son, Jack. A former forest firefighter and rodeo circuit rider, Danny has been working odd jobs and drifting around the region near Pendleton, Oregon. When his ex-wife is killed in an accident, her sister Pudge demands that Danny reclaim his son from Nebraska and bring him home. Danny tries, but before he can deal successfully with the universal problems of adolescent resistance and rebellion, he must first come to grips with the problems in his own life. With the help of an old salmon fisherman and a medicine woman—plus his dreams, courage, and honesty—he untangles the torn web of his Nez Perce heritage, faces past and present violence, and comes home himself. **BK**

460 Lesley, Craig, ed. ***Talking Leaves: Contemporary Native American Short Stories****. Dell 1991, $10.00 (0-440-50344-2). 385pp. Fiction.

This anthology brings together excerpts from novels and previously published short stories by most of the major contemporary Native American fiction writers today. Craig Lesley, himself an important Native American author, offers readers a full range of the themes and styles of the literature.

Most of the selections examine the ways in which Native Americans draw upon religion and cultural traditions for the strength needed to cope with exploitation from white Americans and, simultaneously, to resist the allure of the dominant culture. Other works explore the solemn beauty and the sometimes fatal dangers that together mark the natural world within which Native Americans traditionally live. All stages of the life cycle are included in this collection. Through the many-faceted prisms of Native American cultural motifs and values, the various authors examine such universal themes as birth, maturity, love and marriage, old age and death.   LML

461   Momaday, N. Scott. ***House Made of Dawn.*** Repr. of 1968 ed. HarperCollins 1989, $12.00 (0-06-091633-8). 192pp. Fiction.

This first novel, winner of the 1969 Pulitzer Prize for fiction, brought national prominence to its Kiowa author. Abel, a young Navajo and a World War II veteran, returns at the end of the war to his community and to the grandfather who raised him alone after his mother's death. When Abel kills a white man whom he believes is an evil spirit, he goes to prison and is then relocated to Los Angeles, where he gradually sinks into alcoholism and despair. In Los Angeles, Abel befriends Benally, a Kiowa whose memory of the stories, prayers, and chants he heard as a child have helped to sustain him far from his home, his culture, and the people he loved. Gradually, Benally's words sink in, and as Abel struggles for life after being badly beaten in a fight, he realizes he must go back home. In his grandfather's final days, Abel cares for him and begins his own healing process.

This poetically written novel explores the fate of young Indian men who faced the death of their traditional way of life in the post–World War II. Many were destroyed by loneliness and alcohol, but Momaday shows how some, sustained by their memories and by the sacred values of their culture, have survived, helped others to survive, and contributed to the rebirth of their people. Among Momaday's other acclaimed works of fiction are *The Ancient Child* (Doubleday, 1989), *The Way to Rainy Mountain* (Univ. of New Mexico Pr., 1976), *The Names* (Univ. of Arizona Pr., 1977), and *The Gourd Dancer* (HarperCollins, 1976). Momaday has also published a volume of poetry, *The Angle of Geese and Other Poems* (o.p.).   LML

462   Ortiz, Simon J. ***Woven Stone.*** Univ. of Arizona Pr. 1992, $45.00 (0-8165-1294-9); $19.95 (0-8165-1330-9). 365pp. Poetry.

Woven Stone is an omnibus edition containing the poet's three previous works, *Going for the Rain* (1976), *A Good Journey* (1977), and *Fight Back: For the Sake of the People, For the Sake of the Land* (1980). Ortiz's thirty-page introduction is an autobiographical look back through his intellectual development and spiritual and emotional growth—as a writer, a Native American, a man, a recovering alcoholic struggling to find the strength to face reality, and an active citizen with the courage of his convictions.

Writer, teacher, and storyteller, Ortiz seeks to demystify language, to make it an accessible means of sharing perceptions, consciousness, intimacy, and creativity. He creates his poetry out of contemporary experience and recognizes the realities and responsibilities of the relationships we share with everything—each other, ourselves, and the world around and beneath us.

Drawing on the strong oral traditions of his Acoma heritage, he instills a sense of deep continuity. He imbues his poems with a love of the land, of community traditions, and of language itself.

Jack Dykinga's striking photograph of water-sculpted sandstone provides a fitting cover.   BK

463 Seals, David. *The Powwow Highway*. NAL 1990, $10.00 (0-452-26377-8). 300pp. Fiction.

Three unlikely heroes embark on a quest to rescue a beautiful princess. Cool, competent Buddy needs dumb, 300-pound Philbert because fat Phil has just acquired a new "war pony"—a dilapidated 1964 Buick LeSabre named Protector. Buddy needs to get from their Northern Cheyenne reservation in Montana to the jail in Santa Fe, where his long-lost sister is being held. He isn't prepared for the miraculous transformations Philbert undergoes, nor for the delays they cause, but despite whirlwind mini-adventures along the way, trusty Protector gets them to Bonnie's jail cell in the nick of time.

The first two chapters of this book are wonderfully funny, with lots of startling insights and great nonsense. The next two chapters deteriorate into slapstick, but it's well worth the reader's trouble to keep going, because in later chapters further insights, engaging characters, and an improbably successful mix of high and low humor rescue the fast-moving story and keep pace with it until the novel's satisfying conclusion. This is an underground classic, laced with profanity and rowdy jokes, its characters fueled by copious amounts of booze and shared joints. The author handles these elements so naturally and easily that they seem almost tasteful—if such a thing is possible.

Seals has written a sequel, *Sweet Medicine* (Crown, 1992), which takes itself a little more seriously as it follows Buddy and Philbert (plus Bonnie and Rabbit, minus Protector) back to Montana.   BK

464 Silko, Leslie M. *Ceremony*. Viking 1986, $9.00 (0-14-008683-8). 272pp. Fiction.

After watching his cousin, Rocky, die on a Pacific battlefield, Tayo, sick both emotionally and physically, returns from World War II to his Auntie's home on a New Mexico reservation. He has already spent months in a mental hospital, and his aunt, who has raised him ever since his mother abandoned him at the age of four, calls a spiritual healer out of sheer desperation. Although Tayo is only half-Indian, he comes to recognize that only a spiritual ceremony will cure him. Spurning the overtures of his Indian friends, who spend their days and nights drinking and fighting, he becomes the student of old Betonie. Betonie has adapted the traditional ceremonies to changing times, and he helps Tayo to come to terms with his own mixed-race identity and to draw upon the strengths of Navajo culture in rebuilding his life after the death of his closest friends and his abandonment by the U.S. government, which used the Indians to fight their wars but deprived them of their land.

Silko's first novel is a gripping portrait of a young man fighting for survival in a ravaged community. Like N. Scott Momaday, Silko includes traditional folklore and poetry within the story, which contains a political edge as well. Silko is also the author of *Storyteller* (orig. pub. 1979; Arcade, 1989) and *Almanac of the Dead* (Viking, 1992).   LML

465 Trafzer, Clifford E., ed. ***Earth Song, Sky Spirit: Short Stories of the Contemporary Native American Experience.*** Doubleday 1993, $25.00 (0-385-46959-4); $12.95 (0-385-46960-8). 495pp. Fiction.

This anthology of prose selections—most of them short stories but some excepts from novels—features the works of thirty Native American authors. Among them are the well-known authors contained in virtually every collection—N. Scott Momaday, Michael Dorris, Louise Erdrich, James Welch, Leslie Marmon Silko, and Paula Gunn Allen—but this volume also includes a large number of new and emerging authors. At least half of the works have not been published elsewhere. Editor Trafzer, a Wyandot Indian whose fiction appears in other anthologies, has not included his own stories here. His introduction describes the traditions from which the authors come and the basic plot and themes of their contributions. This is a well-balanced collection in terms of the authors' heritage and the content of their works; included are historical and contemporary stories, humorous and serious tales. All of the works are united by the characters' search for identity and for the bonds of tradition, community, and family.

There are a number of anthologies of Native American literature currently in print. These are especially useful for high school and college classes. Alan R. Velie's *The Lightning Within: An Anthology of Contemporary American Indian Fiction* (Univ. of Nebraska Pr., 1991) contains mostly excerpts from novels by major authors, all of which are recommended in this chapter. LML

466 Vizenor, Gerald. ***Earthdivers: Tribal Narratives on Mixed Descent.*** Illus. by Jaune Q. Smith. Univ. of Minnesota Pr. 1981, $14.95 (0-8166-1048-7). 203pp. Fiction.

Members of many tribal cultures in North America, North Asia, and Europe tell tales about animals diving through primal seas in search of mud or sand from which the Creator forms the Earth. Vizenor uses these "earthdivers" as metaphors for Native American mixed-bloods, survivors who must find their own "urban connection, a place to dive back into the tilted Earth, a way back to the sacred." He explains in his preface that both dreaming and interpretation are creative processes, essential and imaginative; the same can be said for the writing and reading of these twenty-one stories of modern mixed-blood earthdivers and urban shamans.

The memorable characters include Captain Shammer, who is appointed chairman of a college department of American Indian studies and who promptly puts it up for sale—only to be out-trickstered by his audience when the bids are opened. Another is journalist Clement Beaulieu, assigned to cover the story of thirteen-year-old Dane Michael White, whom we never get to meet because he has already hanged himself after spending forty-one days in jail for skipping school. Also here is sweet, innovative Justice Pardone Cozener who, evicted from his reservation, opens the world's first public chicken-plucking center in California, a remarkably successful venture. The modern tricksters who people Vizenor's stories do not always succeed, but the author's clever, unrelenting satire does.

Among Vizenor's other published works, both fiction and nonfiction, are the novel *The Everlasting Sky* (o.p., 1972); *The People Named the Chippewa: Narrative Histories* (Univ. of Minnesota Pr., 1984), and the essay collection *Crossbloods: Bone Courts, Bingo, and Other Reports* (Univ. of Minnesota Pr., 1990). BK

467   Waters, Frank. ***The Man Who Killed the Deer***. Pocket 1984, $4.99 (0-671-55502-2). 224pp. Fiction.

Martiniano, a young Pueblo man forcibly educated in the white world, has returned home. Unable to accept and, therefore, unwilling to obey the full set of rules of either world, he makes of himself a partial outcast. His marriage to an Arapaho/Ute woman eases the emptiness while widening the gulf, and he must still struggle to make his own living and find his own answers.

As the elders know, "there is no such thing as a simple thing." Every thought and action eventually affects the whole. "We are all one, indivisible," they tell him; but Martiniano must discover this truth for himself. When he breaks the laws, the consequences spread gently, like ripples across the sacred lake. He and the other people of the divided pueblo must each discover a harmony in which they can have faith, for only therein lies freedom.

The author paints the inner and outer landscapes of consciousness as beautifully as he does pueblo, mountain, and foothills. His rare ability to understand the many meanings of silence, and to convey the individual and collective need for spirituality, give unusual strength and depth to this finely crafted story. Continuously in print since 1942, this novel remains an American classic.   **BK**

468   Welch, James. ***Fools Crow***. Viking 1987, $11.00 (0-14-008937-3). 400pp. Fiction.

Welch departs from his customary focus on contemporary Native Americans in this highly acclaimed historical novel. White Man's Dog, an eighteen-year-old Blackfoot warrior living in the late 1800s, is renamed Fools Crow after showing both courage and intelligence in defeating warriors from another Indian Nation. Over the years, his wisdom, visions, and leadership earn the respect of his people. The years of Fools Crow's reign as chief are tumultuous and tragic ones for the Blackfeet, as white settlers are encroaching upon ancestral lands and killing the animals that have been the source of their food. Many bands have already been wiped out by soldiers, and the children are being sent to mission schools where they are stripped of their culture. Fools Crow must choose: either resistance and physical death, or negotiation and likely cultural death. He elects to negotiate so that his people might live. He communicates his vision that they are "chosen," that they will retain their culture and identity in the face of all obstacles.

This novel is a reaffirmation of Welch's own heritage and of the continued cultural survival of the Blackfeet people. Woven throughout, as stories within the larger story, are legends and folktales, visions, songs, and poetry, all of which give the reader a powerful sense of the Native American life before the arrival of white settlers.   **LML**

469   Welch, James. ***The Indian Lawyer***. Viking 1991, $9.00 (0-14-011052-6). 352pp. Fiction.

Born and raised on the Blackfeet reservation in Montana, Sylvester Yellow Calf is on the way to major success. After playing on the all-conference basketball team at the University of Montana, he attends Stanford Law School and is now a respected lawyer and member of the State Parole Board. Democratic Party leaders want him to run for Congress. His middle-class life contrasts with the lives of the convicted (white) armed robber Jack Harwood and his wife, Patti Ann, who concoct a scheme to blackmail Yellow Calf and gain Harwood's early release. Patti Ann makes overtures to Yellow Calf, playing into his own insecurities—his failing marriage with Shelley, a rancher's daughter with two children by a previous marriage; his guilt at having succeeded when so many of his high school teammates did not; and his fear of selling out his people in his quest for wealth and power. Pursued by his enemies, his adultery about to be revealed, and confronted with a request to represent *pro bono* a Sioux group whose land rights are under attack, Yellow Calf must eventually decide on the direction of his life.

Like two of the author's other works, *Winter in the Blood* (Viking, 1986) and *The Death of Jim Loney* (Viking, 1987), this is a contemporary novel about Indian life. In focusing on a middle-class Indian trying to navigate two worlds, it shows the diversity of contemporary American Indian experiences and the conflicts facing those who have attained success in the dominant society. LML

470 Wood, Nancy C. ***Many Winters: Prose and Poetry of the Pueblos***. Illus. by Frank Howell. Doubleday 1974, $10.95 (0-385-02226-3). 80pp. Poetry.

"The Earth is what I speak to when I do not understand my life." Through these poems, Wood conveys some of the wisdom of the old people of Taos Pueblo. Beautifully complemented by the artwork of Frank Howell, the rich flow of ideas and images evokes a sense of timelessness, of belonging, and yet of solitude at peace with oneself.

The inner freedom that soars through this book is balanced by the comfort of having deep roots in the natural world. In these poems people rejoice in nature's cycles and celebrate beginnings and endings. The many aspects of human nature are recognized, encouraged, and balanced within the circle of a full life. Although the world has never been perfect and life will forever bring pain and broken dreams, those who have grown old in wisdom can choose those memories that echo, as nature does, "the wholeness of my song."

The book features a brief, interesting introduction along with earth-tone portraits and black-and-white sketches by Howell. BK

NONFICTION

471 Ambler, Marjane. ***Breaking the Iron Bonds: Indian Control of Energy Development***. Illus. with photos by Sarah Hunter-Wiles. Univ. Pr. of Kansas 1990, $14.95 (0-7006-0518-5). 352pp. Nonfiction.

Ambler's contribution to the interdisciplinary Development of Western Resources series is a thorough, readable treatment of the complex issues surrounding Indian development and control of nonrenewable resources. Focusing on fifteen Western reservations, she places the energy development issue in its larger context. A useful history traces changing public-land policies and types of ownership that have applied to tribal lands (excluding those in Alaska) since 1871. Ambler discusses general economic and political factors on modern reservations and how they combine with historical precedents and factors to influence current tribal efforts to control energy development in their territory. The book explores the specific attitudes and purposes of tribes and the people granted development rights and the different paths they took as they attempted to increase and implement their control in the 1960s and 1970s. From extensive research, the author includes many of the personalities and groups involved. For example, she describes the inception and maturation of the Council of Energy Resource Tribes.

Black-and-white photographs were taken by Sara Hunter-Wiles, the author, and others. Included are maps, tables, a list of acronyms, a timeline, extensive notes, bibliography, and index. **BK**

472 *America's Fascinating Indian Heritage* Repr. of 1978 ed. Illus. Reader's Digest 1990, $30.00 (0-89577-372-4). 416pp. Nonfiction.

This colorful and appealing volume provides an excellent introduction to the history and cultural diversity of the first Americans. Covering all of North America, including Canada and Mexico, the text stresses the interrelationships among climate, topography, flora, fauna, and human beings in the never-ending process of adaptation. The reader is swept along by the fascinating story, which covers events from the arrival of the first Asian hunters and the dispersal and development of an amazing variety of distinct cultures to the decline of native populations following European contact to their modern renaissance. Generously illustrated with over 700 paintings, photographs, sketches, maps, and diagrams of daily life and art forms, it concludes with a list of museums, reconstructed villages, archaeological sites, and so on. The text and illustrations are well indexed. **BK**

473 Anderson, Susanne. *Song of the Earth Spirit*. Illus. with photos by the author. Friends of the Earth 1973. o.p. Nonfiction.

Susanne Anderson is primarily a photographer, but this book shows that she is an artist with both her camera and her words. She has recorded experiences and conversations with rural Navajo friends around Rough Rock in northeastern Arizona. Like her photographs, Anderson's text is warm, poetic, uncontrived, funny, serious, and very human.

Having shared daily life with several extended families over the years, she writes insightfully about herding, children, punning, blizzards, lambing, schools, courting, medicinal plants, branding, ghosts, mining, rodeos, healing, clans, and harmony. Illustrated throughout by full-page photographs, the book ends with "The Song of the Earth Spirit," a lyrical blend of word and image.

Rarely is a book this successful in combining black-and-white with color photography. The black-and-white plates are so sensitive, strong, and appealing that a reader may find as many favorites among them as among the color plates. The simple text is equally successful. Together they evoke the many moods and rhythms not just of Navajo life but of all life. **BK**

474 Bancroft-Hunt, Norman. *People of the Totem: The Indians of the Pacific Northwest*. Illus. with plates and photos by Werner Forman. Univ. of Oklahoma Pr. 1988, $22.95 (0-8061-2154-9); Bedrick $24.95 (0-87226-199-9). 128pp. Nonfiction.

In the mild, rainy coastal regions of the Pacific Northwest, an unusual group of cultures developed. Because the rich variety of natural resources was difficult to reach or utilize, the people depended for their livelihood on the sea and on extensive trade networks. As a result, high concentrations of people became possible, along with sophisticated arts, crafts, dance, theater, and social organization. Much about the prehistory of the area remains unknown; this text focuses on the 1770s to the 1880s. Intriguingly, the author makes the point that early trade contact with Europeans during this era tended to intensify rather than change the indigenous cultures.

As with the other titles in the Echoes of the Ancient World series, fine color plates of landscapes and artifacts by series editor and internationally known photographer Werner Forman grace every page. Included are a map, bibliography, and index. BK

475   Bierhorst, John. *The Mythology of North America: Introduction to Classic American Gods, Heroes, and Tricksters*. Illus. Morrow 1986, $13.00 (0-688-04145-0); $6.95 (0-688-06666-6). 272pp. Nonfiction.

Bierhorst's book rivals the work of Joseph Campbell as a definitive guide to the folklore and mythology of Native America before Columbus. Since the turn of the century, entire archives of Native American lore have come to light. Bierhorst presents them in this clearly written, well-organized book for introductory readers. Many of these stories convey a message of renewal and conservation of resources that the modern world would do well to heed.

Bierhorst is also the author of *The Sacred Path* (Morrow, 1983), a collection of classic and adapted folktales from Native North American cultures. EG

476   Brown, Dee. *Bury My Heart at Wounded Knee: An Indian History of the American West*. Henry Holt 1971, $27.50 (0-8050-1045-9); $14.95 (0-8050-1730-5). 488pp. Nonfiction.

It is said that history books are written by the winners. Here, however, Dee Brown uses primary-source documents to create a definitive history of the American West from the perspective of Native Americans, who lost the battle of the frontier. Brown uses the Indians' own words to convey their perspective on the coming of the white settlers, the result of which was loss of traditional lands, destruction of their culture, and death. The survivors of the massacres and parties to treaty negotiations tell how their people struggled to carry on in spite of betrayal by the whites—and at times by their own people. The *Washington Post* called this book a "shocking" look at history. EG

477   Bruchac, Joseph. *Survival This Way: Interviews with American Indian Poets*. Univ. of Arizona Pr. 1990, $16.95 (0-8165-1178-0). 363pp. Essays.

This collection of interviews with contemporary Native American poets offers insights into the authors' perspectives, describes their motivations for writing, and includes samples of their work. When N. Scott Momaday's 1969 Pulitzer Prize–winning book *House Made of Dawn (see main entry)* was published, many budding Native American authors were inspired to tell the story of a people caught between two cultures. For these authors, writing became a means of confronting and transcending the pain of the past in a process of spiritual healing. Bruchac's collection addresses the theme of survival on several levels: personal survival, survival of the old ways, survival of individual tribes and of Indian Nations as a whole. The writers included here—Momaday, Louise Erdrich, Peter Blue Cloud, Simon Ortiz, and seventeen others—offer poignant personal histories and observations on a number of cultural and political issues. The struggle to find their own voices, while connecting to their family circles and the traditional culture, is evident in this powerful work. EG

478 Burch, Ernest S., Jr. *The Eskimos*. Illus. with photos by Werner Forman. Univ. of Oklahoma Pr. 1988, $26.95 (0-8061-2126-2). 128pp. Nonfiction.

The "Eskaleuts"—Inuit, Yupik, and Aleuts—are scattered in small, shifting communities across the Arctic barrens. The author proves that their environment may be hostile, but it is certainly not barren. These indigenous peoples, occupying land from Greenland to the Bering Sea, have refined the techniques of survival to such a sophisticated level that they are able to inhabit the region year-round. Those techniques include an intimate knowledge of the plants, animals, and weather around them; hunting and gathering skills for land and sea; efficient use of meats, skins, and other natural resources; intense family and community relationships; and a complex set of beliefs and customs that enable them to thrive in spite of harsh environmental conditions. Burch explores the great ingenuity and diversity that characterize these survival techniques and admires the beauty, subtlety, intelligence, breadth, depth, warmth, and joy he finds there. Particularly fine photographs by Werner Forman illustrate each page. Maps, a bibliography, and an index are included. BK

479 Burger, Julian. *The Gaia Atlas of First Peoples: The Future for the Indigenous World*. Illus. Doubleday 1990, $24.95 (0-385-26652-9); $15.95 (0-385-26653-7). 191pp. Nonfiction.

This valuable reference tool catalogues the indigenous peoples of the world, including North America. The first section explains what and who the first peoples were. The second section describes the first contact between these people and the Europeans and explains the devastating impact of colonialization on native cultures. Section three explores the efforts of native peoples to preserve their cultures and independence. This unique publication demonstrates that, like many animal species, indigenous populations are threatened with extinction because their habitats are being destroyed through such environmental threats as deforestation by developers. The book also includes a list of indigenous organizations and peoples, a list of resources, and an index. EG

480 Caduto, Michael, and Joseph Bruchac. *Keepers of the Animals: Native American Stories and Wildlife Activities for Children*. Intro. by Vine Deloria, Jr. Illus. by John K. Fadden. Fulcrum 1991, $19.95 (1-55591-088-2). 288pp. Nonfiction.

Parents and teachers are often at a loss when it comes to introducing activities on Native American cultures to children. Many of the activities currently used are superficial and filled with stereotypes. In this book Caduto and Bruchac, respected storytellers and scholars, offer an alternative. Bruchac, of Abenaki

heritage, is a publisher of Native American fiction and folklore and an author in his own right. This volume and its companion, *Keepers of the Earth: Native American Stories and Environmental Activities for Children*, offer not just folktales adapted for children but a wealth of explanatory information for adult readers on the origins of the tales and ways they can be used with young people. A special teacher's edition contains a workbook and lesson plans. Among the topics covered in these two volumes are caring for animals; animal habits and habitats; the self-sufficiency of man and nature; and folklore related to animals and nature. Parents and teachers receive instruction in the art of storytelling and how to use these tales to teach about indigenous peoples. The authors provide lists of activities for adults and children that present aspects of nature and Native American life in more detail. This is an indispensable work for any adult who works with young people and who wants to raise their awareness of both the environment and Native American cultures.
EG

481   Campbell, Joseph. *Way of the Seeded Earth: Mythologies of the Primitive Planters, Vol. 2, Pt. 2; Vol. 2, Pt. 3.* 2 vols. HarperCollins 1989, $50.00 each (0-06-055158-5; 0-06-055159-3); $24.95 each (0-06-096351-4; 0-06-096352-2). Nonfiction.

This massive series of atlases of world cultures and mythology is the culmination of Joseph Campbell's life work and was completed shortly before his death. Campbell, the leading authority on the subject, devotes an entire volume in two parts to Native North American mythologies. The book first describes the two agricultural systems of the New World, then explores the unique but related mythologies of the Northeast woodland tribes and the Southeast tribes. Maps and illustrations convey the spirit and power of the agricultural rites and stories.   EG

482   Conn, Richard. *Circles of the World: Traditional Art of the Plains Indians.* Illus. Denver Art Museum 1982, $24.95 (0-914738-27-5). 152pp. Nonfiction.

Although designed as an exhibition catalogue of traditional Plains Indian art, Conn's book provides an in-depth look at the overall context in which these unique art forms developed. The exhibition was based on the concept of the circle, a form that has neither beginning nor end, a unity that was integral to Plains life. The circle was used in building homes, setting up camps, and making utensils. It was a vital element of social and intellectual perceptions, religious ceremonials, and views of the universe. All Plains Indian art forms had some integral function in society, whether they were used as tipi linings, children's toys, dress clothing, horse equipment, vision or dream art, or military art. Such art, therefore, mirrored society as a whole, reflecting the warmth of extended family relationships, the importance of reciprocal giving, the high value placed on skill and creativity, the sophistication of household arts, and the affirmation of tribal harmony and identity.

Old photographs are interspersed with the text on sepia-tone pages. In a separate section, the clear black-and-white and color plates of artifacts, photographed by Lloyd Rule and assistants, are carefully identified. The book includes a biography. Conn's *Robes of White Shell and Sunrise* (o.p., 1974) covers a wider cultural area, but it is out of print.   BK

483 Coolidge, Grace. *Teepee Neighbors.* Repr. of 1917 ed. Intro. by George L. Cornell; Frwd. by Alice Marriot. Univ. of Oklahoma Pr. 1985, $11.95 (0-8061-1889-X). 200pp. Nonfiction.

Originally published in 1917, and now back in print, this collection of reminiscences is a disturbing document of a threatened way of life. It was written at the turn of the century by a spirited woman from Boston who was married to Sherman Coolidge, a full-blooded Arapaho and an ordained minister. The book's twenty-nine sketches of daily life on Wyoming's Wind River Reservation show many facets of humanity—by turns mischievous, confused, clever, desperate, joyous, foolish, kind, thoughtless, funny, proud, awkwardly embarrassing, quietly courageous, calmly resigned—in short, very real. The brief, unsentimental vignettes are small and personal, and the elegant writing is so spare and delicate that their deep power slowly draw the reader into the reality of another time and place. Coolidge's descriptions are few and skillful, her opinions and explanations rare. Two transcendent qualities infuse the author's writing: respect for the people who are her neighbors, both as individuals and as a group, and appreciation for the resilient humor and dignity with which they live their lives.

Coolidge's vignettes portray the unrelenting poverty, the unceasing hunger, the constant dying, and the cruelty and failure of Indian education. She also portrays the resignation of purposeless men who no longer are allowed to support their families by hunting, yet who are not allowed to succeed as farmers or ranchers; the suffering of women who keep bearing children only to watch them die; and the determined survival of self-respecting adults confined to the reservation as helpless "wards," noncitizens of a faraway, uncaring government.

The introduction to the 1984 reprint is by George L. Cornell, whose grandparents, educated in government Indian schools, drew his attention to this book. He briefly outlines the lives of Grace and Sherman Coolidge, both of whom were unusual and interesting people. Reverend Coolidge, however, undoubtedly struggling with additional burdens of his own, decried much of the "barbarous Indian life" that his empathetic wife accepted on a deeper level and that she saw fit to preserve in these unassuming memoirs.   BK

Crosby, Alfred W., Jr. *The Columbian Exchange: Biological and Cultural Consequences of 1492.*
See entry 731.

484 Curtis, Edward S. *Selected Writings of Edward S. Curtis.* 3rd ed. Barry Gifford, ed. Creative Arts 1976, $6.95 (0-916870-00-6). 192pp. Nonfiction.

At the turn of the century, Edward S. Curtis realized that the traditional way of Indian life was fast disappearing. He worked diligently all of his life to capture this vanishing phenomenon, studying and photographing over eighty tribes. Much of their culture had already been lost through the demise of the oral tradition. In many cases, his is the only record of tribes of this period—their culture, folklore, religion, language, music, and ceremonies. This book contains comprehensive selections from Curtis's monumental masterpiece, a twenty-volume history of Native America, which was published privately between 1907 and 1930 as part of the J. P. Morgan Library.   EG

485 Deloria, Vine, Jr. *Custer Died for Your Sins: An Indian Manifesto*. Univ. of Oklahoma Pr. 1988, $13.95 (0-8061-2129-7). 296pp. Nonfiction.

Sioux author and scholar Vine Deloria, Jr. utilizes the words of the Indians who were witness to their own demise and rebirth to describe the Native American fight for land and survival. Indians, writes Deloria, are cursed above all other people because they have anthropologists. Anthropologists have dissected the Indian's heritage, culture, and his very existence—but only the Indian can describe his own anguish.

Deloria takes the words of prominent Native American leaders, past and present, to describe what the Indian has experienced at the hands of the whites in his own country. He describes how the land was wrested from Indian control and how treaty after treaty was broken by the U.S. government. This is a passionate and eloquent work that looks at American history from an Indian perspective. Over the years, it has become a classic and a must-have for any high school, college, or public library collection.   EG

486 Dooling, D. M., and Paul Jordan-Smith, eds. *I Become Part of It: Sacred Dimensions in Native American Life*. Intro. by Joseph Bruchac. Illus. Harper SF 1992, $15.00 (0-06-250235-2). 304pp. Nonfiction.

This volume contains traditional tribal tales, legends, and sacred stories from a number of tribes, including the Iroquois, Abenaki, Blackfeet, and Pawnee. Noted Native American writers such as Oren Lyons and Vine Deloria, Jr. interpret these stories, making them accessible to readers who are unfamiliar with the oral and written tribal traditions.   EG

487 Downs, James F. *The Two Worlds of the Washo: An Indian Tribe of California and Nevada*. Harcourt 1966, $13.50 (0-03-056610-X). 104pp. Nonfiction.

Although the writing is uneven and somewhat repetitive, this study of the past and present of the Washo is interesting and informative. A subsistence lifestyle based on the seasonal cycles of fishing, gathering, and hunting produced a loosely organized culture of small, highly mobile family units that were remarkably adaptable, that took advantage of new opportunities, and that possessed a great deal of individual freedom. This unusual background, combined with an uncharacteristic pattern of Indian-white contact, led the Washo on a path far different from that of most Native Americans. A map and bibliography are included.   BK

488 Ehle, John. *Trail of Tears: The Rise and Fall of the Cherokee Nation*. Doubleday 1989, $30.00 (0-385-23953-X); $11.95 (0-385-23954-8). 432pp. Nonfiction.

Ehle, an eighth-generation North Carolinian, grew up on land once inhabited by the Cherokee. *Trail of Tears* portrays the life and culture of the Cherokee Nation and some of its people, including Sequoyah, author of the Cherokee alphabet, John Ross, statesman and villain, and John Ridge, a visionary leader.

In 1838 federal agents forced 20,000 Cherokee to relocate; the forced march, during which 4,000 Indians died, became known as the Trail of Tears. Ehle's book is filled with the pain and despair of that march, but it also expresses the hope for a bright future envisioned by Cherokee folklore and culture. He illustrates his book with maps and copies of original documents created by the Cherokee in their struggle for survival.   EG

489   Erdoes, Richard, and Alfonso Ortiz, eds. *American Indian Myths and Legends.* Pantheon 1985, $18.00 (0-394-74018-1). 527pp. Nonfiction.

This volume includes 166 myths and legends from a broad sampling of Indian Nations of North America. The stories, grouped by theme, include creation myths, transformation tales, trickster tales, coming-of-age stories, and apocalyptic tales. In their introductory and explanatory materials, the authors discuss common threads from the myths and legends of geographically diverse peoples. An appendix gives historical and cultural information about each Nation.

Approximately one third of the myths and legends have been retold by the authors. One third are nineteenth-century legends, and the remaining third are classic tales as told by Native Americans interviewed for the book. The authors identify and describe their sources clearly. This work gives an overview of the richness of Indian tradition and is an excellent source for those seeking an introduction to American Indian folklore and mythology.   EG

490   Farr, William E. *The Reservation Blackfeet, 1882–1945: A Photographic History of Cultural Survival.* Illus. with photos. Univ. of Washington Pr. 1986. o.p. Nonfiction.

Like many Northern Plains tribes, the Blackfeet were able for a long time to maintain their traditional culture and economy in dealing with white settlers. Eventually, however, the loss of freedom and resources destroyed their economic parity and interdependence turned to dependence. From the 1830s until 1881 the Blackfeet engaged very successfully in the commercial buffalo robe trade. Then, with the last of the buffalo herds finally gone, they were forced to cope with shrinking boundaries, a burgeoning white population, and the sudden lack of any viable economic base. The ensuing changes are vividly recalled in the images and the accompanying text and captions contained in this book.

Originally conceived as a way to interest Blackfeet high school students in their own history, this remarkable collection of black-and-white photographs is the cooperative result of five years of diligent searching by many people in Montana and elsewhere. These people scoured their homes, attics, family albums, small rural libraries, and major museums and then helped again by identifying the places and faces in the pictures. Over 170 photographs have been reproduced with great care. The images reveal both persistence and loss of traditional ways, as well as adaptations to the new life on the reservation between the 1880s and the 1940s. Although this treasury of images is surprisingly complete and alive, the author's preface warns of its limitations: There was no systematic attempt to record transitional life on the reservation, and even this painstaking piecing together of random photographs leaves gaps and questions. Also, while many of the photographs hint at family closeness, pride of craftsmanship, individual feelings, and other intangibles, they can do no more than record surface realities. Nevertheless, this book is a valuable offering, well researched, well written, and well designed.

There is a foreword by the acclaimed novelist James Welch, whose *Fools Crow (see main entry)* is a fictional account of Blackfeet history. Also included are maps, a selected bibliography, and an index. **BK**

491   Fedullo, Mick. *Light of the Feather: Pathways Through Contemporary Indian America*. Morrow 1992, $22.00 (0-688-11559-4). 256pp. Nonfiction.

In 1979, Nick Fedullo became writer in residence at Sacaton School in Arizona, where his job was to teach poetry. He was surprised to discover that all the students were Pima Indians and that many of them were bilingual. Through his work with the children, he became more and more involved with families and communities, and gradually Indian education became his life's work.

These true stories of teaching, learning, and friendship took place between 1979 and 1990. Arranged chronologically, they reveal the warmth, humor, tragedy, love, suspicion, prejudice, and spirit of sharing he experienced among many Native Americans, including the Hualapai, Cheyenne, Apache, and Mountain Crow. Liberally sprinkled with dialogue, insights, and unique personalities, this book is both worthwhile and easy reading. **BK**

492   Fejes, Claire. *Peoples of the Noatak*. Intro. by Iggiagruk William Hensley. Illus. Volcano Pr. $15.95 (1-884244-00-9). 370pp. Nonfiction.

Between 1958 and 1966, Alaskan artist Claire Fejes made a series of extended visits to the whaling village of Point Hope and the seasonal hunting camps of the Noatak River Eskimos, or Inupiat. Seeing them first as an artist and then as a woman, Fejes found the land, the people, and their movements strikingly beautiful; her admiration and growing love shine through. The verbal sketches are highly visual, as brief and profoundly evocative as the spare line drawings that decorate and enhance the strong flavor of the book.

Fejes felt a continuing need "to paint the Eskimos to show the spirit of love in man," and with each visit she and the reader are drawn more deeply into their lives—sometimes gently, sometimes harshly—gradually absorbing their tremendous strengths, philosophy, history, music, joys, and sorrows. The narrative and different types of artwork become correspondingly more detailed and explanatory, yet rarely does she presume to judge or generalize about Eskimo life. She relies instead on reporting the conversations and opinions of the people themselves, while retaining her own sense of wonder and delight. Iggiagruk William Hensley wrote a personal foreword for the 1994 edition, and Fejes wrote a new preface; maps and a list of main personalities are quite helpful. The book remains an important, readable, and warmly appreciative chronicle of traditional and transitional Inupiat cultures. **BK**

493   Feldman, Susan. *The Storytelling Stone: Traditional Native American Myths and Tales*. Dell 1991, $5.99 (0-440-38314-5). Nonfiction.

Feldman was a curator of the Columbia University holdings of the Bush Collection of Religion and Culture. Drawing on that valuable resource, this book compiles creation myths, trickster myths, tales of heroes, supernatural journeys, and other stories from such tribes as the Iroquois, Blackfeet, Winnebago, Inuit, Comanche, and Cheyenne. Carefully documenting the sources to authenticate the folklore and mythology, the author shows how

Native American cultures reveal their values and structures through stories that tell how the world came about, how human institutions came to be, and how people should conduct themselves.

EG

494 Fowler, Loretta. ***Arapaho Politics, 1851–1978: Symbols in Crises of Authority***. Frwd. by Fred Egan. Illus. with photos. Univ. of Nebraska Pr. 1982, $35.00 (0-8032-1956-9). 373pp. Nonfiction.

Anthropologist Fowler musters evidence showing that the Northern Arapaho were historically unusual among the Plains tribes and that some of those differences contributed significantly to their ability to adapt to profoundly new and stressful political situations and processes. For example, she notes that age-based organizations and the integration of religious ritual into economic and political decisions were critical to the process of consensus building. These factors were also involved in the creation, manipulation, and evolution of traditional symbols. She discusses the kaleidoscope of personalities, pressures, and tactics that permanently changed the Northern Arapaho from nomadic hunters to co-owners of a relatively large and resource-rich reservation. This detailed account reads almost like a novel and is based on extensive, meticulous research drawing on primary, secondary, and oral history sources. Two sections of black-and-white plates include historic photographs from the years 1859 to 1937 plus contemporary portraits by Sara Hunter-Wiles. Helpful maps, notes, references, and an index round out this work.

BK

495 Garbarino, Merwyn S. ***Big Cypress: A Changing Seminole Community***. Waveland Pr. 1986. o.p. Nonfiction.

At first it seems ironic that a community of the Seminole, the "newest" of tribes, was able to retain its language and keep its traditional culture relatively intact far longer than most well-established Native American groups. Geographic isolation, few lines of communication, a spirit of independence, and a loose support system of nonauthoritative, nonjudgmental extended families allowed an amalgam of remnant tribes and runaway slaves to find safety, sustenance, and compatible lifestyles in the swamplands, plains, and pine-palmetto forests of the Florida peninsula. These same conditions then served to minimize their contact with the outside world, thereby mitigating the effects of its influence. The author provides a brief but interesting history of the tribe. She then describes some of the changes that occurred beginning in the 1960s, when paved roads reached the Big Cypress Reservation and a revolving-credit plan altered participation in the cattle program. Her clear, well-written study of a community with problems as well as promise is warm, personal, and insightful while at the same time objectively analytical. The book includes maps, black-and-white photographs, and a bibliography.

BK

496 Grobsmith, Elizabeth S. ***Lakota of the Rosebud: A Contemporary Ethnography***. Harcourt 1981, $13.50 (0-03-057438-2). 160pp. Nonfiction.

Briefly and succinctly, the author presents the facts of life on a modern reservation. Although she focuses on two communities on the Brulé (Sioux) reservation in South Dakota, the same conditions can be found on many other reservations. The traditional culture has evolved and blended into a distinctly contemporary lifestyle, combining native and nonnative elements to different degrees, in different combinations, and with varying degrees of success. Grobsmith describes the cycle of instability, unemployment, and alcoholism that plagues residents of the reservation. She also discusses the major issues of education and health, tribal political structure and dynamics, relationships with the Bureau of Indian Affairs, land use and other economic realities, community life, bilingualism, and the role of schools. She concludes that the most characteristic aspect of modern Lakota life is its overwhelming heterogeneity. The book includes black-and-white photographs, maps, diagrams and charts, and a bibliography. BK

497 Gulick, Bill. *Chief Joseph Country: Land of the Nez Perce.* Illus. Caxton 1981, $39.95 (0-87004-275-0). 316pp. Nonfiction.

Culling from a variety of historical resources, the author has written a well-documented yet very accessible history of the beautiful Northwest, home of the Nez Perce. After discussing briefly the prehistory of the area and the changes wrought by the horse, Gulick then concentrates on the chronology, personalities, and conflicting forces of Indian-white contact, from encounters with Lewis and Clark in 1805 and 1806 to the death of Chief Joseph in 1904. The last chapter follows the Nez Perce from 1905 to 1980. The entire book is liberally spiced with direct quotes and illustrated with numerous historical photographs and sketches. The author presents a number of viewpoints, but he gives most weight to available Native American accounts. He also refers readers to L. V. McWhorter's *Yellow Wolf: His Own Story* (orig. pub. 1940; Caxton, 1984) and *Hear Me, My Chiefs!* (orig. pub. 1952; Caxton, 1984) for more about the Nez Perce War itself. He credits Alvin M. Josephy, Jr. with having written the most comprehensive history of the tribe: *The Nez Perce Indians and the Opening of the Northwest* (Univ. of Nebraska Pr., 1979). Maps, a bibliography, and an index are included. BK

498 Hungry Wolf, Beverly. *The Ways of My Grandmothers.* Illus. with photos. Morrow 1981, $9.95 (0-688-00471-7). 256pp. Nonfiction.

Born on the largest Indian reservation in Canada, the author spoke only the Blackfeet language until she started school. Then, over the years, she adopted modern ways. Only after college, travel, and returning to the reservation to teach did she develop a serious interest in learning about and practicing her cultural heritage. Eventually she began collecting the wisdom and knowledge of the oldest grandmothers among her people to preserve this lore for future generations and to offer a more balanced insight into the daily lives and perspectives of these women. She tells about their personal lives, myths and legends, marriage customs, creative roles, women's societies and status, and even offers domestic hints and recipes. Throughout, she emphasizes the importance of religious ritual in every phase of daily life and indirectly shows the individual freedom allowed in nonreligious matters. The message of this book, written in simple language, is in its own way a reflection of the kindness and generosity valued so highly among the Blackfeet women. Black-and-white photographs and an index are included. BK

The culmination of thirty-five years of collecting, photographing, and writing on Native American art, this sumptuous book is as thoughtful and informative as it is beautiful. The stunning photographs by Jerry Jacka and the elegantly flowing text deal with the wide spectrum of fine-art forms being created by Native American artists today. Although Southwestern artists receive most of the focus, many artists from other regions who display in Southwestern museums and galleries are included.

The introduction by Clara Lee Tanner traces the prehistory of traditional arts and crafts of the Southwest, including weapons, textiles, ceramics, basketry, and jewelry. She continues with the later introduction of sheep and silver, the effects of traders and tourism, and the beginnings of easel art. The Jackas then explore the elemental dilemmas with which each individual artist must struggle in melding the inspiration, techniques, and constraints of heritage with talent, personal vision, and creative freedom. The authors continue with discussions of enduring traditions and new horizons, both in the abstract and in numerous personal examples. The artists' own comments and poetry add passion and promise to an enlightening book.   **BK**

500   Josephy, Alvin M., Jr. *The Indian Heritage of America.* Enlarged ed. Illus.
          Houghton 1991, $11.70 (0-395-57320-3). 448pp. Nonfiction.

This new edition of the noted historian's work on Native American history contrasts the stereotypes of the Indian versus the "real" Indian. The author also covers the pre-Columbian life of Native Americans and discusses the way they preserved natural resources. He covers Indians of all geographic areas in the Americas before and after the whites came to the hemisphere and discusses the impact of their arrival on the Indians and the conquerors alike. The centuries-long Indian struggle for survival in a hostile white world is recounted, and the author paints a vivid picture of the Native American today, five hundred years after Columbus.

In addition to this detailed, comprehensive work, Josephy has written a popular history of the Plains Indians titled *Now That the Buffalo's Gone* (Knopf, 1982), as well as numerous other works.   **EG**

Katz, William L. *Black Indians: A Hidden Heritage.*
See entry 166.

501   Keithahn, Edward L. *Monuments in Cedar.* Illus. Anderson 1945. o.p. Nonfiction.

The author discusses two conflicting theories about the origin of the Northwest Coast totem poles—the "monuments in cedar." One theory is that they evolved in prehistoric times; the other is that they emerged only after contact with Europeans. He briefly explains the evidence supporting each theory, emphasizing that such earlier artworks as chiefs' staffs, ivory pendants, Chilkat blankets, and so on prove that the highly sophisticated art style, the advanced carving and inlay techniques, and the unique cultures that supported them were available before the development of the totem poles. Although the author lacks understanding of other Native American groups, he greatly admires the highly civilized coastal people, the richness of their culture and oral literature, and their utilization of professional artists. Detailed chapters discuss the art and craft of the cedar poles, restoration projects of the 1920s and 1930s, the heraldic screens of the North, prehistory, history, legends, and culture.

Reproduced here is an extensive, carefully identified collection of early drawings and old photographs of totem poles and house pillars, most of which have long since been lost to the ravages of a rainy climate and the fires of idol-destroying missionaries. A map, linguistic chart, and bibliography are included. **BK**

502 Kelton, Elmer. *The Art of Howard Terpning*. Illus. Bantam 1992, $60.00 (0-553-08113-6). 160pp. Nonfiction.

An impressive work of art in itself, this beautifully designed book is a brief, well-written history of the Plains Indians as narrated by Elmer Kelton and interpreted through the remarkable paintings of Howard Terpning. The paintings—more than sixty of which are reproduced here—are magnificent, and the collection glows with Terpning's masterly use of lighting. The artist has an uncanny ability to capture both mood and moment. The design of the book emphasizes this compelling quality through the use of numerous two-page spreads and several plates of details. His works are also noteworthy for their well-researched accuracy and the effective mixture of impression and reality. Creating beauty and feeling without sacrificing authenticity of situation or detail, Terpning focuses on the daily lives of men and women of the Great Plains: Blackfeet, Cheyenne, Apache, and many others. There are high-quality reproductions on almost every page, carefully arranged to illuminate the easy-flowing text. Captions are very informative, if occasionally repetitive, and they complement the text by increasing the reader's appreciation of the artist and of each particular subject. Kelton's graceful writing is accurate, balanced, and eminently readable.

As explained in the fine introduction by Darrell R. Kipp, tribal histories, traditions, and values have been preserved and handed down to succeeding generations by gifted storytellers and artists. Howard Terpning fits admirably into that natural tradition, bringing the heart of Plains Indian history to life with truth and power. **BK**

503 Kroeber, Theodora. *Ishi in Two Worlds: A Biography of the Last Wild Indian in North America*. Illus. Univ. of California Pr. 1961, $35.00 (0-520-03153-9); $12.00 (0-520-00675-5). 262pp. Nonfiction.

On August 29, 1911, a Yahi Indian was discovered near a farm in Oroville, California. Four decades earlier his family and virtually everyone else in his small tribe had either been murdered by whites or had perished in the woods, leaving him, a boy perhaps nine years old, to wander alone. Almost fifty when he was found, he was placed under the care of the University of California Museum of Anthropology. The author's husband, anthropologist Alfred Kroeber, befriended the Yahi, whom he named Ishi (the Yahi word for man), and studied him until Ishi's death of tuberculosis five years later.

This book is not so much a biography of Ishi as an exploration of the world in which he lived and which disappeared forever after his death. Kroeber describes the life and customs of the Yahi, such as hunting, food, craft, family life, and ceremonies. Also receiving attention is the sad history of the extermination of Ishi's tribe and of the other Indian Nations of the Americas. Kroeber explores Ishi's life in the museum—his personal habits, his friendships, and the ways in which he helped the anthropologists learn more about his people. That aspect of the book is moving and compelling, allowing the reader to get to know a stoic and tragic figure who embodied the fate of his people.   EG

504   Kroeber, Theodora, and Robert F. Heizer. **Almost Ancestors: The First Californians.** Illus. with photos. Sierra Club 1968. o.p. Nonfiction.

Well-chosen quotations from Alfred L. Kroeber's *Handbook of the Indians of California* (orig. pub. 1925; Reprint Services, 1988) are smoothly integrated into the gracefully succinct narrative and into the overall design of this book, which includes 117 historic photographs. The book provides a brief, general introduction to the variety of Californian native cultures that thrived for ten thousand years until disrupted by the coming of the Spaniards in the 1700s and their final elimination by white encroachment during the 1800s.

The photographs cover the years from 1851 to 1939; most were taken between 1900 and 1910. An unusual and creative decision was made to eliminate backgrounds from most of the pictures and to crop the portraits to show only the heads of the subjects. In this way the reader focuses directly on the faces—young, old, handsome, homely, serious, smiling, shy, curious, sad. The photographs encourage the reader to look into those faces again and again and see, not just the last remnants of tribes forever gone, but people, real people whose own lives mattered, and continue to matter, even beyond death.   BK

505   Laubin, Reginald, and Gladys Laubin. **The Indian Tipi: Its History, Construction, and Use.** 2nd ed. Frwd. by Stanley Vestal. Illus. Univ. of Oklahoma Pr. 1977, $17.95 (0-8061-2236-6). 384pp. Nonfiction.

In this expanded version of their 1957 classic, the authors emphasize that the Plains tipi was not only the most convenient and comfortable of the world's all-weather tents, but a real home as well. Like other articles of Native American material culture, tipis were as beautiful as they were functional and adaptive. Following Stanley Vestal's foreword and a discussion of the history of the tipi, the Laubins explain the design, construction, decoration, and pitching of both three-pole and four-pole tipis and describe their years of personal experience living in their own tipi year-round. They also tell of their visits among different Plains tribes.

The book discusses how tipis are made, the lining used, and the various furnishings. The unusual chapter "Living in the Tipi" also discusses tipi etiquette, child care, food, cooking, and household hints. Other chapters introduce specific types of tipis, sweat lodges, transportation (then and now), camp circles, and design symbolism. The book also includes diagrams, photographs, appendix, bibliography, and index.

The Laubins have also authored the highly respected *Indian Dances of North America: Their Importance to Indian Life* (Univ. of Oklahoma Pr., 1977) and *American Indian Archery* (Univ. of Oklahoma Pr., 1991).   BK

506 Lavender, David S. *Let Me Be Free: The Nez Perce Tragedy*. Doubleday 1993, $14.00 (0-385-46867-9). 403pp. Nonfiction.

"Let me be a free man—free to travel, free to stop, free to work, free to trade where I choose, free to choose my own teachers, free to follow the religion of my fathers, free to think and talk and act for myself—and I will obey every law, or submit to the penalty." Aided by a translator, Chief Joseph spoke these words in 1879 as part of a speech given before a large audience in Lincoln Hall in Washington, D.C. He received a thunderous ovation and considerable publicity—but not his wish. At his death in 1904, he was still confined—both legally and physically—to a reservation, having failed to arrange for a Nez Perce reservation in the Wallowa Valley, which his people knew as their homeland.

In fascinating detail, Lavender describes the cultural, political, religious, and economic forces that swirled through this period of history. He paints telling portraits of the many strong characters involved and of the ways in which they influenced—and were influenced by—those forces and by the unpredictable flow of events. He questions numerous historical assumptions, often proposing more logical interpretations.

Lavender concludes that, although he became famous as a military genius, Joseph's true greatness lay elsewhere. A natural leader, young Joseph was a camp chief, the peace chief of the Wallowa Nez Perce, and never a war chief. Decisions on the tribe's fateful flight toward Canada were made in council, by consensus, as decisions had always been made; Joseph provided the unifying strength that allowed the band to carry out the decisions. Even after the surrender, however, Joseph continued to be an important symbol—and a stubborn man. Tall, handsome, and dignified, he determinedly sought opportunities to use his formidable oratorical gifts, experience in statesmanship, and persuasive personality to obtain help for his people on various issues over the next quarter century. Sometimes successful, often not, he refused to give up. As his friend Yellow Bull declared at Joseph's funeral, "Joseph is dead, but his words will live forever."

The book includes maps, black-and-white photographs and sketches, extensive notes, a bibliography, and an index.   BK

507 Lincoln, Kenneth, and Al Logan Slagle. *The Good Red Road: Passages into Native America*. HarperCollins 1989, $10.95 (0-06-250517-3). 271pp. Nonfiction.

College professor Lincoln journeys back, physically and emotionally, to his childhood home in the Nebraska-Dakota heartland, intent on reaffirming and expanding his circle of friends among the Lakota and deepening and broadening his perspective. He is accompanied by his small daughter and four students, one of whom is Slagle, who seeks to understand the medicine traditions of his Cherokee ancestors. Although the first two chapters sometimes detour into eloquent exercises in descriptive virtuosity, the authors soon settle down to record the group members' experiences and reactions, individually and collectively, as they meet different people and explore different aspects of modern Lakota life.

The authors write powerfully and well. Dialogue flows smoothly throughout the luminous text and rings so true that the reader is a silent participant in each interview, informal conversation, and argument. Personal insights, both subtle and profound, are offered simply and without adornment. The result is deeply moving, a thought-provoking look through "the heart's eye" at the inner and outer lives of many Sioux.

Alfonso Ortiz, in his foreword, praises the book's openness, sensitivity, and freshness of vision. Logan Slagle's afterword, written eleven years farther down the road, sheds the light of deeper wisdom, greater perspective, and hope.   BK

Littlefield, Daniel F., Jr. *Africans and Seminoles: From Removal to Emancipation*.
See entry 174.

508   Lyons, Oren, and others. *Exiled in the Land of the Free: Democracy, Indian Nations, and the U.S. Constitution*. Frwd. by Peter Matthiessen; Pref. by Daniel K. Inouye. Illus. Clear Light 1992, $14.95 (0-940666-50-2). 427pp. Essays.

Oren Lyons, John Mohawk, Vine Deloria, Jr., and others have contributed to this definitive work. According to the authors, the irony of democracy as it evolved in the United States is that it was a concept borrowed in large measure from the five Iroquois tribes—the Seneca, the Oneida, the Onondaga, the Mohawk, and the Cayuga. What had been labeled "democracy" in Europe had been in fact been merely plutocracy—rule only by the white, wealthy, landed gentry. Some Native American Nations had practiced true democracy long before the Europeans arrived, and the Iroquois system of democracy influenced Thomas Jefferson and the framers of the Constitution and the Bill of Rights. Yet, the authors note, the same revolutionary thinkers who framed these documents also enslaved, murdered, or forcibly removed the very peoples whose ideas they had drawn upon as a model for American economic and political development. The people who had been here before the Europeans and who had maintained the natural world without destroying it were thus displaced form their ancestral lands. The authors also describe how Indians enabled Washington to survive the winter at Valley Forge and helped the rebels win the war of revolution against England.   EG

509   Macgregor, Gordon, and others. *Warriors Without Weapons: A Study of the Society and Personality Development of the Pine Ridge Sioux*. Ed. by Roma K. McNickle. Univ. of Chicago Pr. 1946. o.p. Nonfiction.

The Indian Education Research Project, carried out between 1941 and 1946, was designed to investigate, analyze, and compare the development of personality among five Native American tribes in the context of their total environmental setting. Its ultimate goal was to evaluate systematically the whole Indian administration program, in hopes of increasing sensitivity to the peoples' social and psychological needs as well as the more visible economic and material ones. Although some of the research and interpretations may be dated, most of the insights are not. Many of them, in fact, could well be applied to contemporary non-Indian communities, such as factory towns, in which the majority of men have lost their means of livelihood.

Well-organized family life and communities survived on Pine Ridge until loss of the cattle economy in 1916 and 1917; the resulting demoralization, starvation, and dependency caused widespread personal, family, and community disorganization. The study's designers hoped that knowledge of the patterns of adjustment and dysfunction among the young might lead to improved local programs and conditions. As Willard W. Beatty writes in the foreword, the study might suggest ways "to a wiser and better pattern of relationship between all people, and . . . teach us how to conserve human values rather than destroy them."

The book includes maps, an appendix, a bibliography, and an index.

BK

510 Mander, Jerry. *In the Absence of the Sacred: The Failure of Technology and the Survival of the Indian Nations*. Sierra Club 1991, $25.00 (0-87156-739-3); $14.00 (0-87156-509-9). 400pp. Nonfiction.

Most readers of this book will find points with which they would like to argue, perhaps vehemently, but that in itself fulfills part of the author's purpose—to encourage active thinking, an appropriate vocabulary, and productive dialogue for assessing modern technology and its basic assumptions and examining the philosophical and practical directions we must embrace in order to survive.

Mander describes the technical changes experienced by the industrialized nations that result in negative effects on individuals, society, and the Earth. Subsequent chapters document the traumatic impact of those changes on various indigenous peoples around the world. Mander suggests that our worldviews and our supporting value systems are so internally consistent yet so diametrically opposed that reconciling them may not be possible. A high-powered realist, Mander recommends that we recognize the failure of the relatively modern belief that the Earth is merely another machine to be exploited to the maximum and return to our older beliefs and fuller, more leisurely lifestyles. He observes that by listening to native peoples who have never lost these ways and heeding their message, Westernized societies can get back on track and rediscover healthier, more fulfilling lives.

The book includes an appendix of organizations and periodicals, a bibliography, and an index.

BK

511 Matthiessen, Peter. *In the Spirit of Crazy Horse*. Aftwd. by Martin Garbus. Viking 1991, $27.50 (0-670-83617-6); $14.00 (0-14-014456-0). 628pp. Nonfiction.

First published in 1983, this book offers an intense investigative account of the American Indian Movement (AIM), events at Wounded Knee, South Dakota, and the trial of AIM leader Leonard Peltier on charges of murdering federal agents. The book explains the complex background of regional history, including the government's role in forcing Native Americans onto reservations situated on what seemed to be arid wastelands—only to find that more than half of the continent's uranium and much of its petroleum and coal lie beneath Indian holdings. Indians thus found themselves in the way again, an irony that contributed to the tragic (and ongoing) events documented here.

When he began work on this book, Matthiessen was more sympathetic to the older "traditional" Indians who objected to the young AIM troublemakers. Eventually, though, he decided that, despite excesses and mistakes, AIM's "warrior spirit" had restored much-needed identity and pride to thousands of Native Americans. His book solidly supports AIM without glorifying the movement. The author questions the reactionary traditionals and the tribal councils, which he sees as dominated by the Bureau of Indian Affairs (BIA). Drawing heavily on personal interviews and letters, interrogation records, and court transcripts, the author indicts the FBI and BIA and argues passionately for justice, for keeping tribal lands intact, and for a new, fairer trial for Leonard Peltier.

The book contains a good background introduction by Matthiessen and lengthy notes with comments, ending with an eloquent defense of AIM written to other American Indians by Janet McCloud in 1981. The book includes maps and an index.   BK

512   McReynolds, Edwin C. ***The Seminoles***. Illus. Univ. of Oklahoma Pr. 1975, $15.95 (0-8061-1255-7). 397pp. Nonfiction.

This volume, part of the excellent Civilization of the American Indian series, is the history of the tribe that made a landmark peace with the U.S. government. Some of the story of the Seminole Wars was not revealed until the publication of this book. McReynolds recounts the origins of the tribe in Florida, the military prowess of the Seminole people, and their fierce determination to survive. This is the story of a free, independent, and able tribe told empathetically and expertly by a skilled historian.   EG

513   Medicine Crow, Joseph. ***From the Heart of the Crow Country: The Crow Indians' Own Stories***. Crown 1994, $9.00 (0-517-88220-5). 138pp. Nonfiction.

Crow storyteller, historian, and World War II veteran Joseph Medicine Crow has offered here a portrait of the Crow people, both through his own narratives and through adaptations of tribal legends. He covers a range of topics, including Crow history, his own family's history, and the way life and traditions have changed in the twentieth century. Among the snippets of information he offers are instructions for luring buffalo over cliffs (with drawings included) and a discussion of what happened to the Crows' horses after the tribe was resettled onto reservations. He also describes the techniques used by the Crows to determined social status over the years. Other topics include medicine men and Indians with medical degrees, intertribal warfare, ceremonies, and key figures in Crow history. The book concludes with a discussion of Crow humor, much of which is evident throughout the book. This is a readable, entertaining, and lively work that reflects an essential optimism about Crow survival and adaptation to changing times.   LML

514   Merton, Thomas. ***Ishi Means Man: Essays on Native Americans***. Illus. by Rita Corbin. Unicorn 1976. o.p. Essays.

Poet and philosopher Thomas Merton spent much of his life in a Trappist monastery in Kentucky, but his spirit, intellect, and vision transcended the confines he chose for himself. In fact, he was freed by his lack of connection to worldly things to comment on the life of the intellect and the spirit.

Works by this prolific author include *The Seven Storey Mountain* (orig. pub. 1948; Buccaneer, 1991) and *Love and Living* (Harcourt, 1985). *Ishi* is the tragic story of relations between the Indians and the whites. To say that this conflict was inevitable, Merton argues, is to overlook the myriad choices we have as free men. It was not the "destiny" of the white man to defeat the spirit of native peoples. In fact, it is the antithesis of both the Indian and Christian philosophies that one race or part of nature should be conquered by another. The essays in this book speak eloquently about the dignity of man and the dignity of nature.   EG

515   Nabhan, Gary P. *The Desert Smells Like Rain: A Naturalist in Papago Indian Country.* Farrar 1987, $10.95 (0-86547-050-2). 192pp. Nonfiction.

The overture and ten chapters of this enjoyable book are literal and figurative journeys into friendship with the Desert Papago Indians, also known as the Tohono O'odham. Nabhan discusses experiences from his years as an ethnobiologist, writer, researcher, and teacher in the Arizona Writers on the Road Program. A student of the desert, he is fascinated by the individual adaptations made by, and the complex interrelationships among, the plants, animals, people, soil, and weather of the Sonoran Desert. His enthusiasm transfers to the reader, as does his special affection and respect for the few O'odham who still farm and gather in the traditional ways, fine-tuned to the unpredictable rhythms of a surprisingly productive desert.

He raises a number of questions as well—botanical, anthropological, ethical, legal, nutritional, and political—and invites readers to ponder creative solutions that address the multifaceted problems. The writing flows easily; it is sometimes poetic and often funny.

The notes at the end, which expand on the ideas presented, research being done, and sources of information available, are almost as interesting as the main text itself. The book includes a helpful map and a chart of O'odham sounds.   BK

516   Nabhan, Gary P. *Enduring Seeds: Native American Agriculture and Wild Plant Conservation.* Frwd. by Wendell Berry. Farrar 1991, $11.95 (0-86547-344-7). 250pp. Nonfiction.

Following publication of *Gathering the Desert* (Univ. of Arizona Pr., 1985), which explores the unique plants of the Sonoran Desert and the agricultural traditions of six tribes of the region, author Nabhan expanded the geographical and cultural scope of his plea for diversity. *Enduring Seeds* encompasses the entire Western Hemisphere, particularly the United States, Mexico, and Guatemala.

The first six chapters are largely distillations of Nabhan's lectures and papers. He presents various theories of the evolution of the flowering plants, animals, and peoples of the New World; the remarkable diversification of each; their adaptations to each other; and the gradual loss of biological diversity due to population pressures and monoculture farming. Far from being a dry scientific treatise, this book is beautifully written. The author's intense, information-packed overview argues passionately for acceptance of the lessons to be learned from persistent Native American agricultures and from the enduringly successful plants of the region.

The second half of the book is more anecdotal, based on visits to such varied locations as Wisconsin, North Dakota, and Florida. Nabhan clearly relishes the uniqueness of the plant and human communities he finds, but he also provides sound scientific and practical reasons for encouraging both diversity and wildness, which he sees as critical to our long-term survival. The concluding section of bibliographic essays directs interested readers to a wealth of additional resources. BK

517 Nabokov, Peter, ed. ***Native American Testimony: A Chronicle of Indian and White Relations from Prophecy to the Present, 1492–1992.*** 2nd ed. Frwd. by Vine Deloria, Jr. Illus. Viking 1991, $27.50 (0-670-83704-0). 512pp. Nonfiction.

Anthropologist Peter Nabokov has updated his seminal work on the history of five centuries of contact between Indians and whites. He cites a series of contemporary documents and treaties to present historical events through the Indians' own words and from their own perspective. In the process the reader learns of the public outrage and private humiliations of a people treated so badly that many books are reluctant to tell the true story.

The book conveys the impact of historical events on tribes, leaders, and individuals. The legacy of ancient peoples—a legacy of spirit, human values, and dignity—is also chronicled thoroughly and artfully in this moving book, which includes many illustrations and photographs. EG

518 Niethammer, Carolyn. ***Daughters of the Earth: The Lives and Legends of American Indian Women.*** Macmillan 1977, $16.00 (0-02-096150-2). 281pp. Nonfiction.

Drawn from a wealth of historical research, mythologies, and oral history, this book vividly describes the regional and tribal variations in the daily lives of Native American women. Chapters on childhood, puberty, courtship, homemaking, politics, medicine, crafts, recreation, and aging illustrate the human universality of these events and activities, as well as the creative individuality with which different peoples express them. The author makes the point that a gender-based division of labor was used to enhance a group's economic well-being. While the actual division of tasks and the rigidity with which that division was maintained varied from tribe to tribe, all roles were usually considered complementary and valuable. The author skillfully conveys the strong supportive bonds, hard work, independence, fun, dignity, and sense of purpose as women moved securely through the predictable stages of life. Historic photographs, notes, an extensive bibliography, and an index round out this work.

Niethammer's *American Indian Food and Lore* (Macmillan, 1974) provides 150 authentic recipes, descriptions, and illustrations of more than fifty edible wild and domesticated plants. The book offers harvest and preparation hints and gives the reader a feeling for the lives and spirit of the generations of Southwestern women who discovered these foods and these unique ways of preparing them. BK

519 Ohiyesa (Charles Alexander Eastman). ***The Soul of an Indian and Other Writings from Ohiyesa.*** Ed. by Kent Nerburn. New World Library 1993, $12.95 (1-880032-23-6). 96pp. Essays.

Kent Nerburn edited this collection of writings by Ohiyesa, the poet-philosopher who spoke eloquently for his people. As a boy, Ohiyesa was adopted by a white family and his name was anglicized to Eastman. Later, however, he returned to his roots and rediscovered the Indian wisdom of his grandparents. Ohiyesa's ideas convey the true value of life and describe the most effective ways people can conduct themselves toward others and toward nature. For readers who feel they live in a world empty of values and vision, this powerful book offers wisdom that is much needed today and that can also enrich the lives of future generations. **EG**

520 Oxendine, Joseph B. *American Indian Sports Heritage*. Illus. Human Kinetics 1988, $38.00 (0-87322-120-6). 352pp. Nonfiction.

Shedding considerable light not just on sports but on many aspects of life, this well-rounded book is highly recommended for the general reader and for all educators. Oxendine, a Lumbee Indian and a successful athlete, educator, and author, begins with an exploration of sports and games in traditional Native America. He celebrates each tribe's uniqueness, but he also discovers the many things they share in common: playfulness; a fondness for humorous anecdotes, joking, and teasing; a deep ritual and cultural relationship to sports; extensive preparation for competitions; commitment to winning; and avid betting. Five chapters detail types and variations of games played by adults and children.

The author then discusses the emergence and decline of Native American athletes in modern sports and ends with some hopeful signs for the future. His discussions of numerous American Indian athletes range from a one-sentence mention of all-star lacrosse player Jay Silverheels (who as an actor portrayed Tonto on the Lone Ranger series) to a full chapter on Jim Thorpe. Two chapters of brief biographies honor stars of the twentieth century, such as Oren Lyons and Billy Mills. The book includes a bibliography and an index. **BK**

521 Page, Susanne. *A Celebration of Being*. Illus. with photos by the author. Northland Publishing 1989. o.p. Nonfiction.

This photographer published *Song of the Earth Spirit* in 1972 (under the name Susanne Anderson) and *Hopi* in 1982. An exhibition of her photographs of the Hopi and Navajo was mounted by admirers in 1984. Showings were so successful among the Hopi and Navajo, indeed among all audiences around the United States, that the exhibit was reproduced in this special book. The high-quality images, combined with brief, telling captions, affectionately present real people living the varied facets of their lives.

The foreword by Robert Redford, active in both the Sundance Institute and Futures for Children, and the afterword by Jake Page, Susanne Page's author-husband, contribute to this warm, satisfying portrayal of contemporary Navajo and Hopi people. The book is a gentle, eloquent ode to the unity, diversity, and individuality of all people. **BK**

522 Paul, Doris A. *The Navajo Code Talkers*. Illus. Dorrance 1973, $13.95 (0-8059-1870-1). 160pp. Nonfiction.

This book is the most complete source of information available on the Navajo Code Talkers, an elite group of Marines whose work was essential to American success in the Pacific in World War II. The 420 Code Talkers used their complex native language as the basis for a military message transmission system. Other Native Americans, particularly Choctaws and Comanches, had occasionally been used for similar purposes during World War I and in some earlier campaigns of World War II. But under the guidance of Philip Johnston, the Navajo group devised, memorized, and continually adapted a special code so intricate as to be indecipherable, not only to the enemy but even to other Navajos. The code permitted transmissions that were so fast and accurate that the demand for these specialists eventually exceeded the supply.

Although somewhat dry in places, the narrative is extensively researched and meticulously accurate. Full documentation is provided in the appendices. The author generally manages to avoid stereotyping the Navajo Marines, their Anglo comrades-in-arms, or the Japanese. Personal anecdotes from letters, reports, and interviews add life to the narrative, describing feelings and incidents during training and combat, including such harrowing experiences as being captured by other American units and nearly executed as Japanese. Humorous anecdotes sprinkled throughout the text add a welcome dimension—one too often ignored by researchers and many writers. The last two chapters, covering the postwar era, describe the Navajo Code Talkers' impact on the communities to which they returned. This material is now somewhat dated, but it does not detract from the overall value of the book. An appendix and a bibliography are included.   BK

523   Pijoan, Teresa. *White Wolf Woman: And Other Native American Transformation Myths*. August House 1992, $17.95 (0-87483-201-2); $8.95 (0-87483-200-4). 160pp. Nonfiction.

Indian heroes and heroines have the power to transform themselves into other forms, especially such animals as birds, snakes, bears, and wolves. The meaning of these transformations reveals much about the cultural life of Native American peoples: their history, their sense of values, their image of themselves. In this book, noted storyteller Pijoan has collected forty of these myths from thirty Indian Nations. She regards these tales as windows into the common spirit that binds together people from different Native American tribes—and indeed, all members of the human family.   EG

524   Pike, Donald G., and David Muench. *Anasazi: Ancient People of the Rock*. Frwd. by Frank Waters. Illus. with photos by David Muench and Adam Clark Vroman. Crown 1986, $17.00 (0-517-52688-3); $17.00 (0-517-52690-5). 192pp. Nonfiction.

Following the rich, multidimensional introduction by Frank Waters, Donald Pike draws us deep into the homeland and history of the Anasazi. As he details the evolution of the peoples of Chaco Canyon, Mesa Verde, and Kayenta, he also explains the development and contributions of the neighboring Mogollon and Hohokam cultures, culminating in the rapid rise and spread of the young, vigorous, and highly adaptable Anasazi civilization.

Each short chapter is followed by a color portfolio from master photographer David Muench. His full-page and double-page spreads effectively capture both the majesty and the mystery of Anasazi ruins, dramatically conveying the emotional impact of their functional beauty, mute spirituality, and hard-won harmony with a difficult land. A selection of black-and-white photographs taken by Adam Clark Vroman between 1899 and 1904 concludes the book.

The author explains the various theories of Anasazi origins, changing ways of life, and disappearance so carefully that the reader becomes convinced that what Pike is saying is indisputably true. Only then does the author reveal the conflicting evidence, alternate interpretations, and contradictory arguments. In this entertaining way, Pike stresses that most of what we thought we knew about the Anasazi is actually nothing more than conjecture. The narrative is sometimes excessively wordy and the information repetitive; the organization of the middle chapters can be confusing. However, Pike's writing is picturesque, with generous slices of humor, and the book provides an interesting, thought-provoking, and quite comprehensive look at an intriguing culture. Muench's sensitive photographs speak for themselves.

BK

525   Rea, Amadeo M. *Once a River: Bird Life and Habitat Changes on the Middle Gila*. Illus. Univ. of Arizona Pr. 1983, $35.00 (0-8165-0799-6). 285pp. Nonfiction.

Although primarily ecological and ornithological in its focus, *Once a River* is also useful as a work on American cultures for several reasons. It focuses on a narrowly defined stretch of river, the Middle Gila, and traces its changes from prehistoric times through 1982. In the process, the author discusses the complexity of plant and animal life in and along the river, temperature cycles, rainfall patterns, groundwater levels, and human utilization.

During nineteen years of research on the Gila River Reservation, Rea gathered considerable information from the Pima Indians. He notes that birds have been an important element in the lives of the Gila River peoples for over a thousand years. He offers a discussion of Pima lore and culture in general as well as in relation to their knowledge of the birds and the river. As Bernard Fontana states in his impassioned foreword, inclusion of such information is a first for the Southwest. Finally, Rea makes stunningly clear in concrete terms how even such peaceful tribes as the notably prosperous Riverine Pima, friendly and generous to all travelers, were still nearly destroyed, not by military action, forced removal, or deliberate government policies, but by inadvertent destruction of their delicately balanced environment and the resulting economic impoverishment. Much of the damage is profound and irreversible, but Rea suggests actions that the tribal government (and others in similar situations) might yet take to prevent further deterioration.

The brush paintings by Takashi Ijichi are based on the bird designs and techniques of Hohokam pottery. Extensive maps, tables and charts, black-and-white photographs, a bibliography, an index, and a glossary of Pima words complete this study.   BK

526   Reyhner, John, ed. *Teaching American Indian Students*. Frwd. by Ben Nighthorse Campbell. Illus. Univ. of Oklahoma Pr. 1994, $26.95 (0-8061-2113-0); $14.95 (0-8061-2674-4). 344pp. Nonfiction.

Although written by and for professional educators, this book nonetheless includes a number of chapters that will also be of interest to the general reader, especially parents of all cultural backgrounds. It includes multicultural philosophy, educational theory, hard research, readable history, controversial viewpoints, and practical applications.

The brief foreword by Colorado senator Ben Nighthorse Campbell is personal and hopeful. Extensive appendices add considerably to the value of the book. Maps, lists of organizations and children's periodicals, a resource guide to books and articles, and an index are included. **BK**

527 Ruby, Robert H., and John A. Brown. ***Indians of the Pacific Northwest: A History***. Frwd. by Alvin M. Josephy, Jr. Illus. Univ. of Oklahoma Pr. 1981, $21.95 (0-8061-2113-0). 204pp. Nonfiction.

The authors have collected a vast array of information from primary and secondary sources and organized it into a comprehensive regional history of the coastal, mountain, and plateau peoples of the Pacific Northwest. The time period covered, roughly 1775 to 1900, was noted for the conflict within and among the diverse Native American and white groups who struggled over ownership and use of the land. The wealth of detail lends a suspenseful immediacy to the sequence of events.

The book contains a foreword by Alvin M. Josephy, Jr., an epilogue, a good selection of contemporary and historic black-and-white photographs and sketches, maps, notes, a bibliography, and an index. **BK**

528 Sandoz, Mari. ***Cheyenne Autumn***. Repr. of 1953 ed. Illus. Univ. of Nebraska Pr. 1992, $25.00 (0-8032-4223-9); $9.95 (0-8032-9212-0). 282pp. Nonfiction.

Many people are familiar with the tragedies of the Cherokee Trail of Tears and Chief Joseph's thwarted attempt to lead his people, the Nez Perce, to freedom in Canada in 1877. Fewer, however, are familiar with another epic tragedy that unfolded in 1878 when Little Wolf and Dull Knife led the Northern Cheyennes on a remarkable flight from Indian Territory, Oklahoma, back to the Yellowstone country of Montana, 1,500 miles away. They started out unarmed, most of them on foot, many of them sick and weakened from starvation. What's more, their long path took them through white-settled territory, dotted by towns and homesteads, criss-crossed by telegraph and railroads, and heavily fortified by the military.

Mari Sandoz weaves their engrossing tale of triumph and tragedy, courage and doubt, loyalty and betrayal, shrewdness and recklessness, hope and despair. Drawing heavily on oral tradition, primary research, and her intimate knowledge of Cheyenne culture, the author skillfully recreates the personalities, decisions, and suspenseful sequence of events, placing them in the framework of Cheyenne life and thought as well as within the overall context of the times. The book includes a section of historic photographs plus chapter notes, maps, and an index. **BK**

529 Shaffer, Lynda Norene. ***Native Americans Before 1492: The Moundbuilding Centers of the East Woodlands***. Frwd. by Kevin Reilly. Illus. M. E. Sharpe 1992, $35.00 (1-56324-029-7); $15.95 (56324-030-0). 160pp. Nonfiction.

In this work, historian Shaffer looks at North American prehistory from a refreshing and exciting global perspective. Through her readable and authoritative text, she recreates the unique conditions that allowed three mound-building epochs to flourish over a period of 4,000 years. She examines the life and culture of the mound-building tribes, focusing on their vast economic and cultural exchange networks that stretched from the Rocky Mountains to Florida and from Ontario to the Gulf of Mexico. The unusually extensive riverine network, combined with the mild climate and the abundance of wild foods, contributed to the rise of populous inland civilizations. The author notes how the native peoples along the narrow Eastern seaboard tended to be more scattered and that they were separated from inland cultures not only by mountain ranges but by river drainage systems that flowed east to the Atlantic, rather than west to the Mississippi or south to the Gulf of Mexico. Powerful and cohesive enough to defeat several Spanish invasions, the interior peoples were finally conquered by epidemics of new diseases, such as malaria and smallpox, and by the European population explosion. The book includes maps, illustrations, notes, a bibliography, and an index.   BK

530   Spicer, Edward H. *Cycles of Conquest: The Impact of Spain, Mexico, and the United States on Indians of the Southwest, 1533–1960*. Illus. Univ. of Arizona Pr. 1962, $19.95 (0-8165-0021-5). 609pp. Nonfiction.

A great deal has been written about the native cultures of the greater Southwest. Spicer attempts to synthesize the descriptive accounts and historical narratives into a meaningful interpretation of the cultural processes operating during the 400-year period in which inhabitants of the region were forced to deal with Spanish, Mexican, and Anglo-American expansion.

After briefly describing the native peoples of northern Mexico and the southwestern United States, the author describes the attempts by three successive conquering forces to "civilize" the tribes in the area and the inherent expectations and inconsistencies of each attempt. He then examines the dynamics and courses of cultural change (and continuity), including the growth of economic interdependence, alternative family patterns, community reorientation, political incorporation, and religious diversification. He shows that not one of the ambitious plans for the Native Americans turned out as planned—either for the dominant peoples or for the indigenous ones. Maps, bibliographic notes, and an index are included.   BK

531   Spivey, Richard L. *Maria*. Rev. ed. Frwd. by Dennis Lyon. Illus. Northland 1989, $45.00 (0-87358-499-6); $19.95 (0-87358-484-8). 172pp. Nonfiction.

Written by an acknowledged expert on contemporary Pueblo pottery, this unusual book is a combination biography, history of the craft, and art catalogue. After setting the stage with a brief history of San Ildefonso Pueblo, Spivey discusses the development and changes in its ceramic arts, and the near extinction of its pottery-making by 1907. Then, giving due credit to other people who also contributed significantly, he traces the renaissance in ceramics led by Maria and Julian Martinez. The instructive yet readable text includes divergent viewpoints and is enlivened by extensive quotes from Maria about her life and work, as well as by shorter quotes accompanying the black-and-white photographs that cover the years 1904 to 1952 and that appear throughout the book. Full-color plates of high-quality photographs showcase the different types of San

Ildefonso ceramic wares, from the late 1800s through the more recent innovations devised by Maria's grandson, Tony Da.

The book includes a map, genealogy chart, bibliography, and an index. Interested readers should also consult Alice Marriott's classic biography, *Maria: The Potter of San Ildefonso* (orig. pub. 1948; Univ. of Oklahoma Pr., 1987).

BK

532   Suzuki, David, and Peter Knudtson. ***Wisdom of the Elders: Honoring Sacred Native Visions of Nature***. Bantam 1992, $22.50 (0-553-08862-9); $12.95 (0-553-37263-7). 274pp. Nonfiction.

In this work Suzuki and Knudtson persuasively demonstrate the parallels among the world views of a very diverse section of wise teachings, with specific emphasis on the environmental ethic embedded within them. Juxtaposing the thoughtful views of respected "elders" of the scientific world with the tribal knowledge, beliefs, and shared values of old and new indigenous peoples, they create an illuminating dialogue among traditions that have arrived at the same place from different directions. With exceptionally fine writing and deep insight, the authors show the uniqueness of each perspective while underscoring the commonalities in the enduring philosophies of peoples from many times and places. Each way of seeing has its own validity, internal coherence, and adaptive dynamics and needs no comparisons to legitimize its existence. Yet taken together, they complement each other powerfully and impart vitality to a more holistic way of perceiving and believing, of accepting humankind's responsibility for restraint, reverence, and balance.

An appendix excerpts the 1991 United Nations draft Universal Declaration on the Rights of Indigenous Peoples. Also included are notes and an index.

BK

533   Thornton, Russell. ***American Indian Holocaust and Survival: A Population History since 1492***. Illus. Univ. of Oklahoma Pr. 1990, $32.95 (0-8061-2074-6); $15.95 (0-8061-2220-X). 352pp. Nonfiction.

Sociologist Thornton has written extensively on the impact of population issues among Native Americans. In this, his most important work, he traces the origins of the migration across the Bering land bridge between Asia and North America, and he details the Indian's early population growth and settlement. He examines how scholars have been able to estimate with credibility the Indian population before 1492. After the arrival of European conquerors and settlers, the Indian population declined drastically, the result of disease, war, starvation, alcoholism, intermarriage, and other factors. Thornton's discussion of the devastating impact of white settlement and Indian dispossession occupies the bulk of the study. Accompanying his text are clearly presented charts and tables that make his conclusions even more dramatic. Thornton also describes Native American ceremonies and their importance. His description of the Ghost Dance ceremonies is particularly eloquent.

The twentieth century has seen a resurgence of Native American populations. Thornton tries to answer how and why these cultures have survived against all odds. His writing is clear, the evidence is dramatic and well documented, and the visuals contribute to the reader's understanding of the impact of white settlement upon Native American communities.   EG

534   Trenholm, Virginia Cole, and Maurine Carley. ***The Shoshonis: Sentinels of the Rockies.*** Illus. Univ. of Oklahoma Pr. 1964, $17.95 (0-8061-1055-4). 367pp. Nonfiction.

In following the eventful history of the Shoshone tribes from prehistory to 1960, this colorful narrative makes it clear that not only did the tribes produce two of the most famous Native Americans of the 1800s—Sacajawea and Washakie—but that the tribes were integrally involved in all the stages of westward development.

In prehistoric times, the Northern Shoshones split off from the Western bands who lived in the Great Basin. They acquired the horse and rapidly became undisputed rulers of the Rocky Mountain region, sweeping from the northern plains of Canada to the southwestern territory of their Comanche cousins. Famous for their huge herds of carefully bred horses, the Northern Shoshones adopted many aspects of Plateau and Plains Indian cultures. When British and French traders began providing guns and ammunition to the Blackfeet and other tribes, deliberately keeping them from the Shoshones, the tide swiftly turned. At some point, the beleaguered Northern Shoshones split again; the Lemhis retreated to plateau country, while the Eastern Shoshones moved to the less accessible reaches of the Rockies. During their encounters with Lewis and Clark in 1805, the Shoshones discovered that the white Americans were willing to trade guns and ammunition for their horses and furs. This established a tradition of friendship between whites and the tribe that was seldom broken over the next hundred years. This friendship and the trade in horses that resulted were crucial factors in the subsequent history of the American West.

This well-researched, well-written book is Volume 74 in the Civilization of the American Indian series. It includes black-and-white portraits, maps, interesting footnotes, a preface, a bibliography, and an index.   BK

535   Vanderwerth, W. C. ***Indian Oratory: A Collection of Famous Speeches by Noted Indian Chieftains.*** Repr. of 1971 ed. Frwd. by William R. Carmack. Univ. of Oklahoma Pr. 1979, $14.95 (0-8061-1575-0). 292pp. Essays.

As noted in the foreword by William R. Carmack, formal oratory reflects the major issues, values, and decisions of a people at a given time and place. The speeches contained in this volume range chronologically from Teedyuscung (1758) to Quanah Parker (1910). They were delivered mostly in councils with the whites who were encroaching on their land, and so they deal primarily with the concerns and conflicts of that struggle. Vanderwerth has collected the most reliable records and translations available. Because delivery is such a vital aspect of sophisticated oratory, the author includes notes on the pauses and gestures used during the speeches. Vanderwerth also provides a portrait and a brief biography of each speaker. Unfortunately, no written record exists of the long and honored heritage of early Native American oratory, but these late-period selections attest to the eloquence, logic, and wit of the oral tradition and to the persuasive styles and remarkable memories of the speakers.

The appendix contains the full text of Chief Joseph's "An Indian's View of Indian Affairs" (1879). A bibliography is included.   BK

Vecsey, Christopher. *Imagine Ourselves Richly: Mythic Narratives of North American Indians.* Illus. Crossroad 1988, $24.95 (0-8245-0878-5). 272pp. Nonfiction.

This work is an invaluable overview of Native American mythic narration. Chapters address such topics as ethnography; emergence and maintenance of the Hopi people, Ojibwa creation myths, the story and structure of the Iroquois Confederacy, the heroic tales of the Navajo, an American Indian monomyth, and the genesis of Phillip Deere's sweat lodge.

According to the author, the stories in this book reveal the values native cultures hold concerning the environment, society, and the spiritual realms. To read them is to rediscover—and thus to gain a deeper understanding of—the Native American consciousness that forms such an important part of the American national psyche. EG

536 Viola, Herman J., and Carolyn J. Margolis, eds. *Seeds of Change: A Quincentennial Commemoration.* Illus. Smithsonian Inst. 1991, $39.95 (1-56098-035-4); $24.95 (1-56098-036-2). 280pp. Nonfiction.

This oversized volume contains articles and full-color illustrations covering aspects of the Columbian exchange, particularly as it affected aboriginal peoples. There are articles on the exchange of crops between the Old World and the Americas, Africans as slaves in the New World, and the cultural fusion of African, American, and European peoples throughout North, Central, and South America. The article by George P. Horse Capture, "An American Indian Perspective," examines the myths that surround encounters between Amerinds and Europeans, from the original contact to the American Indian Movement of the last twenty years. Original illustrations and maps complement the text, which combines expert research with excellent information on the cultural clashes between Indian and European and the efforts of Native Americans to retain their cultural heritage. EG

538 Wallace, Anthony F. *The Death and Rebirth of the Seneca.* Random 1972, $7.16 (0-394-71699-X). 416pp. Nonfiction.

Until the end of the eighteenth century, the Seneca were the largest of the Five Nations of the Iroquois Confederation. (The other four were the Cayuga, the Onondaga, the Oneida, and the Mohawk.) The Confederacy occupied most of present-day New York, southern Quebec and Ontario, northern Pennsylvania, and eastern Ohio. By the seventeenth and eighteenth centuries, the Nations of the Iroquois Confederation had a highly developed political, social, and economic system, one that virtually collapsed at the end of the American Revolution.

Wallace examines the culture, values, and rituals of the Seneca. He points out that, along with developing an advanced system of government, the Seneca had highly ritualized procedures for torturing captured enemies. They were effective in playing off the British against the French until they made a disastrous alliance with the British against the rebelling colonials. After the colonists' victory, the Confederation collapsed and the Seneca were confined to reservations, where poverty, disease, and alcoholism reduced their numbers. Others of the tribe survived by assimilating into white society. Wallace describes the Seneca rebirth between 1800 and 1815. This rebirth resulted from a vision by spiritual leader Handsome Lake, who combined ancient traditions with the ways of neighboring Quakers. The new religion has helped the remaining Seneca to retain their culture and to survive and prosper up to the present day. Wallace's exhaustive, well-documented study is essential to an understanding of the history and lives of a principal Indian Nation in the northeastern United States.   LML

539   Williamson, Ray A. *Living the Sky: The Cosmos of the American Indian*. Illus. by Snowden Hodges. Univ. of Oklahoma Pr. 1987, $19.95 (0-8061-2034-7). 404pp. Nonfiction.

According to the author, the complicated Mayan calendar "far exceeded the Old World calendar in its accuracy and long-term predictive power." Like the equally intricate lunar calendar of the Incas, the Mayan calendar controlled the daily and ceremonial lives of the people. Historians have long assumed that the less-centralized Native American cultures north of Mexico lacked the interest and skill required to establish systematic yearly calendars and the heavenly observatories needed to implement them. Williamson argues persuasively that sophisticated astronomies, cosmologies, and observatories did in fact exist and were used as important aids to living in balance with the rhythms and cycles of the natural and supernatural worlds.

He briefly traces the somewhat rocky beginnings of archaeoastronomy, its scientific maturation, and the critical growth of its interdisciplinary focus. He explains that scientists examining a possible astronomical site today measure the area carefully and analyze the site within the larger framework of its makers' mythologies, rituals, and environment. Such care and insight is important, he explains. For example, one known site happens to align with the rising of the sun eleven days before the winter solstice. That apparently random fact becomes significant when it is combined with the knowledge that the people who erected the site had for centuries conducted ceremonies that lasted eleven days—and that had to be completed precisely on Midwinter's Day.

Although skeptics may dispute some of Williamson's findings, it would be impossible to deny the overall import of the amassed evidence he presents so clearly. Tables, diagrams, maps, and attractive line drawings by Snowden Hodges contribute to the reader's understanding. There are also two sections of color and black-and-white photographs, useful notes, a bibliography, and an index.   BK

540   Wilson, Edmund. *Apologies to the Iroquois.* Orig. pub. 1959. Intro. by William Fenton. Illus. Syracuse Univ. Pr. 1992, $15.95 (0-8156-2564-2). 356pp. Nonfiction.

William Fenton's new introduction to the latest edition of a 1959 classic states: "By all odds the greatest man of letters to confront the vast Iroquois literature and to observe and interview their living descendants in the field was Edmund Wilson (1895–1972), America's foremost critic and essayist in this century."

During his visits to the various Iroquois reservations in New York and Quebec, Wilson explored both the past and the present, discovering a unique cultural mix and a resurgence of pride, manifested in the revitalization of the Iroquois League, the Handsome Lake religion, and far older ceremonials. A number of damaging congressional bills and engineering projects in the 1950s sparked a new nationalistic activism and internal political dissension as well, and Wilson's explanations are particularly valuable for their contemporary perspective.

The book begins with Joseph Mitchell's essay "The Mohawks in High Steel." The tone Mitchell sets is continued by Wilson throughout the remainder of the study. Clear and simple, with a touch of humor, the writing seems surprisingly brief and almost offhand, yet it provides a great deal of information with considerable insight. Wilson neither glamorizes, condescends, nor pities. Instead, he shrewdly analyzes; the people he meets become our own acquaintances, individuals to be respected and remembered.   BK

541 Wilson, Gilbert L. ***Buffalo Bird Woman's Garden: Agriculture of the Hidatsa Indians.*** Repr. of 1917 ed. Intro. by Jeffrey R. Hanson. Illus. Minnesota Historical Society 1987, $8.95 (0-87351-219-7). 129pp. Nonfiction.

Wilson, a Presbyterian minister, first visited the Fort Berthold Reservation in 1906, intending to write books for children. But he also felt it important that stories of Indian life be written from the Indian point of view. Thus began his long-lasting friendship with Buffalo Bird Woman and her family. Deciding to enter graduate school as an anthropology student, he returned to the reservation for his fieldwork, not with a thesis to prove or disprove, but with a desire to record as fully and carefully as possible the agricultural practices and philosophy of the Hidatsas, whose economy had thrived for at least 800 years. Rather than interview many Hidatsas, select the most typical responses, and then organize and interpret them himself, he made the innovative decision to personalize the information by concentrating on one traditionally knowledgeable, highly competent informant—a practicing woman agriculturalist—and let her interpret her experiences her own way. The result, originally published in 1917 as *Agriculture of the Hidatsa Indians: An Indian Interpretation*, is unusual in another respect as well. According to the brief preface, it made available "certain varieties of maize of apparently great value to [modern farmers] in the semi-arid areas west of Minnesota."

Unusual characteristics aside, the book is extremely informative technically, wise in garden lore, and interesting historically and ecologically. Yet, most of all, it is human. At one point Buffalo Bird Woman speaks with simple elegance of Hidatsa women singing to the gardens they love; she then laughingly sings some teasing songs made up for passersby. At such points the lilting narrative gradually reveals the fullness and rich texture of daily life in the gardens.

The new introduction by Jeffrey R. Hanson is particularly valuable. The book also includes a preface, introduction, maps, black-and-white photographs, and helpful diagrams.   BK

Wright, Ronald. ***Stolen Continents: The Americas Through Indian Eyes since 1492.***
See entry 786.

542　Bataille, Gretchen M., and Kathleen M. Sands. *American Indian Women: Telling Their Lives*. Univ. of Nebraska Pr. 1984, $9.95 (0-8032-6082-2). 209pp. Autobiography.

The authors begin and end with analyses of American Indian women's autobiographies—past, present, and future—as a genre. The literary distinctions they make may be of little importance to the general reader, but their discussions of Native American women's status, the purposes and methodologies of collecting and producing finished narratives, and the common differences between men's and women's autobiographies are of considerable interest. Drawing on those understandings, the remaining chapters explore a number of diverse examples with sensitivity and perception.

The extensive bibliography has helpful annotations and includes relevant articles, pamphlets, books, and chapters of books; there are also extensive notes and an index. BK

543　Crow Dog, Mary, and Richard Erdoes. *Lakota Woman*. Illus. with photos by Richard Erdoes. Grove 1990, $18.95 (0-8021-1101-7); HarperCollins $12.00 (06-097389-7). 272pp. Autobiography.

From the perspective of her thirty-seven years, Mary Brave Bird looks back on the events, feelings, and transformations of her tumultuous life. With honesty, forthrightness, and flowing simplicity, she recounts her early childhood on the Rosebud Reservation; her boarding school days; her time of alienation, wandering, and drug use; her commitment to and participation in the American Indian Movement (AIM); marriage to medicine man Leonard Crow Dog; motherhood; and the long, difficult process of maturing from a wild, aimless, half-blood loner into a committed, spiritually traditional Lakota woman.

Her intelligence shines through in the text, with valuable insights illuminating each stage, yet she maintains a discreet distance from the reader—just enough to preserve her privacy and to make the more painful revelations bearable. This book provides a unique and highly recommended look at a modern Native American life. Included is a section of black-and-white photographs by Richard Erdoes. BK

544　Dorris, Michael. *The Broken Cord: A Family's Ongoing Struggle with Fetal Alcohol Syndrome*. Frwd. by Louise Erdrich. HarperCollins 1989, $18.95 (0-06-016071-3); $12.00 (0-06-01682-6). 288pp. Biography.

In 1971 Michael Dorris became one of the first single men in the United States to adopt a child. His son, Adam, was a full-blooded Sioux whose biological mother had died of acute alcohol poisoning. As the author began to rediscover his own Native American roots through Adam, he also began to realize that Adam's increasingly obvious mental and physical disabilities were the result of the alcohol the child had been exposed to in his mother's womb. Dorris's experience led him to dozens of Indian reservations and to countless substance abuse counselors and youth workers. He concludes that alcohol abuse and fetal alcohol syndrome are decimating many Native American communities.

Dorris's account of his own family's struggle and of the efforts to combat alcohol abuse among reservation youth is moving and thought-provoking. It casts new light as well upon the debate surrounding the rights of pregnant women and the rights of the unborn.   **LML**

545   Eckert, Allan W. *A Sorrow in Our Heart: The Life of Tecumseh*. Illus. Bantam 1993, $6.99 (0-553-56174-X). 862pp. Biography.

His beloved wife's long, difficult labor on the eve of a great council meeting allows a waiting Shawnee war chief time to ponder his tribe's long and illustrious history. Forty pages later, the panther comet announces the arrival of his new son—Tecumseh, whose name means Panther Passing Across.

Through this dramatic style the author inserts into the narrative flow a great deal of cultural and historical information, gathered over thirty years of research and writing about the Middle American frontier. Told from the Shawnee point of view, this somewhat romanticized "narrative biography" reads like a novel, full of carefully reconstructed dialogue, thoughts, and action. Historical figures become real people, with real lives, loves, disappointments, and joys. The traditional view of the relationship between Tecumseh and his younger brother, the Shawnee Prophet, provides part of the ongoing drama. (See also the main entry for *The Shawnee Prophet* by R. David Edmunds.)

Maps, diagrams, nearly 200 pages of amplification notes, sources, index, and an extensive bibliography are included.   **BK**

546   Edmunds, R. David. *The Shawnee Prophet*. Illus. Univ. of Nebraska Pr. 1983, $30.00 (0-8032-1850-8); $9.95 (0-8032-6711-8). 272pp. Biography.

While researching another topic, historian Edmunds was surprised to discover that primary materials on the Shawnee dating from 1805 to 1810 were more likely to mention the figure known as the Shawnee Prophet than his more famous brother, the war chief Tecumseh. Intrigued, the author dug further and emerged with a picture of these Shawnee brothers quite different from the historically accepted one

After an unhappy childhood, Lalawethika grew into an unsuccessful, alcoholic adult. In 1805, however, he had a dramatic vision and awoke with messages from the Master of Life. To symbolize his new role, he adopted the name Tenskwatawa—the Open Door. He constructed a comprehensive religious and moral doctrine, drawing on both traditional Shawnee culture and the realities of the contemporary world. Espousing nonviolence, he began passionately preaching, trying to revitalize, purify, and unify the tribes of the Old Northwest, while urging avoidance of contact with whites, whom he saw as a source of contamination. Gradually he was forced to add political and economic solutions to his religious ones, laying the foundation upon which Tecumseh built his war confederacy. The Prophet continued to lead an unusual life until his death in Kansas in 1836.

Edmunds's scholarship has finally elevated the misunderstood Tenskwatawa from an inaccurately minor role—as a drunkard turned religious fanatic who only embarrassed Tecumseh—to his rightful place in history as a charismatic architect of pan-Indian unity.

The book includes maps, illustrations, extensive notes, a bibliography, and an index. Also recommended are Edmunds's *Tecumseh and the Quest for Indian Leadership* (HarperCollins, 1987) and *American Indian Leaders: Studies in Diversity* (Univ. of Nebraska Pr., 1980). For more on Tecumseh, readers might want to consult Allan W. Eckert's *A Sorrow in Our Heart: The Life of Tecumseh* (*see main entry*).   **BK**

547   Gridley, Marion E. **American Indian Women**. Hawthorn 1974. o.p. Biography.

Adequately written and largely free of stereotyping, this collection of biographies represents notable Indian women who lived from the 1600s to the 1900s. As the author points out, there are rarely any early records of Native American women (or men, for that matter) unless they happened to affect the lives of the white colonists. Despite this limitation, Gridley is able to present sketches of a variety of female figures, including politically powerful women, artists, prima ballerinas, teachers, a best-selling poet, and the first Indian woman physician. The author obviously admires her chosen subjects as women of courage and deep conviction, whether they are "saviors" responsible for the very survival of European settlements, "warrior queens" responsible for the deaths of hundreds of settlers, or "peacemakers" seeking harmony with justice.

Gridley's brief studies of these fascinating people whet the reader's appetite for more. The book includes black-and-white portraits, a bibliography, and an index.   **BK**

548   Linderman, Frank Bird. **Pretty-shield: Medicine Woman of the Crows**. Illus. by Herbert Morton Stoops. Univ. of Nebraska Pr. 1974, $10.95 (0-8032-5791-0). 256pp. Biography.

Pretty-Shield, a Crow medicine woman in her seventies, agreed to narrate her life story for cowboy-ethnographer Frank Linderman. "Young people know nothing about our old customs, and even if they wished to learn there is nobody now to teach them. I believe that you know more about our old ways than any other man of your age, Crow or white man. This is the reason why I hide nothing from you . . . and . . . tell you truthfully, Sign-talker." Her stories will delight the modern reader as much as they delighted the admiring Linderman.

Pretty-shield related the events and feelings of her childhood and youth—both personal and tribal—from the free-roaming days on the plains to the disappearance of the buffalo and the beginning of reservation life, giving us one of the first accounts of Plains Indian life from a woman's perspective. As mischievous and strong as she was wise and kind, Pretty-shield was able to share practical jokes, battles, buffalo hunts, healings, adoptions, loving families, death, and birth. The stories reflect her love of the nomadic life and great pride in her womanhood. And, as she merrily admits, "[My best friends and I] loved fun, and did not let our hearts grow old too soon."

"Her ready wit and contagious laugh," combined with fluent sign language, transcended the limitations inherent in communicating tribal information, through an interpreter, to a non-Crow white male: Their partnership produced this fast-paced, easy-reading classic that retains its zest today. Also recommended is Linderman's *Plenty-Coups: Chief of the Crows* (John Day, 1930; Univ. of Nebraska Pr., 1962).

549   Neihardt, John G. ***Black Elk Speaks: Being the Life Story of a Holy Man of the Oglala Sioux.*** Univ. of Nebraska Pr. 1979, $25.00 (0-8032-3301-9); $9.95 (0-8032-8359-8). 311pp. Biography.

While working on the fifth song of his epic poem, the stirring *Cycle of the West*, Neihardt amassed a great deal of information on the Messiah, or Ghost Dance, Movement from many sources and points of view, but he felt he lacked an adequate feel for its deeper spiritual significance. He returned to the familiar Pine Ridge Reservation and was introduced to Black Elk (a second cousin of Crazy Horse), who had witnessed the Battle of the Little Big Horn, participated in the Messiah belief and its tragic conclusion, and had been a healer, visionary, and important holy man for most of his life.

Black Elk's story of his early life presents those times of trouble from a unique viewpoint, that of a young Oglala boy, from his birth in 1863 to the final surrender in 1891. Neihardt recorded the narrative, "not only in the factual sense—for it was not the facts that mattered most—but rather to recreate in English the mood and manner" of Black Elk's telling.

First published in 1932, the book was reissued in 1961. It became popular worldwide and has been considered an important classic ever since. Included are a preface, postscript, and a brief life of Neihardt, as well as a section of black-and-white and color plates by Oglala artist Standing Bear.   BK

550   Parker, Dorothy R. ***Singing an Indian Song: A Biography of D'Arcy McNickle.*** Illus. Univ. of Nebraska Pr. 1992, $35.00 (0-8032-3687-5); $13.00 (0-685-75056-6). 317pp. Biography.

The subject of this book was an author, Bureau of Indian Affairs (BIA) administrator, anthropologist, musician, university professor, historian, and founding member of the National Congress of American Indians (NCAI). D'Arcy McNickle was an active intellectual proud of his Native American heritage, but as a young man he denied his Métis background and his painful childhood on the beautiful Flathead Reservation of western Montana. He sold his allotment and traveled widely, settling for a while in New York City. During the more than five years he struggled with his first novel, the semiautobiographical *The Surrounded* (orig. pub. 1936; Univ. of New Mexico Pr., 1978), he gradually came to terms with his own past and developed a deep interest in Native American history.

In this biography, Parker follows McNickle's life through the Depression years, the Federal Writers Project, his appointment to John Collier's BIA during the heady days of the Indian New Deal, the founding of the pan-tribal NCAI, and on through his full life, sudden death, and rich legacy. Parker's own thorough research and the cooperation of many other people resulted in a valuable collection of primary resource materials—voluminous correspondence, articles, reviews, school and tribal records, his parents' divorce proceedings, successive revisions of his novels, a diary, and so on, all of which permitted considerable insight and enabled her to include many personal touches. Careful analysis and good writing complete the effort to do justice to the many facets of this singular life.

The book includes an important foreword and prologue by Parker, black-and-white photographs, notes, a bibliography of McNickle's published works, and an index. The work is part of the American Indian Lives series.   BK

551 Qoyawayma, Polingaysi. ***No Turning Back: A True Account of a Hopi Indian Girl's Struggle to Bridge the Gap Between** the World of Her People and the **World of the White Man**. Illus. Univ. of New Mexico Pr. 1977, $11.95 (0-8263-0439-7). 187pp. Autobiography.

Born into the loving security of a traditional Hopi community, Polingaysi was an inquisitive child and natural leader. Through her contact with white missionaries and her attendance at a day school, Polingaysi's restless spirit and her unquenchable thirst for knowledge led the small, determined girl to rebel against her family and all things Hopi as she made a series of decisions that led down an unusual, painfully difficult path. Outstanding student, talented musician, and zealous convert to Christianity, she anglicized her name to Elizabeth and achieved her dream of becoming a missionary to her own people. Still restless and unfulfilled, often rejected, and feeling increasingly torn, she seized the opportunity to teach primary children at a government school—and found her true calling. For over thirty years, this self-doubting rebel taught hundreds of Navajo and Hopi children and fought to advance and humanize Indian education. Her own successful example contributed to major shifts in national policy.

Finally returning to her own home below the mesa where she was born, she pursued her work as a prize-winning potter and educational consultant, and established a national scholarship fund for Hopi students. In the mellowed wisdom of her seventies, she dictated the story of her lifelong struggles, her doubts, and her coming to peace with herself and with the many facets of her life.   BK

552 Sandoz, Mari. ***Crazy Horse: The Strange Man of the Oglalas.*** Repr. of 1942 ed.; 50th anniversary ed. Intro. by Stephen B. Oates. Univ. of Nebraska Pr. 1992, $11.95 (0-8032-9211-2). 428pp. Biography.

An exceptional biography of an exceptional man, Sandoz's *Crazy Horse* is an enduring classic that, once read, will not be forgotten. As a child of the frontier, the author knew the contemporaries of the great Lakota war chief and listened to their stories; much later, she interviewed his surviving friends and fellow tribesmen to glean as much additional information as remained. Then, with consummate storytelling skill, she brought all those personalities and their changing times vividly to life in this heroic saga of Northern Plains history.

Everyday life, customs, personal interactions, and beliefs form the backdrop as the young Lakota develops from a quiet, thoughtful boy to a reluctant warrior to a brilliant visionary and military genius, honored with the old name Crazy Horse. This leader was most noted for engineering the Sioux defense, including the victory over Custer at the Little Big Horn. Although his dreams and courage could not ultimately save either himself or his way of life from defeat and death, this powerful book remains a moving affirmation of a great life.

A chronology, bibliography, notes on controversial points, and a map are included. Also recommended is Sandoz's brief, informative *These Were the Sioux* (orig. pub. 1961; Univ. of Nebraska Pr., 1985), containing warm recollections from her childhood.   BK

553 Standing Bear Luther. *My Indian Boyhood.* Repr. of 1931 ed. Illus. Univ. of Nebraska Pr. 1988, $6.95 (0-8032-9186-8). 200pp. Autobiography.

The Lakota are a Western Sioux tribe located in present-day South and North Dakota. Under the military leadership of Crazy Horse, the Lakota defeated Custer at the Little Big Horn in Montana.

Luther Standing Bear was for many years chief of the tribe. This account of his Indian boyhood on the Great Plains reflects the mythology, folklore, and mysticism of the Lakota people. Raised to become a Sioux warrior and a useful member of the Sioux society, he was given the Plenty Kill as a sign that his tribe was ready to defeat all foes, Indian and white. However, the luck of the Indians ran out. Their claim on traditional lands was challenged and defeated many times before his people were completely subdued. This account describes a social organization and a way of life that all but disappeared; today, the Lakota are struggling to keep part of that tradition alive.   EG

554 Wagner, Sallie R. *Yazz: Navajo Painter.* Illus. Northland 1983. 76pp. Biography.

Family man, talented artist, Code Talker, active community member, and recovering alcoholic, Jimmy Toddy—also known as Beatien Yazz—comes across in this biography as a multidimensional, evolving person. The first section of the book is a warm, motherly account of his life and art by Sallie Wagner, who recognized and encouraged his talents from the time he was seven or eight years old and who became part of the motherless boy's extended family. The paintings reproduced here span a period of over forty years, from 1939 to 1982. The works trace Yazz's development as an artist from early boyhood to middle age. In the second section of the book, J. J. Brody provides a critical analysis of that art and the various stages and influences it reflects. In the last section, Toddy/Yazz himself reminisces about important people and events that have affected his life and career.

For other extensive books on the artist's first thirty years, Alberta Hannum's *Spin a Silver Dollar* (o.p., 1944) and *Paint the Wind* (o.p., 1958) are recommended.   BK

555 Wallace, Anthony F. C. *King of the Delawares: Teedyuscung, 1700–1763.* Repr. of 1949 ed. Syracuse Univ. Pr. 1990, $16.95 (0-8156-2498-0). 328pp. Biography.

Meticulously reconstructed from an unusual number of available primary sources, this unromanticized life of Teedyuscung presents him as a particularly intelligent man, complex and inconsistent, the frustrated product of Delaware/Lenni Lenape societal disintegration and Colonial unrest—and an important man who influenced the course of American history. He was probably never officially appointed a sachem by the woman chief-maker of his lineage, but the Indian societies were becoming highly disorganized because of their constant removal by the whites and the people cried out for leadership. Teedyuscung's gift of oratory and his negotiating and military skills eventually helped him become the leader of the pivotal Wyoming Valley Delawares and the primary spokesman for many others native groups.

Little is known about Teedyuscung, other than his whereabouts and his oratorical ability, until about 1755. Wallace describes the world in which he moved, carefully explaining the shifting social and political forces of the time. Because of this painstaking care, the narrative does not flow easily, but neither is it dry or cumbersome because of the good writing, good oratory, and the wealth of rather surprising information. The biographer confines himself primarily to Teedyuscung's well-documented public life, but occasionally he makes important, cautiously reasoned inferences as to Teedyuscung's personality and motives.

Murdered in 1763, Teedyuscung was avenged by a major uprising. He had felt inferior throughout his life, partly because he could not read or write, had no personal *manito* (totem) until he adopted the Moravians' "Lamb of God," could not match the material wealth and technology of the Europeans, and was unable to preserve the successive homelands of his people from white encroachment. Yet he was, in Wallace's estimation, the only person, Indian or white, "able to sense the heart of the problem: to grasp the principle that while the 'civilizing' of the Indian was inevitable, it had to be a process undergone peacefully, in security, on Indian land, in Indian communities, at the Indian's pace." The book includes a map, bibliographical references, and an index.   BK

556   Waters, Frank. ***Brave Are My People: Indian Heroes Not Forgotten.*** Intro. by Vine Deloria, Jr. Illus. Clear Light 1993, $24.95 (0-940666-21-9); $14.95 (0-940666-51-0). 160pp. Biography.

This book, which earned its author nearly universal praise, contains "flashing glimpses" of men whose lives, over a period of half a millennium, have enriched the history of the United States. From the legendary Deganawidah and his partner, the orator Hiawatha, to Sequoyah and Seattle and less well-known individuals such as Irataba and White Antelope, the author quickly sketches the time and setting of each life, then focuses on the difficult, critical decisions each person made and presents the results of those decisions—often in the subject's own eloquent words.

In his preface, Waters pays tribute to a personal hero, his part-Cheyenne father. As Vine Deloria, Jr. states in the foreword, Waters has provided us with much-needed models of nobility and integrity, real people who believed in their missions and who devoted their lives to them.

Black-and-white portraits and a bibliography round out this work, which offers a powerful introduction to significant Indian figures for both general readers and students at the secondary level.   BK

5

CANADA

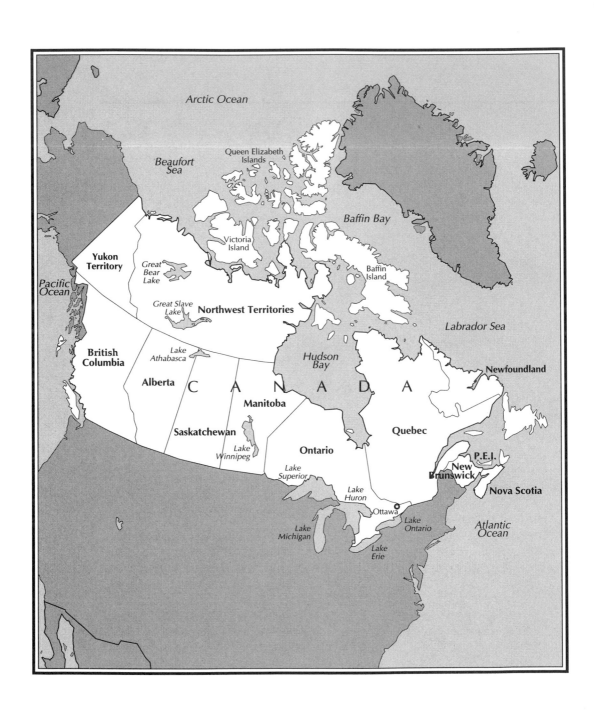

5

CANADA

by Jaswinder Gundara

The sun here must be a different sun
From the one under which
I could live no longer.
The sun here has heard the cry of eagles. . . .

—*Walter Bauer, A Different Sun*

The vast Canadian landscape spreads out like a fresh page that invites the strokes of a pen. Driven by the search for creative fulfillment in a new land, many have taken up that invitation. The burgeoning literature by and about the native peoples of Canada and about those who adopted this place as their home possesses undeniable power, depth, and eloquence. It is the literature of transculturalism, of expansion and aspirations, of emotional and political tension. These works speak of identity, of uprooting and estrangement, of hurt, of questioning. Ultimately they are about the transformation of the Canadian social reality. The new horizons they explore are reshaping the edges of the Canadian literary map—indeed they are redefining what Joel Des Rosiers has called the "moving borders of culture."

The Canadian psyche has been molded by the experiences of Polish, Ukrainian, and Italian homesteaders lost on the prairies, of Chinese laborers on the railroads, of Canadian Japanese interned in their own homeland during World War II, and of the aboriginal peoples who first set foot on this pristine land. For long decades the voices that would tell of these experiences have been largely silent. Now, however, those voices are gradually being heard; the stories they tell are becoming vital components of our culture and literature, of our thinking and dreaming. This bittersweet literature, born of hope and despair, articulates new perspectives on the issues of race, gender, class, language, culture, history, and politics.

But the task of recouping the past and expressing the immense diversity of the present is a daunting one for the Canadian writer or artist. Despite the promise of the new land, "minority" writers in Canada—that is, those who deal primarily with racial, linguistic, or cultural themes and issues—are struggling to prevent their work from becoming marginalized. They must swim against the tide of so-called "mainstream literature," the Canadian canon

251

dominated by Margaret Atwood, Robertson Davies, and a handful of other internationally known figures.

Critics, educators, publishers, and librarians often place writers who fall outside the mainstream into convenient pigeonholes identified with simplistic labels: this author is a "multicultural writer," that one an "ethnic writer." On one level these labels purport to place the writers within a context. In fact, however, such labels become invidious codes that at the very least distract from the universality of their work and that at worst conceal their relevance to society as a whole. Many mainstream writers from the dominant social group are praised for presenting their unique and individual perspectives on the human condition. Why is it, then, that so often "minority" writers are all lumped together by their skin color or their cultural background and assumed to speak with one voice? Like any stereotypes, literary labeling undermines the value of creative work; it assumes uniformity, and that in turn implies mediocrity, which is anathema to any creative endeavor.

Fortunately, as the works in this bibliography reveal, the situation is changing. Increasingly, the works of writers such as Michael Ondaatje and Josef Skvorecký are receiving enthusiastic recognition and are significantly helping to shift public perceptions. Books by Joy Kogawa and Austin Clarke contain stories told through the eyes of the colonized, the immigrant, the dispossessed. The key issue here is one of perspective, of looking at things from points of view other than those of the dominant group. Works by these authors, especially those written in languages other than English, help resist the trend toward "cultural appropriation," the absorption and domination of smaller cultures by the homogenizing forces of the mainstream. Being able to assert their history and culture in their own language is deeply meaningful for such poets and novelists as Marlene Nourbese Philip and Dionne Brand. For them, writing is a form of liberation, an opportunity to redraw the social map, to heighten the consciousness of the reader. It may be argued, too, that the emergence of new voices, speaking in languages that until now have only rarely been heard, results in incalculable gain for the English language because, as Des Rosiers states, "the strength of a language is not to push back what is strange but to assimilate it." Furthermore, the works listed in this chapter that were written by sociologists, historians, and politicians document important aspects of Canadian life that until now have been marginalized or have gone unrecorded. Such works are helping to render the invisible visible.

The future of Canada and the Canadian identity are inextricably entwined with the destiny of the Francophones—the French-speakers who live in Québec. French is the language of one of the founding peoples of Canada, and thus it holds the status of an official language. The survival of the distinctive Québecois identity and culture has been a key issue for decades and has contributed to political and social tensions throughout the nation. The literary writings of Gabrielle Roy and Marie-Claire Blais transcend political divisions to speak to the human heart about this conflict. Also discussed in this bibliography are works of social commentary that provide insight into this ongoing drama and that compel Canadians to ask searching questions about themselves and their future.

Here, too, are works by and about the aboriginal peoples of Canada, those who were first to inhabit this vast and varied land. Before the arrival of white settlers, these peoples lived in highly developed cultures with viable economies founded on principles of respect for the land and for nature. The whites, however, imposed the Western concepts of land ownership and dominance over nature. In doing so, according to Heather Robertson in *Reservations Are for Indians* (James Lewis & Samuel, 1970), they dismantled the aboriginal ways of life but offered no viable alternatives in their stead. With their cultures devastated, and robbed of their wealth, the aboriginal peoples existed in a poverty that was both material and spiritual. Beginning in the 1960s, however, Canada's aboriginal peoples began reasserting themselves and their culture. Today many people realize the wisdom of regarding the planet as a sacred world, one that must be cared for and nurtured. The survival of our planet is now a compelling agenda item for the international community. As Beatrice Culleton writes in *In Search of April Raintree*:

> White Man, you have our land now
> Respect it. As we once did.
> Take care of it. As we once did.
> Love it. As we once did.

Many of these peoples have made self-government their goal. In their struggle to regain their proper place in Canada, the aboriginal communities contend with prejudice rooted in ignorance. The books discussed in this chapter, selected for their balance and perspective, will help the sensitive reader replace ignorance with insight.

Many of the works here—including novels, collections of poetry, oral histories, and biographies—deal with women's struggle to achieve equality within society. These books, like volumes that explore the lives of other racial and national groups, help to dispel entrenched myths and stereotypes and cultivate a deeper understanding.

As one of the world's last frontiers, Canada has served as a haven to people who are fleeing the horrors of war, political turmoil, or crippling poverty in their countries of origin. The nation's official policy of multiculturalism encourages cultural and linguistic diversity. Though tensions exist, this spirit of mutual respect has allowed vibrant and confident new voices to emerge. The ineffable beauty of Canada and the promise of hope held out by life in a new land inspire the search for fulfillment. But this quest is often accompanied by a sense of loss, of yearning. This dilemma, which epitomizes the human condition, finds special expression in the literature of Canada. For the writer, arrival in Canada is not the journey's end. The journey and the search continue.

Another feature of Canadian literature is the sheer number of small presses that have emerged since World War II. These publishers, which mirror the country's multicultural social milieu, are usually devoted to articulating the views and interests of a particular group, whether feminist, philosophical, regional, or cultural. They are often the first to publish writers who then go on to win acclaim within the mainstream. Among these enterprises are Toronto South Asian Review, which emphasizes the complexities of multiculturalism in modern Canadian writing; Williams-Wallace, which began as an outlet for black Canadian writers; Fifth House, which focuses on material by and about aboriginal peoples; and Mosaic Press, which brings to light works from ethnocultural writers who might otherwise never have been read by Canadians. Small presses are integral to the Canadian social fabric. Equally important, they serve as an alternative to large publishers in the United States and Great Britain, who notoriously overlook not just multicultural Canadian works but Canadian writing in general. Most of the books described in this chapter were published originally by small or medium-sized Canadian presses; some are out of print and others are available only directly from their Canadian publisher.

It must be emphasized that, as a highly selective bibliography, this list cannot do justice to the full range and depth of global literature from Canada. At best, the titles discussed here can only whet the reader's appetite. Embedded in the mother lode that is Canadian literature are many prize jewels. This chapter will serve as a starting point for exploration; the reader who experiences these treasures and who is inspired to dig further will be richly rewarded.

About the contributors

This bibliography is the product of a team of staff members from the Metropolitan Toronto Reference Library who, believing the importance of such a work, have volunteered to share their expertise. The contents reflect the views of the contributors and not necessarily those of the library.

Mary Anne Tessaro, the Canadiana Librarian, and Tadeusz J. Uranowski, the Regional Multilanguage Librarian, participated in compiling the overall list. They also served as major contributors of the annotated entries. Without their expertise and generous assistance, the compilation of this bibliography would not have been possible.

Other contributors from the Languages and Literature Department are Catherine Cook, Alexandra B. Günther, Beatriz Hausner, Irina Hedman, Anda Liberis, Susan Martin, Romana Sanocka, Christine Smijak, and Laura Soto-Barra. Contributors from the Business and Social Sciences Department are Marci MacKinnon, Albertine MacNair, and Anna Zanardo. The contributor from the History Department is Gwen Ing.

The participation of all these people made this project truly rewarding.

JG

LITERATURE

557 Armstrong, Jeannette C. *Slash*. Theytus 1984, $12.95 (0-919441-29-1). 215pp. Fiction.

This novel documents the painful experience of the aboriginal peoples of Canada and their struggle to survive in the aftermath of the colonialism that destroyed their traditional ways of living. The story centers on the difficult transition of Slash, a young Okanagan Indian, from childhood to manhood. Slash enters the world beyond the reservation with the irrepressible enthusiasm of youth, but once there he encounters virulent prejudice and racism. To ease the pain of rejection he turns to drugs and alcohol. In his wretched state, he ultimately returns to his own roots and people, seeking healing for his wounds. The beating of the Indian drum symbolizes the awakening of his soul. The road leads him to join the Indians' political struggle; he discovers that when people have to fight, "their pride returns and with it inner strength." This struggle offers him a way to refurbish his psyche and regain his self-worth. His path is one that leads from personal trial marked by tragedy to the rediscovery of the inner strength that he derives from the pristine land and from his heritage.

The author is an Okanagan Indian recognized for her contribution to creative writing. As a keen observer of the changes experienced by her people, she raises important questions in this novel, questions that must be resolved by aboriginal people in determining the future of their descendants.

558 Bauer, Walter. *A Different Sun*. Trans. from German by Henry Beissel. Oberon 1978, $25.95 (0-88750-165-6). Poetry.

Having witnessed the horrors of Nazi Germany, poet Bauer moved to Canada in 1952, but the nightmares from that experience continue to pursue him in his new land. His poetry is haunted by the pain of his predicament: caught between the old world and the new, between a wounded past that will not be forgotten and the allure of a future that brings new promise, by the pain of dislocation and the severing of bonds with his much-beloved homeland.

His poems are fragile; they float across the page as gentle as bubbles glistening in the sun. He is questioning, tentative, probing, and—most of all— intensely evocative. Canada, under a different sun, offers sweet hope amidst the ravages of war-torn Europe. In his verse we meet the emigrant who pines for a country that no longer exists; the traveler who has seen too much but who must tell his story in the new land; the child who beholds a new blossom. We wander through the streets of Toronto as the poet reminds us of the original meaning of that name: a meeting place. In the crossroads of Toronto, the poet finds, to some degree at least, space for reconciliation with himself.

559 Beauchemin, Yves. *The Alley Cat*. McClelland & Stewart 1989, $14.95 (0-7710-1150-4). Fiction.

When Florent, a young salesman, witnesses a near-fatal accident on the street, he rushes to the aid of the victim. His good deed is observed by a strange old man who rewards him with the tip that a small but highly profitable restaurant nearby is selling for a song. Florent buys the restaurant, and at first he enjoys great success. But his guardian angel turns out to be an evil force intent on his downfall, and the young restaurant owner soon becomes involved in a spiral of treachery and deceit.

Beauchemin, a popular French-Canadian author, skillfully treads a fine line between fantasy and reality as he follows the struggles of Florent through his final triumph over his adversary.

560 Bissoondath, Neil. *On the Eve of Uncertain Tomorrows*. Crown 1991, $18.95 (0-517-58233-3). 224pp. Fiction.

Born in Trinidad in 1955, Neil Bissoondath, who immigrated to Canada in 1973, has become one of Canada's more accomplished young writers. Although his previous work focused on the spiritual and material plight of immigrants to Canada, in this collection of stories his view has become darker and more powerful. For most of the characters, Canada represents a broken dream, or at least one that has gone unfulfilled; fluctuating between hope and fear, their only certainty is uncertainty.

In the title story, a man awaiting his immigration hearing divides his time between a Toronto safe house filled with other refugees and torture victims and a rundown cafe frequented by illegal immigrants. In "The Power of Reason," a cleaning lady angry with her undisciplined, drug-dealing sons brings home a packet of poison, the purpose of which remains uncertain. In "Security," once-wealthy Mr. Ramgoolan tries to deny his sense of disorientation in a new culture by the obsessive observance of Hindu rituals he had previously ignored. Neil Bissoondath has created a memorable gallery of characters responding in different ways to life in a new country.

561 Blais, Marie-Claire. ***Mad Shadows***. McClelland & Stewart 1990, $5.99 (0-7710-9867-7). 212pp. Fiction.

Isabelle-Marie is ugly and cruel; her brother, Patrick, is beautiful but simpleminded; their mother is a shallow, vain woman obsessed with the physical perfection of her son. This obsession intensifies as she ages and becomes progressively disfigured by a malignant facial cancer. These three tormented souls inhabit a distorted reality interwoven with elements of myth and fairy tales, a world devoid of moral imperatives and ruled by extreme emotions and wild passions. Matricide, insanity, and disease feature prominently in this tale of greed and obsession, in which Blais's characters ultimately destroy themselves and each other. Some readers may find *Mad Shadows* harrowing; certainly the author's view of the universe is disquieting. But the beauty of the book lies in the clear, simple style used to convey this surrealistic nightmare. The result is a haunting story of great charm and despair, one of the preeminent works of Québecois literature. Blais is also the author of *Deaf to City* (Overlook, 1987).

562 Brand, Dionne. ***Sans Souci and Other Stories***. Firebrand 1989, $18.95 (0-932379-71-0); $8.95 (0-932379-70-2). 150pp. Fiction.

The main characters in Brand's stories are typically black women of inordinate tenacity and complexity who pursue their lives with dignity despite the twin challenges of racism and sexism. The wrenching division of their two worlds—"away" in Canada and "home" in the Caribbean— has a profound influence on their dreams, longings, and aspirations. They are driven by a need to make something of themselves. But the mean and lonely streets of Toronto exact such a heavy price that, as one character puts it, "all the sugar gone outa the thing." Through the juxtaposition of stories set in Canada and the Caribbean, Brand skillfully weaves the themes of "home" and "away," of belonging and alienation. In one story, for example, the reader experiences the bitter irony of the black woman who is hired as child-minder in Toronto but who, as a mother, is forever estranged from her own offspring. For many blacks in Toronto, life means being invisible. Nonetheless, there are moments of hilarity, enclaves of friendship, and sources of support. Brand's characters, complex and restless, possess the will not merely to survive but to live. These stories speak about the predicament, not only of black women, but of all women.

Brant, Beth, ed. *A Gathering of Spirit: A Collection by North American Women.*
See entry 446.

257

CANADA

563 Cameron, Anne. *Daughters of Copper Woman.* Inland 1988, $9.50 (0-88974-022-4). 150pp. Fiction.

The Nootkas, an Indian tribe on Vancouver Island, were decimated by previously unknown diseases following the arrival of the Europeans in 1776. Many who died had served as the official "memorizers" of Nootka history. The irreparable communal loss was reflected in songs and stories of great pathos. This unique book, a collection of stories narrated by Nootka women, contains only a fragment of the vast Nootka oral tradition.

The stories form a cycle of myths and legends that recount the origin of the human race, the mother of which, the Copper Woman, epitomizes feminine vision and wisdom. According to legend, all the races that inhabit the earth are related, because "we all come from the belly of the Copper Woman." The tales feature themes of birth, death, and sexuality. They also recall the coming of the Europeans. The imposition of Western values led to conflict and turmoil, shattering the traditional matriarchal structure of Nootka society. The myths collected by Anne Cameron carry a message for all women about their special role in the social order of the world. Cameron is also the author of *The Journey* (Spinsters Ink, 1986) and *Child of Her People* (Spinsters Ink, 1987).

564 Carrier, Roch. *La Guerre, Yes Sir!* Trans. from French by Sheila Fischman. Anansi 1970, $12.95 (0-88784-410-0). 113pp. Fiction.

The body of a young man is brought back to his native village in rural Québec for burial. His wake and the events that ensue capture the essence of the conflict between English Canadians and French Canadians during the time of World War II. The episodes are alternately gruesome and hilarious. A man amputates his hand so as to avoid conscription; children use his frozen hand as a hockey puck. A woman shares her bed with her lover, who is a draft-dodger, and her husband, a military deserter; she suddenly begins giving birth incessantly to one set of twins after another. The characters are presented with a simplicity often associated with folk tales, while the action moves forward at the breakneck speed of an adventure story. Carrier has succeeded in producing a compact, humorous novel that entertains through its satire of Canadian society and Anglophone-Francophone relations.

565 Clarke, Austin. *Storm of Fortune.* Little, Brown 1973. o.p. Fiction.

This is the second and in many ways the best novel in Clarke's trilogy, the other titles of which are *The Meeting Point* and *The Bigger Light*. These novels chart the fortunes of a group of five friends from Barbados during their slow and eventful adaptation to Canada's social values and conventions.

Bernice fights loneliness and bitterness in the home of her wealthy employers, the Burrmanns. Her sister Estelle, made pregnant by Mr. Burrmann, heads in desperation for northern Ontario to live with a woman she believes to be a friend. A fellow domestic, Dots, carefully plots her climb up the educational and social ladder, dragging along her husband, Boysie, who is reluctant until he also awakens to the seductive power of ambition and success. Their friend Henry, however, suffers an erratic decline and eventual destruction following his marriage to his wealthy girlfriend, Agatha.

Through the mingling of their stories, Clarke explores the entire social fabric encountered by this vital but isolated group, especially the prejudice toward and exploitation of immigrants within polite Toronto society. The novel is saved from bitterness by Clarke's humor, his wonderful gift for dialogue, and the indomitable spirit of his characters.

Craven, Margaret. *I Heard the Owl Call My Name.* See entry 451.

566   Crusz, Rienzi. *Elephant and Ice.* Porcupine's Quill 1980. o.p. Poetry.

Born in Sri Lanka, Rienzi Crusz emigrated to Canada in 1965. In this collection of poems, Crusz combines brilliantly textured and passionate elegies for his lost homeland with elegant and ironic hymns of resignation about life in the new land. "Culture" and "place" as Canadian realities have seldom been expressed as poignantly and with as much resonance as they are here.

Crusz's poetry is rich with laughter and irony. He sees East and West in one clear glance. Totally contrasting elements—such as elephants and ice—are reconciled by his delightful sense of wit. Critics regard his Sun-Man poems as major artifacts of a new Canadian sensibility, important reflections of the realities of national selfhood. Ferocious though the heat may be, the light that the Sun-Man sheds upon the world lingers in the mind with a lovely afterglow. By speaking of the displaced self, these poems articulate and transcend the experience of the newcomer. Crusz conveys a sensibility that is at once primitive and sophisticated, intense and subtle. His previous works include *Flesh and Thorn* (1974), *Singing Against the Wind* (1985), and *A Time for Loving* (1986), and his collection of poems *Still Close to the Raven* was published by the Toronto South Asian Review in 1989.

567   Culleton, Beatrice. *In Search of April Raintree.* Repr. of 1983 ed. Peguis 1992, $6.95 (1-895411-46-7). 228pp. Fiction.

This is an autobiographical novel of unflinching honesty written by a Métis woman. Métis are people of mixed race, combining Native American and French-Canadian ancestry. Born in 1949, Culleton became a ward of the Children's Aid Society of Winnipeg at the age of three. She grew up in foster homes away from her real family and people. Her own experience in these homes was positive, but both of her older sisters committed suicide.

In Search of April Raintree is a searing indictment of Canada's tragic treatment of its aboriginal people. We experience the anguish of two Métis sisters as they try in different ways to carve out a life in a society that despises them. Defying social rejection, Cheryl asserts her native identity, only to pay the ultimate personal price. Her sister, April, hopes to pass as a white person to evade the label "half-breed" and the inevitable destiny of poverty. But her temporary escape into the world of the whites turns into imprisonment. If she hopes to live with herself, she must confront the ruins of her own life. The novel ends on a positive note of individual reassertion. Although the road ahead seems uncertain, April seeks to redeem her sister's death through her reconciliation with the past and with her own identity.

568   Dabydeen, Cyril, ed. ***Another Way to Dance: Asian Canadian Poetry***. Williams-Wallace 1990. o.p. Poetry.

Although the writers in this anthology share some elements in common—such as Asian heritage, history, culture, geography and immigration—the tie that most truly binds them now is that they are all Canadian. Among the poets included are Himani Bannerji, Rienzi Crusz, Joy Kogawa, Michael Ondaatje, and Jim Wong Chu. They bring to their work a rich and diverse heritage of words; their vision and creativity find full rein as they write of family, displacement, and feelings of "otherness." Along with the sense of discovery, they affirm the diversity within Canadian society and the quest for a collective sensibility shaped by an unpredictable destiny.

While changing and being changed by the Canadian landscape and milieu, these writers also add to the inevitable evolution and diversity around them. The traditional literary styles of their ancestry no longer constrict them; the choreography of change and evolution will always find another way to dance.

Dabydeen is also author of *Elephants Make Good Stepladders: Poems (see main entry)*.

569   Dabydeen, Cyril. ***Elephants Make Good Stepladders: Poems***. Third Eye 1982. o.p. Poetry.

Born in Guyana, Cyril Dabydeen immigrated to Canada in 1970. A writer, editor, and college instructor, he serves as national coordinator of readings by Asian-Canadian writers, sponsored by the Canadian Asian Studies Association. Hailed by reviewers as an important voice in contemporary poetry, he was Poet Laureate of Ottawa from 1984 to 1987. His empathy for the poor and displaced, along with his understanding of the humdrum existence of the ordinary worker, have prompted comparisons of his works with those of noted Latin American poets Pablo Neruda and Nicolás Guillén.

Dabydeen's poems deal with the experience of living within two cultures, exploring the themes of immigration, discrimination, and expanding consciousness. Even as he records his growing immersion in Canadian life, memories of Guyana surface with stubborn persistence, feeding his complex sensibility. In his poems he contrasts his past life in the tropical poverty and disorder of the Corentyne district in Guyana with the present reality of his life amid the cool landscapes and growing security of Canada.

Elephants Make Good Stepladders combines his acute sense of social reality with his desire to explore the "bottomless pool of origins." His search for the "elemental man" takes him beyond the urban immigrant experience of Canada and the experience of the rural settlers from Guyana, all the way back to images of ancestral India.

570   Foon, Dennis. ***New Canadian Kid***. Pulp Pr. 1989, $9.95 (0-88978-215-6). Drama.

This play originated in a school workshop in Vancouver in 1980. Students, mostly immigrants, interviewed other New Canadians about their experiences. The students adapted these interviews into a script, *Immigrant Children Speak*, which Dennis Foon used as the basis for this work, intended for production by adult professional actors.

New Canadian Kid tells the story of Nick, a young boy from a fictional country called "Homeland" who immigrates to Canada with his family. During his first day in a Canadian school he tries very hard to grasp the language and culture of the other children. Some of the children are hostile and some are friendly; Nick understands he must learn to live with both.

In the play, the Canadian characters speak gibberish, and the immigrants from Homeland speak English. This convention allows the audience to experience and understand events through the eyes of the immigrants—a dramatic twist that carries an enormous impact. Visual effects are also important. Homelanders dress in green, Canadians in primary colors. As Nick becomes more comfortable in Canada, he symbolically integrates more colors into his costume.

The second play included in this volume, *Invisible Kids*, is the story of George, whose friends at school organize a petition drive, which they hope will force the Canadian authorities to allow George's sister to emigrate from Jamaica. The play reaffirms the power and promise of Canada's children, who are overcoming prejudice to build a truly multiracial society.

571 Froese, Tiessen, and Peter Hinchcliffe, eds. ***Acts of Concealment: Mennonites Writing in Canada***. Univ. of Waterloo Pr. 1992, $18.00 (0-88898-106-6). 244pp. Fiction.

Like members of other minority cultures in Canada, the Mennonites live in a world defined by such terms as *marginality, difference,* and *otherness*. Mennonite writing in Canada is flourishing, as it explores various aspects of identity—cultural, political, ecclesiastical, theological, familial. The essays, stories, and poetry of Canadian Mennonites collected in this anthology explore questions of influence and continuity, of familiar and forbidden discourses, of identity and homelessness, of self and other. Among the poets represented are Rudy Wiebe, Sarah Klassen, David Waltner-Toews, Di Brandt and Patrick Friesen.

These works chronicle and explore the productive tension between revelation and concealment, a tension found not just in Mennonite writing but in all good literature. Such tensions contribute to one of the most energetic and successful strands of contemporary Canadian writing. A few lines by poet Robert Kroetsch capture one of the main themes of this anthology:

> To reveal all is to end the story.
> To conceal all is to fail to begin the story.

572 Galay, Theodore A. ***After Baba's Funeral***. Playwrights Canada 1981. o.p. Drama.

This play takes place in the kitchen of the Danischuk family home in Manitoba, shortly after the funeral of the *baba*, or grandmother. Relatives make small talk about baba's last days of life, about their own families, and about death.

Ted Galay's writing for the theater reveals the profound influence of Ukrainian culture and tradition. Everyday sayings of the older generation assume tremendous importance, providing enduring values for younger people born in a new country. The author creates his characters with great insight into individual dignity as well as deep compassion for human foibles. The family relationships in the play epitomize warmth and tenderness, while small quarrels make for comic relief. The richness of personalities and emotions and the easy spontaneity of the dialogue provide the audience ample opportunity to identify and empathize with the characters. By dealing with intimate familial relationships and the process of coming to terms with difficult situations, the play achieves universality.

573   Gelinas, Gratien. ***Yesterday the Children Were Dancing***. General Distribution Services 1967, $6.95 (0-7720-0210-X). Drama.

The setting of this play is Montréal. A federal election is pending, and political tensions are running high. Following the Minister of Justice's sudden death, Pierre Gravel, eminent lawyer, federalist, and longtime Liberal Party worker, is asked to run in his district and is assured that, if elected, he will be given a cabinet position. For Gravel, the post would mean the fulfillment of his lifelong ambition. To his utter shock, however, he discovers that his older son, André, is not only a separatist but also the leader of the terrorist movement that is responsible for a series of bombings across the province. In fact, that very evening, André plans to set off a bomb and then turn himself in to the police.

The second act dramatizes the confrontation between the generations. André and his girlfriend, Nicole, confront Pierre and his long-time partner in the law firm. The battle shifts from the theoretical to the emotional plane with the arrival of Louise, who is André's mother and Pierre's wife. Her love goes out equally to her husband and to her son. The intractable logic of the situation dictates the outcome: André must act according to his beliefs, while Pierre, only partly defeated, writes a campaign speech in which he sets down the unshakable principles that govern his own political morality.

The themes of federalism versus separatism, of the older generation making way for the younger, reveal the Canadian psyche at a particular moment of its national history. In the universal context of such human tragedy, love and goodwill are not enough to bridge the gap between generations. By setting the play within a familial context, Gelinas underlines the tragic inevitability of a conflict that arises from forces outside the control of the protagonists but that is a natural part of the human condition. In this play, especially in the character of André, Gelinas reflects certain aspects of his own life.

574   Gunnars, Kristjana. ***Settlement Poems 1 and 2***. Turnstone 1980, $10.00 (0-88801-033-8); $6.00 (0-88801-032-X). Poetry.

These poems voice the inner thoughts of imaginary Icelandic settlers who came to Manitoba a hundred years ago. Through her use of spare, stark language, the author effectively conveys the feelings of these settlers and paints vivid images of their fight for survival.

The author was born in Reykjavik, Iceland, in 1948. At sixteen, when she came to Canada, she did not speak English, a fact that undoubtedly contributed to her poetic freedom in creating new rhythms and structure in the use of her acquired language. Gunnars learned about the Icelanders in Canada through diaries and manuscripts found in archives. Her short stories, published in *The Axe's Edge* (Press Porcepic, 1983), draw from the same material. These works also deal with the immigrant experience and reveal the lives of settlers who try to cope with cultural shock.

575 Hébert, Anne. ***Kamouraska***. General Publishing 1970, $5.95 (0-7736-7419-5). 250pp. Fiction.

This passionate romance is based on historical events. Sixteen-year-old Elizabeth d'Aulnieres leads a comfortable, if uneventful, existence until her marriage to Antoine Tassy, an egotistical libertine and member of the local gentry. After several desperately unhappy years with this cruel and unfaithful man, she flees and returns home. There she meets and falls in love with a foreign doctor, with whom she conspires to murder Antoine. The attempt fails, the couple part, and Elizabeth attempts to regain her lost honor by marrying a respectable but dull lawyer.

Hébert skillfully elevates this tale of conjugal infidelity and unhappiness to the level of high tragedy through her vivid portrayal of a woman trapped by the inexorable grip of events beyond her control. The Northern setting further intensifies this powerful romance; the desolate snowy wilderness of Québec reflects the spiritual isolation of the characters.

576 Highway, Thompson. ***Dry Lips Oughta Move to Kapuskasing***. Fifth House 1989, $9.95 (0-920079-55-5). Drama.

Winner of the 1989 Dora Mavor Moore Award for best new play and outstanding production, *Dry Lips Oughta Move to Kapuskasing* is a companion piece to *The Rez Sisters (see main entry)*. It features seven men from the Wasaychigan Hill Indian Reservation who are as obsessed with the game of hockey as the Rez sisters were enthralled by bingo. This play also explores the role of the aboriginal people in contemporary white Canadian society. The supernatural figure Nanabush, appearing in this play in female form, is often the catalyst for the action.

The playwright uses humor and harsh language to present the reality of life on the reservation. Moments of terrible violence, including a brutal rape and a shooting, reveal the rage and frustration that simmers beneath the surface of the story. A mood of despair dominates the play. But the author chooses to end the action on a high note, a peaceful domestic scene with mother, father, and baby, signifying that there is hope.

577 Highway, Thompson. ***The Rez Sisters***. Fifth House 1988, $9.95 (0-920079-44-X). Drama.

Thompson Highway is a Cree Indian from the Brochet Reserve in northwestern Manitoba. Author of many scripts and musical scores produced in theaters across Canada, he served as artistic director of Native Earth Performing Arts, the only professional theater company in Toronto dedicated to the development of drama that presents the concerns and viewpoint of Canada's aboriginal peoples.

Winner of the 1988 Dora Mavor Moore Award for best new play and outstanding production, *The Rez Sisters* is the story of seven women who live on the imaginary Wasaychigan Hill Indian Reservation—the "Rez." On the surface the plot of the work is simple. The seven bingo-mad women decide to travel to Toronto to attend the world's largest bingo game. Each woman dreams of how she will spend the prize money. Through these dreams and the interaction among the women, their lives on the reservation are revealed. Each character in the play is an individual with her own strong voice. At one point during the trip down to Toronto, their car breaks down, and with the stage plunged into blackness, the audience must understand the action and identify the women by voice alone. The only male figure in the play is Nanabush, the trickster, who brings an element of mysticism into the drama. The language of the play, often gritty and harsh, is never inappropriate. Through humor, violence, patience, and community, the women help each other to survive in the often harsh, unwelcoming world that has been created for them by white society.

The sequel to this work is *Dry Lips Oughta Move to Kapuskasing (see main entry)*.

578 Iwaniuk, Waclaw. ***Evenings on Lake Ontario: Poems***. Hounslow 1984, $7.95 (0-888205-42-3). 60pp. Poetry.

Iwaniuk is a much published, Polish-born poet who writes in English. This volume brings together poems that reveal his thoughts on Canada, himself, poetry, Italy, history, and other topics. The poet's style is quite unusual, at times jarring and difficult to follow. Readers may be impressed with his attempts to create a new poetic idiom even if he does not always succeed. His poems touch upon matters of humanity and history, on the problems of peace and war, on the longing for freedom, and on the new Canadian reality. His work transcends national and linguistic boundaries, showing Iwaniuk to be both a Canadian poet of consequence and a commanding voice in Polish poetry.

579 Iwaniuk, Waclaw, and Florian Smieja. ***Seven Polish Canadian Poets: An Anthology***. Polish Canadian Publishing Fund 1984. o.p. Poetry.

This is a collection of poems, some of which are already recognized as classic contributions to national Canadian literature. The seven Polish-Canadian poets included here represent several generations and schools of creativity and reflect different views of human fate in our time: displacements and deportations; families together and families separated; young boys deported for forced labor; transports through the tundras of Siberia; landscapes ranging from the sands of the desert to the mountains of Persia and India; and a migration of epic proportions.

In her melodious, rhythmic stanzas and impressionist imagery, Zofia Bohdanowiczowa represents the turn-of-the-century style of the young Poland and its later continuation by the "Skamander" group. The poetry of Janusz Ihnatowicz, while often abstract and reflective, reveals a strong sensitivity to nature and the people around him. At their best, his verses (such as "Internal Landscape" and "Children at the Window") contain evocative imagery and philosophical insight, traits revealing a strong affinity with the early poetry of Czeslaw Milosz. Bogdan Czaykowski's poems reflect his profound love of the rich landscape of British Columbia, a region that, after his immigration, became his "here." The works of Waclaw Iwaniuk, who also coedited this volume, reveal how, despite his loneliness and estrangement, he has become an active part of the Canadian literary scene: "I was not born here," he writes; "I do not know the splendour of this land, but my voice trembles when I speak of it." Iwaniuk is also the author of *Evenings on Lake Ontario* (*see main entry*).

580   Kelly, M. T. *A Dream Like Mine*. Warner 1992, $4.99 (0-446-36308-1). Fiction.

In this powerful story, told by a white journalist, aboriginal land and water has been destroyed by a paper mill. The death of the ancient forest spells the decimation of a traditional way of life. But during a sweat ceremony, an Indian named Arthur, who verges on insanity, has a vision: Someone must pay for the violation. Arthur kidnaps the unrepentant manager of the paper mill and demands that he atone for the crime; the wound dealt the aboriginal people must be cauterized. Against the pristine backdrop of the Canadian wilderness, Arthur's pent-up rage is unleashed and events take an inevitably tragic course. (The novel is prophetic: In 1991, a few years after the book was published, the Oka Indians in Ontario staged a violent confrontation with the authorities in defense of their forestland.)

Kelly's terse and elemental style conveys the dark tragedy with a nightmarish brilliance. In the words of Peter Matthiessen, this is a "wonderful novel of obsession, terror, and wild strangeness by a man with a strong sense of the Indian people and the Indian way. The main character is an extraordinary creation, unforgettable."

581   King, Thomas. *Medicine River*. Viking 1991, $5.95 (0-14-012603-1). 272pp. Fiction.

This accomplished first novel by the aboriginal writer Thomas King introduces us to the engaging inhabitants of Medicine River, a small Albertan town just outside a Blackfeet reservation. The narrator, Will, is a Blackfoot who does not have official status as a member of the tribe but who has returned to Medicine River to attend his mother's funeral. During his visit he meets the irrepressible Harlan Bigbear, the local basketball coach, matchmaker, business consultant, and all-round meddler. Will is persuaded—against his better judgment—to remain on the reservation and open a photography business. Gradually, Will is drawn back into full participation in the community he had planned to leave behind forever. He becomes a reluctant member of the Medicine River Friendship Center Warriors basketball team, manages to avoid the machinations of Martha Oldcrow, the local marriage doctor, and becomes a surrogate father to a baby named South Wing. Interspersed among these tales are Will's memories of his own often troubled childhood. Despite a light, often humorous touch, Thomas King also deals with deeper issues of the aboriginal experience and identity. Medicine River emerges as an appealing place to visit.

Among King's other highly regarded works are *Green Grass, Running Water* (Houghton, 1993) and *All My Relations: An Anthology of Contemporary Canadian Native Fiction* (Univ. of Oklahoma Pr., 1992).

Kinsella, W. P. *The Moccasin Telegraph: And Other Tales*.
See entry 458.

582 Kogawa, Joy. *Obasan*. Godine 1981, $14.95 (0-87923-429-6); Doubleday $9.00 (0-385-46886-5). 256pp. Fiction.

Joy Kogawa was born in Vancouver in 1935. Like many other Japanese Canadians, her family was interned and persecuted during World War II. *Obasan* is a novel based on the author's experience, historical events, letters and documents of the time.

Events in the story are seen through the eyes of five-year-old Naomi, who lives in a comfortable Vancouver neighborhood. There are flowers in the window. The elegant house echoes with music. Naomi loves the rustle of soft silk as her mother moves around the house and enjoys the hot baths lovingly administered by Grandma Kato. But the attack on Pearl Harbor shatters Naomi's comfortable world. Separated from her mother, evicted from her home, Naomi watches bewildered as her family become enemy aliens, persecuted and despised in the land of her birth. Compelled to leave British Columbia, the family is sent to Alberta, where they find work on a beet farm. They must live in a chicken coop and endure their hardship and humiliation in silence because there is no recourse to justice. With his delicate constitution, her father cannot tolerate the rigors of a work camp for men. Her mother returns to Japan, where ironically she dies in a bombing raid by the Allies.

The novel is a moving testament to the physical and mental anguish suffered by Japanese Canadians, for which there can be no adequate compensation.

583 Kupczenko-Frolick, Gloria. *The Chicken Man*. Williams-Wallace 1989, (0-88795-080-9). o.p. Fiction.

This novel is the reminiscence of a lonely, elderly prairie farmer in his last few days of life. Like most children of poor pioneers, young John Babich grew up in a world dominated by hard work, discipline, and religion. The struggle for survival left little room for "nonsense" such as emotional expression, affection between parents, or parental approval, which the small boy needed desperately. His dreams, hopes, and aspirations as a young man are extinguished when his beloved wife dies. Emotionally and spiritually broken, forgotten by others, Babich finds strength in his work in the field. He awaits the solace in death so that he may be reunited with his wife.

Babich's story reflects the dilemma of old age in modern society. The all-consuming pursuit of material aspirations leaves the elderly on the periphery of our world. In a society obsessed with youth, perfect physical health, and success, there is little tolerance for failure, for the helplessness and pain of loneliness and old age. *The Chicken Man*, a meditation on old age and the tragic frailties of life, reveals much about pioneer culture in Canada and the changes that have left many rural Canadians behind.

584 Laferrière, Dany. *How to Make Love to a Negro*. Trans. from French by David Homel. Coach House 1987, $11.95 (0-88910-305-4). 117pp. Fiction.

Written originally in French, Laferrière's provocative novel is a cryptic and satirical treatment of sexual and racial stereotypes. It is also a novel about an immigrant who covets the culture into which he has moved and who will not be satisfied by crumbs. Throughout his adventures, however, he consciously retains his critical perspective as a bemused outsider.

The protagonist is a nameless black man who spends sweltering days in a tiny Montréal slum apartment, discoursing endlessly with Bouba, a black Freudian philosopher whose couch is his ultimate mistress. The white women who wander into the world of these two French-speaking men are from the upper-class bastions of Anglophone Montréal. The question of identity lies at the heart of this work, as it does for all people in Québec. The fact that this story involves a black man gives an old theme a new twist. Laferrière's novel has been described as being full of "manic energy" emanating from the pen of a former Haitian journalist. Revealing its creator's flair for words, this novel has opened new doors for a writer of promise.

585   Lee, Sky. ***Disappearing Moon Café***. Seal 1991, $18.95 (1-878067-11-7); $10.95 (1-878067-12-5). 237pp. Fiction.

Sky Lee's novel illuminates the dilemmas of being Chinese in Canada. She speaks for a culture that thrives in the shadows, highlighting its good elements—familial loyalty, industriousness, an absence of cynicism—while exposing such problems as misogyny and violence within the community.

The novel traces the lives of five generations of women within the Wong family. In 1892, a young Chinese immigrant named Wong Gwei Chang walks the tracks of British Columbia's Canadian Pacific Railway, retrieving the bones of his dead countrymen to save their ghosts from limbo. Several generations later, in 1986, Gwei Chang's great-granddaughter, Kae Ying Woo, embarks on her own search for bones. A new mother at age 36, she digs deep to uncover the secrets buried by her great-grandmother, whose obsession with providing her husband with a grandson has trapped his descendants into a series of adulterous and unwittingly incestuous pairings.

This ambitious novel deftly sets the puzzle of Kae Ying's parentage against the history of the Chinese in their adopted country and traces the growth and development of Vancouver's Chinatown to reveal a family and its complexities. Trapped in a labyrinth of duty and guilt, the members of the Wong family fulfill a destiny in search of their ancestors' bones. The men struggle with taboo, necessity, and the safety of the Chinese community, while the women try to fit themselves into this jigsaw puzzle. They are all constrained by the strategies they must adopt to survive. This widely acclaimed novel was a finalist for the 1990 Governor General's Award.

586   Lysenko, Vera. ***Yellow Boots***. Ryerson 1954. o.p. Fiction.

Writer, social historian, translator, poet and playwright, Vera Lysenko was born to Ukrainian parents and raised in Winnipeg, Manitoba. This novel tells the compelling story of Lilli Landash, a young Ukrainian girl in rural Manitoba in 1929. Struggling against a tyrannical father and enduring the physical hardships of prairie pioneer life, Lilli turns to nature as a source of inspiration and strength. Blessed with a beautiful voice, Lilli finds release in singing. When her father arranges to have her married to a man she finds repulsive, Lilli flees to the city. There she is befriended by two teachers who help develop her exceptional vocal abilities.

Even as Lilli begins to move into the larger Canadian community, she manages to hold on to her cultural heritage. Through song, Lilli preserves her own rich Ukrainian cultural background while sharing it with others. The story unfolds against the backdrop of the brutal realities of early pioneer and immigrant life in Canada.

Yellow Boots has a distinct place in Canadian literature as a work that reflects the dignity and value of immigrant life. The novel also makes an important contribution to Canadian feminist literature by presenting a strong protagonist who triumphs over adversity and who does not let her gender stand in the way of achieving self-fulfillment and personal happiness.

587   Maillet, Antonine. ***Pélagie-la-Charrette***. Trans. from French. Riverrun 1987, $11.95 (0-7145-3966-X). 314pp. Fiction.

At the heart of Maillet's novel is a tragic episode of Canadian history. The early Acadians were seventeenth-century French settlers in what is now Nova Scotia on Canada's eastern seaboard. Brutally expelled by British troops in the eighteenth century, they scattered to different places throughout the globe. Many found their way to Louisiana, where they became known as "Cajuns," while others sought to return to their Canadian home.

Winner of France's most prestigious literary prize, the Goncourt, in 1979, *Pélagie-la-Charrette* follows a band of exiled Acadians as they attempt to regain their homeland. After surviving fifteen years of destitution in the southern swamplands, Pélagie, her family, and others set out on a journey that spans more than ten years. The exiles endure famine, drought, and epidemics as they trek northward through a country torn apart by civil war. The story is moving, but the telling of it is often comic; the language is imbued with a subtle lyricism. Rather than simply retell the past, the author recounts a mythical, humorous, and magical epic of a people in diaspora.

588   Marlyn, John. ***Under the Ribs of Death***. McClelland & Stewart 1957. o.p. Fiction.

Born in Hungary, John Marlyn was brought to Canada as an infant and grew up in Winnipeg's north end, a setting that features prominently in much of his fiction. *Under the Ribs of Death* is one of the earliest novels to deal with the life of an ethnocultural group outside the Canadian mainstream.

In Part One, set in the early years of the twentieth century, twelve-year-old Sandor Hunyadi, torn between affection and contempt for his idealistic Hungarian immigrant parents, yearns to become "English," a state of being that he associates with wealth and power. He writes an award-winning essay on the meaning of Victoria Day, but not even this success spares him the humiliation of being tormented by the English gang at school. This pattern of disillusionment is repeated in the second part of the novel. The adult Sandor has transformed himself into Alex Hunter, a successful and ruthless businessman. Ruined in the stock market collapse of 1929, Sandor/Alex eventually returns to his family and rediscovers the more humanistic values they represent. A powerful examination of the hardships and prejudice endured by immigrants, the novel also explores their susceptibility to the false values that can cause a more damaging dislocation.

589 Moore, Brian. *No Other Life*. Doubleday 1993, $21.00 (0-385-41515-X). 224pp. Fiction.

Moore, who was born in Northern Ireland but who spent most of his adult life in Canada, has written a number of novels that deal with social and spiritual conflicts. In this novel, told from the perspective of Father Paul Michel, a French-Canadian priest, he explores these issues in the context of a fictional Caribbean country, Ganae.

Father Paul brings a malnourished but brilliant thirteen-year-old boy from his village to the capital to attend the Catholic secondary school on a scholarship. The boy, Jeannot, soon distinguishes himself by writing radical leaflets that his classmates, most of whom come from Ganae's best families, helped distribute. Two decades later, Jeannot, now himself a parish priest, spearheads a revolution against the oligarchy and the military that rule and repress his country, and he becomes the president of Ganae. Many call Jeannot the Messiah, but Father Paul recognizes that within Jeannot's campaign are the seeds of division, anarchy, and violence. Ironically, however, Father Paul finds himself defending the priest-president against the Catholic hierarchy and ultimately aids his escape when the military reasserts its authority.

Inspired by real events and people in Haiti, Moore's novel is a dialogue between the First World and the Third, between the forces of tradition in the Catholic Church and the forces of radical liberation. Moore raises questions about both revolution and faith. As Father Paul's mother states on her deathbed, even heaven is an illusion: "There is no other life."   LML

590 Nomez, Nain. *Burning Bridges: Poems*. Trans. from Spanish by Cristina Shantz. Cormorant 1987, $8.95 (0-920953-28-X). Poetry.

The poems in this volume explore new literary forms to express a variety of subjects, including the psychology of exile. In poems that range in tone from melancholy and whimsy to bitterness, Nomez writes elegantly about emotional fragmentation, the effort required to assimilate a new language, and the unfinished business of his former life. He also casts a discerning and critical eye on his adopted land, Canada.

Nomez, who lived in Toronto, now lives in Santiago, Chile. He is editor of *Chilean Literature in Canada (see main entry)* and serves on the editorial board of *El Espiritu del Valle*. He is the author of *Historias del Reino Vigilado/Stories of a Guarded Kingdom* (1981). Poems from *Burning Bridges* won first prize in the Spanish writing competition organized by the University of Alberta.

591 Nomez, Nain, ed. *Chilean Literature in Canada: A Bilingual Anthology*. Bilingual (Spanish-English) ed. Ediciones Cordillera 1982. o.p. Fiction.

This anthology presents the various forms, styles, and themes found in the writings of Chileans now living in Canada. In Chile, creation is a part of daily existence; writing is not a profession but a way of life. Many of the writers represented in this volume were forced to leave their country, while others went into self-imposed exile after the 1973 overthrow of Marxist president Salvador Allende. They offer a multifaceted, diverse panorama that demonstrates the profound contribution one culture can make to another.

The book is designed not so much to showcase completed work but to present writings in various stages of development. The purpose is to demonstrate the problems encountered by the culturally divided artist who is obliged to reconstruct his world with fragments of memory and bits of everyday experiences. The central theme of much of the work is the difference between "here" and "there": the experience of being uprooted and the resulting frustration, cultural separation, disillusionment, and solitude. Many of the writers are obsessed with the trauma of dictatorship and repression. Their work exhibits the pessimism of a "lost generation," lost to the history of their nation. At the same time, this collection represents the exiles' attempts to preserve and continue to develop their original culture, efforts that are supported by institutions, organizations, groups, and activities within the Chilean community in Canada and abroad.

592 Ondaatje, Michael. ***In the Skin of a Lion***. Viking 1988, $8.95 (0-14-011309-6). 256pp. Fiction.

Michael Ondaatje, a writer of mixed Dutch, Sinhalese, and Tamil ancestry, is one of Canada's most accomplished and original talents. He surprises readers with each new work. His novel *In the Skin of a Lion* describes the building of Toronto, especially such great public works as the Bloor Street Viaduct and the water filtration plant, during the 1920s and 1930s. Ondaatje provides a voice for the nameless immigrants— the Macedonians, the Italians, and the Finns; the tanners, dynamiters, and tunnellers—who sacrificed their health and even their lives to create the modern city.

The central character is the gentle and alienated Patrick Lewis, who leaves behind his northern Ontario childhood for a new life in Toronto. Hired to search for a missing millionaire, Patrick finds a new identity within the Macedonian community. A heady mixture of documentation and imagination, social criticism and mythology, the novel weaves together the real and invented histories of such characters as a daredevil bridge builder, an elusive actress, and a charming thief.

Ondaatje is also a highly acclaimed poet. This novel, written with grace, passion, and a sense of wonder, provides the reader with a string of haunting images and a transformed vision of the city. Ondaatje has also complied *From Ink Lake* (Penguin, 1992), a valuable anthology of Canadian literature whose selections represent many regions and cultural traditions.

593 Ostenso, Martha. ***Wild Geese***. McClelland & Stewart 1925. o.p. Fiction.

Born in Bergen, Norway in 1900, Ostenso immigrated to Canada as a child and settled in Manitoba. This novel chronicles the events of a single summer in the small northern Manitoba farm community of Oeland. Told mainly through the perceptions of Lind Archer, a schoolteacher boarding with the Gare family, the story centers on Caleb Gare. A malevolent and life-denying tyrant, Caleb keeps his family in a state of fear and submission and blackmails his wife with the threat of revealing to her illegitimate son, Mark Jordan, the facts of his humble origins. When Mark arrives in Oeland to manage the homestead of an ailing neighbor, his ensuing love affair with Lind Archer forms a counterpoint to the twisted relationships within the Gare family. Caleb is opposed only by his daughter Jude, a willful and sensual beauty whose pregnancy provides the catalyst for her escape and for the liberation of the entire family. Though the novel contains many elements of romanticism and even gothic perversity, its psychological depth and detailed portrayal of immigrant life represent a major development in the Canadian literary movement towards realism.

594   Paci, Frank G. *Black Blood*. Oberon 1991, $15.95 (0-887508-63-4). 199pp. Fiction.

Set in Sault Ste. Marie in the 1950s and 1960s, this autobiographical novel traces the boyhood of a displaced Italian who resists growing up. The artless style of this book reflects the simplicities of childhood, which the narrator feels are replaced in adulthood by the dishonesties surrounding love and sex.

The narrator encounters the oppressive and dark adult world at an early age. His slowness in growing toward the "dark" that attracts his friend causes him to lapse into a state of nostalgic retardation. Yet his attitude seems justified when violence and envy lead to tragedy.

Reflecting his themes, the author describes the physical and political impact on the town of the presence of the huge International Bridge. The grimy industrial landscape is stitched with railway tracks; slow freight trains move heavily along predetermined lines to their inevitable destinations. The temptation of escape is represented by the characters of the Esposito brothers, whose success in the world of hockey contrasts strikingly with the desperate youngsters who are forced to accept their less glamorous futures.

595   Philip, Marlene Nourbese. *Harriet's Daughter*. Heinemann 1988, $7.95 (0-435-98924-3). 150pp. Fiction.

Marlene Nourbese Philip was born in Tobago in the West Indies in 1947. She has been a writer and poet since 1968; her first book of poetry, *Thorns*, was published in 1980. *Harriet's Daughter* is her first novel. In it she adopts a positive approach to the problems faced by young adults in a multiracial society, including immigration, feelings of exile, and the language barrier. In 1988, Nourbese Philip was awarded both the Casa de las Americas literary award and the Tradewinds Journal prize for her poetry and short-story writing.

Margaret, the protagonist of this novel, is determined to be someone, to be "cool," to have style and class—and to have darker skin. More than anything, she wants to help her best friend, Zulma, escape from Canada and fly back to Tobago to live with her grandmother. She compiles a list she calls "Things I Want Changed in My Life" and sets about methodically achieving her objectives. But at the age of fourteen, coming to terms with growing up, relationships, and responsibilities is not quite so straightforward as she believes, and the parental threat of old-fashioned West Indian discipline is always present. In this charming, humorous, and perceptive story of adolescence, the author explores the friendship of two young black girls and throws into sharp relief the wider issues of culture and identity so relevant to teenagers of all races and colors.

Philip is also the author of a book of poems called *She Tries Her Tongue, Her Silence Softly Breaks (see main entry)*.

596   Philip, Marlene Nourbese. *She Tries Her Tongue, Her Silence Softly Breaks*. Ragweed 1989, $9.95 (0-921556-03-9). 104pp. Poetry.

In this moving volume, the author reminds readers that the enslavement of the African peoples was possible partly because their native languages were suppressed. Without words—one's own words—can there be history? How is it possible to give expression to one's heart and soul when one must speak in a foreign tongue? Such questions, which reverberate in all of Philip's writings, are relevant for all people on the margins of dominant culture, but they are especially profound for black and native peoples who experienced colonialization by Western Europeans.

The book is a set of prose poems that begins with the symbolic search by the mother for the daughter. The mother exists on many levels, physical as well as spiritual and historical. She finds that her child has been beaten and raped—a metaphor for the damage inflicted by oppression and the theft of language. Each poem takes words, sources, and roots and finds the poetry in them—quoting, erasing and rewriting, recontextualizing. The author raises difficult and troubling questions, exhibiting an intensity rarely achieved in poetry.

Marlene Nourbese Philip is the first woman and the second Canadian to win the prestigious Casa de las Américas Prize, which she received in 1988. She is the author of a novel, *Harriet's Daughter (see main entry)*.

597   Ricci, Nino. **The Book of Saints**. McKay 1991, $18.50 (0-679-40118-0). 240pp. Fiction.

Nino Ricci was born in Leamington, Ontario, and first visited Italy in 1971. This novel is a coming-of-age story about a seven-year-old boy and his free-spirited mother in the small Italian village of Valle de Sole in the Apennines in 1960. Vittorio Innocente lives with his mother, Cristina, and his grandfather, the mayor of the village. Vittorio's father left the village four years ago with the understanding that the family will be reunited in North America. In this interval Cristina becomes pregnant and is isolated by her own fury and the shame imposed on her by the villagers. She eventually packs up her hopes, her dreams, and her son and travels across the ocean to Canada. The tragedy that occurs during the ocean voyage quells any notion that the New World might be any kind of paradise.

The title of the novel comes from the school text with which Vittorio's teacher consoles him after his classmates have bullied him. Vittorio would like to embody the significance and possibilities of the lives of the saints. The pattern of the novel is cyclical. What is to become of Vittorio Innocente? How will he survive as he embarks on a new life in Canada—without the love of his mother or his father?

A sequel, called *In a Glass House*, chronicles the life of Vittorio Innocente from age seven to twenty-eight, while the third part of the trilogy portrays his life as an adult.

598   Richler, Mordecai. **The Apprenticeship of Duddy Kravitz**. Viking 1991, $9.95 (0-14-015296-2). 320pp. Fiction.

This novel follows an ambitious teenager from his roots in a poor Jewish neighborhood of Montréal through his efforts to achieve financial success to his ultimate ruin, which leads him to reflect upon his life. Raised in a down-and-out but strictly religious family, young Kravitz wants nothing more than money, power, position, and a comfortable life. He loves money for the status it offers and is willing to sacrifice everything—family, friends, his religious and moral upbringing, everything he knows is right—to achieve it. Ultimately, he loses everything and ends up back where he started: on the streets of his shabby Montréal neighborhood, a lesson for others who might follow in his path.

This highly acclaimed novel, originally published in 1959, was made into a successful feature film starring Richard Dreyfuss. It has much to say about the Jewish community of Montréal and a younger generation that is struggling with the elders' traditional way of life. While Richler's witty, ironic style appeals to a wide readership, this is a particularly good novel for older high school and college students, for whom Kravitz's struggles may strike a chord. Richler is more recently the author of *Solomon Gursky Was Here* (Knopf, 1990), a humorous, fantastic novel about a missing former bootlegger and liquor industry magnate; it offers a satiric look at Jewish Canadian history and all aspects of Canadian society. Also out in paperback is an earlier Richler novel, *Joshua Then and Now* (Viking, 1991).   LML

599   Roy, Gabrielle. *The Road Past Altamont*. Trans. from French by Joyce Marshall. Univ. of Nebraska Pr. 1993, $7.95 (0-8032-8948-0). 147pp. Fiction.

This is an immensely moving novel by one of Québec's great women writers about a young French Canadian girl. Roy writes from her own deeply personal experience about the mystery of growing up and discovering the "still sad music" of the world. It is an utterly Canadian novel, steeped in the Canadian landscape; the preoccupations of its characters spring from the vastness of this continent.

The first episode portrays Christine's visit to her magnificent grandmother, who lives in the expanse of the Manitoba prairie, a landscape that highlights both the ethereal beauty and the limits of human life. Through her grandmother she tastes the wisdom of age. She stands in awe of her grandmother's mountain of housework, her kitchen crammed with jellies and pickles, her cupboards of starched linens, her tranquillity, her solitude as vast as the space stretching outside her front door. The child is filled with inexplicable wonder and sorrow.

The next section describes the enchanting and gentle friendship between the eight-year-old Christine and a very special old man. Through this magical friendship she sees her future, and the vision spurs her on to her extraordinary journey in life, helping her to develop both as a woman and as a creative artist. A trip to Lake Winnipeg provides her first encounter with the wider world, placing her on the threshold of a great and glittering adventure, filled with trepidation and the quivering excitement of discovery. *The Road Past Altamont* is a road that leads Christine away from the limits of her family life and into the fulfilling interior world of the writer's mind.

600   Roy, Gabrielle. *Streets of Riches*. Trans. from French by Harry Binsse. Univ. of Nebraska Pr. 1994, $8.95 (0-8032-8947-2). 176pp. Fiction.

Gabrielle Roy is one of a handful of Canadian writers whose works are as highly acclaimed and appreciated in translation as they are in their original language. Her first novel, *Bonheur d'Occasion* (*The Tin Flute*), has become a Canadian classic and has received international recognition.

Set in the Montréal slum of Saint-Henri, the novel examines the nature and impact of poverty, war, and the present century on the lives of members of the Lacasse family. The plot focuses on the daughter Florentine Lacasse, who yearns to rise above her bleak situation. She is seduced and made pregnant by a ruthless social climber; later she reluctantly marries his shy friend. But the center and heart of the novel is Rose-Anna Lacasse, the stoically enduring mother of twelve, who trudges through the snowy streets in search of a yet cheaper flat, binding her family together with tenderness and courage. Only the advent of World War II offers an escape from this grinding cycle of poverty and despair. Roy enters the lives of her characters with understanding and compassion to create an authentic portrait of a particular chapter in Canada's history.

601 Salverson, Laura G. *The Viking King*. McClelland & Stewart 1923. o.p. Fiction.

The child of Icelandic immigrant parents, Salverson (1890–1970) was one of the first Canadian novelists to chronicle the drama of immigration in Canada, particularly the Scandinavian experience in the West. In this novel, generally considered her best work, Salverson traces the struggles and fortunes of four generations of the Lindal family from the mid-1870s until World War I. As the novel opens, the future matriarch Borga and her family are driven from Iceland by the volcano that claims her brother's life. They settle in an Icelandic community near Gimli, Manitoba, where, despite harsh conditions, they and most members of their community gradually prosper but never quite assimilate. These Icelanders learn to reconcile pride in their ancestral heritage with a genuine love for the new country, including its imperfectly realized dream. Almost epic in scope and intent, this classic offers a wide emotional range, an interesting array of characters, and a wealth of description about an important chapter in Canada's history.

Salverson is also the author of an autobiography, *Confessions of an Immigrant's Daughter* (Univ. of Toronto Pr., 1981), which chronicles her experience growing up as the first generation in her family to be born in a new land.

602 Sapergia, Barbara. *Foreigners*. Coteau 1984, $7.95 (0-919926-35-5). Fiction.

In this novel, the Canadian Dream deteriorates into a nightmare; a Paradise Sought becomes a Paradise Lost. The author's first novel seeks to make sense of what happens psychologically to a Romanian family that immigrates to Canada, the land of their dreams. Like other books on the same theme, the immigrants come to the country with great expectations of opportunities that will lead to wealth, comfort, and security—opportunities denied them in their own land. What they often do not realize is that such opportunities exact a price. They discover that their new-found freedom is not free.

The Dominescu family moves to Canada to escape the oppressiveness and exploitation of the Romanian aristocratic land-owning class. Under the policies of the Homestead Act of 1872, they settle in the badlands of southern Saskatchewan. But in 1912, Stefan Dominescu loses the land because of the relentless drought and is driven to rent land from the arrogant and racist Chisholms. He faces further tragedy with the death of his four-year-old son. Stefan's high hopes and dreams crumble. He realizes he is simply another foreigner in a land he cannot comprehend, a land that has ruthlessly brought him full circle from his humble beginnings. No longer are the family's traditions secure or well defined; the old ways must somehow coexist or evolve with the new ways of the new world.

There is bigotry and oppression, a harsh landscape and a cruel climate, isolation and alienation. But there are also good times: the warmth and comfort of a mother's love, family, friends and their stories, youthful romances, Romanian strudel, roasted lamb and plum brandy, and wedding feasts and music and dancing. All of these are described with a sense of joy.

603 Skvorecký, Josef. *The Engineer of Human Souls*. Trans. from Czech by Paul Wilson. Knopf 1984, $17.95 (0-394-50500-X); Pocket Books $9.95 (0-685-18025-5). 576pp. Fiction.

A central figure in the postwar cultural renaissance in Czechoslovakia, Skvorecký immigrated to Canada in 1968, following the Soviet invasion of his homeland. A number of his novels form a loose cycle featuring Danny Smiricky, a thinly disguised alter ego of the author and a lover of jazz, women, and life in general.

In this book, Danny appears as a middle-aged émigré writer and English professor now comfortably ensconced in the sheltered world of Edenvale College in Toronto. But Danny remains tormented by his inability to reconcile his constant awareness of the past, full of tyrannies of fascism and communism, with his present life of ease and affluence. He is charmed and annoyed by Canadian political innocence, amused by the counterrevolutionary schemes of a bumbling group of compatriots, and sadly aware that he is committed to a past and to a society that exist only in his memory. This huge, sprawling novel, teeming with characters, subplots, and allusions, covers two continents and a period of thirty years. But beneath this exuberant activity and the determinedly comic tone of the writing lies the sorrow and nostalgia of a heart in exile.

604 Smieja, Florian. *Not a Tourist*. Third Eye 1986. o.p. Poetry.

Smieja was born in Poland in 1925. After being educated in Ireland and England, he came to Canada in 1969. His is a poetic voice that has been seasoned by its experience, a voice at once passionate and wry, bitter and reverential. Smieja's poems combine terse irony with an embattled humanism, delicately turned passion with tough political skepticism. They express the burdens of exile as much by their tone and emotional coloration as by their overt content.

Like the hyphen in the term Polish-Canadian, the act of translating these poems is a symbol of separation as much as it is one of connection. Such works as "I Am Not a Tourist" and "Spring in Canada" remind readers of the difficult, multiple existence of the émigré. Other works present images of the pain of modern Poland, crisply though fiercely rendered in poems like "Polish August" and "Patriots." The powerful piece "For Alicja Martyred by the Immigration Office" presents the image of a victim wrapped in red tape who will forever haunt the bureaucrats who destroyed her.

With deft poetic insight, Smieja embraces the hyphens each of us inherits as citizens of our own lands and as citizens of the world.

605 Suknaski, Andrew. *The Ghosts Call You Poor*. Macmillan 1978. o.p. Poetry.

The *Globe and Mail* stated, "If Canada ever needed an argument in defense of the regional writer, Andrew Suknaski is it." In one of his poems, Suknaski states: "It was the faith and humanity inside me and the way it has grown" that inspired him to write. Suknaski reveals his deep interest in people and humanity in this collection of poems. Topics include the early European explorers, aboriginal and Métis culture, the Chinese in British Columbia, and Rumanian and Ukrainian settlers in Saskatchewan and Manitoba. Using stories and images, the author looks for the roots of culture and helps the reader to understand that the past is a great part of our present. Beautifully written, with rich natural language and gently but precisely drawn characters, *The Ghosts Call You Poor* leaves a deep impression.

606 Thériault, Yves. *Agaguk*. Trans. from French by Gwendolyn Moore. McGraw-Hill Ryerson 1992, $10.95 (0-7700-6016-1). 229pp. Fiction.

Set among the Inuit people half a century ago, *Agaguk* recounts the struggles of a young couple who withdraw from the solidarity of communal life to forge their destiny in the bleak wilderness of the tundra. The fight for self-determination and survival brings Agaguk and his wife, Iriook, into conflict with white traders, who routinely cheat and steal from the Inuit. Unable to tolerate injustice, the young Inuit seeks revenge. Agaguk is able to elude the law, but he is finally unable to escape his own conscience. Although there are some inaccuracies in Thériault's portrayal of Inuit life, *Agaguk* is a fast-paced adventure story, vividly told.

607 Valgardson, David. *What Can't Be Changed Shouldn't Be Mourned*. Douglas & McIntyre 1990, $24.95 (0-88894-698-9); $16.95 (0-55054-404-7). 160pp. Fiction.

Valgardson, the author of several novels, many short stories, and collections of poetry, was born in Manitoba in 1939. His father was of Icelandic descent, and Valgardson has never lost touch with his roots. In his short stories he presents a dark vision of the life of Icelandic immigrants, portraying the harsh and cruel struggle for survival in the stark landscape of Manitoba. The author draws on childhood memories of Gimli, an Icelandic-Canadian fishing community in "New Iceland," to create his settings. His characters are in conflict not only with their new environment but also with themselves. The stories deal with the immigrants' vacillating emotions toward the old land and their adopted land, their forefathers and their search for roots, and the difficulty of cultural assimilation while struggling to establish a strong cultural base. Valgardson's skill as a writer lies in his ability to present stories with themes that are both regional and universal.

608 Vanderhaege, Guy. *Homesick: A Novel*. McClelland & Stewart 1989, $17.99 (0-7710-8695-4). 292pp. Fiction.

This is a rich, deeply felt, and spirited novel that explores the curious power of family bonds to both destroy and heal. In his old age Alec Monkman has disturbing dreams and has taken to wearing his fedora inside the house. His daughter, Vera, is coming home to Saskatchewan. He has not seen her since she left home seventeen years earlier, nor has he ever met his grandson, Daniel. This is an uneasy reunion, during which the stories of the characters' lives gradually unfold. As they do, the past confronts the present in unexpected ways.

For Vera and her father, the past is full of bitterness and misunderstanding. There is an unbroken silence concerning her younger brother, Earl. The reader learns that when she was nineteen, Vera left home to join the army. Later, in Toronto, she meets her husband through a series of strange events. Following her husband's death, she finds that the big city is no place to raise her troublesome twelve-year-old boy. For his sake, she is compelled to return home and face her father. Alec, Vera, and Daniel form an unlikely triangle. The truth of what took place during Vera's lengthy absence is revealed, leading to the novel's dramatic and moving conclusion.

Guy Vanderhaege has given distinct voices to his characters and has infused their story with an ingenious blend of tenderness, sardonic humor, and unforgettable emotional power. Born in Saskatchewan in 1948, Vanderhaege is recognized internationally as one of Canada's leading writers of fiction. Among his other important works are *My Present Age* (Houghton, 1985).

609   Vassanji, M. G. *No New Land*. McClelland & Stewart 1991, $12.99 (0-7710-8720-9). 224pp. Fiction.

In this novel, an Asian family travels from Dar-es-Salaam in Tanzania to Don Mills, Ontario. With humor and compassion, the author opens a window to a specific community in an unfamiliar set of circumstances and depicts the challenges faced by an ordinary man, Nurdin, and others who relocate from East Africa to Canada. Although they live in a new country, members of the older generation try to cling to their old ways. Several stories woven into the main narrative tell of the gatherings of the community and of conflicts between these newcomers and the Canadians. Nurdin's transition from one society to another is handled with insight; the process of acclimatization is gradual and credible. Perhaps the author's greatest achievement in this book is his vivid description of the life of the inhabitants of an old apartment building overlooking the Don Valley. M. G. Vassanji was born in Nairobi, Kenya in 1950 and moved to Toronto in 1980. He has also edited an anthology of South Asian Canadian literature titled *A Meeting of Streams* (South Asia Books, 1985).

610   Zeller, Ludwig. *When the Animal Rises from the Deep the Head Explodes*. Trilingual (Spanish-English-French) ed. English trans. by John Robert Colombo and Susana Wald; French trans. by Thérèse Dulac. Illus. with collages by the author. Mosaic 1976, o.p. Poetry.

Of the several full-length collections of poetry Ludwig Zeller has published since coming to Canada from Chile in 1970, this one best captures the impact of changing cultures and language. In it, he introduces to Canadian literature his exuberant poetic universe. Zeller blends the traditions of the Spanish baroque with the rich vein of Latin American surrealism, a movement in which Zeller has played a crucial role. The poems appear in their original Spanish as well as in English and French translations.

A sense of despair permeates the twelve poems and the collages that illustrate them. Zeller describes man's inability to change the course of his destiny. He expresses feelings of alienation through a complex system of metaphors; images of desert sand from his native Chile come together with images of snow and ice from his new land. Through his masterly handling of language, Zeller expresses contradictory sensations of displacement and astonishment when confronting the Canadian landscape, which he sees as endowed with endless possibilities of transformation. Dream images juxtaposed with the reality of everyday life paint a clear, if painful, picture of exile. For this poet, accepting the sense of exile symbolizes the metaphysical condition of anyone who questions the limits of reality.

NONFICTION

611   Abella, Irving. *A Coat of Many Colors: Two Centuries of Jewish Life in Canada*. Illus. with photos. Lester & Orpen Dennys 1990, $12.99 (0-88619-251-X). Nonfiction.

This is a very readable popular history of Jews in Canada from 1738 to 1990. Containing over 300 black-and-white photographs, this volume was published in conjunction with "A Coat of Many Colors," a touring exhibition from the Canadian Museum of Civilization. The author, Irving Abella, a professor of history at York University in Toronto, is the author of several books. He is coauthor of the prize-winning *None Is Too Many: Canada and the Jews of Europe 1933–1948*.

The book traces the lives of members of the Jewish community in Canada, describing settlements from coast to coast, the struggle for political rights, and the establishment of synagogues and other Jewish community organizations. It takes a special look at Jews in the garment industry and their activities in and contributions to the labor movement. Most important, this work outlines how Canadian Jews worked for passage of human rights legislation, such as fair employment and fair housing. Their struggle has benefited all Canadians, leading to tolerance and respect for other ethnocultural groups seeking an equal role in Canadian society.

612   Aun, Karl. *The Political Refugees: A History of the Estonians in Canada*. Illus. McClelland & Stewart 1985. o.p. Nonfiction.

Dr. Karl Aun, Professor Emeritus of Political Science at Wilfrid Laurier University in Waterloo, Ontario, was educated in Estonia, Germany, the United States, and Canada. In this book, he documents the lives of the Estonians in Canada. The volume is part of the series called Generations, A History of Canada's People. The series was commissioned by the Citizenship Branch of the Department of the Secretary of State to stimulate interest in Canadian social history, including immigration and ethnic history.

Popular and scholarly at the same time, Aun's study presents a comprehensive account that aids in understanding not just the Estonians, who form one of the smallest immigrant groups in Canada, but the broader concepts that underline the multiethnic, multicultural structure of Canadian society. This book provides background information about Estonia, the process of Estonian immigration, and adjustment to life in Canada. It also profiles Estonians as a distinct ethnic community, one that has developed an active cultural life as well as a support network of Estonian organizations. Archival photographs complement the text; statistical tables are included in the appendix. The author summarizes the experiences, problems, and challenges faced by Estonians in dealing with both cultural and generational conflict and in meeting the demands of a changing future.

For a brief discussion of the introductory volume to the Generations series, see *Coming Canadians: An Introduction to a History of Canada's Peoples*, edited by Jean R. Burnet and Howard Palmer (*see main entry*).

613   Bagnell, Kenneth. ***Canadese: A Portrait of the Italian Canadians***. Macmillan of Canada 1989, $27.95 (0-7715-9386-4). 287pp. Nonfiction.

The author weaves together people, places, and events in this engaging and informative social history of Italian Canadians in this century. To depict the participation of these immigrants in every aspect of Canadian life, Bagnell presents a scrapbook of biographical portraits of laborers, professionals, and entrepreneurs. He describes the "Little Italies"—Italian communities, such as the Ward in Toronto, that are found in many cities across Canada; he also describes Camp Petawawa, where 500 Italian men and three women were interned during World War II. He discusses the violent strike by Italian freight handlers in Port Arthur and Fort William in October 1906 and the fire at Hogg's Hollow in North York, events that led to major changes in Ontario's labor laws during the 1960s.

614   Bassler, Gerhard P. ***German Canadian Mosaic Today and Yesterday***. German-Canadian Congress 1991, $14.95 (0-9695486-0-5). Nonfiction.

By depicting historical episodes in reverse chronological order, Gerhard Bassler takes a nontraditional approach in this comprehensive overview of German-speaking immigrants in Canada. He begins with a discussion of the German-Canadian mosaic today, then traces its origins back several centuries to the time of exploration. In doing so, he covers all major waves of German immigrants, including such ethnoreligious groups as the Mennonites and the Hutterites. He describes the development of major settlements across Canada, including the first German Canadian community in Lunenburg County, Nova Scotia, in the eighteenth century. In passing, he chronicles such events as the renaming of the Ontario town of Berlin to Kitchener in 1916, at the height of political tensions during World War I.

This text acknowledges the experience of German Canadians and their contributions to Canadian society dating back more than three centuries. It is organized into thirty chapters and includes a detailed bibliography.

615   Borenstein, Sam. ***Sam Borenstein***. Texts ed. by William Kuhns and Leó Rosshandler. Illus. by the author. McClelland & Stewart 1978. o.p. Nonfiction.

Born in Lithuania in 1908, Borenstein came to Canada with his family in 1921. Despite his impoverished circumstances, he defied the odds to pursue his lifelong dream of becoming an artist. His zest is evident in the compelling surges of vigor and passion that spill from his canvas. His rapid brush strokes possess an energy driven by an inner vision. Sensuous and volatile images explode in vibrant colors and shapes, and the thick paint, expertly shaped and manipulated, lends a tactile texture to his work. His expressionistic cityscapes of Montréal and the landscapes of the St. Laurent region are handsomely reproduced in this volume. Also included is a vivid biographical sketch and a critical assessment of his work. In their text, William Kuhns and Leo Rosshandler provide an insight into Borenstein's extraordinary mindset and spirit. Sadly, Borenstein received little acclaim during his lifetime. He struggled to make a living and support his family by taking whatever odd jobs he could; at different times he was an antique dealer and a taxi driver. The pursuit of his passion as a painter has left Canadian art a lasting legacy.

616   Borovilos, John. ***Breaking Through: A Canadian Literary Mosaic.*** Prentice 1990, $21.77 (0-13-083072-0). 318pp. Nonfiction.

This textbook collection of short stories, poems, and essays examines Canada's literary mosaic to help students look with pride on their diverse backgrounds. Forty-two authors, representing the "third voice" in Canadian literature, explore the experience of Canadians of different cultures and heritages. Among the writers represented are Joy Kogawa, Lillian Allen, Guy Vanderhaege, Mary diMichele, Joseph Pivato, and C. D. Minni.

The selections help validate the experience of students who do not come from a white, Anglo-Saxon background by providing deeper understanding, insight, and reconciliation. Themes explored include what it means to be a Canadian, the issue of multiculturalism, racism in Canada, confrontations between the recent immigrant and members of the dominant culture, and the problem of assimilation. For people of various minority ethnic or cultural groups, the book helps answer the important question, "What is *our* history in this land?" The book's primary audience is educators in Canada, and its goal is to help them understand the experiences of indigenous peoples and new immigrants. But the anthology also provides a worthwhile literary overview that reflects Canada's changing ethnic mix.

617   Brand, Dionne. ***No Burden to Carry: Narratives of Black Working Women in Ontario, 1920-1950s.*** Women's Pr. 1991, $17.95 (0-88961-163-7). 282pp. Nonfiction.

Dionne Brand, a black poet and writer in Toronto, embarked on this oral history project to make the voices of black working women heard and to fill the gaps contained in previous histories of blacks in Canada. The narratives of fourteen women, most of them over the age of sixty and all but one of whom were born in Canada, offer rare glimpses of life in some of Ontario's towns and cities from the 1920s to the 1950s.

The stories are fascinating time capsules. Readers learn details about daily life in black neighborhoods and about the work blacks found on farms, as domestics, and in munitions factories. The women interviewed speak of segregation in their social and work life and discuss their political affiliations, especially activities within the Marcus Garvey movement and labor organizations. Brand is particularly interested in the survival of black women in a predominantly white, male-oriented society during the Depression and other times of economic hardship. Her collection proves that marginalized women can speak with authority. Their observations are insightful and instructive, revealing aspects of Canadian life that have at long last become part of recorded history.

Burger, Julian. *The Gaia Atlas of First Peoples: The Future for the Indigenous World.*
See entry 479.

618 Burnet, Jean R., and Howard Palmer, eds. *Coming Canadians: An Introduction to a History of Canada's Peoples.* McClelland & Stewart 1988. o.p. Nonfiction.

In the 1970s the Citizenship Branch of the Department of the Secretary of State commissioned a series of books called *Generations, A History of Canada's Peoples.* The books, aimed at the general reader, present an objective and analytical account of the immigration and ethnic experiences of Canadians. In this introductory volume, series editors Jean R. Burnet and Howard Palmer offer a comprehensive survey of the immigrant experience from the time of exploration to 1980. They chronicle such major incidents as the Vancouver race riots of 1907 and the Komagata Maru incident of 1915 and discuss such themes as settlement and employment patterns, social institutions, and the role of the media and voluntary associations in helping to maintain the ethnic identity. Chapters are organized by chronology and region.

Other titles in the Generations series offer more-detailed studies on specific ethnic groups and include a wealth of facts, statistics, and extensive bibliographies. Another series title discussed in this chapter is *The Political Refugees: A History of the Estonians in Canada* by Karl Aun *(see main entry).*

619 Burnet, Jean R. *Looking into My Sister's Eyes: An Exploration in Women's History.* Multicultural History Society of Ontario 1986, $14.95 (0-919045-27-8). 245pp. Essays.

This work is a collection of thirteen articles that were presented at a conference on immigration and ethnicity in Ontario in 1985 and deal with the largely neglected history of ethnocultural women in Ontario. Eleven different groups are featured in essays exploring the various roles women played in the process of immigration and in the subsequent adjustment of immigrant groups to life in Canada. Gathered from oral histories and autobiographical writings and set in their historical context, the stories convey the experiences of immigrant women. Forced at first into traditional female roles as wives and mothers, they gradually broke free of these restrictions to seek opportunities as paid workers. Invariably, women played essential roles as transmitters of culture, language, and religion and were actively involved in ethnic organizations, schools, and church groups.

This volume, one of the first to highlight Canadian ethnic women's experiences, is rich in detail and is a valuable source of information for those interested in multiculturalism in Canada

Biography

620 Campbell, Maria. *Halfbreed.* Repr. of 1973 ed. Univ. of Nebraska Pr. 1982, $6.95 (0-8032-6311-2). 157pp. Autobiography.

This book is a remarkable and passionate account of a young Métis woman. Born in northern Saskatchewan in 1940, Campbell recounts her happy childhood among a proud and vibrant people with a strong, close-knit society. But with the passage of years, her people become dispirited by poverty, discrimination, and government indifference.

Hoping to escape the hardships and hopelessness of the Métis community, Campbell marries a white man. But she soon learns that life in white society is even harder to bear because of its virulent discrimination against all aspects of aboriginal life. Her alcoholic husband abuses and ultimately abandons her. Left penniless and with a child to support, she is driven to prostitution, seeking solace from the pain and shame of her existence through use of drugs and alcohol. Eventually, however, Campbell emerges from her desperate straits. She returns to her Métis roots and the healing power of her culture, becoming an activist who fights for the rights of her people.

This important autobiography reveals the harsh reality of growing up as a Métis in Canada and exposes, without bitterness, the harm done to Canada's aboriginal people. At the same time it speaks powerfully about the strength of spirit that underlines the enduring aboriginal culture.

621   Cardinal, Harold. ***The Unjust Society: The Tragedy of Canada's Indians***. Hurtig 1969. o.p. Nonfiction.

This book, a classic by an aboriginal writer, outlines incisively the painful neglect and betrayal of Canada's aboriginal people. Written in part as a response to the Trudeau government's proposal to do away with the Indian Act and assimilate Native Canadians into mainstream society, Cardinal delineates point by point the wrongs suffered by these people and outlines a strategy for change.

The author touches on all aspects of aboriginal history over the last century. He dissects the Indian Act and various treaties, exposing the callous government bureaucracy that almost succeeded in eliminating native languages and traditions. He reveals the humiliations suffered by natives under the welfare system and describes the devastating impact of unemployment and banishment to reservations that lacked running water and electricity. He laments the way residential schools and missionaries indoctrinated the Indians to believe that their religion, culture, and language are of no value. He traces the early beginnings of native organizations that were formed to combat these forces and describes their successes and failures.

A later work by the same author is *The Rebirth of Canada's Indians*, (o.p., 1977). This book is more hopeful in its depiction of the future of Native Canadians and discusses their increased involvement in the fight for justice and self-determination, a struggle that continues to this day.

622   Charon, Milly. ***Worlds Apart: New Immigrant Voices***. Cormorant 1989, $14.95 (0-920953-11-5). 428pp. Nonfiction.

Having spent her childhood in a Montréal ghetto in the mid-1930s and 1940s, Milly Charon is well acquainted with the varied experiences of immigrants in Canada. To document these experiences and promote a greater understanding of the newcomer in Canadian society, she collected interviews, manuscripts, articles, and essays from immigrants. The material provided the basis for this book and its companion, *Between Two Worlds: The Canadian Immigrant Experience* (1983).

The book contains over fifty personal histories, each a testimony to the courage and determination of individuals. The countries of origin span all continents, and the reasons for coming to the new land range from the social to the economic to the political. Expressed in their own words, the newcomers' dramatic accounts reveal their fears and aspirations, the hardships encountered in trying to adjust, and their contributions to Canadian society. These personal snapshots allow the reader to become better acquainted with the realities of immigrant life.

623 Cruikshank, Julie, and others, contribs. *Life Lived Like a Story: Life Stories of Three Yukon Elders*. Illus. Univ. of Nebraska Pr. 1990, $50.00 (0-8032-1447-2); $14.95 (0-8032-6352-X). 404pp. Autobiography.

This book records the lives of three very special native women from the southern Yukon. Drawing on the Athapaskan and Tlingit oral traditions, Angela Sidney, Kitty Smith, and Annie Ned record their life stories and their genealogies, reflecting a unique perspective on such catastrophes as the influenza epidemic of 1919. Each author determines the structure and direction of her biography; the interviewer, Julie Cruikshank, a lecturer in anthropology at the University of British Columbia, simply comments on the cultural context and provides background material. This use of oral narrative allows the interviewer to step back so that the reader can enjoy the full flavor of the stories while gaining a better understanding of the culture that produced them.

Aboriginal women are perhaps the most marginalized group in Canadian society. By allowing their stories to be heard fully, Cruikshank provides a basis for comparing their experiences with those of aboriginal men as well as members of other Canadian groups. *Life Lived Like a Story*, a fine example of groundbreaking use of oral history for an ethnographic study, is a thoroughly enjoyable book.

Daniels, Roger. *Concentration Camps: North American Japanese in the United States and Canada During World War II*.
See entry 303.

624 Danys, Milda. *DP Lithuanian Immigration to Canada after the Second World War*. Illus. Multicultural History Society of Ontario 1986, $16.75 (0-919045-30-8). 365pp. Nonfiction.

The author was born a year after her parents came to Canada from the Augsburg displaced-persons (DP) camp in Germany. She lives in Montréal, where she maintains close contact with the Lithuanian community. Danys interviewed two hundred Lithuanian men and women across Canada who, like her parents, arrived here as displaced persons from refugee camps in western Europe after World War II. She also researched Canadian Immigration and Labor Department documents dating from the late 1940s and the 1950s. Her book skillfully combines vivid oral histories of the struggles and achievements of Lithuanians who rebuilt their lives in Canada with an illuminating account of the official postwar Canadian immigration policies and attitudes.

The first part of the book explores the impact of war on the Lithuanians. In the second part she discusses the contract system, which allowed unskilled laborers and domestic servants to work in Canada. The final part describes how immigrants overcame obstacles in their quest for a better life and provides a brief look at Lithuanians in Canada thirty years after the end of the war.

625 Davis, Ann. ***Christiane Pflug: Her Art and Life***. Illus. Oxford Univ. Pr. 1991, $39.95 (0-19-540857-8). 352pp. Biography.

Ann Davis has written a moving biographical account of one of Canada's most important realist painters. Born in Berlin in 1936, Christiane escaped Nazi Germany and was sheltered with an austere family in the Austrian Tyrol. Later, in Paris, she met Michael Pflug, a strong and often overpowering influence in her life and her art. After they married they lived in France, Tunisia, and eventually Toronto. Christiane found the North American continent cold and alien and desolate. Michael urged her to pursue painting to balance the tedium of housekeeping and childbearing.

Like her personal life, Pflug's art is replete with contradictions, tensions, questioning, and self-doubt. The war experiences, her separation from her mother as a child, the conflicts in her life as a woman and an artist find expression in her beautifully crafted images, colors, and themes. In her work she repeatedly symbolizes the isolation and imprisonment of the individual; for example, vistas are often seen through picture frames, window frames, or doorways that define the boundaries between exterior and interior worlds. Images of dead birds, cages, dolls, and lifeless landscapes convey an ever-present sense of death. Unable to escape her own demons, Christiane took her own life in 1972, cutting short a promising career in which she had already achieved considerable success.

Fathi, Asghar, ed. ***Iranian Refugees and Exiles Since Khomeini***. See entry 1169.

626 Gloade, Harold W. ***From My Vantage Point***. Borealis 1991, $27.95 (0-88887-118-X); $12.95 (0-88887-120-1). Autobiography.

The author, a Micmac Indian from Annapolis County, Nova Scotia, uses a native storytelling style to describe his life and that of his family, recounting their struggles, their joys, and their times of sadness. His reminiscences date to the 1920s, when Micmacs were no longer nomadic but had settled permanently. Gloade describes a childhood marked by poverty and hardship, but also by the intense family bonds that characterize native culture. Gloade vividly recalls the people he encountered on the reservation during the 1920s and 1930s. He recounts stories of hunting and the traditional craft of basket making, evoking an era when people maintained a genuine interest in the lives of others, enjoying a level of social activity and a communal bond that has become rare in modern life.

The book closes in 1942, as Gloade describes the early effects of World War II on the people of his reservation and his pride in the young Micmacs who leave Canada to fight overseas for security and democracy.

627 Gratton, Michel. ***French Canadians***. Key Porter 1992, $26.95 (1-55013-438-8). Nonfiction.

The author is a journalist and former press secretary to Prime Minister Brian Mulroney. His book demonstrates that French Canadians constitute a nation—a people in their own right, divided but distinct. He does not predict whether they will separate from Canada or remain a part of it, but he makes it very clear that he wants to be both French and Canadian.

Using an anecdotal approach, he combines his personal story of growing up French in Ontario with the larger story of the French-Canadian people. Along the way, he explores such issues as language, education, religion, politics, and culture. He skillfully describes the forces—the events and the individuals—that have brought the French people to the present political crossroads. An emotionally intense and humorous account that is a pleasure to read, this is an important book for all Canadians and for anyone wishing to understand French Canadians.

628 Hill, Daniel G. ***The Freedom Seekers: Blacks in Early Canada***. Stoddard 1981, $19.95 (0-7737-5558-6). Nonfiction.

In this book, the author covers the early history of slaves, refugees, and black loyalists in Canada. He traces the decline of slavery from the passage of a bill prohibiting the import of slaves into Canada in 1793 to the British Imperial Act of 1833, which abolished slavery throughout the British Empire. The legendary underground railroad and the major routes to freedom from the United States to Canada are discussed, as are the chief areas of early black settlement. The author includes readable and informative personal accounts of early black settlers. Organized thematically, the book deals with such topics as blacks and the law, blacks and education, and black societies and culture. The final chapter contains biographical information on many black freedom-seekers in early Canada. This lucid, informative, and revealing account is a good starting place for the reader who is exploring this topic for the first time.

629 Hillel, Edward. ***The Main: Portrait of a Neighborhood***. Frwd. by Hugh MacLennan. Illus. Key Porter 1987, $26.95 (1-55013-046-3). Nonfiction.

This book presents images of the square-mile district around boulevard St. Laurent, the "Main Street" that divides Montréal into the English section to the west and the French quarter to the east. Edward Hillel, an immigrant from Iraq who moved into "the Main" as a student in 1971, has a deep understanding of the diverse inhabitants and the forces that shape this unique community. He documents immigrants' experiences as they try to synthesize their old world with that of Montréal's English and French milieu. For the most part, his subjects speak for themselves; their moving narratives provide insight into the process of assimilation.

Hillel's powerful black-and-white photographs offer rare glimpses into the personal and social lives of people in rooming houses, shops, and other settings in the region, which one of the subjects describes as "Nouveau Shtetl." These images, realistic and unromanticized, create a vibrant mosaic of busy street scenes and unforgettable portraits of people from many nationalities.

Hungry Wolf, Beverly. *The Ways of My Grandmothers*.
See entry 498.

630 *Identity: The Black Experience in Canada*. Gage 1979, o.p. Nonfiction.

This work is divided into three sections. The first, Canadian Black History, is based on the television documentary *Fields of Endless Day*, which traces the history of the black community in Canada and emigration from the West Indies from the seventeenth century to the mid-twentieth century. Of special interest is the discussion of racial discrimination and how people challenged that policy through the courts and through the actions of the Human Rights Commission. Part II, Contemporary Black Canada, contains fiction and nonfiction by various authors who discuss immigration, education, and the role of black organizations in community life. The first-person accounts of black life are down-to-earth and illuminating. The third section contains a resource guide that is largely out of date.

631 Itawaru, Arnold Harichand. *The Invention of Canada: Literary Text and the Immigrant Imaginary*. Tsar 1990, $15.95 (0-920661-13-0). 146pp. Nonfiction.

This eloquent, incisive, and provocative analysis is a major contribution to Canadian literary criticism. Examining twenty-one novels by ten Canadian writers from other nations, the author explores the tensions arising from the quest for identity as experienced by immigrants in a new land. Among the authors discussed are Henry Kreisel, Ethel Wilson, Austin Clarke, Brian Moore, and Ved Devajee, whose works deal with such themes as racism, cultural conflict, colonialism, alienation, displacement, and domination.

Itawaru argues that Canada has no fixed identity; instead, it is an arena for contesting cultural forces that shift over time. He maintains, however, that despite the adoption of multiculturalism, the Anglophone culture is being perpetuated as the "genuine" culture of Canada. One result is that immigrants are under enormous pressure to become assimilated. Itawaru explores the issues of color, the rejection of blacks in Canada, and the feelings of rootlessness and negation in a country that the newcomers had seen as a welcoming haven. In response to those experiences, Itawaru states, writers search for their connection with the past, with their history. Often these writers express that search in a language that distinguishes their culture from the dominant culture. In resisting assimilation, the immigrant clings to his or her mother tongue, which then takes on a special role as the language of personal anguish and loneliness. Itawaru's work, a critical analysis of a vibrant writing tradition, offers an alternative to notable literary critics such as Atwood and Frye.

Jensen, Joan M. *Passage from India: Asian Indian Immigrants in North America*.
See entry 313.

632 Kanungo, Rabindra N., ed. *South Asians in the Canadian Mosaic*. Kala Bharati 1984, $10.00 (0-920289-00-2). Nonfiction.

This volume brings together articles by social scientists focusing on the lives of South Asian immigrants in Canada. Although the book is somewhat more academic in tone than other works discussed in this bibliography, it is included here because there are few works on the subject available for the general reader. Topics covered include South Asian women, accommodation and adaptation, the challenge of maintaining one's cultural heritage in a new land, and racial discrimination in employment. A typical chapter examines the educational challenges and opportunities for South Asian children in Canada and the importance of such factors as motivation, sense of identity, and language development in achieving academic excellence.

633 Kostash, Myrna. *All of Baba's Children*. Hurtig 1977. o.p. Nonfiction.

In 1975 Myrna Kostash, a second-generation Ukrainian Canadian, traveled to Foothills, Alberta, ninety miles east of Edmonton, to interview the local residents of a predominantly Ukrainian-Canadian community. These narratives, combined with other records, both personal and official, relate the life experiences of the families who left western Ukraine at the turn of the century to homestead in western Canada. The first-generation Ukrainian Canadians, torn between their own minority culture and the dominant one, tell about their interactions with educators and priests and share the feelings of vulnerability they experienced during the years of the Depression. They also describe the importance of their sense of community, a sense that was heightened by their shared culture but also by their shared hardships.

This social history dispels a popular myth that an immigrant need only work hard and be a good citizen to gain acceptance in mainstream Canadian society. The narratives in this book reveal that immigrant status—combined with a persistent foreign accent—leads to second-class citizenship in a society intent on assimilation.

634 Kurelek, William. *Kurelek's Canada*. Illus. by the author. McGraw-Hill 1975. o.p. Nonfiction.

At his death in 1977, William Kurelek was acclaimed as one of Canada's most original artists. His work is now represented in all the great museums of the continent. He was born to Ukrainian-Canadian parents on a farm in Alberta in 1927 and studied in Manitoba, Toronto, and abroad. At his death he lived in Toronto with his wife, Jean, and their four children.

His work as a painter and as a writer is intensely autobiographical, revealing a love for the grandeur and vastness of Canada and the life of simplicity and vision it offers. Kurelek's unique experience raises the personal to the universal. His kaleidoscopic impressions possess intensity of color, simplicity of form, and a fervor that speaks of his love of mankind and his country. This book, unfortunately out of print, contains full-color reproductions of Kurelek's scenes of daily life throughout the provinces.

635 Lindstrom-Best, Varpu. *Defiant Sisters: A Social History of Finnish Immigrant Women in Canada.* Multicultural History Society of Ontario 1988, $14.95 (0-919045-36-7). 205pp. Nonfiction.

This powerful account of Finnish immigrant women in Canada between 1890 and 1930 provides insight into their indomitable spirit as they fought to realize their political and economic dreams in Canada. These women brought to Canada their longstanding tradition of literacy and liberal humanism. They had been extensively educated in Finland, but those who did not know English were barred from most occupations. Instead, they worked as cooks or laundresses in logging camps and rooming houses; some became bootleggers and prostitutes. Most of the women settled in towns and cities where the demand for domestic labor was high. The domestic workers took pride in their work, but it was poorly paid and involved long hours. In 1925, a group of Finnish socialist women formed the first Maid Organization. Similar groups mushroomed in other parts of Canada; devoted to promoting the interests of maids, these groups set up cooperative homes and established employment exchanges. *Defiant Sisters* is an invaluable book that brings to light the hardships, conflicts, and struggles that confronted a remarkable ethnic group in the Canadian mosaic.

Mander, Jerry. *In the Absence of the Sacred: The Failure of Technology and the Survival of the Indian Nations.*
See entry 510.

636 Porter, Jessie, ed. *New Canadian Voices.* Wall & Emerson 1991, $23.95 (1-895131-05-7). 312pp. Essays.

This unique anthology includes journals, biographies, and autobiographies by students in English as a second language classes at Jarvis Collegiate Institute in Toronto. Accompanying these writings are activities to encourage interaction with the text and develop both oral and written language skills. The book is also of interest to anyone wishing to explore issues related to immigration and multiculturalism. Themes explored include the effect of war on families, the problems of adjustment to the Canadian way of life, the need to integrate two cultures, discrimination in Canada, the help society should offer to immigrants, and the importance of family roots and cultural heritage.

Many of the authors come from countries in political or social turmoil, and many are haunted by troubled memories of childhood. Still, these new Canadian voices generally express a positive outlook for themselves, their friends, and their families. The writings in this book speak simply, honestly, and vividly about young people as they meet the challenges of adjusting to life in their new homeland.

637 Regush, Nicolas M. *Pierre Vallières.* Dial 1973. o.p. Nonfiction.

To understand the separatist movement in Québec today, one must examine critically the events that took place in October 1970. This highly readable and popular account by a noted sociologist details the role played by Pierre Vallières, who was chief theorist for the Front de Libération de Québec (FLQ). Regush discusses the revolutionary activities in Québec, the bombings, and the political kidnappings that led the Canadian government to invoke the War Measures Act.

The book includes a brief biography of Vallières, interviews, and excerpts from *White Niggers of America*, Vallières's polemic about discrimination against the Québecois. Regush also includes letters and a number of official documents of the FLQ to trace the birth of the Parti Québecois as well as Vallières's evolution from terrorist to an advocate of peaceful change through the democratic process.

638   Ruprecht, Tony. *Toronto's Many Faces: A Guide to Restaurants, Shops, Festivals, Museums and Monuments of More than 60 Cultural Communities in the City*. Whitecap 1990. o.p. Nonfiction.

A guide for natives and visitors alike, this publication opens an enchanting window on Toronto's rich cultural diversity. Over sixty cultural groups are featured through brief accounts of their historical past, their settlement in Toronto, profiles of their neighborhoods, and an overview of how their communities developed. In brisk prose, the authors describe the various cuisines, shops carrying specialty goods, and important landmarks. Restaurants and cultural centers are listed with useful snippets of information gathered through firsthand encounters. The material is presented in a readable, succinct, and easy-to-access format. There are lists of major associations, religious centers, and schools, as well as media outlets for the various groups. A calendar of festivals and holidays gives a bird's-eye view of the cultural and social life of different groups. The book leads visitors around unexpected corners into small neighborhoods, where they can discover the charms of a hurly-burly city made vibrant by different peoples from around the world.

Suzuki, David, and Peter Knudtson. *Wisdom of the Elders: Honoring Sacred Native Visions of Nature*.
See entry 532.

639   Tyman, James. *Inside Out: An Autobiography by a Native Canadian*. Fifth House 1989, $6.95 (0-920079-49-0). Autobiography.

This book chronicles the tumultuous experiences of James Tyman, a Métis who as an abused toddler was adopted by a white family in Saskatchewan. Labeled with the pejorative term "apple"—someone who is red on the outside but white on the inside—he suffers from an identity crisis constantly fed by racism. As his self-esteem plummets, he becomes increasingly belligerent and self-destructive, acting out his anger through violence and abuse of drugs and alcohol. He is confined to prison for a number of terms, which only accelerates his downward spiral.

A knife attack leaves him seriously wounded, causing him to reassess his life. He is also changed when he falls in love with a woman. He tries to rebuild his life, but fails, and ends up in jail again. During his prison stay he begins writing his autobiography. He wants to tell his story, he says, not to earn pity or forgiveness, but simply "to ask for understanding and acceptance for myself and all native people." His book provides an unvarnished look at the life of a young aboriginal Canadian. Tyman does not describe emotions in depth; instead, his behavior speaks for itself and reveals the depth of his feelings.

The reader develops a profound understanding of the extraordinary pressures Canadian aboriginal youth suffer in a world controlled by white values.

Wilson, Edmund. *Apologies to the Iroquois*.
See entry 540.

640 Women's Book Committee. *Jin Guo: Voices of Chinese Canadian Women*. Illus. with photographs. Women's Press 1992, $19.95 (0-88961-147-5). 353pp. Autobiography (Collective).

Through oral accounts, this book preserves the hitherto ignored history of Chinese women in Canada. The interviews, accompanied by a small selection of photographs, feature women from all walks of life, ranging in age from nineteen to eighty-five.

The book provides several moving life stories that tell of hardships overcome, experiences of racism, the isolation encountered through the language barrier, and the difficulty of gaining acceptance in Canadian culture. There are also success stories of women who contributed much to the Chinese community and to society at large. Vignettes of life and struggle, told with humor and pathos, focus on such themes as education, work, and the daily life in Chinatown. The stories convey a strong sense of history and reveal the tenacity, hard work, and self-reliance of these women in the face of sexism, prejudice, and isolation.

641 Zucchi, John E. *Italians in Toronto: Developments of a National Identity, 1875–1935*. Univ. of Toronto Pr. 1988, $34.95 (0-7735-0653-5); $16.95 (0-7735-0782-5). 255pp. Nonfiction.

This book explores the history of Italian settlement in Toronto from the 1870s to the 1930s. The author traces the origins of the Italian immigrants, examines the means by which they traveled, notes their patterns of settlement, and discusses their participation in social institutions and local economies. According to the author, the first immigrants tended to create "Little Italies," enclaves inhabited by people from their own villages or regions. Such enclaves helped them maintain strong links with their homelands, easing transition to the new world by providing vital services, including shipping, labor agencies, and lodging. When Italy was reunified in the late nineteenth century, the immigrants began to undergo a change in their sense of identity. The links to one's village became less important than one's identification with the Italian nation as a whole. Furthermore, once they had settled in Toronto, people began to intermingle, not just with fellow Italians from other regions but also with other Canadians, through employment, church activities, and social clubs. This social history of Italians tells an important part of the story of Toronto.

6

LATIN AMERICA
AND THE CARIBBEAN

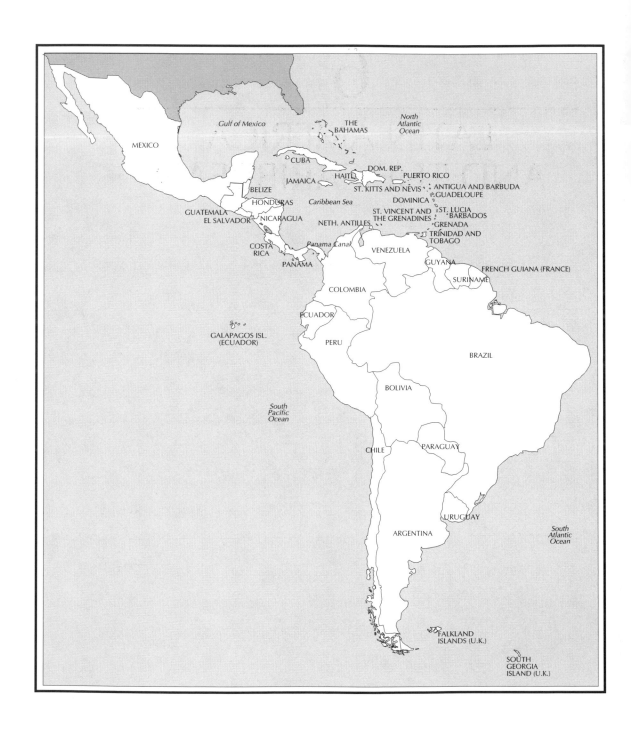

MEXICO

Gulf of Mexico

THE
BAHAMAS

North
Atlantic
Ocean

CUBA

DOM. REP.

PUERTO RICO

HAITI

BELIZE

JAMAICA

ST. KITTS AND NEVIS

ANTIGUA AND BARBUDA

GUADELOUPE

HONDURAS

Caribbean Sea

DOMINICA

GUATEMALA

NICARAGUA

NETH. ANTILLES

ST. VINCENT AND
THE GRENADINES

ST. LUCIA

BARBADOS

EL SALVADOR

GRENADA

COSTA
RICA

Panama Canal

TRINIDAD AND
TOBAGO

PANAMA

VENEZUELA

GUYANA

FRENCH GUIANA (FRANCE)

SURINAME

COLOMBIA

ECUADOR

GALAPAGOS ISL.
(ECUADOR)

PERU

BRAZIL

BOLIVIA

South
Pacific
Ocean

CHILE

PARAGUAY

URUGUAY

ARGENTINA

South
Atlantic
Ocean

FALKLAND
ISLANDS (U.K.)

SOUTH
GEORGIA
ISLAND (U.K.)

6

LATIN AMERICA AND THE CARIBBEAN

by Heather Caines, Christine McDonald,
Lyn Miller-Lachmann, and Patricia Rubio

Latin America and the Caribbean are culturally rich and diverse regions that encompass many racial, ethnic, and language groups. Tens of thousands of years ago these areas were settled by the Indians, who crossed the land bridge that once existed between Asia and North America (in what today is the Bering Sea) and who migrated southward. When Columbus landed on the island that he named Santo Domingo (in the area now known as the Dominican Republic), he entered a world inhabited by people with many different languages and cultures. Some of these indigenous civilizations were extensive and highly organized; among them were the Aztecs of present-day Mexico, the Maya of Mexico and Central America, and the Inca of Peru. The Spanish, Portuguese, French, and English explorers and settlers who followed Columbus brought to the region their own cultures and languages.

Soon after the arrival of Europeans, war and disease wiped out many of smaller indigenous groups. The story of Columbus is told from the perspective of indigenous Americans in books such as Kirkpatrick Sale's *The Conquest of Paradise* and Ronald Wright's *Stolen Continents*. Eventually the indigenous people intermarried with the Europeans, creating the *mestizo* (mixed-race) population that occupies most regions of Spanish America. In the Caribbean and on the Atlantic coast of Central and South America, the colonialists from Spain, Portugal, France, and England imported slaves from Africa to work on the plantations. In those areas, one finds the confluence of three racial groups and traditions. Harsh conditions on the plantations of the Caribbean led slaves to join with the remaining Indians in a revolt against their French masters in Haiti at the end of the eighteenth century. In 1803, this revolt culminated in the first and only successful slave rebellion, leading to the independence of Haiti. C.L.R. James's classic work, *The Black Jacobins*, documents this momentous event, which also receives coverage in Maya Deren's study of the vodun (voodoo) religion, *Divine Horsemen: The Living Gods of Haiti.*

293

DEVELOPMENT OF LITERATURE IN THE REGION

Latin and South America

Strictly speaking, Spanish-American writing began with the diaries of Columbus and the many chronicles written by conquistadors and soldiers. True Spanish-American literature, however, did not arise until the end of the nineteenth century. Until that time authors, with a few exceptions, had followed Spanish models, contributing little that was original to the development of literature in Spanish. Rubén Dar'o (the founder of *modernismo*), José Martí, and other poets from Uruguay, Argentina, Colombia, Cuba, and Ecuador were the first ones to depart from the Spanish literary tradition. They looked for new inspiration and models in Europe, especially France. They were also heavily influenced by Asian themes and their reconsideration of the classical tradition. They were elitist in that their main concerns were aesthetic: Believing in "art for art's sake," they distanced themselves from the parochialism of Spanish-American social, political, and economic concerns. Beauty, rhythm, melody, ornament, the pursuit of the perfect form — these were their primary preoccupations. *Blue* (1888) and *Profane Prose* (1896) by Dar'o of Nicaragua are probably the most representative books of the modernismo movement.

The proponents of modernismo demonstrated that Spanish-American literature could determine its own course, independent from its mother country. Writers addressed such topics as the mores of the people, the social, economic, and political development of their republics, and above all, the relationship between individuals and nature. The most important current in this literary regionalism was *mundonovismo* (new-worldism), which explored the dichotomy between civilization and barbarism. The former was associated with economic development, Western culture, and urban life; the latter with untamed nature, lack of formal education, and the hinterland. Civilization was the ideal to be pursued and fostered; barbarism needed to be tamed or destroyed. Rómulo Gallegos of Venezuela and José Eustasio Rivera of Colombia wrote the most important works of the period. In Gallego's *Do–a Barbara*, civilization has the upper hand, but in Rivera's *The Vortex* (not yet available in English), the protagonist is literally devoured by the jungle.

The two world wars determined much of the development of Spanish-American literature throughout this century. The intelligentsia lost faith in the political, economic, and social models proposed by Europe. Such events as the Spanish Civil War, the rise of fascism, and the Holocaust demonstrated that European societies had run amok. In the absence of credible models of society from abroad, Latin American authors and thinkers looked inward and began to define the unique identity of the Central and South American region and its cultures. Ethnic differences were for the first time considered an asset, not a liability. Both indigenous and African-American contributions to Latin America (which includes Brazil as well as Spanish America) were recognized not merely as something positive, but indeed as crucial to this rising sense of identity. Alejo Carpentier and Nicolás Guillén in Cuba and José María Arguedas in Peru, for example, describe syncretic worlds where the magical dominates over the rational, where African-American and indigenous myths are of paramount importance.

Standard history texts that emphasize the contributions of Europeans in the development of Spanish America downplay or ignore the contributions of other ethnic groups. In contrast, many of the works annotated in this chapter take a new look at history, offering alternative interpretations of significant events. Carpentier's *The Kingdom of This World*, for example, proposes a fresh vision of Haiti's slave uprisings, while *El Señor Presidente* (*Mr. President*) by Miguel Angel Asturias presents a frightening portrait of a fictional, but nevertheless very real, dictator. Similarly, Abel Posse's *Dogs of Paradise* questions the veracity of the traditional characterizations of Columbus.

Often Spanish-American writers discover that the creative tools they have inherited are insufficient for the portrayal of their multilayered reality, a world that is at once modern and traditional, developed and underdeveloped, rational and magical. Confined by linguistic norms, poets César Vallejo and Octavio Paz and fiction writers Juan Carlos Onetti, Severo Sarduy, Guillermo Cabrera Infante, and Julio Cortázar question the validity of language as a reliable means of communication and search for new structures, even for a new language or languages, to express that reality. Through surrealism, many of these authors discovered the hidden dimensions in reality, finding that sensory perception reveals merely the first layer of a rich and complex world. Dreams, the subconscious, the instinctual, and the fantastic are also legitimate, if less evident, means of expression. What differentiates Spanish-American authors from the surrealists, however, is that they do not need to produce the surreal artificially because in Spanish America it is part of everyday life, as demonstrated by *One Hundred Years of Solitude* by Gabriel García Márquez and the masterly short stories of Jorge Luis Borges and Julio Cortázar.

Many of these works are structurally complex. They destroy the chronology of the story, transcend the limits of space, engage in linguistic games, and use multiple narrative voices (many of which are frequently unreliable). To make sense of this world, readers must often grope their way through a labyrinth that forces them to think in creative ways as they constantly encounter new enigmas. In so doing they discover thought processes that in turn enable them to question their own reality—and to understand it more fully. This style is a feature in such works as *Pedro Páramo* by Juan Rulfo, *Time of the Heroes* by Mario Vargas Llosa, and *The Death of Artemio Cruz* by Carlos Fuentes.

Critics often examine writers from Brazil, Latin America's largest nation, separately from those from Spanish America. Colonized by Portugal, Brazil gained its independence in 1822 but did not become a republic until 1889, an event chronicled in Nelida Piñon's *The Republic of Dreams*. Writing in Portuguese, Brazil's greatest twentieth-century literary figures—among them Clarice Lispector, Jorge Amado, and Piñon—share much in terms of style and themes with their Spanish-speaking counterparts. Authors face similar social and political problems, and the intermingling of indigenous, European, and African cultures has certainly influenced Brazil's writers.

Perhaps the most important literary development in this region during the past two decades has been the increase in the number of published works by women writers. Innovative in both form and content, their fiction, poetry, and drama explore the plight of women in patriarchal societies, offering profound analyses of their oppression and the silencing they have experienced. Many authors explore women's contributions to the historical, economic, social, and political development of Latin America, correcting the existing record, which had largely ignored them. Works by María Luisa Bombal, Elena Garro, and Isabel Allende deal with the situation of women in the elite classes, while other works, such as the fiction and nonfiction of Elena Poniatowska, describe the experiences of women in marginalized groups. Much of this literature legitimizes women's erotic feelings and their rebellion against male domination; works by Luisa Valenzuela are good examples of these themes. Twenty years ago discussion of Latin American literature would have included only a handful of women writers. Today that would be impossible. Women's voices not only have become a presence in the literature of Latin America but have also determined its development in new and important ways.

The Caribbean

Like other parts of Latin America, the Caribbean has produced a large and unique body of literature. Readers in the United States who want to explore works by island writers are often stymied, however, because most of these books are published only in the Caribbean or in Europe. One key source is the publishing firm of Heinemann, whose Caribbean Authors series is aimed at secondary-school and college students. The few works that are widely available, however, are vibrant and noteworthy.

Caribbean literature is rich and complex, reflecting the cultural heritage of a number of ethnic strands: English, African, French, East Indian, Portuguese, and Hispanic. Works from the English- and French-speaking countries of the Caribbean are quite different in style and content from the literature produced in the Spanish- and Portuguese-speaking regions. In selecting the items for this bibliography, the editors worked to achieve balance among works from the nations of both areas. An attempt was also made to include works by major authors who produced literature of distinction in more than one genre.

While established authors are highlighted in this bibliography, attention is also given to budding writers who are breaking into the mainstream. A prime example is Caryl Phillips, a native of St. Kitts now living in England, whose1991 novel *Cambridge* received a glowing reception. As is true elsewhere in Latin America, the growing chorus of women writers from the Caribbean after years of exclusion is also a recent development that bears mentioning. Among the notable newcomers included in this chapter are Jamaica Kincaid, Maryse Condé, Michelle Cliff, and Opal Palmer Adisa. Some of their works appear in the short story anthology *Green Cane and Juicy Flotsam* edited by Lizabeth Parravisini-Gebert and Carmen Esteves. Other emerging female authors include Michelle Nourbese Philip, Zee Edgell, and the poet Lorna Goddison. Because of space considerations, these authors are not annotated here, but cross-references direct the reader to discussions of their work that appear in other chapters.

The themes with which many of these authors grapple are central to the Caribbean region: slavery; plantation life; colonialism; the complexities of class, race, and language; and the search for a meaningful West Indian cultural identity. Caribbean society has been a largely patriarchal, and women writers are now bringing a female voice and perspective to these established themes.

Notable works that investigate the topics of slavery and early colonialism include Caryl Phillips's *Cambridge*, Orlando Patterson's *Die the Long Day*, and Jean Rhys's *Wide Sargasso Sea*. Another outstanding novel is George Lamming's *In the Castle of My Skin*. In this work, the social hierarchy of the Caribbean, with its penchant for division by race, class, and skin color, is skillfully rendered.

The quest to formulate a unique racial and cultural identity is another prevalent concern in Caribbean literature. The works of Derek Walcott, especially his play *Dream on Monkey Mountain*, notably explore this theme. V. S. Naipaul, a Trinidadian author of East Indian heritage, focuses on the struggles of mixed-race people as they search for, and struggle to preserve, a sense of self. The quest for an individual personhood, separate and apart from a West Indian identity, is a motif found in Jamaica Kincaid's *Annie John*, Roy Heath's *The Murderer*, and Naipaul's *A House for Mr. Biswas*.

Several works of Caribbean literature trace the region's cultural roots in the folklore, traditions, and daily life of the people of West Africa. Consciousness of forced separation from African ancestors figures prominently in the works of Walcott, Phillips, Condé, Patterson, and others. In French-speaking Haiti, this theme is perhaps best expressed in Jacques Roumain's *Masters of the Dew* and Philippe Thoby-Marcelin's *The Beast of the Haitian Hills*. These men were leaders of the Negritude Movement, which sought to extol the African strands of Caribbean heritage. Their works celebrate the life, beliefs, and culture of black Haitian peasants, many of whom maintain strong emotional links to Africa.

This feeling of kinship with Africa is reflected more in works from the English- and French-speaking Caribbean than it is among works from the Spanish-speaking islands, whose writings reveal more of a connection to the European and indigenous influences. Still, many Cuban and Puerto Rican writers have acknowledged their debt to Africa. Most notable of these is Nicolás Guillén, a Cuban poet who embraced the Negritude Movement and who serves as a bridge between the two main literary trends in the region.

Identity and language are inseparable. Most of the authors discussed here draw on the patois or creole languages of their respective islands. This use of dialect is used to great effect in the works of George Lamming, V. S. Naipaul, and Jamaica Kincaid.

In summary, through story, place setting, and characterization, these writers bring to life the culture, landscape, and experiences of the Caribbean, both past and present. Experiencing their writing brings the reader joy and enrichment.

Nonfiction and Biography

The nonfiction and biographical works about Latin America and the Caribbean included in this chapter address a variety of topics and themes. Given the proximity of the region to the United States, it is not surprising that many of these books look at Latin America and the Caribbean from the point of view of U.S. geopolitical concerns. Led in part by small presses, however, a growing number of books present the region from the Latin American perspective. Some of the most compelling works of nonfiction to come out of this region are the personal testimonies of those who lived through the tumult and terror of recent decades.

In 1992 Rigoberta Menchú received the Nobel Peace Prize. Her personal account, *I, Rigoberta Menchú*, describes the Guatemalan government's brutal treatment of the nation's indigenous population and the daily life of the Mayan people in the twentieth century, a way of living that changed little over the centuries until recently. Her powerful book, among the best examples of "witness" literature in Latin America, gives voice to people who have long been silenced when trying to speak out against the "official" history as published by government-controlled media. Another work that presents this unofficial view is *Voice of the Voiceless* by Archbishop Oscar Arnulfo Romero. In this collection of sermons, essays, and other writings, he speaks of repression in El Salvador, especially of the Catholics who embrace radical Christianity and devote their lives to helping the poor and powerless. Romero himself was murdered by death squads tied to El Salvador's powerful military. In her classic nonfiction work *Massacre in Mexico*, novelist Elena Poniatowska records the words of those who participated in the 1968 uprising by students and workers that culminated in the Army massacre of unarmed demonstrators in the Plaza de las Tres Culturas in Mexico City, an event that was hushed up in the country's supposedly free press. *Let Me Speak! Testimony of Domitila, a Woman of the Bolivian Mines* is a moving chronicle of the extreme poverty of the miners and its effect upon their families. In 1975, the author, Domitila Barrios de Chungara, was chosen to speak at the UN-sponsored International Women's Year Tribunal. In *Prisoner Without a Name, Cell Without a Number*, Jacobo Timerman, an Argentine newspaper editor in Buenos Aires, writes about the oppression arising from anti-Semitism. He was imprisoned and tortured because, at the time, to be a Jew in Argentina was officially listed as a "category of guilt." A testimonial by Cuban author Heberto Padilla, *Self Portrait of the Other*, reveals the many forms of prejudice and repression experienced by dissidents in Castro's Cuba. As Padilla describes it, the pain of repression was even greater because initially many of these idealistic individuals had been among Castro's most ardent supporters.

Most of these personal accounts, like much of the nonfiction works about Latin America in general, deal with the issue of political repression and torture. The region is just beginning to emerge from the darkness of dictatorship and to confront the horrors of its past. In *A Miracle, a Universe*, Lawrence Weschler uses interviews with human rights activists and ordinary citizens in Brazil and Uruguay to examine how societies and individuals come to terms with the past. His book explores the concerns of the victims, the guilt of the torturers, the complicity of society as a whole, and the need to do something to prevent such horrors from happening again. Essential steps in the healing process are discovery and publication of the truth and the national soul-searching that follows. Books that contributed to this process include *Nunca Más (Never Again): The Report of the Argentine National Commission on the Disappeared* and *Torture in Brazil: A Shocking Report on the Pervasive Use of Torture by the Brazilian Military Governments, 1964–1979*. They are among the most difficult works to read and comprehend because of their first-person accounts of systematic torture, yet they demand to be included, just as any account of World War II must include works on the Holocaust. Chile's experience under the Pinochet dictatorship and its aftermath is covered in several works: *Chile from Within: 1973–1988*, with text by Ariel Dorfman and Marco Antonio de la Parra and many photographs documenting the repression; *Scraps of Life: Chilean Arpilleras*, Marjorie Agosín's account of how women created quilts to tell of their family members' disappearance; and *A Nation of Enemies: Chile under Pinochet* by Pamela Constable and Arturo Valenzuela, which explores the polarization of Chilean society and how Chileans of virtually all parties and social classes came together to defeat Pinochet in the 1988 plebiscite.

Despite the emergence of democracies in many Latin American nations, economic problems persist. Brazil, for instance, is a nation of enormous wealth but enormous inequality. *Death Without Weeping: The Violence of Everyday Life in Brazil* by Nancy Scheper-Hughes documents this harsh truth by focusing on the lives of the poorest Brazilians, who live in such misery that almost half of all babies born do not survive to their first birthday. In *Across the Wire: Life and Hard Times on the Mexican Border*, Luis A. Urrea describes the poverty and despair of Tijuana, the Mexican border town only twenty minutes from downtown San Diego. He observes the effects of Central American repression as thousands of the displaced seek asylum only to be faced with unimaginable economic deprivation as they attempt to cross over. Ronald Fernandez's *The Disenchanted Island* and Alfredo Lopez's *Doña Licha's Island* focus on poverty in Puerto Rico, which, despite its special relationship to the United States, offers few opportunities for its residents. In Haiti, enormous turmoil has grown out of widespread official corruption and the disenfranchisement of the vast majority of people, who endure the lowest per capita income in the Western Hemisphere. Life in Haiti has been the subject of a number of important books, including Amy Wilentz's journalistic treatment in *The Rainy Season: Haiti Since the Duvaliers* and *Haiti: State Against Nation: The Origins and Legacy of Duvalierism*, a more scholarly analysis by Haitian-born anthropologist Michel-Rolph Trouillot.

Although many people in the United States view the island nations of the English-speaking Caribbean merely as a vacation paradise, several writers and scholars from the region describe the poverty and inequality that lie behind the idyllic image. In *A Small Place*, novelist Jamaica Kincaid, a native of Antigua, discusses the island's racism and the bleak economic opportunities that drove her to the United States. A study by Clive Thomas, *The Poor and the Powerless*, examines the legacy of slavery and the present-day exploitation of the English-speaking Caribbean by the developed nations of North America and Western Europe. Michael Manley, two-term president of Jamaica, has offered a thought-provoking analysis of poverty and dependence among the nations of the Caribbean and throughout the Third World. Two of his books, *The Politics of Change: A Jamaican Testament* and *The Poverty of Nations*, are included here; they show how his thinking evolved during his years of service to his nation. Manley's socialist perspective contrasts with the free-market outlook championed by Peruvian businessman Hernando De Soto, whose book *The Other Path* argues for deregulation and free enterprise as the way out of poverty for Latin Americans and their countries.

Another important theme in books about Latin America and the Caribbean is the environment. In his compelling work *Bird of Life, Bird of Death: A Naturalist's Journey Through a Land of Political Turmoil*, Jonathan Maslow uses the metaphor of two birds — the quetzal (the sacred bird of the Maya) and the vulture — to show how political decisions are resulting in the destruction of the habitat and the people of Guatemala. The encroachment on the Amazon rain forest, which includes parts of Brazil, Peru, Ecuador, Bolivia, Colombia, and Venezuela, is described in *The Burning Season*, Andrew Revkin's biography of slain Brazilian labor leader and environmentalist Francisco (Chico) Mendes, and in *The Last New World: The Conquest of the Amazon Frontier* by Mac Margolis. The encroachment on the rain forest destroys trees, which not only threatens the supply of oxygen in the world but signals as well the destruction of indigenous groups in the Amazon Basin. In *Tristes Tropiques*, published in 1955, anthropologist Claude Lévi-Strauss wrote of the developing "monoculture" in the world that has accompanied the disappearance of indigenous cultures.

Despite poverty, oppression, and the destruction of the environment and many indigenous cultures, Latin America and the Caribbean offer rich and vibrant cultures that have given much to the world as a whole. The ancient traditions of the Maya were recorded in alphabetic language in the middle of the sixteenth century; known as the *Popol Vuh*, the stories were first translated from Quiché into Spanish in the eighteenth century. The themes of the *Popol Vuh* recur in the writings of Menchú and in *The Labyrinth of Solitude* by poet and essayist Octavio Paz, which explores the roots of Mexican culture. Paz argues that Mexicans must return to their indigenous origins and to the myths that inform their history so that they might integrate the past with the present and restore their fractured community. Another acclaimed Mexican author, Carlos Fuentes, describes the confluence of Spanish and indigenous cultures in *The Buried Mirror: Reflections on Spain and the New World*. One of the most prolific writers on the political and cultural realities of Latin America from a Latin American perspective is the Uruguayan essayist Eduardo Galeano. His *Open Veins of Latin America* looks at all of the Americas—North, Central, and South—and describes the ways in which the North has ignored or exploited the rest of what is also America. Galeano's history of the people of the Americas from 1492 to 1986 in the trilogy *Memory of Fire* is a classic that defies classification by genre.

Although this chapter highlights the works of Latin American and Caribbean authors, several exemplary works by writers not native to these regions also deserve mention. Journalist Stephen Kinzer has produced two highly respected works: *Bitter Fruit: The Untold Story of the American Coup in Guatemala* (written with Stephen Schlesinger) and *Blood of Brothers: Life and War in Nicaragua*. The classic general overview of the region is *Modern Latin America* by Thomas Skidmore and Peter H. Smith, now in its third edition. More critical of the U.S. role in Latin America is James Cockroft's *Neighbors in Turmoil: Latin America*, which focuses on the political history of the region since 1948. Finally, *Distant Neighbors*, Alan Riding's thorough exploration of Mexican society, politics, and culture, offers a solid introduction to the works of Paz, Fuentes, and other commentators from the region.

LITERATURE

642   Agosín, Marjorie, ed. ***Landscapes of a New Land: Short Fiction by Latin-American Women***. Trans. from Spanish. o.p. Fiction.

This useful anthology includes works from ten Latin American women writers. Some of them are well known, such as María Luisa Bombal (Chile), Elena Poniatowska (Mexico), Clarice Lispector (Brazil), and Luisa Valenzuela (Argentina), but others are usually absent from anthologies: Bedregal (Bolivia), Rendic and Balcells (Chile), Hilst (Brazil), and Naranjo (Costa Rica).

These stories, according to the introduction, are "the images and voices that reflect the eclectic nature and energy of these women." The preface places each author in the context of the development of Latin American literature and underscores the salient features of her work.   PR

643   Alegría, Claribel. ***Ashes of Izalco***. Trans. from Spanish by Darwin J. Flakoll. Curbstone 1989, $17.95 (0-915306-83-2); $9.95 (0-915306-84-0). 192pp. Fiction.

Politics and the situation of women in rural patriarchal El Salvador are two of the main topics of Alegría's poetry and prose. In this book, the eruption of the volcano Izalco coincides with the peasants' massacre in 1952, which the author witnessed as a child. The novel weaves together the unrest affecting the country with the protagonist's search for the meaning of her mother's life.

Carmen, the main character of the story, returns to El Salvador to attend the funeral of her mother, who left a diary in which she reveals her frustrations and describes a love affair that she ended on account of her children. Reading the diary, Carmen finds many similarities between their lives. They both married men with whom they cannot communicate, and the roles of wife and mother became traps that stifled their individual development. Paralleling the unrest in the country, behind the apparent stability in Carmen's life are destructive forces waiting to be unleashed.

Other works by Alegría that explore similar topics are *Family Album* (Curbstone, 1990), a collection of short stories, and *They Won't Take Me Alive* (Interlink, 1987), a nonfiction work dealing with one woman's participation in the Salvadoran guerrilla movement. Alegría is also the author of several volumes of poetry, including *Flowers from the Volcano* (Univ. of Pittsburgh Pr., 1982).   PR

644 Allende, Isabel. ***The House of the Spirits***. Trans. from Spanish by Magda Bogin. Knopf 1985, $27.50 (0-394-53907-9); Bantam $5.99 (0-553-27391-4). 400pp. Fiction.

One of the most popular Spanish-American novels of the 1980s, this novel emphasizes the importance of women in Chilean society. Four generations of women—Nina, the suffragette; Clara, whose notebooks constitute the core of the narrative; Blanca, her daughter; and Alba, the granddaughter, who is brutally tortured by the military dictatorship—abandon the traditional upper-class roles of mother and housewife as they become more politically aware. Clara's husband and the family patriarch is the authoritarian Esteban Trueba, who as an influential right-wing politician and supporter of the military contributes to their victimization by opposing their dreams and their political struggles. In the end, however, Clara's notebooks remain, and with them survives the power of women's word and presence.

Allende's second novel, *Of Love and Shadows* (Bantam, 1988), features a woman journalist who risks her life to expose the horrors unleashed by the dictatorship in Chile.   PR

Alvarez, Julia. ***How the García Girls Lost Their Accents***.
See entry 358.

645 Amado, Jorge. ***Gabriela, Clove and Cinnamon***. Trans. from Portuguese. Avon 1988, $11.00 (0-380-75470-3). 425pp. Fiction.

This wry tale is set in Ilheus, a coastal village in northeastern Brazil in the mid-1920s. Told from the point of view of Nacib, a bar owner of Syrian heritage, it chronicles the process of change occurring there and in Brazilian society as a whole. One day Nacib's cook quits, and he hires the beautiful and capable Gabriela, a young biracial woman, to replace her. That day the town is rocked by an even larger scandal: A wealthy landowner kills his wife and her lover. Because the local code of honor stipulates that the landowner must kill the adulterers or be laughed at as a cuckold, the villagers expect him to be acquitted. The code of honor also affects a political matter: An importer, a newcomer to the village, wants to dredge the sandbar and build a port, but he is opposed by the town's traditional leaders, who conspire to kill him. Eventually Nacib falls in love with Gabriela and marries her, only to find himself in a dilemma when he catches his wife in bed with the mayor's son. The importer outmaneuvers the traditional leaders; similarly, Nacib's clever solution to his personal problem symbolizes the triumph of the modern over the traditional.

The foibles of human relationships are the subject of several of Amado's novels, most notably *Doña Flor and Her Two Husbands* (orig. pub. 1969; Avon, 1977). He is also the author of *The Violent Land* (orig. pub. 1965; Avon, 1988), *Home Is the Sailor* (Avon, 1979), *Sea of Death* (Avon, 1984), and *The War of the Saints* (Bantam, 1993), which explores Brazil's multiracial culture.   LML

646   Arenas, Reinaldo. ***The Ill-Fated Peregrinations of Fray Servando***. Trans. from Spanish by Andrew Hurley. Viking 1994, $11.95 (0-14-024166-3). 256pp. Fiction.

First published in French in 1968, this novel, like most of Arenas's fiction, focuses on situations of oppression, persecution, and the struggle for freedom. The protagonist, the Spanish friar Servando Teresa de Mier, falls victim to the Inquisition's persecution of dissenters in the New World. The restrictions imposed by the Church on seventeenth-century Mexican society parallel those imposed by the Cuban revolutionary government on its population and its ideological dissenters. The novel is written in a neobaroque style; its structural intricacies and linguistic games reflect Arenas's idea that writing is a means of attaining freedom, of escaping the forces that constantly try to suppress it.

Other lesser-known works by this author include *Farewell to the Sea* (Viking, 1985), *The Graveyard of the Angels* (Avon, 1987), and *Singing from the Well* (Viking, 1987). Arenas died in 1990; his autobiography, *Before Night Falls*, was published by Viking in 1994. This compellingly written work explores the author's childhood in rural Cuba, his absent father, his growing awareness of his homosexuality, his hopes for the revolution, the dashing of those hopes as Castro's regime relentlessly persecutes him for his political beliefs and his sexual orientation, and his escape from Cuba in the 1980 Mariel boatlift.

PR

647   Argueta, Manlio. ***One Day of Life***. Trans. from Spanish. Univ. of Texas Pr. 1995, $40.00 (0-292-70836-X); $19.95 (0-292-70830-0). 224pp. Fiction.

For Guadalupe, a Salvadoran grandmother in her forties, the day begins early. As she watches the sun rise through the cracks in her tiny house, she thinks of her husband, who must sleep in the mountains with the other farmworkers to avoid capture by the army. She remembers the old priests who did nothing while the children died of dehydration and thinks about the new priests, who are helping the *campesinos* (peasants) struggle for a better life. In the late morning, she sends her thirteen-year-old granddaughter Adolfina to the store with her three younger children, but while they are gone, soldiers come looking for the teenager to interrogate her. The soldiers stay for hours, terrifying Lupe, while Adolfina visits a friend. When Adolfina and the children return, there is a confrontation and a shocking revelation.

Interspersed with Lupe's narrative are snippets from the point of view of Adolfina, her mother (whose own husband has "disappeared"), Adolfina's friend, and the confused teenage boys who have joined the army, to be trained and turned against their own people by the United States. Through this gripping and horrifying story, Salvadoran author Argueta gives the reader a sense of the courage, sacrifice, imagination, and wisdom of the ordinary people in his war-torn country.

Argueta is the author of *Cuzcatlan: Where the Southern Sea Beats* (Random, 1987), the saga of five decades in the life of a *campesino* family and community in El Salvador. **LML**

648 Asturias, Miguel. ***El Señor Presidente***. Trans. from Spanish by Frances Partridge. Macmillan 1975, $11.00 (0-689-70521-2). 286pp. Fiction.

This is one of the first important novels to deal with the issue of dictatorship, a recurring theme in Latin American fiction. Other authors who have developed the subject include Alejo Carpentier (Cuba), Gabriel García Márquez (Colombia), Augusto Roa Bastos (Paraguay), and Luisa Valenzuela (Argentina).

With a complex plot that parallels the web of schemes and distortions the dictator uses to maintain his stronghold, the novel explores the effects of totalitarian power on society as well as the individual. The social fabric is destroyed by the terror of this ominous, bloody, and destructive force, which annihilates all human relationships. Individuals become isolated entities, grotesque puppets of a dictator who is always present but who rarely shows his face. Even his most loyal associates fall prey to his unpredictable schemes. General Canales, a potential political rival, and Miguel Angel Face, the dictator's closest and most trusted aide, are both assassinated. In depicting the ambiguity and grotesquery of such a world, language becomes an instrument that Asturias plays in all its voices: poetic and popular, literary and vulgar.

This Guatemalan author received the Nobel Prize in literature in 1967. His other translated works include *Men of Maize* (Routledge, 1988), a long, complex, and challenging novel that incorporates Indian mythology into the narrative. **PR**

649 Azuela, Maríano. ***The Underdogs***. Trans. from Spanish by Frederick H. Fornoff. Univ. of Pittsburgh Pr. 1992, $49.95 (0-8229-3728-X); $14.95 (0-8229-5484-2). 184pp. Fiction.

The revolution of 1910 has been a recurrent topic in twentieth-century Mexican literature. Azuela, a medical doctor who served under Pancho Villa, wrote this, the first and still the most highly esteemed novel about the event. Writing from his perspective as a disillusioned participant, Azuela presents a brutal and unforgiving picture of the movement. It was fought in the name of poor, landless peasants to give a new beginning to the country and its people. In reality, however, the revolution became merely a mean of enrichment for politicians and the military elite, while for the peasants, the outcome was further degradation, suffering, and poverty.

Most of the characters in the novel are criminals escaping the law or individuals in pursuit of their own material, military, or political gain. Ironically, the only two positive characters in the novel fall victim to the violence. Solís, a young intellectual, is hit by a stray bullet, and Camila, an innocent peasant girl, is killed by a jealous camp follower. In contrast to the prevailing human brutality and deprivation, Azuela presents the Jaliscan countryside in beautiful, pristine images. The novel generates interest not only through its treatment of its subject matter but also through its stylistic quality.   PR

Barreiro, José. **The Indian Chronicles**.
See entry 366.

650   Bombal, María Luisa. ***House of Mist***. Trans. from Spanish; Frwd. by Naomi Lindstrom. Univ. of Texas Pr. 1995, $19.95 (0-292-70830-0). 245pp. Fiction.

One of the first feminist pieces of twentieth-century Spanish-American fiction, this short novel by the Chilean author explores with elegance and skill a bourgeois woman's dissatisfaction with a world that does not respond to her aspirations and needs. Raised to believe that the path to a woman's fulfillment lies in marriage and motherhood, the childless protagonist is trapped by boredom and frustration in a predictable and loveless marriage. She escapes into a dreamlike, misty world where she finds erotic pleasure in a sexual encounter with an imaginary lover. As she ages and as her reveries disintegrate, she realizes the wastefulness and futility of her life.

Other Bombal stories, such as "The Tree," are equally interesting and expertly written. Her work had a profound influence on later women's Spanish-American fiction.   PR

651   Borges, Jorge Luis. ***Labyrinths: Selected Short Stories and Other Writings***. Ed. by Donald A. Yates and James E. Irby; Pref. by André Maurois; Trans. from Spanish. Random 1984, $16.00 (0-394-60449-0); New Directions $9.95 (0-8112-0012-4). 251pp. Fiction.

Borges is the founder of Spanish-American contemporary narrative. He wrote essays and poetry but is best known for his short stories. *Labyrinths* develops topics that recur in many of his other stories, including *The Aleph and Other Stories*, his other major collection of works in English. The labyrinth, the solution to which involves choice, trial and error, and, above all, chance is one of the structures (or puzzles) that Borges uses to construct many of these stories, including "Tlön, Uqbar, Orbis Tertius" and "The Library of Babel." In the latter, the library is infinite, and all the rooms and floors are identical to each other. Finding a book or leaving the library becomes an impossible task.

Time and its actualization in memory and imagination is also a recurring theme, as reflected in "Funes, the Memorious" and "The Secret Miracle." "Pierre Menard, Author of Don Quixote" and "An Examination of the Work of Herbert Quinn" develop Borges's concept that the act of writing is an act of repetition and that all works of literature maintain a constant dialog with each other.

The stories, many of which resemble essays, are deceptively simple. To understand them thoroughly, however, requires a background in both Western and Eastern philosophical traditions.   PR

Brand, Dionne. *Sans Souci and Other Stories*.
See entry 562.

652 Cardenal, Ernesto. *Zero Hour and Other Documentary Poems*. Ed. by Donald D. Walsh; Trans. from Spanish by Paul W. Borgeson, and others. New Directions 1980, $6.95 (0-8112-0767-6). 106pp. Poetry.

A former priest and Sandinista politician, Cardenal is considered Nicaragua's most famous poet after Rubén Darío. In contrast to Darío, who emphasized form and beauty above all else, Cardenal's poetry is characterized by its political commitment. Among his influences are Pablo Neruda and the Trappist monk and philosopher Thomas Merton.

This volume, containing seven long poems and one short one, chronicles Nicaragua's history and the long revolution that brought the Sandinistas to power. Several poems are set in real places—the Atlantic coast in "Mosquito Kingdom" or the impoverished urban barrio of Acahualinca on the shores of Lake Managua in "Oracle Over Managua"—and describe the destruction of the indigenous population or the nation's enslavement to the U.S. empire. Spiritual themes and imagery are woven throughout the poems. In Cardenal's view, Catholicism is a religion of the poor, of humble farmers and workers struggling for liberation in the present rather than salvation in the future. The poems are accessible, and the translations retain the eloquence of Cardenal's fiery pronouncements and his vision of hope. Other volumes of Cardenal's poetry include *Apocalypse and Other Poems* (New Directions, 1977), *Psalms* (o.p.), and *Flights of Victory/Vuelos de Victoria* (Books on Demand, 1985). His collection of essays, *In Cuba* (New Directions, 1974), is a sympathetic (though not totally uncritical) portrait of the Cuban Revolution and its effects upon the lives of ordinary Cubans. **LML**

653 Carpentier, Alejo. *The Kingdom of This World*. Trans. from Spanish by Harriet De Onis. Farrar 1989, $10.00 (0-374-52197-2). 150pp. Fiction.

This novel deals with Haiti's struggle against tyranny, beginning with the first slave uprising against the French colonials and ending with death of its first black king, Henri Christophe. The author, a Cuban, adds a touch of magic to these otherwise real events; the characters of Mackandal and Ti Noel are able to metamorphose into animals when they encounter physical danger. Through this ability, they keep alive the people's faith in their ability to lead the fight against tyranny.

In this as in other works, such as *Ecue-Yamba-O* (o.p.) and *Lost Steps* (Farrar, 1989), Carpentier maintains that myth and magic are part of Latin American reality. Unlike the European surrealists, who create a marvelous reality by juxtaposing disparate elements, magical realism is a defining element of Latin American culture, revealing the enchantment that lies within everyday events. **PR**

654 Carpentier, Alejo. *The Lost Steps*. Trans. from Spanish by Harriet De Onis. Farrar 1989, $12.00 (0-374-52199-9). 278pp. Fiction.

The protagonist is a disenchanted musicologist who travels from a big city somewhere in the Western world (the city is not identified, but it resembles

New York City) to the rain forest of Venezuela in search of new musical instruments. As he penetrates the rain forest, he discovers a reality that suspends his rational, "civilized" understanding of the world. Magic, myth, and ritual prevail, and primitive, animistic beliefs are key to its understanding. In the jungle the protagonist discovers that the Paleolithic era is still part of the present and that discovery and colonialism are events of the future. His journey turns into an exploration of Latin American reality and its history, as well as a journey of self-discovery. His contact with nature, with the primitiveness of the few inhabitants he encounters, liberates him from the conventions that mask his inner being. After he finds the musical instruments that were the object of his quest, he leaves the jungle enriched by an understanding of himself and a holistic understanding of reality, which includes the rational and the nonrational, the objective and the magical, the material and the mythical.

Undoubtedly Carpentier's most important novel, *The Lost Steps* successfully articulates his ideas about magical realism and history. Other major works include *The Kingdom of This World* (orig. pub. 1967; Farrar, 1989) and *Explosion in a Cathedral* (orig. pub. 1963; Farrar, 1989), both set in the Caribbean. *The Rite of Spring* (not yet translated into English), the only one of his works that deals with the 1959 revolution in his native Cuba, juxtaposes historical events with the music and dance of the spring carnival.   PR

655   Castro-Klarén, Sara, and others, eds. ***Women's Writing in Latin America: An Anthology***. Trans. from Spanish. Westview 1992, $64.00 (0-8133-0550-0); $19.95 (0-8133-0551-9). 362pp. Fiction/Essays.

One of the most important anthologies of Latin American literature written by women, this book includes fiction, poetry, essays, and testimonies from authors of ten countries. The editors each contribute a chapter with selected texts that reflect a certain theme: "Women, Self, and Writing," "Female Textual Traditions," and "Women, History, and Ideology." Each part contains a lengthy essay that discusses the authors and their work, a brief essay offering biographical and bibliographical information, and a statement regarding the author's importance within women's writing in particular and within Spanish-American letters as a whole. This is a valuable background text for anyone interested in reading or teaching Spanish-American literature at the high-school level or beyond.   PR

Condé, Maryse. ***Segu***.
See entry 1232.

656   Condé, Maryse. ***Tree of Life: A Novel of the Caribbean***. Trans. from French by Victoria Reiter. Ballantine 1992, $17.50 (0-345-36074-5); $10.00 (0-345-38469-5). 384pp. Fiction.

Condé's novel follows the Louis family from Guadeloupe to Panama, the United States, Jamaica, and Paris. At the center of the saga are Albert Louis and his son Jacob—cold, disillusioned men who make their fortune from the misfortune of others and who in turn suffer the death and betrayal of their loved ones. Contrasted with them are the idealistic members of the family: Albert's older son, Bert, who dreams of living in Paris but who dies there broken-hearted, leaving behind his "lost" son, Bebert; Albert's younger son,

Jean, who gives up his inheritance to work among the poor; and Jacob's daughter, Thecla, who travels the world with a succession of men in search of her place in life.

Through her poignant and lyrical writing, Condé draws memorable portraits of a family torn between self-interest and their mission as Africans cut loose in the New World. Albert Louis worships the Jamaican black nationalist Marcus Garvey; this love contrasts sharply with his decision to exploit others. The legacy of Garvey has power over Louis's children and grandchildren as well. Most of Condé's fiction, including *Segu* (Ballantine, 1988), *The Children of Segu* (Ballantine, 1990), and *Heremakhonon* (Three Continents, 1982), features West African settings, themes, and issues, but she returns to her native country of Guadeloupe in *Crossing the Mangrove* (Anchor, 1995).   LML

657   Cortázar, Julio. ***All Fires the Fire, and Other Stories***. Trans. from Spanish by Suzanne Jill Levine. Pantheon 1973. o.p. Fiction.

Cortázar is one of Spanish America's most skillful short story writers. Heavily influenced by surrealist art and literature, much of his writing makes use of the fantastic to reveal the dimensions of reality hidden behind normal appearances and everyday experiences. In "The Thruway," for example, a routine traffic jam near Paris during the last day of a long weekend triggers unexpected events: Time changes direction; humans merge with their different types of cars and transform into objects; individuals die and are born again. In "The Other Heaven," two different places and historical times (Buenos Aires in the twentieth century and Paris in the nineteenth) communicate as the narrator goes back and forth through the Güeme Arcade in Paris. The transition not only affects traditional definitions of time and space, but also redefines syntax and verbal communication: The beginning of one sentence might refer to one reality, while the end refers to a different century and place. In all of these stories, the unexpected looms behind the obvious; the nonrational becomes another way to explore and understand the world. Other works by Cortázar exploring similar topics are *End of the Game and Other Stories* (1967; published in Spanish as *Final de Juego*, French & European, 1987), *Cronopios and Famas* (o.p.), and *Change of Light and Other Stories* (o.p.).   PR

658   Cortázar, Julio. ***Hopscotch***. Trans. from Spanish. Pantheon 1987, $16.00 (0-394-75284-8). 576pp. Fiction.

One of the most experimental, interesting, and influential novels of Spanish-American literature. *Hopscotch* has been frequently compared to Joyce's *Ulysses*. The novel is at least two books. It can be read conventionally by following its chapters from beginning to end. But the writer also invites the reader to explore the work another way, beginning in the middle and skipping around to other chapters in the manner of a game of hopscotch.

Unlike the structure, the plot is very simple. Like much recent Spanish-American literature, this book deals with the individual's quest for identity. The first part of the story, set in Paris, follows Oliveira, an Argentinean intellectual who perceives life to be absurd and who is searching for a meaning to his existence. In the second part, Oliveira goes to Buenos Aires, where he meets his friend Traveler. They work in a circus and later in a sanitarium for the insane. Both settings take on symbolic meaning in Oliveira's search for self-understanding.

Cortázar is the master of games; as its title reveals, this novel is itself a game, albeit a very serious one. The author constantly interrupts the narrative with self-referential commentary on the plot, meditations on the theory of the novel, fragments from other books and newspaper articles, and so on. *Hopscotch* is a riveting and challenging experience for the sophisticated reader.

PR

Dabydeen, Cyril. *Elephants Make Good Stepladders: Poems*.
See entry 569.

659 Darío, Rubén. *Selected Poems of Rubén Darío*. Intro. by Octavio Paz; Trans. from Spanish by Lysander Kemp. Univ. of Texas Pr. 1988, $6.95 (0-292-77615-2). 149pp. Poetry.

This is a solid, representative selection of the author's poetry and prose. Darío is the founder of *modernismo*, the first Spanish-American literary movement active at the beginning of the twentieth century, which sought to reinvigorate the Spanish-language literary tradition by breaking with stale models from the Old World. The influence of Darío and other proponents of *modernismo*, such as José Martí from Cuba, revitalized the Spanish language, redefined the poetic idiom, and defined a new aesthetic. Formal concerns became a centerpiece of their poetics, and the pursuit of beauty and the perfect form was their obsession. In such poems as "Sonatina," "The Swan," and "For One Moment, Oh Swan," Darío created new rhythms and introduced verse structures never before used in Spanish-language poetry. Eroticism was one of Darío's recurrent themes. In his later work, such as "Thanatos" and "Fatality," the passage of time and the threat of death are overriding preoccupations. He explored his deepening religious feelings in such works as "Poem of Autumn," "Evening," and "St. Helena of Montenegro."

PR

Day, A. Grove, ed. *The Sky Clears: Poetry of the American Indians*.
See entry 452.

660 Donoso, José. *A House in the Country*. Trans. from Spanish by David Pritchard with Suzanne Jill Levine. Knopf 1984. o.p. Fiction.

This novel is an allegory of Chile's political history during the Allende and Pinochet regimes. As in most of the author's work, the grotesque becomes an important instrument in the development of characters and description of events. A group of upper-class children, left alone for a weekend, explore their parent's country house, communicate with people from whom they have been isolated, and delve into spaces usually off limits to them. In time, a leader emerges; some of the children ally with the leader and become the oppressors, while others become the oppressed. Tragedy inevitably ensues.

The novel poses questions about power and its effect on groups and individuals and explores the perceived immutability of the material world. Time expands, losing its fixed chronological value; the weekend of the parents' absence turns into a year. The real becomes unreal and ambiguous; the ordinary becomes menacing. Such techniques characterize most of Donoso's work, including *Coronation* (o.p.), *The Obscene Bird of Night* (orig. pub. 1973; Godine, 1979), *Sacred Families* (o.p.), and *Curfew* (Grove, 1988).

661 Dorfman, Ariel. ***Death and the Maiden***. Viking 1992, $7.50 (0-14-048238-5). 64pp. Drama.

Like many other Chilean contemporary writers, Dorfman deals with the deeply disturbing realities of political torture and the difficulty of healing after such an experience. Paulina Salas is a victim of torture. Her husband is a lawyer appointed to the commission investigating the government's violations of human rights. One night his car breaks down and he is helped out by a doctor. When the doctor comes to their apartment, Paulina recognizes him as her former captor, a Schubert-loving sadist who directed her torture to make sure she did not die in the process. Although her husband tries to dissuade her, she avenges her suffering by torturing the doctor to extract a confession, then killing him.

This highly successful play ran for several years in London; in the United States it was received less enthusiastically. A 1994 film version starred Sigourney Weaver and Ben Kingsley. Other works by Dorfman include *Widows* (Viking, 1983) and *The Last Song of Mañuel Sendero* (Viking, 1987).   PR

662 Esquivel, Laura. ***Like Water for Chocolate: A Novel in Monthly Installments, with Recipes, Romances, and Home Remedies***. Trans. from Spanish. Doubleday 1992, $19.95 (0-385-42016-1); $5.99 (0-385-47401-6). 281pp. Fiction.

The release of its critically acclaimed film version helped make this novel a highly popular Spanish-American novel in translation. The story is set in the time of the Mexican revolution. Tita and Pedro love each other and want to marry, but her mother demands that Tita remain single so that she can look after the mother in her old age. Pedro marries Tita's oldest sister so that he can remain close to Tita. Meanwhile, Tita uses cooking to communicate with Pedro, to extract revenge against her mother, and to rebel against the forces of tradition that arbitrarily control women's destinies. Preparing food, which brings Tita into contact with herbs and many of nature's secrets, becomes her primary way of dealing with the outside world.

This funny and fascinating work loosely follows the structure of a cookbook—each chapter begins with a Mexican recipe—and is well suited for popular reading and for introductory courses of Spanish-American fiction.

PR

663 Ferré, Rosario. ***Sweet Diamond Dust***. Trans. from Spanish. Ballantine 1988, $5.95 (0-345-34778-1). 197pp. Fiction.

The work includes the title novella plus three shorter pieces: "The Gift," "Isolda in the Mission," and "The Unusual Death of Captain Candelario." The stories stand separately, but they all explore events in Puerto Rico from the perspective of those who have been largely excluded from official accounts of its history: people of color, gays, women, and the poor. Using irony, humor, and the grotesque, Ferré skillfully undermines the power of institutions that represent the interests of wealthy white or *mestizo* (mixed-race) men. In another collection of short stories, *The Youngest Doll* (Univ. of Nebraska Pr., 1991), Ferré also explores the experience of women—both white and of color—in a patriarchal society. Her writing is imaginative, vibrant, and resourceful.   **PR**

664   Fuentes, Carlos. *The Death of Artemio Cruz*. Trans. from Spanish by Alfred MacAdam. Farrar 1991, $30.00 (0-374-13559-2); $11.00 (0-374-52283-9). 406pp. Fiction.

At the beginning of the novel, Artemio Cruz is on his deathbed. During the agony of his final twelve hours he recapitulates his life, drifting between the past and the present. Events of the past, told in the third person, focus on Artemio as a young, ambitious, and ruthless man. The first-person account indicates the present-time ordeal of the dying man and his reactions to those who visit his hospital bed: his hated wife, the daughter who despises him, his trusted but corrupt secretary, and so on. Intriguingly, there is also a second-person voice, of primary importance in the novel, that speaks to Artemio and forces him to come to terms with his own past actions. It is the voice of his conscience, exposing his degradation, his lust for power, his shady deals—and his treason.

In this book, as in many of his works, Fuentes explores issues of Mexican identity and examines the consequences of the revolution's failure: purposelessness, irresponsibility, and hedonism. As a corrupt member of the governing elite, Artemio embodies all of the revolution's broken promises. At the end, his life seems devoid of purpose; his ruthlessness and lust for power have damaged everyone who has crossed his path.

The novel is structurally challenging: Artemio's life does not unfold chronologically, and the three narrative perspectives overlap. Other works by Fuentes that explore similar topics are *Where the Air Is Clear* (orig. pub. 1960; Farrar, 1988), *The Good Conscience* (orig. pub. 1961; Farrar, 1987), the two-volume *Terra Nostra* (orig. pub. 1975; pub. in French by French & European, 1989), and many of his excellent short stories.   **PR**

665   Gallegos, Rómulo. *Doña Barbara*. Trans. from Spanish by Malloy. Peter Smith 1948, $14.00 (0-8446-1194-8). 440pp. Fiction.

This book by the Venezuelan author Gallegos, originally published in 1929, is a landmark in twentieth-century Spanish-American fiction. The story focuses on the conflict between civilization and barbarism, a common topic of the movement known as *mundonovismo* (new-worldism). The positive forces of progress, embodied by one of the main characters, Santos Luzardo, are associated with the city. In the remote Venezuelan plains, however, Luzardo meets Do-a Barbara, the incarnation of the evil, untamed, uncivilized forces of nature. In time, though, progress and culture prevail over the dark forces of magic and instinct. After Do-a Barbara dies, Luzardo marries her daughter, whom he saved from her mother's diabolical influence. The symbolism of the novel reveals the author's beliefs about the need to develop both the central and hinterland regions of the country.   **PR**

Gambaro, Griselda. *The Camp.*
See under entry 690.

García, Cristina. *Dreaming in Cuban.*
See entry 377.

666   García Márquez, Gabriel. *No One Writes to the Colonel and Other Stories.*
Trans. from Spanish by J. S. Bernstein. Borgo 1991, $26.00 (0-8095-9054-9);
HarperCollins $11.00 (0-06-090700-2). 175pp. Fiction.

Set in 1956 during the period known as *la violencia* (the violence), this novella
tells the story of an old colonel whose two motivations in life are the weekly
expectation of his pension check, which will enable him to pay off his debts
and repair the leaky roof of his house, and the victory of his rooster at the next
cockfight. The colonel's optimism and cheerfulness contrast with the pessimism of his wife, who has been embittered by poverty and the hardships
caused by the violence in the region. The author was influenced by Heming-
way's style, and this novella is stylistically concise, with few omniscient psychological descriptions. It is a good representation of García Márquez's earlier
fiction and style. Other works in the same stylistic vein include the stories in
In Evil Hour (orig. pub. 1979; HarperCollins, 1991), which also take place
during *la violencia*. Because it is short and less difficult to read than other
works by this Nobel Prize–winning Colombian author, this work is particularly well suited for high school students and introductory courses in Spanish-
American fiction.   **PR**

667   García Márquez, Gabriel. *One Hundred Years of Solitude.* Trans. from Spanish by Gregory Rabassa. HarperCollins 1970, $30.00 (0-06-011418-5); $13.00
(0-06-091965-5). 432pp. Fiction.

The most important novel of the Spanish-American "boom," this lengthy
work by the Colombian Nobel laureate tells the saga of the Buend'a family, a
family that is predestined to last one hundred years. The founders of the clan,
Ursula Iguarán and José Arcadio, are cousins. A prophecy foretells that incestuous relationships will produce deformed offspring, but the prophecy goes
unfulfilled for three generations, until Aureliano Babilonia and Amaranta
Ursula produce a child with a pig's tail and the village of Macondo is swept
away by the elements.

The novel can be read as a metaphor for Western civilization; the plot
combines historical fact with the biblical stories of Genesis and the Apocalypse. It can also be read as an attempt to outline the history and "in-
trahistory" of Spanish America from pre-Columbian times to the present-day
evils of neocolonialism. The expansive world depicted in the novel includes
the objective and the mythical spheres and embraces both linear and circular
time. Its unforgettable characters, many of whom possess extrasensory and
magical powers, are frequently outrageous: Ursula, who manages to keep the
world in order; Remedios la Bella, who rises to heaven; Melquíades, the gypsy
who brings magic and technology to Macondo; and the string of characters

named Aureliano and José Arcadio, who fight wars, engage in bizarre acts, and contribute both to the development and destruction of Macondo.

Other well-known works by García Márquez include *Autumn of the Patriarch* (orig. pub. 1976; HarperCollins, 1991), *Chronicle of a Death Foretold* (Knopf, 1983), *Love in the Time of Cholera* (Knopf, 1988), and the biographical novel of Simón Bolívar's last days, *The General in His Labyrinth* (Knopf, 1990).   PR

668   Garro, Elena. ***Recollections of Things to Come***. Repr. of 1969 ed. Trans. from Spanish by Ruth L. Simms and Alberto Beltran. Univ. of Texas Pr. 1986, $12.95 (0-292-77032-4). 299pp. Fiction.

Time, the uncanny, and violence are the main thematic threads of this novel, the author's first and still her most meaningful work. The story takes place during the Cristero war, which pitted the Mexican Catholic Church against the state. The town of Ixtepec has been occupied by military forces whose mission is to control the influence of the church in the town. The military leaders occupy the city with their lovers, young kidnapped women who are trapped in the rooms of a local hotel. The crackdown on the local *mestizo* (mixed-race) people parallels the villagers' own violence against the local indigenous peasants.

The people's only means of escape is through the imagination. Although forced to participate in the struggle against the state, the Moncada family, especially the father and the three adolescent children, engage in drama, poetry, and reverie. The brothers die; the sister tries in vain to save her eldest brother's life by becoming the lover of the enemy captain.

Garro also explores the themes of oppression and the search for freedom in her later works, such as the short stories collected in *Lola We Are Running Away* and her novel *Testimonies about Mariana*, neither of which is yet available in English translation.   PR

Goldman, Francisco. ***The Long Night of White Chickens***.
See entry 379.

669   Guillén, Nicolás. ***Man-Making Words: Selected Poems of Nicolás Guillén*** Bilingual (Spanish-English) ed. Univ. of Massachusetts Pr. 1972. o.p. Poetry.

The Cuban poet Nicolás Guillén, who died in 1980, is considered one of Cuba's most prominent twentieth-century poets and a major figure in Latin American literature. Many other writers, musicians, and artists, among them the Chilean Nobel laureate Pablo Neruda, have acknowledged their debt to Guillén. As a Spanish-American writer of African heritage and a participant in the Negritude movement, Guillén serves as a bridge between Spanish-American literature and the literature of the English- and French-speaking Caribbean.

This bilingual collection offers a sampling of Guillén's work from throughout his career. Included are his experiments with form and rhythm, his poems about his own land, and his odes to black heroes and martyrs around the world. His use of language, rhythm, rhyme, and even musical forms combine to make Guillén an exceedingly difficult poet to translate; in many respects this translation does not do justice to his work. By offering the original Spanish, however, the editors allow those with some knowledge of the language to

appreciate the author's writing. An introduction and an extensive section of 313
notes add to the usefulness of this volume.   LML/HC/PR

LATIN AMERICA AND
THE CARIBBEAN

670 Güiraldes, Ricardo. ***Don Segundo Sombra*** Rev. ed. Trans. from Spanish by
Patricia O. Steiner. Univ. of Pittsburgh Pr. 1994, $49.95 (0-8229-3851-0);
$22.95 (0-8229-5524-5). 392pp. Fiction.

One of the most interesting coming-of-age novels of early twentieth-century
Latin American fiction, this work is part of the *mundonovismo* (new-worldism)
movement that explored the relationship between individuals and nature. Its
main character is a fourteen-year-old orphan boy who follows Don Segundo,
a seasoned *gaucho* (cowboy), as he roams across the *pampas* (plains) of Argentina. In the novel, this journey becomes a metaphor for life. The protagonist
matures and grows as he confronts and overcomes various difficult situations;
with the help of his mentor, he also develops his spiritual strength. At the end
of the two-year journey, the boy returns to his home town as a mature young
adult, equipped to face his own destiny.

Güiraldes presents an idealistic vision of the cattle herder as a man close to
nature, which is the source of his strength and vision. In Spanish America this
classic novel is still widely read by both young and adult readers alike.   PR

671 Heath, Roy. ***The Murderer***. Persea 1992, $19.95 (0-89255-168-2); $9.95 (0-
89255-169-0). 190pp. Fiction.

Set in Guyana, this is the story of Galton Flood, a young man who grows up
under enormous psychological and cultural burdens. Overshadowed by his
elder brother and emasculated by his overprotective mother, he feels trapped
and develops a debilitating sense of inferiority. Fighting against these sensations, Galton struggles to gain his independence. When his parents die, he
strikes out on his own, leaving his home in Georgetown and heading for the
remote townships of Wismar and MacKenzie. There he meets Gemma, a
woman who fascinates him and whom he eventually marries. But as secrets
from her past begin to emerge, Galton again feels trapped. The pressure
eventually leads him to commit a murder. Although that killing is foretold by
the title, it is not the whole story. In the end, Galton, his personality already
fractured, is overcome by remorse and descends into madness. In this intriguing novel, Roy Heath has created a stunning character study as well as an
incisive portrait of colonial Guyana.   HC

672 Howes, Barbara, ed. ***The Eye of the Heart: Short Stories from Latin America***.
Trans. from Spanish. Avon 1990, $12.50 (0-380-70942-2). 576pp. Fiction.

This excellent anthology of forty-four short stories is organized chronologi-
cally according to date of publication. The works begin with an excerpt from
The Psychiatrist by Machado de Assis and ends with Mario Vargas Llosa's
"Sunday, Sunday." In between, the anthology offers a good cross-section of
the various literary movements and aesthetics: *modernismo*, represented by
Rubén Darío and Leopoldo Lugones; *mundonovismo*, as demonstrated in
works by Rómulo Gallegos and Ricardo Güiraldes; magical realism (Alejo
Carpentier and Miguel Asturias), indigenism (Arguedas and Miguel Astu-
rias), and the "boom" (Jorge Luis Borges, Julio Cortázar, Juan Carlos Onetti,

José Donoso, and Mario Vargas Llosa). It includes important works by women authors such as Gabriela Mistral, María Luisa Bombal, Clarice Lispector, and the lesser-known Armonia Sommers, whose works deserve a wider readership. A section of notes on the contributors places the authors and their works in the context of the historical development of Latin American literature and provides information on available translations. The book is an excellent choice for the beginning and intermediate college and advanced high school levels.

PR

673 Infante, Guillermo Cabrera. ***Three Trapped Tigers.*** Trans. from Spanish. Faber 1993, $10.95 (0-571-15370-4). 487pp. Fiction.

Critics have deemed this work one of the most humorous and inventive Spanish-American novels of the 1960s. Because the humor is largely linguistic, the author collaborated closely in the translation of the novel. At one level the story deals with Havana's night life before the revolution in Cuba. Juxtaposed with no apparent order or structure are a number of elements: music, Afro-Caribbean rhythms, broken conversations between friends or on the phone. At another level, however, this is a novel about the Cuban dialect, which Infante knows intimately and which gives him occasion for play and incessant punning. On yet a third level, the novel is about the lack of communication among individuals. They meet in bars, listen to music together, watch shows, but they never establish meaningful relationships.

Havana is also an important setting in the author's other long novel, *Infante's Inferno* (HarperCollins, 1984). *Three Trapped Tigers* marked a milestone in Spanish-American fiction, and it undoubtedly still is Infante's highest achievement.

PR

674 Kincaid, Jamaica. ***Annie John.*** Farrar 1985, $18.95 (0-374-10521-9); NAL $8.00 (0-452-26016-7). 160pp. Fiction.

Set in Antigua in the 1940s, this novel chronicles in vivid , sparkling detail the life of Annie John from childhood to early adolescence. This personal portrait is set against the backdrop of West Indian culture, mores, and society. In vivid prose, Kincaid captures the flavor and rhythm of daily activities, from a belief in *obeah* (a type of witchcraft) to the relationships in and structure of family life, from the neighborhood and society to descriptions of the plants and animals that are vital parts of the Antiguans' lives. The author also portrays effectively a young girl's coming of age as she ventures into a new world— England—and pursues the study of nursing, eventually discovering a new life for herself. While the growing pains of adolescence are universal, the author roots them in the drama and verve of life in the Caribbean, making these experiences concrete, unique, and personal.

HC

675 Kincaid, Jamaica. ***At the Bottom of the River.*** Farrar 1983, $15.00 (0-374-10660-6); NAL $7.00 (0-452-26754-4). 96pp. Fiction.

Kincaid, a native of Antigua, artfully recalls her childhood and adolescence in this short story collection. Although quite personal, these memories are also highly universal and could belong to almost any inhabitant of the West Indies. Some of the stories are written as streams of consciousness, which gives them the character of entries in a diary. Others are more direct and more grounded in standard narrative form.

A number of these pieces deal with the relationships between mothers and daughters, while others relate the carefree yet confusing experiences of childhood. Additional themes are the social customs, beliefs, and mores of West Indians, dream world of the protagonist, and the power and beauty of nature. The writing is many-faceted, catching and reflecting the light in its own way.

HC

676   Laferrière, Dany. *An Aroma of Coffee*. Trans. from French by David Homel. Coach House 1993, $11.95 (0-88910-439-5). 176pp. Fiction.

The author is a Haitian journalist now living in Canada. This autobiographical novel focuses on a ten-year-old boy living in a small town outside of Port-au-Prince in the early 1960s. Forced to stay home over the summer because of a persistent fever, he sits on the porch of his grandmother Da's house, watching the villagers pass by and listening to their gossip. Over the summer he becomes infatuated with Vava, a young girl who lives nearby. Another child, Sylphise, dies suddenly at the same moment that her father, Big Simon, wins the lottery. Villagers speculate that Big Simon sold her soul to the devil. The boy also tells stories of his family: his grandfather, a businessman who went bankrupt; his mother and her four sisters, who moved to Port-au-Prince; and his grandmother, who takes care of him and serves coffee to the passers-by. Among the other characters are the well-dressed Baron Samedi, who beats his wife, Legype, and who lost part of his arm to a dogfish while swimming in the Caribbean Sea; the narrator's friend, Auguste, a bad student who is publicly beaten by his illiterate mother for skipping school; and Galbaud, who drives his car into the sea. All in all, Laferrière offers a sympathetic and engaging portrait of village life in Haiti in the middle of the century.   LML

677   Lamming, George. *In the Castle of My Skin*. Univ. of Michigan Pr. 1991, $42.50 (0-472-09468-8); $14.95 (0-472-06468-1). 314pp. Fiction.

Set in a fictional village in Barbados from the 1930s through the 1950s, this narrative—part autobiographical, part fictional—traces the development of the main character, referred to simply as "G," from age nine to nineteen, when he leaves the island to accept a teaching position in Trinidad.

This artfully crafted novel reveals the inner workings of Barbadian village: the landscape, cultural mores, family relationships, and schooling with its British influence. The underpinnings of the social hierarchy, with its penchant for division by race, class, and skin color, are presented in vivid and authentic detail. Another noteworthy work by this author is *Natives of My Person* (Univ. of Michigan Pr., 1971), which explores early colonial Caribbean history.

HC

678   Lispector, Clarice. *Family Ties*. Trans. from Portuguese by Giovanni Pontiero. Univ. of Texas Pr. 1984, $9.95 (0-292-72448-9). 156pp. Fiction.

The stories in this collection, which show the influence of the existentialist writers Albert Camus and Jean-Paul Sartre, explore the themes of human aloneness and alienation, of the anguish caused by the ultimate meaninglessness of life. Compared to the human characters, the animals in Lispector's stories ("The Chicken," for example) live instinctually and thus, the author argues, are closer to the essence of life.

The author frequently tells about housewives who lead isolated and predictable lives. A common event, however, such as the breaking of eggs in the story called "Love," can shatter the routine, leading to the experience of the uncanny, of meanings subsumed under the boredom of the daily routine. Such revelations free the characters from their limited worlds. However, these characters often discover that they prefer the security of their limited lives and desire to return to their prescribed roles of wives, mothers, and housewives.

These well-written stories are stylistically and structurally refined. Lispector, who deservedly is Brazil's best-known woman writer, has written other works that have been translated into English, including *The Passion According to G. H.* (Univ. of Minnesota Pr., 1988), *The Stream of Life* (Univ. of Minnesota Pr., 1989), and *The Hour of the Star* (New Directions, 1986).   PR

679   Lovelace, Earl. *The Schoolmaster*. Repr. of 1968 ed. Intro. by Kenneth Ramchand. Heinemann 1983, $7.95 (0-435-98550-7). 171pp. Fiction.

The remote Trinidadian village of Kumaca, inaccessible to the outside world except by a mountain road, decides to establish an elementary school. Father Vincent, the parish priest, fears the corruption of traditional ways that could ensue, but the village elders prevail. When the schoolmaster arrives, things begin to go awry. He infects this orderly and honorable community with his sophistication and vice. He secretly rapes his assistant, who is already promised to a youth she loves. Distraught when she learns she is pregnant, she drowns herself. After a frenzied search for the missing girl, her lifeless body is finally discovered in the river. Learning to their horror that the esteemed schoolmaster is the culprit, the villagers exact revenge for his deed, realizing too late the high price of progress.

Lovelace has painted a portrait of idyllic island life with its lush scenery, simple ways, and colorful speech patterns, a way of life that suffers from the encroachment of modern civilization. Another of his novels, *While Gods Are Falling* (o.p., 1966), addresses the same tension between traditional ways and the temptations of modern life.   HC

McKay, Claude. *Banana Bottom*.
See entry 76.

680   Menton, Seymour. *The Spanish American Short Story: A Critical Anthology*. Trans. from Spanish. Univ. of California Pr. 1980, $16.00 (0-520-04641-2). 496pp. Fiction.

This is a classic anthology of the Spanish-American short story, compiled by one of the leading experts in the United States. The authors (all men except for María Luisa Bombal of Chile) and their texts are organized by their literary periods and movements: romanticism, naturalism, modernism, *criolismo*, cosmopolitanism, neorealism, and the "boom." The movements and the authors who participated in them are introduced by essays that consider the main characteristics of each period and that offer biographical and bibliographical information. What makes this anthology especially valuable, however, are Menton's brief but useful commentaries appearing after each story that analyze the narrative's principal components and place the author in his or her historical and literary contexts.

PR

681 Mistral, Gabriela. *Selected Poems of Gabriela Mistral*. Bilingual (English-Spanish) ed.; Ed. and trans. from Spanish by Doris Dana. Johns Hopkins Univ. Pr. 1971, $35.00 (0-8018-1197-X). 235pp. Poetry.

This collection includes selected poems from the author's four classic works: *Desolation* (orig. pub. 1922; French & European, 1972), *Tenderness* (o.p., 1924), *Felling* (o.p., 1938), and *Wine Press* (o.p., 1954). Although in 1945 Mistral became the first Spanish American to win the Nobel Prize for literature, her poetry is not well known in the United States; but it has profoundly influenced the development of Spanish-American poetry, especially among women authors. Although her poetic style and tone vary greatly from book to book, her verses always return to the same themes. Principal among those themes is love in all its forms: erotic love in *Desolation*; in later works, love of God, children, and the downtrodden, especially Spanish America's indigenous populations. Mistral also writes frequently about her preoccupation with death, which she struggles to understand as part of the continuum of life; about her fascination with Spanish America as a physical (natural), linguistic, and cultural entity; and about her mission as a teacher, which became her way of compensating for her own childlessness. This well-edited volume represents all aspects of Mistral's creativity by including some works that are highly accessible and others that are more demanding.

PR

682 Monegal, Emir Rodríguez, and Thomas Colchie, eds. *The Borzoi Anthology of Latin American Literature*. 2 vols. Trans. from Spanish. Knopf 1977, $19.95 each (0-394-73301-0; 0-394-73366-5). 982pp. Fiction/Essays.

In selecting works for these collections, the editors have taken a holistic approach that is both wide and deep. The material is arranged chronologically, and each part of the book is preceded by an introduction outlining the particular period. Brief essays precede each selection, providing biographical and bibliographical information about the author and placing the work within its historical context.

The first volume includes fifty authors, opening with excerpts from Columbus's diary and closing with poems by Alfonso Reyes, the twentieth-century Mexican poet and intellectual. The second volume is entirely devoted to the twentieth century. This volume also includes a general presentation and individual essays for each of its two parts and each of the authors. Some of the writers—for example, Idea Vilari–o, Juan Gelman, Homero Aridjis—have had no works, or only a few works, translated into English, and are likely to be unfamiliar to a general readership in the United States. This is a useful anthology by two leading critics of Spanish-American literature. Cochie has also assembled a collection of Spanish-American and Brazilian short stories titled *A Hammock Beneath the Mangoes: Stories from Latin America* (NAL, 1991).

PR

Morales, Alejandro. ***The Rag Doll Plagues***.
See entry 396.

683 Murguia, Alejandro, and Barbara Paschke, eds. ***Volcan: Poems from Central America***. Bilingual (Spanish-English) ed. City Lights 1984, $6.95 (0-87286-153-8). 159pp. Poetry.

For young writers experiencing the turmoil of life in Central America during the 1970s and 1980s, poetry became a vital means of literary expression. Many of these writers actively participated in guerrilla movements, and the revolutionary life—often spent in the mountains, in safe houses, or on the run—did not lend itself to the kind of quiet reflection necessary for producing novel-length (or even short story–length) works. Several of the poets—including the Salvadoran Roque Dalton, the Guatemalan Otto-Rene Castillo, and the Nicaraguan Leonel Rugama—were killed before this collection was published.

This bilingual collection offers a cross-section of styles and themes. Many of the works, however, focus narrowly on the region's history, its people, and its political struggles. Poems are arranged by their author's country of origin: El Salvador, Guatemala, Honduras, or Nicaragua. Among the most notable works are Dalton's "Poem of Love," a compelling, tragic vision of his fellow Salvadorans; Castillo's "Prayer for the Soul of My Country," which is steeped in Mayan symbolism; and David Macfield's "Black Is Black," a multilingual statement of identity that connects people with African ancestors who now live in places scattered throughout the world. For the most part, the editors have selected the best and most accessible works by a generation of poets for whom politics was the most important concern.   LML

684 Mutis, Alvaro. ***Maqroll: Three Novellas***. Trans. from Spanish by Edith Grossman. HarperCollins 1992, $20.00 (0-06-016623-1); $10.00 (0-06-092444-6). 288pp. Fiction.

These three interrelated novellas tell the story of Maqroll, the *gaviero* (lookout), on his journeys through the darker side of Latin America. As a sailor, Maqroll has traveled to many places. His tales recall the memories of people he encountered and the events in which he played a role, often unwittingly. Many of those events involve violence and death: Two of his captains commit suicide, and a woman with whom he has fallen in love is killed in a suspicious and horrible accident. Maqroll, a marginal figure filled with shame and despair, describes his work as a dealer in stolen goods, an owner of a fashionable house of prostitution, and an arms smuggler.

Known best in his native Colombia as a poet, Mutis offers here an original and engrossing work of fiction, written in dreamy, lyrical prose.   LML

685 Naipaul, V. S. ***A House for Mr. Biswas***. Viking 1993, $11.95 (0-14-018604-2). 576pp. Fiction.

Naipaul is a third-generation Trinidadian descended from East Indian immigrant grandparents. In the mid-nineteenth century many people from India came to the island, where they worked in the cane fields as indentured laborers. Since then the East Indians have largely resisted assimilation into Creole society, which they consider inferior to their own Hindu culture. The largest non-Creole group in Trinidad, they represent about two-fifths of the population.

This novel, one of the finest to emerge from the West Indies, tells the story of an East Indian family in Trinidad. Life is unkind to the hero, Mohun Biswas, who is buffeted by one misfortune after another. He suffers especially during conflicts with the oppressive Tulsi family into which he has married. To establish his own identity he buys a house in Port of Spain, the ultimate symbol that, socially speaking, he has arrived. But burdened with debts and in imperfect health, he dies in middle age, a broken man. The novel, which Naipaul wrote in London, is based on the author's recollections of his own extended family.   RP

686 Naipaul, V. S. ***Miguel Street***. Heinemann 1974, $7.95 (0-435-98645-7). 172pp. Fiction.

This novel contains a series of vignettes about the inhabitants of a back street in Port of Spain, Trinidad, during the 1940s. Through the perceptions of a young unnamed boy, the street life of this slum comes to life. As the boy observes, "A stranger could drive through Miguel Street and just say 'Slum!' because he could see no more. But we, who lived there, saw our street as a world where everybody was quite different from everybody else. Man-man was mad; George was stupid; Big Foot was a bully; Hat was an adventurer; Popo was a philosopher; and Morgan was our comedian." These and many other colorful characters inhabit Naipaul's world.

In this, the third of his early novels set in Trinidad, the author brings to life members of the East Indian and mixed communities that he remembers from childhood. In lively prose, splashed with humor and salted with Trinidadian dialect, Naipaul creates a truly amusing and enjoyable work.   HC

687 Naipaul, V. S. ***The Mystic Masseur***. Viking 1977, $10.00 (0-14-002156-6). 214pp. Fiction.

This work, the first of Naipaul's three early Trinidad novels, was written in 1957. It tells the story of Ganesh Ramsumair, an East Indian who evolves from lowly masseur to enlightened mystic, from shameless entrepreneur to high-ranking politician and one of the most popular men in the country. Ganesh's metamorphosis is recounted by a young narrator who begins by recalling his first encounter with this now-famous man. Naipaul's work introduces the reader to the flavor of Trinidad's East Indian community. On discovering the many vibrant characters in this tale—some of them quite funny—the reader gains insight into their daily routines, beliefs, culture, and family relationships. The multiracial mix of Trinidad's population is described, as are the contrasting cultural values and beliefs of these groups and their clashes with the British colonial rulers.

Although this work (one of Naipaul's three early Trinidad novels) is humorous in tone, his later Caribbean-oriented novels, such as *Guerrillas* (1990), create a more a somber mood.   HC

688 Neruda, Pablo. ***Canto General***. Trans. from Spanish by Jack Schmitt; Intro. by Roberto G. Echevarria. Univ. of California Pr. 1991, $38.00 (0-520-05433-4); $15.00 (0-520-08279-6). 418pp. Poetry.

This is the major work of epic poetry by Neruda of Chile, who won the Nobel Prize for literature in 1971. Its fifteen cantos deal with the history of the New

World from its most remote past—the beginning of time and the development of pre-Columbian cultures—to the poet's individual present and his candidacy for the Chilean Senate. This progression corresponds to the evolving tone of his poetic voice. In the beginning it is authoritative and full of biblical overtones, while toward the end it becomes more intimate and personal. The first five cantos present the history of the Americas, while the second five focus more on the history of Chile itself. Because the work represents both Neruda's search for America's identity and his own political views, it has been the subject of considerable criticism and widely different interpretations.

Many critics consider the second section, "Heights of Macchu Picchu," to be Neruda's finest work. This section contains twelve poems of different metrical form and length. Two visions give poetic life to this section. The first is the poet's retracing of his own journey in a world consumed by meaningless violence. In its second vision, the poet ascends to Macchu Picchu, the ancient Inca city high in the Andes, where he rediscovers his American roots. The glories of the pre-Columbian empire and the natural setting of the city enable him to recover his sense of belonging and predict the liberation of all humanity from oppression, injustice, and suffering. He expresses the view that poetry will play a critical role in the attainment of such an ideal. A Marxist, Neruda offers the possibility of a classless society where the moving forces are fraternity, not confrontation; solidarity, not competition; and human goals, not material ones. PR

689 Neruda, Pablo. *Residence on Earth and Other Poems*. Trans. from Spanish and Intro. by Donald D. Walsh. New Directions 1973, $12.95 (0-8112-0467-7). 359pp. Poetry.

Residence on Earth is a poetic cycle encompassing three books. *First Residence* includes poetry written between 1925 and 1931, in which the author breaks with the aesthetics of the *modernismo* movement as embodied in the works of Rubén Darío and his followers. Neruda's poetry of this period was influenced by existentialist philosophy and other intellectual trends that arose following World War I. It is cryptic, studded with fragmented imagery and addressing subjects that are not always well defined.

The poems of the *Second Residence*, written between 1931 and 1935, are more optimistic in tone and more narrative in style. They represent a new dimension of Neruda's poetic quest, which recognizes and underscores the material world, as shown in "Walking Around," one of the most important poems of the collection.

Third Residence collects poems Neruda composed between 1935 and 1945. Influenced by the events of the Spanish Civil War, these works are often dismissed as "propagandistic." Although the poems clearly express Neruda's Marxist political views, they need to be read, as one critic proposes, from the perspectives of both art and culture, poetry and politics. PR

Nomez, Nain. *Burning Bridges: Poems*.
See entry 590.

Nomez, Nain, ed. *Chilean Literature in Canada: A Bilingual Anthology*.
See entry 591.

690   Oliver, William I., ed. ***Voices of Change in the Spanish American Theater: An Anthology***. Trans. from Spanish by William I. Oliver. Univ. of Texas Pr. 1971, $20.00 (0-292-70123-3). 312pp. Drama.

The sole anthology of Spanish-American theater in translation, this volume contains works by E. Carballido (*The Day They Let the Lions Loose*), G. Gambaro (*The Camp*), C. Maggi (*The Library*), E. Buenaventura (*In the Right Hand of God the Father*), L. J. Hernandez (*The Mulatto's Orgy*), and S. Vodanovic (*Viña: Three Beach Plays*). The introduction discusses the political, economic, and social circumstances that have contributed to the development of Spanish-American theater and its acceptance among Spanish-speaking audiences and analyzes why these works remain largely unknown among mainstream theatergoers. The most well known of these plays is Argentine writer Griselda Gambaro's *The Camp*. Reflecting the camp's dual connotation of a place of incarceration and amusement, every character plays two roles. The SS officer is Francisco Franco with a kind face, and Emma is an accomplished pianist whose appearance and garb correspond to that of a prisoner in a concentration camp. In this play, as in Gambaro's other works, life is portrayed as a cruel experience; individuals are pathetic in their inability to establish meaningful relationships. Heavily influenced by Artaud's theater and his aesthetic of cruelty, Gambaro's characters find fulfillment by inflicting pain and causing suffering and despair. Her fiction in translation includes *Bitter Blood* (o.p., 1988) and *The Impenetrable Madam X* (Wayne State Univ. Pr., 1991).

Each play is preceded by a short essay offering general information on the author and the work. More than two decades after this work's publication, the playwrights included here remain at the forefront of Spanish-American drama. There is a need, however, for published translations of more-recent works.   PR

691   Onetti, Juan Carlos. ***The Pit***. Trans. from Spanish. 1939. o.p. Fiction.

This was the first published work by Onetti, a writer from Uruguay, and it signals a turning point in Spanish-American fiction. The novella departs from the constraints common to regional fiction and its characterization of social types. Similarly, it is not bound by the conventional linear and chronological rendition of events. The plot develops at multiple levels; free associations and fragmented discourse abound.

As with most of Onetti's characters, Eladio Linacero, the protagonist, is a marginal individual who is isolated from his fellow human beings. He inhabits a room in a boarding house, and in writing his memoirs he attempts to transcend his alienation. Imaginary acts (like the act of creating a novel) become the only alternative for finding answers to the futility of life. But even those acts are doomed to failure.

Onetti's fiction is characterized by its pessimism, as demonstrated by his other major works, which include *The Shipyard* (orig. pub. 1968; Serpent's Tail, 1993), *A Brief Life* (orig. pub. 1976; Serpent's Tail, 1994), *Goodbyes and Stories* (Univ. of Texas Pr., 1990), and *The Body Snatcher* (Pantheon, 1991).   PR

692   Paravisini-Gebert, Lizabeth, and Carmen Esteves, eds. ***Green Cane and Juicy Flotsam: Short Stories by Caribbean Women***. Rutgers Univ. Pr. 1991, $34.00 (0-8135-1737-0); $11.95 (0-8135-1738-9). 220pp. Fiction.

This anthology features twenty-seven vibrant tales, some of which were originally written in English and others in French, Dutch, or Spanish. There is a sampling of works from the various islands, including Guadeloupe, Jamaica, Trinidad, Puerto Rico, Antigua, Haiti, and Cuba. Internationally known writers such as Jamaica Kincaid, Maryse Condé, and Jean Rhys are included, as are a number of talented newcomers, among them Opal Palmer Adisa, Michelle Cliff, and Phyllis Shand Allfrey. Some of the stories deal with women's traditional roles; others present women's perspectives on the history of Caribbean slavery and colonialism; and still others capture the magic hidden behind everyday occurrences. All resonate with the beautiful cadences of the language of Caribbean women. The anthology is an excellent overview of the variety of styles, themes, and linguistic and cultural traditions found in the Caribbean. A critical introduction, biographical notes preceding each story, and a bibliography are included.   HC

693 Patterson, Orlando. **_Die the Long Day_**. Morrow 1972. o.p. Fiction.

Set on a Jamaican sugar plantation in the eighteenth century, this novel balances a dramatic plot against a detailed and informative portrait of slave life. The story opens as Quasheba, a slave, is found to be missing from her quarters. Many suspect that she seeks revenge against the syphilitic plantation owner who has made advances toward her daughter Polly. Quasheba is alone in her rebellion; the other slaves are immobilized by fear. Her strength and their weakness define the pivotal question of the novel: Should one defy and die or accommodate and live? Quasheba chooses the former to save her daughter from a slow, painful death. But her attempt to kill the plantation owner fails, and she is slain by slaves sent to track her down.

This well-crafted and gripping novel illuminates the past and brings it to life. Another work that explores the theme of slavery in its modern guise of humiliating economic deprivation is _The Children of Sisyphus_ (1964). Patterson, a sociologist now living in the United States, has also written several academic studies and essay collections on the issues of race and slavery in the Americas.

HC

694 Paz, Octavio. **_Sunstone—Piedra de Sol_**. Repr. of 1963 ed. Trans. from Spanish by Eliot Weinberger. New Directions 1991, $18.95 (0-8112-1197-5); $8.95 (0-8112-1195-9). 64pp. Poetry.

This long poem is the culmination of a poetic search that began with "Libertad Bajo Palabra," which appears in the author's _Early Poems 1935–1955_ (New Directions, 1973). The Aztec calendar stone, or "sunstone," symbolizes the poem's central theme: the exploration of time as history. It also juxtaposes two antithetical conceptions of time: circular time, which informed the thinking and world view of Mesoamerican peoples, and linear time, which has determined Western thought and historical development.

In the poem, the speaker finds himself in a world in ruins and chaos, in the middle of a void, at which time he meets his beloved. The erotic experience is the only way he can transcend his solitude and sadness, overcome violence and chaos, and end his alienation from the world.

Other important poetic works by Paz include _A Tree Within_ (New Directions, 1988). There are also several editions of his collected poems. Considered to be Mexico's foremost poet and essayist, Paz was awarded the Nobel Prize for literature in 1990.   PR

Philip, Marlene Nourbese. *Harriet's Daughter*.
See entry 595.

Philip, Marlene Nourbese. *She Tries Her Tongue, Her Silence Softly Breaks*.
See entry 596.

695 Phillips, Caryl. *Cambridge*. Knopf 1992, $18.50 (0-679-40532-1); $10.00 (0-679-73689-1). 192pp. Fiction.

Set on a fictitious West Indian island during the early 1880s, this novel reveals the details of life on a sugar plantation from the vantage point of two characters: Emily, daughter of the plantation owner, and Cambridge, a slave. Emily leaves England for the West Indies, chronicling her experiences in a journal. At first she feels nothing but disgust for this "backwater of the Americas." Eventually, though, her feelings are transformed into understanding and acceptance. Central to this change is her interaction with and eventual attraction to Mr. Brown, the brutal estate manager, and to Cambridge, the proud slave. The novel closes as Cambridge tells the stirring story of his life and the events that brought him to the island.

This is a distinctive and stunning novel. Phillips is also the author of *Final Passage* (Viking, 1990), which deals with the experiences of Caribbean emigrants in England, and *Crossing the River* (Knopf, 1994), the story of an African father and the children he sells into slavery.   HC

696 Piñon, Nelida. *The Republic of Dreams*. Trans. from Portuguese by Helen Lane. Knopf 1989, $22.95 (0-394-55525-2); Univ. of Texas Pr. $17.95 (0-292-77050-2). 669pp. Fiction.

In 1913, Madruga, a restless thirteen-year-old, leaves the impoverished village of Galicia against his family's wishes and heads for Brazil, where he intends to make his fortune. On the journey he befriends another teenager, Venancio. Over the next seven decades their lives intertwine; the practical Madruga prospers while his idealistic, dreamy companion fails, but the two always remain close friends. Madruga returns to Galicia to marry Eulalia, the daughter of the well-to-do Dom Miguel, and he takes her to Brazil, where eventually they have six children and many grandchildren. Joy is mixed with sadness as one child dies in infancy; another, alienated from her father, dies in an auto accident; and the children fail to live up to their father's hopes for them. Granddaughter Breta, with whom Madruga feels a special closeness (and to whom he entrusts his stories), must leave the country for political reasons, and both Venancio and Madruga's youngest son, Tobias, get mired in lost political causes.

Piñon's first publication in English is an epic work, complex in its portrayal of the characters and the lands they call home. The author followed this work with another highly regarded novel, *Caetana's Sweet Song* (Knopf, 1992).
LML

697 Poniatowska, Elena. *Until We Meet Again*. Trans. from Spanish. Pantheon 1987. o.p. Fiction.

Although this novel should be read as fiction, it is based on the true story and testimony of Jesusa Palancares, a woman of the Mexico City slums. The work presents the life experiences of poor women who are often relegated to the fringes of Spanish-American literature or ignored altogether. Jesusa loses her mother at a young age. She marries an abusive man and joins the revolution as a camp follower. Deprivation, physical violence, and sexual abuse characterize her married life. After her husband dies she overcomes her passivity and submissiveness and refuses to remarry, thus challenging the roles and behaviors traditionally assigned to Spanish-American women. Although she is unable to overcome the class barrier imposed on her by a rigidly stratified society, she is able to determine her own future within the limitations of her class. The book is a tribute to Mexican working-class women, whose strength and determination often are invisible in a world dominated by powerful men.   PR

Portillo-Trambley, Estela. *Trini*.
See entry 406.

698 Posse, Abel. *The Dogs of Paradise*. Trans. from Spanish by Margaret S. Peden. Macmillan 1990, $19.95 (0-689-12091-5). 196pp. Fiction.

The 500th anniversary of Columbus's voyage to the New World prompted many Spanish-American writers to reassess what was commonly known as the "Enterprise of the Indies." Posse, a writer from Argentina, has written a novel about the event that is both funny and tragic. Columbus, the central character, is portrayed as a megalomaniac who believes that his trips are divinely inspired. As the envoy of God, he believes his mission is to find paradise on Earth. Columbus is also seen as a liar and a sex maniac, a pawn of the European powers whose greed and callousness lead the deaths of millions of indigenous people. The novel is also a serious meditation about the mendacity of historical discourse, which until recently inevitably portrayed Columbus as an exemplary individual.

Spanish-American colonial history has been one of Posse's interests. His novel *Daimon* (Macmillan, 1992) features as its central character Lope de Aguirre, the psychopathic conquistador of the Amazon.   PR

699 Puig, Manuel. *Kiss of the Spider Woman*. Trans. from Spanish by Thomas Colchie. Random 1991, $11.00 (0-679-72449-4). 288pp. Fiction.

Adapted both for film and for a Broadway musical, this novel has become Puig's most popular work in the United States. As is true of his other fiction, the novel integrates cinematic elements to provide structure and meaning. The characters represent two groups that have been historically oppressed and persecuted in Spanish America. Molina, who is gay, challenges the traditional mores of the social order. Valentín is a revolutionary whose ideology is a direct threat to the economic and political status quo. They both share a prison cell, and their conversations about films and about their dreams and experiences become a process of liberation from the labels imposed on them by society. At the end of the novel, they have both broken the surface of their roles and recognized their deeper identities. Other recommended works by Puig include *Heartbreak Tango* (orig. pub. 1973; Viking, 1991), *Tropical Night Falling* (Norton, 1991), and *Pubis Angelical* (o.p., 1986). **PR**

700 Ramírez, Sergio. ***To Bury Our Fathers: A Novel of Nicaragua***. Trans. from Spanish by Nick Caistor. Illus. with woodcuts by Dieter Mashur. Readers International 1985, $11.95 (0-930523-03-2). 250pp. Fiction.

Although Ramírez served as the vice president of Nicaragua during the twelve years of Sandinista rule, he will probably best be remembered as a writer of fiction about his native land. This novel, narrated through six interrelated story strands, covers the period from 1934 to 1960. Each of the strands is identified by a woodcut. One strand tells of Catalino López, a National Guard officer who is kidnapped and humiliated by three opponents of the Somoza dictatorship. Two of the kidnappers are themselves former Guardsmen; the third is the grandson of a prominent doctor whose political career ended in a stolen election. Other strands give the histories of these men and describe what happened to them after the kidnapping.

Ramírez's novel portrays a cross-section of Nicaraguan society, captured in a moment of time. His narrative is rich with irony and with the experiences and feelings of his three guerrilla protagonists. A selection of Ramírez's short stories has been published under the title *Stories from Nicaragua* (Readers International, 1987). **LML**

701 Rhys, Jean. ***Wide Sargasso Sea***. Norton 1993, $8.95 (0-393-31048-5). 192pp. Fiction.

Set in Jamaica and Dominica during the 1830s, this novel deals with the personality development of Antoinette Cosway Rochester, the mad wife in *Jane Eyre*. The author reconstructs the early years of this troubled woman, depicting her as a character who is "alienated, menaced, and at odds with life." Her story unfolds against the backdrop of the landscape, mores, and social fabric of West Indian culture. In addition, the author examines the effects of emotional suffocation on women in a patriarchal society.

The novel is divided into three parts. The first is told in the heroine's own words as she recollects her troubled childhood and early adolescent years. In the second part, the young Mr. Rochester describes his arrival in the West Indies, his marriage to Antoinette Cosway, and the marriage's disastrous outcome. The last part is once more narrated by Antoinette, but the setting is England; now a deranged woman, she speaks from the attic room in Thornfield Hall. Within the large body of work by Jean Rhys, *Wide Sargasso Sea* is the only novel that reflects her Caribbean background. **HC**

702 Roumain, Jacques. ***Masters of the Dew***. Trans. from French. Heinemann 1978, $9.95 (0-435-98745-3). 192pp. Fiction.

Manuel Delivrance, the protagonist, returns to Fonds Rouge, Haiti, his birthplace, after years spent cutting cane in Cuba. He is confronted by a drought-stricken landscape, one that is tragically different from the lush scenery he remembered from before his departure. Undiscouraged by this barren vista, Manuel attempts to locate a new water source for his village. Upon finding the source, he organizes the feuding villagers to irrigate their land. However, he is knifed by a jealous rival who is angered by Manuel's success. On his deathbed, hoping to prevent the peasants from descending once again into a state of war, Manuel refuses to identify his attacker.

This well-written work draws upon the experiences of peasants in the author's land. Critics have hailed Roumain's literary treatment of his country, its culture, and the African roots that make Haiti a unique place, rich in language and tradition. Roumain's daring presentation of Haiti's problems and conflicts gives this book a singular power. An additional work that portrays Haitian culture and its African influences and demonstrates Roumain's interest in the Negritude movement, is his collection of poems, *Ebony Wood* (o.p., 1972).   HC

703   Rulfo, Juan. *Pedro Páramo*. Trans. from Spanish by Margaret S. Paden. Grove 1990, $11.00 (0-8021-3390-8). 128pp. Fiction.

This work by the noted Mexican author is structurally difficult. The plot lacks a clear nucleus and the story is not developed linearly. As in much of contemporary Spanish-American fiction, the reader is challenged to participate actively in reconstructing the story. The challenge is increased by the fact that the author constantly crosses the boundaries of space and time; the objective and the imaginary intertwine, and the world of the living and that of the dead coexist. The novel questions the notion that the rational, sensory mind is adequate for comprehending the world.

Juan Preciado arrives in Comala looking for his father, Pedro Páramo. He discovers a dead town, filled with noises and spirits, and he soon dies of fright. In his tomb he listens to the story of Pedro Páramo as told by the ghosts of those who became victims of his greed. Their voices intertwine with Páramo's own monologue as he remembers his past and explains why he destroyed the town. The novel's vision is one of extreme pessimism, offering no redeeming factors for human life, which the author portrays as devoid of sense and purpose. Social institutions fail the people, who have no protection from the predatory actions of their landlord. The characters are condemned to a life of poverty and deprivation with no hope for relief.   PR

704   Sánchez, Luis Rafael. *Macho Camacho's Beat*. Trans. from Spanish by Gregory Rabassa. Pantheon 1980. o.p. Fiction.

In this, the first novel by the well-known Puerto Rican playwright, Sánchez satirizes modern-day Puerto Rico, especially its loss of identity through its wholesale acceptance of the worst aspects of U.S. culture.

The novel juxtaposes the monologue of Vicente Reinosa, a corrupt pro-American politician who is stuck in a traffic jam, with that of his mistress, a young mulatto singer-hooker who fantasizes about relationships with younger men. The lyrics of a song sung by Macho Camacho are interwoven with the words of the characters and the narrators, establishing a rhythm that is both overpowering and nightmarish. The novel is filled with noise, creating a suffocating atmosphere. Through its use of humor and irony, the book offers a serious critique of Puerto Rico and its lack of a strong culture independent of U.S. influence.   PR

705 Sarduy, Severo. ***Cobra and Maitreya***. Trans. from Spanish by Suzanne J. Levine. Dalkey Archive Pr. 1995, $13.95 (1-56478-076-0). 288pp. Fiction.

Fiction by this Cuban author is technically sophisticated and thematically demanding. The reader is plunged into the underground existence of transvestite prostitutes and other marginal individuals who inhabit worlds where the rules that govern mainstream reality dissolve. The theatrical setting of *Cobra* (the name of the principal character) underscores the story's main concerns: the falsehood of defined identities, on both the individual and the national levels, the hypocrisy of social conventions, and the general fluidity of reality. Language, like theatrical makeup, costume, and speech, is artificial and lacks the power to communicate fully; its main function is to mask the speaker's real identity. Although not accessible to every reader, *Cobra* is one of the most intriguing works of Spanish-American fiction, one that has profoundly influenced many writers. Other works by Sarduy include *Colibri* (Ediciones del Norte, 1984) and *For Voice* (Latin American Literature Review Pr., 1985).

PR

706 Skarmeta, Antonio. ***Burning Patience***. Trans. from Spanish by Katherine Silver. Graywolf 1994, $10.00 (1-55597-197-0). 128pp. Fiction.

The story of this novel begins just before Salvador Allende's inauguration as president of Chile and concludes with the military coup in 1973. The Nobel Prize–winning author Pablo Neruda is one of the main characters. Neruda is mentor to Mario Jiménez, a young mailman who wishes to be a poet. Jiménez has fallen in love with a waitress and asks the poet's help in expressing his feelings. Impressed by the young man's naiveté and freshness, Neruda agrees. The novel explores the relationship between the poet and the people and between the people and poetry. Humor abounds, and there are some insightful and realistic scenes, especially regarding Chile's political situation after the coup. This is a short, accessible novel, less rich and complex, perhaps, than the masterworks of Latin American literature, but nonetheless a good choice for older high school students and general readers who are beginning to explore the continent and its writing.

The novel has been adapted for film and the stage. Skarmeta is also the author of *I Dreamt the Snow Was Burning* (Readers International, 1985), a novel set amid the chaos of Allende's last days in power.   PR

Suárez, Virgil. ***Latin Jazz***.
See entry 412.

707 Thoby-Marcelin, Philippe, and Pierre Marcelin. ***The Beast of the Haitian Hills***. Repr. of 1946 ed. Trans. from French by Peter C. Rhodes. City Lights 1990, $6.95 (0-87286-189-9). 176pp. Fiction.

This novel tells the story of a Haitian mulatto, Morin Dutilleul, who after the death of his wife leaves Port-au-Prince to live in the hills above the city. Always enamored of peasant life, Morin looks forward to the bucolic pleasures of farming and life among the simple folk. Repulsed, however, by the rustics' backward ways, belief in voodoo, and crude mannerisms, he becomes alienated from his neighbors. Through his callous disregard for the inner workings of society in the country, he sets in motion a chain of events that ultimately result in his death.

The book warns urban, upper-class, mixed-race Haitians not to ignore the power and significance of voodoo and not to sever themselves from the roots of their cultural heritage. In doing so, the authors underscore the central tensions in Haiti that arise from issues concerning class, race, urbanization, and the country's unique history. Other works by Thoby-Marcelin that deal with similar themes are *The Pencil of God* (o.p., 1951) and *All Men Are Mad* (o.p., 1970). HC

708 Triana, José. ***The Criminals***. Reprinted in *The Drama Review*, vol. 14, no. 2 (1970): 105-129. Trans. from Spanish. Dutton 1971. o.p. Drama.

The play, which won the prestigious 1965 Casa de las Américas Award, has been acclaimed by audiences in Latin America, Europe, and the United States. The characters—two sisters and a brother, closer to adolescence than adulthood—reminisce about their murdered parents and their stultifying and destructive family life. The characters shift roles to reenact the murder and the incidents leading to it. This play-within-a-play becomes more and more complex as it portrays the family as a decaying institution. The parents are seen as cruel and repressive, harsh in their behavior to each other and insensitive to their children's needs. The children, in turn, are selfish, constantly pursuing their own gratification, and oblivious to the increasing frustrations in their parents' lives. As the plot unfolds, the children's vicious games grow increasingly irrational, cruel, and violent. PR

709 Valenzuela, Luisa. ***Other Weapons***. Trans. from Spanish by Deborah Bonner. Ediciones del Norte 1985, $10.00 (0-910061-22-X). 135pp. Fiction.

The five stories in this book, each narrated by a female voice, explore the ways in which women resist the images, values, and codes of behavior imposed on them by a society ruled by men. The title refers to the violence of the military dictatorship in Argentina during the mid-1970s and early 1980s, a dictatorship that declared liberated women to be one of its primary targets. It also indicates the resources available to women as they struggle for survival, express their sexuality, seek freedom, and search for their identity. In the title story, torture reduces the protagonist, a former member of the revolutionary forces, to a vegetable-like state devoid of memories and volition. "Fourth Version" shows how the political and the erotic can intertwine to become a source of conflict between the sexes. In "Rituals of Rejection," the author explores the question of whether women can extricate themselves from the seductive power of men, even though the punishment imposed on liberated women by patriarchal power can be brutal. These stories reflect the author's view that in the struggle against traditional passivity and submission, women need to chart new ground and explore the untapped resources—the other weapons—of their imagination and their erotic impulses.

Other works by Valenzuela exploring similar topics are *Strange Things Happen Here* (o.p., 1979), *Open Door Stories* (o.p., 1988), *The Lizard's Tail* (Serpent's Tail, 1983), and *The Censors* (Curbstone, 1992). PR

710   Vallejo, César. ***The Complete Posthumous Poetry***. Trans. from Spanish by Clayton Eshelman and José R. Barcia. Univ. of California Pr. 1979, $16.00 (0-520-04099-6). 339pp. Poetry.

The work of the Peruvian poet César Vallejo has greatly influenced the development of contemporary Spanish-American poetry. These verses, with their deep human content, offer profound meditations on the meaning and capabilities of language. Questioning whether human language can represent reality, Vallejo sometimes uses his poems to show how words mislead and conceal. For example, in *Human Poems*, one of the most significant works in this anthology, he explores the importance and meaning of the names we give to things. By redefining common words, Vallejo demonstrates the untrustworthiness of language. Two of his other books, *Trilce* (Marcilio, 1992) and *Spain, Let This Cup Pass from Me* (Invisible City/Red Hill, 1978), also explore the shortcomings of language as a means of communication. His poetry embodies the contradictions that rational discourse frequently ignores.   PR

711   Vargas Llosa, Mario. ***The Time of the Hero***. Trans. from Spanish by Lysander Kemp. Farrar 1986, $14.00 (0-374-52021-6). 409pp. Fiction.

Vargas Llosa's first novel, still considered one of his best works, earned him the prestigious Biblioteca Breve Prize and brought him wide recognition. The story takes place in a military academy, a microcosm of Peru, and explores the impact of machismo on the members and institutions of society. To maintain their identity, honor, and status, males need to prove their masculinity through robbery, rape, animalism, victimization of others, even murder.

The plot is simple. A group of students in their senior year decide to steal a copy of the chemistry final exam. When they are caught, their leader, Jaguar, suspects that the gentle and humble Arana (alias the "Slave") has turned them in. During a military exercise Arana is shot in the head and dies. One of the members of the group implicates Jaguar, but the institution prefers to blame the victim for his own inability to deal with military life. In so doing, the school and its leaders avoid facing responsibility for their failure.

As in *The Real Life of Alejandro Mayta* (Farrar, 1986), *Green House* (Farrar, 1985), and *The Storyteller* (Farrar, 1989), Vargas Llosa uses multiple narrative voices to present the story, challenging the reader to participate actively in its reconstruction. The author has also written several humorous and satirical works, of which the best known is *Aunt Julia and the Scriptwriter* (Avon, 1985).   PR

Villaseñor, Victor. ***Macho!***
See entry 421.

712   Walcott, Derek. ***Dream on Monkey Mountain, and Other Plays***. Farrar 1970. o.p. Drama.

The play opens in a West Indian jail where Makak, the protagonist, is being interrogated for his drunken and disorderly conduct. In his inebriated state, the elderly islander displays confusion about his cultural identity and the meaning of his life. Following this jail scene, reality fades; the remainder of the play takes place in Makak's dream, in which he undertakes a messianic mission to purify his people by leading them back to Africa, where they will regain their true heritage and culture. Within the dream Makak suffers greatly, but he awakens with a clear sense of self and identity and abandons his fear and hatred of whiteness. The confusion that West Indians face in dealing with the clashing African and European influences that underlie their cultural and racial identity is the theme that is central to the play's denouement.

Walcott received the Nobel Prize in 1992. His works include the poetry collection *The Star-Apple Kingdom* (1979) and an anthology of plays, *Remembrance and Pantomime* (1980). His epic poem *Omeros (see main entry)* tells the story of *The Iliad* and *The Odyssey* in an island setting.   HC

713   Walcott, Derek. ***Omeros***. Farrar 1992, $12.00 (0-374-52350-9). 336pp. Poetry.

Nobel laureate Derek Walcott's poem *Omeros* endows the inhabitants of the Caribbean island of St. Lucia with the names and the heroic spirit of characters in the Greek epics *The Iliad* and *The Odyssey*. One of the work's many narrative threads involves the daily lives of the islanders, including Helen, a maid; her husband, Achille, a fisherman and the hero of the book; Helen's lover, Hector; and their friend Philoctete. Other strands involve Achille's imaginative journeys through history and reflections on the historical events that shaped St. Lucia in particular and the Caribbean region in general. The intertwining of these narrative threads creates the fabric that is *Omeros*.

Walcott's poem is a complex and intriguing work, made even more stunning by his lyrical use of language and his ability to describe St. Lucia's landscape, its flora and fauna, and the sparkling Caribbean Sea. Other noteworthy collections of poems by this author include *The Gulf* (o.p.) and *Midsummer* (Farrar, 1989).   HC

714   Wolff, Egon. ***Paper Flowers***. Trans. from Spanish. Univ. of Missouri Pr. 1971. o.p. Drama.

Wolff is one of Spanish America's best playwrights. Although he has staged and published many successful plays, only *Paper Flowers* has been translated into English. In most of his works, Wolff deals with the absurdity of reality, reflected in the ease with which an established state of affairs can disintegrate. Eva, a middle-class widow, allows El Merluza, a vagrant, to help her carry her groceries. He enters her apartment; instead of accepting a tip and leaving, he requests a cup of tea. Eva accedes without realizing that she has given in to him and that she will not be able to evict him. Within a week he totally changes and destroys her apartment—and obliterates Eva's individuality in the process. After a week they leave together to live in the slums across the river. Eva, secure and comfortable in a predictable world, has surrendered to chaos because she can neither stop Merluza's crazy actions nor defend herself against his impeccably coherent reasoning. The play questions the foundation of bourgeois life, which finds security in material possessions but which disintegrates under the slightest challenge.   PR

Zeller, Ludwig. ***When the Animal Rises from the Deep the Head Explodes***. See entry 610.

715 Abbott, Elizabeth. *Haiti: The Duvaliers and Their Legacy*. Rev. updated ed. Simon & Schuster 1991, $12.95 (0-671-68620-8). 416pp. Nonfiction.

Abbott, wife of Haitian hotelier Joseph Namphy, provides an inside account of the Duvaliers, François ("Papa Doc") and his son Jean-Claude ("Baby Doc"), and their thirty-year dictatorship. In this revised and updated edition, she presents a chronological history that begins with the U.S. occupation and ends with the installation in 1988 of Haiti's forty-third president, Ertha Pascal Trouillot. Abbott points out how the occupation, along with the rise of the Pan-Africanism movement, which opposed the U.S. presence, affected François Duvalier's political development. The author then details his rise to power and the murderous regime that he established and that Jean-Claude perpetuated. The book explores the political, economic, religious, and social forces that shaped the turbulent era. This is a gripping narrative that brings the country and the Duvaliers to life. An extensive index and a source listing round out this excellent work. HC

716 Agosín, Marjorie. *Scraps of Life: The Chilean Arpilleras: Chilean Women and the Pinochet Dictatorship*. Trans. from Spanish by Cola Franzen. Illus. Red Sea Pr. 1987, $29.95 (0-932415-28-8); $9.95 (0-932415-29-6). 190pp. Nonfiction.

Arpilleras, traditional craft objects found throughout much of South America, are three-dimensional tapestries that feature small figures in scenes from daily life. During the Pinochet dictatorship in Chile, arpilleras took on a political meaning. The Vicariate of Solidarity—the Catholic Church's human rights organization—organized poor women, most of them relatives of detained, murdered, and "disappeared" people, to sew arpilleras for sale abroad. Besides providing economic sustenance, these humble artworks also alerted people outside Chile to the poverty and oppression within the country.

Agosín's study focuses on the women: their stories, the making of the arpilleras, and the history of the women's movement in Chile in general. She points out the underlying sexism of Popular Unity activists and shows how their inattention to women's issues contributed to their downfall in 1973. She also describes the alliances Pinochet made with women's groups for the sole purpose of enforcing personal and political submissiveness. An extensive bibliography completes this useful and readable study. LML

717 Anderson, Marilyn, and Jonathan Garlock. *Granddaughters of Corn*. Illus. with photos by the authors. Curbstone 1988, $35.00 (0-915306-64-6); Curbstone $19.95 (0-915306-60-3). 120pp. Nonfiction.

As part of a master's degree program in photography at the Visual Studies Workshop in Rochester, New York, photographer Anderson and her husband, Jonathan Garlock, traveled to Guatemala in 1975 to document traditional weaving techniques, especially backstrap weaving. Worked with an 8x10 camera, Anderson spent hours with each weaver to provide an in-depth record of her individual technique. Many of the women allowed Anderson to take portraits of them wearing traditional clothes. Three projects resulted from this effort: a book, *Guatemalan Textiles Today*; a photographic exhibit,

"Granddaughters of Corn: Women and Repression in Guatemala," and this work, based on that exhibit.

A few years after Anderson's visit, the political situation in Guatemala worsened and these portraits took on an even greater significance. Many of the villages where the photographs were taken were destroyed; many of the weavers who were not murdered or "disappeared" fled to Mexico. This book juxtaposes the beauty and grace of the pictures with text that describes the horror of the situation in Guatemala. A narrow gray band below the photographs lists just some of the 40,000 people—many of them women—who have disappeared since 1965. The history of repression documented on every page contrasts sharply with the extraordinary and beautiful portraits of an indigenous people who are faced with destruction.   CM

718   Barrios de Chungara, Domitila, and Moemar Viezzer. *Let Me Speak! Testimony of Domitila, a Woman of the Bolivian Mines*. Trans. from Quechua by Victoria Ortiz. Monthly Review 1979, $12.50 (0-85345-445-0); $8.50 (0-85345-485-X). 235pp. Nonfiction.

In 1975, Barrios, mother of seven children and wife of a tin miner, was invited to speak at the UN-sponsored International Women's Year Tribunal because of her work in the Housewives' Committee of the Siglo XX mine. Barrios was the only working-class representative at the tribunal. Her testimony, translated from her native Quechua language, describes the experiences of ordinary people who are struggling for a better life for their children and their country. Miners have a life expectancy of thirty-five years; their last years are spent fighting silicosis, a miner's disease that destroys the lungs. Living and working conditions are primitive. Children must work to help support the family, so they receive only limited education. As part of the "new politics" that has emerged in Latin America in the last three decades, women have begun to accept that their roles must extend beyond care of the home and children. Improving conditions in the broader society is the only route by which they might improve life for their own families and for their people.

The plight of Bolivian tin mine workers has not changed much since this account was published over a decade and a half ago. Despite years of activism, the workers still experience poverty and dreadful working conditions, although they have been organized with some success and some reforms have been enacted.   CM

719   Bellegarde-Smith, Patrick. *Haiti: The Breached Citadel*. Westview 1989. o.p. Nonfiction.

After a brief overview of the land and society, this book then reviews the history of Haiti from Columbus's arrival in the Caribbean to the fall of General Henri Namphy in late 1988. Bellegarde-Smith, a Haitian who teaches at the University of Wisconsin, Milwaukee, discusses the Haitian revolution, the pattern of trade in the eighteenth and nineteenth centuries, the U.S. occupation of Haiti between 1915 and 1934, the birth of modern Pan-Africanism, and the rise and fall of the thirty-year Duvalier dynasty. Throughout, he points out the contributions of women to the economic, cultural, and religious life of Haiti. In addition, the historical and contemporary role of the vodun (voodoo) religion in Haitian culture is examined. A useful bibliographic essay at the end of the work, maps, photographs, and an index are provided. Other books in the same series, Westview Profiles: Nations of Contemporary Latin America, examine the history and society of Bolivia, Nicaragua, Venezuela, Paraguay, Cuba, Uruguay, Ecuador, Mexico, Belize, Colombia, and the Dominican Republic.   HC

720   Bode, Barbara. *No Bells to Toll: Destruction and Creation in the Andes.* Illus. Macmillan 1989. o.p. Nonfiction.

On May 31, 1971, an earthquake registering 7.7 on the Richter scale caused major devastation in a region of Peru. The quake also touched off an avalanche and a mud slide, or *aluvión*. In less than five minutes a huge chunk of the 21,860-foot Andean mountain Huascaran hurled through the Callejón de Huaylas valley at 200 miles an hour. The town of Yungas was buried under the debris. Over 75,000 people in the area, most of them indigenous Peruvians, died as a result of the quake.

Bode, an anthropologist, whose child had died recently, decided to go to a place to work where grief and disaster were a part of daily discourse. She wrote her account of the earthquake's aftermath after a year of living with and interviewing residents of the area. She sought to understand the meaning of this catastrophe from the testimonies of the survivors. Her account is detailed and often lyrical; it includes some of her own poetry. Bode examines the political, religious, social, and spiritual effects of the disaster as well as the changes forced upon indigenous peoples and their culture by the Peruvian government.   CM

721   Boeker, Paul H., ed. *Lost Illusions: Latin America's Struggle for Democracy, As Recounted by Its Leaders.* Markus Weiner 1990, $29.95 (1-55876-023-7); $12.95 (1-55876-024-5). 360pp. Essays/Interviews.

To understand the Latin American perspective on democratic issues, Paul Boeker, president of the Board of the Institute of the Americas and former U.S. ambassador to Bolivia under President Jimmy Carter, traveled throughout Latin America in 1988. He interviewed ten current heads of state, ten former presidents, and six opposition leaders in Chile, Argentina, Uruguay, Costa Rica, Mexico, Venezuela, Peru, Colombia, Ecuador, Brazil and the Dominican Republic. This book contains those interviews plus brief profiles of each leader. Two bookend essays by Boeker define and explain the issues.

In the 1970s, military dictatorships dominated Latin America, but as the 1990s approached, freely elected democracies became the norm. Overwhelming civilian rejection of military regimes sustains these new democracies. The leaders Boeker spoke to often fault the United States for its failure to assist them in escaping the dual problems of economic stagnation and declining standards of living. However, they also realize that the solution to their problems does not lie in the United States alone. Similarly, the majority of these citizens don't expect miracles from their presidential elections, but they do expect human rights protection, guarantees of basic freedoms of the press and speech, economic stability and controlled inflation. The leaders interviewed understand that the basis of continued citizen support rests on these premises.   CM

722 Buckley, Kevin. *Panama*. Rev. ed. Simon & Schuster 1992. o.p. Nonfiction.

This book chronicles the events that led to the U.S. invasion of Panama in December 1989 and the arrest of military strongman Manuel Noriega on drug charges. Buckley's account begins in 1985 with the brutal murder of Dr. Hugo Spadafora, an outspoken opponent of Noriega. Rather than drawing a complete biographical portrait of Noriega, Buckley casts him as the wily villain in a gripping political drama. In his geopolitical battle, Noriega played off all sides to his own advantage, offering favors to—and taking them from—Fidel Castro, the contras, Oliver North, and the Medellín drug cartel. Buckley details Noriega's dealings with George Bush, who first embraced him as an opponent of the left-wing Sandinistas and then turned on him when he became a political liability after the Iran-Contra scandal and before the 1988 U.S. presidential election. How Noriega initially outfoxed the Bush administration receives attention, as does the dictator's self-destructive behavior and the mistakes he made that triggered the invasion. Among the cast of characters receiving sympathetic attention are Spadafora's brother, who is determined to obtain justice, and a dedicated female assistant to Senator Jesse Helms, who found herself harassed by the general and his allies. This well-documented account reads like a work of fiction and will appeal to a broad audience, from high school students on up.   LML

Burger, Julian. *The Gaia Atlas of First Peoples: The Future for the Indigenous World*.
See entry 479.

723 Carrigan, Ana. *The Palace of Justice: A Colombian Tragedy*. Four Walls Eight Windows 1993, $22.95 (0-941423-82-4). 303pp. Nonfiction.

On November 6, 1985, members of the Colombian guerrilla group M-19 attacked the Palace of Justice in Bogotá, seat of Colombia's Supreme Court and Council of State. The guerrillas demanded that then-President Belisario Betancur be put on trial for violating a 1984 peace agreement between the government and M-19. The guerrillas held about 300 civilians hostage, including a number of Supreme Court justices. Within a day, the army attacked with gunfire and artillery; in the wake of the palace's recapture, more than 100 hostages, including eleven judges, lay dead.

Carrigan, the author of *Salvador Witness: The Life and Calling of Jean Donovan* (Ballantine, 1986) (which became the basis for the TV movie "Choices of the Heart"), offers a detailed and gripping account of the guerrilla attack, the government counterattack, and the aftermath. While criticizing the guerrillas for their part in the massacre, she reserves most of her criticism for the Betancur government, which, she argues, did not explore less-violent alternatives and which was guilty of subsequent human rights abuses. (In fact, she tells the reader, some of the civilians who survived were later "disappeared" by the government.) Carrigan places the events in a broader context, discussing the country's turbulent history and politics, the origins of M-19 and other guerrilla groups, and the complex and often misinterpreted relationships among the government, the guerrillas, and the drug cartels.   LML

724 Chatwin, Bruce. *In Patagonia*. Viking 1988, $8.95 (0-14-011291-X). Nonfiction.

Chatwin became interested in Patagonia as a boy for two reasons. His family thought it would be the best place on Earth to escape the effects of nuclear annihilation, which, during the Cold War years, seemed inevitable. The other reason, though, is more intriguing. A relative of Chatwin's, a sailor, brought back to England a mysterious patch of brown leathery skin with reddish hair. The skin belonged to the mylodon, or giant sloth, which lives in caves just north of Puerto Natales in Chilean Patagonia. Still curious about this remote land as an adult, Chatwin traveled throughout Patagonia in Argentina and Chile in the 1970s. He also explored the literature of fact and imagination and the histories, most of which were written by European authors. Chatwin weaves history and fantasy about the region together with stories of his hundreds of encounters with residents of the region.

This is the land of the Ona Indians, who wrapped their feet in furs for treks across the snowy mountains. When the Portuguese explorer Magellan saw the enormous animal-like prints, he referred to the Indians as the *Patagonas* ("paw-footed Indians"). Chatwin believes that Shakespeare based his half-man, half-beast character Caliban (*The Tempest*) on descriptions of the Patagons by Magellan's chronicler. Here, too, is where Darwin voyaged on the *H.M.S. Beagle* to research his theories of evolution. Chatwin casts doubt on the story that Butch Cassidy and the Sundance Kid lived in Patagonia before they were gunned down in Bolivia. He also compiles what little information exists about the indigenous peoples of the region—the Ona, Tehuelche, Haush, Alakaluf and Yaghan—Indians who were systematically destroyed by the English settlers in the late 1800s. The book includes a substantial bibliography. An outsider's view of this land, Chatwin's work is an eclectic and fascinating example of travel writing. CM

725 Clarke, Colin, ed. *Society and Politics in the Caribbean*. St. Martin 1991, $65.00 (0-312-06583-3). 312pp. Nonfiction.

This work is a collection of papers by specialists in the politics and sociology of the Caribbean. The book examines all five of the nations that make up the Greater Antilles—Cuba, Haiti, the Dominican Republic, Puerto Rico, and Jamaica—and it also explores most of the Lesser Antilles—Trinidad and Tobago and the southeastern Caribbean states. In addition, there is a separate chapter on Grenada, the two French insular departments, and the two mainland states of Belize and Venezuela.

In the introduction, the editor makes the point that the subject matter of the book eludes easy generalizations: "All Caribbean states bear the traces of extreme social inequality based upon differences of race, class, and culture. . . . [T]he relationship between these variables and political organization . . . depends upon historical and geographical circumstances, coupled to the leadership and managerial skills of the population." The articles in this book then go on to explain and analyze these complex variables and their impact on life in the region. HC

335

LATIN AMERICA AND
THE CARIBBEAN

726 Clements, Charles. *Witness to War: An American Doctor in El Salvador.* Bantam 1984, $4.50 (0-553-26779-5). 288pp. Nonfiction.

In 1982 Clements, a U.S. doctor and former Air Force pilot in Vietnam, secretly entered El Salvador to offer medical services to civilians and guerrilla fighters in rebel-held territory near the Guazapa Volcano. His patients suffered from malnutrition, diarrhea, and other illnesses as well as from the results of war—gunshot wounds, shrapnel, and burns from aerial bombardment. Readers of this affectionate portrait of the people with whom Clements lived and worked will come to admire their resilience and hope in the face of adversity. The author describes the harrowing evacuations of civilians in advance of rumored government offensives. He also offers an intimate portrait of the guerrillas and their organization in the area. Although his sympathies clearly lie with the rebels, he does not flinch from honest discussion of their mistakes and internal divisions. This book is most valuable for its first-person observations concerning health conditions in rural El Salvador and the impact of war upon innocent civilians.   LML

727 Cockcroft, James D. *Neighbors in Turmoil: Latin America.* HarperCollins 1989. o.p. Nonfiction.

Cockcroft examines the history of Latin America country by country. He is especially critical of U.S. foreign policy since 1948, which generally has regarded the region as the nation's "backyard." Such a policy tended to perpetuate the notion that change, revolution, or reform will only foster the rise of communism. In a historical overview, the author examines the origins of turmoil and the emergence of new political structures that develop as Latin American nations reject dictatorships and establish basic human rights. These countries, awakening to the consequences of long-standing U.S. policies, are moving away from simply blaming foreign intervention for their problems and are beginning to discover more practical solutions.

Organized by region and country, the book provides brief but useful histories and political analyses. Although events since 1948 are emphasized, Cockcroft includes essential background material covering the entire colonial era. The political parties, the labor unions, death squads, guerrillas, and other major groups involved in the political process of each country are named and described. The chapter bibliographies are so extensive as to include films, while a section of documents provides excerpts from primary source material, including the Arias Peace Plan, the 1986 World Court decision condemning U.S. policy toward Nicaragua, congressional hearings on the Iran-contra scandal, and U.S. policy documents from the Kissinger Commission. This comprehensive history is invaluable for its passionate concern for human rights, its careful documentation of U.S. involvement in sophisticated government repression against citizens, and its thorough analyses of each country's problems. At this writing, there are plans for the book to be updated and republished by Nelson Hall.   CM

Cockcroft, James D. *Outlaws in the Promised Land: Mexican Immigrant Workers and America's Future.*
See entry 426.

728   Constable, Pamela, and Arturo Valenzuela. *A Nation of Enemies: Chile under Pinochet*. Norton 1993, $12.95 (0-393-30985-1). 368pp. Nonfiction.

In spite of its long tradition of democracy, Chile has always been a divided society, both economically and politically. These divisions came to a head with the election of the country's first openly Marxist president, Salvador Allende, in 1970 and in the 1973 coup that toppled Allende and brought Army General Augusto Pinochet to power. In this book the authors examine the chaos of the Allende years and the brutal repression under Pinochet from the perspectives of the army, Pinochet and his junta colleagues, the secret police, the clandestine opposition, the judiciary, the free-market technocrats known as the "Chicago Boys," the wealthy, the poor, the politicians, and the young people who grew up under dictatorship. They chronicle the process by which the country's defeated political leaders put aside their differences to reclaim their democracy from the stubborn Pinochet.

This is a balanced, insightful account of a nation's trauma, growth, and eventual triumph. Offering interviews with people from all sectors of Chilean society, the book reads in many places like a work of fiction. It is the best general analysis of this period in Chile's history.   LML

729   Cortázar, Julio. *Nicaraguan Sketches*. Trans. from Spanish by Kathleen Weaver. Norton 1989, $7.95 (0-393-30642-9). 142pp. Essays.

Best known for his experimental fiction, Cortázar was born in Brussels but raised in Argentina. He held dual citizenship in Argentina and France, where he lived in exile after becoming disgusted with the Perón dictatorship. His short story "Blow Up" was the basis for the film by Michelangelo Antonioni; his novel *Hopscotch (see main entry)* is considered a classic of Latin American literature. Cortázar, an advocate for human rights, worked for UNESCO for thirty years. In his last decade of life he turned much of his political attention to Nicaragua. This book contains fifteen essays, lovingly written, about a country subjected to ruthless rule by the dictator Anastasio Somoza. Rebels led by Daniel Ortega conducted a revolution that on July 19, 1979 succeeded in ousting Somoza. Before then, Cortázar visited the country clandestinely three times; he returned again after the revolution.

The author's essays are quite different from his fiction. These intimate works reveal his deepest feelings about the Somoza regime, the revolution, and the way Nicaragua was treated by the West. In the piece entitled "Apocalypse in Solentiname," we get an insider's look at Father Ernesto Cardenal, leader of a religious and cultural community in which radical Christianity developed into political action. Cortázar also chronicles the impressive literacy campaign by the Sandinistas, which increased the literacy rate in Nicaragua from fifty percent to eighty-eight percent. A year before his death, Cortázar received Nicaragua's highest honor, the Rubén Darío Award; his essay about this event is among the most emotional of the pieces contained in this volume. Also included are extensive notes with bibliographical and other information.   CM

730   Crassweller, Robert O. *Perón and the Enigmas of Argentina*. Illus. Norton 1988, $14.95 (0-393-30543-0). 432pp. Nonfiction.

Crassweller provides a compelling portrait of Argentina, focusing on its most controversial leader, Juan Domingo Perón; his wife, Eva ("Evita"); and their lasting effect on the nation's politics and public policy. The book is divided into sections that present a short history of Argentina from 1516 to 1943; the rise of Perón to ruler during the years 1946 to 1955; and Perón's decline, exile, and return in 1973 and his death in 1974. A postscript covers the short presidency of Perón's third wife, Isabelita, after his death until she was overthrown in a coup in 1976. It also examines the subsequent repressions and trials of the military government and events during the reformist presidency of Raúl Alfonsín.

The book shows how Juan Perón understood the need to attend to the social problems of the people. Through the emotional power of propaganda and the muscular power of the armed forces and the unions, Perón was perceived as an advocate for workers; ultimately—almost in spite of himself—he did improve conditions.

Crassweller examines the often prickly relationship between the United States and Argentina under Perón. He argues that tensions arose partly through misunderstanding about the complex nature of Argentina and partly because of the refusal by the United States to import Argentine goods. The author notes that while as a ruler Perón never used Nazi tactics, he nonetheless admired their ideology and laced his rhetoric with elements of fascism. Despite Crassweller's attempt to be even-handed, Perón detractors will probably find this evaluation to be too generous.   CM

731   Crosby, Alfred W. **The Columbian Exchange: Biological and Cultural Consequences of 1492**. Greenwood 1973, $45.00 (0-8371-5821-4); $9.95 (0-8371-7228-4). 268pp. Nonfiction.

The voyages to the Americas by Columbus and later explorers had profound ecological consequences for both the Old and New Worlds. This book provides a clear account of the major effects of the transfer of crops, animals, disease-bearing microorganisms, and peoples between Europe and the Americas. The opening chapter contrasts the ecologies of the two regions, and subsequent chapters deal with the devastating effects upon Amerindians of the introduction of European diseases to the Americas. The decimation of the native populations opened the Americas to European settlement.

The author devotes a chapter to a study of syphilis, believed by many to be the one disease transmitted to Europe from the Americas. The mixing of Old and New World crops benefited all, playing a major role in expanding world food production and supplies. Although this book is more than twenty years old, it still provides an excellent overview of historians' and ecologists' knowledge of this important aspect of the European colonization of the Americas.   LML

732   Delano, Jack. **Puerto Rico Mio: Four Decades of Change, in Photographs by Jack Delano**. With essays by Sidney Mintz, Alan Fern, and Arturo M. Carrion. Illus. with photos. Smithsonian Inst. 1990, $24.95 (0-87474-389-3). 224pp. Photos/Essays.

In 1941, at the end of the Depression, the Farm Security Administration sent U.S. photographer Jack Delano to Puerto Rico to document the conditions of residents. More than forty years later, in 1982, Delano returned to the island to see how the land and people had changed. This book contains a collection of Delano's black-and-white photographs from the two journeys. The images are positioned on facing pages to emphasize the extent of transformation.

Four essays expand on the pictures. "The Island," by Sidney Mintz, places Delano's photographs in their historical context. Two other essays discuss the federal project of which Delano's work was a part. A final essay by Delano discusses his search in 1982 for the subjects and scenes he had filmed decades earlier.   LML

733   Deren, Maya. ***Divine Horsemen: The Living Gods of Haiti.*** Repr. of 1952 ed. Frwd. by Joseph Campbell. Illus. McPherson 1984, $24.00 (0-914232-64-9); $15.00 (0-914232-63-0). 350pp. Nonfiction.

Deren, a filmmaker, traveled to Haiti in 1947 to make a documentary about the vodun (voodoo) religion. Four years and three trips later, she completed a book based upon what she had learned. She describes vodun as "the religion, primarily African in origin, of the vast majority of the inhabitants of the Republic of Haiti." In the text, she traces elements of vodun—myths, deities, symbols, and rituals—to specific regions in West Africa; the religion as a whole, she argues, grew out of the amalgamation of these elements in the New World. She sees vodun as an open religion, one that has successfully incorporated elements of both Christianity and Native American spirituality as well. Within vodun, there is a strong aggressive current that at the end of the eighteenth century contributed to the successful slave rebellion that culminated in Haiti's independence. Deren details the multiple roles of the *houngan* (minister), the various rituals and rites of passage, and the key symbols. The book's title comes from the archetype of the horseman, the spirit *loa*, that can mount an individual and temporarily take possession of his or her body. Despite the book's outdated language, this is a thorough and sensitive account of a religion that holds enormous spiritual power for many Haitians.
                                                                                           LML

734   De Soto, Hernando. ***The Other Path: The Invisible Revolution in the Third World.*** Pref. by Mario Vargas Llosa. HarperCollins 1989, $22.95 (0-06-016020-9); $14.00 (0-06-091640-0). 288pp. Nonfiction.

De Soto, a Peruvian businessman and the director of the Institute for Freedom and Democracy (ILD), offers a fresh look at the underground economy in Peru. An advocate of free-market capitalism, De Soto is critical of government regulations that have hampered economic growth and made it impossible for the poor to buy homes and start businesses. In response to these pressures, he notes, poor people have created a parallel economy: They take over unused land to build makeshift shelters, set up stands as illegal street vendors, and run informal bus lines. In some cases, public health and safety have been jeopardized (particularly by the illegal buses), but these enterprises have also demonstrated the creativity and resilience of impoverished migrants to the city who manage to carve out a life for themselves and their families. Extrapolating from his case study in Lima, De Soto calls for reduced government regulation, less dependence upon the United States, and increased support for local free-market initiatives.

De Soto makes a powerful argument, one that is remarkably free of polemics. He takes into account both left-wing and right-wing positions and shows that, while each side has contributed something to the debate, together they have ultimately fallen short of devising a workable solution and new approaches are needed. For those looking to understand Latin American development, as well as the situation of the poor in urban areas, his book cannot be ignored.   LML

735   Ferguson, James. ***Dominican Republic: Beyond the Lighthouse***. Monthly Review 1992, $10.00 (0-85345-853-7). 150pp. Nonfiction.

The lighthouse mentioned in the title is a monument built to commemorate the five hundredth anniversary of Columbus's landing on the island of Hispaniola, which the Dominican Republic shares with Haiti. In this book, however, the author takes the reader beyond the pleasing facade of tourist spots to survey the current status of Dominican politics and economics. The island nation's economy has been hampered by its dependence upon foreign capital and markets, especially in the sugar industry and in tourism, its two most important sources of revenue. Many Dominican families are supported by remittances from relatives living in the United States.

The author traces the history of the Dominican Republic from the nation's wars of independence against Haiti and then Spain, its occupation by the United States, the long and brutal dictatorship of Trujillo, and the domination of politics since 1961 by two men, Joaquin Balaguer and Juan Bosch. Today, both men are elderly and near retirement. The author concludes with a hopeful look at popular movements capable of stimulating real Dominican democracy and forcing the government to build an economy devoted to the well-being of the people.   LML

736   Fernandez, Ronald. ***The Disenchanted Island: Puerto Rico and the United States in the Twentieth Century***. Greenwood 1992, $45.00 (0-275-94096-9). 264pp. Nonfiction.

Puerto Rico has been a dependency of the United States since its conquest in 1898. The relationship between the island and its mainland master has been governed by two often contradictory desires on the part of the United States. First, businesses have seen the island and its people as a source of cheap land and labor, available for exploitation and profit. Second, fearing that it would be branded a colonial power, the U.S. government devised a special "commonwealth" status for Puerto Rico, giving islanders a number of benefits that have made them more prosperous than any other people of the Caribbean.

Yet the price paid for U.S. citizenship, food stamps, and other welfare benefits has been the loss of political autonomy, the suffocation of Puerto Rican identity by U.S. culture, and an imported educational system. Many islanders who have resisted mainland domination have experienced suppression at the hands of U.S. and Puerto Rican officials. The author advocates Puerto Rican autonomy, either through independence or a grant of statehood that respects the islanders' unique heritage.   LML

737   Fuentes, Carlos. ***The Buried Mirror: Reflections on Spain and the New World***. Houghton 1992, $34.00 (0-395-47978-9); $24.95 (0-395-67281-3). 399pp. Nonfiction.

Spain's relationship with the Americas is the subject of this historical and cultural essay by the prominent Mexican novelist, author of *The Death of*

Artemio Cruz (see main entry). Fuentes first focuses on indigenous cultures before the arrival of Columbus and on Spain at the time of his voyage. He then explores interactions between Spain and the Americas over the next four centuries, up to the point at which virtually all of Latin America had won its independence. A brief chapter on Spain, Latin America, and "Hispanic U.S.A." concludes the narrative. Fuentes tells his story through many references to works by Spanish and American artists and writers, providing an intellectual history that is eloquently written and accessible to general readers. Numerous prints and reproductions grace this finely made book. An extensive list of sources, mostly in Spanish, is included. LML

LATIN AMERICA AND THE CARIBBEAN

738 Galeano, Eduardo. ***Memory of Fire: Vol. I: Genesis; Vol. II: Faces and Masks; Vol. III: Century of the Wind***. 3 vols. Trans. from Spanish by Cedric Belfrage. Pantheon 1988, $15.00 each (0-394-74730-5; 0-394-75167-1; 0-394-75726-2). 320+304+320pp. Essays.

In exploring the history of the people of Latin America, Galeano spins a new type of history that defies classification by genre—a literary creation that is a kaleidoscopic amalgam of historical fact, epic, essay, and political narration. He selects, combines, and transforms events recorded in almost a thousand primary sources, over ninety percent of which were originally written in Spanish.

In Volume I, *Genesis*, Galeano begins with the myths of creation as contained in ancient texts. He then covers the period between 1492, when Columbus arrived in the Americas, and 1700, when the death of King Charles II of Spain signaled an end to a dynasty marked by exploration and conquest. Volume II, *Faces and Masks*, covers 1701 to 1900; and Volume III, *Century of the Wind*, addresses the twentieth century up to1986. In this trilogy, Galeano has created a new and original way of approaching Latin America, one that presents the continent's story from the historical perspective of its peoples and cultures. CM

739 Galeano, Eduardo. ***Open Veins of Latin America: Five Centuries of the Pillage of a Continent***. Trans. from Spanish by Cedric Belfrage. Monthly Review 1973, $10.00 (0-85345-308-X). 320pp. Nonfiction.

Born in Uruguay, Galeano has long been a voice of the Americas, a region that, he reminds us, includes all of North, Central, and South America. Written in 1973, this indictment of foreign exploitation has become a classic. The book begins at the moment Columbus lands in the Americas. Subsequent Spanish conquests of the Aztec, Mayan, and Incan civilizations led to the plundering of the natural resources of the continent: sugar, gold, tin, silver, copper, oil, coffee, fruit, and other assets. Galeano shows how the rulers of Spain and Portugal did not believe that the indigenous people were human; their belief legitimized slave labor and economic exploitation. However, in 1537, Pope Paul III issued a Papal Bull declaring that Indians were "true men." With their supply of native slaves cut off, the monarchies authorized the kidnap of blacks from Africa for import to Latin America. Indians, however, remained in bondage through the system known as *encomienda*; their treatment in modern society continues to be deplorable. Latin America, Galeano contends, exists only to serve the market economies of Europe and the United States. His arguments are compelling and serve to reveal, in part at least, the economic straits found today in the countries of Latin America. CM

740   Galeano, Eduardo. ***We Say No: Chronicles 1963–1991***. Trans. from Spanish by Mark Fried. Norton 1992, $22.95 (0-393-03150-0); $11.95 (0-393-30898-7). 296pp. Essays.

The title of this collection of thirty-four essays comes from the 1988 electoral campaign in Chile, when dictator Augusto Pinochet permitted a plebiscite and lost by a wide margin. His opponents mounted a campaign in which the simple word *no* became a battle cry among the people who demanded an end to fifteen years of repression.

The subjects of these essays, only a few of which have appeared previously in the United States, include Pelé, the Brazilian soccer superstar; Pu Yi, the last emperor of China; Che Guevara, the Cuban revolutionary; and Juan Domingo Perón, ruler of Argentina. Galeano also provides his unique perspectives on issues facing Guatemala, Brazil, Venezuela, Bolivia, Argentina, Chile, and Nicaragua. He explores the problems of writers in exile and the rise of fascism in Latin America. He deconstructs Columbus's discovery of the New World, calling it an "invasion," and analyzes how rulers in Latin America have compromised democracy through their reigns of terror. One provocative essay is "Ten Frequent Lies or Mistakes about Latin-American Literature and Culture," and another especially beautiful piece explores the work of Brazilian photographer Sebastião Salgado.

In a previous work, *Open Veins (see main entry)*, Galeano explores five centuries of repression in Latin America. In these essays, he updates his opinions with insightful examples from the present day. This perceptive writer uses biting irony to destroy the fictions that he feels have distorted the truth for too long.   CM

741   Guillermoprieto, Alma. ***Samba***. Knopf 1990, $19.95 (0-394-57189-4); Random $11.00 (0-679-73256-X). 256pp. Nonfiction.

Mexican-born journalist Guillermoprieto writes of the period—almost a year—during which she lived among the residents of the Mangueira *favela* (slum) located on a hillside above Rio de Janeiro. Most of Mangueira's residents work at insecure, low-paying jobs in the city below. For them, the annual Carnival, which takes place just before Lent, is the high point of their lives. This book describes the favela residents as they prepare for Carnival. Each of Rio's neighborhoods puts on a performance of music and dance known as *samba*. All year long, samba schools train the residents, develop a theme for the performance, and select the principal performers. The performances are judged in a competition that participants take very seriously. The themes of the sambas may be political, religious, mythological, or drawn from popular culture.

The author explains how relationships among neighbors during the year contribute to highly charged internal politics at the samba school come Carnival time. At the same time, she reveals the hopes, dreams, and realities of some of Brazil's urban slum dwellers—those who fled drought and poverty in the northeast, only to find few opportunities in their new home. Guillermoprieto describes these people with respect and affection; among her most memorable characters are a struggling young couple eagerly awaiting the birth of their first child. The issue of race, the discrimination against blacks in Brazilian society, and the influence of African dance and music upon the samba are among the issues explored in this appealing ethnographic work.   LML

742 Hebdige, Dick. ***Cut 'n' Mix: Culture, Identity, and Caribbean Music***. Routledge 1987, $37.50 (1-85-178029-7); $11.95 (0-906890-99-3). 177pp. Nonfiction.

This book offers a history and cultural interpretation of reggae and other forms of Caribbean music. The author traces the varied roots of reggae in the music that slaves originally brought with them from West Africa. In modern times this music melded with religious music and with black American rhythms. The lyrics of reggae also have varied sources in Rastafarian religion, in radical Jamaican politics, and in youth cultures from around the Caribbean.

Reggae has had broad influence in the Caribbean and beyond, first among black Jamaican immigrants to the United States and Great Britain, and then, as the music was commercialized, among white youth throughout North America and Europe. The author describes successive waves of innovation and explains the impact of market forces upon the style and quality of reggae from the 1960s to the 1980s. This book offers an informed and sophisticated treatment of the dominant musical form of the Caribbean and reveals its seminal influence upon rap, hip-hop, and other forms of contemporary popular music.   LML

Herskovits, Melville J. ***The Myth of the Negro Past***.
See entry 158.

743 Hillman, Richard S., and Thomas J. D'Agostino. ***Distant Neighbors in the Caribbean: The Dominican Republic and Jamaica in Comparative Perspective***. Greenwood 1992, $45.00 (0-275-93927-8). 197pp. Nonfiction.

Both the Dominican Republic and Jamaica are poor countries that depend on larger and richer nations, especially the United States. Yet they have dealt with their problems of underdevelopment from different traditions. The Dominican Republic, part of the Hispanic Caribbean, has a presidential system, albeit one in which the military has often supported dictators. The weakness of Dominican democracy has made it vulnerable to influence by the United States, including influence through military intervention. Jamaica, by contrast, has a parliamentary system, derived from its history as a British colony. Democracy has been far more stable there; the military plays virtually no role in Jamaican politics.

Despite the differences in their governments, the politics of the two nations have been characterized by elite domination over weak peasant majorities and underorganized middle classes consisting largely of nonunionized workers. In both countries, the governments encourage U.S. investment to foster economic development. This book provides a valuable overview of politics and economics in two of the largest Caribbean nations and shows how cultural, political, and external factors affect their struggle to overcome legacies of dependence and underdevelopment.   LML

Hiro, Dilip. ***Black British, White British***.
See entry 834.

744 Hurston, Zora Neale. ***Tell My Horse***. Borgo 1990, $25.00 (0-8095-9020-4); HarperCollins $12.00 (0-06-091649-4). 304pp. Nonfiction.

Hurston, an African-American novelist who studied anthropology as an undergraduate at Barnard College in the 1920s, spent 1936 and 1937 in Haiti and

Jamaica. This book, first published in 1938, is an account of her impressions of the two islands and their peoples. In her rich narrative, Hurston uses language as powerfully as she does in her novels. She evokes both the lushness and the poverty of the islands, celebrating the strength with which Afro-Caribbeans face everyday life. The book explores in detail the rituals that define the islanders' relationship to divine power and to nature. The detailed descriptions of voodoo practices are presented matter-of-factly though eloquently, without the censorious tone that many writers adopt. This work is a compelling account of voodoo rituals and beliefs that remain a central element in Haitian and Jamaican culture to this day.   LML

745   James, C.L.R. ***The Black Jacobins: Toussaint L'Ouverture and the San Domingo Revolution.*** Random 1989, $14.00 (0-679-72467-2). 426pp. Nonfiction.

This classic work, originally published in 1963, is a history of the Haitian people's struggle to overthrow slavery and free themselves from the oppressive rule of Napoleonic France. The revolution was led by François Dominique Toussaint L'Ouverture, a coachman skilled in the art of warfare. He mustered a disciplined and well-trained fighting force of Africans and, at times, people of mixed race known as mulattoes. This band of revolutionaries defeated not only the French but the Spanish and English forces deployed against them and created for themselves a free and independent democratic state. They accomplished this goal without the support—let alone the blessing—of the United States, the first white democratic nation in the New World. For decades to follow, that lack of U.S. support would haunt the fledgling country. This book compares the institution of slavery as it was practiced in various regions of the Americas and traces Toussaint L'Ouverture's critical role in making it possible for the United States to purchase the Louisiana Territory from France.   AJWM

746   Kincaid, Jamaica. ***A Small Place.*** NAL 1989, $7.00 (0-452-26235-6). 96pp. Nonfiction.

Kincaid, a native of Antigua and a noted fiction writer, rages at the colonial exploitation of her homeland, describing the poverty, political corruption, and racism that have resulted but that the average tourist never sees, let alone considers. This brief book provides a strong sense of the physical beauty of the island's landscape and culture. It also offers insight into the thoughts of the islanders, seldom voiced, about the tourists who invade their land.

                                    HC

747   Kinzer, Stephen. ***Blood of Brothers.*** Doubleday 1992, $14.00 (0-385-42258-X). 368pp. Nonfiction.

New York Times reporter Kinzer describes his years in Nicaragua, from the 1979 fall of Somoza to just before the 1990 election, which saw the Sandinistas, victorious eleven years earlier, voted out of power by an overwhelming majority. Kinzer seeks to explain what the revolution was about, what it accomplished, and why it went sour. He argues that the Sandinistas' dictatorial tendencies were reinforced by the hard-line attitude of the Reagan administration, which tended to interpret all world events in light of Cold War geopolitics. The Reagan administration created and funded the *contras*, whose mission was to seize control of Nicaragua. Reagan staff also choked off internal opposition and silenced those policy makers who sought a middle ground. Kinzer notes that potential advocates for peace, such as Arturo Cruz or Cardinal Obando, abdicated their role by failing to condemn the documented atrocities committed by the contras. In Kinzer's analysis, the Sandinistas come across as inexperienced, dogmatic, and misguided, but the author praises Daniel Ortega and other leaders for their desire to help the Nicaraguan people. He notes, too, that the Sandinistas did what no other Nicaraguan regime had ever done: hand over power peacefully after losing an election. Above all, Kinzer's sympathies lie with the ordinary people of Nicaragua, whose lives were torn apart by war. Kinzer is a sensitive and authoritative writer of history, and his book is a fine discussion of these events.

A well-written though less even-handed account of the Sandinista Revolution is Shirley Christian's *Nicaragua: Revolution in the Family* (o.p., 1985), which portrays the Sandinistas as hard-line Communists from the outset. The essays contained in two books edited by Thomas W. Walker, *Nicaragua in Revolution* (Greenwood, 1981) and *Nicaragua: The First Five Years* (Greenwood, 1986), offer scholarly studies, mostly sympathetic, of the Sandinistas' accomplishments in education, health care, land reform, and other areas.   LML

748   Kinzer, Stephen, and Stephen Schlesinger. ***Bitter Fruit: The Untold Story of the American Coup in Guatemala***. Illus. Doubleday 1983, $11.95 (0-385-18354-2). 336pp. Nonfiction.

The authors, two respected U.S. journalists, explain that the current situation of political violence in Guatemala and Central America is the direct result of U.S. intervention in Guatemala's internal affairs during the Eisenhower administration. In 1945, inspired by democratic principles and the idealism of Roosevelt's New Deal, Guatemala enacted a new liberal Constitution. Its first president implemented much-needed land reforms and increased respect for human rights. When the second president, Jacobo Arbenz, took office in 1953, he enacted swift land reform, including government purchase of private land.

At the time, the United Fruit Company (UFCO), Guatemala's major employer and landowner, had deliberately lowered the assessed value of its land holdings to avoid higher taxes. Yet when the government offered to buy UFCO's property, the company inflated the value.

The conflict between government and business escalated. UFCO fed propaganda to U.S. newspapers linking Arbenz to a few Communists in the government. Added pressure came from Secretary of State John Foster Dulles and his brother Allen Dulles, director of the CIA, who both had financial stakes in UFCO. During this era, dominated by Senator Joseph McCarthy's ruthless campaign against communism, a nervous U.S. government decided to foment a coup. President Eisenhower personally approved the plan to install military strongman Castillo Armas as president. In 1954, the United States launched its assault against Guatemala, nicknamed "Operation Success." After Arbenz was deposed, democracy was destabilized, reforms were abolished, and anti-American sentiment rose. The authors of this well-researched and eye-opening study argue that the bitter fruit resulting from the Guatemalan coup includes a string of dictatorships and unrelenting political violence that continues to this day. CM

749   Knight, Franklin W. *The Caribbean: The Genesis of a Fragmented Nationalism*. 2nd ed. Oxford Univ. Pr. 1990, $45.00 (0-19-505440-7); $17.95 (0-19-505441-5). 416pp. Nonfiction.

This book calls attention to the experiences shared by the peoples of the various Caribbean island nations. These agricultural lands with their wonderful climates are often threatened by natural dangers such as hurricanes and earthquakes. The people here also share a heritage of having to endure the oppression of slavery and colonial rule. Arising from these natural and political forces is a distinctive Caribbean culture. The common people—the peasant farmers and impoverished urban workers—are the main shapers of that culture. In contrast, the elites, who came from the ranks of slaveowners and colonial rulers, tried to distinguish themselves from the masses by emphasizing their European traditions.

On many of the islands, the common people played a crucial role in winning independence from their colonial rulers. The Haitian and Cuban revolutions were propelled, the author argues, by a nationalism that was grounded in Caribbean culture. The political movements throughout the region continue to be marked by struggles between the masses, who draw their inspiration from local culture, and the elites who are more closely aligned with the economies and culture of Europe and the United States. HC

750   Knight, Franklin W., and Colin A. Palmer, eds. *The Modern Caribbean*. Univ. of North Carolina Pr. 1989, $45.00 (0-8078-1825-9); $14.95 (0-8078-4240-0). 382pp. Nonfiction.

The thirteen essays in this collection trace the development in the nineteenth and twentieth centuries of the Caribbean, a region that includes the numerous islands plus certain cultures found in mainland South and Central America. The first essay provides an overview of the historical sources for some of the broad regional similarities in economics, politics, and culture. Other essays discuss the historical developments that shaped the region—the Haitian slave revolution of 1791 to 1803, which inspired slaves throughout the hemisphere; the legacy of British and French colonialism; and the frequent military and economic interventions by the United States throughout the region.

A number of the contributors to this volume discuss the impact of slavery, colonialism, and U.S. domination on the development of Cuba, Puerto Rico, Jamaica, and Trinidad. These authors see Caribbean culture as the product of active efforts by the peoples of the region to come to terms with the class and racial divisions and national aspirations created by long histories of foreign oppression. LML

751   Krich, John. *El Beisbol*. Prentice 1990, $9.95 (0-685-46177-7). 272pp. Nonfiction.

A fanatical baseball devotee, Krich traveled to Mexico, Puerto Rico, the Dominican Republic, Nicaragua, and Venezuela to explore the state of the sport. In Latin America, teams are members of the Palm Tree League and they play their games in winter. As Krich explains, each country puts its unique spin on the sport. Possessing a good command of the Spanish language, Krich uses and explains the local baseball vocabulary in a delightful way. The book is a scattershot selection of free association, information, and a who's who in Latin American baseball, mingled with fast-paced comments on the social and political realities that affect the sport. The author concludes that baseball is truly a sport of all of the Americas.

Krich is also the author of *Why Is This Country Dancing?* (1993), a personal view of Brazilian music and dance. In that book he interviews various musicians and examines the indigenous and African roots of the samba, bossa nova, tropicalismo, and other musical forms.　　　　　CM

752　Lévi-Strauss, Claude. *Tristes Tropiques*. Rev. ed. Illus. Viking 1992, $15.00 (0-14-016562-2). 432pp. Essays.

First published in 1955, twenty years after the author worked as professor of philosophy in São Paulo, Brazil, this popular and unusual work attracted world attention. Lévi-Strauss, the French founder of structural anthropology, takes an eclectic approach in exploring cultures and communication by combining ethnographic exploration of indigenous peoples, first-person reflections, opinions, philosophy, history, and social commentary. The author traveled and lived among the Caduveo, Nambikwara, Bororo, and Tupi-Kawahib Indians and other indigenous groups and came to realize that they were already in danger of extinction. He cautions against what he sees as the development of a "monoculture," a mass civilization that would wipe out the unique characteristics of the peoples of the world. His ideas, developed sixty years ago, are prescient; today we are witnessing the very destruction he predicted. Four chapters omitted in previous translations are included in this edition. Photographs and drawings by the author add significantly to the reader's understanding.　　　　　CM

753　Levine, Barry, ed. *The Caribbean Exodus*. Greenwood 1987, $49.95 (0-275-92182-4); $18.95 (0-275-92183-2). 300pp. Nonfiction.

This collection of sixteen essays examines the migration of Caribbean peoples to the United States, Canada, and Western Europe. Migration began 150 years ago with the emancipation of slaves and increased geographic mobility. Several of the chapters explore how Mexican immigration to the United States set a pattern for later Caribbean immigrants and how recent changes in U.S. immigration laws affect patterns of immigration. Today Caribbean migrants often move back and forth between family homesteads in the Caribbean and jobs in North America and Europe.

Immigration law and opportunities for citizenship have a significant effect on the economic and cultural strategies adopted by migrants and their children. The liberalization of U.S. immigration quotas and policies since 1965 has vastly expanded the scale of Caribbean immigration, creating new communities of Caribbean peoples in many U.S. cities and easing the two-way movement of migrants and their children, not just between their old and new homes but between two cultures.　　　　　LML

754 Lewis, Gordon K. *Growth of the Modern West Indies.* Monthly Review 1968, $12.00 (0-85345-130-3). 512pp. Nonfiction.

This book examines the Caribbean islands that were once British colonies; it also covers Guyana and British Honduras (Belize), on the mainland of South America, which the author sees as being part of the West Indies. The author traces each colony's trek toward independence, beginning in the years after World War I, when the British began assisting the colonies to become viable independent nations. Among the main forces for independence were the political parties, which helped organize the people and which articulated their demands, first for autonomy and then for independence. The British heritage played a key role in determining the form of government adopted by each new nation, but local conditions and class divisions shaped the specific ideologies and programs. Finally, the author examines the efforts between 1958 and 1962 to establish a West Indies Federation; failure of the movement ensured that the new nations of the Caribbean would be small and would have weak governments. LML

755 Lewis, Oscar. *Five Families: Mexican Case Studies in the Culture of Poverty.* Frwd. by Oliver LaFarge. Basic Books 1975, $18.00 (0-465-09705-7). 364pp. Nonfiction.

Lewis, an anthropologist, is noted for his "culture of poverty" thesis, which argues that people in poor communities develop values, mores, and modes of survival that only serve to undermine their chances for success in mainstream society. The thesis has been a source of controversy; Lewis himself has questioned it in recent years.

In this early work, Lewis offers an intimate view of five families who came to Mexico City from rural areas; four live in poor urban slums, and the fifth moved away after becoming wealthy. In most cases, the families are in transition, unable to find a place in society to replace what they have lost. Lewis observes the breakdown of traditional religion, morality, and ways of life. The stories, which read like fiction, instantly draw the reader into the lives of the families. The author does not dwell on the lack of economic opportunities and the Mexican government's chronic neglect of the poor. Instead he focuses on individual foibles and community failures, providing insight into the sense of dislocation experienced by those who move from rural areas to the urban slums.

Lewis continued his explorations into the culture of poverty with *The Children of Sanchez* (orig. pub. 1961; Random, 1979), *A Death in the Sanchez Family* (o.p., 1969), and *La Vida: A Puerto Rican Family in the Culture of Poverty— San Juan and New York* (o.p., 1965). LML

756 Lopez, Alfredo. *Doña Licha's Island: Modern Colonialism in Puerto Rico.* South End 1987, $30.00 (0-89608-258-X); $12.00 (0-89608-257-1). 200pp. Nonfiction.

This book presents the history of Puerto Rico since its conquest by the United States during the Spanish-American War in 1898. The story is largely one of colonialism and exploitation. After being used as a U.S. military base, by the 1920s Puerto Rico had become the provenance of U.S. sugar companies. Many peasants lost their land; either they became poor laborers or they could find no work at all. Discontent among the people over the relentless poverty and the ongoing U.S. control spawned a formidable independence movement in the 1930s, but the movement was weakened by a compromise engineered by Luís Muñoz Marín and his Popular Democratic Party. In return for accepting commonwealth status, Puerto Rico received generous aid and tax benefits from the U.S. corporations that built factories there.

Much of the book is devoted to describing the results for Puerto Rico of its modern dependence on the United States: It is the richest island in the Caribbean, but living standards are still far below those on the mainland. Furthermore, political debate is largely stifled, and advocates of independence are often repressed. The author advocates Puerto Rican independence as the only real solution to the island's political and economic problems.   LML

Mander, Jerry. *In the Absence of the Sacred: The Failure of Technology and the Survival of the Indian Nations.*
See entry 510.

757 Manley, Michael. *The Politics of Change: A Jamaican Testament.* Rev. ed. Howard Univ. Pr. 1990, $15.95 (0-88258-029-9). 223pp. Nonfiction.

In this book, written in 1973 during his second year as Prime Minister of Jamaica, Manley outlines his program for reform. The first part describes his belief that change requires an activist government that fosters equality through social welfare measures and, above all, provides an excellent education for all children. Once young people are offered the opportunity to succeed, he says, they will become self-reliant members of society with a desire to contribute to the public good and a willingness to set aside differences of class and race.

In the second part, Manley discusses issues of political strategy, explaining how multiparty democracy can mobilize both the dispossessed and the better-off people through a devotion to ideals of equality. Manley addresses the question of how to overcome the legacy of colonialism and the problem of continued interference by great powers in small nations such as his. This work is a compelling vision of political philosophy and action by an author who has played a central role in Jamaican politics as leader of its main socialist party since the 1960s. He is also the author of *The Poverty of Nations (see main entry)*.   LML

758 Manley, Michael. *The Poverty of Nations.* Westview 1991, $42.00 (0-7453-0314-5); $12.95 (0-7453-0449-4). 122pp. Nonfiction.

Michael Manley, who twice served as Prime Minister of Jamaica, attempted to forge a democratic socialist path to economic development for his nation. In this book, he provides a clearly written overview of academic and practical political approaches to the causes of underdevelopment in the Third World. He analyzes various strategies for improving conditions in countries that still suffer from the legacies of colonialism and from continuing economic domination by Europe, Japan, and the United States.

Manley views colonialism as only the most overt form of a worldwide system of capitalist exploitation of the Third World. The struggle for independence from colonial powers is one step in a longer process to win economic as well as political freedom. Defining a New International Economic Order as a precondition for genuine development, he finds fault with strategies that assume and encourage continued exploitation. He concludes with an agenda for change, reporting with modesty his own considerable role in Jamaican and international socialist politics. Manley is also the author of *The Politics of Change: A Jamaican Testament (see main entry).*   LML

759 Margolis, Mac. **The Last New World: The Conquest of the Amazon Frontier.** Norton 1992. o.p. Nonfiction.

Much of the recent interest in the Amazon has centered on the burning of the rain forest and its environmental impact. Among the books published on the subject are several biographies of Francisco "Chico" Mendes, the president of Brazil's rubber tappers union and an internationally acclaimed environmentalist, who was assassinated in 1988. In this book Margolis takes a broader view, looking at the conflicts over the rain forest as the culmination of centuries of exploration and settlement in the frontier regions of the Americas. Unlike the pioneers who developed the western United States more than a century earlier, the Amazon's developers must contend with environmentalists who want to save what is left of the continent's original ecosystem.

In weighing the issues, Margolis attempts to balance the planet's needs with those of a developing nation. Consequently there are few villains in his story. The author cites examples of ecologically sustainable development, which he feels represents the one source of hope for the future. His study, which reveals the problems Brazilians of all classes face, is a valuable contribution to the current debate over the preservation and use of the Amazon rain forest.   LML

760 Maslow, Jonathan. **Bird of Life, Bird of Death.** Dell 1987, $6.95 (0-440-50708-1). 249pp. Nonfiction.

In 1983, naturalist Maslow and photographer Michael Kienitz traveled to Guatemala in search of the nearly extinct quetzal, the iridescent green bird with long plumage and red breast that is sacred to the Maya and is a symbol of liberty to people in the region. The bird is increasingly difficult to locate because its habitat in the cloud forest—the upper layer of the rain forest—is being destroyed. Maslow sees the threatened extinction of the quetzal as a metaphor for the destruction of indigenous populations, who for centuries have revered the bird as a supernatural protector. The author describes his book as "political ornithology," a combination of Mayan and Spanish history, travelogue, political observations, and detailed descriptions of quetzal sightings. Maslow also contrasts the quetzal, the bird of life, with the vulture or *zopilote*, the bird of death; the vultures' number is increasing dramatically as they vie with children for food in dumps and feed on human carrion, the result of slaughter by the brutal Guatemalan regime.

Maslow analyzes the current political situation and the human rights abuses reported by Amnesty International, which has branded Guatemala as the country with the worst human rights record in the Western Hemisphere. His encounters with Indians include their stories of terrifying repression, torture, disappearances, and murder in a country that can no longer be represented by the Mayan symbol of freedom, the quetzal.   CM

McWilliams, Carey. **North from Mexico: The Spanish-Speaking People of the United States**.
See entry 428.

761   Meiselas, Susan, ed. **Chile from Within, 1973–1988**. Texts by Ariel Dorfman and Marc Antonio de la Parra. Illus. with photos. Norton 1989, o.p. Photos/ Essays.

Seventy-five photos by sixteen photographers, all Chilean except for one from the United States, document life and events in Chile. The book covers the era from the election of President Salvador Allende in 1970 through the September 11, 1973 coup by the military junta and the subsequent dictatorship under Augusto Pinochet, ending with the plebiscite in 1988 in which Chileans repudiated Pinochet and fifteen years of repression. During the dictatorship, the photographers witnessed and documented horrific and tragic daily scenes: police abductions, the ubiquitous military presence, the homeless, soup kitchens, the results of torture, demonstrations against repression, and vigils for the "disappeared." Extensive notes accompany the photos. Ariel Dorfman's essays from the *New York Times*, the *Los Angeles Times*, *The Nation*, the *Washington Post*, and the *Village Voice* are included along with excerpts from two novels and an epilogue. These texts were written by authors in exile, which adds to the sense of hopelessness, disbelief, and horror arising from the suspension of democracy, the imposition of a police state and curfew, and the loss of human rights. The photographs evoke the events and the emotions of life in Chile under the dictatorship.   CM

762   Morales-Carrion, Arturo. **Puerto Rico: A Political and Cultural History**. Norton 1984, $12.95 (0-393-30193-1). 400pp. Nonfiction.

This volume explores the emergence of the Puerto Ricans as a people with a distinct identity, one that was forged in part as its residents resisted the efforts of outsiders to subordinate the island. As a Spanish colony, Puerto Rico's cultural and political heritage was largely molded by Spain. But it was also profoundly influenced by the struggles of African slaves for freedom and the quest by the people of neighboring islands to win their own independence from Spanish rulers.

Twentieth-century Puerto Rican history has seen the evolution of a mixed-race, dependent society under the rule of the United States. North American aid has transformed the island economically while creating a multifaceted culture that absorbs powerful influences from the United States and struggles to sustain an independent identity. This volume is unique among histories of Puerto Rico in its emphasis on culture as a source both of national identity and of political action.   LML

Nabhan, Gary P. **Enduring Seeds: Native American Agriculture and Wild Plant Conservation**.
See entry 516.

763   **Nunca Más: The Report of the Argentine National Commission on the Disappeared**. Farrar 1986, o.p. Nonfiction.

Argentina's history of repression began under Juan Perón, who set up a modern police state during his years of rule (1946–1955 and 1973–1974). After his death and a brief presidency by Perón's widow, Isabelita, a military junta took over in 1976, leading to an era of political and economic instability. The junta leaders dissolved the Congress, appointed their own justices to the Supreme Court, ignored Argentine law, suspended human rights, and declared a "dirty war" against terrorists and "subversive thinkers." Tens of thousands of ordinary citizens were systematically abducted, thousands were tortured, and almost nine thousand were "disappeared" (secretly murdered) by a state that many described as morally depraved and out of control.

This book compiles thousands of graphic accounts of abduction, torture, and murder into what Ernesto Sábato, chairman of the Argentine National Commission on the Disappeared, calls an "encyclopedia of horror." The commission was established by Argentine president Raúl Alfonsín, who was elected in 1983 after the military lost the war with Britain over the Malvinas (Falkland) Islands. This loss, coupled with economic stagnation and the rising chorus of human rights protests, brought about the restoration of democracy. The book is frightening to read, and the enormity of the brutality against human beings is difficult to comprehend. By exposing the truth, the commission sought to ensure that torture and murder would never again be used by Argentina or any other country.

More recently, *Uruguay: Nunca Más* (Temple Univ. Pr., 1992), a similar report on human rights abuses in Uruguay, has been published in English.

CM

764 Oppenheimer, Andres. *Castro's Final Hour*. Simon & Schuster 1993, $13.00 (0-671-87299-0). 480pp. Nonfiction.

This book interprets events in Cuba from 1986 to 1992. The author argues that the collapse of the Soviet Union as the leading Communist world power has fatally undermined Castro's regime in Cuba, making inevitable his downfall and the failure of communism in the island nation. The author interviewed Cuban government officials, dissidents, and common people. In addition, he spoke with many Cuban exiles in Miami and with allies of Cuba from the Sandinista government of Nicaragua and Manuel Noriega's regime in Panama.

The interviewees blame Cuba's troubles on Castro's rigid communist ideology. They also note his grandiose sense of self-importance, which led him to eliminate capable subordinates, most notably General Arnaldo Ochoa Sánchez, the hero of Cuban military intervention in Angola. Castro's inability to tolerate dissent and his execution of Ochoa, a popular proponent of liberalization, on trumped-up charges of corruption and drug trafficking have undermined support for the Cuban leader and his policies. This well-written and absorbing work presents one side of the debate over Castro and the Cuban revolution.

LML

765 O'Shaughnessy, Hugh. *Grenada: An Eyewitness Account of the U.S. Invasion and the Caribbean History that Provoked It*. Dodd 1984. o.p. Nonfiction.

In 1983 the United States invaded Grenada, a tiny Caribbean island that had won independence from Great Britain nine years earlier. Grenada's movement toward independence was led by Eric Gairy, who became increasingly erratic and dictatorial after rising to become the new nation's prime minister. Gairy was opposed by the socialist New Jewel Movement, led by Maurice

Bishop and Bernard Coard, who deposed Gairy in a coup in 1979. Seeking to reduce Grenada's economic dependence upon the United States, Bishop's government accepted aid from Cuba, most notably to expand the island's airport in hopes of increasing tourist traffic.

In the process, Grenada earned the unrelenting hostility of the Reagan administration. Pressure from the United States weakened the island's economy, exposing tensions between Bishop and Coard and their factions in the New Jewel Movement. Intraparty conflict culminated in Coard's arrest and murder of Bishop. The United States used Bishop's death as the grounds for invading the island. The author, a British journalist, provides a vivid and comprehensive history of the island and concludes by arguing that the U.S. invasion not only served to retard economic development and democracy in Grenada but was illegal under international law. LML

766 Parry, J. H., and others. *A Short History of the West Indies.* 4th ed. Illus. St. Martin 1988, $29.95 (0-312-00442-7); $27.99 (0-312-00443-5). 352pp. Nonfiction.

The modern societies of the West Indies were built by imported peoples from Europe and Africa who cultivated plants and animals brought from the Old World. Well into the twentieth century, the islands remained tied to, and dependent upon, Europe, and they became increasingly dependent on the United States. The island economies prospered only insofar as they could produce goods marketable in Europe and North America. With the exception of Haiti, the islands remained colonies of great powers through the nineteenth century, and even after independence they retained the political forms bequeathed by their former rulers and were subject to various forms of intervention by the United States.

This book provides a clear and comprehensive history of the islands from Columbus's arrival to the 1960s. The narrative is punctuated with wars, revolutions, and political transitions from colonialism to independence. The authors present the ecological, economic, and social contexts in which the great events of Caribbean history occurred and explain how societies with a high degree of cultural diversity emerged out of the struggles with foreign political dominance and economic dependence. LML

767 Paz, Octavio. *Labyrinth of Solitude: The Other Mexico, Return to the Labyrinth of Solitude, Mexico and the U.S.A., The Philanthropic Ogre.* Trans. from Spanish by Lysander Kemp. Grove 1989, $11.95 (0-8021-5042-X). 398pp. Essays.

Born in 1914, Paz became one of Mexico's and Latin America's most important literary figures. Poet, essayist, critic, writer, and diplomat, he was influenced by the Mexican revolution of 1910, the Spanish Civil War, surrealism, Marxism, existentialism, Buddhism, and Hinduism. His essays, metaphysical in style, pose major questions about the character, history, culture, and politics of Mexico. Many of them explore what it means to be a Mexican.

His writing can be difficult, especially when he combines the metaphysical and the poetic to frame an issue. However, much of his work is accessible. He addresses such issues as the "otherness" of Mexico; the need to criticize the country in order to bring about change; and the need to return through the labyrinth to the indigenous origins of Mexico and to its myths so as to integrate the past with the present. He examines as well the horrible effects of racism on the culture. The importance of the revolution to Paz is that it acknowledged the pre-Columbian Indian past of Mexico. He views artistic creativity, tolerance, freedom of the spirit, and love as radical forces that can overcome solitude and lead to the restoration of community.   CM

768 Poniatowska, Elena. *Massacre in Mexico*. Intro. by Octavio Paz; with poems by Rosario Castellanos; Trans. from Spanish by Helen R. Lane. Univ. of Missouri Pr. 1991, $16.95 (0-8262-0817-7). 352pp. Nonfiction.

On October 2, 1968, police and the army in Mexico City opened fire on a student protest in the Plaza de las Tres Culturas in Tlatelolco, killing dozens of protesters and bystanders. Poniatowska, a noted Mexican novelist, chronicles this tragedy through interviews with student leaders, witnesses to the shootings, and ordinary Mexicans. The book traces the repression to events that occurred long before the shootings, including the imprisonment and torture of protest leaders and the fomenting of violence by government provocateurs. Through the interviews, the reader comes to know some of the principal people involved—idealistic youngsters from poor families, the first in their family to attend university; mothers who took pride in their children's accomplishments, only to see their children imprisoned or killed; and teachers who found themselves incarcerated alongside their pupils. A variety of Mexican and foreign journalists offer their insights; their witness is contrasted with the official Mexican government version of what happened. Poems by Rosario Castellanos (written especially for this book), by other major Latin-American poets, and by the prisoners round out this gripping documentary presentation.   LML

769 *Popol Vuh: The Definitive Edition of the Mayan Book of the Dawn of Life & the Glories of Gods and Kings*. Trans. and edited by Dennis Tedlock. Illus. Simon & Schuster 1986, $10.95 (0-671-61771-0). 416pp. Nonfiction.

The *Popol Vuh* is considered the most important text in the original native language in the Americas, a masterpiece of religious and philosophical writing that guides the Quiché Indians to this day. Known as the *Mayan Book of Counsel,* it is critical to a complete understanding of the Mayan people. This translation is unique: During his research in the Guatemalan highlands, the editor became an apprentice to a Mayan "daykeeper" who instructed him in the *Popol Vuh*. Tedlock's introduction clearly explains the meaning and purpose of the book. The original text was written in hieroglyphics; the first alphabetic version was created by indigenous authors between 1554 and 1558. The work reemerged two centuries later when a friar named Francisco Ximenez translated the Quiché text into Spanish. In this translation, hieroglyphics copied from Mayan funerary vases and other sketches and photographs by the translator provide a visual-element text that brings it closer in feeling to the original hieroglyphic version.

The *Popol Vuh* tells the story of the Mayan gods and the creation of the Earth, plants, animals, and humans, who are formed from corn, the basis of all life. It provides a clear vision of the universe and a way to foresee the future, understand the past, and perceive the divine in all human activity. The alphabetic manuscript of *Popol Vuh* has been in the collection of the Newberry Library in Chicago since 1911.   CM

770   Riding, Alan. ***Distant Neighbors: A Portrait of the Mexicans.*** Random 1989, $11.00 (0-679-72441-9). 352pp. Nonfiction.

Riding, a U.S. journalist, has written an overview of Mexico's history, culture, and society. He begins with the pre-Columbian era, arguing that the ethos of the Aztecs and other ancient indigenous groups continues to affect this *mestizo* (mixed-race) nation, although Spain's legacy also continues to hold powerful sway. Much of the book examines Mexico's political history, exploring, for example, how the revolution that began in 1910 became institutionalized, giving Mexico an extraordinarily stable one-party system. Finally, Riding examines the rise of the mass media and the influence of the United States, forces that portend change in Mexico's future.

Riding's work is comprehensive and readable, offering a strong introduction to a study of Mexico. It is also a critical look at the Mexican character. Many of its insights are based on Octavio Paz's classic *The Labyrinth of Solitude (see main entry)*, a work that can profitably be read in conjunction with *Distant Neighbors*. A bibliography of books in English and Spanish and an index are included.   LML

771   Rogozinski, Jan. ***A Brief History of the Caribbean: From the Arawak and the Carib to the Present.*** Illus. Facts on File 1992, $24.95 (0-8160-2451-0); NAL (0-452-01134-5). 256pp. Nonfiction.

Beginning with the first known islanders, the Arawak and the Carib Indians, this book traces the complex and colorful history of the region. The author reexamines Columbus's arrival, European domination, the islands' ongoing struggle for political and economic independence, and U.S. intervention in Cuba, Grenada, Haiti, and the Dominican Republic. The highly readable narrative offers information about the colonial plantation system, the pirates who frequented the area, the natural environment, and tourism today. This information is complemented by numerous black-and-white photos, maps, tables detailing economic and demographic change, and a section of suggestions for further reading. It is a comprehensive, though at times rambling, study of the Caribbean area and its people, one that will appeal to general readers.   HC

772   Romero, Oscar. ***Voice of the Voiceless: The Four Pastoral Letters and Other Statements.*** Trans. from Spanish by Michael J. Walsh; Intros. by Ignacio Martin-Baro and Jon Sobrino. Orbis 1985, $14.95 (0-88344-525-5). 208pp. Essays.

On March 24, 1980, Archbishop Oscar Arnulfo Romero of El Salvador was assassinated while delivering a homily during a Mass commemorating the death of a friend a year earlier. Under the leadership of Colonel Carlos Umberto Romero and José Napoleón Duarte, El Salvador's record of violence and human rights violations was escalating, rivaled only by the bloody events in Guatemala. At one point the government began targeting the Catholic Church for repression, and Romero became an enemy of the state.

This book includes the major writings and homilies of Archbishop Romero from the time he was elevated by the Vatican to Archbishop of San Salvador in 1977, the year Carlos Romero rose to power, until his death a few years later. Because Oscar Romero had not been a political gadfly prior to 1977, it was widely believed that he would remain neutral on political issues. On attaining the status of archbishop, however, Romero became an advocate for the poor and oppressed and demanded that his government curb the death squads and end the horrifying torture and violence. Included in this collection are four pastoral letters to his congregation in San Salvador; his address at Georgetown University on receiving an honorary doctorate for human rights work; a pastoral message to the National Council of Churches; the Louvain Address; his letter to then-President Jimmy Carter asking that the United States stop contributing to the violence by cutting off military aid and stopping all direct or indirect intervention in El Salvador; and the final homily on the day of his death. The simplicity with which Archbishop Romero delivered his message of truth gave voice to those who had been silenced through murder, torture, and repression, not just in his country but in all of Central America.   CM

773   Rosenberg, Tina. ***Children of Cain: Violence and the Violent in Latin America.*** Viking 1992, $12.50 (0-14-017254-8). 404pp. Nonfiction.

Despite the title, which implies an intrinsic connection between Latin Americans and violence, this is an even-handed, readable introduction to a variety of interrelated political problems. Rosenberg takes the unusual approach of exploring the broad issues by interviewing individual Latin Americans, who reveal, in their own words, their personal hopes and failings and those of their societies.

The six chapters address a series of topics: the drug war in Colombia and the government's inability to stop it; the psychology of a torturer in Argentina; the poverty and government neglect in Peru that has sparked a fanatical guerrilla movement; the hedonistic, walled-off lives of the "Fourteen Families" in El Salvador; an idealistic Sandinista who found the burdens of governing to be far more complex than winning the revolution; and a former socialist in Chile who, while enjoying the economic boom under Pinochet, shut his eyes to continued poverty and human rights abuses. While other works go into more detail on individual countries, Rosenberg conveys a great deal of complexity and insight in a few pages, thus offering a solid overview of the problem of violence in the region.   LML

774   Sale, Kirkpatrick. ***Conquest of Paradise: Christopher Columbus and the Columbian Legacy.*** Knopf 1990, $30.00 (0-394-57429-X); NAL $14.00 (0-452-26669-6). 453pp. Nonfiction.

Columbus's arrival in the Americas transformed both Europe and the New World. Wealth from the Americas allowed a number of European nations—most notably Spain, France, and England—to become world powers and to launch a sort of capitalism that eventually made a majority of their citizens wealthier than any people in human history. European culture moved to the forefront to dominate the Americas and then the world.

The Americas, however, were transformed even more profoundly by these events. The author traces the ways in which the vast wildernesses were destroyed, plant and animal species wiped out, and the pre-Columbian natives largely exterminated and their cultures obliterated by the invading Europeans. In the process, the new settlers created new civilizations for themselves. As they began conceiving of themselves as Americans, they honored the memory of Christopher Columbus, turning the history of his voyages into a legend of the discovery of paradise. Sales's book— one of several revisionist histories that challenge long-established perceptions of Columbus's voyage— is written for a general audience and offers a readable, powerful, and highly opinionated narrative. LML

775 Scheper-Hughes, Nancy. ***Death Without Weeping: The Violence of Everyday Life in Brazil.*** Univ. of California Pr. 1992, $29.00 (0-520-07536-6); $15.00 (0-520-07537-4). 614pp. Nonfiction.

The author, an anthropologist, first traveled to Brazil in 1964 as a Peace Corps volunteer. She returned to Alto do Cruzeiro, a town in Brazil's northeast, in 1982 and again in 1989. In this book she describes the lives of the town's poorest inhabitants and the social forces that have kept them poor.

Scheper-Hughes challenges the "culture of poverty" thesis advanced by Oscar Lewis, author of *Five Families (see main entry)*. She argues that poor Brazilians, migrants from rural areas, have a culture that preserves their community and offers some emotional protection for their harsh lives. The core of the book focuses on child death and its meaning for the women. Fated to lose half of their children because of unsanitary water, insufficient food, substandard housing, and inadequate care (most of the women have to work soon after giving birth), mothers perceive certain babies as "wanting" to die. Children do not receive names or command the affection of their parents until they have survived the first year. This book documents the cruel consequences of a society based upon inequality. Scheper-Hughes is passionate and compelling in her portrayal of the misery of those left out of Brazil's economic "miracle." LML

776 Shumway, Nicolas. ***The Invention of Argentina.*** Univ. of California Pr. 1991, $38.00 (0-520-06906-4). 352pp. Nonfiction.

After an era of great prosperity, Argentina became a poor and despotic country again during the twentieth century despite its vast lands, agricultural potential, natural resources, and highly literate population. The author attributes the country's many political and economic problems today to the myths about Argentina created by nineteenth-century intellectuals.

This book focuses on the period between 1808 (just prior to Argentina's independence in 1816) and 1880. Written for an English-speaking audience that does not have specialized knowledge of Argentina, Shumway's book adds much to our knowledge about the current realities of that country with a thorough examination of its intellectual and political leaders. Through careful research, the author supports his "guiding fictions" theory and depicts the leading intellectual leaders and political leaders—with all their strengths and their faults—in a highly readable manner.

Shumway begins with Mariano Moreno, staunch advocate of independence from Spain. He discusses the "gauchesque poets" Bartolomé Hidalgo and José Artigas, who championed the idea of separate and equal provinces that could trade and flourish and that would be governed through a radical democracy in which leaders derived power from the people they served. Other key figures include Bernardo Rivadavia, who established economic policies that concentrated land in the hands of a few, built up foreign debt and dependence on foreign capital, and identified with the high culture of Europe; Juan Manuel de Rosas, the nineteenth-century dictator who prefigured Juan and Eva Perón; Juan Bautista Alberdi and Domingo Faustino Sarmiento of the "Generation of 1837"; and Bartolomé Mitre, whose written history of Argentina ensured that certain myths and historical figures would be firmly entrenched.   CM

777   Skidmore, Thomas E., and Peter H. Smith. *Modern Latin America*. 3rd ed. Oxford Univ. Pr. 1992, $19.95 (0-19-507649-4). 480pp. Nonfiction.

In the latest edition of this classic work, Skidmore and Smith present a history of the Americas from the 1880s to the early 1980s. They theorize that definable economic and social patterns will generally predict typical political outcomes, at least in the larger countries profiled: Argentina, Chile, Mexico, Cuba, Peru, and Brazil. Examining Latin America in terms of its dependency and modernization, the authors link the United States and other First World nations to the development of the middle class and to democratic reforms in the region. U.S. interests are a recurring theme, and there is discussion of the NAFTA agreement, which the authors argue will strengthen ties between North and South America. Though not as detailed as *Neighbors in Turmoil* by James Cockcroft *(see main entry)* and written from a different perspective, this country-by-country analysis discusses such critical issues as Latin America in a post–Cold War context, emerging democracies, and capitalism. This edition also expands on the roles and contributions of women, the Church and its "theology of liberation," and the stereotypes and realities of Latin America and its people.
      CM

Spicer, Edward H. *Cycles of Conquest: The Impact of Spain, Mexico, and the United States on Indians of the Southwest, 1533–1960*.
See entry 530.

Steady, Filomena C., ed. *The Black Woman Cross-Culturally*.
See entry 1337.

Suzuki, David, and Peter Knudtson. *Wisdom of the Elders: Honoring Sacred Native Visions of Nature*.
See entry 532.

778   Thomas, Clive Y. *The Poor and the Powerless: Economic Policy and Change in the Caribbean*. Monthly Review 1988, $28.00 (0-85345-743-3); $14.00 (0-85345-744-1). 416pp. Nonfiction.

The vast majority of the people in the independent nations of the English-speaking Caribbean are poor. This book explains why those nations have developed economies dependent upon—and exploited by—the United States and Western Europe. The legacies of slavery and imperialism have been accentuated by forms of foreign investment and "aid" from the United States. Such aid, the author argues, is designed to keep the islands as sources of cheap labor and raw materials for multinational corporations from the richest nation.

The author explores various alternative development policies. He explains what the radical strategies proposed by socialist governments in Jamaica and Grenada attempted to accomplish. He also shows how underdevelopment, combined with U.S. political and economic intervention, helped sabotage those strategies. More-conservative approaches, fostered with U.S. aid, promote development that does little to ameliorate the poverty and the political powerlessness of most citizens of the island nations of the region.   LML

Thompson, Vincent B. *The Making of the African Diaspora in the Americas, 1441–1990.*
See entry 197.

779 Timerman, Jacobo. *Cuba: A Journey.* Trans. from Spanish by Toby Talbot. Knopf 1990, $18.95 (0-394-53910-9); McKay $9.00 (0-679-73631-X). 125pp. Nonfiction.

Timerman, a leading Argentine journalist who was imprisoned and tortured by that nation's military government, has been a long-time supporter of Cuba's right to develop without interference by the United States. He also spoke out against Castro's suppression of political opposition and took up the cases of several men imprisoned by the Cuban regime. In 1987, Timerman visited Cuba for the first time. This book records his impressions of that brief trip.

Timerman found a cynical Cuban public. Although the Cuban government had created an educational system that has eliminated illiteracy, only a limited range of books, mostly imported from the Soviet Union, were sold in Cuba, and writers were severely censored. At the time of Timerman's visit, the Soviet Union was demanding that Castro reform his regime. Yet, few Cubans believed that even the threat of losing Soviet subsidies would affect Castro. Cuba, to Timerman, appears mired in a stalemate created by the Cuban public's passivity and Castro's rigidity. The possibility of peaceful reform that preserves the best of Cuban socialism appears remote, both to Timerman and to the Cubans to whom he gives voice in this well-written book.

Earlier, Timerman traveled to Chile to record life in that country under the Pinochet dictatorship; his thoughts during the trip appear in *Chile: Death in the South* (Knopf, 1987).   LML

780 *Torture in Brazil: A Shocking Report on the Pervasive Use of Torture by Brazilian Military Governments, 1964–1979, Secretly Prepared by the Archdiocese of São Paolo.* Ed. with Intro. by Joan Dassin; Trans. from Spanish by Jaime Wright; Frwd. by Philip Potter, General Secretary of the World Council of Churches, 1972–1984; Pref. by Archbishop of São Paulo, Cardinal Paulo Evaristo Arns. Random 1986. o.p. Nonfiction.

Published in 1986 by the Archdiocese of São Paulo, this book draws on transcripts from over seven hundred cases that were tried in the Brazilian military courts between 1964 and 1979 to document how 1,843 people were subjected to torture. When a dictatorship was installed in 1964, Brazil's military waged a war against any opposition. Torture became a state-authorized means of repression, taught in military classrooms and sanctioned by the courts. This horrifying account, intended to promote democracy and to stop any reoccurrence of torture, murder, and the abridgment of human rights, was completed by thirty-five researchers who worked in secret to prevent government retaliation.

The book is divided into five parts: an explanation of the 283 methods of torture by 444 individual torturers; description of the origins of the military dictatorship; a profile of those tortured; the illegal use of the courts; and the 242 places of torture. The report also contains indexes listing the names of those who died under torture and of "the disappeared." In 1979 an amnesty was declared by the government to prohibit investigation into the use of torture. This book makes the point that there cannot be a moral amnesty.

An account of how this book came into being and the heroic actions of those involved is the subject of Lawrence Weschler's *A Miracle, a Universe (see main entry)*.   CM

781   Trouillot, Michel-Rolph. ***Haiti: State Against Nation: The Origins and Legacy of Duvalierism***. Monthly Review 1989, $28.00 (0-85345-755-7); $12.00 (0-85345-756-5). 288pp. Nonfiction.

Trouillot, a Haitian and a professor of anthropology at Johns Hopkins University, efficiently covers a broad range of Haiti's history, from the period before independence through the country's ill-fated elections of 1987. He develops the thesis that the Duvalierist state emerged from a long-term historical process, marked by a widening gap between political and civil society. This split reached its apex during the Duvalier era, creating a polarized society divided into two parts: the authorities and everyone else. Trouillot maintains that in this environment the peasants, who make up the bulk of Haitian society and provide the bulk of the labor, were the most disenfranchised group.

The book also explores the mechanisms through which the Duvaliers ruthlessly won and held onto power for twenty-nine years. Trouillot documents the damage that their regime inflicted on Haitian society and assesses its legacy since their departure. He ends with a plea to integrate the soul of Haiti—the peasantry—more closely into the nation's political life.

This well-written and convincing scholarly study contains an extensive bibliography, index, and notes.   HC

782   Urrea, Luis A. ***Across the Wire: Life and Hard Times on the Mexican Border***. Illus. with photos by John Lueders-Booth. Doubleday 1993, $9.00 (0-385-42530-9). 190pp. Nonfiction.

Tijuana, the chaotic Mexican border town twenty minutes from San Diego, is the setting for this book. Urrea focuses on poverty—unromanticized, terrifying, revolting, putrid, and relentless. For some people, such as those who live in the garbage dumps, the poverty persists for a lifetime.

Born in Tijuana to a Mexican father and an American mother, Urrea is a bilingual, bicultural Chicano. From 1978 to 1982 he worked with a Baptist missionary, Father Von, whose philosophy was to act, not to preach. They brought food, delivered clothing, built houses and churches, washed children, provided emergency medical care, and listened to—and made friends with—the poor. Many of Tijuana's residents will never be able to cross the border into the United States. Most are Mexican, but there are thousands of refugees from poverty, war, and repression in other countries of Central America. Urrea's prose is blunt, direct, and compassionate. The author regards every person as valuable and worthy of time and attention. These are narratives of ordinary people who wanted their stories to be told so their lives would not be forgotten, so they would not remain invisible simply because they live in poverty. The myths people hold about the poor, and about Mexican and illegal aliens, are shattered by the mirror of this book, a mirror from which we cannot look away.   CM

Viola, Herman J., and Carolyn Margolis, eds. *Seeds of Change: A Quincentennial Commemoration*.
See entry 537.

783   Weschler, Lawrence. *A Miracle, a Universe: Settling Accounts with Torturers*. Pantheon 1990, $22.95 (0-394-58207-1); Viking $9.95 (0-14-015844-8). 304pp. Nonfiction.

The question of what to do with former torturers and how to achieve justice for their victims has dogged a number of democratically elected Latin American governments in recent years. Weschler recounts two attempts to address this issue. One is the clandestine publication in 1986 of *Torture in Brazil*, a report on the atrocities of the military government between 1964 and 1976, compiled by the Archdiocese of São Paulo *(see main entry)*. Weschler's account of the difficult publication process focuses on Presbyterian minister Jaime Wright, who is the work's translator, one of its principal compilers, and the brother of an activist killed by the military. The second attempt is the 1989 referendum in Uruguay on the government's amnesty for human rights violations between 1972 and 1985. Through interviews with Uruguayans on all sides, Weschler examines what happened during the years of military dictatorship and why the referendum ultimately failed.

This is a movingly written, well-documented, and thoughtful account of a complex issue. Weschler reveals the tragedy of those years and, in the voices of the Latin Americans themselves, offers insights into the recovery, not only of individual victims, but of the society as a whole, to prevent such crimes against humanity from happening again.   LML

784   Wilentz, Amy. *Rainy Season: Haiti Since the Duvaliers*. Simon & Schuster 1990, $9.95 (0-671-70628-4). 427pp. Nonfiction.

Amy Wilentz, a young writer and reporter, provides a journalistic account of the events in Haiti prior to the fall of the Duvalier government in 1986 and after Jean-Claude "Baby Doc" Duvalier's departure. She describes how the Haitians' hope for change turned first to disappointment and then to despair when it became clear that the dictator's fall was leading not to reform but to chaos and stagnation. Moving on to 1989, Wilentz covers the political, economic, social, and religious developments on the island. Central to her discussion is Jean Bertrand Aristide, the radical Catholic priest and spiritual leader of the opposition (and who, in 1994, was installed as president of the country). Amy Wilentz also points out the significance of voodoo in Haiti and the impact that it has on all areas and levels of society.

This is a personal account of her visits to Haiti and what she saw there, interspersed with historical background that fleshes out the events, people, and places of the drama that is Haiti. A bibliography and index are included.

HC

Williams, Eric. *Capitalism and Slavery*.
See entry 205.

785   Williams, Eric. *From Columbus to Castro: The History of the Caribbean, 1492–1969*. Illus. Random 1984, $16.00 (0-394-71502-0). 608pp. Nonfiction.

This work emphasizes the differences among the various Caribbean nations and the resulting fragmentation of the region into political units that the author regards as being too small to foster the necessary economic development. The Caribbean's diversity is a result of its settlement by various European powers, each of which ensured that settlers could profit only by providing for the particular needs of their colonial rulers. Although slavery was the dominant form of labor on most of the islands well into the nineteenth century, the slave systems and the postemancipation forms of labor control varied with the types of commodities produced on each island. National politics developed first to emancipate slaves and then to win independence for each island. Today, the opportunities for economic development are still limited by the legacy of slavery, by racial conflict in the islands, by the continued intervention of the United States (although that has helped Puerto Rico and some of the other islands to achieve rapid growth during the 1960s), and by political fragmentation. According to Williams, only if and when the Caribbean nations overcome racism and unite will the region achieve economic and political modernization.   LML

786   Wright, Ronald. *Stolen Continents: The Americas Through Indian Eyes Since 1492*. Illus. Houghton 1992, $22.45 (0-395-56500-6); $12.70 (ISBN 0-395-65975-2). 448pp. Nonfiction.

At the time of Columbus's arrival, the Americas were inhabited by perhaps a hundred million people who populated cities and formed kingdoms that rivaled in scope and power those of their European invaders. The Amerindians were defeated by diseases that the Europeans brought with them and for which the indigenous people had no immunity. Within a century waves of epidemics killed more than half the population. The indigenous people lost control of their lands and of their destinies.

The book's three sections tell the history of the European conquest, of the Amerindians' life under Spanish and British colonialism, and of their life in the twentieth century in the nations established by the settlers' descendants. Each part of the book has five chapters, one each devoted to the Aztec, Maya, Inca, Cherokee, and Iroquois. This work is notable for presenting history from the perspectives of five Amerindian peoples. Making use of extensive sources written by and about Amerindians, the author spins a compelling narrative that draws together much recent scholarship and rarely accessed documents of peoples and cultures suppressed—but not fully eliminated—by the European conquest of the Americas.   LML

BIOGRAPHY

787 Cabezas, Omar. *Fire from the Mountain: The Making of a Sandinista.* Frwd. by Carlos Fuentes; Aftwd. by Walter LaFeber. NAL 1986, $9.00 (0-452-26276-3). 240pp. Autobiography.

Cabezas, a former Sandinista guerrilla and government official, tells how he became a guerrilla fighter and describes his experiences in the mountains battling the Somoza regime. His account is frank, lively, and filled with humor. He traces the events that led him to convert to the Sandinista cause while a university student. When his commanders ordered him to go into the mountains, he was excited at first, but soon he discovered cold, hunger, poison ivy, and mountain leprosy. He also met *campesinos* (peasants) who welcomed him into their modest homes and gave him the courage to keep fighting for the cause that would make their lives better.

Cabezas's work is one of the most readable accounts of life as a guerrilla. He explores the process by which one detaches himself from the everyday world of family, friends, and personal concerns to enter a dangerous realm where the collective struggle outweighs the needs of the individual and the only goal is victory. Although set in Nicaragua in the 1970s, this book offers insight into the minds of rebels and warriors everywhere. LML

Cofer, Judith Ortiz. *Silent Dancing: A Partial Remembrance of a Puerto Rican Childhood.*
See entry 435.

788 Herrera, Hayden. *Frida: A Biography of Frida Kahlo.* Illus. HarperCollins 1984, $20.00 (0-06-091127-1). 528pp. Biography.

Wife of the great Mexican muralist Diego Rivera and an accomplished painter in her own right, Frida Kahlo was a central figure among Mexican intellectuals in the mid-twentieth century. Active in the Communist Party, she had a brief affair with Leon Trotsky during his exile in Mexico. Her paintings reflected themes of violence and mutilation that sprung from personal experience: When she was nineteen, Frida was badly injured in a bus accident in Mexico City. The accident left her in constant pain and unable to bear children. Her body slowly deteriorated, and she died in 1954 at the age of forty-seven.

Herrera's biography, deeply felt and vividly written, includes a number of Frida's personal letters. Also featured are black-and-white and color plates of her work, which the author analyzes extensively in the context of the artist's life. Although he does not discuss her husband Rivera's work to any extent, Herrera does offer information about their social circle and the life of Mexico's intellectuals in the first half of the twentieth century.

Readers seeking more information about Rivera should read his autobiography, *My Life, My Art* (Dover, 1992) or Bertram D. Wolfe's adulatory biography, *The Fabulous Life of Diego Rivera* (Madison, 1990). LML

Galarza, Ernesto. *Barrio Boy.*
See entry 436.

789 Menchú, Rigoberta. *I, Rigoberta Menchú: An Indian Woman in Guatemala*.
Trans. from Spanish by Ann Wright. Routledge 1985, $44.95 (0-86091-083-0);
$13.95 (0-86091-788-6). 252pp. Autobiography.

Recipient of the Nobel Peace Prize in 1992 and now living in exile in Mexico,
Menchú, a Quiché Indian, recounts the birth of her political consciousness
and commitment to protecting the way of life of Guatemala's twenty-two
indigenous groups. Her account begins in 1978, when she was twenty. The
government-sponsored terror of the time resulted in the torture and murder
of her brother, mother, and father in separate army actions.

At the time of the government's war against its Indian citizens, Menchú
spoke only Quiché, but eventually she learned Spanish so that she could
defend her people in the language of their oppressors. After leaving Guate
mala and fleeing to Paris, Menchú conducted twenty-four hours of taped
interviews in Spanish with anthropologist Elisabeth Burgos-Debray. She sees
her testimony as representative, not just of the Indians in Guatemala, but of
all indigenous groups throughout the Americas who suffer under a government policy of genocide. Reading the *Popol Vuh (see main entry)* will enhance
the reader's understanding of Menchú's narrative. She recounts the daily life
and customs of the Indian in Guatemala for whom corn (maize) is the basis of
life and for whom relationships with nature are crucial.   CM

790 Padilla, Heberto. *Self-Portrait of the Other: A Memoir*. Trans. from Spanish by
Alexander Coleman. Farrar 1990, $19.95 (0-374-26086-9). 220pp. Autobiog-
raphy.

Padilla, a prominent Cuban poet and novelist, was an early supporter of
Castro. When the revolution triumphed in 1959, Padilla was living in exile in
New York. He returned immediately and was given diplomatic posts that took
him to London, Paris, and Moscow. In Moscow he befriended antiestablish-
ment poet Yegveny Yevtushenko and had many discussions about Stalinism,
freedom, and the direction of Castro's Cuba. He began to see the totalitarian
direction of Castro's rule, his cult of personality, and his whims that destroyed
lives. Upon his return to Cuba, he published a controversial volume of poetry
and finished the manuscript of a novel, which police alleged he gave to a
Chilean diplomat who was expelled from Cuba in 1971. This was the beginning of seven years of imprisonment, house arrest, and persecution, culminating in Padilla's own expulsion from his beloved land. Padilla describes in
harrowing detail his torture in prison and Castro's visit while he was in the
hospital recovering from his injuries. He also details the international campaign of writers that led to his release. Although the narrative begins slowly,
Padilla's self-portrait offers insight into the leftist Latin American literary
scene and the dilemmas that idealistic writers faced when Cuba's struggle for
liberation turned out to be merely another form of oppression.   LML

791 Perera, Victor. *Rites: A Guatemalan Boyhood*. Harcourt 1986, $15.95 (0-15-
177678-4); Mercury House $12.95 (1-56279-065-X). 192pp. Autobiography.

Perera is a Guatemalan-American journalist and the author of *Unfinished Conquest: The Guatemalan Tragedy* (Univ. of California Pr., 1993), a chronicle of
human rights abuses under the Guatemalan military. Here he offers the story
of his childhood in Guatemala City, told in a series of thematically related

vignettes. As the child of a wealthy Jewish family, the author, renamed Jaime Nissen (real names have been disguised to protect the people discussed in the book), is aware of his status as an outsider. He must defend himself against the taunts of anti-Semitic classmates; at one point he is "baptized" by the drunken father of a friend. He also becomes aware of the class distinctions separating his family from the mass of poor Guatemalans, most of whom he only sees as servants in his family's household but with whom he occasionally has more uncomfortable encounters. Dictatorship and revolution figure in his childhood consciousness, from the military regime that is imposed upon his elite private school to family members and school friends who join the opposition. Tragedy is never far from view. His younger sister goes insane. One of his best friends dies of leukemia, and another commits suicide after the Arbenz government falls. A younger cousin, who becomes an outspoken right-wing figure, dies in a gruesome boating accident that some suspect to be the work of leftists. This slender, well-written, and accessible work describes what it was like to grow up Jewish and wealthy in Guatemala in the middle of the twentieth century.   LML

792   Quirk, Robert E. *Fidel Castro.* Norton 1993, $35.00 (0-393-03485-2). 898pp. Biography.

This massive biography presents Fidel Castro as an elemental figure, a man whose unquenchable desire for attention and acclaim propelled him into politics. From an early age, Castro was a demanding person with a magnetic personality. However, his early efforts in sports, in society, and in school politics were failures. Castro achieved success in what initially seemed a quixotic effort to overthrow Cuba's long-time dictator, Fulgencio Batista. Once he became the "maximum leader" of Cuba, he pursued his vision that his people would achieve a degree of communist reform and economic development unequaled by any other nation in the world.

Coming to power at the height of the Cold War, Castro received ample Soviet backing for his plans to raise Cuban educational levels and health standards and to make Cuba a major military power. However, his economic-development movement was largely a failure. Opposition to Castro, even from sympathetic friends, was met with repression. With the fall of the Soviet Union, the weaknesses of Castro's regime were exposed. The book provides considerable background on Cuba and its place in world events; nonetheless, the author attributes all of that nation's present problems to flaws in Castro's character.   LML

793   Revkin, Andrew. *The Burning Season: The Murder of Chico Mendes and the Fight for the Amazon Rain Forest.* NAL 1994. o.p. Biography.

Francisco "Chico" Mendes, a third-generation rubber tapper in Brazil's southwestern Amazon province of Acre, rapidly rose in the 1980s to become the leader of the rubber tappers' union and an internationally acclaimed environmentalist. In December 1988, he was killed by a violent family of ranchers whose attempts to slash and burn the rain forest he had thwarted.

Revkin's biography traces the events of Mendes's life and his accomplishments as a political activist. It places those events in the context of the broader issue of the destruction of the Amazon rain forest. He explores the rain forest's importance, both for the rubber tappers and for the world as a whole, and he embraces Mendes's personal cause: the creation of protected reserves. Although this well-written book is largely sympathetic to its subject, it presents Mendes as a multidimensional figure with flaws as well as strengths.

After Mendes's death, several other books about his work were rushed into print. Adrian Cowell's *Decade of Destruction* (Doubleday, 1991) was written to accompany his excellent documentary film on the destruction of the Amazon rain forest. The book, which devotes considerable space to the making of the film, is more of interest to the film's viewers than to readers who want information about Mendes or the environmental issue. Alex Shoumatoff's *The World Is Burning: Murder in the Rain Forest* (Avon, 1991) offers another perspective on Mendes's life but is marred by an excessive focus on the biographer's own life, travels, and thoughts. LML

794 Timerman, Jacobo. ***Prisoner Without a Name, Cell Without a Number***. Trans. from Spanish by Toby Talbot. Knopf 1981, $12.50 (0-394-51448-3); Random $10.00 (0-679-72048-0). 176pp. Autobiography.

Born in 1923 in Ukraine, Timerman and his family moved to Argentina, a nation of many immigrants, in 1928. Eventually he became a distinguished journalist and the editor/publisher of *La Opinión*. His newspaper, which confronted many factions of the complex political scene in Argentina, advocated democracy, human rights, tolerance, and an end to all terrorism. In 1976, President Isabel (Isabelita) Perón was ousted in a military coup. Having been in power previously, between 1966 and 1973, the military was already primed to unleash a terrifying repression based in part on Nazi beliefs. According to military officials, the start of World War III was at hand and Argentina was to be the main battleground. Estimates are that from 1976 to 1982 as many as 30,000 people were murdered in what became known as the government's "dirty war." Argentina became a country where being a Jew was defined as a "category of guilt." Timerman, targeted as an outspoken critic of the military junta, was abducted in 1977, tortured, and detained for two years in three clandestine sites, two legal prisons, and under house arrest. He was never convicted of any crime, and the Supreme Court found no basis for his arrest. During his detainment he endured anti-Semitic acts at the hands of his interrogators and torturers. In 1979 his Argentine citizenship was revoked and he was exiled to Israel. His book allows readers to understand in a limited way the horror of Argentina during these years and Timerman's double victimization as both a government opponent and a Jew. CM

Villaseñor, Victor. ***Rain of Gold***.
See entry 443.

795 White, Timothy. ***Catch a Fire: The Life of Bob Marley***. Rev. ed. Henry Holt 1989, $13.95 (0-8050-1152-8). 400pp. Biography.

Bob Marley, the preeminent figure in reggae music, was an enigmatic individual. However, through in-depth interviews, research, and skillful writing, author White paints an intimate portrait of the man and his work. Coverage begins with the events surrounding Marley's birth and continues to the full flowering of his manhood and his musicianship. His creative legacy, perpetuated largely by his son Ziggy, is also examined. In the first two chapters, the author discusses in depth the milieu that informed Marley's thinking and his music, including Jamaican culture and belief systems, the influence of Marcus Garvey, and the cultlike religion of Rastafarianism that arose around King Haile Selassie I of Ethiopia. Interwoven throughout the book is a discussion of Jamaica's troubled music business and of reggae's influence on politics. All of this material is presented in rich prose grounded in White's ability to catch the flavor and essence of the Jamaican dialect. The reader comes away with a deep sense of Marley the man as well as a great deal of information about reggae music. This is a riveting and compelling biography. A discography, an extensive bibliography, and an index are included. HC

7
BRITAIN AND IRELAND

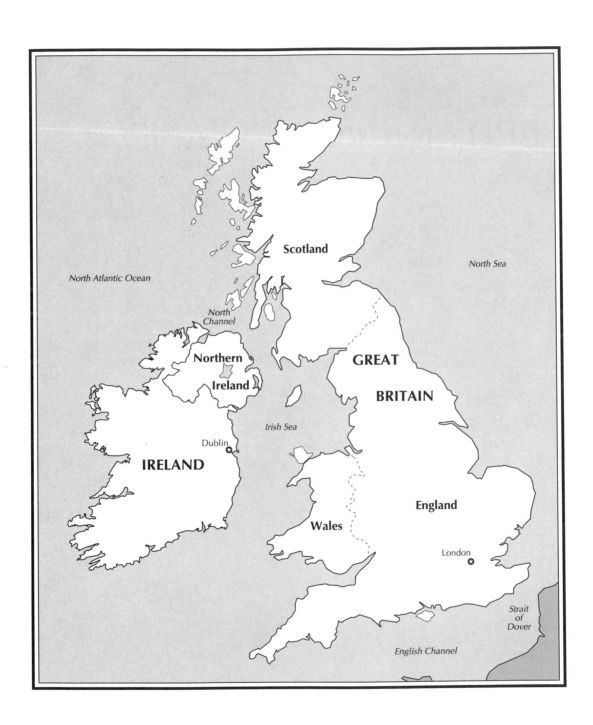

7

Britain and Ireland

by Anju Kapur

During the twentieth century, Great Britain granted independence to many of its colonies. As a consequence, there have been tremendous shifts in population. People from far-flung regions that were formerly part of the British Empire migrated to and settled in Great Britain. This influx is producing significant changes in the cultural landscape. For example, multicultural writing has become an established and vital part of British publishing. Much of this work reexamines the history of the empire from the hitherto suppressed perspectives of the people who had been colonized. In the process, two goals are achieved. First, the writers retrieve their people's own history from the obscurity to which it had been consigned. Second, they challenge the notion that domination by foreign powers always, and in all ways, results in progress and the rise of "civilization." The title of Remi Kapo's book, *The Savage Culture*, reflects this attitude; the book takes an ironic look at what the author calls the savagery that often resulted from imperialist conquest by a supposedly enlightened nation. Similarly, much of the writing by multicultural authors challenges and redefines the concepts of Britain and Britishness.

Until the latter part of the twentieth century, the general homogeneity of Britain's population meant that little attention was paid to interethnic concerns or relationships among races. In contrast, writers in Ireland have long recognized that ethnic differences and hierarchies deeply affect their culture and their politics. Moreover, recent writings by immigrants have fostered awareness of issues of race, class, and ethnicity. In addition, the increased availability of writing by women authors has brought the dimension of gender to this debate.

As Britain's first colony, Ireland has a political history that is closely intertwined with its cultural politics. The colonial experience—a central issue in books about Irish history, society, and culture—is a theme that connects the works of Irish writers with those of other immigrant authors now living in Britain. However, it is an oversimplification to regard the Irish as a marginal or oppressed people in the way that immigrants to Britain from Pakistan or Jamaica might be so considered. The presence of these latter groups in Britain is a result of the disruptive forces of colonialism. In contrast, the Irish were essentially a conquered people who continued to live in their original country, alongside their conquerors, as subjects of the victorious nation. As such, they had much in common with other groups such as the Native Americans, whose land was taken over by white settlers; the Mexicans, whose territory north of the Rio Grande was annexed by the United States during the war of 1848; and the black South Africans, who constitute a majority of the people but who, until the dismantling of apartheid, had little power or autonomy within their native land. For most of the Catholic Irish, this situation changed with independence in 1921, but the conflict continues in British-controlled Northern Ireland.

Similarities and differences among immigrant and colonized groups provide a thematic framework that permits a revealing evaluation of multicultural works. These issues map out the political terrain on which a battle to redefine British identity is taking place. Such issues include colonialism, postcolonialism, and neocolonialism; nationhood and national identity; race and ethnicity; political mobilization; and gender and sexuality. The texts described in this chapter are divided into fiction, nonfiction (primarily history, political science, and sociology), and biography and autobiography. Much of this writing takes a revisionist approach, challenging traditional perceptions of British life and society.

FICTION, POETRY, AND DRAMA

The stories and themes found in the typical English novel, which began to blossom in the late eighteenth and early nineteenth centuries, were products of several factors. Industrialization and colonialization led to increased economic wealth and the rise of a middle class. Increasingly, there was conflict between the middle class and the aristocracy above it and the working class below. This class struggle is reflected in the works of Charles Dickens and many other nineteenth-century writers and is also found in the works of George Orwell a century later. In contrast, the Irish novel emerged out of a climate of social and political upheaval. Rather than depicting the struggle between aristocrat and bourgeois, these works explore the cultural impact of political events. Stories by writers such as Liam O'Flaherty, Edna O'Brien, and Julia O'Faolain unfold against the backdrop of the Irish resistance movement, the problems within the Catholic Church in Ireland, and the situation of women in a society where divorce and birth control are still matters of enormous controversy. Bernard MacLaverty's *Cal* offers a poignant look at "the Troubles" and the tragic dilemmas they continue to pose in Northern Island. There are also writers like John Banville, a cosmopolitan writer whose novels explore the connections between Ireland and the rest of Europe. The novels of Mary Lavin often downplay the turbulent struggles within Ireland and instead explore the life of the settled middle classe.

Novels by immigrant writers focus on such themes as the experience of racism and the challenges of surviving in a hostile social environment. The women in Buchi Emecheta's novel *Second-Class Citizen* confront a social structure based not only on colonial oppression but also on local patriarchal domination. Such writers transform their experience of racism into fictional form, thereby exploring the concept of nationalism and challenging the image of British civilization. However, exploring the conflict with British society is not the exclusive focus of these novels. The works of George Lamming, Samuel Selvon, Buchi Emecheta, and Joan Riley reveal the immigrant world and at the same time reflect its relationship to the larger society.

NONFICTION

In writing their own histories and questioning the standard narratives of imperialism, the Irish and the immigrants in Britain are redefining the boundaries of society. Works that present an Irish perspective on such issues and events as the Irish Republican Army (IRA), the Easter Rising of 1916, independence, partition, religious divisions, and cultural chasms reveal the role of colonial intervention in shaping the Irish psyche. These books destroy the negative stereotypes about the Irish, stereotypes that were fomented by colonialists as part of the effort to justify and maintain their subjugation of the people. Similarly, books such as *A Savage Culture* analyze the links between the breakup of the empire and the rise of modern British nationalism. In this book—essentially a political psychology of British racism—Kapo argues that the loss of imperial power has fostered in many Britons a nostalgia for their former glory; that nostalgia is expressed as domination over the ethnic peoples now living within their own borders. Under such circumstances, nationalist ideology easily becomes confused with racial ideology; "British" becomes synonymous with "white." But, as Paul Gilroy argues in *There Ain't No Black in the Union Jack*, it is indeed possible to be both British and black. (It's worth noting here that, in Britain, the term "black" is sometimes used to refer to people from India and Pakistan as well as those from Africa. This chapter will also use the term in that way, unless a distinction needs to be made.)

In challenging the imperialist mentality, Kapo and other authors, including Rozina Visram, Amrit Wilson, and Dilip Hiro, have written histories of blacks in Britain. These writers agree that colonization created a huge reservoir of cheap local labor that Britain tapped for its industrial development. The black diaspora is a legacy of the dissolution of that empire. In *Ayahs, Lascars and Princes*, Visram describes how the Indian community in Britain emerged and developed between 1700 and 1947, the year that India gained its independence. During this period, many Indians came to England as servants (*ayahs*) and sailors (*lascars*) or as students and visiting princes. Many returned to India, but others remained. In *Black British, White British*, Hiro describes how, after independence, large numbers of Africans, Afro-Caribbeans, and Indians moved to Britain as cheap labor, often taking jobs that the white British refused to accept at such low wages. In *Finding a Voice*, Amrit Wilson points out that most immigrants were men who intended to return home after making enough money to survive in their native countries. However, because they could only find low-paying jobs, they were forced to stay longer than they had planned. Those who were married and had children sent for their families to join them. British racist attitudes prevented the immigrants from assimilating into mainstream society, so those who wished to start families while living in England had to send for women from home. Paradoxically, the author argues, racist British attitudes were responsible for an influx of Asian women and children and thus an increase in the immigrant population.

The permanent presence of blacks in British society, argues Paul Rich in *Race and Empire in British Cities*, shaped internal patterns of race relations and led to the rise of segregation in the cities. As Trevor Carter shows in *Shattering Illusions*, these patterns also led to the equation of race with class. It is often true, he argues, that, by many measures, being black in Britain is synonymous with membership in a lower social class. But he points out that such a simplistic formula ignores the gaps that also exist between the white working classes and the immigrants. Although these groups live at the same social level, the relationship between them is uneasy at best. The essays in Peter Braham's anthology *Racism and Antiracism* resist the temptation to oversimplify the links between race and class. Instead the writers in this volume examine such complex issues as the presence of racism within trade unions, union policy on immigration, and the unions' complicity in confining black workers to poorly paid and less-desirable jobs. A study by Trevor Jones, *Britain's Ethnic Minorities*, reveals that, even thirty years after their arrival, the first wave of immigrants from the Caribbean and the Indian subcontinent still have a lower standard of living than the white population. The author also points out, however, that immigrant groups are increasingly taking advantage of educational opportunities as a means of escaping the ghetto.

The availability of books dealing with these and other issues has raised public awareness and prompted government action. In *Communities of Resistance*, Ambalavaner Sivanandan analyzes the impact of that intervention. According to the author, one consequence is that the ideologies of the left have been co-opted by the establishment. As a result, the fight against racism has moved from the streets to the town halls and committee rooms. The struggle became a fight for culture and ethnicity; the battleground shifted from racism on the institutional level to racism on the personal level.

The essays in Bhiku Parekh's collection, *Colour, Culture, and Consciousness*, examine the role of the immigrant intellectual. In their home countries, these intellectuals often identified with British culture. As residents of Britain, however, they often encounter racism, despite their high levels of education and their contributions to the nation's economy and culture. In consequence, they become critical of British society and develop a stronger identification with their own people. In his contribution to Parekh's book, Dilip Hiro contends that immigrant intellectuals develop a "minority-mindedness," an increase in consciousness that helps them identify with all minority groups and work toward creating a unified approach to their common problems.

Similarly, Irish historians have begun to focus on global colonial patterns and to present the Irish situation within this larger framework. Richard Rose, in *Northern Ireland: Time of Choice*, points out the similarities in Britain's colonization of Ireland and America; for example, Ulster and Virginia were both settled as plantations chartered by the English crown in the same year, 1607. In *The Unresolved Question*, Nicholas Mansergh shows how the creation of partitions within countries is a chief characteristic of British imperial withdrawal from such colonies as India, Nigeria, Canada, Cyprus, and South Africa.

J. Bowyer Bell, in *The Irish Troubles: A Generation of Violence*, discusses Ireland between 1967 and 1992 in light of other regions of world conflict, such as Palestine and South Africa. From this large overarching framework, he examines the Anglo-Irish Agreement and the resulting institutionalization of violence. He wisely cautions against oversimplifying the situation; Belfast, he argues, is not Beirut. Thomas Gallagher's *Paddy's Lament* further enlarges this framework. Gallagher's research reveals that Irish peasant resistance to British rule did not arise in isolation but instead drew inspiration from revolutions in France and the United States. In contrast to the stereotype that portrays Irish peasants as passive and unconcerned about world events, books like Gallagher's reveal that the peasants were indeed aware of, and participants in, global political movements.

BIOGRAPHY AND AUTOBIOGRAPHY

The biographical and autobiographical works annotated in this chapter reflect an effort to revisit and reinterpret history through the actions of prominent individuals. In *Selections from Cultural Writings* (David Forgacs and Geoffrey Nowell-Smith, eds.; Harvard Univ. Pr., 1985), Antonio Gramsci points out that autobiography can stand alongside the political or philosophical essay: "Autobiography certainly has a great historical value in that it shows life in action and not just as written laws or dominant moral principles say it should be." Vivid and personal views of events, such as the Irish resistance movement, can be found in the autobiographies of Sean O'Casey and Sean O'Faolain and in the memoirs of Kathleen Clarke. Such works do not regard the individual as the sole agent of history. Instead, the individual and history are intertwined, each acting upon and reacting to the other. Similarly, the life stories of Eamon de Valera, Michael Collins, Charles Parnell, Kitty O'Shea, Maud Gonne, Douglas Hyde, Roger Casement, James Conolly, and Eoin MacNeill reexamine the concept of self. These works increase insight into Irish history because they analyze, often in minute detail, events and issues that may have been ignored in traditional histories. For example, the political relationship between de Valera and Collins and the role it played in the formation of the Irish nation comes across more vividly in biographies of these men than it does in most standard history texts.

To date, black-immigrant writing from Britain has produced comparatively few autobiographical and biographical works. Remi Kapo's *A Savage Culture*, Ved Mehta's continuation of his life story in *Up at Oxford*, and *The Scarlet Thread*, an immigrant woman's account narrated to Rachel Barton, are the only three such texts described in this chapter. These works explore the life of the individual within the contexts of nation, state, and empire, and address the related issues of race, class, and gender.

Many books by mainstream Western authors are written in the voice of an impersonal narrator who purports to be speaking objectively. In contrast, postcolonial texts often reject this literary device; instead, the authors place value on identifying and speaking from their own specific historical and cultural perspectives. The use of an obviously partisan narrator is a device that serves to blur rigid distinctions of genre. Sivanandan's *Communities of Resistance* addresses the larger topic of black cultural studies, but the author begins the book with a personal account of his life in Sri Lanka, his immigration to Britain, and how he began his immigrant life as a tea boy in the same library where he is now a librarian. By drawing no boundaries between the events of his life and his theoretical position, political activism, and intellectual activity, the author thus produces a work that blends autobiography with history and social commentary.

Readers will no doubt notice that many mainstream works of British fiction, poetry, history, and biography are virtually absent in this chapter. Such works are more than adequately covered in other sources that do not have a multicultural focus. Occasional exceptions to this rule include Bill Bryson's amusing and popular history of the English language, *The Mother Tongue*, and Martin Gilbert's biography of Winston Churchill, who was himself a highly regarded mainstream historian and who is considered to be twentieth-century Britain's greatest political leader.

Unless otherwise indicated, all annotations in this chapter are by Anju Kapur.

LITERATURE

796 Banville, John. *The Book of Evidence*. Warner 1991, $8.99 (0-446-39253-7). 219pp. Fiction.

John Banville has been described as Ireland's most cosmopolitan writer. His work—particularly this novel—offers a view of Ireland that is often lost sight of in literature about the Irish struggle: a view of the settled, leisurely class in which the struggle has been peripheralized. This book explores the strong connections between the Irish people and the Irish-American community and depicts the world of Irish art collectors in California and on the Riviera. The story reminds the reader that Ireland exists outside the context of its historical struggles, that a cosmopolitan, urban, bourgeois Ireland is very much a reality.

Some critics claim that the Irish novel is still in its infancy. But Banville manages his craft in a mature and capable manner. In true Irish tradition, he chooses an unreliable narrator to tell the story; such playfulness leaves the reader wondering whether a murder indeed occurred or whether it is yet another of the narrator's fancies. This is a highly sophisticated work marked by a high degree of craftsmanship and experimentation with the elements of the genre.

Banville's other recent works include *Birchwood* (o.p., 1973), *Doctor Copernicus* (orig. pub. 1976; Random, 1993), *Kepler* (orig. pub. 1983; Random, 1993), *The Newton Letter* (Godine, 1987), and *Mefisto* (Godine, 1989).

797 Casey, Linda M., and Daniel J. Casey, eds. *Stories by Contemporary Irish Women*. Syracuse Univ. Pr. 1990, $32.95 (0-8156-2489-1); $14.95 (0-8156-0249-9). 160pp. Fiction.

The world of nineteenth-century story writers was one dominated by belief in the virtues of the rural world, of the security of marriage and family, of peasants dancing on Big House lawns. This world has vanished; the world of contemporary story writers is one of computerized offices, chic boutiques, fashionable lounges, and fast cars.

The pace of writing by Irish women increased in the mid-1960s. This development coincided with a change in women's self-perception and a questioning of traditional roles spurred by political, economic, and social upheaval. Two of these events were the ongoing civil war in the North and an unsettling alliance with the European Community, both of which accelerated the traumatic clash of traditionalism and modernism. The stories in this collection, which depict the impact of those changes on women and families, includes work by Helen Lucy Burke, Ita Daly, Mary Beckett, F. D. Sheridan, Clare Boylan, Anna Devlin, Mary Lavin, Maura Treacy, Rita Kelly, Lucille

Redmond, Una Woods, Emma Cooke, Fiona Barr, Julia O'Faolain, and Edna O'Brien. These writers tell stories about society in a state of flux, a nation that has experienced profound changes and that has yet to fully confront the taboo issues of divorce and contraception.

798 Dabydeen, David. *Disappearance*. Secker & Warburg 1993. o.p. Fiction.

This novel is a provocative and accomplished look at postimperial Britain, a rewriting of British history from the viewpoint of the colonized people at the margins of society. A Guyanese engineer, enthralled by his notions of British "civilization" and "antiquity," arrives in the village of Dunsmere to help shore up a stretch of the crumbling Kent coast. In time he becomes disillusioned by his encounter with a Britain in an advanced stage of social decay, a society that fails to fulfill his expectations. The pathos is supplied by the contrast between his hopes and his actual experiences. This is Dabydeen's second novel. His first, *The Intended*, was published in Britain in 1991.

799 Delaney, Shelagh. *A Taste of Honey*. Grove 1989, $8.95 (0-8021-3185-9). 87pp. Drama.

The author wrote this play at the age of eighteen; it earned rave reviews, was a huge success in London, won several national awards, and was made into a film. The story focuses on Jo, a working-class adolescent, and her relationship with the black sailor who gets her pregnant; the homosexual art student who moves into her apartment to take care of her during her pregnancy; her saloon-frequenting, fun-loving mother; and Peter, her mother's new husband. Jo moves within this economic and emotional whirlpool in a way reminiscent, according to Graham Greene, of another classic play of this era, John Osborne's *Look Back in Anger*.

800 Doyle, Roddy. *Paddy Clarke Ha Ha Ha*. Viking 1994, $20.95 (0-670-85345-3). 288pp. Fiction.

The narrator of this novel is ten-year-old Paddy Clarke, through whose eyes the author convincingly portrays life in a bleak and anonymous working-class Irish neighborhood. As the fighting between his Ma and his Da escalates, Paddy escapes by spending more and more time with his friends. He doesn't get along with his younger brother, Sinbad, but neither is he able to escape him. Paddy's verve and insight seem destined to be crushed by the narrow religious and social attitudes of his neighborhood and by the difficulties of escaping the poverty that afflicts his family and his neighbors.

The book won Britain's prestigious Booker Prize in 1993. Two of the author's earlier novels, *The Commitments* (Random, 1989) and *The Snapper* (Viking, 1992), were adapted for film. All of Doyle's writing has the cinematic qualities of vivid and engaging dialogue and rich and convincing descriptions of their Irish settings and characters.

801 Emecheta, Buchi. *Second-Class Citizen*. Braziller 1983, $8.95 (0-8076-1066-6). 175pp. Fiction.

This is the poignant story of a resourceful Nigerian woman for whom the term "second-class citizen" has many meanings. As a female child in Lagos, she must fight to overcome her mother's belief that girls do not need an education. Later she builds a career as a librarian in the American Consulate, but she must struggle against her husband's fears about having an educated wife. He then moves by himself to London to be educated, but he repeatedly fails his exams. The protagonist clashes with her in-laws, who are unwilling to let her join her husband. At last, she moves to London. There her black skin adds yet another meaning to her second-class status, but ironically, it is also in Britain where she is able to establish an independent life for herself.

The novel gives a vivid account of the race, class, and gender oppression encountered by black women both in Africa and in Britain. It introduces the reader to the lives of black immigrants in London, particularly to the life of the Nigerian community, and presents their perceptions of British society.

Emecheta's other novels include *The Bride Price* (Braziller, 1976), *The Joys of Motherhood* (Braziller, 1979), and *The Family* (Braziller, 1990).

802   Ishiguro, Kazuo. ***Remains of the Day***. Knopf 1989, $18.95 (0-394-57343-9); Random $11.00 (0-394-25134-2). 256pp. Fiction.

This novel was described by the *New York Times Book Review* as "one of the finest books of the year" and by the *Boston Globe* as "one of the best books of the decade." It is a compelling portrait of Stevens, a perfect English butler, and his fast-disappearing insular world in postwar Britain. After three decades of devoted service to the lord of Darlington Hall, Stevens takes his first motoring vacation through the country. On reflection, he comes to realize the political corruption, racism, and fascism that permeated Lord Darlington's life and life at the manor in general. He tries to reassure himself that he had been serving "a great gentleman," but doubts persist, leading him to reexamine his own life and his role in events at the manor.

Narrated with compassion and humor, the novel makes insightful observations on the persistence of aristocratic values in British society, the class clashes that result, and the ruthless way these political struggles can be suppressed.

Ishiguro's other works include *A Pale View of the Hills* (orig. pub. 1982; Random, 1990) and *An Artist of the Floating World* (orig. pub. 1986; Random, 1989).

803   Lamming, George. ***The Emigrants***. Repr. of 1954 ed. Univ. of Michigan Pr. 1994, $14.95 (0-472-06470-3). 280pp. Fiction.

The first part of the novel recounts the sea journey from the West Indies to England by a group of immigrants. The second part narrates the experiences of these newcomers to London, living in basement flats, banding together, fighting for respect. The third part is narrated by one of the group and provides a moving account of the immigrants who first moved to Britain following decolonization, hoping to find acceptance a new land.

George Lamming's other works include *The Pleasures of Exile* (orig. pub. 1960; Univ. of Michigan Pr., 1992) and *In the Castle of My Skin* (orig. pub. 1953; Univ. of Michigan Pr., 1991).

804   Lavin, Mary. ***The House in Crew Street***. Originally published in 1945. Viking 1987. o.p. Fiction.

This author is considered to be the originator of the bourgeois Irish novel. Her fiction has always skimmed over Ireland's turbulent struggles to focus on the lives of the settled middle classes. The tension in her works lies in the character's personal relationships and are set against the backdrop of class, property, and a religion that demands social conformity.

In this novel, Lavin explores the strange forms that love assumes if it is not expressed—Theresa's hardness, Sara's meekness, Onay's willfulness. The house in Crew Street, known as Castle Rampart, is a world unto itself; as its name suggests, it is a protected place, a fortress that permits few ties to the universe outside. The harshness and isolation of the women's lives is reflected in the fact that Castle Rampart becomes an important and dominating "character" in the story.

Lavin has a long list of honors and awards to her credit. She has been awarded two Guggenheim Fellowships, the Katherine Mansfield Prize, the Eire Society Gold medal, the Literary Award of the American Irish Foundation, and the Gregory Medal, founded by William Butler Yeats as the supreme literary award of Ireland. Her other works include *A Likely Story* (o.p., 1957), *The Great Wave* (o.p., 1961), *The Second Best Children In The World* (o.p., 1972), *Mary O'Grady* (Viking, 1989), and several volumes of short stories.

805   MacLaverty, Bernard. *Cal*. Braziller 1983. o.p. Fiction.

The story begins in an abbatoir (slaughterhouse), which symbolizes the butchery of the struggle in Northern Ireland. Cal, an aimless nineteen-year-old growing up in a Catholic slum, reluctantly takes part in the Irish Republic Army (IRA) killing of a Protestant militiaman. Later, by chance, he meets the militiaman's young widow, Marcella. Consumed with guilt, he cannot tell Marcella what he has done, nor can he forget her. Eventually, Cal and Marcella become romantically involved. His problems deepen when the IRA asks him to assist in even more violent acts.

Forced to grow up at an early age, Cal is emotionally stunted and incapable of an honest relationship. He has allowed himself to become a participant in a conflict in which everybody loses, and through him the author explores the human tragedy of violence in general and of "the Troubles" in particular. As MacLaverty shows in this poignant and poetic novel, the war in Northern Ireland is made up of countless human tragedies and dilemmas for which there seem to be no solutions.   LML

806   Maddy, YuLisa Amadu. *No Past, No Present, No Future*. Heinemann 1973. o.p. Fiction.

This novel describes the changes in, and the eventual breakdown of, a friendship among three boys. When we first meet them, they are studying at mission school in Sierra Leone. Joe Bengoh is an orphan; Santigie Bambolai is the son of the chief; and Ade John, son of a Bauyan civil servant, is a member of the elite class. In a series of richly detailed vignettes about adolescent life, the boys drop out of school one by one to work at the railway freight office. Eventually they collect enough money to move to England. Once there, confronted by the pressures of immigrant living—lack of money, an unfriendly racist environment, and isolation—their bonds start to fray. Santigie repeatedly fails his examinations and takes revenge against the hostile British culture by having numerous affairs with white women. Ade falls in love with a Danish woman, but weaves a web of lies about his life. Joe goes heavily into debt and is expelled from drama school; he has a nervous breakdown, but eventually becomes the most mature of the three when he learns to accept both his homosexuality and the loss of his friends.

Naipaul, V. S. *A House for Mr. Biswas.*
See entry 685.

807   O'Brien, Edna. *A Pagan Place.* Graywolf 1984, $8.00 (0-915308-59-2). 234pp. Fiction.

O'Brien is one of the most widely read women writers internationally. Her stories explore the world of the petty bourgeoisie in small-town semirural Ireland. The social boundaries of this world are clearly delineated, as the opening sentence of this novel shows: "Anny Parker was a Botanist, out in all weathers, lived with his sister that ran the sweetshop, they ate meat Fridays, they were Protestants." On the surface the Parkers' world seems like a static, never-changing place. But change does come, in the form of World War II. Many Irish support the Germans—the enemy of their enemy, the British. The small town with its strict social and moral codes is buffeted by the winds of international warfare and local political strife. The impact of change on an unsuspecting population is conveyed through poignant vignettes and lyric language.

Other works by this author include *Lantern Slides* (Farrar, 1990), *Time and Tide* (Farrar, 1992), and *House of Splendid Isolation* (Farrar, 1994).

808   O'Faolain, Julia. *No Country for Young Men.* Carroll & Graf 1986, $8.95 (0-88184-354-7). 416pp. Fiction.

The title is an ironic inversion of a line from "Sailing to Byzantium" by William Butler Yeats: "This is no country for old men." In Yeats's view, Byzantium represents a civilization blessed with perfect balance and harmony. But in this novel, the setting is the very imperfect state of Ireland, torn by political strife, a country where young men are sacrificed at the altar of political resistance. Elements of the plot include an unsolved 1922 murder witnessed by a nun who has gone mad; internal church politics; a passionate love affair; and the targeting of an American citizen for elimination by the Irish Republican Army (IRA), an act that threatens to trigger violence on an international scale. This is an extremely intense work that exposes the malaise and corruption in the church and that sweeps the reader into the complexities of Irish life.

809   O'Flaherty, Liam. *The Informer.* Repr. of 1925 ed. Harcourt 1980, $7.95 (0-15-644356-2). 188pp. Fiction.

The author of this novel was active in the Irish movement for independence. In January 1922, soon after the creation of the Irish Free State, O'Flaherty and a band of unemployed dock workers seized and occupied the Rotunda in Dublin, over which they raised a red flag. After a few days he ended the occupation and fled to Cork. When the civil war started he joined the Republican side, opposing the treaty between Ireland and England; but before the war ended in 1923 he had moved to London and was trying to make a living as a writer.

This novel of political betrayal, originally published in 1925, is set in the aftermath of the civil war against the backdrop of the conflict that continues to divide Ireland. Gypo Nolan, a brute of a man in need of a night's shelter, has informed on a friend who is wanted by the authorities. He spends his reward money, twenty pounds, on a rampage through Dublin's public houses and brothels. Soon, though, he is hunted down and brought to secret trial by the outlawed revolutionary organization. A contest between two wills ensues—between animal passion and rigid ideology—that in the end brings both retribution and salvation.

810 Orwell, George. ***Keep the Aspidistra Flying***. Repr. of 1956 ed. Harcourt 1969, $8.95 (0-15-646899-9). 250pp. Fiction.

In this biting view of England between the two world wars, Orwell shows the moral emptiness of capitalism. Gordon Comstock, the hero, is an aspiring poet who abandons a promising career as an advertising copywriter because he wants to escape "the money world" of middle-class respectability. Falling ever deeper into poverty, he becomes bitter and estranged from his family and his only friend, the socialist Ravelston. His girlfriend, Rosemary, is unwilling to marry him unless he can support her, but, constantly worrying about money, Comstock finds it difficult to write. A hopeful ending suggests the possibility of a humanistic alternative to the bleakness of working-class deprivation. This powerful realistic novel is a worthy counterpoint to Orwell's more famous later works, *Animal Farm* (orig. pub. 1945) and *Nineteen Eighty-Four* (orig. pub. 1949).   RL

Phillips, Caryl. ***Cambridge***.
See entry 695.

811 Randhawa, Ravinder. ***A Wicked Old Woman***. Interlink 1990, $8.95 (0-7043-4078-X). Fiction.

The author, a woman of Indian origin now living in Britain, is a founding member of the Asian Women Writer's Collective. This, her first novel, is the story of Kulwant, a Punjabi woman living in Britain. Divorced from her husband, Kulwant is shunned by her sons and her disapproving daughters-in-law. Wearing National Health Service spectacles and a coat donated by a charity, she masquerades as an old woman. In this disguise, she leads the reader through scenes of life in the Asian community and its uneasy interactions with the dominant British culture. She encounters a number of colorful characters: Bahadur, a Punjabi punk; Caroline, a gregarious friend from her schooldays; Maya, who cannot see beyond her weeping heart; and Shanti, whose daughter runs away but returns to the fold. The novel provides a rich and witty description of Indian life in Britain.

812 Riley, Joan. ***The Unbelonging***. Rev. ed. Interlink 1993, $10.95 (0-7043-3959-5). 160pp. Fiction.

Eleven-year-old Hyacinth, who lives with an aunt in Jamaica, is summoned to London by a father she has never met. When she arrives, she realizes hers is the only black face in a sea of white faces, all of them hostile. As time goes by, she longs increasingly to exchange the gloom of inner-city London for the warmth and exuberance of the back streets of Kingston.

In school, where she is one of only eight black children, she is constantly confronted by white animosity. At home, her father's violence is an ever-present threat. Despite these challenges, Hyacinth refuses to be a passive victim. She excels academically, which helps her to face problems at home and at school. This is a moving story of a child who grows up in a fragmented family and who must deal with racial hostility in a strange country.

Joan Riley's other works include *Romance, Waiting in the Twilight,* and *A Kindness to Children*, all of which are out of print.

Rushdie, Salman. ***The Satanic Verses***.
See entry 1387.

813   Salkey, Andrew. ***Escape to an Autumn Pavement***. Hutchinson 1960. o.p. Fiction.

This novel describes the life of immigrants in London. Living in a single-room "bedsitter" are Jonny Sorbet and Shakuntala Goolam, an unmarried couple who collect rent for their landlady. They also sometimes cook for the old lady, spy for her—and hate her. Others living in the house include Trado, Sandra, Biddy, and Du Bois B. Washington. Their world is tinged with racism, so much so that one character claims living in London is like living in a hick town in the southern United States. These immigrants try to create a life for themselves in alien surroundings, a task made more difficult when their traditional patterns of social behavior and relationships are disrupted by the events in the story.

This is Andrew Salkey's second novel; his first was *A Quality of Violence* (o.p.), and he is also the author of a folktale collection, *Brother Anancy and Other Stories* (Longman, 1993).

814   Selvon, Samuel. ***The Lonely Londoners***. Longman 1956. o.p. Fiction.

This is a novel about West Indian immigrants to Britain in the early 1950s, when immigration and racism were nascent issues. In the hopeful aftermath of World War II, waves of West Indians flocked to Britain looking for a prosperous future. The comedy of this story lies in the contradictions between their expectations and their actual experiences. They find a cool reception, bone-chilling weather, and bleak prospects. Yet friendships take root among these "lonely Londoners," and eventually they grow to love their new home.

The novel's characters include Galahad, who never feels the cold; Big City, who dreams of fame and fortune; Harris, who likes to play la-de-da; Moses, who hates his own soft heart; and Captain, who has a way with women. Through these characters the reader is introduced to London life from the perspective of the immigrants.

NONFICTION

815   Akenson, Donald H. ***The United States and Ireland***. Facsimile ed.; Repr. of 1973 ed. Books on Demand 1973, $87.00 (0-7837-4444-7). 322pp. Nonfiction.

Although part of the American Foreign Policy Library, this book is aimed at the general American reader and is intended to present a cohesive and unromanticized view of Irish history and the relationship between the United States and Ireland. The author has focused on the rise of Irish nationalism, the events leading to the partitioning of the country, and the controversial gaining of independence by the Republic of Ireland. Akenson presents the complex subject from a variety of perspectives and illustrates how events in Ireland have affected people and events in the United States. This is a useful beginning book for anyone interested in Irish history.

816   Anwar, Muhammad. *Race and Politics*. Routledge 1986, $32.50 (0-422-79840-1). 256pp. Nonfiction.

This is perhaps the only book-length study to examine the extent of participation in mainstream British politics by ethnic minorities. The author argues that active minorities involvement—not mere token representation—is essential for the political process to function democratically. For this study, he monitored Asian participation in the 1972 parliamentary by-election and conducted thirteen years of additional research. He makes a compelling case for minority involvement at the decision-making level. In addition, he analyzes the response of the political parties to minority participation and makes suggestions about ways in which minorities could improve their roles in the future. The range of subject matter this work covers makes it useful for both the general and the specialized reader.

817   Arthur, Paul, and Keith Jeffery. *Northern Ireland Since 1968*. Blackwell 1988, $34.95 (0-631-16141-4); $19.95 (0-631-16061-2). 128pp. Nonfiction.

This book, written for British high school students, is also a useful beginning book for all lay readers. The authors use a thematic approach, rather than a chronological one, to analyze the conflict in Northern Ireland, the conflict that has come to be known as "the Troubles."

This work explores the salient issues, beginning with a discussion of the main political developments in the province, especially the events of 1968–1969, 1974, and the years following the Anglo-Irish Agreement of 1985. It then presents an analysis of the social and economic aspects of the situation, a summary of Nationalist and Unionist politics (especially the parties' relationship with paramilitary activities) and a discussion of the responses by various factions to security challenges. Next, it reviews the international aspects, particularly Anglo-Irish relations and U. S. involvement. The authors conclude with an assessment of proposed solutions and an unflinching assessment of the most realistic policy options.

The themes covered make this an extremely useful introduction to the issues involved. The bibliography provides a list of other works that discuss the chronology of events.

818   Barton, Rachel. *The Scarlet Thread: An Indian Woman Speaks*. Virago 1987. o.p. Nonfiction.

This work, a mixture of autobiography and sociology, is the narrative of an Indian woman who migrates to England. A tale of suffering and courage, it shatters the stereotype of the silent, passive Asian. Rachel Barton met the narrator, who uses the pseudonym Sita Devi, by chance. As the two women became friends, Barton encouraged Devi to tell her life story. Together, they turned this narration into a book.

Devi recounts her marriage at the age of fifteen to Nirmal, a man she had never met before. He lived in London, and Devi left India to travel there alone. The marriage was a mistake. The book describes how Nirmal beat and abused her and took all the money she earned from her job in a factory. By the time she was eighteen, she had two children to care for, but, in an act of tremendous courage, she walked out of the marriage.

This eminently readable book provides an excellent portrayal of the plight of many Asian working-class women who immigrate to Britain.

819 Bell, J. Bowyer. *The Irish Troubles: A Generation of Violence, 1967–1992*. St. Martin 1993, $35.00 (0-312-08827-2). 944pp. Nonfiction.

As a historian of contemporary "colonies" in different locations around the globe, Bell compares and contrasts events in Northern Ireland with events in Palestine, Beirut, and South Africa, although he cautions against drawing too many parallels. He argues, for example, that Belfast is not a combat zone like Beirut; comparatively few die in "the Troubles," and only a small minority of the population is involved in the politics or in the armed struggles. Few—though these few are too many—live on the dangerous edge.

It is from this context that Bell interprets the history of Ireland from 1967 to 1992. He notes how the struggle has the delayed economic progress of both parts of Ireland, and he discusses the divisions within the Irish Republican Army (IRA), the escalation of the armed struggle, Protestant power in Northern Ireland, the Protestant backlash, and the hunger strike of 1980–1981. He then presents an analysis of the Anglo-Irish Agreement and the resulting institutionalization of violence.

This book is valuable to both academics and lay readers, in large part because of its unusual sources: In his years of research, Bell interviewed people in London, Ireland, and Philadelphia and talked to arms merchants in the Middle East, journalists in Italy, and functionaries in South Africa and Israel.

820 Blackett, R. J. *Building an Antislavery Wall: Black Americans in the Atlantic Abolitionist Movement, 1830–1860*. Louisiana State Univ. Pr. 1983, $32.50 (0-8071-1082-5); Cornell Univ. Pr. $14.95 (0-8014-9624-1). 264pp. Nonfiction.

This book assesses the presence and role of African Americans who visited Britain between 1830 and 1860. This group included virtually all the noted figures in antebellum black America, men and women committed to the destruction of slavery: Nathaniel Paul, James McCune Smith, Robert Purvis, and Moses Roper in the 1830s; Charles Lenox Remond, J.W.C. Pennington, Frederick Douglass, Henry Highland Garnet, and Alexander Crummell in the 1840s; Josiah Henson, William and Ellen Craft, William G. Allen, Henry "Box" Brown, John Brown, Martin Delany, Sarah Parker Remond, Robert Campbell, and Samuel Ringgold Ward—to mention only a few—in the 1850s. The author explores their contributions in keeping the abolition movement unified and in winning the support of the British working class.

821 Braham, Peter, and others, eds. *Racism and Antiracism: Inequalities, Opportunities and Policies*. Sage 1992, $55.00 (0-8039-8581-9); $19.95 (0-8039-8582-7). 320pp. Nonfiction.

This collection of articles is one of three volumes that constitute a major component of an Open University course called Race, Education, and Society. Although the books have been prepared specifically for Open University students, each can be read independently by readers who wish to acquaint themselves with the social and cultural dynamics of race in Britain.

The essays challenge the simple equation of race with class as they explore the links between racism and immigration, the presence of racism within trade unions, the unions' stand on immigration, and union complicity in restricting immigrants to the poorly paid and less-desirable jobs for which they had been recruited in their home countries. The articles also examine the impact of colonization on the assignment of roles by gender and the consequences on the labor market of the influx of women of South Asia and Africa.

822 Bryson, Bill. *The Mother Tongue: English and How It Got That Way*. Morrow 1990, $18.95 (0-688-07895-8); Avon $11.00 (0-380-71543-0). 288pp. Nonfiction.

This book details the origins of language in general and of the English language in particular. Bryson describes the nascent language among the Angles and the Saxons and traces the impact of successive invasions of Celts, Normans, Germans, and others. The author is at his most amusing in describing the development of various dictionaries and other attempts to codify English. He offers delightful vignettes of linguists, from the learned Dr. Samuel Johnson to the self-trained philologist James Augustus Henry Murray, who directed the massive Oxford English Dictionary (OED) project, even enlisting his eleven children to help him as soon as they learned their letters.

The book will be of more interest to high school students and general readers than to those with a background in the subject. Unfortunately, it is somewhat marred by its superior attitude toward English, which Bryson, an American living in England, regards as the premier world language. Such an approach reflects the tendency toward ethnocentrism on the part of many British linguists who, until recent years, would not even admit American expressions into the OED. EG/LML

823 Carlson, Julia, ed. *Banned in Ireland: Censorship and the Irish Writer*. Univ. of Georgia Pr. 1990, $13.95 (0-8203-1235-5). 192pp. Nonfiction.

The editor prepared this work under the auspices of Article 19, the International Center on Censorship, which is a human rights organization that campaigns on behalf of the right to freedom of expression worldwide. The organization exists independently of any government's controls and independently of all political ideologies and religious beliefs. It takes its name from the nineteenth article of the Universal Declaration of Human Rights, drafted in 1948, which proclaims freedom of opinion and expression as a basic human right.

Banned in Ireland gives voice to a group of novelists whose work, at one time or another, has been officially banned in their own country. It includes interviews with Benedict Kiely, John Broderick, John McGahern, Edna

O'Brien, Lee Dunne, Maurice Litch, and Brian Moore. These writers, from both Northern Ireland and the Republic of Ireland, articulate their experiences with feeling and humor and describe the effect that isolation from their reading public has had on their writing.

An appendix presents the opinions of some of the best known Irish writers—W. B. Yeats, George Bernard Shaw, Liam O'Flaherty, Samuel Beckett, Sean O'Faolain, and Frank O'Connor—who have protested censorship over the years, and a bibliography lists the key works denouncing censorship.

824 Carter, Trevor. *Shattering Illusions: West Indians in British Politics*. Humanities Pr. 1986, $17.50 (0-85315-674-3). 158pp. Nonfiction.

This book analyzes the history of racial and class tensions in Great Britain in the years after World War II. The author argues that black struggle and working-class struggle overlap and are interdependent. Blacks, he contends, are not merely allies of the working class; they are part of it. Carter urges them to create intraracial alliances based on class identity. He further argues that black politics should strive for socialist goals because, in his view, only socialism can help blacks forge the class links that in turn lead to a redefinition of mainstream society, a new definition that includes people who today live on the margins.

Cham, Mbye, and Claire Andrade-Watkins, eds. *Blackframes: Critical Perspectives on Black Independent Cinema*.
See entry 1286.

825 Cohen, Phil, ed. *It Ain't Half Racist, Mum: Fighting Racism in the Media*. State Mutual Book & Periodical 1982, $36.00 (0-906890-31-4); $25.00 (0-906890-30-6). 119pp. Essays.

In the 1980s, protests rose over racially biased news coverage in Britain. Two of the events that triggered the protests were the war with Argentina over the Falkland (Malvinas) Islands and the hostile media reaction to the plight of two Asian families with British passports who were expelled from Malawi and who were living on social security in London. The protests led a group consisting mostly of white journalists to launch the Campaign Against Racism in the Media (CARM). The campaign's first publication, *In Black and White: Racist Reporting and How to Fight It* sold 2,500 copies within months. *It Ain't Half Racist, Mum*, a television documentary that exposed TV's own form of racism, was seen by over 300,000 people. Among the results of CARM's campaign was the creation of the Black Media Worker's Association. This book contains essays by members of the two organizations that address the question of how journalists of all races can educate the public about racism.

826 Coogan, Tim P. *The IRA: A History*. Rinehart, Roberts 1993, $27.95 (1-879373-67-X); $16.95 (1-879373-99-8). 500pp. Nonfiction.

This books examines the role of the Irish Republican Army (IRA) in the larger pageant of Irish history, a history involving tangled issues of conquest, land, religion, politics, and the struggle for the soul of a people. Coogan traces the evolution of the IRA from its roots in the Fenian tradition to its formation on the day the First Dail met in 1916. The book also examines how policies of the IRA have changed over time as pressures mount to make peace with political reality and recognize the parliaments of Dublin, Belfast, and London. The author explores the IRA's controversial links to foreign powers, its bombing campaigns, its support of the Nazis, and the sometimes explosive internal political battles.

In constructing this history, the author conducted more than 500 interviews with people who were either members of the IRA or sympathetic to its cause. He has also used the wealth of Republican publications: IRA directives, regulations, proclamations, pamphlets, newspapers, records of court martial proceedings and of county brigade activities, letters, and personal statements of various kinds. He also had access to material not usually available to the general public, such as the ritual (adopted 1931) and Constitution (adopted 1946) of the Clann na Gael.

Cross, Malcolm, and Hans Entzinger, eds. ***Lost Illusions: Caribbean Minorities in Britain and the Netherlands***.
See entry 924.

827 Gallagher, Thomas. ***Paddy's Lament—Ireland 1846–1847: Prelude to Hatred***. Harcourt 1987, $10.95 (0-15-670700-4). 348pp. Nonfiction.

This book investigates the causes and consequences of the Irish famine of 1846–1847. The author's research convinced him that the famine was not an isolated event of Irish history, but it was certainly the low point. Yet the voice of the Irish peasant on the experience of the famine has been little heard, if indeed it was heard at all. Gallagher shows how the famine affected the farmer's daily life, his family, his institutions, his beliefs, his very existence. The author reconstructs these life experiences using Irish, British, and American government documents, essays, letters, theses, contemporary printed sources, interviews, and folklore.

The book notes that the silencing of peasant voices has been a key theme throughout the colonial history of Ireland, from the reign of Queen Elizabeth I to the takeover by the British Parliament under the Act of Union in 1800. Inspired by international movements, such as the American and French revolutions, Irish peasants arose to resist the takeover. That protest offers a stark contrast to the stereotype of the Irish peasant as a static and uncommitted group.

828 Gilroy, Paul. ***There Ain't No Black in the Union Jack: The Cultural Politics of Race and Nation***. Univ. of Chicago Pr. 1991, $13.95 (0-226-29427-7). 280pp. Nonfiction.

Often, in writings about immigration, blacks are represented either as "problems," to use W.E.B. Du Bois's term, or as victims. The goal of this book is to establish a black identity outside of those limited categories. Gilroy explores the ways African and Afro-Caribbean immigrants to Britain express their cultures in their new homeland. He urges that class analysis be substantially reworked to take race into account and cautions against defining race and ethnicity as cultural absolutes.

Through his analysis of the expressive culture of black Britain, the author reveals how culture develops. He argues that culture does not grow along purely ethnic lines. Instead it produces complex, dynamic patterns of syncretism in which new definitions of blackness emerge from raw materials provided by black populations elsewhere in the diaspora. This is essential reading for students of culture, both specialist and lay readers, who want to learn about the process by which cultures form and grow.

829   Glassie, Henry. ***All Silver and No Brass: An Irish Christmas Mumming***. Illus. Univ. of Pennsylvania Pr. 1976, $17.95 (0-8122-1139-1). 224pp. Nonfiction.

Mumming is an ancient Irish oral tradition that thrives even today. During the cold, bleak winter months, men wander from house to house, brightening country homes with their comical drama. The play—brief, poetical and musical—traces the life of a character through death and resurrection.

Glassie, a folklorist, has researched the tradition and the mummers who still practice it. In the village he studied, all the mummers in the village were men in their sixties and seventies who were exceptionally energetic, outgoing, and articulate.

The first part of the book draws on conversations with the mummers. These conversations also record the texts of the plays, which appear in their original form. But mumming is a performance art, and a written text does not do it justice. To give the reader a clearer picture, the second part of the book consists of other conversations that offer background information as well as the author's insights on linguistic and theoretical issues.

830   Gmelch, Sharon, ed. ***Irish Life and Traditions***. Illus. Syracuse Univ. Pr. 1986, $34.95 (0-8156-2367-4). 256pp. Nonfiction.

The editor, a cultural anthropologist, presents a comprehensive look at the history and habitat of Ireland, its people, and their complex culture. The first part of the book is devoted to a discussion of the land, from the rugged coastline and the abundant boglands and the plants and animals that live there to the man-made environment, both ancient and modern. Essays in the second part, "Growing Up," written by a historian, a Protestant archbishop, a Gaelic-speaking writer, and a feminist, give a vivid picture of an Irish upbringing and reveal the country's diversity across regional, religious, class, and generational lines.

The third section features essays on ancient fairs, religious pilgrimages, modern festivals, and sports. The final section, "Words," reflects the Irish interest in people, conversation, and social life and focuses on the enduring power of tradition in everyday life. The concluding chapter places Irish nationalism, the Easter Rising of 1916, the public life of Ireland, and the economic situation in a contemporary perspective. This book is an excellent introduction to Ireland

831   Hall, Stuart. ***The Hard Road to Renewal: Thatcherism and the Crisis of the Left***. Verso 1986. o.p. Essays.

This is a collection of articles written between 1978 and 1988 by a prominent Jamaican-born sociologist. The essays explore the political goals of British Prime Minister Margaret Thatcher and the crisis of the Left that her administration precipitated. The book describes how Thatcher, a Conservative, attempted to dismantle the welfare state to restore the prerogatives of ownership and profitability for the effective use of capital, and to create a climate that favored business and encouraged market solutions to social problems.

The book is divided into three parts. The first discusses the events that led to the development of Thatcher's policies, the second frames these events within a larger historical context, and the third focuses on the crisis of the Left. Hall asserts that a radical reshaping of the class structure of British society is under way, transforming the material basis, the occupational boundaries, the gender and ethnic composition, the political culture, and the social imagery of class. The Left, according to Hall, has not grasped how completely this restructuring is undermining its power.

832   Hancock, Ian. *The Pariah Syndrome: An Account of Gypsy Slavery and Persecution*. Illus. Karoma 1986, $17.95 (0-89720-079-9). 203pp. Nonfiction.

The author, a Gypsy living in Britain, spent ten years ferreting out the material for this study of Gypsy slavery. The text traces the history of the Gypsies from the time of their exodus from India to Iran and Egypt to their settlement in Eastern Europe. Two events dominate this history. The first is the enslavement of Gypsies in Eastern Europe. Gypsies were also victims of Western European slave traders, who transported them as unpaid laborers to Africa, the Americas, and India. Yet the enormous extent of Gypsy suffering is not acknowledged in any books or studies about the Atlantic slave trade.

The second key event is the Nazi attempt to destroy the Gypsies during the Holocaust of World War II. Hancock has discovered that Hitler's policy against the Gypsies was even more vicious than his policy toward the Jews, yet virtually every history of the war omits any discussion of Gypsy genocide.

A major part of Hancock's book deals with the current situation of Gypsies in Britain. There is also a section on Gypsies in America and the discriminatory laws regarding Gypsies currently on the books in many European countries. This work is recommended for readers interested in the situation of small minority communities.

Harris, Geoffrey. *The Dark Side of Europe: The Extreme Right Today*.
See entry 934.

833   Hebdige, Dick. *Subculture: The Meaning of Style*. Routledge 1987. o.p. Nonfiction.

The author defines *subculture* as the culture of revolt, of resistance against the power of the dominant culture. He analyzes the expressive forms and rituals of the subcultures that have emerged in Britain since the 1960s, such as the teddy boys, the mods and the rockers, the skinheads, and the punks. He also discusses how mainstream reactions to these groups reflect the fears and concerns of the established order.

The text explores the style of subcultures to show how mundane objects—a safety pin, a pointed shoe, a motorcycle—become symbols of a self-imposed marginalization. Hebdige describes the process by which these objects acquire their meaning and how style becomes a form of revolt, of refusal. Although there is little discussion of class inequality as a factor in the rise of subcultures, this study is readable and useful in its discussion of youth culture in Britain, a culture that has had enormous influence on teens in the United States and elsewhere. Hebdige is also the author of *Cut 'n' Mix: Culture, Identity, and Caribbean Music (see main entry)*.

834   Hiro, Dilip. ***Black British, White British***. Facsimile ed. Books on Demand 1973, $98.90 (0-7837-3899-4). 366pp. Nonfiction.

Hiro presents a history of how the Afro-Caribbeans, the Africans, and the Asians came to Britain. He reviews British imperial history from the perspective of the people subjected to colonialization and creates a single thread that ties the stories of these minority people together. In the process he discusses how white racism fostered black consciousness, citing such examples as the rise of Enoch Powell and other politicians on the radical right, the hostile environment in which the children of immigrants grow up, and the backlash of the "White Power" movement. The book does not aim to influence government policy. Instead, the goal is to provide fresh insights into the broad historical and theoretical framework that is so crucial in understanding the race situation.

835   Jones, Trevor. ***Britain's Ethnic Minorities: An Analysis of the Labour Force Survey***. Policy Studies Institute (London) 1993. o.p. Nonfiction.

Through its analysis of data from the Labour Force Survey conducted in Britain between 1984 and 1990, this book presents both a detailed description of Britain's ethnic minority populations at the end of the 1980s and a statistical comparison with the white community. The research in previous decades showed that Britain's ethnic minorities from the Caribbean and the Indian subcontinent had a substantially lower standard of living than whites. Three decades later, those patterns persist. The study also identifies a powerful dynamic among minority communities, one that drives them to develop beyond the social and economic level they occupied during their first years in Britain. The drive toward educational achievement is particularly strong. The report evaluates the new situation in the light of the progress made in education and its expected impact on the future of these communities. This is the first survey to cover minority communities throughout England, Scotland, and Wales and is also the first to include other ethnic communities, such as the Chinese and blacks from African countries.

836   Kapo, Remi. ***A Savage Culture***. Quartet Books 1981. o.p. Nonfiction.

Kapo has written a passionate account of British colonization and the use of racism as a means of domination. The narrative is informed by the author's own ethnic and racial situation—he came to Britain from Nigeria in 1953 at the age of seven—and provides a carefully thought-out and well-researched analysis. He places his assessment of racial issues against the background of the 1981 race riots that occurred in Brixton and elsewhere and examines these events in the broader context of the history of the British empire. His thesis is that the Britons suffer from nostalgia for their nation's former glory; they are experiencing withdrawal symptoms and are clinging to an "empire mentality."

Kapo criticizes the fragmented approach to race-related problems in housing, education, and the law, arguing that that the common denominator in these problems is racism. The book provides valuable insights into the workings of British race relations and is useful for all types of readers.

837 Kenny, Herbert A. *Literary Dublin*. Rev. ed. Irish Books & Media 1991, $19.95 (0-7171-1828-2). 288pp. Nonfiction.

Kenny traces the long history of cultural and intellectual activity in Dublin, a heritage that led Queen Elizabeth I to establish Trinity College there in 1592. He makes the point that the literary history of Dublin is often synonymous with that of Ireland as a whole. Exploring the symbiotic relationship between culture and politics, the author weaves together the history of Irish literature with the political history of the country and its people. The city is not only the capital of the Republic of Ireland, it was once the "second city" of the British Empire, renowned for its architecture and famous as a capital of literature, finance, art, music, and education.

838 Mansergh, Nicholas. *The Unresolved Question: The Anglo-Irish Settlement and Its Undoing, 1912–1972*. Yale Univ. Pr. 1991, $40.00 (0-300-05069-0). 384pp. Nonfiction.

The theme of this book is the making, working, and ultimately the dismantling of the political settlement between Ireland and Britain between 1920 and 1925. Neither a narrative history nor a constitutional treatise, the book contains essays of political and historical analysis. The essays unravel the origins of the settlement; discuss the concepts, interests, and personalities that led to its creation; define its goals; assess its successes and failures; and trace the circumstances that led to its undoing.

The Anglo-Irish Settlement was based on three key documents. The first was the Government of Ireland Act of 1920, which divided Ireland into two parts: Southern Ireland, with twenty-six counties, and Northern Ireland, with six. The second document was the Anglo-Irish Treaty of 1921, which created an Irish Free State as a dominion within the British Commonwealth of Nations; the Free State embraced the whole of Ireland, but it permitted Northern Ireland to opt out of the agreement—which it did. The final document was the agreement of 1925, which settled certain financial and boundary issues.

The text analyzes the new balances and alliances that were created and their implications for subsequent independence movements. Partition became a recurrent model for British imperial withdrawal from India and elsewhere.

839 Mirza, Heidi S. *Young, Female and Black*. Routledge 1992, $65.00 (0-415-06704-9); $16.95 (0-415-06705-7). 224pp. Nonfiction.

In a book titled *Learning to Labour* (Columbia Univ. Pr., 1981), author Paul Willis investigates a group of white and Jamaican school children to answer the question "By what process do working-class children get trapped in working-class jobs?" His answer lay in the notion of the "counter-school culture." These children, he argued, were motivated by a culture that fostered resistance to the authority of school.

Mizra's book, published a decade later, studies young black females who drop out of school. Like Willis, she analyzes the factors that influence their job choices to determine how those choices perpetuate racial inequality. Mirza challenges Willis's "romantic" notions about the subculture of resistance, pointing out that using culture as the sole determinant for a sociological analysis obscures the roles that racial and sexual discrimination can play. She traces the experiences of young black British women as they leave school to enter the work force. Her theoretical approach moves away from an emphasis on cultural identity toward a more structural understanding of the process of inequality. This book complements Willis's work and is a useful study in its own right.

840   Moore, Robert. *Racism and Black Resistance*. Pluto 1975. o.p. Nonfiction.

The author, who spent ten years working in the field of race relations, bases his findings on a historical and a theoretical overview of race and on interviews with blacks in Britain from various socioeconomic classes. Beginning with a look at the factors that cause workers and their families to leave their homes and emigrate to Britain and Europe, the author then examines the process by which black immigrants from British Commonwealth countries have come to be defined as a "problem" in their adopted land. He describes the political campaign waged against them by politicians of the radical right, such as Enoch Powell, and explains how legislation was enacted that eroded immigrant rights, stripped them of the automatic citizenship to which many Commonwealth residents had been entitled, and drastically curtailed the rate of immigration. The book also examines the role of British immigration authorities and the courts in oppressing people of color. A closing chapter analyzes the effects of racism and shows how it damages both the perpetrators and the victims.

841   O'Brien, Conor Cruise. *States of Ireland*. Pantheon 1972. o.p. Nonfiction.

The author, an Irish politician, describes this work as "an inquiry in the form of a discursive essay; an inquiry into certain aspects of Irish history, consciousness, and society, as part of an effort to understand what has been happening in the two parts of Ireland in recent years." His focus is the relationships between Catholics and Protestants and the political entities created by this religious divide. O'Brien is eminently qualified to write about this bifurcation in Irish society: He grew up Catholic, but was educated at Protestant schools. He challenges what he calls the dangerously distorted and simplistic maneuver of equating the Catholic perspective with the politics of the Left and the Protestant position with the politics of the Right.

He also examines the Catholic/Protestant divide in the light of the relationship of these two communities with Britain and America and analyzes trends in Ireland within the broader context of global politics and economics. The decline of Britain as a world power and the effects of this change on its political relations with Ireland are examined at length. This is a useful book for all readers, especially because the author treats the Irish question in relation to larger politics of power.

842   O'Farrell, Patrick. *Ireland's English Question: Anglo-Irish Relations, 1534–1970*. Schocken 1971. o.p. Nonfiction.

O'Farrell analyzes the history of Anglo-Irish relations through the theme of religion. The author, an Australian of Irish ancestry, contends that, given the relationship between the two countries, all answers to the Irish question so far have been British in origin; couched in the vocabulary of secularism, these solutions draw on the language of political power and economic development. Irish nationalism responded, in turn, along the structures and language dictated by the British. This secular approach, he argues, has ignored the importance of religion in the discussion and accounts for a great deal of the ongoing enmity of these countries.

According to the author, the quarrel between the Irish and the British is also about a different world view, a view that is determined by culture, historical experience, and economic development. He devotes special attention to the question of religion and argues that the English, who often relate to other nations through power politics, tend to interpret the Irish expression of faith as a political activity. One consequence of that attitude is the proliferation of stereotypes about the Irish. The author attempts to correct those stereotypes by focusing on the close kinship between culture and politics. Including the cultural dimension makes it possible to reexamine Anglo-Irish relations and discover fresh historical insights about the events that have shaped the destinies of the two nations.

843 O'Malley, Padraig. *Biting at the Grave: The Irish Hunger Strikes and the Politics of Despair*. Beacon 1991, $14.00 (0-8070-0209-7). 344pp. Nonfiction.

During 1980 and 1981, ten Irish Republican Army (IRA) prisoners at the Maze/Long Kesh Prison in Belfast died during a hunger strike called to protest prison conditions. The main issue was the British government's refusal to treat them as political prisoners rather than as common criminals. One of the strikers, Bobby Sands, became an international symbol of resistance and was elected to the British Parliament shortly before his death on May 5, 1981.

O'Malley, a journalist, cuts through the romantic images of the strikers to offer an even-handed analysis of why the strike took place and what it accomplished. He examines the backgrounds of the ten prisoners and argues that, in large part, the strike fulfilled a death wish. He presents the reactions to the strike in Northern Ireland, in the Republic of Ireland, in Britain, and in the rest of the world, including the United States, home to many people who sympathize with the IRA. He also explores the role of the Catholic Church. O'Malley sees the hunger strike, and indeed much of IRA terrorism, as the suicidal response of people who have internalized their status as victims and who see no way out except through the most extreme means. His analysis reaffirms the religious basis of the conflict, underscoring the role of religion as a source of zealous commitment and a means of defining one's culture and community.   LML

844 O'Malley, Padraig. *The Uncivil Wars: Ireland Today*. Beacon 1991, $18.00 (0-8070-0215-1). 532pp. Nonfiction.

Written before the Anglo-Irish Agreement of 1985, this work explores the segregation between Catholics and Protestants. The topic is not new or unusual, but what is different about this work is the author's approach to his analysis. The book is based largely on interviews conducted with various Irish and British political activists and politicians.

O'Malley takes up such topics as the "Anglo-Irish Process"; the involvement in the South; the Social Democratic Party and the Labour Party; the Protestants and their organizations, leaders, and positions; the often inconsistent actions of the British government; the Irish Republican Army (IRA) and its political arm, Sinn Fein; the 1982 elections in Northern Ireland; and prospects for peace. He provides the historical and theoretical framework for each of these topics. The interviews provide some rare insights, making this a valuable book for both lay and academic readers.

845   Parekh, Bhiku, ed. *Colour, Culture, and Consciousness: Immigrant Intellectuals in Britain*. Allen & Unwin 1974. o.p. Essays.

This volume is divided into two parts. The first contains essays by nonwhite intellectuals who live in Britain. The contributors, born and raised outside the United Kingdom, reflect on their life in England and on the problems they have encountered. They also analyze the tensions generated by the conflict between their own cultures and the dominant British culture and comment on the distinctive characteristics of British life and society. These discussions range from highly personalized accounts to analyses of race and politics.

The second part consists of responses by sociologists, philosophers, and students of English character to the questions raised by the interviewees.

Although this collection is very useful as far as it goes, it has some limitations: No women or Arab intellectuals are included, and only one African is interviewed.

Phillips, Caryl. *The European Tribe*.
See entry 955.

846   Rich, Paul B. *Race and Empire in British Politics*. Cambridge Univ. Pr. 1990, $22.95 (0-521-38958-5). 288pp. Nonfiction.

This work examines British racial thought during the last phase of empire, from the 1890s to the early 1960s. The author shows that the decline in imperial power did not bring about a concomitant decline in racism. On the contrary, black immigration during the 1940s and 1950s created a new phase of racial tension and hostility in British society and politics, tension that erupted in race riots in Bristol, Liverpool, and London.

The objective of this work is to examine the legacy of imperial tradition, specifically the political concepts of race and how those concepts affect British thinking today. This work presents a lot of statistical data; readers accustomed to more theoretical analyses of racial issues may find this challenging reading. However, the book contains much useful factual evidence of the workings of the British political system and its administrative structure.

847   Rose, Richard. *Northern Ireland: Time of Choice*. Illus. Books on Demand 1976, $48.10 (0-8357-4515-5). Nonfiction.

The author places the Irish political situation into context for readers in the United States. He points out analogies between the British colonization of Ireland and the colonization of America. Ulster (the region containing modern-day Northern Ireland and several counties in the south) and Virginia were both chartered as plantations by the English Crown in 1607. The United States, Rose argues, has fewer residual "problems" from the past because the American settlers were more ruthless in clearing native people from the land than were the Scots and English who settled Ireland.

The object of this study is to outline the dominant features of politics in Northern Ireland and to better understand the choices ahead for this province. The author explores the nature of political authority, and Northern Ireland—with its history of both Protestant and Catholic challenges to political authority—provides the ideal political backdrop for this philosophical and ideological research. The philosophical dimension makes this a useful work for scholars of political theory, while its readable style makes it useful for the nonscholarly reader.

848 Ryan, John. *Remembering How We Stood: Bohemian Dublin at the Mid-Century*. Gill & Macmillan 1976. o.p. Nonfiction.

Ryan has written a fascinating memoir about literary life in Dublin, based on his acquaintance with the group of writers active between 1945 and 1955. This was the period immediately following the deaths of Ireland's greatest literary figures, W. B. Yeats and James Joyce; their deaths sparked a great deal of writing in their honor. More important, this was the period during which Ireland was emerging from its insularity during the wartime years; Irish intellectuals began interacting with the world once more.

Ryan's literary Dublin is peopled by such writers as Edna O'Brien, J. P. Donleavy, and Brendan Behan, who were then just beginning their literary careers but who would become internationally known. Others like Patrick Kavanaugh and Myles na Gopaleen (Flann O'Brien) were making a late debut because of the war. It was a world of tremendous creative energy, one that thrived on the unique camaraderie among the various artists, who shared a number of experiences in common: critical neglect, financial worries, and the challenge of making their marks during what Ryan calls a "literary skinhead age."

849 Shivers, Lynne, and David Bowman. *More Than the Troubles: A Common Sense View of the Northern Ireland Conflict*. New Society 1984, $24.95 (0-86571-025-2); $12.95 (0-86571-061-9). 240pp. Nonfiction.

This book is especially recommended to introduce readers in the United States to the situation in Northern Ireland so they can more accurately understand and interpret events there. So as not to lose sight of the human experience in the maze of factual information, the authors begin with their subjective impressions of the situation. They then present factual information on history and economics, describe conflicting views, outline chronologies, and provide profiles of the people and organizations involved in the conflict.

The authors, who declare their commitment to nonviolence, also describe and profile the many groups in Northern Ireland that follow a nonviolent strategy. The detailed profiles of various organizations that have attempted to heal Northern Ireland since 1968 give a very different picture of the region from the one that most people see. The authors also discuss the numerous ways in which American people and organizations are involved in this process.

850 Sivanandan, Ambalavaner. ***Communities of Resistance: Writings on Black Struggles for Socialism***. Routledge 1990, $55.00 (0-86091-296-5); $18.95 (0-86091-514-X). 225pp. Nonfiction.

This is an excellent work that explores issues of race in neoimperial, postindustrial Britain. Sivanandan reexamines the fight against racism and the turns that the struggle took after the government intervened. He analyzes how ideologies of the Left have been co-opted by the establishment. After the inner-city rebellions of the 1980s, the established Left took up the "black cause." The fight against racism moved from the street to the town halls and committee rooms, where bureaucrats sought neatly packaged solutions to throw at the problems and to mollify their vocal spokespeople. As a result, the definition of the problem and the objectives of struggle underwent a major change. The fight against racism became a fight for culture and ethnicity, and personal racism rather than institutional racism became the site of struggle. In addition to his study of Britain, the author offers an assessment of race, class, and state in postcolonial societies, using Sri Lanka as the model.

851 Solomos, John. ***Race and Racism in Britain***. 2nd ed. St. Martin 1993, $18.95 (0-312-09980-0). 209pp. Nonfiction.

This book provides an overview of race, racism, and immigration in postwar Britain. In includes detailed discussion of the historical context of British politics, the political responses to immigration after the war, the pressures for legislative controls and restrictions, the development of national and local policies on discrimination, and the shifts in racial ideology that took place from the 1940s to the 1980s.

The author also explores the most important aspects of the racialization of contemporary British politics. He analyzes the growth of ideologies that focus on race as an important political symbol, the role of both antiracist and of ethnic-minority mobilization, and the impact of social and economic restructuring on ethnic and national identities in British society.

852 Stewart, Anthony. ***The Narrow Ground: Aspects of Ulster, 1609–1969***. Faber 1977. o.p. Nonfiction.

The author shows that events in Irish history are just one of the influences on the present political situation in Northern Ireland. Other pressures and problems of the contemporary world have had their effect. Stewart argues that the outbreak of guerrilla warfare in Ulster in 1968 was more closely linked with the student riots in May that year in Paris, for example, than it was with the Penal Laws or the Battle of Boyne. The mass protests in the streets of Ulster find an echo in the Czechoslovakian uprising or the protests against the war in Vietnam that were taking place in the United States. According to the author, history determined the form and course of the conflict, but contemporary trends fed the fire.

Seeing this interaction between history and contemporary world politics is useful in enlarging our knowledge of political processes and the connections between nations and cultures. By cautioning against reductive, linear evaluations of history, this valuable work corrects many previously held suppositions.

More recently, Stewart is the author of *A Deeper Silence: The Hidden Origins of the United Irishmen* (Faber, 1993), a more specialized work that builds on the theoretical approach he uses in this book.

853 Sword, Keith, and others. *The Formation of the Polish Community in Great Britain, 1939–1950*. o.p. Nonfiction.

This work by the M. B. Grabowski Polish Migration Project Report will appeal to specialists in the field. It contains a broad survey of the history of the Polish presence in Britain. The report is divided into three parts. The first deals with the chronology of the arrivals and departures of the various groups of Poles. The second analyzes the political problems caused by the establishment of the Polish government in London during World War II and the decision at the end of the war to resettle large numbers of Poles in Britain. The third section deals with the administrative and sociological problems involved in the process of resettlement.

854 Visram, Rozina. *Ayahs, Lascars and Princes*. Pluto 1986. o.p. Nonfiction.

In this account of Indians in Britain from 1700 until the granting of Indian independence in 1947, the author argues that one of the legacies of imperialism was the transplanting of Indians to sites throughout the British empire. Many of those who came to Britain in the eighteenth and nineteenth centuries were servants or *ayahs* (nannies) brought over by British families returning from India, or they were sailors (*lascars*) employed by the East India Company. Some settled permanently in Britain. A third group of migrants—students— came as a direct result of the British policy to impose English culture on India. As English education became widespread, students flocked to Britain to study law, medicine, or other professions. Many of these also remained in Britain. Another group of Indians included Indian princes and maharajahs who visited London on several occasions and who attracted a great deal of notice.

This book provides interesting reading and is useful for both the general and the specialized reader.

855 Ward, Alan J. *The Easter Rising: Revolution and Irish Nationalism*. Illus. Harlan Davidson 1980 (0-88295-803-8). 192pp. Nonfiction.

In the revisionist intellectual tradition that has emerged as a result of the political and military crisis in Northern Ireland, Ward examines one significant event, the Easter Rising of 1916, to raise pertinent questions: Why did the uprising occur, and how did it influence the course of Irish history? Instead of offering a comprehensive review of twentieth-century Northern Ireland, Ward uses the Easter Rising as a lens through which to focus on a few important themes and events and explore them in detail.

Above all, Ward confronts the controversy surrounding the Easter Rising, study of which has been revived in Northern Ireland. This is a useful work that provides a deeper understanding of the changing Northern Irish perspective.

856 Watson, James, L., ed. *Between Two Cultures: Migrants and Minorities in Britain*. Blackwell 1977. o.p. Nonfiction.

This is a collection of writings by twelve anthropologists who have studied ethnic minorities in Britain, including Sikhs, Pakistanis, Montserratians, Jamaicans, West Africans, Chinese, Italians, Poles, Greeks Cypriots, and Turkish Cypriots. The juxtaposition of European and non-European minorities provides a more complete picture of migrant communities and an opportunity for comparison.

All the contributors have had field experience at both ends of the migration chain—in the migrant's country of origin and in Britain. Some of the studies started in Britain and moved to the home countries. Other authors began their projects as conventional village studies in widely scattered parts of the world; after following some of the villagers abroad, they realized the close connection between the new immigrant communities and the communities in their land of origin.

Although this study is intended for the general reader, bibliographies at the end of each chapter direct the specialized reader to other resources.

857   Wilson, Amrit. *Finding a Voice: Asian Women in Britain*. Virago 1978. o.p. Nonfiction.

Wilson wrote this book to provide Asian women with a forum through which they could discuss their life experiences. Based on interviews with Indian, Pakistani, and Bangladeshi women, this work presents different facets of their lives—their loneliness in an alien culture and environment, the monotony and long working hours, concepts of shame and honor that clash with those of their adopted nation, and the racism the women encounter from British people and institutions.

In an introduction, the author discusses immigration patterns and links colonialism to changes in family structure and other aspects of rural society in the former colonies. For example, economic deprivation increased the desirability of sons and led to the devaluation of daughters. Wilson then traces the history of South Asian immigration to its colonial past. Colonialism had created a vast army of labor in the former colonies. Whenever British industry needed workers, it could draw on this vast reserve, and this is how postwar emigration from Punjab, Gujerat, and Bangladesh began.

Most immigrants came to Britain intending to earn money and then go back. The economic hardships faced by immigrants—hardships that arose to a large degree because of racism in the workplace—forced them to stay on longer than they had anticipated. They therefore had to send for wives from home, which led to an increase in the numbers of Asian women in Britain. This is a book for all readers.

858   Wilson, Tom. *Ulster: Conflict and Consent*. Illus. Blackwell 1989, $56.95 (0-631-16245-3); $21.95 (0-631-17006-5). 330pp. Nonfiction.

In this book, the author questions whether Irish nationalism played the central role in events in Northern Ireland. He makes the case that two other political issues are equally important. One is the differences between the situation in Ireland and that in Scotland and Wales, which were also invaded by England but which coexist as independent ethnic units within Britain. From this example, the author argues that partition might have been the ideal solution had the majority population of Ulster been a homogeneous group of Protestant unionists. But given the fissured Protestant situation and the presence of militant Irish nationalism, such a solution was impossible.

The other issue involves the status of minorities in Ulster. Wilson looks at the treatment of minorities from a number of angles: recruitment and promotion in both public and private employment, the geographical location of new industries, housing policy, and education in an area where the churches have insisted on denominational segregation.

BIOGRAPHY

859 Clarke, Kathleen, and Helen Litton, ed. ***Revolutionary Woman***. Dufour 1991, $33.00 (0-86278-245-7). 240pp. Autobiography.

Kathleen Clarke was an activist, a dedicated feminist, and a member of the Sinn Fein executive committee. She took part in the 1916 Easter Rising and was imprisoned along with two other female revolutionaries and associates, Maud Gonne and Countess Markievicz. Her husband, Tom Clarke, was executed for his part in the rising. During the municipal elections of 1919, she was nominated for two wards by Sinn Fein—Wood Quay and Montjoy—and was elected alderman for both. She also served as president of the Children's Court and the Court of Conscience.

She wrote these memoirs at the urging of the Reverend Father Albert Bibby, a Catholic priest who attended several of the 1916 executions. The stories had to be reconstructed completely from memory. During the years of the struggle for freedom she kept no documentary evidence for fear it might fall into enemy hands, but she had been trained to memorize all details. After the rising, her home was constantly raided by British military authorities. The few letters and things she had were put into storage.

Clarke provides a woman's perspective on the revolution. She was an outspoken critic of the role in the struggle for independence played by Eamon de Valera, a patriot and Ireland's first president. She also denounced the Irish leadership's attitude toward women, questioning the significance of a revolution that did not allow women full participation. The memoir ends in 1943, when she retired from public life. The editor has filled in the years from 1943 to Clarke's death in 1972 at the age of ninety-four.

860 Coogan, Tim P. ***The Man Who Made Ireland: The Life and Death of Michael Collins***. Illus. Rinehart, Roberts 1992, $24.95 (1-879373-23-8); $14.95 (1-879373-71-8). 480pp. Biography.

This biography assesses the political career of Michael Collins and his controversial role in the creation of the Republic of Ireland. It begins with his involvement in the Easter Rising of 1916 and describes how he fomented revolution at the grassroots level. He soon realized that "static warfare" would only continue to hand victories to the British, so he devised a new form of guerrilla warfare, based on the capture of enemy information, a tactic eventually adopted by guerrilla leaders all over the world. When the British dispatched spies to infiltrate and snuff out independence movements, Collins created a counter-network of inconspicuous men and women to spy on the spies.

Coogan has meticulously researched Collins's life and has confronted the controversy surrounding the partition of the country, Eamon de Valera's duplicitous role in accepting partition, and the scapegoating of Collins as the man chosen to conduct the final negotiations with Lloyd George. The author has also delved into other controversial areas, such as the power struggles within Sinn Fein and the de Valera family's alleged misuse of funds earmarked for the revolution.

861 Dunleavy, Janet E., and Gareth W. Dunleavy. *Douglas Hyde: A Maker of Modern Ireland*. Illus. Univ. of California Pr. 1991, $35.00 (0-520-06684-7). 475pp. Biography.

In 1938, at the age of seventy-eight, Douglas Hyde, a Protestant, was elected as the first president of the Republic of Ireland, a post he held until 1945. A man with varied interests, he had an equally varied career as a poet, playwright, philologist, scholar, and college professor. He was an authority on Irish folklore, an activist, and a nationalist—in short, an Irish institution.

The authors undertook this book at the urging of Sean O'Luig, a colleague and friend of Hyde, who brought them two bags full of materials—letters, cuttings, manuscripts, notes—that he had gathered over the years. In addition, the biographers corresponded with scores of people acquainted with Hyde, his life, his times, and his achievements. The also interviewed local people in north Roscommon and Sligo, where Hyde grew up.

Straddling the realms of scholarly work, creativity, and politics, Hyde was responsible for shaping the modern Irish presidency. This book reflects that blend, making it an important work, not only as a biography but also as a reflection of the unique alignment of politics and culture in Irish history.

862 Edwards, Owen D. *Eamon de Valera*. Catholic Univ. of America Pr. 1988, $22.95 (0-8132-0665-0); $9.95 (0-8132-0666-9). 160pp. Biography.

The author describes this as a psychobiography of de Valera's life, but such a label does not do justice to the book's other dimensions. The biography does discuss de Valera's early life: his Spanish father, who died when de Valera was still an infant; his subsequent arrival in Ireland; his upbringing by his maternal grandmother and an uncle; his mother's refusal to send for him after she remarried; and his constant search for a father figure. But in the process, Irish history, contemporary world events, and Irish–American relations are all woven into the fabric of de Valera's life.

The author handles the contradictory and the controversial aspects of de Valera's life well. Many have criticized de Valera for taking credit for the achievements of others. He claimed he had been the leader of the Irish struggle, when in fact he spent most of the time in jail, cut off from the ongoing movement. Edwards also explores the extent to which de Valera left the bulk of the work on the Treaty of 1921 to Michael Collins. Even so, Edwards presents de Valera's achievements and contributions sympathetically, making this an immensely readable biography, particularly for the nonspecialist reader.

This book is part of the Political Portraits series produced by the Catholic University Press of America.

863 Foster, Robert F. *Charles Stewart Parnell: The Man and His Family*. Harvard Pr. (England) 1976. o.p. Biography.

Although Parnell's work as a politician has been widely researched and written about, little is known about his personal life because there are virtually no documents about the Parnell family. Foster reconstructs Parnell's life through an analysis of nineteenth-century Wicklow and its society, then proceeds to a study of the Parnell family, and finally deals with the man himself. This approach, known as "contextual biography," challenges the assumptions of earlier biographers who had attributed Parnell's political activism and nationalism to his American mother's dislike of British imperialism. Examining Parnell's development as a political activist within the specific political consciousness of Wicklow society, Foster sees Parnell's evolution as a logical extension of the social milieu in which he grew up. This method not only weaves Parnell's life into the fabric of Irish history, it also acknowledges the role of regional politics in shaping national history.

864   Gilbert, Martin. *Churchill: A Life*. Illus. Henry Holt 1991, $34.50 (0-8050-0615-X); $19.95 (0-8050-2396-8). 1,088pp. Biography.

Winston Churchill was prime minister of Great Britain from 1940 until 1945 and again from 1951 to 1955. He served in Parliament for decades as a member of both the Conservative and Liberal parties and in various Cabinet offices. His reputation as Britain's greatest twentieth-century statesman rests on his years of service during World War II. As prime minister he rallied his nation and inspired the allies in a series of speeches so eloquent that after they were published he was awarded the Nobel Prize for literature in 1953.

This biography relates all the key events in Churchill's long political and literary career while providing useful background about the historical events in which he played such a key role. However, it is as much a study of a vital and colorful personality as it is a work of history. Readers will learn what it was like for Churchill to grow up as a child of privilege in late Victorian England, how he inspired respect but also disdain from his less-able political allies, and why his personality was uniquely suited to lead Britain in time of war. Churchill emerges as a historical figure with many human frailties and failings in this exciting and well-written biography.

865   Marlow, Joyce. *The Uncrowned Queen of Ireland: The Life of Kitty O'Shea*. Weidenfeld & Nicholson 1975. o.p. Biography.

Marlow's account of Kitty O'Shea's life, her marriage, her adulterous relationship with Irish nationalist politician Charles Stewart Parnell, her involvement with Irish politics, and her divorce and remarriage to Parnell make compelling reading. This book also provides glimpses of Victorian Irish society and history. The author explores in detail the issue of the Irish Home Rule and its implications for Irish society. The biography is thus inextricably woven with the unfolding of Irish history.

Kitty O'Shea's tumultuous personal life reflects the revolutions then going on in Ireland's social and domestic sphere. Her relationship with Parnell reveals the role of the church in the life of Irish women and the status of women in Irish society. The biographer uses O'Shea's journals, letters, and family documents to produce a fascinating and readable study.

866   Martin, F. X., and F. J. Byrne, eds. *The Scholar Revolutionary: Eoin MacNeill 1867–1945 and the Making of Modern Ireland*. Irish Univ. Pr. 1973. o.p. Biography.

The title of the book affirms the close links between cultural and political revolutions. The editors have assembled a collection of essays that explore the various facets of Eoin MacNeill's life. He was a scholar, historian, and editor; a linguist involved in the renaissance of the Irish language; and a professor for whom teaching itself was an act of political activism. Furthermore, he outlined the purpose and organizational structure of the Irish Volunteers, a citizen militia of Irish nationalists, in 1913.

The first five essays in the collection focus on MacNeill as a scholar: his work in the Irish language, his place in Celtic studies, his achievements as a historian, his expertise in the Ancient Irish Laws. The other essays deal with his political activism, his court martial, his imprisonment, his work with the Boundary Commission, and his political offices.

Although the author's academic background might deter lay readers, this is an interesting book for anyone interested in the connection between teaching and political activism and in the creation of cultural identities through revolution.

867   Mehta, Ved. *Up at Oxford.* Norton 1993, $25.00 (0-393-03544-1). 432pp. Autobiography.

This is the seventh volume in the author's memoirs, a series that begins with his early childhood in India and continues with his move to the United States to attend a school for the blind in Arkansas, and then his attendance at Pomona College in California. This volume begins in 1956, when he attends Oxford University's Balliol College on a scholarship.

At Oxford, Mehta lives among students from around the world. He expresses his thoughts about being at one of the academic centers of the English-speaking world, at the university where many of the colonial masters who ruled his native India were trained. Mostly, Mehta feels admiration for the superior learning of the British students and extols the virtues of a classical education, but he also notes the emotional immaturity of many of his fellows.

His return to Oxford decades later allows Mehta to learn what has happened to his young friends, so full of promise. The sad fates of several of the most privileged students provides a poignant end to this beautifully written work.

868   Morgan, Austen. *James Connolly: A Political Biography.* St. Martin 1989. o.p. Biography.

The author sets himself the task, which apparently no other writer has yet tackled, of resolving the paradox of James Connolly's life: How could a man who lived as a socialist die as an Irish nationalist? Morgan focuses on this duality to critique the antinationalist Marxism that arose during the Ulster "troubles" of the 1970s.

This work contests the view propounded by C. Desmond Greaves in *The Life and Times of James Connolly* (o.p., 1971), an influential work that describes Connolly as a would-be Lenin. Morgan contends instead that Connolly lived in two worlds simultaneously: the world of international socialism and the world of militant nationalism. A supporter of syndicalism, Connolly believed in attaining socialism by organizing skilled workers, many of whom were committed nationalists. It was this narrow view of socialism that led Connolly in the last two years of his life—from 1914 to 1916—to join the Dublin revolutionaries, whom he led in a failed attempt at national revolution during the First World War.

869 O'Casey, Sean. *Autobiographies*. Vols. 1 & 2. Carroll & Graf 1985, $10.95 each (0-88184-049-1; 0-88184-075-0). Autobiography.

Dramatist Sean O'Casey's *Autobiographies* evoke the oral-narrative traditions of Gaelic folk tales and myth. Originally there were six volumes; although only the first two are in print as of this writing, this discussion will cover the complete set.

The series was originally published between 1939 and 1954. *I Knock at the Door* (1939) covers the first ten years of his life in Dublin (1880–1890); *Pictures in the Hallway* (1942) takes up the period from 1891 to 1903; *Drama under the Windows* (1945) covers the years 1903 to the Easter Rising of 1916; *Inishfallen, Fare Thee Well* (1949) looks at the era from 1916 through the civil war period to his departure from Ireland as a successful dramatist; *Rose and Crown* (1952) covers the spring of 1926 to the end of 1934, when he returned from New York; and *Sunset and Evening Star* (1954) covers the years up to 1953.

Myth, romance, and the rhythms of the Gaelic language interweave with history, politics, Protestantism, O'Casey's growing stature as a dramatist, his increasing sense of political commitment, and his political and cultural disagreements with William Butler Yeats to reveal the fabric, not just of his life as an artist but also of the life of an entire nation caught in the throes of political and social struggle.

870 O'Faolain, Sean. *King of the Beggars: A Life of Daniel O'Connell*. Viking 1938. o.p. Biography.

This biography was published in 1938, but its style of narration and its success in capturing the rhythms of Gaelic make it a classic. It is in equal measure a biography of O'Connell, the early-nineteenth-century political agitator, and an account of the history of the Irish people.

To explain O'Connell's pivotal role in the political and religious revival and Ireland, the author explains that, during early British history, Irish political life and institutions had fossilized. That process began in the miserable days after the fall of the old Gaelic state in 1691. The great majority of the population then—just over a million people—were very poor. Their conquerors treated them as helots (serfs) under the infamous code known as the Penal Laws. By the first quarter of the nineteenth century, this helot population increased to eight million.

It was these people—without hope, without modern political institutions, without a leader, slaves in their own country—whom O'Connell fashioned into a culturally conscious populace, capable of seeking democracy and self-rule. The biography is an account of O'Connell's political contribution to a modern, independent Ireland.

871 Sawyer, Roger. *Casement: The Flawed Hero*. Routledge 1984. o.p. Biography.

This work focuses on areas of Lord Casement's life that previously have been neglected because of a lack of sources. Recently, however, caches of his letters to friends have come to light, and other previously unpublished letters have become available. These new documents give a more complete picture of the man, especially at crucial points in his development. These letters reveal the workings of Casement's mind as he approached his decision to commit himself wholly to Irish nationalism.

Born of mixed religious parentage—his mother was Catholic, his father a Protestant—Casement worked as a British consular officer. He was consul at Lisbon and then a consul general in South America, where he carried out two sets of antislavery negotiations. This biography traces the growth of his concern for vulnerable groups who lacked basic human rights and describes his divided loyalties. Part of this interest in human rights developed within the framework of British imperialism, which he tried to modify to suit his humanitarian impulses; the other involved the renunciation of the empire in emphatic terms.

As an Irish revolutionary, Casement conducted negotiations with Germany, seeking German support for the 1916 Easter Rising, an act for which he was tried and executed.

872   Ward, Margaret. ***Maud Gonne: A Biography***. Rev. ed. Harper SF 1994, $22.00 (0-04-440889-7). 320pp. Biography.

In a biography of Maud Gonne published in 1976 and now out of print, the author, Samuel Levenson, states: "Though Maud Gonne was deeply and energetically involved all her life in Irish public affairs, she is remembered because of her *private* affairs and most of all for a private affair in which her participation was minimal." This biography paints a more complete and compelling picture of this complex and fascinating woman. To be sure, Ward presents the best-known aspects of Gonne's life: wife (and then widow) of Easter Rising hero John McBride; mother of Nobel Peace Prize winner Sean McBride; the romantic inspiration for William Butler Yeats, one of the greatest poets of the twentieth century. But the book also deals with other aspects of her being: her love for Ireland and hatred of British domination; her deep and energetic political involvement; her unconventional life in Paris; her affair with a French politician; her illegitimate children; her imprisonment; and her marriage to John McBride and the scandal of her separation from him. This dynamic portrayal reveals Gonne's role in extending the revolution in Ireland beyond its political significance and into the daily lives and homes of people, especially women. Ward's biography is well researched and written in a lively manner that will appeal to general readers.

873   Yeats, William Butler. ***Autobiography of William Butler Yeats: Consisting of Reveries over Childhood and Youth***. Macmillan 1987, $50.00 (0-02-632710-4). 344pp. Autobiography.

William Butler Yeats won the Nobel Prize for literature in 1923 and is generally acknowledged as the greatest English-language poet of this century. His autobiography was written in several parts over a number of years. The first volume, "Reveries over Childhood and Youth," traces his early years as the son of John Butler Yeats, a painter and mystic who repeatedly moved his family between London and Ireland. William also trained as a painter, and although he abandoned that career, his poetry reflected the sharp visual sense he developed under his father's tutelage. Later parts of the autobiography discuss his central role as a playwright in founding Ireland's national theater.

The autobiography is valuable as a document of Irish history. Yeats knew, observed, and sympathized with the key figures in Ireland's independence movement. This vividly evocative work reveals Yeats as a person, a writer, and a man who lived during a vital era in English and Irish history. Among his poetic and prose works in print are several poetry and drama collections, as well as his adaptations of Irish folklore .   RL

8

WESTERN EUROPE

ICELAND

Norwegian Sea

SWEDEN

FINLAND

NORWAY

Gulf of Bothnia

North Atlantic Ocean

North Sea

DENMARK

Baltic Sea

NETH.

GERMANY

English Channel

BELGIUM

LUX.

FRANCE

SWITZERLAND

AUSTRIA

Bay of Biscay

ANDORRA

ITALY

PORTUGAL

Adriatic

SPAIN

Tyrrhenian Sea

GREECE

Aegean

Ionian Sea

Mediterranean Sea

8

Western Europe

by Barbara Walden

In an area stretching from the islands of the North Atlantic and the Arctic to the Mediterranean, from the shores of France and Portugal to the eastern borders of Austria and Germany, Western Europe presents a diverse mosaic of regional and national languages, geography, customs, and peoples.

The people of Western Europe speak a wealth of languages: French, German, Italian, Spanish, Swedish, Danish, Norwegian, Dutch, Greek, and Portuguese, as well as Basque, Catalan, Occitan (Provençal), Frisian, Sami, Faeroese, Icelandic, Breton, Turkish, Arabic, Vietnamese, Hindi, and Chinese. They are Christians, Jews, Muslims, Buddhists, and Hindus. In language, ethnicity, religion, geography—indeed, in all of the ways that define "multicultural"— Western Europe is and has been throughout its long history a meeting ground of cultures and peoples. Sometimes that meeting has been peaceful; more often, however, it has not.

This chapter attempts to provide a balanced overview of the diversity of Western Europe. Although some books discussed here are included because they provide a broad historical framework for understanding the present, the focus is very much on the twentieth century. This is not meant to suggest that cultural diversity or the clash of cultures in this part of the world is by any means a new phenomenon. Readers who wish to take a closer look at the religious and class-based conflicts of the Middle Ages and the Early Modern eras in France, for example, can consult books such as Emmanuel Le Roy Ladurie's *Montaillou, the Promised Land of Error: Cathars and Catholics in a French Village 1294–1324* (Random, 1979) and *Carnival in Romans* (Braziller, 1979). Historical works about Italy include Carlo Ginzburg's *Night Battles: Witchcraft and Agrarian Cults in the Sixteenth and Seventeenth Century* (Johns Hopkins Univ. Pr., 1992) and *The Cheese and the Worms: the Cosmos of a Seventeenth-Century Miller* (Johns Hopkins Univ. Pr., 1992). Such works provide carefully researched, well-written, and engrossing historical accounts of the impact of religious and cultural conflicts on the lives of earlier Europeans. These have not been included in this bibliography because they focus exclusively on a short time frame in the distant past.

However, other works that cover a longer time frame have been included

407

to introduce the reader to the subject in its current manifestations. Thus, Jerry Bentley's *Old World Encounters* and Leslie Moch's *Moving Europeans* provide the historical background for the twentieth-century migrations described in Robert Marrus's *The Unwanted: European Refugees in the Twentieth Century*. John Boswell's history of homosexuality in Western Europe, *Christianity, Social Tolerance, and Homosexuality: Gay People in Western Europe from the Beginning of the Christian Era to the Fourteenth Century* expands the time line of contemporary German gay culture that is described in the novels of Hubert Fichte. In Spain, Moorish influence is still felt, and the flowering of Basque and Breton culture in the Middle Ages is even today a source of ethnic pride and identity. These cultural cross-currents are described in *Sephardim: The Jews from Spain* by Paloma Dias-Mas, *The Basques* by Roger Collins, and *The Bretons* by Patrick Galliou.

Twentieth-century Western Europe was the scene of two devastating and divisive world wars. The aftermath of those conflicts—population upheavals, tragic memories of death and destruction—continue to affect lives and events today, more than half a century after the close of World War II. The end of the Cold War era, with the collapse of Communism and the opening of boundaries between nations, brought further waves of immigrants into the nations of Western Europe. In addition to these continent-wide cataclysms, political and cultural differences have also led to more-localized upheavals, including destructive civil wars in Greece and Spain and acts of terrorism by ethnic minorities seeking an end to their oppression. In some cases, only recently have the wounds from these conflicts begun to heal. Much of the historical literature written about these events continues to be largely partisan. For that reason it has fallen to novelists and anthropologists to capture the human drama through books that speak in the individual voices of the people who witnessed these events and who were affected by them. This bibliography includes documentary accounts from both sides of the Greek Civil War. To tell the story of the Spanish Civil War, the editors chose to include *Homage to Catalonia*, the classic account by English novelist George Orwell, who fought on the Republican side, and anthropologist Neil MacMaster's *Spanish Fighters: An Oral History of War and Exile*, the story of a couple whose lives were caught up in this cause. Other works annotated in this chapter include short histories that introduce and outline the modern events, causes, and conflicts currently going on in these countries.

In countries such as France, Italy, the Netherlands, and especially Germany, the event that defines and overshadows virtually all other discussions of cultural interaction in the twentieth century is the Holocaust. Despite the huge body of literature devoted to it, the full horror of the systematic destruction of millions of people—Jews, Poles, Gypsies, homosexuals, and others—remains beyond rational comprehension. This bibliography makes no attempt to discuss every book devoted to the topic. Instead the reader is referred to other more comprehensive lists, including Harry James Cargas's *The Holocaust: An Annotated Bibliography* (American Library Assn., 1985) and a more selective work, *The Schocken Guide to Jewish Books: Where to Start Reading about Jewish History, Literature, Culture, and Religion*, edited by Barry W. Holtz (Pantheon, 1992). Similarly, for the related general subject of anti-Semitism in Western Europe, the available literature is too large to be represented fully in a selective bibliography such as this one. The bibliographies just named provide a good beginning point for readers who would like to go beyond what is presented here.

Instead of attempting to be comprehensive, therefore, this chapter provides a judicious selection of books about different facets of the Holocaust. Preference has been given to the more recently published works, and an attempt has been made to represent a range of experiences. Readers thus will find here a biography of Rabbi Leo Baeck, an important Jewish resistance leader in war-time Berlin, as well as Peter Wyden's sensitive biography, *Stella*, the story of a Jewish woman who survived the war by acting as a "catcher" of other Jews. Also included is the classic memoir by philosopher Gershom Scholem, who grew up in an educated German Jewish family in Berlin around the time of World War I; Susan Neiman's *Slow Fire*, the journal of a Jewish-American woman of German descent who spent seven years as a graduate student of philosophy in modern-day Berlin; Harry Mulisch's *The Assault*, a meditation in the form of a novel on the impact, both in the past and the present, of the Nazi occupation; Anne Frank's classic diary; and the story of Miep Gies, who sheltered Anne and her family. These works and the others described serve as starting points from which the reader's journey can begin.

Among the works by and about Italians are books by Primo Levi, who survived Auschwitz and who created some of the most eloquent chronicles and meditations on the Holocaust yet published, as well as the delicate novels of Natalia Ginzburg and Giorgio Bassani, who tell the story in other ways. Books that explore culture in Italy—for example, the differences between northern and southern Italy, or the contrasts between peasant life and life in modern cities—include nonfiction titles by Ann Cornelisen, Carlo Levi, and Pino Arlacchi and novels by Ferdinando Camon, Giuseppe Tomasi di Lampedusa, and Grazia Deledda.

The regional, political, and class differences that figure in the literature of Spanish multiculturalism are perhaps reflected most eloquently in the works of novelists, poets, and playwrights: Federico García Lorca, Bernardo Atxaga, Camilo José Cela, and others. Several of the contemporary Spanish novelists discussed here launched their careers with works dealing with the Spanish Civil War and its aftermath; more recently, some of these authors have addressed the differences between rural and urban life in Spain. Several spent time in exile during the regime of the dictator Francisco Franco, who died in 1975; their books look at Spain from a perspective of distance and isolation.

Regrettably, some aspects of Western European multiculturalism can be only partly represented in this bibliography. For example, the migration of people from North Africa to France has resulted in a vibrant literature that reflects several generations of immigrant experience, much of it painful. Only a handful of these novels, along with some autobiographies and other works that deal with the experience of people from North Africa living in France, have been published in English.

In Germany, immigration from Turkey, Italy, and Eastern Europe has led to new clashes of culture and social tensions. The books by Tahire Kocturk and Jorgen Nielsen listed here offer eye-opening general sociological studies of Turks and Muslims in Western Europe. Immigrants from these regions have produced novels, poetry, plays, and works of nonfiction, but very few of these titles have been translated into English. The pivotal events of 1989 and 1990—the tearing down of the Berlin Wall and the subsequent unification of

East and West Germany—have generated a large number of books; some of the ones available in English are noted here. Perhaps firsthand accounts by new German immigrants will be made available in translation soon.

Understandably, fewer works are written about the peaceful interactions of cultures than about more dramatic events: the upheavals of war, genocide, and ethnic conflict. Nevertheless, two fine descriptions of the Sami (Lapps) are available in English: *Greetings from Lappland*, by Nils-Aslak Valkeapaa, a Sami activist, and *A Year in Lapland: Guest of the Reindeer Herders*, by American anthropologist Hugh Beach. Two writers of fiction, Hesin Brú and William Heinesen, tell about the unique and gradually evolving culture of their native land, the isolated Faeroe Islands off the coast of Denmark; their books are available in English. The proud and peaceful Frisians of the Netherlands are described by anthropologist Cynthia Mahmood in *Frisian and Free*. At this time, however, no novels or sociological studies are available to the general reader in English that deal with the ethnic, political, and linguistic tensions between the Flemish and the Walloons of Belgium.

In summary, there are gaps in the English-language literature about many of the diverse cultures within Western Europe. The picture that emerges in those works that are available is one of many contrasts. Sometimes different peoples can intermingle peacefully; more often, however, clashes erupt based on deep-rooted historical animosities or differences of language, ethnicity, political and social goals, philosophy, or religion. The books described in this chapter have much to teach about Western Europe's experience of cultural diversity, an experience that ranges from the deepest acts of human depravity to soaring acts of courage and nobility.

LITERATURE

874 Appelfeld, Aharon. ***Badenheim, Nineteen Thirty-Nine***. Trans. from Hebrew by Dalya Bilu. Godine 1980, $9.95 (0-87923-799-6). 160pp. Fiction.

Appelfeld was born in 1932 to Polish-Jewish parents in Bukovina, now part of Ukraine. When the Germans overran his city during World War II, he became separated from his parents. He spent his childhood and early adolescence wandering the countryside or living in refugee camps. He emigrated to Palestine in 1947 and now lives and teaches in Israel.

Appelfeld's novels, which he writes in Hebrew, concern the assimilated world of Central European Jews just before the Holocaust. His calm, elegiac style has been compared to that of Thomas Mann and Franz Kafka. One of his main themes is the self-delusion of the emancipated, assimilated Jew.

Badenheim Nineteen Thirty-Nine describes a Jewish resort near Vienna whose guests try to enjoy their holiday while the sinister Department of Sanitation gradually rounds up and deports all the Jews. In the first part of *The Age of Wonders* (Godine, 1989), a boy describes with eerie calm the relentless chaos of his childhood in Austria and the destruction of his family and his world. In the second part, the boy, now a man, returns to his Austrian hometown and discovers that little has changed, even though all the Jews are gone. Other novels by Appelfeld that have been translated include *The Retreat* (o.p.), *Tzili* (o.p.), *To the Land of the Cattails* (HarperCollins, 1987), *For Every Sin* (Random, 1990), *The Healer* (o.p.), and *The Immortal Bartfuss* (HarperCollins, 1989).

875 Atxaga, Bernardo. ***Obabakoak: A Novel.*** Trans. from Spanish by Margaret J. Costa. Pantheon 1993, $22.00 (0-679-42404-0); Random $12.00 (0-679-74958-6). 226pp. Fiction.

Winner of Spain's National Prize for Literature, this novel is a tribute to the language and culture of the Basque people. It has been translated into English from the author's own Spanish translation of his original Basque text.

This loosely structured novel contains a series of interdependent and inter-related stories that introduce the reader to a cross-section of society in the town of Obaba and its environs. The novelist peoples this world with a variety of absorbing characters, including a lovelorn schoolmistress; a cultured but self-hating dwarf; a schoolboy whose father, a mining engineer, tricks him into growing up; and an environmentalist who now spends his time rescuing lizards after having tortured them when he was a youth.

876 Ayala, Francisco. ***The Usurpers.*** Trans. from Spanish. Schocken 1987. o.p. Fiction.

Ayala was born in Granada, Spain, and became a professor of political science at the University of Madrid. He went into exile following the Spanish Civil War and returned to Spain in the 1960s. In the 1940s, he began to write novels and stories centered on contemporary events. During his long career he has produced many works, some dealing with the Spanish Civil War and others examining more-contemporary aspects of Spanish society. *The Usurpers*, a collection of short stories based on historical events and legends of Spain's past, has as its central theme the nature of power in society.

877 Bassani, Giorgio. ***The Garden of the Finzi-Continis.*** Trans. from Italian by William Weaver. Buccaneer 1994, $27.95 (1-56849-255-3); Harcourt $7.95 (0-15-634570-6). 200pp. Fiction.

Bassani is the son of a Jewish family from Ferrara in northern Italy, and his novels are suffused with sights and sounds of the city of his birth. *The Garden of the Finzi-Continis* is his most famous work. The story, drawn from the experiences of real people, depicts the members of a wealthy Jewish family and their neighbors as the horrors of the Holocaust gradually permeate their quiet, idyllic community and the walls of the garden that isolate them from the reality of the outside world. The book was made into a successful film in 1971. Another Bassani novel, *The Gold-Rimmed Spectacles* (o.p.), is the story of a respected Jewish physician driven to ruin by his passion for a homosexual thief.

878 Ben Jelloun, Tahar. ***With Downcast Eyes.*** Trans. from French by Joachim Neugroschel. Little, Brown 1993, $19.95 (0-316-46059-1). 297pp. Fiction.

This is a novel of two cultures, Moroccan and French. A Berber girl in Morocco is given the secret of a hidden treasure, a treasure that one day is expected to save her family's community. The girl emigrates with her family to France, where over time she becomes increasingly aware of her enormous sense of separation, both from her adopted country and from her homeland. Twenty years later she returns to her destitute village in Morocco to fulfill her mystical destiny and come to terms with her divided nature.

Ben Jelloun, a novelist and poet who was born in Morocco, lives in Paris and writes in French. He won the Prix Goncourt in 1987 for his novel *La Nuit Sacrée* (*The Sacred Night*) (Ballantine, 1991). His novel *Solitaire* (o.p., 1988) also addresses the lives of people from the former French protectorates in North Africa who, encouraged by the French government, flooded into France by the thousands, only to experience poverty, bigotry, and alienation.

879   Böll, Heinrich. ***Billiards at Half-Past Nine***. Trans. from German. Viking 1994, $9.95 (0-14-018724-3). 288pp. Fiction.

Heinrich Böll (1917–1985), novelist and short-story writer, won the Nobel Prize in 1972 for his contribution "to a renewal of German literature." Along with Günter Grass, he is considered the most important of the West German "Gruppe 47" authors. The writers advocated a rebirth of the German literary and linguistic tradition, which they felt had been perverted under Nazism. The ideals of Gruppe 47 included acknowledgment of the moral guilt of Germany and social involvement in purging that guilt.

Böll was born in Cologne and was conscripted into the German army. He served on the Russian front and was captured by the Americans. After his release from prisoner camp he began to write. His early works, which dealt with the war and its aftermath, include *And Where Were You, Adam?* (Northwestern Univ. Pr., 1994), *The Silent Angel* (St. Martin, 1994), *Acquainted with the Night* (o.p.), and *And Never Said a Word* (Northwestern Univ. Pr., 1994). In *Billiards at Half-Past Nine*, the action is confined to a single day, during which the history of the Faehmels family—and of Germany—is re-created through the recollections of the principal characters.

As West Germany rebuilt and become prosperous, Böll's work reflected with humor and sarcasm his dislike of the nation's growing materialism and his distaste for its increased demands for political conformity. *Group Portrait with Lady* (Avon, 1976), *The Lost Honor of Katharina Blum* (Viking, 1994), and *Safety Net* (o.p.) offer commentary on the injustices of the German social system. During the 1980s, Böll's short stories also appeared in English translation; one such collection is *The Casualty* (Farrar, 1987). Although always controversial, at his death Böll had earned a reputation as a great humanist of the post–World War II era.

880   Brecht, Bertolt. ***The Jewish Wife and Other Short Plays***. Trans. from German by Eric Bentley. Grove 1965, $9.95 (0-8021-5098-5). 176pp. Drama.

Brecht (1898–1956), a dramatist, poet, and novelist, was born in Augsburg, where his socialist political activities quickly earned him a prominent place on the Nazi's list of political criminals. From 1933 to 1949, he lived in exile, mainly in Denmark and the United States. Eventually he moved to East Berlin where he built a famous drama company, the Berliner Ensemble. His plays reflect his deep engagement in political activities.

Among the anti-Nazi plays are *Fears and Miseries of the Third Reich* and *The Private Life of the Master Race*. His best-known works, *The Threepenny Opera* (with music by Kurt Weill), *The Caucasian Chalk Circle*, *Mother Courage and Her Children*, *Galileo*, and *The Good Woman of Szechuan* deal with the struggle for survival in a society dominated neither by justice nor intelligence.

The Jewish Wife and Other Short Plays, one of few collections of Brecht plays currently in print, includes three short works (the title play plus "A Sense of Justice" and "The Informer") that depict life under the Nazis in the mid-1930s. These miniatures are typically Brechtian: They portray monstrous human behavior with pathos, but also with a sense of the comic and the grotesque.

881　Brú, Hesin. *The Old Man and His Sons*. Trans. from Faeroese by John F. West. Eriksson 1970, $15.95 (0-8397-8412-0). 203pp. Fiction.

The Faeroe Islands in the North Atlantic have a distinctive language and a rich literary life descended from an earlier oral tradition. The change in Faeroe society from traditional fishing villages to a more modern and less isolated existence is reflected in works by Faeroese writers.

This novel by one of the leading writers from the islands explores the generation gap as experienced by the Faeroese. Written in 1940 and widely translated into European languages before finally appearing in English, it deals with the change from a traditional subsistence economy to a market economy. The positive aspects of the old ways—rectitude, courage, and a sense of community—are embodied in Ketil and his wife, who support themselves through their farming and fishing. Their son, Kalv, who fishes for profit, is his parents' ambassador to the outside world; he speaks on their behalf to the officials and other outsiders who come into their small community. Kalv personifies the peaceful change to new ways, ways that manage to preserve the strong ties between the generations. Told with gentle humor and irony, this story is at once a picture of a vanishing way of life and a testament to changing folkways that retain the best of the old along with the new.

882　Camon, Ferdinando. *The Fifth Estate*. Trans. from Italian by John Shepley. Marlboro 1987, $16.95 (0-910395-29-2); $9.95 (0-910395-30-6). 176pp. Fiction.

This is the first novel in a trilogy dealing with Italian peasant culture of the Veneto. The books grew out of the author's desire to memorialize a way of life he remembered from his early years and how it changed over the course of the twentieth century. *The Fifth Estate* tells of the heroism and resignation of a peasant people whose story had never been told. It is a portrait of peasant imagination, custom, and myth, a world untouched by the changes that had revolutionized the rest of Europe. It is, Camon says, a testimony from within, and it is told in a first-person, stream-of-consciousness style reminiscent of, but more accessible than, the works of James Joyce.

Life Everlasting, the second volume, focuses on World War II, which wrenched the peasants into the twentieth century. Thoughts, myths, and speculations are interwoven with the narrative about the occupation and the peasant resistance, the coming of the "Mericans" (the Americans), and the peasants' efforts to return to the old ways after war's end. In a postscript, the author notes that it was the advent of the electric light and television after the war, and not the war itself, that ultimately wrought changes in an age-old way of life. *Memorial*, the final book in the trilogy, is more personal and semiautobiographical, as Camon relates the death of his mother and the building of an altar to her memory by his father. Here again, myths and folkways are filtered through the thoughts of the author.

883 Cela, Camilo Jose. ***Mazurka for Two Dead Men***. Trans. from Spanish by Patricia Haugaard. New Directions 1992, $21.95 (0-8112-1222-X); $10.95 (0-8112-1277-7). 272pp. Fiction.

Cela, a prolific and influential novelist, short-story writer, and travel memoirist, won the Nobel Prize for literature in 1989. Like many of his novels, this one explores life among the rural lower class. *Mazurka for Two Dead Men* is not a closely plotted novel; instead, it is a fascinating character study and a portrait of peasants in the Galicia region of Spain. The deaths of two men lead the other characters to remember them in various ways as they carry on with their lives. Mixed in with the present are memories and fantasies of both the near and the distant past.

Cela's best-known novels are *La Familia de Pascual Duarte* (*The Family of Pascual Duarte*; Little Brown, 1990), a bloody and disturbing story of a man who can be viewed as either a criminal or a victim of a destructive social environment, and *La Colmena* (*The Hive*; Farrar, 1990), a portrait of post–Civil War Madrid.

884 Charef, Mehdi. ***Tea in the Harem***. Trans. from French by Ed Emery. Serpent's Tail 1991, $10.95 (1-852421-51-7). 176pp. Fiction.

Born in Algeria in 1952, Mehdi Charef moved to Paris in 1964. After leaving school he worked in a factory until he achieved success as a writer. This book, which became a rallying point for second-generation Algerians and Moroccans, brought the author to the attention of film producer Henri Costa-Gavras, for whom Charef directed a prize-winning film based on the story.

The book is set in a public housing complex in the Paris suburbs. As Majid, a teenager, grows up, he struggles to deal with a France that rejects and insults Arabs, with his own Arab family, and with his impoverished immigrant world. General readers will sympathize with Majid's attempts to break away from his strict parental upbringing, his adolescent sexual encounters, and his rebellion against school authorities who look down upon him and refuse to recognize his intelligence. The title, a pun in French on the Theorem of Archimedes ("le thé au harem d'Archi Ahmed"), is the author's comment on the irrelevance of traditional schooling in the life of Majid and his friends.

885 Chraibi, Driss. ***The Butts***. Repr. of 1955 ed. Trans. from French by Hugh Harter; Pref. by Germaine Bree. Three Continents 1983, $18.00 (0-89410-324-5); $11.00 (0-89410-325-3). 124pp. Fiction.

Driss Chraibi, born in Morocco, moved to Europe in 1945. He is perhaps the best known of the writers of the first wave of North African immigration to France. This work, first published in 1955 during the brutal Algerian War, is an excoriation of France and the Western world that seemed to promise so much to the Islamic immigrants but that delivered so little. The "butts," or scapegoats, refers to the people who are destined to be sacrificial victims, those who may assimilate into a society but who never truly become part of it.

Chraibi's later novels, including *Mother Comes of Age* (Three Continents, 1984) and *The Mother Spring* (Three Continents, 1989), have been more restrained and humorous, and they are set in Morocco as well as in France.

Condé, Maryse. *Tree of Life: A Novel of the Caribbean.*
See entry 656.

Cortázar, Julio. *All Fires the Fire, and Other Stories.*
See entry 657.

Cortázar, Julio. *Hopscotch.*
See entry 658.

886 Daeninckx, Didier. *Murder in Memoriam.* Trans. from French by Liz Heron.
Serpent's Tail 1992, $13.95 (1-85242-206-8). 176pp. Fiction.

In a demonstration in Paris in 1961, hundreds of Algerians are killed by the
police. During the demonstration, Roger Thiraud, a young history teacher of
French extraction, is also murdered. Twenty years later, his son, Bernard, is
murdered in Toulouse after visiting the local reference library. Inspector Cadin
can only solve the puzzling murder of the son by solving the murder of the
father. And to do this he must follow a trail that links powerful people of
today with their murky pasts during the German occupation of France in
World War II.

First published in France in 1984, *Murder in Memoriam* won that country's
Detective Fiction Prize. This is the first English translation of a novelist who is
a leading figure in the new wave of European writers of crime fiction dealing
with political themes and issues.

887 Deledda, Grazia. *Cosima.* Trans. from Italian by Martha King. Italica 1988,
$10.50 (0-934977-06-2). 153pp. Fiction.

Deledda's works are noted for their realistic Sardinian settings and their portrayals of peasant life. Largely self-educated, Deledda led a conventional
woman's life in Italy while continuing to write. She was awarded the Nobel
Prize for literature in 1926.

Many of her novels have been translated into English; of these, *Mother*
(Cherokee, 1982) is perhaps the best known. *Cosima* is a semiautobiographical
novel of the growth into adulthood of a young Sardinian girl who loves to write.
She lives in a privileged, upper-class family in the late nineteenth century and is
allowed to develop her talents under almost idyllic circumstances.

888 Di Lampedusa, Giuseppe. *The Leopard.* Trans. from Italian by Archibald
Colquhoun. Knopf 1991, $15.00 (0-679-40757-X); Pantheon $12.00 (0-679-
73121-0). 320pp. Fiction.

Di Lampedusa was an Italian prince who spent most of his life in Sicily. He
lived, for the most part, a withdrawn and quiet life; the posthumous publication in 1959 of *The Leopard*, his only novel, was greeted with surprise as well as
praise. This is a novel of Sicilian life during the Risorgimento, the period of
Italian unification during the late nineteenth century. Events of the novel,
seen through the eyes of Prince Fabrizio, chronicle with irony and sensitivity
the passing of a feudal way of life. The novel continues into the twentieth

century, when life among the alienated and ineffectual next generation suggests that not all of the new ways are better—conclusions that sparked controversy when the novel was first published.

The Leopard was adapted for a 1963 film directed by Luchino Visconti and starring Burt Lancaster.

889   Döblin, Alfred. ***Berlin Alexanderplatz: The Story of Franz Biberkopf.*** Trans. from German by Eugene Jolas. Continuum 1984. o.p. Fiction.

Döblin was born in Pomerania in 1878 of Jewish parents. Taken as a boy to Berlin, he served as a doctor in World War I. After the war he practiced medicine in a poor section of eastern Berlin and also worked as a journalist and writer. His socialist views made him unpopular with the Nazis, who burned and banned his works. Döblin lived in exile in France and the United States from 1933 to 1945, when he returned to Germany. While in exile, in 1941, he converted to Catholicism. Döblin left Germany again in 1953, believing that, although Hitler was gone, little had changed. He died in 1957.

Berlin Alexanderplatz, his most famous novel, depicts the bleak despair of ordinary lives in lower-class Berlin after World War I. It covers eighteen months in the life of Franz Biberkopf, beginning with his release from prison in 1927 and ending in 1929 with his release from an insane asylum. During that time he struggles to earn a living, is duped into acting as a lookout for thieves, and is himself blackmailed and robbed. His girlfriend is murdered by a man he had befriended. At the end he once again struggles to put his life together. The book was adapted into a long film of the same name by Rainer Werner Fassbinder.

Among Döblin's other works translated into English are *Journey to Poland* (Paragon, 1991), a sensitive account of a Poland that vanished during World War II, and the novels *Karl and Rosa* (Fromm, 1983) and *A People Betrayed* (Fromm, 1983), which depict the upheavals of the socialist revolution in Germany at the end of World War I. His autobiographical account of his years in exile has been translated as *Destiny's Journey* (Paragon, 1992).

890   Feuchtwanger, Lion. ***The Jew Süss.*** Trans. from German. Carroll & Graf 1984. o.p. Fiction.

Feuchtwanger, a playwright and novelist, was born in 1884 in Munich, the son of a wealthy Jewish industrialist. He earned a doctorate in German literature and began work as a writer and critic. *Jud Süss* (*The Jew Süss*; sometimes given the alternate title *Power*) was written in 1921 and was a great success. The protagonist of this melodramatic historical novel set in the eighteenth century is Joseph Süss Oppenheimer, a Jew who is the confidant and finance minister to the princes of Württemberg. In a plot involving seduction, betrayal, treachery, revenge, intermarriage, and conflict between Catholics and Protestants, Süss holds fast to his Jewish faith and dies bravely on the gallows.

In 1933, Feuchtwanger's house and fortune were confiscated by the Nazis and his works were banned. He went into exile in France, where he wrote *Die Geschwister Oppenheim* (*The Oppermanns*; Carroll & Graf, 1983). This novel deals with the fate of a German-Jewish family caught in the Nazi web of prejudice and oppression. Its thinly veiled satire of Hitler especially angered the Nazis. When France capitulated to the German army, Feuchtwanger was interned in a French concentration camp. He managed to escape and go to the United States, where he died in 1958.

891 Fichte, Hubert. ***Detlev's Imitations***. Trans. from German by Martin Chalmers. Serpent's Tail 1992, $14.99 (1-85242-167-3). 256pp. Fiction.

Fichte (1935–1986) grew up near Hamburg and left school at sixteen to work at a series of jobs ranging from actor to shepherd. He studied agriculture and began to support himself by writing during the 1960s. During the 1970s he became interested in anthropology and traveled to Bahia (now Salvador, Brazil), Haiti, and Trinidad. His writings describe these experiences from his perspective as a writer and anthropologist. His works include novels, essays, short stories, journalism, radio plays, and documentary interviews with people from the subcultures of Hamburg.

In *Detlev's Imitations*, Detlev, half Jewish and fatherless, survives the Hamburg firestorm of 1943 to become a child actor in the hungry postwar years. The boy Detlev becomes the man Jacki, who lives in Hamburg in 1968, a city that has a thriving gay culture and that is wracked by student revolt. *The Orphanage* (Serpent's Tail, 1991), set in 1942, recounts the story of one of the "mixed-race" children who found themselves hurriedly handed over to nuns for protection from the Nazis. Both of these novels are coming-of-age stories that include investigation of the possibilities and limits of language, the development of sexual and religious identity, and an ethnography of sexual cultures, as well as depictions of postwar Hamburg and Germany.

892 García Lorca, Federico. ***The Rural Trilogy: Three Plays by Federico García Lorca***. Trans. from Spanish by Michael Dewell and Carmen Zapata. Bantam 1987, $8.95 (0-553-34434-X). 272pp. Drama.

Poet and playwright García Lorca is probably the most widely read Spanish writer of the twentieth century. He was born in Andalusia, and his works are steeped in the popular traditions of Granada. His premature death at the hands of Fascist partisans during the Spanish Civil War made his name one of the great symbols of the fight against totalitarianism. Many of his plays deal with the struggles of minority or impoverished people, such as Gypsies or peasants, to maintain personal integrity and exert their right to freedom. Often the most memorable characters in his plays are women, and the tensions between the sexes and the consequences for women who do not fulfill the rigid demands of their gender roles play an important part in his works.

Each of the plays in this anthology derives from a real-life incident. *Blood Wedding* grew from García Lorca's interest in a famous crime of passion in which a bride ran off with her cousin on the day of her wedding, only to be pursued by the bridegroom; the two men killed each other. The kernel of the play *Yerma* is the spring pilgrimage that barren wives and their husbands undertake to a mountain village near Granada; the play addresses the harsh lot of childless women in a peasant society in which childbearing is a woman's only true destiny. A woman much like the title character in *The House of Bernarda Alba* lived near García Lorca and was the model for the vicious widow whose embittered daughters have been stunted by their spinsterhood and their hatred. Federico's brother, Francisco García Lorca, has written an affecting memoir of his brother, *In the Green Morning* (New Directions, 1986).

893   Ginzburg, Natalia. *All Our Yesterdays*. Trans. from Italian by Angus Davidson. Arcade 1989, $8.95 (1-55970-026-2). 300pp. Fiction.

Born into a Jewish academic family, Ginzburg began to write when she was an adolescent. She is among the foremost Italian writers influenced by the Fascist era; her husband was active in the antifascist movement and died in prison in 1944. Her novels, which often center on family life, are written in a style that is thoughtful and deceptively simple.

A complex work filled with interlocking relationships, *All Our Yesterdays* details the lives of children of two neighboring families from the 1930s through World War II. Gradually coming to the center is Anna, who lives in a middle-class household in northern Italy. She and her friends become active in antifascist activities. At age sixteen Anna is made pregnant by a neighbor's son, but she marries an old family friend who takes her to his home in the south. There she finds a new world of poverty and misery, but a world filled with warm and generous people. To this small village come waves of Jewish refugees followed by occupying German troops. After the war Anna returns to the north and an uncertain future.

Voices in the Evening (Arcade, 1989) also deals with the Fascist past; it is an attempt to reconstruct the history of the author's own generation, which came of age under Fascism. Other works by this author currently in print include *Family Sayings* (Arcade, 1989), *The City and the House* (Arcade, 1989), and *The Road to the City* (Arcade, 1990).

894   Goytisolo, Juan. *Juan the Landless*. Trans. from Spanish by Helen R. Lane. Serpent's Tail 1991, $14.95 (1-85242-192-4). 268pp. Fiction.

Goytisolo, the author of short stories, travel fiction, literary criticism, and fiction, is one of Spain's most important living novelists. Born in Barcelona, Goytisolo was profoundly affected by the Spanish Civil War, in which his father was imprisoned and his mother killed. In 1956 he moved to Paris; many of the works he wrote there were banned in Franco's Spain. His novels typically concern the lives of the poor and describe the brutality of a society in which public order has collapsed.

Among his works available in English are a trilogy of novels. *Marks of Identity* (Consortium, 1992), originally published in 1966, is an attack on the Franco regime that presents stories of suffering in a Spanish police state where men are beaten, arrested, and killed for having defended the Republic. *Count Julian* (Serpent's Tail, 1990), written in 1971, is a meditation on exile and betrayal and offers a harsh portrayal of the author's native land. The third part of the trilogy, *Juan the Landless*, was written in 1975 and is often considered to be his finest work. This gripping portrayal of peasant life marks the end of the author's undiluted hostility toward Spain and celebrates Muslim contributions to Spanish culture.

Goytisolo's stream-of-consciousness style and his references to the Spanish past in history and literature make his novels challenging, but they repay the persistent reader with their passionate intensity. In addition to his novels, two volumes of memoirs were translated into English: *Forbidden Territory* (o.p.), covering the years from 1931 to 1956, and *Realms of Strife* (o.p.), which covers the author's life up to 1982.

895   Grass, Günter. ***The Danzig Trilogy: The Tin Drum, Cat and Mouse, The Dog Years***. Trans. from German. Pantheon 1987, $29.95 (0-15-123816-2). 1,030pp. Fiction.

Grass, a poet, novelist, essayist, and playwright, is perhaps the best-known German writer to emerge since World War II. He was born in the Free City of Danzig (now the Polish city of Gdansk), which is the setting for several of his novels, including the ones in this collection. He was drafted into the Labor Service late in World War II. After his release from an American prisoner-of-war camp in Bavaria, he worked for a time as a farm laborer and tombstone carver in West Germany. He studied painting and sculpture before beginning to write.

The Tin Drum, his first novel, established his reputation in Germany and abroad. It is a huge, irreverent, multilayered novel that surveys the Nazi era through the eyes of Oscar, a dwarf who grows up in Danzig. *Cat and Mouse* is a short novel about a Danzig boy set apart from his peers by his grotesque Adam's apple. *The Dog Years* traces the relationship of two young people from 1917 to 1957; the story also follows a line of Alsatian dogs, including one named Prinz, who was Hitler's favorite.

Grass has been a forceful campaigner for the Social Democratic Party and a critic of West German politics, as well as a voice of dissent in the German rush to reunification. Some of his more recent novels, such as *Headbirths: Or the Germans Are Dying Out* (Harcourt, 1990), as well as his essays, reflect his satirical and committed political viewpoint.

896   Heinesen, William. ***Laterna Magica***. Trans. from Danish by Tiina Nunnally. Fjord 1987, $15.95 (0-940242-22-2); $7.95 (0-940242-23-0). 160pp. Fiction.

This is a collection of short stories set in a small community in the Faeroe Islands. Heinesen, who writes in Danish rather than his native Faeroese, combines a sensitivity to nature with a strong social awareness and a sense of the fantastic. In many of his works, the heroes are ordinary Faeroese people. Novels currently in print in English translation include *The Kingdom of the Earth* (Irvington, 1974), *The Lost Musicians* (Irvington, 1971), and *Tower at the Edge of the World* (Univ. of Toronto Pr., 1982). Also available is a collection of stories, *The Winged Darkness* (Irvington, 1983). Another novel about the Faeroe Islands is *The Old Man and His Sons* by Hes in Brú *(see main entry)*.

897   Hofmann, Gert. ***Our Conquest***. Trans. from German. Fromm 1985. o.p. Fiction.

Gert Hofmann wrote fiction and plays for the stage and for radio. He was born in East Germany and moved to West Germany in 1951, where he was a professor of German literature. His works, reflective in tone, often deal with the qualities—both good and bad—of people who are confronted with illness, fear, and death. Several of his early novels have not been translated into English; these include *Die Denunziation*, *Leute in Violett*, and *Veilchenfeld*, which deal more or less directly with the nazification of Germany.

A novel that has been translated into English, *Our Conquest* (o.p.), deals with the impact of World War II on German schoolchildren. All the events take place in a small town during a single day just after the German defeat in May 1945. "Our conquerors"—the Allied troops—are nearby, but they are never seen. The boys of the Imbach family and their companion, the orphaned Edgar, vacillate between the prejudices they have learned from their Nazi parents and their desire to uncover the truth about their father's role in the death of a Czech prisoner. Poignantly, they see the grotesque situations in which they find themselves as normal.

Another novel by this author is *Before the Rainy Season* (Grove, 1991), the story of a former Wehrmacht officer who has moved to Bolivia and who tries to repress a past that nevertheless returns to haunt him.

898 Kazantzakis, Nikos. ***Zorba the Greek***. Trans. from Greek by Jonathan Griffin. Buccaneer 1993, $26.95 (1-56849-178-6); Simon & Schuster $9.95 (0-671-21132-3). 311pp. Fiction.

Kazantzakis, a novelist, essayist, dramatist, poet, philosopher, and translator, was born into a peasant family on Crete. He studied philosophy at the Sorbonne and traveled extensively in Europe and the Soviet Union. He became immersed in the revolutionary and communist ideas of the 1920s, then was active in the civil war that followed the liberation of Greece after World War II. He moved to France when the Royalists returned to power in Greece. He wrote many of his novels between 1942 and 1947. His belief in communism and his antireligious heroes made Kazantzakis the subject of controversy both during his life and afterward.

Zorba the Greek is the story of Crete and its people as personified by Zorba, a miner whose passion for life even in the face of death forms the core of the story. Other novels by Kazantzakis include *Freedom or Death* (o.p.), an epic novel about the Cretan uprising against the Turks in 1889, and *The Fratricides* (o.p.), a story about the Greek civil war.

899 Keneally, Thomas. ***Schindler's List***. Simon & Schuster 1994, $25.00 (0-671-51688-4); $12.00 (0-671-88031-4). 400pp. Fiction.

In 1940, Oskar Schindler, a German-speaking Czech and an early Nazi supporter, received weapons contracts from the Nazis and went into business in the Jewish ghetto of Cracow, Poland. He borrowed money from Jews to buy factories and hired skilled Jewish laborers to work for him. Unlike others who never repaid their Jewish investors and who beat and starved their Jewish workers, Schindler behaved honorably, never taking advantage of the powers that gentiles had over Jews under the Nazi regime. Schindler, notorious as a womanizer who organized lavish parties for Nazi officials, used his profits to free Jews from death convoys. By 1943 he had become a conduit of money from Jews throughout Europe to ransom their relatives.

Keneally, an Australian novelist, studied documents describing the exploits of the real-life Schindler to create this vivid historical novel, which was made into an Academy Award–winning feature film in 1993. The personality of the novel's Schindler is largely an invention of Keneally's imagination, created to explain how a self-centered and decadent businessman was able to rise above the evil of the Nazi world and become a true hero. This is a powerfully written and exciting novel that gives the reader a realistic portrayal of life for the Jews and their exploiters in the Nazi era.   RL

900 Lessing, Gotthold Ephraim. ***Nathan the Wise, Minna Von Barnhelm and Other Plays and Writings***. Trans. and ed. by Peter Demetz; Frwd. by Hannah Arendt. Continuum 1991, $29.50 (0-8264-0706-4); $14.95 (0-8264-0707-2). 324pp. Drama.

A dramatist, philosopher, essayist, and translator, Lessing is considered the greatest writer of the German Enlightenment. His play, *Nathan the Wise*, explores issues concerning religious tolerance. In Jerusalem at the time of the Crusades, Nathan, a Jew, recounts the parable of the three rings, which represent Christianity, Judaism, and Islam. When members of the three faiths accept each other's differences, all prosper, but when they try to conquer or convert the other, mutual destruction follows.

901 Levi, Primo. ***If Not Now, When?*** Trans. from Italian by William Weaver. Viking 1986, $11.00 (0-14-008492-4). 352pp. Fiction.

This historical novel of World War II is based on the experiences of an actual Yiddish-speaking partisan military unit. Written in part to counter the idea that the Jews offered no resistance to their Nazi oppressors, it is both an adventure story and a character study. In the book, some peaceful Jews take up arms to fight in a cause they know to be hopeless and end up battling their way across Eastern Europe. At war's end they are in Italy, hardened and exhausted, their homes and people destroyed, but with their dignity and humanity intact.

Primo Levi, who also fought in a partisan group in northern Italy, was one of the most eloquent chroniclers of the Holocaust. During the war he was captured and sent to Auschwitz, where for the first time he came in contact with Eastern European Jews such as those he describes here.

902 Maron, Monika. ***Flight of Ashes***. Trans. from German by David N. Marinelli. Readers International 1986, $16.95 (0-930523-22-9); $8.95 (0-930523-23-7). 188pp. Fiction.

Monika Maron was born in Berlin and lived in East Berlin until the East German authorities allowed her to go to Hamburg in 1988. She studied theater arts and worked as a reporter until her first novel, *Flugasche* (*Flight of Ashes*), was published in 1981. This is a powerful political story about a young reporter who writes an honest and sobering account of the East German industrial city of Bitterfeldt—perhaps the most polluted region in Europe. The reporter describes the gray, empty lives of the alienated, cynical workers, many of whom are made ill by their work. For her efforts in exposing the workers' condition, the young journalist is harassed and threatened by the Communist authorities.

Another of Maron's works, *The Defector* (Readers International, 1988), portrays the despair of a young woman who, unable to escape her circumscribed and arid existence, "defects" through the power of her imagination. *Silent Close No. 6* (Readers International, 1993) concerns a retired East German high official who hires a disaffected journalist to transcribe his memoirs. His life is seen through the critical consciousness of the journalist. This book won the Heinrich von Kleist Prize in 1992; despite flaws in its English translation, it offers a subtle reassessment of Communist rule.

903 Mulisch, Harry. *The Assault*. Trans. from Dutch by Claire White. Pantheon 1986, $13.00 (0-394-74420-9). 162pp. Fiction.

Mulisch, a novelist, poet, playwright, and essayist, is one of the Netherlands' foremost writers. *The Assault*, which earned him an international reputation, is the story of a family in Haarlem and the consequences of an act of violence—the assassination of a Nazi collaborator—that took place outside the family's home during the German occupation. In the course of several episodes, a young—and then increasingly aging—survivor must confront new facets and viewpoints of the event. This work is a study of human nature and the nature of evil.

904 Multatuli. *Max Havelaar: Or the Coffee Auctions of the Dutch Trading Company*. Trans. from Dutch by Roy Edwards; Intro. by D. H. Lawrence; Aftwd. by E. M. Beekman. Univ. of Massachusetts Pr. 1982, $35.00 (0-87023-359-9); $18.95 (0-87023-360-2). 400pp. Fiction.

Multatuli is the pseudonym of Eduard Douwes Dekker, a novelist, essayist, and satirist who was one of the foremost Dutch writers of the nineteenth century. Born in Amsterdam, he was sent to Java in 1838 as an officer in the Dutch colonial bureaucracy. After he began to protest the abuses by the colonial administration, he was forced to return to Holland in 1857. His first novel, *Max Havelaar*, appeared in 1860; its theme is the abuses of labor in the Dutch Indies. The story concerns a young, idealistic administrator—a character obviously based on the author—who experiences profound disillusionment about his country's actions, motives, and ideals in the East Indies. The book was read all over Europe. Multatuli's later writings continued to attack Dutch colonial administration and conventional Dutch society.

905 Nexo, Martin Andersen. *Pelle the Conqueror: Vol. 1: Childhood; Vol. 2: Apprenticeship; Vol. 3: The Great Struggle*. Trans. from Danish by Steven T. Murray and Tina Nunnally. Fjord 1989; 1991, $19.95 each (0-940242-41-9; 0-940242-49-4; 0-940242-64-8); $9.95 each (0-940242-40-0; 0-940242-48-6; 0-940242-63-X). 244+ 224+ 256pp. Fiction.

This trilogy, part of which was adapted into an award-winning film, traces the development of a boy growing up during the turbulent changes of the late nineteenth century. In Volume 1, the Swedish boy Pelle arrives on the Danish island of Bornholm with his father, Lasse, in search of work and a better life. In Volume 2, Pelle becomes an apprentice shoemaker and dreams of leaving the island. The third volume of the series was slated for publication at the time of this writing. An ongoing tale, this work is already a classic of European literature, one filled with humor and warmth and peopled by diverse and interesting characters.

906 Perec, Georges. *Things: A Story of the Sixties and A Man Asleep: Two Novels in One Volume*. Trans. from French. Godine 1990, $19.95 (0-87923-857-7). 221pp. Fiction.

Perec (1936–1982) was born in Paris of Polish-Jewish parents. After a traumatic childhood, which he recorded in his autobiographical work *W: Or the Memory of Childhood* (Godine, 1988), he decided to become a writer. *Things: A Story of the Sixties*, written after his return from a year in Tunisia, reflects some of this experience as well as the unrest of the young intellectuals in 1960s Paris, the first postwar generation to confront mass consumerism. The work is written as a series of vignettes, often filled with irony or satire, in which Perec portrays youngsters who reject their parents' materialistic values while at the same time embracing the new consumer products geared to their generation. *A Man Asleep* deals with the theme of serious depression.

Perec's television film and book *Recits d'Ellis Island* (*Stories of Ellis Island*; not translated) profoundly explores his Jewish identity. His most famous novel is *La Vie, Mode d'Emploi* (*Life, A User's Manual*; French and European, 1980), which describes the lives of occupants in a Parisian apartment building as though the outer walls had been removed.

Ricci, Nino. **The Book of Saints.**
See entry 597.

907 Schwarz-Bart, André. **The Last of the Just.** Repr. of 1960 ed. Trans. from French by Stephen Becker. Bentley 1981, $22.00 (0-8376-0456-7); Macmillan $15.95 (0-689-70365-1). 202pp. Fiction.

Schwarz-Bart was born the son of Polish Jews in France in 1928. When he was thirteen, his parents were taken by the Nazis and deported to extermination camps; at fifteen he joined the Resistance. This novel, his first, was published in 1960. It is the epic and passionate history of the persecution of the Jews, beginning in England in 1185, addressing the bigotry and pogroms in France, Spain, Poland, and Russia, and ending in the gas chambers of Auschwitz. Giving unity and meaning to this inhumanity is the Jewish legend of the thirty-six just men, one of whom, it is said, emerges in each generation to receive upon himself the world's grief. The last of these just men is Ernie Levy, who goes voluntarily to the gas chamber. His reasons are not made clear, but he feels connected to past horrors and feels it is his duty to submit to the fate awaiting him. This philosophical novel is a classic that should be read by everyone who wants to learn more about the Jews' tragic history in Europe.

908 Sebbar, Leila. **Sherazade.** Trans. from Arabic by Dorothy S. Blair. Interlink 1991, $19.95 (0-7043-2778-3). 264pp. Fiction.

Leila Sebbar, born in Algeria of a French mother and an Algerian father, is a novelist and journalist now living in Paris. This semiautobiographical novel has a female protagonist, Sherazade, who lives a marginalized existence in the working-class districts of Paris with friends and acquaintances who are children of the immigrant proletariat from North Africa, the Caribbean, and Poland. These young adults are independent, unassimilated, intelligent factory workers, drug addicts, revolutionaries, and dropouts. Sherazade writes poetry, loves to read, and gradually discovers her Algerian inheritance. She moves out of her parents' home into a building taken over by squatters. When the building explodes, she disappears entirely, and the French authorities refuse to investigate because they do not consider her to be "French."

Walker, Scott, ed. **Stories from the New Europe.**
See entry 1038.

909 Wolf, Christa. ***Patterns of Childhood***. Trans. from German by Ursule Molinaro and Hedwig Rappolt. Farrar 1984, $15.00 (0-374-51844-0). 407pp. Fiction.

Wolf, a novelist, essayist, and screenwriter, is perhaps the most famous of all East German authors. Her works achieved great popular success in both Germanies, though often without the support or approval of East German authorities. She was born into a comfortable, pro-Nazi household in the extreme eastern part of Germany, now part of Poland. After fleeing as refugees from the Soviet army in World War II, her family settled in East Germany, where she was educated and where she began to write. Following German unification, Wolf has come under criticism for not having been sufficiently critical of the East German regime.

Patterns of Childhood is a semiautobiographical novel based on the author's childhood in a family of Nazi supporters. The protagonist, a young girl, joins the Nazi youth organizations and learns to hate and fear Jews. No one in the family protests when a feeble-minded aunt becomes a victim of the Nazi euthanasia program. By 1946, everything the girl had grown to believe in has collapsed. Paralleling this is the story of a visit by the protagonist, now a woman, to her old home in 1971. She is accompanied by her own teenage daughter, to whom she attempts to explain how these things could have happened.

What Remains and Other Stories (Farrar, 1993) collects Wolf's short fiction from her early work to the title story, which stirred considerable debate when it appeared in Germany in 1990. In this story, the writer portrays how secret police surveillance destroys all normalcy in life, making even close friends suspect each other of being informants. Wolf's essays on literature and politics have been collected in a volume entitled *The Author's Dimension* (Farrar, 1993).

NONFICTION

910 Abrahamsen, Samuel. ***Norway's Response to the Holocaust: An Historical Perspective***. Holocaust Publications 1991, $21.95 (0-89604-116-6); $13.95 (0-89604-117-4). 200pp. Nonfiction.

Nearly half of Norway's Jewish population was killed during World War II. In this clear and objective account, the author contends that while only a few Norwegians were members of the Nazi party, there were enough anti-Semites and bureaucrats who collaborated with them to make the extermination of Jews in that country a near success. He discusses Norway's long tradition of anti-Semitism and Norway's restrictive interwar immigration policies, which kept out refugees from Nazi terror elsewhere. In counterpoint, the author notes that thousands of ordinary Norwegians helped hundreds of Jews escape, mostly into Sweden.

911 Arlacchi, Pino. ***Mafia Business: The Mafia Ethic and the Spirit of Capitalism***. Trans. from Italian by Martin Ryle. Routledge 1987, $44.95 (0-86091-135-7); $13.95 (0-86091-892-0). 239pp. Nonfiction.

Arlacchi, a sociologist, is one of Italy's leading authorities on the Mafia. In this book he examines the culture of the Mafia, its belief systems, and its role in

Italian society since World War II. Arlacchi is also the author of *Mafia, Peasants and Great Estates: Society in Traditional Calabria* (Cambridge Univ. Pr., 1983), a scholarly economic and social history of the southern region of Italy before the transformations of the war.

912   Bar-On, Dan. *Legacy of Silence: Encounters with Children of the Third Reich.* Harvard Univ. Pr. 1990, $35.00 (0-674-52185-4); $12.95 (0-674-52186-2). 384pp. Nonfiction.

Bar-On is an Israeli psychologist of German origin. These interviews with the children of some of the major Nazi war criminals reveal them to be people who are coming to terms with their past in various ways: Some deny the enormity of the Holocaust; others align themselves with antifascist left-wing causes; still others refuse to have children for fear of passing on the "bad gene." One of the interviewees even converted to Judaism. These sensitive interviews also illustrate some of the complexity of contemporary Germany's involvement with its recent past.

913   Beach, Hugh. *A Year in Lapland: Guest of the Reindeer Herders.* Illus. Smithsonian Inst. 1993, $24.95 (1-56098-230-6). 280pp. Nonfiction.

An American anthropologist tells of his first year among the Sami reindeer herders of Swedish Lapland. He describes their way of living, one that follows the ancient traditions of herding and grazing while incorporating the technology of the modern world. Combining travelogue and anthropological detail, humor and poignancy, this readable and attractively illustrated book documents one of Europe's most unique peoples.

914   Bentley, Jerry H. *Old World Encounters: Cross-Cultural Contacts and Exchanges in Pre-Modern Times.* Illus. Oxford Univ. Pr. 1992, $37.00 (0-19-507639-7); $15.95 (0-19-507640-0). 240pp. Nonfiction.

Well before modern times, Asian, African, and European peoples were regularly interacting and intermingling with each other. Their encounters rank among the most effective agents of change in all of world history, fostering the spread of technologies, ideas, beliefs, values, and religions. This study examines processes that determined cross-cultural encounters before 1492. It explores several eras, from the age of the ancient silk roads that linked China with the Roman Empire, through the Mongol Empire, up to the early transoceanic ventures of Europeans during the fifteenth century. Taking a global rather than a Eurocentric approach, the author examines the dynamics that brought populations in contact with each other and identifies the distinctive patterns of conversion, conflict, and compromise that emerged from these encounters.

915   Björgo, Tore, and Rob Witte, eds. *Racist Violence in Europe.* St. Martin 1993, $59.95 (0-312-10297-6); $18.95 (0-312-12409-0). 260pp. Nonfiction.

To create this book, fifteen experts in the field of racism and racist violence each contributed a chapter based on their expertise. Included are chapters on Germany, the Netherlands, Scandinavia, Britain, France, and Turkey, as well as more general treatments of the international dimensions of neo-Nazism, the role of the media, and general policy concerns. The emphasis is on current conditions, with a brief introduction that provides historical background. The chapters are well written and accessible to general readers and students and provide a good basis for further reading and discussion of European racism.

916 Blanke, Richard. ***Orphans of Versailles: The German Minority in Western Poland, 1918–1939***. Univ. Pr. of Kentucky 1993, $39.00 (0-8131-1803-4). 328pp. Nonfiction.

The lands Germany ceded to Poland after World War I were home to more than one million ethnic Germans for whom the change meant a sharp reversal of roles. The Polish government now had to deal with a German minority in the region—a complete reversal of the way things had been for more than a century. Many factors combined to create a national conflict without parallel in recent European history, a conflict that was one of the underlying triggers of World War II. This book examines the complex psychological and political situation of Germans consigned to Poland, their treatment by the Polish government and society, their diverse strategies for survival, their place in international relations, and the impact of Nazism. This even-handed analysis treats the contributions of both the Polish state and the German minority to the conflict that culminated in their mutual destruction.

917 Boswell, John. ***Christianity, Social Tolerance, and Homosexuality: Gay People in Western Europe from the Beginning of the Christian Era to the Fourteenth Century***. Univ. of Chicago Pr. 1981, $35.00 (0-226-06710-6); $18.95 (0-226-06711-4). 424pp. Nonfiction.

This is a history of the experiences of homosexuals in Europe over the past millennium and a half. Tracing the origin and evolution of overt intolerance of homosexuals, which arose in the thirteenth century, the author draws parallels to the rise in intolerance toward other minorities: heretics, Muslims, and Jews. He also argues that prejudice against homosexuals cannot be traced to Christian texts found in the Bible, but rather to later writers such as St. Augustine. This is a clearly written, classic work that debunks many myths in analyzing the fear of homosexuals so prominent in Western and Western-influenced societies today. Boswell is also the author of *Same-Sex Unions in Premodern Europe* (Random, 1994).

Bredin, Jean-Denis. ***The Affair: The Case of Alfred Dreyfus***.
See under entry 919.

918 Burleigh, Michael, and Wolfgang Wipperman. ***The Racial State: Germany, 1933–1945***. Illus. Cambridge Univ. Pr. 1991, $44.95 (0-521-39114-8); $19.95 (0-521-39802-9). 416pp. Nonfiction.

During the Nazi era, Germany tried to construct a society of social classes structured along racial lines. This book describes the origins of the Nazi racial ideology, the thoroughness with which it was put into action, and the effectiveness of its execution. The book deals not only with the systematic persecution of Jews but also with the fate of Gypsies, the mentally handicapped, the "asocial," and homosexuals. Finally, it examines the racially motivated social policies that affected all Germans. This is a useful encyclopedic treatment of a vast topic.

Readers wishing more information on specific aspects should consult such sources as Richard Plant's *The Pink Triangle: The Nazi War Against Homosexuals* (Henry Holt, 1988), Robert Jay Lifton's *The Nazi Doctors: Medical Killing and the Psychology of Genocide* (Basic Books, 1986), George Mosse's *Nazi Culture* (Schocken, 1981), and Claudia Koonz's *Mothers in the Fatherland: Women, the Family, and Nazi Politics* (St. Martin, 1988).

919   Burns, Michael. *Dreyfus: A Family Affair, 1789–1945*. Illus. HarperCollins 1991, $30.00 (0-06-016366-6); $15.00 (0-06-092345-8). 576pp. Nonfiction.

The Dreyfus affair is perhaps the most famous and symbolic act of French anti-Semitism before the Holocaust. It is the subject of many books; this one and a related title—Jean-Denis Bredin's *The Affair: The Case of Alfred Dreyfus* (Braziller, 1987)—represent the most successful recent attempts to understand and synthesize its history and denouement. Bredin's book focuses on Captain Dreyfus, a Jew, and the forces surrounding his persecution. In his book, Burns traces the history of the Dreyfus family from the eighteenth century through the end of World War II, viewing the history of this family as both typical and emblematic of the history of the Jews in Europe. The Burns work thus adds to the dimensions of the story by placing the Dreyfus affair in its broader historical context.

920   Calvino, Italo. *Italian Folktales*. Repr. of 1956 ed. Trans. from Italian by George Martin. Illus. Harcourt 1990, $27.95 (0-15-145770-0); $19.95 (0-15-645489-0). 800pp. Nonfiction.

Noted Italian author and storyteller Calvino has selected and adapted 200 folktales from throughout Italy. In each case, he identifies the region from which the story comes. Extensive notes at the end offer additional information on the origins of the tales and about other known versions and variations. A useful introduction provides a history of Italy's folk traditions, identifies the criteria the author used in selecting the tales, and includes a few personal touches. The introduction also outlines the major recurring themes of the stories in the collection, such as the relationship between kings and commoners. Calvino notes how the tales paint a picture of Italy as a center of worldwide commerce, a meeting ground between Europe and the Middle East. The influence of other European and Middle Eastern traditions on these tales is evident. Many of the stories depict Italians as hosts of foreign travelers or as guests in other lands. This is a definitive and comprehensive collection, of interest to students of folklore and general readers seeking to learn about Italian culture.   LML

921   Cheles, Luciano, and M. E. Vaughan, eds. *Neo-Fascism in Europe*. Illus. Longman 1991, $23.95 (0-582-03951-7). 368pp. Nonfiction.

Each essay in this collection is written by specialists in the political analysis of the resurgence of the radical right in Italy, Spain, France, West Germany, Greece, and Portugal. This is an accurate and detailed description and analysis that provides deep insights to readers with an interest in the subject.

922 Collins, Roger. *The Basques*. Illus. Blackwell 1990, $19.95 (0-631-17565-2). 288pp. Nonfiction.

This book and another volume, Marianne Heilberg's *The Making of the Basque Nation* (Cambridge Univ. Pr., 1989), together form a comprehensive study of the Basques of Spain and France. Both authors are anthropologists. Collins's book is a history of the Basques from their earliest origins through the end of the Middle Ages. Knowing the long history of the Basque people and the richness of their culture is crucial for understanding the modern issue of Basque nationalism, which is the focus of Heilberg's book.

923 Cornelisen, Ann. *Women of the Shadows: A Study of the Wives and Mothers of Southern Italy*. Illus. Viking 1991, $9.95 (0-14-014785-3). 256pp. Nonfiction.

In 1954 Cornelisen, a worker for the Save the Children Fund, went to Italy to build and administer a nursery school in Lucarnia, a small farming community that had changed little since feudal days. She remained in Italy and has written eloquently of the people she met. *Torregreca* (o.p.), her first book, tells about life in the Italian villages in the Abruzzi, Lucania, and Calabria regions and the struggle to bring the benefits of modernity to children. For *Strangers and Pilgrims* (o.p.), Cornelisen traveled to northern Italy and to Germany to visit the families she had known in the south. Most of them had done well, with far better jobs and housing than they had before, yet they had paid a price in the pain and bitterness of being uprooted from their traditional homes and living as outsiders in their new communities. *Women of the Shadows* describes the lives of five peasant women who stay home struggling to care for their families while their husbands seek work.

924 Cross, Malcolm, and Hans Entzinger, eds. *Lost Illusions: Caribbean Minorities in Britain and the Netherlands*. Routledge 1988, $55.00 (0-415-00628-7). 224pp. Nonfiction.

In this collection of articles, sociologists look at issues of assimilation and social mobility among Caribbean minorities in the Netherlands and Great Britain. The situations in these countries are examined both individually and comparatively. Included are discussions of the recent history of immigration, as well as articles on labor, education, economic development, and the role of ethnicity in Dutch politics. On the whole, the essays are clearly written and readable, offering insights to students or to general readers with interest and some background in the subject.

925 Dias-Mas, Paloma. *Sephardim: The Jews from Spain*. Trans. from Spanish and ed. by George K. Zucker. Univ. of Chicago Pr. 1992, $27.50 (0-226-14483-6). 292pp. Nonfiction.

Dias-Mas provides an account of the Sephardic Jews, including their culture, history, religious practice, language, and literature. Most of the Sephardim originally settled in Mediterranean Europe, the Low Countries, North Africa, and the Turkish Empire. In the nineteenth century, a second diaspora brought the Sephardim to the United States, South America, Israel, and Western Europe. After detailing the various causes of the second diaspora, Dias-Mas addresses the specific impact of the Holocaust on the Sephardim and reviews the involvement of the Sephardim in Spanish politics through the years of the Republican government and into Franco's time and the present. The final chapter focuses on the situation of the Sephardim throughout the world today.

A related book by Jane Gerber, *The Jews of Spain: A History of the Sephardic Experience* (Free Pr., 1992), traces the history of the Sephardim from their emergence as a distinctive community in the second century to the present. Special focus is given to the great flowering of Jewish culture under Moorish rule.

926   Ellwood, Sheelagh M. ***The Spanish Civil War***. Illus. Blackwell 1991, $10.95 (0-631-16617-3). 112pp. Nonfiction.

The Spanish Civil War is the subject of a large, complex, and often controversial body of literature. This book is a clear and nonpartisan introduction to, and overview of, the war. The author describes all of the parties involved, the origins of the conflict, the chronology of events, and the immediate aftermath. Included is an extensive guide to further reading. Readers wishing a more detailed account should consult Hugh Thomas's *The Spanish Civil War* (HarperCollins, 1986).

927   Enzensberger, Hans Magnus. ***Europe, Europe: Forays into a Continent***. Trans. from German by Martin Chalmers. Pantheon 1990. o.p. Nonfiction.

In a book that was very well received in Europe, one of Germany's leading authors offers an insider's tour of Europe in the recent past. Focusing on Italy, Poland, Hungary, Sweden, Spain, and Portugal, he describes how Europe has been moving toward a new identity. By delving into surprising corners and byways and through his revealing interviews with people of many backgrounds, he suggests that Europe's strength lies not in size and regimentation but increasingly in its ability to embrace diversity and improvise new solutions to its problems.

928   Fraser, Angus. ***The Gypsies***. Illus. Blackwell 1992, $24.95 (0-631-15967-3); $19.95 (0-631-19605-6). 352pp. Nonfiction.

Broadly speaking, the Gypsies are a single distinct ethnic minority with communities in many European countries. But they are also a diverse and varied people. This work provides an up-to-date history and description of the Gypsy peoples of Europe, describing and documenting both the common elements of their history and the ways in which they have come to differ. It is a history of change, resilience, and continuity despite prejudice and persecution at the hands of governments as well as individuals.

Fuentes, Carlos. ***The Buried Mirror: Reflections on Spain and the New World***. See entry 737.

929   Galliou, Patrick, and Michael Jones. ***The Bretons***. Illus. Blackwell 1991, $29.95 (0-631-16406-5). 240pp. Nonfiction.

The Bretons, an ancient people, struggle to preserve their own language, ethnicity, and cultural distinctiveness within modern France. This book discusses the historical development of Breton culture over a very long span, from its earliest beginnings to the end of the Middle Ages. Another theme is the changing relations between the Bretons and their neighbors.

930   Gay, Ruth. *The Jews of Germany: A Historical Portrait*. Intro. by Peter Gay. Illus. Yale Univ. Pr. 1992, $40.00 (0-300-05155-7); $20.00 (0-300-06052-1). 336pp. Nonfiction.

Lavishly illustrated with paintings, photographs, and excerpts from letters and other historical documents, this lively and affirming history covers the period between the fall of Jerusalem in A.D. 70 and the rise of Hitler in 1933. The emphasis is on the day-to-day life of the Jews who lived in the German lands. A portrait emerges of a vibrant and changing culture.

Gerber, Jane S. *The Jews of Spain: A History of the Sephardic Experience*. See under entry 925.

931   Grass, Günter. *Two States, One Nation?* Helen Wolff and Kurt Wolff, eds.; Trans. from German by Krishna Winston with A. S. Wensinger. Harcourt 1990, $18.95 (0-15-192270-5). 66pp. Essays.

In addition to being one of Germany's foremost novelists, Grass is also deeply involved in politics. This collection of political essays and speeches is particularly timely because Grass has been one of the most eloquent critics of the rush to unification of the two Germanies. Essentially, he argues that Germany has not fully shed its Nazi past and is not yet ready to become a large nation that, one day, may pose a danger to the rest of Europe. Several of the speeches and interviews translated here sparked enormous controversy when they first appeared in Germany. Other collections of his political speeches and writings include *On Writing and Politics 1967–1983* (Harcourt, 1985). Grass is also the author of *The Danzig Trilogy (see main entry)*.

932   Hallie, Philip P. *Lest Innocent Blood Be Shed: The Story of the Village of Le Chambon and How Goodness Happened There*. Repr. of 1979 ed. Illus. HarperCollins 1994, $13.00 (0-06-092517-5). 303pp. Nonfiction.

The author of this book, a professor of ethics, discovered this story in the course of researching Nazi atrocities. In the tiny Protestant village of Le Chambon in southern France, the villagers, led by their pastor, risked their lives to shelter and protect the Jewish refugees who fled there during the Nazi occupation of France. To understand how and why such acts occurred, Hallie traveled to Le Chambon and spoke to the villagers, who have a long tradition of pacifism and nonviolence. This portrayal explores the deceptively simple acts of human kindness that occurred in the privacy of people's homes and examines in detail the central role that women played in sheltering the refugees.

Hancock, Ian. *The Pariah Syndrome: An Account of Gypsy Slavery and Persecution*.
See entry 832.

933   Hargreaves, Alec G. *Voices from the North African Immigrant Community in France: Immigration and Identity in Beur Fiction*. St. Martin 1991, $49.50 (0-85496-649-8); $15.95 (0-85496-335-9). 184pp. Nonfiction.

"Beur" is the name given to the new generation of North Africans in France. These sons and daughters of the original North African immigrants are creating a striking new body of literature, and this book is the first English-language treatment of their work. Aimed at the general reader, it explores the themes, sources, and people that make up this new wave. These writers are passionately concerned with issues of identity in a society that does not fully accept them.

934   Harris, Geoffrey. *The Dark Side of Europe: The Extreme Right Today*. 2nd ed. Barnes & Noble 1994, $64.50 (0-389-20924-4); Columbia Univ. Pr. $25.00 (0-7486-0466-9). 205pp. Nonfiction.

This is a scholarly but accessible account of the growth and current status of the extreme right in Europe. In recent years rightist political movements have produced a wave of intolerance against immigrants and other racial, religious, and cultural minorities. Each chapter in this book is devoted to a different aspect of the problem, including the dimensions of right-wing politics, terrorism, the extreme right in countries such as Britain and France, and efforts by the European Community to deal with this phenomenon.

Heilberg, Marianne. *The Making of the Basque Nation*.
See under entry 922.

935   Hilberg, Raul. *The Destruction of the European Jews*. 3 vols.; Rev. ed. Holmes & Meier 1985, $99.50 (boxed set) (0-8419-0832-X); $16.95 (abr. ed.) (0-8419-0910-5). 1,312pp. Nonfiction.

In this massive work, the author shows in riveting detail the processes by which the Jews of Europe were slaughtered. The definitive history of the mechanisms of genocide, this book details the bureaucratic organizations and structures established by the Nazis for the efficient and total destruction of Jews and other "undesirables," including the Poles, the Gypsies, homosexuals, and the mentally retarded. The author explores all facets of this organization, from the administrative offices to the local sites where the killings were carried out. He also examines the responses to the genocide among victims and bystanders and explores the ways people organized themselves for survival. Packed with information, including tables and graphs, this majestic three-volume work heightens the reader's sense of the horror of this carefully planned and meticulously carried out carnage. Also available is a single-volume abridged edition.

Another work by the same author, one perhaps more directly accessible to the lay reader, is *Perpetrators, Victims, Bystanders* (HarperCollins, 1992). In this work Hilberg offers short biographies of the people who caused, suffered from, and witnessed the Holocaust. This book reveals the impact of the Holocaust at every level of society.

936   Hughes, Robert. ***Barcelona***. Knopf 1992, $27.50 (0-679-41085-6); Random $14.00 (0-679-74383-9). 496pp. Nonfiction.

This is an appreciation of Barcelona, tracing the evolution of the city from its ancient origins to its contemporary identity as the center of Catalan culture and identity. The author, a noted critic of art and culture, intended at first to write an architectural history of late nineteenth-century Barcelona. He soon discovered, however, that to tell the story fully required exploring the entire context of Catalonia's long history, especially the interrelationship of the region's art and architecture with its literature and music as well as with its political and social history. Thus, although on one level the book is an urban history, the author also presents a loving view of all aspects of Barcelona, past and present. Aimed at the nonspecialist, this is an enjoyable introduction to one of Spain's most distinctive places and cultures.

937   James, Harold, and Marla Stone, eds. ***When the Wall Came Down: Reactions to German Unification***. Routledge 1992, $59.95 (0-415-90589-3); $17.95 (0-415-90590-7). 464pp. Essays.

This collection of articles from various sources documents the views of observers from Europe and America who reacted as the unification of Germany proceeded with what seemed to be astonishing speed. Included are several pieces that carefully analyze the process through which the two German states became one. Some of the opinions expressed here are controversial, others seem misguided, and still others appear prescient. This is a useful documentation of the reaction of non-Germans to the phenomenon of unification.

Kaplan, Robert D. ***Balkan Ghosts: A Journey Through History***. See entry 1058.

938   Katz, Jacob. ***Tradition and Crisis: Jewish Society at the End of the Middle Ages***. Trans. and Aftwd. by Bernard D. Cooperman. New York Univ. Pr. 1992, $40.00 (0-8147-4637-3); Schocken, $17.00 (0-8052-0996-4). 416pp. Nonfiction.

Katz's works are classic studies in the history of European Jewish society. *Tradition and Crisis* traces the origins of modern Judaism through two movements, Enlightenment in the West and Hasidism in the East. Katz examines the question of how two Jewish traditions could evolve so differently, and he examines the social contexts that led to the existence of two distinct types of Judaism—one liberal and willing to embrace the secular and the other highly orthodox and strongly traditional.

Another of this author's books, *From Prejudice to Destruction* (Harvard Univ. Pr., 1990), is a carefully written and well-informed social history of European anti-Semitism before the Nazi period.

939   Kocturk, Tahire. ***A Matter of Honour: Experiences of Turkish Women Immigrants***. Humanities Pr. 1992, $49.95 (1-85649-075-0); $19.95 (1-85649-076-9). 204pp. Nonfiction.

More than three million Turkish workers, largely from rural areas, have migrated to Western Europe, where they provide a cheap source of labor. Nearly all of them arrived in the 1960s and 1970s. This book examines the social and cultural impact of life in Western industrial society on these Muslim immigrants. Special focus is given to gender and family relations.

Kocturk provides a historical overview of Turkish women's lifestyles from ancient times to the 1920s, when they first were granted equal rights. In examining modern Turkey, the author describes the lives of upper- and lower-class women in both urban and rural settings, including the slums that surround the big cities. Through interviews with Turkish immigrants, especially the women and their daughters, the author explores how these families, nurtured in a rural Islamic tradition, have reacted to living in secular Western Europe.

940 Krause, Axel. *Inside New Europe*. HarperCollins 1991, $27.50 (0-06-039101-4). 367pp. Nonfiction.

This is a lively, journalistic account of the Western European movement toward economic and political unity as demonstrated by the growth of the European Community. The author describes both the history and the current state of European unity and the resurgence of the European economy. Also included here is discussion of the role of the United States in European economic affairs. Anecdotal and sometimes irreverent, the author brings life to a subject more often discussed in academic terms.

941 Lewin, Rhoda G. *Witnesses to the Holocaust: An Oral History*. Illus. Macmillan 1989, $20.95 (0-8057-9100-0); $12.95 (0-8057-9126-4). 240pp. Nonfiction.

This book contains forty-four evocative narratives mostly collected by the author in Minnesota during the 1980s. People who were caught up in the Holocaust reflect upon their experiences and tell their stories in their own words. Sections of this book focus on various groups: survivors of concentration camps, survivors who were not in concentration camps, and American liberators. In addition to memories about life in the camps, there are reminiscences by people who had been slave laborers, by resistance fighters, by those who survived in hiding, and by witnesses to the liberation of the camps.

942 Lewis, Rand C. *A Nazi Legacy: Right-Wing Extremism in West Germany*. Greenwood 1991, $42.95 (0-275-93853-0). 184pp. Fiction.

This work examines the ideas, personalities, and events that have led to a resurgence of right-wing neo-Nazi politics in Germany. The first half, which deals with the development of the German right from the 1920s to the 1960s, contains information that is widely available in other sources. The second half, however, gives detailed coverage of radical right-wingers and neo-Nazis from the late 1970s until German unification in 1990. The author describes the leading contemporary personalities, the connections between German neo-Nazis and their counterparts abroad, and the background, character, and philosophy of the "skinheads."

943 Mahmood, Cynthia. ***Frisian and Free: Study of an Ethnic Minority of the Netherlands***. Illus. Waveland Pr. 1989, $8.50 (0-88133-418-9). 111pp. Non-fiction.

This portrait by an anthropologist looks at an ethnic group that has proudly retained its linguistic and cultural identity for generations. The author examines the success of the Frisians in maintaining cultural autonomy in the light of current conditions and raises the question of how deeply rooted this autonomy will actually prove to be in the decades to come. Included are sections on history, village and rural life, and the prospects for the survival of Frisian culture.

944 Malino, Frances, and Bernard Wasserstein, eds. ***The Jews in Modern France***. Illus. Univ. Press of New England 1985, $40.00 (0-87451-324-3). 368pp. Nonfiction.

This collection of essays focuses on the encounters between Jews and French society and culture in the period since the French Revolution. In addition to pieces detailing the history of the Jews of France, there are several works exploring anti-Semitism and the general status of Jews in present-day France. Although the essays vary in quality and readability, many of them provide thoughtful overviews of their subjects and are ideal for students and others who are beginning to explore this area.

945 Marrus, Michael R. ***The Unwanted: European Refugees in the Twentieth Century***. Illus. Oxford Univ. Pr. 1987, $30.00 (0-19-503615-8); $10.95 (0-19-505186-6). 371pp. Nonfiction.

Although refugees have been part of European history since time immemorial, only in the twentieth century have they become an important problem of international politics. This book is a survey of the refugee migrations in Europe since the 1880s. As the size of the European refugee population became greater than any the world had ever known before, new problems of refugee displacement and permanent statelessness also grew. This book traces Europe's growing consciousness of the refugee phenomenon and the attempts by various governments to deal with it from the period of the Balkan crises before World War I to the present. Among the people discussed are the vanquished Armenians and the stateless persons created by the changes in national boundaries that resulted from the two World Wars.

946 Marrus, Michael R., and Robert O. Paxton. ***Vichy France and the Jews***. Schocken 1981. o.p. Nonfiction.

This work documents the active collaboration between officials of occupied France (the Vichy government) and Nazis in the persecution of the Jews. More troubling is evidence that the Vichy government also initiated anti-Semitic acts of its own. To explain the origin of this activity, the authors, both well-known historians, describe the tradition of anti-Semitism in Europe generally and in France in particular. This is an important work, accessible to both general and specialist readers.

947 McElvoy, Anne. *The Saddled Cow: East Germany's Life and Legacy*. Faber 1992, $22.95 (0-571-16591-5). 288pp. Nonfiction.

The author, a British journalist, covered East Germany both before and after the Berlin Wall came down. In this book she provides an excellent overview of four decades of East German history, then examines the thoughts about unification expressed by people representing different aspects of East German society, including an author, a politician, and the former head of the East German intelligence agency. She concludes that while the unification of *Germany* was easy, the unification of *Germans* will be more difficult, a conclusion that seems to be borne out by recent events in the region.

948 Moch, Leslie P. *Moving Europeans: Migration in Western Europe Since 1650*. Indiana Univ. Pr. 1992, $35.00 (0-253-33859-X). 320pp. Nonfiction.

This book about the vast migrations of people within Western Europe examines the impact of human mobility on life in the region. The author describes major population shifts from the preindustrial era to the modern day, including changing patterns of work, landholding, and population in rural and urban areas. Examining these events in the context of the social and political forces that helped to shape them, Moch looks at a broad range of issues, from gender and family practices to the regulations imposed by nineteenth-century nation states, and describes the different experiences of men and women and of the propertied and the poor.

Moore, Robert. *Racism and Black Resistance*.
See entry 840.

949 Mosse, George L. *Toward the Final Solution: A History of European Racism*. Illus. Fertig 1978, $40.00 (0-86527-941-1); Univ. of Wisconsin Pr. $16.95 (0-299-10184-3). 324pp. Nonfiction.

George Mosse is a prolific intellectual historian who here presents a summary of European racial ideas from the Enlightenment to the Holocaust. This work traces the rise of European racism from its beginnings to what Hitler called the "final solution to the Jewish question." The author's thesis is that racism evolved into a fully developed system of thought and ideology with its own structure and language. He also argues that, although European racism was not at first exclusively anti-Semitic, it became more so as time went on.

950 Neiman, Susan. *Slow Fire: Jewish Notes from Berlin*. Schocken 1992, $22.50 (0-8052-4112-4). 320pp. Nonfiction.

The author, an American Jew of German descent, is a philosopher and student of Kant. She is also a keen and thoughtful observer of the West German process of *Vergangenheitsverarbeitung*, or "working through the past," and the contradictions that process can create. This book, a memoir of her six years as a graduate student in today's Berlin, offers not just a portrait of the city but a look at Berlin's tiny Jewish community and its efforts to work through its past. Her reminiscences encompass such subjects as nightclubs and bohemian life, the housing shortage, and life in East Berlin and East Germany. In one of the most poignant examples of *Vergangenheitsverarbeitung*—or the lack of it—she describes why she decided to apply for a job with a Jewish community group and why the job was given to a non-Jew with fewer qualifications.

951 Nielsen, Jorgen. *Muslims in Western Europe*. Illus. Columbia Univ. Pr. 1992, $42.50 (0-7486-0309-3); $27.50 (0-685-61122-1). 192pp. Nonfiction.

Aimed at the interested general reader, this is a sociologist's succinct and encyclopedic introduction to the origins, ethnic composition, distribution, and organizational patterns of Western Europe's Muslim communities and to the political, legal, and cultural context in which they exist. The main chapters explore Islam as practiced in individual countries, and other chapters discuss history and issues that transcend national boundaries. A bibliographic essay completes the volume.

952 Pauley, Bruce F. *From Prejudice to Persecution: A History of Austrian Anti-Semitism*. Univ. of North Carolina Pr. 1992, $55.00 (0-8078-1995-6). 426pp. Nonfiction.

This study of Austrian anti-Semitism focuses on the period from the end of the nineteenth century to the present, ending with a discussion of the "Waldheim affair" and the state of affairs in the country today. Included are discussion of the myths that fueled anti-Semitism; the political, religious, cultural, and social factors involved; and the Austrian-Jewish response to anti-Semitism.

Readers interested in more information about the scandals involving former UN Secretary General and Austrian President Kurt Waldheim will find a detailed discussion in Richard Mitten's *The Politics of Antisemitic Prejudice: The Waldheim Phenomenon in Austria* (Westview, 1992).

953 Payne, Stanley G. *The Franco Regime, 1936–1975*. Illus. Univ. of Wisconsin Pr. 1987, $30.00 (0-299-11070-2). 704pp. Nonfiction.

This book, by a well-known historian of modern Spain, is a general political history of the Franco regime, one of the longest-lived right-wing authoritarian systems in history. Although the focus is on politics, this is a balanced and detailed account of a major episode of Spanish history of the twentieth century, one whose political aftermath remains an important part of Spanish life today.

954 Philipsen, Dirk. *We Were the People: Voices from East Germany's Revolutionary Autumn of 1989*. Duke Univ. Pr. 1992, $49.95 (0-8223-1282-4); $19.95 (0-8223-1294-8). 432pp. Nonfiction.

This is an oral history recalling the experiences of members of dissident groups in East Germany who petitioned and demonstrated against the police state. Most, however, are disappointed with the results of German unification. They generally feel overwhelmed by West German politicians and policies, and they regret that they are not being allowed to reform their country themselves, as they had hoped. In searching for what is going wrong with the process, the author finds answers in the lack of political skills and the gap between workers and intellectuals in what is theoretically a classless society. This fascinating and readable account will appeal to general readers and scholars alike.

955 Phillips, Caryl. *The European Tribe*. Faber 1993, $10.95 (0-571-19803-1). 135pp. Essays.

In this book, Phillips, an English novelist of African-Caribbean descent, records here his impressions of a year's journey through Europe. His observations and experiences as he meets and reflects upon the lives of the Europeans in Britain, Spain, Italy, and elsewhere are both thoughtful and thought provoking. These essays reflect the interactions between Europe's dominant cultures and those of its minorities, and the author does not hesitate to bring the experiences of his own life to bear on the subjects he addresses. Phillips is the author of the novel *Cambridge (see main entry)*.

956 Rittner, Carol, and Sondra Myers, eds. *Courage to Care: Rescuers of Jews During the Holocaust*. New York Univ. Pr. 1989, $35.00 (0-8147-7397-4); $18.95 (0-8147-7406-7). 176pp. Nonfiction.

In this chronicle of human decency during the Holocaust, oral histories and essays attest to the bravery and righteousness of Europeans who risked their own lives to save the life of a Jewish man, woman, or child. One thread that ties these narratives together is the rescuers' belief that what they did was not special or extraordinary; they simply did what strong values and a sense of duty to their fellow human beings required. Several of the individuals discuss the pervasive anti-Semitism in their countries during this time and ask the reader to try to understand why, in such a poisoned atmosphere, others could not do as they had done to save the Jews.

957 Salamander, Rachel. *The Jewish World of Yesterday, 1860–1939*. Illus. with photos. Rizzoli 1991, $65.00 (0-8478-1415-7). 320pp. Nonfiction.

A European best-seller, this is a stunning portrait of a vanished world. Through photographs and literary texts, interspersed with essays by contemporary scholars, all aspects of Jewish life are explored. With sections devoted to religion, work, home life, school, sports, culture, and fashion, the entire range of Jewish life—from the elite sophistication of Vienna to the rustic villages of East Central Europe—is eloquently conveyed.

958 Schneider, Peter. *The German Comedy: Scenes of Life After the Wall*. Trans. from German by Philip Boehm and Leigh Hafrey. Farrar 1991, $21.00 (0-374-10201-5); $11.00 (0-374-52358-4). 212pp. Nonfiction.

In a number of vivid sketches about the reunification of Germany, this book brings home to the reader the strains and conflicts that flow from the sudden union of the poor and the rich, the weak and the strong. This is a guide through the psychological complexity of German identity. Schneider's approach is humorous and readable; he uses the techniques of fiction and drama to give the reader insight into a society as it undergoes profound change. There are many ironies here, as two societies with very different economic systems, political cultures, and value systems come into contact with each other after more than four decades of separation.

959   Sichrovsky, Peter. ***Born Guilty: Children of Nazi Families***. Basic Books 1989, $8.95 (0-465-00741-4). 192pp. Nonfiction.

This book distills the author's interviews with fourteen people born after World War II whose parents had been Nazis. As their comments reveal, these individuals cope with their heritage in a variety of ways. Some are indifferent; others are ambivalent. Some work through their sense of guilt by espousing left-wing political causes. A few say they refused to have children of their own for fear of passing on a terrible genetic legacy.

An earlier work by Sichrovsky, *Strangers in Their Own Land* (Basic Books, 1986), deals with the other side of the equation: children of Jews who continue to live in contemporary Austria and Germany. Here, too, is ambivalence, but these honest narratives also reveal signs that anti-Semitism is still active in German and Austrian society.

960   Stern, Frank. ***The Whitewashing of the Yellow Badge: Antisemitism & Philosemitism in Postwar Germany***. Trans. from German by William Templer. Pergamon 1991, $53.00 (0-08-040653-X). 455pp. Nonfiction.

The central themes of this book are the attitudes, behavior, and actions of non-Jews toward Jews in postwar Germany. Beginning with the period immediately after the war and ending in the present, the author, a historian, discusses both continuing anti-Semitism and its surprising counterpart, the emerging "philo-Semitism"—an embracing of Jewish culture, especially by university intellectuals but also by workers, politicians, and other groups in German society.

961   Stille, Alexander. ***Benevolence and Betrayal: Five Italian Jewish Families under Fascism***. Illus. Viking 1993, $12.00 (0-14-017715-9). 368pp. Nonfiction.

This is an oral history of the complex experience of Italy's Jews under Fascism. Through the words of five families of different socioeconomic and geographic backgrounds, the tragedy of the Holocaust in Italy is revealed. The experiences of these people ranged from fervent belief in Fascism, through courageous resistance, to the horrors of Buchenwald. Tying these stories together is the author's clear and dispassionate historical narrative.

962   Valkeapaa, Nils-Aslak. ***Greetings from Lappland: The Sami, Europe's Forgotten People***. Zed 1983. o.p. Nonfiction.

The author, one of the founders of the World Council of Indigenous Peoples, is a Sami musician and artist. He believes that the cultural existence and traditional ways of life of the Sami—the original inhabitants of the Nordic countries—are seriously threatened. In this book he discusses the impact of tourism, development, technology, and an educational system that is unsuited to the needs of the Sami. In his analysis, he links the situation of his people to that of other indigenous peoples of the world. To date, this is only the second book by a Sami author to appear in English.

963 Wallraff, Günter. *Lowest of the Low*. Trans. from German by Martin Chalmers. Illus. with photos. Freundlich 1987, $16.95 (0-317-62634-5). Nonfiction.

Wallraff is a prolific German journalist and writer who has become famous for his crusading reports on Germany's treatment of its minorities, particularly the Turks. Invited in as "guest workers" during the period of economic expansion in the 1960s and 1970s, many Turks have lived in western Germany for as long as two generations, but they continue to enjoy only marginal status within the German state. For this book, Wallraff disguised himself as a Turkish worker and documented firsthand, in words and photographs, the abuse and exploitation he encountered. Although Wallraff's articles and books are widely read and discussed in Germany, few of his writings have been translated into English. They deserve a wider readership.

964 Woodhouse, C. M. *Modern Greece: A Short History*. 5th ed. Faber 1992, $12.95 (0-571-16122-7). 400pp. Nonfiction.

Modern Greece, carved from the remains of the Ottoman Empire, was ravaged in the twentieth century by two world wars and by a fierce civil war. Its people have cultural roots in both Western and Eastern Europe. The story of the country, then, is a study of identity. This book is one of the few up-to-date short histories of Greece available. Another is Richard Clogg's *A Concise History of Greece* (Cambridge Univ. Pr., 1992).

965 Yahil, Leni. *The Holocaust: The Fate of the European Jewry, 1932–1945*. Trans. from Hebrew by Ina Friedman and Haya Galai. Oxford Univ. Pr. 1990, $39.95 (0-19-504522-X); $19.95 (0-19-504523-8). 832pp. Nonfiction.

This book, winner of Israel's Shazar Prize for Jewish History, is perhaps the most comprehensive recent one-volume history of Hitler's war against the Jews. Written over a twenty-year period, it is a massive yet carefully constructed and approachable description of all aspects of the Holocaust, from the beginnings of Nazi rule until 1945. Included are sections on resistance, rescue, and other Jewish attempts to survive, as well as discussion of the Nazis' plans and activities.

BIOGRAPHY

966 Baker, Leonard. *Days of Sorrow and Pain: Leo Baeck and the Berlin Jews*. Illus. Oxford Univ. Pr. 1980, $9.95 (0-19-502800-7). 396pp. Biography.

Leo Baeck was a rabbi who worked with the Reichsvertretung, an organization of German Jews who faced the Nazis and tried to mitigate their policies. He negotiated with emissaries from abroad to help Jews emigrate, and although he himself could have fled, he chose to remain in Berlin. Eventually he was sent to the concentration camp at Theresienstadt. After the war, he worked for reconciliation between Jews and non-Jewish Germans.

In addition to being the biography of an exemplary spiritual leader, this book offers a broader context, telling the story of the Jewish community of Berlin and its response to the growth of Nazi anti-Semitism.

967   Djura. *The Veil of Silence*. Trans. from French. Quartet 1992, $25.00 (0-7043-7033-6). 158pp. Autobiography.

This is the autobiography by the lead singer of a French-Algerian rock band called Djurdjura. Djura's story is one of an idyllic early childhood in Algeria, followed by uprooting and immigration to France, poverty, violence, abduction, and finally success.

Lured to France by the promise of employment, Djura's father brought his family and thirteen children to Paris in the 1950s. When Djura's talent for acting was noticed, she was admitted to the School of Performing Arts and then to a university to study filmmaking, There she also began dating a French boy, but she encountered strong resistance from her family. She returned to Algeria to escape her family, but she was abducted and imprisoned by her brother. After escaping, she returned to France, where she found success as a filmmaker and became the family breadwinner—but when she married a Frenchman, family members tried to kill her.

This is a gripping story of an exile torn between her longing for assimilation in the new society and the need to maintain her cultural roots. It is a true tale of the violent clash of cultures and the resilience of one woman.

968   Fallaci, Oriana. *A Man*. Trans. from Italian by William Weaver. Simon & Schuster 1980. o.p. Biography.

Fallaci is an Italian journalist and novelist whose candid, aggressive interviews and sometimes controversial nonfiction have made her famous. *A Man* is the powerful account of her love affair with Alexandros Panagoulis, the poet and Greek Resistance leader who was killed in 1976. The biography—told in the second person, as if Fallaci is addressing her dead lover—reads like a work of fiction. Gripping and compelling, it explores Panagoulis's complex career, revealing his experience of torture and imprisonment, his difficult adjustment to freedom, and his total commitment to economic and social justice in his country. Their stormy relationship receives a great deal of attention; Fallaci shows in detail the difficulties of living with one so committed to a cause. A best-seller when it was published in English, this biography will appeal especially to general readers.

969   Fourtouni, Eleni. *Greek Women in Resistance*. Illus. Lake 1986, $25.00 (0-941702-13-8); $11.95 (0-317-43473-X). 225pp. Biography (Collective).

This collection of first-person narratives covers the period of anti-Nazi resistance (1940–1944) and the Greek Civil War (1945–1950). The author conducted interviews as the Greek dictatorship of the 1970s was collapsing and the floodgates of memory were opened. These testimonies are courageous, and the stories they tell are both inspiring and horrifying. The author provides a historical narrative to link the sections, and a photographic essay is included. Fourtouni has documented another side of the story recounted in Nicholas Gage's *Eleni* (*see main entry*).

970   Frank, Anne. *The Diary of Anne Frank: The Critical Edition*. Ed. by the staff of the Netherlands State Institute for War Documentation; Trans. from Dutch by Arnold J. Pomerans. Doubleday 1989, $40.00 (0-385-24023-6). 283pp. Autobiography.

This diary of a teenage Jewish girl, written while she and her family were hiding from the Nazis in the occupied Netherlands, is perhaps the best-known and most widely read of all personal accounts of the Holocaust. The diary is constantly in print and available in many versions, of which the most definitive is this critical edition, prepared by the Netherlands State Institute for War Documentation and translated by Arnold J. Pomerans.

971   Friedlander, Saul. *When Memory Comes*. Trans. from French by Helen R. Lane. Farrar 1991, $8.95 (0-374-52272-3). 186pp. Autobiography.

Friedlander, a Czech-Israeli historian who writes in French, was born in Prague's German-speaking Jewish community. His parents fled with him to Paris. After the Nazis invaded France, he was sent to a home for Jewish children and then to a Catholic boarding school, where he was baptized and even began studying for the priesthood. Uprooted again at the end of the war, he discovered Zionism and relocated to Israel.

In this memoir, first published in 1978, he used his parents' letters, conversations recalled, fragments of memories, and his diary entries of 1977 to work through his past and rediscover his identity. The result, a moving meditation on what it meant to be Jewish in Hitler's Europe, also reveals the author's consciousness of the lingering aura of Nazism in contemporary Europe.

972   Gage, Nicholas. *Eleni: A Mother's Love and a Son's Revenge: A Personal Story*. Random 1983, $19.95 (0-394-52093-9); Ballantine $5.95 (0-345-32494-3). 472pp. Biography.

In this poignant dramatic narrative, the author tells the story of his mother Eleni's murder by Communist guerrillas in her peasant village. He weaves together the major strands of recent Greek history: World War II, the Civil War, and the life of Greek peasants and their resistance. He also intertwines threads from his own childhood memories to describe how his journey evolved from a search for vengeance to a quest for understanding. A marriage of fiction and fact, this is an affecting personal tale that documents the aftermath of World War II in Greece

In a subsequent book, *A Place for Us* (Simon & Schuster, 1990), Gage tells what happened to Eleni's children as they escaped from their Greek mountain village and went to join their father in the United States. A film version of *Eleni* was released in 1985.

973   Gies, Miep, and Alison L. Gold. *Anne Frank Remembered: The Story of the Woman Who Helped to Hide the Frank Family*. Simon & Schuster 1988, $10.00 (0-671-66234-1). 252pp. Autobiography.

Miep Gies and her husband hid Anne Frank and her family from the Nazis during the occupation of the Netherlands. Yet she begins her autobiography by saying "I am not a hero," noting that twenty thousand other Dutch people performed similar acts of courage. She laments that her actions were not enough. This affecting memoir illuminates the upheaval of the war and its effects on ordinary Dutch people, and it sheds light on Anne Frank's story from the perspective of those who tried to help.

974   Glückel. *The Memoirs of Glückel of Hamelin*. Trans. from German by Marvin Lowenthal; Intro. by Robert Rosen. Illus. Schocken 1987, $15.00 (0-8052-0572-1). 295pp. Autobiography.

Glückel of Hamelin was a lively and literate Jewish businesswoman of the seventeenth century. In this, one of the earliest autobiographies by an "ordinary" person, Glückel provides a highly readable, detailed, and often humorous account of childbearing, business, politics, religion, and all the other aspects of a Jewish woman's life of the time. Glückel worked on these memoirs throughout most of her life, and they form a fascinating chronicle from youth to old age. Originally written in Yiddish, her memoirs were first translated and published in English in 1932.

975   Hillesum, Etty. ***An Interrupted Life: The Diaries of Etty Hillesum, 1941–1943***. Trans. from Dutch by Arnold Pomerans. Pocket Books 1991, $5.95 (0-671-74555-7). 226pp. Autobiography.

Unlike Anne Frank, Etty Hillesum was an adult when World War II began. A talented member of a talented Jewish family, she went to work for the Jewish Council and later was consigned to Westerbork prison camp. She and her parents died in Auschwitz

Hillesum's diaries reflect first her inner spiritual world and then, increasingly, the developments of the outer world. Her work is notable for its spiritual reflections; her commitment to her faith informs her perceptions of the Holocaust. She refused to flee because she believed there were things she could only accomplish, both for her own development and for others, by remaining.

This moving testimony complements both *The Diary of Anne Frank* and André Schwarz-Bart's philosophical novel *The Last of the Just (see main entries)*. In the latter book, the spiritually committed Jewish protagonist goes voluntarily to his death.

976   Labro, Philippe. ***Le Petit Garçon***. Trans. from French by Linda Coverdale. Farrar 1992, $23.00 (0-374-18448-8). 320pp. Autobiography.

The narrator of this autobiography remembers his childhood years in a rural village in southwestern France during World War II. His parents extended what help they could to the refugees who passed through the village. When the German forces occupied his village, his parents revealed to the children that all those "old friends of the family" who had supposedly been visiting were actually Jews and others who were fleeing the Nazis. The narrator and his siblings accepted the need for secrecy. Even when the German Brigadeführer took up residence in the house, the family continued to hide six Jews. This is a story of village life, a portrait of a strong and loving family, and a picture of the impact of the Nazi occupation on people who quietly refused to cooperate.

977   Levi, Carlo. ***Christ Stopped at Eboli***. Trans. from Italian by Frances Frenaye. Farrar 1947, $10.00 (0-374-50316-8). 268pp. Autobiography.

This is a famous account of peasant life in Southern Italy, the loving and eloquent story of the author's stay among people whose lives were filled with disease and deprivation. The title refers to a local legend among the villagers that Christ never came to their remote, mountainous location—he stopped at Eboli, a hundred kilometers to the north—and so no real message of salvation ever reached them. It is a community of superstitious and oppressed people, neglected by their government, who nonetheless were capable of great endurance and devotion.

Levi wrote the book, first published in 1945, while sentenced to internal exile for his anti-Fascist activities.

978 Levi, Primo. ***The Drowned and the Saved***. Trans. from Italian by Raymond Rosenthal. Random 1989, $10.00 (0-679-72186-X). 203pp. Autobiography.

Since their first publication in the 1970s and 1980s, Primo Levi's memoirs have been among the most widely read and frequently quoted of all the great Holocaust personal narratives. Levi, a chemist, spent time at Auschwitz; after being released, his journey back home to Turin—by truck, train, and cattle car—took nine months. These events are the subjects of *Survival in Auschwitz* (Macmillan, 1986) and *The Reawakening* (Macmillan, 1987).

The Drowned and the Saved, completed shortly before his suicide, is a collection of meditative essays. One of the themes is the ongoing presence of the Holocaust in the minds of its survivors. His memoirs are detached, dispassionate, and restrained, marked by an absence of bitterness and anger, yet full of a stark intensity that has produced a powerful impact on readers around the world.

979 MacMaster, Neil. ***Spanish Fighters: An Oral History of War and Exile***. St. Martin 1991, $45.00 (0-312-04738-X). 260pp. Biography.

Based on interviews conducted between 1979 and 1982, this book presents the story of David and Consuela Granda, a Spanish couple who grew up in the poverty of Asturias, fought against fascism in the Spanish Civil War, went into exile in France, and were imprisoned during World War II. They returned to Spain in the late 1970s after Franco's death, only to find that they could no longer consider their native country home. The Grandas are compelling storytellers who command the reader's sympathy and interest.

An earlier work, Ronald Fraser's *Blood of Spain: An Oral History of the Spanish Civil War* (o.p.), contains 300 interviews dealing with the events of that conflict.

980 Orwell, George. ***Homage to Catalonia***. Repr. of 1952 ed. Harcourt 1969, $7.95 (0-15-642117-8). 232pp. Autobiography.

This is a classic firsthand account of the Spanish Civil War. An established writer, Orwell went to Spain in 1936 to observe and write about the Civil War. Caught up in the passion of the conflict, he decided to fight as a soldier for the Republic and was stationed in Aragon and Barcelona. He was especially sensitive to the nuances of politics on the Leftist side. This memoir is both a soldier's account and a report from a politically committed observer of the agonies of this war.

981 Richarz, Monika, ed. ***Jewish Life in Germany: Memoirs from Three Centuries***. Trans. from German by Stella P. Rosenfeld and Sidney Rosenfeld. Illus. Indiana Univ. Pr. 1991, $39.95 (0-253-35024-7). 496pp. Autobiography (Collective).

This collection of fifty-one autobiographical accounts by German Jews between 1780 and 1945 includes memoirs by people from all social strata, from the city and from the country, holding a range of religious and political views.

The writers report on all aspects of daily life, and their texts provide the reader with a picture of German-Jewish society from the beginning of their emancipation through their expulsion and the Nazi attempt to exterminate them during World War II. A well-written introductory essay by the editor briefly outlines the social history of the Jews of Germany.

982   Scholem, Gershom Gerhard. ***From Berlin to Jerusalem: Memories of My Youth***. Trans. from German by Harry Zohn. Schocken 1988. o.p. Autobiography.

Scholem was a Jewish philosopher and scholar. This classic memoir tells of his early years in Berlin, his awakening to his Jewish heritage, his education during World War I, and his commitment to Zionism, which resulted in his emigration to Palestine in 1923. The Zionist movement and its profound effect upon a generation of Jewish youth receives a great deal of attention as well. For the contemporary reader, this book chronicles the development of a philosopher and also provides a vivid picture of the life of an elite, assimilated Jewish family in Berlin before the Nazi era.

983   Smith, Denis Mack. ***Mussolini: A Biography***. Random 1983, $18.00 (0-394-71658-2). 464pp. Biography.

This is a classic portrait of the Italian dictator Mussolini—"Il Duce"—and the rise of Italian fascism. Colorfully written, it presents Mussolini as a clever manipulator whose presentation of fascism to a gullible world masked corruption and disorganization. The author also discusses Mussolini's influence on emergent Nazism. A useful companion to this book is Victoria De Grazia's *How Fascism Ruled Women, 1922–1945* (Univ. of California Pr., 1992).

984   Wyden, Peter. ***Stella***. Simon & Schuster 1992, $23.00 (0-671-67361-0); Doubleday $12.95 (0-385-47179-3). 384pp. Biography.

This book is part autobiography and part biography. Peter Wyden tells of growing up in Nazi Berlin and attending a school for Jewish children, which was founded when "non-Aryans" were no longer allowed to attend German schools. One of his classmates there was Stella Goldschlag. When Wyden returned to Germany in 1945 he discovered that Stella had survived the Holocaust by becoming a "catcher"—someone who hunted down Jews in hiding and betrayed them to the Nazis. Many years later Wyden returned again to find out more about Stella and her fate. He tracked her down and found that she was willing to speak freely of her past. This is a nightmare story of a world in which survival through any means was paramount. It is also a compelling reminder of the fallibility of human beings under intolerable stress.

9

EASTERN EUROPE

Norwegian
Sea

Gulf
of
Bothnia

RUSSIA

ESTONIA

LATVIA

Baltic
Sea

LITHUANIA

RUSSIA

BELARUS

POLAND

UKRAINE

CZECH REP.

SLOVAK
REP.

MOLDOVA

HUNGARY

ROMANIA

SLOVENIA

CROATIA

Black
Sea

Adriatic

BOSNIA

SERBIA

BULGARIA

MONTENEGRO

MACEDONIA

ALBANIA

Aegean

Mediterranean Sea

Ionian
Sea

9

EASTERN EUROPE

by Edward Ifkovic

Aleksandr Solzhenitsyn, Russian émigré and Nobel laureate in literature, has dramatically summed up the radical shifts occurring now in Eastern Europe: "Having lived through these seventy lethal years inside communism's iron shell, we are crawling out, though barely alive. A new age has clearly begun, both for Russia and for the whole world." This emphatic declaration reflects both the nightmare of life in Eastern Europe during recent decades and a dream for the future. Throughout the former Soviet Union and all of Eastern Europe—the world hidden behind what Churchill called the Iron Curtain—the twentieth century has been marked by repression, misery, and cruelty. Somehow, despite the obstacles, individuals have struggled to maintain their self-respect in the face of numbing bureaucratic mindlessness. With the collapse of Communism, a new world did, indeed, begin. In many ways, the 1990s are proving to be a decade of redefinition, rededication, and renewal.

The old guard is gone—or, at least, it is assuming a new guise. As of this writing, in the middle of the decade, it is still too early to understand fully the implications of the changes of the 1980s. What we do know is that the moribund political and social systems established by the Soviet Union, systems mimicked to greater or lesser degrees in the captive nations of the Soviet bloc, no longer work—if, indeed, they ever worked. The international spread of Communist rule, the mass export of Communist ideology, is largely extinct. In some instances, however, the decay or disappearance of Communist structures—including the military machines used to crush dissent—has led to a backlash of regression. In Russia, for example, old-guard hardliners and zealous nationalists threaten the fledgling democracy. Worse still is the resurgence of ethnic factionalism, which is reviving cruel hatreds that are centuries old. The specter of violence and misery experienced in the broken-down Yugoslav state is a staggering tragedy. Serbian hardliners, ostensibly anxious to maintain a Yugoslav federation, in effect used the chaos of secession to settle old scores. Terms such as *ethnic cleansing* emerge to describe the devastation in Bosnia, as Europe sees its first important war since World War II. The roots of that conflict are vividly portrayed in Ivo Andric's classic novel *The Bridge on the Drina*.

Doubtless, the next few years will see the emergence of a new generation

447

of writers who grapple with this new and different world. What will be their creative response to new-found freedom in a world where democracy is still a novelty—and a source of puzzlement and confusion? Even as these new writers develop, however, it is important to remember that, during the dark decades of Communist rule, writing has been going on—important, often brilliant, memorable, landmark writing. Poets, playwrights, novelists, essayists, historians, and philosophers have dedicated themselves to describing, explaining, dramatizing, and amplifying their experiences. One of the more delicious ironies of the Iron Curtain was that dictatorial regimes may have censored newspapers and publishing houses, and they may have jailed, exiled, or shot writers—but the writing went on. Truth was driven underground, but it continued to flourish. The creative imagination was everpresent—and, in its way, omnipotent. The phenomenon known as *samizdat* (self-publishing) resulted in the circulation, usually by hand, of mimeographed or typed manuscripts. Poetry and fiction flourished; Pasternak and Solzhenitsyn even received the Nobel Prize, but they were prevented from accepting the award.

Not surprisingly, much of the literature generated during this time was political in content. The Polish poet Wislawa Szymborska expressed the fact that life in a totalitarian state is governed by the dynamics of politics:

> We are children of an age;
> it's a political age.
> All day long, all through the night
> all affairs—yours, ours, theirs—
> are political affairs.

To review the body of recent writing produced in the Soviet Union and Eastern Europe, especially those works available in translation, is to see a disproportionate listing of satire and political commentary marked by sharp, acerbic, biting ridicule. Novel after novel presents stories of an individual battling the bureaucratic machine. A pervasive theme in the works of Vladimir Voinovich— *Moscow, 2042*, for example—is "Little man, what now?" But contemporary satire is not the only vein that runs through this literature. Poets such as Vasko Popa and Anna Akhmatova and novelists including Milan Kundera and Ivan Klíma mine the ore of universal humanity and in the process create refined works of enduring importance.

As the dark, forbidden countries are opening up, books of commentary and review, such as *Iron Curtain Rising* by Peter Laufer, bring us perspective and insight. These works reveal that Eastern Europe has had a wealth of intriguing characters and personalities throughout the twentieth century, from the tsars, Lenin, and Trotsky to Gorbachev, Yeltsin, Havel, and Walesa; in between are Stalin, Khrushchev, Tito, Masaryk, Sakharov, and many lesser-known men and women who became memoirists or who were the subjects of biographers. Together, these individuals led millions in dictatorship or dissent, in rebellion or compliance. The rebellious and their insurgencies became the stuff of legend: the Yugoslav break with Stalin, the Hungarian Revolution of 1956, the Prague Spring of 1968, and others. These events are triumphs of the individual in the face of crushing military dictatorship. Inevitably, historians and sociologists, poets and novelists take their turns at interpreting these riveting moments of history.

The creative writers express the hearts and the minds of whole peoples at defining moments in time. In their way, these writers become the constant soul, the vibrant conscience, the lasting truth. They—or, more accurately, the ideas to which they give voice—are the true and stalwart enemies of totalitarian states. In democracies, where writers routinely publish whatever they wish, even the most outrageous notions cause others to do little more than blink. Strangely, in these free nations, few citizens see the pen as powerful enough to effect revolution. But in Eastern Europe, dictators have always had a greater respect for the power of the pen. Clearly, they know something about the power of ideas that democracies have yet to grasp, because they dedicate such enormous amounts of energy to persecute and prosecute writers. When a state erects around itself a rigid, brittle shell, that shell is often very easily cracked. And so the writer—the embodiment of flexibility, the cracker of shells—is feared by the tyrant and revered by the reader. No wonder that even in this dark era the Eastern European love for literature thrived and the underground press and its outlet, the underground bookstore, flourished. If the bookstores were shut down, then the poetry of dissent was passed hand to hand, friend to friend.

Following the death of Stalin, when government controls seemed to relax somewhat under the new Soviet premier Nikita Khrushchev, writers began to push the state-sanctioned boundaries of what was allowed. They were tired of the official "socialist realism" that had been the norm since 1932. As Marc Slonim notes in his book, *Soviet Russian Literature*, socialist realism demanded that poets, novelists, and artists help build communism "in the same way that workmen or engineers do." In 1954, Ilya Ehrenburg published his aptly named novel *The Thaw*. By 1957, just one year after the Soviets crushed the revolution in Hungary, Ehrenburg and his colleagues felt emboldened enough to petition the government for closer literary ties with the West. A few years later, Stalin's daughter, Svetlana Alliluyeva, came to the West to be free to write as she pleased. In 1963, the writer Valeriy Tarsis, whom officials had silenced by confining him to a mental hospital, was released (although he was sent into exile). In that same year Khrushchev allowed publication of Solzhenitsyn's *One Day in the Life of Ivan Denisovich* and Yevgeny Yevtushenko's *A Precocious Autobiography*.

But the "thaw" proved to be slight and short-lived. In 1966, the sham trials of Andrewi Sinyavsky ("Abram Tertz") and Yuri Daniel ("Nikolai Arzhak") resulted in prison terms of five and seven years, respectively, for publishing their works abroad. Ninety-five writers signed a petition for their release, and Lidiya Chukorskaya sent a damning letter to a Soviet official saying that "ideas should be fought with ideas, not with camps and prisons." Transcripts of the mock trials were smuggled out of the country; when writers around the world read them, they launched a loud protest. But the thaw was definitely over. One victim of the new freeze was future Nobel laureate Joseph Brodsky, who spent twenty-one months in a Soviet labor camp for being a "parasite"— that is, a poet and a critic. The war against words had begun anew.

Of course, the political landscape of Eastern Europe involved more than the familiar dictates of Marxism and attendant repression of personal and literary liberty. Writers dealt with, and gave voice to, all the burgeoning issues of the twentieth century, such as the role of women in society. The form of feminism that emerged in Eastern Europe reveals much about the cultures in the region. Biographies of early Bolshevik feminist Alexandra Kollontai describe the failed attempts to integrate women's issues into the fabric of socialist agendas. Since the end of the Cold War, however, there has been a renewed examination of the role of women. Russian feminist Tatyana Mamonova, a fighter for women's rights since the 1960s and a deportee since 1979, now lives in the United States, where she publishes a journal called *Women and Earth*. In that publication, and in her books such as *Russian Women's Studies: Essays on Sexism in Soviet Culture*, she chronicles the life of women in Russia. According to Mamonova, attitudes are shifting; the shaky political reforms in the former Soviet Union have been accompanied by a new, and in some ways equally shaky, form of feminism. Groups like Grandmothers for Peace have sprung up; so have battered women's centers, rape crisis centers, and so forth. Such movements are not without backlash; the Russian Orthodox Church, for example, sponsors a "Women Go Home" movement, whose goal is to push women back into their traditionally prescribed domestic roles.

The continued progressive reforms in Eastern Europe, at least in part, are the result of the émigré culture and its maintenance of an Eastern European sensibility in the West. Many writers, unable to be published at home, became self-exiles in the West, where they could give voice to their thoughts. For example, the Nobel laureate Czeslaw Milosz, author of *The Bells in Winter*, writes from the United States about the passion he carried from his native country, Poland. A few Western publishing houses have published a large body of émigré and underground literature. Thus, these writers send messages back to their native land; the messages circulate, often in the form of mimeographed handouts. Other media, too, such as Radio Free Europe, help fan the flame of reform. And writers still trapped in these repressive societies somehow find courage—and write.

Solzhenitsyn is a classic example of this spirit. In November 1962, all Moscow was buzzing about the latest issue of a magazine called *Novy Mir* (New World), which contained the short novel *Odin den Ivana Denisovicha* (*One Day in the Life of Ivan Denisovich*). Khrushchev had approved the publication, which revealed for the first time the abuses under Stalin; a preface by the magazine's editor, Aleksandr Tvardovsky, stated: "[The novel] echoes the unhealthy phenomena in our life associated with the period of the personality cult." The book galvanized an entire society. But with Khrushchev's fall in 1964, Tvardovsky lost his job, and Solzhenitsyn, left without his official protection, was expelled from the Soviet Writers' Union—which meant he no longer had an income. Solzhenitsyn's manuscripts were smuggled out of the country; the larger his reputation grew abroad, the worse life became for him at home. Solzhenitsyn was another chapter in the long history of Soviet repression of writers. In 1929 Boris Pilnyak had published *Mahogany* abroad; after he was officially attacked, he recanted his subversive views. Pilnyak is represented in this bibliography by *The Chinese Story and Other Tales*. In 1957 Pasternak also published abroad; his book was the epic *Doctor Zhivago*, for which he won the Nobel Prize a year later, an honor he was forced to decline. When Sinyavsky and Daniel were sentenced to prison, Solzhenitsyn attacked the verdict publicly, a position that made him increasingly dangerous in the eyes of Soviet officials. In 1970 Solzhenitsyn, too, won the Nobel Prize, but he could not travel to Sweden to accept it, fearing he would be unable to return to the Soviet Union. Eventually censorship and continued humiliation forced him to emigrate; he lived as a near-recluse for two decades in the United States. This brief survey of his battles as a writer in the Soviet Union reflects the lot of all independent Eastern European writers. The works these artists produce reveal their vision of the world. Equally important, they are documents of courage and truth. The writer in Eastern Europe was, and in many ways continues to be, constantly tested. Some succumbed and became mere mouthpieces for the system. But many, like Solzhenitsyn, became the voices that kept the sound of truth alive.

The winds of change have blown—and continue to blow—through Eastern Europe and the former Soviet Union. It is too early to know for certain what seeds these winds carry. But the listing that follows, containing more than 125 books from the region, will give some idea. There is a very heavy concentration of books from the post-1960s period, especially from the most recent years of change. Some classics are included, dating from as far back as the turn of the century, but most had to be omitted because such works are already widely known and much information about them is available elsewhere. As extensive as it is, this list offers a mere sampling that only suggests the rich and varied body of writing done during this century. In providing this recommended list, the editors hope that readers who enjoy these works will be inspired to read other writings on similar themes or other works by the same authors. More information can be found in other bibliographies, including *Books in English on the Soviet Union, 1917–73* by David Lewis Jones (Garland, 1975) and *The Soviet Union and Eastern Europe: A Bibliographic Guide to Recommended Books for Small and Medium-Sized Libraries and School Media Centers* by Stephen M. Horak (Libraries Unlimited, 1985).

In 1993, Solzhenitsyn was awarded the medal of honor for literature by the National Arts Club. Accepting the award, the writer, who was soon to return to his beloved motherland, warned: "Denigrating the past is deemed to be the key to progress. And so it has once again become fashionable in Russia to ridicule, debunk, and toss overboard the great Russian literature, steeped as it is in love and compassion toward all human beings, and especially toward those who suffer." Heeding his caveat, we now look to discover modern Russian and Eastern European writing of value and integrity, books that provide glimpses of the human heart in conflict with itself. The listing that follows will guide the reader on that marvelous journey.

LITERATURE

985 Aczél, Tamás. ***The Hunt***. Little, Brown 1991. o.p. Fiction.

The time is the 1950s, and the setting is a totalitarian country probably patterned on the author's native Hungary. In this novel, the author crafts a full-scale allegory of half a century of Communist oppression. A newly installed prime minister invites three of his cronies—a corrupt general, a corrupt chief justice, and a questionable Catholic prelate—to a hunting lodge. As the three await their host, uncertain of his intent, they review their long lives in the political arena.

In this novel—as in his previous works, such as *The Ice Age* (o.p., 1965)—Tamás chronicles the onerous burden of power in a totalitarian state. His thesis is that in corrupt political systems, like those of Eastern Europe, any man coming to power inevitably compromises his integrity. The price for that compromise can be terrible. The author tends to overwrite and to indulge his sometimes ponderous style. But his writing is often rich and full of images, conveying a compelling and at times frightening portrait of life under a dictator's iron fist.

986 Ageyev, M. ***Novel with Cocaine***. Trans. from Russian by Michael Heim. Northwestern Univ. Pr. 1991, $10.95 (0-8101-0998-0). 212pp. Fiction.

This curious novel, originally written in the 1930s, first appeared in Paris in an émigré magazine called *Chisla*. Its melodramatic story focuses on the passage of a young and gifted student, Vadim, from total innocence to degradation and death following drug use. The idea may seem dated, but the novel is written with a compelling clarity and verve. The author places Vadim's descent into moral and physical ruin against the larger backdrop of the Russian Revolution, which serves as a fitting metaphor for the struggle and decline of the young man himself.

There is some question about the authorship of this confessional novel; one scholar suggested it may be an early work by Vladimir Nabokov. Whatever its provenance, it is a fascinating read, offering a brief, gaudy glimpse into a moment of Russian history.

Agnon, S. Y. ***A Simple Story***.
See entry 1113.

987 Akhmatova, Anna. ***Poems***. Trans. from Russian by Lyn Coffin; Intro. by Joseph Brodsky. Norton 1983, $15.50 (0-393-01567-X); $9.95 (0-393-30014-5). 268pp. Poetry.

In this volume, translator Lyn Coffin serves the great Russian poet well. Her sensitive, riveting renditions give English-language readers a deep sense of Akhmatova's breadth and lyrical power. The selections include poems from her major works, including *Evening* (orig. pub. 1912), *The Willow* (orig. pub. 1940), and, most important, excerpts from *Requiem* (orig. pub. 1963), her poetic response—long banned in the Soviet Union—to the notorious Stalin purges.

Akhmatova, one of the most lauded and revered of Russian poets, in many ways reflected the soul of the evolving Soviet Union. A brave yet sensitive poet, she produced verses that range from lyric descriptions of quiet moments to harsh and noisy struggles against full-scale Soviet atrocities. She rendered both themes superbly, and this collection is a perfect introduction to a major voice in world literature.

988 Andreyev, Leonid. ***Visions: Stories and Photographs***. Trans. from Russian and edited by Olga Carlisle. Illus. with photos. Harcourt 1987. o.p. Fiction.

The seven short stories in this volume were all written between 1902 and 1908; all but one of them were translated by the author's granddaughter. At the turn of the century Andreyev earned his reputation with the now-classic "Seven Who Were Hanged," which is included here and which is widely regarded as a minor masterpiece. The other stories, while readable and entertaining, do not always reflect the same degree of mastery. Nevertheless, the volume is valuable, not only for its most famous story but for "The Abyss," a harrowing tale about gang rape. Included, too, are interesting photographs and an introduction that places Andreyev in the context of the Russian literary tradition.

989   Andric, Ivo. ***The Bridge on the Drina***. Trans. from Serbo-Croatian by Lovett F. Edwards; Intro. by William H. McNeill. Univ. of Chicago Pr. 1977, $10.95 (0-226-02045-2). 314pp. Fiction.

This novel, part of the author's Bosnian trilogy, is the crowning achievement by the Serbian Nobel laureate. It is an epic fiction that captures the pageantry of life in Visegrad, a village on the river Drina that forms the boundary between Serbia and Bosnia. The invading Turks built the bridge in the sixteenth century, and life in the village evolved around it. This novel chronicles events in the region over three and a half centuries, ending around World War I.

The bridge is the crucial symbol around which Andric develops his story. The characters—Turks, Serbians, Bosnians, and outsiders—are not so much fully realized people as they are representatives of the dramatic social and cultural currents that sweep people along, victimizing them and subjecting them to a relentless fate. By 1914, the railroad has replaced the bridge as the village's lifeline. As the bridge begins to crumble, the lives of the people of the region change. The novel has an epic sweep that captures the folklore, the history, and the power of a victimized people.

Appelfeld, Aharon. ***Badenheim, Nineteen Thirty-Nine***.
See entry 874.

990   Baranczak, Stanislaw, and Clare Cavanagh, eds. ***Polish Poetry of the Last Two Decades of Communist Rule: Spoiling Cannibals' Fun***. Trans. from Polish; Frwd. by Helen Vendler. Northwestern Univ. Pr. 1991, $29.95 (0-8101-0968-9); $12.95 (0-8101-0982-4). 204pp. Poetry.

This is a lively, eclectic collection that fittingly summarizes the literary and intellectual climate of Poland in the 1970s and 1980s, near the end of totalitarian rule. Not surprisingly, these poems are often heavily political and topical, but their lyrical power and fresh vision give them universal appeal. The editors (Baranczak is himself a superb poet) have introduced English-reading audiences to some gripping verses culled from officially approved publications as well as from the vibrant underground and émigré presses. There is also an excellent introduction by Helen Vendler.

The poets and their works embody the stubbornness of the lyric impulse despite repeated attempts by a numbing dictatorial government to squelch the human soul. As his verses clearly show, despite the oppression, Zbigniew Herbert never let go of his imagination. And Wislawa Szymborska expresses his belief that, in a totalitarian state, life—and poetry—are suffused with politics: "All affairs," he writes, "are political affairs."

991   Borowski, Tadeusz. ***This Way for the Gas, Ladies and Gentlemen***. Trans. from Polish by Barbara Vedder; Intro. by Jan Kott. Viking 1992, $9.95 (0-14-018624-7). 192pp. Fiction.

The author, a Polish writer, was a prisoner-laborer in the death camps at Auschwitz and Birkenau. The twelve grim, realistic short stories in this collection are vignettes—only somewhat fictionalized—about life in the camp. Incidents are made even more horrific by the author's flat, reportorial style, an alarming stripped-to-the-bone realism that conveys a deepening sense of dread. The translator conveys Borowski's almost poetic simplicity with fierce truthfulness.

The stories are filled with striking images, each more horrific than the last. In one, for example, a weeping little girl who has lost an arm is hurled atop a truckload of corpses; her terror is almost impossible to imagine. Although not for the squeamish, this collection is both necessary and important. Eloquent, never dogmatic, always riveting, the stories reveal the dark side of the human soul.

992   Capek, Karel. *R.U.R.* Trans. from Czech. Baker 1923. o.p. Drama.

The initials in the title stand for "Rossum's Universal Robots." In this delightful and satirical drama, Capek describes a world where only one human being still lives; all the others have been replaced by hordes of mechanized automatons, creatures for which the author coined the term "robots."

Capek—one of Czechoslovakia's most distinguished playwrights, novelists, and political commentators—created a number of clever, witty stage pieces that dramatized the growing mechanization of society and the resulting loss of personality and humanity. Most of his other stage pieces, including *The Insect Comedy* (o.p.), are almost forgotten, but *R.U.R.* remains a classic of its kind. Still staged in theaters all over the world, the play enchants viewers with its satiric sting and its futuristic vision of a society that values the machine over the soul.

A number of other works by Capek have recently come back into print, including his 1937 novel *War with the Newts* (Catbird, 1990) and *The Gardener's Year* (Univ. of Wisconsin Pr., 1984), originally published in English in 1929. A collection, *Three Novels* (Catbird, 1990), is also available.

993   Cosic, Dobrica. *Reach to Eternity*. Trans. from Serbo-Croatian by Muriel Heppell. Harcourt 1980, $14.95 (0-15-175961-8). 480pp. Fiction.

In 1915, as Austro-Hungarian forces bombard independent Serbia, a new and even deadlier menace suddenly appears: a typhus epidemic that virtually paralyzes both military and civilian populations. In the small town of Valjevo, in the isolation ward of the small hospital, a drama of life and death begins. The author portrays the agonies of this epidemic through interwoven stories of patients and doctors.

Cosic's book is philosophic and slow-moving in places; some readers may be put off by its deadpan presentation of certain characters, who at times seem to be more symbolic than creatures of flesh and blood. Still, some characters are quite memorable, such as the doctor who experiments on his own body. Despite its flaws, the novel paints a riveting panorama of man in turmoil—the good and the bad, the despicable and the noble.

994   Daniel, Yuli. *This Is Moscow Speaking, and Other Stories*. Trans. from Russian by Stuart Hood, and others. Dutton 1969. o.p. Fiction.

This book earned its author five years in a Soviet labor camp. Brave, satiric, and caustic, the stories in this appealing collection capture the essence of the

Soviet state gone mad with bureaucracy and self-importance. In the title story, leaders announce a Public Murder Day during which people over eighteen can kill anyone they desire—except, of course, officials and the police. This sharp-edged satire on irrational political agendas won Yuli Daniel much acclaim in the West.

The author, a master of language, has a gift for turning a phrase. What is most ingratiating about these often grim tales, aside from their obvious political and social context, is their humor and spiritedness, which at times bubbles over into full-scale hilarity.

995 Demetz, Hana. ***The House on Prague Street***. St. Martin 1980. o.p. Fiction.

In this autobiographical novel, the protagonist, Helene Richter, endures life in wartime Czechoslovakia. She attempts to maintain a childlike innocence while the world around her, and the people in it—including her relatives—seem to be losing their minds. Her beloved house on Prague Street, usually a refuge of serenity and hope, becomes less and less so as the madness of the Holocaust penetrates even the house's idyllic sanctity.

This haunting work centers on Helene's quest for peace in the midst of abject horror. Although it tells a familiar story, it does so in a powerful way. The author's careful delineation of the people in the book underscores the spreading cancers of discrimination, hatred, and terror that eventually touch the lives of every main character.

996 Djilas, Milovan. ***Under the Colors***. Trans. from Serbo-Croatian by Lovett F. Edwards. Harcourt 1971. o.p. Fiction.

Djilas, a Yugoslav dissident and former vice president, has fictionalized peasant life in Montenegro during the late nineteenth century. The Radaks, a fierce and noble clan, fight to maintain their Serbian identity in the face of Turkish oppression. Theirs is a saga of ruthless tribal bloodletting, of unmitigated racial pride, of bravery in the face of gruesome slaughter. In this novel, the landscape of Montenegro becomes a major character in itself, because the land gives birth to the peasants who draw their life from it and, as repayment, defend it to the death.

Although the novel seems drawn out in spots, the sheer force of the narrative makes the story compelling. Djilas also reveals a part of the world—the mountainous terrain of Yugoslavia—that remains unfamiliar to many Western readers. In a subsequent work, *The Stone and the Violets* (o.p., 1972), containing thirteen short works, Djilas further develops his nationalistic themes. The author is best known for his essays, collections of which include *Conversations with Stalin* (Harcourt, 1963), *The New Class: An Analysis of Communism* (Harcourt, 1982), and *Of Prisons and Ideas* (Harcourt, 1986).

997 Donchev, Anton. ***Time of Parting***. Trans. from Bulgarian by Marguerite Alexieva. Morrow 1968. o.p. Fiction.

Some Western readers are put off by the classic Eastern European epic style and the myriad details that must be explained in glossaries and footnotes. But readers who stay with this long saga will be rewarded with a gripping story focusing on the seventeenth-century conversion of parts of Bulgaria to Islam.

Rounding out the narrative are two parallel stories—one about a French noble-man and the other about a provincial priest—showing how the people were maneuvered and deceived into conversion.

The author brings another century to life through descriptions of the ambi-ance of the villages, the mountainous terrain, and the vibrant and colorful folk customs. Donchev won Bulgaria's highest literary award for this work, a chronicle of Bulgarian peasant life in a previous time.

998   Dovlatov, Sergei. ***The Compromise***. Trans. from Russian by Anne Frydman. Academy Chicago 1990, $7.95 (0-89733-353-5). 148pp. Fiction.

The author, who worked for years as a journalist in Estonia, has written a delightful satire of the decaying Communist state. Each chapter begins with a brief news item, followed by the elaborate "true" story. As the reporter be-comes more and more successful, the pressure mounts on him to "compro-mise" his integrity. He finds it increasingly difficult to end each newspaper item with the obligatory happy or positive conclusion that the Party demands.

The novel works because of its caustic barbs and its irreverent jabs at such topics as bureaucratic ineptitude and sex in a socialist state. Events are seen through the jaundiced eye of an offbeat and cynical reporter. A slight work of fiction, the novel is very much in the grain of contemporary Eastern European satire in which breezy surface humor masks the horror below.

999   Dumitriu, Petru. ***Incognito***. Trans. from French. o.p. Fiction.

Dumitriu, long considered the dean of Romanian literature, headed the State Literary Society of Romania until he escaped to the West in 1960. His fiction, written first in French, has been highly esteemed in the West, largely because he has transcended the traditional limitations of art produced in a totalitarian state to create works with universal appeal. His stories often explore the struggle of the human soul to flourish in a repressive social context. An earlier novel, *Meeting at the Last Judgment* (o.p.), combines Christian symbolism with socialist reality to paint Romania as a land of the damned.

In similar fashion, *Incognito* fuses traditional Christian imagery with bu-reaucratic horror. The main character, Sebastian Ionesco, a Christ-like figure, writes an autobiography that triggers a state investigation of conspiracy. Through allegory, Dumitriu uses Ionesco's words to comment on the univer-sal nature of salvation.

1000   Ehrenburg, Ilya. ***The Thaw***. Trans. from Russian. o.p. Fiction.

This popular novel, published at the height of the Cold War in the 1950s, galvanized a whole generation of young Soviet artists. In fact, the title became the name of the entire movement that arose following the death of Stalin in 1953: a "thaw" in the cultural censorship and oppression that long plagued Soviet artists. On a more literal level, the title refers to the fact that the central characters in the novel leave the constraints of a long winter and "warm up," psychologically speaking, in their own lives.

The novel was revolutionary in its time. Its theme was that, after Stalin, the Soviet Union had no choice but to thaw—to loosen the reins of repression that had hampered the artist during the Stalin regime. It is the story of Dmitri Koroteyev, an engineer and a successful Soviet citizen whose life is intricately interwoven with others in his small Russian city, especially a Soviet official's wife, whom he loves and who loves him in return. The characters experience the coldness of life under the Communist system and recognize their nagging need to loosen up, to grow, to flower—to thaw.

1001 Eliade, Mircea. **The Forbidden Forest**. Trans. from Romanian by Mac Linscott Ricketts and Mary Park Stevenson. Univ. of Notre Dame Pr. 1978. o.p. Fiction.

This novel by one of the world's great thinkers and scholars is dense, philosophical, and serious. Imbued with mythic structures and larger commentaries on universal truths, it demands a close—perhaps even a second—reading to savor its story and theme. The central character, economist Stefan Viziru, lives through the chaos afflicting his native Romania, from the rise of fascism to the advent of communism following World War II. Later scenes shift to émigré colonies in France and elsewhere, where the characters attempt to resolve their longings for their homeland with their new life abroad.

Written between 1949 and 1955, it is, according to the author, his most significant fiction, epitomizing in many ways the complex observations about mankind found in his other more philosophical works. It is an intellectual novel, with all the joys and problems that that term suggests: rich ideas embodied by characters who sometimes live more in the realm of myth and symbol than in the real world. A challenging read, *The Forbidden Forest* was a milestone for the author, who has also edited the massive *Encyclopedia of Religion* and other scholarly works on myth and spirituality and who is the author of a two-volume autobiography *(see main entry)*.

1002 Fink, Ida. **A Scrap of Time and Other Stories**. Trans. from Polish by Madeleine Levine and Francine Prose. Pantheon 1987. o.p. Fiction/Drama.

This collection of twenty-two stories and a one-act play was written by a Holocaust survivor who now works at Yad Vashem, the Holocaust Memorial, in Jerusalem. These short pieces—some little more than character sketches—explore the day-to-day lives of Polish Jews who struggle to survive during World War II despite the oppressive horror of the Holocaust. Although brief, the works in this volume convey a powerful and almost unrelenting sense of horror.

Fink, who has a good eye for detail, manages to convey simple truths through sharp, lyrical sentences and taut characterizations. To write about horror quietly is to made that horror all the more dreadful; the author's measured style converts the Holocaust from a dark memory to a chilling reality. She has also written a novel, *The Journey* (Farrar, 1992), using the same settings and themes.

Grass, Günter. **The Danzig Trilogy: The Tin Drum, Cat and Mouse, The Dog Years**.
See entry 895.

1003 Hašek, Jaroslav. **The Good Soldier Svejk**. Trans. from Czech by Cecil Parrott. Illus. by Josef Lada. Knopf 1993, $20.00 (0-679-42036-3); Viking $9.95 (0-14-018274-8). 784pp. Fiction.

This uproarious satire, written by a Czech and first published in English translation in 1930, has become a classic of the twentieth century. Svejk (some editions render the name "Schweik"), a professional dog trader, is a bumbling, errant, feeble-minded hero whose comic misadventures mock the obsession with the military found in many cultures. Although expelled from the army, Svejk is drafted anew at the outbreak of World War I. During a series of chaotic and complicated journeys, this happy-go-lucky misfit's innocent cheer and jovial earnestness create havoc wherever he goes. There is a series of classic scenes in which little man confronting a large and oppressive bureaucracy, a theme beloved by satirists. Despite calamities, and as the world falls apart around him, Svejk goes blithely on.

Hašek had been a prisoner in Russia for a number of years, an experience that inspired him to begin his gentle mockery of military life. He died in 1923, having completed only four of the projected six Svejk volumes. The translation in this edition restores the deliciously bawdy humor and the robust language of the original—essential flavors that were missing from earlier English versions.

1004 Holub, Miroslav. *Poems Before and After: Collected English Translations*. Trans. from Czech by Ian Milner, and others. Dufour 1990, $40.00 (1-85224-121-7); $19.95 (1-85224-122-5). 274pp. Poetry.

Holub is a Czech scientist; his curiosity and his willingness to experiment are evident in this collection. Born in 1923, he first made a name for himself as a pathologist, only to discover his gift for poetry at age thirty. After his works appeared in print he rapidly became one of the most celebrated poets of his homeland. In his words: "There is no deep difference between the scientific mind and the artistic mind: Both include the maximum creativity with the maximum freedom." An antitraditionalist, Halub has experimented constantly with the shape and content of his verse.

Although he writes from the perspective of an avowed Marxist, he often puts an ironic spin on the ideology, especially in those works that explore the connections between science and art. In "Pathology," for example, the speaker sees a link between the world revealed by a microscope and the political state he calls home:

Here too are cemeteries
farms and snow.
And I hear the murmur
the revolt of immense estates.

This energizing and intelligent collection reflects the influence of such American masters as William Carlos Williams.

1005 Hrabal, Bohumil. *I Served the King of England*. Trans. from Czech by Paul Wilson. Harcourt 1989, $17.95 (0-15-145745-X); Random $12.00 (0-679-72786-8). 256pp. Fiction.

Hrabal, a popular Czech writer, has written a freewheeling, spirited satire that covers the full range of twentieth-century Czech history. His picaresque hero, Ditie (a word that means "child"), is a low-level hotel worker who drifts from job to job and who becomes involved in myriad unpredictable experiences, some of them poignant, many of them hilarious. During World War II he marries a Nazi; after the war he becomes incredibly wealthy, only to see his fortune disappear when the Communists take over.

The author writes with gusto, easily satirizing the various political regimes through his fantastic, bizarre characters. Always exploring the grotesque, whether through his studies of people or their ideologies, he reflects a fairy tale–like sensibility in this story of a rambling and, ultimately, a failed life. Another recent novel is *Too Loud a Solitude* (Harcourt, 1990).

Iskander, Fazil. ***Sandro of Chegem***.
See entry 1126.

Iwaniuk, Waclaw. ***Evenings on Lake Ontario: Poems***.
See entry 578.

Keneally, Thomas. ***Schindler's List***.
See entry 899.

1006 Kiš, Danilo. ***Garden, Ashes***. Trans. from Serbo-Croatian. Harcourt 1975. o.p. Fiction.

This fragmentary novel is narrated by Andreas Scham, a young boy who lives in an equally fragmented world. In World War II Yugoslavia, his family is compelled to leave their idyllic home and hole up in a rundown building near the decaying railyards. Eduard, the eccentric father, is a visionary and a classic original. His hobby is assembling railroad timetables from around the world, complete with departure times and fares. He is a wanderer, reappearing throughout the story in one fantastic guise or another.

Giving the novel its chaotic rhythm of life is Andreas, who muses about his wartime life and tries to integrate his bizarre father into his vision of things. The boy knows he must construct a life of his own; as the title suggests, where some see ashes, he envisions gardens. Other works by this author include *A Tomb for Boris Davidovich* (Viking, 1980), *Encyclopedia for the Dead* (Farrar, 1989), and *Hourglass* (Farrar, 1990).

1007 Klíma, Ivan. ***My First Loves***. Trans. from Czech by Ewald Osers. HarperCollins 1988, $14.95 (0-06-015866-2); Norton $7.95 (0-393-30601-1). 176pp. Fiction.

Klíma is a strangely evocative writer who draws on fragments of his autobiography to portray universal experience. This book is a collection of four short stories, all set in Czechoslovakia (where, ironically, publication of the book was forbidden). Written in the first person, the stories follow the protagonist as he goes from adolescence through sexual maturity and discovers writing as his vocation.

Obsessed with the underbelly of Czechoslovakian life, Klíma often places his naive heroes in such settings as seedy barrooms, dark, deserted neighborhoods, and isolated rooms where the bitter, ugly specter of communism is ever present—and ever menacing to the human spirit. There is a rawness to his frank autobiographical fictions; sometimes they skirt too close to his actual experiences, as though Klíma could not distance himself from his source of inspiration. A similar power is found in his *My Merry Mornings: Stories from Prague* (Readers International, 1985).

1008 Koestler, Arthur. ***Darkness at Noon***. Macmillan 1987, $35.00 (0-02-565210-9); Bantam $5.99 (0-553-26595-4). 267pp. Fiction.

This classic condemnation of totalitarianism, a major bestseller in the 1940s, remains one of the major testaments to failed idealism. In the novel, an old-guard Bolshevik publicly confesses sins he never committed to the ruling party. His "error" of judgment, it seems, was the simple but heretical act of thinking for himself. This novel is a readable, penetrating study of the effects of political agendas that destroy the soul.

Koestler had been a Communist, but later in life he came to despise the way that system exalted the state at the expense of the individual. The author declared that his novels were inspired by his "quarrels with the human condition" and that they usually grapple with a central theme: Does a noble end justify an ignoble means?

1009 Konrád, György (George). ***The Loser***. Trans. from Hungarian by Ivan Sanders. Harcourt 1982, $10.95 (0-15-653584-X). 320pp. Fiction.

In 1975, the West lauded *The Case Worker* (o.p.), the first work of fiction by Konrád available in that part of the world. The novel was a brilliant portrait of a middle-aged bureaucrat enmeshed in the political machinery of Budapest. *The Loser*, published a few years later, added to his growing reputation as an important Hungarian writer.

In this novel, a fifty-five-year-old "patient" in a state psychiatric hospital tells his own story. Once a high-ranking government leader, he has become a social "loser." While undergoing treatment, he reviews his family's history, starting with his Jewish grandfather in the late nineteenth century and moving through the story of his sex-crazed father. He then details his own bizarre romances and ends by describing the circumstances that led to his current isolation. His personal drama unfolds against the background of rising socialism, the 1956 rebellion in Hungary, and the tragedies that followed. Konrád is a master stylist, an artist who can create portraits of entire generations of people and who can limn entire eras with a few deft turns of phrase.

1010 Kosinski, Jerzy. ***The Painted Bird***. 2nd ed. Random 1983, $6.95 (0-394-60433-4). 224pp. Fiction.

This gripping, explosive novel caused a furor, especially in Eastern Europe, where it was seen as an attack on the state. Critics in one country even suggested that the United States paid Kosinski, who was born in Poland, to write it as an act of propaganda.

The story deals with the effects of war and struggle on a young child. A dark-haired, olive-skinned boy—perhaps a Gypsy or a Jew—is abandoned by his parents during World War II. The boy is compelled to wander from one village to another in some unnamed Slavic land. In his struggle to survive, he encounters deadly bias, harrowing brutality, and numbing indifference to human suffering. Yet the boy is determined to live—at any cost. Whatever the nightmare, says the author, the "urge to survive is inherently unfettered." Speaking of his novel, Kosinski said: "Can the imagination, any more than the boy, be held prisoner?"

1011 Kosmac, Ciril. *A Day in Spring*. Trans. from Slovenian. o.p. Fiction.

In this bittersweet, charming romance, a prominent Slovenian novelist celebrates the life and spirit of his little-known people (fewer than two million in number). The setting for the story is the Slovene Litteral, an area where the Slovenes were compelled to live under Italian rule between the two World Wars. After 1945, the area was incorporated into Yugoslavia. The violent interethnic tensions in this borderland region are reflected in the troubled psychological states of Kosmac's characters.

In the novel, a writer returns to Slovenia after fifteen years in exile. He recounts the melodramatic story of Bozena, a young woman born during World War I, the product of an unhappy romance between a Czech soldier and a local girl. Twenty years later Bozena falls in love with a young Italian; history, it seems, is about to repeat itself.

Kosmac, born in Slovenia in 1910, clearly has an abiding love for his land. His lush, elegant prose and his romantic characters make the book a charming Slovene idyll.

1012 Krleza, Miroslav. *The Return of Philip Latinovicz*. Trans. from Croatian by Zora G. Zepolo. Lincoln-Prager 1959. o.p. Fiction.

During his long career, Krleza, who was president of the Yugoslav Union of Writers, produced numerous plays, essays, and works of fiction. He was a master at evoking the ambiance of old-fashioned provincial life in the era between the two World Wars. With his keen eye and sharp pen, he caught the decadence of a society jaundiced by political indifference and world-weary philosophies of life. He was considered the dean of Croatian novelists, and this work is his avowed masterpiece.

The story concerns an internationally renowned painter who one day returns to his home, a small village on the Danubian plain of Croatia. As Philip Latinovicz struggles with his past—with his confused paternity, with sexual questioning, with the nature of artistic talent and fame—he gradually discovers, and comes to grips with, his true identity.

1013 Krotkov, Yuri. *The Nobel Prize*. Trans. from Russian by Linda Aldwinckle. Simon & Schuster 1980. o.p. Fiction.

Krotkov has fictionalized the compelling story of the Soviet novelist Boris Pasternak. Publication of Pasternak's most famous work, *Doctor Zhivago*, was forbidden by Soviet censors because of its "anti-Marxist" content. Despite this, the work was published in the West, where it earned its author the Nobel Prize. Soviet officials, however, forced Pasternak to reject the award; furthermore, out of fear of expulsion from his beloved homeland, he agreed to publicly renounce his own writings.

In recasting this engrossing story, Krotkov demonstrates his skill at fictionalizing real-life figures, including Pasternak and Soviet Premier Nikita Khrushchev. This result, far from being a dry polemic dressed up as fiction, is a readable, fast-paced narrative that dramatizes the life and dilemmas of the conscientious artist in a society that despises and fears the creative spirits who give voice to the truth.

1014 Kundera, Milan. ***The Unbearable Lightness of Being***. Trans. from Czech by Michael Heim. HarperCollins 1984, $19.95 (0-06-015258-3); $13.00 (0-06-091465-3). 320pp. Fiction.

Kundera is one of the most celebrated Czech novelists of his time. This novel, set in Czechoslovakia after the 1968 Soviet invasion, is the story of Tomas, a Prague surgeon and a notorious lover of women. Ostensibly the plot involves Tomas's attraction to a barkeep, Tereza, and their eventual marriage and emigration to Zurich. In fact, however, the story line is simply a device that allows Kundera to expound on deep truths—from digressions about the meaninglessness ("lightness") of life to philosophic and ironic ruminations on the vagaries of life. In the process of spinning his tale, Kundera experiments with structure, design, and technique, continually surprising the reader with both his lyricism and his profundity.

Kundera has been widely translated. Other important works are the novels *The Book of Laughter and Forgetting* (Viking, 1981) and *The Joke* (rev. ed., HarperCollins, 1992) and the short story collections *Laughable Loves* (Viking, 1988), *Life Is Elsewhere* (Viking, 1986), and *The Farewell Party* (Viking, 1987). Any of these works serves to introduce English-reading audiences to this master storyteller, a profound artist and a speaker of universal truths.

1015 Kuniczak, W. S. ***The March***. Doubleday 1979. o.p. Fiction.

Kuniczak fictionalizes the tragic consequences of the Russian invasion of eastern Poland in 1939, the so-called liberation of Poland. He vividly depicts this grim and shocking historical event, which resulted in the murder of 10,000 Polish soldiers in the Kayn Forest and the drowning of 7,000 Polish officers in the Lara Sea. These events are contrasted with the equally grim fate of a small group of exiles from the town of Lwów as they inch along in their death march to Siberia.

The author creates some vivid and tragic characters, including Abel Abramowski, a young poet, and Mendeltort, a Jew. The lives of these characters parallel Poland's national tragedy to convey the author's bleak vision of humanity. The long novel, full of anecdotes and vignettes, may be difficult for some readers, but it is rewarding nonetheless. Although it continues the story of an earlier work by the same author, *The Thousand Hour Day* (o.p., 1967), it can be read independently.

1016 Liehm, Antonin, and Peter Kussi, eds. ***The Writing on the Wall: An Anthology of Contemporary Czech Literature***. Karz-Cohl 1983. o.p. Fiction.

In the days—not so long ago—when Czech writers could not get their works published because of oppressive political regimes, they passed their stories and poems covertly from hand to hand, creating a culture of underground literature. This wonderful collection brings together over three dozen short stories by eighteen such writers, introducing readers in the West to many superb works that are at last emerging into the light. Given the repressive culture in which these works were written, it is amazing to experience their spiritedness and humor, to discover their authors' abiding faith in the joys of life and the power of the pen.

This readable, important collection includes some standard names. Václav Havel's "The Trial" explores the criminal trial of a band of underground Czech rock musicians. Eda Kriseova contributes a tale of a peasant who battles the official order to "collectivize" his farm. Works by other, lesser-known writers are equally satisfying.

1017 Limonov, Eduard. *Memoir of a Russian Punk*. Trans. from Russian by Judson Rosengrant. Grove 1991. 320pp. o.p. Fiction.

The previous volumes in this autobiographical series, *It's Me, Eddie* (o.p., 1987) and *His Butler's Story* (o.p., 1987), dealt with a character called "Eddie-baby" after his emigration to New York. Limonov finishes his trilogy with a story, set in Russia, recalling Eddie-baby's experiences as a fifteen-year-old boy. Although he is a sensitive poet, he becomes involved in a vicious gang in the deadened city of Khartov. The events in the novel take place in the span of only two days, the holiday celebrating the Glorious October Revolution.

Some readers may be put off by Limonov's brutal, mechanical style, his seemingly casual discussion of a gang rape that involves a murder, and Eddie-baby's own rape of his girlfriend. There is a great deal of adolescent bravado here, and it is not always attractive. But Limonov tells a compelling story, and his account of a wayward youth—a thug, a reveler, a ne'er-do-well with the soul of a poet—is always fascinating.

1018 Lustig, Arnošt. *Night and Hope*. Trans. from Czech by George Theiner. Northwestern Univ. Pr. 1985, $9.95 (0-8101-0702-3). 219pp. Fiction.

Lustig, a Holocaust survivor, has chosen the short story as his vehicle for recounting his experiences as a young boy in concentration camps during World War II. The stories are collected in a three-volume series known as *Children of the Holocaust*; the other volumes are *Darkness Casts No Shadow* (Northwestern Univ. Pr., 1985) and *Diamonds of the Night* (Northwestern Univ. Pr., 1986). These important tales—dark and sinister, depressing and menacing—are told in simple, graphic terms and narrated by young boys. From their perspective, readers witness key events, such as daily life in the death camps and the liberation of Prague. Such a recounted journey is hardly pleasant, to be sure, but it is both necessary and galvanizing.

The unmitigated severity of Lustig's tales makes it difficult for the reader to stay with them for a long period. The author's dark vision leaves little room for the glimpses of humanity and the occasional flashes of wit sometimes seen in writings by other Holocaust survivors. Nevertheless, many of his tales satisfy deeply, because he has vividly captured small moments in the life of a boy caught in a madness he can barely understand.

1019 McLaughlin, Sigrid, ed. *The Image of Women in Contemporary Soviet Fiction: Selected Short Stories from the U.S.S.R.* Trans. from Russian by Sigrid Mc-Laughlin. St. Martin 1989, $45.00 (0-312-02823-7); $16.95 (0-312-02824-5). 256pp. Fiction.

This is an important collection of twelve short stories—five by men, seven by women—written in the Soviet Union between the 1960s and the late 1980s.

Some fairly familiar current writers are represented, including Tatyana Tolstaya and Valentin Rasputin, and the overall level of quality is high.

Despite the title, this is not a work of feminist literary criticism; instead, the volume simply presents some excellent, intelligent fiction that grapples with the issue of women's roles in what was then the Soviet Union. The stories also provide insight into the relationships between men and women living in a Communist state. The work is made even more valuable by the editor's comprehensive introduction, her supplementary materials, and her seasoned, sophisticated translations. A good companion volume is Helena Goscilo's *Balancing Acts: Contemporary Stories by Russian Women* (Indiana Univ. Pr., 1989).

1020 Milosz, Czeslaw. *The Bells in Winter*. Trans. from Polish by Lillian Vallee. Ecco 1978. o.p. Poetry.

Milosz, born in Lithuania and raised in Poland, is now an American citizen. But his poetry, fiction, and essays, for which he was awarded the Nobel Prize, still bear the indelible mark of a man haunted by a search for personal salvation in a world gone mad and cruel. Milosz writes as if he knows he can never escape his role as a seer for nations blinded by their political choices.

The pieces in this volume, drawn from five decades of writing, are exquisite, eloquent, and memorable. Those wishing to read more of this Polish master's works in English have available to them a number of options. *The Issa Valley* (Farrar, 1982) is a novel set in the author's native Lithuania. *Native Realm: A Search for Self-Definition* (Univ. of California Pr., 1981) and *The Captive Mind* (Peter Smith, 1992) contain brilliant essays. Another important poetry collection is *The Separate Notebooks* (Ecco, 1986). All these works reveal one of the consummate artistic voices of this century.

1021 Nowakowski, Marek. *The Canary and Other Tales of Martial Law*. Trans. from Polish by Krystyna Bronkowska. Dial 1984. o.p. Fiction.

This is a collection of thirty-six brief but powerful short stories that chronicle reactions to the imposition of martial law in Poland in December 1981. Originally published by underground Polish presses in France between 1982 and 1983, they constitute a dark and bitter chapter in Polish life.

Nowakowski's style is particularly fascinating: sharp, colloquial, acerbic, ironic. His short pieces are so abbreviated that they seem to have been written on his way to the police station. Their reportorial, almost throwaway tone provides memorable snapshot glimpses into people's lives; taken together, these vignettes create a vivid mosaic of a fragmented, troubled society. The title story is exemplary: An old woman's telephone conversation about her pet canary leads to her interrogation by police, who assume such an innocuous conversation must be a form of subversive political code.

1022 Ostrovskii, Nikolai A. *Born of the Storm*. Repr. of 1939 ed. Trans. from Russian by Louise L. Hiler. Hyperion 1975, $20.00 (0-88355-175-6). 251pp. Fiction.

Ostrovskii was a young Ukrainian partisan during the bloody, turbulent civil wars that followed the Russian Revolution, and this fictional rendition of his experiences is written with candor and often stark realism. His novel, hugely popular in the Soviet Union, depicts the life of the common man in the days immediately following the revolution. The exuberant young student Paul Korchagin battles with his cleric teachers until he is expelled. In time he becomes caught up in the changing political ideology of the new Russia. His life changes when he reads political tracts and embraces the agendas of organizations such as the Young Communist League. As he puts it, "I do stand for the type of revolutionary for whom individual things are nothing in comparison with the general cause."

The book was originally entitled *How the Steel Was Tempered*, and the author intended to follow it with a sequel called *Korchagin's Happiness*, but in 1927 he was struck by a paralyzing disease that led to blindness and, a decade later, to death.

1023 Pasternak, Boris. **Doctor Zhivago**. Trans. from Russian; Intro. by John Bayley. Buccaneer 1991, $36.95 (0-89966-839-9); Pantheon $14.00 (0-679-73123-7). 544pp. Fiction.

Pasternak was widely known for his poetry, but that reputation was eclipsed by the international furor over the publication of this novel. He was awarded the Nobel Prize, but the Soviet government forced him to refuse the honor. The ensuing controversy made *Doctor Zhivago* an overnight sensation; its popularity increased following the release of a successful film adaptation.

But the virtue of the novel is not its profundity—which it largely lacks—or its stylistic brilliance—which it displays only in spots. Its true strength lies in its engrossing story and its characters: Dr. Yuri Zhivago, healer, poet, humanitarian; and others, including Lara, Pasha, Tonia, and the memorable Uncle Kolia. Events take place from the turn of the century through the middle of World War II, in the harsh yet beautiful landscapes of Moscow, Siberia, and the Eastern Front. Pasternak has captured an era now gone, a generous people now compromised, in a memorable story that has given the world characters entrenched forever in the popular imagination. A biography is available: *Boris Pasternak* by Guy de Mallac *(see main entry)*; a fictionalized version of Pasternak's struggle can be found in Yuri Krotkov's *The Nobel Prize (see main entry)*.

1024 Pekic, Borislav. **The Houses of Belgrade**. Repr. of 1978 ed. Trans. from Serbo-Croatian by Bernard Johnson. Northwestern Univ. Pr. 1994, $12.95 (0-8101-1141-1). Fiction.

This highly regarded novel tells the story of Arsenie Negovan, a rich but eccentric landowner, who believes that the rental homes he owns in Belgrade are to be loved as passionately as if they were women. In fact, he gives them women's names. The terrors of World War II drive him inside; panic-stricken and frightened, he does not leave his home for twenty-seven years. Still, he keeps watch on his property with binoculars and a blizzard of official papers.

The eccentric Negovan's ruminations and fixations become a metaphor—at once comic and satiric—for many human foibles. The reading is at times challenging, with many circumlocutions, off-beat tangents, and archaic meanderings. Pekic's intricate, almost fussy style takes getting used to, but once the reader latches onto Negovan's personality, he stays with him until Negovan finally emerges from his isolation.

1025 Pilnyak, Boris. *The Chinese Story and Other Tales*. Trans. from Russian by Vera T. Reck and Michael Green. Univ. of Oklahoma Pr. 1988. o.p. Fiction.

Pilnyak was a great master storyteller of the 1920s. Many of these stories, written between 1915 and 1927, are famous in the West, particularly "The Tale of the Unextinguished Moon." In this work, a popular leader dies as the result of an unnecessary operation ordered by party officials. Pilnyak's writings offended the Soviet bureaucrats, who vilified him and forced him from the chairmanship of the All-Russian Union of Writers. Arrested during the purges of the 1930s, he was apparently executed in 1937.

At times melodramatic, his stories fuse a nineteenth-century flair with a darker twentieth-century sensibility. Pilnyak can become lyrical in his descriptions of rather dreadful people, and his characters seem destined to grapple with displacements—both physical and psychological   over which they have no control. He is also the author of *The Volga Falls to the Caspian Sea* (orig. pub. 1931; A M S, 1971).

1026 Popa, Vasko. *Homage to the Lame Wolf: Selected Poems*. 2nd ed. Trans. from Serbian by Charles Simic. Oberlin College Pr. 1987, $9.00 (ISBN 0-932440-22-3). 125pp. Poetry.

Popa is a poet who cultivates a tight, controlled imagery. His sharp poetic lines often belie the humorous or casual theme. This anthology shows the evolution of a significant poet, immensely popular in Yugoslavia, who has begun to acquire considerable reputation in the Western world. His work is easily accessible to the general student of world literature.

1027 Sholokhov, Mikhail. *Quiet Flows the Don*. 2 vols. Trans. from Russian by Robert Daglish. State Mutual Book & Periodical 1988, $130.00 (0-569-09106-3). 1,612pp. Fiction.

Sholokhov, born into the tradition of the Don Cossacks, began writing his massive epic in 1926. The first part, *And Quiet Flows the Don*, tells of a young Cossack, Gregor Melekhov, through whose eyes the reader sees how war pervades the life of the peasant village, how soldiers shift allegiances in utter confusion, how warring factions turn a serene world into chaos. Throughout the turmoil, there is an abiding love of the land, a faith in the power of the rural life to bring salvation.

The second part, *The Don Flows Home to the Sea*, follows Gregor from 1917 through the coming to power of the Communists. This book, like the first, reveres and exalts the Cossack tradition, which represents a threat to newly powerful Soviets. Both volumes are rich sagas of inviolable traditions and enduring peasant faith in the soil that makes them whole. Sholokhov received the Nobel Prize for literature in 1965.

1028 Simic, Charles, ed. *The Horse Has Six Legs: Contemporary Serbian Poetry*. Graywolf 1992, $12.00 (1-55597-165-2). 222pp. Poetry.

This collection, assembled by a Pulitzer Prize–winning poet, is a rich and varied one, filled with both the exuberance and tragedy of life. It is particularly satisfying because the editor, Charles Simic, is such a faithful and lyrical translator. His selection of works by eighteen poets is generous and eclectic, ranging from early oral verse and women's songs to the internationally known writing of poets such as Vasko Popa.

This collection is a lyrical treat. Several of the works, such as Lalic's "Love in July," celebrate life; others, including Beckovic's "Yevtushenko," take the form of tributes. Nevertheless, underlying much of the poetry—Nastasijevic's "Burial" for example—there is a haunting sadness, a dark and often startling sensibility. The reader comes away from the volume with a bittersweet taste of Eastern European darkness and fatalism. Simic's own poetry has been collected in various volumes, most notably *Selected Poems, 1963-1983* (Braziller, 1990).

1029 Singer, Isaac Bashevis. ***The Brothers Ashkenazi***. Trans. from Yiddish by Joseph Singer; Intro. by Irving Howe. Viking 1993, $11.95 (0-14-039086-3). 448pp. Fiction.

This epic novel follows the lives of two brothers in Poland at the turn of the century. Jacob is honest and friendly, Simcha withdrawn and manipulative. The novel is also a tapestry of Jewish life in Lodz, Poland, at a time when the forces of socialism, anti-Semitism, and nationalism all affect the lives of ordinary citizens.

As the inhabitants of Lodz begin to prosper with the growth of the textile industry, their traditional Jewish values become threatened. Simcha, wooed by the appeal of economic gain, becomes a negative force in the novel, a symbol of what Singer regarded as "the failed Jew." Ultimately, though, his brother Jacob offers him a path to redemption. The novel, a classic of social realism, is matter-of-fact, gritty, and clinical in its execution of detail and plot.

Among Singer's other works are *The Family Moskat* (1988) and *The Certificate* (1992), the latter of which is set in post–World War II Poland. He is also the author of numerous short story collections that focus on Jewish folklore and Jewish life throughout the world in the nineteenth and twentieth centuries.

Škvorecký, Josef. ***The Engineer of Human Souls***.
See entry 603.

1030 Škvorecký, Josef. ***The Swell Season***. Trans. from Czech by Paul Wilson. Ecco 1986, $8.50 (0-88001-090-8). 226pp. Fiction.

Škvorecký's trilogy, which ideally is read in its entirety, tells the story of Danny, a Czech youth living under Nazi occupation. *The Cowards* (orig. pub. 1970; Ecco, 1980) deals with Danny in 1945, when he is in his early twenties. *The Bass Saxophone* (orig. pub. 1979; Ecco, 1994) shifts back in time to when Danny was eighteen. Although *The Swell Season* was written last, it returns to a time when Danny is younger yet. All three books together create a picture of a typical young man out in the world, romping through life and bitter times in a rollicking sex comedy of manners.

In rambling, fun-filled prose, Škvorecký recounts his hero's mishaps and sexual gameplaying. Danny, a classic womanizer, is caught up in the world of the 1940s youth culture. The sound of jazz permeates his nightlife. Yet his bright escapades contrast starkly with the darkening shadows of Nazism. This is sex farce at its most inviting—humorous, bawdy, farcical in places. The author is a master storyteller, and the three novels together create a multilayered portrait of Danny—a young man in a hurry, living in a world that is changing as fast as he is.

Smieja, Florian. ***Not a Tourist***.
See entry 604.

1031 Solzhenitsyn, Aleksandr. ***One Day in the Life of Ivan Denisovich***. Trans. from Russian by H. T. Willetts. Farrar 1992, $24.95 (0-374-22643-1); $13.00 (0-374-52195-6). 148pp. Fiction.

This autobiographical novel, which first introduced Western audiences to Solzhenitsyn's work, describes the plight of a Russian citizen trapped in a Stalinist labor camp. The novel first appeared, with the permission of Soviet Premier Khrushchev, in the magazine *Novy Mir* (*New World*); publication of a work that dared criticize the revered Soviet leader was a landmark event in the Soviet Union. Aside from the political impact, the novel is a stunning literary achievement. Ivan Denisovich, struggling to survive just one more day, is a galvanizing character, one whose battles with destiny are universal and unforgettable.

When Solzhenitsyn received the Nobel Prize in 1970, his citation read: "For the ethical force with which he has pursued the indispensable traditions of Russian literature." *Ivan Denisovich*—the first of many English-language publications by the writer—explores this very theme. Solzhenitsyn was prevented from traveling to Oslo to accept the award; his undelivered Nobel lecture is a moving testimony to the power of the artist to transcend the limitations of his given state. As Solzhenitsyn wrote, "The only salvation of humanity lies in everyone concerning himself with everything everywhere." Among Solzhenitsyn's other works in recent editions are *The Gulag Archipelago, Vols. 1 and 2* (HarperCollins, 1992), *The Cancer Ward* (Random, 1989), and *August, Nineteen Fourteen* (Viking, 1992).

1032 Sorescu, Marin. ***The Biggest Egg in the World***. Dufour 1988, $11.95 (1-85224-021-0). 80pp. Poetry.

This is a curious book of poetry. Working from sketches translated from the Romanian by Joana Russell-Gebbett, eight British and Irish poets have rendered Sorescu's poetry into English. In some cases, several versions of a particular poem have been created by different poets. There is even one printed in the original Romanian. Sorescu has been well served by this process; his important poetry, often reflecting the troubled nation he writes about, is engaging and evocative, especially in the renditions of celebrated English poet Ted Hughes.

Sorescu is a challenge to translate, given his intricate and bitter ironies and his experiments with illogic and the bizarre. This is a slight volume, but it is one that provides intriguing glimpses of the writer's talent. Another collection is *Selected Poems*, translated by Michael Hamburger (Dufour, 1983).

1033 Sorokin, Vladimir. ***The Queue***. Trans. from Russian by Sally Laird. Readers International 1988, $16.95 (0-930523-44-X); $8.95 (0-930523-45-8). 198pp. Fiction.

This novelistic *tour de force* takes place entirely in a queue—one of those endless lines, so emblematic of the Soviet economy, where people waited for hours to purchase meager goods. In this novel, we do not know what these various speakers are trying to purchase. Instead, the focus is their wide-ranging conversations on such topics as the Jews, Stalin, romance, Ronald Reagan, Yevtushenko, rural life, and so on. The main character is Vadim Alekseyev, a part-time student at Moscow State University, and we follow his rambling musings as he shuffles along in the queue.

The novel is fun to read because of Sorokin's keen satiric wit, strong sense of the bizarre, and a sharp ear for dialogue. The characters endure delays that stretch into the night, but patiently they wait to purchase some unidentified foreign import—one that everyone wants simply because it is, indeed, foreign.

1034 Tolstaya, Tatyana. ***On the Golden Porch***. Trans. from Russian by Antonina Bouis. Knopf 1989, $17.95 (0-394-57798-1); Random $11.00 (0-679-72843-0). 208pp. Fiction.

This collection of thirteen short stories, set in Leningrad and Moscow, is a brilliant introduction to the vivid and offbeat imagination of this author. Tolstaya is not concerned with socialist realism; indeed, unlike so many of the stories written in Eastern Europe, these works appear to have no political agenda. The central characters do not seem plagued by communism; they do not seem destined to play out their destinies against a domineering ideology. Rather, they are characters of fancy: misfits, dreamers, losers, errants, people on the curious edge of a moment in time.

Her stories are often lushly metaphoric exercises that fuse figurative language with strange characterizations. They may not appeal to every reader, yet they are worth the effort. Tolstaya creates her own fictional world, and the landscape she explores is refreshing. She is also the author of the short story collection *Sleepwalker in a Fog* (Knopf, 1991), which develops many of the same themes that are found in this volume.

1035 Trifonov, Yuri. ***Another Life and The Houses on the Embankment***. Trans. from Russian by Michael Glenny. Simon & Schuster 1983. o.p. Fiction.

These two novellas, beautifully and faithfully translated by Glenny, demonstrate why Trifonov is considered a masterly contemporary Russian writer. His economy of phrase, coupled with an acute psychological sense of human endeavor, suggest that, in this rare instance, the artistic dictates of socialist realism could actually work to produce worthwhile literature. These are late pieces of fiction (the author died in 1981), and they are lively reading indeed.

In *Another Life*, a biologist reminisces about the sixteen years she spent with her delightful, if wimpish, mate. In *The House on the Embankment*, Vadim Glebov, a literary critic, recalls how as a young man he betrayed his mentor, a man whose daughter was Glebov's fiancée. As the critic muses on how his youthful manipulations led to his later success, the reader becomes aware of an irony: The mentor himself, it turns out, rose to prominence in a similar fashion.

Trifonov is also the author of the novel *Disappearance* (Ardis, 1991), a complex and challenging work set in the Soviet Union during the late 1930s. Also back in print is *The Exchange* (Random, 1991), a collection of short stories.

1036   Tsvetayeva, Marina. *Selected Poems*. Trans. from Russian by David McDuff. Dufour 1988, $18.95 (1-85224-025-3). 160pp. Poetry.

This collection of Tsvetayeva's poetry is a new translation of a previous collection by the same name, edited by Elaine Feinstein (Oxford Univ. Pr., 1982). McDuff has deleted some poems from the earlier volume and added others, including some written during the years when the poet resided in the Soviet Union. The translations evoke the writer's power and demonstrate clearly her reputation as a consummate love poet.

Tsvetayeva (sometimes spelled Tsvetaeva) perhaps is best represented here by her careful evocations of love in a hostile, dark world. But another side of her work emerges in such offerings as excerpts from her early work, "Ratcatcher" (1925). Here she uses her satiric edge to turn the story of the Pied Piper into an allegory of oppressed lives. Readers wishing to know more can look for the bilingual collection *The Demesne of the Swans* (Ardis, 1980), the nonfiction *A Captive Spirit: Selected Prose* (o.p., 1980), and *Marina Tsvetaeva: A Pictorial Biography*, edited by Ellendea Proffer (Ardis, 1980).

1037   Voinovich, Vladimir. *Moscow, 2042*. Trans. from Russian by Richard Lourie. Harcourt 1990, $12.95 (0-15-662165-7). 432pp. Fiction.

This imaginative novel deals with a Russian writer, Vitaly Nikitich Kartsev, living in Munich, who gets on an airplane and ends up in Moscow sixty years into the future. A prominent satirist, Voinovich writes with keen wit and delicious humor, and his goal in satire—"to herd all the sacred cows into a blind alley"—is achieved in this engaging volume.

Voinovich omits no one in Russia from the gaze of his acerbic eye. He uses the biggest weapons in his arsenal of wit to batter bureaucratic and stereotypical Communists, but he also lambastes the monarchists, those tired Russians who have a lingering, if misguided, affection for the old days. Voinovich's characters tend toward the one-dimensional—a typical occupational hazard for any satirist—but his novel, full of clever turns of phrase, is richly satisfying. Voinovich is also the author of the humorous novels *The Life and Extraordinary Adventures of Private Ivan Chonkin* (o.p., 1977), *The Fur Hat* (Harcourt, 1989), and *The Ivankiad* (o.p., 1976), an autobiographical tale describing the author's frustrating odyssey in search of a larger apartment.

1038   Walker, Scott, ed. *Stories from the New Europe*. Graywolf 1992. o.p. Fiction.

This superb, one-of-a-kind anthology offers a variety of short stories written by lesser-known "ethnics" of Europe, both Eastern and Western: Baltic, Catalan, Croat, Slovak, Euzkadi (Basque), Icelandic, and Czech. Some of the writers, such as Danilo Kiš of Serbia, have been internationally known for years. But the lesser-known writers are what make this work especially useful.

The editor has included stories from a number of forgotten or ignored peoples, half of them from Eastern Europe. There are works from Estonia (by Teet Kallas), Latvia (Regina Ezera), and Lithuania (Juozas Aputis), as well as from Croatia, Serbia, the Czech Republic, and Slovakia. These unknown authors and stories cannot be found elsewhere, which makes this anthology—now unfortunately out of print—a especially rare treasure.

1039 Wiesel, Elie. *Night*. Trans. from French. Bantam 1982, $4.99 (0-553-27253-5). 128pp. Fiction.

This classic work describes Wiesel's harrowing experiences in concentration camps. Brought up in the Hungarian village of Sighet, young Eliezer received a traditional Jewish education; his commitment to his heritage was to be sorely tested in the years that followed. In 1944, with the tide turning against the Nazis, the Jews of Sighet were rounded up and moved to the ghetto and then sent to Auschwitz. Eliezer's mother and younger sister were separated from him and his father; they never saw them again. Eliezer and his father lied about their ages so as to qualify for labor camps and thus were spared the ovens of Auschwitz. They were transferred to Birkenau and then to Buna and Buchenwald, where they toiled under horrible conditions and experienced the arbitrary brutality of camp officials. Observing the suffering of innocent people—and suffering a great deal himself—the young Wiesel began to question his religious beliefs and the goodness of God. Less than three months before the war's end, his father fell ill and died. Liberated from the camp in 1945, Eliezer, then sixteen, was near death, without family, faith in humankind, home—or hope. This is a grim and pessimistic work, but it has much to say about evil, survival, and the destruction of innocence. **LML**

1040 Yevtushenko, Yevgeny. *Collected Poems*. Trans. from Russian. Henry Holt 1991, $29.95 (0-8050-0696-6). 576pp. Poetry.

During the 1960s, the popular press doted on Yevtushenko, depicting him as the youthful voice of a new Soviet generation. His works are well represented in this brief collection. Born in 1933, Yevtushenko matured at a time when Soviet policies was deeply entrenched. Even so, he was able to observe the political landscape with a skeptical eye and to convert his observations into trenchant verse. In the process he led the way for others who wanted to write honestly, without compromise. Of mixed peasant birth—Russian, Ukrainian, Tartar—he spent a childhood in Siberia; his "Zima Junction" is an evocative, powerful account of his return home after twenty years.

Like most poets of his time, Yevtushenko embraces not only the simple lyricism so vital to Russian verse, but also the requisite grappling with political ideology. This collection ranges in tone from the easy humor of "On a Bicycle" to the somber intensity of "Babi Yar," his bitter assault on anti-Semitism in the Soviet Union. Today his works appeal to a general audience for the insight they give the poetic soul of a generation of Soviet youth.

1041 Zalygin, Sergei, ed. *The New Soviet Fiction*. Illus. Abbeville 1989, $9.95 (0-89659-881-0). 397pp. Fiction.

Zalygin, an editor of the magazine *Novy Mir* (*New World*), has selected a variety of short fiction that represents the best of 1980s writing from the Soviet Union. His only criterion, it seems, has been literary excellence, for this volume displays a vast artistic landscape, ranging from such well-known writers as Valentin Rasputin and Irina Grekova to some obscure but worthwhile authors.

There is not a failure in the collection. Some entries, like Andrei Bitov's futuristic meditation "Pushkin's Photograph (1799–2099)," are masterpieces. Zalygin avoids the pitfalls of many similar collections: He does not choose pieces simply because they deal with life in the collectivist world—a world that seems destined to breed satire. Instead, he choose stories that tell stories of real people, universally recognizable, who—like the rest of humanity—are caught in the vortex of everyday human dilemmas.

NONFICTION

1042 Abel, Elie. *The Shattered Bloc: Behind the Upheaval in Eastern Europe*. Houghton 1990. o.p. Nonfiction.

Abel is an accomplished journalist, a former NBC reporter and dean of the Columbia University School of Journalism. In 1988 he visited virtually every Eastern European country that was undergoing massive political and social change. His account is not a full-blown historical perspective, but it is valuable for a general reader who wants a coherent, intelligent overview of the upheavals occurring in that part of the world at the dawn of the 1990s. His detailed analyses of the tremendous shifts in the region are on target and worthwhile. Of course, developments continued swiftly in the years following publication of this book. Abel anticipated some of these, which he describes presciently in his text.

There is a breezy, reportorial tone to the work; it is probably not of value for the serious scholar. Yet there is also a first-hand immediacy to his writing, a sense of "you-are-there" that goes beyond the story captured in newspaper headlines.

1043 Adamic, Louis. *The Native's Return*. Repr. of 1934 ed. Greenwood 1975, $55.00 (0-8371-7965-3). 358pp. Nonfiction.

Louis Adamic emigrated from Carniola, Slovenia, at fourteen years of age. In 1934, then thirty-three and an American citizen and a noted author, he traveled back to his native land. His lively, witty account became an immediate best-seller. Adamic became an advocate of Tito's Yugoslavia and a spokesman for Yugoslav policy in the United States after World War II. Here he tells his story with fresh observation and delightful anecdotes.

He chronicles the life of his family and friends in their small Yugoslav village, filling in his narrative with fascinating bits of folklore and custom. He also surveys life in such cities as Zagreb, Croatia, and Belgrade, Serbia. His portrait is important reading today because it defines the political and social framework that underlies both the revolution in the region that followed World War II and devastating ethnic rivalries that plague the dissolved state of Yugoslavia in the 1990s. His is an insider's tale, told from the perspective of one who has come back to observe.

1044 Batt, Judy. *Economic Reform and Political Change in Eastern Europe: A Comparison of the Czechoslovak and Hungarian Experiences*. St. Martin 1988, $49.95 (0-312-01196-2). 384pp. Nonfiction.

Recent changes in both Hungary and Czechoslovakia may suggest that this volume is already dated, but such is not the case. By focusing on the different eras of economic reform in both countries, beginning with Hungary in 1968, the author, a noted British lecturer on Eastern European politics, explains the historical and philosophical background of what is happening in the region in the 1990s.

She focuses on the problems of both these socialist nations experienced when they began to implement the difficult reforms required for a transition to a market-based economy. Now, as virtually all of Eastern Europe scrambles to make such a transition, it is interesting to note how the scenarios described by Batt are playing out in other nations as they struggle to balance market forces against decaying political ideologies. Batt also explores the fascinating paradox that arises when ruling socialist parties use the leverage of the market-place to guarantee their own survival.

Blanke, Richard. *Orphans of Versailles: The German Minority in Western Poland, 1918–1939.*
See entry 916.

1045 Brodsky, Joseph. *Less Than One: Selected Essays of Joseph Brodsky.* Farrar 1986, $30.00 (0-374-18503-4); $12.95 (0-374-52055-0). 501pp. Essays.

This eclectic collection of pieces shows that Brodsky, a renowned poet, is also a master essayist. The first entry is an autobiographical look at his early days in Leningrad, and the last discusses his parents in a beautiful, evocative elegy. In between he analyzes Russian and non-Russian writers and ruminates on such thorny topics as ethics and politics. In all, he reveals himself to be a writer of engaging wit and intellectual verve, in full control of his adopted English language.

His extended analysis of W. H. Auden's "September 1, 1939" is important both for its fine, intelligent reading of the British master and for the way Brodsky relates it to his own verse. The author states, in fact, that he started writing in English as a desire "to please the shadow" of Auden, whom he so admired. Included, too, is a commencement address Brodsky delivered at Williams College; the speech is surprisingly original, compelling, and fresh.

1046 Brokhin, Yuri. *Hustling on Gorky Street: Sex and Crime in Russia Today.* Trans. from Russian by the author and E. B. Kane. Dial 1975. o.p. Nonfiction.

Brokhin, who emigrated to the United States in 1972, paints a curious, sordid picture of Soviet underworld life, one filled with Hogarthian rogues and sinners, as well as buffoonish TV sitcom–inspired con artists. This is an uneven book, given the clearly manufactured conversations. Nevertheless, it provides insight into another side of the Soviet empire, a world quite unlike the glowing official portrayals generated by government propagandists. Admittedly, too, there is tabloid-like fascination in this rogue's gallery of harlots, drug addicts, sleazy money men, tramway pickpockets, and other common criminals.

The author claims to have been a respected mining engineer as well as a TV writer, but he also talks of his days as a gypsy cab driver. He seems to revel in his participation in life's darker side; for example, he refers to his cab as his "brothel on wheels." The book works best when Brohkin indulges his taste for broad humor; it fails when he waxes sociological, because his observations are familiar and trite. Still, this slight work gives us a glimpse into a culture we seldom see, a symptom of a failed political system.

1047 Cullen, Robert. ***Twilight of Empire: Inside the Crumbling Soviet Bloc***. Atlantic Monthly 1991. o.p. Nonfiction.

The author recounts the last days of the crumbling Soviet empire by focusing on events in two of the Baltic States, Latvia and Lithuania, as well as the drama in Romania that unfolded between August 1989 and December 1990. Not a scholarly study, this book combines anecdotes and dramatic moments to illuminate the incredible changes occurring in the twilight of a great empire.

With his reporter's eye and instincts, Cullen understood the coming decline of the empire. He shows how states on the fringes of the empire began to tire of the violence and irrational cruelty they had suffered under a moribund political system and how, inevitably, dissatisfaction and rebellion would spread. This is a good popular account of historic events.

1048 Dawisha, Karen. ***Eastern Europe, Gorbachev, and Reform: The Great Challenge***. 2nd ed. Cambridge Univ. Pr. 1990, $44.95 (0-521-38498-2); $17.95 (0-521-38652-7). 240pp. Nonfiction.

Although the reforms Dawisha discusses in her book have wrought unbelievable and unanticipated changes, this volume nevertheless is not wholly outdated. It describes the machinations and deliberations that led to the dissolution of the Soviet Union and the wholesale shifting of politics in Eastern Europe. To provide perspective, the author explores the evolving relationships of the Soviet Union with other parts of Eastern Europe, as well as the Soviet Union's relationship to the West, throughout the 1980s. The text addresses the problems that sparked reform, analyzes Gorbachev's role, and predicts the fallout from the shakeup.

In the last few years many astounding events have occurred: the collapse of Communism, the breakup of the Soviet Union, the reunification of Germany. Dawisha's book analyzes in detail the roots of these changes. Although the author predicted much of the chaos that would follow the democratization of Eastern Europe, she nonetheless remains optimistic about the future for the region.

1049 Dedijer, Vladimir. ***The Battle Stalin Lost: Memoirs from Yugoslavia***. Trans. from Serbo-Croatian. Coronet 1978, $57.50 (0-85124-223-5). 341pp. Nonfiction.

In the spring of 1948, the icebound silence of Eastern Europe was shattered in the West by the news that Stalin had denounced Tito and called for the Yugoslavs to overthrow him. Dedijer, Director of Information and close friend of Tito, was actively involved in the tense, dreadful period when the whole world waited to see whether the Soviet Union would crush Tito's Yugoslavia. This is a gripping, page-turning story.

What makes the volume valuable is Dedijer's powerful insights into the violent events that redefined Eastern Europe for the rest of the world following World War II. What is maddening about his account, however, is the rambling, disheveled style, the incomplete interpretations, and the careless attention to detail. Despite these flaws, the drama of the upheaval rivets the reader's attention, and Dedijer's insights are necessary for a complete understanding of these events. When read today, it is clear that many of the reforms occurring in Eastern Europe during the 1990s were foreshadowed by Tito's defiance of Stalin.

1050 Dobroszycki, Lucjan, and Barbara Kirshenblatt-Gimblett. *Image Before My Eyes: A Photographic History of Jewish Life in Poland Before the Holocaust.* Illus. with photos. Schocken 1994, $25.00 (0-8052-1026-1). 269pp. Nonfiction.

This stunning collection of 300 photographs is drawn from the YIVO Institute for Jewish Research's collection of over 10,000 images of Jewish life in Poland. There are three divisions: "Persistence of the Past," "The Camera as Chronicler," and "Creating a Modern Resistance." The photographs open a window on life from the days of the tsars through the period just before World War II.

Despite the haunting, melancholic tone of this book, it is a visual feast that documents and celebrates the vibrant, thriving culture among the largest Jewish population in Europe before it was destroyed in the Holocaust. The accompanying text is brief, and the bibliography and other supplementary materials add to the book's value.

1051 Doder, Dusko. *The Yugoslavs.* Random 1978. o.p. Nonfiction.

Given the enormous upheaval in the Yugoslav region in the past quarter century—the death of the defiant Tito in 1980, the dissolution of the Yugoslav state beginning in the 1990s—much of what Doder has to say may have been rendered hopelessly out of date. Nevertheless, this study has continuing merit. Despite the headlines emanating from Yugoslavia in recent years, many readers remain unfamiliar with the ethnic mix of the population: Serbs, Croats, Slovenes, Macedonians, Montenegrins, Bosnians, Muslims, and others. Through conversation and anecdote, Doder carefully and persuasively delineates the similarities and differences among these various cultures to paint a rich and complex portrait.

The author explains in detail how Tito managed to run a dictatorship and at the same time encourage Western-style market policies. He also offers a profile of the dissident Vladimir Dedijer, author of *The Battle Stalin Lost (see main entry).* The tragedies attending the breakup of Yugoslavia are made all the more poignant in this author's loving, impassioned account of the people he met and talked with throughout the entire country.

1052 Drakulic, Slavenka. *How We Survived Communism and Even Laughed.* Norton 1992, $22.95 (0-393-03076-8); HarperCollins $12.00 (0-06-097540-7). 288pp. Nonfiction.

In 1990 *Ms.* magazine commissioned this celebrated Yugoslav novelist to investigate the status of women and feminism in the changing Eastern European nations. For her report Drakulic traveled to Hungary, Poland, Czechoslovakia, Bulgaria, and East Germany. Despite its bizarre title, this account is grim and sober—no laughing matter at all.

A superb writer, Drakulic creates vivid portraits of women who hunger for something other than the drudgery that defines their lives. This book is a damning account of the failure of socialist regimes to help women discover rewarding roles beyond the traditional ones inherited from the peasant culture of the nineteenth century. Drakulic fills her book with lively and amusing anecdotes as well as bittersweet stories of young and old women struggling against a system that would deny them their individuality. Ironically, Western women reading this book may discover echoes of their own struggles since the 1960s. Drakulic is also the author of *Balkan Express: Fragments from the Other Side of War* (Norton, 1993), another work, similar in style, about her native land.

1053 Echikson, William. ***Lighting the Night: Revolution in Eastern Europe*.** Morrow 1990. o.p. Nonfiction.

As Eastern European correspondent for the *Christian Science Monitor* in the 1980s, Echikson saw firsthand the rapid and vital changes in the region. This overview, written in a breezily reportorial but nonetheless authoritative style, summarizes events during the author's five years in the field. His observations are lively, sometimes witty, and generally well informed. At times he categorizes countries through superficial thumbnail sketches or classifies people according to arbitrary labels. Even so, for the student who wishes an easy entry into the complex and changing face of Eastern Europe, this is probably it.

Through his quick eye, we meet the prime figures involved in key events, including Lech Walesa of Poland and Václav Havel of Czechoslovakia. Perhaps more important, however, is the chance to hear the voices of common people, especially the dissidents in the street who have suddenly become empowered with a vision of democracy and freedom many thought they would never attain. This is an immensely readable account, fast-paced and engaging.

Enzensberger, Hans Magnus. ***Europe, Europe: Forays into a Continent*.** See entry 927.

1054 Fél, Edit, and Tomás Hofer. ***Proper Peasants: Life in a Hungarian Village*.** Illus. with photos. Aldine 1971. o.p. Nonfiction.

For their ethnographic survey of a Hungarian peasant life in collectivist society, the authors used the village of Atany. During their fourteen years of research, they focused on the social organization of the village to draw a portrait of family, neighborhood, and the changing stratification of village life in the post–World War II period.

The authors are particularly adept at depicting the traditional values that give the village its sense of coherence. Readers of this book, which is intended for English-speaking audiences, come to understand the power of folklore, tradition, and habit in helping the villagers resist government agendas imposed on them from above. Bringing the text to life are a number of engaging and evocative photographs.

1055 Havel, Václav. ***Open Letters: Selected Writings, 1965–1990*.** McKay 1991, $22.00 (0-679-40027-3); Random $12.00 (0-679-73811-8). 415pp. Essays.

Havel was a dissident Czech playwright; after the collapse of communism he became president of the republic and later the head of the separated Czech state. He is represented here, not by his works for the stage, but by twenty-five articles and public letters. In one piece he discusses the famed Charter 77, the human rights declaration that he spearheaded. Another important essay,

"The Power of the Powerless," deals with the abuses of power in the repressive political state.

Havel is a powerful writer who uses simple language to convey weighty thoughts on the nature of freedom and oppression. A companion volume, *Václav Havel, Or Living in Truth* (Faber 1987), contains twenty-two essays, six by Havel, the rest dedicated to him. He is also the author of an autobiography in interview format, *Disturbing the Peace: A Conversation with Karel Hvizdala* (Knopf, 1990).

1056 Hoffman, Eva. ***Exit into History: A Journey Through the New Eastern Europe***. Viking 1993, $23.00 (0-670-83649-4); $10.95 (0-14-014549-4). 432pp. Nonfiction.

Hoffman is a Polish Jew who emigrated to Canada as an adolescent. In this book she uses the travel genre to create insightful portraits—sometimes painfully dark, sometimes wonderfully lyrical—of five Eastern European countries after the 1989 revolutions and the fall of Communism. On her journeys through Poland, Romania, Bulgaria, Hungary, and Czechoslovakia, she met and talked with people still in the throes of social change, and in this book she tells their stories in a series of vivid sketches. She is especially forceful and poignant when discussing her native Poland, which, she says, "remained for me an idealized landscape of the mind . . . land of childhood sensuality, lyricism, vividness, and human warmth."

She dispels the comfortable Western stereotype of Eastern Europeans who "walked bent under the leaden weight of an awful System." Instead, she reveals the vibrant day-to-day life in the region. She offers portraits of a people who despised—but eventually became conditioned to—the communist worldview that was forced on them; these portraits are galvanizing and at times a little frightening. In this book Hoffman does not cover some countries, such as the former Yugoslavia, where the change is ongoing, the process more complex, and the results less certain. Instead, she concentrates on countries permeated by what she calls the "melancholy of transition."

As reflected in her previous autobiographical work, *Lost in Translation: A Life in a New Language* (Viking, 1990), Hoffman is an elegant and witty stylist, able to generate perceptive single sentences that summarize and define an entire lifetime. Hers is an essential book for those who want to recognize the new and changing face of Eastern Europe.

1057 Juric, Ilija. ***The Fall of Yugoslavia***. Trans. from Croatian by Dorian Cooke. Harcourt 1974. o.p. Nonfiction.

This is an important chapter in the history of Yugoslavia covering the period from 1941, when Hitler conquered the country, to 1945, when the Communists under Tito assumed control. Juric was involved with the royal Yugoslav government that was forced into exile; not surprisingly, his account has a decidedly royalist, anticommunist bias. Nevertheless, he provides valuable background information concerning this complex and still-troubling episode in Balkan history: the full-scale empowerment of a socialist regime with the help of Western allies.

Juric faults the inept royal government for not conceiving and executing a political agenda that would have fostered a reconciliation between the Chetnik forces under Mihailovic and the Communists under Tito. The results of this weakness included civil war, wholesale slaughter of natives by natives, the reemergence of centuries-old ethnic hostilities, and a simmering violence that boiled over again in Bosnia in the 1990s. Juric, a Croat, spares no one in his damning assessment of the disaster in the region. This is a valuable work, whose graphic and saddening portrayals of slaughter differ little from today's headlines about struggles in the shattered Yugoslav republic.

1058 Kaplan, Robert D. ***Balkan Ghosts: A Journey Through History***. St. Martin 1993, $22.95 (0-312-08701-2). 307pp. Nonfiction.

In this lively, witty book, Kaplan recounts his wanderings through the violent, passionate Balkan States—Greece, Romania, Albania, Bulgaria, and the shattered remains of the Yugoslav republic. As a journalist covering the Balkans for such publications as the *New Republic*, Kaplan had a firsthand view of the major political shifts in the post-1990 period. Writing with a keen, sharp-edged literary style, he evokes the marrow-deep fanaticism that is so manifestly part of the spine of the Balkans.

What is particularly important about the book is Kaplan's ability to grapple with the complex history of the region—history that, for the people, is actually vivid contemporary memory. He shows, for example, how the present crisis in Bosnia—as well as the political movements in Greece and elsewhere—are outgrowths of past injustices and slights. In the process he makes it clear that nothing is ever forgotten in the Balkans; children today avenge injustices perpetrated hundreds of years ago. Kaplan's interviews and pithy descriptions make for galvanizing reading in this book that is as up-to-date as today's headlines.

1059 Kapuscinski, Ryszard. ***Imperium***. Knopf 1994, $24.00 (0-679-42619-1). 331pp. Nonfiction.

This author's previous books explored the corruption and depravity of imperial rule in Ethiopia under Haile Selassie (*The Emperor*; Random, 1989) and in Iran under the Shah (*Shah of Shahs*; Random, 1992). During the years of Communist rule and Soviet domination, many Poles read Kapuscinski's works and saw reflections of their own situation. In this book, the author examines the Soviet Union as its empire was breaking up and evolving into a set of unstable and declining countries. Kapuscinski begins by describing the Soviet occupation of Poland at the end of World War II and his first visits as a young Polish journalist to the seemingly invincible Soviet Union, which he calls "the Imperium."

The main section of *Imperium*, however, consists of sketches of the disintegrating empire between 1989 and 1991. Particularly interested in what happened to the non-Russian parts of the Soviet Union, the author chronicles the heady explosion of democracy in the region as well as the vicious prosecution of ethnic and political vendettas. Writing about Moscow, Kapuscinski contrasts the supreme power and secrecy of the Kremlin during the heyday of Soviet power with its current status as the capital of a shaky and impoverished Russian republic. He also analyzes the reasons for the breakup of the Soviet Union and speculates about the future of Russia. RL

1060 Karpinski, Jakub. ***Countdown: The Polish Upheavals of 1956, 1968, 1970, 1980***. Trans. from Polish by Olga Amsterdamska and Gene M. Moore. Karz-Cohl 1982. o.p. Nonfiction.

This book is perhaps the most cogent analysis available of the birth of the Polish Solidarity Movement in August 1980. It was written by one of the student leaders of the 1968 demonstrations at Warsaw University; because of his participation, Karpinski was imprisoned for three years. He is currently a professor at the State University of New York in Albany.

Karpinski examines the political climate that led to Solidarity, tracing the growth of rebellion from the post–World War II era through the major crises that rocked the nation: the 1956 "Polish October"; the 1968 student protests; and the Workers' Riots of 1970 and 1976. Drawing on his own firsthand experience, he recounts the efforts of students and workers to bring about real economic reform despite military and political repression. He also describes the growth of the free trade-union movement. Although at times dry in execution and awash in minute detail, *Countdown* is nevertheless a vital work for understanding the recent seismic changes in Poland.

1061 Király, Béla, and Paul Jónás, eds. ***The Hungarian Revolution of 1956 in Retrospect***. Columbia Univ. Pr. 1978. o.p. Nonfiction.

In 1956 the world was galvanized by the media images of Soviet tanks crushing the rebellion in Hungary. For many people, the event was the epitome of Cold War cruelty and despair. The fourteen essays in this collection place events in perspective, placing special emphasis on the domestic consequences of the rebellion. Many of the works also relate the uprising to parallel developments in neighboring countries, such as Czechoslovakia and Yugoslavia, and explore its significance in the West.

The central theme is that the Hungarian Revolution revealed more than the peoples' chronic opposition to Soviet control. It also showed that totalitarian rule could be challenged—that even in defeat, important moral victories could be claimed. Surprisingly, in the aftermath of the uprising, the Soviets relaxed their iron grip, a fact reflected in the more progressive lifestyle the Hungarians maintained in the decades following.

1062 Kollontai, Alexandra. ***Selected Writings of Alexandra Kollontai***. Trans. from Russian by Alix Holt. Hill and Wang 1978. o.p. Essays.

Kollontai was an important early Soviet feminist. This collection of excerpts from her essays, written between 1909 and 1948, expresses her opinions on such topics as feminism, communism, and sex and love in a Bolshevik world. Particularly interesting is the image her essays generate of the young, evolving Soviet Republic. Kollontai, the U.S.S.R.'s first minister of social welfare, sought to integrate women into the larger fabric of socialist life. Though she often denounced "bourgeois feminists," women's issues were clearly high on her own social agenda.

These writings also provide a look at a dynamic, colorful figure, long respected in the Soviet Union, whose positions on issues of sexuality and women were advanced and radical for the time. Her writing is often pedestrian and labored—and quite serious. But the ideas themselves show us a singular woman who had a powerful influence on her people and their world.

1063 Laufer, Peter. *Iron Curtain Rising: A Personal Journey Through the Changing Landscape of Eastern Europe*. Illus. by Robert Schwarzenbach; Frwd. by Rainer Hildebrandt. Mercury House 1991, $19.50 (1-56279-015-3). 215pp. Nonfiction.

Between 1989 and 1990 the author traveled throughout East Germany, Poland, Czechoslovakia, Hungary, Romania, Yugoslavia, Bulgaria, and Albania. This book is his insightful account of the tremendous changes in those areas since the fall of the Berlin Wall. After listening to ordinary people in all these countries, he has painted a panorama of change. As the old ideology disappears, what emerges is new factionalism (as in parts of Yugoslavia) anti-Semitism (as in Poland), or a general confusion about what is to come. "The same crooks are in charge," one Hungarian scoffs; the sentiment reveals the distrust that continues to plague the region.

This breezy, readable overview of the shifting currents in Eastern Europe is a good starting point for the reader in the West who wishes to understand what is happening now that the Iron Curtain has lifted.

1064 Logoreci, Anton. *The Albanians: Europe's Forgotten Survivors*. Westview 1977. o.p. Nonfiction.

Logoreci was educated in Albania and was a short story writer there. Later he studied at the London School of Economics. Although this book is out of print and probably hard to locate, it is a valuable resource for any student of Eastern Europe. One major reason is that few other intelligent works discuss this little-known and little-analyzed ethnic population. Because it was published in 1977, the book obviously does not discuss the grudging changes in Albania since the end of the Cold War. Nevertheless, Logoreci's articulate, comprehensive account of the history and culture of the Albanian people does much to explain the long-standing isolation and rigid distrust of outsiders that persists even today.

The author describes the earliest history of the Albanians, beginning with the prehistoric Illyrian civilization that was overrun by the Romans in 35 B.C. The main focus, however, is on the twentieth century, particularly the Communist influence after World War II. His final chapter, "Totalitarian Isolation," is a revealing study of the national psyche.

1065 Mamonova, Tatyana. *Russian Women's Studies: Essays on Sexism in Soviet Culture*. Pergamon 1988, $45.00 (0-08-036482-9); $17.95 (0-08-036481-0). 198pp. Essays.

These short pieces discuss topics that concerned women in the former Soviet Union and that were long ignored or forbidden, such as feminism, homosexuality, pornography, and emigration. Mamonova was exiled because of her work as a feminist and as a writer for underground journals that addressed women's concerns. With much to say on these topics, she has become a significant voice on the role of sexism in the socialist state.

Her essays are noted for their integrity, their commitment to change, their wholesale embrace of the need to reform. Because they are not fully developed critical studies, they may dissatisfy some readers. Mamonova makes no claim to being a serious scholar; her style is to toss out ideas and let others run with them. An earlier and more scholarly work that Mamonova edited,

1984), is a collection of speeches from 1984 to 1987 describing the progress and the lessons of feminist reform to that point.

A useful complement to Mamonova's work is *Moscow Women: Thirteen Interviews* (o.p., 1983). Though somewhat flawed by the interviewers' transparently feminist agenda and their almost exclusive focus on young, educated women, this volume offers the women's own words on the contradictions between Soviet officialdom's claims about the "liberation" of women and the traditional, confining, stereotyped roles in which they were still cast.

1066 Medvedev, Grigori. ***The Truth about Chernobyl***. Trans. from Russian by Evelyn Rossiter; Frwd. by Andrei Sakharov. Basic Books 1991, $22.95 (0-465-08775-2); $12.00 (0-465-08776-0). 288pp. Nonfiction.

Russian nuclear expert Medvedev reviews the circumstances surrounding the worst accident in history to occur at a civilian nuclear facility: the April 1986 explosion at the Chernobyl nuclear power plant in Ukraine. He provides a minute-by-minute account of the accident and the events that followed. He interviewed many of the plant's operators even as they were dying of radiation sickness. Medvedev examines the key factors that led to the disaster, especially the Soviet government's ignorance and complacency, an attitude fostered by a political system that controlled information and permitted little dissent.

In places, Medvedev's explanations are quite technical. However, most of the book is devoted to human-interest stories about the people involved. Medvedev judges senior officials harshly, but he writes compassionately about those who made mistakes and risked their lives to contain the damage. His book is both a testimony to a changing society and a condemnation of totalitarianism, which he sees as being destructive to all life.

Medvedev is also the author of *No Breathing Room: The Aftermath of Chernobyl* (Basic Books, 1993), a somewhat less interesting but still valuable account of the former Soviet government's persistent refusal to publish works critical of its nuclear policy. LML

1067 Mihailovich, Vasa, and others, eds. ***Modern Slavic Literatures: Bulgarian, Czechoslovakian, Polish, Ukrainian, and Yugoslav Literatures, Vol. 2***. Ungar 1976. o.p. Essays.

Volume 1 of this title dealt with Russian literature; this volume deals with lesser-known Slavic writing and thus is crucially important for the student wishing to learn something about several of the undeservedly obscure writers from Eastern European nations.

The quality of discourse in the volume is very high. Included are significant critical pieces by major writers from the Slavic countries, such as Ivo Andric, Miroslav Krleza, Karel Capek, and Witold Gombrowicz. There are also important essays by some of the leading names in Western literature. For example, Stephen Spender discusses Czeslaw Milosz, Philip Roth analyzes Milan Kundera, and Ted Hughes appraises Vasko Popa. This is an important basic reference for the student of these various literatures.

1068 Moroz, Valentyn. ***Boomerang: The Works of Valentyn Moroz***. Trans. from Ukrainian. Smolsky 1975. o.p. Essays.

Moroz, a famous Ukrainian historian and dissident, was long an advocate of Ukrainian independence and an avowed critic of the Soviet Union. He is represented here by a collection of his most important writings. Included are "Amid the Snows," "A Chronicle of Resistance," and "A Report from the Beria Reserve," a highly regarded piece he wrote while in prison. In fact, Moroz was incarcerated several times, but his political commitment remained unshaken.

His central thesis is simple but highly dangerous to totalitarian thinking: He believes that progress can only be made through the freedom of the individual. The collective state is the antithesis, the natural enemy of progress. And he depicts the KGB as the consummate hater of any individual spirit. Only when the individual is allowed to develop, Moroz argues, can society benefit.

1069 Narkiewicz, Olga A. ***Eastern Europe, 1968–1984***. Barnes & Noble 1986, $57.00 (0-389-20607-5). 288pp. Nonfiction.

By focusing on political and economic reforms in Eastern Europe between 1968 and 1984, the author provides an overview of an enigmatic and complex part of the world. Much of the book's worth arises from Narkiewicz's forthright, insightful discussion of the political-economic agendas of the Eastern European countries. However, the scope of the book is limited because she opts not to discuss other important elements, including cultural, military, and social trends. There is also curiously little about changes in Romania, Bulgaria, and a few other countries.

Nevertheless, because the book is aimed at a general readership, it fulfills its purpose. The student wishing to gain insight into the evolving political economy of the region will find plenty of material here. The style of writing is at times heavy-handed, but the information is solid and intelligent.

1070 Niezabitowska, Malgorzata. ***Remnants: The Last Jews in Poland***. Trans. from Polish by William Brand and Hanna Dobosiewicz. Illus. with photos by Tomasz Tomaszewski. Friendly 1986. Nonfiction.

This is a melancholic work, beautiful yet sad. There are only four or five thousand Jews left in Poland, and most are sickly, dying, isolated, and forgotten. They live in small, cramped apartments, and the memory of their once-thriving and rich Jewish way of life is fading fast. Here, in text and seventy marvelous photographs, we see a dying breed. These are the casualties of prejudice, the remnants of a culture that the Nazis systematically and ruthlessly destroyed.

There is some text in the book, but for the most part the photographs tell the story. An essay attempts to understand the chronic anti-Semitism that still persists among many Poles, but no satisfactory answer is possible.

1071 Pavlychko, Solomea. ***Letters from Kiev***. Trans. from Ukrainian by Myrna Kotash; Annotations by Bohdan Krawchenko. St. Martin 1992, $35.00 (0-312-07588-X). 150pp. Nonfiction.

This fascinating collection of letters chronicles the important political and cultural events that ultimately led to Ukrainian independence from the Soviet

Union. Pavlychko, a specialist in English and American literature, was an exchange professor in Canada; she returned home to find her native Ukraine in turmoil. Her letters to Bohdan Krawchenko (who provides excellent annotations) offer a detailed, day-by-day account of the changes taking place.

The letters were written between May 12, 1990 and March 25, 1991. The author was deeply involved in the political scene; she worked at the Institute of Literature of the Ukrainian Academy of Sciences and is the daughter of a prominent opposition member of Parliament. The story has a happy ending: Ukraine became an independent republic in August 1991. Written with verve and intelligence, her letters recount the growing excitement as dissident Ukrainians begin to realize that their long-sought dream of freedom was about to come true.

1072   Remnick, David. *Lenin's Tomb: The Last Days of the Soviet Empire*. Random 1993, $25.00 (0-679-42376-1); $14.00 (0-679-75125-4). 512pp. Nonfiction.

This comprehensive, readable story of the decline and fall of the corrupt and flagging Soviet empire was written by a reporter for the *Washington Post* who covered the Soviet Union from 1988 through 1991—from the early days of perestroika through the collapse and the rise of the Russian state under Boris Yeltsin. Remnick has a sharp, reportorial eye, and his thumbnail characterizations of key figures like Mikhail Gorbachev, Andrei Sakharov, and Nina Andreyeva, among many others, are excellent. But the achievements of these historic figures are dwarfed by the mountainous failures of the regime. For contrast, Remnick also describes both the peasant on his collectivist farm and the transplanted peasant who struggles to find a meaningful life in the enervating, decaying, socialist city.

The author's account is one of the most thorough and intelligent summations of the end of an era. He weaves the historical tapestry against which local events are played out and traces the threads of the elusive, enigmatic Soviet soul.

1073   Ryback, Timothy W. *Rock Around the Bloc: A History of Rock Music in Eastern Europe and the Soviet Union, 1954–1988*. Illus. with photos. Oxford Univ. Pr. 1990, $25.00 (0-19-505633-7). 304pp. Nonfiction.

Excuse the pun, but this book about rock music is an important volume. Ryback explores the close relationship between the music of rebellion and political events in Eastern Europe. Somewhat surprisingly, the author shows that rock has been an important force in the region since the 1950s—indeed, music evolved there in much the same manner as it did in the West. Moreover, he says, changing tastes in music can be examined as an index of evolving political consciousness among the young, and thus music is both a precursor to and a reflection of the dissent that burst into the mainstream in the late 1980s.

Written in a lively, engaging style, the book is filled with anecdotes and fascinating cultural vignettes. At the same time it is very much a serious work. The chapter on the Beatles, for example, discusses the incredible importance of that group in giving new direction to youth in socialist regimes. With its authoritative indexes and well-chosen photographs, it surpasses in scope an earlier study by Artemy Troitsky titled *Back in the U.S.S.R.: The True Story of Rock in Russia* (Faber, 1988).

1074 Sakharov, Andrei D. *Sakharov Speaks*. Trans. from Russian; Ed. by Harrison E. Salisbury. Knopf 1974. o.p. Essays.

The famous dissident and high-ranking Soviet physicist expands on the ideas he developed earlier in *Progress, Coexistence, and Intellectual Freedom* (o.p., 1969). The works in this volume, culled from his major statements and interviews between 1968 and 1974, continue his warning to the West about the growing duplicity and dangerousness of the Soviet Union. Harrison Salisbury's introduction is an excellent overview that places Sakharov and his achievements in the context of his time.

Given the astounding changes in the former Soviet Union, much of what Sakharov says has been rendered irrelevant. Still, this volume is important because it reveals a major thinker at work, a man whose courage and dedication inspired an entire generation of dissidents in the Soviet Union. Also of interest are Sakharov's autobiographical works, *Memoirs* (Knopf, 1990) and *Moscow and Beyond, 1986-1989* (Knopf, 1991).

Salamander, Rachel. *The Jewish World of Yesterday, 1860–1939*. See entry 957.

1075 Shklovsky, Iosif. *Five Billion Vodka Bottles to the Moon: Tales of a Soviet Scientist*. Trans. from Russian by Mary Fleming Zirin and Harold Zirin. Norton 1991. o.p. Essays.

Born in 1916, Shklovsky eventually became an eminent Soviet astrophysicist, hobnobbing with the likes of Carl Sagan, Aleksandr Solzhenitsyn, and Andrei Sakharov. Before his death in 1985, he had acquired a worldwide reputation. These delightful observational essays, geared toward an English-speaking audience, are witty, informed, and infectious.

The author has a keen eye, not only for the humorous and satirical, but for the quirks of human nature, which he skillfully sketches in miniature. His commentaries about the brutality of life during World War II and under the Communist regime reflect his abiding sense of ethics and justice. These essays reveal Shklovsky as a man who looked up to read the stars, but who also looked inward to read the human soul.

1076 Spiegelman, Art. *Maus: A Survivor's Tale*. 2-vol. set; each vol. also available separately. Illus. by the author. Pantheon 1993, $25.00 (0-679-74840-7). 136+144pp. Nonfiction.

These innovative and revolutionary books tell the story of Vladek Spiegelman, a Jew who survived the Holocaust. At the same time, they tell about Vladek's son, who, like the author, is a famed cartoonist. What makes this book original is that the entire story is told in comic book format—starkly stylized graphics complete with thought balloons. Nazis are cats, Jews are mice. The scene shifts in time and place, from past to present, from Auschwitz, Poland, to Rego Park, New York. The son interviews the father, who tells of his suffering. The younger Spiegelman then interprets the words as pictures. In time, some of the emotional shadows between the two men lift, offering hope that they will heal the wounds they caused each other.

Volume 2 continues the story. Again the action shifts from the barracks of Auschwitz to the comfortable cabins of the Catskills. By turns funny and frightening, uplifting and depressing, the book dramatizes two games of cat-and-mouse, one played out in the global arena, the other in the still-evolving relationship between father and son. Brilliant, different, these "cartoons" are unlike anything published on the subject. The work is also available as an interactive CD-ROM.

1077 Tischner, Josef. ***The Spirit of Solidarity***. Trans. from Polish by Marek B. Zaleski and Benjamin Fiore. HarperCollins 1984. o.p. Essays.

This is a book of sermons—a "cycle of reflections"—by the priest who served as chaplain to the Solidarity movement in Poland. Simple and evocative, these brief, interlocking homilies provide a unique perspective on the complex dynamics of Polish reform. They chronicle the spiritual underpinnings of one of the most important social and political movements in history.

Father Tischner's sermons reveal philosophy in action. Streetwise and smart, these models of practical theology reveal how our moral choices can affect events in the everyday world. Tischner, who draws on ideas from the fields of economics, politics, and social justice, nourished the growing democratic spirit of Solidarity, which soon dismantled the socialist state.

A companion volume is *The Birth of Solidarity* by Anthony Kemp-Welch (2nd ed., St. Martin, 1991), containing full transcripts of the accords between Solidarity and the Polish government plus other key documents.

1078 West, Rebecca. ***Black Lamb and Grey Falcon: A Journey Through Yugoslavia***. Viking 1994, $20.00 (0-14-018847-9). 1,181pp. Nonfiction.

This classic travel narrative tells of the author's journeys through Yugoslavia in the 1930s. Guided by a friend from the region, West explored the territory and wrote about the people she met: their beliefs and customs, their lives and personalities. But this book is more than a simple travelogue. It captures images of a world that would soon be wiped out by war.

As she moved through remote provinces and modern cities, West commented on literature, politics, architecture, psychology—anything that caught her attention, including her friend's Marxist principles. A consummate stylist, she interprets the mysteries of the Balkans for Western readers with wit and humanity.

1079 Zeman, Z.A.B. ***The Prague Spring***. Hill and Wang 1969. o.p. Essays.

The author returned to his native Prague in 1968, intending to study the effects of two decades of Communist rule. He got more than he bargained for when, a few months into his research, he witnessed the famous 1968 Czech uprising. This short, bittersweet essay, written just after the event, describes his conversations with the people he met: their culture, their politics, and especially their attitudes before and after the crisis.

The book elegantly reveals the minds and hearts of an oppressed people on the edge of rebellion, people who can foresee both disaster and reform.

1080 Amalrik, Andrei. *Notes of a Revolutionary*. Trans. from Russian by Guy Daniels. Knopf 1982. o.p. Autobiography.

Amalrik was a prominent Soviet dissident, a founder of the Soviet Democratic Movement in the late 1960s. In 1980, as he headed for an international conference to testify about conditions in the Soviet Union, he was killed in a bizarre automobile crash near Madrid. These memoirs show what Amalrik described as "the conflict between the individual person and the system in a country where the individual is nothing and the system is everything." He maintains that this is not an evolved discussion of ideas or theories; rather, it is simply his own story, the autobiography of a dissident.

This volume is no grim epitaph to a dead social reformer. Instead, it is testimony to the power of justice and truth. Amalrik is always witty, intelligent, and optimistic. His account of exile to Siberia as a "parasite," his tales of protest and arrest, his refusal to compromise, his steadfast courage in the face of official condemnation and dismissal all attest to the unflagging human spirit. The book stands as Amalrik's own best elegy.

1081 Arnothy, Christine. *I Am Fifteen—And I Don't Want to Die*. Repr. of 1956 ed. Scholastic 1993, $2.95 (0-590-44630-4). 128pp. Autobiography.

This gripping, stunning memoir recounts events in 1944, when the author, then fifteen, and her family were trapped in Budapest, Hungary. Arnothy left Hungary four years later, moving to Belgium, where she began writing both fiction and nonfiction based upon her wartime diaries. *I Am Fifteen* shocked readers with its grimly realistic portrayal of the adolescent girl's terror and yearning—as well as her abiding faith in tomorrow. It won the Prix de Veritas, a French award for nonfiction. She followed up her memoir with a popular, if dark and fatalistic, novel, *God Is Late* (o.p.).

With her incisive, almost deadpan writing style, Arnothy tells of life in a cold cellar of a bombed-out building and reflects almost mechanically on the horror going on in the streets above her. The book is particularly compelling because it stresses the plight of a young girl who wanted only the things any typical teenager wants—fun, school, games, a happy life—but who was now struggling to keep alive a kind of desperate hope. "How good that would be," she concludes, "to be born."

1082 Azbel, Mark Ya. *Refusenik: Trapped in the Soviet Union*. Trans. from Russian. Houghton 1981. o.p. Autobiography.

A theoretical physicist in the Soviet Union, Azbel saw firsthand how anti-Semitism hindered not only advancement in his career but events in his daily life as well. His request for an exit visa began a six-year period of KGB surveillance and abuse. The ordeal finally ended in 1977 when he and his family boarded a plane for Israel, where he now lives.

This account reads like a novel, filled with bizarre twists and shocking turns as Azbel gradually realizes the price he is paying for dissent: loss of friends, official condemnation, and personal doubts. His book was written for those he left behind: the thousands of nameless dissidents who were, indeed, trapped in the Soviet Union by the force of their belief in freedom. A convincing writer, Azbel tells a page-turning story.

1083 Bukovsky, Vladimir. ***To Choose Freedom***. Trans. from Russian. Hoover Inst. 1987, $11.95 (0-8179-8442-9). 188pp. Autobiography.

Bukovsky, a political dissident, was exiled from the Soviet Union in 1976, after years of confinement in various psychiatric hospitals and prisons. He tells his story with intelligence, wit, and an array of anecdotes that illuminate the peculiar agonies he experienced in the post-Stalinist period.

Like other books of its kind, *To Choose Freedom* recounts past horrors, condemns Soviet oppression, and issues a cry for justice. What makes it especially valuable, however, is that it clearly chronicles the evolution of a dissident: the slow progression of questioning, doubt, investigation, and the battle of wills against mindless bureaucratic stupidity. His memoir shows how dissent emerges from within the corrupt system, fed by a potent mixture of indignation and injustice. This is the testimony of a brave, intrepid individual who took a stand against tyranny.

1084 Clements, Barbara E. ***Bolshevik Feminist: The Life of Aleksandra Kollontai***. Repr. of 1979 ed.; facsimile ed. Illus. Books on Demand 1979, $102.10 (0-7837-1746-6). 370pp. Biography.

This is a lively biography of the famous early Russian feminist, a member of Lenin's Central Committee, which carried out the 1917 Revolution. As an official with the new regime, Kollontai's main agenda was the "woman question" in the Soviet Union. Eventually, however, she fell out of favor with Stalin, largely over her avocation of the feminist agenda that she saw as crucial to the survival of Marxism, and drifted into obscurity. At her death in 1952 she had become a mere footnote to the history of revolutionary idealism.

Clements resurrects Kollontai as a major figure in Soviet life, documenting her influence and presence and describing the evolution of feminist ideals, which are still largely unrealized in Eastern Europe. This biography, as well as Beatrice Farnsworth's *Aleksandra Kollontai: Socialism, Feminism, and the Bolshevik Revolution* (Stanford Univ. Pr., 1980) are excellent companions to Kollontai's own *Selected Writings (see main entry)*.

1085 Codrescu, Andrei. ***The Life and Times of an Involuntary Genius***. Braziller 1975. o.p. Autobiography.

This book traces the evolution of a distinguished Romanian Jewish poet who eventually resettled in the United States. Its piecemeal, disjointed approach is unusual for autobiography, but it reflects the poet's lyricism and his gift for imagery. The story of Codrescu's childhood in a castle in Transylvania is exotic and fascinating, especially so because it is played out against the backdrop of a repressive Communist regime.

The specter of Stalin haunts these memoirs, but even after emigrating to Paris, Rome, Detroit, New York City, and ultimately California, he cannot escape his lingering nostalgia for the frightening land he left behind. There is a poet's touch here, especially in his anecdotal characterizations of people he meets during this long and emotional journey.

In 1989 Codrescu returned to Romania, commissioned by National Public Radio to report on the revolution there. His account of those events, *The Hole in the Flag: A Romanian Exile's Story of Return and Revolution* (Avon, 1992), is lively, ironic, and bittersweet. Now living in Louisiana, Codrescu is a teacher, writer, editor, and radio commentator.

1086 Craig, Mary. ***Crystal Spirit: Lech Walesa and His Poland***. Continuum 1987. 471pp. o.p. Biography.

This biography of the famed Polish trade unionist is also a detailed account of the rise of the Solidarity movement. Intended for general readers, it depicts of Walesa as superhero and superpatriot. Although this laudatory, somewhat simplistic approach may put off the serious scholar, the book offers a readable, accessible account that is faithful to its sources and that provides a detailed background for understanding a complex situation.

Walesa comes off as a complex man, a seemingly simple electrician who was thrust into greatness by the forces of chance and circumstance. At times he seems to want to exaggerate his own importance, as if he himself does not truly realize the enormous impact of what he did. The author also seems cavalier in dismissing—or at least downplaying—the ongoing problem of Polish anti-Semitism.

More scholarly students should look at Tim Garton Ash's *The Polish Revolution* (o.p., 1984). Lech Walesa's first autobiography, *A Way of Hope* (o.p., 1987), is fragmented and somewhat simplistic, but it provides a readable firsthand history of the Solidarity movement, written while Walesa was still under police surveillance. A later work, *The Struggle and the Triumph: An Autobiography* (Arcade, 1992), discusses the events and personalities that led to Walesa's election as president of Poland, with special emphasis on the roles played by the Catholic Church and by Pope John Paul II, a fellow Pole.

1087 De Jonge, Alex. ***Stalin***. Illus. Morrow 1987, $15.00 (0-688-07291-7). 544pp. Biography.

Building a biography from secondary sources and the recollections of émigrés has its limitations, but De Jonge has managed to create a readable, fascinating portrait of the Soviet dictator, a man both hated and revered. The author capably describes Stalin's enormous power over the lives of the Soviet citizens.

Stalin still holds an appeal for some Russians, who seem unable to free themselves from their almost mythological fascination with oppressive leaders. De Jonge helps us to understand something of this continuing fascination. The "why" of any crushing bureaucracy always is intriguing, and De Jonge's book contributes another piece of the puzzle. Stalin the man still remains enigmatic; how, for example, is it possible to account for his full-scale brutality, the many gruesome purges carried out against his own people?

1088 De Mallac, Guy. ***Boris Pasternak: His Life and Art***. Intro. by Rimvydas Silbajoris. Illus. Univ. of Oklahoma Pr. 1981, $35.00 (0-8061-1660-9). 476pp. Biography.

One of the best-known and most influential Russian writers of the twentieth century, Pasternak has found his ideal biographer in De Mallac. Twenty years in the making, this biography is divided into two parts. The first part gives us a thorough and highly readable story of Pasternak's life, often drawing on previously unknown sources. Part Two is more esoteric, providing a detailed analysis of his writings.

Most Westerners know Pasternak as the author of the classic novel *Doctor Zhivago (see main entry)*. This biography places that seminal work in its full historical and biographical context. De Mallac also deftly discusses the entire Nobel Prize controversy, in which pressure from Soviet officials forced Pasternak to refuse the award. A fictionalized version of these events can be found in *The Nobel Prize* by Yuri Krotkov *(see main entry)*. However, anyone with even a casual interest in the true story of the genesis and aftermath of *Zhivago*'s publication will benefit from reading this biography. Pasternak's mistress, Olga Ivinskaya, describes her relationship with the writer in *A Captive of Time (see main entry)*.

1089 Djilas, Milovan. ***Tito: The Story from Inside***. Trans. from Serbo-Croatian by Vasilije Kojic and Richard Hayes. Harcourt 1980. o.p. Biography.

Djilas worked with Tito in the Yugoslav Communist Party before World War II and fought alongside him during the war. He became Tito's vice president and was being groomed as his successor. In 1954, however, believing Tito had created a "new class," Djilas became Yugoslavia's preeminent dissident. This personal perspective on Tito should be read in conjunction with Djilas's *Wartime* (Harcourt, 1980), for the two books present a coherent portrayal of the enigmatic dictator. Also a novelist, Djilas wrote *Under the Colors (see main entry)*.

Tito was the classic working-class hero who, once enthroned in power, reveled in luxury and grandeur. He also became obsessed with removing any factions that championed views contrary to his own. Djilas's books reflect his lingering respect for Tito, an attitude that at times can color his interpretation of events. Tito, of course, had the support of his people in challenging Stalin, and Djilas tries to grapple with the paradox of a man so committed to an independent Socialist Yugoslav state that he executed thousands of dissidents to maintain it.

1090 Dubček, Alexander, and Jiri Hochman. ***Hope Dies Last: Dubček by Dubček: The Autobiography***. Paul Angelis, ed. Illus. Kodansha 1993, $27.50 (1-56836-000-2). 352pp. Autobiography.

Leader of Czechoslovakia during the Prague Spring of 1968 (and forcibly deposed that August by Soviet tanks), Alexander Dubček remained a symbol and a hero to those who continued to struggle for democracy in Eastern Europe. In the aftermath of the 1989 Velvet Revolution in Czechoslovakia, Dubček became an elder statesman, advising President Václav Havel until Dubček's death in a car accident in 1992.

Published posthumously, Dubček's memoir details his family's roots in Slovakia and his upbringing in Russia. He describes how his pro-Communist parents joined an industrial cooperative in Central Asia and then moved to Gorky when the cooperative failed. He also discusses the impact of Tiso's pro-Nazi regime upon Slovakia and his own participation in the Communist Party of Czechoslovakia at the end of World War II. As he rose through the party ranks in the 1950s and 1960s, he retained his optimism, expecting that the ideal society, one that combined a socialist economy with freedom of expression, could be attained. His idealistic vision, like that of his father, led him to be the catalyst of the 1968 liberalization.

Dubček offers a compelling account of the Prague Spring's end. Without bitterness, he describes his humiliating and disillusioning encounter with Moscow and his eventual reassignment to manual labor, far from the centers of power. Even here, he looked to the positive side, seeing his work as a way of returning to his and his family's roots. LML

1091 Eliade, Mircea. ***Autobiography***. 2 vols. Trans. from Romanian by Mac L. Ricketts. Illus. Univ. of Chicago Pr. 1988, 1990, $15.95 + $19.95 (0-226-20407-3, 0-226-20411-1). 336 | 240pp. Autobiography.

The first volume, *Journey East, Journey West, 1907–1937*, traces Eliade's life from birth in Bucharest, Romania through his years in India, ending with his return to Romania. The second volume, *Exile's Odyssey* starts where the other left off and covers World War II, the years of his exile in France after the war, and his 1956 move to the United States. When Eliade died in 1986, the manuscript for the latter volume was unfinished, which explains its piecemeal and somewhat haphazard construction. For example, the years dealing with Eliade's tremendous international fame as a novelist and as an expert in spirituality and religion are treated mechanically; he devotes more attention to his achievements than to his ideas.

However, the earlier volume, as well as the initial chapters of the second, are truly significant. Indeed, there is a long diary excerpt from 1937 that has much to say about his years before the war, the formation of his ideas, and his linguistic skills. We also get a perspective on the man who would eventually convert so much of his experience into both philosophy and fiction. Eliade edited the multivolume *Encyclopedia of Religion* (Macmillan, 1993), and his novels include *The Forbidden Forest (see main entry)* and *Bengal Nights* (Univ. of Chicago Pr., 1994).

1092 Fluek, Toby. ***Memories of My Life in a Polish Village***. Illus. with drawings. Random 1990, $19.95 (0-394-58617-4). 110pp. Autobiography.

Through words and drawings, this magnificent book depicts the life of the author from her early childhood in Poland through the destruction of her family at the hands of the Nazis. Fluek lyrically evokes the serene life of a young Jewish girl: her participation in custom and religion, her laborious yet idyllic farm life, and her devotion to family. All of this was crushed by the devastation of war.

The author's careful, evocative drawings counterpoint the horrible story she tells. Through her renderings we see the coming of the Nazis, feel the full weight of Russian occupation, and experience her escape to the United States, where she found peace and safety. This book captures a time, a place, and a people now gone.

1093 Gladilin, Anatoly. ***The Making and Unmaking of a Soviet Writer: My Story of the "Young Prose" of the Sixties and After***. Trans. from Russian by David Lapeza. Ardis 1979. o.p. Autobiography.

This memoir of the Soviet Union in the 1960s was written by one of the most popular and influential writers of that period. In simple, sometimes rambling prose, Gladilin recounts life after The Thaw—the relaxation of Stalinism under Khrushchev—until his own emigration to Paris in 1976. Particularly fascinating is his insightful account of the well-regarded journals with which he was associated with, such as *Yunost* (*Youth*) and *Novy Mir* (*New World*), and their special connection to the shifting political and social currents in the Soviet Union, including The Thaw, the removal of Khrushchev, and the rebellion in Czechoslovakia.

Gladilin shows how The Thaw turned out to be little more than a facade. Increasingly aware of the growing constraints on his writing and publishing, he came to believe that little, if any, truly honest writing could appear in his homeland. He describes how censorship ultimately sapped the creative and intellectual soul of the Soviets. His awareness of this trend compelled him to leave the U.S.S.R. and reestablish his career in France. This memoir is an important document in understanding the complex machinations of Soviet literary life in the 1960s.

A novel that deals with this era—in fact, that lent its name to the movement—is *The Thaw* by Ilya Ehrenburg *(see main entry)*. Ehrenburg himself is the subject of a biography by Anatoly Goldberg *(see main entry)*.

1094 Goldberg, Anatoly. *Ilya Ehrenburg: Revolutionary, Novelist, Poet, War Correspondent, Propagandist: The Extraordinary Epic of a Russian Survivor.* Viking 1984. o.p. Biography.

Goldberg's biography, the first in English of the celebrated Russian writer, explores the various contradictions surrounding the man whose 1954 novel *The Thaw* coined the phrase that summed up the relaxed political climate in the Soviet Union after Stalin. Acclaimed for his writing, Ehrenburg was also denounced for his anti-German politics; his propaganda sparked some horrific atrocities against German citizens.

Goldberg manages to give a balanced, reasonable look at the multitalented Ehrenburg. Like his subject, Goldberg is a middle-class Russian Jew, able to assess Ehrenburg's life and work within the sociopolitical context of his time. The anecdotes he recounts, some of them culled from Ehrenburg's own memoirs, *People, Years, Life* (o.p., 1962), are poignant and revealing. Goldberg does not rely on scholarly sources; rather, he draws on published works by and about Ehrenburg. But the result is an appealing, readable, and informative biography. Ehrenburg, who died in 1967, remains a crucial figure in Russian cultural life, and a biography in English has been long overdue.

1095 Gorky, Maxim. *My Childhood.* Trans. from Russian by Ronald Wilks. Viking 1966, $4.95 (0-14-044178-6). 232pp. Autobiography.

Gorky was a proletariat Soviet writer, apologist for the Bolshevik revolution, and author of such classic works as *Mother* (orig. pub. 1907; Carol Publg., 1992), which was an early celebration of the working-class hero who would bring about revolution. Gorky's autobiography appears in three volumes: this one, *In the World* (orig. pub. 1916; o.p.), and *My Universities* (orig. pub. 1923; Viking, 1979) (also published as *My Apprenticeship: My Universities*, Beekman, 1975 and *My Apprenticeship*, Viking, 1990). All three books celebrate his abiding faith in the artist's ability to make sense of an often chaotic and despairing world.

One of the most popular Soviet authors, Gorky in 1932 received the Order of Lenin to commemorate his forty years of literary achievement. His autobiographies trace the life of the artist before and after the revolution; his insights, told with novelistic skill, are illuminating.

1096 Grigorenko, Petro. ***Memoirs***. Trans. from Russian by Thomas P. Whitney. Illus. Norton 1983, $19.95 (0-393-01570-X). 462pp. Autobiography.

Petro Grigorevich Grigorenko, born in the Ukraine in 1907, was a loyal member of the Communist Party and a much-decorated general during World War II. Yet he became the highest-ranking military officer ever to be exiled from the Soviet Union. His break with Soviet officialdom came after the death of Stalin; he was isolated in psychiatric hospitals, imprisoned for five years, and in 1977, while sojourning in the United States, he lost his Soviet citizenship.

The author tells his story in a simple, matter-of-fact style, but the events he describes are profound and shocking. He traces the arc of his life, from fiercely loyal party member to war hero, from the first glimmerings of doubt to grueling days spent in horrendous "psychoprisons." Grigorenko comes across as an intelligent, courageous dissident, a man who shook the Soviet system to the core by refusing to conform to ideas he came to believe were not only false but destructive to the human spirit.

1097 Gurevich, David. ***From Lenin to Lennon: A Memoir of Russia in the Sixties***. Harcourt 1991, $21.95 (0-15-149825-3). 307pp. Autobiography.

Gurevich's memoir begins in the Russian town of Syzran, continues to his emigration to the United States in 1975, and ends with his dramatic return to the Soviet Union in 1989. A young man with a gift for languages, he became a tour guide. But as a Jew, he increasingly found himself the target of anti-Semitic outbursts. Well-educated and versatile, he tells his story with many breezy anecdotes and wry, cynical observations. Yet this autobiographical piece is more than a casual look at the Soviet Union in 1960s. It depicts the numbing effects of repressive regimes, the day-to-day humiliation of having to maintain personal dignity in a system that undermines it at every turn. Cleverly written, sparkling in style, its crowning moment is the final, moving reunion of son with father after years of distance and isolation.

1098 Ivinskaya, Olga. ***A Captive of Time***. Trans. from Russian by Max Hayward. Doubleday 1978. o.p. Biography.

Ivinskaya, who was the mistress of poet and novelist Boris Pasternak during the last fourteen years of his life, served as the model for the character of Lara in Pasternak's masterpiece novel, *Doctor Zhivago (see main entry)*. These memoirs recount the triumphs and failures of their relationship. The work tends to ramble in spots; chronology is not a prime concern for the author, and her narrative is marred by occasional inane or careless remarks. Nonetheless, it is important for the personal insights it offers into the day-to-day life of a great writer. In spite of its style, the book sheds light on Pasternak, who is quoted at length on such topics as Stalin, the art of poetry and translation, and his fellow writers. As such, it is a readable companion to the great writer's own work.

Interested readers can learn more by consulting *Boris Pasternak* by Guy de Mallac *(see main entry)*. A fictionalized version of the controversy surrounding the publication of *Doctor Zhivago* can be found in *The Nobel Prize* by Yuri Krotkov *(see main entry)*.

1099 Khrushchev, Sergei. ***Khrushchev on Khrushchev: An Inside Account of the Man and His Era, by His Son***. Trans. from Russian and ed. by William Taubman. Little, Brown 1990, $24.95 (0-316-49194-2). 423pp. Biography.

The son tells the story of his father, the pivotal Soviet politician during the period from 1953 to 1964, including Khrushchev's downfall and his sad final years. It is a son's loving portrait, to be sure, but it is also an attempt to give a fair, reasonable portrait of this key figure in world politics.

Sergei's account is significant because he provides anecdotes and family memories to create a more personal and complete picture of his father than that available in most other biographies. His detailed recounting of the plot to overthrow his father is told with suspense, economy, and rich investigative reportage. His depiction of the growing power of Leonid Brezhnev, Khrushchev's successor, gives an important glimpse of this chapter in Soviet history, one told with drama and impartiality.

1100 Koestler, Arthur. ***Arrow in the Blue***. Madison Bks. 1984. o.p. Autobiography.

The distinguished novelist (*Darkness at Noon*; *see main entry*) and essayist recounts his life story from his birth in Budapest, Hungary, to his close involvement with the Communist Party in 1931. Koestler led a varied, exciting life. Half-Jewish and educated in Vienna, he traveled broadly to Germany and Palestine. He wrote insightfully about many of the most important events in world history. While covering the Spanish Civil War, for example, he was captured and sentenced to death. He also described the founding of the modern nation of Israel.

His autobiography reflects the same attention to detail and acute observation that are the hallmarks of his fiction and his essays. The story of his life continues in *The Invisible Writing* (o.p., 1984), which covers the years 1931 through 1938, as he grew disaffected with the Communist Party.

1101 Markov, Georgi. ***The Truth that Killed***. Trans. from Bulgarian by Liliana Brisby. Ticknor & Fields 1984. o.p. Autobiography.

In this disturbing, often horrific book, Markov, a brave but doomed dissident, tells his tragic story. A novelist and playwright who was trained as a engineer, he fled Bulgaria in 1969. Living in London, he continued to fight for freedom in his native land. He learned to ignore the threatening warnings he received, demanding that he stop working for Radio Free Europe.

Markov's abiding love of his homeland permeates these memoirs. He depicts a country numbed by Communist irrationality and violence. His description of the brutal labor camp at Belene is the stuff of nightmares. Filled with riveting anecdotes, this biography sheds interesting light on the day-to-day workings of citizens trapped in a world without light.

The author met a bizarre end. In 1978, on his way to work, he was stabbed by someone carrying an umbrella, the tip of which had been sharpened and dipped in poison. Markov died four days later.

1102 Medvedev, Roy A., and others. ***Khrushchev: The Years in Power***. Trans. from Russian by Brian Pearce. Columbia Univ. Pr. 1976, $38.00 (0-231-03939-5); Norton $8.95 (0-393-00879-7). 197pp. Biography.

Roy Medvedev is a devoted Marxist and admirer of Khrushchev. Nonetheless, he and his coauthors manage to write a fair, albeit largely favorable, portrait of the Soviet leader. At the time he wrote, Roy Medvedev was a dissident who had fallen out of favor with the new Soviet hierarchy. In this book he explores Khrushchev as a power broker who sought to reverse Stalin's "cult of personality," a leader who—while perhaps not an enlightened statesman—nevertheless did much to improve the lot of the ordinary Soviet citizen.

Khrushchev is a difficult subject to write about, especially since his ignominious downfall in 1964 is still clouded in mystery and speculation. (For more on this, readers can consult *Khrushchev on Khrushchev* by Sergei Khrushchev; *see main entry*). The official accounts of his fall, which Medvedev summarizes, are dubious. Throughout the book the authors stress Khrushchev's achievements rather the details of his personal life. Still, their meticulous use of detail helps the reader to realize the tremendous power and influence of this important leader—an influence still felt in the renascent republics of the former U.S.S.R.

Roy Medvedev has written a number of other important works of history and biography. Among them is his now-classic study of Stalin, *Let History Judge: The Origins and Consequences of Stalinism* (Columbia Univ. Pr., 1989), originally published in the late 1970s and revised to include new archival research.

1103 Medvedev, Zhores A. ***Gorbachev***. Trans. from Russian. Norton 1987, $8.95 (0-393-30408-6). 288pp. Biography.

The author of this book is an agronomist by profession, so he approaches his biography of the important Soviet leader from a unique angle. He is particularly illuminating in discussions that describe the important links between agriculture and public policy. At the same time he provides a detailed, compelling account of how Gorbachev's long rise to power laid the foundation for his pivotal role as the reformist leader of what was then the Soviet Union.

The book was written when Gorbachev had been in office only one year, and thus it is limited in its vision. It does not, for example, discuss fully the startling changes resulting from perestroika ("restructuring") and glasnost ("openness"), nor does it cover the attempted coup by party hardliners in 1991. Yet the background information it provides, coupled with the author's unique interpretation of the Soviet political machine, makes it a valuable tool for understanding a man who altered forever the face of Eastern Europe. Although its style is pedestrian in places, the book still offers a penetrating look into the thinking and agendas of a powerful politician.

1104 Money, Keith. ***Anna Pavlova, Her Life and Art***. Illus. with photos. Knopf 1982. o.p. Biography.

This beautifully written biography presents a fully realized portrait of the great artist, covering her career from her early days at St. Petersburg Imperial Ballet School in 1899 to her international acclaim. While performing all over the world, she logged an astounding 400,000 miles of travel. The author uses previously unavailable Russian sources to produce a book both thorough and inviting. Pavlova remains a mysterious, elusive ballerina, yet Money manages, through detail and insight, to illuminate this glorious artist and her time.

This oversize book is all the more laudable because of its stunning array of photographs, many of which have never been published before. The volume should appeal not just to students of the dance but to anyone interested in the complex life and methods of a superlative artist.

1105 Morrison, John. ***Boris Yeltsin: From Bolshevik to Democrat.*** NAL 1991, $20.00 (0-525-93431-6); $12.00 (0-452-26906-7). 303pp. Biography.

This is a readable biography of the first president of the Russian Republic, a pivotal politician who struggled to engineer many of the democratic reforms in the former Soviet Union. Morrison attempts to portray Yeltsin against the shifting backdrop of changes in the region and focuses on his dealings with Gorbachev, his redefinition of perestroika ("restructuring"), and his intricate game-playing with the Russian Parliament.

Yeltsin is still very much an ill-defined character. There are so many conflicting assessments—he is seen as a drunken madman, a patriot, a visionary—that it is hard to fully understand him. His own memoir, *Against the Grain* (o.p., 1990), presents events from his perspective but is largely self-serving. Yeltsin has also written *The Struggle for Russia* (Random, 1994). In the meantime, Morrison's biography will have to satisfy until enough time has passed so that history can better define this important figure on the world stage.

1106 Nabokov, Vladimir. ***Speak, Memory: An Autobiography Revisited.*** Random 1989, $12.00 (0-679-72339-0). 240pp. Autobiography.

Born in St. Petersburg in 1899, Nabokov, author of *Lolita* and many other works, was one of the twentieth century's premier literary stylists. He studied French literature and Russian literature at Cambridge, lived in Paris and Berlin, and then moved to the United States in 1940. In 1961 he moved to Switzerland, where he died in 1977. *Speak, Memory*, first published in 1951 as *Conclusive Evidence*, was revised in 1966.

His autobiographical account covers the period from 1903 to 1940, "with only a few sallies into later space-time," as Nabokov put it. These are intimate, casual, and personal recollections, charming and evocative, and they help illuminate the personality of man behind the classic—and often controversial—novels. Particularly interesting are his memories of life as a child of privilege in old St. Petersburg, before the onslaught of the Russian Revolution.

A useful companion to this biography, which is currently out of print, is *The Letters of Vladimir Nabokov*, edited by his son Dmitri (Harcourt, 1989). Most of the letters deal with the period after 1940, when the writer was living in the United States.

1107 Scammell, Michael. ***Solzhenitsyn: A Biography.*** Illus. with photos. Norton 1984. o.p. Biography.

This huge biography—over 1,000 pages—attempts to reconstruct every facet of the life of the famed Russian dissident writer: his poor boyhood, his years in war and in labor camps, his apprenticeship as a writer, his disagreements with the ruling powers of the Soviet Union, his expulsion, the media hoopla surrounding his move to the United States, and his ultimate withdrawal to the backwoods of Vermont.

Scammell has clearly done his homework, and this volume, richly illustrated with photographs, serves his subject well. He delves beyond Solzhenitsyn's image in the media, beyond the "disinformation" that the Soviets spread about him, to present a riveting portrait of this important writer and human rights advocate. Because the book was not conceived as a critical biography, it does not analyze his major writings; instead, it places them in the context of author's life.

1108 Sharansky, Natan. *Fear No Evil*. Trans. from Russian. Random 1989, $19.95 (0-394-55878-2); $10.95 (0-679-72542-3). 480pp. Autobiography.

After he applied for an exit visa from the Soviet Union, Sharansky, a prominent Jewish human rights activist, was subjected to years of harassment, including the loss of his job. In March 1977 he was arrested, tried, and sentenced to thirteen years in prison, of which he served nine. Freed after Gorbachev's rise to power in 1986, he emigrated to Israel.

In this autobiographical account, Sharansky describes his arrest and trial and the conditions in the work camps and prisons where he spent nearly a decade of his life. He details how he managed to maintain his dignity under the most degrading conditions and how his spiritual beliefs helped him to survive. He portrays the other activists he saw in prison—those who resisted and maintained their solidarity and those who were broken by the Soviet regime of relentless psychological manipulation and torture. His critique of the Soviet legal system reveals the twisted logic that forms the foundation of many totalitarian societies. Despite the breakup of the Soviet Union, this remains an incisive commentary and an inspiring portrait of one of the past decade's most courageous individuals.   LML

1109 Ulam, Adam B. *Stalin*. Beacon 1989, $18.00 (0-8070-7005-X). 760pp. Biography.

Ulam's first-rate biography of the brutal, enigmatic Soviet dictator is comprehensive and thorough. In reconstructing Stalin's life, the author also provides a complex history of the Soviet Union itself. The book traces Stalin from his early years, through his complex relationship with Lenin and the diplomatic machinations of World War II, to the purges that lasted till his death in 1953. There are other books available on Stalin, including Robert C. Tucker's *Stalin as Revolutionary* (Norton, 1992), but in this volume Ulam is especially adept at untangling the paradoxes of dictatorship as practiced by a sly and menacing tyrant.

Ulam debunks the myths that Stalin was merely a powerful psychopath; instead, he analyzes the shrewd workings of a deliberate, maniacal leader— whose influence, the author believes, continued to dominate Soviet policies and structure even two decades after his death. This book was written when Soviet archives were still off-limits to most researchers, so many unanswered questions remain. But this volume provides a fascinating and gripping portrayal of an important figure in twentieth-century history.

1110 Werbell, Frederick E., and Thurston Clarke. *Lost Hero: The Mystery of Raoul Wallenberg*. McGraw-Hill 1982. o.p. Biography.

Raoul Wallenberg was a member of a prominent Swedish banking family. In 1944, when he was thirty-two, Wallenberg, a Christian, was sent to Hungary in an attempt to rescue Jews. When he arrived, nearly a half million people were imprisoned at Auschwitz, but a quarter million still remained in Budapest. By January 1945, when the Russians captured the city, there were 120,000, and Wallenberg is credited with saving the lives of 100,000 of them. Immediately afterward, he was arrested and consigned to the *gulag* (the network of Soviet forced-labor camps). To this day his fate has remained a mystery. After interviewing a number of reliable sources, the author of this book maintains that Wallenberg survived another twenty years in the gulag

Even though it deals with a selfless hero of near-mythic proportions, Werbell's book is balanced and readable, its story rooted in documented historical facts. Less successful books on the same subject include John Bierman's *Righteous Gentile: The Story of Raoul Wallenberg* (Anti-Defamation League of B'nai B'rith, 1982) and Kati Marton's *Wallenberg* (o.p., 1982).

1111 Zeman, Zbynek. *The Masaryks: The Making of Czechoslovakia*. St. Martin 1990, $16.50 (0-685-38704-6). 230pp. Biography.

This is a dual biography of Thomas Masaryk, founder of the state of Czechoslovakia after World War I, and his son, Jan, who served as foreign minister after World War II. The Masaryks helped define the nation they loved and are regarded as near-deities by many of their countrymen and by other biographers. But in this work, the author is intent on portraying his subjects, not as the subject of myth, but as real people. Through Zeman's careful interpretations, we come to understand the creation and evolution of an Eastern European nation. The author devotes considerable space to an analysis of Czechoslovakia's special relationship with the Soviet Union.

Zeman also tackles the issues surrounding Jan Masaryk's controversial and still-debated death. Officially, he was declared a suicide, but rumors persist that he was victim of Communist rivalry. After weighing the evidence, Zeman is inclined to accept the official verdict, but the arguments he musters to support that decision seem weak. Whatever the truth, the volume stands as a comprehensive overview of the powerful family that helped construct and rule a troubled nation.

10

THE MIDDLE EAST

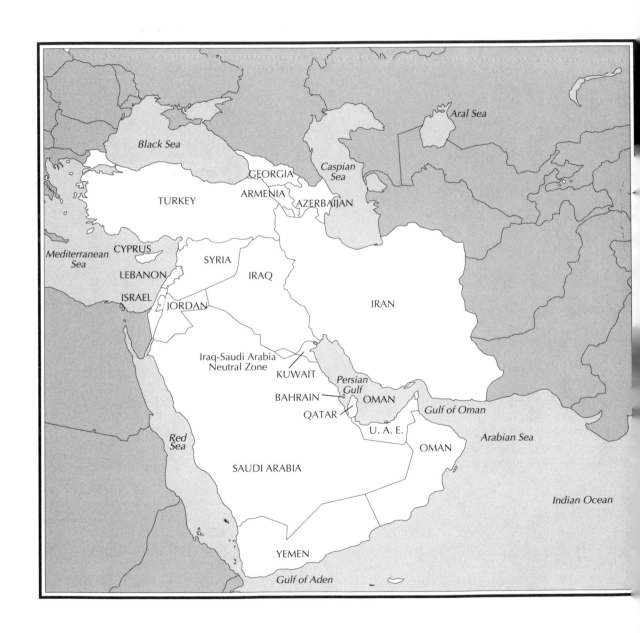

10

THE MIDDLE EAST

by Mohammed A. Bamyeh

The Middle East, sometimes called the Near East, is the area encompassing western Asia and North Africa. While the intermixing of the region's populations across the centuries has made it impossible to speak of "pure" ethnicities, the majority of the people are considered ethnic Arabs. Consequently, the Arabic language, culture, literature, and political concerns provide a significant degree of commonality among the inhabitants.

The Arab League lists twenty-one states in the region among its members, including countries as diverse as Iraq, Morocco, Yemen, Mauritania, Syria, and Djibouti. In addition, the area contains other significant ethnocultural entities, such as the Iranians and the Turks, who have historically shared the Muslim Empire with the Arabs. The area arguably includes as well the newly reemergent states of Georgia, Azerbaijan, and Armenia, formerly part of the Soviet Union, and many stateless population groups such as the Kurds, the Berbers, and other smaller Caucasian ethnicities. Since antiquity, Jews have also lived in various urban centers across the region. In 1948, the state of Israel was founded in what was Palestine. Many Jews emigrated from nations around the world, including the war-torn countries of Europe. This influx introduced into the region a new Ashkenazi Jewish presence, and it also concentrated the presence of Sephardic Jews who had been living elsewhere in the Middle East and North Africa.

Broadly speaking, the politics, culture, and history of western Asia must be studied in relationship to the area's connection to North Africa. Most of the books annotated in this chapter, however, pertain primarily to the Asian part of the Middle East. Readers are also urged to consult Chapter 11 of this bibliography, which is devoted to works from African nations, including those in North Africa.

Problems of Multicultural Understanding of the Middle East

The Middle East, a region that plays a pivotal role in world events, is little understood in the West. Negative images and stereotypes abound—terrorists, harems, oil sheiks wallowing in untold wealth. Such images are fortified by the news media, Hollywood, and by a pervasive belief that the people of the Middle East are inscrutably foreign in culture, manners, and mentality.

There are several reasons this perception persists. First, only a small number of Westerners are familiar with the languages and cultures of the Middle East. First-rate educational programs devoted to the region are rare in schools and colleges, so the supply of trained scholars is low, especially when compared to experts in European area studies. As a result, many Western journalists who cover the Middle East have little or no background in its languages or cultures. They may rely on questionable sources for their information, or they may lack the perspective needed to analyze events fully. Government policymaking bodies, such as the U.S. State Department, bemoan the chronic shortages of Arabic-speaking staff and experts with knowledge of the region acquired through other than formal diplomatic channels.

A second reason for Western misunderstanding is that, for much of history, the dominant cultures of the Middle East and those of Europe have been at odds, often defining themselves as opposites—and enemies. The two-hundred-year history of the Crusades, whose purpose was to rout the Islamic "infidels" from the Holy Land, caused deep animosity between Christians and Muslims. Hostility continued in new guises throughout the era of the Ottoman Empire (from the thirteenth century to World War I) and on into the twentieth century, with its decades of colonialism. Such issues as the support of the West for Israel since 1948, Western assistance given to various local dictators, the bitter struggle against colonization, and the Gulf War in 1991 all contribute to the already wide gap between the Muslim world and the West. The result is a legacy of deep-seated mutual suspicions and distrust.

A third reason for tension is the Arab-Israeli conflict, one of the most persistent and vexing ongoing dramas played out on the modern world stage. Despite incremental steps toward peace, the marrow-deep animosity between these groups—coupled with U.S. support of Israel—has made it difficult at times to obtain objective information about the Middle East in many Western countries. The situation has improved in recent years, but popular prejudices, formed over the course of centuries, will take a long time to disappear.

Another barrier to understanding is the sheer complexity of the Middle Eastern world. Penetrating that complexity can be a huge challenge for the uninitiated. Although one can glean certain large common themes, interests, and cultures in the region, one must also wrestle with vast diversities and divisions. Most readers who seek to explore the region's multicultural affairs would perhaps begin by demanding straightforward and easy-to-digest narratives, but few such works are available.

The last reason has to do with the fact that communities of people of Middle Eastern ancestry in North America are largely invisible in most of North America. Arab immigration—particularly from the eastern Mediterranean area known as the Levant—began in the late nineteenth century and continues today from other parts of the Arab world. There was also a significant growth of an Iranian-American community in the 1980s, following the Islamic revolution in Iran. Many Arab-Americans, lacking sufficient resources to combat negative stereotypes, have chosen to assimilate or hide their identities. There are some signs that this state of affairs is changing slowly, especially in urban areas where there is a large presence of recent immigrants and communities from the Middle East.

The Gulf War again demonstrated—though in fact no such demonstration was needed—the importance of the region in international politics and economics. The problems that led to that war, as well as to the wars before it, still exist. Solving such problems requires an urgent and broad educational effort about the Middle East. The first step is to make available quality books about its culture, economics, politics, and history. To that end this chapter recommends the best contemporary works for college students and general adult readers.

In addition, the Middle East has been defined by various U.S. administrations as crucial for national interests. The United States has been deeply involved in the region since the early 1950s, and now it has established a military presence there while at the same time it is scaling back its military bases in Europe. At the same time, however, there is a clear lack of even an elementary public education about the region, its inhabitants, their cultures, religions, habits, and sensitivities. On the contrary, what little knowledge is available serves largely to dehumanize or demonize the vast majority of the peoples of the region.

Despite the problems, there are reasons for guarded optimism. The signing of an accord between Israel and the Palestine Liberation Organization in 1993, granting mutual recognition and limited Palestinian self-rule, was meant as a "first step" in a frustratingly slow and fragile peace process, a process that has a long way to go before it could fulfill its promise of peace and prosperity. Similarly, the media and the educational community have a long way to go before the American people have access to a better understanding of the Middle East.

Selecting the Best Books

In light of the above, this list is a modest step toward furnishing a minimum foundation for understanding the region from a multicultural perspective. True to that end, the list also strives to include less familiar aspects and points of view, along with those that are better known. Furthermore, the list emphasizes peoples and traditions and is less concerned with biographies of major personalities and leaders. One reason is simply that few reliable and balanced biographies are available about these figures. The bitterness of the conflicts of the region and the controversial or dictatorial nature of many contemporary leaders has meant that biographies tend to be propagandistic—either too flattering or too damning to be of much value. The general works described here discuss in passing the most important leaders and their impact on the region. As editor of this chapter, I have strived to exclude works that glorify any particular personality or group and have been especially wary of those not written by objective bystanders or neutral observers. Instead, the emphasis here is on stories told by and about ordinary people, stories largely missing from the standard image of the Middle East.

Finally, selecting the best books about a politically volatile part of the globe meant weeding out volumes that were little more than polemics and propaganda. It required considerable effort to find books written about the Middle East that could not be considered "partisan." Unfortunately, many writers and readers approach that region with already formulated opinions, seeking only to confirm their existing biases. Most of the books listed here do not promote a single-minded political agenda; instead they provide stimulating and thought-provoking reading. Another criterion for inclusion was that the books should present original but accessible perspectives that generally improve public understanding of the region. Additional preference was given to those works that reflect a multicultural perspective.

There are a number of key themes in the nonfiction concerning the Middle East. I have emphasized books that present the many cultural and religious groups in the region. Some of these books are quite general, encompassing many groups and spanning North Africa as well as western Asia. Among the best is Albert Hourani's *History of the Arab Peoples*, an extensive and well-written social history that presents the urban experience as well as rural life. The Sephardic Jews, who have roots in the Middle East, North Africa, and Southern Europe, are discussed in Ammiel Alcalay's *After Jews and Arabs: Remaking Levantine Culture*. (Books about the Ashkenazi Jews from Central and Eastern Europe, many of whom relocated to Israel after World War II, are discussed in Chapter 8, Western Europe, and Chapter 9, Eastern Europe.) The Kurds, an ethnic minority that has come under attack both by Iraq's Saddam Hussein and by the Turks, are portrayed in *Kurdish Ethnonationalism* by Nadar Entessar and the collection *The Kurds: A Contemporary Overview*, edited by Philip Kreyenbroek and Stefan Sperl. The genocide of the Armenians, an act that foreshadowed the devastation of the Holocaust, is documented in *The Slaughterhouse Province: An American Diplomat's Report on the Armenian Genocide of 1915–17* by Leslie A. Davis. The continued survival of the Armenian people and the rebirth of the independent state of Armenia in 1990 are the subjects of *Armenia: The Survival of a Nation* by Christopher J. Walker. The history and beliefs of Shiite Muslims—the dominant group in Iran and a significant religious minority in many other Arab countries—are explored in Roy Mottahedeh's *The Mantle of the Prophet: Religion and Politics in Iran*. Fazlur Rahman's classic work, *Islam*, is perhaps the best current study of Islam and its various sects, including the dominant Sunni Muslims, the Shiites, and the Sufis. Other works on this list are included because they present other aspects of Islam or are written for readers with little knowledge of Islam or its early history.

The rise of religious fundamentalism has intensified traditional conflicts and brought them to the attention of the West. Nazih Ayubi's *Political Islam* and Habib Boularès's *Islam: The Fear and the Hope* offer clearly written, even-handed analyses of the phenomenon. Both trace the roots of Islamic fundamentalism to the cultural dislocations resulting from economic development and in the poor quality of leadership in the Arab countries. In his book, Ayubi focuses more on the leaders' inadequate challenge to Israel and the West, while Boularès blames dictators for not allowing ordinary citizens other outlets for self-expression. As Samuel Heilman discusses in *Defenders of the Faith: Inside Ultra-Orthodox Jewry*, Judaism has not been immune to the spread of fundamentalism in the Middle East.

Other conflicts in the region have been political and economic as much as religious. The flashpoint of the Gulf War was Iraq's 1990 invasion of Kuwait following a long-standing border dispute. *Beyond the Storm* by Phyllis Bennis and Michel Moushabeck offers the commentaries of Middle Eastern scholars and political activists, while *The Gulf War Reader* by Micah Sifry offers a number of primary documents and is geared to introductory-level students. Upon intervening in the Gulf crisis in 1991, the United States imposed strict controls on journalists covering the war. The response of the journalists is contained in two works on the list, John Fialka's *Hotel Warriors: Covering the Gulf War* and John MacArthur's *Second Front: Censorship and Propaganda in the Gulf War*. The compliance of journalists with the "official" attitudes toward Islam and the Arab world in general is the subject of Edward W. Said's classic, penetrating, and highly controversial study, *Covering Islam.*

The most persistent and bloody conflict in the Middle East has been that between Israel and its neighbors. The establishment of the state of Israel in 1948 in what was known as Palestine dispossessed the Arabs living in that territory. Successive wars between Israel and neighboring Arab countries brought new territories under Israeli control. Among these were the West Bank and Gaza, areas already inhabited by Arab farmers, townspeople, and refugees. These Palestinian Arabs chafed under Israeli occupation, and their resentments exploded in the Intifada. A number of books on this list chronicle the hostility between Israel and its Arab neighbors and between Israelis and Palestinians, as well as attempts to reconcile the differences. Former Israeli Foreign Minister Abba Eban presents the Israeli perspective in his autobiography. Among the most eloquent accounts from a Palestinian perspective is Sami Hadawi's *Bitter Harvest: A Modern History of Palestine.* Historian Ritchie Ovendale offers an analysis of Israel's conflicts with the neighboring Arab states in *The Origins of the Arab-Israeli Wars,* and Keith Kyle's *Suez* is already a classic work on the 1956 crisis over the Suez Canal. Deborah Gerner's *One Land, Two Peoples: The Conflict over Palestine* is an excellent historical work about the Israeli-Palestinian conflict from an outsider's perspective. Sources of hope and reconciliation appear in several works by Israeli and Palestinian commentators. Uri Avnery, an Israeli peace activist once prosecuted by the Israeli government for his "illegal" contacts with PLO leaders, tells his story in *My Friend, the Enemy.* Israeli writer David Grossman has offered two moving works of nonfiction. The *Yellow Wind* contains Grossman's interviews with Palestinians and Israeli settlers in the occupied territories, while his subsequent work, *Sleeping on the Wire,* offers the point of view of Palestinians living within Israel's borders.

Finally, the role of women in the Arab world is a major theme of both nonfiction and literature. Although they are often portrayed in terms of stereotypes, women have maintained a complex and significant place in Arab society. Religion, class differences, and the degree of Westernization have all affected women's roles within and outside marriage and in the society as a whole. Arab woman scholars and creative writers have sought to redefine the roles and the image of women. Some of those authors are included in the collection *Opening the Gates: A Century of Arab Feminist Writing,* edited by Margot Badran and Miriam Cooke. Fatima Mernissi's *Beyond the Veil: Male-Female Dynamics in Modern Muslim Society,* which disputes the belief that Islam subjugates women; instead, the author argues that the real roots of oppression lie in repressive social and political institutions. The interviews in Bouthaina Shaaban's *Both Right and Left Handed: Arab Women Talk About Their Lives* show how women achieve power, an expanded role for themselves, and even a measure of liberation despite restrictions and taboos.

Literature provides another window into the world of the Middle East. The Iranian writers Simin Daneshvar and Nahid Rachlin, the Lebanese writer Emily Nasrallah, and the Saudi-Lebanese novelist Hanan Al-Shaykh are among the women whose distinguished works of fiction examine the role of women in Arab society and offer a compelling portrait of war, politics, and the society as a whole. In addition to exploring and critiquing gender relations and roles, Middle Eastern literature reveals life in the different areas of the region. Iran has contributed a number of renowned writers, among them Daneshvar, Rachlin, Jalal Al-E Ahmad, Samad Behranqi, and Hadi Khorsandi, whose fiction touches upon Persian folklore, the Koran, and life under the Shah and the mullahs. Writing about the region of Abkhazia—now seeking its independence from Georgia—is Fazil Iskander, whose *Sandro of Chegem* is one of the few works from this region that have been translated into English. The Lebanese civil war serves as the background for many poignant works of literature. Among the best are Nasrallah's short story collection, *A House Not Her Own: Stories from Beirut*; Elias Khoury's *Little Mountain* and *Gates of the City*, which describe life in Beirut before and during the war; and the poetry of Khalil Hawi. Ghassan Kanafani and Sahar Khalifeh have chronicled the lives of Palestinians in the West Bank and Gaza and in exile, while Emile Habiby and Anton Shammas explore the contradictions, ironies, and cultural dislocations facing Arabs who have chosen to live in Israel. Many of the recommended works on this list are anthologies that offer an overview of the writing of a country or an ethnic group. These collections, with their copious explanatory material, offer an introduction for readers with little background and are well suited to introductory classes on the high school and college level. In some cases, they are the only sources in English for examples of literature from a particular nation or region. The anthologies annotated here include literary works from Turkey, Lebanon, Saudi Arabia, Iran, the Palestinians, and from throughout the Arab world.

Modern Israeli literature has up until now been dominated by a few highly acclaimed and prolific writers. In poetry, Yehuda Amichai and T. Carmi stand out. Their works, as well as those by less-well-known poets, are contained in the anthologies *The Modern Hebrew Poem Itself* and *The Penguin Book of Modern Verse*. A principal theme explored in such anthologies is the revitalization of Hebrew as both a spoken and a written language, due in large measure to the Zionist movement and the establishment of the State of Israel. Israeli poets juxtapose biblical imagery with images of modern Israel as they celebrate the Jews' return to their biblical land. In fiction, Nobel laureate S. Y. Agnon serves as a transitional figure; his works deal with such themes as Jewish life in Eastern Europe, Zionism, and the experiences of Jewish settlers in Palestine. The novelists Amos Oz, Meir Shalev, and A. B. Yehoshua offer a vision of contemporary Israel, focusing on the tensions between the nation's European founders and their Israeli-born children. In general, conflicts among the generations figure heavily in Israeli fiction, as do war and relations with the Palestinians. All three of these themes come together, to powerful effect, in Yehoshua's *The Lover* and Oz's *My Michael* and *A Perfect Peace*.

Clara Lazimy provided the list for Israeli literature, and Richard Lachmann annotated those works. Unless indicated by the initials of another contributor, all annotations were written by the chapter's principal contributor, Mohammed A. Bamyeh.

LITERATURE

1112 Agnon, S. Y. *Shira*. Trans. from Hebrew by Zeva Shapiro. Schocken 1989, $24.95 (0-8052-4043-8). 585pp. Fiction.

Agnon, winner of the 1966 Nobel Prize for literature, was the first major twentieth-century novelist to write in Hebrew and is viewed as the founder of modern Hebrew literature. Born in 1888 in Galicia, a region ruled by Austria, he emigrated to Palestine as a young man. He then spent ten years in Germany and returned to Palestine in 1924. He witnessed the founding of Israel in 1948 and died in 1970.

The dangers confronting Jews in Palestine and abroad is a recurring theme of this novel. Manfred Herbst is an aging professor of Byzantine art and archaeology at Hebrew University in Jerusalem in the late 1930s. Jewish settlers in Palestine are experiencing ever-more-frequent violent attacks from their Arab neighbors, and Herbst's in-laws, who still live in Germany, are trying to emigrate to escape Nazi persecution. Herbst has two grown daughters, the eldest of whom is active in the armed Zionist underground.

Besides dealing with political dangers and tensions, Herbst is obsessed with the promise of regaining his youthfulness through an affair with a woman named Shira. She is mainly an object of Herbst's fantasies, although he does consummate his relationship with her. When not thinking of himself and his love life, Herbst muses on literature and painting. The ample references to European writers serve to link this novel of Palestine to the literary and scholarly tradition from which the fictional Herbst and Agnon, his creator, come. Herbst uses art to break out of the ordered academic and social world in which he has lived. He also struggles to discover more-elemental truths in his love for Shira and in his dreams of personal and Jewish renewal. Agnon is also the author of *A Simple Story (see main entry)*. RL

1113 Agnon, S. Y. *A Simple Story*. Trans. from Hebrew by Hillel Halkin. Schocken 1985. o.p. Fiction.

Much of Agnon's early work evokes the Eastern European Jewish ghettos in which he grew up. *A Simple Story* is set in the fictional town of Szybusz. Hirshl, son of a wealthy storeowner, is in love with his impoverished cousin, Blume. Hirshl's parents arrange a marriage to Nina, daughter of wealthy farmers. Hirshl is too passive to resist his parents, even though many of his Jewish contemporaries in turn-of-the-century Eastern Europe are defying theirs by marrying for love, embracing socialism, or becoming Zionists who migrate to Palestine. Agnon adopts a humorous tone in describing Hirshl and his relatives and neighbors. At the end the novel, Hirshl finds contentment in his marriage to Nina and as a shopkeeper and father. The outcome expresses Agnon's empathy and love for the secure though doomed world of Eastern European Jews. Agnon is also the author of *Shira (see main entry)*. RL

1114 Ahmad, Jalal Al-E. *By the Pen*. Trans. from Persian by M. R. Ghanoonparvar. Univ. of Texas Pr. 1988. o.p. Fiction.

Ahmad, who died in 1969, is considered one of the key figures in modern Persian literature. This work, which was banned during his lifetime, is one of his best. Set in late premodern Persia, this is the story of two scribes, one driven by honesty and professionalism, the other by the urge for material gain and worldly power. The compact plot employs many allusions to folktales in a thinly veiled critique of the political culture of modern Iran, a culture that laid the foundations for the rise of the mullahs and a return to Islamic fundamentalism. The reader who is new to the literature and themes of Iran will greatly benefit from a well-informed introduction by Michael Hillman, who situates the author and the novel in the proper context.

1115 Behranqi, Samad. ***The Little Black Fish and Other Modern Persian Short Stories.*** 2nd rev. ed. Trans. from Persian by Mary Hegland and Eric Hooglund. Three Continents 1987, $10.00 (0-89410-621-X). 106pp. Fiction.

Five stories represent the work of this Iranian folklorist and storyteller. Behranqi's stories are deeply embedded in the culture of Irani Azerbaijan and are loaded with social critique, which is often conveyed through the voices and perspectives of children. The book includes a memorial essay and an afterword, both of which seek to provide basic information about the author's life and work during the Shah's reign, his political philosophy, and his mysterious death in 1968.

1116 Burnshaw, Stanley, and others, eds. ***The Modern Hebrew Poem Itself: Twenty-Four Poets in a New Presentation.*** Rev. ed. Harvard Univ. Pr. 1990, $17.00 (0-674-57925-9). 231pp. Poetry.

Poems by twenty-four nineteenth- and twentieth-century Hebrew poets are presented in several versions: in the original Hebrew; in Hebrew transliteration so that readers who can't read Hebrew can at least hear the sound of the language; and then in an annotated translation with a commentary that explains the biblical, literary, and historical allusions. Readers will be impressed with the diversity of poetic expression in modern Hebrew literature.

The nineteenth-century poets represented here, most of whom lived in Europe, wrote on biblical themes and on the yearning of Jews in exile for a return to their ancient homeland. In this century, many poets were immigrants to Palestine or they are native-born Israelis. Initially, the dominant themes of their verses were Zionist—celebrations of the return to the homeland, explorations of the struggle to build a new nation, and defending the nation in war. More recently, Israeli poets have often turned away from political themes to explore other themes and to work with new structures and linguistic devices. An afterword to this edition discusses the evolution of Hebrew poetry from 1965 to 1988. The examples reveal a new interest in social and political themes along with a celebration of present-day Hebrew language and Israeli expression. RL

1117 Carmi, T. ***At the Stone of Losses.*** Trans. from Hebrew by Grace Schulman. Illus. Univ. of California Pr. 1983, $13.00 (0-520-05107-6). 192pp. Poetry.

T. Carmi is one of Israel's leading contemporary poets as well as a scholar and the editor of the *Penguin Book of Hebrew Verse (see main entry).* Carmi has done much to remind Israelis of their biblical literary heritage and the ways in which Jews in exile sustained and developed their ancient tradition through medieval times to the modern Zionist revival of Hebrew as a spoken language.

Carmi illuminates the range of Hebrew expression in his own poetry. Thoroughly modern in his form and imagery, he draws on the long written tradition in Hebrew and incorporates biblical images, characters, and landmarks to give a Jewish focus to his work. In many poems the narrator is an active presence, acutely aware of his obligations to give voice to the sad history of mankind and of Jews in particular. At the same time he laments the limits of what an author can express, even when using this rich and ancient language. RL

1118 Carmi, T., ed. ***The Penguin Book of Hebrew Verse.*** Bilingual (Hebrew-English) ed. Viking 1981, $16.95 (0-14-042197-1). 448pp. Poetry.

This anthology offers a comprehensive selection of Hebrew poetry from the Bible to present-day works written in modern Hebrew by Israelis. The first Hebrew poems are the books of the Old Testament, composed and compiled from the thirteenth to the second century B.C. These were followed by commentaries on the Bible and religious meditations written by Jewish poets throughout the Middle East. By the ninth century A.D., Jews had scattered into exile throughout Europe and North Africa as well as the Middle East, and Hebrew poetry began to address secular subjects, although many Jewish poets abandoned their ancient language for the tongues of their new countries.

Hebrew poetry was revived in the nineteenth century by Zionists seeking to resurrect the language of the Torah as the language of the homeland they envisioned. In the twentieth century, a number of poets, mostly from Israel, have given new depth to the language while drawing upon classical idioms in their poetry. This anthology reprints each poem in both Hebrew and English. An annotated table of contents describes each work, gives its date of composition and author (if known), and discusses its religious and social meaning. The history of Hebrew poetry is explored in an introductory essay. Carmi is also the author of *At the Stone of Losses (see main entry).*   RL

1119 Daneshvar, Simin. ***Daneshvar's Playhouse: A Collection of Stories.*** Trans. from Persian and Aftwd. by Maryam Mafi. Illus. Mage 1989, $22.00 (0-934211-19-1). 184pp. Fiction.

The five stories included in this collection introduce to the reader of English a representative sample of the work of this talented and eminent Iranian writer. The author is an established figure in contemporary Persian literature. Through her confident style, she reflects upon the social reality and the events of the past two decades in the political and cultural life of Iran. The handsomely produced book contains a foreword by the author and a critical and biographical afterword by the translator.

1120 Galin, Muge, ed. ***Turkish Sampler: Writings for All Readers.*** Univ. of Indiana Pr. 1988. o.p. Fiction/Poetry.

This book is both a collection of literary samples and an educational tool for learning the Turkish language. With its broad scope, including folk mythology and modern literature, the book is a microcosm of modern Turkish culture. The selections are organized in four sections based on their ease and accessibility. Also included are excellent supporting materials, such as biographies of authors, maps, explanations, vocabulary questions, and tips for students of Turkish.

1121 Gibran, Kahlil. ***The Prophet.*** Illus. Knopf 1923, $30.00 (0-394-40426-2); $14.00 (0-394-40427-0). 96pp. Poetry.

The best known work of this Arab-American author, *The Prophet* continues to generate interest because of its romantic rendition of mystical tradition and wisdom. Gibran, who wrote in both English and Arabic, considered his work to be a distillation of a cultural synthesis, even though his background in

Eastern mysticism has rarely been acknowledged in the West. Since the book first appeared in 1923, the clear and evocative tone with which it addresses some deep universal themes has attracted many readers who seek guidance in wrestling with their everyday lives and problems.

1122 Green, John, and Mohammad R. Ghanoonparvar, eds. ***Iranian Drama: An Anthology***. Trans. from Persian. Mazda 1989, $24.95 (0-939214-63-6). 332pp. Drama.

The editors have selected seven important plays, one each by a modern Iranian playwright. The book includes an informative introduction by the editors describing the author's position as a dramatist in the overall context of Persian culture and literature. The collection has some historical value as well because the era in which most of the works were written and performed—between 1960 and 1979—largely corresponds to the reign of the last Shah of Iran, and thus they reflect events and ideas circulating before the advent of the Islamic Revolution.

1123 Habiby, Emile. ***The Secret Life of Saeed the Pessoptimist***. Trans. from Arabic by Salma Khadra Jayyusi and Trevor LeGassick. Readers International 1989, $9.95 (0-930523-08-3). 170pp. Fiction.

This is one of the most influential novels in modern Palestinian literature. Habiby, an Israeli Arab, tells the story of Saeed, a young Palestinian who returns secretly to the region that became Israel. Saeed marries a Palestinian woman who is soon to be deported, then marries another who lands both of them in trouble with the authorities. Meanwhile, Saeed is recruited by the Israelis to spy on a union of Palestinian workers. Later, when the authorities find out that his son had become a resistance fighter, Saeed is imprisoned and interrogated. Throughout the novel, Saeed is portrayed as a half-educated innocent—in some ways, the author seems to be suggesting that his character represents the still-forming sense of Palestinian unity. However, in 1967—the year of the six-day Arab-Israeli war—that innocence is lost. In this wildly imaginative story, Saeed disappears altogether with the aid of extraterrestrial beings with whom he had been in contact through tunnels constructed by the Crusaders under the port of Acre. This beautiful novel is full of political allegories, symbolism, proverbs, and mythology, and it could very well be read as a dream-like rendition of the Palestinian collective psyche during a crucial period in modern history.

1124 Hawi, Khalil, and Nadeem Naimy. ***From the Vineyards of Lebanon: Poems by Khalil Hawi and Nadeem Naimy***. Trans. from Arabic with Pref. and Intro. by Fuad S. Haddad. Syracuse Univ. Pr. 1992, $11.95 (0-8156-6085-5). 161pp. Poetry.

This translation introduces two significant Lebanese poets to the English-speaking audience, one of whom, Khalil Hawi, is considered to be one of the leading poets of the Arab world. The selections in this volume are flavored with philosophical undertones. The verses reflect improvisational techniques as well as more traditional forms and deal with such themes as human destiny, the meaning of life, and possible harmony between Eastern and Western civilizations.

1125 Heinrichsdorf, Ava M., and Abu Bakr Ahmed Bagader, eds. ***Assassination of Light: Modern Saudi Fiction***. Trans. from Arabic by the editors. Three Continents 1990, $24.00 (0-89410-598-1); $11.00 (0-89410-599-X). 87pp. Fiction.

The first anthology of Saudi literature to appear in English, this book takes an important step toward filling an enormous literary gap. It contains sixteen short stories by an equal number of authors. Most of the stories are rooted in the realistic tradition, and their characters—often family members in exaggerated stereotypical roles—are easy to identify with. They portray social reality and modern transformations among a people that Western visitors rarely encounter. Two prefaces, short biographies, and a glossary of terms guide the reader through this unfamiliar, often strange landscape. The anthology includes many works from established writers, but it also introduces many new authors.

1126 Iskander, Fazil. ***Sandro of Chegem***. Trans. from Russian by Susan Brownsberger. Vintage 1983. o.p. Fiction.

Set in Abkhazia, at the eastern end of the Black Sea, this novel by the immensely popular Iskander (himself an ethnic Abkhazian living in Moscow) is a rollicking feast of humor, folklore, and realistic storytelling. The adventures of Uncle Sandro, a picaresque hero much in the tradition of Gil Blas or Lazarillo de Tormes or even Huckleberry Finn, take us from the 1880s through the 1960s. Sandro, a classic rogue with innate and endearing humanity, begins as a dancer in a folk-dancing troupe and eventually becomes a noted toastmaster.

What makes the novel so appealing is the author's robust sense of life as reflected in his clear-cut enjoyment in recounting the misadventures of the errant Sandro. The novel is episodic and disjointed; rather than hurting the book, that structure gives the book—like its title character—an even greater sense of movement, adventure, and randomness. A more serious element is the political message, carried through the author's sentimental portrayal of a disappearing village life that is contrasted with the encroaching political agenda of the Soviet Union.   EI

1127 Jayyusi, Salma K., ed. ***Anthology of Modern Palestinian Literature***. Columbia Univ. Pr. 1992, $34.95 (0-231-07508-1); $20.00 (0-231-07509-X). 740pp. Fiction/Drama/Poetry.

Jayyusi continues here her admirable work producing resources to facilitate the study of Arab culture and literature. This anthology focuses on contemporary Palestinian authors, seventy of whom are represented, including Israeli Arabs, Palestinians living in the occupied territories, and Palestinians from the diaspora. They comment on traditional themes of loss, nostalgia, and exile, as well as love, honor, social relations, and individualism. This anthology is an essential guide to Palestinian literature as a whole.

1128 Jayyusi, Salma K., ed. ***The Literature of Modern Arabia: An Anthology***. Intro. by Shukry Ayyad. Univ. of Texas Pr. 1989, $24.95 (0-292-74662-8). 560pp. Fiction/Drama/Poetry.

A sampling of literature from the modern Arabian peninsula, a body of work virtually unknown in the West, is presented in distinguished translations.

Three generations of poets, dramatists, and story writers—ninety-five in all—from Saudi Arabia, Yemen, and the Gulf states, have contributed to this volume. The themes that permeate their work involve the search for the self amid the onslaught of technological modernity and the struggle against well-entrenched social conservatism. The anthology includes an incisive introduction by the Egyptian literary scholar Shukry Ayyad, a glossary, and short biographies of the contributors.

1129 Jayyusi, Salma K., ed. ***Modern Arabic Poetry***. Columbia Univ. Pr. 1991, $15.00 (0-231-05273-1). 526pp. Poetry.

Poetry, more than any other genre, has always been a central literary medium in the Arab world, and this collection is a great contribution to literature in translation. As part of an ongoing and collaborative work, several translators worked carefully to render into English nearly 300 poems by ninety-three modern Arab poets. These include some of the best-known poets as well as a few newcomers. The book's comprehensiveness, superb translations, and biographic segments make it an ideal candidate for reference and introductory bookshelves.

1130 Kanafani, Ghassan. ***All That's Left to You: A Novella and Other Stories***. Trans. from Arabic by May Jayyusi and Jeremy Reed. Univ. of Texas Center for Middle Eastern Studies 1990. o.p. Fiction.

This collection brings to the English-reading audience some of the best works of this Palestinian writer. In the skillfully written novella, Kanafani tells the story of an escape from the oppression of Gaza—oppression generated both by Palestinian and Israeli culture—into the neighboring desert. Through their existential dialogues, the characters undertake a rich journey that leads to self-discovery and a recognition of the power of fate. These themes are explored further in ten other short stories that, like all of Kanafani's work, involve meditations on scenes of Palestinian life. The characters confront life under occupation, as refugees, and also as individuals who are vulnerable to intergenerational conflicts and who are looking for meaning in life.

1131 Kanafani, Ghassan. ***Men in the Sun.*** 3rd ed. Trans. from Arabic by Hilary Kilpatrick. Three Continents 1992, $10.00 (0-89410-392-X). 90pp. Fiction.

Published in Arabic some thirty years ago, *Men in the Sun* has never lost its timeliness and relevance. Three characters, who generally represent three generations of Palestinians, attempt to smuggle themselves into Kuwait in a tanker truck, whose driver may be seen as symbolizing ineffective Palestinian leadership. The delays caused by the security guards at the borders, whose callousness and corruption reflect the author's attitudes about certain Arab rulers, trigger the novel's horrible outcome. This highly symbolic book is one of the best expressions of the Palestinian dilemma in modern times. In addition, this edition includes extracts from Kanafani's later novel *Umm Saad*, which depicts Palestinian adaptation to refugee life and the growth of the resistance movement in the late 1960s, though the eyes of a traditional and elderly Palestinian woman.

1132 Kanafani, Ghassan. ***Palestine's Children***. Trans. from Arabic by Barbara Harlow. Three Continents 1984. o.p. Fiction.

The fifteen stories in this collection are set between 1936 (the year the author was born) and 1967, when the Arab armies were defeated by Israel and the Palestinians lost what had remained of their historic homeland. The collection includes significant longer novellas, such as *Return to Haifa*, set in the immediate aftermath of the 1967 war; the story was widely acclaimed for its penetrating critique of the traditional nostalgic conception of "return" as espoused by the older generation of Palestinians. Other scenes in the stories address historical and human situations, such as life under the British mandate, peasant mentality, resistance, and refugee life. Kanafani, who spent much of his relatively short life as a teacher, often tells the stories from the point of view of children, whose psyche he keenly observed.

1133 Kemal, Yashar. ***They Burn the Thistles***. Trans. from Turkish. Writers and Readers 1972, $6.95 (0-906495-47-4). 412pp. Fiction.

Kemal is considered to be one of the greatest contemporary writers in Turkey, and many of his works have been translated into English. This one stands out as an example of his preoccupation with the depiction of social tension, especially in rural settings. It portrays a struggle between the landless poor of Anatolia and their feudal landlords. Against this background, common traditions, individual eccentricities, and everyday routines are sketched out in full details.

1134 Khalifeh, Sahar. ***Wild Thorns***. Trans. from Arabic by Trevor LeGassick and Elizabeth Fernea. Interlink 1989, $9.95 (0-940793-25-3). 207pp. Fiction.

This well-written novel by an increasingly important Palestinian writer from the occupied territories portrays daily life under occupation in an Arab town. With each new humiliation suffered by a character at the hands of the Israeli occupiers, the novel becomes increasingly direct and urgent. Yet the author is likewise critical of the Palestinians and their society. The realism of this novel leads to a pessimistic worldview that, like the *Zeitgeist* of the contemporary Middle East, is cynical about the power of resistance yet derisive about the effects of collaboration.

1135 Khorsandi, Hadi. ***The Ayatollah and I: Iran's New Satire***. Trans. from Persian by Ehssan Javan. Readers International 1987, $7.95 (0-930523-37-7). 160pp. Fiction.

This book offers a hilarious selection of political humor from the Iranian satirical journal *Asghar Agha*, which the author edits in London. He realized that the state of affairs in his homeland had become so disastrous that it was ripe for reinterpretation through pointed satire. Here we find extracts from the "wisdom" of the mullahs, "interviews" with Iranian citizens, parodies, and faked news that comments on the unbelievable nature of the "real" news spewed out by government-dominated media in Iran. Hardly anyone associated with the Iranian regime is spared. The undertone of this witty rendition of contemporary sociopolitical reality is a deep sense of sadness at the retrograde nature of the modern rulers. Sadness, however, is powerless to produce change; a more effective creative response, as this editor shows, is humor.

1136 Khoury, Elias. *Gates of the City*. Trans. from Arabic by Paula Haydar. Univ. of Minnesota Pr. 1993, $15.95 (0-8166-2224-8). 112pp. Fiction.

Set in an unidentified war-torn city that in many ways resembles Beirut, this story tells of a series of wanderings of a man in the city. Along with his footsteps, we hear a tale of the city's past, its present conflicts, and its possible future. The man's memories are as full of pain as the city's recent past. The author delivers a highly focused literary rendition of the cultural and historical factors that conspired to destroy the city over a span of sixteen years.

1137 Khoury, Elias. *Little Mountain*. Trans. from Arabic by Maia Tabet; Frwd. by Edward Said. Univ. of Minnesota Pr. 1989, $24.95 (0-8166-1769-4); $9.95 (0-8166-1770-8). 124pp. Fiction.

In this beautiful novella, Khoury recounts his early years in "Little Mountain," the predominantly Christian sector of East Beirut, before the outbreak of the Lebanese civil war. The author, who now lives in Paris, is also a literary critic, journalist, translator, and editor. He was a guerrilla fighter during the first year of the war (1975), and his leftist sympathies got him expelled from Little Mountain, where he grew up. His description of that place is passionate and existential, revealing a sense of loss and a psyche tormented by the horrors of battle. An introduction by Edward Said situates this work properly in the context of the Arabic novel.

1138 Kishon, Ephraim. *Wise Guy, Solomon*. Trans. from Hebrew by Yohanan Goldman. Macmillan 1973. o.p. Fiction.

Kishon, Israel's leading comic writer, here offers a collection of short pieces lampooning various aspects of life in contemporary Israel. Kishon's Israelis try desperately to overcome the traditions and habits their parents and grandparents brought from the ghettos of Eastern Europe to the new nation

For his objects of humor, Kishon uses many occupations and practices. He describes in exaggerated terms the demands religious political parties make of the government to force all Israeli Jews to conform to Orthodox restrictions, which "even the Lord finds too burdensome." Tourists from the United States gape in awe at even the most trivial Israeli accomplishments and sights. Modern technological innovations such as the telephone and automobile are described in hyperbole of near-biblical proportions. Kishon lampoons Israelis who rush to travel abroad yet who make other Jews feel guilty for not living in Israel, and he especially casts his critical eye on Jews who live in New York. References to politicians and events sometimes date the pieces in this book, but overall Kishon presents a vivid, often riotous view of life in Israel.

Kishon's other satirical works include *The Funniest Man in the World* (Shapolsky, 1989) and *More of the Funniest Man in the World* (Shapolsky, 1990).

RL

1139 Nasrallah, Emily. *A House Not Her Own: Stories from Beirut*. Trans. from Arabic by Thuraya Khalil-Khouri. Gynergy 1992, $12.95 (0-921881-19-3). Fiction.

This collection contains translations of seventeen short stories by an eminent Lebanese writer. The stories, based on the experiences of war, deal with the physical and emotional destruction of society and the transformations that ordinary citizens undergo as they witness their country being torn asunder by civil war. Nasrallah, who vowed to stay in Beirut throughout its long ordeal, is uniquely qualified to register the emotional and existential pulses of the people who clung to life in the city. As in most of her previous work, Nasrallah flavors these stories of this collection with impressions from the south Lebanese village in which she grew up, offering a rich range of integrated snapshots of contemporary Lebanon.

1140 Oz, Amos. *My Michael*. Random 1992, $11.00 (0-679-72804-X). 287pp. Fiction.

Michael Gonen, a geologist working on his dissertation, is a reserved and shy man, and his wife, Hannah, a kindergarten teacher, is excitable. Their marriage lacks emotional depth. In their first year together, Hannah becomes pregnant unexpectedly. Michael is a warm father to their son, Yair, but Hannah finds it difficult to communicate with her child.

This novel takes place during the 1950s in Jerusalem. Oz offers a harrowing display of two emotionally stunted people trapped in a loveless marriage. Although the focus is on Hannah and Michael, Jerusalem is a vivid background for the story, and Israel's conflicts with its Arab neighbors continuously intrude upon the lives of the characters. At the end of the novel, the 1956 war between Israel and Egypt breaks out. Israel is victorious, but for Michael and Hannah the most important development of that year is their move to a new and larger apartment. Hannah and Michael's self-centeredness leaves them unable to communicate adequately with any of their friends and family or to participate fully in the life of their country.

Among Oz's other novels in print are *Black Box* (Harcourt, 1988), *Elsewhere, Perhaps* (Harcourt, 1985), and *Unto Death* (Harcourt, 1978). For discussion of another novel, *A Perfect Peace*, and a work of nonfiction, *In the Land of Israel*, see their main entries.   RL

1141 Oz, Amos. *A Perfect Peace*. Trans. from Hebrew by Hillel Halkin. Harcourt 1985, $16.95 (0-15-171696-X); $11.95 (0-15-671683-6). 400pp. Fiction.

The novel opens at the end of 1965, as Arab attacks heighten tension throughout Israel. The main character is Yonathan Lifshitz, who was born and raised on Kibbutz Granot. His father, Yolek, is the founder and leader of the kibbutz, as well as a one-time member of the Israeli cabinet and long-time friend of the current prime minister. Yonathan, tired of his father, of his wife, Rimona, and of life in the small, closed community of the kibbutz, is planning to run away from them all. Oz ably conveys the mixture of arrogance on the part of the old founders and claustrophobia on the part of some of their children in the intertwined worlds of Israeli politics and the kibbutzim of that era.   RL

1142 Rachlin, Nahid. *Veils: Short Stories*. City Lights 1992, $8.95 (0-87286-267-4). 180pp. Fiction.

This is a collection of ten short stories by the author of two acclaimed novels, *Married to a Stranger* (City Lights, 1993) and *Foreigner* (Norton, 1979). Rachlin, an Iranian woman living in North America, re-creates scenes of migration and loss, seeking to show the continuity of a rich cultural heritage among exiled Iranian Americans. One of the author's greatest accomplishments is her ability to convey the value of this heritage without excessive romanticizing. The scenes are typical of the general experience of Iranian Americans, whose community grew steadily throughout the 1980s. These experiences include exposure to negative media images, losses through war, and the conflicts that arise when people try to maintain their traditions while living in a new country.

1143 Shalev, Meir. *The Blue Mountain: A Novel*. Trans. from Hebrew by Hillel Halkin. HarperCollins 1991, $22.95 (0-06-016691-6); $13.00 (0-06-099503-3). 352pp. Fiction.

Baruch, orphaned at age two, has been raised by his grandfather, Ya'akov Mirkin, who is one of the founding settlers of an agricultural collective in the Jezreel Valley of Israel. This novel tells many poignant and amusing tales of the early development of a Jewish farm settlement in Palestine and its growth and transformation by the children and grandchildren of the founders in contemporary Israel. Baruch is the keeper of the village cemetery. As he learns new details about the loves and feuds among his ancestors, he digs up and reburies their bodies so as to separate enemies and to bring lovers together again in death.

The early history of the farming village is told through the eyes of Ya'akov and his friend Pinness, who sways people's opinions by making up biblical quotations and scientific "facts." As the older people die, their descendants leave the village for a more exciting life in the city. Only a few young people remain, united by their love for the land and respect for the elders. Although devoid of the biblical and historical references common in much Israeli literature, this novel conveys love Israelis have for their land through rich descriptions of nature and its connections to settlers dead and living.   RL

1144 Shammas, Anton. *Arabesques*. Trans. from Hebrew by Vivian Eden. HarperCollins 1988, $16.95 (0-06-015744-5); $11.00 (0-06-091583-8). 256pp. Fiction.

This novel appeared originally in Hebrew and quickly became a rare and widely acclaimed expression of hope for a multicultural way of seeing and being. The author, an Israeli-born Christian Arab, draws on his heritage to weave together an eloquent autobiographical narrative. The themes of *Arabesques* are a people's connection to the land, homelessness, dispossession, and hope—elements that are an important part of both his Israeli and his Arab ancestries.

1145 Al-Shaykh, Hanan. *Women of Sand and Myrrh*. Trans. from Arabic by Catherine Cobham. Doubleday 1992, $10.00 (0-385-42358-6). 288pp. Fiction.

This is the fifth book of fiction by this increasingly prominent Arab feminist writer and the second to be translated into English. The novel consists of a thread of images taken from the daily lives of four women in an unnamed Gulf country (ostensibly Saudi Arabia). One is a well-educated woman who flees the ravages of the war in Lebanon with her husband; in her new land, however, she discovers that her potential as a woman is curtailed by the patriarchal conservatism of the society. Another character is an independent-minded seamstress who uses her limited work potential to create a niche for herself beyond the traditional domain. A third character is rich enough to enjoy travel and the possibility of overseas adventure. The last major thread in the story involves a middle-aged American housewife who compensates for her unsatisfying relationship with her expatriate husband by seeking out thrills in her new country. The novel is not structured to provide a traditional linear tale with a clear beginning, middle, and end; instead it offers a panorama of women's daily lives in an extremely conservative society. Also in print by this author is *The Story of Zahra* (Doubleday, 1994).

1146 Sullivan, Soraya P., ed. ***Stories by Iranian Women Since the Revolution***. Trans. from Persian by Soraya P. Sullivan; Frwd. by Elizabeth W. Fernea. Univ. of Texas Pr. 1991, $8.95 (0-292-77649-7). 150pp. Fiction.

This anthology of short stories includes contributions from established authors as well as from a younger generation of women writers. The overall tone is markedly influenced by the clash between resistance to patriarchy and the uneasy adaptation to the new conditions facing Iranian women since the Islamic revolution. These engaging stories offer delightful and richly diverse readings drawn from daily experiences. They go a long way toward dispelling widely held stereotypes about the subjugation of Iranian women under the uniformity of the veil.

1147 Al-Udhari, Abdullah, ed. ***Modern Poetry of the Arab World***. Trans. from Arabic by Abdullah Al-Udhari. Viking 1986. o.p. Poetry.

This anthology is an ambitious undertaking, bringing to the English-speaking reader a well-rounded collection of modern Arabic poetry in superb translations. The book emphasizes the post-traditional poets who have dominated the poetic scene in the Arab world since the late 1940s. Selections are arranged in roughly chronological order and further divided according to a number of features. Some, for example, reflect unusual poetic styles, such as metric innovations, while other poems are grouped together because they deal with similar themes, such as the aftermath of war. An appendix provides relevant dates and information.

1148 Walker, Barbara K. ***The Art of the Turkish Tale, Vol. 1 and 2***. Frwd. by Talat S. Halman. Illus. by Helen Siegel. Texas Tech Univ. Pr. 1990, $25.00 (0-89672-228-7); $17.50 (0-89672-316-X); 1993 $27.50 (0-89672-265-1); $18.50 (0-89672-317-8). 280+286pp. Folktales.

These are remarkable collections. Volume 1 contains fifty-one tales selected from thousands of folktales, fables, and legends the editor has collected over the years. Readers will discover, to their delight, that the compiler has strived to respect the Turkish oral tradition by re-creating in her deft translations the sounds and nuances of the original language. Each story is illustrated with beautiful collagraphs by Helen Siegel, and the text is accompanied by a glossary of Turkish terms. The introductory essay is a rich source of information about folklore and Turkish literary traditions.

A second volume of this work, published in 1993, contains eighty tales and expands the scope of the previous title by including religious and historical stories. Featuring its own useful foreword and introduction, as well as a glossary and pronunciation guide, the volume stands on its own and at the same time complements its excellent predecessor.

1149 Yehoshua, A. B. *A Late Divorce*. Trans. from Hebrew. Harcourt 1993, $12.95 (0-15-649447-7). 354pp. Fiction.

This work, by one of Israel's most acclaimed authors, chronicles the disintegration of an Israeli family as related by three generations of family members. The story takes place in the days preceding and during the Passover holiday. Yehuda Kaminka, the grandfather, has arrived from the United States to finalize his divorce from his insane wife, Naomi, so that he can marry his American girlfriend, who is expecting a baby. Two of his children are also involved in loveless marriages, and the third is gay but unable to establish a healthy relationship with the businessman who loves him. Yehuda's six-year-old grandchild—an obese, socially inept boy—also narrates part of the story. Told through the voices of the characters, the story builds to its tragic conclusion—an "accident" at the mental hospital that brings full circle the events that drove Yehuda to the United States and Naomi to madness.

Yehoshua's novel explores interpersonal and intergenerational relationships. His characters find no love or happiness within marriage, but they long for intimacy nonetheless. The Israeli setting is fully realized as Yehoshua describes the landscape of three cities—Jerusalem, Tel Aviv, and Haifa—and the preparations for the Passover celebration. Through Yehuda and his girlfriend, the tensions between Jews in Israel and those in the United States are also revealed.

Yehoshua is also the author of *Five Seasons* (NAL, 1990) and *The Lover* and *Mr. Mani (see main entries)*. **RL**

1150 Yehoshua, A. B. *The Lover*. Trans. from Hebrew by Philip Simpson. Harcourt 1993, $12.95 (0-15-653912-8). 352pp. Fiction.

Adam and Asya share a loveless marriage, mourning their son who died in childhood and raising a defiant and lively daughter, Defi. To cope with his grief, Adam searches for a substitute son. He first finds Gabriel, a Jew who recently returned to Israel from France to care for his dying grandmother. Gabriel becomes Asya's lover, and Asya rediscovers her zest for life through the affair. Adam breaks into the grandmother's house to learn more about Gabriel's past. When the 1973 war begins, Gabriel is called up by the army; by the end of the war, however, he has disappeared. Adam searches for him, aided by a young Palestinian, Na'im, who works in the garage that Adam owns. Na'im finds himself attracted to Defi and repeatedly uses a key to enter his boss's apartment, where he can see and touch Defi's clothes and books. At the conclusion of the novel, Adam and Asya find Gabriel, who has deserted the army and who is hiding as an Orthodox Jew in Jerusalem. Defi and Na'im discover and consummate their attraction to each other.

Defi, Gabriel, and Na'i each reflect aspects of Israel's present and future. The ambiguities of Jews and Arabs in Israel are played out through the characters and plot of this gripping story. **RL**

1151 Yehoshua, A. B. *Mr. Mani*. Trans. from Hebrew by Hillel Halkin. Harcourt 1993, $12.95 (0-15-662769-8). 369pp. Fiction.

519

THE MIDDLE EAST

This unusual novel tells the stories of ten generations of the Mani family. The Manis are Jews who have been living in Palestine since the eighteenth century. The adventures of the Manis are traced—in reverse chronological order—through a series of five conversations, of which the reader hears only one speaker: Someone whose life was changed by a member of the Mani clan. The conversations are preceded by introductory biographies of the speakers and their unheard interlocutors. Also included are "supplements" that tell what happens to the characters after these revealing conversations.

Only in the final conversation does a Mani actually narrate the story, telling about the family's arrival in Palestine in the 1700s and its affinity for certain fields of interest, such as obstetrics, and its recurrent problems, such as suicide. In the other conversations, a Polish Zionist, a British Jew serving in the British army during World War I, a Nazi soldier, and a young woman who has left her kibbutz for the first time describe how they were transformed by their encounters with a Mani. The Manis reveal their Jewishness through their affection for the holy sites of ancient Judaism in Jerusalem. They and other characters express their religion and ethnicity in terms of geography. As obstetricians with a spiritual attachment to their land, the Manis give birth to children and at the same time engender a broader Zionist consciousness.   RL

NONFICTION

1152 Alcalay, Ammiel. *After Jews and Arabs: Remaking Levantine Culture*. Univ. of Minnesota Pr. 1992, $44.95 (0-8166-2154-3); $16.95 (0-8166-2155-1). 288pp. Nonfiction.

This is one of the more difficult books in this list, but because of its remarkable originality and significance, the added effort required to read it will be greatly rewarded. Alcalay argues that the contributions of Middle Eastern and Sephardic Jewish thinkers have been neglected by both the Western cultural paradigm and by Eurocentric Zionism. In reconstructing the cultural history of the Levant (the region of the eastern Mediterranean, from Turkey to Egypt), the author shows the historic interplay between Arab and Jewish cultures from the medieval era to modern times. Alcalay shows that Middle Eastern Jews are firmly rooted within the other traditions of the Levant. That concept stands in sharp contrast to the myth of the eternally wandering and excluded Jew, an image more appropriate for describing the Jewish experience in Europe. The book is also valuable in introducing the works of hitherto little-known Sephardic authors.

1153 Altorki, Soraya. *Women in Saudi Arabia: Ideology and Behavior Among the Elite*. Columbia Univ. Pr. 1986, $46.50 (0-231-06182-X); $15.50 (0-231-06183-8). 224pp. Nonfiction.

This book, based on the author's survey of women from thirteen elite families in Jeddah, provides rare insights into the domestic lives of women, their adjustments to traditional expectations, and their changing role within the nuclear family. Altorki shows how sexual segregation affects daily life by prescribing women's roles, defining for them what is allowed and what is forbidden. She also describes marriage not as a romantic relationship between partners but as the outcome of a negotiated agreement between families. This work is recommended for anyone interested in seeing the reality of Saudi women beyond the anonymity of the veil.

1154 Ashabranner, Brent. *An Ancient Heritage: The Arab-American Minority.* Illus. with photos by Paul Conklin. HarperCollins 1991, $14.89 (0-06-020049-9). 160pp. Nonfiction.

Although Arabs have immigrated to the United States since the late the nineteenth century, they continue to be greatly misunderstood in this country. Many Arab-Americans, confronted with prejudice and misunderstanding, opted to conceal their heritage and seek complete assimilation. The author shows how, through a kind of "guilt by association," Arab-Americans have suffered because of fallout from conflicts in the Middle East. This, he argues, accounts for the hostility that many of them feel toward American Jews, who many Arabs believe are responsible for defaming them in the West. The book humanizes the Arabs and identifies their similarity to other immigrant groups by showing the continuity of cultural traditions among them, such as close family ties, a strong work ethic, and devotion to educational attainment. This book was written for teenage readers, but it is one of the best sources about Arabs in America for readers of any age.

1155 Ayubi, Nazih. *Political Islam.* Routledge 1991, $59.95 (0-415-05442-7). 224pp. Nonfiction.

Ayubi offers a well-researched and very readable analysis of the array of contemporary Islamic movements known collectively as "fundamentalism." He rejects commonly held Western misconceptions—both scholarly and popular—about Islam, as well as the arguments of Muslim revivalists. Ayubi argues that Islam has always been a *social* rather than a *political* religion. For that reason, he suggests, it is vulnerable to becoming politicized when secular authorities fail to address social problems. The author identifies two main contributing factors: the mediocrity of official Arab challenge to Israel and the West, and the failure of modern reform and development movements to create a deeply rooted and viable identity for twentieth-century Muslims. Without these contemporary problems, Ayubi suggests, Islam could easily coexist with secular or liberal governments, as it frequently did in the past. The author provides an abundance of historical and textual evidence to support this point of view.

1156 Badran, Margot, and Miriam Cooke, eds. *Opening the Gates: A Century of Arab Feminist Writing.* Indiana Univ. Pr. 1990, $39.95 (0-253-31121-7); $17.95 (0-253-20577-8). 448pp. Essays.

This is one of the first anthologies of writings by Arab women about their lives and concerns. The book contains nearly fifty contributions organized around three fluid categories: "Awareness," "Reflection," and "Activism." One of the strengths of this work is the diversity of the genres represented: fiction, memoirs and recollections, drama and poetry, essays, interviews, and speeches.

As a general introduction to Arab women from their own point of view, this book will be very helpful in dispelling widely held stereotypes regarding their roles in, and attitudes toward, modern Arab society.

1157 Barakat, Halim. ***The Arab World: Society, Culture, and State***. Univ. of California Pr. 1993, $30.00 (0-520-07907-8); $15.00 (0-520-08427-6). 339pp. Nonfiction.

This valuable book attempts to portray the people, culture, and political systems of the twenty-one Arab countries from an Arab point of view. The author, an exiled Syrian scholar, is primarily preoccupied with improving human conditions in the Arab world. His perspective is clear and his analyses encompass political life, modern history, and cultural practices. Many books on this subject emphasize biographies of leaders and recaps of diplomatic maneuvering. In striking contrast, Barakat's work brings to the discussion the human dimension so often overlooked.

1158 Bennis, Phyllis, and Michel Moushabeck, eds. ***Beyond the Storm: A Gulf Crisis Reader***. Frwd. by Edward Said; Intro. by Eqbal Ahmad. Illus. Interlink 1991, $29.95 (0-940793-87-3); Interlink $14.95 (0-940793-82-2). 480pp. Nonfiction.

In this book, knowledgeable commentators, including Eqbal Ahmad, Steve Niva, Sheila Ryan, Naseer Aruri, Penny Kemp, and many others offer a good antidote to common misconceptions about the history of the Gulf War. Chapters survey Kuwaiti and Iraqi history and provide a chronology of the crisis. There is insightful discussion of the role of U.S. aid to Israel, post—Cold War U.S. policy in the Middle East, human rights, and environmental damage, the "American Century," and the antiwar movement. Contributors provide historical analysis of the Pentagon's perspectives on—and its strategy for dealing with—the Gulf. Compared to other essay collections on the Gulf War, this one stands out because it eschews echoing the "official" story and resists the temptation to present narrow-minded ideological interpretations of events.

1159 Bickerton, Ian J., and Carla L. Klausner. ***A Concise History of the Arab-Israeli Conflict***. 2nd ed. Illus. Prentice 1990, $19.95 (0-13-292038-7). 276pp. Nonfiction.

An easy-to-read narrative of the Arab-Israeli conflict, this book also offers a comprehensive and open-minded interpretation of events from the onset of Ottoman rule over Palestine in 1516 through the Gulf War in 1991 and beyond. It discusses many key events in the twentieth century: the rise of Arab and Jewish territorial nationalism; the British mandate; the impact of the Jewish immigration in the 1930s and 1940s on communal relations; the creation of Israel; the wars of 1956, 1967, 1973, 1982; and the Palestinian Intifada, which began in 1987. The book does not advocate any specific political perspective; instead, it offers several interpretations and leaves conclusions to the reader. The text is supported by photos, maps, chronologies, and suggestions for further reading.

1160 Boularès, Habib. *Islam: The Fear and the Hope*. Humanities Pr. 1990, $45.00 (0-86232-944-2); $15.00 (0-86232-945-0). 192pp. Nonfiction.

In a reflective book of twelve short chapters, Boularès, a former Tunisian minister of culture, offers an articulate and liberal view on the contemporary Islamic revival. The author traces the roots of the revival to the social and economic conditions and blames various dictatorships for having left their citizens no other outlets for venting their deep-seated frustrations. This eye-opening presentation reveals that the misleading term *fundamentalism* is often casually used to lump together a wide range of movements. Generally, though, he perceives two main types of movements. One is based on fear; it is the intolerant form of fundamentalism with which Iran's Khomeini has become synonymous. The other is based on hope and is, he argues, a reformist and more enlightened trend, one that has been part of important Islamic doctrines, societies, and experiences throughout history.

1161 Boullata, Kamal. *Faithful Witnesses: Palestinian Children Recreate Their World*. Illus. Interlink 1990, $19.95 (0-940793-26-1). 120pp. Nonfiction.

This is an excellent collection of, and commentary on, paintings by Palestinian children. In this book, aimed at adults, drawings are analyzed to reveal the ways children use them to convey their everyday social reality and to express feelings that transcend the written or spoken word. In addition, the collection reveals aspects of the psychological development of children under conditions of conflict, war, and foreign occupation. The photos of the drawings were originally commissioned for an exhibition at the UN Secretariat in New York, and proceeds from the sale of the book go to the Tamer Institute, whose mission involves furthering the art education of Palestinian children.

1162 Brynen, Rex. *Sanctuary and Survival: The PLO in Lebanon*. Westview 1990. o.p. Nonfiction.

This is the first book to describe fully the long history of the PLO in Lebanon, especially since 1970. The author also details the demographic and geographic complexities of Lebanon, the role and history of Palestinian refugees there, and the process by which the PLO built a large constituency within the country, up to and including the Lebanese civil war. The book includes an excellent account of the Israeli invasion of 1982 and the subsequent relocation of the PLO's leadership to Tunis and of its main constituency to the West Bank and Gaza, where the Intifada (Palestinian uprising) would begin a few years later. The author's chronological narrative is informative and lucid.

1163 Bulloch, John. *The Persian Gulf Unveiled*. Congdon & Weed 1984. o.p. Nonfiction.

This survey of four small Arab states in the Gulf (Kuwait, Qatar, Bahrain and the United Arab Emirates) is intended as a guide for Western travelers, businessmen, and students. Transcending the stereotypical images of the region, the author includes information on economics, society, and politics in these countries. In a final and somewhat prophetic chapter, the author detects in the Gulf the seeds of a future world war; in fact, the Gulf War that shattered the region a few years after the book was written fulfilled many of Bulloch's predictions. Given the pace of events, more updated books are needed. Until that niche is filled, this one continues to be recommended.

1164 Chomsky, Noam. ***The Fateful Triangle: The United States, Israel and the Palestinians***. South End 1983, $40.00 (0-89608-188-5); $18.00 (0-89608-187-7). 481pp. Nonfiction.

In this well-documented and straightforward book, Chomsky traces the history of U.S.-Israeli relations. The author, a well-known pacifist, aims some of his critiques at Arabs and Palestinians, but he devotes much of the book to a scathing denunciation of the way the Israeli-U.S. relationship has developed over the years. He argues that unlimited U.S. support was the factor that allowed Israel to achieve military superiority in the Middle East, to occupy more land, and to expand settlements in the occupied territories. At the same time, he argues, this support renders Israel less likely to make concessions in exchange for peace and, in the long run, will reduce U.S. influence on a country whose very might was created by U.S. taxpayers' dollars. Chomsky examines the way Congress as well as official and academic circles grant Israel a "unique immunity from criticism" and accountability for human rights.

1165 Davis, Leslie A. ***The Slaughterhouse Province: An American Diplomat's Report on the Armenian Genocide of 1915–1917***. Ed. and with an Intro. by Susan Blair. Illus. Cartazas 1989, $30.00 (0-89241-458-8). 216pp. Nonfiction.

This eyewitness report on the Turkish slaughter of the Armenians was only recently discovered in the National Archives. It was subsequently edited and published by Susan Blair, who wrote an introduction. Davis was the U.S. consul in remote Harput in eastern Turkey from 1914 to 1917. As a neutral observer who reported only what he saw, Davis described in harrowing detail the onset of Armenian deportation and subsequent massacre by Turkish authorities. During that time, Davis offered refuge to some of the Armenian inhabitants. He describes the rapid deterioration of Turkish-Armenian relations from friendly to violent following the insistence of Turkish nationalists— who had assumed power—on accomplishing one of the first models of "ethnic cleansing" in this century, a model copied less than three decades later in the Holocaust.

1166 Dwyer, Kevin. ***Arab Voices: Human Rights and Culture***. Univ. of California Pr. 1991, $45.00 (0-520-07490-4); $14.00 (0-520-07491-2). 350pp. Nonfiction.

This survey is an important antidote to a widely spread belief that the notion of "human rights" emanates primarily from a liberal Western tradition. Dwyer's book comments on a representative selection of Arab writings, drawn from both secular and religious traditions, on human rights in the Arab world. The author traces the evolution of the concern with human rights through several periods of contemporary Arab history: from the period of anticolonial movements and independence in the 1950s, to the period of experimentation with socialist and capitalist models of development in the 1960s to late 1970s, and into the current period of religious revivalism.

1167 Emerson, Gloria. *Gaza: A Year in the Intifada: A Personal Account.* Grove 1992, $10.95 (0-87113-466-7). 266pp. Nonfiction.

The author, a prize-winning journalist, devotes her skills to this moving account of the Palestinian uprising that started in Gaza in 1987. One of the poorest, most populous, and most harshly treated of the occupied territories, Gaza has been a scene of almost continuous contention for the past three decades. In this powerful report, Emerson allows ordinary Gazans to speak for themselves and recount stories of torture, house demolitions, imprisonments, collective punishment, and other human rights abuses that sparked the uprising.

1168 Entessar, Nader. *Kurdish Ethnonationalism.* Rienner 1992, $34.00 (1-55587-250-6). 208pp. Nonfiction.

Entessar addresses the growth of Kurdish nationalist feelings and the subsequent history of this ethnic group in the Middle East. Chapters are devoted to the Kurds' relation to and conflicts with state authorities in Iran, Turkey, and Iraq. In addition, there is a chapter on the Iran-Iraq and Gulf wars and a final chapter on the status of the Kurds within the political structures of the countries now in control of territory that historically had been Kurdistan. The book does not cover Kurdish culture per se in much detail. Nonetheless, it is a good source of the local and international political dimensions of the Kurdish issue.

1169 Fathi, Asghar, ed. *Iranian Refugees and Exiles Since Khomeini.* Illus. Mazda 1991, $16.95 (0-939214-68-7). 295pp. Nonfiction.

The editor has put together a number of papers on various facets of the experience of exile among Iranian refugees—mainly in the West—since the establishment of the Islamic Republic. The essays in this volume examine various exile communities, analyze their literature and experiences in North America, and trace the growth of a diverse Iranian-American community since the revolution.

1170 Fialka, John J. *The Hotel Warriors: Covering the Gulf War.* Frwd. by Peter Braestrup. Woodrow Wilson Center Pr. (Johns Hopkins Univ.) 1992, $9.75 (0-943875-40-4). 80pp. Nonfiction.

The author, a *Wall Street Journal* correspondent, provides a lively day-by-day account of the difficulties faced by most journalists who sought to cover the Gulf War. The title refers to the inadequacy of much of the reporting, which was not based on direct knowledge of events in the battlefield but instead was transmitted from the comforts of hotels in Riyad and Dhahran and through military briefings. The author blames the military for excessive distrust of the media, feelings that apparently stemmed from coverage of the Vietnam War, and accuses the military of obstructing attempts at independent newsgathering. Further, Fialka hints that there was collusion between the media and the Pentagon, a situation that meant that many journalists' words and pictures were never made available to the American public.

1171 Gerner, Deborah J. *One Land, Two Peoples: The Conflict over Palestine*. Illus. Westview 1994, $49.95 (0-8133-2179-4); $14.95 (0-8133-2180-8). 220pp. Nonfiction.

This is an excellent historical book, with maps, a glossary, and a list of available videos, that examines the development throughout the twentieth century of claims and counterclaims to the land known as Palestine. It offers a solid review of the ramifications of the dismantling of the Ottoman Empire following World War I, the firm convictions of Zionist Jews, and the attitudes of Palestinian Arabs, including both Muslims and Christians. The author manages to keep the book wonderfully readable, without oversimplifying the complexities of the issues involved.

1172 Giannou, Chris. *Besieged: A Doctor's Story of Life and Death in Beirut*. Illus. with photos. Interlink 1991, $29.95 (0-940793-80-6); $12.95 (0-940793-75-X). 288pp. Nonfiction.

The author, a Canadian doctor, recounts his experiences and encounters during his work in PLO-run hospitals in Beirut during the 1980s. Giannou was a witness to several assaults during his tenure—the siege of Beirut by the Israeli army in 1982, the siege of Palestinian refugee camps by Shiite groups in 1985, and attacks on the same camps by warring Palestinian factions in 1988. In addition to providing medical assistance, Giannou became acquainted with leaders of various PLO factions and members of the Shiite Hizbollah militia. Following this daring sojourn amid so much death and destruction, the author renders the story of human suffering in places that were inaccessible to most Western observers. The book includes a number of photos.

1173 Golan, Matti. *With Friends Like You: What Israelis Really Think about American Jews*. Trans. from Hebrew by Hillel Halkin. Free Pr. 1992, $22.95 (0-02-912064-0). 144pp. Nonfiction.

This book offers a rare glimpse into the little-suspected and seldom-discussed tensions between some Israelis and American Jews. Backed by a number of important Israeli politicians and written from a right-wing perspective, the author questions the credentials of American Jews who either criticize Israel or who do not provide enough support to it, offering once more the familiar argument that Jews who choose to live outside of Israel do not enjoy the same latitude to criticize it as do its Jewish inhabitants. Although the arguments are presented from an admittedly slanted perspective, some readers may enjoy the book for its many anecdotes that shed light on some dimensions of Jewish thoughts and attitudes.

1174 Graham, Douglas F. *Saudi Arabia Unveiled*. Kendall/Hunt 1991, $13.95 (0-8403-6461-X). 176pp. Nonfiction.

Written by a former reporter for the Saudi-based *Arab News*, this book provides basic and general information about diverse facets of Saudi society. Different chapters discuss such issues as politics, security, religion, culture, women, industry, and the importance of water. This is a good primer on the country, although readers who want more background information should consult other sources.

1175 Grossman, David. ***Sleeping on a Wire: Conversations with Palestinians in Israel***. Trans. from Hebrew by Haim Watzmann. Farrar 1993, $22.00 (0-374-17788-0); $10.00 (0-374-52400-9). 192pp. Nonfiction.

Continuing the framework of provocative questions and bold answers that he developed in his earlier book, *The Yellow Wind (see main entry)*, Grossman reproduces conversations with many Israeli Arabs, who constitute about one sixth of the population of Israel. Grossman is sympathetic to many of the experiences of Arabs living within the Jewish state: their treatment at the hands of the Israeli Army and domestic intelligence agents, the seizure of their land, and the exclusion of their culture from the mainstream Israeli society. On the other hand, many Arabs criticize their own society as much as they do Israel. This makes for a lively book, original in its perspective, bold in its questions, and far different from the predictable nature of much of the available writing about the Arab-Israeli conflict.

Grossman is also a highly acclaimed novelist in Israel. His first novel, translated and published in the United States as *The Smile of the Lamb* (Farrar, 1991), juxtaposes the narratives of four characters—an elderly Arab, an Israeli Jew of Iraqi descent, a military commander who is a Holocaust survivor, and a psychologist who is married to one character and is carrying on an affair with another. The novel describes one day in the lives of these people. Events are set against the backdrop of the Arab-Israeli conflict and a miscarriage of justice that raises concerns about the occupation. Another Grossman novel, *See Under: Love* (Farrar, 1989), examines the legacy of the Holocaust for the younger generation in Israel.

1176 Grossman, David. ***The Yellow Wind***. Trans. from Hebrew by Haim Watzmann. Farrar 1988, $17.95 (0-374-29345-7); Dell $11.95 (0-385-29736-X). 188pp. Nonfiction.

In a beautifully written account of his conversations with Palestinians of the occupied territories as well as with Israeli settlers, Grossman conveys everyday feelings and worries, sources of hatred and conflict, and other realities of existence. The author demonstrates the admirable and rare ability to see things from the perspective of the other side in times of war. That courageous act alone suggests that peace might one day be possible. For a description of *Sleeping on a Wire: Conversations with Palestinians in Israel*, a later book by Grossman, see the main entry.

1177 Hadawi, Sami. ***Bitter Harvest: A Modern History of Palestine.*** 4th rev. and updated ed. Illus. Interlink 1991, $29.95 (0-940793-81-4); $14.95 (0-940793-76-8). 384pp. Nonfiction.

This comprehensive history of the contemporary Palestinian problem has been published in several editions since its original appearance in 1967. The book begins with the key events of World War I: the British pledge of Arab independence, the Balfour Declaration, and the subsequent division of the Levant between Britain and France. Hadawi draws important historical distinctions between Judaism and Zionism and shows how these differences affected events in the region. The period of Jewish immigration, the establishment of Israel, and the strained Arab-Jewish relations in Palestine are covered in more detail than is found in most books on the subject. Another strength lies in the weight the author places on the refugee problem; he discusses the social conditions from which the Intifada, the Palestinian uprising, arose. The book also has specific chapters on U.S.-Israeli relations, United Nations resolutions, and the Camp David accords. Sixteen maps help to fortify the text, and numerous appendices provide the text of various historical documents.

1178 Heilman, Samuel. ***Defenders of the Faith: Inside Ultra-Orthodox Jewry.*** Illus. Schocken 1992, $27.00 (0-8052-4095-0); Pantheon $18.00 (0-8052-1007-5). 416pp. Nonfiction.

In this accessible sociological study, Heilman documents the practices, beliefs, and celebrations of separatist ultra-Orthodox Jews in Jerusalem. Heilman's observations reveal the intensity of faith among adherents and the often astounding extent of their knowledge of the Talmud. But he also shows the ambivalence of their relation to the state of Israel and to politics in general. Through its patient documentation of their everyday life and marital relations, the book humanizes ultra-Orthodox Jews without excessively romanticizing their culture.

1179 Holden, David, and Richard Johns. ***The House of Saud: The Rise and Rule of the Most Powerful Dynasty in the Arab World.*** Holt 1981. o.p. Nonfiction.

Although somewhat dated, this book remains one of the best primers on the royal Saudi family and its long relation to the United States. The authors' highly readable account credits the royal family with establishing stable rule and pursuing a friendly policy toward the United States. At the same time, the book describes the family's corruption and its fanatic religious conservatism.

1180 Hourani, Albert. ***A History of the Arab Peoples.*** Illus. Harvard Univ. Pr. 1991, $27.50 (0-674-39565-4); Warner $14.99 (0-446-39392-4). 576pp. Nonfiction.

Albert Hourani, who was born in south Lebanon, is one of the leading historians of the Arabs in the United States. In this book, which became an instant best-seller upon publication, Hourani's scholarly skills and breadth of knowledge render accessible almost fifteen centuries of Arab history. The strengths of the book, beyond its graceful style, are many. The author discusses important urban issues, demonstrates how history still affects the present, and devotes attention to cultural and economic forces while downplaying political issues. The book's completeness and thoughtful presentation make it a rare treasure in its genre, a long-overdue successor to Philip Hitti's history of the Arabs, which was published in the 1930s.

1181 Khalidi, Walid. ***Before Their Diaspora: A Photographic History of the Palestinians, 1876–1948.*** Rev. ed. Illus. with photos by the author. Institute for Palestine Studies 1991, $49.00 (0-88728-219-9); $29.00 (0-88728-228-8). 351pp. Nonfiction.

This interesting book by a distinguished Middle East historian unearths many old photographs that document, more than any words could, the lives of Palestinians before the establishment of Israel in 1948. The visual record is deeply humane and captivating, devoid of the usual bitterness and recriminations commonly found in works of this kind. This book, combined with Said and Mohr's *After the Last Sky (see main entry)*, provides a full visual history of the Palestinians in the twentieth century.

Kocturk, Tahire. *A Matter of Honour: Experiences of Turkish Women Immigrants.*
See entry 939.

1182 Kreyenbroek, Philip G., and Stefan Sperl, eds. *The Kurds: A Contemporary Overview*. Routledge 1991, $47.50 (0-415-07265-4). 224pp. Nonfiction.

The clearly written essays in this book provide a great deal of information about the Kurds throughout history and up to the present. The reader learns that, although the Sunni form of Islam predominates, the twenty million Kurds are in fact a diverse cultural entity, with four distinct dialects and many religions. The political history of the Kurds is detailed as well, showing the role played by the allied powers after World War I, in collusion with nationalist Turkey, in denying Kurdish self-determination and dividing their territory among Turkey, Iran, Iraq, Syria, and the Soviet Union. Some essays explore the history of Kurdish conflict with the various states of the region, and others discuss intra-Kurdish conflicts and their present status. The book includes a comparative account on human rights in various countries.

1183 Kyle, Keith. *Suez*. St. Martin 1991, $35.00 (0-312-06509-4); $21.95 (0-312-08422-6). 672pp. Nonfiction.

In 1956, a tripartite alliance of Britain, France, and Israel attacked Egypt. The mission was to regain control over the Suez Canal, an essential shipping lane that the Egyptian government had nationalized. That action precipitated an international crisis, one that continued until massive pressure from the United States and the threat of Soviet intervention forced the alliance powers to withdraw. That crisis marked the beginning of U.S. influence and, ultimately, the decline of British and French colonial power in the region. Kyle draws on declassified documents to reconstruct the chain of events that led to the crisis and its aftermath. In the process, he reveals the machinations of the diplomatic world and shows how government officials—operating freely because the public was largely unaware of events—managed to miscalculate the situation, with sometimes fatal consequences.

1184 Lustick, Ian S., and Barry Rubin, eds. *Critical Essays on Israeli Society, Politics, and Culture*. State Univ. of New York Pr. 1991, $49.50 (0-7914-0646-6); $16.95 (0-7914-0647-4). 205pp. Nonfiction.

This collection of reviews and articles offers a synopsis of different ways of seeing Israeli society and politics from Israeli perspectives. These include revisionist accounts of the founding of Israel, the origin of the Palestinian refugee problem, public opinion regarding Israel and the United States, Israeli leadership, and questions about democracy. Although the articles are not uniformly accessible to all kinds of readers, they present good recaps of the major issues.

1185 MacArthur, John R. *Second Front: Censorship and Propaganda in the Gulf War.* Frwd. by Ben Bagdikian. Hill & Wang 1992, $20.00 (0-8090-8517-8); Univ. of California Pr. $10.00 (0-520-08398-9). 224pp. Nonfiction.

This history of the Gulf War was written by a researcher and journalist who had to deal with propaganda and censorship in his attempt to gather information on the course of the war and the motives behind it. In particular, the author demonstrates a great deal of knowledge about connections between the media and policy makers at every level. He also describes the adjustments that reporters had to make in order to deal with the dearth of uncensored news and plethora of "official" interpretations of events. In the process, he explains how a uniform public understanding of the war, its causes, and its course came to be.

1186 Mauger, Thierry. *The Bedouins of Arabia.* Illus. Routledge 1990, $45.00 (0-7103-0366-1). 139pp. Nonfiction.

This beautiful book is the fruit of a rich photographic journey into the Empty Quarter (*Ar-Rub' Al-Khali*) in southeastern Arabia, one of the most formidable deserts on Earth. In pictures and text, the book seeks to document the faces and lifestyle of the nomadic Arabs known as Bedouins. The text accompanying the color pictures conveys the spirit of the author's encounters with Bedouins and explains the recent changes in their lifestyle. In addition, the pictures describe the vital elements of Bedouin existence, such as natural scenes, animals, and the adaptation to modern times.

1187 Mernissi, Fatima. *Beyond the Veil: Male-Female Dynamics in Modern Muslim Society.* Rev. ed. Indiana Univ. Pr. 1987, $25.00 (0-253-31162-4); $8.95 (0-253-20423-2). 224pp. Nonfiction.

This is one of the most renowned books by Mernissi, who is a prominent Muslim feminist. Mernissi refutes the argument that Islam opposes equality of the sexes. Like other critics, including some males, she makes the case that equality of human potential is one of the fundamental principles, the essence, of Islam. Acknowledging that inequality is pervasive in many Muslim countries, the author goes on to blame specific social institutions and official interpretations of Islam. She shows that such institutions repress women not because of any belief in their inferiority, but rather due to a fear of what she calls "social chaos."

1188 Minns, Amina, and Nadia Hijab. *Citizens Apart: A Portrait of the Palestinians in Israel.* St. Martin 1990, $34.50 (0-685-38700-3). 250pp. Nonfiction.

The book is based on field reporting by the authors, conducted between 1987 and 1989, in their effort to document the experiences and expectations of the Palestinians, who constitute nearly one sixth of the population of Israel. The book describes today's efforts by grassroots organizations to reverse a long history of official neglect and discrimination against Israeli Arabs. The authors provide a readable account of the confiscations of Arab land since 1948. They also describe the official red tape that has effectively prevented Arab towns and villages from developing and that has denied them much-needed social services, thereby relegating Arabs to second-class citizenship. Another problem they identify is the prohibition against teaching Arab culture and heritage in schools. The solutions proposed by the authors are geared toward the creation of a bicultural state that would treat all its citizens with greater equality.

1189 Mottahedeh, Roy. *The Mantle of the Prophet: Religion and Politics in Iran.* Pantheon 1986, $14.95 (0-394-74865-4). 416pp. Nonfiction.

One of the most accessible works about Iranian politics, culture, and intellectual life, Mottahedeh's book is a compassionate treatise and a reference work at the same time. The author offers a good account of the views, outlooks, and intellectual traditions of the *ulama*, or religious authorities. A substantial portion of the book is devoted to the biography and thought of the mullah Ali Hashemi, as well as to the lives of key figures in Iranian intellectual history, such as Ibn Sina and Rumi in the classical age of Islam, and Musaddiq, Al-e Ahmad, and Khomeini in modern times. The book is a reliable source on the doctrines and practices of Shiite clerics. Notably, the author describes Khomeini's particular interpretation of Islam as a reaction to such external factors as colonialism and foreign intervention.

1190 Muslih, Muhammed, and Augustus R. Norton. *Political Tides in the Arab World.* Illus. Foreign Policy Association 1992, $5.95 (0-87124-142-0). 72pp. Nonfiction.

This short volume introduces a number of major themes in the recent history of the Arab world, such as twentieth-century history, governmental systems in seven Arab states, the Gulf crisis, and other issues. Its value consists in a surprisingly fruitful combination of broad scope and brevity. The book concludes with an annotated reading list.

1191 Al-Naqeeb, Khaldoun H. *Society and State in the Gulf and Arab Peninsula.* Routledge 1991, $65.00 (0-415-04162-7). 240pp. Nonfiction.

Though written before the Gulf War of 1991, Al-Naqeeb's book, steeped as it is in history, is still the best one available in English for anyone interested in understanding the Gulf region, its politics, and its societies. The author, a professor at Kuwait University, tells how, from the sixteenth century to the present, Western powers—particularly Britain—became increasing involved in the affairs of the region. He shows that such intervention put an end to a natural cycle of indigenous tribal migrations and manipulated tribal conflicts. One critical consequence of foreign intervention was that those chiefs who agreed to sign treaties with Britain in the nineteenth century were rewarded with legitimacy and protection. Further institutional developments after World War I resulted in the redrawn borders, the prevention of peoples' movements, and the increase in political control. Al-Naqeeb's main thesis is that this system, to which foreign protection and authoritarian rule are central, remained in place after the discovery of oil. This highly recommended book is well written, richly documented, and infinitely informative about a region that is so important yet about which so little is known.

1192 Nassar, Jamal R. ***The Palestine Liberation Organization: From Armed Struggle to the Declaration of Independence***. Illus. Greenwood 1991, $49.95 (0-275-93779-8). 256pp. Nonfiction.

Nassar writes about the history and structure of the PLO with clarity and authority. Emerging from Palestinian history and the unique predicament of the Palestinian people, the PLO came to play a significant role in regional and international politics. In the process, it listed a number of accomplishments and a number of failures as well. Nassar traces the evolution of the PLO into a form of quasi-government in exile and outlines the structures of its policy-making and legislative bodies. He pays specific attention to the important sessions of the Palestine National Council, which Palestinians commonly consider a "parliament in exile." The author also provides a clear account of the history and nature of infighting within the organization, its relationships with various Arab governments, and its outreach to the international community.

1193 Ovendale, Ritchie. ***Britain, the United States, and the End of the Palestine Mandate, 1942–1948***. Boydell 1989, $71.00 (0-86193-214-5). 344pp. Nonfiction.

Ovendale, a respected historian of the Middle East, reconstructs in detail the role that Anglo-American diplomacy played in the creation of Israel in 1948. The author uses declassified documents as well as published sources to document the path of that diplomacy. Part of this story involves a coalition in the United States between Zionists, Anglo-Saxon Protestants, and religious organizations—some of whom were motivated partly by religious beliefs and partly by anti-Semitism—to channel European Jews into Palestine, mainly by closing off their escape route to the United States. The author also explores the details of the decisive (and no longer so secret) negotiations between Zionist leaders and king Abdullah of Jordan on the eve of the British withdrawal from Palestine. Overall, the book is a riveting, well-researched, and nonjudgmental account of the daily machinations of policy making at a crucial point in Middle Eastern history. The author has also written a book titled *The Origins of the Arab-Israeli Wars (see main entry)*.

1194 Ovendale, Ritchie. ***The Origins of the Arab-Israeli Wars***. 2nd ed. Longman 1991, $23.95 (0-582-06369-8). 264pp. Nonfiction.

This second, updated edition of Ovendale's book came out after the first edition, published in 1984, went through seven printings in as many years. Meticulously researched, even-handed, and well presented, this is perhaps the best available source in English about the many Arab-Israeli wars. The book is also distinguished by the fact that, unlike many military historians, Ovendale goes beyond the battlefield to look at the cultural and broader historical factors contributing to tensions. One especially important section discusses the role of the United States. Ovendale is also the author of *Britain, the United States, and the End of the Palestine Mandate, 1942–1948 (see main entry)*.

1195 Oz, Amos. *In the Land of Israel.* Harcourt 1993, $11.95 (0-15-648114-6). 272pp. Nonfiction.

Amos Oz is one of Israel's leading novelists and an activist in the Peace Now movement, which advocates mutual recognition and reconciliation between Jews and Palestinians. In 1982, following Israel's invasion of Lebanon, Oz traveled through Israel and the occupied territories to discuss Israel's past and future with fellow peace activists, militant Jewish settlers on the West Bank, and Palestinians. This book brings together Oz's accounts, previously published in an Israeli magazine, of his travels and conversations.

The Palestinians with whom Oz spoke are moderates who advocate the kind of mutual recognition between Israel and the Palestine Liberation Organization that eventually occurred in 1993. They also support a two-state solution to the fight between Jews and Arabs for control of their shared homeland. The peace activists, along with elderly pioneers who settled in Israel decades before its independence in 1948, share an antipathy toward both the "soft," "cosmopolitan" Israelis—who they feel have forgotten the hard past and yearn only for normalcy—and the Bible-quoting members of Gush Emmunim, who want to colonize the entire West Bank and expel the Palestinian Arabs who live there. Oz allows the religious settlers and Orthodox students in Jerusalem to speak for themselves, exposing their hatred of nonreligious Jews and Arabs alike. These interviews expose the fierce divisions among Jews that persist to this day and explore the possibilities for reconciliation between Jews and Arabs.   RL

1196 Pipes, Daniel. *Greater Syria: The History of an Ambition.* Oxford Univ. Pr. 1990, $35.00 (0-19-506021-0); $16.95 (0-19-506022-9). 256pp. Nonfiction.

This unique book traces the events after World War I that led to the division of greater Syria into the nations of Syria, Lebanon, Jordan, and Palestine. Much of the book is dedicated to proving the thesis that Syrian policy, especially since 1974, can be understood as driven by the ambition, not always publicly expressed or acknowledged, to reunify the historic region.

1197 Rahman, Fazlur. *Islam.* 2nd ed. Univ. of Chicago Pr. 1979, $11.95 (0-226-70281-2). Nonfiction.

This is perhaps the best book by the late Fazlur Rahman, who was one of the world's most renowned authorities on Islam. Here, fourteen centuries of Islamic teaching and history are woven together in a concise and thoughtful work. The author discusses such important themes as Mohammed's role in Islam; the Koran; Islamic rituals, or *sunna*; the status of the recorded sayings of the prophet (*hadith*); and Islamic law and theology. He also surveys the growth of various Islamic sects and schools of thought, devoting particular attention to the Sufis.

1198 Rahman, Habib U. *A Chronology of Islamic History, 570-1000 C.E.* Macmillan 1989, $45.00 (0-8161-9067-4). 256pp. Nonfiction.

This book, a handy and detailed survey of the first four centuries of Islam, presents its material in a straightforward, if somewhat dry, manner. Written from a traditional Islamic point of view, the book is adequate for readers with little or no knowledge of that period.

533

THE MIDDLE EAST

Robinson, Francis. *Atlas of the Islamic World Since 1500*.
See entry 1421.

1199 Rodinson, Maxime. *The Arabs*. Trans. from French by Arthur Goldhammer. Illus. Univ. of Chicago Pr. 1981, $14.00 (0-226-72355-0); $10.95 (0-226-72356-9). 208pp. Nonfiction.

This book, largely factual but sometimes impressionistic, is based on the author's lifetime of study of the Arabs and provides a much-needed general look at Arab culture, politics, and history up to the contemporary period. The author's unparalleled knowledge of the Middle East is coupled with many insights into Arab society, making this book a joy to read. Rodinson is also the author of *Israel and the Arabs (see main entry)*.

1200 Rodinson, Maxime. *Israel and the Arabs*. Trans. from French by Michael Perl and Brian Pearce. Viking 1982. o.p. Nonfiction.

This book by a prominent French orientalist adds a different perspective of the Arab-Israeli conflict. Here, Rodinson brings to bear his immense knowledge of the history and internal dynamics of Middle Eastern societies. In this straightforward book, Rodinson places into context the conflict over Israel and Palestine in terms of colonial history and in light of the changing ambitions of the Arab states. In his assessment, the author blames both sides for initiating and perpetuating what has become the most entrenched territorial conflict in modern times. Rodinson is also the author of *The Arabs (see main entry)*.

1201 Rouchdy, Aleya, ed. *The Arabic Language in America*. Wayne State Univ. Pr. 1992, $44.95 (0-8143-2283-2); $19.95 (0-8143-2284-0). 345pp. Nonfiction.

This book contains fourteen chapters on the use, teaching, and prospects of the Arabic language in the United States and on alternative approaches to teaching, including the use of computers. The essays are grouped under three major headings: "Language Contact and Language Change," "The Use of Arabic: Aspects and Attitudes," and "Teaching and Learning." This is a good source for learning, not just about the use of Arabic in the United States, but about lives of Arab Americans as well, such as the large Arab community in Cleveland. The author provides insight into the difficulties and potential involved in the teaching and learning of this critical but undertaught language.

1202 Said, Edward W. *After the Last Sky: Palestinian Lives*. Illus. with photos by Jean Mohr. Pantheon 1986, $20.00 (0-394-74469-1). 174pp. Essays.

In this collaboration between a renowned literary critic and an accomplished photographer, the everyday reality of the Palestinians and their history are presented through images of faces and landscapes. The photographs and the text complement each other to present the human dimension of a people who are largely misunderstood in the West. The main chapters of the book are organized around large themes of space and time, such as "States," "Interiors," "Emergence," and "Past and Future." A short introduction discusses Palestinian ways of life, and a postscript addresses the consequences for the Palestinians of the Israeli invasion of Lebanon in 1982.

1203 Said, Edward W. *Covering Islam*. Pantheon 1981, $12.00 (0-394-74808-5). 192pp. Nonfiction.

It is unfortunate that this book continues to be as relevant today as it was upon its original publication a decade and a half ago. Largely based on the media coverage of the American hostages in Iran from 1979 to 1980, the book shows how and why the media distorts Islam and events in the Middle East for the American public. The author notes that most American journalists in the region have little training in the languages, traditions, or history of the countries they are covering. Instead, they often rely on those academic experts who are most likely to confirm their biases. He argues, too, that the American media play into the hands of U.S. policy makers when it comes to Muslims and Arabs. Further, he accuses the media of resorting too often to generalizations and oversimplifications—some of which, he says, are not, entirely innocent, because in many instances the objective is not to report on the cultures and peoples of the region but on events deemed detrimental to U.S. interests. This creates a general and self-perpetuating state of ignorance about the Muslims, which in turn makes it easy for policy makers in this country to demonize them and wage war against them whenever they see fit. They can do so, Said says, without fear of censure by a public that continues to be hopelessly undereducated about Islam and the people who practice its teachings.

1204 Schimmel, Annemarie. *Islam: An Introduction*. State Univ. of New York Pr. 1992, $29.50 (0-7914-1327-6); $9.95 (0-7914-1328-4). 166pp. Nonfiction.

This is a short, lively, and well-written introduction to the religion of Islam. Although organized in a rather conventional way, it manages to look at Islam from a number of relevant perspectives. In an even-handed manner, it explains the differences between the various Islamic sects, schools, and practices.

1205 Segev, Tom. *The Seventh Million: Israel Confronts the Holocaust*. Trans. from Hebrew by Haim Watzman. Hill & Wang 1993, $27.50 (0-8090-8563-1). 580pp. Nonfiction.

This relatively large book provides a history of the Holocaust's effects on contemporary Israeli psyche and politics. The author argues that, from its inception in the nineteenth century, Zionism had Eurocentric roots and biases, which only intensified the significance of everything that happened in the European scene in the twentieth century. To support his argument, he accounts for the dealings with Germany that resulted in the so-called "transfer" agreement. The author comments on a number of episodes after the establishment of Israel in which the Holocaust was used as an educational tool for the new generation and as an element to further legitimize the Jewish state.

1206 Shaaban, Bouthaina. ***Both Right and Left Handed: Arab Women Talk about Their Lives***. Indiana Univ. Pr. 1991, $35.00 (0-253-35189-8); $12.95 (0-253-20688-X). 252pp. Nonfiction.

This book, highly acclaimed for its courage and scope, is the most remarkable book about Arab women to appear in English and a must-read for anyone seeking further knowledge about Arab women that transcends commonly held stereotypes. The editor has collected a large number of interviews, spanning the entire Arab world and all levels of society. Her comments and her writing style are as engaging as the interviews themselves. In addition to describing their expected roles in society, the women tell how they adjust to and fulfill such roles. Encouraged by the author, they sometimes explore taboo sexual subjects, providing a fascinating glimpse of the Arab way of life.

1207 Sifry, Micah, and Christopher Cerf., eds., ***The Gulf War Reader: History, Documents, Opinions***. Random 1991, $15.00 (0-8129-1947-5). 326pp. Nonfiction.

This collection strives to offer a balanced presentation of opinions about the origins and consequences of the Gulf War. The antiwar camp is represented in essays by Joe Stark and Martha Wegner, Noam Chomsky, Edward Said, Michael Klare, and Rashid Khalidi, while the prowar camp is represented through essays and statements by George Bush, Henry Kissinger, A. M. Rosenthal, and Charles Krauthammer. This is a particularly good source for advanced high school students as well as for introductory courses on the college level.

1208 Timerman, Jacobo. ***The Longest War: Israel in Lebanon***. Trans. from Spanish by Miguel Acoca. Random 1983, $11.95 (0-394-53022-5); $4.95 (0-394-71471-7). 192pp. Nonfiction.

Timerman's work is a critical commentary on the Israeli invasion of Lebanon in 1982, during which the Israeli army was bogged down in a long siege of Beirut. Timerman's reflections are important in that they represent a pacifist sentiment and a widespread opposition to the war in Israel at the time.

The author is best known for his autobiographical account of imprisonment in his native Argentina, *Prisoner Without a Name, Cell Without a Number (see main entry)*. Timerman emigrated to Israel in 1979; because of his stand against the Israeli invasion, he was vilified and harassed; eventually, he returned to Argentina.

1209 Toubia, Nahid, ed. ***Women of the Arab World: The Coming Challenge***. Humanities Pr. 1988. o.p. Essays.

This collection of essays by women activists and scholars in the Arab world emerged from an Arab women's conference in Cairo in 1986. Among the wide-ranging issues addressed are the living conditions of women in Arab countries, problems of inequality, and the relation of women's issues to larger questions of human rights.

1210 Walker, Christopher J. *Armenia: The Survival of a Nation.* 2nd rev. ed. St. Martin 1990, $35.00 (0-312-04230-2). 500pp. Nonfiction.

In this book, perhaps the most complete history of Armenia and the Armenians to appear in English, Walker depicts the relationship of the Armenians to various empires throughout the ages, illustrating the internal developments within Armenian society in the process. The 1990 edition includes new materials to bring the book up to date in light of such developments as perestroika, the rebirth of modern independent Armenia, and the region's ongoing conflict with Azerbaijan over the territory known as the Karabagh.

1211 Weir, Shelagh. *Palestinian Costume.* Illus. Univ. of Texas Pr. 1989, $45.00 (0-292-76514-2). 288pp. Nonfiction.

This survey of Palestinian costume includes some one hundred black-and-white photographs along with a substantial text. Weir explains the historical transformations of Palestinian traditional costume in various regions, the relationship of dress to nationalism, differences between Bedouin and peasant costumes, and regional variations in embroidery. The study of costume not only provides a feast for the eyes, it also serves as a unique point of entry into a more general discussion of the cultural history of the Palestinians.

1212 White, Patrick. *Let Us Be Free: A Narrative Before and During the Intifada.* Illus. Kingston 1989, $19.95 (0-940670-32-1); $12.95 (0-940670-35-6). 150pp. Nonfiction.

In this short book written while he was teaching at Bethlehem University in the West Bank, White seeks to explore the human and personal dimensions of the Palestinian uprising known as the Intifada. Going above and beyond the political generalities and slogans, he tells stories, reports his impressions, and records events during a unique moment in time, as the attitudes and life goals of his friends and acquaintances metamorphosed during the general upheaval. Unlike other commentators, who visited the occupied territories only after the fact, White had lived in the area prior to the Intifada and continued living in it afterwards. Besides its commentary on Palestinian lives, expectations, and experiences, the book includes many digressions on the possibilities of peace and explores issues of concern to Israelis.

BIOGRAPHY

1213 Avnery, Uri. *My Friend, the Enemy.* Lawrence Hill 1987, $12.95 (0-88208-213-2). 320pp. Autobiography.

The author, a peace activist in Israel, offers the story of his contacts with a number of PLO figures since 1973. These contacts culminated in his meeting with Yasir Arafat in Beirut in 1982 as the Israeli army lay siege to the city. In this and other meetings, Avnery sought to convince the PLO leadership to undertake a number of concessions that would, in theory, make the work of the peace camp in Israel somewhat easier. The types of concessions Avnery sought indeed were later placed on the negotiating table, and they bore fruit in the 1993 peace talks between Israel and the PLO.

1214 Eban, Abba. *Abba Eban: An Autobiography.* Random 1977. o.p. Autobiography.

Abba Eban was a central figure in Israeli politics and government during the 1960s and 1970s. In his capacity as foreign minister from 1966 to 1974, he represented Israel before the world during and after the 1967 and 1973 wars, negotiating the ceasefire and disengagement with Egypt in 1974. After leaving public office that year, Eban continued to travel the world as a spokesman for Israel. His books, *My People* (Behrman House, 1968) and *My Country* (o.p., 1972) are widely read portrayals of the emergence of Israel as both a haven for Jews and a dynamic twentieth-century nation.

Eban's autobiography is a well-written account of the life of one of the proud Zionists who helped establish Israel as a viable nation. Eban recounts his childhood as an assimilated Jew in England, his developing Zionist beliefs, his diplomatic activities as Israel's first representative at the United Nations, and his subsequent rise to high office in Israel. Eban presents himself and his nation as under constant siege from implacable and brutal Arab enemies. Israel survived, he says, due to the selfless dedication of the many Jews who were determined to create and preserve a nation for themselves in the land of their ancestors. His attitude, understandably biased, reflects the beliefs of most Zionists and Israelis of that time. Although one may criticize his views and his statements about the Arabs, they must be read for a complete understanding of the political turmoil in the Middle East. RL

1215 Hart, Alan. *Arafat: A Political Biography.* Indiana Univ. Pr. 1989, $39.95 (0-253-32711-3); $18.95 (0-253-20516-6). 560pp. Biography.

This generally reliable biography of the Palestinian leader is based largely on the author's interviews with Arafat and with other major figures in the PLO. Hart's journalistic skills, sense of humor, and knowledge of recent history make for smooth reading. The author has managed to avoid the pitfalls of other biographies, which are either written without a personal knowledge of the person involved or else from a perspective that often seems too flattering.

1216 Mattar, Philip. *The Mufti of Jerusalem.* Rev. ed. Columbia Univ. Pr. 1991, $14.50 (0-231-06463-2). 176pp. Biography.

Amin Al-Husayni, who lived from 1895 to 1974, was the highest Muslim scholarly authority (or *mufti*) and the most prominent Palestinian leader during the period that culminated in the establishment of the state of Israel and the commencement of the Palestinian diaspora in 1948. In this biography, the author offers a balanced account of the Mufti's life and role. He detects a shift around 1936, when the Mufti fled into exile and began a policy toward the authorities who carried out the British mandate that was marked by misguided rigidity. That position, the author argues, was as calamitous to the Palestinians as was the Mufti's earlier policy toward the British, which was marked by too much collaboration and caution. These critical assessments, however, still allow the author to draw a sympathetic picture of the man and place him in the context of his times.

1217 Musaddiq, Muhammad. ***Musaddiq's Memoirs***. Trans. from Persian and with an Intro. by S. H. Amin and Homa Katouzian. JEBHE 1988. o.p. Autobiography.

When Khomeini came to power in Iran in 1979, many observers saw the event in a larger historical context that went back to the attempt made by nationalist Iranians in 1953 to rescue their country from the grip of Western oil concerns and the ex-colonial masters. That attempt was led by Musaddiq, Iran's liberal nationalist prime minister, who was overthrown in a well-orchestrated plot involving the Shah, the Iranian military, and the CIA. In these memoirs, Musaddiq recounts the events leading to his downfall, emphasizing palace machinations and external conspiracies. He does not express a sense of glory about his mission, nor does he immodestly claim a place in history. Rather, his story reveals the human dilemma faced by an ordinary member of an established Iranian family, a man whose growing popularity derived from the tremendously challenging task he set for himself. Even after accounting for the biases and deletions that invariably accompany autobiographical writings, these memoirs offer some of the best history of that decisive juncture in modern Iranian history. They have a great deal to say about the political structure of the elites in Iran, which the Shah ultimately used to augment his own power. This book is also an important document on the beginning of the modern involvement of the United States in Iran's internal affairs. The excellent introduction puts many of these themes and issues into perspective.

1218 Renda, Gunsel, and C. Max Kortepeter. ***The Transformation of Turkish Culture: The Ataturk Legacy***. Kingston Pr. 1986. o.p. Biography.

In this book of essays, various Turkish commentators explore the changes in different spheres of Turkish culture during the 1920s and after, following the collapse of the Ottoman Empire and the subsequent founding of the modern Turkish republic by Kemal Ataturk. The authors comment on changes in areas such as opera and ballet, language, film, sculpture, literature, mass media, music, the press, painting, drama, and architecture. Throughout the essays, the authors strive to highlight Ataturk's opinions and role in these changes.

1219 Rodinson, Maxime. ***Muhammad***. Trans. from French by Anne Carter. Pantheon 1980. o.p. Biography.

In retelling the life story of Mohammed, the founder of Islam, through a very readable and fluent style, Rodinson's book strives to correct many misconceptions. At the same time, the author provides a good account of the growth of the Koran and of its teachings, which he connects to various stages of Mohammed's life. The author delves occasionally into psychological explanations and devotes considerable attention to the prophet's political and tribal activities, as well as to his marital and sexual life.

Scholem, Gershom Gerhard. ***From Berlin to Jerusalem: Memories of My Youth***.
See entry 982.

11

AFRICA

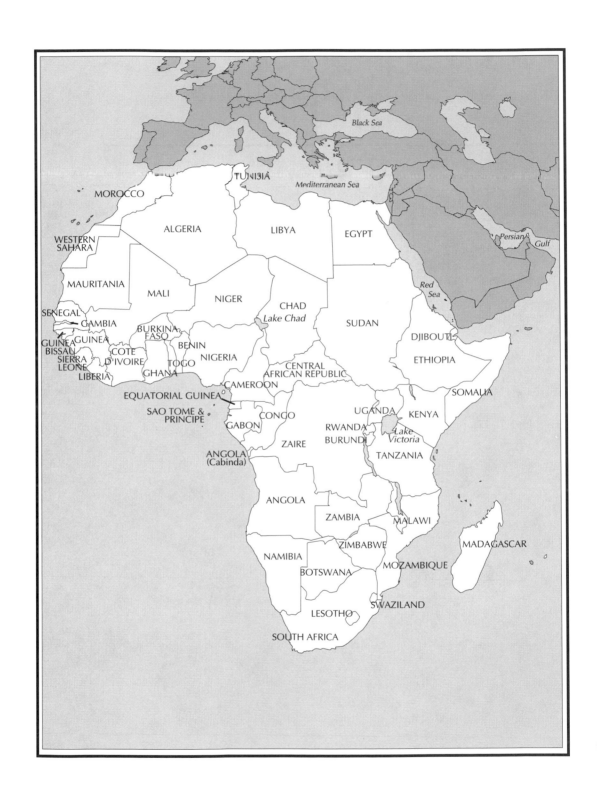

11

AFRICA

by Brenda Randolph, Ruby Bell-Gam,
Robert Cummings, and Razia Nanji

Africa, the world's second largest continent, is a vast and diverse land. The United States, Europe, India, China, Argentina, and New Zealand could all comfortably fit within its borders. Africa contains huge deserts, craggy mountain ranges, and varying climatic zones. The popular image of Africa as a vast, hot "jungle" is grossly inaccurate. Africa has fewer rain forests than South America or Asia, and they cover only a small percentage of the land. Most of Africa is savanna woodlands and grasslands that support a rich variety of plant and animal life. Below the ground lies a dazzling array of valuable minerals and other natural resources.

Africa's peoples also reflect the continent's diversity. They speak approximately one thousand languages, live in more than fifty countries, represent a broad range of ethnic groups, and pursue various lifestyles. Their history is the oldest in the world. Human life began in Africa, many of the basic features of human culture developed there, and the continent is the site of several of the world's oldest and most successful societies.

Africa's immense size, diversity, and long history are often ignored in Western literature. Myths and stereotypes inherited from the period of the European slave trade continue to dominate Western perceptions of Africa. Recent tragedies involving drought, famine, and war have added to the distorted image of Africa in the West. In her book *Africa's Media Image*, Beverly Hawk characterizes press coverage of Africa in the United States as merely a collection of Western metaphors created and shaped to confirm stereotypes of Africa that Americans already hold.

The books recommended in this chapter provide a more balanced view of Africa. In selecting titles for inclusion, we placed special emphasis on books that provide African perspectives of events and issues. Excellent scholarship, the significance of a work within a body of literature, and readability were primary in the selection process. Diversity of opinion was another important criterion. Titles are drawn primarily from history, the social sciences, literature, and biography. All are original English-language titles or translations. Classic titles have been included as well as newer works that reviewers and scholars have found exceptional. A few out-of-print classics are noted, but the bulk of the titles are still in print and easily available from U.S. publishers. We have also included outstanding books available from African publishing houses. (These titles can be obtained with U.S. dollars from African Books Collective, a company in England that represents African publishers; the address is The Jam Factory, 27 Park End St., Oxford OX1 lHU, England.)

The titles cited in this chapter represent a wide range of topics and subjects. To clarify and illuminate important commonalities and trends, this introduction will highlight titles within the following thematic headings: Human Origins in Africa; Ancient Africa; Africans in the Diaspora; Enslaved Africans; Conquest and Colonization; Independence and Neocolonialism; and New Directions. Publishing information is provided for titles that are mentioned in passing but that do not appear in the annotated list.

Human Origins in Africa

One of the most important themes to emerge in the literature on Africa is the continent's role in the evolution of human life. Skeletal remains unearthed in eastern and southern Africa indicate that human life originated in Africa millions of years ago. In recent years, new dating techniques and DNA evidence have added weight to the "out-of-Africa" hypothesis that describes Africa not only as the birthplace of hominids (early human forms) but as the first home of our own kind, *Homo sapiens sapiens*.

Today, virtually every general history text on Africa provides information on human evolution in Africa. A good overview of recent research can be found in Brian Fagan's in-depth but highly readable book *Journey from Eden: The People of Our World* (Thames & Hudson, 1990). He reviews both the "out-of-Africa" theory of human evolution and the competing "candelabra" theory. The latter confirms Africa as the home of early humans but describes a multiregional origin for *Homo sapiens sapiens*.

Ancient Africa

Early humans occupied Africa for thousands of years, developing knowledge and skills. As a natural consequence, some of the world's first highly centralized societies arose on the continent. Egypt was one of the first of these societies. It emerged about 5,000 B.C. and lasted until 332 B.C. The knowledge accumulated by ancient Egyptians led to achievements in various fields, including medicine, agriculture, religion, science, engineering, and architecture. This knowledge stimulated and expanded the thinking of individuals and groups within Africa and beyond.

In recent years there has been a resurgence of the acrimonious debate concerning the ethnic identity of ancient Egyptians. The debate first arose in the nineteenth and early twentieth centuries. At that time some Western-trained Egyptologists held the view that ancient Egyptians were dark-skinned whites and that Egyptian civilization was more closely linked to Mediterranean and Asian countries than it was to societies in Africa. Africans in the Americas were prominent in early efforts to demonstrate the African origins of Egypt. Martin R. Delany, Edward Blyden, and W.E.B. Du Bois were early defenders of an African Egypt. Du Bois, for example, discussed the issue in *Black Folks Then and Now: An Essay in the History and Sociology of the Negro Race* (Kraus, 1975). In more recent times, the subject has been tackled in such books as *The Destruction of Black Civilization* by Chancellor Williams, *Stolen*

Legacy by George James, *Black Man of the Nile and His Family* by Yosef Ben-Jochannan, *Afrocentricity* by Molefi Asante, and *The Golden Age of the Moors* by Ivan van Sertima, all reviewed in this chapter. One of the most definitive studies of the topic has come from Africa. In the 1970s and 1980s, Senegalese scholar Cheikh Anta Diop emerged as the primary proponent of a "Negro" Egypt. He detailed his theories in *African Origin of Civilization: Myth or Reality*. (His findings are the subject of vigorous debate. See, for example, Ronald Oliver, "The African Rediscovery of Africa" in the *Times Literary Supplement* [March 20, 1981: 29].)

Of course, interest in Africa's past extends beyond ancient Egypt and beyond a narrow focus on centralized societies. British scholar Basil Davidson has made a major contribution to popular knowledge of a broad range of African societies in his numerous articles and books, such as *African Civilization Revisited*. Of great interest are the growing number of works on precolonial African history that are being produced by indigenous African scholars, such as Elizabeth Isichei, D. T. Niane, L. D. Ngcongco, and B. A. Ogot, to name a few. One of the most important of these books, reviewed in this chapter, is *The Africans: A Triple Heritage* by Ali Mazrui.

Africans in the Diaspora

As noted above, Africans in the Americas were prominent in early efforts to correct distortions about African history. Black scholars responded to a barrage of myths and pseudoscientific theories about black inferiority promulgated by some Western academics. In *A Study of History* (Oxford Univ. Pr., 1939), for example, Arnold Toynbee claimed that Africa and the black "race" had produced no great civilizations. In defending Africa, vindicationist scholars often emphasized the great kingdoms of Africa. Less attention was paid to small-scale decentralized African societies, many of which were just as successful as the great states and that typically were more egalitarian and peaceful.

Vindicationists also worked to demonstrate the ways African culture was retained and expressed in American culture. In *Africanisms in the Gullah Dialect* (Ayer, 1969), Lorenzo Turner identified numerous African words and phrases in the Gullah dialect of blacks from the Sea Islands of Georgia. Melville Herskovits, a white anthropologist and author of *The Myth of the Negro Past* (Beacon, 1941), uncovered a rich heritage of Africanisms in American religious and social life. More recently, Joseph E. Holloway and other contemporary scholars have continued the Turner-Herskovits tradition in a recently published volume entitled *Africanisms in American Culture (see main entry)*.

One of the most persistent preoccupations of Africans in the American diaspora has been the desire to return to Africa. Edward W. Blyden and the Rev. Alexander Crummel were prominent figures in early repatriation efforts. The work of these and other Pan-Africanists is described in *Global Dimensions of the African Diaspora*, edited by Joseph Harris, and *The African Diaspora*, edited by Martin Kilson and Robert Rotberg (Books on Demand, 1976). In his thought-provoking book *The Invention of Africa*, Zairean philosopher V. Y. Mudimbe discusses Edward Blyden at length, describing his Pan-African goals as a quixotic mix of paternalism and black nationalism. Sylvia Jacobs reaches similar conclusions about diasporan blacks in *Black Americans and the Missionary Movement in Africa*. As these scholars point out, the development plans of many diasporan blacks revealed a lack of knowledge about Africa and often smacked of the same cultural arrogance evidenced in European plans.

It is important to note, however, that the diasporan vision for Africa differed from that of the Europeans in fundamental ways. As they saw the tentacles of Western power creeping around Africa, Africans in the diaspora were determined to maintain (and later to secure) Africa's independence. As Elliott Skinner concludes in *African Americans and U.S. Policy Toward Africa 1850–1924*, many African Americans invested their limited political power in Africa, believing that a strong, respected Africa would benefit African people the world over.

In the decades prior to World War II, Africans in the diaspora continued to assert an interest in Africa's welfare. John Henrik Clarke provides a detailed look at Garvey's Africa agenda in *Marcus Garvey and the Vision of Africa*. William Scott documents the efforts of African Americans to halt Italy's disruptive intrusion into Ethiopia in *The Sons of Sheba's Race: African Americans and the Italo-Ethiopian War, 1935–1941*. Robert Edgar provides a valuable look at the work of one African American in his edited volume *An African-American in South Africa: The Travel Notes of Ralph J. Bunche, 28 Sept. 1937–1 Jan. 1938*. The period of involvement by African Americans before and after World War II is ably summarized by Henry Jackson in his classic work *From the Congo to Soweto*. In a recent work, *Pan-Africanism in the African Diaspora: An Analysis of Modern Afrocentric Political Movements* (Wayne State Univ. Pr., 1993), Ronald Walters describes the role diasporan blacks have played since the 1960s.

Slave Trade

The enslavement of Africans figures prominently in any discussion on Africa. Beginning in the seventh century A.D. and continuing through the nineteenth century, Africa was ravaged by slave merchants. Other peoples and nations found themselves enslaved during these centuries, but no other continent endured the scope and the intensity of the trade in humans that was perpetrated in Africa.

The African slave trade involved three geographical zones: the Sahara, the Indian Ocean, and the Atlantic Ocean. Arab slavers preceded those from the West by several centuries, but the extent of their trade was smaller in volume. The Arabs were the primary slave merchants in the Saharan and Indian Ocean regions, funneling Africans into the Arabian peninsula, Persia, and India, where they worked as soldiers, servants, concubines, and ship laborers. In the nineteenth century, many were forced to labor on plantations in Zanzibar and the French colonies of Mauritius and Reunion.

Perceptions of the roles Arabs have played in African history vary. In *The Africans: A Triple Heritage*, Kenya's Ali Mazrui, who is a descendant of Arabs and Africans, describes the Arabization of Africa — through such means as the Arabic language, Islam, and intermarriage — in rather neutral terms. In *Africa 2001*, Nigeria's Herbert Ekwe-Ekwe stresses the de-Africanization process and violence that accompanied Arab conquest. He charges that Arabs launched a holocaust in Africa, a cataclysmic process that was pushed even closer to a "final solution" by European slavers.

Spanish and Portuguese companies initiated the Atlantic slave trade in the fifteenth century. They were quickly joined by traders and financiers from Dutch, British, and French companies. Estimates of the actual number of Africans affected by the slave trade vary. In *The Atlantic Slave Trade: A Census*

(Univ. of Wisconsin Pr., 1972), American historian Philip Curtin gives an estimate of six million for the Atlantic trade and eleven million for trade to all geographical areas. Joseph E. Inikori challenges these figures in *Forced Migrations*. He posits a figure of fifteen million for the Atlantic trade and thirty million overall. Contributors to Inikori's book describe the motives and actions of the European and Arab instigators of the trade, but their primary emphasis is on Africans as both victims and manipulators of the trade. This Africa-centered approach owes much to the innovative work of Nigerian historian Kenneth O. Dike. In the 1950s, Dike revolutionized the study of the slave trade when he authored *Trade and Politics in the Niger Delta, 1830–1885*, reviewed below. Dike avoided conventional Eurocentric approaches to the study of the slave trade, which focused largely on external issues, and focused instead on the impact of the trade on West African societies. Another innovative work on this period is *King Jaja of the Niger Delta: His Life and Times, 1821–1891* by Sylvanus J. S. Cookey (NOK, 1974). Jaja, a former slave-boy, rose to become king of the city-state that he helped establish.

Other useful accounts of the slave trade can be found in *The Africans and Their History* by Joseph E. Harris (Viking, 1987) and *African History* by Philip Curtin and others (Little, Brown, 1978). Personal accounts of enslavement, particularly those of West Africans, are collected in Curtin's *Africa Remembered: Narratives by West Africans from the Era of the Slave Trade* (Univ. of Wisconsin Pr., 1968). One account that stands out in Curtin's book is the riveting description provided by Olaudah Equiano, an Igbo who was captured when he was eleven years old. A more detailed account of Equiano's story is available in his autobiography, *The Life of Olaudah Equiano*, edited by Paul Edwards (Longman, 1988).

Conquest and Colonization

In 1833 Britain abolished slavery, and the United States followed suit in 1865. Antislavery activists in the Western Hemisphere were prominent in the struggle to end slavery, but British and U.S. industrialists played the primary roles. As the industrial mode of production gained primacy in Britain and the United States, slavery became obsolete. With the end of slavery, European powers scrambled to establish colonies in Africa. They sought direct access to Africa's agricultural and mineral wealth, more effective control of African labor, protection of strategic trade routes, markets for manufactured goods, and, in the temperate parts of the continent, land for European settlers.

The establishment of European rule did not occur without a struggle. African resistance to European colonization was lengthy and bloody. Prior to African independence, Western academics typically ignored examples of African resistance or described such efforts as irrational struggles against vastly superior powers. Pioneering research efforts by scholars such as George Shepperson, Terence Ranger, Gilbert Gwassa, Yves Person, I. N. Kimambo, and A. J. Temu changed the image of African resistance.

Despite strong resistance efforts, by 1900 most of Africa was occupied by European powers. Only Ethiopia and Liberia remained completely independent. As Belloc's famous lines indicate, European technology ultimately won the day: "Whatever happens, we have got /The maxim-gun, and they have not."

European conquest and colonization had profound and complicated results for Africans. The major result was the incorporation of Africa into a world-capitalist system dominated by Europe. Walter Rodney describes this process and the harnessing of Africa's resources for European development in his seminal work, *How Europe Underdeveloped Africa*. Chinweizu builds on and extends Rodney's analysis in *The West and the Rest of Us*, a brilliant and provocative analysis of the international scope of Western imperialism and conquest.

In *African Perspectives on Colonialism*, Ghanaian historian A. Adu Boahen highlights the specific consequences of European conquest for Africa. He notes the dramatic altering of the African economic landscape, with cash crops for export replacing Africa's domestic-oriented economies. He also points to changes in the political realm, describing a shift in power from kings and priests to a Western-educated elite. This reallocation of power drastically changed Africa's governing systems, many of which had been relatively egalitarian and democratic.

A major political and social consequence of conquest was the partition of Africa. In *Partitioned Africa: Ethnic Relations Across Africa's International Boundaries, 1884–1984*, A. I. Asiwaju and other contributors examine the social, cultural, and economic cost borne by populations disrupted by the partition.

Another important consequence of colonialism was the reduction of indigenous checks on male power. As Europeans reshaped African systems to mirror European views of the appropriate relations between male and female, African women lost political power, status, and, in many cases, the primary roles they played in the economic life of their societies. European writers who described African women as drudges of their husbands seemed blissfully unaware of the part Europeans played in creating this new reality. In an article entitled "The 'Status of Women' in Indigenous African Societies," published in *Women in Africa and the African Diaspora*, Niara Sudarkasa describes the position of precolonial African women and notes the destabilizing effects of European colonialism and its economic correlate, capitalism.

One of the most insidious results of conquest was the damage done to the African psyche. The loss of land and the denigration of African values and religious beliefs left many Africans bereft of spiritual sustenance, prey to false prophets, and open to extreme solutions. The Xhosa cattle killing is a tragic example of the latter. Conquered in war and alarmed by the settlement of whites on their land, the Xhosa of Ciskei followed the millenarian vision of a young Xhosa girl named Nongqause. She had prophesied that a great wind would sweep the whites into the sea if the Xhosa slaughtered all their cattle. Noel Mostert retells the events of this tragedy in *Frontiers* (McKay, 1992) a lengthy but highly readable history of the Xhosa people of South Africa's eastern Cape.

African novelists and poets have brilliantly captured the experiences of conquest and colonization. Some have modeled their works on European literary forms, while others have made conscious efforts to employ African idioms and literary devices. Writing in the early twentieth century, the South African writer Sol Plaatje blended Shakespearean and Tswana literary traditions in *Mhudi*, a suspenseful novel that describes the rising tide of warfare in South Africa following European settlement.

In the pioneering work *Things Fall Apart*, Chinua Achebe skillfully weaves Igbo proverbs into his tale of the historic encounter between the Igbo and the British in eastern Nigeria. Wole Soyinka, another Nigerian writer, uses his mastery of English syntax and Shakespearean styles to tell of the clash between the Yoruba and British values in his brilliant play *Death and the King's Horseman*, which appears in his *Collected Plays II*. In *Radiance of the King* (Random, 1989), Camara Laye employs the French language and African symbols as he chronicles the transformation of a smug white racist into a man who eventually embraces African traditions. Laye is also the author of *The Dark Child*, reviewed below. Ferdinand Oyono provides a bitter slice of French colonialism in his satirical novel *Houseboy*. White colonialists are absent in Okot p'Bitek's praise poem *Song of Lawino and Song of Ocol*; instead, the impact of the West is seen in the dialogue between a traditional Acoli wife and her Western-educated husband.

Independence and Neocolonialism

Colonial rule ended in most of Africa in the 1950s and early 1960s. Independence brought great optimism about Africa's future in Africa as well as abroad. Kwame Nkrumah's dictum, "Seek ye first the political kingdom," embodied the general view that political sovereignty was the key to African freedom and prosperity. However, as ethnic struggles, corruption, and military dictatorships spread throughout the continent, early optimism changed to disillusionment and despair.

A host of writers have captured the disappointment and frustration of the postcolonial period, including Sembene Ousmane, Ngugi wa Thiong'o, Nuruddin Farah, and Ama Ata Aidoo. Characters in their works are frustrated by inept bureaucracies and angered by politicians who live opulent lives while the common folk endure poverty and hopelessness. These novelists hold African leaders accountable for problems occurring in contemporary Africa. In some countries, criticism of people in high places has resulted in imprisonment of authors. Ngugi wa Thiong'o and Wole Soyinka have both been incarcerated for their political writings. Ngugi describes his prison experiences in *Detained: A Writer's Prison Diary*, while Soyinka's *The Man Died* records his two years' imprisonment during Nigeria's civil war.

While highly critical of African leaders and the African elite, many writers also point to the part Western powers have played in creating Africa's current problems. The hidden (and sometimes not-so-hidden) hand of the West is detailed in *The Crisis in Zaire: Myths and Realities*, edited by Nzongola-Ntalaga, *Conflict and Intervention in Africa: Nigeria, Angola, Zaire* by Herbert Ekwe-Ekwe, and *In Search of Enemies: A CIA Story* by John Stockwell (Norton, 1984).

The winds of change that swept post–World War II Africa failed to bring freedom to blacks in South Africa, Rhodesia (now Zimbabwe), and the Portuguese-held territories of Angola, Mozambique, and Guinea-Bissau. In *The Political Economy of Race and Class in South Africa*, Bernard Magubane attributes the tenacity of white minority rule to the support these countries obtained from the West. His claim is substantiated in other books, including Elliott Skinner's *Beyond Constructive Engagement: United States Foreign Policy Toward Africa* (Washington Inst. Pr., 1986).

South Africans Peter Abrahams, Es'kia Mphahlele, and Bloke Modisane were the first authors to give a personal face to apartheid through their early autobiographical writings. In recent decades we have witnessed the continuation of the autobiographical genre in southern African literature. Ellen Kuzwayo, John Ya-Otto, and Phyllis Ntantala provide remembrances of their African childhoods while detailing the disruptive force of apartheid. The novels of Lewis Nkosi and Alex LaGuma and the poetry of Dennis Brutus protest the intrusive and exploitative nature of apartheid. The rising tide of black consciousness in South Africa is captured in Steve Biko's *I Write What I Like*. Chenjerai Hove's extended praise poem *Bones* (Heinemann, 1970) celebrates the sacrifices made by a peasant woman during the Zimbabwean liberation struggle. *Mayome* (o.p., 1983) by Pepetela explores the realities of Angola's guerrilla war against Portuguese colonialism. These writings provided an agenda for action and a healthy escape valve for feelings of rage and humiliation engendered by apartheid and Portuguese colonialism.

New Directions

In recent years, a number of African writers have turned inward for additional themes. Njabulo Ndebele describes these introspective journeys as liberating and necessary: "You see, too much obsession with removing oppression in the political dimension soon becomes in itself a form of oppression. And then mostly all it calls for is that you thrust an angry fist into the air." African writers remain rooted in the political and economic realities of their societies, but the themes they address today represent more than an angry fist. In the short story "Fools," from his anthology *Fools and Other Stories*, Ndebele moves away from a descriptive documentation of suffering to create fiction that explains—not merely describes—apartheid. An acrimonious relationship between a disreputable teacher and an idealistic young activist becomes his springboard for examining human dilemmas and the impact of apartheid. In *The Famished Road*, Ben Okri tells a fanciful tale about an *abiku* (a spirit-child) who, in the Nigerian tradition, comes into the world to challenge the mental, financial, and physical health of its parents .

One of the most exciting changes in African literature is the growing body of writings by African women. Prominent in the past in oral literature, today women are breaking the hold male authors have held in the realm of the written word. They write on a wide range of topics, including family life, urbanization, male-female relationships, the subjugation of women, and the impact of war. Their work builds on earlier writings by pioneers Grace Ogot, author of *Promised Land* (East African Publg., 1966), and Efua Sutherland, author of *Edufa* (Three Continents, 1969). An important title reviewed here is *One Is Enough* by Flora Nwapa.

In her multifaceted novel *The Joys of Motherhood*, Nigerian author Buchi Emecheta explodes myths of African motherhood. She also addresses the alienation imposed by a hostile urban life and the impact of economic stress on the family. Senegalese author Mariama Ba touches universal chords in *So Long a Letter*, a novel that reveals the inequities inherent in polygamous marriages. A strong similarity between African polygamy and Western divorce and remarriage patterns can be discerned in this heart-rending story. *The Heinemann Book of African Women's Writing* provides a sampling of new works by African women, including Zimbabwe's Tsitsi Dangarema, Kenya's Awuor Ayoda, and Egypt's Nawal El Saadawi. As editor Charlotte Bruner notes, each writer "reflects her unique perspective on her own time and culture." Margaret Busby combines old and new works in *Daughters of Africa*, a comprehensive anthology of oral and written literature by women of African descent.

In the realm of nonfiction, women have authored and edited several outstanding works. Carole Boyce Davies and Anne Adams Graves have made a major contribution to the field of literary criticism with their edited volume *Ngambika: Studies of Women in African Literature*. Irene Staunton's riveting accounts of war experiences in *Mothers of the Revolution* show the contributions of women to the liberation of Zimbabwe and the special risks to which they were exposed by virtue of their gender. *Women in Africa and the Diaspora*, edited by Rosalyn Terborg-Penn and others, focuses on the unique strategies black women have developed to resist various forms of oppression. In *Black Women Cross-Culturally*, Filomina Steady argues that in their daily lives African women are often more feminist than their Euro-American counterparts.

Collectively, the works of women writers foster new and deeper understandings of African life. Some African male authors are unnerved by the words of their female counterparts. However, as Carole Boyce Davies notes in *Ngambika*, "a number of male authors are able to envisage female emancipation without terror." As evidence, she cites the work of Mongo Beti, Ferdinand Oyono, Sembene Ousmane, and Henri Lopes, all of whom view the liberation of women as part and parcel of the liberation of Africa.

A spate of new writings by African philosophers adds another dimension to the reader's understanding of Africa. At some point, most of these works confront the often-repeated charge that there is no African philosophy. Tsenay Serequeberhan, an Eritrean philosopher, rejects this idea in *African Philosophy: The Essential Readings*. Working within and beyond European philosophical constructs, he identifies the four major themes in African philosophical thought: ethnophilosophy, philosophic sagacity, national ideological philosophy, and professional philosophy. Operating strictly within European-defined frameworks, Paulin Hountondji of the Republic of Benin accepts only professional philosophy as appropriate intellectual matter for philosophical discourse. In *African Philosophy: Myth and Reality*, he analyzes the writings of Anton-Wilhelm Amon, an eighteenth-century Ghanaian philosopher who wrote principally in Latin. He also examines philosophical aspects of Kwame Nkrumah's thought. Kwame Appiah analyzes ethnophilosophy, Pan-Africanism, and other subjects in his provocative book *In My Father's House: Africa in the Philosophy of Culture*. A primary question for Appiah is "what it means to be African" in a multicultural world. In *African Philosophy: Traditional Yoruba Philosophy and Contemporary African Realities*, Segun Gbadegesin of Nigeria also covers a variety of topics, including the relevance of religion in modern Africa, Senghor's concept of Negritude, and Julius Nyerere's theory of African socialism.

An intriguing work on African philosophy is V. Y. Mudimbe's *Invention of Africa: Gnosis, Philosophy, and the Order of Knowledge*. Mudimbe turns on its head the Western assumption that Africa has no philosophical roots by questioning whether Westerners can actually comprehend African philosophical concepts, grounded as they are in the African gnosis (system of knowledge). Moreover, he questions whether the European structure of knowledge, which he describes as decidedly ethnocentric, can be seen as universal. As Mudimbe notes, in the nineteenth century, Europeans defined themselves as normal and "civilized" by constructing a category of so-called non-Europeans (the other) as abnormal and "uncivilized." Europeans, Mudimbe asserts, created the concept of "Africa" and imposed it on the peoples of the continent. He challenges African intellectuals to tackle the task of unraveling what is European, what is "African," and what is universal.

Among the most provocative discussions on Africa today are those that focus on African development strategies. Basil Davidson, Fantu Cheru, Herbert Ekwe-Ekwe, and Ngugi wa Thiong'o offer radical—but some would argue necessary—solutions to Africa's problems. In his recent book *The Black Man's Burden: Africa and the Curse of the Nation-State* (Random, 1992), Davidson questions the effectiveness of the nation-state and suggests that Africa's redemption lies in the decentralization of political power, mass participation in decision-making, and development strategies that focus on the rural many rather than the urban few. Cheru, the author of *Silent Revolution in Africa*, describes Western and most contemporary African plans for Africa's development as mere blueprints for the recolonization of Africa by imperialist forces. He advocates disengagement from Western economic systems so that African countries will be forced to cooperate collectively and become self-reliant. "A self-reliant and united Africa," he argues, "will eventually be able to reestablish relations with the North without surrendering its sovereignty." Herbert Ekwe-Ekwe also advocates detachment from Western-dominated economic systems. He argues further that the nation-state that Europeans foisted on people such as the Yoruba, Asante, Kikuyu, and Hutu merely serves as "a lever to transfer Africa's wealth to the West." He proposes a retreat to Africa's "precolonial homelands of social formations to begin the arduous task of reconstructing a battered heritage." Ngugi wa Thiong'o advocates a similar position when he challenges African authors to abandon European tongues and use local languages as the primary vehicle for their writings.

There are many Africans who do not agree with these propositions. In *The Challenge of African Economic Recovery and Development* (Cass, 1991), Adebayo Adedeji, the former executive secretary of the United Nations Economic Commission for Africa, expresses his belief that Africa can achieve economic self-reliance without completely severing ties to the West. Chinua Achebe admits that the nation-state is artificial, but he views it as essential to Africa's development. In *Morning Yet on Creation Day: Essays* (Doubleday, 1976), he states that the English language belongs to him no less than his British counterpart because language is not bound by geography.

The most appropriate strategies for Africa's regeneration will continue to be debated in the years to come. One hopes that the debate will lead to a collective plan that, as Ekwe-Ekwe puts it in *Africa 2001*, will release "the phoenix of African genius that set the pace of human creativity in antiquity."

LITERATURE

1220 Achebe, Chinua. **Anthills of the Savannah**. Doubleday 1988, $16.95 (0-385-01664-6); $8.95 (0-385-26045-8). 240pp. Fiction.

This novel is Achebe's indictment of military dictatorships in Africa and the persistent problems of corruption and unaccountability among leaders who are barely familiar with the demands of their office. It is a story of love and violence, power and disillusionment, as ordinary people struggle with change. Modern-day Africa is presented here in a narrative that is strengthened by its use of everyday speech. Achebe exposes the inner workings of the military government of a fictitious African country where jobs, lives, and the wellbeing of its citizens depend completely on the mood of the military dictator. The author reveals the acrimonious debates and contentions, scheming and intrigues, directed violence, murders, and betrayals within the government and among the country's top ministers.

After losing a referendum to be President-for-Life, the military president becomes suspicious and distrustful of his ministers, and he depends on his security officers to eliminate his critics. A growing disenchantment with the leadership engulfs ordinary citizens in a confrontation with government. Students, taxi drivers, and market women risk their lives to save the country from anarchy. College campuses are invaded by the military and the students are arrested, beaten, and detained. The wit and resolve of the ordinary citizen are the weapons that Achebe provides them for use against the military machinery. Students and displeased ministers form unexpected alliances and standards are compromised as surviving the military becomes the preeminent goal of a people groping for freedom.

1221 Achebe, Chinua. *Girls at War: And Other Stories.* Doubleday 1991, $8.95 (0-385-41896-5). 186pp. Fiction.

Achebe wrote some of the works in this collection of thirteen short stories while a student in Ibadan, Nigeria; others are based on his experiences during the Nigerian civil war. The title story, about the tragic effects of war on the civilian population, focuses on a girl whose high ideals and expectations fizzle as the war drags on. In "Gladys and Nwankwo," Achebe tells the story of the hard life and the need to survive behind the lines of the civil war. Gladys is transformed from an idealistic participant in the crusade to just another citizen seeking to survive by dabbling in casual sex and the promises of the black market, while Nwankwo compromises his rectitude in the civil service by getting a little more than his share of government food relief. Nwankwo's character contrasts sharply with that of Gladys, who for all her faults is seen to be more fully human than her high-minded companion. It is Gladys who, in the end, embodies the ideals of the war as she sacrifices her life attempting to save a soldier she barely knows. In "Civil Peace," Achebe captures the irony of a people whose quest for peace and rebuilding their lives after the war must be achieved and negotiated within the cloak of incivility, threat to lives and property, and a scorn of law enforcement.

1222 Achebe, Chinua. *A Man of the People.* Doubleday 1989, $8.95 (0-385-08616-4). 141pp. Fiction.

Odili, an ordinary schoolteacher, tells the story of his fight against the politics of greed and self-exaltation, a central theme of this author's political satire. In this story, Honorable Chief Dr. M. A. Nanga, M.P., LL.D, finds himself in the enviable position of his country's Minister of Culture. At his disposal are the resources he needs to command the unquestioning loyalty of his constituents. From this powerful position, Nanga influences the distribution of government benefits, ruthlessly suppresses all forms of opposition, has his pick of the local maidens—and still remains a hero among his people. His uncontrollable greed and his willingness to trample his opponents bring him into confrontation with Odili, who joins a group of young intellectuals to form a political party and challenge the chief and change the system. But there is another level to Odili's actions: Rather than seeking political change, Odili may be trying to seduce Chief Nanga's fiancee in revenge for Nanga's seduction of his girlfriend. Unprepared for the complexities of politics, Odili is humiliated by Chief Nanga during the political campaign.

Achebe resolves the story when the country's military dismisses the government and puts itself in power. Both Odili and Nanga lose the political battle, but with Nanga under arrest, Odili wins the battle of romance by capturing the love of the Chief's fiancée.

1223 Achebe, Chinua. *Things Fall Apart*. Knopf 1992, $15.00 (0-679-41714-1); Doubleday $4.95 (0-385-47454-7). 150pp. Fiction.

This book, Achebe's first novel, has become a classic work in the teaching of southern Nigerian cultures in colleges. Besides being one of the few books that conjure up an image of precolonial Nigeria, it also fills the gap created by the lack of ethnographies on southern Nigeria by revealing Nigerian rural culture and the precolonial Igbo cultural environment.

The narrative tells of Obi Okonkwo, the "Roaring Flame" of Umuofia, whose bravery and uncompromising resolve make him disdainful of less ambitious folks. In the process, he brings punishment upon himself for intentional and unintentional mishaps against his society and is temporarily banished. Although he violates some of his society's norms, he also maintains a strong desire to preserve the values of his society. But his challenge of the introduction of Christianity to his community conflicts with the changes sweeping through other parts of Igboland and leaves Okonkwo mourning for "the warlike men of Umuofia, who have so unaccountably become soft like women."

The story of Obi Okonkwo's family continues in *No Longer at Ease* (Astor-Honor, 1960), which focuses on Okonkwo's grandson and his move to Lagos to become a government official under the British.

1224 Aidoo, Ama Ata. *No Sweetness Here*. Longman 1970. o.p. Fiction.

The stories in this book by one of Africa's leading women writers focus on men and women caught up in the wrenching confrontations between traditional ways of life and the sweep of modern change: the eye-opening impact of getting a Western education, the shock and uncertainty of living in a city, and the growing assertion of human rights. There are many poignant and dream-like moments in this book. A man searching for his missing sister accidentally meets her in a sleazy hotel where she plies her trade as a prostitute and hardly acknowledges him. The title story tells of Maami Ama, who is the first wife of her polygamous husband and who is disliked by her in-laws. Unlike the younger wives, she always gets "the smallest, thorniest plot" of land. Eventually she divorces, seeking comfort in the vitality of her only son, Kwesi. Later, her grief is compounded when Kwesi dies from a snake bite. Mourners tell her harshly: "Life is not sweet!" Indeed, the author seems to be saying that there can be no sweetness here when Western education puts African people in conflict with their traditional ideals, when we lose our loved ones, and when the highest castles we build come tumbling down.

A recent work by Aidoo published in the United States is *Changes: A Love Story* (Feminist Pr., 1993).

Al-Udhari, Abdullah, ed. *Modern Poetry of the Arab World*.
See entry 1147.

1225 Ba, Mariama. *So Long a Letter*. Trans. from French by Modupé Bodé-Thomas. Heinemann 1989, $8.95 (0-435-90555-4). 96pp. Fiction.

Winner of the 1980 Noma Prize for Publishing in Africa, this book was Mariama Ba's first published novel. Written in the form of an intimate letter, it is an emotional exposé of two women caught between love and polygamy. The central characters in the novel, Rammatoulaye and Aissatou, are sophisticated, Western-educated Senegalese women. In their youth, both women avoided prearranged marriages and wed for love. Yet, in their middle years, their husbands abandon monogamy and choose second wives. Aissatou refuses to participate in such a relationship. She leaves her husband and Senegal to pursue a career in New York. In contrast, Rammatoulaye acquiesces, hoping that her husband will follow the traditional custom of treating each wife equally. When he fails to do so, a disappointed and humiliated Rammatoulaye attempts to find dignity by confronting her loneliness, fears, and hopes.

The fact that this book has been translated into sixteen languages attests to its universal appeal. It depicts the social inequities and hardships women in many types of societies are forced to face.

Ben Jelloun, Tahar. *With Downcast Eyes*.
See entry 878.

1226 Brink, Andre. *A Dry White Season*. Viking 1984, $10.00 (0-14-006890-2). 320pp. Fiction.

Ben Du Toit is an Afrikaner (white) schoolteacher who is roused to political action by the murders of the school's black custodian and his son by the South African police. Du Toit demands an investigation, but his wife and eldest daughter turn against him and his friends advise him to be silent. He turns for solace to a sympathetic journalist with whom he subsequently has an affair. But authorities mail pictures of their trysts to his wife and to the school's headmaster. Du Toit is fired and abandoned by his wife and both his daughters; only his son supports him. As the police continue to stonewall on the murders, each of the black characters whom Du Toit contacts also dies; he is tortured by the realization that his attempts to gain justice have led to so much suffering.

This gripping novel was made into a feature film in 1990. Brink is also the author of several other highly acclaimed historical and contemporary novels set in South Africa, including *A Chain of Voices* (Penguin, 1983), a fictional account of the 1824 slave revolt in Cape Town, and *On the Contrary: A Novel: Being the Life of a Famous Rebel, Traveller, Explorer, Reader, Builder, Scribe, Latinist, Lover, and Liar* (Little, Brown, 1994).   LML

1227 Bruner, Charlotte, ed. *The Heinemann Book of African Women's Writing*. Heinemann 1993, $10.95 (0-435-90673-9). 211pp. Fiction.

This volume is a companion to the author's earlier work, *Unwinding Threads* (Heinemann, 1983). Like its predecessor, the new book contains short fiction by African women from various parts of the continent. With a few exceptions, it includes writers who were not featured in the earlier work. It draws its stories from a generation of African women who, as Bruner puts it, "know the

Africa since independence, since 'modernization,' since westernization, since the feminist movement." Some of the stories were written expressly for this volume; others were culled from previous anthologies. The stories are grouped according to the author's region of origin (western, eastern, southern, and northern Africa). Bruner introduces each section by highlighting the works of significant women writers from each region. The writers explore a variety of topics, including family life, male-female relationships, politics, economic conditions, and war. At the conclusion of the stories, Bruner provides a literary biography of each contributor.

Another Heinemann work that will be of interest to readers is *The Heinemann Book of Contemporary African Short Stories* (1992), edited by Chinua Achebe and C. L. Innes. This collection contains short works of fiction by African writers, female and male, that were published in the interval since the editors' earlier anthology, *African Short Stories* (1980).

1228 Brutus, Dennis. *A Simple Lust: Collected Poems of South African Jail and Exile*. Heinemann 1973, $11.95 (0-435-90115-X). 176pp. Poetry.

Brutus, an award-winning South African poet, is a long-time foe of apartheid. In the 1960s, the Pretoria government banned his writings and he was imprisoned on South Africa's notorious Robben Island. Upon his release, the authorities permitted him to leave South Africa on the condition that he never return. He lived in England for a time and ultimately settled in the United States. On university platforms, boycott lines, poetry gatherings—any place he could find a forum—Brutus continued to denounce apartheid. Currently, he is a tenured professor at the University of Pittsburgh.

This book includes selected poems from the author's other well-known but out-of-print volumes, including *Sirens, Knuckles, and Boots*; *Letters to Martha*; *Poems from Algiers*; and *Thoughts Abroad*. Although his prison experience is the dominant theme in much of his work, Brutus is a poet with many facets. As a protest poet, he speaks passionately of the oppression of South Africa's masses and exhorts people to take up the fight for their own liberation. As a romantic troubadour, he woos and excites a lover. The praise poet heralds the "valour" of Luthuli and "smoldering anger" of Biko. The poet-in-exile laments the life of the outsider. Sometimes complex and ponderous, sometimes simple and terse, Brutus has used his poetic voices with versatility and verve. A master wordsmith, he is a poet for many seasons.

1229 Busby, Margaret, ed. *Daughters of Africa: An International Anthology of Words and Writings by Women of African Descent and from the Ancient Egyptian to the Present*. Pantheon 1992, $35.00 (0-679-41634-X); Ballantine $19.95 (0-345-38268-4). 1,152pp. Poetry/Fiction.

Lovers of prose and poetry are indebted to Margaret Busby for this massive literary tour de force, the most comprehensive anthology ever produced of oral and written literature by women of African descent. The volume includes short stories, excerpts from novels, essays, and poems. Each selection is preceded by introductory notes that provide biographical information about the writer and her works.

The anthology begins with anonymous poems and songs from Africa. The selections that follow are arranged in chronological order according to the author's date of birth. A few selections are included from ancient times; most come from the period between the eighteenth century and today. Diversity is a hallmark of this collection, which tallies over one thousand pages. Although all the authors are of African descent, they hail from many parts of the globe and focus on a variety of themes.

The useful appendix includes sources and individual works by the authors, a bibliography for further reading, and a geographical listing of authors. If funds are available for only one anthology of black women's writings, this is the volume of choice.

1230 Chinweizu, ed. ***Voices from Twentieth-Century Africa: Griots and Town Criers***. Faber 1989, $14.95 (0-571-14930-8). 416pp. Fiction.

The editor argues that students of African literature have too readily accepted a Eurocentric emphasis and have neglected myriad other African cultural expressions. Chinweizu redraws the map of African literature by allowing traditional and contemporary African voices from different parts of the continent to speak. This anthology includes myths, fables, songs, riddles, short stories, epics, and essays from Azania (South Africa) to Zimbabwe. About half of the collection consists of traditional literature originally written in, or translated to, English. The collection is grouped into eleven thematic sections that express the variety of African writing.

Another work edited by Chinweizu and others, *Toward the Decolonization of African Literature* (Howard Univ. Pr., 1983), examines the effect colonialism has had on the development of African literature.

Chraibi, Driss. ***The Butts***.
See entry 885.

1231 Coetzee, J. M. ***Waiting for the Barbarians***. Viking 1982, $9.00 (0-14-006110-X). 156pp. Fiction.

This novel, based on events of the Boer War, offers a metaphorical vision of the dehumanizing effects of apartheid upon both the colonizers and their victims. Coetzee, an Afrikaner opponent of white rule in South Africa, tells the story through the unnamed Magistrate of a frontier town in an unnamed country. The rulers of the town exploit the inhabitants in the countryside. Despite their power and prosperity, the townspeople are consumed with fear of an invasion by "barbarians." In actuality, the only violence they witness is carried out by Colonel Joll, the security expert sent from the capital to command the Civil Guard defending the town. The Magistrate, sickened by the torture of captured barbarians, cares for a blinded girl. The townspeople scoff at the Magistrate's remorse, and he is removed from office. In the end most of the townspeople have fled in panic to the capital. Many die from the harshness of the journey; ironically, they never encounter the feared "barbarians." This powerfully written novel expresses the dilemma faced by liberal-minded colonists, such as the Magistrate and Coetzee, who benefit from an inhuman regime that they loathe but from which they cannot remove themselves.

RL

1232 Condé, Maryse. *Segu*. Trans. from French. Ballantine 1988, $14.50 (0-345-35306-4). 499pp. Fiction.

Set in Mali and spanning nearly a hundred years in the late eighteenth and early nineteenth centuries, this novel describes the final years of the slave trade and the expansion of Islam as seen by several generations of a powerful Bambara family. The fictional Dousika Traore family is held together by loyalty, even when one son, Tiekoro, converts to Islam and subsequently tries to convince all the Bambara to give up their animistic beliefs. After his violent death, Tiekoro is worshipped as a hero, but the reader sees as well his all-too-human qualities. The novel, which is based upon extensive historical and anthropological research, offers both a panoramic history of a people and a set of memorable and multidimensional characters.

Conde, who is originally from Guadaloupe, continues the saga of the Traore family in *The Children of Nya* (Viking, 1989). Another of her novels, *Heremakhonon* (orig. pub. 1982; Three Continents, 1992), is also set in part in Africa; it portrays a Caribbean-born intellectual living in Paris who journeys to an unnamed West African country in the midst of a revolution and has a brief and disillusioning relationship with a revolutionary leader.   LML

1233 Diop, Birago. *Tales of Amadou Koumba*. Trans. from French. Oxford Univ. Pr. 1966. o.p. Fiction.

Senegalese storyteller Diop recounts the intricate narratives of Koumba the griot, whose fables feature the exploits of animal characters such as the hare, the jackal, the monkey, and the lion. The world of these characters is intertwined with human nobility and weakness, good and evil, and the supernatural realm of spirits and ancestors. These various qualities humanize the characters and imbue them with familiar experiences, effectively blurring the boundaries between the real and the imaginary. At the end of the griot's tale, there is always a moral and ethical message, a postscript imparting elderly wisdom or instilling appropriate social behavioral code. These tales are also available in a French-language edition.

1234 Emecheta, Buchi. *The Joys of Motherhood*. Braziller 1979, $8.95 (0-8076-0950-1). 244pp. Fiction.

Emecheta traces the life of a young woman who leaves her home in the Igbo area of Nigeria to find love and happiness in the city with a husband whom she is meeting for the first time. Her tribulations in Lagos intensify with the loss of a child, a subsequent suicide attempt, and a polygamous marriage. She manages to maintain a tenuous link with folks back home and to remain resourceful in the face of the adversities of city life. Her perseverance and a strong entrepreneurial spirit help her survive an often troubling marriage and successfully plan for her children's future.

This book shows the author in firm control of a story that reflects the lives of African women of diverse social and economic circumstances. It is set against the background of World War II, when Nigeria and other countries sent troops to fight alongside allied forces abroad. Emecheta delves into history to succinctly recount some of the social problems that resulted from the wartime separation of families and the loss of friends. But even more poignant is her scathing portrayal of a tradition in which the worth of the woman is measured by the number of male children she gives to the extended family. The second wife, Adaku, falls short of this expectation by having two daughters; she jeers at custom by becoming a prostitute. Emecheta's characters fall in and out of love, try to keep their families together, cope with rumors, and form new relationships. "The joy of being a mother was the joy of giving all to your children," one character says. Unfortunately, in this story, the gift is never requited because the children are not there at the end to show their love to their mother.

Among Emecheta's other acclaimed works about women's experiences in Nigeria are *The Moonlight Bride* (Braziller, 1983) and *The Family* (Braziller, 1989).

Emecheta, Buchi. ***Second-Class Citizen***.
See entry 801.

1235 Farah, Nuruddin. ***Sweet and Sour Milk***. Graywolf 1992, $12.00 (1-55597-159-8). 241pp. Fiction.

Since Farah began publishing in the 1970s, critics have described him as the most talented of the younger African writers. His first novel, *From a Crooked Rib*, looked at the ways women in Somali society are exploited.

This novel is part of a loosely conceived trilogy in which the author explores life in a state under dictatorial control. The other two parts of the trilogy are *Sardines* (orig. pub. 1981; Graywolf, 1992) and *Close Sesame* (Graywolf, 1992). As the protagonist investigates the apparent murder of his brother, he uncovers totalitarian forces that have reduced Somalia to a petrified state of anarchy and repression. The novel can be compared with others that portray the horrors of political repression and expose the forces (internal and external) stifling the political, social, and economic development of African societies. Another highly regarded work by Farah is *Maps* (Pantheon, 1987).

1236 Fugard, Athol. ***Blood Knot and Other Plays***. Theatre Communications Group 1991, $22.95 (1-55936-019-4); $10.95 (1-55936-020-8). 226pp. Drama.

Athol Fugard, a playwright from Port Elizabeth, South Africa, has been hailed as one of the best dramatists of our time. The offspring of an Afrikaner mother and an English-speaking father, Fugard began life with his feet in two cultures. In the 1950s, he encountered other cultural streams when he opened the African Theatre Workshop in the multiethnic township of Sophiatown. There he met a number of Africans, including writers Lewis Nkosi and Can Themba and jazz musician Zakes Mokae. His friendship with Mokae blossomed into a creative relationship when the two performed in Fugard's play "The Blood Knot."

The four plays in this collection are all set in Port Elizabeth. The title play explores family and power relationships between whites and blacks. Other works in this collection, including "Hello and Goodbye" and "Boesman and Lena," deal with the themes of family and race relations.

Fugard's best-known play to date is *Master Harold . . . and the Boys* (Penguin, 1984), about a lonely white adolescent and his changing relationships with the black employees of his father's restaurant who had been his closest companions as a child. Other notable Fugard plays are *Sizwe Bansi Is Dead* (o.p., 1974) and *A Lesson from Aloes* (Theatre Communications Group, 1989).

1237 Gordimer, Nadine. ***Burger's Daughter***. Viking 1980, $11.00 (0-14-005593-2). 362pp. Fiction.

One of Nobel laureate Gordimer's pivotal works, this novel offers a complex portrait of an activist family's private struggles. As the story begins, white teenager Rosa Burger stands outside a South African jail, waiting to deliver a parcel to her imprisoned mother. Her father, a noted antiapartheid leader, will soon be arrested again, this time to die in prison. Having experienced surveillance, police raids, and the arrest of her parents as part of her upbringing, Rosa chooses exile and a life of sensual pleasure. Yet she cannot escape her memories of the past or the people—especially a black youth her age, the son of one of her family's servants—whom she left behind. Rosa Burger is a complex character, one who embodies the tragedy and nobility of those trying to change an unjust society. Gordimer's thoughtful, elegant storytelling makes this one of the great novels of our time.

Among Gordimer's other acclaimed novels are *The Conservationist* (orig. pub. 1974; Viking, 1983), which established her international stature as a writer. *July's People* (Viking, 1982), a novel set in the postrevolutionary future in which a black former servant and his fellow villagers help a white family to survive; *A Sport of Nature* (Viking, 1988), which portrays a Jewish woman activist who joins the black struggle; and *My Son's Story* (Farrar, 1990), the tale of an activist father of mixed race and his teenage son, who is struggling to come to terms with his own identity and values. For a discussion of her short story collection *Crimes of Conscience*, see main entry.   LML

1238 Gordimer, Nadine. ***Crimes of Conscience: Selected Short Stories***. Heinemann 1991, $8.95 (0-435-90668-2). 121pp. Fiction.

Highly praised for such novels as *Burger's Daughter (see main entry)*, Nadine Gordimer is also a gifted short story writer. This collection contains some of her best work. All of the pieces are set in Africa, and most take place in her native South Africa. Gordimer explores various themes in these tales, but the dominant one is the impact of apartheid. In a detached and restrained fashion, she reveals the tensions that develop between individuals and groups in South Africa's stratified, race-conscious, and increasingly violent society. Included among the eleven tales are several outstanding works, including "A City of the Dead, A City of the Living," "Crimes of Conscience," and "Oral History." Pensive and subtle, the stories challenge existing stereotypes and myths about life in South Africa. Gordimer has authored numerous other collections of short stories, including *A Soldier's Embrace* (Viking, 1982) and *Jump and Other Stories* (Viking, 1992).

1239 Head, Bessie. ***The Collector of Treasures***. Heinemann 1994, $8.95 (0-685-62974-0). Fiction.

Head, a South African, is best known for her novels, all of which are more or less autobiographical. However, readers delving into her fiction for the time may want to sample her short stories first, and this collection is a good place to begin. The anthology is the creative outgrowth of a series of interviews Head conducted while researching her semidocumentary work *Serowe: Village of the Rain Wind* (Heinemann, 1981). In these stories, Head explores numerous themes, including male-female relationships, family, colonialism, and the African past.

Head, the child of a white mother and a black father, often used her fiction to examine the feelings of exile, alienation, and madness, all of which she experienced firsthand in her foreshortened life. Her first novel, *When Rain Clouds Gather* (Heinemann, 1987), describes the life of an idealistic South African refugee who seeks to bring about change in his new land. The character experiences many of the tensions Head herself felt as a refugee in Botswana. Her second novel, *Maru* (Heinemann, 1988), focuses on a young teacher who belongs to the Masarwa, a minority group oppressed by Botswana's Tswana majority. Head draws analogies between the oppression of the Masarwa and her own experiences as a "colored" person in South Africa. *A Question of Power* (Heinemann, 1974), her challenging and highly praised third novel, mirrors the author's downward spiral into mental confusion and collapse.

Head died suddenly in Botswana in 1986. In *The Tragic Life: Bessie Head and Literature in South Africa* (Africa World, 1990), editor Cecil Abrahams extols her literary contributions, describing her work as "an important and vibrant presence in the continuing development of African literature."

1240 Kane, Cheikh Hamidou. *Ambiguous Adventure*. Trans. from French by Katherine Woods. Heinemann 1972, $10.95 (0-435-90119-2). 178pp. Fiction.

This book explores the cultural conflict between Africa and the West. The protagonist, Samba Diallo, observes that Western educators have tried to "transform me in their image." But, he adds, "I have chosen the itinerary which is most likely to get me lost," an itinerary that threatens to turn this African man into a hybrid, someone who is out of place in both his native culture and his adopted one. According to Katherine Woods, who translated this book from French, "*Ambiguous Adventure* is the recital of a tearing to pieces, of the crisis of conscience which for the 'Europeanized' African accompanies the grip of science upon himself. Certain ones among them escape from it, too easily, by interrupting their studies." Woods notes that the author has put a bit of himself into the story, but it is a presence conditioned by his environmental, religious, and other diverse experiences. The policy of assimilation was the basis of French colonial policy, which purported to make Africans an integral part of the French colonial system. The failure of this system is examined in the cultural conflict facing religious Senegalese aristocrats who must choose either to accept or to discard Western ways.

1241 Kunene, Mazisi. *Emperor Shaka the Great: A Zulu Epic*. Trans. from Zulu by the author. Heinemann 1979, $14.95 (0-435-90211-3). Poetry.

This epic is often described as the African counterpart to *The Iliad* and *The Odyssey*. An extended praise-song, it glorifies the achievements of the Zulu king Shaka. In the early eighteenth century, Shaka built a formidable army of some 70,000 soldiers, extending Zulu rule beyond its narrow boundaries to cover a broad expanse of southern Africa. Disgruntled commanders who broke ranks with Shaka—such as Mzilikazi of the Ndebele—pushed Zulu rule even further. Charismatic and brilliant, Shaka revolutionized military, social, and political systems in southern Africa. Fifty years after his death, the military structure he created delivered the British army the most crushing defeat it suffered in its colonial history.

Originally written in Zulu, this epic work was translated into English by Kunene himself. As sources of information, he drew heavily on Zulu oral literature and history (including historians in his own family). The work is studded with Zulu imagery and concepts of life. The author provides background information for readers who are unfamiliar with Zulu history, language, and genealogy.

1242 LaGuma, Alex. *A Walk in the Night and Other Stories.* Northwestern Univ. Pr. 1967, $9.95 (0 8101 0139-4). 129pp. Fiction.

In 1973, South African–born Alex LaGuma won the Afro-Asian Writers' Association's Lotus Prize for literature. The author of several books and numerous short stories, LaGuma has been praised by critics for his colorful dialogue and his ability to evoke the mood and atmosphere of a place and time. His better-known novels include *And a Threefold Cord* (o.p.), *In the Fog of the Seasons' End* (Heinemann, 1972), and *Time of the Butcherbird* (Heinemann, 1989).

This book is a collection of short works. The title novella is set in Cape Town's District Six, a simmering ghetto where the realities of white exploitation and racism surface in daily scenes of poverty, hunger, fear, and crime. The protagonist is Michael Adonis, a young "colored" man, who has been fired from his job for a cheeky response to a white boss. Later, an angry and resentful Michael lashes out at his white neighbor, a kindly, booze-guzzling actor who has fallen on hard times. In a flash of rage, Michael kills the old man and escapes. Another man is blamed for Michael's crime and pays the ultimate price. In the space of less than a hundred pages, LaGuma brilliantly captures the complexity of race relations in South Africa under apartheid. His multidimensional characters depict the conflicts inherent in a repressive state that uses race as its organizing principle. Like LaGuma's other works, *A Walk in the Night* was banned in his native country. LaGuma and his wife were arrested and confined to solitary imprisonment. Eventually he left South Africa and lived in exile in London and Cuba. He died in the late 1980s.

1243 Laye, Camara. *The Dark Child.* Trans. from French. Farrar 1980. o.p. Fiction.

In this English translation of *L'Enfant Noir* (French & European, 1976), the Guinean writer Camara Laye portrays his African childhood as a world of wonder, mystery, and love, a world built on the comforting rituals of family and community life. In simple but subtle language, the author presents the crucial events of initiation, the preparation to adopt future responsibilities of adulthood, and the new possibilities that the world holds.

The protagonist is accepted at a French technical college in the city of Conakry. While acquiring new learning, he maintains contact with his family by observing old traditions. He also increases his knowledge of his Islamic faith and practices. After graduating, he continues his studies in France despite his mother's misgivings. In this essentially autobiographical novel, the author brings to life the social vigor and cultural dynamism of a traditional African upbringing and the transition from childhood to adult life.

1244 Lefanu, Sarah, and Stephen Hayward, eds. *Colors of a New Day: Writing for South Africa*. Pantheon 1991, $12.95 (0-679-73094-X). 416pp. Fiction.

In the late 1980s, editors Lefanu and Hayward invited writers from around the world to express their opposition to apartheid and their support for the African National Congress by donating a piece of writing. This anthology is the result. Of the thirty-eight writers represented, a number were born in Africa, including Margaret Busby, Naomi Mitchsen, Ben Okri, Nadine Gordimer, Mbulelo Mzamane, and Nuruddin Farah. A partial listing of writers from other continents includes Margaret Atwood, June Jordan, Joyce Carol Oates, Dennis Scott, Han Suyin, Aamer Hussein, Bapsi Sidhwa, Edward Upward, Raymond Williams, Nicole Ward Jouve, and Marina Warner.

Some of the pieces included focus directly on apartheid. June Jordan's "Poem to Free Nelson Mandela" laments the suffering of Winnie Mandela, the murder of Victoria Mxenge, and the oppression endured by the nameless many in South Africa. The title of the book comes from Lewis Nkosi's tale of violence and resistance in South Africa. Other writers draw on their own experiences of injustice, alienation, and loneliness. This is a solid collection of stories and poems. The paperback price makes it an affordable choice.

Maddy, Yulisa Amadu. *No Past, No Present, No Future*.
See entry 806.

1245 Mahfouz, Naguib. *Midaq Alley*. Trans. from Arabic. Doubleday 1992, $21.50 (0-385-26475-5); $9.00 (0-385-26476-3). 304pp. Fiction.

In 1988 Mahfouz's work gained worldwide attention when he was awarded the Nobel Prize for literature. Mahfouz had already won numerous Egyptian literary awards during his career, which spans forty years. The earliest of his forty-plus novels described life in the time of the Pharaohs, but he is more widely known for his more recent novels of contemporary Egypt.

This is his best-known work. Set in the early 1940s, it provides insight into Egyptian life during a period of rapid change, a transition that continues today. Its central character, a young girl named Hamida, represents the tragic attraction of modernity for those who try to escape from the oppressive forces of life in "the Alley." Hamida dreams of a better life in Cairo, only to end up in extreme degradation.

Another popular novel is *Miramar* (orig. pub. 1978; Doubleday, 1993). Zahra, a young peasant woman, escapes an arranged marriage and flees to Alexandria. There she and three men occupy a building called Miramar. The male characters provide differing but illuminating perspectives on Zahra's life. Mahfouz uses this structure to trace the vagaries of modern Egyptian life, such as the contradictions of its politics and the population's feelings as their country makes the sometimes painful transition to independence and modernity. In his later works, Mahfouz explores the social problems created by modern life and outlines the political action needed to correct them. His novels are never bitter or despondent. In fact, it is the humanity of his characters that gives his fiction universal appeal. Mahfouz is also the author of *Palace Walk (see main entry)*.

1246 Mahfouz, Naguib. ***Palace Walk***. Trans. from Arabic by William M. Hutchins and Olive E. Kenny. Doubleday 1990, $22.95 (0-385-26465-8); $11.00 (0-385-26466-6). 498pp. Fiction.

This novel is a study of contrasts between tradition and modernity, the old and new generations, and the world of Western values and those of traditional Egyptian culture. The story, which traces the lives of members of the Al-Sayyid Ahmad family over a span of fifty years in Cairo, symbolizes Egypt's transition from colonialism to independence. The main character, Al-Sayyid, is a successful merchant who adheres to Islamic custom and who expects utter obedience from his family. Within this suffocating environment, the family members gradually rebel; each act of defiance mirrors the changes taking place throughout Egypt and among its people. The slow evolution of Egypt into a modern nation appears complete when the youngest child, Kamal, fills the house with loud, forbidden music, symbolizing to the patriarch the intrusion of alien voices and the disruption of Egyptian traditions.

1247 Maja-Pearce, Adewale, ed. ***The Heinemann Book of African Poetry in English***. Heinemann 1991, $9.95 (0-435-91323-9). 224pp. Poetry.

This anthology of African poetry includes poems written in English by various African authors over the last thirty years. The collection is not meant to be representative or inclusive; instead, the pieces were chosen for their excellence as well as the depth of their authors' political and social commitment. Works by such poets as Dennis Brutus, Wole Soyinka, Jack Mapanje, and Frank Chipasula mourn the loss of African tradition and condemn the oppression of colonial and postcolonial times. All of these writers envision an Africa in which indigenous values blend with modern values to create a new and just society. Many of the poets in this volume have been involved in the struggles for national self-determination and have challenged nondemocratic forms of rule after independence. Many have also suffered imprisonment or have been exiled from their countries. Readers will benefit from the detailed biographical notes on each poet.

The collection offers a comprehensive and diverse view of Africa poetry. What's more, it breaks new ground by including writers from certain countries in central and southern Africa, whose literary output is often overlooked. A valuable companion work is *The Penguin Book of Modern African Poetry* (Viking, 1984), edited by Gerald Moore and Ulli Beier.

1248 Mda, Zakes. ***The Plays of Zakes Mda***. Intro. by Andrew Horn. Ohio Univ. Pr. 1989, $24.95 (0-86975-389-4). 256pp. Drama.

A South African by birth, Zakes Mda left his homeland for Lesotho when his father became a political refugee in the 1960s. Mda began writing plays while in Peka High School in Lesotho. The first professional presentation of his work was the production in Johannesburg in 1979 of "Dead End," one of the five plays in this anthology. Rather than confronting apartheid directly, the author explores the problems of racial subjugation through the personal weaknesses of the central characters. A black pimp betrays his "decent type" girlfriend, only to find that he, in turn, has been betrayed by one of his sleazy white associates. A more explicit look at apartheid is found in such works as "Dark Voices Rising" and "The Hill," in which Mda explores the inhumane treatment of farm and migrant labor in South Africa. "We Shall Sing for the Fatherland" examines neocolonialism in independent Africa, while the fifth play in the anthology, "The Road," is a "seriocomic parable" about the link between sexual politics and South Africa's migrant labor system. Several of Mda's plays have been performed in the United States. At this writing he is a teacher at the University of Vermont.

1249 Ndebele, Njabulo S. *Fools and Other Stories.* Readers International 1986, $11.95 (0-930523-20-2). 280pp. Fiction.

In the 1970s, Njabulo Ndebele emerged as a major figure in the Black Consciousness Movement in South Africa. He is part of a new generation who urged South African writers to go beyond the "descriptive documentation of suffering" to create fiction that digs deep to explain apartheid. The five stories collected here take place in South Africa's black townships, settings that allow the author to explore the complex social, economic, and psychological dimensions of apartheid as revealed in events and relationships. Whites do not play roles as central characters in the title story. Instead, the author uses an acrimonious relationship between a disreputable older teacher and an idealistic young activist as his springboard for examining human dilemmas and the impact of apartheid.

In 1983, this book won the prestigious Noma Award for Publishing in Africa. In addition to short story writing, Ndebele is a poet of some note. His work has been published in numerous journals in South Africa and abroad. After growing up in Johannesburg and Charterston Location, Nigel, he studied at Cambridge University and at the University of Denver, where he received a doctorate. He is currently rector of the University of the North in South Africa.

1250 Ngugi Wa Thiong'o. *Petals of Blood.* Viking 1991, $13.00 (0-14-015351-9). Fiction.

This novel has been described as Ngugi's most ambitious and representative work. An overtly political story, it critiques Kenya in the postcolonial period by drawing on the analysis of colonial history that the author offered in his trilogy, the first part of which is *Weep Not Child (see main entry).*

Using the framework of a murder mystery and a workers' struggle, Ngugi reaches into the immediate past to expose political and economic corruption in independent Kenya. In the opening chapter, three directors of a prominent Kenyan brewery are found burned to death following a "no-nonsense-no-pay-rise decision." Four suspects, three men and a woman, are arrested. In a series of flashbacks, Kenya's history and the interlocking lives of the suspects are revealed. Each suspect, it seems, had strong motives for the killings. The characters and the murders are Ngugi's vehicle for analyzing the oppressive and inequitable conditions that prevail in Kenya's essentially neocolonial state.

1251 Ngugi Wa Thiong'o. *Weep Not Child.* Heinemann 1988, $8.95 (0-435-90830-8). 136pp. Fiction.

This novel is the first in a trilogy that re-creates through a fictive lens the clash between Kenyan and British culture during the colonial period. The story depicts the Gikuyu (Kikuyu) people and their resistance to the British seizure and appropriation of their traditional lands. Events take place during the rise of the Mau Mau resistance and the subsequent emergency declared by the colonial government. The central figure is Njoroge, a young Gikuyu student whose hopes for an education are dashed when his father is arrested as a Mau Mau suspect. Young Njoroge is propelled into the independence struggle and the strife and violence that ensue. An award-winning book, *Weep Not Child* was the first novel written and published in English by an East African writer.

In *The River Between*, the author challenges the imposition of Christianity and British values on Gikuyu society. The story revolves around Waiyake and his lover, Nyambura. The two are separated not only by the river between their villages but by the different beliefs and backgrounds of their families. Waiyake's family sends him to a missionary school, where he acquires a European education. He soon finds himself caught between conflicting world views. In this tragic tale of love and loss, Ngugi suggests that a return to traditional ways rather than a synthesis of old and new is the solution to Waiyake's dilemma.

A Grain of Wheat portrays the dilemmas and struggles of life in the period preceding Kenyan independence. The central figure is Mugo, a man regarded as a hero by the local villagers. During Uhuru celebrations, Mugo is asked to speak in honor of his slain and martyred friend, Kihika. Mugo's refusal is initially interpreted as modesty. Ultimately the people learn that Mugo had betrayed Kihika to the British colonialists.

Ngugi's skill lies in weaving together the various strands of these three novels into a complex and continuous narrative. He is also the author of *Petals of Blood* (see main entry).

1252 Niane, D. T. *Sundiata: An Epic of Old Mali*. Humanities Pr. 1979, $9.95 (0-685-62276-2). Poetry.

Mali was one of the great Sudanic empires of West Africa. At the peak of its power in the fourteenth century, the empire stretched from the shores of the Atlantic to the city of Timbuktu. Strategically located along the trans-Saharan trade route, Mali gained its wealth and power through control of long-distance trade, particularly trade in gold. Mali began about A.D.1230, following the dissolution of Ghana, the first of the great Sudanic kingdoms.

In this book, the author presents a griot's account of the origin of Mali. He begins by noting the importance of oral accounts in precolonial Africa and the position of griots as repositories of history. Part legend, part history, this epic tale recounts the story of Sundiata, the crippled son of a hunchback princess, who grew up to fulfill the prophecies of soothsayers that he would unite the twelve kingdoms of Mali into one of the most powerful empires in Africa and the world. Often compared to *The Iliad* and *The Odyssey*, this griot's tale provides a fascinating look at a medieval Africa.

1253 Nkosi, Lewis. *Mating Birds*. HarperCollins 1987, $5.95 (0-06-097085-5). 192pp. Fiction.

Like Richard Wright's *Native Son (see main entry)*, this novel sweeps the reader into a sexually and racially charged drama. The setting is Durban, South

Africa, and the main character is Ndi Sibiya, who in many ways recalls Wright's character, Bigger Thomas. As the novel opens, Sibiya is awaiting execution for the rape of a young white woman, a charge that Sibiya vigorously denies. He describes instead a strange courtship in which the supposed victim was a willing, even eager, participant. In sensual and beautifully written prose, Nkosi uses his characters to explore power relations and the "forbidden fruit" syndrome. He also provides an illuminating portrait of Zulu village life. Some critics are bothered by Nkosi's image of a "corrupting female"; others wonder if too much blame for the character's shortcomings is ascribed to the apartheid system. Few, however, question Nkosi's ability to create a powerful drama.

1254 Nwapa, Flora. ***One Is Enough***. Africa World 1992, $24.95 (0-86543-322-4); $9.95 (0-86543-323-2). 157pp. Fiction.

Amaka is a young married woman in a Nigerian society where the wife takes the blame for her husband's failure in business or in life generally. Amaka is made to feel guilty because she cannot bear children for her husband, who has secretly proven his manhood by having two children outside their marriage. Her dilemma is complicated by the mysterious death of two earlier marriage prospects. Making things worse, her mother sees little connection between love and marriage. As she puts it, "You children got the idea of love into your heads when you went to school and read those books." Hounded by a mother-in-law who never approved of her and humiliated when her husband marries the mother of his sons, Amaka leaves her home and heads out to Lagos, where she quickly learns the mechanics of city survival. The story follows Amaka through her success in business, the failure of her love affairs, and ultimately her relationship with a priest, who abandons the church and agrees to marry her. This aspect of the story was a daring move by the author, who is writing in a culture where the love dalliances of priests are barely whispered about. Although the priest impregnates her, there is no marriage because he is overcome with guilt. Amaka bears twin sons, proving to the world that "I am a mother as well as a woman."

Among Nwapa's other works are *Efuru* (Heinemann, 1966), *Wives at War and Other Stories* (orig. pub. 1984; Africa World, 1992), and a testimony about the Nigerian civil war titled *Never Again* (orig. pub. 1975; Africa World, 1992).

1255 Obradovic, Nadezda, ed. ***Looking for a Rain God: An Anthology of Contemporary African Short Stories***. Simon & Schuster 1990, $9.95 (0-671-67177-4). Fiction.

This collection of short stories explores a variety of topics ranging from traditional customs to madness. Written primarily in English by twenty-six African authors, it includes such well-known names as Chinua Achebe, Ngugi wa Thiong'o, and Alex LaGuma. The book also highlights a number of women authors, including Bessie Head, Ama Ata Aidoo, and Grace Ogot. The authors and stories provide insight into the everyday life of a representative sampling of African cultures. Each story is followed by a short biography of the author as well as a bibliography of the author's publications. Obradovic has also edited *African Rhapsody: Short Stories of the Contemporary African Experience* (1994).

1256 Okri, Ben. *The Famished Road*. Doubleday 1992. o.p. Fiction.

Many Nigerian cultures tell stories about children who did not want to be born, but who come into the world anyway to challenge the mental, financial, and physical health of their parents. Ben Okri's book is an excellent illustration of this traditional theme.

Azaro, a spirit-child who strides both the spirit and human worlds with apparent ease, is "an unwilling adventurer . . . into the dreams of the living and the dead." Azaro sees things other humans cannot and participates in events that others could not comprehend. His companions in the spirit world constantly demand his return; that demand is made manifest in the human world through Azaro's occasional bouts of ill health and the resulting economic and physical stress on his parents. Caught between two worlds, Azaro negotiates for life rather than death as he attempts to untangle the duality of his existence. This novel was the recipient of the 1991 Booker Prize.

Okri wrote his first novel, *Flowers and Shadows* (o.p., 1980), at the age of nineteen. That story, set in Lagos, portrays an upper-class teenager's coming of age while his corrupt businessman father is exposed and prosecuted. Other works by Okri include *The Landscapes Within* (o.p., 1981), the short story collection *Stars of the New Curfew* (Viking, 1990), and a sequel to *The Famished Road* titled *Songs of Enchantment* (1993).

1257 Osundare, Niyi. *Waiting Laughters*. Malthouse 1990. o.p. Poetry.

The poems in this collection address the process of waiting, a condition in which Africa and her people often seem to find themselves. Osundare draws imagery from the daily lives of ordinary citizens involved in commonplace experiences. Consider, for example, these lines about the predicament of Africans applying for travel papers abroad: "Waiting /the anxious fumes of the visa awe-ffice /thick with queries, thick with fear /and stamps which bite trembling papers /with purple fangs and seals pompous /like a mad phallus." Still, the author finds relief even in the midst of all the despair—"Lofty shadows cast shadows of lengthy laughters"—hinting that something positive will emerge from the gloom. Another poem deals with an African despot who is merely waiting to celebrate the seventeenth year of his rule. The poet is particularly adept in the use of metaphors that vibrate with color. An example: faces that are "a mask of wrinkles / The voices wounded by a battalion of edicts."

1258 Ousmane, Sembene. *God's Bits of Wood*. Repr. of 1962 ed. Trans. from French by Francis Price. Heinemann 1987, $8.95 (0-435-90892-8). 245pp. Fiction.

Set during the period of French colonialism, this novel is a fictionalized account of the 1947 strike by workers on the Dakar-Niger railway line. The rebellious workers are depicted as struggling not only to unionize but to lift the yoke of oppressive foreign rule from their shoulders. The author was well acquainted with the events and circumstances of this period, having worked as a manual laborer in Dakar during the early 1940s and on the docks in Marseilles following World War II. *God's Bits of Wood*, viewed by many as Ousmane's finest literary achievement, has been praised not only for the dynamism of the story but for the insight it provides into family life and Islamic culture. One of the most riveting parts of the book is the protest march led by the wives of the workers. Their courageous stance defies the stereotype of the passive and controlled Islamic woman.

Ousmane is the author of several other highly praised fictional works. His first novel, *The Black Docker* (orig. pub. 1956; Heinemann, 1987) is a semiautobiographical account of his experiences as a docker and union leader. Other titles include *The Money-Order with White Genesis* (Heinemann, 1987) and Xala (Lawrence Hill, 1983). He is also a gifted and internationally known filmmaker.

1259 Oyono, Ferdinand. ***Houseboy***. Trans. from French by John Reed. Heinemann 1991, $9.95 (0-435-90532-5). 140pp. Fiction.

Oyono tells the story of Toundi Ondoua, a houseboy who serves in the home of a French colonial couple in Cameroon. He is privy to the web of pretense, deceit, and adultery that the mistress of the house weaves around her husband. The game of wits between the houseboy, his master, and the mistress is left unresolved, a reflection of the failure of the colony's foreign administrators to understand the simple needs and the honesty of their African hosts.

The story begins when Toundi is discovered close to death, coughing, his shirt covered in blood. Summing up his experience at the hands of his French masters, Toundi asks his rescuer, "Brother, what are we? What are we black men who are called French?" In flashbacks, the reader sees how Toundi loses favor with his French master, after which local officials frame him for abetting a theft. Stripped of his liberty, he is detained, whipped, and brutalized in jail. Suffering from broken ribs and punctured lungs, he is hospitalized until he is well enough for punishment. Toundi, however, manages to escape from his captors. Toundi records the crisis of colonialism in a diary, a document that becomes a powerful indictment of foreign administrators, who saw faults where there were none and punished friends to satisfy their enemies.

1260 p'Bitek, Okot. ***Song of Lawino and Song of Ocol***. Repr. of 1966 ed. Intro. by G. A. Heron. Illus. by Frank Horley. Heinemann 1984, $9.95 (0-435-90266-0). 151pp. Fiction.

This author, Uganda's best-known poet, wrote several poetic novels, the most famous of which is *Song of Lawino*. In this powerful poetic song, an Acoli woman, Lawino, laments the loss of her husband, Ocol, to Western ways and to a Westernized Ugandan woman. Lawino staunchly defends Acoli culture and heaps scorn on her husband and his mistress. In *Song of Ocol*, the second part of the volume, Ocol defends himself against his wife's accusations. Through the character of Lawino, p'Bitek raises issues about colonialization and its impact on African societies. Throughout the book, he contrasts the grace of traditional African ways with the artificiality of modern educated Africans, as represented by Ocol. p'Bitek uses Acoli songs to show that Africans possess a rich heritage and to make the point that aping an alien culture's practices diminishes Africa's own vibrant heritage. His songs are voices of complaint against the erosion of traditional values and an affirmation of the cultural heritage that Africans might unwittingly lose. p'Bitek is also author of *White Teeth (see main entry).*

1261 p'Bitek, Okot. ***White Teeth***. Trans. from Acoli by the author. Heinemann 1989. o.p. Fiction.

This novel, first published in 1953 as *Lak Tar Miyo Kinyero Wilogo*, was written in the Acoli language of Uganda. It represents one of the few efforts in Uganda to create a modern indigenous tradition of literature. Okot p'Bitek translated the novel into English before his untimely death in 1982. Like his other works, including *Song of Lawino and Song of Ocol (see main entry)*, *White Teeth* is a comment on tradition and its role in the changing society of modern Uganda. The central character is Atuk, who lacks the required bridewealth that would enable him to get married. Like many young men, he sets out for the big city to earn enough money to pay the bridewealth. Unfortunately, life in the city proves treacherous, and Atuk returns home penniless. In telling the story, the author weaves together traditional songs, customary expressions, colloquial terms, and Acoli words, many of which are left untranslated because the author felt they would lose their essence if rendered in another tongue. The story reveals the vitality and richness of Acoli culture and the pressure put on it by changing conditions and needs.

1262 Plaatje, Solomon. ***Mhudi: An Epic of South African Native Life a Hundred Years Ago***. Heinemann 1917. o.p. Fiction.

His biographer describes Solomon Tshekisho Plaatje as "one of the most talented South Africans of his generation." Plaatje was a tireless spokesman for a free South Africa, an astute politician, a linguist who mastered eight languages, and a gifted writer. *Mhudi* is his only novel. It took the author ten years to find a publisher in South Africa; four decades would pass before the book was published abroad. These delays were not due to any lack of literary merit but rather to publishers' general lack of interest in African perspectives.

The book presents a slice of South African history through African eyes. A blend of Tswana oral tradition and English literary form, the novel features three major South African groups, the Barolong (Plaatje's own Tswana-speaking people), the Matabele (a Zulu-speaking people), and the Boers. Set in the nineteenth century, the events in the novel are precipitated when a Barolong villager kills two Matabele tax collectors. An impetuous son of the Matabele king retaliates by launching a scorched-earth attack against the offending village. Mhudi, a brave Barolong maiden, escapes the slaughter. Afterward, in the Matabele kingdom, there is jubilation. A wrong has been avenged and there is booty (Barolong cattle) to share. The reveling briefly ceases when Gubuza, the respected commander of the Matabele army, wonders aloud whether the punishment has exceeded the crime and warns of retributions to come. In time Mhudi meets and marries Ra-Thaga, another Barolong survivor. As they rebuild their lives, they rail against the murderous Matabele. Eventually they organize the Barolong to avenge their loss, doing so with the assistance of newcomers on the Tswana plains, the Boers. The Barolong see the Boers as allies in the struggle against a common enemy, not as the usurpers and destroyers they would become.

This lyrical and majestic novel succeeds on many levels. A thrilling, fast-paced adventure story, it reveals Plaatje's political savvy, his knowledge of history, and his ability to transcend the conventions of his time. He shatters gender and racial stereotypes by making a woman the hero of his novel and by depicting the immigrant Boers as vulnerable and dependent on Africans.

Rich in the Tswana idiom and Shakespearean in its approach and style, *Mhudi* is a blend of the best in both literary traditions. It is truly a treasure.

For a biography of the author, see *Sol Plaatje: South African Nationalist 1876–1932* by Brian Willan (Univ. of California Pr., 1984).

1263 Salih, Tayeb. ***The Wedding of Zein and Other Sudanese Stories***. Trans. from Arabic. Heinemann 1991, $8.95 (0-435-90047-1). 120pp. Fiction.

This book includes three short stories, originally written in Arabic, that portray village life in a predominantly Muslim region of the Sudan. "The Doum Tree of Wad Hamid" deals with the intrusion of bureaucracy, government, and so-called progress into village life. The resistance of the villagers is resolved when it is recognized that the Doum tree—the most important symbol in the village—can coexist with modernity. "A Handful of Dates" describes the awakening of a child into the real world. During the harvesting of dates, the boy sees his grandfather's ruthless treatment of a field owner who is in debt to him. This harsh, business side of village life shatters the child's sense of innocence, and in a highly symbolic gesture, he vomits up the dates he has just eaten. The title story captures the excitement, emotion, and activity generated by a traditional Sudanese wedding.

1264 Samkange, Stanlake. ***On Trial for My Country***. Heinemann 1967, $8.95 (0-435-90033-1). 150pp. Fiction.

This spellbinding novel, drawn from historical events and based on African oral history, letters, and documents, tells of the clash between Lobengula, king of the Ndebele people, and the empire-building Cecil Rhodes, founder of Rhodesia. Rhodes coveted the Ndebele kingdom, located in what is now Zimbabwe. He saw its temperate climate as ideal for European settlement and was convinced that vast mineral wealth lay beneath the land's surface.

In the novel, readers are transported to the hereafter, where the ancestors of Lobengula and Rhodes stage a trial in which the two men are called to account for their actions on earth. Lobengula's incredulous father asks him: "What witch, what wizard, and what medicines, then, could have made you sell my people, my cattle, and my land to these whitemen?" In similar fashion, the Rev. Francis William Rhodes queries his son, Cecil: "Some say you have . . . unscrupulously dealt with other men and cheated them out of their money and land . . . [that] you drove an African monarch named Lobengula out of this country, usurped his land, burnt his kraals, massacred his people, took their cattle, and enslaved those of his subjects who survived. . . . Say now in this the Lord's house . . . whether these evil things we hear about you are true or false." In the balance of the book, Lobengula, Rhodes, and other historical figures plead their cases. This unusually structured, compelling, and dynamic book is not to be missed.

1265 Senghor, Leopold S. ***Leopold Sedar Senghor: The Collected Poetry***. Bilingual ed.; Trans. from French with Intro. by Melvin Dixon. Univ. Pr. of Virginia 1991, $40.00 (0-8139-1275-X). 598pp. Poetry.

Leopold Sedar Senghor was born over eighty years ago in Joal, a small fishing village some seventy miles from Dakar, the capital of Senegal. From inauspicious beginnings he rose to great heights, serving as Senegal's first president. Also hailed as a great poet, he was the only black writer invited to join the 350-year-old French Academy. Senghor, who began publishing poetry during his student days in Paris, was greatly influenced by African Americans and Caribbean Americans who were living in Paris at the time. Together with Aime Cesaire, Leon Damas, and the Nardal sisters, Senghor is credited with launching a literary movement known as Negritude, a movement that defied French racism by validating black culture and experiences.

This volume provides an excellent introduction to his poetry. The poems, printed in both the French original and in English translation, represent the broad range of Senghor's poetry by including excerpts from his first book of poems, *Shadow and Song* (o.p., 1945), as well as his more recent works. The reader will be captivated by the rhythms, passion, and imagery of Senghor's multifaceted world. There are joyous poems that celebrate Senghor's idyllic Senegalese childhood; sensuous poems that praise the beauty of the black woman; somber, angry poems that mourn the loss of Senegalese soldiers in World War II who sacrificed their lives for an ungrateful France; and measured elegies that acknowledge Senghor's family, friends, and heroes. The elegies include a heartbreaking farewell to Senghor's dead son, Phillippe, a boy whose "smile was dawn." In his introduction, translator Melvin Dixon provides a succinct overview of the man, his life, and his poetry.

In addition to this volume, readers will want to explore Sylvia Ba's *The Concept of Negritude in the Poetry of Leopold Sedar Senghor* (Books on Demand, 1973) and Janet Vaillant's superb biography, *Black, French, and African : A Life of Leopold Sedar Senghor (see main entry).*

1266 Sepamla, Sipho. ***A Ride on the Whirlwind***. Heinemann 1984, $8.95 (0-435-90268-7). 244pp. Fiction.

At the beginning of this fast-paced novel, Mzi, a guerrilla trained in the Eastern bloc, slips into Soweto. His assignment: to kill a brutal black policeman. His contacts lead him to a group of high school students who are participating in the school boycott and demonstrations. The youngsters, led by the handsome, charismatic Mandla, are fascinated by this professional guerrilla and join him in his mission. Soon they are helping to carry out assassinations of local traitors and manufacturing homemade bombs as the struggle for liberation takes a new, more violent turn.

Sepamla's novel explores the issue of terrorism used as a weapon against a society that was founded upon terror. As the children's eyes are opened to the inner workings of their society, they must choose between being passive victims or active participants in the struggle; the latter course leads them into the world of violence, betrayal, and moral ambiguity. This little-known novel was published clandestinely in South Africa in 1981 and later republished by Readers International, which specializes in fiction originally banned in its country of origin. LML

1267 Soyinka, Wole. ***Collected Plays, Vol. 1 and Vol. 2***. Oxford Univ. Pr. 1973, 1974, $12.95 each (0-19-281136-6; 0-19-281164-9). 307+276pp. Drama.

These two volumes bring together ten of Soyinka's most important plays. Volume 1 contains "A Dance of the Forest," "The Swamp Dwellers," "The Strong Breed," "The Road," and "The Bacchae of Euripedes."

Volume 2 offers "The Lion and the Jewel," in which a crafty and resourceful tribal chief lures the virgin, Sidi, to bed. Soyinka plays the innocence of this youthful maiden against the wiles of the chief, who cleverly spreads the false news of his impotence in the hope that "other maids will hear of it, /And go to mock his pride." "Kongi's Harvest" is a political satire that shows the conflict between a present-day dictatorship and an eroding traditional system. But Oba Danlola, the traditional king, remains powerful even in confinement because "Ogun is still a god /Even without his navel." In order to capture the Oba's spiritual authority, President Kongi manipulates him into presenting the harvest yam to him in public. The shattering climax punctuates the play of wits between these clashing personalities. In "The Trials of Brother Jero" and "Jero's Metamorphosis," Soyinka makes a moral indictment of power politics. These plays capture the religious fervor of a prophet and his flock in their mutual quest to survive a difficult economic environment. The prophet says their chances of success depend on how well some of the female converts are able to "shake their bosoms in spiritual ecstasy," because even in the prophet's business "one must move with modern times. Lack of color gets one nowhere." Also in this collection is the allegorical play "Madmen and Specialists," which grew out of the author's two-year imprisonment in Nigeria. Another play by the same author is *The Road (see main entry).*

1268 Soyinka, Wole. ***The Road***. Oxford Univ. Pr. 1965, $7.95 (0-19-911084-0). 101pp. Drama.

This play describes the world of motor mechanics, drivers, and hangers-on and the carnage on the roads that has become part of their lives. Soyinka uses a remarkable range of language in this play, making his characters equally at home in Yoruba, pidgin, and standard English. From their discussion we get a sense of their shared experiences, their despair, and the hopelessness that marks the lives of the generally destitute. Relief for their plight comes via their hope in the Professor, who is first introduced as a forger of documents and a necessary evil within this cluster of desperate beings. The Professor is obsessed by his quest for the elusive Word, an object he is unable to find and even less able to explain to his lowly dependents. Their complex relationship climaxes in a confrontation in which one of them stabs the Professor. As he wrestles with the pain, it is the driver's dirge that accompanies him in his last moments.

1269 Tutuola, Amos. ***The Palm-Wine Drinkard and His Dead Palm-Wine Tapster in the Dead's Town***. Repr. of 1953 ed. Greenwood 1970, $38.50 (0-8371-4044-7); Grove $12.00 (0-8021-3363-0). 130pp. Fiction.

With only a few years of formal education, Tutuola was inspired to become a writer by an elementary schoolteacher who helped shape his immense talent as a storyteller. He does not have the literary command of Soyinka or Achebe, but his plot exposition is no less gripping. In this work, Tutuola delves into Yoruba oral narrative to tell the story of the sudden death of the palm-wine drinkard's favorite tapster (bartender) and the series of events that set the drinkard on an uncertain journey to the land of the Dead to find him. His quest straddles the human and the supernatural worlds. A series of adventures facilitates his reunion with his tapster, who, having spent two years in death training, has "qualified as a full dead man" and can no longer return to the land of the living. But the tapster gives the drinkard a magic egg that is later crucial in solving the world's famine crisis, although his benefactors then turn against him. In this story, Tutuola explores a popular Nigerian folk theme that cautions against greed: Only by sharing our fortune, helping, and respecting others can we attain true happiness.

NONFICTION

1270 Abu-Lughod, Lila. *Veiled Sentiments: Honor and Poetry in a Bedouin Society*. Illus. 1987, $42.50 (0-520-05483-0); Univ. of California Pr. $14.00 (0-520-06327-9). 317pp. Nonfiction.

In this aptly titled work, the author collects, analyzes, and brings to life the experiences of Bedouin women who live in a small settlement in the western desert of Egypt. Her pathway into their social world is the uniquely Bedouin form of oral poetry called *ghinnawa* (or, as the word is sometimes spelled, *ghannawa*).

The first segment of the book includes discussions of Bedouin perspectives on love, marriage, honor, family hierarchy, modesty, and sexuality. The second part explores these themes as expressed through the women's poetry. Abu-Lughod's insight is that, in everyday discourse, the women's speech suggests that they are adhering to the traditional social norms. But through ghinnawa, the women share their true feelings. This study of nomadic Arab culture, poetry, women, and gender roles is anthropological yet accessible to the general public.

1271 Abun-Nasr, Jamil M. *A History of the Maghrib*. 2nd ed. Books on Demand 1975, $108.00 (0-317-26070-7). 416pp. Nonfiction.

The term *Maghrib*— literally, "the West"—refers generally to the countries in the northwest part of Africa: Algeria, Libya, Morocco, and Tunisia. Though diverse, these nation-states have in common enough history and tradition that in many ways they constitute a discrete region. In this new edition of a work first published in 1971, the author traces the history of the area from the spread of Islam to the early postcolonial period. Describing the impact of various dynasties on the people and their society, the author focuses on the role of the Berbers, who he says appropriated the Islamic faith and Arabic culture. There are chapters dealing with dynastic rule, the Ottoman era, the onset of European colonization, the rise of nationalism, the emergence of independence, and development. The theme of the book is the conflict between the forces of ethnicity and those of the state. Although there is little here about other aspects of life in the region—the economy and the agriculture, for example—the book is a good introduction in English to the history of Africa's northwest.

1272 Achebe, Chinua. *Hopes and Impediments: Selected Essays*. Doubleday 1990, $9.95 (0-385-41479-X). 166pp. Essays.

In this collection of previously published essays, Achebe argues that writers are teachers and that literature is a social force. As a negative example, the author cites Joseph Conrad's *Heart of Darkness*, a novel that is often taught in schools but which is marred by a distorted—even racist—view of Africa. Other essays celebrate African writers such as Amos Tutuola, Christopher Okigbo, and Kofi Awonoor. As Achebe notes, works by these dynamic poets and storytellers make their cultures come alive. The book ends with a tribute to an African American, James Baldwin, for enlisting his pen in the fight against racism. Readers will develop with a deeper understanding of African culture and a solid grounding in Achebe's own literary philosophy.

For a discussion of Achebe's fiction—including *Anthills of the Savannah*, *Girls at War*, and *A Man of the People*—see their main entries.

1273 Afigbo, A. E., and others. ***The Making of Modern Africa: Vol. 1: The Nineteenth Century; Vol. 2: The Twentieth Century.*** 2nd ed.; 2 vols. Illus. Longman 1986, $22.95 each (0-582-58508-2; 0-582-58509-0). 352+352pp. Nonfiction.

This updated version of a two-volume work by five prominent historians, first published in 1971, is an excellent choice for both students and the general reader.

Volume 1, *The Nineteenth Century*, opens with an overview of the geography, peoples, and history of the continent, including a discussion of external influences on Africa before 1800. Eschewing the traditional view that regarded the African past as a mere extension of European history, the authors place Africa at the center of African history. They summarize major events and processes in the nineteenth century, including the formation of nations, long-distance trade, foreign intrusion, African resistance, and European conquest. The essays are grouped geographically to cover four major regions: western, northern, southern and central, and middle Africa.

Volume 2, *The Twentieth Century*, covers the era of European administration, the rise of nationalism, and the period of independence through the mid-1980s. Among the topics discussed are the evolution of the one-party state, the frequency of military coups, apartheid, and the search for economic stability. Succinct and highly readable, the books provide a solid introduction to the history of the continent over the past two hundred years. Tightly captioned black-and-white photographs, drawings, and maps complement the text.

1274 Ajayi, J.F.A., and Michael Crowder, eds. ***A History of West Africa.*** 2 vols. Columbia Univ. Pr. 1972. o.p. Nonfiction.

This two-volume work provides a general background for studies in West African history. The first volume covers the period from earliest times to 1800 and emphasizes state formation and the development of political institutions in West Africa. It features contributions from scholars trained in different disciplines and specializing in different geographical regions and historical periods. The second volume covers the nineteenth and twentieth centuries, when external influences exerted significant effects in the lives of West African peoples. Special attention is given to the roles of Christianity and Islam in shaping life on the continent.

The ongoing events of history would not wait for completion of this work. Instead, events continuously shaped the content of both volumes. For example, the Nigerian civil war resulted in changes of authors and delays in publication. The final product is worth the time that went into the project.

1275 Appiah, Kwame Anthony. *In My Father's House: Africa in the Philosophy of Culture.* Oxford Univ. Pr. 1992, $38.00 (0-19-506851-3); $10.95 (0-19-506852-1). 232pp. Essays.

Reviewers have both praised and criticized Kwame Anthony Appiah's book. His primary focus, what it means to be African in a multicultural world, is open to different interpretations. Appiah begins the book with glimpses of his upbringing in Kumasi, Ghana. He is a member of both a prominent Ghanaian family and an equally prominent English family. Appiah's world thus included relatives of different hues and different cultural backgrounds. Yet, as Appiah notes, his child's eye saw these worlds as strikingly similar: "If my sisters and I were 'children of two worlds,' no one bothered to tell us this; we lived in one world, in two 'extended' families divided by several thousand miles and an allegedly insuperable cultural distance, that never, so far as I can recall, puzzled or perplexed us much. . . . I am used to seeing the world as a network of points of affinity. "

Appiah divides the nine chapters in his book into four clusters. The first explores the role of race ideology in the development of Pan-Africanism and closely examines the ideas of two well-known Pan-Africanists, Alexander Crummel and W.E.B. Du Bois. The second cluster analyzes African identity in African literature, with particular reference to the writing of Nigeria's Wole Soyinka (some of whose books are reviewed in this chapter). The third cluster focuses on philosophical issues. The fourth and final cluster recapitulates and amplifies Appiah's questions about politics and identify.

The book is not an easy read. Appiah's writing is often dense, and references may be unfamiliar to the general reader, yet many have found the intellectual journey worth the effort. *In My Father's House* received the Melville Herskovits Award for the best book on Africa and was named a Notable Book of the Year by the *New York Times*. The book will cause many to rethink their concepts about the African world. Readers interested in learning more can consult *Joe Appiah: The Autobiography of an African Patriot* (Praeger, 1990) by Kwame Appiah's father.

1276 Apraku, Kofi K. *African Émigrés in the United States: A Missing Link in Africa's Social and Economic Development.* Greenwood 1991, $45.00 (0-275-93799-2). 162pp. Nonfiction.

This volume is a comprehensive study of recent African emigrants to the United States. It is a valuable source for understanding the direct relationship between the social and economic factors of Africa's development. The book, based on an informative national study, discusses many key topics: the reasons skilled Africans immigrated to the United States, the factors influencing whether or not they returned, the benefits from emigration for African states, and the influence of Africans living outside the continent on foreign policy and foreign aid. The question of "reverse transfer of technology" or the "brain drain" phenomenon in Africa is delineated with precision and clarity. The volume argues forcefully that African leadership must recognize the range of potential contributions that emigrants in the United States can make toward Africa's development. It shows that African professionals are willing to return home if certain policy and democratic changes are made.

1277 Asante, Molefi K. *Afrocentricity: The Theory of Social Change.* 2nd ed. Africa World 1990, $9.95 (0-86543-067-5). 145pp. Nonfiction.

The author, professor and chair of the Department of African-American Studies at Temple University, is one of the most well-known proponents of Afrocentrism. As described by Asante, Afrocentrism is more than a scholarly paradigm; it is a full-blown ideological system with its own language, values, heroes, and religion. Building on the intellectual heritage of scholars such as Cheikh Anta Diop and Maulana Karenga, Asante develops a philosophical base and a practical program for the regeneration of black people. He introduces, for example, such concepts of Ebonics (the language spoken by black Americans), Afrology (which the author defines as "the study of concepts, issues, and behaviors with particular bases in the African world, diasporan and continental"), and Njia (the collective expression of the Afrocentric world view, one that is grounded in the historical experience of African people). Asante states that a Njia meeting consists of libation to the ancestors, poetry, music, discussion, positive reinforcement, and other actions designed to raise the level of awareness among African people and reinforce a collective sense of responsibility. The author also discusses the relevancy of Islam, Christianity, and Marxism to African peoples. Provocative and visionary, this book is must reading for anyone interested in understanding Afrocentricity.

Asante has elaborated and refined his thoughts in several other works, including *The Afrocentric Idea* (Temple Univ. Pr., 1988), *Kemet, Afrocentricity, and Knowledge* (Africa World, 1992), and a book coauthored by Kariamu Welsh Asante titled *African Culture: The Rhythms of Unity* (Greenwood, 1985).

1278 Asiwaju, A. I. *Partitioned Africans: Ethnic Relations Across Africa's International Boundaries, 1884–1984.* St. Martin 1985, $29.95 (0-312-59753-3). 350pp. Nonfiction.

In 1884, the major European powers delineated boundaries that carved Africa into spheres of European influence and governance. A number of books have examined European perspectives of the division of Africa, but in this edited volume, the contributors discuss partition from the African perspective. The book's scope goes beyond the usual focus on law and diplomacy to emphasize the human factors involved. In eight case studies, scholars examine the social, cultural, and economic cost borne by border populations that straddle national boundaries. Disrupted family networks, obstructed access to holy sites, broken lines of communication, and thwarted access to valued resources are among the central issues of concern. One Somali poet-herdsman poignantly put his case: "My brother is there, I can hear the bells of his camels when they graze down in the valley. . . . When I pray, he prays, and my Allah is his Allah. My brother is there and he cannot come to me." The individual essays and the concluding section of the book propose solutions to the thorny problems generated by the partition.

1279 Ben-Jochannan, Yosef. *Black Man of the Nile and His Family.* Black Classic 1990, $24.95 (0-933121-26-1). 381pp. Nonfiction.

A Nile Valley historian, Ben-Jochannan is the revered mentor of many black students. Western scholars, however, have generally ignored his work, finding him too polemical and one-sided. Making no apologies for his style, Ben-Jochannan describes his approach as necessary to counterbalance the negative, hostile, and often inaccurate depiction of Africa in Western literature. This book, one of his best known, includes discussions on human origins in Africa, the African high cultures of Nubia, Meroe, and Egypt, and the African origins of "Greek" philosophy. A chapter entitled "Questions and Answers on Africa" explores African influences on Christianity. Other books by this author include *Africa: Mother of Western Civilization* (Black Classic, 1988) and *We the Black Jews: Witness to the "White Jewish Race" Myth* (Black Classic, 1992).

1280 Biko, Steve. *I Write What I Like*. Harper SF 1986, $10.00 (0-06-250055-4). 224pp. Essays.

Steve Biko, the dynamic leader of South Africa's Black Consciousness Movement, was killed in 1977 while in police custody. This collection of his writings demonstrates why, years after his death, he is widely revered. His articles, lectures, trial testimonies, and letters reveal an astute intellect and passionate commitment to human rights.

Biko was a major architect of Black Consciousness, which he defined as a positive philosophy that would enable the oppressed blacks of South Africa to infuse themselves with pride and dignity and "rid themselves of the shackles that bind them to perpetual servitude." Knowledge of black history was an important element of the ideology. As Biko put it: "A people without a positive history is like a vehicle without an engine." Biko's ideas echoed those of an earlier generation of South Africans, especially Anton Lembede, A. P. Mda, and Robert Sobukwe. Readers who wish to consult an excellent summary of these individuals, their ideas, and the early development of Black Power should see Gail Gerhart's *Black Power: The Evolution of an Ideology* (Univ. of California Pr., 1978).

Critics have proclaimed *I Write What I Like* a classic that provides a window into Biko's mind and the philosophy of Black Consciousness that he articulated so well. For additional information on Biko, see Donald Woods's *Biko* (Peter Smith, 1983) and *Bounds of Possibility: The Legacy of Steve Biko and Black Consciousness* by Barney Pityana and others *(see main entry)*. A movie based on Biko's life and starring Denzel Washington is called *Cry Freedom*.

1281 Blyden, Edward W. *Christianity, Islam, and the Negro Race.* Repr. of 1887 ed. Intro. by Raye G. Richardson; Contrib. by Samuel Lewis. Julian Richardson 1990, $34.95 (0-685-45610-2); $21.95 (0-685-45611-0). 408pp. Nonfiction.

Edward Blyden was born in St. Thomas, Virgin Islands, in 1832. Denied an education in the United States, he settled in West Africa, living first in Liberia and later in Sierra Leone. A prolific writer, Blyden expressed his views in over a hundred articles and several books, including *Vindication of the Negro Race* (1857) and *The Negro Race in Ancient History* (1869). Many scholars consider *Christianity, Islam and the Negro* to be his most important work.

In this book, Blyden focused his attention on Western motives in Africa. He also described the condition of colonized Africans and articulated his own program for the transformation of the continent. Blyden argued that the regeneration Africa should be in the hands of "civilized" blacks from the Americas, not whites. He described this "civilizing" mission as beneficial not only to

Africans but to the immigrant blacks as well. As he put it, "Only in Africa will they find the sphere of their true activity." Although he was an ordained Christian minister, Blyden viewed Islam rather than Christianity as the force most capable of organizing African communities and supporting an African identity.

Blyden left an important legacy of thought. He has been called the "first Pan-Africanist," the "foremost precursor of Negritude," and the "Father of the Black Cultural Nation." Numerous scholars and political activists have identified him as the guiding force in their work. Readers seeking further information about Blyden will want to read Hollis Lynch's masterly biography *Edward Wilmot Blyden: Pan-Negro Patriot 1832–1912* (Oxford Univ. Pr., 1967).

1282   Boahen, A. Adu. *African Perspectives on Colonialism*. Johns Hopkins Univ. Pr. 1989, $10.95 (0-8018-3931-9). 144pp. Nonfiction.

This book is a collection of the James S. Schouler Lectures given by the author at the Johns Hopkins University. Boahen's objective is to show "how Africans perceived colonialism, what initiatives and responses they displayed in the face of this colonial challenge, and above all how they reacted after the forcible imposition of colonialism." Although African kings aggressively protected their kingdoms against nineteenth-century European interference, they were also willing to cooperate at certain levels. However, they were no longer dealing with a fifteenth-century Europe, in which mutual exchange flourished, but with a Europe that "had witnessed the industrial revolution and was desperately in need of markets as well as raw materials." Boahen notes that the partitioning of the African continent by the Europeans resulted from the economic conditions that led to the search for new investment opportunities as well as from political and social conditions in Europe in the last two or three decades of the nineteenth century. Increasing competition for international trade made European businesses conservative and restrictive of trade boundaries, leading to the search for new colonies outside Europe that would serve as the exclusive providers of raw materials and markets for goods. Boahen also examines the legacy of colonialism in Africa and the significance of colonialism for Africa and Africans. He concludes that the African economic landscape has been significantly altered with a cash economy permanently replacing the barter economy, while power has shifted from kings and priests to an educated elite.

1283   Bunche, Ralph J. *An African-American in South Africa: The Travel Notes of Ralph J. Bunche, September 28, 1937–January 1, 1938.* Ed. by Robert R. Edgar. Illus. Ohio Univ. Pr. 1992, $40.00 (0-8214-1021-0). 405pp. Essays.

In 1950, Ralph Bunche won the Nobel Peace Prize for his role as mediator in the Middle East. Thirteen years prior to this honor, his mettle was tested in another conflict-ridden part of the world. In 1937, Bunche surmounted numerous hurdles to secure a visa to visit South Africa. For three months, he traveled throughout the land recording his observations and impressions in candid and copious notes. Bunche had planned to use this material to write a book about South Africa, but events and responsibilities intervened. Fortunately, historian Robert Edgar has accomplished this task. Edgar's edited volume of Bunche's research notes is valuable for several reasons. First, it provides a wealth of information on black life in South Africa during the 1930s. Second, it gives us one of the few accounts of South Africa by an African American. Third, it provides an unguarded look at Bunche, a man who scrupulously concealed his private thoughts and emotions. Bunche looked at a variety of issues during his sojourn in South Africa, including race relations, black living conditions, African organizations, health, education, sports, business, and the legal system. A warrior seasoned by years of battle with American racism, Bunche was well equipped to analyze the complexities of racism, South African style. He provides an astute and revealing portrait of this time period.

1204 Cabral, Amilcar. ***Return to the Source: Selected Speeches by Amilcar Cabral.*** Facsimile ed. Books on Demand 1973, $29.70 (0-7837-3918-4). 110pp. Essays.

For this author, returning to the source means a conscious effort to contest foreign economic and political domination. Cabral, who comes from Guinea-Bissau, sees this process as being more difficult for indigenous elites isolated from their people because of their ambiguous role. One of the speeches in this book was part of a series Cabral gave in Syracuse University, New York, in which he defined the revolution as "a struggle both for the preservation and survival of the cultural values of the people and for the harmonization and development of these values within a national framework." Cabral also addressed the United Nations in 1962 and 1972, calling the attention of the world body to the atrocities committed against his people by the Portuguese. This book opens with the text of his second address to the UN in which he chastised Portugal for flouting the resolution calling on it to give up its role in Guinea. He denounced the intransigence of some NATO countries, whose economic assistance to Portugal made them neglect the rights of Africans. Defining the terms of the struggle, Cabral notes that the fight is not against the Portuguese people but against Portuguese colonialism. According to the editors, this collection of Cabral's speeches is "a vital part of the study, analysis, and application which made it possible for the people of Guinea-Bissau, and their comrades in Mozambique and Angola, to achieve what they have achieved in the face of numerous difficulties."

1285 Cabral, Amilcar. ***Revolution in Guinea: Selected Texts.*** Books on Demand 1969, $45.80 (0-318-34961-2). 174pp. Essays.

Cabral, along with a small group of dedicated followers, founded the liberation group known as PAIGC, whose aim was to free Guinea-Bissau from Portuguese colonial domination. This effort served as a model for liberation struggles in much of Africa because of its sheer tenacity, political strategy, and the certainty of victory. The speeches in this collection go beyond the specific issue of Guinea to question all forms of colonialism in Africa and to suggest a political theory of class participation in the struggle for change. The author also urges the oppressed to "the struggle against our own weaknesses," which he acknowledges is an even more difficult battle than one fought against the oppressor. He identifies those weaknesses as the economic and social contradictions in which colonized peoples find themselves. One unique feature of Cabral's revolution was that he traveled all through his country to get a sense of the physical and demographic characteristics of the land and people he fought so hard to liberate. Another volume of Cabral's speeches is *Return to the Source (see main entry)*.

1286 Cham, Mbye, and Claire Andrade-Watkins, eds. ***Black Frames: Critical Perspectives on Independent Black Cinema***. Illus. MIT Pr. 1988, $9.95 (0-262-53080-5). 116pp. Nonfiction.

This book highlights the historical and cultural expressions of filmmakers of African descent in the United States, Africa, and Britain. The discussions are not limited to the aesthetic and cultural components of the films, but also extend to the problems of production and distribution of independent films by Africans. Many of the articles are based on critical perspectives that are both historical and contemporary, placing the films within the context of the politics of race and delineating ways in which they conflict with or complement the Hollywood code.

1287 Cheru, Fantu. ***Silent Revolution in Africa: Debt, Development, and Democracy***. Humanities Pr. 1989, $49.95 (0-86232-890-X); $17.50 (0-86232-891-8). 160pp. Nonfiction.

African intellectuals are making their perspectives known, often to the chagrin of Western development experts. In this book, the author analyzes the role of the Bretton Woods institutions—the World Bank and the International Monetary Fund (IMF)—in maintaining Africa's economic underdevelopment. He dismisses both the African-developed Lagos Plan of Action and the World Bank's Berg Report as simply blueprints for the recolonization of Africa. Cheru argues that Africa needs to disassociate itself from Western-led economic strategies and retreat from export-led development programs that continue to govern Africa.

Additionally, he faults the African elite for focusing on short-term solutions (such as servicing the foreign debt) rather than building Africa's capacity for self-sustained development. The book is divided into seven chapters: "The Garden of Eden Revisited," "Africa: Debt—Bondage or Self-Reliance?," "Tanzania: Suffering with Bitterness," "Kenya: A Tarnished Miracle," "Ethiopia and Sudan: The Fabrication of Hunger," and "Zambia: The IMF's Newest Bantustan." The final chapter, "Rethinking Development: Conditionality or Democracy?," recommends a more dignified and democratic alternative to economic development.

1288 Chinweizu. ***The West and the Rest of Us: White Predators, Black Slavers, and the African Elite***. NOK 1978, $21.95 (0-88357-015-7); $9.95 (0-88357-016-5). 544pp. Nonfiction.

In this masterly overview of the past five hundred years of African exploitation, Chinweizu exposes the greedy and the ambitious West. He describes his book as "a long letter to the Third World, and especially to those who fancy themselves to be the African elite, pleading for a moment to listen closely and analyze the tunes being played to us by the Pied Pipers of progress from the West, before we decide whether and how we should march out after them."

The first section of the book is a excellent summary of the history of European expansion and conquest from the fifteenth century to the end of World War II. Subsequent sections focus more closely on the methods and means by which the West accomplished this feat. Central factors in the conquest of Africa were those Africans who became handmaidens to Western interests. As the title suggests, these Africans receive their share of castigation. The final section of the book describes the steps Africa should take to recapture control of its destiny.

1289 Chirimuta, Richard, and Rosalind Chirimuta. *AIDS, Africa, and Racism*. Columbia Univ. Pr. 1989, $16.00 (1-85343-077-3). 192pp. Nonfiction.

This book is a response to Western media and health researchers who promote the theory that the deadly disease AIDS first arose in Africa. The authors discuss what they identify as erroneous claims, bad science, and wasted human, material, and media resources invested in perpetuating what the authors consider to be a racist lie. General and specialty readers interested in reviewing primary data associated with the origins of AIDS and the related debate will find this work both fascinating and highly informative. The book also offers a valuable guide to AIDS terminology, origin theories, and the real AIDS situation in Africa.

1290 Clarke, John Henrik, ed. *Marcus Garvey and the Vision of Africa*. Random 1974, $10.00 (0-394-71888-7). 496pp. Nonfiction.

A Jamaican, Garvey was the twentieth century's most prominent advocate of black emigration to Africa. He followed in the footsteps of "back-to-Africa" advocates such as Paul Cuffee, Martin Delany, and Bishop Henry McNeal Turner. However, as editor John Henrik Clarke notes, a physical return to Africa was only one aspect of Garvey's plan. His was a vision of "total African redemption." This volume includes Marcus Garvey's own writings and interpretative analyses of Garvey by well-known scholars, including W.E.B. Du Bois, E. Franklin Frazier, Kelly Miller, and Edwin Redkey. Amy Jacques Garvey, Marcus's wife, also provides valuable documentary analyses and an insightful and useful summary of Garvey's early years.

Clarke allows Garvey to speak for himself and set forth his vision of Africa and for Africa's people. He has organized Garvey's speeches and writings—labeled "Marcus Garvey in His Own Words"—in six of the volume's seven parts. These primary data are central to understanding the historical logic of Garvey's life and the mass movement he led. Integrated into each part are valuable interpretative analyses of Garvey from the perspective of the community he served. An honest and balanced treatment, the book conveys Garvey's strengths and weaknesses, his intellectual prowess, and, as the title indicates, his vision of Africa and its peoples. For additional information on Garvey, readers can consult *Marcus Garvey: Life and Lessons* (Univ. of California Pr., 1987), written by Garvey and edited by Robert A. Hill and Barbara Bair. Hill is also the editor of a multivolume series, *The Marcus Garvey and Universal Negro Improvement Association Papers*, published by the University of California Press.

1291 Davidson, Basil. ***African Civilization Revisited: From Antiquity to Modern Times.*** 2nd, rev. ed. Africa World 1990, $39.95 (0-86543-123-X); $14.95 (0-86543-124-8). 460pp. Nonfiction.

Davidson is one of the best and most prolific chroniclers of African history. Over half of his twenty-three books on Africa are still in print. This volume, a historical anthology, is a collection of primary source material from antiquity to the nineteenth century plus a few selections from the twentieth century. Dissatisfied with the usual anthologies that focus on European exploration of Africa rather than on African life, Davidson aims in this work to "reflect the deeper truths of African life, its long passage and unfolding through the years." Of the more than 120 authors included, a significant number are African. Each document is preceded by an illuminating narrative by Davidson. Collectively, the selections and narratives provide a valuable guide to the African past.

Among Davidson's better-known works are *Africa in History* (Macmillan, 1992), *The African Genius: An Introduction to Social and Cultural History* (Little, Brown, 1970), *Let Freedom Come: Africa in Modern History* (Little, Brown, 1979), and *Lost Cities of Africa* (Little, Brown, 1988). A recent work, *The Black Man's Burden* (Random, 1992), draws on the author's long experience in Africa and his knowledge of the Balkans, where he served as a British agent with anti-Nazi forces during World War II. Here he draws historical and contemporary parallels between Africa's nation-states and those of the Balkans. He concludes that Africa's redemption (and that of the Balkans) lies in the decentralization of political power, mass participation in decision-making, and development strategies that focus on the rural many rather than the urban few. He cites Cape Verde and Eritrea as models worth emulating.

1292 Davies, Carole B., and Anne A. Graves, eds. ***Ngambika: Studies of Women in African Literature.*** Africa World 1986, $125.00 (0-86543-017-9); $40.00 (0-86543-018-7). 256pp. Essays.

The word *ngambika*, from the Tshiluba language of Central Africa, means "help me to balance this load." The term is thus a fitting title for this study, which attempts to restore balance by analyzing often-overlooked writings by and about African women.

The essays in this collection assess the image of women in the works of African writers. The essays are grouped into three parts. Part 1 examines the depiction of women from the male or societal perspective as demonstrated by the writings of authors such as Sembene, Ngugi, and Soyinka. The articles in Part 2, by contrast, examine the rise of African feminism and feminist consciousness. The authors analyze the African woman in her traditional roles and as an individual who questions and challenges herself and others. They also examine the forces that shape the lives of women in African societies. Discussion focuses on some well-known authors, including Mariama Ba, Buchi Emecheta, and Flora Nwapa, whose works are reviewed elsewhere in this chapter. Part 3 focuses on the impact on women of such political and social institutions as marriage and motherhood.

Although the collection is not intended to be comprehensive, the authors manage to cover a variety of topics, geographical areas, and perspectives.

Included is a useful bibliography of literary criticism by and about African women.

1293 Denoon, Donald, and Balaam Nyeko. **Southern Africa Since 1800.** 2nd ed. Longman 1984, $22.95 (0-582-72707-3). 246pp. Nonfiction.

This volume is a revised edition of a popular 1972 text. Written specifically for secondary school, college, and university students, the book serves as an informative introduction to South African history since 1800. It is particularly useful for those seeking African perspectives of South African history. Many older histories of South Africa focused almost exclusively on South Africa's white settler population. Information on Africans was included only as it pertained to the lives of whites. Also, in the older texts, conflict between black and white is often described as the inevitable result of contact between "racial" groups that differed in physical appearance, culture, and technological development. Denoon and Nyeko depart from older historical traditions by incorporating significant information on South Africa's black population. Moreover, they describe the economic problems that they identify as key factors in the struggle between classes.

There are several other historical works that students and general readers will find useful. Paul Maylam's *A History of the African People of South Africa: From the Iron Age to the 1970s* (St. Martin, 1986) is a dynamic and comprehensive survey that places Africans at the center of South African historiography and refutes the notion that black history has been static and simply reactive to white initiatives. Similar in its approach is Kevin Shillington's *The History of Southern Africa* (Longman, 1987). The author describes African societies before European settlement in southern Africa and keeps the African population squarely in focus throughout the text. Neil Parson's recently revised *A New History of Southern Africa* (Holmes & Meier, 1993) is another excellent work. Written for secondary school students in Africa, the book provides a comprehensive and easy-to-read history of southern Africa from the later Stone Age to the 1990s. Another resource that is well worth acquiring is J. D. Omer-Cooper's *History of Southern Africa* (Heinemann, 1987). This text analyzes the interaction between black and white people in South Africa and explores political, economic, legal, and social issues and their implications for South Africa's future. *The Reader's Digest Illustrated History of South Africa: The Real Story* (Reader's Digest, 1988) is a surprisingly good history text. Coherently written and illustrated with numerous color plates, it also pays significant attention to African perspectives of history. Finally there is Leonard Thompson's liberal interpretation of South African history, *A History of South Africa* (Yale Univ. Pr., 1992).

1294 Diawara, Manthia. **African Cinema: Politics and Culture.** Illus. Indiana Univ. Pr. 1992, $29.95 (0-253-31704-5); $10.95 (0-253-20707-X). 208pp. Nonfiction.

This is one of the few books that specifically address African cinema. It traces the historical development of film production and distribution in Africa and the monopoly of African cinema by foreign companies. Diawara discusses the different facets of film production from earlier colonialist interest to the attitude of governments and individuals toward African films. He writes that early filmmakers believed that distributing commercial films in Africa would be harmful because it would introduce Africans to the power of films. "Such films were held to be technically too sophisticated for African minds and also damaging because they depicted the negative aspects of European and North American lives." In the last chapter of the book, Diawara discusses and notes several themes. One theme is the social realist films that draw on contemporary experiences and that oppose tradition in favor of modernity; a second is the theme of colonial confrontation that depicts the conflict between Africans and their European colonizers; finally, there is the theme of a return to the source and to the perspective of the subjects—ordinary Africans—themselves. There is a major focus on films by French-speaking Africans because, according to the author, Francophone filmmaking dominates the cinema in Africa.

1295 Dike, Kenneth O. *Trade and Politics in the Niger Delta, 1830–1885: An Introduction to the Economic and Political History of Nigeria.* Repr. of 1956 ed. Greenwood 1982, $52.50 (0-313-23297-0). 250pp. Nonfiction.

The publication of this book by a Nigerian historian in the 1950s sparked a major revolution in African studies. The author eschewed conventional approaches to the study of the slave trade, which typically focused on the organization of the trade, middle passage, abolitionist movements, and European policies and personalities. Instead he examined the impact of the trade on West African societies. Most specifically, he looked at the fifty-year period between 1830 and 1885, when West African societies made the transition from predominantly slave-trading economies to commodity exchange economies based on the export of raw materials, primarily forest products such as palm oil and ivory. Adjustments to the new economy were nothing less than revolutionary for Africans who, for centuries, had depended on the sale of human beings. Dike describes these adjustments in fascinating detail. His seminal study influenced numerous works and reshaped the debate on slavery in Africa.

1296 Diop, Cheikh Anta. *The African Origin of Civilization: Myth or Reality.* Trans. from French and Intro. by Mercer Cook. Illus. Lawrence Hill 1974, $11.95 (1-55652-072-7). 336pp. Nonfiction.

The author, a Senegalese historian, argues that the base of Egyptian civilization is African and that its cultural heritage is the fount of Western civilization. Using material drawn from various disciplines, compiled by some of the most noted and respected writers on Egypt, Diop directs his attention to what he considers to be gross misrepresentations of Egyptian history. Diop alleges that these interpretations were fostered by Western writers who, in their eagerness to "whiten" ancient Egypt, perpetrated "the most monstrous falsification in the history of humanity." The author's multidisciplinary approach brings together what he considers to be evidence supporting the idea "that Egyptian civilization was produced by black Africans and that Egyptian civilization played a major role in the shaping of classical Mediterranean civilization and, therefore, lies at the root of much of what is worthwhile in European history."

A related work is Marin Bernal's two-volume *Black Athena* (Rutgers Univ. Pr., 1987 and 1991), in which the author argues that an "Aryan model" was used by nineteenth-century historians to disguise any traces of African and Judaic influence on the rise of Greco-Roman society.   AJWM

1297 Drake, St. Clair. ***Black Folk Here and There: An Essay in History and Anthropology.*** 2-vol. boxed set. Illus. Univ. of California, Los Angeles, Center for Afro-American Studies 1991, $58.95 (0-934934-28-2); $35.95 (0-934934-29-0). 757pp. Essays.

Is the color black universally viewed as undesirable? Does the devaluation of the color black always lead to prejudice and discrimination of persons defined as black? What factors are decisive in changing attitudes and behavior toward blacks? These are just three of the important questions the late African-American scholar St. Claire Drake addresses in this seminal two-volume work on the black experience and color prejudice. Drake's analysis covers a broad spectrum of time and several geographical regions. Volume 1 includes an overview of scholarly and popular thought on color prejudice, an in-depth discussion on the role of the "Negro" in the development of Egypt, and previously ignored information on relations between ancient Egypt and Ethiopia. Volume 2 continues the investigation with an analysis of the experiences of blacks in the Judeo-Christian world and the Islamic world. Scholars use terms such as "breathtaking," "tour de force," and "brilliant" to describe this comprehensive and thorough work that is destined to become a classic.

1298 Du Bois, W.E.B. ***The World and Africa: An Inquiry into the Part Which Africa Has Played in World History.*** Repr. of 1965 ed. Kraus 1965, $21.00 (0-527-25340-5). 352pp. Essays.

This volume, first published in 1946, was expanded in 1965 to include a section titled "Andromeda," which included Du Bois's commentaries on the "future of the darker races and their relation to the white peoples" and his "Writings on Africa, 1955–1961."

Du Bois used these essays to further the ongoing debate about Africa's role in world history. The work was a response to racially driven and ethnocentered nationalists, primarily from Western Europe and the United States, who unrelentingly denied African contributions to world history. Du Bois challenged the authority of those who dared to treat black people throughout the world as though they did not exist or were unimportant.

Flawed in places due to the limited knowledge base available at the time, this volume nevertheless makes a seminal contribution to the central debate regarding Africa and world history. The book remains a valuable document precisely because historical realities have substantiated most of Du Bois's original claims. He provides critical insights into what is wrong with Euro-centered versions of world history.

A valuable recent work on Du Bois's life is David L. Lewis's masterly two-volume *W.E.B. Du Bois: Biography of a Race (see main entry)*. The first volume covers the years from 1868 to 1919, and the second covers the period up to Du Bois's death in 1963.

1299 Ekwe-Ekwe, Herbert. ***Africa 2001: The State, Human Rights, and the People.*** International Inst. for Black Research 1993. o.p. Nonfiction.

In this book, the author provides a penetrating analysis of Africa. He begins Part 1 with a provocative overview of the Asian-European conquest of Africa, a process that began in the seventh century with the Arab invasion of North Africa and continued in the fifteenth century with the European invasion. This section also includes assessments of the work of Ali Mazuri and Basil Davidson, two well-known figures in African studies. He criticizes Mazuri for his "proselytizing" efforts on behalf of the Arab-Muslim world and castigates Davidson for a lack of vigor in his analysis of British colonialism. In Part 2, Ekwe-Ekwe gives a brief description of the foundations of neocolonialism, including the role that the United States has played in Africa since World War II. In Part 3, the author outlines strategies for Africa's redevelopment. Another work by this author is *Conflict and Intervention in Africa (see main entry)*.

1300 Ekwe-Ekwe, Herbert. ***Conflict and Intervention in Africa: Nigeria, Angola, Zaire***. St. Martin 1990, $59.95 (0-312-04617-0). 170pp. Nonfiction.

This slim but informative book describes civil war and foreign intervention in the author's home country of Nigeria and in Angola and Zaire. Although Nigeria is given appropriate analytical attention in this volume, the work is a particularly useful source of information in English on the other countries, because most works about them by African writers are either in Portuguese or French.

As the author notes, Angola has been racked by civil war since the country achieved political independence in 1975. The primary intervening powers in this conflict include the United States, South Africa, the former Soviet Union, and Cuba. In Zaire, the United States, France, and Belgium have intervened—on more than one occasion—to prevent the overthrow of President Mobutu Seso Seko. In a clear and balanced style, Ekwe-Ekwe analyzes the nature of foreign intervention, paying particular attention to the type, extent, motivations, and consequences of intervention for the African people.

He follows his analysis with a comparative survey and some shocking statistics; for example, more than six million Africans have died in internal conflicts since 1960. This figure is about three times the number of Africans who died confronting European colonialism. While lambasting the silence of certain African governments in the face of this carnage, Ekwe-Ekwe also points an accusatory finger at the hypocritical behavior of Western governments, which lecture Africa on human rights abuses while continuing the policies that laid the foundation for the current crises.

Persons interested in the topic of foreign intervention in Africa will want to consult Ekwe-Ekwe's extensive bibliography. Among the titles he has included on Angola are Gerald Bender's authoritative *Angola Under the Portuguese: The Myth and the Reality* (Univ. of California Pr., 1978), John Stockwell's revealing study of CIA activity in *In Search of Enemies* (Norton, 1984), and Basil Davidson's classic *In the Eye of the Storm: Angola's People* (Doubleday, 1972). Also recommended are David Birmingham's elegant and concise study *Frontline Nationalism in Angola and Mozambique* (Africa World, 1992) and Elaine Windrich's detailed study *The Cold War Guerrilla: Jonas Savimbi, the U.S. Media, and the Angolan War* (Greenwood, 1992). Jonas Savimbi's version of events in Angola is available in Fred Bridgland's *Jonas Savimbi: A Key to Africa* (Mainstream, 1986).

1301 Fanon, Frantz. ***The Wretched of the Earth***. Trans. from French by Constance Farrington; Pref. by Jean-Paul Sartre. Grove 1988, $12.00 (0-8021-5083-7). 320pp. Nonfiction.

In this classic work, first published in 1965, Fanon presents the worlds of colonizing Europe and of colonized Africa and the Caribbean as total opposites. This dualistic perspective paints a grim picture of the human, political, and cultural impact of European imperialism on the many indigenous peoples whose lives have been reduced to utter wretchedness. The work draws on the author's experiences as a psychiatrist in Algeria during its war of independence against France. He argues for massive resistance and armed conflict, not just against colonial aggression, but also against the authoritarian new regimes that stand in the way of a just independence and true liberation of colonized peoples.

In a earlier work, *Black Skin, White Masks* (orig. pub. 1967; Grove, 1988), Fanon analyzed the dual existence of blacks living in a white-ruled world. Since their first publication, Fanon's writings have influenced social scientists and political activists throughout the world.

Fredrickson, George W. *White Supremacy: A Comparative Study in American and South African History.*
See entry 145.

1302 Gbadegesin, Segun. *African Philosophy: Traditional Yoruba Philosophy and Contemporary African Realities.* Peter Lang 1992, $27.95 (0-8204-1770-X). 298pp. Nonfiction.

The author, a professor of philosophy originally from Nigeria, provides an accessible study of past and contemporary facets of African culture and philosophy. As the title indicates, Gbadegesin's focus is Yoruba culture and philosophy. However, he also draws on his knowledge of other thought systems, particularly that of the Akan of Ghana. The book covers traditional thought, the ideas of contemporary politicians, and the writings of professional philosophers.

The book is divided into two parts: "Traditional Yoruba Philosophy" and "Contemporary African Realities." Each chapter begins with a clear statement of the questions or issues under analysis. For example, the chapter titled "Individuality, Community, and the Moral Order" begins with the question: "What is the relationship between individuality and the community in traditional African thought systems?" By framing the central issue at the outset, Gbadegesin engages readers and keeps them focused on the topic at hand (no mean feat in a philosophical treatise). Persons interested in contemporary issues will find a wealth of interesting topics in Part II, including the relevance of religion in the modern Africa; Senghor's concept of Negritude; African socialism as articulated by both Senghor and Nyerere; postcolonial society and culture (with particular reference to Nigeria); the neocolonial state; the work ethic; and the nature and goals of development plans in Africa. Throughout the discussion, Gbadegesin describes and critiques the work of other well-known thinkers, including Joseph Mbiti, Kwasi Wiredu, and Paulin Hountonjdi. The general reader will find this work a useful introduction to African philosophical thought.

1303 Harris, Joseph E., ed. *Global Dimensions of the African Diaspora.* 2nd ed. Howard Univ. Pr. 1993, $24.95 (0-88258-149-X). 532pp. Nonfiction.

In 1979, Howard University—through the efforts of Joseph Harris—convened the First African Diaspora Studies Institute (FADSI), the primary goals of which were to determine the status of African diaspora studies and to foster linkages between African and American scholars. This book is a collection of the papers read at the conference. A few of the essays are lengthy and are concerned with scholarly issues. Most, however, are brief discussions on topics of interest to the general public. The section entitled "Assimilation and Identity" includes essays on Africanisms in American culture, blacks in Britain, and relations between African Americans and French-speaking Africans. The section entitled "The Return" begins with an essay on Marcus Garvey's impact on Africa. Other chapters in this section describe the return of diasporan Africans (from the United States, Britain, and Brazil) to Africa. Comprehensive and innovative, these essays provide rich sources of information.

Somewhat similar in scope is *The African Diaspora: Interpretive Essays* (Books on Demand, 1976), edited by Martin L. Kilson and Robert Rotberg, which among other topics includes discussions on blacks in the ancient Greco-Roman and Islamic worlds. Readers wishing more information on Harris's research on Africans in Asia can consult *The African Presence in Asia: Consequences of the East African Slave Trade* (o.p.). Harris is also the author of a useful general survey, *Africans and Their History* (Dutton, 1972).

1304 Harris, Joseph E., ed. *The William Leo Hansberry African History Notebook: Vol. I: Pillars in Ethiopian History; Vol. 2: Africa and Africans as Seen by Classical Writers.* 2 vols. Howard Univ. Pr. 1981, $9.95 each (0-88258-090-6; 0-88258-089-2). 154+160pp. Nonfiction.

The late historian William Leo Hansberry has often been called the father of African studies. In 1921, this pioneer Africanist traveled to numerous schools and colleges in the United States to help teachers and students learn about ancient African kingdoms. In 1922 he began the process of institutionalizing a series of courses on African history on his own campus, Howard University. Between 1916 and 1954, Hansberry marshaled a voluminous amount of evidence to demonstrate Africa's achievements and role in history. Historian Joseph Harris has organized and edited these findings in this two-volume set.

The first volume, *Pillars in Ethiopian History*, focuses on ancient and medieval Ethiopia. The pillars, which constitute the basic roots of Ethiopian unity, include the legend of the Queen of Sheba, the development of Christianity in Ethiopia, and Ethiopia's foreign relations in medieval times. The second volume, *Africa and Africans as Seen by Classical Writers*, includes comments by Greek and Roman poets, playwrights, and geographers about Africa and its people. Hansberry refutes the claim of some scholars that African contacts with ancient Greece and Rome were minimal. His work complements, rather than duplicates, Frank Snowden's research on blacks and the ancient Greco-Roman world as reported in *Before Color Prejudice: The Ancient View of Blacks (see main entry)*. Hansberry died before he could publish his extensive and valuable research, and Harris is to be commended for organizing his papers and bringing his work to light. Harris is also editor of *Global Dimensions of the African Diaspora (see main entry)*.

1305 Hawk, Beverly G., ed. *Africa's Media Image*. Greenwood 1992, $49.95 (0-275-93796-8). 268pp. Nonfiction.

Editor Beverly Hawk has assembled nineteen essays that examine media coverage of Africa in the United States. The initial essays set out the central debate between Africanist scholars and U.S. journalists. The former argue that the media present essentially negative and distorted images of Africa, while reporters reply that they are simply reporting the facts. Other essays take a closer look at news reporting. Among the stories analyzed are the Mau Mau rebellion, the Algerian war of independence against France, the Nigerian civil war, the Cold War, food aid, African-American press coverage of Africa, and an extended look at press coverage of southern Africa. The concluding section examines trends and suggests changes for the future.

Herskovits, Melville J. *The Myth of the Negro Past*.
See entry 158.

Hiro, Dilip. *Black British, White British*.
See entry 834.

Holloway, Joseph E., ed. *Africanisms in American Culture*.
See entry 160.

1306 Hountondji, Paulin. *African Philosophy: Myth and Reality*. Trans. from French. Indiana Univ. Pr. 1983. o.p. Nonfiction.

Hountondji, a philosopher from Benin, is a major contributor to philosophical thought. This volume was originally published in French in 1976 with the subtitle "A Critique of Ethnophilosophy." Hountondji defines African philosophy as "the set of texts written by Africans and described as philosophical by their authors themselves." This definition excludes ethnophilosophy and all other oral traditions from philosophical discourse.

In Part 1, Hountondji articulates his view of the appropriate matter for African philosophical discourse and evaluates the approaches of others, including Placide Tempels and Alexis Kagame. In Part 2, he first analyzes the philosophical writings of Anton-Wilhelm Amo, a Ghanaian who was born in the eighteenth century, who studied and taught in Germany, and who wrote principally in Latin. He then examines philosophical aspects of Kwame Nkrumah's thought in his works generally and devotes a whole chapter to Nkrumah's Consciencism. He follows this discussion with a critique of cultural pluralism. Those who claim that there is no African philosophy will find much that deserves attention in these essays.

1307 Inikori, Joseph E., and Stanley L. Engerman, eds. *The Atlantic Slave Trade: Effects on Economies, Societies, and Peoples in Africa, the Americas, and Europe*. Duke Univ. Pr. 1992, $48.00 (0-8223-1230-1); $18.95 (0-8223-1243-3). 418pp. Nonfiction.

For over a thousand years, Africans were enslaved and forced to migrate to, and labor in, other lands. This traffic in Africans began in early Christian times and continued through the nineteenth century. The trade traversed three geographical areas: the Sahara, Indian Ocean, and the Atlantic Ocean. Following the lead of Kenneth O. Dike, author of *Trade and Politics in Niger Delta, 1830–1885 (see main entry)*, Inikori and others continue the debate on the impact of the trade on Africa. In the introduction, Inikori argues that the trade in enslaved Africans had significant demographic, political, and economic consequences for Africa. He also challenges American historian Philip Curtin's estimate of the number of persons enslaved; Inikori posits a figure of fifteen million, in contrast to Curtin's estimate of six million for the Atlantic trade, and gives an estimate of thirty million for all geographical areas. The ten essays in this volume cover East, Central, and West Africa, and each one examines the impact of the trade on African peoples and historical processes.

Readers interested in exploring this topic in greater depth will want to consult Philip Curtin's *The Atlantic Slave Trade: A Census* (Univ. of Wisconsin Pr., 1972) and W.E.B. Du Bois's *Suppression of the Atlantic Slave-Trade to the United States of America* (Amereon, no date; reprint of 1896 edition).

1308 Jackson, Henry. *From the Congo to Soweto: U.S. Foreign Policy Toward Africa Since 1960.* Morrow n.d. o.p.

This book challenged the monopoly of U.S. foreign policy analyses by "mainstream" scholars and experts and questioned their tendency to view Africa almost solely within the U.S.–Soviet Union cold war context.

Jackson argued that the cold war approach to Africa reduced U.S. credibility in Africa as well as the U.S. world leadership role. He called on the United States to rethink its foreign policy–making strategies in light of new international realities, such as the enlarged and influential role of Africa in international forums, e.g., the United Nations. He demonstrated that Africa is a legitimate U.S. policy and national-interest priority for the same reasons as Asia, Europe, or the Middle East. Moreover, he argued that this claim is substantiated by the importance of Africa's abundant natural resources, its central location to American strategic interests, and Africa's historic links to its politically and economically awakening African-American descendants.

The chapters "Afro-Americans and Africa: The Unbroken Link" and "U.S. Economic Reliance on Africa: Petroleum and the 'Persian Gulf of Minerals' " are especially useful for studying the continent's significance to the larger international community. "Soweto: Decision Time for U.S. Policy in South Africa" is invaluable for its insightful contribution to understanding South Africa's contemporary apartheid history. Jackson's untimely death stilled a vital voice. His book stands as testimony to the ongoing role African Americans have played in analyzing U.S. foreign policy. Readers may also consult Elliott Skinner's *African Americans and U.S. Policy Toward Africa (see main entry)* for another view of this role.

1309 Jackson, John G. *Introduction to African Civilization.* Intro. by John Henrik Clarke. Carol Publg. 1974, $10.95 (0-8065-0420-X). 384pp. Nonfiction.

In the 1930s, a New York city school educator, Dr. Willis N. Huggins, and a self-educated scholar, John G. Jackson, authored a volume entitled *An Introduction to African Civilization.* The book was an early attempt to address distortions in existing works on Africa. In the 1970s, Jackson authored this more extensive volume with the same title. He portrays African history and culture as having long and complex traditions, comparable and at times even superior to other histories and cultures. The book covers prehistory to the early part of the twentieth century and highlights contributions by Africans to various fields, including art, religion, and literature. Jackson also discusses the negative impact of colonization and European invasion on Africa and its peoples. Although dated, the book remains a useful introductory text on Africa.

1310 Jacobs, Sylvia M., ed. ***Black Americans and the Missionary Movement in Africa***. Illus. Greenwood 1982, $55.00 (0-313-23280-6). 255pp. Nonfiction.

This edited volume examines the role of African Americans in the evolution of the Christian missionary movement and the drive to "civilize" continental Africans. It reviews the history of missionary activities, the goals of early leaders, and the impact of colonization and race on missionary movements in Africa.

The contributors are guided by the belief that African Americans have an ambiguous alliance with Africa. Historically, African Americans have been willing to accept the reality of their African heritage, but at the same time they have often endorsed the Western perception of Africa as a "Dark Continent" desperately in need of "civilizing" influences. The volume acknowledges that reality and addresses fundamental conflicts that existed between and among the various missionary societies. These conflicts influenced the work of missions and sparked ideological confrontations that defined and often split the movement into factional religious entities.

This book demonstrates the active role of African-American missionaries in education and government, with special focus on the role of women from the nineteenth to the early twentieth century. Its four sections include eleven chapters plus a bibliographic essay. Jacobs is also the author of the related book *African Nexus: Black American Perspectives on the European Partitioning of Africa 1880–1920* (Greenwood, 1981). Readable and informative, it covers an often neglected topic.

1311 James, George G. ***Stolen Legacy: Greek Philosophy Is Stolen Egyptian Philosophy***. Africa World 1992, $24.95 (0-86543-361-5); $9.95 (0-86543-362-3). 90pp. Nonfiction.

In this book, originally published in 1954, the author presents evidence to support the theory that Egyptians were the true authors of Greek philosophy. Citing the work of ancient historians, who documented the travel of many Greek thinkers to Egypt, James argues that these Greeks came to Africa not as teachers but as pupils. From the Egyptians they learned religious, philosophical, and mathematical concepts that were subsequently passed off as "Greek." According to James, for example, the Pythagorean Theorem is actually the Egyptian theorem of the square of the hypotenuse. Furthermore, Plato's four cardinal virtues (justice, wisdom, temperance, and courage) were copied from the Egyptian Mystery system, which was also the source of Aristotle's doctrines.

James is not the only scholar to claim non-Hellenic roots for "Greek" achievements. More recently Martin Bernal, in his scholarly two-volume work *Black Athena* (Rutgers Univ. Pr., 1987 and 1991), identified African antecedents in Greek language, religion, and culture. Other scholars have emphasized Asian roots in many "Greek" accomplishments. James's book has provoked much scholarly debate.

1312 Johns, Sheridan, and R. Hunt Davis, Jr., eds. ***Mandela, Tambo, and the African National Congress: The Struggle Against Apartheid, 1948–1990—A Documentary Study***. Illus. Oxford Univ. Pr. 1991, $15.95 (0-19-505784-8). 376pp. Nonfiction.

This valuable collection of documents chronicles the role of South Africa's African National Congress (A.N.C.) and its two most illustrious leaders, Nelson Mandela and Oliver Tambo. The work is similar in many respects to *The Struggle Is My Life* (o.p., 1986), a volume produced as a tribute to the then imprisoned Nelson Mandela. Like that collection, this volume includes speeches and other writings by Mandela, comments about Mandela by his fellow prisoners, and documents related to the A.N.C. However, this book includes speeches by Tambo, and the editors have provided introductions for each section that provide background information to deepen the reader's understanding of the documents in the context of the antiapartheid struggle.

The documents are grouped into historical periods beginning with the formation of the A.N.C. Youth League in 1948 and ending with Mandela's release from prison in 1990. The historical structure reveals the political evolution of the A.N.C. and the dynamic roles played by Mandela and Tambo. A chronology and a useful guide to further reading complete the volume.

1313 Jordan, A. C., ed. ***Tales from Southern Africa.*** Repr. of 1973 ed. Frwd. by Z. Pallo Jordan; Intro. and commentaries by Harold Scheub. Illus. by Feni Dumile. Books on Demand 1973, $78.30 (0-685-23973-X). 301pp. Nonfiction.

Jordan, a Xhosa-speaking scholar, was an expert on the Xhosa language and literature of South Africa. In the foreword to this collection of Xhosa tales, Jordan's son Pallo tells how his father traveled into rural and urban areas of South Africa seeking Xhosa storytellers, particularly women, who were renowned for their oral narrative skills. Jordan chose thirteen of their tales to retell. He re-creates the Xhosa *ntsomi* performance, which utilizes call-and-response clicks that alert the audience to the beginning of the story and invite their participation. The stories pass on the wisdom, wit, and ways of the Xhosa people. For most of the tales, Jordan has included introductory notes that illuminate the events in the story to follow.

Jordan is also the author of two other highly praised works. *The Wrath of the Ancestors* (o.p.) is a classic novel that, like Achebe's *Things Fall Apart (see main entry)*, describes the disruption of African values by European intrusion. *Toward an African Literature: The Emergence of Literary Form in Xhosa* (Univ. of California Pr., 1973) is a book of essays tracing the development of Xhosa literature, including oral narrative, songs, poetry, riddles, and proverbs. Recently, Jordan's widow, Phyllis Ntantala-Jordan, wrote *A Life's Mosaic*, an autobiography that includes information on their life together *(see main entry)*.

1314 Katjavivi, Peter H. ***A History of Resistance in Namibia***. Illus. Africa World 1990, $35.00 (0-86543-143-4); $11.95 (0-86543-144-2). 168pp. Nonfiction.

Part of UNESCO's Apartheid and Society series, this book is a good introduction to Namibia. The author, a historian and former member of the Namibian resistance movement, begins with a brief history of Namibia before European intrusion. He then discusses the wars of resistance against German occupation in the nineteenth century and the various forms of nonviolent resistance Namibians mounted against South African rule in the first half of the twentieth century.

American readers will be particularly interested in the book's discussion of Garveyism in Namibia. Garvey's belief in "Africa for the Africans" proved to be a useful resistance slogan and an organizing principle for Namibians. The first branch of Garvey's Universal Negro Improvement Association (UNIA) was established in Luderity, Namibia in 1921 by S. W. Ncwana, a South African. Other branches quickly sprung up in Windhoek and other urban centers. The balance of the book describes Namibian resistance in the post–World War II era, with particular attention to the role of SWAPO (South West Africa People's Organization) in the liberation struggle. Another good introductory work is *Namibia: The Nation After Independence* by Donald L. Sparks and Reginald Green (Westview, 1992).

1315 Keller, Edmond J. *Revolutionary Ethiopia: From Empire to People's Republic.* Illus. Indiana Univ. Pr. 1989, $35.00 (0-253-35014-X); $12.95 (0-253-20646-4). 320pp. Nonfiction.

Among the African nations, Ethiopia is especially meaningful to general readers in the West. In addition to its connections with the biblical era, Ethiopia stands out as a politically independent state at a time when almost all the rest of Africa was colonized. In this book, Keller analyzes another Ethiopia, revolutionary Ethiopia. After discussing the formation of the Ethiopian bureaucratic state in the late nineteenth century, he reviews the rise and fall of several Ethiopian regimes to demonstrate how and why the bureaucratic Ethiopian empire was created. In this context, he gives special attention to the ever-changing relationships between the king, the ruling nobility, and the Ethiopian church. The history of Ethiopian politics is presented through an analysis of the feudal state, colonialism, ethnic nationals, and the formation of socioeconomic classes. Haile Selassie's emergence, rule, and fall are carefully presented.

Similar care is given to the analysis of the September 1974 revolution and radical efforts by the Derg to create a Marxist-Leninist Ethiopian state. Keller's explanation for the failures by the Derg in its attempts to implement changes is enlightening. Most of the main topics—the national question, international alliances, institutional changes, agricultural developments, famine, population resettlement, social myths—are clearly discussed in readable prose.

Other recent works on Ethiopia that are recommended to complement this work are John Harbeson's *Ethiopian Transformations: The Quest for the Post-Imperial State* (Westview, 1987), Christopher Clapham's *Transformation and Continuity in Revolutionary Ethiopia* (Cambridge Univ. Pr., 1988), and Bereket Selassie's fictional work *Riding the Whirlwind: An Ethiopian Story of Love and Revolution* (Africa World, 1993).

1316 Kenyatta, Jomo. *Facing Mount Kenya: The Tribal Life of Gikuyu.* Repr. of 1953 ed. Intro. by B. Malinowski. AMS 1975, $36.00 (0-404-14676-7); Random $6.36 (0-394-70210-7). 326pp. Essays.

This book, first published in 1938, is a classic among early African writings. The author, Jomo Kenyatta, was Kenya's first president. He wrote the book during his schooling in London as a way of studying African societies from an

African point of view. Kenyatta traces the origins, history, social life, and traditions of his own Gikuyu people, bringing vividly to life a pattern of human relationships, values, beliefs, and continuity that defy Western stereotypes of African societies. Kenyatta's was the first among many African voices that spoke with pride about and on behalf of African peoples

1317 Keto, C. Tsehloane. ***Africa Centered Perspective of History***. K. A. Rubins 1991. o.p. Essay.

Keto is a historian and senior faculty member in the African American Studies Department at Temple University. In this fifty-three-page essay, he provides an introduction to the "centrist" perspective in general and to the Afrocentric perspective in particular. He believes that a Eurocentric approach can be valid, provided it is "nonhegemonic" in its analysis. His quarrel is with those Eurocentric scholars who exclude other world views and conceal their biases by using terms such as "global," "international," and "cosmopolitan." He also takes issue with Afrocentric scholars who "claim all progress in all regions is due to African presence alone." Having set out the parameters of the centrist position, Keto builds the case for the acceptance of the Africa-centered perspective in African and African American Studies. He then applies the paradigm in two case studies, African-American and South African historiography. Keto has provided a succinct and useful work for those seeking to understand and employ Afrocentrism.

1318 Knappert, Jan. ***The A-Z of African Proverbs***. Karnak House 1989. o.p. Nonfiction.

This collection of nearly 1,500 African proverbs is a valuable resource. The author has assembled the proverbs deemed "the very best, the wisest, the most poetic" from peoples and nations throughout the continent. His purpose is "to prove that the people of Africa do possess original proverbs, very beautiful and very wise ones." A retired professor of Swahili literature, Knappert collected many of the proverbs himself and selected others from the writings of scholars and missionaries. The entries are grouped under headings that pertain to daily life, such as "Courtesy and Manners," "Life and Fate," and "Greed and Abstinence." The meaning of most of the proverbs is obvious, and the author provides explanations for those that are more obscure.

Another useful though slimmer volume is *African Proverbs* by Charlotte Leslau (Peter Pauper, 1985).

Kyle, Keith. ***Suez***.
See entry 1183.

1319 Magaia, Lina. ***Dumba Nengue: Run for Your Life: Peasant Tales of Tragedy in Mozambique***. Trans. from Portuguese by Michael Wolfers; Intro. by Allen Isaacman. Illus. Africa World 1988, $14.95 (0-86543-073-X); $6.95 (0-86543-074-8). 115pp. Nonfiction.

According to Mozambican author Lina Magaia: "There is no civil war in Mozambique. In Mozambique there is genocide perpetuated by armed men against defenseless populations." The phrase *dumba nengue* is a Mozambican proverb that literally means "Run with your feet." It is also the name of a once-prosperous region of southern Mozambique that has been devastated by war. In a series of vignettes, Magaia describes the fate of individuals who have suffered torture and death at the hands of the RENAMO (Mozambique National Resistance). In his introduction, Allen Isaacman provides a brief history of RENAMO, which was created in 1976 by a coalition of Rhodesian, Portuguese, and South African security forces. RENAMO has also received considerable support from members of the U.S. Congress. Isaacman, who played a major role in bringing this critically acclaimed book to American readers, states: "I agreed to write this introduction in the hope of creating a bridge between readers in Mozambique and in America, whom I felt would share my sense of outrage."

1320 Magubane, Bernard. *The Political Economy of Race and Class in South Africa.* Monthly Review 1980, $12.00 (0-85345-506-6). 364pp. Nonfiction.

Magubane, a professor of sociology and anthropology at the University of Connecticut at Storrs, is also a member of South Africa's dispossessed. His account of the conquest of his homeland exposes the racist foundation of South African society. Like the eminent African-American sociologist Oliver Cox, author of *Caste, Class and Race* (Monthly Review, 1970), Magubane identifies modern capitalism as the primary factor in the development of oppressive racism in South Africa. Magubane's book is not a detailed history of South Africa. Rather, it is an analytical interpretation of the processes by which black South Africans were stripped of their land and forced to serve white interests. Magubane is particularly concerned with the exploitation of African labor by the settler community and its Western allies. Powerful and passionate, this is an excellent account of the conquest of South Africa and the means by which white rule has been sustained.

Another insightful work is William Minter's in-depth analysis of Western capital in southern Africa, *King Solomon's Mines Revisited: Western Interests and the Burdened History of Southern Africa* (Basic, 1986). Minter's study begins with South Africa's mineral discoveries and includes an analysis of U.S. foreign policy during the Nixon-Kissinger and Reagan eras. An analysis of the role of Western capital in South Africa can be found in Luli Callinicos's three-volume social history *Gold and Workers, 1886–1924* (Ohio Univ. Pr., 1985), *The Working Life, 1886–1940: Factories, Townships and Popular Culture on the Rand* (Ohio Univ. Pr., 1987), and *A Place in the City: The Rand on the Eve of Apartheid* (Ohio Univ. Pr., 1993). Teachers and students will appreciate the volumes' accessible formats and the numerous excerpts from primary source documents.

1321 Magubane, Peter, and Carol Lazar. *Women of South Africa: Their Fight for Freedom.* Intro. by Nadine Gordimer. Illus. with photos by Peter Magubane. Bulfinch 1993, $40.00 (0-8212-1928-6); $24.95 (0-8212-1934-0). 128pp. Nonfiction.

Peter Magubane has been taking photographs in his native South Africa for almost forty years. His poignant and vivid photo essays have earned him numerous awards, including the 1992 Missouri Honor Medal for distinguished service in journalism. Magubane's previous books include *Soweto: The*

Fruit of Fear (Africa World, 1987), *Black Child* (Knopf, 1982), and *Soweto: Portrait of a City* (State Mutual Book & Periodical, 1989).

In this work, Magubane combines his photos with the words of South African journalist Carol Lazar. Women of all major racial and economic groups are featured. One encounters the familiar faces of Winnie Mandela, Helen Joseph, Albertina Sisulu, as well as many lesser-known individuals. The common thread is the struggle of these women against apartheid. The text and photographs provide an excellent introduction to the history of South Africa since the 1940s and the roles women have played.

1322 Mazrui, Ali A. ***The Africans: A Triple Heritage***. Illus. Little, Brown 1987, $24.95 (0-316-55201-1). 336pp. Nonfiction.

The author, a well-known political scientist, has taught in East Africa, Nigeria, and the United States. This volume is the companion to a nine-part public television series, narrated by Mazrui, broadcast in 1986. Mazrui argues that Africa is the product of three major cultural influences: indigenous traditions, Western culture, and Islamic culture. He considers such subjects as religion, technology, sports, and oral tradition in the dynamic and sometimes controversial context of this triple heritage. The book is not a detailed history of Africa; instead, it is a well-argued personal analysis of African themes. Some criticize Mazrui's eclectic approach to African history and his tendency to digress. Others describe his approach as bold and his digressions as eloquent and informative. Provocative and challenging, Mazrui is always a good read.

There are several other general histories of Africa that are well worth acquiring: Phyllis M. Martin and Patrick O'Meara's *Africa* (Indiana Univ. Pr., 1986), *African History* by Philip Curtin and others (Little, Brown, 1978), and Kevin Shillington's *History of Africa* (St. Martin, 1989).

1323 Mbiti, John S. ***Introduction to African Religion***. 2nd, rev. ed. Illus. Heinemann 1992, $18.50 (0-435-94002-3). 216pp. Nonfiction.

The author, an Anglican priest originally from Kenya, is currently a professor of religion and philosophy at the University of Bern, Switzerland. This book is a revised and expanded version of a work, first published in 1975, that has been widely used as an introductory text. In addition to an expanded bibliography, this edition includes an entirely new section on African proverbs.

Mbiti breaks the study of African religion into small, digestible topics: the nature of African religions, views of God, festivals, the roles of religious leaders, and healing. In addition to discussing indigenous African religions, Mbiti examines the impact of Christianity, Islam, Judaism, Baha'i, and Hinduism.

Some reviewers have criticized this work as too simplified to educate readers about complex African religious systems. Others appreciate its simple style and concise handling of topics. Those interested in Mbiti's more in-depth studies will want to consult his *African Religions and Philosophy* (Heinemann, 1990) and *Concepts of God in Africa* (Praeger, 1970). More recently, Jacob Olupona and Sulayman Nyang have edited a volume celebrating Mbiti's contributions, titled *Religious Plurality in Africa: Essays in Honour of John S. Mbiti* (Mouton de Gruyter, 1993). An additional resource on religion, one especially written for a Western audience, is Benjamin Ray's *African Religions: Symbol, Ritual and Community* (Prentice, 1976).

1324 Mudimbe, V. Y. *The Invention of Africa: Gnosis, Philosophy, and the Order of Knowledge.* Indiana Univ. Pr. 1988, $39.95 (0-253-33126-9); $14.95 (0-253-20468-2). 256pp. Nonfiction.

The author, originally from Zaire, usually writes in French. The publication of this volume gave the English-reading public access to his work. The book also earned Mudimbe the prestigious Melvin J. Herskovits Award in 1989 for the best book on Africa published that year. It is a complex, weighty, and provocative work that has challenged the thinking both of Western scholars and of African intellectuals.

Mudimbe critiques Western interpretations and assessments of African conceptual systems. He questions whether minds shaped by Western concepts can adequately translate African philosophical concepts, which are grounded in African languages and African gnosis (a term that refers to secret systems of knowledge controlled by the elders). For general readers, the most accessible chapters are "Power of Speech" and "E. W. Blyden's Legacy." In the former, the author discusses missionary and anthropological intrusions into Africa and African responses to these forays. In the latter, Mudimbe questions Leopold Senghor's designation of E. W. Blyden as "the foremost precursor both of Negritude and of the African Personality." Mudimbe reveals Blyden's quixotic mixture of African nationalism and colonialism. Parts of the book may be difficult for those who lack background in philosophical discourse and Francophone intellectual traditions.

Since its publication, *Invention of Africa* has generated much scholarly debate. In 1989, an entire panel at the African Studies Association's annual conference was devoted to the book, and two years later, the literary journal *Callaloo* devoted a special section to Mudimbe's ideas, which clearly are a force to be reckoned with.

1325 Nyerere, Julius K. *Freedom and Development—Uhuru Na Maendeleo: Selections from Writings and Speeches, 1968–1973.* Illus. Oxford Univ. Pr. 1973, $8.95 (0-19-519772-0). Essays.

Nyerere served as president of Tanzania from independence in 1963 to his retirement in 1985. This book is the third volume in the collected series of his writings and speeches; previous titles were *Freedom and Unity* (o.p., 1967) and *Freedom and Socialism* (o.p., 1968). Together these works comprise the main body of Nyerere's political philosophy during the period 1957 to 1973. They contain his various attempts to define the form of African socialism that he believed necessary if Tanzania hoped to develop into an economically and culturally self-reliant modern nation. In retrospect, the idealism and eloquence reflected in the writings and speeches represent the first phase in Tanzania's attempt to work out an ideological basis for its development. In hindsight, given the realities and vagaries of geopolitical development in the Third World, Nyerere's idealism turned out to have been misplaced. That fact, however, does not detract from the passion and sincerity of purpose that engendered it.

1326 Nzongola-Ntalaja, ed. *The Crisis in Zaire.* Africa World 1988, $32.00 (0-86543-023-3); $11.95 (0-86543-024-1). 327pp. Nonfiction.

Despite great wealth in natural resources, Zaire has been unable to generate and sustain economic growth and development. In 1984, a conference at

Howard University examined the reasons for this failure in an effort to generate problem-solving strategies. This book of conference papers provides useful analyses of the causes and consequences of the crisis in Zaire. Although some of the essays are rather scholarly, others are accessible to the general reader. The volume is valuable both because it represents a wide range of views and because it makes available to the English-language reader essays by prominent scholars, a number of them from Zaire, who usually write in French. Initial essays focus on the crisis from historical and contemporary perspectives, and later contributions describe the strategies ordinary people have developed to survive the crisis. Also included are discussions on development issues and the role international agencies play in Zaire's economic development.

1327 Olaniyan, Richard, ed. *African History and Culture*. Illus. Longman 1982, $22.95 (0-582-64369-4). 259pp. Nonfiction.

This is an impressive multidisciplinary effort that fulfills the interest of Africanist scholars and students beyond the mandate set for the project by its editor. Originally conceived as a general handbook for the study of African history and culture, this collection evolved into a definitive and wide-ranging treatise. The articles on culture, for example, address African art, language, religion, politics, and social organization; and the contributions on history survey earlier as well as contemporary conditions. These topics are loosely organized around three main themes: the African sense of history, which is an interwoven continuum of the past, the present, and the future; the sources of African history, including oral narratives and early literary traditions; and the African peoples' relationship to their environment, which, as one author notes, incorporates both the visible and the invisible realms.

In his contribution to the text, the noted dramatist Wole Soyinka sees African art as firmly connected to its physical environment. Akin Euba explains how African music reflects changes in the social environment. Examining the reasons for military intervention in Africa, one critic concludes that the soldiers are more corrupt than the civilians they drove out of office. In one of his two contributions, Solanke discusses traditional social and political institutions and examines social mechanisms of stability and control. One helpful feature of this book is the suggestions for further reading provided at the end of each article.

1328 Olupona, Jacob K., ed. *African Traditional Religion in Contemporary Society*. Paragon 1991, $24.95 (0-89226-077-7); $12.95 (0-89226-079-3). 212pp. Nonfiction.

The fourteen essays in this volume focus on the positive role that traditional religions are playing in the development of African society. A broad range of disciplines is represented: anthropology, sociology, history, the arts, literature, and theology. Most of the contributors are continental Africans; a few are Americans. Among the issues explored are the role of women, encounters between traditional religions and Christianity and Islam, methods and theories in the study of indigenous religions, and ethics in African religions. This book does much to counteract the misinformation and myths that predominate in the West about traditional religions.

1329 Pfaff, Francoise. *The Cinema of Ousmane Sembene: A Pioneer of African Film.* Illus. Greenwood 1984, $49.95 (0-313-24400-6). 207pp. Nonfiction.

This book is the culmination of the author's ten-year study of the films of Ousmane Sembene. Interpreting the director's works, Pfaff notes the various changes Sembene has introduced into African cinema and how those changes reflect the historical circumstances of the films. The author shows that Sembene's main characters tend to be types, rather than individuals; as such, they often mirror collective social attitudes. Sembene himself maintains that the "myth of the hero is a European creation," so he redefines heroism, not according to the Western concept of individual bravery, but according to the hero's role within society. In a film called *Ceddo*, for instance, Princess Dior is able to kill the Imam because of her status as a woman, which is accorded little importance or recognition in a male-controlled society. Although the primary focus is Sembene's films, the introductory chapter gives a good background of the constraints African films and filmmakers face in the course of fulfilling their art.

Robinson, Francis. *Atlas of the Islamic World Since 1500.* See entry 1421.

1330 Rodney, Walter. *How Europe Underdeveloped Africa.* Rev. ed. Howard Univ. Pr. 1982, $9.95 (0-88258-096-5). 312pp. Nonfiction.

This is an engaging analysis of the historical roots of Africa's inability to maintain sustained economic growth in the twentieth century. The author, from Guyana, traces the problem to Afro-European contacts, beginning as far back as the fifteenth century. Rodney contends that Europe has always maintained its monopoly over technological and economic ideas and that ever since its initial contacts has refused to share those ideas with African states. After centuries of unequal trade, diplomatic duplicity, and intrigue, the inevitable result was Africa's conquest and colonization. The author concludes that the only solution is for African nations to make "a radical break with the international capitalist system." AJWM

1331 Samatar, Ahmed. *Socialist Somalia: Rhetoric and Reality.* Humanities Pr. 1988, $49.95 (0-86232-588-9); $17.50 (0-86232-589-7). 224pp. Nonfiction.

This book focuses on the political economy of Somalia since the 1969 coup that brought General Mohammed Siyaad Barre to power. The author, a Somali, evaluates Barre's effort to create a participatory socialist state, independent of Western influences. The first part of the book presents a short overview of Somali history, concentrating on colonial history during the eighteenth and nineteenth centuries and ending with a brief review of politics since World War II. The volume also discusses the struggle for independence and the civilian regimes from 1960 to 1969. The second part deals with the military regime, which came to power in 1969. Under Barre's rule, Somali policy concentrated on military expansion. This led to a stagnating economy and dependence on both the Soviet Union and the oil-rich Arab states. In the concluding chapters, the author argues that the trend of economic stagnation continued into the mid-1980s, with the United States replacing the Soviet Union as the supplier of arms.

Another useful volume, although one that is unfortunately out of print, is *Somalia: Nation in Search of a State*. Written by David Laitin and Said Samatar, two renowned Somali scholars, the book provides information that helps to elucidate the crisis in Somalia that prompted U.S. intervention in the waning days of the Bush administration. One of the most penetrating works on Somalia by an outsider is I. M. Lewis's *A Modern History of Somalis: Nation and State in the Horn of Africa* (Westview, 1988). Written by a political anthropologist with twenty-five years of experience in Somalia, this ethnohistory analyzes past and contemporary events through the 1980s.

1332 Scott, William R. *The Sons of Sheba's Race: African Americans and the Italo-Ethiopian War, 1935–1941*. Illus. Indiana Univ. Pr. 1992, $42.50 (0-253-35126-X). 384pp. Nonfiction.

Benito Mussolini, the fascist leader of Italy, invaded Ethiopia in October 1935 and rekindled a fire in the African-American community. Ethiopia had been an inspiration to the American diasporan community since the late 1700s. African Americans had idealized and idolized the Ethiopian state, seeing hope and inspiration in its struggle for freedom and its history of independence. Outraged by Italy's intrusion into Africa, African-American leaders urged the U.S. government to act against the invasion by an international bully.

In precise and captivating prose, William Scott presents a detailed study of African-American reactions to the Italo-Ethiopian conflict. The volume contains twelve chapters grouped into three parts: "The Call of Ethiopia," "Black Activism," and "Ethiopian Brotherhood." The book concludes with an exceptional analysis of the war's influence on what African Americans thought and felt about fascism, the Western powers, the Ethiopian people, world race relations, and internationalism.

1333 Serequeberhan, Tsenay. *African Philosophy: The Essential Readings*. Paragon 1991, $13.95 (1-55778-309-8). 250pp. Essays.

This volume is valuable because it draws together eleven important essays written by African philosophers. The editor's aim is to provide these writers with a forum "to formulate their differing positions in confrontation and dialogue and on their own, that is, minus foreign mediators."

The introductory essay identifies the main themes of the essays—ethnophilosophy, philosophic sagacity, national-ideological philosophy, and professional philosophy—and traces the major debates these ideas have provoked. Serequeberhan sees these themes as constituting a continuum rather than rigid and distinct schools of thought. The contributors flesh out their ideas concerning the appropriate domain of African philosophical thought and in passing offer critiques of Western philosophy. Among the contributors are Innocent Onyewuenyi, Henry Odera Oruka, Peter Bodunrin, Kwasi Wiredu, Paulin Hountondji, Lansana Keita, Oyenka Owomoyela, Marcien Towa, Okonda Okolo, and E. Wamba-Dia-Wamba. Lucid, readable, and provocative, their essays provide a good introduction to the ideas of contemporary African philosophers. Readers interested in pursuing the subject further might consult *African Philosophy: An Introduction* by Paulin Hountondji (*see main entry*).

Shaaban, Bouthaina. **Both Right and Left Handed: Arab Women Talk about Their Lives.**
See entry 1206.

1334 Skinner, Elliott P. *African Americans and U.S. Policy Toward Africa: In Defense of Black Nationality, 1850–1924.* Howard Univ. Pr. 1992, $34.95 (0-88258-142-2); $24.95 (0-88258-159-7). 555pp. Nonfiction.

This volume is the result of the author's frustration with the ignorance that abounds in the United States and Africa regarding the influence of African Americans on U.S. policy toward Africa. The fruit of Skinner's frustration is nourishing indeed. Comprehensive yet highly readable, this volume provides an extensive look at the roles African Americans have played in U.S. foreign policy toward Africa despite their general lack of political leverage in their own country. Among the topics included are the partition of Africa, Pan-African initiatives, assisting black South Africa, imperialism in the Congo, and the impact of W.E.B. Du Bois and Marcus Garvey. Skinner concludes that African Americans used their limited political power in Africa's interest believing that a strong, respected Africa would benefit Africans the world over. He challenges the idea that African-American interest in Africa might not be in America's national interest and rejects the description of African Americans as too emotionally involved to be "objective."

Another informative foreign policy title by *Skinner Is Beyond Constructive Engagement: United States Foreign Policy Toward Africa* (Paragon, 1986). The essays in this edited work examine the conduct of U.S. foreign policy toward Africa during the Reagan administration.

1335 Snowden, Frank M., Jr. *Before Color Prejudice: The Ancient View of Blacks.* Illus. Harvard Univ. Pr. 1991, $14.95 (0-674-06381-3). 224pp. Nonfiction.

An earlier work by this author, *Blacks in Antiquity: Ethiopians in the Greco-Roman Experience* (orig. pub. 1970; Harvard Univ. Pr., 1990), is considered a classic in the field of ancient history. This book covers a similar topic, but with broader geographic and chronologic scope as the author discusses Mediterranean societies beyond Greece and Rome. Snowden cites two aims for this study: to trace the image of blacks as seen by whites from Egyptian to Roman times, and to explore the rationale for the attitude toward blacks during this period. He characterizes the ancient view of blacks as "highly favorable" and describes white-black relations as "markedly different from those that have developed in more color-conscious societies." He rejects the view that ancients bore color prejudice merely because some of them made uncomplimentary comments about blacks. The volume includes four chapters: "Who Were the African Blacks?," "Meetings of Blacks and Whites," "Images and Attitudes," and "Toward an Understanding of the Ancient View." A generous selection of excellent black-and-white illustrations completes the volume.

1336 Staunton, Irene, ed. *Mothers of the Revolution: The War Experiences of Thirty Zimbabwean Women.* Illus. Indiana Univ. Pr. 1991, $35.00 (0-253-35450-1); $12.95 (0-253-28797-9). 320pp. Nonfiction.

Books on the war for independence in Zimbabwe often overlook the contributions of women. Yet, as editor Irene Staunton notes, "Without the women the war could not have been won." Assisted by several Shona and Ndebele translators, Staunton traveled throughout Zimbabwe recording the war experiences of women. Most of the thirty women she interviewed were farmers.

Each woman begins her story with a brief overview of her life before the war. These vignettes give the reader a sense of the woman's place in her family and in the socioeconomic structure of colonial society. One of the common themes in the women's stories of war is fear. Threats, beatings, torture, murder, and separations were common during the war years. The infamous Selous Scouts (crack troops of the Rhodesian army) meted out these punishments, but African freedom fighters sometimes used tough tactics as well. Often the women had little or no knowledge of the war until it erupted on their doorsteps. As they learned more about the struggle, most of the women willingly fed and protected the guerrillas. Some courageously carried supplies to them right under the noses of the Rhodesian forces. Others openly organized political activity and risked imprisonment. Many were the sole support of their families when their husbands, sons, and daughters went off to war. For a number of these women, the war exacted the supreme sacrifice, the loss of a loved one. Years after their loss, they speak of their grief and pain. Yet most of them maintain that independence, however flawed, is worth the price.

1337 Steady, Filomina C., ed. ***The Black Woman Cross-Culturally***. Schenkman 1985, $24.95 (0-87073-346-X). 640pp. Nonfiction.

The increasing attention being paid to feminist literature has tended to subsume the fragmented writings on black women within the general category of gender scholarship. Consequently, the dynamics of feminist change within Africa and among people of African descent are rarely analyzed within the purview of black women's experience. This book's editor observes a gendered polarization in the analysis of social malaise, even when survival struggles affect the genders equally and cross-culturally. "Rather than seeing men as the universal oppressor, women will also be seen as partners in oppression and as having the potential of becoming primary oppressors themselves." With this in mind, she organizes the materials into four parts—Africa, United States, Caribbean, and South America—and draws on contributions from feminist scholars in those regions to understand the complexity of social oppression.

1338 Terborg-Penn, Rosalyn, and others, eds. ***Women in Africa and the African Diaspora***. Howard Univ. Pr. 1988, $19.95 (0-88258-171-6); $12.95 (0-88258-177-5). 256pp. Nonfiction.

Western feminists have taken a keen interest in the roles and status of women in African societies. However, their conclusions have not always squared with those of black scholars. In the fourteen essays in this collection, African and African-American scholars from various disciplines present their perspectives on the challenges black women have faced.

The book focuses on the unique strategies that women in Africa and the diaspora have developed to resist and survive threats to their well-being and development. In the first essay, anthropologist Filomina Chioma Steady theorizes that racism is a crucial factor in the oppression of African women. She describes African feminism as "combining racial, sexual, class, and cultural dimensions of oppression to produce a more inclusive brand of feminism through which women are viewed first and foremost as human, rather than sexual, beings." She reminds Western feminists that the world economy (which is dominated by whites) has subordinated both black men and black women. Steady is editor of *The Black Woman Cross-Culturally (see main entry)*. Other essay topics include women in religious life, the role of the extended family, and black women in folk culture and literature. Historian Sharon Harley concludes the volume with an essay on research priorities for the future. This collection is an important contribution to gender and diasporan studies. Other useful works on women in Africa include *Female and Male in West Africa* by Christine Oppong (Unwin Hyman, 1983); *African Women South of the Sahara* (Longman, 1984), edited by Margaret Jean Hay and Sharon Stichter; and *Women In Africa: Studies in Social and Economic Change* (Stanford Univ. Pr., 1976), edited by Nancy Hafkin and Edna Bay.

Toubia, Nadia, ed. **Women of the Arab World: The Coming Challenge**. See entry 1209.

1339 Tutu, Desmond. **Crying in the Wilderness: The Struggle for Justice in South Africa.** American ed.; Ed. by John Webster. Books on Demand 1986, $36.00 (0-7837-8095-8). 124pp. Essays.

Winner of the 1984 Nobel Peace Prize, Archbishop Desmond Tutu of South Africa has devoted much of his life to nonviolent social change. This collection of his sermons, speeches, articles, and press statements reflects his philosophies and beliefs. Tutu begins with a discussion of the activist nature of Christ and the need for a church that reconciles differences while fearlessly fighting for justice. Other chapters address the explosive situation in South Africa and strategies for change. For the most part, the selections are addressed to whites. Tutu speaks frankly and passionately, imploring whites to act before violence consumes the country. He describes the unjust laws and wretched conditions blacks have been forced to endure and outlines strategies that will ensure justice. Whites are urged to agree to majority rule (as opposed to black rule, which he rejects), to redistribute wealth, and to avoid the folly of "engaging in a charade with leaders whom most blacks repudiate." The South African Broadcasting Corporation receives his severe rebuke for functioning as a propaganda machine for the apartheid government. The affluent Northern Hemisphere countries are also chastised and warned. As Tutu puts it: "The hungry masses will [not] forever just look on at the groaning tables of their wealthy neighbours." Of course, with the release of Nelson Mandela from prison, the dismantling of the apartheid system, and the implementation of majority rule in South Africa, some of the issues have changed. Much that Tutu says, however, remains relevant and timely.

Another important work in this vein is Allan Boesak's *Black and Reformed: Apartheid, Liberation, and the Calvinist Tradition* (Orbis, 1984). An ordained minister in the Dutch Reformed Mission Church, Boesak has written several books on the Christian church, apartheid, and the condition of blacks in South Africa. This work is a collection of addresses delivered between 1974 and 1983. Articulate and passionate, Boesak challenges Christians to bring their faith and actions into conformity with God's Word.

1340 UNESCO General History of Africa. 8 vols. Illus. Univ. of California Pr. 1980-1993. Nonfiction.

This eight-volume series, prepared under the auspices of UNESCO, includes the following titles: Vol. 1, *Methodology and African Prehistory*, edited by G. Ki Zerbo (1980); Vol. 2, *Ancient Civilizations of Africa*, edited by G. Mokhtar (1980); Vol. 3, *Africa from the Seventh to Eleventh Century*, edited by M. F. Fasi (1988); Vol. 4, *Africa from the Twelfth to Sixteenth Century*, edited by D. T. Niane (1984); Vol. 5, *Africa from the Sixteenth to Eighteenth Century*, edited by B. A. Ogot (1992); Vol. 6, *Africa in the Nineteenth Century Until the 1880s*, edited by J. F. Ade Ajayi (1990); Vol. 7, *Africa Under Colonial Domination, 1880-1935*, edited by A. Adu Boahen (1985); and Vol. 8, *Africa Since the Ethiopian War, 1935-1975*, edited by A. A. Mazrui (1993).

The books were prepared by an international committee with the express purpose of dispelling or correcting myths, omissions, and inaccuracies about Africa. The planning and preparation for the series began some sixteen years before the first two volumes appeared in 1980, and the latest volume appeared in 1993. Each volume is edited by a renowned African scholar, and many of the individual chapters are authored by Africans. The contributors are experts in their fields and generally well regarded by their colleagues. Some of the chapters are too complex for beginners, but most are appropriate for the research-oriented student or general reader. As one might expect, some of the volumes and chapters are stronger than others, but the overall result is a valuable and essential resource. Numerous maps, excellent etchings, and photographs are included. The UNESCO series complements and extends the information and perspectives found in the older, well-known multivolume series *The Cambridge History of Africa*.

1341 Van Sertima, Ivan, ed. **The Golden Age of the Moor.** Transaction 1991, $20.00 (1-56000-581-5). 256pp. Nonfiction.

In 1978, a group of African-American and African-Caribbean scholars launched the *Journal of African Civilization*. For the past fifteen years, the driving force behind the journal has been Guyanese professor Ivan van Sertima, an anthropologist and associate professor of African studies at Rutgers University. The journal publishes articles that provide African-centered perspectives on historical, economic, political, and social issues. Periodically, related articles by different contributors focusing on a specific theme are drawn together and published in separate volumes. This collection looks at the influence of Moorish culture. Other volumes in the series edited by Van Sertima include *Black Women in Antiquity* (o.p., 1988), *Blacks in Science: Ancient and Modern* (Transaction, 1983), *African Presence in Early America* (Transaction, 1987), and *Nile Valley Civilizations* (o.p., 1985).

Some scholars have criticized the series, dismissing whole volumes as speculative and resting on dubious evidence. Other reviewers have taken the more scholarly approach of judging each essay on its individual worth and soundness. In certain cases, contributors explore highly controversial topics using unconventional approaches that make some scholars uncomfortable (such as drawing evidence from folklore, mythology, and linguistics). But many of the contributors are respected scholars who consistently produce well-documented papers using conventional research methods. On the whole, these volumes have been an important means of disseminating knowledge about Africa to the general public while stimulating vigorous debate.

Van Sertima, Ivan. *They Came Before Columbus: The African Presence in Ancient America*.
See entry 199.

1342 Williams, Chancellor. *The Destruction of Black Civilization.* Rev. ed. Third World Pr. 1987, $29.95 (0-88378-042-9); $16.95 (0-88378-030-5). 384pp. Nonfiction.

The book is an in-depth examination of the peoples of Africa who built some of the most advanced societies in the world prior to the arrival of the Euro-Asians. The book challenges the old myths of Africa as the "dark continent" that was only brought into the light of history with the intrusion of Asians and Europeans, invasions that resulted in the destruction of developed cultures, the rise of trade in African captives, and ultimately the conquest and colonization of the African continent. Williams paints a picture of high achievement in both government and culture that characterized such states as Benin and Asante in West Africa, Uganda/Bunyoro in East Africa, Zimbabwe in the south, and Kongo in Central Africa.   AJWM

1343 Wilson, Francis, and Mamphela Ramphele. *Uprooting Poverty: The South African Challenge*. Norton 1989. o.p. Nonfiction.

In the 1930s, university and church leaders in South Africa, with financial assistance from the Carnegie Corporation of New York, established the Carnegie Committee on the Poor White Problem. The findings from this study were used to develop strategies to raise poor whites (primarily Afrikaners) above the poverty line. As history has shown, these strategies were quite successful. The Carnegie Committee recommended that researchers undertake a second study to assess the extent of poverty among South Africa's black population. However, it was not until 1980, some fifty years after the first study, that the Second Carnegie Inquiry into Poverty and Development in Southern Africa was launched.

The findings of the Carnegie Inquiry—over 300 papers—were presented in 1984 at a six-day conference in Cape Town. This book is a synthesis of these papers. The editors, one black and one white, are both South Africans who are on the faculty of the University of Cape Town. Wilson is an economist, and Ramphele is a physician and a social anthropologist. Together they have assembled a masterly and highly readable overview of the Inquiry's findings. The focus of the volume is primarily South Africa, but the book includes regional and global perspectives on poverty and development issues. *Uprooting Poverty* is a useful resource for activists, students, and the general reader. It provides an excellent overview of the nature and causes of poverty in southern Africa and practical strategies for change. The appendixes include a bibliography, a list of conference papers, and a listing of films shown at the conference. A photo essay of images exhibited at the conference was published under the title *The Cordoned Heart* (o.p., 1986).

Wright, Richard, ed. *African Philosophy: An Introduction.* 3rd ed. Univ. Pr. of America 1984. o.p. Nonfiction.

This edited volume has been a popular choice in many introductory courses on African philosophy. Richard Wright, an American professor and the book's editor, has collected essays that offer various viewpoints regarding the nature and content of African philosophical thought. P. O. Bodunrin begins the discussion by identifying four major themes or approaches to African philosophical thought: ethnophilosophy (myths and folk wisdom), philosophic sagacity (the ideas of African sages), nationalist-ideological philosophy (works of politicians), and professional philosophy (contributions in the areas of logic, metaphysics, ethics, and the history of philosophy).

In the second essay, the French philosopher Henri Maurier argues that there is no African philosophy, at least not yet. Maurier, like many other Western philosophers (and some Africans), argues that Bodunrin's first three themes simply do not qualify as philosophical thought. He credits Placide Tempels, A. Kagame, and Vincent Mulago with ground-breaking efforts in the area of professional philosophy, but he concludes that "we still have not really gotten hold of an African philosophy or even the necessary first steps toward an African philosophy."

Clearly the major debate revolves around the definitions, and several contributors take a broader view than that espoused by Maurier. Ben Oguah analyzes the concept of personhood in Fante society in the essay "African and Western Philosophy: A Comparative Study." In "The African Philosophical Tradition," Lancinay Keita identifies three major chronological periods of African philosophy: classical (ancient Egypt), medieval (Sudanic kingdoms), and modern (Negritude and Pan-Africanism). Among other contributors to the volume are J. E. Wiredu, Kwame Joke, and John A. A. Ayoade.

1345 Wubneh, Mulatu, and Yohannis Abate. *Ethiopia: Transition and Development in the Horn of Africa.* Westview 1987. o.p. Nonfiction.

Ethiopia, one of the oldest countries in the world, has long fascinated scholars, artists, political and religious figures, and others. It has attracted much attention in recent years because of the immense suffering caused by famine and civil war. Until 1974, Ethiopia was ruled by Emperor Haile Selassie I (who traced his lineage to Solomon and Sheba). Opposition to Selassie's imperial rule had been growing since the 1960s, and in 1974 the military overthrew the Emperor and established a socialist government. The new rulers—who accused the Emperor of having covered up the ravages of famine—embarked, in turn, on a policy of repression and war. By 1984, famine and drought plagued the land.

In this work, two Ethiopian professors analyze and explain what happened. After reviewing the history and geography of the country, they focus on the revolutionary government's politics of power and its economic policies. They discuss Ethiopia's international alignment with the Soviet Union and Cuba and the consequences of this decision for the Horn of Africa. They provide the larger cultural context of these and other processes through a discussion of urban development, education, women in society, and the arts.

1346 Yohannes, Okbazghi. *Eritrea, a Pawn in World Politics*. Univ. Pr. of Florida 1991, $34.95 (0-8130-1044-6). 352pp. Nonfiction.

This volume is notable because it exemplifies the fundamental impact of modern Western colonialism on Africa and its people. The author strongly argues that the "Ethio-Eritrean conflict was essentially a function of exogenous forces that had harnessed the future of the former Italian colony to the vicissitudes of power politics." Ethiopia, the African colonial power governing Eritrea, was merely an internal agent of control. The author argues that external forces, principally the former Soviet Union and the United States, conspired to maintain the Ethio-Eritrean status quo to further their own economic, military, and political interests.

Yohannes, an Eritrean scholar, provides a powerful and persuasive analysis of the Eritrean problem. He describes the international efforts, schemes, and conspiracies that exacerbated the situation and that made Eritrea "a pawn in world politics." The book contains a bibliography and an appendix that reprints the UN resolution establishing Eritrea as an autonomous unit federated with Ethiopia under the sovereignty of the Ethiopian Crown.

BIOGRAPHY

1347 Abrahams, Peter. *Tell Freedom*. Faber 1982, $9.95 (0-571-11777-5). 311pp. Autobiography.

Peter Abrahams was born in 1919 in Vrededorp, South Africa near Johannesburg. His autobiography, which received universal acclaim when it was originally published in the 1950s, is still regarded as one of the best of its genre. Critics have praised both its literary merit and its sociological importance. The book re-creates his upbringing in the slums of Johannesburg, and Abrahams tells of his thirst for knowledge and his search for a world beyond the oppressive race-defined society of South Africa.

Prior to this work, Abrahams wrote *Mine Boy* (Heinemann, 1989), a novel that tells the story of Xuma, a young country lad who confronts racism and economic exploitation in Johannesburg. First published in the early 1940s, it had a profound impact as one of the first novels in English to draw international attention to the condition of blacks in South Africa. Other noted works by Abrahams include *Dark Testament* (o.p., 1942), *A Wreath for Udomo* (AMS, 1956), and *Path of Thunder* (orig. pub. 1948; Chatham, 1975).

1348 Atiya, Nayra. *Khul-Khaal: Five Egyptian Women Tell Their Stories*. Frwd. by Andrea Rugh. Illus. Syracuse Univ. Pr. 1982, $29.95 (0-8156-0177-8); $14.95 (0-8156-0181-6). 216pp. Biography (Collective).

The lives of Arabic-speaking women are something of a mystery to Western readers. In this book, five contemporary Egyptian women speak about themselves. The women all come from an urban environment and from diverse socioeconomic classes. They range in age from early twenties to mid-sixties. Through personal accounts, they relate their stories from birth and childhood, to puberty, marriage, adult life, children, and death. They recount their hopes, dreams, fears, disappointments, and tragedies. The author also incorporates folklore, superstition, manners, and customs that are part of the daily rhythms of life in Egypt.

1349 Breytenbach, Breyten. ***The True Confessions of an Albino Terrorist***. Harcourt 1994, $14.95 (0-15-600134-9). 396pp. Autobiography.

607

AFRICA

Breytenbach, a noted South African writer of Afrikaner heritage, lived in exile in Paris for many years. But in 1975, he returned clandestinely to recruit supporters, blacks as well as whites, for a militant exile organization loosely affiliated with the African National Congress. In the airport on his way back to Paris, he was arrested by the South African police. Thus began seven years of imprisonment. Breytenbach describes his trial, in which he was portrayed as a traitor to his family and his people, and the conditions of his imprisonment. His various guards, their ploys, and their machinations receive a great deal of attention. So, too, does his growing sense of paranoia, which ultimately led to a mental breakdown in prison. Much of the memoir is told in stream-of-consciousness style, vividly portraying his deteriorating mental state and his growing awareness of the depravity of humankind. An outstanding work of prison literature, Breytenbach's memoir also conveys the twisted and complex reality of South Africa.

This book is the second and best-known volume in a trilogy of memoirs about Breytenbach's trips back to his homeland. The other titles are *A Season in Paradise* (Harcourt, 1980) and *Return to Paradise* (Harcourt, 1993).   LML

1350 Christie, Iain. ***Samora Machel: A Biography***. Illus. Humanities Pr. 1989, $49.95 (0-901787-51-5); $15.00 (0-901787-52-3). 224pp. Biography.

Christie opens his biography of Samora Machel on the chilling day in October 1986 when the people of Mozambique and the world at large learned that President Machel had been killed in a mysterious plane crash in South Africa. No one knows why Machel's plane veered off course, and, as Christie notes, the circumstances surrounding the crash have never been satisfactorily explained.

Christie, a Scottish-born journalist, has lived in Africa for over two decades, first in Tanzania and since 1975 in Mozambique. Soon after meeting Machel in 1971, Christie resolved to write the life story of this charismatic leader. He includes information on Machel's childhood and his personal life, but his primary focus is Machel's life in its broader historical and political contexts. Christie looks at Machel's development as a military leader and his role in the Mozambican revolution. Machel was an early and close associate of Eduardo Mondlane, the brilliant professor turned guerrilla fighter who organized FRELIMO, the national resistance movement that fought against Portuguese colonialism. For more on this topic, readers can consult Mondlane's book *The Struggle for Mozambique* (o.p.). When Mondlane was assassinated in 1969, the mantle of leadership was placed on Machel's shoulders. He led FRELIMO to victory, but following the defeat of Portugal, there were struggles with Rhodesian forces, South Africa, and RENAMO (a guerrilla group funded by South Africa). Christie reviews this history, providing information on personalities and situations that he gleaned from his travels with Machel. Clearly, the author's sympathies lie with Machel and the goals he had hoped to achieve.

There are several other works that provide insight into Mozambique's history and struggle for independence: *Mozambique: The Revolution and its Origins* by Barry Munslow (Longman, 1983); *Mozambique: From Colonialism to Revolution* by Allen and Barbara Isaacman (Westview, 1985); *A Complicated War: The*

Harrowing of Mozambique by William Finnegan (Univ. of California Pr., 1992); *Mozambique: The Revolution Under Fire* by Joseph Hanlon (Humanities Pr., 1984); *Mozambique: A History* by Thomas Henriksen (Rex Collings, 1979); and a sequel by the same author, *Revolution and Counter-Revolution: Mozambique's War of Independence, 1964–1974* (Greenwood, 1983).

1351 Curtin, Philip D., ed. ***Africa Remembered: Narratives by West Africans from the Era of the Slave Trade***. Illus. Univ. of Wisconsin Pr. 1968, $16.95 (0-299-04284-7). 376pp. Autobiography (Collective).

Most accounts of slavery are contained in the works of early European scholars. These works tend to focus more on the horrors of slavery than on the mechanisms of its operation or the feelings of slaves themselves. In the realm of slave narratives, there have been false accounts given by people who claimed to have been captured at a time when in fact no raiding parties were operating or to have been taken from African villages that never existed in the locations they described.

The importance of *Africa Remembered* is that it contains vivid personal accounts by Africans who suffered and survived the experience of slavery. The introduction admits a number of shortcomings in this kind of collection; for example, these narratives are sometimes tinged with biases, such as the distortions of memory or inadequate familiarity of the translator with the narrator's language. As the editor notes, however, even allowing for such shortcomings, these accounts capture the "feelings and attitudes of many millions whose feelings and attitudes are unrecorded."

1352 Kuzwayo, Ellen. ***Call Me Woman***. Illus. Aunt Lute 1985, $9.95 (1-879960-09-5). 288pp. Autobiography.

Born in South Africa in 1914, Ellen Kuzwayo has played many roles in her lifetime: daughter, teacher, wife, mother, social worker, and activist. Her autobiography describes these roles and, more important, reveals the impact that color and gender have had on her life experiences. In Part 1, Kuzwayo outlines the major features of apartheid and describes its impact on Africans, particularly African women. In Part 2, she describes how her own life and the lives of others in her family have been affected by apartheid. This section also contains Kuzwayo's remembrances of her childhood in the Orange Free State. Readers gain insight into various aspects of Tswana culture and learn to appreciate the strength of the extended African family. It is the extended family that sustains Kuzwayo when her parents divorce and her mother dies prematurely. The family also comes to her rescue when she is forced to flee an abusive husband and leave her two young sons behind. The oppression Kuzwayo suffered at the hands of apartheid and her first husband transformed her into an activist for human rights and women's rights. In the 1960s, Kuzwayo began an illustrious career with the YWCA. By the 1970s, she had become an influential figure and mentor to young activists in the Black Consciousness Movement. Her support of the antiapartheid struggle resulted in her imprisonment in 1976. The final section of the book reaffirms her commitment to the struggles for human dignity and freedom. It also contains a listing of black South African women who are doctors and lawyers. Kuzwayo's story is inspiring and instructive.

Two other first-rate autobiographies of South African resistance leaders are Emma Mashinini's *Strikes Have Followed Me All My Life* (Routledge, 1991) and Helen Joseph's *Side By Side* (Humanities Pr., 1986).

1353 Makeba, Miriam, and James Hall. ***Makeba: My Story***. NAL 1989, $11.00 (0-452-26234-8). 249pp. Autobiography.

This candid autobiography provides a multidimensional portrait of the well-known South African singer. Daughter, music star, mother, activist, and wife (five times), Makeba has experienced much in her sixty-plus years. With candor and modesty, Makeba tells of her life onstage and off. Zenzi, as Makeba was first called, was delivered single-handedly by her mother, Christina Makeba, who was a trained nurse and an *isangoma*, a traditional healer.

The religious and cultural beliefs of her mother and those of her Xhosa and Swazi relatives made deep inroads into Makeba's spiritual fiber. These roots sustained her in troubled and turbulent times. Although Makeba has enjoyed many glorious moments, she also has endured more than her share of problems and personal tragedies. Refused reentry into South Africa following a tour in Europe, Makeba was forced into a life of exile. Success in the American music world ended abruptly following her marriage to Black Power advocate Stokely Carmichael (now Kwame Toure). Record contracts were frozen, stage appearances canceled, and business ventures nixed. Makeba found safe haven in Guinea under the protection of President Sekou Toure, but even there she suffered tragedy. A young grandson died in Conakry; so, too, did her estranged daughter Bongi.

There are juicy slices of gossip in the book about some of Makeba's Broadway and Hollywood pals—she recounts, for example, her feud with her former mentor and "Big Brother," Harry Belafonte. But for the most part, Makeba focuses on her own foibles and follies. Throughout her life and travels, Makeba has remained a daughter of Africa. She is admired for her exciting voice and even more for her courageous stand against apartheid and other forms of injustice.

1354 Mathabane, Mark. ***Kaffir Boy: The True Story of a Black Youth's Coming of Age in Apartheid South Africa***. NAL 1990, $11.00 (0-452-26471-5). 354pp. Autobiography.

This compelling autobiography begins when young Mathabane, then called Johannes, is six years old and his tiny house is raided by the police. His parents are carried away, accused of violating pass laws—the first of many arrests during Mathabane's childhood. His story vividly describes the poverty of life in the township; the temptations of alcohol, prostitution, and gang life; and the self-hatred fostered by a racist system, which almost drove Mathabane to suicide at the age of nine. Mathabane's salvation comes through tennis and the sponsorship of two American tennis players—Stan Smith and Arthur Ashe—who help him to obtain a college scholarship in the United States, where he continues to make his home.

Mathabane's autobiography is controversial for its negative portrayal of his father and traditional African culture. As he recounts in the book, Mathabane was also criticized by black activists for choosing individual betterment over the collective struggle. Nonetheless, his perspective is a valuable one, and its extraordinary presentation makes this a book one is not likely to forget. Mathabane's story continues in his memoir of coming to the United States, *Kaffir Boy in America: An Encounter with Apartheid* (Macmillan, 1990), and *Love in Black and White* (HarperCollins, 1992), which explores his interracial marriage and attitudes toward race in the United States   LML

1355 Meer, Fatima. ***Higher Than Hope: The Authorized Biography of Nelson Mandela.*** Frwd. by Winnie Mandela. Illus. HarperCollins 1991, $10.95 (0-06-092066-1). 456pp. Biography.

South African sociologist Fatima Meer has written a revealing and politically astute biography of her longtime friend Nelson Mandela. Undertaken at the request of Winnie and Nelson Mandela, this authorized biography provides a fuller account of Mandela's childhood and his personal life than other recent works. Meer was able to interview Mandela (albeit behind prison doors) and Mandela himself corrected errors in the first edition of the book. The biography is divided into five parts: "Roots," "The Struggle," "Winnie," "Life-Sentence," and "Letters from Prison."

Despite her closeness to her subjects, Meer has managed to produce a relatively candid and balanced work. Mandela is clearly a man Meer admires, but she also sees him as a very real person who is capable of mistakes and misjudgments. Winnie Mandela and her recent problems are treated with discretion and sympathy. Meers helps readers to understand the enormous pressure Mrs. Mandela has been forced to endure. Comprehensive yet readable, this biography is a useful and worthy companion to Mary Benson's pioneering work *Nelson Mandela: The Man and the Movement* (Norton, 1986). Winnie Mandela's life story, written prior to her legal difficulties and her separation from Mandela, is available in her book *Winnie Mandela: Part of My Soul Went with Him* (Norton, 1986).

1356 Modisane, Bloke. ***Blame Me on History.*** Simon & Schuster 1990. o.p. Autobiography.

Small wonder that this autobiography was banned in South Africa when it was first published in 1963. More than just a soul-searching analysis of Modisane's own personal history, this book is a damning indictment of apartheid and its practitioners. Modisane takes whites to task, individually and collectively, for the horror they have created in South Africa. Whites can expect dispensation, Modisane argues, only if they—like Jesus and John Brown—are willing to align themselves with the downtrodden and dispossessed.

During the 1950s, William "Bloke" Modisane was a journalist for two South African publications, the *Drum* and the *Golden City Post*. He was also a playwright and actor. Modisane begins the riveting story of his life with the razing of Sophiatown. To whites, Sophiatown was a slum that could be improved only by destroying it and replacing it with a white town, but to Modisane and the other occupants, it was home. Modisane resurrects his beloved Sophiatown in all its flawed and beautiful dimensions. Moving backward and forward in time, he re-creates major events in South African history and introduces us to personalities, public and personal. His probing, relentless gaze exposes complexities and contradictions in each situation and relationship. The madness of South Africa drove Modisane into exile in 1959. He died in West Germany in 1986. This republication of his autobiography is testimony to his power as a writer, his brilliant intellect, and the relevant and universal questions he asked about justice and individual responsibility.

Readers who admire Modisane's approach will want to read Joseph Lelyveld's Pulitzer Prize–winning *Move Your Shadow: South Africa, Black and White* (Viking, 1985). Like Modisane, Lelyveld writes with biting wit and has the ability to detect contradictions and double-speak. A journalist with the *New York Times*, Lelyveld was declared "one of South Africa's most notorious enemies" and expelled from the country in 1966. Fourteen years later, he was permitted to return by a government anxious to showcase their "new and improved" South Africa. Lelyveld strips away the veneer of "change" touted by South Africa's spin doctors and exposes the gross inequities that still permeate the system. This is a well-written book, and the impact of its analysis has not diminished with time.

1357 Mphahlele, Ezekiel. ***Down Second Avenue: Growing Up in a South African Ghetto***. Peter Smith 1985, $21.50 (0-8446-4451-X); Faber $8.95 (0-571-09716-2). 222pp. Autobiography.

This is Mphahlele's most praised book. A classmate of the South African writer Peter Abrahams, author of *Tell Freedom (see main entry)*, Mphahlele used the autobiography as a literary form, much as Abrahams did, to describe his search for identity in oppressive South Africa. The book is both a tale of childhood and an indictment of the harsh conditions blacks have endured in South Africa.

Mphahlele grew up in the 1920s and 1930s. Like many South African children, he was forced to endure long periods of separation from his parents while they toiled at jobs in white areas. At the age of five, a bewildered Mphahlele was left with his paternal grandmother in Maupaneng, one of South Africa's poverty-stricken rural reserves. He describes his grandmother as "big as fate, as forbidding as a mountain, stern as a mimosa tree." Following the breakup of his parent's marriage, his mother took him to Marabastad, a Pretoria ghetto, where he lived with his maternal grandmother on Second Avenue. The bulk of the book describes the people of Marabastad and Mphahlele's coming of age. Gradually, he realized that the deprived lives he and other blacks endured were the result of South Africa's carefully constructed policy of racial discrimination and exploitation.

Determined to succeed, Mphahlele overcame enormous obstacles to gain an education and become a teacher. Banned from his profession for his outspoken condemnation of Bantu education, he worked at menial jobs until he began a literary career as a reporter for *Drum* magazine. In 1947, he produced his first collection of short stories, *Man Must Live* (o.p.). Ten years later, he left South Africa for Nigeria. His book *Afrika My Music* (Ohio Univ. Pr., 1986) tells of his life in exile and the talented people whom he encountered during his odyssey. An earlier novel, his award-winning *The Wanderers* (o.p.), also explores the theme of exile. In 1974 Mphahlele moved to the United States and accepted a position as professor of English literature at the University of Pennsylvania. Unable to bear the life of exile, he returned to South Africa in 1977.

1358 Mzala. *Gatsha Buthelezi: Chief with a Double Agenda.* Humanities Pr. 1988. o.p. Biography.

Mangosuthu Gatsha Buthelezi is one of the most controversial figures in South Africa today. He describes himself as an opponent of apartheid, yet as Chief Minister of the Kwazulu bantustan, he was a paid employee of the apartheid government. He passionately advocates the use of nonviolent change, yet Inkatha (the Zulu-based organization he heads) has shown little reticence in using violent tactics against its opponents. In the introduction to this biography, Mzala poses the central question: Is Buthelezi a collaborator and a sellout, or is he simply trying to change the system from within? Mzala examines the evidence and presents his conclusions in this well-researched book.

Equally good and more accessible in the United States is the biography of Buthelezi by Gerhard Mare and Georgina Hamilton, *Appetite for Power: Buthelezi's Inkatha and South Africa* (Ravan and Indiana Univ. Pr., 1987). Buthelezi's own (and less than candid) view of his agenda is available in his *South Africa: My Vision of the Future* (St. Martin, 1990).

1359 Ngugi Wa Thiong'o. *Detained: A Writer's Prison Diary.* Heinemann 1981, $11.95 (0-435-90240-7). 232pp. Autobiography.

Ngugi wa Thiong'o is Kenya's most prolific writer and one of the most important writers on the African continent. Novelist, essayist, playwright, and literary critic, he has been described as a "novelist of the people." His works reflect concern for the ordinary people who have suffered oppression and economic exploitation at the hands of colonialists and neocolonialists. Ngugi's outspoken criticism of the Kenyan government resulted in the confiscation of his work and his arrest in 1977. His books were banned and he was held in detention for a year without charges.

Detained is a collection of essays reflecting on the nature of his imprisonment and the link between his writing and his detention. As he puts it: "I am here because a tiny section of [Kenyan] society . . . has not particularly liked the image of its role in Kenya's history. They have therefore struck with vengeance at the hand that raised a mirror which showed them what they did not like to see, or what they did not like seen by the ordinary folk. To them, the hand which held the mirror and the mirror itself, were what created the reality therein reflected." Ngugi goes on to describe the degradation and humiliation faced by political detainees like himself. He also includes a revealing historical analysis of the reasons for his detention along with a compilation of arrest orders, post-prison reports, and his university correspondence.

1360 Nkrumah, Kwame. *Autobiography.* Humanities Pr. 1973. o.p. Autobiography.

Nkrumah, the first president of Ghana, wrote his autobiography in 1957, when he was in his late forties. This work is important not only because of the personal data that Nkrumah included but also because it provides a window into his early political thought. In the first part of the book, Nkrumah recalls his childhood and his education abroad. With affection, he remembers his years at Lincoln University, a historically black institution in Pennsylvania. The warm and supportive environment at Lincoln provided a refuge from the discrimination Nkrumah experienced in buses, restaurants, and other public places in the United States. Nkrumah uses the remainder of the volume to describe his return to Ghana (then the Gold Coast), his role in his country's struggle for independence, and his election as Ghana's first prime minister. The book reveals an idealistic revolutionary who, like Gandhi, viewed nonviolent resistance (which Nkrumah called "positive action") as the appropriate means of ending colonial rule and achieving self-government.

Nkrumah ultimately altered many of his early ideas. He recorded his changing views in a series of thoughtful and provocative books, including *Africa Must Unite* (Humanities Pr., 1963), *Consciencism* (Humanities Pr., 1970), *Neocolonialism, the Last Stage of Imperialism* (Humanities Pr., 1965), and *Handbook of Revolutionary Warfare* (Humanities Pr., 1968). Scores of books have been written about Nkrumah. Two recent and highly recommended biographies are *Black Star: A View of the Life and Times of Kwame Nkrumah* by Basil Davidson (Westview, 1989) and *Kwame Nkrumah: The Conakry Years* by June Milne (Humanities Pr., 1990)

1361 Ntantala-Jardan, Phyllis. ***A Life's Mosaic: The Autobiography of Phyllis Ntantala***. Univ. of California Pr. 1993, $25.00 (0-520-08171-4); $13.00 (0-520-08172-2). 237pp. Autobiography.

A member of the landed Xhosa of Transkei, South Africa, Phyllis Ntantala grew up in the 1920s and 1930s in comfortable surroundings. Her parents were educated, "modern" Christians who owned a sprawling farm where all sorts of people gathered. The Ntantala household was composed of servants, hired hands, and numerous relatives. Frequent guests included members of the Xhosa elite as well as "red-blanket Africans" (the ochre-covered Xhosa who refused to accept Western education and Christianity). Ntantala describes her "red-blanket" relatives as a "very respectful people" and recalls them sitting gingerly in her mother's home "so as not to stain with their ochre the beautiful things of the school woman." The portrait that Ntantala paints of her world shatters many stereotypes. She describes a doting father who, following his wife's death, ironed his daughters' dresses and raised the girls to be the equal of any man. Independent and brainy, young Phyllis had her choice of suitors. She chose the bookish, mature A. C. Jordan, who went on to become a legend in academia, writing volumes on literature and teaching at home and abroad. The second half of Ntantala's book describes her life with Jordan and their growing fight against apartheid. Ultimately, the Jordans and their four children moved to the United States. Here they also suffered discrimination (a cross was once burned on their lawn, and their politically active son was deported). Ntantala's autobiography reveals an elegant, astute, and proud woman who always expects fair treatment and has the temerity to demand it.

1362 Pityana, Barney, and others, eds. ***Bounds of Possibility: The Legacy of Steve Biko and Black Consciousness***. Humanities Pr. 1991, $49.95 (1-85649-047-5); $17.50 (1-85649-048-3). 288pp. Biography.

In this edited volume, Biko's colleagues and friends analyze his life and political contributions. Almost a third of the book is devoted to a biography of Biko.

Lindy, the author of this chapter, provides a multidimensional portrait of the charismatic leader. She describes him as an exceptional person and powerful leader but a very human man who had weaknesses as well as strengths. As she reminds readers: "Biko must be respected as a man, not a myth."

In a graphic and painful chapter, Biko's close friend Barney Pityana reviews the details of Biko's death in detention. He pillories South Africa's medical establishment for its complicity in Biko's death and the deaths of other political prisoners. Subsequent chapters analyze Biko's political thought, most particularly his Black Consciousness platform. His views are scrutinized within the context of Biko's own time and that of the contemporary period. Readable and informative, this volume provides a good introduction to the man, his ideas, and his legacy.

1363 Russell, Diana E. ***Lives of Courage: Women for a New South Africa***. Illus. Basic Books 1989, $22.95 (0-465-04139-6); $12.95 (0-465-04141-8). 384pp. Biography (Collective).

Books on antiapartheid activists are rare in the United States, and books on women in the antiapartheid movement are even rarer. In recent years, biographies of the Mandelas have appeared in bookstores, but there is little available on other activists. A notable exception has been the work of the International Defense and Aid Fund of Southern Africa. Over the years the IDAF has published several pamphlets that highlight the efforts of activists, including women activists. Unfortunately, these pamphlets are often tucked away in the vertical files of libraries or, worse, never purchased. *Lives of Courage* is thus a welcome and much-needed resource.

The book profiles twenty-four South African women who have been involved in the fight against apartheid. All of the women have engaged in political activities that have put them at significant risk. The women come from various backgrounds. There is diversity in race and ethnicity, social class, age, occupation, and political affiliation. Included are a chronology of major events in South African history, a glossary, and an extensive bibliography.

The author, who was born in South Africa, earned her stripes as a fighter against apartheid when she gave up a comfortable life among affluent whites to join a revolutionary underground group called the African Resistance Movement. Ultimately she left South Africa and became an American citizen.

1364 Saitoti, Tepilit Ole. ***The Worlds of a Maasai Warrior***. John G. Galaty, ed. Marboro 1992, $18.95 (0-88029-686-0); Univ. of California Pr. $11.00 (0-520-06325-2). 144pp. Autobiography.

Although a number of Maasai people have adopted different lifestyles, Westerners remain fascinated with those Maasai who continue the traditional cattle-keeping life. In countless movies, documentaries, and books, Westerners emphasize the more exotic and stereotypical features of Maasai life. In the initial pages of his autobiography, Maasai writer Tepilit Ole Saitoti seems to confirm rather than dispel Western images of his people. However, as the story unfolds, so does the depth and diversity of the culture he is depicting.

Chosen by his father to receive a Western education, Saitoti was soon exposed to worlds beyond his family and community. He reveals the guilt and turmoil he experienced as he broke free to explore new vistas. An early job was as a tour guide in Tanzania's Serengeti National Park. His extensive knowledge of animal life and adroit handling of tourists earned him a featured role in a documentary about the Serengeti. This exposure resulted in travel to Germany and ultimately to the United States, where he earned B.A. and M.A. degrees.

Saitoti writes about his travels beyond East Africa with insight and sensitivity. His chapter on the United States provides a rare look at American culture through African eyes. He describes American generosity, decadence, materialism, and racism. The book is an excellent means of learning about cross-cultural experiences.

1365 Shostak, Marjorie. *Nisa: The Life and Words of a Kung Woman*. Illus. Random 1982, $9.56 (0-394-71126-2). 416pp. Biography.

The !Kung (the exclamation point represents a clicking sound that is not part of the English language) are one of the few groups in the world still practicing the hunting-and-gathering lifestyle. This book focuses on one !Kung woman in particular, Nisa. In Nisa's world, as in many hunting-and-gathering societies, women have high status and wield considerable influence. Their power is rooted in the economic role they play as major food providers. Anthropologist Marjorie Shostak provides background information on the !Kung throughout this book, but then she wisely steps aside and allows Nisa to tell the story of her life. Nisa begins her story with a clear sense of purpose, "Fix my voice on the machine so that my words come out clear. I am an old person who has experienced many things and I have much to talk about." Nisa tells of her childhood, her parents, her loves, her children, and her losses. This is a profound and unforgettable story that provides a window into a different world while conveying the universality of human emotions.

1366 Soyinka, Wole. *Ake: The Years of Childhood*. Random 1983, $14.95 (0-394-52807-7); $12.00 (0-679-72540-7). 230pp. Autobiography.

This classic autobiography of Nigeria's Nobel laureate in literature reveals his life in intimate and humorous detail from a very early age to age eleven. Soyinka—a playwright, poet, novelist, teacher, and activist—delights the reader with a remarkable memoir of his growing up in the urban, Christian, Yoruba home of his parents in western Nigeria during the 1930s and 1940s. Soyinka describes his adventures and delights as a three-year-old and tells about his siblings, his extended family, and his parents. For the nonspecialist, it is a more accessible piece of literature than his novels, and it is a good complement to other African literature about rural community life. Although the book focuses on Nigeria, the author's memories reflect universal childhood experiences.   JS

1367 Soyinka, Wole. *The Man Died: Prison Notes of Wole Soyinka*. Farrar 1988, $9.95 (0-374-52127-1). 317pp. Autobiography.

The strictness with which Nigeria's military government suppressed the news of the publication of Wole Soyinka's prison memo was equaled by the secret enthusiasm with which Nigerian academics guarded and read smuggled copies of the book. Soyinka writes that the "man dies in all who keep silent in the face of tyranny," a stance that he uncompromisingly took in the years of Nigeria's civil war to protest the humiliation of Nigerians by the imposition of military dictatorship. His denunciation of the war in the press contributed to his arrest and imprisonment. In this book, Soyinka details the events that led to his imprisonment and the physical and mental torture he experienced in the hands of top government officials and prison authorities. The book recounts the insensitivity of government bureaucrats consumed with breaking his spirit, the private joy of guards who would have a prisoner "locked in one of the cells, and let him scream till his lungs burst—no one paid the least heed." Soyinka was denied reading materials, was refused visitors, and was continuously moved from one prison to another. In one of the book's appendixes, Soyinka reports a particularly horrific incident that captures the excesses of the military regime of the time, an incident in which a state governor ordered the public flogging of local chiefs.

1368   Vaillant, Janet G. *Black, French, and African: A Life of Leopold Sedar Senghor.* Illus. Harvard Univ. Pr. 1990, $32.50 (0-674-07623-0). 416pp. Biography.

Vaillant has written a superb biography of Senegal's first president. Her work takes its place beside two previous biographies in English, the much-lauded literary biography *Leopold Sedar Senghor* by Janice Spleth (Macmillan, 1985) and an earlier work, *Leopold Sedar Senghor: An Intellectual Biography* by Jacques Hyman (o.p.). The well-chosen title of Vaillant's book represents Senghor's major and sometimes conflicting identities. Senghor was born in Africa, studied in France, and launched the Negritude movement from Paris in the 1930s. After World War II, he returned to Senegal, where he was elected president in 1958. In 1980, he became the first African president to voluntarily leave office.

In a fascinating account, Vaillant explores the life of this cultured and complex man. Her account includes new information on Senghor's childhood and family, particularly the influential role played by his dynamic and sophisticated sister-in-law Helene. This is not a hagiography; Vaillant notes that Senghor had critics as well as admirers, shortcomings as well as triumphs. The result is a measured and highly readable biography that provides a multidimensional portrait of Senghor.

1369   Ya-Otto, John, and others. *Battlefront Namibia.* Lawrence Hill 1981, $12.95 (0-88208-132-2); $6.95 (1-55652-063-8). 168pp. Autobiography.

This gripping autobiography describes Ya-Otto's childhood in Namibia and his transformation from teacher to political activist. Ya-Otto was born in Ovamboland, a rural ghetto for Ovambo people in Namibia. In the post–World War I years, Namibia (then South West Africa) was ruled by a defiant South Africa that refused to relinquish its illegal control of the country. White South Africans ruled Namibia with the same oppressive strategies employed in South Africa. Whites and blacks were rigidly segregated, blacks were removed from their land to make way for whites, and defiant Namibians were imprisoned or banished to remote areas.

Ya-Otto was born into this race-defined world. He describes his supportive family, his school years, and his growing awareness of apartheid. The galvanizing experience for Ya-Otto was the Windhoek Massacre of 1959. In a powerful and well-crafted chapter, Ya-Otto describes the slaughter of protesters by the South African police and his narrow escape from death. Soon after this harrowing experience, Ya-Otto was arrested and imprisoned in South Africa. There he was beaten, tortured, and placed in solitary confinement. Ya-Otto's story is one of the few personal accounts of a Namibian freedom fighter. Compelling and well written, it provides an excellent introduction to preindependence Namibia.

12

SOUTH AND CENTRAL ASIA

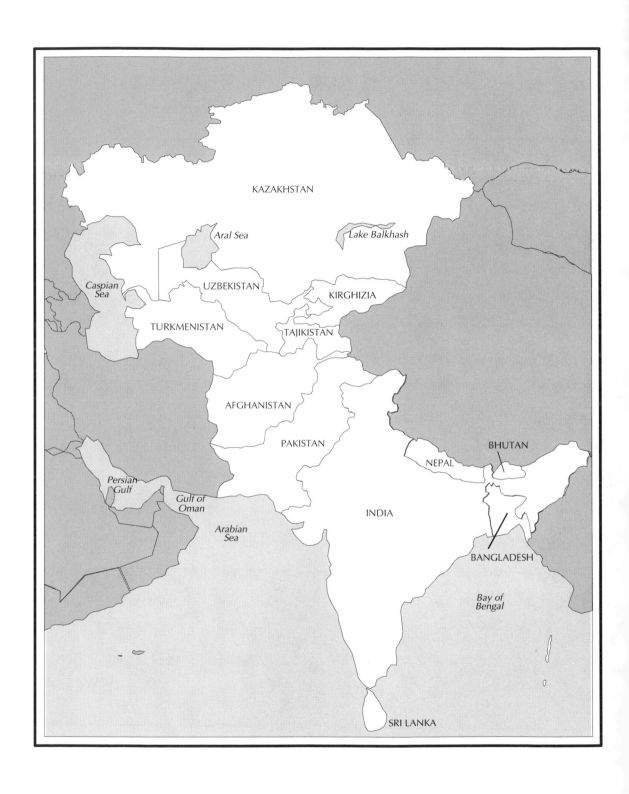

KAZAKHSTAN

Aral Sea

Lake Balkhash

Caspian Sea

UZBEKISTAN

KIRGHIZIA

TURKMENISTAN

TAJIKISTAN

AFGHANISTAN

PAKISTAN

NEPAL

BHUTAN

Persian Gulf

Gulf of Oman

Arabian Sea

INDIA

BANGLADESH

Bay of Bengal

SRI LANKA

12

SOUTH AND CENTRAL ASIA

by Rajagopal Parthasarathy, Shobhan Parthasarathy,
and Maureen Haley Terada

South and Central Asia include the countries of Afghanistan, Bangladesh, Bhutan, India, Kazakhstan, Kirghizia, the Maldives, Nepal, Pakistan, Sri Lanka, Tadzhikistan, and Uzbekistan. (For the sake of brevity, in this chapter the term "India" will sometimes be used to refer to the entire region.) It is the home of one of the oldest civilizations, the Harappa culture. The earliest literary texts of the Indo-Europeans, the Vedas, were composed in India about 1500-1000 B.C, attesting to an unbroken literary tradition of 3,500 years. Sanskrit, Persian, and English have each functioned as a lingua franca throughout the region for centuries.

Seven hundred and fifty years of uninterrupted foreign rule, between A.D. 1192 and 1947, disrupted the continuity of the Indian tradition. However, beginning in the late eighteenth century, European and Indian scholars rediscovered the past and ushered in the Indian renaissance. In contrast, much of modern Indian literature arose in large part as a result of the Anglicization of the Indian languages. Bengali was, in fact, the first language to be heavily influenced by English. Later, however, Bankim Chandra Chatterji (1838–1894) and Rabindranath Tagore (1861–1941) launched a literary revolution, profoundly nationalistic in tone, as an attempt to restore to India her former prestige while at the same time reflecting the changes that were transforming Indian society. Tagore exemplifies the literary response of the Indian mind to European culture, which he experienced through contact with the English colonizers. Vishnushastri Chiplunkar (1850–1882) spoke for all Indian writers when he remarked: "To Indians, English literature was like the milk of a tigress." Another consequence of exposure to English writing was an increasing secularization of Indian literature, which, before the nineteenth century, had been essentially religious in inspiration and content. In sum, the backlash against the influence of English has been instrumental in developing India's national consciousness over the past two centuries.

That being said, it is ironic that Indian literature in English has increasingly come to represent Indian writing abroad, sometimes at the expense of literature in the original languages. Translation is the baptism of fire that Indian writers must go through if they are to earn a reputation in the West. Few writers, however, undergo that transition. Thus, literature written in any of the seventeen major Indian languages (including those spoken in Pakistan) exists largely in a world of its own. Our point is that Indian works available in English—many of which are described in this chapter—represent only the tip of the iceberg, and that the influence of writers who express themselves in English is out of proportion to their actual numbers.

It was Tagore's own English translation of his Bengali poems, *Gitanjali* ("The Offering of Songs") (orig. pub. 1912; Macmillan, 1971), that earned him the Nobel Prize for literature in 1913, making him the first non-Western writer to be so honored and securing his reputation as the greatest Indian writer of the twentieth century. *The Broken Nest* (orig. pub. 1901), also written originally in Bengali, laid the foundation of the modern Indian novel. The story, highlighting the emotional, psychological, and social insecurity of marriage, is Tagore's attack on a culture in which the husband takes his wife's love and fidelity for granted.

The two major writers who followed him, Premchand (1880–1936) and Saadat Hasan Manto (1912–1955), did not enjoy Tagore's good fortune. Neither was translated into English during his lifetime—Premchand's first translated work appeared in 1969, Manto's in 1987—so recognition in the West has been slow to come. Premchand is the greatest figure in modern Hindi literature, and his short stories reflect the world of his native Uttar Pradesh in northern India in the first three decades of the twentieth century. Inspired by Gandhi's efforts to reform Hindu society, Premchand exposes in one story after another the evils plaguing India, such as the caste system and the oppression of women. He portrays village life in India with realism, insight, and compassion.

The partition of the subcontinent into India and Pakistan in 1947 is the backdrop for some of Manto's finest stories. He writes scathingly in Urdu about the horrors committed by Muslims, Hindus, and Sikhs in the wake of independence. Manto's stories are especially relevant today in the context of religious intolerance in the subcontinent.

Faiz Ahmed Faiz (1910–1984), who also wrote in Urdu, is considered the preeminent poet in that language in this century. A Pakistani national after the partition of India in 1947, he was thrice imprisoned by the government on charges of political conspiracy; ultimately he was exiled. Faiz's poetry speaks of the tyranny of dictatorship and laments the sterility of life in Pakistan.

One important novelist who writes in English is Raja Rao (b. 1908), and his works have redrawn the literary map of India. Departing boldly from the European tradition of the novel, Rao has incorporated themes and styles from the Indian literary tradition to explore the metaphysical basis of writing—indeed, of the word itself. He was recognized for his achievement when he was named the tenth laureate of the Neustadt international prize for literature in 1988. Two of his novels, *Kanthapur* (1938) and *The Serpent and the Rope* (1960), are discussed in the annotations that follow.

Also included here are a few titles that are essential for a complete understanding of Indian culture and that are easily available in Western bookstores and libraries. Sanskrit and Tamil, the two classical languages, are represented by the best poems in those two languages. *The Bhagavad-Gita* ("The Word of God," originally composed in the first century A.D.) is a philosophical poem in Sanskrit, one that has often been compared to Dante's *Divine Comedy*. The most influential text in the Hindu religious tradition, it has profoundly shaped every aspect—spiritual, political, and social—of the Hindu way of life through the centuries and into the modern era. The other major poem is *The Cilappatikaram of Ilanko Atikal* ("The Tale of an Anklet," originally written in the fifth century A.D.), which relates the story of Tamil civilization but is also a poem about marriage and family. The Tamil national epic, it describes in unforgettable poetry the issues that humanity has always confronted: love, war, evil, fate, and death.

Most of the fiction and poetry included in this chapter were written in English and are therefore generally accessible to the Western reader. With the exception of R. K. Narayan (b. 1906) and Khushwant Singh (b. 1915), all the English writers live outside India: Rao and Mehta (b. 1934) in the United States; Markandaya (b. 1924), Naipaul (b. 1932), and Rushdie (b. 1947) in England; and Mistry (b. 1944) in Canada. Desai (b. 1937) and Seth (b. 1952) spend part of the year in the United States. Most of the writers are Hindus, and the Hindu worldview informs their work, while the Islamic, Sikh, and Zoroastrian ideologies suffuse the writings of Rushdie, Singh, and Mistry respectively. These writers represent the increasing globalization of English literature, an unexpected fallout from the *Pax Britannica*. In Rushdie's resonant phrase, the empire is "writing back with a vengeance."

As the examples just cited suggest, many noted writers are either exiles who take their language and culture abroad with them or who write in a language other than the one they spoke first. In a way, exile becomes a rite of passage some writers must endure before they earn the "right" to speak. Ironically, the dominance of English in India made some writers exiles in their own homeland; hardly any Indian writer of the last one hundred and fifty years, including Tagore, has escaped the bewitchment of English.

The nonfiction works annotated here offer a panoramic view of the South and Central Asian world, introducing the reader to its history, its religious and philosophical traditions (including Hinduism, Buddhism, Sikhism, and Islam), and its political issues, artistic heritage, music, and anthropology. A number of standard reference works are included to encourage the reader to sample the enormous diversity the region presents. Titles include *The Wonder That Was India* by A. L. Basham, *Sources of Indian Tradition* by Ainslie T. Enbree and Stephen Hay, *Village India* by McKim Marriott, *A Sourcebook in Indian Philosophy* by Sarvepalli Radhakrishnan and Charles A. Moore, *The Cambridge Encyclopedia of India, Pakistan, Bangladesh, Sri Lanka, Nepal, Bhutan, and the Maldives* by Francis Robinson, *A Historical Atlas of South Asia* by Joseph E. Schwartzberg, and histories of India by Romila Thapar and Vincent A. Smith. As this list suggests, scholarly discourse about the region is largely conducted in English, both by South Asian and Western scholars. The prevalence of English has expanded the influence of South Asian scholarship outside the region but has perhaps done so at the expense of scholarly discourse in vernacular languages. When looking exclusively at English-language sources, whether by Western or South Asian scholars, readers should be aware that differing views may be present in vernacular-language materials. As would be expected, South Asia is most likely introduced to Western readers through English books.

India, due to its size if nothing else, dominates South Asia, and it is therefore not surprising that there is a predominance of books on India included in this list. In an effort to include some of the less represented countries in the area, several excellent books on the region as a whole (i.e., titles by Robinson and by Dutt) are included. Only one book on the list, *Central Asia: One Hundred Thirty Years of Russian Dominance*, focuses on the newly independent countries of Central Asia—Kazakhstan, Kirghizia, Tadzhikistan, and Uzbekistan—that until recently were part of the Soviet Union. A collection of scholarly articles, the book was originally published in 1967 and was revised in 1994.

Despite more than a decade of civil war, Soviet intervention, and open U.S. support for the anti-Soviet combatants, there are few accounts of recent events in Afghanistan. The best is by the French analyst Olivier Roy, who observed the Islamic resistance movement firsthand and has updated his *Islam and Resistance in Afghanistan* to cover the period of the Soviet withdrawal. There are no works on the list that focus solely on Bhutan or the Maldives.

Both leaders and ordinary citizens are represented in the essays and autobiographies on this list. Mohandas K. Gandhi and Jawaharlal Nehru—the central figures in India's independence struggle—are represented through their respective autobiographies. These works reveal Gandhi's philosophy of nonviolence, its roots, and its application in the independence struggle as well as the contrasting personalities of Gandhi and Nehru. Nehru's life and ideas are also represented through his historical essay *The Discovery of India* (1946), which was written in prison, and through *Freedom's Daughter* (1989), the collection of letters between Nehru and his daughter, Indira Gandhi, edited by Sonia Gandhi. Pakistan's first female Prime Minister, Benazir Bhutto (1954), has also written an autobiography, titled *Daughter of Destiny* (1989). Among the ordinary Indians telling their stories are Nirad C. Chaudhuri (b. 1897), who explores the nature of British rule in India in his *Autobiography of an Unknown Indian* (1951), Shudha Mazumdar, whose *Memoirs of an Indian Woman* (1989) describes life for a middle-class woman at the time of Indian independence, and Ved Mehta (b. 1934), whose trilogy *Daddyji* (1979), *Mamaji* (1979), and *Vedi* (1982) tell of his family's history and his own experience of growing up blind, the result of a childhood illness his physician father could not cure.

Unless otherwise noted, the literature entries were written by Shobhan and Rajagopal Parthasarathy and the nonfiction and biography entries by Maureen Haley Terada. The introduction was written by Shobhan and Rajagopal Parthasarathy, with revisions by Lyn Miller-Lachmann.

LITERATURE

1370 *The Bhagavad-Gita*. Trans. from Sanskrit and ed. by Barbara Stoler Miller. Bantam 1986, $4.50 (0-553-21365-2). 176pp. Poetry.

The Bhagavad-Gita ("The Word of God"), a philosophical poem in Sanskrit, has often been compared to Dante's *Divine Comedy*. The most influential text in the Hindu religious tradition, it has profoundly shaped every aspect—spiritual, political, and social—of the Hindu way of life through the centuries, and it continues to do so today. Anyone who wishes to understand India should read it.

The poem, which took its present form in the first century A.D., is a dialogue between the warrior Arjuna and his teacher, the god Krishna. It comprises eighteen sections, each of which emphasizes one aspect or another of Krishna's teachings, the most important of which is that one must work without any thought of reward.

1371 Desai, Anita. *Clear Light of Day*. Viking 1989, $6.95 (0-14-010859-9). 192pp. Fiction.

This novel tells the story of Tara, now married to a diplomat and living abroad, as she visits her family in their home in Delhi. Both parents are dead, and the only people living there now are Bim, her sister, a professor of history, and Baba, a younger brother, who has always been withdrawn. An older brother, who is married, has moved to southern India. The two sisters recall their childhood; the events of their lives are interwoven and yet separate. Their travel back in time parallels Bim's interior journey of self-discovery and evaluation. The author manages to keep this journey into the past from deteriorating into sentimentality. Desai's lyrical prose evokes an entire civilization, a way of life, that has all but disappeared.

The author has also written *Baumgartner's Bombay* (Knopf, 1989), the story of a German-Jewish refugee living in Bombay. She begins the novel with his violent death and from there traces his marginal existence as a perennial outsider in Germany, in Calcutta, and finally in Bombay.

1372 Desai, Anita. *Fire on the Mountain*. HarperCollins 1977, $12.95 (0-06-011066-X); Viking $7.95 (0-14-005347-6). 152pp. Fiction.

The novel is set in Kasauli, a Himalayan resort town. Nanda Kaul, widow of a university vice-chancellor, has come here seeking refuge from a life that was once filled with the hustle and bustle of family, servants, and social demands. In Kasauli, Nanda enjoys self-imposed isolation from the outside world. But her tranquillity is interrupted by the arrival of Raka, her boisterous, willful great-granddaughter, who has come to live with her. The two women, though separated by their years, are curiously alike: Both resent their loss of freedom. After a while, Nanda tries to reach out to Raka. She also confides in her old friend Ila Das, whose anxiety presages a violent end to the story. The conflict between Nanda and Raka escalates into a suspenseful climax. The conversation over afternoon tea between Nanda and Ila vividly demonstrates how the lifestyle of upper-class Indians has become Westernized. Raka, Nanda Kaul, and Ila Das are unforgettable characters embodying reckless youth and poignant old age.

This book won the Winifred Holtby Memorial Prize of the Royal Society of Literature and the 1978 National Prize of the Indian Literary Academy.

1373 Faiz, Faiz Ahmed. *The True Subject: Selected Poems of Faiz Ahmed Faiz*. Trans. from Urdu and ed. by Naomi Lazard. Princeton Univ. Pr. 1987, $35.00 (0-691-06704-X); $12.95 (0-691-01438-8). 110pp. Poetry.

Faiz is the preeminent Urdu poet of this century. A Pakistani national after the partition of India in 1947, he was thrice imprisoned by the government on charges of political conspiracy; ultimately, he was sent into exile. Faiz's poetry draws its strength from his emotional involvement with the working classes. In "Lament for the Death of Time," for instance, he speaks of the tyranny of dictatorship and laments the sterility of life in Pakistan, which seems to function in limbo. He associates himself totally with the fate of his country. "Don't Look at Them" is a severe condemnation of "the heroes of pen and sword" who adorn the pages of history. Instead, Faiz's heart goes out to the unknown men and women who freely gave their lives for the country: "Look at those others instead, /the ones who have freely given /the shining coin of their blood /in our streets." Often even his love poetry reverberates with political overtones, but in later poems Faiz becomes more preoccupied with human suffering. In "Do Not Ask Me, My Beloved, Love Like That Former One," the speaker tells his beloved that he cannot offer her the kind of love she has known in the past. Faiz's poetry reflects his dream of freedom from oppression for his people.

1374 Gunesekera, Romesh. ***Monkfish Moon: Short Stories***. New Pr. 1993, $16.95 (1-56584-077-1). 144pp. Fiction.

This collection, Gunesekera's first to be published in the United States, features nine stories set in Sri Lanka or among Sri Lankan immigrants in England. The focus, however, is upon Sri Lanka, its politics, ethnic and class divisions, and family relationships. The title story features a morbidly overweight business tycoon from Colombo who organizes a dinner party that is distinguished by its excess. "A House in the Country" is a dialogue between a British retiree who lives in Colombo and the carpenter who is fixing up the retiree's dilapidated house. The two become close friends, and the retiree plans to help the carpenter finance a small house on a family plot in the country. The carpenter's hopes, however, are dashed when his brother, who has been farming the plot, is murdered by terrorists. Two other stories, "Ullswater" and "Ranvali," portray characters seeking the truth about their fathers, who were activists in the anticolonial struggle and who experienced profound disillusionment and despair.

While the stories in this collection are uneven—most are insightful and poignant, but some are slight and poorly developed—they reveal the perspective of one of Sri Lanka's first major postcolonial authors. LML

1375 Ilanko Atikal. ***The Tale of an Anklet (The Cilappatikaram of Ilanko Atikal): An Epic of South India***. Trans. from Tamil by R. Parthasarathy. Columbia Univ. Pr. 1993, $35.00 (0-231-07848-X). 448pp. Poetry.

This is a new translation in verse of the renowned Tamil poem, one of the world's literary masterpieces and India's finest epic in a language other than Sanskrit. Traditionally believed to have been composed in the fifth century A.D. by Ilanko Atikal, a Tamil prince, *The Tale of an Anklet* is the compelling love story of Kannaki and Kovalan. The anklet is the emblem of the goddess Pattini (chaste wife), and the poem depicts the transformation of Kannaki into the goddess.

The work is divided into three books, named after the capitals of the three Tamil kingdoms that constitute the poem's setting. Love in all its aspects is explored in "The Book of Pukar." "The Book of Maturai" retells the myth of Kannaki's apotheosis into the goddess Pattini. The heroic aspects of kingship are the subject of "The Book of Vanci." *The Tale of an Anklet* relates the story of Tamil civilization, but it is also a poem about marriage and family. Considered to be the Tamil national epic, it spells out in unforgettable poetry the issues that humanity has always confronted: love, war, evil, fate, and death, which have been the special concern of the epic from the beginning of time.

The translator's introduction compares the poem to the Sanskrit and Greek epics and suggests that Ilanko transformed the epic tradition by featuring a woman as its main character. A postscript discusses the poetics of the Tamil epic in the light of the two great categories of Tamil discourse, the erotic and the heroic. To these, Ilanko added a third category, the mythic.

1376 Jhabvala, Ruth P. *Heat and Dust*. Peter Smith 1988, $17.25 (0-8446-6335-2); Simon & Schuster $11.00 (0-671-64657-5). 192pp. Fiction.

An English girl is intrigued by the story of her grandfather Douglas's first wife, Olivia, who is said to have left her husband to elope with an Indian prince in 1923. The episode had created a scandal that none of the family members wishes to remember or talk about. The girl sets off to India to reconstruct the story for herself. Upon her arrival in Bombay, she begins a diary. Her experiences in India surprisingly parallel those of Olivia. Spanning several decades from the 1920s to the present time, the novel vividly contrasts the old India of the princes with the contemporary one. Layers of history peel away to reveal the vast changes that have taken place in the lives of individuals and nations. On another level the contemporary characters' lives are constantly affected by a very palpable past. Through the juxtaposition and interaction of Indian and English characters, Jhabvala reveals the beautiful and the horrible in both cultures. The book won the 1975 Booker Prize.

In addition to this novel, Jhabvala is known for her short stories, of which there are several collections still in print. The title story of *Out of India: Selected Stories* (Simon & Schuster, 1986) was the basis of an Academy Award–winning film of the same title, for which Jhabvala authored the screenplay.

1377 Manto, Saadat H. *Kingdom's End and Other Stories*. Trans. from Urdu by Khalid Hasan. Routledge 1988, $18.95 (0-86091-183-7). 272pp. Fiction.

The short story is the dominant form of Urdu fiction in the twentieth century, and Manto is its undisputed master. The partition of the subcontinent into India and Pakistan in 1947 is the backdrop for some of his finest stories. As tales such as "Toba Tek Singh" reveal, Manto writes scathingly about the horrors committed by Muslims, Hindus, and Sikhs in the wake of independence. His sympathies always lie with the underdog and the oppressed. In "The New Constitution," which questions the legitimacy of British rule, he exposes the underside of the *Pax Britannica* by dramatizing the abusive treatment of the Muslim cabdriver Mangu by an English soldier, who symbolizes the worst aspects of the occupation. For Mangu, all foreign occupations are immoral. As he puts it, "They came for a night, and stayed on as masters of the house." Manto's stories are especially relevant today in the context of religious intolerance in the subcontinent.

1378 Markandaya, Kamala. *Nectar in a Sieve*. NAL 1956, $5.99 (0-451-16836-4). 192pp. Fiction.

This novel of village India tells the story of a peasant woman, Rukmani, who fights against all odds to keep her family together. Her parents marry her off to Nathan, a tenant farmer, when she is only twelve years old. Despite the arranged marriage, the couple grow to love each other and raise a family. The ubiquitous Indian poverty forces their daughter into prostitution, and both Rukmani and Nathan become temple beggars. But Rukmani refuses to despair; in a triumph of the spirit, she accepts her condition cheerfully. As the author suggests through her story, the real India exists in the villages. This is an exceptional first novel that makes a distant civilization intelligible to the English reader. Later novels of Markandaya, such as *Two Virgins* (o.p.), continue the theme of the impoverishment of village India.

1379 Mistry, Rohinton. ***Such a Long Journey***. McKay 1991, $21.50 (0-679-40258-6); Random $11.00 (0-679-73871-1). 384pp. Fiction.

The novel is set in Bombay, the city in which Mistry grew up. The year is 1971, and India is at war with her neighbor Pakistan. Most of the characters in the novel are Parsis, who are members of the small but influential Zoroastrian community that settled in western India at some point after the Islamic conquest of Iran thirteen hundred years ago. The hero, Gustad Noble, is a hardworking middle-class Parsi who is devoted to his family. The war, brief though it is (it lasted just thirteen days), touches Noble's life in several profound ways.

Paralleling the external disruption of life is the domestic chaos. His daughter falls ill, and his rebellious son ruins all hopes for the bright future that Noble has planned for him. An old friend, Jimmy Bilimoria, encourages him to join the Research and Analysis Wing (RAW) of Indira Gandhi's government. Out of a sense of loyalty to Bilimoria, who is already a member, and in the patriotic fervor of the moment, Noble agrees, and unwittingly becomes a pawn in a dangerous political subterfuge full of life-threatening situations. At the end of the novel, a sadder and wiser Noble, who has lost a friend to RAW, rediscovers his true self and becomes reconnected to his family.

Like his collection of short stories, *Swimming Lessons and Other Stories from Firozsha Baag* (Viking, 1990), Mistry's novel is peopled with characters that may seem exotic to the American reader but are entirely credible in their Indian context.

1380 Mukherjee, Bharati. ***Jasmine***. Fawcett 1991, $5.99 (0-449-21923-2). 244pp. Fiction.

Jasmine, the heroine of this novel, grows up in Hasnapur, a typical village in rural India. From the moment of her birth she seems marked for a life utterly different from that of an Indian villager. Already a widow at seventeen, she enlists the help of her brothers to escape the prescribed life of a village widow by emigrating to the United States. Her unpredictable and precarious life as an illegal alien propels the events of the novel. Her survival instinct, so characteristic of many new immigrants, helps her to survive many painful experiences without succumbing to self-pity or regret. As in other works by this author, readers see the American scene through the eyes of an "outsider," and in the process come to look at both India and the United States in a new way.

Strongly etched characters and a fine mastery of the American idiom are Mukherjee's strengths as a writer. These strengths are also on display in *The*

Middleman and Other Stories (Grove, 1988). The principal characters in these stories are all immigrants, mainly from Asia (Afghanistan, India, the Philippines, Sri Lanka, and Vietnam), but also from the Caribbean, Italy, and the Middle East. Most of the stories are first-person narratives recounting different immigrant experiences. The characters are united in the commonality of their vision: the vision of the "outsider" and of the newcomer to the United States. Their encounters with the geographic vastness of the country, and with the sexuality and violence that are a part of the American way of life, ultimately reflect the true American spirit: the restless spirit of an adventurer. The book won the 1988 National Book Critics Circle Award in fiction.

1381 Narayan, R. K. ***The Financial Expert***. Univ. of Chicago Pr. 1981, $15.00 (0-226-56840-7); $9.95 (0-226-56841-5). 224pp. Fiction.

Many of Narayan's novels are set in the imaginary town of Malgudi in southern India, and they center on the lives of ordinary people as they struggle to achieve self-awareness. Not all of them do. However, they accept their fate calmly. Narayan captures in natural and unaffected English the uneven tenor of the Hindu way of life. Malgudi is not only village India in microcosm, but it is also an emblem of the human condition. The title of the novel derives from the occupation of its hero, Margayya, who offers advice on loans and mortgages to peasants in his open-air office under a banyan tree. His business practices are questionable. He amasses a fortune, first as a publisher of a pornographic book and then as a banker, but after an unseemly quarrel with his son, Balu, he goes bankrupt. Despite the literal meaning of his name ("One Who Shows the Way"), Margayya is lost in a maze of self-deception. The novel is an ironic commentary on the realities of life in postindependence India.

1382 Narayan, R. K. ***The Guide***. Viking 1992, $9.95 (0-14-018547-X). 224pp. Fiction.

This comic masterpiece is a story of self-deception. Raju had been a successful tour guide in Malgudi, a town in southern India. His infatuation with the dancer Rosie lands him in prison, from which he emerges unrepentant. He permits an unsuspecting villager, Velan, to regard him as a guru or spiritual guide. The novel skillfully combines two stories: Raju's disreputable life in Malgudi as told to Velan, and his life as a guru in the village of Mangal. It calls into question the Hindu religious tradition, which the author suggests has deteriorated. In an irony for which the author is famous, the villagers invest Raju with all the paraphernalia of the "renouncer," which in Hindu philosophy is the last of the four stages of life (the *ashrama*s). The villagers expect him to save them from drought and famine, but naturally he is uncomfortable with the role. In the end, however, he dies as a result of a fast he undertakes to bring rain. Raju's karma catches up with him, as he turns into a fake god-man incapable of guiding himself or others. The book won the 1961 National Prize of the Indian Literary Academy.

1383 Premchand. ***Deliverance and Other Stories***. Trans. from Hindi by David Rubin. Viking 1988. o.p. Fiction.

Premchand is the greatest figure in modern Hindi literature, and his short stories reflect the world of his native Uttar Pradesh in northern India in the first three decades of the twentieth century. Inspired by Gandhi's efforts to reform Hindu society, Premchand exposes in one story after another the evils plaguing India, such as the caste system and the oppression of women. He portrays life in village India with realism, insight, and compassion.

In one of his best-known stories, "The Chess Players" (the basis of Satyajit Ray's 1977 film), he explores the reasons for the illegal annexation in 1856 of the kingdom of Oudh by Lord Dalhousie, the British governor-general. The ruler of Oudh, Nawab Wajid Ali, is let down by his own nobles, who have abandoned themselves to a life of opulence and sensuality. In "A Coward," Premchand questions the taboo against intercaste marriage and examines the impact of the modernization of Indian society by the British on the status of women. One of the issues the story raises is debated even today: "How might Indian women assume equal status with men in a fundamentally traditional society?" Almost half a century after his death, Premchand's stories continue to illuminate the contemporary Indian scene.

1384 Rao, Raja. ***Kanthapura***. Greenwood 1977, $47.50 (0-8371-9573-X); New Directions $10.95 (0-8112-0168-6). 244pp. Fiction.

This is a classic story of how Gandhi's struggle for India's independence from the British came to change forever life in a village, Kanthapura, in southern India. The struggle takes place on two fronts: nonviolent resistance to the *Pax Britannica* and social protest to reform Indian society. References to specific events in India in the late 1920s and the early 1930s ground the novel firmly in a distinct historical context. Told by an old woman, Achakka, the story evokes the spirit and discourse of India's traditional folk narratives. Like Gandhi, Moorthy, the hero of the story, is committed to ending British rule as well as to ending the inequalities within Indian society, such as "untouchability" and the oppression of women. The Gandhian bias of the novel is obvious: Moral revolution takes precedence over social and political revolutions. Rao's preface to the novel has become a stylistic guide for Third World writers everywhere.

1385 Rao, Raja. ***The Serpent and the Rope***. Overlook Pr. 1986, $22.50 (0-87951-220-2); $9.95 (0-87951-243-1). 408pp. Fiction.

The novel portrays the meeting of the East and West on the most intimate plane. It is the story of Ramaswamy, an Indian, and Madeleine, a Frenchwoman, who meet at the University of Caen in northern France shortly after World War II. Central to their quest is the need to understand the true nature of love. The novel is also a meditation on the nature of existence. Moving in setting from India to France to England, the story traces with rigor and clarity the spiritual progress of its hero from innocence to experience and maturity. The fullest possible expression of a profound Indian sensibility, the novel presents India not merely as a spot on a map but as an idea, with all its traditions intact. Rao's English draws on the nuances of Sanskrit to bring to life traditional India as never before. E. M. Forster described *The Serpent and the Rope* as "the best novel in English to come from India." The book won the 1964 National Prize of the Indian Literary Academy.

1386 Rushdie, Salman. *Midnight's Children*. Viking 1991, $11.00 (0-14-013270-8). 448pp. Fiction.

The novel chronicles the family history of Saleem Sinai, who was born on the stroke of midnight, the first hour of India's independence, on August 15, 1947. The story begins in 1915 with his grandfather and ends in 1978, one year after Indira Gandhi's defeat at the polls and the end of her Emergency. Sinai's personal history is interwoven with the history of postindependence India. At every significant event in that period of India's history, Sinai manages to turn up, showing himself as an ingenious instrument of that change and giving new meaning to the saying "The personal is the political." Rushdie writes vividly and emotionally about the growing pains of a newborn nation. At the heart of the novel is the central Indian question of identity: the individual in relation to his family, community, and nation. On one level, Sinai examines his personal history, trying to find some meaning in his life. At another, the novel explores the fragmented psyche of an entire nation coping with multiple languages, religions, cultures, and races, and yet joined together by a mythical vision of oneness. The book won the 1981 Booker Prize and in 1993 received a special Booker of Bookers for the best British novel of the previous quarter-century.

Rushdie followed this novel with *Shame* (o.p.), a less-polished but still important work that chronicles the independence process in Pakistan and the years under the rule of Zulfikar Ali Bhutto. He is best known, however, for the novel *The Satanic Verses (see main entry)*.

1387 Rushdie, Salman. *The Satanic Verses*. Viking 1989, $19.95 (0-670-82537-9); Consortium $10.00 (0-9632707-0-2). 496pp. Fiction.

Perhaps no novel in this century has caused so much international controversy, political intervention, and religious persecution as *The Satanic Verses*. Even today Rushdie is a fugitive from the wrath of the Iranian ayatollahs, who sentenced the author to death for what they perceived to be his blasphemous writing.

The novel opens with two characters falling from a hijacked Air India airplane that has blown up over the English Channel. On reaching the earth safely, they are magically transformed into an angel and a devil. The angel (Gibreel, a film actor who specializes in "theologicals") experiences vivid dream sequences in which the prophet Mohammed comes to him for advice. It is these dream sequences and the visions of the prophet that so roused the indignation of Islamic fundamentalists. Meanwhile, the devil, Saladin Chamcha, goes through a series of wild adventures. He is branded an illegal immigrant and is outlawed. In the end, Gibreel and Saladin, once close friends but now sworn enemies, meet face to face in a riotous melodramatic sequence. Gibreel becomes Azraeel, the Islamic angel of death. The novel has the characteristic exuberant style, irreverent humor, leaps of the imagination, and allegorical elements that Rushdie previously exhibited in *Midnight's Children (see main entry)*.

1388 Seth, Vikram. *A Suitable Boy: A Novel*. HarperCollins 1993, $30.00 (0-06-017012-3); $15.00 (0-06-092500-0). 1,376pp. Fiction.

In India, marriages arranged by parents are the rule, and those in which spouses choose their own partners are the exception. On the basis of this simple proposition, Seth has spun out one of the longest novels (over 1,300 pages) in the history of English-language fiction.

The story revolves around nineteen-year-old Lata Mehra, a college student, whose mother Rupa insists on picking a suitable boy for her marriage. In the process, the novel encompasses several generations of families: the Mehras, the Kapoors, the Khans, and the Chatterjees. Family trees are provided on the endpapers to help keep the reader on track. The backdrop for this human drama is also vast. It is set in the early 1950s, as India, newly independent, confronts its first major crisis: the first general elections. The American reader may initially compare the novel to a soap opera—multiple characters, complex relationships, intricate subplots—but in the Indian context it is an entirely credible story. The author, however, makes no concessions to Western readers. For example, he provides no glossary for the numerous words in Indian languages scattered throughout the novel.

Seth has depicted with great skill the most subtle and delicate nuances of a complex society. At its core, the novel evokes the gamut of human emotions: love, both fulfilled and unrequited; separation and reconciliation; and ambition. From these powerful feelings this massive and challenging work draws its universal appeal.

1389 Singh, Khushwant. ***Train to Pakistan***. Greenwood 1975, $38.50 (0-8371-8226-3); Grove $8.95 (0-8021-3221-9). 181pp. Fiction.

On August 15, 1947, the Indian subcontinent was partitioned by the British into India and Pakistan. A bloodbath ensued in which thousands of Sikhs, Hindus, and Muslims died. Against this historical background, Singh tells his story of heroism and sacrifice, of a Sikh's love for a Muslim girl in a Punjabi village in northwestern India. Though Sikhs and Muslims had been living in peace for generations in the village, violence erupts between them in the aftermath of the partition.

The novel also evokes the Sikh way of life. Sikhism, founded by Guru Nanak in the fifteenth century, began as a movement to reform Hinduism and bring Hindus and Muslims close to each other. The political situation, however, is far too explosive to be contained by the teachings of either Sikhism or Islam. *Train to Pakistan* is a classic novel drawn from real-life events in the tumultuous history of India.

1390 Tagore, Rabindranath. ***The Broken Nest***. Trans. from Bengali. Asia Book Corp. 1983, $5.50 (0-318-37008-5). 104pp. Fiction.

Winning the Nobel Prize for literature in 1913 helped Tagore establish his reputation in the West as the greatest Indian writer of the twentieth century. Tagore was a prolific writer of poetry, drama, and fiction. Numerous collections of his literary works as well as his essays and lectures are still in print.

The Broken Nest, written in Bengali in 1901, laid the foundation of the modern novel in India. Until 1911, Calcutta was the capital of the British Indian empire. The Bengalis' proximity to the seat of power exposed them to Western cultural influences. Most significantly, perhaps, English displaced Persian as the lingua franca and relegated Indian languages to a subordinate position. For Tagore, the broken nest symbolizes the violation of Indian languages by English. The novel criticizes anglophilia via its portrayal of the character of Bhupati, the editor of an English-language newspaper. As the paper becomes his sole obsession, he becomes estranged from his native language and even from his wife, Charulata. Bhupati's cousin, Amal, steps in to fill the emptiness, and gradually Amal and Charulata fall in love. The knowledge of their relationship devastates Bhupati.

In addition to its political themes, the novel depicts the emotional, psychological, and social insecurity of Hindu women. Married at an early age, they face an uncertain future. Charulata represents the modern Indian woman who risks everything for love. Through Charulata, Tagore criticizes the system of arranged marriages in which the husband takes his wife's love and fidelity for granted. Satyajit Ray's outstanding 1964 film *Charulata* is based on Tagore's novel.

NONFICTION

1391 Allen, Charles. *Plain Tales from the Raj: Images of British India in the Twentieth Century*. Illus. South Asia Books 1992, $10.00 (0-8364-2835-8). 348pp. Nonfiction.

This book was developed from tape-recorded interviews that Charles Allen made for the BBC Radio series of the same name that was first broadcast in 1974. Sixty men and women, referred to by Allen as "survivors of the Raj," discuss many aspects of their lives during the period of British rule in India. The book is an excellent and very readable introduction to the British perspective on colonialism and life in India. Most of the interviewees were born at the turn of the century into British families whose time of service in India stretched back a hundred years or more. Most left India as children to attend school in England and returned after World War I. Allen describes this transition as "the divide between the old Imperial India of the Edwardian age and the newly self-conscious India of the twenties." Material is arranged by subject rather than by region or period. The book is illustrated with photographs, sketches, and reproductions of original documents, and contains a glossary of "Anglo-Indian" terms and slang.

1392 Allworth, Edward, ed. *Central Asia: One Hundred Thirty Years of Russian Dominance, a Historical Overview*. 3rd ed. Illus. Duke Univ. Pr. 1994, $68.50 (0-8223-1554-8); $26.95 (0-8223-1521-1). 664pp. Nonfiction.

This account of the effects of Russian rule on Central Asia begins with the storming of Tashkent by Russian troops in 1865, then briefly looks back in history to earlier encounters. With the fall of Tashkent, religion became a primary issue between the regions, though it had been a factor in their relationship for some time. The encounter is described in terms of military inroads, trade offensives, cultural and intellectual exchanges, diplomatic relations, and government policies. Topics also include discussions of the people, languages, and migrations of Central Asia; population and land issues; historical events; agricultural development and industrialization; intellectual and literary changes; musical tradition and innovation; and art and architecture. The text of this third, revised edition contains many illustrations and tables plus an indexed glossary and index.

1393 Basham, A. L. *The Wonder That Was India: A Survey of the Culture of the Indian Sub-Continent Before the Coming of the Muslims.* Illus. South Asia Books 1992, $14.00 (0-8364-2888-9). 572pp. Nonfiction.

This classic work is an excellent survey of the culture of pre-Muslim India. Intended for the general reader, the book covers most aspects of ancient Indian life and thought. The author introduces India through its geography and the prehistoric sites of Harappa and Mohenjo-Daro. From here he divides the book into large chapters on history, the state, society, everyday life, religion, the arts, and language and literature, ending with an epilogue on the impact of the West and the world's debt to India. The eleven appendixes demonstrate India's contribution to world civilization and include sections on cosmology, astronomy, mathematics, medicine, and other topics. The book is an excellent general reference work, with an easy-to-use index and glossary. Sections of the book, especially the appendixes, can easily stand alone and can therefore be used as supplementary reading for undergraduate classes. Many illustrations and a bibliography are included.

1394 Brass, Paul. *The Politics of India Since Independence.* 2nd ed. Illus. Cambridge Univ. Pr. 1994, $59.95 (0-521-45362-3); $18.95 (0-521-45970-2). 424pp. Nonfiction.

In this valuable introduction to a complex subject, the author explains the organization of India's government and discusses the major issues facing that government since Independence in 1947. According to the author, the central theme of the book "concerns the consequences of increasing efforts by the country's national leaders to centralize power, decision making, and control of economic resources in one of the most culturally diverse and socially fragmented agrarian societies in the world." The introduction provides a background to the discussion by focusing on the continuities and discontinuities between pre- and postindependence India. The rest of the book is divided into three sections: Political Change, Pluralism and National Integration, and Political Economy. This volume is a good choice for undergraduates and general readers seeking an understanding of the ethnic conflicts and, especially, the language-related problems occurring in modern India. A bibliography and index are included.

1395 Bumiller, Elisabeth. *May You Be the Mother of a Hundred Sons: A Journey Among the Women of India.* Random 1990, $19.45 (0-394-56391-3); Fawcett $12.00 (0-449-90614-0). 320pp. Nonfiction.

During her three-and-a-half years as a reporter in India for the *Washington Post*, Elisabeth Bumiller found that writing stories about Indian women touched her most deeply. She chose to write about the women in this book because she was inspired by them, because their lives illustrate important themes, or simply because they had interesting stories to tell. The title of the book is a Hindu blessing bestowed on women at the time of their wedding; Bumiller says, however, that she came to regard these words as a curse.

The introductory chapter discusses women in India generally, while the remainder of the book presents stories exploring various issues touching women's lives. Bumiller writes about the horrendous practice of bride-burning; the Self- Employed Women's Association; women in the Indian film industry; Indira Gandhi and women in Indian politics; the Indian women's movement; population control; and the struggles and accomplishments of women in different strata of society. The book, written for a general audience in a readable, first-person style, includes a bibliography and an index.

1396 Burki, Shahid J. *Pakistan: The Continuing Search for Nationhood.* 2nd rev. and updated ed. Illus. Westview 1991, $53.00 (0-8133-8100-2); $18.95 (0-8133-8101-0). 243pp. Nonfiction.

The author is a former economic adviser to Pakistan's Ministry of Commerce. He has taught at Harvard and has worked as Director of the International Relations Department of the World Bank. In this introductory book, he outlines the political history of Pakistan and the country's economic and social development. He explores the interaction between politics and the economy, and the structural changes in the economy since independence, and the problems of social development, especially the low literacy and high fertility rates among Pakistani women. The nature of Pakistan's foreign policy, especially with bordering countries, is examined. Burki remarks that the foreign relations of a country so preoccupied with its neighbors naturally has a profound effect on both political and economic development. Maps, tables, and illustrations, and a bibliography are included.

1397 Cohen, Stephen P., ed. *The Security of South Asia: American and Asian Perspectives.* Univ. of Illinois Pr. 1987, $29.95 (0-252-01394-8). 304pp. Nonfiction.

This volume, a collection of articles on security issues in South Asia, examines the relationship between India and Pakistan, the region's two militarily important states, and the involvement of the United States. To compare and contrast Indian, Pakistani, and American views, specialists in South Asian strategy from the three nations examine the underlying causes of the India-Pakistan conflict and in some cases suggest policies to improve regional stability.

Part One looks at perceptual and issue-related problems from the standpoint of India, Pakistan, and the United States. In an intriguing intellectual exercise, the authors are asked to place themselves in the position of their counterparts in another country. In Part Two, four strategic analysts speculate on the future of the region. In his concluding chapter, editor Stephen Cohen summarizes the arguments presented in the book and discusses five emerging themes that provide some indication of the prospects for stability in the region. The book has no bibliography, but footnotes at the end of each article suggest further reading.

1398 Conze, Edward. *Buddhism: Its Essence and Development.* Peter Smith 1951, $25.25 (0-8446-1889-6); HarperCollins, $13.00 (0-06-130058-6). 212pp. Nonfiction.

This clear, classic introductory text presents the basic philosophy of Buddhism and follows the development of the Buddhist schools of thought. The book is brief, about 200 pages, but contains an excellent discussion of the Buddhist approach to life. Conze explains the roles of the monks and the laity in early

Buddhism, the development of the Mahayana and Tantric traditions, and the influence of devotionalism. He then briefly surveys Buddhist developments outside India, particularly Zen, Amidism, Tibetan Buddhism, and recent interest in the West. Several charts help the reader to visualize the development of the various schools in the context of historical events. A selected reading list and an index are included.

1399 Coomaraswamy, A. K. ***The Arts and Crafts of India and Ceylon.*** Repr. of 1913 ed. Illus. Scholarly Publications 1987, $19.00 (0-88065-044-3). 265pp. Nonfiction.

Coomaraswamy was born in Ceylon (now Sri Lanka) to a Hindu father and English mother. At an early age he left to be educated in England. The author rightly describes this classic book, originally written in 1913, as "a summary of a vast subject." It briefly covers the Indian arts of sculpture, architecture, and painting as well as the work of the craftsmen in metal, enamel, wood, earthenware, gesso, lac, textiles, and embroidery. He makes a strong point for including the art and culture of Ceylon within the larger Indian tradition. Part One focuses on Hindu and Buddhist art and includes sections on the character and history of art as well as on the various media. Part Two concerns Mughal Art, with an emphasis on architecture and calligraphy. The book includes many illustrations and an index.

1400 Dutt, Ashok K., and Margaret Geib. ***An Atlas of South Asia***. Illus. Westview 1987. o.p. Nonfiction.

The text, maps, diagrams, photographs, and sketches in this atlas illustrate the physical, political, economic, cultural, and historical aspects of the Indian subcontinent. Most of the maps and figures concern India, but Pakistan and Bangladesh are well represented. Sri Lanka, Nepal, and Bhutan are also depicted, albeit on a lesser scale. In the introductory general chapter on South Asia, the authors examine the climate, religion, physical features, and historical developments. The following chapters are divided by country; the India chapter, for example, addresses such diverse themes as intensity of cropping, railroad networks, important temple sites, population density, and five-year plans. The information is easy to locate and to use, and the book is a good quick reference guide as well as a source for more-detailed statistics. A bibliography is included.

1401 Embree, Ainslie T., ed. ***Sources of Indian Tradition: Volume 1: From the Beginning to 1800.*** 2nd ed. Columbia Univ. Pr. 1988, $18.50 (0-231-06650-3). 547pp. Nonfiction.

This work, the first of two volumes on Indian civilization and part of a larger series on Asian civilization, offers an introduction to the intellectual and spiritual life of the Indian through translations of basic documents by leading thinkers of the subcontinent. Background material explains the religious and philosophical developments in the region and traces the evolution of political, social, and economic thought as well. The chapters in this first volume are arranged in sections according to religion: The Brahmanical Tradition; The Vedic Tradition; Jainism and Buddhism; The Hindu Way of Life; Islam in

Medieval India; and Sikhism. For the second edition, some sections were deleted and new material has been added, mostly new translations. Sources are limited to those of the written tradition. A bibliography, an index, and a list of Indic words are included.

1402   Farmer, B. H. *An Introduction to South Asia.* 2nd ed. Illus. Routledge 1993, $49.95 (0-415-05695-0); $16.95 (0-415-05696-9). 192pp. Nonfiction.

In introducing the main characteristics of South Asia, geographer B. H. Farmer begins by stressing the diversity present within the region we call South Asia. He underscores some of the issues facing its people, issues of national unity and types of government, of economic development and social change, and of the reciprocal impact of South Asia and the wider world. He then provides an introduction to the geography of the area. Subsequent chapters concern the history of the subcontinent (particularly the significance of the colonial period), political developments since independence, and international relations. The final, relatively large chapter concerns economic developments since independence. There is no bibliography; Farmer has written a closing section including notes and references that may suggest further readings.

1403   Fischer, Louis, ed. *The Essential Gandhi.* Random 1983, $10.00 (0-394-71466-0). 369pp. Essays.

This anthology includes excerpts, arranged in chronological order, from Gandhi's autobiography; his books, such as *Satyagraha in South Africa* (Greenleaf, 1979); his publications, such as *Young India* and *Harijan*; his letters; his speeches; and his conversations with the editor. Interspersed throughout are bracketed comments by the editor, quotations from the editor's biography of Gandhi, and, occasionally, information from other sources. According to Fischer, Gandhi believed in revealing himself, and through his writings he created a detailed self-portrait. The editor's admiration for the Mahatma is evident; he describes Gandhi, for example, as "perhaps the greatest figure of the past nineteen hundred years." Fischer comments on sources in his concluding section of notes.

1404   Gandhi, Sonia, ed. *Freedom's Daughter: Letters Between Indira Gandhi and Jawaharlal Nehru, 1922–39.* Hodder & Stoughton 1989. o.p. Essays.

Indira Gandhi was prime minister of India for sixteen years; her father, Jawaharlal Nehru, was one of the most important figures in India's independence movement and was India's first prime minister. These letters, exchanged between the young Indira and her father from 1922 to 1939, provide a glimpse into the lives of this prominent family by showing the changing relationship between father and daughter as she matures. The volume is edited by Sonia Gandhi, wife of Indira's son, Rajiv, who was himself prime minister until, like his mother, he was assassinated. In the introduction, the editor describes the place of the Nehru family in Indian politics, beginning with Indira's grandfather Motilal Nehru, and the influence of Gandhi on the members of the family. From the postcard messages her father wrote to her from jail when she was five and six years old, to his later missives commenting on the situation in India and in Europe before the onset of World War II, this affectionate correspondence tells the reader almost as much about India as about the Nehru family.

Goldstein, Melvyn C., and Cynthia M. Beall. *Nomads of Western Tibet: The Survival of a Way of Life*.
See entry 1523.

1405 Hardy, Peter. *The Muslims of British India*. Books on Demand 1972, $79.30 (0-317-27996-3). 306pp. Nonfiction.

This is an excellent account of the British impact on the Muslims of India. According to Hardy, Indian Muslims harbored a deep nostalgia for the time centuries earlier when, as Lord Dufferin, Viceroy of India, put it in a 1888 speech, they "reigned supreme from the Himalayas to Cape Cormorin." This self-image impelled them to demand a special political position in British India and later, during the partition, to demand that a separate nation—what became modern Pakistan—be created for them. Hardy expands on this thesis by suggesting that in the nineteenth century lower-class Muslims did not see themselves as part of a Muslim nation, nor would they have described themselves as members of the ruling class any more than would the British working class of nineteenth-century England. In his final chapter, he presents his theory that, in fact, two partitions took place in 1947. The first was the partition of British India into the modern nations of India and Pakistan. The second was the division of the Muslim community into those who lived in or moved to Pakistan and those who chose to stay in India. The book includes a descriptive bibliography, glossary, and index.

1406 Harle, J. C. *The Art and Architecture of the Indian Subcontinent*. Illus. Viking 1987, $40.00 (0-685-17500-6); Yale Univ. Pr. $26.50 (0-300-05329-0). 528pp. Nonfiction.

This volume was written to update and replace Benjamin Rowland's classic *The Art and Architecture of India: Hindu, Buddhist, Jain*, first published in 1953 as the original volume on Indian art in the Pelican History of Art series. This version adopts the conventional art history approach, emphasizing styles, their character, origins, and development. In passing, the book supplies only as much cultural background as necessary for the reader to understand the basic features of artistic, sculptural, and architectural forms. Harle devotes six chapters to the art of South India and single chapters to the art of Sri Lanka and Nepal. Painting also comprises a distinct section of six chapters, and a segment on Indo-Islamic architecture is covered in four chapters. The book contains many black-and-white photographs, diagrams, and maps, and a bibliography.

1407 Hartmann, Betsy, and James K. Boyce. *A Quiet Violence: View from a Bangladesh Village*. Humanities Pr. 1979, $45.00 (0-86232-171-9); Inst. for Food & Development Policy/Food First Books. $15.95 (0-935028-16-1). 298pp. Nonfiction.

The "quiet violence" referred to in the title is the violence of needless hunger. The authors give names and faces to some of the world's poorest people, the inhabitants of a Bangladeshi village. In the process, they hope to dispel the myths about the poor and challenge the prevailing cynicism about their future. Having lived in northwestern Bangladesh, the authors write about many aspects of village existence, including the lives of village women, class conflict between landowners and peasants, the workings of the market, religion, and the effects of outside aid. The final chapter addresses the problems associated with foreign aid in Bangladesh as a whole, where, by 1979 figures, foreign aid financed roughly half the government budget and three quarters of its development expenditures. The authors see the greatest impact of foreign aid in the capital city of Dhaka, where foreign aid workers congregate and where a Bangladeshi bourgeoisie has been established. Foreign aid that does reach the countryside, the authors explain, simply "lubricates the vast rural patronage machine which links the government in Dhaka to the rural elite."

1408 Hay, Stephen, ed. ***Sources of Indian Tradition: Volume 2: Modern India and Pakistan.*** 2nd ed. Columbia Univ. Pr. 1988, $18.50 (0-231-06414-4). 433pp. Nonfiction.

This work, the second of two volumes on Indian civilization and part of a larger series on Asian civilization, offers an introduction to the intellectual and spiritual life of the Indian subcontinent through translations of basic documents by leading thinkers of India and Pakistan. In both volumes, background material explains the religious and philosophical developments in the region and traces the evolution of political, social, and economic thought. Introductory comments in each section of this second volume focus on social and political thought. Chapters include: The Opening of India to the West; Leaders of Hindu Reform and Revival; Nationalism Takes Root: The Moderates; The Marriage of Politics and Religion: The Extremists; Leaders of Islamic Revival, Reform, and Nationalism in Pre-Independent India; Mahatma Gandhi: Nationalist India's "Great Soul"; Other Nationalist Leaders in the Decades Before Independence; Public Policies for Independent India; and Pakistan: Defining an Islamic State. For the second edition, some sections were deleted and new material has been added, mostly new translations. Sources are limited to those of the written tradition. A bibliography, an index, and a glossary of Indic words are included.

> Hiro, Dilip. ***Black British, White British.***
> See entry 834.

1409 Hopkins, Thomas J. ***The Hindu Religious Tradition.*** Wadsworth 1971, $19.95 (0-8221-0022-3). 156pp. Nonfiction.

In his introductory chapter, the author asks how someone might sort out all the patterns present in India—familial, regional, historical—and concludes that the answer is quite simple: One cannot. Notwithstanding, in this short book, he provides a guide to a better understanding of Hindu tradition through a historical and chronological approach to its thoughts, values, and practices. He discusses where these concepts came from, how they developed, what they are now, and perhaps what they will be in the future. Topics include the Aryans and early civilization; the power of sacrifice; the meaning of the Upanishads; challenges to Brahmanism from such ideologies as Buddhism and Jainism and the Brahmanical synthesis that followed; the religion expressed through the epic poems and Puranas; the development of devotionalism; and the effects of contact with Islam and the West. Also included are several schematic diagrams and a bibliography organized by chapter headings.

1410 Johnson, B. L. C. *Development in South Asia*. Viking 1983. o.p. Nonfiction.

As background to a discussion of development in South Asia, the author provides a brief survey of the region's colonial past, a sketch of the mineral wealth and environmental variety in the area, and a look at the ideological basis for the national agricultural plans. Traditional farming methods are compared to methods introduced since the "green revolution." Details on new irrigation methods and the high-yielding varieties of grains sustained by fertilizers and an assured water supply are highlighted, along with comments about the variable success of the new crops from country to country. Other issues include agrarian reform and the social aspects of agricultural change; various channels for delivering new technology and growing techniques to villages; the colonial legacy of plantation agriculture; and the success of India's industrial development compared to other countries in the region. The concluding chapters summarize the results of three decades of development efforts. Many tables and a brief bibliography are included.

1411 Kapur, Sudarshan. *Raising Up a Prophet: The African-American Encounter with Gandhi*. Beacon 1992, $28.00 (0-8070-0914-8); $14.00 (0-8070-0915-6). 240pp. Nonfiction.

As advocated by Gandhi, the method of nonviolent resistance has been applied in struggles throughout the world. Martin Luther King, Jr.'s interest in and use of Gandhian principles is well known, but in this book the author shows how civil rights leaders prior to King also embraced nonviolence. The author underscores the religious foundations of both movements and describes how African Americans who, encouraged their organizations to practice—Gandhi's philosophy. Kapur makes special note of the importance of the African-American press in this process. A bibliography and index are included.

1412 Kramrisch, Stella. *Art of India Through the Ages*. Illus. South Asia Books 1987. o.p. Nonfiction.

Kramrisch provides an introduction to Indian art, illustrated with extensive plates, some in color. She describes India's artistic tradition as one means of attaining the ultimate aim of *moksha*, or release. Moksha, she explains, is "the realization of the Absolute within one's own living body, a mature communication which some will attain and of which all are aware in some degree, even though their time has not yet come." The narrative flows from one topic to the next, with an excellent discussion of the design and importance of the Hindu temple and the ways it reflects Hindu cosmology. The author has expanded on this concept in another of her many books, *The Hindu Temple* (South Asia Books, 1991). If *Art of India Through the Ages* has a flaw, it is that, like many books on the subject, there is no mention of art produced since the nineteenth century; in fact, there is very little information on art after the medieval era.

The bibliography is organized by media and type of publication. Kramrisch is also the author of *The Art of Nepal* (o.p.).

1413 Kulke, Hermann, and Dietmar Rothermund. *A History of India*. Illus. Dorset 1990, $24.95 (0-88029-577-5); Routledge, $19.95 (0-415-04799-4). 422pp. Nonfiction.

This valuable introductory history of India emphasizes structural patterns rather than chronological events. The authors explain the major political, economic, social, and cultural forces that have shaped the history of the Indian subcontinent. The introduction, for example, focuses on how history and the environment of the region are mutually dependent.

Hermann Kulke, an expert in ancient and medieval India, wrote the first four chapters, which concern early civilization and Aryan immigration, the great ancient empires, regional kingdoms of the early Middle Ages, and the religious communities and military feudalism of the late Middle Ages. The other chapters are by Dietmar Rothermund, a specialist in modern India, and they address such topics as the rise and fall of the Mughal Empire, the colonial period, and the independence movement. The book concludes with a discussion of the internal and external affairs of the modern Republic of India. The bibliography and notes are arranged by headings within chapters. There are also a detailed chronology, maps, and an index.

1414 Marriott, McKim. *Village India: Studies in the Little Community*. Univ. of Chicago Pr. 1955. o.p. Nonfiction.

This classic anthropological work looks at Indian civilization through eight village studies. The contributors address two important questions: How relevant are holistic methods to studies of villages in India, and what relevance do these types of studies have for understanding India as a whole? The essays in the book are: "The Social System of a Mysore Village" by M. N. Srinivas; "The Social Structure of a Tanjore Village" by Kathleen Gough; "The Changing Status of a Depressed Caste" by Bernard Cohn; "Interplay Among Factors of Change in a Mysore Village" by Alan Beals; "A Study of Personality Formation in a Hindu Village in Gujerat" by Gitel P. Steel; "Peasant Culture in India and Mexico: A Comparative Analysis" by Oscar Lewis; "Little Communities in an Indigenous Civilization" by McKim Marriott; and "The World and the World View of the Kota" by David Mandelbaum.

Matsui, Yayori. *Women's Asia*.
See entry 1630.

1415 Moore, Mick. *The State and Peasant Politics in Sri Lanka*. Cambridge Univ. Pr. 1985. o.p. Nonfiction.

This book examines the participation of small landholders in the political process in Sri Lanka and concludes that the country lacks the distinct "agrarian interest" such as is found in Malaysia, India, Japan, North America, and most of Western Europe. The author argues that the small landholders take part in elections on the basis of identities other than that of agricultural producer. The book describes the paradox in Sri Lanka, which has "a highly politicized rural electorate that regularly played a major role in replacing governments at successive general elections, but apparently had not used its electoral power to even place on the national agenda an issue which directly and deeply affected its material welfare." In the first three chapters, crown lands, land reform, and pricing and agricultural services are surveyed. Subsequent chapters discuss the reasons why Sri Lankan landholders have failed to articulate certain kinds of class demands. The book includes tables and a bibliography.

1416 Naipaul, V. S. *An Area of Darkness*. Peter Smith 1992, $20.25 (0-8446-6680-7); Viking $10.00 (0-14-002895-1). 288pp. Nonfiction.

This, the first and most controversial of Naipaul's three travel books on India, records his visit to the subcontinent between 1962 and 1964. The author's grandparents emigrated to the West Indies as indentured laborers in the nineteenth century. During Naipaul's travels in India, he discovers that he has no identity of his own and expresses his anger and frustration at Indian society, which he finds "impotent." He describes his visit as a total failure: He does not find his roots in the ancestral village in Uttar Pradesh in northern India, and he returns to England with an increased awareness of his alienation from both the West Indies and India. Naipaul writes about the two cultures from his own uneasy perspective. As an anglicized West Indian educated at Oxford, he feels unable to enjoy a meaningful relationship to the real India. But Naipaul does not give up. He resumes his dialogue with India in two successive books: *India: A Wounded Civilization* (Random, 1977) and *India: A Million Mutinies Now* (Viking, 1992).   RP

1417 Nehru, Jawaharlal. *The Discovery of India*. Illus. Oxford Univ. Pr. 1990, $19.95 (0-19-562394-0); $11.95 (0-19-561322-8). 584pp. Nonfiction.

This history of India, by the man who was to become India's first prime minister, was written during one of his stays in prison for his actions against the British colonial government. An absorbing work, it makes Indian history accessible to the general reader (who would do well to keep in mind the author's political perspective). In the introduction, Nehru comments on contemporary world events and includes an interesting aside on his philosophy of life. After exploring various sources of Indian culture and the strengths and weaknesses within the diverse region, he offers a survey of Indian history, beginning with the Indus Valley civilizations. Nehru calls on modern Indians to look with pride at their past, but he also warns them against too strong an affection for "a romanticized past to which we want to cling, . . . allowing us to forget our many weaknesses and failings or blunt our longing to be rid of them."

1418 Radhakrishnan, Sarvepalli, and Charles A. Moore, eds. *Sourcebook in Indian Philosophy*. Princeton Univ. Pr. 1957, $18.95 (0-691-01958-4). 807pp. Nonfiction.

In this useful book, source material on Indian philosophy from Vedic to modern times is presented with introductory commentary, chiefly by Sarvepalli Radhakrishnan, a noted philosopher. The book was produced with two goals in mind: to supply Western readers with basic source material on Indian philosophy in an accessible style and to discuss all the major philosophical systems of India, from the earliest to the most recent, from the secular as well as the religious schools of thought. The general introduction provides a concise history of Indian philosophy, and each of the five sections (Vedic Period, Epic Period, Heterodox Systems, Orthodox Systems, and Contemporary Thought) has additional introductory material. This volume is a good overview of the diversity of Indian philosophical thought. An extensive bibliography is divided according to schools of philosophy.

1419   Rahman, Fazlur. *Islam.* 2nd ed. Univ. of Chicago Pr. 1979, $11.95 (0-226-70281-2). 271pp. Nonfiction.

This book on the general development of Islam was written by a noted Pakistani scholar. In clear language, Rahman covers the range of essential themes: Mohammad; the Koran; the origins and development of Islamic traditions; the structure of the law; dialectical theology and the development of dogma; the Shari'a; the philosophical movement; Sufi doctrine, practice, and organizations; sectarian developments; education; premodernist reform movements; modern developments; and Islam's legacy and prospects. Rahman includes a bibliography arranged by chapter headings and an index.

A more recent and equally interesting introduction to Islam, also written by a Pakistani scholar but offering a perspective "tinted by South Asian experience," is *Discovering Islam: Making Sense of Muslim History and Society* by Akbar A. Ahmed (Routledge, 1988).

1420   Rahula, Walpola. ***What the Buddha Taught.*** Rev. ed. Frwd. by Paul Demieville. Illus. Grove 1987, $9.95 (0-8021-3031-3). 192pp. Nonfiction.

The author, a Buddhist monk from Sri Lanka, manages to present the teachings of the Buddha in a clear fashion without forsaking the intricacies of early Buddhist philosophical development. Rahula states in his preface that he has written this book for "the educated and intelligent general reader, uninstructed in the subject, who would like to know what the Buddha actually taught." His discussion of the essential teaching of the Buddha includes the doctrines of the Four Noble Truths, the Noble Eightfold Path, the Five Aggregates, karma, rebirth, conditioned genesis, the doctrine of "no-soul," and the setting-up of mindfulness. He briefly explains the differences between Theravada and Mahayana Buddhism and argues that, although the two schools have differences with respect to certain beliefs, practices, and observances, they unanimously agree on the most important teachings. Excerpts from selected Pali texts make up the latter third of the book. Also included are a short bibliography and a glossary of Buddhist terms.

Richardson, Hugh E. *Tibet and Its History*.
See entry 1555.

1421   Robinson, Francis. ***Atlas of the Islamic World Since 1500***. Illus. Facts on File 1982, $45.00 (0-87196-629-8). 240pp. Nonfiction.

This colorfully illustrated introduction to the history of Islam contains a good percentage of material on Islam in South Asia, of which the author is a well-known authority. Robinson begins with a historical look at Western attitudes toward Islam and then discusses briefly the spread of Islam from A.D. 622 to 1500. Most of the book concerns Islam after the rise of Muslim power in the sixteenth century. The world of the Mughals in India is reflected through examples of its art and architecture. Later chapters deal with cross-regional issues such as decline, reform, and revival in the eighteenth and nineteenth centuries; the rise of Europe; and the response and later reassertion of Islam in the twentieth century. The religious life of Islam is examined through discussion of various key topics: the design and significance of the mosque and shrine; the stages of life; the Islamic calendar; and the central tenet of Islamic belief, the pilgrimage to Mecca. Among the Islamic arts featured are calligraphy, ceramics, and carpets. A final chapter on society and the modern world addresses nomadic life, life in villages and towns, Muslim houses, and the position of women within Islam. Throughout the book, beautiful photographs and other clear illustrations add to the reader's understanding. Robinson includes a short annotated bibliography with suggestions for further study, a glossary, and an index.

1422 Robinson, Francis, ed. *The Cambridge Encyclopedia of India, Pakistan, Bangladesh, Sri Lanka, Nepal, Bhutan and the Maldives*. Illus. Cambridge Univ. Pr. 1989, $55.00 (0-521-33451-9). 520pp. Nonfiction.

The stated aim of this book is to make the world of South Asia accessible to the general reader while at the same time offering new knowledge to the specialist. Sixty-nine experts on South Asia from a variety of disciplines have contributed to the volume, which contains many illustrations, maps, tables, and photographs. The editor defines three themes that emerge in this work: the interaction between South Asia and the wider world; the constant tension within South Asia between urban and rural areas; and the interaction between the preindustrial elements of South Asian civilization and the forms of modern industrial civilization imported from the West. The book is divided into discrete sections: Land, Peoples, History to Independence, Politics, Foreign Relations, Economies, Religion, Societies, and Culture. This is a useful and readable reference book with a comprehensive index that includes all of the countries of South Asia.

1423 Rose, Leo E., and John T. Scholz. *Nepal: Profile of a Himalayan Kingdom*. Westview 1980. o.p. Nonfiction.

This overview of Nepali history and society offers a good introduction to broad themes such as the evolution of Nepal's social, economic, and political institutions and the country's struggle for survival. The authors survey the physical and cultural environment of Nepal and trace its history to illuminate the process of building a modern Nepali political system. Focus is given to the importance of family and kinship ties in this predominantly peasant society and to the Nepali people's strong association with their ethnic identities. The book examines the processes of democratic reforms and Nepal's quest for economic growth. The final chapter addresses the issue of international relations and Nepal's special relationship with India. A brief supplementary bibliography describes other books on Nepal.

1424 Roy, Olivier. *Islam and Resistance in Afghanistan.* 2nd ed. Cambridge Univ. Pr. 1990, $59.95 (0-521-39308-6); $18.95 (0-521-39700-6). 256pp. Nonfiction.

Roy's analysis of the Afghan resistance to the Soviet invasion is based on his six journeys to the area between 1980 and 1985. The book provides general information on the state and society in Afghanistan and Islamic movements from 1947 forward, but it also traces the resistance movement to its roots in popular Muslim uprisings of the past, such as that of Shah Waliaullah, an Indian Sufi reformer in the early eighteenth century. This book increases the reader's understanding of the link between Islam and popular movements. The author points out that the West, long haunted by the specter of Islam, tends to lump together many distinct movements under a single fundamentalist label. To refine that understanding, Roy discusses the difference between traditionalism—"the desire to freeze society so that it conforms to the memory of what it once was"—and fundamentalism, in which "it is of paramount importance to get back to the scriptures, clearing away the obfuscation of tradition." A glossary and bibliography are included.

1425 Schwartzberg, Joseph E., ed. *A Historical Atlas of South Asia.* 2nd ed. Illus. Oxford Univ. Pr. 1992, $250.00 (0-19-506869-6). 416pp. Nonfiction.

This updated edition is a comprehensive cartographic record of South Asia from the Stone Age to the present day. Other regions, including Central Asia and Southeast Asia, are discussed in passing. The atlas (development of which originally took over a decade and a half) is designed to complement more-detailed histories of South Asia. Approximately half of the book consists of maps and the remainder of supporting text. The index at first seems difficult to use, due to the various types of entries and detail: an alphabetized list of all the regions, places, movements, and other mappable features plotted in the atlas; names of people mentioned in both the text and the illustrations; and major subject headings. Once the index is mastered, however, the atlas is very useful. An extensive bibliography is provided, and overlays and chronological charts are included as end cover inserts.

Seth, Vikram. *From Heaven Lake: Travels Through Sinkiang and Tibet.*
See entry 1561.

1426 Singh, Khushwant. *A History of the Sikhs, Vol. 1: 1469–1839.* Illus. Oxford Univ. Pr. 1991, $11.95 (0-19-562643-5). 438pp. Nonfiction.

Singh, an Indian Sikh, is a well-known and widely published commentator on many aspects of contemporary India. He is also author of *Train to Pakistan*, one of the best-known novels about the 1947 partition of India (*see main entry*). In this volume, Singh writes about the birth of Sikhism and the political ascendancy of the Sikhs, who came to dominate the Punjab under Maharaja Ranjit Singh. A recurring theme is the rise of Punjabi consciousness and the quest to establish an independent Punjabi state under Sikh auspices. Volume Two (Princeton Univ. Pr.; o.p.) covers Sikh history from the death of the Maharaja to 1964, including the resettlement of Sikhs in independent India and the renewal of the call for a Sikh state. This volume focuses on the struggle of the Sikhs to survive as a separate community in the face of British expansionism, Muslim domination, and, after independence, absorption by renascent Hinduism. This history provides background for understanding both the recent violence in the Punjab and the calls for the establishment of an independent Sikh nation of Khalistan. A bibliography and index are included.

Sivanandan, Ambalavaner. *Communities of Resistance: Writings on Black Struggles for Socialism*.
See entry 850.

1427 Smith, Vincent A., and Percival Spear, ed. *The Oxford History of India*. 4th ed. Illus. Oxford Univ. Pr. 1981, $13.95 (0-191561-297-3). Nonfiction.

This classic history of India, originally written by Vincent Smith three decades ago, was revised and updated in 1981. The aim of the book is to relate the history of the Indian people as a whole and make plain the unity of texture in the development of Indian society from the Mughal period to the election of Nehru as prime minister and into the modern era. The original version tended to look with favor on the impact of British colonialism in India. As Spear puts it: "India was brought into the Perso-Turkish world by the Mughals and into the western world by the British. She is now taking her place in the new world society into which the west is merging." This newer edition offers a somewhat more objective assessment of developments in India since the country gained independence. A bibliography with comments by the author is included.

1428 Thapar, Romila. *A History of India, Vol. 1*. Illus. Viking 1966, $6.95 (0-14-020769-4). 353pp. Nonfiction.

According to the author, this book is written for readers with a general interest in India who wish to acquaint themselves with the major developments in early Indian history. Beginning with a look at the culture of the Indo-Aryans, the book's fourteen chapters survey in basically chronological order political, economic, social, and cultural developments prior to the coming of the Mughals and the Europeans in the sixteenth century. The author stresses economic rather than religious factors as the key to understanding India's early history. Included are several maps, a chronological table of events, a glossary, and a bibliographic section with notes on sources.

1429 Wade, Bonnie. *Music in India*. Illus. Riverdale 1987, $23.00 (0-913215-25-2). 252pp. Nonfiction.

This is an introduction to the two classical traditions in Indian music: Hindustani (North Indian) and Karnatak (South Indian). In the text, the author discusses the effects of music on the listener and compares and contrasts Indian and Western concepts in classical music. Chapters describe the two main types of instruments: those that produce melody and those that produce rhythm. Other sections explore the distinctive rhythms and meters and the various performance genres. In the final chapter, the author discusses the talents required of an Indian classical musician. The book contains many plates, charts, a guide to source materials (including a somewhat dated discography), a bibliography, and a glossary.

BIOGRAPHY

1430 Bhutto, Benazir. *Daughter of the East*. Simon & Schuster 1989, $21.95 (0-318-40972-0). 394pp. Autobiography.

Benazir Bhutto was the prime minister of Pakistan from 1988 to 1990—the first woman prime minister of a Muslim state—and was reelected in 1993. In the interval she served as leader of the opposition party. In this autobiography, published before she took office, Bhutto recounts the story of her father, Zulfikar Ali Bhutto, who had been prime minister until 1977, when he was overthrown in a coup led by his former chief of staff, General Zia ul-Haq. After two years in prison, Zulfikar was tried and executed by Zia's military government. As a result of the coup, Benazir—who had been a student at Oxford and Harvard—was subjected to seven years of imprisonment and two years of exile. In 1987 she took part in an arranged marriage. The epilogue, written in August of 1988, is her reaction to Zia's death in a plane crash and her thoughts as the November 16 election approaches. She won the election, which also swept her political party into power. The book includes an index but no bibliography.

1431 Brown, Judith. *Gandhi: Prisoner of Hope*. Yale Univ. Pr. 1991, $17.00 (0-300-05125-5). 452pp. Biography.

This superb biography vividly recounts the important political events in Gandhi's life; but equally important, it offers intriguing insights into the inner dilemmas he confronted as a leader. The author explains how Gandhi's spiritual evolution paralleled his political development. Based on newly available historical sources from official as well as private archives, the book, according to Brown, is "a study and interpretation of a man whose life reflected many lasting human dilemmas, who attempted to resolve them in a particular historical situation, but in a way which had considerable significance in his homeland and beyond. . . . It is an invitation to become familiar with an enigmatic figure, both irritating and attractive; to respond to one whose life was sustained by a religious vision which created in him an abiding sense of hope and prompted him to speak and act on issues which have proved crucial to mankind in our century." The author has noted suggestions for further reading.

1432 Chaudhuri, Nirad C. *The Autobiography of an Unknown Indian*. Addison Wesley 1989, $16.30 (0-201-15576-1). 506pp. Autobiography.

Written shortly after India gained her independence in 1947, this autobiography presents a look at the effects of ever-increasing Westernization on the country and its people. At the same time the author explains that his personal development is in no way typical of twentieth-century India and that his book is more of a national history than a personal one. Chaudhuri wants to tell the story of "the struggle of a civilization with a hostile environment, in which the destiny of British rule in India became necessarily involved." He hopes, he says, to reach the English-speaking world, both those "curious about the combination of man and geography which has worn out the British Empire in India" and those "not wholly uninterested in a country which will provide them as likely as not with their most harassing future burden." In the final chapter, he explicates his philosophy concerning the course of Indian history.

1433 Dalai Lama. ***Freedom in Exile: The Autobiography of the Dalai Lama.*** Illus. HarperCollins 1991, $12.00 (0-06-098701-4). 304pp. Autobiography.

The Dalai Lama, who was awarded the Nobel Peace Prize in 1989, states that he wrote this book both because he sensed an interest among many people to learn about his life and because he wanted to set the record straight on a number of historical events. After describing his life as a small boy, he provides a brief explanation of Tibetan Buddhism, describes the search for the fourteenth Dalai Lama that led to his confirmation as the spiritual leader of Tibet, and gives an account of life in Tibet before the Chinese invasion in 1950. In subsequent chapters he describes his relationship with Chinese leaders and with Jawaharlal Nehru of India; his exile from Tibet to India in 1959; the establishment of Tibetan Resettlement areas in India; his travels abroad; and the continuing negotiations with China for Tibetan independence. This book, written for a general audience, is highly readable. It contains an index but no bibliography.

1434 Gandhi, Mohandas K. ***An Autobiography: The Story of My Experiments with Truth.*** Intro. by Sissela Bok. Buccaneer 1990, $35.95 (0-89966-746-5); Beacon $10.95 (0-8070-5909-9). 535pp. Autobiography.

Gandhi interprets the main events in his life from his childhood until the early 1920s, when he had become the leader of the Indian independence movement. In his introduction, Gandhi comments that it is not his purpose to attempt a real autobiography but rather "to tell the story of my numerous experiments with truth, and as my life consists of nothing but those experiments, the story will take the shape of an autobiography. . . . My experiments in the political field are now known, not only in India, but to a certain extent to the 'civilized' world. . . . But I would certainly like to narrate my experiments in the spiritual field which are known only to myself, and from which I have derived such power as I possess for working in the political field." This book presents Gandhi's impressions of his education in England, the beginnings of civil disobedience and passive resistance in South Africa, his return to India, and his involvement with the Indian National Congress and the independence movement. There is an index but no bibliography.

1435 Mazumdar, Shudha. ***Memoirs of an Indian Woman.*** Ed. and Intro. by Geraldine Forbes. M. E. Sharpe 1989, $35.00 (0-87332-520-6). 248pp. Autobiography.

Mazumdar writes about events during the Indian independence movement from a unique perspective: not that of a key player in the political events of the day, but that of an ordinary middle-class Indian woman. She writes about her family, her marriage, the births of her children, and her deepening commitment as a volunteer working to improve the lives of women and children. She experiences firsthand the changes affecting the lives of Indian women in the first half of the twentieth century. Providing a glimpse into the life of one Indian woman and how she adapted to dramatic changes, the book will interest readers concerned with India or with gender studies in general. Geraldine Forbes's introduction provides a lucid background to the story and argues for the inclusion of memoirs such as this one in our study of social history. "This is not the whole story by any means," Forbes writes, "but it is vivid and concrete and it makes it possible for the reader to visualize and feel the texture of the past." The book includes a glossary and an index.

1436 Mehta, Ved. ***Daddyji***. Illus. Oxford Univ. Pr. 1979, $6.95 (0-19-502619-5). 195pp. Biography.

This book, the first in a series of biographical portraits of the Mehta family, is the story of Amolak Ram Mehta, whom his children called "Daddyji" (the suffix "ji" is an honorific attached to names as a mark of affection and respect). Ved Mehta traces the history of his family back to 1815. His great-great-grandfather Gian Chand Mehta settled in the village of Nawankote, about thirty miles northwest of Lahore, in the Punjab. There Mehta's grandfather Bhola Ram—"Lalaji"—was born. Lalaji was a petty government official whose job took him to several villages in the Punjab. Amolak Ram was born in Kathunangal, a nondescript village. From these humble beginnings, Daddyji goes on to attend Government College in Lahore and then King Edward Medical College. In England he earns diplomas in public health and tropical medicine and hygiene, and returns to hold important government jobs. While drawing his father's portrait, Mehta takes the reader on a journey through rural and urban India, presenting revealing vignettes of Hindu customs, rituals, and relationships in an extended family. The book is a celebration of a bygone age in India. Mehta continues the saga in *Mamaji* and *Vedi* (*see main entries*).   SP

1437 Mehta, Ved. ***Mamaji***. Illus. Oxford Univ. Pr. 1979, $17.95 (0-19-502640-3). 384pp. Biography.

In *Mamaji*, the second book in Mehta's biographical trilogy, the author paints a vivid and sensitive portrait of his mother, Shanti Devi Mehta—Mamaji, as her children called her. Though Shanti Devi was born in a high-caste affluent Hindu family, she—like most traditional Hindu women of those days—had little formal education. Instead, living In her father's house, she spent her time in endless household chores, performing orthodox rituals, and practicing ancient herbal medicine. At seventeen she married Amolak Mehta, whom she had never seen until the day of the marriage. After marriage, her life revolves around her husband, their eight children, and a large extended family of in-laws and other relations. The biography introduces Shanti Devi's parents and forebears, as well as friends and contemporaries, thus bringing the reader close to several generations of Indians living in the late nineteenth and early twentieth centuries. American readers will no doubt be fascinated by Mehta's vivid descriptions of a way of life far removed from their own; Indian readers, however, will find *Mamaji* a nostalgic journey into their own past. Other books in this series include *Daddyji* and *Vedi* (*see main entries*).   SP

1438 Mehta, Ved. **Vedi**. Illus. Oxford Univ. Pr. 1982, $18.95 (0-19-503005-2); Norton $7.95 (0-393-30417-5). 272pp. Autobiography.

This book concludes the trilogy of family portraits begun with *Daddyji* and *Mamaji (see main entries)*. At the age of four, Ved Mehta—whose nickname was Vedi—contracted cerebrospinal meningitis, which left him permanently blind. His father, aware of the dismal future awaiting blind children in India, sent him to Bombay, some 1,300 miles from their home in Lahore, to attend the Dadar School for the Blind. This departure from the protective safety of his parents' home when he was barely five years old was the beginning of Vedi's journey to independence. The book is a reconstruction of the years Vedi spent at the school, which was really an orphanage. Almost all the other children in the school were waifs with no known parents. The principal, Ras Mohun, and his wife were astonished that Vedi's father had decided to send so young a boy to a school so far away at such a young age. They took him under their wing, providing him a special soft bed in the dormitory and allowing him to take his meals with them. The social and cultural differences between Vedi and his peers only increased his isolation. Vedi spoke only Punjabi and did not know Marathi, the language of the other children. Yet somehow Vedi adjusted to life in the school. He made friends, and learned to read and write English Braille, do simple arithmetic, and play the games of childhood. When it appeared that World War II might come to India, Vedi returned home to Lahore with the knowledge that the four years he had spent in Bombay had provided him with the opportunity for a meaningful life.

Mehta's autobiography continues with *The Ledge Between the Streams* (Norton, 1985), which describes his childhood after he returned from Bombay, and *Sound-Shadows of the New World* (Norton, 1987), in which, as a teenager, he goes to the United States to attend a school for the blind. SP

1439 Nehru, Jawaharlal. **An Autobiography: Centenary Edition**. Oxford Univ. Pr. 1989, $19.95 (0-19-562395-9); $9.95 (0-19-562361-4). 640pp. Autobiography.

Like his other book, *The Discovery of India (see main entry)*, Nehru wrote this volume in prison during the time of the Indian independence movement, primarily between June 1934 and February 1935. Nehru states in the preface that he undertook the project to occupy himself with a definite task as well as to review past events in India. His mood was one of self-questioning; his intended audience—"if there was one"—was Indian, not foreign; his goal was to trace his own mental development and not to survey Indian history. Through this autobiography, the reader learns about the life and thinking of an extraordinary leader. An interesting comparison between his story and Gandhi's autobiography provides insight into the differences between these two important twentieth-century leaders of India. The book includes a postscript, written five and half years later, commenting on events both inside and outside India at the end of the 1930s, and an epilogue calling for the parting of ways with Britain. The appendixes to this centenary edition include several presidential addresses made by Nehru to the Indian National Congress. A glossary and index are included.

1440 Tandon, Prakash. ***Punjabi Century, 1857–1947***. Frwd. by Maurice Zinkin. Univ. of California Pr. 1968, $14.00 (0-520-01253-4). 274pp. Autobiography.

This is the first and best known of a trilogy of autobiographical books by Prakash Tandon collectively called the *Punjabi Saga*; the other volumes are *Beyond Punjab* (Ind-U.S., 1971) and *Return to Punjab* (o.p.). *Punjabi Century* covers the years from 1857, the year of "The Mutiny," which altered the way the English ruled in India, to 1947, the year of independence and partition. Tandon's story is about growing up in West Punjab, which became Pakistan in 1947. In his introduction, Maurice Zinkin writes, "Mr. Tandon is talking of a past which is over, the flavour of which, had it not been for him, would soon have departed never to be recaptured. His memory, his sense of a scene as a whole, his capacity to recreate the past as it was and not as the present day would have it—these combine to give us the old Punjab as it lived, thought, atc, and enjoyed itself. This is how marriages were made, this is how the Indian backbone of the administration got tired of the British, this is what the houses looked like and how one went out for a walk." A glossary is provided.

13

EAST ASIA

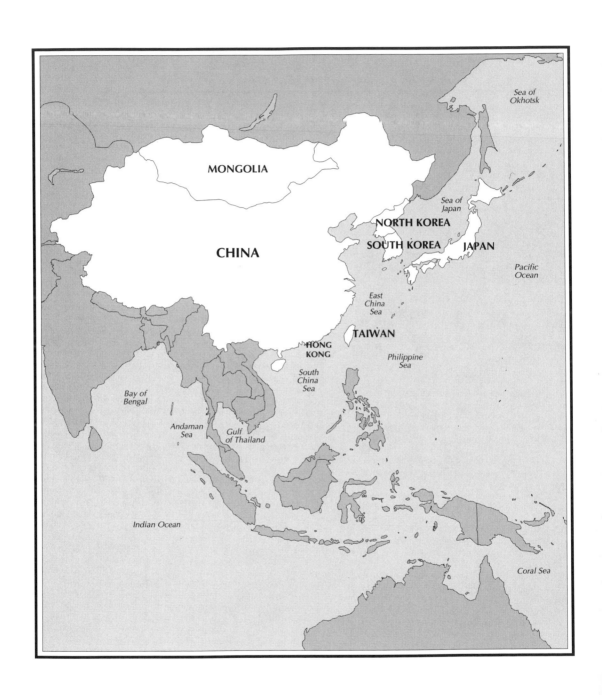

13

EAST ASIA

by Ginny Lee, Suzanne Lo, and Susan Ma

Like other regions of the globe, East Asia has a histtory that is full of conflicts and wars, conquerors, occupations, and displaced peoples. Nonfiction books, novels, and poetry from the region, which includes Japan, Korea, the People's Republic of China, Singapore, Taiwan, and Hong Kong, often reflect the human pain resulting from the birth—and often the violent rebirth—of these nations.

Most of the widely available nonfiction books in English describing these countries are written by Western scholars, travelers, and journalists. Usually there are few surprises in these straightforward descriptive works, which attempt to describe the country to an audience of Westerners who presumably have an open-minded interest in Asia. Often, however, a careful assessment of the book reveals that the text, written by a supposed authority in the field, can in fact be quite biased—if not downright patronizing. Because the author's own ethnocentrism permeates the work, the book does little to promote understanding of Asia; instead it tends to promulgate condescending views that merely reinforce old stereotypes. Our goal in this chapter, as in the rest of this bibliography, is to recommend books that avoid such problems.

With respect to literature, a question arises whether creative writing by a writer who is a native of a certain country will have a higher degree of integrity—an element of validity—that is intrinsically lacking in works by someone who is not a native. In other words, can novels, poems, and stories by authors steeped in a culture tell us more about a country and its people than even the most well-informed and well-intentioned outsider? We would argue that, in some cases at least, the answer is a qualified yes.

Historically and recently, Asian nations have produced a wealth of literature of excellent standing. The problem for bibliographers is to choose those works that are most representative. Much of the fiction set in Asia and written by nonnatives reflects the Western point of view, Western taste in humor, and Western longings and inclinations. For example, *The White Tiger* by Robert Stuart Nathan (Simon & Schuster, 1987) is a competently written tale of political intrigue in China. The story holds the reader's attention like a good whodunit. But its style and tone, even its sense of humor, are far more American than Chinese. A truly Chinese protagonist, for example, would not constantly seek refuge from his troubles in a glass of red wine. For comparison, consider *The Dragon's Village* by Chen Yuan-tsung. This novel, beautifully written in English by a Chinese woman, effectively illustrates the Chinese perplexities and idealisms of the early 1950s. The latter book is included in this list; the former is not.

Many Asian writers, especially from Japan and China, have been exposed to the West and to Western writing styles. These authors are often influenced by such writers as Kafka, Mann, Gide, Nabokov, and Joyce. But another aspect of writing that some Eastern authors have borrowed from the West is the shock of realism, reflected in such elements as sex, violence, and raw language. Books of this kind may be on the cutting edge in a nation like Taiwan, where many people embrace and emulate whatever they perceive to be popular in the West. For instance, the very popular Li Ang won a literary prize for her riveting and graphic novel *The Butcher's Wife*, in which a woman murders her sadistic and violent husband. In our estimation, however, the novel fails to make any clearer to us the true character of Taiwan and its people, and so it does not appear on this list. Instead, insightful writings by Taiwanese women can be found in anthologies such as *Bamboo Shoots after the Rain*, edited by Ann C. Carver and Sung-sheng Y. Chang.

Another source of discomfort in analyses of Asian literature are such novels as those by Lilian Lee, a popular Hong Kong writer of escapist fiction. Two of her recent books, *The Last Princess of Manchuria* (Morrow, 1992) and *Farewell My Concubine* (Morrow, 1993), illustrate her style and themes. Although she portrays China's culture, history, and recent turbulence, in our opinion she is more interested in telling a titillating story than in presenting an accurate picture. There is also the case of Japan's runaway best-seller *Kitchen* by Banana Yoshimoto (Pocket, 1994). The two interlinked stories in this novel discuss the main character's frantic search for comfort following the death of a loved one. The focus of comfort is the kitchen. Easy and entertaining to read, the book tells us a lot about the acceptance of sadness and death as a part of life. But it does not tell us much about Japan, and so, despite its popularity both in Japan and in the West, it does not appear on this list.

Among the important trends in China, Japan, and Korea during this century is the fact that more attention is being paid to women writers. Furthermore, East Asian writers are more able to express themselves and the truth as they see it, rather than serve as mouthpieces for political doctrines and social formulas. Consequently, writers are producing more stories that contain social, economic, and political criticism. Space does not allow a separate discussion for each of the many talented and important writers. Instead we have selected a number of anthologies, the better to introduce their works to readers.

There are far more books in English by Western scholars and journalists about China and Japan than there are about other Asian countries. Countless volumes describe and explain life and culture in Japan, but there are very few comparable works by Western scholars dealing with Korea, and even fewer translations of Korean literature. Thus, many of the books about Korea on this list are by necessity of the tourist and guidebook caliber.

The nonfiction for China and Japan, however, comes in such variety that we found it a challenge to select those that best explain these countries to an outsider. One criterion was that the books on the list had to look at their subjects from new perspectives and to shed new light on them. There was some debate about whether we should deal with certain subjects at all, but in the end we felt that it was worth a try to exorcise some of these ghosts. The stereotypical symbols of these nations thus are represented here in a new light. See, for example, *Setting Sails: A Tribute to the Chinese Junk* by Derek Maitland and *Geisha* by Liza C. Dalby.

Political movements in the Asian countries are ongoing struggles about which much has been written. The attempt here, however, is not to cover political incidents, although these events certainly influence people's lives and what authors write about. Instead we tried to choose books that look beyond events of the nonce to give a broader perspective of the lifestyles and values of the people. Such topics as the Vietnam War, the Cambodian massacre, and the Tiananmen Square incident are discussed. The question we wrestled with, however, was not *whether* to cover the events, but *which* works that arose from them have enough literary or cultural merit to be included here.

Travel in Asia by Westerners naturally generates a large number of personal narratives. Everyone who has spent time in Asia seems to feel a need to expound on the peculiarities of society. Too many of these books, however, are of the "I-went-here-and-I-saw-this" variety. Often these books devote too much attention to irrelevancies such as the number of people on a bus, how long was spent waiting for luggage, or how many times teeth got brushed. These works tend to be written by journalists who stayed for as long as two weeks. More valuable are the works by teachers, doctors, and long-term travelers who lived in an area for at least a year. Among these writers are missionary children born and raised in Asia, scholars who have devoted their careers to studying the languages and literatures of these countries, China watchers who have taken careful note of all the political happenings, and so on. Again, the question is not how to cover all these groups in this chapter, but which of their works have the literary and cultural qualities needed to explain how a country came to be what it is. A good example of works by teachers is the objective and culturally insightful *Teaching China's Lost Generation* by Tani Barlow and Donald Lowe. Though less objective, Mark Salzman's *Iron and Silk* (Vintage, 1987), not reviewed in this list, is also available.

Another type of visitor is the energetic individual who immerses himself in the country to better understand the people firsthand. In Alan Booth's *The Roads to Sata* (Viking, 1986), the author walks the 2,000 miles from the northern tip of Japan to the southern tip. Along the way he encounters some people who welcome him, but he also meets others who refuse to believe what he is doing, or who give faulty directions or otherwise add to his frustration at being a foreigner in an inscrutable land. His resulting book is less than complimentary. However, his posthumous work *Looking for the Lost: Journeys Through a Vanishing Japan* (Kodansha International, 1995) is a magnificent tribute to the remote regions that the Japanese themselves consider "truly Japanese" and merits inclusion here but for the too recent date of publication. Similarly, Pico Iyer's *Video Night in Kathmandu* (Random, 1989), though an entertaining tour of the nightclub scene in various countries, emphasizes the influence of Western culture on countries in what the author calls the "not-so-far East." These two books, interesting as they are, did not meet our criteria for inclusion in a multicultural bibliography. Two that did, however, are very entertaining accounts of nonnatives journeying in Asian countries: *From Heaven Lake* by Vikram Seth and *Journey Across Tibet* by Sorrel Wilby. Seth's book narrates the adventures that befall a student en route from his school in Nanking to his home in India via China's great western province, Xinjiang, and Tibet. Sorrel Wilby is a young Australian woman who achieved fame for ascending Mount Fuji on her bicycle. She also walked across Tibet, staying with nomads, learning their language, and immersing herself in their culture. A work from a past era is *Exotics and Retrospectives* by Lafcadio Hearn, the noted Japanophile and prolific author of books about Asian culture, history, language, and folktales.

A worthwhile book that is now out of print and not included in this list is Lesley Downer's *On the Narrow Road* (Summit, 1989). Downer is an English woman who walked to the north of Japan, following the same route as the seventeenth-century poet Basho, looking for the special places he mentions and reading his poems. Also not reviewed, but still of value, are Alexandra David-Neel's *My Journey to Lhasa* (orig. pub. 1927; Beacon, 1993) and Isabella Bird's *Unbeaten Tracks in Japan* (orig. pub. 1880; Tuttle, 1971). Both are well-written and detailed historical accounts of adventures by older women.

Other works representing a foreign "invasion" into isolated regions include Peter Hopkirk's *Trespassers on the Roof of the World*, which tells about intrepid Western travelers and adventurers from the mid-nineteenth century to the present who were intent on discovering for themselves the secrets of Tibet. Scott Berry's book *A Stranger in Tibet* covers the same territory from a different angle: His "strangers" are not Caucasians but Japanese who entered a Tibet that was just as forbidden but who, by virtue of the fact that they were Asian, attracted less attention than Westerners.

Objectivity is a key feature in our decision to recommend a few of the mushrooming number of works that try to explain Asian countries to Westerners. An early example is Ruth Benedict's classic *The Chrysanthemum and the Sword*. Among the other books of this kind discussed here are *The Compact Culture: The Japanese Tradition of Smaller Is Better* by Lee O-young, *A Taste of Japan* by Donald Richie, and *The Japanese Mind* by Robert C. Christopher. Not reviewed here is David Rearwin's *The Asia Business Book* (Intercultural Press, 1991), a good general guidebook for the businessman in Asia; the book has a few flaws but is otherwise a decent basic book for readers new to the scene.

There are many histories of the nations of Asia. Among the works included here are *The Heart of the Dragon*, Alasdair Clayre's intimate look at the present culture of China; *The Koreans* by Russell W. Howe; and *Tibet and Its History* by Hugh E. Richardson. A new slant on the connections among all the countries on the Pacific Rim appears in Simon Winchester's *Pacific Rising*, an entertaining exploration that is full of interesting anecdotes and background histories. Readers who prefer more scholarly treatises, which lie outside the scope of this chapter, might consult *China: A New History* by John King Fairbank (Belknap, 1992) or *The Rise of the Chinese Republic from the Last Emperor to Deng Xiaoping* by Edwin Hoyt (McGraw-Hill, 1989), which thoroughly covers the twentieth century and is full of readable facts and colorful anecdotes. For an analysis of Hong Kong's uncertain future as it makes the transition to Chinese control, Kevin Rafferty's *City on the Rocks: Hong Kong's Uncertain Future* (Viking, 1989), while a little dry, is somewhat more reliable than other books on the same subject.

A recent publication well worth mentioning is Donald Keene's *Modern Japanese Diaries: The Japanese at Home and Abroad as Revealed Through Their Diaries* (Henry Holt, 1995). This 543-page tome gives insight into recent Japanese attitudes toward foreign cultures.

A great deal of information is packed into some of the popular travel guide series; some of these books also have enough literary merit to warrant a full entry here. Into the same category fall a good number of spectacularly photo-graphed coffee-table books, such as *A Day in the Life of China*, *All Japan*, and *My Tibet*.

This bibliography is not exhaustive, nor does it even attempt to cover all the genres. Instead our goal has been to offer a sampling of the many kinds of writers and writings that represent the many different views of Asia.

(Editor's note: In this chapter, author's names are generally listed with the family name first, reflecting the style of usage in Asian countries. For exam-ple, a book by Lee O-young appears alphabetically under L, not O, and a work by Mishima Yukio is listed under M, without a comma between the family name and the given name. Exceptions include Asian authors in the West or those who use Westernized names, such as Dominic Cheung (listed under Cheung, Dominic) or Helen F. Siu (Siu, Helen F.). Where possible, an attempt has been made to use the modern pinyin style for rendering Chinese names, but in certain cases names appear as they are listed in the books discussed or in *Books in Print*. Readers who are unable to find information about a certain author are urged to check indexes under different permuta-tions of the name.)

LITERATURE

1441 Abe Kobo. ***The Ruined Map.*** Repr. of 1969 ed. Trans. from Japanese by E. Dale Saunders. Kodansha 1993, $13.00 (4-77001-635-2). 320pp. Fiction.

Abe Kobo's first book to appear in English, *The Woman in the Dunes* (orig. pub. 1964; Random, 1991), dealt with the feeling of being caught in a senseless, purposeless, meaningless life. His subsequent novels deal with personal iden-tity, its definition and its loss.

In this story, a detective is hired by an intriguing woman to locate her missing husband. Her brother enters the scene, but we are never sure whether he is helping the search or concealing vital information. He states that one needs a good reliable map to find one's way through life. But the map these characters follow is dangerously flawed; the brother and a col-league of the husband are murdered, and the detective is beaten up. At all times the sinister influence of the underworld is sensed. Finally the detective begins to lose track of who is looking for whom, as he identifies more and more with the husband, who may have engineered his disappearance to escape from a stifling society. This novel is less an everyday whodunit than it is a political drama about the search for identity. The author depicts a very Westernized Tokyo, barely recognizable as a Japanese city. Particularly intrigu-ing is Abe's description of modern inner-city street life.

Other novels of Abe Kobo deal with similar questions of identity. In *The Face of Another* (orig. pub. 1966; Kodansha, 1992), a badly burned man gets a new face and wonders whether he belongs to it. *The Box Man* (orig. pub. 1970; Farrar, 1991) tells about a man who decides to live on the street in a cardboard box. *Secret Rendezvous* (orig. pub. 1975; Kodansha, 1993) is the story of a man who searches for his missing wife in a bizarre hospital; meanwhile he ponders such issues as the elements of civilization, the definitions of *healthy* and *sick*, and the place of misfits in society.

1442 Ahn Junghyo. *Silver Stallion: A Novel of Korea*. Trans. from Korean. Soho 1993, $12.00 (0-56947-003-0). 269pp. Fiction.

This is the story of what happens to a small village in Korea that is happily minding its own business when the Korean War breaks out and American soldiers march in, set up camp, and ruin everyone's life. It is told from the point of view of a small boy living with his single mother. There is perhaps too much explicit sex and violence for this book to make it onto a purely literary list. It is included here because it reveals the impact of war between peoples of different cultures, especially events between soldiers and local women. It also offers insight into the psychology of young boys in gangs and what happens to a member once he is ousted. The tragedy of villagers caught up in the war and forced to flee their homes is vividly portrayed.

1443 Anderson, Jennifer, and Theresa Munford, eds. *Chinese Women Writers: A Collection of Short Stories by Chinese Women Writers of the 1920s and '30s*. Joint Publg. 1985. o.p. Fiction.

The 1920s and 1930s in China were decades of political upheaval and cultural change. With the end of the last Chinese Dynasty (the Qing, also called the Ching or Manchu) in 1912 and the introduction of Western ideas, people began questioning old traditions. The role of women in Chinese society had been subservient and confining. Now women began tenuously exploring new roles.

The young intellectuals who wrote the stories in this volume were the liberals daring enough to say "yes" to a university education and "no" to immediate and arranged marriages. As these works reveal, writing evolved from rigid, stylized formats to more creative expressions and explorations of real-life problems. Many of these stories are autobiographical in inspiration and deal with the author's own feelings and experiences. Themes include the loneliness of independence; a distaste for polygamy; chastity versus sexual freedom; corruption of the wealthy under the old feudal system; the terrible working conditions of the poor laboring classes; prostitution; education; and single-parent families.

A personal background and discussion of the author's works and style precedes each selection. The reader learns that some of these writers enjoyed the support of their families in their careers, but many others endured ostracism because of their decision to write. Each of these intriguing stories provides its own insight into the mind of a Chinese woman.

1444 Ariyoshi Sawako. *The Twilight Years*. Trans. from Japanese by Mildred Tahara. Kodansha 1988, $8.00 (0-87011-852-8). 216pp. Fiction.

In this novel, members of a family gather on the occasion of an elderly woman's death. The interactions vividly reveal the differences between the stoic, responsible, silently enduring Meiji women—unsung heroines of the last generation—and the young, modern feminists, who, much like their American counterparts, are impatient with social traditions and protocols and who demand equal treatment. In the course of the book, the dead woman's husband degenerates from being merely senile to becoming helplessly infantile. The daughter-in-law, Akiko, who works in an office full time, must wait on him as he becomes an incapable, mentally deteriorating, and even disgusting old man. Akiko must see to his care day and night, but she gets little help or sympathy from her husband or her son.

In ancient times, so the old tales say, there was a mountain called Obasteyama where families took the elderly and left them there to die. Each culture has its own ways of dealing with old people. Akiko discovers that in Japan, as in the West, these ways are changing. This finely written novel, ringing with overtones of Japanese culture and perceptions, portrays the universal issues of youth dealing with old age and of middle-aged people confronting their own imminent old age.

1445 ***Best Chinese Stories, 1949–1989***. Trans. from Chinese. China Books 1989, $17.95 (0-8351-2066-X). 501pp. Fiction.

This lengthy collection of stories represents the development of Chinese writers in the decades since the beginning of the Communist era in the People's Republic. An enlightening preface gives a background of the problems of writing in China for most of this century. Among the authors represented are Wang Meng, Wang Anyi, Zhang Xianliang, and Shen Rong, as well as lesser-known writers from different backgrounds and regions. Some of the works are translated by well-known Western scholars of China, others by Chinese translators. The variety in this collection provides readers with an impressive look at China's inner thoughts and creative soul.

Generally, the stories written before the late 1970s reflect Communist ideology and describe political events at different stages in China's evolution. Most of these stories, however, were written in the 1980s, when writers felt freer to express their own artistic and creative talents, even if their ideas and styles clashed with the official party line.

1446 Bing Xin. ***The Photograph***. Chinese Literature Pr. 1992. o.p. Fiction/Poetry.

Bing Xin—born at the turn of the century and a contemporary of another noted Chinese author, Ding Ling—was part of the student movement of 1919. The literature she produced during the ensuing years is fresh, full of life, and devoted to exploring issues of individuality and personal and political liberty. The three parts of this book include nonfiction, poetry, and fiction selected from various times in the author's life. Bing Xin's works explore the tiny daily emotional happenings that are important to her. She gives readers an idea of what she and her contemporaries have gone through in their lives, allowing them to see "the innermost workings of (their) heart and mind."

The nonfiction writings are small, somewhat maudlin pieces of personal description of wonder in which she expresses her appreciation of life's gifts. The small section of poetry is equally simple and innocent. In various stories, Bing Xin describes the tender feelings of a young boy who has lost his cousin, an old woman who has lost her country, and others who experience the sweet, sour, bitter, and pungent feelings of love, loss, and separation.

1447 Bo Yang. ***Secrets: A Collection of Short Stories***. Trans. from Chinese by David Deterding; Intro. by Howard Goldblatt. Cheng & Tsui 1984, $12.95 (0-88727-037-9); $8.95 (0-88727-051-4). 293pp. Fiction.

A prolific and highly honored writer, poet, and historian from Taiwan, Bo Yang has produced many volumes of prose, poetry, and historical criticism as well as translations of historical writings from China's history. Jailed in the early 1970s for swaying people's opinion away from the government, he is now back in Taipei and still writing as ferociously as ever.

In the author's own foreword to these impeccable stories, he confesses his preoccupation with life and death, love and hate—large and profound themes that are sometimes so intertwined as to be indistinguishable. His pieces of fiction explore his suspicions about the nature of love and how it can be tainted by money, status, title, and other consequential forces of ordinary life. Accused of being cynical in his stories, he claims he is "just trying to figure things out." In any case, his thought-provoking stories explore weighty themes and offer the reader much to think about.

1448   Bokushi Suzuki. ***Snow Country Tales: Life in the Other Japan***. Trans. from Japanese by Jeffrey Hunter with Rose Lesser. Illus. with photographs and drawings. Weatherhill 1986, $32.50 (0-8348-0210-4), 400pp. Fiction.

This amazing and unusual book is the result of the combined efforts of the translator and a Western woman, Rose Lesser, who survived World War II in Japan. For seven years Lesser was separated from her family as she lived in Echigo, a remote area on the "backside" of Japan known as the Snow Country, where winter lasts most of the year. While there, she happened across this classic written by a man who lived all his life in Echigo. She wanted the world to know about these hardy, courageous, and enduring people who brave life in the Snow Country, and so she arranged to have the book translated and published.

The tales describe people being saved by a bear, digging tunnels through the snow to get around the village, and other local sights and events. Although Bokushi set the stories in the years between 1800 and 1840, the tales are not so far removed from life in the Snow Country today. A few modernities have been added—electricity, tractors for some, kitchens—but the land is just as raw and the people are just as abiding as ever.

A few black-and-white photographs show that the snow is no joking matter. The rest of the illustrations come from Bokushi's original classic, which was written originally to make Japanese city dwellers aware that "another Japan" exists. His book became a bestseller in old Edo (Tokyo).

1449   Buck, Pearl S. ***The Good Earth***. Ed. by Donna Ng. Pocket 1994, $5.99 (0-671-51012-6). 272pp. Fiction.

Some readers of this bibliography may find it strange that Buck's novel appears among the listings. Admittedly, there is always a danger that readers who encounter a classic novel—even one as beautifully written as this—will assume that the people, places, and events in the story reflect the present-day reality. But part of the goal in this bibliography is to present books that portray not just the way things are but how things came to be. On the basis of that criterion, this classic work, for which the author was awarded the Nobel Prize, is worthy of inclusion. It is the story of a man's life in the late 1800s, his marriage to a plain but sturdy woman, his beautiful and pouty concubine, and his children, who both serve him and plot behind his back.

Buck's writing reveals the obviously tender feelings for the country she adopted as her home. Having lived in China for many years, she is able to delve deeply into its spirit and its soul. Although her style is somewhat dated, her works are considered fine literature and they rank high on many reading lists about China. She also wrote novels about other Asian countries: *Mandala* (Moyer Bell, 1995), for example, is about India.

1450 Carver, Ann C., and Sung-sheng Y. Chang, eds. ***Bamboo Shoots after the Rain: Contemporary Stories by Women Writers of Taiwan***. Trans. from Chinese. Feminist Pr. 1990, $35.00 (1-55861-017-0); $14.95 (1-55861-018-9). 264pp. Fiction.

This collection of works by popular authors in Taiwan represents three generations of women struggling to present the reality of women in society as they see it. The stories challenge the reader who comes from a very different society and perspective to identify with each heroine on her own terms. Many of the stories deal with woman's place in the home, in the affections of family members, and in society. Lin Hai-yin, for example, writes of a noble lady whose husband takes a concubine. Yu Li-hua writes of the effect of a woman's rape on her strongly traditional family.

The Taiwanese understanding of their women's status has changed through the generations and is also very different from perceptions of woman in the West. As the editors note, it is often necessary to recognize the walls of difference before we can see through them. An article by the editor titled "Can One Read Cross-Culturally?" points out the pitfalls of trying to do so. An extended bibliography of writers, collections, critiques, and relevant journals is included.

1451 Chen Yuan-tsun. ***The Dragon's Village***. Trans. from Chinese. Viking 1981, $8.95 (0-14-005811-7). 285pp. Fiction.

Although this novel was written in Chinese, it has no ring of a "translation." The writing, flowing and easy, draws the reader in. The characters are well rounded, partly, perhaps, because they are all based on real people. In fact, although it is presented as fiction, the story itself is real and provides an intimate picture of what it was like to be young and naive in 1949 in China on the eve of the Communist takeover.

The main character is Ling Ling, a teenager who lives the luxurious, idyllic—and bored—life of the affluent. She is jolted out of her complacency when she gets caught up in the urgent mission of idealistic Communist youth, the same young people who had been her friends at school. Like the other determinedly idealistic young people, she heads for the distant countryside to help with land reform. Traveling far, both literally and figuratively, from the comforts of city life, Ling Ling finds herself in a tiny, remote village trying to adjust her values so as to fit into her new surroundings and to carry out the mission embraced by her new friends and compatriots.

1452 Cheung, Dominic, ed. ***The Isle Full of Noises: Modern Chinese Poetry from Taiwan***. Trans. from Chinese by the editor. Columbia Univ. Pr. 1986, $38.50 (0-231-06402-0). 272pp. Poetry.

A fine editorial board including noted Sinologists Donald Keene and C. T. Hsia has selected these poems from modern Taiwan written between 1949 and the 1970s. Some of the thirty-two poets represented are from Taiwan; others were raised in Macao, Hong Kong, or the Philippines and later moved to Taiwan. Still others have never set foot in Taiwan, but their poetry frequently appears in Taiwanese publications.

Major poets include those who founded the three—sometimes clashing—poetry societies in Taiwan. Chi Hsien, who brought from Mainland China his love of French poetry, began the Taiwanese Modernist School, whose writers are interested in exploration, sensitivity, purity—and anti-Communism. Next comes Yu Kuang-ching, a founder of the Blue Star poetry society, and Chang Mo, who began the Epoch Society. Some of the authors represented write in the Taiwanese vernacular, claiming that this dialect is a more valid tool for describing Taiwanese places and feelings. Some, like Lung Ying-chung, are also very successful short story writers.

Themes include eulogies to political figures, teachers, family members, and friends; expressions of longing for comradeship, home, and family on the mainland; descriptions of life abroad; and subtle political statements. A lengthy introduction discusses the historical and political backgrounds of the poets, and a brief biography appears before each author's works. An appendix of poets' names, poem titles, and a topical index complete the book.

1453 Dai Hou-ying. *Stones of the Wall*. Trans. from Chinese. St. Martin 1985. o.p. Fiction.

This is a decently written novel whose characters are realistic and life-size, unlike the cardboard representatives of current social or political values that so often populate works produced in totalitarian societies. The setting is Shanghai just after the end of the Cultural Revolution. Both the "villains" and the victims of the massive changes in China had been caught inextricably in the wheel of fortune. Intellectuals were criticized, killed, tortured, and driven to the countryside—or to suicide. Many of those who harassed and tortured these intellectuals did so against their better nature and in fear of their own lives should they refuse to comply. Now, as the dust of revolution settles, all the characters find themselves back in the workaday world, having to get along with each other despite their antagonisms and the suffering of the past ten years.

All this is background to a love story in which the author explores the true, deep meaning of marital love—something beyond friendship and certainly beyond mere physical attraction. A pair of high school lovers marry, divorce, marry other people, and continue in the same world with each other. This happens all the time in the West, but in China it is a rare phenomenon. The allegorical imagery in the story is sometimes painfully obvious, but at least the author succeeds in offering an artistic portrayal of universal human feelings.

1454 Dalai Lama, and Galen Rowell, ed. *My Tibet: Text by His Holiness the Fourteenth Dalai Lama of Tibet*. Illus. with photographs by the editor. Univ. of California Pr. 1990, $40.00 (0-520-07109-3). 168pp. Essays.

Many captivating Tibetan faces peer out from the pages of this large book of exquisite photographs. The text consists of philosophical statements contributed by the Dalai Lama. In six essays interspersed among the masterly photos, the spiritual leader of the Tibetan Buddhists discusses the relation of compassion and universal responsibility to world peace and explains why these qualities are even more needed in today's shrinking world.

Many of the photos present the flora and fauna of Tibet, and the accompanying essays discusses ecology and environmentalism. Other passages explore Tibetan Buddhism and its injunction to contribute to human society. The Dalai Lama tells about Lhasa, the city of his childhood, and describes the Tibet he knew before becoming an exile in India in 1959.

Galen Rowell has created a number of splendid photographic volumes, including *Mountains of the Middle Kingdom: Exploring the High Peaks of Tibet and China* (Sierra Club, 1983). For a description of the Dalai Lama's autobiography, see the main entry in Chapter 12.

1455 Dazai Osamu. ***Self-Portraits: Tales from the Life of Japan's Great Decadent Romantic***. Ed. by Shaw Pockell; Trans. from Japanese by Ralph McCarthy. Illus. Kodansha 1991, $18.95 (0-87011-779-3); $8.00 (4-77001-689-1). 208pp. Fiction.

Dazai Osamu was born into a large, rich family and grew up in the early part of the twentieth century, at a time when Japan promulgated in its citizens a fanatic ideological patriotism. Even as a teenager, Dazai began his plummet into drug addiction, alcoholism, sex, and rejection of society. He survived the deaths of several young brothers and his parents before he reached his twenties, and he was only thirty-nine when he committed love-suicide.

Dazai's stories, nearly all autobiographical, reflect the full passion and tragedy of human relationships and represent some of the best literature to come from Japan in the 1930s and 1940s. His bitterness and hopelessness could not help but affect his writing and yet they also engendered in him a devil-may-care attitude that allowed him to resist the political demands Japan made on other writers. Instead he wrote what was closest to him and what concerned him. His stories are mostly transparent versions of events that happened to him and his family and friends. Over time, he saw suicide as the only way out and attempted it twice with two lovers before he was finally successful with a third.

This collection has a biographical feeling to it; sprinkled throughout are black-and-white photographs of Dazai and his family and friends as well as some of the more important sites in his writing. The introduction by Ralph McCarthy clarifies Dazai's life, although it is Dazai himself who says it all best. Little though the reader may approve of the man himself, one cannot help but admire his way of expressing himself.

1456 Ding Ling. *I Myself Am a Woman: Selected Writings of Ding Ling*. Trans. from Chinese and ed. by Tani Barlow and Gary Bjorge. Beacon 1990, $16.00 (0-8070-6747-4). 364pp. Fiction.

Ding Ling began to write earlier this century when it was not considered appropriate for a woman to do anything but serve her mother-in-law and her husband. She was inspired by her own widowed mother, who rebelled at the notion that a woman's life ends with the death of her husband and who passed her own lively spirit on to her daughter.

Ding Ling's writings are full of feminist sympathies and left-wing idealism. She explores facets of society that seem to have the same name in the East as they do in the West—such as motherhood, democracy, individualism, and privacy—but which in fact have strikingly different implications in Asia. Consequently, feminism in the West is very different from feminism in the East. Ding Ling was one of the first writers—and is by many standards the most important, writer—to address this concept.

Her writings describe women in various situations that arise because of their sex. Her subjects include romance, marriage, motherhood, widowhood, revolution from a woman's point of view, and the struggle between men and women. A recurring theme in her stories is that, because traditional solutions are no longer appropriate for the dilemmas modern women confront, women are called on to think for themselves.

In addition to a generous selection of her writings, the book contains a lengthy introduction that traces literary development in China, with particular reference to feminism in its various definitions. It also gives a biography of Ding Ling and analyzes her growth as a writer. A preface spells out some of the problems of translating these works. Notes on each selection and a few lines of description of each translator are offered at the end.

1457 Duke, Michael S. ***World of Modern Chinese Fiction: Short Stories and Novellas from the People's Republic, Taiwan, and Hong Kong***. Trans. from Chinese. M. E. Sharpe 1991, $55.00 (0-87332-757-8); $16.95 (0-87332-758-6). 360pp. Fiction.

This hefty collection of stories, mostly written in the 1980s, represents a group of writers who are trying out new wings. Previously, writers from China were bound by political constraints, but in the 1980s they were finally able to relinquish the government-enforced belief that they were writing for "the masses" and began their own experimental writings, which, while not always successful by literary standards, were at least individually expressive.

Themes in these works include a search for something in the past that might be relevant to the present, quite a few romances, and meditations on the meaning of love. A few of the stories contemplate what the future might bring to Chinese society, while others deal with minority groups in China's far western region.

Literary styles of the stories reflect the variety of translators as much as the variety of original authors. Notes on authors and translators are found at the end of the book.

1458 Enchi Fumiko. ***The Waiting Years***. Trans. from Japanese by John Bester. Kodansha 1994, $9.00 (0-87011-424-7). 204pp. Fiction.

In Japan only a generation or so ago, a woman of distinction in society was expected to put family, household, and husband before anything else—certainly before her own comfort and happiness. In this novel, the protagonist, determined to live an exemplary life, stubbornly embodies the binding social code of human conduct. In the process, she disregards the even stronger sense of special relationship between people. Throughout her marriage, she puts up with her husband's immorality and license, achieving for herself the tempering that comes from suffering. In her final moments, she apologizes to her husband for having been unable to trust him. That astounding act of generosity strikes him more deeply than it would have had she devoted their married years to protesting his lack of love.

Many novels, both Western and Eastern, detail the unhappiness of unrequited love and unfairness in marriage. This one offers a portrayal of the traditional Japanese woman's point of view, her priorities, and her uniquely Japanese way of dealing with crises.

1459 Feng Jicai. *Chrysanthemums and Other Stories*. Trans. from Chinese. Harcourt 1985. o.p. Fiction.

Each person alive in China during the Cultural Revolution has a horror story to tell. Feng Jicai wrote copiously during that period, but his manuscripts have all been lost or destroyed. The present collection of short stories represents his work from 1976 to the present. Published at a time when the government was cracking down on what it referred to as "spiritual pollution," these stories represent a daring excursion into the humanistic writings that Feng Jicai is known for worldwide. Themes range from beauty and guilt and human-heartedness to political misadventures. Many of his stories have an O. Henry–style twist at the end.

Still writing today, Feng Jicai maintains a strong sense of social commitment, though the suffocating political atmosphere that permeated his earlier works now appears more as a background. A recent work is *The Three-Inch Golden Lotus* (Univ. of Hawaii Pr., 1994).

1460 Gao Yang. *Rekindled Love and Purple Jade Hairpin: Stories by Gao Yang.* Bilingual (Chinese-English) ed. Chinese Univ. Pr. 1989. o.p. Fiction.

From Taiwan comes this popular and prolific writer of histories, classics, and fiction based on historical characters. These two novellas are retellings of stories, one from the Qing Dynasty (1644–1912) and one from the Tang (618–907). This is a bilingual edition, with Chinese on one page and English on the facing page.

In the first story, a young man is heading to the capital to take the imperial exams that will allow him to become an official. Along the way, he is tempted to commit adultery, but he is prevented from this distraction by a loud thunderclap issued from Heaven. Without this divine message, he would never have passed the exam.

In the second, a loyal woman is rejected by her lover. She dies in sorrow and returns to haunt him and drives him crazy. Before, the man's desire was to be known for his poetry. In the end, however, he is known only for being crazy.

1461 Gessel, Van C., and others, eds. *The Showa Anthology: Modern Japanese Short Stories*. Trans. from Japanese. Kodansha 1993, $10.00 (4-77001-708-1). 452pp. Fiction.

The term *Showa* signifies an age of enlightenment and peace that began in Japan in 1926. Many fine authors who emerged during this time are already known in the West. Among those represented in this collection are Dazai Osamu, Abe Kobo, Mishima Yukio, Shono Junzo, Inoue Yasushi, and Kawabata Yasunari. But the book also presents works by a host of other lesser-known writers. Thus, this volume has two goals: to present little-known sides of those whose names are already familiar and to introduce for the first time other important writers who are also a part of Japan's literary scene.

The quintessential Japanese literary form, known as the "I-novel," is represented in several of the stories. This first-person approach allows authors to itemize—in sometimes laborious detail—their social agonies and critiques. Other themes include the advance (some call it the invasion) of modern technology, the worker hero, the war, and life in the countryside. Fantasy and science fiction are represented, as are a few experimental styles. Six women writers are among the authors.

Notes on the authors appear before each story, and there are a few lines on each translator along with a selected bibliography of translations at the end.

1462 Go Shizuko. **Requiem**. Trans. from Japanese by Geraldine Harcourt. Kodansha 1992, $7.00 (4-770-01618-2). 122pp. Fiction.

In the instant of death, they say, one's whole life passes before one's eyes. This is the life story of a sixteen-year-old girl who is lying in a shelter, in pain and alone, after the indiscriminate bombings of the heavily populated areas between Tokyo and Yokohama during World War II. Her life passes before her memory's eye in the time it takes her to die.

In the novel, past and present intertwine. The scene shifts back and forth between her present reality, her dreams, and her haunting memories of her family and friends. In the process, the author chronicles the last few months of the war—not chronologically, but in the helter-skelter fashion of a feverish dream. The girl is a vessel holding the conflicting emotions of anguish at the loss of family members, one by one, and her desire to stand by her country and her Emperor—her god—until the last Japanese citizen has died. Now, though, she knows that the Emperor has surrendered, and she must deal with her conflicting feelings: joy that more people need not die and agony that so many died needlessly. If only, she thinks, they had been born in an age without war.

The author vividly describes the horror of the bombed villages and the pain of family losses, the conversations and letters between schoolmates, the tenderness of people trying to help each other in a nightmarish time. On another level the protagonist explores such deep questions as the inscrutability of the reasons for war and for surrender. In the end, the book transcends questions of patriotism and loyalty to explore the deepest chasms of human suffering.

1463 Hsu, Vivian L., ed. **Born of the Same Roots: Stories of Modern Chinese Women.** Facsimile ed. Trans. from Chinese. Books on Demand 1981, $85.60 (0-7837-6101-5). 317pp. Fiction.

This volume offers stories that focus on Chinese women and that were written by both women and men. Authors include such well-known names as Lao She, as well as many lesser-known but still important writers. They all reflect the changing social and political scenes of the twentieth century. Many explore the horrors of torture and separation during eras of unrest in China. Other themes include prostitution, separation from family members, romance, marriage, and the contrast of family life with the life of the working world.

A biography of each author precedes the selections, and a selected bibliography describes further reading.

1464 Hyon Joongshik, and Han Hakjoon, ed. **Modern Korean Short Stories**. Larchwood 1981. o.p. Fiction.

The three decades following World War II were not happy ones for Korea. Close on the heels of the global conflict came the Korean War. In the 1960s there was a military revolution. The country enjoyed an economic surge in the 1970s, but the gap between rich and poor only grew wider. All these events and more are reflected in the stories that emerged from Korea during that era.

Themes of the works in this volume include human kindness even in the midst of war, the effect of war on children, and the loneliness of poor and backward places. Some of the stories experiment with symbolism. Authors include Song Byungsoo, who describes the North Korean Communist invasion; Park Yunhee, who writes of the dark sociopolitical times of the 1970s; Oh Youngsoo, who writes with sympathy of the loneliness of women in a fishing village; and a handful of other authors who are well known in Korea but little known outside. A brief introduction gives historical and literary background.

1465 Inoue Yasushi. ***Tun Huang***. Trans. from Japanese by Joan O. Moy. Kodansha 1993, $9.00 (0-87011-576-6). 216pp. Fiction.

For historical interest, this book is, so far, one of a kind. It recounts the turbulent era of the Chinese Song Dynasty (960–1279), during which the Hsi-Hsia, a non-Chinese people to the north, periodically invaded the Chinese border towns.

Tun Huang is the name of a present-day town in the middle of what used to be known as Chinese Turkestan. The town bears the same name as the nearby caves where scrolls were hidden. Also in these caves are many frescoes of Buddhist drawings and replicas of the Buddha. It was considered good fortune to place a Buddha in these caves, so travelers and merchants took care to place one there on every trip back and forth along the Silk Road to ensure safety from brigands, ruffians, and inclement weather.

The details of how, why, and when the scrolls were hidden are unknown, but the author has created a good story. There are lengthy descriptions of the battles, strategies, and circumstances surrounding the several royal houses and the barbarians who constantly threatened to invade the "civilized world" (China). The hero, whose name was inspired by one of the scrolls, is a Chinese (Song) citizen who becomes a soldier who battles the invading armies. He becomes part of a triangle vying for the affections of a princess, though his attention is divided by his own intense interest in the writing system of the Hsi-Hsia, then newly created and based on the Chinese writing system. Even today this system is not thoroughly understood.

The Japanese author began as a newspaper reporter; if the book has a flaw, it is that much of the writing in this novel sounds like reportage or descriptions of film footage. (In fact, a film was made from the book.) However, he has won several coveted literary prizes for other works, including *Wind and Waves* (o.p.), a historical novel set in Korea, and *The Roof Tile of Tempyo* (Columbia Univ. Pr., 1982), set in Japan in the seventh century.

1466 Ishiguro Kazuo. ***Artist of the Floating World***. Random 1989, $10.00 (0-679-72266-1). 206pp. Fiction.

Delicately written, this novel is full of the subtle Japanese nuances of emotion and cautious demonstration of feelings, even among family members.

Now an old man, Mr. Ono, a retired, renowned artist, gradually discovers—or rather reveals—the character flaws that prevented him from realizing his artistic potential. An undercurrent of benign mystery begins to engulf the reader: What is it about Mr. Ono that is blemished, culpable? What is so unacceptable in his paintings that they must be "tidied away" for the time being?

The author explores the nature of patriotism and the elusive definition of war crimes by scrutinizing the lives of several characters. The pacifist undercurrent of this book is revealed in a statement about war—in which, a character says, "brave young men die for stupid causes"—and in the ruminations of Mr. Ono, who "was not a bad man, just someone who worked very hard doing what he thought was for the best."

Subtle and elegant, the writing draws the reader into this reminiscence of a vanishing Japan and a struggle to cope with the demands of society. Ishiguro Kazuo has also written *A Pale View of the Hills* (Random, 1990), set in Japan, and *The Remains of the Day* (Random, 1993), set in England, where the author now lives.

Ishiguro Kazuo. ***Remains of the Day***.
See entry 802.

1467 Jia Pingwa. ***Turbulence: A Novel by Jia Pingwa***. Trans. from Chinese by Howard Goldblatt. Louisiana State Univ. Pr. 1991, $22.95 (0-8071-1687-4). 592pp. Fiction.

Mao Zedong's death in 1976 signaled the end of the Cultural Revolution, which had effectively stripped ten years from many people's productive life in China. In the bitterness and confusion of trying to get things to run normally again, officials found it easy to abuse their privileges; a short while later, the "classless" society was again divided into the haves and the have-nots.

In this novel, Golden Boy, an idealistic young man, becomes a journalist who attempts to expose the local political corruption in his own rural village. A romantic subplot shows how political and social circumstance can keep people apart. Through graphic detail and a sense of humor, the novel portrays pettiness, gossip, corruption, tradition, idealism, hope for the future, and love in this small rural town, which serves as a microcosm for what is happening throughout China today.

This novel won the Pegasus Award in 1988 as a distinguished work from a country whose literature is not often represented in English.

1468 Kang Sok-kyong, Kim Chi-won, and O Chong-hui. ***Words of Farewell: Stories by Korean Women Writers***. Trans. from Korean by Bruce Fulton and Ju-chan Fulton. Seal 1989, $20.95 (0-931188-77-6); $12.95 (0-931188-76-8). 274pp. Fiction.

Korean women, like women of other parts of Asia, have traditionally been relegated to domestic roles. Because literature was considered a public occupation, it was therefore a task for men only. But Korea has not been spared the political and social upheavals of this century. One result is the gradual emergence of women writers. Because of the wars and the economic challenges Korea has endured, literature from the region has tended to be depressing, pessimistic, and fatalistic. However, contemporary writers—those who established their careers in the 1970s and 1980s—are branching out into new concerns.

Three women writers have contributed the stories in this collection: Kang

Sok-kyong, Kim Chi-won, and O Chong-hui. Their themes include a concern for social problems; women interacting with men; the frustrations of modern family life as members try to change to fit the times; loss of loved ones; and the need to loosen family bonds to achieve personal independence.

A few pages of introduction give us a historical background, a brief biography, and an overview of the literary development of each of the authors represented here.

1469 Kawabata Yasunari. ***Palm-of-the-Hand Stories***. Trans. from Japanese by Lane Dunlop and J. Martin Holman. Farrar 1990, $9.95 (0-86547-412-5). 256pp. Fiction.

One of the most widely read Japanese novelists, Kawabata is the author of the acclaimed works *Thousand Cranes* (orig. pub. 1969; Berkley, 1981), *Snow Country* (orig. pub. 1969; Berkley, 1981), *Beauty and Sadness* (orig. pub. 1975; Berkley, 1981), *The Master of Go* (orig. pub. 1972; Berkley, 1981), and *The Lake* (orig. pub. 1974; Kodansha, 1993). In his youth, when everyone else was writing poems, he wrote his "palm-of-the-hand stories"—brief and delicate pieces so small they could "fit" into the palm of your hand.

Ranging in theme from memories of his grandparents to brief encounters with a beautiful girl on the beach or in the woods, these literary pearls immortalize the many tiny bits of love, immortality, sadness, and joy of which life is made. Like the bonsai tree, they incorporate the wisdom of age and the perfect, simple beauty of the small and delicate. These stories will appeal to a broad audience and are especially valuable to introductory-level students of Japanese literature.

1470 Kita Morio. ***The House of Nire***. Trans. from Japanese by Dennis Keene. Kodansha 1991, $7.95 (0-87011-859-5). 772pp. Fiction.

Also renowned as a masterly and prolific short story writer, Kita Morio is perhaps most famous for this novel. The "house" of the title is actually a mental hospital, which the author uses as a subtle metaphor for Japan, its people, and its way of life. The long, involved story—painfully funny in spots—is told in two volumes. The first tells about the hospital and its myriad characters. The second, *The Fall of the House of Nire* (Kodansha, 1985), follows the story after the war years. So well translated is this edition that readers, forgetting that they are reading about Japan, will realize the universal meaning behind the author's comments about society.

Kita Morio is also author of *Ghosts* (orig. pub. 1954; Kodansha, 1991). In this novel, a young man searches for something significant in his past—in his childhood—that will dignify and signify his life and his future. In the process, he discovers the importance of everyday, ordinary events. The author explores similar themes in *The House of Nire*, revealing the influence of Thomas Mann, André Gide, and Vladimir Nabokov.

1471 Kizaki Satoko. ***The Phoenix Tree and Other Stories***. Trans. from Japanese by Carol A. Flath. Kodansha 1990, $18.95 (0-87011-982-6); $9.95 (4-7700-1790-1). 192pp. Fiction.

The author was born in Japanese-occupied Manchuria and lived for fifteen years in the West. These cultural influences contribute to the sense of displacement in her stories. Awarded the coveted Akutagawa Prize, the title story in this collection probes the concept of disease and death as a part of the self that must be accepted and endured. The story explores the question of whether it is wise to intervene medically in cases of terminal illness. A young woman, struggling to understand and accept her own position within her adoptive family, nurses her ailing aunt in the last days of her fight with cancer. They are determined to avoid doctors, hospitals, and all help except tender, loving care and moral support. The author examines complicated family relationships through those subtly nuanced emotions—shame, concern with the opinion of others, and the struggle to express the self without unnecessarily burdening others—that are the subject of so much Japanese writing.

In many of Kizaki's stories, a lonely or orphaned adult seeks some fulfillment or wholeness related to something felt to be lost in childhood. Her tales are rich both in prose style and in the complex explorations of interpersonal relationships.

1472 Lao She. *Rickshaw*. Trans. from Chinese and Intro. by Jean M. James. Univ. of Hawaii Pr. 1979, $12.00 (0-8248-0616-6); $8.95 (0-8248-0655-7). 249pp. Fiction.

This is a new and more faithful translation of a classic Chinese novel originally serialized in a Chinese periodical in 1936. (The earlier version was titled *Rickshaw Boy*.) Thoroughly researched and impeccably translated by Jean James, who provides an illuminating introduction, this edition omits the Hollywood-style features that marred the earlier work and renders the original story complete with all its eloquent portraits of life in old Peking, the frustration of the poor trying to better themselves, and the unthinking exploitation and oppression of the lower classes.

Lao She, who lived in England for five years, became an admirer of Dickens, whose works describe the details of the downtrodden of London and whose social consciousness is reflected in this, the author's eighth and most important novel.

The story tells of a rickshaw puller whose name presages good fortune but who is anything but fortunate. Trying to put aside enough money to buy his own rickshaw, he struggles and works hard, but, due to a series of bad choices, bad company, bad habits, and ignorance, he squanders his money and falls into a life of drinking, drugs, and relationships with prostitutes. Finally, his spirit broken, he fades away— old, stricken with disease, and caring about nothing. He is a pitiful portrait of the society of the time, a society, according to the author, that is in need of radical change.

1473 Lau, Joseph S., ed. *The Unbroken Chain: An Anthology of Taiwan Fiction since 1926*. Trans. from Chinese. Indiana Univ. Pr. 1984, $35.00 (0-253-36162-1); $12.95 (0-253-20489-5). 298pp. Fiction.

This anthology represents not only the styles and themes of Taiwanese writers but the sweep of the country's modern history as well. The Japanese occupied the island until 1945; during that era little literature of note was produced. The four works in the first section by such authors as Lai Ho and Yang Kuei represent that time.

The thirteen works in the second section reflect the great changes in Taiwan's political and economic life during the last half-century. Stories deal with the shift from the extreme poverty of the countryside to the rapid economic growth that catapulted Taiwan into the world market scene. Other tales explore the evolution of feelings among the Chinese exiles, many of whom clung to the belief that they would soon be able to return to the mainland but who gradually came to adjust to life in their new land.

Political events also affect events and people in these stories. Some characters, for example, express discomfort over Nixon's visit to the People's Republic of China, feeling that the United States might not be as friendly to Taiwan as before. Themes of loneliness and homesickness and commentary on social ills are also found here. An essay on the authors and their works precedes each story. Translators include both Western scholars of China and Chinese writers.

1474 Li, Leslie. *Bittersweet*. Tuttle 1992, $12.95 (0-8048-3036-3). 388pp. Fiction.

The story of modern China is reflected in this fictionalized account of the author's grandmother, Li Xiu-wen (1889–1992), who lived for nearly a century and who was the wife of Li Tsung-jen, acting president of China from 1948 to 1949.

The heroine, called Bittersweet (whose name truly reflects her life), is a feisty young girl who is just bold enough to resist tradition in small ways yet who is also a shining example of Chinese virtues. For example, she expresses the importance of filial piety in Chinese society and exemplifies the values of tolerance, forbearance, forgiveness, and family harmony.

Her husband is so completely devoted to his political career that he often ignores her and their children. When he takes a second, younger wife, she mutters to herself, "Honor, respect, and good fortune aren't everything in life . . . especially for a woman." She accepts his decision gracefully so as to save face and maintain peace in the family. Although she struggles to contain her own fury and bitterness, she never gives people cause to accuse her of pettiness or jealousy.

Increasing in wisdom, inner peace, and status in society, Bittersweet becomes a model citizen and wife and a pillar of whatever society she finds herself in. Her contacts with foreigners reveal a none-too-flattering portrait of Westerners as seen through Chinese eyes. The reader becomes so absorbed in the story that the hundred years of time covered in the novel melt away quickly.

1475 Link, Perry, ed. *Roses and Thorns: The Second Blooming of the Hundred Flowers in Chinese Fiction, 1979–80*. Trans. from Chinese. Illus. Univ. of California Pr. 1984, $14.00 (0-520-04980-2). 300pp. Fiction.

In 1942, at the Yanan Conference on Literature and Art, Mao Zedong called for "a hundred flowers" to bloom together. He meant that artists and writers should pour out their souls in expressing themselves. That artistic freedom did not last long, but while it did, a good deal of interesting material was created. Eventually the politically repressive Cultural Revolution in China once again imposed restraints on creative individuals. After Mao's death, the Revolution abated, and once more—as the title of this anthology suggests— the flowers of creativity could bloom. These stories reflect the sense of relief from the stress and oppression that so clouded the atmosphere during the previous era.

Another collection of short stories, plays, and poems of the 1980s edited by Perry Link is *Stubborn Weeds: Popular and Controversial Chinese Literature after the Cultural Revolution* (Univ. of Indiana Pr., 1983).

1476 Lippit, Norika M., and Kyoko I. Selden, eds. ***Japanese Women Writers: Twentieth Century Short Fiction****. Trans. from Japanese by the editors. M. E. Sharpe 1991, $42.50 (0-87332-859-0); $16.95 (0-87332-860-4). 312pp. Fiction.

The authors of these fourteen pieces of short fiction are keen observers of life. Their stories deal with the range of human life and emotions, examining the experiences both of great people and of the weak and insignificant. Social consciousness, new lifestyles for modern women, and the search for a common humanity are some of the many themes explored in these works.

The introductory essay presents a brief history of Japanese literature with special focus on the prominent place of women in mainstream Japanese writing. Also included is a brief commentary on each author. At the end, a glossary of Japanese terms is followed by a biography of each writer and a listing of major works.

1477 ***Love That Burns on a Summer's Night****. Trans. from Chinese and other languages. Chinese Literature Pr. 1990. o.p. Fiction.

The majority of Chinese people belong to a distinct ethnic group that calls itself Han, after the dynasty that reigned from 206 B.C. to A.D. 220. In fact, however, China is a multinational country, home to at least fifty-six ethnic nationalities. The population of these minorities totals many millions. There are, for example, thirteen million Zhuang.

Each minority has its own body of literature; among some groups, stories exist only in oral form, but among others, the literature is not only written but is highly developed. Many folktales from these individual peoples have been lumped together under the single label "Chinese." This volume, however, presents works by ten minority authors, eight of whom are blossoming young writers and two of whom are well established.

The title story, from Mongolia, deals with the love between a Mongolian and a Han woman. In this and another Mongolian tale, the vastness of the grassland becomes an integral part of the story, and descriptions of the land reveal to the reader just how important a sense of place is to the Mongolians. A story from Tibet was written by Dawa Tashi, who won a national award in 1985 for *A Soul in Bondage* (China Books, 1992). Other minority nationalities represented include Mulam, Manchu, Ewenki, Korean, and Tujia. Notes on the authors are found in the back of the book.

1478 Lu Hsun. ***The True Story of Ah Q.*** 5th ed. Trans. from Chinese by Hsien-yi Yang and Gladys Yang. Cheng & Tsui 1990, $3.95 (0-917056-93-0). 68pp. Fiction.

Lu Hsun (also spelled Lu Xun) (1881–1936) is the one Chinese writer who is claimed by both the Nationalists of Taiwan and the Communists of the People's Republic. A revolutionary spirit in his youth, he decided to pursue a medical career because he wanted to help people. However, after witnessing the massacres of wartime, he felt it would be futile to heal people's bodies if their minds were still full of the stupidity and ignorance that would only rouse them to take up arms and get themselves killed. So he became a writer—to heal men's minds.

One of the leaders of the revolution that led China out of the last century, Lu Hsun was incensed by nothing so much as the insensitivity of the people and the corruption of the old society. The stories he wrote depict the old society in a harshly bitter and sarcastic vein. In a story collected in *Diary of a Madman* (Univ. of Hawaii Pr., 1990), for example, he states that the Chinese of his day are all "people-eaters." It's a dog-eat-dog, people-eat-people world. But he still believed there was hope, and that it lay in the children: "Save the children!" became his rallying cry. *The True Story of Ah Q* is a little booklet, describing with sympathy and sorrow the simple ignorance, humiliation, and persecution of an old peasant who refuses to acknowledge the oppression and exploitation of the lower classes by the bourgeoisie. In the author's view, the peasant represents China's old society with its blinders on.

His other works include several volumes of short stories, sixteen volumes of essays, and *A Brief History of Chinese Fiction* (Hyperion, 1990).

1479 Mao Dun. ***Rainbow***. Trans. from Chinese by Madeleine Zelin. Univ. of California Pr. 1992, $38.00 (0-520-07327-4); $13.00 (0-520-07328-2). 255pp. Fiction.

Mao Dun is the pen name of Shen Yanbing (1896–1981), one of the finest writers China has produced. This novel, written in 1929 and recently republished, is the story of changing political times. New ideas were sweeping China in the wake of the May 4th movement for political freedom. Some observers have compared that movement, which was a milestone in Chinese literature as well as politics, to the Tiananmen Square incident.

In the story, a young woman, Mei, leaves home to escape an arranged marriage. Venturing outside traditional family life, she immerses herself in the modern movement of "individualism, sexual equality, and political responsibility," terms that were repeated over and over on the streets and in the new literature. She represents the many young women of her day who dared take their lives into their own hands and enter the political arena.

1480 Maruya Saiichi. ***Singular Rebellion***. Trans. from Japanese by Dennis Keene. Kodansha 1990, $6.95 (0-87011-989-3). 420pp. Fiction.

Maruya, born in 1925, had been a longtime admirer of such Western novelists as James Joyce before he finally began writing in the 1960s. This novel, which first appeared in 1972, itself represented a singular form of artistic rebellion, because it challenged the traditional assumption that a novel must be serious, somber, and self-confessional. Instead, the light, comic style and risqué, slightly vulgar subject matter makes it sound more like a piece of Western writing than a Japanese one. In the story, a middle-aged widower has an affair with a dashing young model whose "granny," fresh out of jail for murder, is also having an affair.

This work was a big hit among Maruya's Western readers and earned many literary prizes in Japan. The stories in his collection *Rain in the Wind: Four Stories* (Kodansha, 1990) echo the themes and characters of the novel:

There is a middle-aged man, a bar girl, a scholar, and a novelist in a search for something in the past, something elusive. Although light-hearted, the stories make some telling satirical jabs at the foibles of Japanese society.

1481 Mishima Yukio. ***The Sea of Fertility: Spring Snow; Runaway Horses; Temple of Dawn; Decline of the Angel.*** 4 vols. Trans. from Japanese. Random 1990, $12.00; $13.00; $14.00; [o.p.] (0-679-72241-6; 0-679-72240-8; 0-679-72242-4; [o.p.]). 400+421+330+236pp. Fiction.

In 1970, Mishima finished the last novel in his tetrology, *The Sea of Fertility*. Then, aided by the military society he had set up, he committed ritual suicide. His act astonished the literary world.

Much of his prolific writing over his thirty-year career was an attempt to explore and explain his fascination with death, homosexuality, the loss of traditional Japan, and a certain indebtedness to his country, a debt he felt could only be paid by his death. Each of the four novels that constitute this final work involves the same character, who is reincarnated into different people. In each case the character is recognizable by the three moles under his—or her—arm and is destined to live only twenty years. These stories explore the personal, social, and political meanings of death, war, transition of society, persistence of the soul, freedom, virility, and, perhaps most of all, of beauty—beauty of the male, of muscle, of sun and masculine strength, and the beauty of suicide for a noble cause.

Other Mishima works also plumb these concepts. Titles include a long autobiographical essay, *Sun and Steel* (Kodansha, 1994), in which Mishima lays out his philosophy, and many novels and novelettes, including *Confessions of a Mask* (New Directions, 1968), *Forbidden Colors* (Berkeley, 1981), *The Sound of Waves* (Random, 1994), *The Temple of the Golden Pavilion* (Random, 1994), and *The Sailor Who Fell from Grace with the Sea* (Random, 1994), which was adapted into a motion picture in 1976. *Mishima*, a film based upon the author's life, was released in 1985.

1482 Mo Yan. ***Red Sorghum***. Trans. from Chinese by Howard Goldblatt. Viking 1993, $23.50 (0-670-84402-0); $10.95 (0-14-016854-0). 384pp. Fiction.

This is a tale of atrocity and horror. The Japanese occupy a farming village in the remote northeast part of China. They have come to conscript men and donkeys to destroy the wheat (red sorghum) fields that are the lifeblood of the farmers in order to build a road for use by the Japanese occupying army. The villagers' naiveté and disbelief lead to many gruesome deaths. The author seems to be suggesting parallels to what some regard as the passivity of the Jews during the Holocaust.

Peppered with flashbacks and flashforwards, the times and places and characters are all given at once. The reader puts together the picture gradually, like pieces of a puzzle. (This technique was originally used by Gabriel García Márquez.)

The book is notable for its depiction of the treatment of women in the 1930s. They were considered more as possessions than as human beings, although strong women could be found there. The heroine of the novel is just such a woman because she defies both tradition and the oppression for the sake of love.

1483 Mori Ogai. *The Incident at Sakai and Other Stories.* Trans. from Japanese; Contrib. by Richard Bowring. Illus. Books on Demand 1977, $62.40 (0-8357-6154-1). 240pp. Fiction.

Mori Rintaro (1862–1922), who used Ogai as his pen name, became one of Japan's most noted writers. He is best known for his novel *The Wild Geese* (Tuttle, 1974), which was first translated into English in 1959. That novel describes the unfulfilled love between a young student and the daughter of a candy maker who is unhappily married. The novel beautifully portrays student and street life in Tokyo and explores Japanese social paradigms.

Mori is one of the first Japanese writers who studied and lived in the West. As a result, Western ideas and ways of thinking, as well as the influence of such writers as Turgenev, first appear in Japanese writing in the works of Mori. He also was classically trained in Chinese literature and poetry. As a result his style is brilliant but it can make for heavy reading in English, as is the case with some of the historical narratives contained in this collection.

In the title work, a group of twenty Japanese are forced by the French to commit suicide. Other stories in the collection also deal with suicide. Another story tells of a constable who is taking another man in for a "murder" that he did not commit. In the course of the story, the men ride in a boat and discuss an old Buddhist legend about children sold into slavery and the passage of a boy into manhood. Other tales deal with nuns and priests. Some acquaintance with Japanese history and social mores is helpful in appreciating these stories, but all are engrossing and somewhat disturbing. These stories explore the nature of public duty, as opposed to personal glory; the rebellion inherent in self-sacrifice; and the reasons (proper or improper) for committing suicide.

1484 Morin, Edward, ed. *The Red Azalea: Chinese Poetry Since the Cultural Revolution.* Trans. from Chinese by Edward Morin, Fang Dai, and Dennis Ding; Intro. by Leo O. Lee. Univ. of Hawaii Pr. 1990, $35.00 (0-8248-1256-5); $14.95 (0-8248-1320-0). 256pp. Poetry.

Modern Chinese poetry had its beginnings with the May 4th movement in the early part of this century. Students were eager to establish new political, cultural, and social guidelines and mores. Decades later, after the singularly confining and debilitating Cultural Revolution, artistic creativity manifested itself in writings dedicated to the search for self. Examples of these later poems are collected in this book.

Older writers like Ai Qing and Zheng Min spent time living and studying abroad. Ai Qing, who has been considered the leading poet of China, studied in France and was influenced by the French symbolists. Coming of age during the Cultural Revolution were poets like Bei Dao, who has also written a collection of short stories (*Waves*; New Directions, 1990) and several poetry anthologies, such as *The August Sleepwalker* (New Directions, 1990). The two dozen poets represented here are seeking a new language of self-expression. At times that language appears very simple or superficial, but it was not so long ago that an attempt to deviate from the official party doctrine could lead to trouble.

1485 Morris, Ivan, ed. ***Modern Japanese Stories: An Anthology***. Trans. from Japanese by Edward Seidensticker, George Saito, Geoffrey Sargent, and Ivan Morris. Illus. with woodcuts by Masakuzu Kuwata. Tuttle 1977, $16.95 (0-8048-1226-8). 512pp. Fiction.

This fat and very thorough collection of stories was selected by a panel of prominent scholars of Japanese literature. Many of the important writers who were prominent before the 1960s are represented in this volume, the official UNESCO entry in the Japanese Translation series, which has gone through more than twenty reprintings.

A lengthy historical introduction traces the development of Japanese literature in modern times. Japanese literature is unique among Asian countries. Until the Meiji Restoration in 1868, men wrote poetry or plays; prose writing was considered the domain of women and was not held in high esteem. But under the influence of the Western world, fiction, especially in the form of the novel, became popular.

Major authors represented here include Mori Ogai, one of the first Japanese writers to create pieces in the style known as lyrical romanticism. His stories represent a break with the naturalists, who, influenced by such Western writers as Zola, were writing cold, pessimistic descriptions of "reality." Active in the early 1900s, the naturalist school is represented here by Tokuda Shusei. Other notable authors include Japan's favorite, Tanizaki Junichiro, as well as Akutagawa Ryunosuke, Kawabata Yasunari, Inoue Yasushi, Dazai Osamu, and Mishima Yukio.

These selections present a broad look at Japan's society in the first half of the century; in the process, they incorporate much of history as well. Themes include social relationships between men and women; the state of the lower classes; the effects of war on the human psyche; contact with the West; and the sometimes ludicrous attempt to translate everything Western into Japanese culture. This excellent collection is punctuated with stark and beautiful woodcuts. A biographical account of each author examines the writer's life and connects it to the style and themes of his story. A selected bibliography of additional works in translation by the authors is found at the end.

1486 Oe Kenzaburo. ***Teach Us to Outgrow Our Madness***. Trans. from Japanese by John Nathan. Grove 1977, $11.00 (0-8021-5185-X). 261pp. Fiction.

After the end of World War II, the Japanese had to deal with tremendous changes in the structure of their society. On the one hand, they had to accept the humiliating revelation that their Emperor was not, after all, a god but was merely as human as anyone else. On the other hand, they had expected that the American soldiers who occupied their land would rape their women and pillage the country, when in fact the Americans seemed to bring with them a rain of Hershey bars and chewing gum. The generation of young Japanese, witnesses to the ravages of the atomic blasts at Hiroshima and Nagasaki, had to deal with their conflicting emotions of disbelief, anger, humiliation, and relief. Fearful that their fury would turn to apathy, writers like Oe Kenzaburo used their emotions as a catalyst within themselves to produce stories like the ones in this volume.

Oe's characters deal with sickness, madness, deformity, and death in various guises. They want to come to terms with their own disease—their own "dis-ease." The stories are about their pursuit of a lost childhood innocence and past identity and the struggle to preserve hope and "forbearance."

Other works by Oe include novels dealing with the alienation of the self and the search for human meaning in what seems to be a meaningless society. *A Personal Matter* (Grove, 1969) describes such a man, in his twenties, whose wife gives birth to a deformed baby; the father sees in the child a reflection of his own spiritual deformity. *The Silent Cry* (Kodansha, 1974) presents two brothers, very different in character, who stand for different facets of Japanese history. They go back to the village where they grew up, only to find and take part in an ongoing drama of passion. Oe Kenzaburo was awarded the Nobel Prize for literature in 1994.

1487 Roberts, R. A., and Angela Knox, eds. *One Half of the Sky: Stories from Contemporary Women Writers of China*. Trans. from Chinese. Dodd 1988. o.p. Fiction.

It has not been easy for Westerners to know the personal feelings of China. Through fiction more than in factual books and newspapers, China begins now to reveal itself. These eight stories reflect the development of the writing of Chinese women writers in this century. These works are drawn from many important eras: the 1920s, when women writers such as Ding Ling were just beginning to emerge; the struggle in the 1940s between the Nationalists and the Communists; the idealism of the 1950s; the horror of the Cultural Revolution in the 1960s and 1970s; and the new generation that has experienced none of China's "feudal" past.

There is a saying in China that "women hold up half the sky." Although women have not always held a place in the literary limelight in China, this small volume is an attempt to honor the struggle of women writers to make a place for themselves in the Chinese literary scene.

1488 *Seven Contemporary Chinese Women Writers: Ru Zhijuan, Huang Zongying, Zong Pu, Shen Rong, Zhang Jie, Zhang KangKang, Wang Anyi*. Trans. from Chinese; Intro. by Gladys Yang. Panda 1982. o.p. Fiction.

The seven authors represented in this small but important collection include some of the most popular and well-known women writers in China. All these authors are members of the Chinese Writers' Association, which boasts 220 women among its ranks.

Women in China are just beginning to come into their own. Some of their work is controversial because they dare to write about human feelings, injustice, social inequality, and political corruption in a country where such things are not supposed to exist. In fact, in their revolutionary fervor, writers in the past have turned a blind eye to these problems. The stories in this volume still contain that modern Chinese quality of socialist idealism, but their authors are not afraid to go inward and examine their lives.

Several of these stories describe the plight of women in the professions who must try to advance their careers while struggling with household drudgery. A key theme in some of the other works is the problems of young people who have recently moved from the countryside and who must forge a new life in the city. The youth, idealistic in their own way, seem flippant and materialistic to their intellectual parents, who lost the best years of their lives in the

Cultural Revolution. Romance also finds its way into the stories, but it is colored differently from romance as presented in works by Western writers.

1489 Shono, Junzo. *Still Life and Other Stories*. Trans. from Japanese by Wayne P. Lammers. Stone Bridge 1992, $11.95 (1-880656-02-7). 264pp. Fiction.

Shono is one of the leading writers in Japan today. The short stories in this collection are characteristic of his work—short interlinked pieces written in what he calls his "snapshot" style, as though the whole book were a family album—a phrase that is, in fact, the title of one of his stories.

The reader of these works senses that, under the placid surface of seemingly ordinary family life, something is terribly wrong. Often the problem is revealed, not in a cathartic dramatic explosion, but almost as an aside in something someone says offhandedly. In Kafkaesque fashion, Shono gives us an ominous vision of what he sees is going on in Japan today. His snapshots capture dark images of the Japanese soul.

1490 Siu, Helen, and Zelda Stern, eds. *Mao's Harvest: Voices from China's New Generation*. Trans. from Chinese; Frwd. by Jonathan Spence. Illus. with photos. Oxford Univ. Pr. 1983, $21.95 (0-19-503274-8); $10.95 (0-19-503499-6). 231pp. Fiction/Poetry.

In a lengthy introduction, the editors present a thoughtful literary history of the century and present the various influences on this new generation of writers. These authors, mostly born during the 1940s and the 1950s, are particularly interesting because they were raised during the height of Mao Zedong's influence over the thoughts of the Chinese people. In their works, these individuals, notably Bei Dao and Zhang Jie, present something other than social protest or the political line of the day.

This generation knew nothing of the "old society" that was the object of such disgust during the Cultural Revolution. It was their parents who were the idealistic participants in the new China of the 1950s. How would these young people find the zeal to carry on the flame? Mao wanted to encourage in them a communal spirit.

The noted China commentator, Jonathan Spence, has written an informative foreword to this volume. The works are grouped by themes, which include love, family, politics, faith, and work. A biography and a photograph are included for each author.

1491 So Chongju. *Unforgettable Things: Poems by So Chongju*. Trans. from Korean and Intro. by David R. McCann. International Communication Foundation 1986. o.p. Poetry.

More than just a collection of poems, these brief writings collectively tell a story of a man's life from his childhood in a Korean village to his school boy years, through the Japanese occupation to a larger view of Korea in the world today.

Personal, impressionistic, free-verse translations and a few poetic essays describe minute events in the poet's life: the girl he first saw washing vegetables and who later became his wife; setting off to become a teacher and making the journey in a trailer pulled by a pony whose harness was bedecked with a jangling bell; a treasured set of rosewood chests that he and his wife were obliged to sell in their poverty in the 1940s; a lichen-covered stone that he found and kept and watered every morning; the tears of a young girl as she read a poem that he had written; two high school students who had frequented his house, one of whom was killed in the April Revolution of 1960; the Buddhist monk who advised him to "study the philosophers and poets, and then become a poet." These poems, sprinkled with Western as well as Korean literary allusions, are deceptively simple. Through them we see Korean daily life through Korean eyes.

1492 Soseki Natsume. ***Grass on the Wayside***. Trans. from Japanese and Intro. by Edwin McClellan. Univ. of Michigan, Center for Japanese Studies 1990, $8.95 (0-939512-45-9). 169pp. Fiction.

Soseki is considered the definitive writer of the modern Japanese realistic novel. Born in 1867, he lived much of his childhood with an adoptive family before he returned to his own aging parents. The resulting feelings of being passed around unwanted—or at least feeling unwanted—provide the main thematic matter for this novel.

As in many Japanese autobiographical novels, guilt, shame, self-pity, an atmosphere of moroseness, and introspective monologues predominate. However, Soseki's characters are real and moving. Kenzo, the character who represents Soseki, is not an entirely likable person. The story revolves around his personal interactions with his family—his parents, his foster parents, his brother and sister, and later his wife, who at one point finally confronts him with a stark and revealing accusation: "There isn't anybody in this world you approve of, is there? Everybody is a fool as far as you are concerned."

Tan, Amy. ***The Kitchen God's Wife***.
See entry 291.

1493 Tanaka Yukiko, ed. ***To Live and to Write: Selections by Japanese Women Writers, 1913–1938***. Trans. from Japanese by Tanaka Yukiko, Elizabeth Hanson, and Hirolo M. Malatesta. Seal 1987, $16.95 (0-931188-44-X); $12.95 (0-931188-43-1). 225pp. Fiction.

This is the first volume of the three collections of short stories by Japanese women that, taken together, describe the development of women's literature in Japan in this century. The subsequent volumes in the series are *This Kind of Woman* and *Unmapped Territories* (*see main entries*).

These years in Japan (1913–1938) were characterized by the first real social liberalism Japan had seen. The women of that time sought freedom to explore their own lives, to interact in politics, to work, to be something to themselves besides complacent objects keeping house for their husbands. Nine courageous women who stood up to be counted have written the stories in this volume.

1494 Tanaka Yukiko, ed. ***Unmapped Territories: New Women's Fiction from Japan***. Trans. from Japanese by the editor. Women in Translation 1991, $10.95 (1-879679-00-0). 162pp. Fiction.

The three volumes of stories collected and edited by Tanaka Yukiko represent Japanese women's literature in each of three major eras of this century. This volume, the third, consists of stories written by Japanese women in the 1980s. It is important for reflecting the changing society and the changes in the status of women in Japan in the last decade.

Old legends, reexamined and readjusted, appear here in the very modern and liberated lives of young women and older women exploring their sexuality. The writers also explore women's desires and roles within the family, in the workplace, and in the rapidly changing society at large. Japanese society is coming to resemble Western society in many ways, and yet it also retains qualities of its own. These stories ponder the relative values of the secure but confining old and the exciting but sometimes misguided new.

1495 Tanaka Yukiko, and Elizabeth Hanson, eds. ***This Kind of Woman: Ten Stories by Japanese Women Writers, 1960–1976***. Trans. from Japanese by Mona Nagai. Stanford Univ. Pr. 1982, $35.00 (0-8047-1130-5); Univ. of Michigan, Center for Japanese Studies, Write for price info (0-939512-66-1). 320pp. Fiction.

This is the second of three volumes of collected stories of Japanese women by Tanaka Yukiko. Together, they explore the development of Japanese women in literature and society in this century.

In this volume, an extensive introduction traces the development of women in literature and their social roles throughout Japanese history. The editors argue that the 1960s marked a new era in Japanese literature, one that reflected the economic success of Japan and at the same time revealed the sense of loss and insecurity at the changing traditions. These stories explore those feelings, some blatantly, some merely describing the subtle, almost imperceptible changes in daily life away from the traditional and toward a new Japanese reality.

1496 Tanizaki Junichiro. ***A Cat, a Man, and Two Women***. Trans. from Japanese by Paul McCarthy; Intro. by John Updike. Kodansha 1990, $18.95 (0-87011-755-6). 192pp. Fiction.

One of the best-loved writers in Japan, Tanizaki has written a number of hefty novels, including the famous *The Makioka Sisters* (Berkley, 1981), which tops the list of must-read novels from Japan. He has also written in other genres: essays, such as those collected in *In Praise of Shadows* (Leete's Island, 1977), through which he expresses admiration for traditional Japanese attitudes about beauty; a book of memoirs, *Childhood Years* (Kodansha, 1990); a masterly translation of the twenty-six-volume literary classic *The Tale of the Genji* (not available in English) and a number of short stories, including the three in this volume.

The title story is about a tantalizing cat who provides the third leg of two love triangles. Both amusing and pitiful, as are many of his stories, the great delight of this one is his portrait of the elegant and beautiful cat, whose name is Lily. "A Little Kingdom" is a little masterpiece about a well-bred, perhaps too-tender schoolmaster who meets his match in a quiet but charismatic student who sets up his own society within the school. The third story, "Professor Radio," consists of dialogues between an intrusive newspaper reporter and an eccentric old professor with a taste for masochism.

Tanizaki's first novel to appear in English, *Some Prefer Nettles* (orig. pub. 1965; Berkley, 1981), relates the struggle of a young man who is tempted by the frivolities and apparent freedoms of Western society. At the same time he struggles to retain his loving dedication to his family and to his past—both his childhood and his country's ancient traditions. *The Makioka Sisters*, first published in Japan in 1948, is considered his masterpiece. It is the long, involved tale of four sisters in Tokyo who try to find a husband for one of them so that the youngest one will be free to marry. The novel, more of an exercise in mood and style than a traditionally plotted work, paints an absorbing picture of family life, values, and social tradition in old Tokyo.

1497 Ueda Makoto, ed. ***The Mother of Dreams and Other Short Stories: Portrayals of Women in Modern Japanese Fiction***. Trans. from Japanese by John Bester. Kodansha 1986, $19.95 (0-87011-775-0); $9.00 (0-87011-926-5). 280pp. Fiction.

This volume of works about women arranges the stories into five sections reflecting women's traditional and developmental status in Japan: Maiden, Wife, Mistress, Mother, and Working Woman. Although the categories are familiar, the Japanese attitudes toward them do not always parallel attitudes about women in the West.

In this full and well-edited volume, readers will find some of Japan's best-known authors. Kawabata Yasunari is a Nobel Prize winner with a reputation for writing probing works about the feminine psyche and the search for ideal beauty long cherished in traditional Japanese culture. Inoue Yasushi, a novelist especially popular among women readers, is represented here by a story that sheds new light on the traditional family meeting between two marriage prospects. Dazai Osamu, Japan's infamous decadent poet, regards tenderness and sympathy as the highest moral virtues; the work included here is a poignant description of a married woman. Abe Kobo, representing the existentialist school, contributes a story written early in his career about the poverty of a young factory girl.

One of the six women writers included is Enchi Fumiko, whose novel *The Waiting Years (see main entry)* describes several women who cannot seem to escape from the uncomfortable roles imposed on them by society. Her story in this collection portrays a girl who follows her mother into the life of a geisha. The stereotyped Japanese view of motherhood is one of unconditional tenderness, protection, sacrifice, and love for her children. The pheasant's shrill cry is said to reflect the mother's concern for her children. Setouchi Harumi explores this image in her story "Pheasant."

Biographical notes are included before each story. A thoughtful introduction describes in detail the Japanese views on the five categories into which the stories are divided and follows the literary and historical development of the authors' works.

1498 Wang Anyi. ***Baotown***. Trans. from Chinese by Martha Avery. Norton 1989. o.p. Fiction.

Rare among the stories and novels of China chosen recently for publication in English, this novel is set far away from the free-for-alls and fanaticisms of political events in big cities like Beijing and Shanghai. Instead it presents a vivid and glowing picture of the joys and tragedies of the very human lives of a small country village.

A handful of poignant portraits are painted; the characters have their own tales to tell, each of which fits into the others like pieces of a puzzle. One episode explores the special relationship of a grandfather and a young boy who die trying to save each other from a flood. There is a young woman who goes north in hard times to look for food and who returns two years later with a two-year-old boy that she "picked up" somewhere. Another incident reveals how the Chinese villagers begin to develop a new consciousness as rumors circulate about a new society, one that threatens to confound the mores and ideals of their traditional life.

The villagers are depicted as merciless in their teasing—a form of social pressure that is usually loving and that can become tantamount to ostracism. But they are also well grounded in tradition, which helps them define their roles and keeps everyone in place. A more recent work by this author is *Brocade Valley* (New Directions, 1992).

1499 Ya Ding. *The Earth Sings*. Trans. from Chinese by Jon Rothschild. Harcourt 1990, $21.95 (0-15-176140-X). 261pp. Fiction.

The story is set in China in the middle of the century, at a time when Mao Zedong is regarded as the Great Helmsman. A young boy goes from the city with his family to live in a small rural village. His father, a loyal and strong party member, is a respected leader. The boy is proud of him and wants to be just like him someday.

Then comes the Cultural Revolution. Everyone has to find someone else to criticize for fear of being criticized himself. The boy's father is accused of putting too much importance on production and growth and not enough on the Revolution. "Does he want us all to turn into bourgeois?" complain the villagers. The father is disgraced and sent away. Such were the consequences of Mao's "Revolution," when people lost their families, their homes, their honor and pride—even their lives. Told through the eyes of an innocent and confused young boy, this poignant novel reveals life in a Chinese small town during a time of tremendous upheaval.

1500 Zhang Chengzhi. *The Black Steed*. Trans. from Chinese. Panda 1990. o.p. Fiction.

The title story is woven around a simple Mongolian folk song, which says that it is possible for a horse to change color after many years. The larger meaning is that a lover met again after many years may also seem to be a different person. The eight verses of the folk song appear as preludes to each tale.

The bittersweet quality of the beauty of love characterizes the first story, in which a girl is sent away to another place to be married while the boy who really loves her stays behind. A similar mood permeates the second tale, "Rivers of the North." In both stories, the Mongolian love of the vastness and beauty of the land seems to provide hope and to melt away the bitterness of lost love.

1501 Zhang Jie. *Heavy Wings*. Trans. from Chinese by Howard Goldblatt. Grove 1989. o.p. Fiction.

Sometimes translated as *Leaden Wings*, this novel exposes the corruption of the Communist Party and the members of the higher echelon who cling to a rigid old ideology to maintain their own positions of privilege, power, and security. Struggling against them are the reformers who want to implement the freedom, justice, and equality that socialism promised to provide.

A staunch socialist, the author feels it is her duty to expose corruption in the party and in society so that socialism can achieve its goals. Also a spokeswoman for women's rights, she comments on women's roles in society and deals with the problems of those changing roles. The story presents people at all levels of society who struggle with problems of romance, politics, and industry, all institutions that were set up to work wonderfully and give people satisfaction but that have become corrupt. As one of her characters says of squabbling next-door neighbors, "They started their lives loving. Why do they now argue all the time?" On many levels, their story is the story of China.

1502 Zhang Jie. *Love Must Not Be Forgotten*. Trans. from Chinese and Intro. by Gladys Yang. China Books 1986, $16.95 (0-8351-1699-9); $8.95 (0-8351-1698-0). 244pp. Fiction.

Zhang Jie is one of the most courageous and popular writers in China today—courageous because she dares to expose the corruption of those in power, and popular because she writes graphically and touchingly about the human side of problems. A fierce speaker on women's issues, she writes with great concern about women and their roles in society today. She believes that much of human misfortune and misery is caused by our lack of ability of communicate and understand each other.

Traditionally in China, women were expected to marry and have children—especially sons—if they hoped to be fulfilled in life. The experience of love outside of marriage was unthinkable. When it was first published, the title story in this collection provoked enormous controversy because in it the author suggests that love—not family, status, or money—is the most important thing in a marriage. Adding fuel to the fire, she further claims that women are within their rights to choose not to marry at all.

Another collection of Zhang Jie's powerful and controversial stories, called *As Long as Nothing Happens Nothing Will* (Grove, 1988), offers more insights into the workings of Chinese society.

1503 Zhang Xianliang. *Half of Man Is Woman*. Trans. from Chinese. Ballantine 1991. o.p. Fiction.

This gripping novel is drawn from events in the author's life. Like the hero, who is a writer, the author spent the decade of China's Cultural Revolution in jail sentenced to hard labor. During this time, the government attempted to control every last aspect of people's lives, including their thoughts; understandably, such conditions obliterated an author's desire and ability to write anything but the "confessions" demanded of prisoners.

This is also a love story. Over the course of a decade, a relationship blooms between the protagonist and a beautiful woman prisoner. Impotence, both as a man and as a poet, threaten his sanity. Struggling with his desire to create but confronted with his inability to succeed, he blames the regime that tells him, "Snuff out this desire to create, . . . know your place and abide by the rules they set." Without his creative power, he knows he will be easier for the regime to control.

Zhang Xianliang has also written a novel, *Getting Used to Dying* (HarperCollins, 1991), in which a similarly autobiographical character must deal for the rest of his life—in China and in the United States, in and out of various women's beds—with "that bullet of fear . . . lodged in his brain." As in *Half of Man Is Woman*, the hero struggles to maintain his creativity even in the face of death. Controversial in China for his frank discussion of feelings, politics, and sexuality, Zhang Xianliang has dared in his writing what few Chinese writers have dared.

1504 Zhu Hong, ed. *The Chinese Western: An Anthology of Short Fiction from Today's China*. Trans. from Chinese. Ballantine 1991, $4.99 (0-345-37358-8). 224pp. Fiction.

The great "West" of China consists mainly of Xinjiang, formerly referred to as Chinese Turkestan. The region was once important for its Silk Road, but in later centuries it fell into economic decline. It is inhabited by central Asian peoples who in culture and language are more Middle Eastern than Chinese; for one thing, they practice Islam. To be sure, there have been ethnic Chinese (known as Han) living in the region for many generations. Many of these residents are descendants of people who were exiled to this Chinese equivalent of Siberia. Other regions considered part of China's West include Tibet, Mongolia, and other areas; each has its own ethnic mix, languages, and customs.

Remote from control by the bureaucracy of Beijing, these regions are comparatively unaffected by the great injunctions and the massive "campaigns" and "struggles" initiated by the central government. Life is a little freer, a little more varied, and a little more lonely for the gregarious Han Chinese, who generally like noise and laughter and large crowds.

These stories, some written by local residents, some by visitors from elsewhere in China, still have a very Chinese tone to them. The characters are concerned with tradition, what the neighbors will think, the suffering of the peasants due to exploitation by various official groups, and their struggle to survive and to discover their dignity. A glossary of terms is appended.

1505 Zhu Hong, ed. *The Serenity of Whiteness: Stories by and about Women in Contemporary China*. Trans. from Chinese. Ballantine 1992. o.p. Fiction.

The women authors represented in this volume have in common their experiences of the years of struggle and transition in the 1930s and 1940s, the idealism of the 1950s, and the disillusionment that followed the Cultural Revolution of the 1960s and 1970s. Most of these stories were written in the 1980s, when even the staunchest Communists were beginning to open up to other ways of thinking and writing.

Before 1949 and the dawn of the Communist regime, depictions of women in Chinese literature were rare. Ding Ling, who began writing in the 1920s, was one of the few authors who created well-rounded female characters; her works are still widely read in China today. After the 1949 Communist victory, however, women characters in literature tended to be reduced to mere symbols and metaphors.

In striking contrast, the women depicted in these gentle, serene stories define what it means to be a human being. They incorporate all the sadness, suffering, and loss that come from enduring hard times. They also reveal what it means to be a woman, especially in dealing the men in their lives. These are not symbols cut from cardboard; they are recognizable people who experience life as human beings and who talk not just about political events but about feelings and ideas.

Many of the writers represented here generally write for a Chinese audience and are not widely known in the West. The translator is a professor of literature and a writer known for her concern with women's issues. A glossary lists special terms used during the Cultural Revolution.

NONFICTION

1506 Barlow, Tani, and Donald N. Lowe. ***Teaching China's Lost Generation***. China Books 1987, $8.95 (0-8351-1818-5). 267pp. Nonfiction.

Early in the 1980s, China began inviting foreign experts to teach in the universities there. The authors of this book are teachers who worked together in Shanghai. During their year-long tenure, they carefully noted all their cultural insights and conversations with locals, sprinkled in some history, and wrote detailed newsletters home. On returning, they turned these letters into a book, with an interesting postscript written in 1987.

Many returning teachers have written this kind of personal account of a Westerner's encounter with Chinese culture. This one seems more comprehensive than most, with fewer accounts of such quotidian minutiae as personal hygiene and greater emphasis on the people encountered.

1507 Barme, Geremie. ***New Ghosts, Old Dreams: Chinese Rebel Voices***. Random 1992, $29.50 (0-8129-1927-0). 515pp. Essays.

The interesting format of this thick book immediately catches the eye. The reader can dive in almost anywhere and find interesting speeches, essays, stories, anecdotes, and poems about the political pros and cons of democracy, socialism, and rebellion.

Conceived as a sequel to Barme's previous work, *Seeds of Fire: Chinese Voices of Conscience* (Farrar, 1990), this collection of voices from the Chinese people contains an even greater variety of story, song, commentary, and protest. The author compares China to a pendulum, swinging back and forth between anarchy and totalitarianism, trying but never quite succeeding to find a system that represents the true voice of the people.

All walks of modern Chinese life are represented here, ranging from teenage break dancers to respected elderly poets. Other themes include dissatisfaction with the cultural scene, political problems, and economic unrest. Even the problem of what to do with Hong Kong is addressed.

A list of translators, an extensive and useful chapter-by-chapter bibliography of recent publications, a detailed list of sources for each chapter, and an index are included.

1508 Belleme, John, and Jan Belleme. ***Culinary Treasures of Japan: The Art of Making and Using Traditional Japanese Foods***. Illus. by Akiko A. Shurtleff. Avery 1992, $17.95 (0-89529-509-1). 248pp. Nonfiction.

To these authors, selecting and preparing food is both an art and a source of worldwide "health, longevity, peace, and social stability." Each of the fourteen chapters in this book is dedicated to the history, development, and preparation of a particular food, from mochi to sashimi; a fifteenth chapter examines traditional food containers. The book presents an array of traditional Japanese cuisine, complete with anecdotes. Each explanatory essay brings us a little closer to an understanding of how food reflects the Japanese way of life.

A large-format paperback with pen-and-ink sketches and a handful of color photographs that illustrate and explain, the book offers a few select recipes for each item discussed.

1509 Benedict, Ruth. ***The Chrysanthemum and the Sword: Patterns of Japanese Culture***. Intro. by Ezra Vogel. Houghton 1989, $10.95 (0-395-50075-3). 324pp. Nonfiction.

The 1989 introduction by Ezra F. Vogel explains the great popularity of this book since it was first published in the 1940s. Benedict wanted to know the whys and wherefores of Japanese behavior and cultural assumptions about propriety, especially during wartime. The appeal to readers of the original edition, Vogel states, lay in the apparent paradox between Japanese politeness, loyalty, and concern for beauty (symbolized by the chrysanthemum) and the perceived Japanese insolence, treachery, and willingness to die (as reflected in the sword). Benedict's main focus was Japanese attitudes toward guilt and shame. She obtained most of her information through painstaking, exacting interviews with Japanese immigrants.

After the war, American attitudes toward Japan became more kindly. The author's descriptions of determined soldiers bound by duty and discipline began to seem exaggerated. But, in retrospect, her study maintains its historical value and continues to offer insights into the Japanese character.

1510 Berry, Scott. ***A Stranger in Tibet: The Adventures of a Wandering Zen Monk***. Illus. Kodansha 1989, $19.95 (0-87011-891-9); $6.95 (0-87011-858-7). 304pp. Nonfiction.

This book is both a biography of an unconventional Japanese Zen Buddhist monk and a description of life in Tibet in the early 1900s. Kawaguchi Ekai was a bit more of an individualist than was tolerable in his Japanese monastery, so early in his career—after teaching himself basic medicine, both Japanese and Western—he began wandering around India, planning eventually to head for the mysterious, alluring—and very forbidden—Tibet.

He knew it would be difficult to enter that realm. So, disguised as a Chinese monk, he spent several years in India and Nepal studying the Chinese and Tibetan languages and preparing himself for his lone and secret invitation; his weapons would not be soldiers and spears but language and culture. His mission succeeded.

In Tibet, word quickly spread of his medical talents, and he was invited to visit many places, both as a doctor and as a monk. He thus was able to make his way around much of Tibet, his route determined only by his own curiosity. Fascinated with the people, the culture, and the religion, he spent fifteen years in Tibet, poking his nose into every corner and recording every detail of the people's lives. In many instances, his descriptions of places or events in Tibet were the best—or the only—ones available until very recently. This book dwells chiefly on Kawaguchi's years in Tibet, although he later returned to Japan, where he spent the last thirty years of his life.

1511 Besher, Alexander. *Pacific Rim Almanac*. Illus. HarperCollins 1991, $19.95 (0-06-273065-7). 512pp. Nonfiction.

This hefty volume contains many things that belong in an almanac: statistics, tables, market charts, and so on. But its real delight lies in the lengthy and anecdotal articles on nearly everything about life in Asia. These highly entertaining, amusing, and informative tidbits range from medical wonders to odd food (for example, no *durian*—a notoriously smelly fruit—is allowed on airlines), from elephants and tigers to smoking and environmental concerns, and unusual ways of dealing with smugglers, criminals, and drug addicts.

Nine appendixes give addresses of universities and Pacific Rim research organizers and lists of investment guides, Asian advertising, marketing and public relations firms, government offices, and so on. An index provides the vital key to this staggering wealth of information on Asia.

1512 Blumberg, Rhoda. *Commodore Perry in the Land of the Shogun*. Illus. Lothrop 1985, $14.95 (0-688-03723-2). 128pp. Nonfiction.

Here is the gift that Robert Burns asked for: "to see ourselves as others see us." In the mid-1800s Japan had been a closed nation for a very long time. Insiders had stayed in, outsiders had stayed out. Then came Commodore Perry, the wedge that eventually broke open Japan to the West.

In the reproductions of contemporary Japanese drawings, black-and-white sketches, and historical photos, we see the Westerner through the eyes of the Japanese. These images are revealing, amusing, and priceless. The text of the work details the arrival of Perry's black ships and gives a blow-by-blow description of the encounter of East and West, the plentiful doubts, accusations, fears, and faux pas on both sides.

Appendixes range from details of gifts and letters to the concluding treaty of Kanagawa. Chapter notes provide much helpful information, and a bibliography and index complete the book.

1513 Blunden, Caroline, and Mark Elvin. *Cultural Atlas of China*. Illus. Facts on File 1983, $45.00 (0-87196-132-6). 240pp. Nonfiction.

Tables, charts, graphs, and well-chosen photographs, as well as many varied maps, fill this beautiful encyclopedic atlas. Detailed essays of every description abound, with topics ranging from the land and its peoples to the art of prehistory. Thorough histories of the dynasties are accompanied by analyses of the cultural achievements of each: language, calligraphy, poetry, philosophies, medicine, mathematics, music, and more. An extensive bibliography in essay form, a gazetteer, and an index complete this comprehensive array of cultural and historical detail about China.

1514 Bo Yang. *The Ugly Chinaman and the Crisis of Chinese Culture*. Trans. from Chinese by Don Cohn. Paul & Co. 1992, $19.95 (1-86373-116-4). 224pp. Essays.

Controversial among Chinese both on the mainland and in Taiwan, and much discussed in the United States as well, this series of articles and lectures by the Chinese poet, historian, and short story writer grew out of a talk he gave at the University of Iowa.

Using the "ugly American" syndrome as his point of departure, the author dredges up all the criticisms of China and its people that have occurred to him in the past several decades. Having spent nearly eight years in a Taiwanese prison for antigovernment activity, he has much to say. His main premise, which he explores in a variety of ways, is that the Chinese people are self-centered and overly concerned with position and face. He claims that they are too narrow-minded and boorish to enter the world scene as a sophisticated, democratic nation. The final third of the book is devoted to responses, pro and con, from other writers. Somewhat surprisingly, perhaps, many commentators not only agree with him but add to his list their own critiques of the Chinese character. On one level, the book is 162 pages of grumbling. On another, the author hopes that the Chinese may take the criticisms to heart and improve their behavior. (Incidentally, just as one does not need to be American to act in an ugly way in another's country, so also one does not need to be Chinese to find oneself described in the pages of this book.)

1515 Bordewich, Fergus M. *Cathay: A Journey in Search of Old China*. Prentice 1991. o.p. Nonfiction.

The author traveled throughout China during his year-long assignment in Beijing as an English-language consultant to a daily newspaper. Having also traveled through much of the Middle East and South Asia, his comparative observations of China bear the marks of a seasoned traveler.

Bordewich provides details about his friends and traveling companions while describing his visits to mountaintop temples and historical sites. Enough anecdotes, history, and local color are included to make this book more than just a personal diary. A useful and lengthy bibliography includes many old and hard-to-find sources as well as more recent ones. There is no index.

1516 Brick, Jean. *China: A Handbook in Intercultural Communication*. National Center for English Language Teaching and Research, Macquarie Univ. (Australia) 1992 (0-85837-719-5). 170pp. Nonfiction.

This intriguing work from Australia is a companion volume to one by Koyama Tomoko *(see main entry)*. The author examines the important differences in Australian and Chinese cultures. Topics covered include how to make friends, how to begin a conversation with a new acquaintance, how to visit the sick, and other aspects of daily life.

Designed as a textbook, the book is divided into sections with classroom tasks involving cultural knowledge quizzes and comparative interviews of Australian and Chinese citizens. Essays on such subjects as friendship, family relationships, position of women, health, concept of history, learning and teaching, and so on provide unusual insight into some of the hidden aspects of China's culture. Even outside the classroom, the cross-cultural issues addressed in the book are interesting to ponder.

1517 Chow, Kit, and Ione Kramer. ***All the Tea in China***. Illus. China Books 1990, $14.95 (0-8351-2194-1). 160pp. Nonfiction.

Tea, and the rituals associated with drinking it, are central to life in China and Japan. Several books have appeared recently that discuss tea and what it reveals about the culture of these countries, their history, and their people.

In this book, maps, drawings, and reproductions of historic prints are sprinkled throughout. Chapter topics include the story of how tea spread all over the world, Chinese tea customs, poems, the teahouse as the center of life, Japanese tea and customs, tea paraphernalia, tea in relation to health, and ways to prepare and serve it. Fifty Chinese teas are described; appendixes include a glossary and an annotated bibliography.

1518 Christopher, Robert C. ***The Japanese Mind***. Fawcett 1984, $10.00 (0-449-90120-3). 320pp. Nonfiction.

This highly readable commentary on what makes the Japanese the way they are is one of the best on this subject, comparable to Ruth Benedict's probing classic *The Chrysanthemum and the Sword (see main entry)*. Christopher's well-researched analysis of Japanese culture includes a comparative discussion of educational systems, family structures, and values. The author examines the way Japan adopts elements of Western culture and addresses the geisha issue, social protocols, class attitudes toward foreigners, and myriad other topics.

1519 Clayre, Alasdair. ***The Heart of the Dragon***. Houghton 1985. o.p. Nonfiction.

In 1980 the British Broadcasting Corporation began work on a film documentary of China. Just at that time, China was beginning to open up to foreign presence after the Cultural Revolution. The resulting 200-plus hours of film footage were condensed into eleven hour-long programs for TV. This book incorporates photographs from that series plus a text that expands on the script.

Each chapter of the book parallels one of the episodes and explores an important aspect of life in modern China. For example, the chapter called "Remembering" presents a historical and a geographic tour of important places. "Believing" discusses Buddhism, Taoism, and Confucianism and examines the place of religion in society. Other chapters include "Marrying," "Eating," "Living," "Working," "Correcting" (which deals with the penal system), and "Creating" (describing the fine arts). The chapter on "Mediating" discusses the care of children and old people and the ways that members of society are controlled, while "Trading" involves China's historical and modern-day ventures into the world beyond its borders.

In all the chapters, the general descriptions are brought to life through pictures and interviews with individuals and families. The result is a personal glimpse into the mind and heart of a vast and complex country. A detailed chronological table places events in their global context. Notes to the chapters and an index complete the work.

1520 Colcutt, Martin, and others. ***Cultural Atlas of Japan***. Illus. Facts on File 1988, $45.00 (0-8160-1927-4). 240pp. Nonfiction.

This book first details Japan's geographical regions, then examines the main historical periods. Each section is accompanied by various maps and well-selected color photographs of modern scenes and of paintings, sculpture, and ceramics. The section on Kamakura (medieval times) illustrates the world of the samurai and Zen gardens. The premodern age of Edo is also well illustrated with photos. Essays address many aspects of Japanese culture, including the tea ceremony, netsuke, Kabuki theater, castles, and woodblock prints from the Floating World. An extensive bibliography in essay form, a list of Japan's rulers, a glossary, a gazetteer, and an index complete this beautiful reference work.

Conze, Edward. ***Buddhism: Its Essence and Development***.
See entry 1398.

1521 Dalby, Liza C. ***Geisha***. Illus. Univ. of California Pr. 1983. o.p. Nonfiction.

One of the most stereotyped and misunderstood images of Japan in the West is the geisha. To understand the geisha and her role within society, Dalby, an English woman, spent fourteen months in Japan interviewing geisha—and ultimately became a geisha herself. This account, including history, culture, and photographs, helps to dignify the image of the geisha in Western eyes.

Literally, the term *geisha* means "artist." The first geisha, in the 1600s, were men—jesters or drummers hired to entertain at parties with their lively and risqué banter. Today, of course, the geisha are women, but in many ways they fulfill a similar and integral role. To explain that role, the author provides commentary on many aspects of Japanese society, such as the importance of humor, male-female relationships (which differ from those in the West), dress, food, business, and religion.

Within geisha society today, the students and elders have a familial relationship. The girls refer to themselves as sisters and to their elders as mothers. They study long hours every day and are "on stage" with their performances every night. They must learn to play the shamisen and they take lessons in drumming, singing, and dancing lessons. They also study poetry. The schedule is rigorous and the life is not easy. But, as the author indicates, times are changing; suffering in the name of art—even the art of being a geisha—is no longer so fashionable these days.

1522 Davis, Hadland F. ***Myths and Legends of Japan***. Repr. of 1913 ed. Illus. Gordon 1976, $59.95 (0-8490-2328-9); Dover $9.95 (0-486-27045-9). 432pp. Nonfiction.

Despite its title, this encyclopedia of essays and art criticism, originally published in 1913, is not limited to the mythology of Japan. It also addresses such topics as expression in the faces of women portrayed in Japanese prints, the Japanese love of nature and gardens, human sacrifice in ancient times, trees, dolls, the legends behind festivals, the tea ceremony, and many versions of historical legends. The sources of many of Lafcadio Hearn's famous stories can be found here. (See the main entry for Hearn's *Exotics and Retrospectives*.) A list of gods and goddesses, a bibliography, and an index complete the book.

1523 Goldstein, Melvyn C., and Cynthia M. Beall. ***Nomads of Western Tibet: The Survival of a Way of Life.*** Illus. with photos. Univ. of California Pr. 1990, $52.00 (0-520-07210-3); $20.00 (0-520-07211-1). 200pp. Nonfiction.

This volume combines photography with a general text about the Pala nomads of Western Tibet. The authors offer a first-person narrative, beginning with a description of their arrival in nomad country. In subsequent chapters, they discuss nomadic pastoralism, the nomadic economy and the cycle of annual migration, the importance of horses and livestock in this community, and the lifestyle of these people. They also describe the changes that have occurred since the nomads came under the rule of China in 1959, the economic and social effects on the region of China's Cultural Revolution, and China's policy toward Tibet since 1976, when the Revolution ended. The photographs are exquisite. Included are notes, a glossary, and an index.

MHT

1524 Hartzell, Richard W. ***Harmony in Conflict: Active Adaptation to Life in Present Day Chinese Society.*** Caves 1991 (957-606-001-X). 713pp. Nonfiction.

This lengthy but fascinating and highly readable book explores popular Chinese philosophy, linguistics, and daily life in fine and well-researched detail. Chapters address such intriguing subjects as eating and banqueting. The art of being a guest contains a score of subdivisions, including dieting in China and Chinese sanitary habits. The chapter on "Opportunities and Obstacles" addresses money problems, smog problems, problems of translating poetry, and problems teaching English to locals. Other topics include "Comparative Ideals of Obedience" and "Face Saving as a Way of Life." This great array of cultural topics will appeal to the general reader as well as to the more serious scholar or traveler.

An explanatory appendix of confusing terms, chapter notes, a bibliography, and an index are included.

1525 Hearn, Lafcadio. ***Exotics and Retrospectives.*** Repr. of 1898 ed. Illus. Irvington 1972, $36.50 (0-8398-0774-0). 299pp. Essays.

Shunning the hustle and bustle of the capitalistic world, Hearn retreated to a place devoted to quiet beauty: Japan at the turn of the century. Among his many writings are journalistic essays recording his thoughts and experiences while ensconced in that country, which at the time was much farther away from the West, geographically and psychologically, than it is now. He also wrote original stories as well as many retellings of Japanese folk and fairy tales, such as his popular *Kwai Dan* (*Strange Tales*), which was adapted into a successful film.

In this book of essays, Hearn describes his trek to the summit of Mount Fuji, and tells the stories of other pilgrims, including a meteorologist who was determined to spend the winter on Fuji's peak in a wooden hut with no fire. The custom of keeping crickets caged to enjoy their music is described, along with a variety of poets, poems, and folktales about the insects. Drawings of the critters are helpfully provided.

There are other gems here as well. A Zen tale from China prompts Hearn to meditate on the nature of his soul. A nearby temple inspires a discourse on Buddhist thought and writings. A chapter on frogs expresses the Japanese appreciation of the small things of nature. Other essays on beauty, youth, sadness, the aesthetics of a certain shade of blue, and the forces of the supernatural all reflect Hearn's complete immersion in the world of Japan.

1526 Herdan, Innes. *The Pen and the Sword: Literature and Revolution in Modern China*. Pref. by Brian Power. Humanities Pr. 1992, $49.95 (0-86232-329-0); $17.50 (0-86232-330-4). 192pp. Nonfiction.

In previous eras, literature in China was traditionally considered an individual pursuit whose purpose was to further the Buddhist quest for perfection of self. Any involvement of literature with politics or other mundane matters was considered unwholesome. In the twentieth century, however, and especially since the Communist victory in 1949, literature was pressed into the service of political ends. Individual creativity was jettisoned in favor of promulgating official doctrine. A somewhat scholarly treatise, this compact history of and commentary on Chinese literature and its authors is a valuable contribution to the field.

1527 Hidaka Rokuro. *The Price of Affluence: Dilemmas of Contemporary Japan*. Kodansha 1984. o.p. Nonfiction.

Written by a Japanese man who was born and raised in China, this book is a warning of the consequences of Japan's embrace of the materialism that came with Western industrialization and technology.

He identifies an intriguing pattern: Japan's shift after the war from nationalistic patriotism to what he terms "economic patriotism." According to the author, this shift caused Japan to evolve quickly into a controlled society. Under such a structure, people are not oppressed by an iron-fisted government but by their own perceived need to follow the path laid out for them by society so that they might obtain "the good life." This, he observes, has led to a lack of creativity and choice and has made life in Japan relatively uniform. Because of the narrow range of lifestyles, he says, a sense of purposelessness is growing among the Japanese. The author parallels Japan's fate to that of other technologically advanced countries that seem interested primarily in the consumption of material goods. He describes vividly the consequences of having too much and offers a discussion of social alternatives. In the process, he paints a picture of what a well-adjusted society should be, thus giving his book universal importance.

1528 Hopkirk, Peter. *Trespassers on the Roof of the World: The Secret Exploration of Tibet*. Kodansha 1994, $13.00 (1-56836-050-9). 288pp. Nonfiction.

Tibet has long had a reputation for being intriguing, mysterious, and very forbidden. This century and the last have been one long tale of outsiders trying to get in and insiders trying to keep them out. This book tells those tales.

The prologue hints at the variety of intrepid adventurers whose stories are told in this book. The first chapter gives geographical, historical, anthropological, cultural, and religious background. The rest of the book consists of tales of travelers, soldiers, spies, and missionaries from the mid-nineteenth century to the present. The first to open Tibet to Western eyes were Indian spies (*pundits*) who were hired by the British to collect geographic information; these spies generated the first maps of the area.

The various American, French, British, Russian, and Japanese adventurers who later explored the region were each intent on being the first to reach the fabled city of Lhasa. Later came a six-nation scramble to possess the Buddhist art treasures of the monasteries along the old Silk Road. Several middle-aged British women undertook the journey so that they might preach the Christian gospel to the Tibetans.

A few black-and-white photographs of the explorers accompany their tales. The book ends with the Chinese occupation and the invasion of the Red Guards. There is a bibliography of principal sources and an index. The whole book provides most entertaining reading as well as information on a country about which, even today, little is known.

1529 Howe, Russell W. *The Koreans: Passion and Grace*. Illus. Harcourt 1988, $12.95 (0-15-647185-X). 272pp. Nonfiction.

This conversational description of South Korea begins with a detailed account of a typical day in a Korean family. A few surprises no doubt await Western readers: For example, the daughter-in-law, barely out of high school, is seen to be essentially a servant for her husband's mother. Seniority, status, and protocol seem, as in Japan, to hold a far greater place in Korean society than in the West.

The author's goal is to show how Korea differs from other East Asian cultures. Each minute aspect of life in Korea is analyzed and compared to life in Japan and the United States. The author underscores the fact that the Korean systems of values and beliefs are dramatically different from those in neighboring countries. Some rather dry black-and-white photographs appear here and there. The text is marred by occasional generalizations that thoughtful readers will take with a grain of salt. At different times, for example, the author labels Koreans as "a nation of hypochondriacs," as "a nation of footloose people," and as "a polite but not inherently a modest people." Nevertheless, the book is written with humor and style and gives us a graphic idea of the Korean character, at least from one writer's point of view.

The chapters include analyses of the contrasts between city life and country life, the relationships between men and women, commentary on the importance of alcohol in the culture, as well as studies of art, acupuncture, and the place of animism (nature worship). A bibliography and an index are appended.

1530 Ishikawa Takashi. *Kokoro: The Soul of Japan*. East Publications 1986. o.p. Essays.

These thirteen essays on Japanese history, religion, and culture are somewhat more serious than the recently popular and playful books that try to explain Japan to Westerners. The author begins with theories about the origins of the Japanese people and the Japanese language, which are still subjects of dispute. Also included in this historical section is a discussion of the many man-made hills that turned out to be the tombs of ancient local rulers. Ishikawa examines the contents of the tombs as a way to describe the beliefs and values of bygone eras.

One chapter explains the origins of Shinto ("The Way of the Gods"), the ancient traditional Japanese religion. The author describes in detail the *kami* (spirits) and the shrines at which they are worshipped, and explains *matsuri*, which are the ceremonies for inviting *kami* or other honored guests to the village. This is followed by chapters on Buddhism and Taoism, Japan's other prominent religions.

The last third of the book contains probing essays on artistic subjects such as the traditional use of color, flower arranging (*ikebana*), the tea ceremony (*chanoyu*), gardens, and music. Two appendixes include commentary on Noh drama by Zeami, a fifteenth-century master, and the oldest description of Japan, written by a Chinese historian in the third century A.D.

1531 Kataoka, Hiroko C. *Japanese Cultural Encounters and How to Handle Them*. NTC 1990, $9.95 (0-8442-8531-5). 119pp. Nonfiction.

This is an amusing, clever, and useful collection of fifty-six brief vignettes about recently arrived Americans who try to fit into Japanese society. Each potentially embarrassing situation or social blunder is presented in a paragraph or two. Then, in multiple-choice format, four possible actions or responses are given. One is the Japanese socially correct choice, and the others are common wrong assumptions or mistakes that Westerners are prone to make. Some of the answers are downright ridiculous, even to the untrained eye, but a sense of humor is a necessary tool for Westerners as they attempt to understand and adapt to another culture. A brief and enlightening discussion of each possibility is given in the last part of the book.

1532 Kim Jae-un. *The Koreans: Their Mind and Behavior*. Trans. from Korean by Kim Kyong-dong. Kyobo Book Centre 1991. o.p. Nonfiction.

The author and the translator, brothers and university professors who have studied and taught extensively in the United States and Korea, are also prolific writers in the fields of sociology and psychology. In their opinion, the material available on Korea and Koreans in English is sadly lacking, and so they offer this book as an introduction to the subject. The work describes cultural traits and values and presents the results of psychological studies and surveys. Historical anecdotes help explain present-day Korean behaviors and beliefs. An extensive bibliography includes books in Korean, English, and Japanese. These readable articles will be informative for readers hoping to develop their understanding of the Korean people.

1533 Klein, Leonard S. *Far Eastern Literature, Twentieth Century*. State Mutual Book & Periodical 1989, $59.00 (0-685-45093-7). 197pp. Nonfiction.

Essays, historical commentary, and literary critiques of writings from all over East Asia are arranged alphabetically by country. Biographical sketches are included, as well as complete lists of works and bibliographies for each author. Although scholarly and a bit pedantic, this book is nevertheless recommended for its usefulness as an overview reference.

1534 Koyama Tomoko. *Japan: A Handbook in Intercultural Communication*. National Center for English Language Teaching and Research, Macquarie Univ. (Australia) 1992. 170pp. Nonfiction.

This Australian book, a companion to *China* by Jean Brick, compares Australian and Japanese cultural differences in making friends, talking with new acquaintances, offering gifts, apologizing, expressing gratitude, and other important behaviors that people usually perform without thinking but which can be fraught with peril when they involve individuals from different backgrounds.

Designed as a classroom text, each section presents learning exercises involving cultural knowledge quizzes and comparative interviews of people from Australia and Japan. There is a large section on features of the Japanese language. Other essays compare such topics as living in society, defining self in society, the importance of age, education, and family. The book will be enlightening to many general readers, whether or not they are Australian and whether they use the book in a classroom setting.

1535 Kristof, Nicholas, and Sheryl Wu Dunn. *China Wakes: The Struggle for the Soul of a Rising Power*. Random 1994, $25.00 (0-8129-2252-2). 501pp. Nonfiction.

The authors are a husband-and-wife team of correspondents for the *New York Times* who covered China between 1988 and 1993. They won a joint Pulitzer Prize for their coverage of the 1989 Tiananmen Square democracy demonstrations and the subsequent massacre of students by the army. This book is an account of their years in China.

The authors believe that China is in the midst of a revolutionary transformation from an essentially fascist regime, in which the state restricts individual freedom and heavily participates in a market economy, to a society in which individuals are able to assert control over the economic, sexual, and intellectual aspects of their own lives without state interference. They document the continuing brutalities of the government and the brave efforts of dissidents to press for democratic alternatives. Through an engaging series of biographical sketches, the authors tell stories of Chinese men and women who are in effect undermining state power by making money, producing innovative art, or living hedonistically. Other parts of the text highlight the obstacles to China's continued progress toward economic prosperity and political reform. The authors conclude with an optimistic vision of a wealthy, democratic, and militarily powerful China of the twenty-first century. **RL**

1536 Kuck, Loraine. *The World of the Japanese Garden: From Chinese Origins to Modern Landscape Art*. Illus. with photos by Takeji Iwamiya. Weatherhill 1968, $52.50 (0-8348-0029-2). 416pp. Nonfiction.

This large volume is recommended for its copious information on the importance of gardens in Japanese culture, its historical notes, and its illustrative photographs. Based on a 1941 edition, the book was expanded in 1968 to include changes in Japan following World War II. A number of more recent how-to and coffee-table books are available, but this one includes so much historical and cultural commentary that it remains a major work on the subject.

The introductory chapter begins with a discussion of the development of the garden in the world at large. Readers are shown the reasons behind the differences in the development of the European garden and the garden in ancient Egypt, in the Near East, and in India. The next three chapters detail the development of the garden in China and include general history and a brief history of art and painting as well. The section on Japanese gardens begins with a discussion of islands and lakes, which some styles of gardens imitate. To these are added rocks and "mountains." There are chapters on meditative Zen gardens, on tea gardens, and on the Western influence during the Meiji period (1867–1912), which introduced straight lines into the design of Japanese gardens. Following are many pages of black-and-white photographs. Color photographs are sprinkled liberally throughout the book. A section of notes, a bibliography, and an index add to the usefulness of this classic tome.

1537 Lee O-young. *The Compact Culture: The Japanese Tradition of Smaller Is Better*. Trans. from Korean by Robert N. Huey. Illus. Kodansha 1992, $6.95 (4-77001-643-3). Nonfiction.

This compendium of essays explores Japan's fascination with the miniature. In passing, it discusses many items of daily life, including cars, bowls, toys, parts of houses, poems, the Noh mask, bonsai, and modern technology, including computer parts, TVs, and transistor radios.

The author, who is Korean, describes some telling differences between Korean and Japanese culture. In the Korean language, for instance, there is a word similar to *king*, as in *king-size*, which is used to indicate something overly large. But there is no corresponding word to describe something that is smaller than usual. In contrast, the Japanese language has many such words. Also from Japan come many fairy tales about miniature heroes, such as those who go to sea in a bowl using chopsticks for oars but who nevertheless are powerful and crafty beings. There are a few black-and-white photographs and an index.

1538 Lee, Peter H., and others, eds. *Sources of Korean Tradition*. Columbia Univ. Pr. 1993, $49.50 (0-231-07912-5). 640pp. Nonfiction.

Although presented as a scholarly work, this book is highly readable and full of interesting historical, social, and religious facts and anecdotes about Korea. Arranged in chronological order, the brief and conversational essays discuss historical figures, the invention of rain gauges and the Korean alphabet, Korean medicine, and stories revealing the origins of cultural practices that continue to the present day.

1539 Lindquist, Cecelia. *China: Empire of Living Symbols*. Trans. from Swedish by Joan Tate. Merloyd Lawrence 1991. o.p. Nonfiction.

Using written Chinese characters as the springboard for her discussion of Chinese history and daily life, the author has gathered an immense amount of information and anecdote. The book is also a serious study of the Chinese written word. Organized somewhat like a dictionary, a page or two is devoted to each character, which is printed in different shades of black and brown to indicate the historical period in which the character first appeared. Black-and-white photographs of objects or scenes of daily life support the description of the character and elucidate its definition. For example, the mountain peak in one photograph is clearly reflected in the written character that represents the word "mountain." Similarly, seeing a picture of a cart makes it easier to understand how the pictograph that means "cart" evolved.

Not every character has such a direct one-to-one relationship with its referent. Etymologies can be somewhat speculative. However, they allow an easier access to the study of these elusive characters, especially for Westerners. A section of color photos toward the end adds to the book's value. Both scholarly and yet of great appeal to a lay reader interested in present-day China, the book is both well documented and attractively produced. An extensive bibliography and index complete the book.

1540 Lord, Bette B. *Legacies: A Chinese Mosaic.* Knopf 1990, $19.95 (0-394-58325-6). 245pp. Nonfiction.

This book contains what its author describes as "the most precious gifts a writer could receive . . . the uncensored stories" of her friends' lives. Lord, who lived in China for over three years as the wife of an ambassador, passes along these poignant, heart-wrenching stories and adds to them her own insights. The life stories, anecdotes, and confessions range from comments on the Tiananmen Square incident to harrowing tales of the injustices perpetrated against innocent victims during the uncertainty and terror of the Cultural Revolution.

1541 McFarland, H. Neill. *Daruma: The Founder of Zen in Japanese Art and Popular Culture.* Illus. with photos. Kodansha 1987. o.p. Nonfiction.

This book presents the evolution over the centuries of the Daruma, the physical representation of the founder of Zen. The story begins with the great Indian patriarch Bodhidharma, who brought Buddhism first to China, where it was known as *Chan*, and then to Japan, where the word evolved into *Zen*. Eventually the Daruma became the ubiquitous roly-poly figure found in Japanese toy stores. His image is used as a good luck symbol on kites, in logos, and on other folk objects. The Daruma has been represented historically in prints, paintings, and sculpture. He is even found in the temples, such as the famous Shao Lin Temple in China, where martial arts are taught

This book looks beyond the whimsical image to explore the historical personage, the legends, and the symbolism in serious paintings and in folk crafts. The author also describes the movement in Japan to restore the Daruma's ideals and values as relevant to modern society. Black-and-white photos throughout and a few color photos enhance and clarify the text in this large, beautiful volume. References and an index are included.

1542 Maitland, Derek. *Setting Sails: A Tribute to the Chinese Junk.* Illus. 1981. o.p. Nonfiction.

Long a symbol of China, the distinctive boat known as the junk is presented in this large, beautiful book. Through its use of historical and cultural detail, the wide-ranging text describes the boat's origins, features, and advantages. Photographs reveal the design and construction of junks that are used on rivers, lakes, or the open sea.

The author reviews the history of seafaring China, focusing on the use of the junk as a sailing ship capable of traversing vast distances. Readers learn that Cheng Ho, a sailor in the 1400s, maneuvered his gigantic vessels to sites as remote as Africa. A lively section describes the exploits of junk-piloting pirates.

Color and black-and-white photos depict both historic ships and those of the present day and reveal the patterns of life and work on board. A bibliography and an index complete the work.

1543 Martin, Helmut, and Jeffrey Kinkley, eds. ***Modern Chinese Writers: Self-Portrayals***. M. E. Sharpe 1992, $55.00 (0-87332-816-7); $22.00 (0-87332-817-5). 424pp. Essays.

This book offers a scholarly overview of the literary development and philosophies of over forty modern authors of Chinese descent. Some of the writers live in China, but others are natives or residents of other countries around the world. This book is not an anthology but a collection of interviews and interpretive essays on such topics as the nature of the creative process and the role of reportage as literature.

The editors provide an overview and an introductory look at the impact of twentieth-century political forces on Chinese writing. A brief biography and a list of major works precede each essay.

1544 Merson, John. ***The Genius That Was China***. Illus. Overlook 1990, $29.95 (0-87951-397-7). 288pp. Nonfiction.

Until a few centuries ago, China was far ahead of Europe technologically. This large, visually attractive book reveals how China and her monarchs failed to maintain that lead. With the depth of a reference work, the volume discusses the political and cultural forces that contributed to China's technical stagnation. The reader learns, for example, that in Chinese culture there was no parallel to the Western concept of "progress."

Beautifully illustrated with historical paintings, period drawings, and modern color photographs, the text features excerpts from literary and historical sources, Oriental as well as Occidental.

1545 Morrison, Hedda. ***A Photographer in Old Peking***. Illus. with photos by the author. Oxford Univ. Pr. 1986, $29.95 (0-19-584056-9). 278pp. Photos/Essays.

The masterly black-and-white photographs in this large book were taken in Beijing (then called Peking) between 1933 and 1946 by Hedda Morrison. In the introduction, the reader learns that Morrison worked in a photo studio in the Chinese capital for five years. She stayed in the country another decade, during which time she traveled widely.

These artistic images present portraits of people from all walks of life: toy sellers, litter collectors, beggars, vendors pulling carts loaded with fruit or dumplings, merchants spreading their wares on a cloth on the ground. Here, too, are temple carvings, streets crowded with men in long gowns, rickshaws, and weddings—priceless shadows of a now-vanished way of life.

The informative captions and essays offer additional insight into the culture of Beijing. Chapters focus on such features as walls, palaces, parks, temples, street life, food and entertainment, calligraphy and other arts, and views of life in the countryside. The book is a tribute both to a wonderful city and to a fine photographer.

1546 Nahm, Andrew C. *A Panorama of Five Thousand Years: Korean History.* 2nd rev. ed. Hollym 1989, $24.50 (0-930878-23-X). 123pp. Nonfiction.

Easy reading and lots of photos and other illustrations make this wide-ranging survey of historical information suitable for the junior high or high school level. It is also interesting general reading for the lay person.

1547 Nelson, Randy, ed. *The Overlook Martial Arts Reader: Classic Writings on Philosophy and Technique.* Overlook 1989, $19.95 (0-87951-347-0); $14.95 (0-87951-459-0). 416pp. Essays.

The essays in this unique collection are from the pens of such writers as Lafcadio Hearn, the nineteenth-century folklorist; Curt Singer, a noted observer of Asian culture; and Maxine Hong Kingston, the popular novelist. The pieces primarily explore the martial arts in Japan, but there is also some reference to Chinese forms such as Tai Ji Chuan. Through analyses of the history and development of the various disciplines, the essays address such topics as the impact of *bushido*—"the warrior way"—on Japanese attitudes over the past seven centuries, the preference for swords over firearms, and the role of women.

The book presents many historical anecdotes regarding the learning and practice of the various martial arts, about the masters and the students, and about the truths expressed through the practice. Paradoxically, the essence of most martial disciplines is to *avoid* fighting. The names of the styles translate into such surprisingly mild terms as "the gentle way," "spiritual harmony," and "giving way." The training students receive applies to social interactions, business, education—virtually every aspect of life. Even today, businessmen study the ancient classic *The Book of Five Rings* by Musashi, a Japanese swordsman and folk hero, to pick up pointers on strategy.

An extensive topical bibliography provides a useful, though somewhat dated, reading list.

1548 Osamu Mizutami. *Japanese: The Spoken Language in Japanese Life.* Trans. from Japanese by Jane Ashby. Japan Times 1990 (4-7890-0161-X). 180pp.

Culture is like oxygen—a vital element of life that constantly surrounds us and that we take in without thinking. In any culture, people share certain assumptions about what constitutes good or bad behavior. This intriguing book shows that, in Japan, many of those cultural assumptions derive directly from the structure and use of the Japanese language.

The author, a longtime teacher of Japanese as a foreign language, describes different social situations in which language plays a critical role. Not surprisingly, many of these situations involve consideration for others. For example, people in Japan tend to express their choices indirectly, whereas people from the Western countries are usually more outspoken. Other linguistic issues involve humility and respect, social status, and saving face.

While readers with some knowledge of Japanese will benefit from the author's analysis, even those who have no prior knowledge of the language will find the book readable and interesting and will come away with a deeper understanding of Japanese society.

1549 Pan Ling. *In Search of Old Shanghai*. Joint Publg. 1983 (962-04-0195-6). 143pp. Nonfiction.

Although the author claims this is not a guidebook, it has many similar elements, such as maps, historical photos, modern color photos, a section on history, advice on where to go and what to see, and descriptions of how the city has changed.

In the century prior to the Communist victory of 1949, Old Shanghai was an odd mixture: licentious, cosmopolitan, avant garde, and corrupt—thrilling, but not very Chinese. Today, much of what gave Shanghai its wild reputation on the world scene is gone, swept away by the winds of Communist change. Shanghai also suffered during the Cultural Revolution, along with the rest of the country. This book describes the city as it was and compares it to the way it is now. The text regales us with historical anecdotes, and black-and-white photos present a picture of life in Shanghai today. A note on sources is followed by an index.

Pan Ling (whose name is sometimes rendered as Pan Lynn) has written a number of other books on China, including *Sons of the Yellow Emperor: A History of the Chinese Diaspora* (Kodansha, 1994), *Tracing It Home: A Chinese Journey* (Kodansha, 1994), and *Shanghai: The Paris of the Orient* (NTC, 1993). Many of her writings are based on her own experiences, but her impressions are more historical and factual than personal.

1550 Parsons, Frances M. *I Didn't Hear the Dragon Roar*. Illus. by Ahn Vu. Gallaudet 1988, $17.95 (0-930323-41-6). 251pp. Nonfiction.

This is as much a portrait of a remarkable woman as it is a travelogue through China. Middle-aged and hearing impaired, Parsons traveled in China—alone and "not first class"—in the years when the country was just beginning to open up again to foreign travelers. Warned to try only three weeks, she decided on six and stayed for twelve.

Honest observations of China's tourist spots are intermingled with tales of frustration at being a single traveler. She makes new friends and meets many types of people, the helpful as well as the apathetic. Having located schools for the deaf and other hearing-impaired people, she compares the various signing differences, intricacies, and problems in communication she found in different parts of China.

Her travels took her as far west as Kashgar (near the Afghanistan border in Xinjiang), Tibet, and Mongolia, as well as all through China proper and then out through Nepal. She maintains throughout her travels the three P's of vital importance to any lone traveler in China: politeness, persistence, and patience. An edition of this book is available in Braille (William A. Thomas, Braille Bookstore, 1990).

1551 Picken, Stuart D. B. ***Buddhism, Japan's Cultural Identity***. Kodansha 1982. o.p. Nonfiction.

Tracing Buddhism from its birth in India to its passage through various places in China and its transformation in Japan, this large-format, thin book of fine photographs and essays provides a detailed history of Buddhism and its present-day practice.

Essays include descriptions of the various sects, funeral rites, grave visiting, family altars, temples, and the basis of the Japanese character in Buddhism. The author explains Buddhist philosophy, literature, and art; describes the Buddhist saints; and reveals the connections between Buddhism and the traditional animistic Japanese religion of Shinto (The Way of the Gods). The ancient message of Indian Buddhism is echoed in the modern Japanese form: "We can learn to enjoy life in this world while retaining only a limited attachment to it." Most interesting are the discussions that explore the connections between Buddhism and the Japanese character. The book includes a bibliography, index, and glossary.

1552 Pihl, Marshall R., ed. ***Listening to Korea: A Korean Anthology***. Praeger 1973. o.p. Essays.

This book brings together writings of different genres—short stories, articles, essays, personal narratives—to explore the hearts and minds of the Korean people. The first part is a political statement about the attitudes of Koreans about their own history and about neighboring countries, particularly Japan and China; Korea has a special affection for China, which it sees as the "bearer of our culture."

Succeeding parts discuss the role of the press and writers in Korean society. Intellectuals have always spoken out on social issues, though usually they have little influence within the political sphere. Some of the well-written fictional works deal with the Korean War or with the changes the war produced during the decade that followed. Later stories present the attitudes of Koreans toward the loud and expensive but opportunity-laden city and the rustic, peaceful countryside of their ancestral homes. Others present the traditional and changing concerns of youth and old age, which are different from those of the West. An introduction gives a good historical overview. Biographical sketches at the end introduce the scholars, writers, and poets who contributed these essays and stories.

Pihl is also an editor of a newer anthology, *Land of Exile: Contemporary Korean Fiction* (M. E. Sharpe, 1993).

Rahula, Walpola. ***What the Buddha Taught***.
See entry 1420.

1553 Reid, Daniel P. ***Chinese Herbal Medicine***. Illus. Shambhala 1987, $20.00 (0-87773-398-8). 180pp. Nonfiction.

Chinese herbal medicine is a discipline over 5,000 years old. In the West, interest in this field has grown steadily over the past several decades. Herbalists and acupuncturists now work alongside Western practitioners in some hospitals, and private clinics devoted to Eastern medical ways are springing up all over. Often, when Western doctors shrug their shoulders, Chinese medicine may offer an alternative.

This large-format book gives a historical survey of herbalism as practiced in China from the dawn of its history. A separate chapter outlines the premises and principles of herbal medicine, which are quite different from anything practiced in the West. Other chapters describe the practice of herbal medicine today, including the growing and processing of the herbs, acupuncture, suction cups, and moxibustion (the burning of moxa, a soft downy material, on the skin for therapeutic purposes).

Nearly half the book discusses the herbs themselves, the effects of their use, and the ailments they treat. A few sample prescriptions and recipes for teas and food follow. Intriguing sketches, historic prints, and color photographs of herbs are sprinkled throughout the text, and a bibliography and index are included.

1554 Reischauer, Edwin. ***My Life Between Japan and America***. HarperCollins 1986, $22.95 (0-06-039054-9). 416pp. Nonfiction.

Besides being the most highly respected spokesman for Japan in America today, Reischauer's life of devotion to Japan is a truly inspiring story. Born in Japan to missionary parents, he spent his childhood there, coming to the United States only in his late teens to attend college. After earning his doctorate degree from Harvard, he served as U.S. ambassador to Japan for five years during the early 1960s. Since then he has been a professor of Japanese studies and a non-professional diplomat who has played an important role in cementing the friendship between the Japanese and the Americans. His goal has been to present the Japanese point of view to the American public to increase understanding and good will.

This book is more a personal statement than a political or historical analysis and is readable and accessible to a general audience. Other books by Reischauer, including *The Japanese Today: Change and Continuity* (Harvard Univ. Pr., 1995) delve more deeply into Japanese culture.

1555 Richardson, Hugh E. ***Tibet and Its History***. Shambhala 1984. o.p. Nonfiction.

Straight history written with a clever twist—scholarly though very readable—this long book is accompanied by a sprinkling of rather unusual black-and-white photographs. The book begins with a general background discussing geography, climate, religion, social organization, and government. There is also a brief review of Tibetan history up to the eighteenth century. The bulk of the work, however, describes events since 1720 and devotes considerable attention the modern relationship of Tibet with China and India. The appendix includes various treaties and agreements; a chronological table comparing historical events and dynasties in Tibet, Mongolia, and China; notes to chapters; a select bibliography; and an index.

1556 Richie, Donald. ***A Taste of Japan***. Illus. Kodansha 1993, $13.00 (4-77001-707-3). 112pp. Nonfiction.

Based on a series of magazine articles, this book presents the context of Japanese cuisine, how it has developed in Japanese history, how it fits into modern Japanese life, and what it reveals about the people and their culture. The Japanese regard the presentation of food as a fine art. They pay great attention to the balance of color and shape. Round foods, for instance, are presented in square dishes. The texture, as distinct from the taste, of the food is carefully considered and must be balanced.

The book describes both daily fare and delicacies, presenting their histories, steps in preparation, and the cultural amenities involved. Sketches and photographs in color and black and white enhance the reader's understanding of Japanese eating habits and culture relating to food.

1557 Salisbury, Harrison E. ***The New Emperors: China in the Era of Mao and Deng***. Little, Brown 1992, $24.95 (0-316-80910-1); Avon $12.50 (0-380-72025-6). 576pp. Nonfiction.

This work presents the personalities and private lives of the Chinese Communist leaders, concentrating on Mao Zedong and Deng Xiaoping, who governed China much as did the emperors of old. He exposes many of the failings of Mao and explores the complex relationship between Mao and Deng.

The book notes that, like some other Chinese rulers, Mao emerged from the peasant class. Although certain emperors were able to rise above their rude origins, Mao's peasant background contributed to his failings and shortcomings as a leader. For example, he was more interested in the "mobilization of the masses" than in running the country efficiently. His dabblings in drugs and pornography were notorious. His paranoia (probably well-founded) of his colleagues and fellow leaders led to strained relationships and a bizarre succession of power.

In preparing to write this book, Salisbury interviewed many people and consulted documents, memoirs, and other writings. As a journalist, he has developed a writing style with wide popular appeal, and his reporter's instincts allow him to recognize and take advantage of political opportunity. His writing is all the more convincing for being so well researched, and it is fascinating to watch the emperor being dethroned. One of the major Western commentators on China and the Soviet Union, Salisbury has authored a number of other works, including *The Long March* (HarperCollins, 1985) and *Tiananmen Diary: Thirteen Days in June* (Little, Brown, 1989).

1558 Sands, William Franklin. ***At the Court of Korea***. Intro. by Christopher Hitchens. Century (London) 1987 (0-7126-1765-5). 216pp. Nonfiction.

A few years before the turn of the century, the author, barely twenty-five years old, was sent to Korea by the U.S. government to learn the language and familiarize himself with the ways of the people. Within three years, he had learned his lessons so well that he was invited to become counselor to the Korean emperor. He was groomed to be one of the new breed of diplomats. This chronicle of his stay in East Asia indicates how familiar he became with the people and their ways.

Before entering Korea, he stayed for a while in Japan. That sojourn grounded him in the techniques of European-style diplomacy and gave him some insight into the nature of the differences between cultures of the East and those of the West. Today, many decades later, many of his observations still hold true.

From a discussion of *bushido* ("the warrior way") in Japan to a lyrical description of old Korea, the author regales us with anecdotes that portray the character of these countries as well as personal stories of the diplomatic corps and the political intrigues that swirled around the emperor. For example, he recounts the story of a queen who, on the public demand for her death, was rescued and carried off by a burly miner. Later, her spunky serving maid turned heroine tricked the palace guards and initiated a revolution. These stories are the stuff of which good novels are made.

1559 Schell, Orville. ***Mandate of Heaven: A New Generation of Entrepreneurs, Dissidents, Bohemians, and Technocrats Lays Claim to China's Future***. Simon & Schuster 1994, $24.50 (0-671-70132-0). 464pp. Nonfiction.

In staging prodemocracy protests in 1989, Chinese students demanded political liberalization to match the Communist government's openness to private enterprise and foreign investment. However, the government's murderous crackdown on the political protesters who occupied Tiananmen Square in the center of Beijing led to a reversal of both economic and political liberalization. Orville Schell, a long-time American commentator on Chinese affairs, vividly recounts the events of 1989 through the eyes of protesters, government officials, and foreign observers.

Later parts of this book describe the exile and imprisonment of protest leaders after 1989 and the fear and resignation of ordinary Chinese. Schell explains how Deng Xiaoping, the de facto leader of China's government, maneuvered to resume economic reform and regain foreign investment in the 1990s. In a series of biographical sketches, Schell reveals how ordinary Chinese have used economic freedom to make their fortunes, while enjoying the chance to indulge in material pleasures without directly challenging government authority. This book ably presents China's political history over the past decade, while giving a sense of the disappointments and opportunities faced by ordinary Chinese.   RL

1560 Schodt, Frederick L. ***Inside the Robot Kingdom: Japan, Mechatronics, and the Coming Robotopia***. Illus. Kodansha 1990, $12.95 (0-87011-918-4). 256pp. Nonfiction.

What is the connection between man and technology, and why is that connection different in Japan than it is in the United States? This book explores these and other questions to understand how Japan has been able to overcome some of the technical problems that have hampered the U.S. economy.

The book begins with the history and development of the robot, East and West. The introduction of the robot to the West began with Karel Capek's 1921 satirical play *R.U.R* ("Rossum's Universal Robots") *(see main entry)*, in which robots who can think for themselves take over the world. The word *robot* derives from the Czech word for "work." Hand in hand with the development of the robot go the development of attitudes toward robots, the concept of making a machine to replace human labor, and the concept of creating a mechanical creature in the image of human beings. Since robots first clanked onto the industrial scene, the West seems never to have quite let go of its fear of a robot takeover, or at least of robots stealing jobs from people. In Japan, however, there is little of that fear and animosity toward technology. Both popular and official attitudes have encouraged the Japanese to exploit the potential of machines.

The author devotes some space to the difficulty of definition. Just exactly what is a robot? Developments in robot technology are also traced, along with their political and economic implications. A lengthy bibliography including periodicals and symposium papers is included at the end.

1561 Seth, Vikram. *From Heaven Lake: Travels Through Sinkiang and Tibet.* Random 1987, $11.00 (0-394-75218-X). 184pp. Nonfiction.

Nearly everyone who visits China is at some point taken with the notion of a journey into Tibet, the forbidden country. For many years, Tibet was pointedly prohibited to all outsiders, and even today only the most intrepid travelers manage to scale the walls of bureaucracy to get there.

Vikram Seth is a poet and novelist originally from India and now living in the United States. While a student in Nanjing, he learned Chinese and traveled around China. It struck him that he would be able to return to his native India via Tibet, an adventure not to be passed up.

With lyrical prose, a novelist's eye for detail, and a rich sense of humor, Seth recounts his journey into the far reaches of China, Xinjiang (Sinkiang), and Tibet. He describes his many humorous and intriguing encounters with people to paint for the reader a portrait Tibet, one of unusual clarity and beauty.

1562 Shapiro, Michael. *The Shadow in the Sun: A Korean Year of Love and Sorrow.* Atlantic Monthly 1990. o.p. Nonfiction.

Part of the intent of this book is to portray a Third World nation in the process of becoming a major influence in the modern world. In 1987 Korea made the transition from dictatorship to democracy with peaceful free elections. Suddenly the nation's technological prowess mushroomed. The jump in such exports as computers and cars led to radical political and economic changes that the average Korean citizen, even today, might find difficult to absorb.

The book seeks to explain the psychology of the people, which the author sums up as a cross between *han* ("bitterness") and *jong* ("contentment"). Shapiro analyzes the political events of 1987 and 1988, including the student protest movement and ideological battles within it, all the while focusing on his overall themes.

1563 Sivin, Nathan, ed. *The Contemporary Atlas of China.* Illus. Houghton 1988, $39.95 (0-395-47329-2). 200pp. Nonfiction.

This beautiful atlas is much more than a collection of maps. It includes discussions of each major region of China, followed by intricate essays on every subject imaginable. The detailed cultural and historic discussions are each accompanied by striking photographs. Among the many topics are plant and animal life, the Great Wall, the emperors, the Cultural Revolution, the role of women, the Chinese language, silk and lacquer, and economics and industrial technology in China today. An index to the maps and a general index are appended.

1564 Spence, Jonathan D. ***Chinese Roundabout: Essays in History and Culture***. Illus. Norton 1992, $24.95 (0-393-03355-4); $12.95 (0-393-30994-0). 384pp. Essays.

This collection of essays on various subjects was written over many years and was recently collected in one volume. Each essay pertains to a significant aspect of Chinese culture; together, like spokes in a wheel pointing to the hub, they point to the central issue of what defines China today. By examining the ordinary events and small details, the author draws large and spirited conclusions.

The book covers selected historical events as they shed light on present-day China. Social and economic aspects of daily life today are examined. Two sections are devoted to studies of Chinese food and medicine. The author analyzes the Tiananmen Square incident, examines the impact of film on politics, and evaluates the modern poetry of Bei Dao as a commentary on the nation's politics. The final section discusses the great China scholars and teachers of this century, including Arthur Wright, Arthur Waley, John King Fairbank, and Fang Chao-ying.

Spence has written several other notable books, among which are *The Search for Modern China* (Norton, 1990) and *The Gate of Heavenly Peace: The Chinese and Their Revolution* (Penguin, 1982).

1565 Spry-Leverton, Peter, and Peter Francis Kornicki. ***Japan***. Illus. Facts on File 1988, $22.95 (0-8160-1845-6). 192pp. Nonfiction.

This photographic essay of Japan covers its recent history, its image in the West, how information and technology are sweeping it into the modern world, items of importance to the Japanese, such as the tea ceremony and theater, and lifestyles in town and country. Thoughtful as well as descriptive essays complement the excellent selection of photographs. A detailed bibliography and index are included.

1566 Stalberg, Roberta, and Ruth Helmer. ***A Mini-Encyclopedia of Chinese Crafts: Nesi***. Times Books 1983. o.p. Nonfiction.

Black-and-white photos and drawings accompany the technical, detailed descriptions of China's many arts and crafts. The history of art development is included. There is a glossary of Chinese terms, a list of crafts, and addresses in China where the crafts are made. An index is included.

1567 Statler, Oliver. ***All Japan: The Catalogue of Everything Japanese***. Illus. Morrow 1984, $15.95 (0-688-02530-7). 224pp. Essays.

Though the title of this elegant book says "everything," these sixteen essays focus on well-selected topics central to life in Japan. Not actually a catalogue, this is a series of artistic presentations with tasteful color plates reflecting the Japanese flair for beauty in simplicity and clean lines.

The essays address such themes as crafts and design, both ancient and modern; dance and the theater; flower arranging and the tea ceremony; literature and film; games and toys; ritual travel and the public bath; and the intricate Japanese language. Appended are a bibliography and index plus lists of museums, schools, businesses, and other sources of things Japanese.

1568 Statler, Oliver. *Japanese Pilgrimage*. Morrow 1983. o.p. Nonfiction.

709

EAST ASIA

A number of Westerners have been inspired to take a walking journey through an Asian country in order to better understand the people and the culture. In this book, the author describes a trek undertaken for a different purpose: to make a religious pilgrimage around the Japanese island of Shikoku—along with hundreds of Japanese journeying on foot or by bus—to honor Kobo Daishi, an eighth-century Japanese artist, poet, scholar, and monk who founded the Shingon sect of Buddhism.

Sandwiched between the vivid descriptions of the author's pilgrimage around the island is the story of the monk in whose path he travels, as well as commemorations of other famed travelers through the centuries. Illustrations of the route in traditional woodblock prints, woodcuts, paintings, sketches, and black-and-white photographs abound.

A list of over one hundred temples is given at the end. There is also a postscript by the author and an index. Statler is the author of *Japanese Inn: A Reconstruction of the Past* (Univ. of Hawaii Pr., 1982)—about his stay along the famous Tokkaido road between Tokyo and Kyoto immortalized by the painter and wood print artist Hiroshige—and is the editor of *All Japan: The Catalogue of Everything Japanese (see main entry)*.

1569 Stepanchuk, Carol, and Charles Wong. *Mooncakes and Hungry Ghosts: Festivals of China*. China Books 1992, $14.95 (0-8351-2481-9). 145pp. Nonfiction.

This book describes all kinds of Chinese national and local festivals and celebrations. The authors explore the stories behind the festivals, explain common customs surrounding them and discuss the games and special foods associated with them. Poems recited during the festivals are included, and there is a special chapter on celebrations among China's many ethnic minorities. Photographs are mostly black and white, with one section in color. Appendixes and an index are included.

1570 Sumii, Sue. *The River with No Bridge*. Trans. from Japanese by Susan Wilkinson. Tuttle 1990, $19.95 (0-8048-1590-9). 359pp. Nonfiction.

One of the most valuable books to come out of Japan, this human rights plea is the story of members of an occupational minority that has experienced ridicule and discrimination from other Japanese. The victims are called the *burakumin*; their occupations, such as sandal-making, involve the use of sulfur, the yellowish element that makes everything and everyone smell like rotten eggs. The work is passed from one generation to the next.

The author makes her case by focusing on the story of a small boy, Koji, and his slightly older brother, Seitaro. Called names like "smelly" and "dirty," the boys gradually come to realize their low place in society. Their innocence and suffering will stir feelings of shame and outrage in many readers, who will learn how it feels to be the object of irrational disgust.

This translation is the first volume of six, published in Japan between 1961 and 1973. The whole has been made into a feature film in Japan. The fine translation is accompanied by thoughtful notes in the back of the book.

1571 Sun Tzu. *The Art of War*. Ed. and Intro. by James Clavell. Dell 1989, $9.95 (0-385-29985-0). 197pp. Nonfiction.

In recent years, this Japanese classic from the sixth century B.C. has been retranslated several times and has become popular with market management strategists and other achievement-oriented groups. It is now hailed as a modern classic of market strategy. There is an edition available for every taste. There is a straight, no-nonsense account by Chinese translators T'ao Hanchang and Yuan Shibing. A popular coffee-table version by R. L. Wing (Doubleday, 1988) contrasts with the scholarly account, with history and appendixes by Samuel B. Griffith (Oxford Univ. Pr., 1963). This neat little package with commentary for the layperson was edited by James Clavell, author of *Shogun* (Dell, 1983) and other novels set in Far Eastern countries.

Sun Tzu offers strategy on how to overcome the enemy and emerge as victor, such as "do the unexpected" and "pursue the indirect approach." But the main thrust of his philosophy is not to put a premium on killing. As he puts it, "There has never been a protracted war from which a country has benefited." Instead, Sun Tzu suggests ways to "subdue the enemy's army without engaging it, and overthrow his state without bloodying swords." He also urges that victors treat captives well so that they can be put to use.

1572 Tatsuno, Sheridan M. *Created in Japan: From Imitators to World-Class Innovators*. HarperCollins 1990, $21.95 (0-88730-373-0); $12.95 (0-88730-492-3). 244pp. Nonfiction.

Full of tables, figures, diagrams, computer jargon, and acronyms, the thrust of this book is to alter the Western image of Japan as a mere imitator. It is technical though not scholarly, and it is laced with enough human interest anecdotes to make it lively and readable.

Beginning with discussions of traditional crafts and the special Japanese appreciation of smallness, Tatsuno describes how traditional skills apply to modern electronic and computer enterprises. Each chapter has its own extensive bibliography, which serves as an excellent source for further reading. Also included is a detailed index.

1573 Temple, Robert. *The Genius of China: 3,000 Years of Science, Discovery, and Invention*. Simon & Schuster 1986. o.p. Nonfiction.

According to the author, the West owes China a huge debt for its contributions to the worlds of science and technology. This book presents fascinating and detailed descriptions of Chinese achievements and inventions, some of which were developed in Asia thousands of years before they appeared in the West. Temple's stated goal is to encourage the West to recognize the contribution to world knowledge made by the East and to see each other as "true and full partners" in the quest for progress.

The author credits the Chinese with discovering essential mathematical concepts. They also developed the fields of magnetism, seismology, and medicine; amazingly, the reader learns, the Chinese discovered the principle of immunization against smallpox. Other achievements include advances in metallurgy, such as the discovery of cast iron, and in industrial technology, such as the development of lacquer, the first plastics, and the use of petroleum and natural gas as fuel. Ancient Chinese scientists studied sunspots and solar winds. And of course the Chinese are credited with creating kites, gunpowder, paper, and printing.

Endpapers present a historic chart comparing the time lags between the invention of a technology in China and its discovery in the West. There is also a bibliography for further reading.

1574 Thubron, Colin. ***Behind the Wall: A Journey Through China***. Illus. HarperCollins 1989, $9.95 (0-06-097256-4). 320pp. Nonfiction.

Here is a personal account of travels through nearly all of China just after the nation cracked open its doors to foreign visitors. The author traveled alone through China at a time when hardly anyone was traveling in China at all. Conversations with local people give the book its spice. The discussions cover everything from differences in bathing styles East and West to political intrigue. Quite a bit of history finds its way into the text, adding to its scope and usefulness. Amusing accounts of personal situations as well as historical and social commentary are highly readable. An index is appended.

1575 Trager, James. ***Letters from Sachiko: A Japanese Woman's View of Life in the Land of the Economic Miracle***. Macmillan 1982. o.p. Essays.

This is a collection of letters from "Sachiko," who is actually a composite of several sisters in Japan, to their sister who lives in the United States with her American husband. The correspondence presents an intimate look at the problems and concerns of ordinary women in Japan and address such issues as position, status, and daily life. The letters are long and elegantly written, seeming to hail from the age of the literary letter in the last century. They are readable and fascinating in the way they reveal Japanese women's attitudes toward their men, their families, and their lives. The author furnishes extensive notes that highlight and clarify aspects of the letters. An index adds to the usefulness of the book.

1576 Whittaker, Clio. ***Oriental Mythology***. Chartwell 1989. o.p. Nonfiction.

This large-format, thin, and beautiful volume contains a selection of myths and legends from China, India, and Japan. It does not purport to be encyclopedic in scope; instead it offers detailed essays that delve more deeply into selected subjects. An introduction provides the cultural background of the myths and discusses the function of myth in a society. Color photos of paintings, sculptures, and scenes of modern life fill the pages with life and spirit. A brief bibliography and an index complete the work.

1577 Wilby, Sorrel. ***Journey Across Tibet***. Contemporary Books 1988. o.p. Nonfiction.

This is a gracious and affectionately written account of a trek through Tibet by a sensitive and perceptive observer. Wilby is a young Australian woman who became famous as the first woman to climb Mount Fuji by bicycle. She then went on to travel all over China. After her first brief tour of Lhasa, she developed a thirst to learn more about Tibetan life. She wanted to know every brick in every monastery and to understand the significance of every cup of tea. To savor the Tibetan culture and to get to know the people, their customs and language, their religion, and their land, she decided to walk the breadth of the country.

She seems to have been in physical pain and misery most of the time. Her graphic descriptions of the beauty of the country and the friendliness of the people contrast sharply with her tales of constant blisters, aching feet, broken bones, and encounters with unseen but powerful microbes. Nonetheless, her exhilaration at the hospitality of those she met, their constant good cheer, laughter, and smiles, their sincerity and their spirituality kept her going.

Not surprisingly, Wilby is unsupportive of China's claim to Tibetan territory. She reports the stories she hears in the more populated areas about the horrific impact on Tibet of the Cultural Revolution in China. But in the remote districts, she revels in becoming as completely Tibetan as it is possible for a twentieth-century Westerner to become.

1578 Winchester, Simon. *Korea: A Walk Through the Land of Miracles*. Illus. Prentice 1991, $10.95 (0-13-517244-6). 256pp. Nonfiction.

In this book, world traveler Winchester recounts his trek across South Korea. He begins his journey at the monument to Hendrick Hamel, an intrepid adventurer who wrote the first Western account of Korea in 1668; a quote from Hamel introduces each chapter. Eventually he makes his way to the northern border. Along the route Winchester pauses to describe landscapes of inspirational beauty and to report revealing conversations with the people he meets—some of whom, he notes, risked political reprisals for the critical comments they made.

From these people he collects tales of Korea's past, accounts of personal problems, and insights into societal issues. To these comments he adds his own perceptive remarks. As a Korea scholar and an intrepid traveler, Winchester offers essays that are packed with eye-opening information about this little-researched country. The combination of thoughtful essay and personal anecdote combine to produce a book that is easy to read and absorb. Far more than just a walking tour of the land, this beautifully written journal is also a political commentary, social treatise, and fine literature. Winchester is also the author of *Pacific Rising: The Emergence of a New World Culture (see main entry)*.

1579 Winchester, Simon. *Pacific Rising: The Emergence of a New World Culture*. Illus. Simon & Schuster 1992, $14.00 (0-671-78004-2). 512pp. Nonfiction.

This book, which describes each of the Pacific Rim cultures, explores the premise that these diverse countries will become the center of the world in the next century, as the United States and Western Europe were in the last. Readers must set aside the ethnocentric world view of the author, who is British. After all, for several thousand years, China has held the view that *China* was the kingdom in the center of the universe, and that every place else was merely savage, barbaric wasteland. Nonetheless, the book contains a series of interestingly detailed portraits of these nations. Beyond such high-profile places as Japan and China, Winchester describes the lesser-known native cultures of the Pacific, Russian, and Alaskan islands, as well as those of South American countries on the Pacific side.

Punctuated by the author's own personal observations—he comments on his white rental cars and seems to enjoy breakfasts of café au lait, pineapple, and hard rolls—the essays are interesting and informative, although sometimes he seems unaware of his Western biases. (To Winchester, for example, Singapore is "all Somerset Maugham and Joseph Conrad, all heat and mystery) Even so, the stated intention of the book is "to sketch the faces, color the landscapes of the mosaic of Pacific rim cultures." It does that in a way that will appeal to readers just beginning to explore the area.

1580 Wong How Man. ***Exploring the Yangtze: China's Longest River***. China Books 1989. o.p. Nonfiction.

This book reports on National Geographic expeditions to the Yangtze undertaken by Chinese-American adventurers. Over a period of two years, the explorers spent a total of ten months tracing Asia's longest river from its mouth to its source. The glory of the book lies in its quality color photographs and the descriptive captions.

The introduction describes the land along the Yangtze and the various ethnic peoples who inhabit the region. Although packed with the detail of traveling, the text also presents information about daily life, work, and play among the inhabitants. At the lower reaches of the river are fisheries, dams, and locks. Beyond the spectacular gorges are the upper reaches, populated by many minority peoples. Enough history of the various areas is added to make the book more than just another travelogue. There is added drama in the author's report of how the explorers discovered a previously unknown source of the Yangtze, hidden in the hinterlands of Qinghai Province.

1581 Yip, Jacky, and Judy Bonavia. ***The Silk Road***. Illus. with photos. Chartwell 1988. o.p. Nonfiction.

This thin coffee-table book is well stocked with large, beautiful photographs from all along the old Silk Road, tracing its old route through Xinjiang province, which used to be called Chinese Turkestan. An introduction describes the geography of the region and mixes in bits of culture and history. For the rest of the book, captions enhance and explain the photos, some of which tell stories and others of which are purely artistic in intent. All of them, however, evoke life in the outer reaches of China.

The book vividly portrays the highlights of the landscape, including the vast deserts with their ruins of ancient cities, and the Tun Huang caves, resplendent with ancient Buddhist frescoes, where priceless and sacred manuscripts were hidden for 800 years. Here, too, are striking images of people: the colorful natives of Xinjiang, where Chinese is not much spoken; the laughing children; the old gentlemen with their long-stemmed pipes; the young mothers.

A reader of the novel *Tun Huang* by Inoue Yasushi *(see main entry)* would do well to look through this book first so as to become better acquainted with the land, the people, and the history.

1582 Yoo Yushin. ***Korea the Beautiful: Treasures of the Hermit Kingdom***. Illus. Golden Pond 1987, $24.95 (0-942091-01-9). 226pp. Nonfiction.

This large coffee-table book contains many beautiful full-page glossy photographs with detailed descriptions of Korean art, culture, history, religion, music, lifestyles, temples, and natural wonders.

1583 Zee, A. *Swallowing Clouds*. Illus. Simon & Schuster 1991, $15.00 (0-671-74724-X). 384pp. Nonfiction.

It is difficult to say whether this book deals more with language, culture, or cuisine. Not a cookbook—although it does contain some recipes—its purpose is to explain the origins of the characters in the Chinese language that are used to represent foods. The author shows how some of these pictographs resemble the object that they represent; fire, mountain, and water, for instance, are pretty easy to recognize. The text then traces the evolution of that character into its modern form and lists the names of foods and dishes that might contain the character.

In between the language lessons are anecdotes, both historical and present-day, about various foods, drinking games, and dictionaries. Discussions of Buddhism, bamboo, children, and tea are interspersed along with other related topics. The book includes chapter notes, bibliographies for both English and Chinese books, tables of dynasties, and lists of characters by chapter. Although the topic sounds somewhat formidable, the book is actually playful as well as informative and very easy to get lost in.

1584 Zhang Xin Xin, and Sang Ye. *Chinese Lives: An Oral History of Contemporary China*. Trans. from Chinese; Intro. by Studs Terkel. Pantheon 1987. o.p. Nonfiction.

In the manner of oral historian Studs Terkel, who wrote the preface and in fact inspired this work, two interviewers traveled through China and talked with people from all walks of life. These monologues, which read for the most part like verbatim transcriptions of taped interviews, offer intriguing and sometimes provocative glimpses into the minds and feelings of ordinary people in China in the 1980s.

Subjects interviewed include street vendors and university professors, bankers and newlyweds, editors and gold miners, actresses and stage managers, young people and old. They discuss their lives and feelings and comment on controversial aspects of changing life in China today, such as attitudes about when and whether to marry, the importance of higher education, the relative values of wealth and happiness, and changing political beliefs.

BIOGRAPHY

1585 Chang Jung. *Wild Swans: Three Daughters of China*. Doubleday 1992, $14.00 (0-385-42547-3). 524pp. Biography.

More than just a biography, this is the poignant story of three strong, independent-minded women: the author, her mother, and her grandmother. The story of these three generations reflects the historical situation of China and the women's changing cultural environment.

As a young girl at the end of the Qing Dynasty (around 1911), the grandmother was forced to marry a local wealthy warlord. Unhappy, she eventually fled with her infant daughter. The daughter grew up to become active in the Communist underground. She married a guerrilla fighter who became a senior official under Mao Zedong. Despite his loyalty, which called on him to value the Communist party above his own family, he was branded a rightist and sentenced to years in a labor camp. His wife (the author's mother) was also jailed separately; she later spent years in exile in the Himalayas. The instability of the times made it difficult for anyone to know who was truly loyal to what, and it was common practice for innocent people to serve years in the labor camps of the very parties they had thought they were trying to support.

The author herself was a member of the Red Guards, which she joined as a survival tactic. Adherence to party policy required citizens to think of country and society first and the individual last. In this world, a desire for privacy was tantamount to selfishness. Privately, however, Chang Jung rebelled at the inhumane treatment of those hapless souls who were branded as rightists. Eventually she graduated from a university, received a scholarship to London, married a professor, and stayed there.

This moving story of women sustained by family ties sheds light on qualities of human endurance. Other autobiographies whose stories reveal life in China in this century include Nien Cheng's *Life and Death in Shanghai* (Grove, 1986), which emphasizes the cruelty of the regime and the author's own bitterness. *Wild Swans*, though, has a literary style that attracts the reader's attention and engagement like iron filings to a magnet.

Dalai Lama XIV. ***Freedom in Exile: The Autobiography of the Dalai Lama***.
See entry 1433.

Hyun, Peter. ***Man Sei! The Making of a Korean American***.
See entry 338.

Kingston, Maxine Hong. ***China Men***.
See entry 342.

Kingston, Maxine Hong. ***The Woman Warrior: Memoirs of a Girlhood Among Ghosts***.
See entry 343.

1586 Liu Binyan. ***A Higher Kind of Loyalty: A Memoir by China's Foremost Journalist***. Trans. from Chinese. Pantheon 1990. o.p. Autobiography.

This autobiography, originally published in Taiwan, is popular and widely read in its original Chinese version, but it has been banned in China. Liu Binyan's story is in many ways the story of China for most of this century. The author describes his life as a promising young journalist and gives an account of life under the Japanese occupation in the 1930s and under the Communist regime from the 1950s on. As a journalist for the leading official Communist newspaper in China, he attempted to write with courage and integrity but was twice arrested and sentenced to prison, where he suffered humiliation and torture. He now lives in the United States.

Liu Binyan has also written a collection of essays, *China's Crisis, China's Hope* (Harvard Univ. Pr., 1990), which criticizes the Chinese Communist regime. After the Tiananmen Square incident, he wrote *Tell the World What Happened and Why* (Pantheon, 1989), in which he describes the struggle among the leaders of the party and how they manipulated each other. His highly readable style and swift reportage of events has led him to be called the Harrison Salisbury of China.

Minatoya, Lydia. *Talking to High Monks in the Snow: An Asian-American Odyssey*.
See entry 346.

Pai, Margaret K. *The Dreams of Two Yi-min*.
See entry 349.

1587 Rittenberg, Sidney, and Amanda Bennett. *The Man Who Stayed Behind*. Illus. Simon & Schuster 1993. o.p. Autobiography.

In the 1940s Sidney Rittenberg went to China as a young draftee. Idealistic and a bit naive, he had an overwhelming desire to fight the injustices of the world and create a better society, one dedicated to the welfare of the people. To further that end, he stayed in China after the war and joined the Communist Party. Because the Chinese language came easily for him, he was accepted early on as a friend of China. Lured by a sense of adventure, his excitement for his new friends who became the leaders of the new China, and their exhortations to help their cause, he stayed.

But idealism got caught up in political power struggles. Rittenberg was arrested for espionage in China and placed in solitary confinement for six years. During the Cultural Revolution (1967–1977), he was jailed again, this time for ten years, because of his association with the notorious Gang of Four. Theirs had seemed to him a democratic movement. But the Red Guards were being used in a political struggle by Mao against Liu Shaoqi. Like a moth walking on an oriental carpet, Rittenberg says, he couldn't see the whole pattern. He couldn't see that the political winds had changed and that the game had become more a political struggle than a true concern for the people.

Here is an insider's view of the lives of the leaders of China and a poignant and thought-provoking personal journal of what has happened in China in the last half century.

1588 Seagrave, Sterling. *Dragon Lady: The Life and Legend of the Last Empress of China*. Knopf 1992, $30.00 (0-679-40230-6); Random $16.00 (0-679-73369-8). 601pp. Biography.

What is truth? Once a life has passed into history, can its objective reality ever be known? The last empress of China, Tzu Hsi—popularly called the Dowager—and also known as the "Dragon Lady"—was one of three women who had a long, successful reign in China. But what was her true personality? Was she the evil, grasping, power-hungry despot of popular report? Or was she the most misrepresented woman in recent centuries?

The author based this biography in part on the writings of Hugh Trevor-Roper, whose *Hermit of Peking* (o.p.) explored the life of Tzu Hsi's principal detractor, Sir Edmund Backhouse. Other principal sources were the diaries of Dr. George Morrison, who "knew everybody in Peking." Through his research, the author weaves a fascinating tale. Seagrave makes it his personal mission to discredit Backhouse, the man held chiefly responsible for the public perception of Tzu Hsi as the Dragon Lady and to restore her reputation. In Seagrave's account, Sir Edmund is revealed as a sex pervert, con man, and secret agent. Tzu Hsi, meanwhile, is exonerated. Intent on documenting the biography as thoroughly as possible, Seagrave's chapter notes consume nearly one hundred pages, and he adds an extensive bibliography and a detailed index.

Seagrave has also written several other epic historical biographies, such as *The Soong Dynasty* (HarperCollins, 1985) and *The Marcos Dynasty* (HarperCollins, 1988).

1589 Wu Ningkun. *A Single Tear: A Family's Persecution, Love, and Endurance in Communist China*. Contrib. by Yikai Li. Little, Brown 1994, $11.95 (0-316-95639-2). 367pp. Autobiography.

In an account notable for its author's stoic acceptance and lack of bitterness, Wu Ningkun describes his twenty-two years as a "class enemy" in China. A teacher at the University of Chicago at the time of the Communist victory, he returned to his native land in 1951 to accept a position at a university in Beijing, joining thousands of other overseas Chinese who responded to a call from the motherland to "return home" and help China evolve as a new country.

The idealism of the era quickly ebbed as many innocent people were "purged" and jailed or sent to labor camps for being "rightist" or "bourgeois." Any bit of wealth, special privilege, or intellectual creativity was enough to brand one as an enemy of the state. Wu—labeled a "counterrevolutionary" because he owned Western teaching materials—was confined to prison in the 1950s during the Great Leap Forward. Again in the 1960s and 1970s, during the Cultural Revolution, he was jailed as an intellectual and separated from his family.

Wu knows what he believes and what he stands for. His willingness to come to terms with his fate indicates a high level of spiritual attainment. He likes to quote Shakespeare and T. S. Eliot, whose verses, he says, sustained him through his suffering. It may be of interest to Western readers that a Chinese found intellectual comfort and refuge in Western literature. This inspiring work is one of the best testimonials to emerge from China during this grim period, a powerful exploration of how Mao's regime affected one caring and idealistic man and his family.

1590 Xiao Hong. *Market Street: A Chinese Woman in Harbin*. Trans. from Chinese by Howard Goldblatt. Illus. Univ. of Washington Pr. 1986, $17.50 (0-295-96266-6). 133pp. Autobiography.

Published in Chinese in 1936 and only recently translated into English, this autobiographical account of two poverty-stricken years in the author's early life is strikingly simple and touching. Xiao Hong lived hand-to-mouth with her lover in Harbin in what used to be called Manchuria. Small vignettes of ordinary life reveal the couple's struggle to earn a living and survive in difficult times.

Although the pair manage to leave Harbin and head back to "their own country" (China proper) at the end of the book, an epilogue reveals that the author succumbed to ill health and poverty and died in Hong Kong of a throat infection only ten years later. However, her lyrical writings and plea for attention to the plight of Chinese women live on.

1591 Zhai Zhenhua. *Red Flower of China*. Soho 1993, $24.00 (0-939149-83-4); $13.00 (1-56947-009-X). 245pp. Autobiography.

The author describes her childhood in Shandong province. A precocious and inquisitive child, she peppered her relatives with relentless questions: "Why did women suffer the pain of 'golden lilies' [bound feet] just for the sake of being considered beautiful?" "Why doesn't father just ignore second uncle if he's a pain?" "How can a woman's ONLY name be her maiden name?"

As she grows up, she becomes caught up in the political changes sweeping China. Watching the approach of the Cultural Revolution through the eyes of a naive middle-school girl, the reader can feel the forces that drew millions of Chinese young people like Zhai into the flow that later became unstoppable. This firsthand account of what it was like to be a Red Guard is horrifying because of the extreme measures that even a thinking, rational, feeling human being can take in going along with the tide, especially when, like Zhai, she is afraid for her life.

When the Red Guards fell into disfavor, Zhai was sent to the countryside for hard labor and "thought reform." Later she had a chance to attend university. Now living in Canada, she "ambivalently" loves China—the country that robbed her of her youth and innocence—and hopes that it will change for the better. More readable than many such accounts, this one is both fascinating and disturbing.

14

SOUTHEAST ASIA

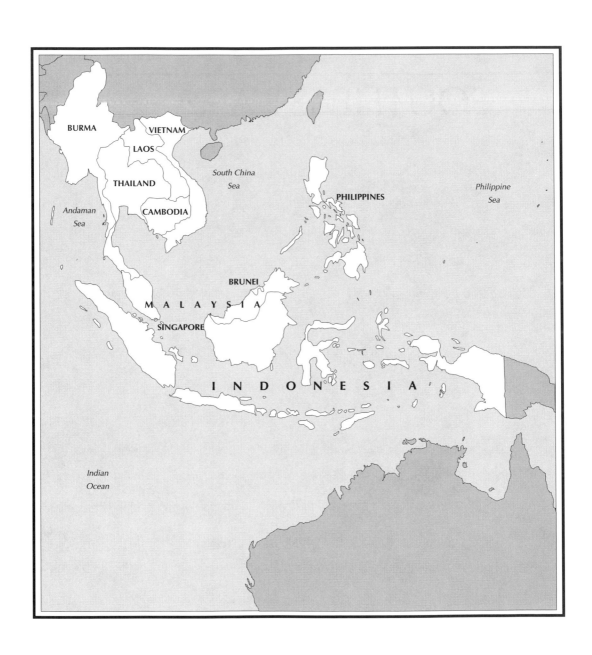

14

SOUTHEAST ASIA

by Ginny Lee, Suzanne Lo, and Susan Ma

Southeast Asia in this century has been a site of political turmoil and social change, marked by heart-wrenching stories of violence, family separations, and personal loss. Whether fiction or nonfiction, recent books about the region reflect this turbulence.

Nonfiction works from Southeast Asia—a region that includes Vietnam, Laos, Cambodia, the Philippines, Singapore, Myanmar (formerly Burma), Malaysia, Thailand, and Indonesia fall into two main categories: travel and autobiography. Travel books, whether practical guides or elaborate coffee-table volumes with large glossy photos, are designed to tell about a country's history, geography, and the social setting in such a way as to entice the reader to visit. Sometimes these are promotional books put out by national organizations, such as ministries of culture or education, or by tourist agencies. In contrast to these books are the autobiographical accounts of excruciating trauma and terror following political upheavals. Examples of such books reviewed in this chapter include two firsthand accounts of escaping the Cambodian massacre: *To Destroy You Is No Loss: The Odyssey of a Cambodian Family*, coauthored by Joan D. Criddle and Teeda Butt Mam, and *Stay Alive My Son* by Pin Yathy and John Man. Personal stories of Vietnam during and after the war include *When Heaven and Earth Changed Places* by Le Ly Hayslip and *The Will of Heaven: The Story of One Vietnamese and the End of His World* by Noc Ngan Nguyen.

A number of book series, such as World Leaders, offer biographies of prominent figures including Ho Chi Minh of Vietnam and Pol Pot of Cambodia. And although some of the history and geography series, including Country Study, Enchantment of the World, and Discovering Our Heritage, were designed for use by schools, they contain enough interest and information to be of value to the general adult reader. Selected titles in these series are discussed in the following list. Other titles available include the Area Handbook series, produced in part by the U.S. State Department. These books tend to reflect the American government's perspective, but nonetheless they contain much useful information.

The countries of Southeast Asia are continuing and developing their long tradition of literature, particularly drama and poetry. Writers in some of these countries are now beginning to explore such Western literary forms as the short story and the novel. In some cases, as in the Philippines and Indonesia, the body of creative writing is especially rich and extensive. Unfortunately, at this time there are few translations of these writings available in English for the Western reader.

From a critical perspective, one could make the case that, overall, works by Western writers about Southeast Asia may be more sophisticated and well rounded than those by regional authors. Styles are more refined, fictional characters are better developed, and so on. Even so, in certain cases Western-ers tend to use Asia simply as a backdrop for their stories. Their goal is largely to hold the reader's attention by spinning tales set in exotic locales. An example is *The North China Lover* by Marguerite Duras (which was adapted for the film *The Lover*). Although the novel is beautifully written and romantically evocative, in our opinion the book does not tell the reader enough about Vietnam or its people to merit inclusion here. On the other hand, works by Southeast Asian people about their own countries offer one thing that books by non-Asians, for all their technical skills, often lack: an unmistakable quality of verisimilitude. In our opinion as editors, much of the fiction about Asia written by Westerners is often little more than a collection of interesting or amusing tidbits. In contrast, the Asian writers are—sometimes literally— writing as if their lives depended on it.

Most of the fiction chosen for this list consists of translations of works by native writers. One recurring problem in making selections has been the quality of available translations, which can run the gamut from impeccable to execrable. Also, because such literary forms as novels and short stories are relatively new to Asian writers, some of these works, measured by Western standards, contain such flaws as weak plotting or shallow characterizations. Of additional concern is the question of whether, despite its shortcomings, the book has anything valuable to say about the country and its people. In selecting fiction for this bibliography, we have tried to pay more attention to the latter criterion without completely ignoring the technical aspects.

For a number of reasons, Philippine writing has matured faster than writing in other Southeast Asian countries. This is due in part to early exposure of the Filipinos to Western society. Also, there is a very active writers' community in the Philippines. Many leading authors, in addition to producing numerous volumes of prose and poetry, are busy leading writers' workshops, teaching courses, and establishing literary magazines. One magazine that is not available in the West but that deserves wider attention is *Solidarity* (531 Padre Faura, Ermita, Manila, Philippines). Many popular writers from all over Southeast Asia appear in its pages.

A significant percentage of writing by Filipino authors is in English; because these works avoid the pitfalls of translation, some of these works have been exported to the United States. Major writers of influence represented in this bibliography are F. Sionil José, author of *Three Filipino Women*; Bienvenido N. Santos, author of *The Praying Man*; Edilberto K. Tiempo, author of *To Be Free* (Tiempo's wife, Edith, is herself a noted poet and novelist); Alfred Yuson, a young experimental writer strongly influenced by James Joyce and who wrote *Great Philippine Jungle Energy Cafe*; N.V.M. González, who wrote *The Bamboo Dancers* and a more recent work, *The Bread of Salt and Other Stories* (Univ. of Washington Pr., 1993); and Linda Ty-Casper, whose *Dread Empire* is reviewed here. Undoubtedly, though, the giant of Philippine novelists remains the national hero of 1898, Dr. José Rizal, author of *The Lost Eden* and other important works.

Another hero of both literature and revolution is Pramoedya Ananta Toer from Indonesia, author of *This Earth of Mankind*. Readers will be seeing more of his name in the near future. Mochtar Lubis, also from Indonesia, is represented in the collection *ASEAN Short Stories*, edited by Robert Yeo, and also by the nonfiction *Indonesia: Land Under the Rainbow*. Until recently, very little of the vast Indonesian-language literature has been translated into English. For glimpses into the country, readers must turn to the factual and descriptive books by Westerners of their adventures in the region. The beauty of Indonesia especially lends itself easily to the coffee-table book format.

Women writers are represented in *ASEAN Short Stories*. Two from Singapore are Catherine Lim and S. Kon. Also in that small but representative anthology are a few authors from Malaysia and Thailand whose works are difficult to find anywhere else. A rising young author from Thailand who deserves special mention is Minfong Ho. Her novels for young adults, including *Rice Without Rain* (Lothrop, 1990), and her books for younger children, including *The Clay Marble* (Farrar, 1991), have been well received in the United States. Perhaps from this trickle of examples, a wave of works in translation will soon wash up on Western shores.

The few available collections of short stories from Vietnam reveal the tremendous impact of decades-long wars, including poverty, depression, and general dissatisfaction with life. Perhaps by some standards the writing styles of these authors are not polished, but clearly their hearts are in the writing. The emotions they express and the images they convey stay with the reader long after the book has been closed. As is true of other Southeast Asian countries, travel guides, cultural studies, and beautiful coffee-table books are available for armchair travelers curious about Vietnam.

LITERATURE

Bacho, Peter. *Cebu*.
See entry 255.

1592 Banerian, James, and Chinh Hoa Nguyen, eds. ***Vietnamese Short Stories: An Introduction***. Trans. from Vietnamese by the editors. Sphinx 1986. o.p. Fiction.

As a teacher says in one of these stories, "Although their assignments were not very well written, I gave everyone a high grade." The teacher made the award because the students, troublesome and slow and struggling with their desire to be anywhere but Vietnam, had finally written some honest essays about their real lives at home. Similarly, these stories receive high grades, not because they rival the works of O. Henry or Guy Maupassant, but because they honestly struggle to portray reality in Vietnam: the poverty, the shackles of tradition, and the reality of a war that tore the country and families apart.

The Vietnamese language is lyrical, and it lends itself well to oral poetry, legend, and song. But the Western short story is a relatively new art form in

Vietnam. Also new is the artistic freedom with which writers can explore their own ideas and feelings. No Communist writers are represented here, as the translator states acidly in his introduction, but ten, well-known authors from the South write about history, culture, and life in Vietnam today.

1593 Casper, Leonard. ***New Writing from the Philippines: A Critique and Anthology***. Books on Demand 1966, $107.30 (0-317-52002-4). 411pp. Literature.

This collection represents twenty-one authors and poets—some of them people of Filipino descent now living and writing in the United States—by bringing together a collection of their best stories and poems. A third of the book is devoted to the author's critical assessment of the writers and their contributions to literature from the Philippines.

1594 Collis, Maurice. ***She Was a Queen.*** Repr. of 1937 ed. Intro. by Louise Collis. New Directions 1991, $12.95 (0-8112-1169-X). 304pp. Fiction.

Burma, which officially changed its name to Myanmar in 1989, has been so isolated from the rest of the world for so long that, although this tale is set in the thirteenth century, it still reflects the contemporary landscape and feeling of the country. The descriptions of the lives of the peasants, the hills, the elephants and the tigers, and the spirit world would not have been terribly different had the book been written in the 1990s.

The novel was written in 1937 by an Englishman who had spent twenty-two years in Burma absorbing its flavor. Recently reprinted, it is one of the few books on the market today that capture the essence of Burma and tell a rollicking good story at the same time.

Full of supernatural symbolism, the story reveals what happens when the old pagan world meets the "modern" church (Buddhism). A farmer discovers a deadly snake posturing mysteriously around his baby daughter. This is a sign reserved for royalty. Enter the State: The highly educated old king has abdicated the throne and the vivacious prince has assumed rule. Later the prince fathers two sons. As these rivals grow, they hatch plots in league with the king's chief minister. Meanwhile the Mongols arrive, and the Pagan Dynasty collapses. The farmer's daughter, now grown into a clear-thinking woman full of integrity, overcomes the legacy of the previous kings, holds off the threat by another man who seeks the throne, and becomes queen. Her virtues and triumphs make this novel an interesting statement about women.

1595 González, N.V.M. ***The Bamboo Dancers***. Alan Swallow 1961. o.p. Fiction.

In this novel, two brothers, a sculptor and a physician, both of whom lived and studied in the United States, return to the Philippines with diametrically opposed attitudes toward the materialism of the United States and the "mixed culture" of the Philippines.

González appeared first in English in 1947 with his collection of short stories called *Seven Hills Away*. His novels include *The Winds of April* and *A Season of Grace* (both o.p.). The latter portrays life on the island of Mindoro—simple, a little primitive—reminiscent of the way things must have been when the first European ships bearing "the people who are not our kind" landed there centuries ago. He has also written a volume of short stories,

Mindoro and Beyond (Cellar Book Shop, 1990). His most recent work to appear in the West is a short story collection, *The Bread of Salt* (Univ. of Washington Pr., 1993).

1596 Hagedorn, Jessica. ***Dogeaters***. Viking 1991, $10.00 (0-14-014904-X). 272pp. Fiction.

"Dogeaters" is a none-too-flattering nickname for Filipinos. In this book the reader discovers all levels of Philippine society, its diverse characters and its many ways of living. The story focuses on Rio, a young Filipino girl. As she grows up, she becomes consumed with envy of the West and a longing for things American. Like many residents of Third World countries, the characters in this story are torn between their desire for the material riches of the West and their repugnance over the image of Western culture as cruel, arrogant, and devoid of human feeling. Other characters include Rio's flamboyant cousin, Pucha; the elegant, enviable artist, Clarita; a few decadent politicians, and others.

Neither hopeful nor elegant, Hagedorn's novel nevertheless provides an important picture of the various elements in Philippine society. Scenes in the story deal with everything from poverty to soft porn, from street violence to wild teenage parties. The story is written in the present tense, as if describing scenes in a comic book or in snapshots. A series of narrators, all speaking in the first person, emerge at different times in the book. Through this unusual device, the author presents the reader with multiple viewpoints of the same society.

Hagedorn is the author of a somewhat uneven short story collection titled *Danger and Beauty: Dangerous Music, Pet Food, and Tropical Apparitions and New Writings* (Viking, 1993). She has also edited a collection of writings by Asian-American authors, *Charlie Chan Is Dead (see main entry).*

1597 Huong, Duong Thu. ***Paradise of the Blind***. Trans. from Vietnamese. Morrow 1993, $20.00 (0-688-11445-8); Viking $9.95 (0-14-023620-1). 256pp. Fiction.

This stunning novel begins when Hang, a young Vietnamese woman living as a factory worker in the Soviet Union, receives a message to come to Moscow to see her Uncle Chinh, who is supposedly ill and near death. Although recovering from an illness herself, Hang, consumed by her sense of duty, undertakes the long journey by train. On the way, she remembers her mother's many sacrifices on behalf of her younger brother, who joined the independence movement and became a Communist Party official in North Vietnam. After the death of her father—in part the result of Uncle Chinh's actions—Hang moved with her mother to Hanoi, where her mother gave nearly all her earnings as a market vendor to Chinh's family. Hang grew resentful of her mother's actions; meanwhile, she accepted lavish gifts from her Aunt Tam, who tried to drive a wedge between her and her mother.

When Hang finally arrives in Moscow, she discovers that Uncle Chinh is not ill; instead, he wants to use the girl as a courier in a smuggling racket. This experience helps her to recognize the political and cultural forces that have torn her family apart. Her desire to take control of her own fate allows her to come to terms with both her mother and her aunt. Through her experiences, the reader sees how ancient traditions and modern Communism have combined to stifle and oppress women. While offering the reader a sense of Vietnam's beauty, folklore, and cultural riches, Huong's work (for which she spent nine months in prison) portrays a society turned inside out by Communist rule. LML

1598 José, F. Sionil. *Three Filipino Women*. Random House 1992, $22.00 (0-679-41360-X). 174pp. Fiction.

These three novellas each feature a tender and loving description of an unusual woman as seen by a rather common man who adores her. The plots and the characters who populate them are filled with opportunism, ambition, idealism, and lustful desire. Another thread the stories have in common is that passion often ends in tragedy.

In the first story, "Cadina de Amor," a beautiful and brilliant but unscrupulous young woman politician is murdered for her anti-Americanism. The mistake she made in climbing to the top of the heap was to assume that, once she got there, she would be free of "slimy politicians." But, as her adoring biographer tells her, "The government is not a vacuum. . . . Where there are human relationships, compromises are inevitable."

"Obsession," the second novella, is about a prostitute who is very particular about the company she keeps. The author sardonically suggests that there is more than one way to sell oneself. To dramatize his point, he shows how the prostitute's admirer gets caught up in government corruption. As the author says, "they all wanted . . . loopholes . . . all the information they needed to make profits without sweating."

The third story, "Platinum," describes the violent death of a beautiful political activist, who is the adored wife of the narrator.

All these stories prompt the reader to ponder just what is worth the sacrifice of one's life. Politics seems to be an ignoble cause, and yet it is politics and revolutionary fervor that have engulfed the Philippines for decades and claimed many lives.

Multatuli. *Max Havelaar: Or the Coffee Auctions of the Dutch Trading Company*.
See entry 904.

1599 Nguyen, Huy Thiep. *The General Retires and Other Stories*. Trans. from Vietnamese. Oxford Univ. Pr. 1992. o.p. Fiction.

In the 1930s, the French colonial government in Vietnam permitted a brief period of relatively free expression. During that time a group of fine writers emerged, including Nhat Linh, Xuan Dieu, Ngo Tat To, and Nam Cao. More recently, the Vietnamese government, which had required writers to follow strict political formulas, began granting greater freedom in the choice of subjects. One consequence has been the emergence of writers whose style and themes merit wider familiarity among audiences outside their own country. Nguyen Huy Thiep is one of those new writers.

In this edition, a lengthy introduction gives a biographical sketch of the author's life and works, explores the connections between literature and politics, and discusses other facets of literary criticism relevant to Vietnamese literature. A bibliography of references follows.

The eight stories translated here are full of complex characters. Even the villains are capable of generous acts. In the title story, a retired general, reminiscing about the way he was needed during wartime, struggles to adjust to life in peacetime. In another story, a small boy remembers his mother's soul. A particularly poignant tale is about a beggar who longs to be seen as something more, as a "real" human being. One tale, "A Drop of Blood," incorporates images from the past. All of these stories provide us with further insight into the character of Vietnam and the people who live there.

1600 Rizal, José, and Vicente F. Del Carmen, ed. ***Rizal: An Encyclopedic Collection.*** 2 vols. Cellar Book Shop 1983, $14.50 (971-10-0060-1); Cellar Book Shop $10.00 (971-10-0061-X). 205+205pp. Fiction.

The Philippine national hero, José Rizal, was executed in 1896 because of his writings, especially two novels, *The Lost Eden* and *El Filibusterismo*. Since his death, these novels, both included in this anthology, have been acclaimed as the reflecting the very "soul of nationalism."

Rizal was a talented, multifaceted scholar and a fine and sensitive writer. In *The Lost Eden*—considered by many to be his best work—he aims his satirical barbs at the church, or rather at the corruption and immovability behind it. His purpose in this emotional and involved tale was to open the eyes of his countrymen and show them the injustices committed in the name of stability and religion. He begs for the abuses of society to be corrected by royal decree, calling for "zealous authorities to watch over its execution," and for "freedom of speech to be granted against the excesses of petty tyrants." Readers will naturally wonder whether Rizal meant his hero, Ibarra, to stand for himself, because much of the fate that befalls his character actually came to pass in the Philippines.

1601 Santa Elena, Antonio E. ***Mahinhin: A Tale of the Philippines***. Downey Place 1984. o.p. Fiction.

Although this story is about a girl growing up in the Philippines, it has universal appeal because, to a great extent, the events and characters would be recognizable almost anywhere. The girl—whose nickname is Shy Star—grows up in a family that doesn't have much money. The struggle to put food on the table is an ever-present concern. Shy Star longs to have a doll; instead, she gets a duck for a pet. She grows into a feisty tomboy, big for her age. In time she is called to confront a gang of ruffians. She does so successfully, because her father had taught her *arnis*, a form of self-defense involving fencing. Later she must rescue one of the bullies who is drowning in the river—a formidable stream that always claims its due. And eventually Shy Star must fight and kill a giant six-foot ground lizard who sees her pet duck as a future dinner.

The backdrop of this unassuming tale is a picture of what life was like for a poor family in a small town in the Philippines in the 1950s.

1602 Santos, Bienvenido N. *The Praying Man*. Cellar Book Shop 1982, $7.50 (971-10-0002-4). 172pp. Fiction.

Santos is one of the most popular writers of the Philippines, known for his vivid portrayals of the emotional and political forces in society. In this novel, he explores "the need to pray and the tendency to prey on others." Much of the action takes place in the United States.

An earlier novel, *The Volcano* (orig. pub. 1965; Cellar Book Shop, 1986), is about an American missionary family that has come to spread the gospel to the Philippines. Their presence causes strain among the Filipinos. This novel paints for the reader a picture of nascent nationalism within the Philippines.

Santos, Bienvenido N. *Scent of Apples: A Collection of Stories*. See entry 288.

1603 Sudham, Pira. *Monsoon Country*. Breakwater 1990. o.p. Fiction.

In this novel, Kumjai, a schoolteacher in northern Thailand, holds philosophical views that bring him into conflict with his community. The teacher has a young protégé, Prem, who embraces his teacher's philosophy and follows his lead in exploring deep issues, such as the philosophical ideals needed to lead a Third World country out of poverty, or the value Communism might offer to a backward and ignorant nation. The novel explores several philosophical conflicts: the clash between the Buddhist ideals of detachment and nonmaterialism and the Western concepts of involvement and individualism; the tension between peasants who are devoted to family and land compared to the members of the younger and more educated generation who seek broader horizons; the meaning of liberty; and the importance of fighting against poverty, social injustice, and corruption.

Traveling in England and Germany, Prem acquires as part of his education a host of conflicting feelings and values: the contrast of wealth and poverty, of the educated and the ignorant, of life in his homeland and life abroad.

In the deft hands of its creator, this volume transcends mere philosophizing and becomes a true novel, one whose story tugs at the reader's heartstrings and that offers much food for thought. It also provides rare insight into the life and spirit of the Thai people.

1604 Tiempo, Edilberto K. *To Be Free: A Novel*. Cellar Book Shop 1972. o.p. Fiction.

The American occupation of a small town in the Philippines in 1899 and the interactions of the villagers with the soldiers is part of the sociopolitical background in this novel. The author, a leading Filipino short story writer and novelist, has also written *Cry, Slaughter* and *More Than Conquerors* (Cellar Book Shop, 1981), both of which have won literary prizes. His novel set in World War II, *They Called Us Outlaws*, was so powerful that it was cited as evidence during the prosecution of Japanese war criminals. A more recent novel *The Cracked Mirror*, appeared in 1984. Tiempo also wrote the award-winning novel *The Standard Bearer* (Cellar Book Shop, 1985). His recently published short story collections include *Rainbow for Rima* (Cellar Book Shop, 1988) and *Snake Twin and Other Stories* (Cellar Book Shop, 1992). His wife, Edith, a poet and novelist, has collaborated with him in writing and in directing a popular and well-attended writers' workshop.

1605 Toer, Pramoedya A. ***This Earth of Mankind***. Trans. from Indonesian by Max Lane. Morrow 1991, $20.00 (0-688-09373-6); Avon $10.00 (0-380-71974-6). 448pp. Fiction.

In some respects, this Indonesian author holds a place similar to that of Faulkner or Steinbeck in the West. Toer, a popular spokesman for people's rights, is a novelist of highest skill. He wrote his first novel, *The Fugitive* (Morrow, 1990), between 1947 and 1949 while he was imprisoned as a revolutionary. Since then he has written more than thirty works, both fiction and nonfiction.

This Earth of Mankind, his masterpiece, is the first volume of four, written during a subsequent and longer imprisonment from 1965 to 1979. His books have all been banned in Jakarta, where he is at present still under city arrest.

This novel brilliantly reveals the rise in Indonesian national consciousness. That movement is embodied in a character named Minke, a young Native Indonesian man, the only Native in a Dutch high school. In Indonesia, the term *Native* is a social classification; the other classes are *Mixed-Blood* and *Pure*. Such language is vitally important in the construct of Indonesian society; these labels, for example, conveniently indicate to the Dutch colonial leaders which people are permitted to do what. There are many local dialects in addition to the European languages. In times of upheaval, Natives are forbidden to use Dutch.

Minke gradually realizes the subservient role that Native people play in their own country. Central to the plot is a love story. Minke becomes embroiled in the inner life of an infamous Native concubine who has an amazing mind and equally amazing determination. Why should she need schooling, she asks rhetorically. "Life," she says, "can give everything to whoever tries to understand and is willing to receive new knowledge." So, self-taught, she runs her own large firm, controls her own destiny, and has a beautiful daughter. The characters are so real that it takes some time to grasp that they also represent facets of the drama of social and political upheaval in Indonesia. The translator's note, afterword, and glossary are helpful.

Minke's saga continues in *A Child of All Nations* (Morrow, 1993).

1606 Ty-Casper, Linda. ***Dread Empire***. Heinemann. o.p. Fiction.

This author's novels are passionately political. Feeling strongly that her country greatly needs political reform and moral responsibility, she populates her novels with sensitive characters caught up in the various political happenings of recent decades.

The Philippines have endured a series of foreign occupations. The islands were Spanish territory for 300 years; the Spanish were ejected in 1898 and replaced by American occupying forces. Later, the Japanese tried their hand. These occupations were humiliating to nationalist Filipinos, but even greater humiliation was experienced after the Filipinos established their own government and discovered it to be hopelessly corrupt.

The political backdrop of this novel is marked by urban chaos and rural discontent. The New People's Army, which sprung from a peasant movement, conducts more frequent and more violent attacks, until a military coup follows a student and worker uprising in 1972. This novel is about what these events do to the lives of common people caught up in the eddying currents of their times.

More recent novels by this author include *Wings of Stone* (Readers International, 1986) and *Awaiting Trespass* (Readers International, 1986). They expand on the themes in *Dread Empire*, drawing in journalistic fashion on more recent political events as they unfold. Ty-Casper's books are a strong moralistic plea for the country to right itself. She musters strong evidence showing that, since the foreigners have all gone home, the worst enemy confronting the Philippines is itself.

1607 Van Dinh, Tran. ***Blue Dragon White Tiger: A Tet Story***. TriAm 1984, $14.95 (0-914075-00-4). 334pp. Fiction.

According to Asian lore, everything that happens in the universe is a result of the eternal struggle between the Blue Dragon—symbol of springtime and tenderness—and the White Tiger, the embodiment of winter and force. The Vietnamese New Year, a movable feast called Tet, is a ceremony occurring halfway between winter and spring that honors the truce between these two forces. People celebrate with their families at home. It was at Tet that the Viet Cong made their surprise attack on the American Embassy in Saigon, a turning point in the war.

This long and satisfying novel follows a Vietnamese man who is devoted to his mother but who suffers a life of alienation from family and friends during the war. He spends time in the United States and takes an American wife, but attracted by the high ideals espoused by the Viet Cong, he returns to his country and joins their movement. Later, he experiences the life of a Marxist bureaucrat both in Hanoi and in Paris.

The author is a professor of international politics and communication, and his understanding of these fields pervades and informs the events in the book.

1608 Yeo, Robert. ***ASEAN Short Stories***. Repr. of 1981 ed. Heinemann 1989, Write for price info (9971-64-016-3). 246pp. Fiction.

The twenty stories in this volume hail from the various countries of the Association of Southeast Asian Nations (ASEAN) and represent the best of its fiction writers.

From Indonesia come Pramoedya Ananta Toer, author of *This Earth of Mankind (see main entry)* and Mochtar Lubis, who writes biting satire and who is also author of the nonfiction work called *Indonesia: Land Under the Rainbow (see main entry)*. Catherine Lim from Singapore also writes satirical stories as well as stories for children. S. Kon, one of Singapore's best writers, is represented here with a story about the difference in the contributions to society made by two young schoolboys.

From Malaysia comes Usman Awang, whose lyrical and tragic tales portray the way changing social mores bring out the best and worst human qualities. From the Philippines come Nick Joaquin and F. Sionil José, author of *Three Filipino Women (see main entry)*. Pensri Kiengsiri, from Thailand, contributes an ironic comedy, which he translated, about a village peasant who pokes fun both at modern big-city fashions and the poor folk who desire those fashions.

Robert Yeo, an author in his own right, has written an insightful introduction. Notes are included that list the major writings by each contributor.

1609 Yuson, Alfred A. *Great Philippine Jungle Energy Cafe: A Novel*. Philippine Expressions/Filipiniana Bookshop, Los Angeles. o.p. Fiction.

Yuson is one of the freshest young writers in Philippines. He is highly educated and obviously acquainted with the works of James Joyce, Aldous Huxley, and Virginia Woolf. His stream-of-consciousness style and cinematic devices make his avant-garde writing style a big hit among intellectual readers and his fellow writers.

Set in the days of the Guardia Civil during the Spanish occupation, the novel barrages the reader with a conglomeration of historical figures, all present at once; a dizzying array of literary allusions; and—like the famous monologue by Molly Bloom at the end of Joyce's *Ulysses*—a monstrous seven-page sentence with no period at the end. All of these elements combine to give the reader a dizzying kaleidoscopic picture of the Philippine social, economic, and political scene.

Yuson is the award-winning author of other fictional works as well as two volumes of poetry published in the Philippines, *Sea Serpent* and *Dream of Knives*. This novel, in fact, often reads more like poetry than prose.

NONFICTION

1610 Alegre, Edilberto N., and Doreen G. Fernandez. *Writers and Their Milieu: An Oral History of Second Generation Writers in English*. Philippine Expressions/ Filipiniana Bookshop, Los Angeles 1987. o.p. Nonfiction.

This book is a collection of interviews with nineteen Filipino writers in English, all of whom are in their seventies but are still actively publishing. The authors discuss their personal history, the development of their writing, and their literary theory. Their remarks provide a good overview of the literature as well as insights into the Filipino writer's life during the past fifty years. Included are black-and-white photographs, reprints of newspaper article reprints, and samples of writings.

1611 Alvima, Corazón S., and Felice Santa Maria. *Halupi: Essays on Philippine Culture*. Philippine Expressions/Filipiniana Bookshop, Los Angeles 1989. o.p. Essays.

This book, containing newspaper columns written by two women over the course of three years, is a treasure trove of fun, facts, and fantastic details of life in the Philippines. *Halupi* is the name of the Ifugao gods of collective memory and, by extension, of all natural history, tribal history, culture, and tradition.

Written in fine literary style with a delicate and refined sense of humor, these articles make wonderful casual reading. They also provide information about Philippine history, the land, and folk wisdom. Topics include herbal remedies, recipes, carpenter's tools, ships, botany, dances, saints, love, travel, and the language of flowers. (For example, the authors say that if you receive a papaya leaf, you should feel insulted, because it means the sender is calling you a fool.) There are articles about the wild *pili* nut, a national delicacy; about the ethnic custom of tattooing and the meaning of the designs; and about the idioms of the Tagalog language, including a code of vegetable communication (peanuts served means "surely you jest").

1612 Aung San Suu Kyi. *Freedom from Fear and Other Writings*. Ed. by Michael Aris; Frwd. by Václav Havel. Viking 1991, $25.00 (0-670-84560-4); $12.00 (0-14-017136-3). 338pp. Essays.

The author is the daughter of Burma's national hero and liberation leader, Aung San. Suu Kyi married a British man, lived in England, and bore two sons before returning to Burma in 1988 to care for her dying mother. She never returned to England. Feeling herself called by the people of Burma in the hour of their struggle for democracy, amid student uprisings and bloody reprisals, Suu Kyi traveled around Burma giving supporting lectures and carrying on her father's tradition. The people of Burma embraced her as their spokesperson.

An open election was held, but the results were never acknowledged by the military government. Suu Kyi publicly accused the military of never intending to relinquish control and honor the people's wishes, as expressed at the ballot box.

In July 1989—the same year the country officially changed its name to Myanmar—authorities placed her under house arrest in Rangoon, where she remains today. Nevertheless, her courage in speaking out for her country, calling for unity and nonviolence in the manner of Gandhi, earned her the Nobel Peace Prize in 1991. Her son accepted the award on her behalf.

This book contains her letters and speeches and a section of "appreciations"—writings by her family and friends describing her life and her ideals. A section of black-and-white photographs details some of the events of her life, and a note on the contributors is followed by an index.

1613 Balaban, John. *Remembering Heaven's Face: A Moral Witness in Vietnam*. Illus. Simon & Schuster 1992, $11.00 (0-671-77969-9). 336pp. Nonfiction.

Vignette by tiny graphic vignette, John Balaban pieces together for us—or maybe for himself—the none-too-pretty picture of the American presence in Vietnam during the late 1960s.

Balaban, a conscientious objector, volunteered to work for International Voluntary Service, a private organization not unlike the Peace Corps. His situation in Vietnam was highly unusual. Unlike the soldiers, he was able to mix with the people, speak the language, sing the songs—in general, to look beyond the squabble over words like *Communism* and *democracy* and see the thoughts and lives behind the bright eyes he saw everywhere.

He spent the late 1960s working with wounded children in the hospitals, trying to get permission to send them to the United States for medical help. After the war he returned to Vietnam with his wife to teach English. During that stay he went around the countryside, taping peasants as they sang the old lyric poems that were in danger of being lost.

This insightful personal saga reveals Balaban as one of the few people writing about Vietnam with the sensibility to regard the players in that drama as human beings and to treat them as such. His own journey inward is part of this beautiful story.

1614 Blair, Lawrence, and Lorne Blair. *Ring of Fire: An Indonesian Odyssey*. Illus. Inner Traditions 1991, $24.95 (0-89281-430-6). 272pp. Nonfiction.

More than merely a beautiful photographic essay, this book draws on the journals of two brothers to explore the remote islands of Indonesia and to explain the religious states of mind of the inhabitants. This book is a flowing narrative recounting ten years of adventure and exploration whose goal was to make a film, sponsored by former Beatle Ringo Starr, about a search for the greater bird of paradise. In their quest, the authors cultivated friendships with religious leaders and psychics. They also searched for Michael Rockefeller, scion of the famous family, who disappeared in 1961 at the age of 22, while collecting Indonesian art and artifacts.

Ten years between dream and reality, peppered with startling narrow escapes and sudden insights, this photographic and essay record of the Blairs' journey is a tribute to the vanishing world of Indonesia.

Chan, Sucheng, ed. *Hmong Means Free: Life in Laos and America*. See entry 299.

1615 Chandler, David P. *The Land and People of Cambodia*. Illus. HarperCollins 1991, $19.00 (0-06-021129-6). 224pp. Nonfiction.

Essentially a history of Cambodia, this volume was written for junior high and high school students, but it also has value for the adult general reader. The book begins by describing the ascent to power of the Khmer Rouge forces, a topic further explored in such biographies as *Stay Alive, My Son* by Pin Yathy and *To Destroy You Is No Loss* by Joan D. Criddle and Teeda Butt Mam *(see main entries)*. The Khmer Rouge implemented a policy in which Cambodia was forced to "start all over," which eventually meant the massacre of over two million people. The book details events of history and provides a complete description of the land and the people. Social and economic questions are addressed, and separate boxed essays discuss details of religion, ethnic divisions, historical figures, and chronologies of events. An extensive chapter-by-chapter bibliography offers an excellent source of further reading, and an index is included.

1616 Collins, Joseph. *The Philippines: Fire on the Rim*. Illus. Inst. for Food & Development Policy/Food First Books 1989, $18.95 (0-935028-50-1); $9.95 (0-935028-51-X). 316pp. Nonfiction.

The author interviewed fifty people in the Philippines who represent various walks of life and various political philosophies. The thrust of their conversations is that agrarian reform is sorely needed in the Philippines, even if a revolution is necessary to bring that reform about. Reflecting the tension between tenant farmers and their landlords, the interviewees express their belief that there was no true land reform under President Cory Aquino. Each "voice" heard here represents a lifetime of struggle against poverty and hunger. This collection is a highly charged, personal, poignant, political testimony of a people hoping for a better future for their nation.

> Conze, Edward. **Buddhism: Its Essence and Development**.
> See entry 1398.

1617 Corn, Charles P. **Distant Islands: Crossing Indonesia's Ring of Fire**. Viking 1991, $25.00 (0-670-82374-0). 320pp. Nonfiction.

Many travelers, both intrepid and cautious, have made their way through China, Japan, Korea, and other parts of Asia and have returned home to publish a book of their travels. There have been few such books, however, to emerge from travels in Indonesia. This book is a rare exception. The author spent several months wandering through the largest archipelago on earth, absorbing the traditional wisdom of the people, learning about the forest spirits, and experiencing the strange mix of mysticism and modernity that characterizes Indonesia. Corn seeds his personal adventures with plenty of anecdotes about history and offers the reader generous glimpses of local color by describing the many characters that spice his already flavorful narrative.

A bibliography of further reading is appended, including several recent publications by other intrepid adventurers in Indonesia.

1618 Courtald, Caroline. **In Search of Burma**. Illus. Fredrick Muller 1984. o.p. Nonfiction.

Burma (known officially since 1989 as Myanmar) is a land with an unusual attitude toward outsiders. Tourists, to put it mildly, are not encouraged. There are no tour groups, no tourist hotels, no businesses that cater to tourists. It's not necessarily the case that the Burmese have anything to hide; they are certainly a friendly people. However, the country's policy is simply to block any influence by foreigners. In recent years the limit of a foreigner's stay was extended from twenty-four hours to a week; still, there are no amenities that would encourage so long a visit. Burma may be one of the last places on Earth where one can go, not as a tourist, but merely as a traveler.

Though it is a land of seeming simplicity and gentleness, its history, as described in this book, is full of violence. The people are strongly Buddhist. Every male child goes to the temple at least once in his life to become a monk for a certain length of time; some remain there forever. The author describes life within the temple in some detail. The Burmese are a gregarious people. Of utmost importance to them are their many festivals, theaters, songs, and dances. The book also describes life along the Irrawaddy River, involving peasant farmers, transportation, commerce, farming, and fishing. Historical maps provide the reader with a clearer sense of Burma's relationship with neighboring countries. Ethnic minorities also play an important part in shaping the region's national identity.

Finally, there is a historical chronological chart comparing events in Burma with those in greater Asia and the rest of the world. Suggested reading is given in essay form. There are a list of festivals, a glossary, and an index. This small coffee-table book is laden with beautiful color photographs and provides a good introduction to a country about which little information is available.

1619 Diamond, Judith. *Laos*. Illus. Children's Pr. 1989, $20.55 (0-516-02713-1). 128pp. Nonfiction.

Written for young people, this book will also interest the adult interested in a mostly factual background of Laos. The book provides many illustrations, including color photographs, black-and-white engravings, and maps. In her text, the author also attempts to illustrate Laotian philosophy and frame of mind. Factual sections address such topics as geography, history, economy, the people, education, festivals, art, and literature. Interesting reading can be found in the sections labeled "Mini Facts at a Glance," and a list of important people precedes the index.

1620 Draine, Cathie, and Barbara Hall, eds. *Culture Shock: Indonesia*. Illus. Graphic Arts Center 1991, $10.95 (1-55868-057-8). 280pp. Nonfiction.

In this book, Indonesian culture is described by and for Westerners. One benefit in this approach is that a Western traveler can avoid the social blunders that marred the visits of previous adventurers. Written with humor, but intended to prevent serious misunderstandings, the book offers advice on what to do and what not to do. Valuable sections discuss a range of topics: the various ethnic groups that make up the population of Indonesia; the spoken language (making note, for example, that there are six ways to say "please" and twelve ways to say "no"); a handy list, with descriptions and examples, of Indonesian perceptions that are likely to differ from those of Westerners; long pages of social dos and don'ts; and advice on how visitors can arrange to have their personal needs taken care of while traveling in the region. The editors of this book hope that by sharing knowledge and experience, they can promote tolerance and understanding of people and things that are different.

The same series includes another title, *Culture Shock: Thailand*, by Robert and Nanthapa Cooper (Times Books, 1982). These authors also use a humorous touch in their efforts to help Westerners adapt to and make sense of another culture.

1621 Duldulao, Mañuel D. *The Filipinos: Portrait of a People*. Illus. Philippine Expressions/Filipiniana Bookshop, Los Angeles 1987. o.p. Nonfiction.

This coffee-table book, embellished with beautiful color photos, presents a detailed history and portrait of the people of the Philippines. The writing style is chatty and far from literary, but both the pictorial and the textual presentations of the country are detailed and extensive. The author is at times clearly opinionated, but the reader gets an interesting perspective on this country.

The book begins with a description of the elements that have gone into the formation of the multifaceted profile and character of the Philippines. On the surface, the people seem to chase after the American lifestyle and culture, but the Spanish influence is also still very much present. The influence of its giant neighbor China is felt mainly in the realm of business.

Succeeding sections discuss a range of topics: the natural beauty and variety of the islands; art history and artifacts; a discussion of the various indigenous groups; the debates about language—especially the struggle to establish a single national language; indigenous folk customs and costumes; the daily life of the farmer; and lifestyles of urban workers, who only recently adopted the Western-style work week (9 to 5, Monday through Friday). The last section addresses music, art, dance, crafts, and fiesta, the most joyous occasion of the year.

1622 Freeman, Michael, and Roger Warner. ***Angkor: The Hidden Glories***. Illus. Houghton 1990, $45.00 (0-395-53757-6). 256pp. Nonfiction.

This giant coffee-table volume is filled with dazzling color photographs of the great, mysterious, and beautiful Angkor Wat, the ancient ruins in Cambodia, now largely overgrown with jungle. The carvings and structures clearly reveal influence of the Hindic cultures and the Hindu gods, but the temples also look as though they could be found in the Mayan jungles of Guatemala.

The introduction offers a vivid description of the site and its discovery. Every photograph is accompanied by an insightful and informative caption. History, architecture, and cultural items are included along with the author's lyrical musings about the role and function of the shrine. A glossary and a bibliography are included.

1623 Graetz, Rick, and Fred Rohrback. ***Vietnam: Opening Doors to the World***. Frwd. by Stanley Karnow. Illus. with photos. American World Geographic Publg. 1988, $17.95 (0-938314-57-2). 160pp. Nonfiction.

The authors traveled in a small group from Ho Chi Minh City (formerly Saigon) in South Vietnam to Hanoi and Haiphong in the North to talk with the people and take photographs. This resulting volume is primarily a travelogue that offers a good deal of geographical detail, a few points of culture, some commentary about the war years, and descriptions of the various occupations of this century, but the text has very little historical or cultural insight. Still, the well-selected color photos present captivating faces and a surprisingly great variety of city, country, and village scenes, and make this photographic essay the most illuminating one available of the Vietnamese people.

1624 Herbert, Patricia, and Anthony Milner, eds. ***South East Asia: Languages and Literatures: A Select Guide***. Illus. Univ. of Hawaii Pr. 1989, $18.95 (0-8248-1267-0). 182pp. Nonfiction.

This multilingual bibliography of bibliographies lists works pertaining to the languages and literatures of the various Southeast Asian countries. The book is organized by country, and each chapter offers an introductory essay addressing topics relevant to the region discussed. The book is quite scholarly and is not aimed at the casual reader, but it is included in this listing because it offers a wealth of detailed information not likely to be gathered together anywhere else.

1625 Hess, Martha. ***Then the Americans Came: Voices from Vietnam***. Illus. with photos. Four Walls Eight Windows 1993, $22.95 (0-941423-92-1); Rutgers Univ. Pr., $14.95 (0-8135-2145-9). 300pp. Nonfiction.

In 1989, the author traveled throughout Vietnam to interview people from all walks of life about their feelings and experiences during the Vietnam War, which they naturally refer to as "the American War." The focus of the conversations is on the suffering of the Vietnamese people at the hands of the Americans. Many of the interviewees refer to Americans—not the Northern Vietnamese—as "the enemy." Tales of rape and torture abound, and there are vivid memories of helicopter flights to the hospital with the wounded. Despite the suffering the people describe, they harbor surprisingly little bitterness and express mainly a hope for friendship and peace with their former enemy.

1626 Lewis, Paul, and Elaine Lewis. ***Peoples of the Golden Triangle: Six Tribes in Thailand***. Illus. Thames & Hudson 1984, $40.00 (0-500-97314-8). 225pp. Nonfiction.

This large and detailed book catalogs and describes a full array of cultural information regarding six hill tribes of Thailand: the Akha, the Hmong, the Karen, the Lahu, the Lisu, and the Mien. For each group, parallel topics are presented, ranging from clothing and ornaments to village life. The authors explore such themes as social relationships, courtship and marriage, leaders and family relationships, birth, death, and religion.

Some readers may find the amount and detail of information to be over-whelming. Relief comes from the striking and delightful compilation of color and black-and-white photographs. There are vivid displays of the rich and complex designs in clothing, jewelry, pipes, silver knives, looms and other tools for producing textiles, baskets, musical instruments, carrying bags, and much more. Photographs of people in their environment using these items and interacting with each other are interspersed throughout. This is a delight-ful and definitive work on a topic that, due to the recent immigration of these peoples to the United States, is of growing interest.

1627 Lubis, Mochtar. ***Indonesia: Land under the Rainbow***. Illus. Oxford Univ. Pr. 1991, $22.00 (0-19-588977-0). 236pp. Nonfiction.

Intended as a popular narrative history of Indonesia, this small book is packed with data organized around descriptions of foreign occupations. Chapters include early ships from China, India, and Persia; the arrival of Islam; and occupation by the Portuguese, the Dutch, the British, the Japanese, and fi-nally the Americans. The reading is surprisingly dry for a book aimed at the general reader. Nevertheless the book is highly informative. An epilogue, which is possibly the most interesting chapter, describes the Indonesian reac-tion to all these foreigners in their islands.

The author is also an important novelist and short story writer; examples of his work can be found in *ASEAN Short Stories*, edited by Robert Yeo *(see main entry)*.

1628 Lue Vang, and Judy Lewis. ***Grandmother's Path, Grandfather's Way: Hmong Preservation Project: Oral Lore, Generation to Generation***. Zellerbach Family Fund 1984. o.p. Nonfiction.

This soft-cover, large-format book is an attempt to preserve as much as possi-ble of the Hmong oral culture and traditions. The authors gleaned the informa-tion directly, through interviews with the Hmong people.

The first sections deal with the history and origins of the Hmong, which are rooted so deeply in the distant past that no one is sure just where this group came from. The Hmong migrated through China and spread through-out Southeast Asia, eventually settling in large concentrations in Laos and elsewhere. Religion, language, dress, and social customs are discussed.

A large section of folktales, proverbs, and similes is given both in Hmong and in English, followed by sung poetry, word play, and songs, also in both languages. Traditional needlepoint, clothing, and daily life are discussed in English, and, more intriguingly, in story-cloth drawings. An extensive bibliography lists music, film, videos, and material available in the Hmong language.

1629 Lueras, Leonard. ***Bali: The Ultimate Island***. Illus. with photos by R. Ian Lloyd. St. Martin 1987, $35.00 (0-312-00863-5). 240pp. Nonfiction.

This is a coffee-table book par excellence. The color photos—some full-page, some double-spread—are magnificent, haunting, ethereal, and unusual. There are also some sepia historical photographs and prints. Even the essays and chapters that surround the photos are unusually good for a book of this type, discussing such topics as ritual trance dancing and other religious rites, dancing, theater, music, puppet plays, art, and artists. Various Western photographers are represented. Among the topics explored in the text are early encounters with curious foreigners, patterns, textiles, ceremonies, temples, masks, and the importance of rice to the Balinese culture. As the book reveals, the island paradise abounds with color, natural beauty, and festival. Good maps, historical chronology, discography, filmography, bibliography, and an index are also included.

1630 Matsui, Yayori. ***Women's Asia***. Illus. with photos. Humanities Pr. 1989, $15.00 (0-86232-827-6). 192pp. Nonfiction.

People's movements and human rights endeavors are mushrooming all over Asia. At long last, people and their governments are addressing such important problems as poverty and women's roles. This book—originally aimed at the Japanese, whom the editor perceives as complacent—exhorts readers to open their eyes to the plight of women in less-favored countries. Its publication in English may also produce similar results among complacent readers in the West.

The book exposes the difficulties faced by women in Third World countries, including economic exploitation, environmental pollution, corruption, prostitution, and apathy. Most of the countries discussed are in South Asia and Southeast Asia, although one chapter focuses on Korea.

Black-and-white photographs in a center section enhance the reader's awareness—and hopefully their sense of dismay—at the degrading, often dehumanizing, treatment of women in the region.

1631 Muller, Kal, and Paul Zach. ***Indonesia: Paradise on the Equator***. Illus. with photos. St. Martin 1988. o.p. Nonfiction.

This beautifully photographed coffee-table book contains cultural and historical tidbits as well as the author's anecdotes of travel around the islands of Indonesia. The book offers geographic details about the various ethnic peoples who inhabit the region. Special emphasis is placed on colorful religious ceremonies and festivals. A lengthy and useful bibliography and index are appended. Muller has also produced a related book, *Indonesia in Color* (Periplus, 1990).

Rahula, Walpola. ***What the Buddha Taught***.
See entry 1420.

Robinson, Francis. *Atlas of the Islamic World Since 1500*.
See entry 1421.

1632 Schwaback, Karen. *Thailand: Land of Smiles*. Illus. Macmillan 1991, $14.95 (0-87518-454-5). 128pp. Nonfiction.

Written for children in upper elementary or junior high school, this book can also provide vital information to an interested adult. "Fast Facts" and a rudimentary map precede each of the nine chapters, which discuss geography, the people, history, legends, festivals, families, schools, sports, and emigration to the West. An appendix lists Thai consulates and embassies in the United States and Canada. A glossary gives interesting words and phrases, while a bibliography refers readers to other sources. The text even includes a few recipes.

Suzuki, David, and Peter Knudtson. *Wisdom of the Elders: Honoring Sacred Native Visions of Nature*.
See entry 532.

1633 Thich Nhat Hanh. *The Moon Bamboo*. Trans. from Vietnamese by Vo-Dinh Mai and Mobi Ho; Intro. by Mobi Ho. Illus. by Vo-Dinh Mai. Parallax 1989, $12.00 (0-938077-20-1). 179pp. Essays.

The many popular books by this Vietnamese monk offer philosophies to help readers cope with daily life. In this book he expresses his views on how best to live through the charming device of recounting four of his own modern fairy tales. Each story in this volume contains some elements of traditional Vietnamese myth, but the author has revised and enlarged the original tale to incorporate a political or social statement about Vietnam and its present plight. The stories address the hopes and tragedies of refugees and boat people and offer philosophical thoughts on life and death. Mythological characters mix with modern people to convey to readers the fundamental Buddhist precept that all things are interconnected. Elegantly written and sophisticated, the stories are more complex than first meets the eye, and they will reward repeated readings.

1634 Ulack, Richard, and Gyula Pauer. *Atlas of Southeast Asia*. Illus. Macmillan 1988, $95.00 (0-02-933200-1); $75.00 (0-318-32912-3). 171pp. Nonfiction.

This encyclopedic atlas offers methodical presentations of each country's history, geography, economy, transportation, tourism, people, and culture. In addition to the maps there are charts, graphs, and tables plus a picture or two to enhance understanding. A bibliography and index are appended.

1635 Valencia, Teodoro F. *Over a Cup of Coffee*. Illus. Philippine Expressions/ Filipiniana Bookshop, Los Angeles 1988. o.p. Essays.

For thirty-three years this author wrote a column called "Over a Cup of Coffee." This volume is a commemorative tribute, assembled by his editors and admirers, containing his best writings. These tidbits, rich in humor and revelation about the Philippines, are light and easy to read. Their insights, matched by the journalist's flowing style, present a fascinating and uniquely insightful picture of the Philippines of today and of the past several decades.

On political issues, Valencia wrote: " 'The people should trust their leaders,' President Garcia said. . . . Amen, we say. But we hope the president did not confuse high office with leadership. They're not the same."

On religion, he wrote: "Priests and ministers who have been toying with being politicians should go out and campaign in the coming elections. That would make honest men of them. As it is, feeding churchgoers with hate instead of religion is outright swindling—wasting the time of the faithful."

Education was another of his targets: "Teaching—next only to ditch digging—is one of the most difficult occupations in the world."

A dozen longer columns complete the collection. Not all his writings will seem in good taste to an American reader, who may chafe at the outspoken author's rather low opinion of American involvement in the Philippines. Nonetheless, this popular and influential writer has much to say about the thoughts and feelings of his fellow Filipinos. Nearly forty pages of black-and-white photos illustrate the journalistic life of this popular writer who entered the political scene, made his way into the living rooms of leaders, and lent his name to social groups for backing and prestige. He died in 1987 at the still-youthful age of seventy-four.

1636 Warren, William. *Thai Style*. Illus. by Luca I. Tettoni. Rizzoli 1989, $37.50 (0-8478-1043-7). 224pp. Nonfiction.

This coffee-table book offers a collection of beautiful photographs of Thai art, architecture, and lifestyles. An overview explains the historical background for this civilization, which relied on an extensive—and even beautiful—network of canals. The author and the photographer note how the ancient temples that abound in the region represent various eras of history as well as the influence of many non-Thai population groups. There is also detailed discussion of the decorative arts, Thai architectural forms, spirit houses, palaces, and monks' quarters.

1637 Wilcox, Donald J. *Hmong Folklife*. Illus. with photos. Hmong Natural Assn. of North Carolina 1986. o.p. Nonfiction.

This simple book, graced with a few descriptive photos and simple pen-and-ink sketches, begins with a cultural definition of the Hmong and briefly explores their history. The essays that make up the body of the book address such topics as language, music and musical instruments, traditional clothing, customs, traditional houses, herbal folk remedies, fishing and hunting, food, children's games, stories, and songs. A handful of color photos give life to this very informative book.

1638 Wintle, Justin. *Romancing Vietnam: Inside the Boat Country*. Pantheon 1991, $25.00 (0-679-40621-2). 464pp. Nonfiction.

The author was struck by the fact that American movies about the Vietnam War revealed a great deal about American attitudes and values, but told audiences virtually nothing about Vietnam itself. To achieve a better balance for himself, and to see the country as something other than as a proving-ground for American muscle, Wintle traveled throughout Vietnam. Escorted by his entourage—assigned guides, a driver, an interpreter, and growing peripheral crew—he probably saw more of the country than the top brass wanted him to see—more, in fact, than he expected to see himself. He discovered that, to the Vietnamese, the war had been a matter of pride.

Wintle writes in a style that is witty without being cute, simple without being stupid. He reports engagingly on his own day-by-day travels, discoveries, conversations, and meetings. In the process he packs in plenty of political and historical facts and shares his understanding about the country, the culture, and the people themselves.

1639 Wright, David K. *Burma*. Illus. Children's Pr. 1991, $20.55 (0-516-02725-5). 128pp. Nonfiction.

Presenting something more than "just the facts," the Enchantment of the World series for young people is sprinkled liberally with lively color photos. Color maps are found in the front and in the back. Besides the usual details about geography, history, people, and religion, this book on Burma (Myanmar) also discusses ethnic guerrillas, insurgents, drugs, and the legends associated with the colorful pagodas. The arts and theater are also emphasized, and discussions of cities and foreign influences offer the Burmese point of view on various problems. "Mini Facts" at a glance, a list of important names, and an index complete the book.

1640 Zickgraf, Ralph. *Laos*. Illus. Chelsea House 1991, $14.95 (0-7910-0159-8). 112pp. Nonfiction.

This small book is a strictly factual presentation of the geography, history, people, and religion of Laos, a country that is often called "The Land in the Middle." Black-and-white photographs and a selection of color photos enhance the reader's feel for the country. Like other volumes in the Places and Peoples of the World series, this book includes an initial section of "Facts at a Glance" and a chronology called "History at a Glance." Written for young people, the book has plenty of appeal for the adult interested in a terse, focused description of the country. A glossary and an index are included.

BIOGRAPHY

Bulosan, Carlos. *America Is in the Heart: A Personal History*. See entry 334.

1641 Criddle, Joan D., and Teeda Butt Mam. *To Destroy You Is No Loss: The Odyssey of a Cambodian Family*. Doubleday 1989. o.p. Autobiography.

Contrary to popular belief in the West, the peoples of the various countries of Indochina are not all related by culture or by language or even by love for each other. As an example, the language spoken in Vietnam is more closely related to Chinese, while the languages of Laos, Thailand, and Cambodia are of Hindic origin.

This book offers an elaborate preface with illuminating and straightforward cultural and historical background. The author, a Cambodian refugee, challenges the notion that the American presence in Indochina brought about any good at all. When the Khmer Rouge seized control of the government, the Cambodian people—already tired of five years of their own civil war plus the suffering they experienced because of their proximity to the Vietnam War—were forced into the villages from the cities. The Cambodian Holocaust began; eventually, two million people—one fourth of the population—were killed.

With the intensity of a murder mystery writer, Teeda Butt Nam tells her story to coauthor Joan Criddle. It is the story of her family's move from normalcy to hell. City residents were herded into the countryside; the teenage Khmer Rouge soldiers had no qualms about killing any troublemakers on the spot. Repeatedly, the soldiers told the people how insignificant they were: "To destroy you is no loss!" The author's father died during this horror. Many times during her ordeal, Mam—a mere teenager—contemplated suicide. Still, she found it in her heart to go on living. She married, and together with her husband and other family members, she made the treacherous journey to Thailand—not once but twice—to attain freedom after the Vietnamese invaded Cambodia in 1979. At the end of this excruciating tale, a Cambodian historical timeline is given, which helps put the events of the story in perspective.

Although the book itself is out of print, an adaptation of this story for the theater, written by Dorothea H. Bonneau, is available (Dramatic Publg., 1992).

1642 Crisostomo, Isabelo T. ***Cory: Profile of a President***. Intro. by Heherson Alvarez. Branden 1987, $19.95 (0-8283-1913-8). 340pp. Biography.

The author is strongly pro-Aquino and equally strongly anti-Marcos. Even allowing for bias, this book is one of the clearest pictures available of the great differences between the Marcos family and regime and the Aquino family and regime. Marked by treachery, corruption, and doubletalk, the Marcos regime finally fell because of the will of the Filipino people, who demanded a government that would truly and at last take care of the people. After Benigno Aquino, a prominent opposition leader, was assassinated, his wife, Cory, was talked into taking his place. To the amazement of all, she not only accepted the challenge but won the presidential election. This is her story, from her beginnings through her days as the housewife who supported her husband during his meteoric political career to her ultimate triumph as leader of her people. Appendixes offer speeches as well as a copy of the new Philippine constitution, chapter footnotes, and an index.

Fiffer, Sharon S. ***Imagining America: Paul Thai's Journey from the Killing Fields to Freedom***.
See entry 335.

Hayslip, Le Ly, and James Hayslip. ***Child of War, Woman of Peace***.
See entry 336.

1643 Hayslip, Le Ly, and Jay Wurts. ***When Heaven and Earth Changed Places: A Vietnamese Woman's Journey from War to Peace***. NAL 1993, $12.00 (0-452-26417-0). 368pp. Autobiography.

Americans came to Vietnam largely unarmed with any knowledge of the land, the people, or its recent history. To the Vietnamese peasants, North and

South, the Americans were incarnations of monsters from their worst fairy tales. Their village upbringing taught them to seek strength and comfort by turning to the spirits of their ancestors.

After a century or more of constant occupation by foreign governments, it seemed to the Vietnamese that the Americans, far from being liberators, were merely stepping in to take the place of their recently departed oppressors, the French. Even the Americans' green berets looked the same as the French headgear. The Vietnamese wanted no more foreigners on their soil; they just wanted to be left alone to run their own country and keep it whole. For many of them, the war was not about a struggle between Communism and democracy. Most of them knew nothing of either system. Instead, for them, the war was a struggle of resistance to outsiders, a battle to unify the country and return it to the care of the farmers.

This gripping story—adapted into a film by Oliver Stone—tells the intimate details of a woman living in a war-torn country as she recounts her childhood and youth in a small village in central Vietnam. Le Ly describes her mental and physical torture during the war years, her flight to the United States—the land of the enemy—and her return journey sixteen years later. Stepping nimbly back and forth between memories of the past and her recent return journey, Le Ly describes, in moment-to-moment urgency, her life, her thoughts and feelings about the war, and her insights into the actions of her people.

Le Ly married an American, James Hayslip. She continues her saga in *Child of War, Woman of Peace (see main entry)*.

1644 MacDonald, Peter. ***Giap: The Victor in Vietnam***. Norton 1993, $25.00 (0-393-03401-1). 352pp. Biography.

As a Vietnamese soldier, Vo Nguyen Giap was involved in three separate wars. Gradually he rose in rank to become a general. His story is inspiring for young people because of his self-discipline and diligence, which led to his acceptance as leader of his country. The author is himself a brigadier general in the British army. He interviewed American, French, and Vietnamese officers, including William Westmoreland, commander of American troops during the Vietnam War and Marcelle Bigeard, the French general in command at Dien Bien Phu. He also spoke with Giap himself to gain perspective on how the Vietnamese managed to fend off, and ultimately defeat, the mighty armies from the West. The easy-flowing reading makes this a good biography for high school students and the interested lay reader.

1645 Nguyen, Noc Ngan. ***The Will of Heaven: The Story of One Vietnamese and the End of His World***. Trans. from Vietnamese. Dutton 1982. o.p. Autobiography.

A popular writer in Vietnam, the author dedicates this engrossing tale to the millions of Vietnamese who have also suffered loss of life, family, and culture. He begins his story when he was a schoolteacher in the early years of the Vietnam War. News of the fighting in the countryside was repressed in the city. Still, he knew, from the experience of years of civil war, how corrupt governments can be even while claiming to fight for peace, freedom, and equality for all.

After the Americans left in 1975, Nguyen was sentenced to three years of forced labor in the countryside. He eventually returned to his wife and child, only to experience dismay when he saw how the victorious Communist forces had created a "new" Vietnam, one that confiscated private property and that moved people around according to the convenience of the Communist Party, with no regard for the person's family, interest, or ability. About to be separated again, Nguyen and his family decided to try to escape from "the larger prison"—Vietnam itself. Their tiny boat set out for Malaysia and freedom. But after many frightening days at sea, the vessel was swamped in a storm, and numerous lives were lost, including the author's wife and their four-year-old son.

The author repeats that he speaks for all those who shared in the tragic fate of the end of the old Vietnam, who witnessed the farewell to their beloved old culture and who experienced firsthand the startling inhumanity that power can bring.

1646 O'Brien, Niall. ***Revolution from the Heart.*** 2nd ed. Intro. by Theodore Hesburgh. Oxford Univ. Pr. 1987, $22.95 (0-19-504950-0); Orbis $12.95 (0-88344-765-7). 320pp. Autobiography.

The author, a Catholic priest, left his home in Ireland on a mission to bring the Christian message to the people of Negros in the Philippines. It was 1964, at the height the Marcos regime. The author's intention was to help the farmworkers in their fight against poverty and hunger. He organized small Christian groups, which became so popular that the authorities felt threatened. Fighting bouts of hepatitis as well, O'Brien lasted twenty years in the Philippines, until Marcos jailed him. This book is his report on the state of things in the Philippines. The last part of the book contains stories of visits from friends to his jail cell, as well as discussions of the insights he achieved while a prisoner. The poverty and exploitation of the poor that the author describes is heart-wrenching, and the reader experiences the priest's elation over the people's revolution and the final overthrow of Marcos. A full and useful recent bibliography is included.

1647 Yathy, Pin, and John Man. ***Stay Alive, My Son.*** Free Pr. 1987, $24.95 (0-02-935861-2). 256pp. Autobiography.

The story of one family becomes the story of millions. In the years between 1975 and 1979, the Communist-inspired Khmer Rouge soldiers took over Cambodia. In a misbegotten attempt to create a utopia where only the "right" people would survive, the soldiers massacred a quarter of the nation's people. The few who escaped to Thailand or the United States, sometimes after years of near starvation and persecution, all have similar stories to tell.

As the author recounts, the mostly teenage soldiers seemed to act as if human life had no meaning. The moral values and honored traditions of a noble and ancient land were destroyed virtually in an instant. The Khmer Rouge used key words like *freedom, democracy, independence,* and *national unity* to make the Cambodians believe the soldiers were interested in their welfare and equality. Gradually, inexorably, the truth becomes clear. The soldiers had no goodwill; the only thing on their minds was to murder unmercifully those millions whom they deemed were "not right." The lucky few who understood in time tried to escape through the jungle and over mountains to Thailand. A few survived. In this author's case, he was the only one of his large family to make it. One by one, all the others were killed, or they died, or they were swallowed up by the relentless jungle and lost forever.

Poignant and heartrending, the stories of suffering during this Cambodian Holocaust are comparable to the horror of the Jewish Holocaust in Germany. The world must rely on the bravery of the few survivors, such as this author, to tell the world what happened.

1648 Zaide, Gregoriao F. ***Rizal and Other Great Filipinos***. Univ. of Washington Pr. 1988. o.p. Collective Biography.

This book describes the life stories and accomplishments of a handful of political heroes from the history of the Philippines. They range from early heroes who fought against domination by Spain to the modern hero of people's power, the revolutionary Benigno Aquino. A good portion of the book is devoted to a discussion of Dr. José Rizal, a man of many talents—from physician to educator, from writer to artist—who is widely acclaimed as the Philippine's national hero. Rizal was also an author, whose novels include *The Lost Eden*, which is included in *Rizal: An Encyclopedic Collection (see main entry)*.

15

AUSTRALIA, NEW ZEALAND, AND THE PACIFIC

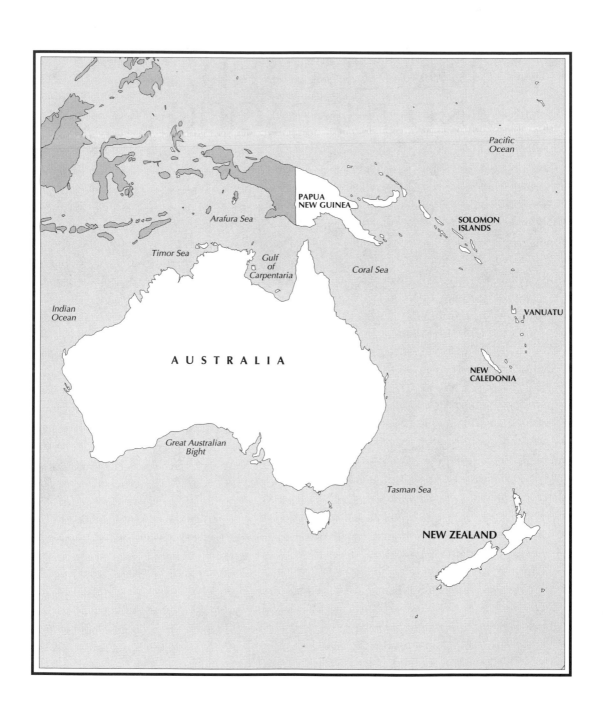

PAPUA
NEW GUINEA

Pacific
Ocean

SOLOMON
ISLANDS

Arafura Sea

Timor Sea

*Gulf
of
Carpentaria*

Coral Sea

*Indian
Ocean*

VANUATU

A U S T R A L I A

NEW
CALEDONIA

*Great Australian
Bight*

Tasman Sea

NEW ZEALAND

15

AUSTRALIA, NEW ZEALAND, AND THE PACIFIC

by Arlen Feldwick

The ideas and issues associated with multiculturalism form a major feature of contemporary social, political, legal, and economic life in Australasia. The reasons for this are complex, and the precise configuration of multiculturalism in Australasia varies with the nation or region in question. It would be a mistake to regard the multicultural scene throughout the South Pacific as homogeneous; the expressions of multiculturalism are as diverse as South Pacific experience itself.

Australia has by far the strongest international profile and national identity among the South Pacific nations. But the dominant Australian self-image has been challenged since the 1960s by two developments. The first involves Australia's Aboriginal population, which has resided on the continent for 40,000 years or more but was only accorded full citizenship in 1967. Recently, the Aborigines have demanded—in an ever louder voice—a much larger role in Australian society as well as a greater share of the country's resources. Not only have the Aborigines found many outlets for expressing their dissatisfaction at centuries of brutal and inhuman treatment, but writers of European origin have sympathized with, and taken an abiding interest in, the Aboriginal plight.

The second challenge to hegemonic Australian identity has come from the huge wave of immigration experienced by the country in the period following World War II. Australian immigrants had generally come from English-speaking countries, especially the British Isles (although during the nineteenth century some immigrants also arrived from non–English-speaking nations in Europe, from China, and from elsewhere). Australia officially endorsed this immigration pattern by a policy popularly known as "White Australia." In more recent times, however, as the result of political debate and pressure, the government has permitted immigrants not only from non–English-speaking sections of Europe and Asia, but also from Southeast Asian nations such as Vietnam. As a consequence, the demographic and cultural mix of Australia has shifted dramatically in a relatively short time, producing a far more multicultural society. Indeed, awareness of this trend has been promoted by Australian government commissions, studies, and departments. Although multiculturalism has by no means been accepted as the new Australian identity by many of its citizens (especially certain of the traditional white segments), the realities of Australia today have made the nation inescapably multicultural in fact.

The issue of multiculturalism has taken on a quite different complexion in New Zealand. Without the large waves of recent immigration that characterize Australia, New Zealand's population and its national identity are in some ways more stable. New Zealand whites of European descent are known colloquially as *Pakeha*, once considered a derogatory term but now in general use. The challenge to the dominance of Pakeha culture has arisen almost entirely from the recent economic and cultural struggle of the nation's indigenous Polynesian community, the Maori, who form about ten percent of the New Zealand population. The Maori have been part of New Zealand society since initial Pakeha settlement in the nineteenth century, and there was for a long time an explicit policy of assimilating the Maori into mainstream New Zealand. In the past several decades, however, Maori leaders have begun to view assimilation as tantamount to cultural genocide and have called for official recognition of Maori culture (Maoritanga) as an equal partner within the country. These cultural claims have been strengthened by successful Maori prosecution (through legal and political channels) of claims to enhanced economic and social rights.

The island states of Polynesia, Melanesia, and Micronesia have dealt with multicultural problems largely within the context of decolonialization and its aftermath. Although the French continue to pursue some of their colonial claims in the region and the United States' strategic interests are never far from view, most of the islands now enjoy the highest degree of autonomy from Western political powers they have had in two centuries. In some places, such as Fiji, this has created conflict, as democratic rights clash with traditional religious and social values. In most of the South Pacific Island states, Western-oriented attitudes and tastes sit in uncomfortable juxtaposition to traditional cultures. Some observers regard the new Western cultural imperialism as a far greater threat to indigenous ways of life than the militaristic and territorial imperialism of earlier days. For many, the main challenge is resisting the lure of Western culture to such a degree that the South Pacific Islanders' own identities can survive and flourish.

Multicultural self-awareness is very much a phenomenon of the last quarter-century. Consequently, multicultural writing is still in relative infancy throughout the South Pacific. This creates special obstacles to the promotion of an understanding and appreciation of Australasian multiculturalism within North America. Some problems are practical. The availability in the United States of writings published in the South Pacific, particularly the works of indigenous authors, is uneven. Many important publishers in the region (for example, the University of the South Pacific Press, Aboriginal Studies Press, and Australian Institute for Aboriginal Studies) do not have regular book distribution agreements in North America. In addition, a great deal of Australasian multicultural writing is still published by small presses or by minor academic presses. This makes it difficult for residents of the South Pacific, let alone of the Northern Hemisphere, to find out about and obtain such works. In addition, many multicultural writers shun mainstream popularity and support alternative publishing ventures (such as Western Australia's Magabala

Books, which publishes only Aboriginal writing) that are committed to the values of cultural enrichment over those of commerce.

As a consequence, some of the most talented and influential authors working in Australasia today do not directly reach an American audience. The problem is especially dire in the case of fiction and biography. A few examples will suffice. Witi Ihimaera is New Zealand's leading Maori novelist and an editor of Maori fiction, yet as of this writing only one of Ihimaera's own books and none of his edited collections are currently marketed in the United States. Similarly, the fictional works of the prominent and prolific Aboriginal writers Mudrooroo Narogin (who once published under his European name Colin Johnson) and Jack Davis have been, until very recently, almost entirely unobtainable. With the exception of the Fijian-Indian writer Subramani and the Samoan Albert Wendt, no authors of fiction from the Pacific Island states have been published in the United States, and the principal works available about the region, such as *Best South Seas Stories* and *The Lure of Tahiti*, tend to feature classic (and somewhat stereotypical) tales by white male European or American authors.

This general problem is compounded by several factors. First, Australasian multicultural authors (from both indigenous and immigrant backgrounds) do not always choose English as their language of expression. One reason is that they fear they will be unable to capture completely their own cultural experiences in what, to them, is a foreign tongue. They resist the dominance of the English language, which threatens to marginalize indigenous languages. Furthermore, they do not necessarily have a strong desire to communicate with English-speaking readers; they tell their stories primarily for an audience of their own people. A multicultural society may well mean a multilingual one as well.

A second factor hindering wider access to Australasian multicultural writing is gender. South Pacific women are (characteristically) underrepresented among the authors from the region who have managed to achieve international publication and distribution. For instance, two important and acclaimed Aboriginal autobiographies by women, *Don't Take Your Love to Town* by Ruby Langford (1988) and *Wandering Girl* by Glenyse Ward (1987) are not distributed in the United States. *Civilized Girl*, a tale from the Pacific Islands by Jully Sipolo, is similarly unavailable. Talented Maori women such as Trixie Te Arama Menzies and Toi Te Rito have failed to make an impact outside their region. The resulting false impression is that the female contribution to Australasian multicultural writings is negligible.

The practical difficulties of accessibility to books are fairly easy to resolve, at least in comparison with the harder conceptual problems posed by Western attitudes toward Pacific culture. In the United States, as in all Occidental societies, there is a tendency to judge different cultures by Western standards. Often, the perceived failure to measure up to these standards becomes equivalent to "inferiority" or "backwardness" or some other negative or condescending evaluation. This perspective is even reflected in some travelogues about the South Pacific by Western authors: Paul Theroux's *The Happy Isles of Oceania: Paddling the Pacific* (Putnam, 1992) is a prime example. This book should be compared to Bruce Chatwin's infinitely more sensitive and absorbing work, *The Songlines*. But the multicultural authors of Australasia are often not trying to imitate or live up to the expectations of Western minds. Consequently, to read and appreciate these works, Western readers must suspend the standards of judgment that apply within their own cultures and instead try to discover the modes of expression that are appropriate to the writers' distinctive cultural milieus. This is not to say that we must suspend critical evaluation altogether. As Norman Simms emphasizes in *Silence and Invisibility*, we can and should continue to make distinctions and formulate critiques of non-Western literature—but we should do so according to standards relevant to the culture from which it derives. This is a cornerstone of reading multicultural writing.

Multicultural authors in the South Pacific have returned to their origins for inspiration in large measure because they have come to regard Western culture and aesthetics as a threat — or even as an enemy. By encouraging assimilation, Eurocentrism is held responsible for undermining cultural difference and identity. This is not simply a theoretical criticism. Many of the leading exponents of South Pacific multiculturalism were initially assimilated, whether by choice or under compulsion, into the dominant Eurocentric culture. In many cases some personal crisis inspired them to return to their roots. One need only read the autobiographical narratives of Sally Morgan or Mihi Edwards to realize how profoundly endangered are the indigenous cultures of Australasia.

One of the most hopeful signs for the perpetuation of multiculturalism throughout Australasia has been a general attitude of support for nondominant cultures by government agencies and programs. Grants of public funds to arts projects, events, and organizations such as publishing ventures and theatrical groups have already aided in diversifying the cultural landscapes of the South Pacific. The threat of hard economic times places the continuation of such funding in danger, of course, but there now seems to be a broad awareness throughout Australasia (admittedly, with some noteworthy exceptions, such as Fiji) that the realities of a multiracial and multiethnic society require the recognition of multicultural programs aimed at encouraging the perpetuation of diverse languages, values, and ways of life. Consequently, in the years to come, readers may expect to see an increase, both in quantity and quality, of multicultural writing emerging from throughout the South Pacific region.

LITERATURE

1649 Astley, Thea. ***Beachmasters***. Viking 1988. o.p. Fiction.

Peace does not always reign in paradise. Kristi is a fictional small tropical island in the South Pacific cast adrift by the governments of Britain and France. After years of colonial domination by uncaring administrators in distant capitals, the indigenous people start to desire self-rule, and like a discontented ship's crew, they plan a mutiny to get it. The revolutionary leaders are unskilled in the finer points of insurrection and the uprising is short-lived. Nevertheless, the revolution transforms many of Kristi's inhabitants, and matters cannot, will not, remain the same.

The revolution affects individuals as well. Gavi Salway, a young boy, discovers secrets about his racial ancestry that touch off an identity crisis. Is he white or black, or — worse yet, perhaps — is he neither? Confused, angry, and vulnerable, he inadvertently aids the fomenters of the revolution. These events, both on the personal and political levels, leave Gavi (and the entire island) with scars that may never heal completely.

Thea Astley is an acclaimed Australian author. *Beachmasters* is a beautifully written, sensitive, and realistic portrayal of contemporary island life and culture. Other recent titles include *A Descant for Gossips* (International Specialized Book Services, 1986) and *Hunting the Wild Pineapple* (Viking, 1992).

1650 Davis, Jack, and others, eds. ***Paperbark: A Collection of Black Australian Writing***. Illus. Univ. of Queensland Pr. 1990, $16.95 (0-7022-2180-5). 369pp. Anthology.

The first volume in a new series, Black Australian Writers, *Paperbark* displays the diversity and vitality of contemporary Aboriginal writing. The voices speaking here are powerful, often angry; they are not just the voices of the present generation but the cries of a people oppressed for more than two centuries and only now able to find expression.

Although most of the contributions are short stories or poems, the editors have also included a novella (Mudrooroo Narogin's *Struggling*), one scene from *Bran Nue Day*, a work considered the first Black Australian rock opera, and a one-act play by Gerry Bostock titled *Here Comes the Nigger*. The book also contains many designs by acclaimed Aboriginal artist Jimmy Pike. Another useful feature of the volume is a bibliography of recent Aboriginal writing in all genres, including nonfiction.

1651 Day, A. Grove, and Carl Stroven, eds. ***Best South Seas Stories.*** Repr. of 1947 ed. Mutual 1985, $4.95 (0-935180-12-5). 320pp. Fiction.

The South Pacific Islands and their peoples have inspired some of the world's greatest writers to compose tales of experience, romance, and adventure. For those wishing to experience the South Pacific as these writers saw it, this is a good place to start.

The editors have compiled a selection of what they consider the best-known and best-written South Pacific stories. Among the writers included are W. Somerset Maugham, Jack London, James A. Michener, Robert Louis Stevenson, Louis Becke, and Herman Melville. Whether by accident or design, the stories are all by Western male authors; a flaw of the collection is its omission of female and indigenous authors. Nevertheless, the stories are of value because they are wonderfully written and contain vivid descriptions of a bygone era. Each story is preceded by a brief biographical sketch that also recounts the author's travels in the South Pacific.

A similar book by the same editor is *The Lure of Tahiti: An Armchair Companion* (Mutual, 1987).

1652 Du Fresne, Yvonne. ***Frederique***. Viking 1987. o.p. Fiction.

It is a common misconception that New Zealand is a bicultural society made up entirely of Maori and descendants of British colonialists and missionaries. On the contrary, Auckland is the largest Polynesian city in the world; what's more, there are many Pakeha (European) people living in New Zealand who claim ancestry from many other places besides Britain.

Frederique is a historical romance about a young Danish Huguenot woman and her immigrant family. Fleeing political persecution in war-torn Europe during the 1860s, they find refuge and anonymity on the great plains of the Manawatu on New Zealand's North Island. As political exiles eking out an agricultural existence among the local Maori and the English missionaries, they are now far removed, physically as well as emotionally, from the opera houses and drawing rooms of Denmark.

This story explores the issue of coexistence and relationships between disparate cultures: Danish Huguenot, English, and Maori. The tripartite association is clearly unequal. The Pakeha are the invaders, as Frederique recognizes. She comes to see herself as little better than the Prussians oppressing Denmark. There is a deeper message, then, woven into this young woman's romantic dreams, for she grapples not only with the affairs of the heart but also with prejudice and notions of racial superiority.

1653   Gawith, Gwen, ed. ***Falling off the Edge of the World: New Zealand Stories***. Viking 1991. o.p. Anthology.

Out of New Zealand—the land the Maori call *Aotearoa* (Land of the Long White Cloud)—there has emerged in the last half century a vital new wave of writers and writing. These writers come from different ethnic, cultural, and social backgrounds. They may be Maori, Polynesian, European, Asian, or from colonialist British stock. Their common bond is that they all call themselves New Zealanders.

With the aim of capturing this distinctive New Zealand voice, the editor has collected her personal favorite authors and stories. The authors represented, all well known in New Zealand, include Witi Ihimaera, Patricia Grace, and Janet Frame. The extracts are all brief, and in both their multicultural content and their essential "New Zealandness" they will appeal to the general reader.

1654   Grace, Patricia. ***Selected Stories***. Viking 1991. o.p. Fiction.

Patricia Grace is an award-winning New Zealand author of Maori descent. Her first collection of stories, *Waiariki* (Three Continents, 1975), was also the first published collection of stories by a Maori woman writer. Grace has published widely in a variety of forms. She has written novels and children's books, and her short stories, in particular, have won wide acclaim.

This collection of stories covers the breadth and depth of Grace's work. The stories are arranged chronologically, reflecting her development as a writer from the earlier, gentler stories that had appeared in *Waiariki* through later pieces that have a sharper, more political edge.

Grace's work is infused with the Maori way of seeing things, of storytelling, and of living. Through her skills as an author, the reader inhabits the minds of her characters and thus gains insight into Maori culture. The Maori tend to live close to the land—spiritually as well as physically. By reflecting this reverence and respect for nature, Patricia Grace's stories speak with a quintessential Maori voice. Other books by this author published in the United States include *The Dreamers and Other Stories* (Viking, 1987), and *The Dream Sleepers* (Viking, no date).

1655 Gunew, Sneja, and Jan Mahyuddin, eds. *Beyond the Echo: Multicultural Women's Writing*. Univ. of Queensland Pr. 1989, $16.95 (0-7022-2085-X). 296pp. Anthology.

This is an anthology of writing by Australian women of all ages who are not of British descent. The epigram by A. Kefala encapsulates the book's purpose: "To find our measure, exactly, not the echo of other voices." The brief selections in this book fall into three general categories. The selections in the first part, "Writing Rather Than Confession," are stylistically and thematically diverse; many of them are autobiographical reflections on the author's ethnic and cultural heritage. Part Two, "What Makes a Real Woman?", contains stories about women and their search for identity. The final part, "English Plus," touches on notions of culture and cultural differences.

As the editors point out, this is not an anthology of immigrant writers; some of the women are second- or third-generation Australians. Nevertheless, the stories and essays reflect their roots. The range of ethnic and cultural heritage represented in this anthology includes many of the nations of Asia, Europe, and the Americas.

Another valuable collection edited by Gunew is *Displacements 2: Multicultural Storytellers* (Deakin Univ. Pr., 1987). This anthology includes short narratives by "new" Australian men and women from diverse ethnic backgrounds. This is a lively volume that features a visually provocative photomontage.

1656 Hall, Rodney. *A Place Among People*. Univ. of Queensland Pr. 1985, $16.95 (0-7022-0963-5). 249pp. Fiction.

This early prize-winning novel by a preeminent Australian author is set in Battery Spit, Queensland, Australia not long after World War II. The small coastal town is home to the eccentric Collocott, still considered a newcomer after eight years, as well as a cast of colorful local characters.

A dominant theme of the novel is the notion of the "outsider." Collocott, a loner, has an uncertain and often uneasy relationship with his adopted community, and it with him. Nevertheless, Collocott has the choice of whether he wishes to live as an outsider. In contrast, Daisy, the sole Aboriginal inhabitant of Battery Spit, is forced to be an outsider because of the town's racial prejudice.

The tension builds to a climax when the seemingly peaceful town erupts into mob aggression against Daisy. Collocott courageously defends her, and although his bravery earns him respect and acceptance, both he and Daisy feel that they cannot remain in Battery Spit. In the end, Collocott prepares to leave, perhaps to a more mainstream existence, but Daisy's future remains cloudy.

Also recommended for their intelligent and sensitive treatment of the relation between whites and Aborigines are two other novels by this author, *Kisses of the Enemy* (Farrar, 1988) and *The Second Bridegroom* (Farrar, 1991).

1657 Hulme, Keri. *The Bone People*. Louisiana State Univ. Pr. 1985, $19.95 (0-8071-1284-4); Viking $9.95 (0-14-008922-5). 450pp. Fiction.

The wild beaches of New Zealand's South Island provide the backdrop for Keri Hulme's first novel, which portrays the powerful interplay between three strong individuals: a part-Maori woman, a Maori man, and his adopted autistic child. Hulme weaves Maori myth and Christian symbolism into the lives and personalities of her characters, all of whom are struggling, in their own ways, to come to terms with their flawed natures. The three compelling central characters are emotionally wounded beings who gradually learn to heal one another.

This is a novel of great intensity and feeling, a story about passion that is told with passion. It is about people—Maori and Pakeha (Europeans)—and about a place, New Zealand. This outstanding novel won the Booker Mc-Connell Prize for 1985, a prestigious annual award for British and Commonwealth literature. Hulme is also the author of *Strands* (Oxford Univ. Pr., 1992), a collection of poems.

1658 Ihimaera, Witi. ***Tangi***. Heinemann 1990. o.p. Fiction.

It is said that when a Maori dies, rain will follow. To mark the passing of a loved one, members of the *whanau* (extended family) gather together, often coming from great distances, to perform a *Tangi*. This funeral ceremony takes place at the *marae* (meeting house) where the deceased lies in state before being buried after the third day. This novel is the story of events surrounding the death and the *Tangi* of Tama's father.

Tama is a twenty-two-year-old Maori brought up near Gisborne, a small town on the east coast of New Zealand's North Island. Tama, like many young Maori, is lured away from his rural community by the bright lights of a large city, Wellington. The sudden death of his father causes him to reevaluate his life and think about his future. He experiences guilt and distress about having left his *whanau*, especially his father, whom he will never see again. As the eldest son, he is expected to return home, look after his mother and his siblings, and run the farm. His ruminations about his loss and his childhood memories traveling around the remote regions of New Zealand are entwined with Maori myth, spirituality, and an abiding sense of the important role that family plays in a Maori's sense of identity. This is a sensitive account of one person's experience of deep personal loss. It is also extremely rich in many aspects of Maori culture. See also *The Matriarch* (1986) and *Into the World of Light: An Anthology of Maori Writing* (1982).

1659 Kalechofsky, Roberta, and Robert Kalechofsky, eds. ***Jewish Writing from Down Under: Australia and New Zealand***. Micah 1984, $12.95 (0-916288-16-1). 292pp. Anthology.

This is a diverse collection of writings, short stories, introspective anecdotes, studies, and poems by Jewish writers from "Down Under." The pieces were written between the 1840s and the present. Because the authors were either born outside New Zealand and Australia or are first-generation Australasians, their writings often reflect the country and culture of their non-Australasian background.

World War II generated huge waves of European Jewish immigrants to Australia and New Zealand, and adjusting to life in the "new country" was not always easy. Many of those experiences, both good and bad, are expressed in these stories.

The entries in this anthology are as diverse in style and content as are the different social backgrounds of the contributors. This diversity adds to the book's value. The overall unity of the work is maintained in the shared challenges of people trying to establish a life in a new country and in their common ethnic and religious bond.

1660 Keneally, Thomas. ***The Chant of Jimmie Blacksmith***. Viking 1972, $6.50 (0-670-21165-6); $6.95 (0-14-006973-9). 178pp. Fiction.

Thomas Keneally narrates the tragic life of Jimmie Blacksmith, a well-meaning half-caste Australian Aborigine raised by missionaries around the turn of the century. Jimmie's teachers see his efforts to assimilate and to reject his tribal ways as marks of future success. Indeed, they hold him up as an example to other young Aborigines. The teachers instill in him a number of goals, which he takes to heart: the ambition to work and complete work, the ambition to own property, and the ambition to marry a white woman. Sadly, in striving to fulfill these ambitions, all he achieves is the loss of his Aboriginal identity. Finally unable to accept repeated instances of gross unfairness and mistreatment at the hands of his white "superiors," this model student explodes and goes on bloody rampages with his uncle and his brother. Jimmie develops a new ambition: to seek out and slaughter past oppressors and tormentors. An outraged and fearful Australian public raises a nationwide manhunt to find the perpetrators of heinous acts against "innocent" white men, women, and children.

Keneally's sensitive yet violent novel has been seen as an expression of white guilt, an attempt to come to terms with his own people's subjugation of others. It is highly recommended for its portrayal of the historic maltreatment of Aborigines at the hands of white Australians.

A recent work by Keneally, set in Australia and featuring white middle-class characters (some of whom are recent immigrants from Europe), is *Woman of the Inner Sea* (Doubleday, 1993). His most acclaimed novel, *Schindler's List (see main entry)*, is set in Poland during World War II and is the story of a real-life industrialist who concocted an elaborate scheme to save over a thousand Jews from the Nazi death camps.

1661 Malouf, David. ***Remembering Babylon***. Pantheon 1993, $20.00 (0-679-42724-4); Random $10.00 (0-679-74951-9). 200pp. Fiction.

Malouf's seventh novel explores the history of the Australian frontier and the prejudice that helped to define the white-settler community. The principal character is Gemmy Fairley, who ran away from an abusive employer in London and ended up in Australia. Abandoned in the bush by equally abusive sailors, Gemmy was adopted by Aborigines, with whom he lived for sixteen years until, at the beginning of the novel, he wanders into a frontier community and is taken in by three children and their family. Gemmy is a "white Aborigine," both like and different from the settlers. He becomes the children's friend and teaches them about nature and life in the bush; in the process, he brings the family closer and teaches them much about themselves. The other villagers see Gemmy as a half-wit or a buffoon. Increasingly, villagers grow suspicious of the strange visitor. Their suspicion turns to hatred when they see Gemmy talking with two other Aborigines. Suddenly, their fear of the Aborigines is transformed into violence against Gemmy, who is beaten almost to death. In portraying the nineteenth-century Australian frontier and the clash between the settlers and the Aborigines, Malouf reflects upon human nature and the ideological underpinnings of Australian society.

LML

1662 Nyoongah, Mudrooroo. ***Wildcat Falling***. HarperCollins 1993, $10.00 (0-207-17446-6). 160pp. Fiction.

Often celebrated as the first Aboriginal novel, *Wildcat Falling* was initially published In 1965 to wide critical acclaim. Its author, then known by his Western name of Colin Johnson, has gone on to become a major figure in Australian letters and one of the guiding lights in the quest to establish an authentic Aboriginal voice and culture.

This tale captures the essence of the Aboriginal predicament in the early 1960s. Its nameless narrator struggles against the standards imposed upon him by Eurocentric society: He is as constrained by the white Australian system of education as he is by its penal institutions. The story's opening and closing scenes are set in prison, but, ironically, the time the protagonist spends in "freedom" is in some ways just as oppressive. The main character drifts aimlessly from one experience to the next, as though his only real purpose were to return to incarceration. The struggle is ultimately fruitless; like so many young Aborigines, he returns to jail and again falls under the control of the white masters from whom he seems unable to escape. Mudrooroo offers a bleak and starkly realistic vision of the Aborigine, trapped in his own land and cut off from his authentic identity.

Nearly three decades after this novel appeared in Australia, the author published a sequel titled *Wildcat Screaming* (HarperCollins, 1993). That work, which portrays Wildcat's experience in prison after shooting a policeman, was published simultaneously in the United States with *Wildcat Falling*. The author has also edited a collection of Aboriginal writing entitled *Writing from the Fringe (see main entry)*.

1663 Shadbolt, Maurice. ***Season of the Jew***. Godine 1989, $12.95 (0-87923-753-8). 383pp. Fiction.

During the nineteenth century, British whites settled in New Zealand in ever-increasing numbers. Many of them used trickery and bribery to take land from the Maori. It was also common for European men to marry Maori women so as to take control of their estates—and after they did so they abandoned their wives. Not surprisingly, by the late 1860s, the Maori had grown angry and had begun to retaliate. There were bloody uprisings by followers of the religious leader Te Kooti, and the colonists had to call on the British Imperial Army for protection. The epigraph to this novel is a fitting excerpt from a speech by the vengeful Shylock, the Jewish moneylender, in Shakespeare's *The Merchant of Venice*: "The villainy you teach me I will execute; and it shall go hard, but I will better the instruction." Thus the bitter years of the late 1860s are considered the "season of the Jew"—a time of revenge—for the Maori of New Zealand.

Drawing on actual historical events and characters, prominent New Zealand novelist Maurice Shadbolt narrates the travails of George Fairweather, a British imperial officer and amateur artist. A veteran campaigner in the Maori Wars, Fairweather's experiences lead him to sympathize with the Maori people. Resigning his commission, he begins to explore and paint the then-untroubled east coast of New Zealand's North Island. Fairweather becomes embroiled in incidents surrounding the return of Te Kooti and his followers from exile. This widely praised novel highlights the evils of British imperialism in early colonial New Zealand.

1664 Subramani. ***The Fantasy Eaters: Stories from Fiji***. Illus. by Max Winkler. Three Continents 1988, $20.00 (0-89410-630-9); $10.00 (0-89410-630-9). 144pp. Fiction.

A century ago, white colonialists brought large numbers of Asian Indians to Fiji to work on plantations as indentured servants. The shifts in population resulted in a multiethnic island state. Today there are more Asian Indians in Fiji than there are ethnic Fijians, and often their traditional cultures continue to clash. In this novel, the author, a Fijian of Indian ancestry, expresses his feelings of alienation and anomie.

Subramani is a prize-winning author whose short stories sensitively convey how cultural dislocation can erode the pleasures of living in a tropical island paradise. His characters—often sober, pessimistic, or ill—are at war with themselves, with their inherited traditions, and with their country of birth. Subramani evokes Fiji's seductive tropical sensuality and contrasts it with the discontent and malaise of his characters. He successfully paints a realistic picture of the Indian predicament in Fiji and the complex problems that arise for those who try to be both traditional Indian and Fijian.

1665 Wendt, Albert. ***The Birth and Death of the Miracle Man and Other Stories***. Viking 1986. 176pp. Fiction.

Through the skilled wielding of his pen, Wendt, the preeminent Samoan writer, brings to life not only his characters but also the lush jungle environment they inhabit. The realistic short stories in this collection present slices of Samoan life, yet the author explores themes of such universal significance that his characters might be found anywhere in the world. As human beings, they struggle alone, wrestling with personal failures and inadequacies; as Samoans, they lament the dwindling—and often the passing—of their culture because of Western domination and influence. To express his feelings, Wendt often uses such literary devices as the internal monologue and revealing psychological description.

Wendt is the most internationally prominent Polynesian author. His stories, novels, and poems are widely distributed and have received worldwide acclaim from both the general public and scholars. His first novel, *Sons for the Return Home*, has been adapted into a celebrated film. Wendt also became the first Polynesian professor of English at Auckland University in New Zealand. Readers interested in other works by this author might want to see the novels *Pouliui* (Univ. of Hawaii Pr., 1980) and *Leaves of the Banyan Tree* (Univ. of Hawaii Pr., 1994) and his volumes of poetry, including *Inside Us the Dead* (orig. pub. 1976; Three Continents, 1993).

1666 White, Patrick. ***A Fringe of Leaves***. Viking 1993, $10.95 (0-14-018610-7); $8.95 (0-14-004409-4). 368pp. Fiction.

This fact-based novel is set both in nineteenth-century England and the far-flung British outpost and penal colony, Australia. Ellen Roxburgh, from Cornwall, marries into the English gentry and sails with her husband to Australia to visit his adventure-seeking younger brother. Although now a lady of some standing, Ellen's humble upbringing enables her to recognize and feel distaste for the pretentious selfishness of the colony's self-styled elite. When her husband falls ill, Ellen suggests they return to England. She does so partly to escape the temptation of the romantic advances of her brother-in-law. A few days into the voyage, however, the ship is wrecked on a reef off the barren coast of northeast Australia. After an arduous time adrift, the survivors reach land, only to be captured or killed and eaten by the Aborigines.

As a captive, Ellen becomes a member of the tribe, but she is accorded the lowest possible status. Her resilience of character helps her to survive. After some time, she is rescued by an escaped convict. She returns to civilization, but her strange new behavior and refusal to honor the social graces leave the colonials perplexed. They do not realize that Ellen's experiences with the Aborigines and the land have transformed her forever.

White, who was born in Australia but educated in England, received the Nobel Prize for literature in 1973. He is also the author of *Voss* (orig. pub. 1957; Viking, 1993), another novel that deals with the emergence of the Australian identity and attitudes toward the Aborigine in the nineteenth century.

1667 Wongar, B. *Barbaru*. HarperCollins 1992, $8.00 (0-207-17069-X). 99pp. Fiction.

This is a recent work by an immigrant author who writes under the Aboriginal pseudonym of B. Wongar. That the author is not in fact an Aborigine (he is married to an Aboriginal woman) does not detract from the work's authenticity. The Aboriginal perspective on Australian society is a common element in all of Wongar's works. His poetic style expands the reader's understanding of the essentially spiritual nature of Aboriginal culture.

The "I" persona in each of the stories in *Barbaru* is different from tale to tale. Although on first reading these stories appear to be distinct and separate, they are united by the themes of family relationships and spirituality. For example, to an Aborigine, the concept of "family" includes the living and the dead, as well as spiritual embodiments in nonhuman but natural objects such as rocks, trees, and insects. Wongar's lyrical prose draws the reader's attention to this essential difference between Aboriginal and European cultures and underscores how the failure of Europeans to appreciate such differences has led to the cultural as well as physical attacks upon Aborigines and the devaluation of their culture.

Similar themes infuse Wongar's other writings, such as *Gabo Djara* (Braziller, 1991), *Karan* (Braziller, 1991), *Walg* (Braziller, 1990), and *Bilma* (Ohio State Univ. Pr., 1984).

NONFICTION

1668 Attwood, Bain. *The Making of the Aborigines*. Illus. with photos. Routledge 1990, $19.95 (0-04-370185-X). 240pp. Nonfiction.

The term by which most people refer to the various indigenous peoples of Australia is *Aborigines*. The name implies that these are a single, unified people. In this book, however, the author dispels the myth that Aborigines are a homogeneous group. Instead, he shows that the myth was created and promulgated by European conquerors. Attwood focuses on what he terms "cultural colonialism"—that is, the definition of indigenous tribal life in Australia in a manner that suited the Western intellectual framework and helped the imperialists to conquer the territory.

Attwood's historical narrative focuses on events in the nineteenth century, especially the spread of Western attitudes and standards of conduct through such social institutions as religion, government, and law. He makes ample use of contemporary documents and reports, but he presents these materials in a nontechnical style. He also includes numerous early photographs of indigenous Australians in the process of cultural assimilation.

1669 Ball, Desmond. *Aborigines in the Defence of Australia*. Pergamon 1991, $31.01 (0-08-034419-4). 240pp. Nonfiction.

Australian Aborigines have played an important and complex role in the military defense of the nation. Even though Aborigines did not enjoy full rights as citizens until 1967, many served with distinction during World War II, providing invaluable aid in defending the country's borders.

The collection of essays, edited by noted military analyst Desmond Ball, acknowledges the Aborigines' contribution to Australian security while examining the problems for the national defense raised by Aboriginal issues. Contributors from a wide range of specialties, including an army officer and a lawyer, examine the military implications of Aboriginal land claims, the role of Aboriginal soldiers in the Australian Defence Force, and the potential security threat posed by Aborigines.

Although the essays are full of fascinating detail, the book generally avoids technical discussions and covers its topic in a refreshingly nondogmatic fashion. It will appeal to military history buffs as well as to readers seeking information about Australia's indigenous peoples.

1670 Barlow, Cleve. *Tikanga Whakaaro: Key Concepts in Maori Culture*. Oxford Univ. Pr. 1991, $24.95 (0-19-558212-8). 208pp. Nonfiction.

Barlow, a leading New Zealand authority on the Maori language, has produced a brief, readable guide (in both Maori and English) to the terminology and ideas central to Maori cultural identity, beliefs, and behavior. In a manner analogous to Raymond Williams's pioneering work *Keywords*, Barlow uses a quasi-dictionary format to reconstruct the basic principles of Maori life.

More than a mere phrasebook, this work is a primer on a rich and complex culture. The previously uninformed reader will come away with a keen appreciation of the structure of Maori kinship, social structures, language, rituals, and moral values. Even knowledgeable readers (especially those fluent in Maori) will find Barlow's reconstruction of Maori culture illuminating and thought-provoking.

1671 Bell, Diane. *Daughters of the Dreaming*. 2nd ed. Univ. of Minnesota Pr. 1993, $16.95 (0-8166-2398-8). 342pp. Nonfiction.

Studies by anthropologists have traditionally placed Aboriginal women in a subservient role to Aboriginal men. It was popularly believed that these women had little control over their own lives and that women's ceremonies were considered of limited value or influence in larger Aboriginal society. Bell's study calls all these assumptions into question. As a woman talking with Aboriginal women and learning from them about their lives and rituals, she explodes the biases and orientations of field studies by previous researchers. For example, in her study, she describes a group of women who are knowledgeable in the ways of the *jukurrpa* ("dreaming law"), the spiritual foundation of Aboriginal culture that addresses the connection between human beings and the cosmos. The women's knowledge of this fundamental principle gives them power, independence, and autonomy that would be envied by their white counterparts.

This is an important work for those seeking to gain a more complete picture of Aboriginal society. It corrects the imbalance engendered by male anthropologists who collected data primarily from male informants. Bell's narrative style is both entertaining and informative.

1672 Bennett, Scott. *Aborigines and Political Power*. Illus. with photos. Unwin Hyman 1989. o.p. Nonfiction.

Although the Aboriginal peoples of Australia have only been given full civil and political rights since the mid–1960s, they have rapidly come to play an important role in Australian politics. In this book the author provides an overview of the organizations, activities, and personalities central to Aboriginal politics in the national arena. He concentrates on the latter half of the twentieth century, the period during which Aborigines gained special prominence.

Bennett considers Aboriginal participation in democracy by examining such topics as federal institutions, political parties, electoral success, representation, impact of the media, and so on. As a result, his book simultaneously presents an introduction to the basics of the Australian national political system.

The book, intended for use by a nonspecialist audience, contains a number of photographs. A bibliography is appended to each chapter.

1673 Betts, Katharine. *Ideology and Immigration: Australia, 1976–1987*. Melbourne Univ. Pr. 1988, $27.50 (0-522-84351-4). 234pp. Nonfiction.

Australia experienced one of its greatest periods of immigration during the decade examined by this study. Large numbers of immigrants from war-torn Vietnam and other countries in Asia, as well as from Europe, significantly changed the face of Australian society. Sociologist Betts argues that the governmental decisions leading to this influx were made by a small cadre of political and intellectual elites who ignored the opinions of ordinary Australian citizens.

Although this volume draws heavily on government documents and public-opinion polls, it is written in a manner accessible to a nonacademic audience. Betts provides a thorough review of the debates over population growth and immigration that preceded the decision to open Australia's shores to multicultural (especially nonwhite) immigration. She also examines the consequences of this decision for the Australian economy and social structure. This work offers an indispensable summary of the social background to the conflicts over multiculturalism (and the nature of Australia itself) that are currently central issues in Australian politics.

1674 Blainey, Geoffrey. *Triumph of the Nomads: A History of Aboriginal Australia*. Overlook 1982, $22.95 (0-87951-043-9); $13.95 (0-87951-084-6). 304pp. Nonfiction.

The Australian Aborigines are an ancient people whose presence on the continent dates back at least 40,000 years. Although some aspects of Aboriginal life have changed considerably with the coming of Western culture, Australia's indigenous peoples have retained many of the central features of their customs and identities.

This book attempts to reconstruct the primary elements of Aboriginal existence by drawing on anthropological, archaeological, and geographical evidence. Blainey rose to prominence in the 1980s during the nationwide debate about the size and composition of Australian immigration. Presenting his findings in a readable, nonacademic style, he covers the full range of Aboriginal history and society to explain how the Aborigines have managed to survive—and even thrive—in the harsh Australian outback for so many millennia.

1675 Brennan, Frank. *Land Rights Queensland Style*. Univ. of Queensland Pr. 1992. o.p. Nonfiction.

Inhabitants of the Australian continent for more than 40,000 years, the Aboriginal tribes enjoy an indisputable claim as the "first peoples" of Australia. Yet since the settlement of the country by Europeans just over two centuries ago, the Aborigines have been systematically excluded from the enjoyment of their lands. Only in the past few decades has this injustice been explicitly recognized by the Australian government, which has since made some attempt to repay the debt.

Frank Brennan, a lawyer, Catholic priest, and social activist, examines the political and legal issues stemming from Aboriginal demands for self-management of their territories in the State of Queensland during the 1980s and early 1990s. He describes the issues at stake and explains the efforts to resolve the conflict. He concludes that, while some progress has been made toward achieving Aboriginal goals, the white power structure still resists making a full-fledged commitment to Queensland's Aborigines.

Brick, Jean. *China: A Handbook in Intercultural Communication*.
See entry 1516.

1676 Brownlie, Ian. *Treaties and Indigenous Peoples*. Oxford Univ. Pr. 1992, $47.00 (0-19-825716-3). 160pp. Essays.

These lectures, delivered in 1991 at the University of Auckland by an eminent human rights lawyer, examine New Zealand's Treaty of Waitangi from the perspective of international human rights principles and legislation. The author believes that the treaty, long regarded as a foundational document of the social compact between Maori and Pakeha (European) cultures, poses some significant difficulties when compared to other human rights charters and international conventions.

In particular, Brownlie points out that interpreting the treaty as granting permanent special group rights to the Maori undermines basic principles of representative democracy, social equality, and nondiscriminatory practices. He argues instead that if the Treaty of Waitangi is interpreted literally, it will create many more problems than it resolves and that it could readily become the basis for claims that he describes as "reactionary" when judged in relation to liberal human rights values.

Burger, Julian. *The Gaia Atlas of First Peoples: The Future for the Indigenous World*.
See entry 479.

1677 Chatwin, Bruce. *The Songlines*. Random 1987, $10.95 (0-224-02452-3); Viking $9.95 (0-14-009429-6). 304pp. Nonfiction.

One of the premiere travel writers of his time, the late Bruce Chatwin transformed his thoughts about the nomadic culture of the Australian Aborigines into a deep meditation on the nature of journeys, roots, and identity. The title of this book refers to the Aboriginal belief that eons ago, in the era called the Dreamtime, legendary creatures walked through the outback singing out the names of all mortal beings and, in doing so, calling them to life. The invisible trails these beings left are called Songlines.

Chatwin has a perceptive eye for detail and a sharp ear for dialogue. He vividly recounts his meetings with the many colorful characters who inhabit the harsh outback: Europeans escaping from the oppression (real or imagined) of Western life, as well as Aborigines connected to their environment by time and culture. Interspersed with Chatwin's narrative are passages copied from his notebooks—quotations from works of literature and philosophy, accounts of discussions and interviews from other journeys, personal observations and musings. This is a sensitively written book, one that reveals as much about the universal human longing to avoid being "too tied down" as it does about nomadic Aboriginal culture.

1678 Collmann, Jeff. *Fringe-Dwellers and Welfare: The Aboriginal Response to Bureaucracy*. Univ. of Queensland Pr. 1988, $29.95 (0-7022-2067-1). 276pp. Nonfiction.

It has long been the systematic policy of the Australian government to "detribalize" the Aboriginal population and integrate it into the political and social mechanisms of the state. The result has been the exchange of one system of control (placing the Aborigines on reservations) for another (wrapping them in the red tape of a welfare bureaucracy). One Aboriginal response to detribalization has been "fringe-dwelling"—that is, the construction by Aborigines of shanty towns on the geographical edges of urban communities throughout Australia.

Jeff Collmann's study rejects the standard and uncritically accepted belief that the fringe camps reflect a kind of degeneracy (moral, cultural or social) among the Aboriginal people. He sees instead that fringe-dwelling is in fact an effective attempt to resist the bureaucratic interference that characterizes the policy of detribalization. He supports this claim with a detailed and extensive study of life in a fringe camp located on the outskirts of Alice Springs.

1679 Connell, John, and Richard Howitt, eds. *Mining and Indigenous Peoples in Australasia*. Illus. Oxford Univ. Pr. 1992, $28.00 (0-424-00177-2). 216pp. Nonfiction.

Mining is a major industry throughout the South Pacific region, and the activities associated with it have profound implications for the indigenous populations of Australasia. This stems in part from the fact that indigenous workers are a primary source of labor for the mining of precious minerals and gems, including such hazardous materials as asbestos and uranium. In addition, given the increase of claims by indigenous peoples to ownership of the land and resources of their nations, mining poses a particular set of problems. Unlike forests and fisheries, which are to some extent self-regenerating and can be restored more or less to their original intact form, minerals and gems are nonrenewing and nonrestorable. The continuation of mining operations is therefore a subject of special concern for advocates of the rights of indigenous peoples.

The essays in this collection are interdisciplinary in scope and cover most of the main mining nations of the Pacific. Although some attention is devoted to Australia and New Zealand, the main emphasis is on smaller island states such as Papua New Guinea, Indonesia, and Fiji. Issues addressed include dispossession, environmental impact, and economic compensation.

1680 Cowlishaw, Gillian K. ***Black, White or Brindle: Race in Rural Australia***. Cambridge Univ. Pr. 1988, $59.95 (0-521-34660-6). 208pp. Nonfiction.

The divisions between races in Australia take different forms in urban communities than they do in rural ones. Aboriginal people in the cities live in essentially "Westernized" territory; out of their element socially and culturally, they are at a significant disadvantage in dealing with other groups of people. In the outback, by contrast, Aborigines interact with white "settlers" on terms that are in some ways more complex and more favorable to the needs of the indigenous population.

In this book, Cowlishaw examines the traditional nature of relations between whites and blacks in rural Australia, paying particular attention to the question of how those relations have been transformed by recent government attempts to eliminate or ameliorate the consequences of racism. To achieve her goal, the author creates a composite Australian country community she calls Brindleton, which is based on several such rural towns in the western region of New South Wales. The picture she paints is not a pretty one for those who had hoped that Australia was moving toward more tolerant and harmonious race relations.

1681 Davidson, Robyn. ***Tracks***. Pantheon 1983, $12.00 (0-394-72167-5). 256pp. Nonfiction.

While in her twenties, Queensland-born Robyn Davidson conceived and undertook a unique expedition (or, as she put it, "a lunatic idea"): to capture and train several wild Australian camels and to ride them—alone—across Australia's Central Desert. An accomplished Renaissance woman, whose studies had embraced biology, music, the Japanese language, and philosophy, Davidson here recounts the obstacles standing in the way of her vision and her firm determination to overcome them.

The first part of the book recounts her preparations for the journey, including her successful solicitation of a commission from the National Geographic Society to write about the expedition. The second section is a first-person chronicle of the trip itself, including her encounters with outback Aboriginal people, her fears and triumphs, and her doubts about whether her adventure would have any impact—or whether she would even survive it. This is a gripping, readable tale of survival and a wonderful evocative account of the relationship between a people and its harsh environment. A multimedia version of Davidson's journey, including an interactive CD-ROM, is available under the title *From Alice to Ocean: Alone Across the Outback* (Addison Wesley, 1992).

Along with Thomas Keneally and others, Davidson is the author of *Australia: Beyond the Dreamtime* (1989), a collection of essays about the various waves of settlement on the continent. She has also written *Ancestors* (Viking, 1991), a commentary for general readers on Australia's complex heritage.

1682 Day, A. Grove. *Mad About Islands: Novelists of the South Seas*. Mutual 1987, $13.95 (0-935180-46-X); $9.95 (0-935180-47-8). 304pp. Nonfiction.

James A. Michener coined the term *nesomaniac*—"mad about islands"—to describe himself as someone smitten with the romance and flavor of the South Pacific. That term fits all the writers included in this book. The Pacific was one of the last areas explored by Europeans and, in a Romantic age, stereotypical tales of happy, uncomplicated people, uninhibited maidens, and a near-paradisiacal setting sparked imaginations and inspired further, more in-depth exploration.

In this book, the author charts the discovery and exploration of the Pacific from its first non-European inhabitants to European expansion and settlement in the present century. The wave of literary exploration of the Pacific began with Daniel Defoe's *Robinson Crusoe* (1719). Since then, many writers have sought to experience and write about life in the South Seas. The author devotes a chapter to each of the most famous of these writers—Herman Melville, Mark Twain, Robert Louis Stevenson, Jack London, W. Somerset Maugham, and James A. Michener. Day offers a well-researched and readable study of those creative souls who were lured to a now-vanished Pacific, during a time when the limpid waters of lagoons reflected the gentle light of the moon shining through the fronds of coconut palms—not the harsh glare spilling from high-rise hotels.

1683 Dean, Eddie, and Stan Ritova. *Rabuka: No Other Way*. Doubleday 1988. o.p. Nonfiction.

In May 1987 a small group of Fijian army officers staged a coup against the elected government of their nation, headed by Dr. Timoci Bavadra. The leader of the coup, thirty-eight-year-old Lieutenant Colonel Sitiveni "Steve" Rabuka, an ethnic Fijian, justified his actions on the basis of two principles: indigenous rule and Christianity.

The Bavadra coalition regime, elected just a month earlier, was dominated by ethnic East Indians, whose numbers constitute a majority of Fijian citizens. In Rabuka's view, however, the rule of such a government would cause a transfer of power and rights from the aboriginal people of Fiji to the Indians, who were relative newcomers to the islands, having been imported as plantation workers by the British during the nineteenth century. Rabuka is also a devout Methodist who was afraid of the secularist (or Hindu and Islamic) tendencies of the new government and who wished to establish Christianity as the official religion of the islands. Soon after the first coup Rabuka returned control of Fiji to civilian hands. But the failure of the new government to pursue his reforms led him to stage a second military takeover in September of the same year.

This volume is Rabuka's own story, as told to two prominent South Pacific journalists. It offers a unique, and not entirely self-aggrandizing, insight into the planning of the two coups as well as the fears and conditions that led to their occurrence.

1684 Dixon, R. M. *Searching for Aboriginal Languages: Memoirs of a Field Worker*. Univ. of Chicago Pr. 1989, $14.95 (0-226-15430-0). 334pp. Nonfiction.

The study of Australian Aboriginal languages and culture is a recent pursuit. Historically, white Australian society (and Eurocentric society in general) held the view that the Aborigines were without significant culture and that their languages were simplistic and rough. In fact, however, the numerous languages of the various Aboriginal tribes and regions display enormous complexity and fluidity.

Dixon, a linguist, chronicles the institutional development of the study of Aboriginal languages during the 1960s and 1970s. At the same time he recounts the experiences he had among the Aborigines while conducting his fieldwork. The resulting book is both a profoundly personal narrative and a eulogy on the death of many indigenous languages and the subsequent passing of some unique cultures. The author offers interesting and important insights into Aboriginal ways of thought that will fascinate any reader.

1685 Edwards, Coral, and Peter Read, eds. *The Lost Children: Thirteen Australians Taken from Their Aboriginal Families Tell of Their Struggle to Find Their Natural Parents*. Doubleday 1989. o.p. Nonfiction.

From the early nineteenth century until the mid-twentieth century, government policy in Australia routinely separated Aboriginal children from their families. As many as 100,000 children were taken away from their ancestral lands. The aim of this massive relocation was nothing less than cultural genocide: Those who devised the policy expected the Aborigines to die out. In the meantime, the children were a cheap and expendable source of labor.

The compelling personal accounts of thirteen "lost" children are included in this book. With the help of an organization in New South Wales called Link-Up, these children, now adults, speak of the personal and often painful search for their natural parents and the anguish they feel over having their identities as Aborigines stolen from them.

The organization of the main body of the book parallels this process, moving from "Growing Up," to "Homecomings," and finally to "Reflections." These accounts enable readers to understand the extent to which Australian Aborigines have suffered in their ancestral home.

1686 Erbacher, John, and Sue Erbacher. *Aborigines of the Rainforest*. Illus. with photos. Cambridge Univ. Pr. 1991. o.p. Nonfiction.

The Erbachers are film producers who have spent nearly two decades visiting, photographing, interviewing, and befriending the Kuku-Yalanji tribe of Aborigines who live in the rainforests of Northern Queensland. This slim volume is a thorough and well-documented introduction to the living conditions of this tribe, the last in Australia to retain its own culture and language.

The intended audience for the book is high school students, but it would appeal to adults who want to know more about the Aboriginal way of life. The volume contains about thirty large color plates depicting everyday tribal life and cultural artifacts. The clear and succinct text explains the major aspects of the history, rituals, practices, and beliefs of the Kuku-Yalanji and offers a glossary and pronunciation guide to the Kuku-Yalanji language.

1687 Evans, Raymond, Kay Saunders, and Kathryn Cronin. *Race Relations in Colonial Queensland: A History of Exclusion, Exploitation and Extermination.* Univ. of Queensland Pr. 1988, $29.95 (0-7022-2099-X). 460pp. Nonfiction.

Queensland has perhaps the most notorious record on relations between white and Aboriginal peoples of any Australian state. Even in recent times, much of the controversy surrounding the long-time Queensland government led by Sir John Bjelke-Petersen was connected with its poor handling of racial issues.

The authors of this book establish the background of recent events by carefully documenting the early history of race relations in Queensland. They concentrate on three important nonwhite groups: Aborigines, Melanesians, and Chinese. Originally published in 1975, the volume was updated in 1988 with additional material. Their study draws heavily on nineteenth-century primary sources such as diaries, letters, and newspapers to paint a fascinating and detailed picture of the systematic exploitation of the three racial groups by the white colonial establishment.

Readers wishing more information can consult *Gender Relations in Australia: Domination and Negation* by Kay Saunders and Raymond Soams (1992).

1688 Fisher, Ron, and others. *Blue Horizons: Paradise Islands of the Pacific.* Illus. with photos. National Geographic 1985. o.p. Nonfiction.

The National Geographic Society assigned three teams of writers and photographers to scour the islands of the Pacific. The result is a beautifully photographed and well-written account of the major Polynesian island chains. Even visitors familiar with Samoa, Fiji, Tahiti, the Cooks, and the other islands may discover new landscapes and peoples in this volume.

In addition to the book's visual appeal, the authors have captured the flavor of everyday life in the South Pacific. The essays that accompany the photographs offer valuable information on the geography, history, culture, and contemporary problems of island life, seen especially from the perspective of the indigenous peoples. *Blue Horizons* offers a reliable basic introduction to Polynesia.

1689 Foster, Lois, and David Stockley, eds. *Australian Multiculturalism: A Documentary History and Critique.* Taylor & Francis 1988, $79.00 (1-85359-008-8); $29.95 (1-85359-007-X). 240pp. Nonfiction.

Foster and Stockley have produced an indispensable book for anyone who wishes to understand the issues at stake in current Australian debates over multiculturalism. The editors present in carefully edited form the important documents associated with each major facet of the issue, including immigration, education, religion, law, the media, social services, labor, and the economy. The documents include newspaper and magazine articles, government reports, and excerpts from books.

The editors conclude that early debates about multiculturalism in Australia were vague and ill conceived. Now, they argue, Australia is entering a period of what they term "post-multiculturalism," in which the questions posed about social and cultural diversity will be more focused and the answers better considered.

1690 Gunew, Sneja, and Kateryna Longley. *Striking Chords: Multicultural Literary Interpretations*. Paul & Co. 1992, $19.95 (1-86373-089-3). 224pp. Nonfiction.

This volume addresses the problem posed by the existence of a hegemonic framework within Australian literature that discriminates against writers whose ancestors did not come from the British Isles. Even though many non-British writers write in English, and even though they come from second- or third-generation immigrant families, these writers are often marginalized or excluded altogether from the national discourse.

Writers and critics from many divergent backgrounds have contributed to this work, which is divided into five parts: "Theoretical Perspectives," "Literary Histories," "Author Studies," "Subversive Rereadings," and "Rewritings." The thirty-three entries, all relatively brief, directly address—and help the reader make sense of—the issues of multiculturalism within the Australian society. For further reference, this volume also includes three selected bibliographies on multicultural writing, Greek-Australian literature, and Italo-Australian literature.

1691 Haas, Michael. *The Pacific Way: Regional Cooperation in the South Pacific*. Illus. Greenwood 1989, $49.95 (0-275-93121-8). 205pp. Nonfiction.

It is tempting to think of the island states and nations of the South Pacific as independent, completely sovereign units whose interactions are relatively limited and insignificant. But, somewhat ironically, because of their small size and geographic isolation, the countries of the South Pacific have learned to cooperate with one another far more effectively than nations in most other regions of the world. An example of this cooperation during the 1980s is the creation of the South Pacific Nuclear-Free Zone under the guidance of New Zealand's Prime Minister David Lange.

Haas reveals the network of relationships that made possible this wide scope of South Pacific interdependency and cooperation. He argues that the breakdown of traditional colonial domination and the relative absence of interference by the superpowers have created a unique opportunity for political collaboration in the South Pacific, a cooperation based less on traditional military alliances than on common interests such as education, trade, justice, and tourism.

1692 Haebich, Anna. *For Their Own Good: Aborigines and Government in the South West of Western Australia, 1900–1940*. Illus. with photos. Univ. of Western Australia Pr. 1992, $24.95 (1-875560-14-9). 413pp. Nonfiction.

The Aboriginal resettlement programs of the early twentieth century were among the harshest and most inhumane actions directed against indigenous

Australians by the white rulers of the nation. Aborigines were removed from their lands and villages without regard for familial or tribal connections and forcibly resettled in encampments that were little more than concentration camps.

Haebich has documented the human costs of this policy as it was pursued in Southwestern Australia from 1900 to 1940. She discusses the resettlement programs in the context of the political push for a uniformly "white" Australia, one in which Aborigines would have no economic or social place. The first-person accounts are made more vivid by the inclusion of numerous photographs documenting life in the Aboriginal camps.

1693 Hanson, F. Allan. *Rapan Lifeways: Society and History on a Polynesian Island*. Waveland Pr. 1983. o.p. Nonfiction.

Rapa is a tiny island of fewer than 400 inhabitants on the southern fringe of French Polynesia. This classic study of Pacific Island culture and society, which first appeared in 1970, presents an exhaustive but readable account of everyday Rapan life, including the geography, economy, kinship structure, rituals, history, and domestic relations of the inhabitants. The author helps readers understand how the tiny population of Rapa can continue to survive largely untransformed despite more than two centuries of contact with the West.

Hanson has also edited several volumes with his wife, Louise, about aspects of South Pacific culture. Most notable is *Art and Identity in Oceania* (Univ. of Hawaii Pr., 1990), a collection of essays on South Pacific folk art and its social context. This book is based on papers presented to the Pacific Art Association's 1984 meeting at New York's Metropolitan Museum of Art, just prior to the opening of the acclaimed exhibition "Te Maori: Maori Art from New Zealand Collections," which was the largest single display of Maori artifacts ever assembled.

1694 Hardy, John, ed. *Stories of Australian Migration*. New South Wales Univ. Pr. 1988, $24.95 (0-86840-155-2). 149pp. Nonfiction.

As part of its contribution to Australia's bicentennial celebrations in 1988, the Australian Academy of the Humanities commissioned these essays on various aspects of the multicultural heritage of immigrants to the country. The essays, contributed by academics, civil servants, and community activists, encompass European and Asian migration from the early nineteenth century to the present day. Readers learn that Australian multiculturalism has deep roots, laid down during the very earliest waves of immigration. For instance, in the Australian state of Victoria, the proportion of the population from non-English-speaking countries is about the same today as it was in the 1850s. Much of this immigration occurred as a result of the Gold Rush, in which Chinese laborers and shopkeepers played a major role.

Some of the contributions have a scholarly slant, but many are impressionistic or biographical in character. These latter essays offer especially interesting and helpful insights into the nature of Australia's efforts to build a multicultural nation.

1695 Healy, J. J. *Literature and the Aborigine in Australia, 1770–1975.* 2nd ed. Univ. of Queensland Pr. 1989, $29.95 (0-7022-2150-3). 314pp. Nonfiction.

The author has produced a useful survey of European knowledge about, and reaction to, Australian Aborigines as viewed through the prism of literature produced between the middle of the nineteenth century and World War II. This book expands the information available about the topic, because few if any of the authors discussed in this volume are well known in the Northern Hemisphere.

Healy detects in these writings, which he calls the "literature of contact," a growing sense of realism about Aboriginal peoples. Early representations depicted Aborigines as a nuisance or, worse, as a pestilence. As later writers learned more about the Aborigines, they began to understand their distinctive ways of thinking and being. The author suggests that European literature helped to build bridges of understanding between the Aborigines and white Australians, many of whom had little direct contact with the indigenous peoples—residents of the continent since the dawn of human history .

1696 Jupp, James, ed. *The Challenge of Diversity: Policy Options for a Multicultural Australia.* Australian Government Publishing Service 1990. o.p. Nonfiction.

This book outlines a coherent policy designed to guide Australia in managing the impact of an increasingly diverse population. Commissioned in the late 1980s by the Office of Multicultural Affairs, the papers address both the costs and the benefits of maintaining a plural society. Examples are drawn from such areas as education, employment, health, and law. Some of the authors are academics, but most are public-policy consultants or social-service practitioners. The book is intended as a resource for policy makers, but for general readers it offers a trove of facts about Australia and the resources available in that country to people whose heritage is other than European.

1697 Kluge, P. F. *The Edge of Paradise: America in Micronesia.* Random 1991, $22.00 (0-394-58178-4); Univ. of Hawaii Pr., $14.95 (0-8248-1567-X). 256pp. Nonfiction.

This is a riveting personal account of the author's journeys through Micronesia. Kluge had just accepted a position teaching creative writing at Kenyon College in Ohio when he learned about the death of his friend Lazarus Salii, a prominent politician on the island of Palau. The men had met during a stint in the Peace Corps and had stayed in touch over the years. Kluge traveled to the island to pay his respects. While there, he retraced the paths he had explored as a much younger man. Revisiting his old haunts, seeing people again after so much time had passed, he discovers how much both he and Micronesia have changed.

This tale of (re)discovery becomes a meditation on Micronesian life and how it has become inextricably linked to the outside world, especially to the United States. Kluge examines shifting American policies toward poor nations and explores the living conditions and attitudes among the people of the South Pacific. In mourning Salii, Kluge laments the loss of Micronesia's inability of people in Micronesia to retain their independence and to escape being caught in the net of international (largely, American-oriented) culture and politics. Kluge is an American novelist, perhaps best known for *Eddie and the Cruisers*, which was adapted into a film.

1698 Kolig, Erich. ***The Noonkanbah Story: Profile of an Aboriginal Community in Western Australia***. Univ. of Otago Pr. 1987, $24.95 (0-908569-37-8). 160pp. Nonfiction.

The story of the Yangura tribe and the Noonkanbah community of Western Australia is both a tragedy and a cautionary tale. Excluded from or marginalized on their historical tribal lands, the Yangura fought for reinstatement and were granted a leasehold in 1976. Yet they were soon to discover that they had been again stripped of full privileges under the terms of the lease, which ceded them the topsoil but not the right to exploit the valuable minerals beneath. In a classic confrontation between indigenous underdog and powerful state and commercial interests, the claims of the Yangura ultimately bowed before the interests of industry.

Kolig narrates the compelling and troubling story of the systematic denial of Aboriginal rights by a white society bent on the pursuit of profit. He spent considerable time in Noonkanbah during the period he chronicles and presents a firsthand account of how the quest for oil proved more important than the Aborigines' economic and civil rights.

Koyama Tomoko. ***Japan: A Handbook in Intercultural Communication***. See entry 1534.

1699 Lawlor, Robert. ***Voices of the First Day: Awakening in the Aboriginal Dreamtime***. Illus. Inner Traditions 1991, $24.95 (0-89281-355-5). 352pp. Nonfiction.

This definitive survey of Australian Aboriginal culture, society, beliefs, and cosmology is unrivaled for its clarity, ease of style, and accessibility. Neither an academic study nor a coffee-table pictorial, the book integrates the author's thorough knowledge of the subject with an appealing design that artfully displays its many photographs and illustrations of artifacts.

Lawlor's account stems from a lifetime of direct experience with Aboriginal peoples. He invites the reader to enter into the thought-world of the Aborigine, yet he is able to set Aboriginal rites and myths into a wider context of human history, deftly drawing connections to the ancient cultures and religions of the East and West and to contemporary popular film and music. *Voices of the First Day* is breathtaking in its scope and revealing in its use of image and detail.

1700 Loh, Morag, and Judy Winternitz. ***Dinki-Di: The Contributions of Chinese Immigrants and Australians of Chinese Descent to Australia's Defence Forces and War Efforts, 1899–1988***. Australian Govt. Publg. Service 1989, $19.95 (0-644-08292-5). 172pp. Nonfiction.

This volume was written to allay fears expressed in the 1980s by some Australians that the waves of new Asian immigrants flooding into the country were a security risk. One specific concern was that the Asians could not be trusted to serve their new nation in time of war. Loh's book describes contributions made by Australians of Chinese descent to the defense of the country throughout the twentieth century.

In Australian slang, *dinki-di* means "loyal" or "true-blue." The author shows how the Chinese troops earned that label. The first and briefer section of the book offers a historical survey of Chinese participation in the Australian Defense Forces, concentrating on the period up to World War II. This section has a great deal of visual appeal, offering photographs as well as reproductions of relevant documents. The second part contains interviews with numerous Chinese Australians who served in the military during war and peace. From Sam Tongaway, who served in World War I, through several young men of the current generation, Loh records the voices of Australians of Chinese origin as they reflect on their experiences in the armed forces. Despite the semiofficial sponsorship of the book, the interviews are not sanitized, as Sam Tongaway and others express some bitterness at the treatment that his people have received from white Australians.

Mander, Jerry. *In the Absence of the Sacred: The Failure of Technology and the Survival of the Indian Nations*.
See entry 510.

1701 Mulvaney, D. J. *Encounters in Place: Outsiders and Aboriginal Australians 1606–1985*. Illus. Univ. of Queensland Pr. 1989, $44.95 (0-7022-2153-8). 263pp. Nonfiction.

Many studies about the contact between Aboriginal Australians and the waves of European settlers are presented from a one-sided cultural perspective. Usually the point of view is that of the "outsiders." In this book, the author adopts a unique perspective by concentrating on the geographic locales at which these contacts have taken place over the course of the last four centuries.

Mulvaney's approach forces the reader to look to the physical conditions under which contact occurred, as well as the environmental consequences of this contact. He consequently raises new types of questions in the ongoing dialogue about Australian multiculturalism. The book is profusely illustrated, including a number of color plates containing both European and Australian depictions of some of the crucial aspects of cultural interaction and reaction. Mulvaney's volume will fascinate and inform the general reader.

1702 Narogin, Mudrooroo. *Writing from the Fringe: A Study of Modern Aboriginal Literature*. Hyland House 1990, $19.95 (0-947062-55-6). 192pp. Nonfiction.

This is a critical assessment of the development of contemporary Aboriginal writing and writers. Narogin, an Australian Aborigine, is an accomplished poet and writer who published several works under the name Colin Johnson. In this book he argues that "it is impossible to write about Aboriginal writing in English without an understanding of the history of Aboriginal people and of the policy of assimilation which cut the linkage to traditional culture and language." The introduction includes a general schema of Aboriginal history to help restore those links.

Narogin's main point is that Aboriginal authors must be true to themselves and to their culture. He criticizes Aboriginal authors who ape the literary styles and mores of the Western canon, but he also condemns critics who dismiss non-Occidental Aboriginal writing. This penetrating analysis recognizes that Aboriginal literature currently exists in the margins and that, culturally speaking, Aboriginal authors are fringe-dwellers. His use of that term has special resonance, because in Australian lingo it denotes the Aboriginal inhabitants of rural town ghettos. Yet, he says, this fringe existence need not be—indeed, should not be—the permanent fate of Aboriginal writing.

Narogin is also the author of *Wildcat Falling (see main entry)*, published under a different rendering of his name (Mudrooroo Nyoongah). For more information about the Aboriginal fringe-dwellers, readers can consult Jeff Collmann's *Fringe Dwellers and Welfare: The Aboriginal Response to Bureaucracy (see main entry)*.

1703 Newbury, Colin. *Tahiti Nui: Change and Survival in French Polynesia, 1767–1945*. Univ. of Hawaii Pr. 1980. o.p. Nonfiction.

The adaptation of Polynesian islanders to the social standards imposed on them by European explorers and settlers depended heavily on the question of whether they would accept the economic principles of modern Occidental society. The author traces the evolution of a market-type economy in the islands of Tahiti. Rather than being a narrow, scholarly investigation, this fascinating account places almost two hundred years of trade and economic relations into a broader context of political and cultural interchange between the new and old peoples of Polynesia. Newbury ends his book by explaining that many of the assumptions of colonialism are just now being subjected to questioning and searching criticism. His history of Tahiti is thus a general account of the rise and the beginning of the fall of Western (specifically, French) hegemony in the Polynesian region.

1704 O'Farrell, Patrick. *Vanished Kingdoms: Irish in Australia and New Zealand*. New South Wales Univ. Pr. 1990, $39.95 (0-86840-148-X). 310pp. Nonfiction.

Although written by an academic historian, this is an intensely intimate book, self-consciously subjective in its vantage point. Yet its lessons serve a more general point. Taking as his starting point his own family's letters, O'Farrell reconstructs the experience of Irish migrants to the Antipodes during the nineteenth and early twentieth centuries. He also describes the settlers' uneasy continuing relationships with their former homeland.

O'Farrell spells out the physical and cultural conditions of the Irish during the colonial and postcolonial eras. What's more, he draws his reader into the very minds of his family and, by extension, those of Irish immigrants generally. To aid in this process, the volume is heavily illustrated with both archival and personal photographs.

Those interested in a more general and scholarly treatment of Irish immigration to the South Pacific should consult O'Farrell's *The Irish in Australia*, (Univ. of Notre Dame Pr., 1989).

1705 Oliver, Douglas L. *Oceania: The Native Cultures of Australia and the Pacific Islands.* 2 vols. Univ. of Hawaii Pr. 1988, $90.00 (0-8248-1019-8). 1,264pp. Nonfiction.

This massive two-volume set represents the culmination of a life's work by anthropologist Douglas Oliver, who is among the preeminent experts on indigenous South Pacific society and culture. Encyclopedic in scope, the book covers the full range of island peoples in Polynesia, Melanesia, and Micronesia. In Volume One, Oliver describes the physical circumstances, artifacts, languages, beliefs, and behaviors of Oceanic inhabitants. Volume Two concentrates on the social systems that characterize the various regions of the South Pacific.

Although *Oceania* is firmly rooted in scholarly research, it is more an introductory than an advanced academic work. It offers in a single source an invaluable reference guide to all aspects of Pacific life. Oliver carefully explains basic concepts and assumptions of the many cultures he surveys, and he does not expect the reader to possess any prior specialized knowledge of Oceanic peoples.

1706 Orange, Claudia. *The Treaty of Waitangi.* Unwin Hyman 1987. o.p. Nonfiction.

New Zealanders generally regard 1840 as the birth year of their nation, because that was when Maori chiefs and representatives of the British government signed the Treaty of Waitangi. The treaty cedes "sovereignty" to the British Crown but also guarantees the political and economic rights of the Maori tribes and their leaders. The treaty did not win unanimous support among the various Maori tribes throughout the country, nor in fact was it ever officially ratified by the British government. But among Pakeha (Europeans) and Maori alike, it is the single most important expression of New Zealand's national identity.

Claudia Orange's book is the standard history of the events surrounding the development of the treaty, as well as the subsequent course of its interpretation and abuse. Orange clearly explains the misunderstandings that have been associated with the document almost since it was signed. Among the valuable features of her book are maps and texts of the central relevant documents (in both Maori and English). All subsequent studies of the treaty have relied heavily upon Orange's research.

1707 Pettman, Jan. *Living in the Margins: Racism, Sexism and Feminism in Australia.* Paul & Co. 1992, $19.95 (1-86373-005-2). 220pp. Nonfiction.

The central aim of this book is to discuss the issues of gender, race, class, and ethnicity, not as the separate and distinct concerns for which they are frequently taken, but as interacting categories. Pettman's work stands on the cutting edge of current scholarship on these issues. Her study examines Australian society from its early colonial beginnings, through the massive migration programs implemented following World War II, to present-day issues and concerns. Although written from an academic slant, it is stimulating, provocative, and eminently readable. The author's groundbreaking analysis of these three areas of oppression in Australian society is readily applicable to other societies in other countries. The text includes an extensive and helpful bibliography.

1708 Pilger, John. *A Secret Country: The Hidden Australia*. Knopf 1991, $22.50 (0-394-57462-1). 305pp. Nonfiction.

John Pilger is an Australian-bred and internationally acclaimed journalist and filmmaker. This book is both a personal reflection on, and a well-documented evaluation of, the flaws and failures of Australia's economic, political, and cultural establishment. In particular, he singles out the Australian elite's attachment to what he terms "matehood" and to the Anglo-Celtic values of the British Isles. In Pilger's view, Australia's inability to follow through on its multicultural promise, both to its newer non-British immigrants and to its indigenous peoples, is a direct result of the lingering Anglophilia of the Australian elites.

The central event of Pilger's narrative is the alleged conspiracy of leading Australia "mates," with the aid of the U.S. Central Intelligence Agency, to destabilize and oust the 1970s Labour government of Gough Whitlam. Whitlam and his supporters proposed policies that ran counter to the cultural assumptions (not to mention the material interests) of the Australian ruling class. The Labour Party seemed destined to prevail. But pressure was brought to bear on the CIA-connected Governor General, Sir John Kerr; soon thereafter, in 1975, Whitlam's government was dismissed. Unsurprisingly, *A Secret Country* was not well received in Australia because it held a mirror to a nation that did not wish to confront its own blemishes. Pilger marshals a great deal of evidence to support his story, although many of the facts he presents are open to debate and interpretation. Nonetheless, the book—a combination real-life thriller and private meditation—makes fascinating reading.

1709 Pomare, Maui, and others. *Legends of the Maori*. 2 vols.; repr. of 1934 ed. Illus. AMS 1976, $75.00 (0-404-14350-4). 607pp. Nonfiction.

First published in the early 1930s, this work is the standard collection of Maori stories, mythology, folklore, and poetry. James Cowan, a noted New Zealand folklorist, wrote the first volume, which is derived from his lifelong work of gathering traditional Maori tales and chants. For the most part, the legends Cowan includes were recounted to him in oral form; this volume represents the first time these narratives have appeared in written form.

The second volume has an altogether different character. It is the work of prominent Maori physician and politician Sir Maui Pomare. He presents a combination of remembered stories, personal reflections on Maoridom, speeches, poems (both his own and others)—in sum, a kind of cultural potpourri of Maori literature, history, and language. Especially striking are Pomare's tales (some recollected, others no doubt in the misty realm between fiction and fact) about the early relations between Maori and Pakeha (Europeans).

Together, the two volumes form a valuable overview of traditional Maori culture both before and after the coming of the Pakeha.

1710 Reynolds, Henry. *With the White People*. Viking 1990. o.p. Nonfiction.

Australian Aborigines responded to white colonization and settlement in one of two general ways: resistance or collaboration. In his widely read book, *The Other Side of the Frontier* (1981), Henry Reynolds examined the first response. *With the White People* completes the discussion by analyzing the so-called Aboriginal pioneers, those indigenous Australians who aided the Europeans in their conquest of the continent.

Filled with many early photographs, the book documents the central role played by Aborigines who worked alongside whites in settling the country. The Aborigines provided many services and performed menial duties during the nineteenth and early twentieth centuries. They also served as guides, diplomats, guards, and, inevitably, friends and lovers to their white masters. Although Reynolds demonstrates that collaborating Aborigines were always "fringe dwellers," the lines of separation were considerably more blurred than one might expect. For a related collection of documents relevant to early contact between Aborigines and whites, see also Reynolds's *Dispossession: Black Australians and White Invaders* (Routledge, 1989).

1711 Rivett, Kenneth, ed. *Australia and the Non-White Migrant*. Melbourne Univ. Pr. 1975, $34.95 (0-522-84078-7). 327pp. Nonfiction.

This is not a dispassionate study but a polemical plea on the part of the influential Immigration Reform Group for a nonracially oriented policy toward prospective immigrants to Australia. The Group, founded in the late 1950s, was an important force behind the challenge to the longstanding official policy of "White Australia." Although immigration patterns did change somewhat during the 1960s and 1970s, the Group continued to be active in monitoring and evaluating immigrant programs.

The Group's report, contained in this volume, is helpful in a number of ways. It contains valuable quantitative and qualitative information about the immigrant composition of Australia. It also sets Australian policies in a more global and comparative context. Finally, it lays out and defends a plan for the future, one that involves a more tolerant and open approach to immigration. Although the plan was formulated in the 1970s, two decades later, it has yet to be implemented in Australia.

1712 Rosenthal, Odeda. *Not Strictly Kosher: Pioneer Jews of New Zealand*. Illus. Starchand 1988, $26.95 (0-910425-07-8). 208pp. Nonfiction.

Many readers, New Zealanders and non–New Zealanders alike, would probably be surprised to learn of the long and important role that Jews played in the creation of the island nation. Jews arrived in New Zealand in the early nineteenth century, and the synagogue in the town of Christchurch, for instance, was constructed in the same year as (and only a few blocks from) the city's famous cathedral.

Rosenthal's history of the Jewish settlement in New Zealand concentrates on the nineteenth century and is aimed entirely at the general reader rather than at an academic audience. She reproduces early photographs, numerous documents, newspaper clippings, and line drawings. Although by no means a weighty tome, Rosenthal's book sketches the outlines of a fascinating aspect of New Zealand's multicultural past.

1713 Scarr, Deryck. *Fiji: The Politics of Illusion: The Military Coups in Fiji.* New South Wales Univ. Pr. 1988, $19.95 (0-86840-131-5). 161pp. Nonfiction.

In Fiji in 1987, two successive military coups, led by the devout Christian and native rights advocate Lieutenant Colonel Sitiveni Rabuka, created a considerable stir in the South Pacific, a region not usually noted for unstable politics. Indeed, troops in Australia and New Zealand were put on alert, ostensibly to ensure the safety of nationals in residence or on vacation there, but more likely in response to requests from Dr. Timoci Bavadra, the ousted leader of the democratically elected government. Scarr argues that what may have halted external interference was the close association between the United States' Central Intelligence Agency and the U.S.-trained military leaders of the coup, including Rabuka himself.

This book by a sometime resident of Fiji recounts the story of the coups and presents a clear survey of their political and social causes and consequences. In Scarr's view, the coups were the result of a (possibly avoidable) set of misperceptions on the part of various ethnic groups struggling for power on the island. Readers interested in expanding their understanding of these events might want to consult *Rabuka: No Other Way* by Eddie Dean and Stan Ritova and *Fiji: A Paradise in Peril* by Pran Seth *(see main entries)*.

1714 Seth, Pran. *Fiji: A Paradise in Peril.* Sterling 1990, $25.00 (81-207-1254-4). 200pp. Nonfiction.

Multiculturalism is often seen as the struggle of an indigenous or minority group against a dominant, usually Western political and cultural power. The situation in Fiji diverges from this model. The British colonial influence in the island state largely ebbed long ago. That left the island with two main groups: the native Fijians, who are a numerical minority, and the immigrant East Indians, who a century earlier had been brought to Fiji by the British to work on the sugar plantations. In the intervening years, the Indians had become prosperous merchants, entrepreneurs, educators, and civil servants. Despite their economic clout, the Indians chafed under Fijian laws that strictly limited their ability to own real estate by deeming property ownership an exclusive right of the indigenous population.

This situation was poised to change in early 1987, when a Labour Party–led coalition government was elected to rule Fiji on a platform that included more equitable distribution of rights to all citizens regardless of ethnic heritage. The promise of reform was squashed, however, by a military coup in May 1987 and reconfirmed by another coup in September of the same year. Pran Nath Seth, an Indian national with a long interest in Fiji, relates the events of 1987 and their aftermath from the perspective of the country's Indian majority, arguing for a return to the democratic political path from which Fiji was forcibly diverted.

Other accounts of the coups in Fiji are available: *Rabuka: No Other Way* by Eddie Dean and Stan Ritova and *Fiji: The Politics of Illusion: The Military Coups in Fiji* by Deryck Scarr *(see main entries)*.

1715 Sharp, Andrew. *Justice and the Maori: Maori Claims in New Zealand Political Argument in the 1980s*. Oxford Univ. Pr. 1990, $19.95 (0-19-558202-0). 320pp. Nonfiction.

The 1840 Treaty of Waitangi between Britain and the Maori chiefs established the terms of New Zealand settlement during the nineteenth century. In the twentieth century, however, especially during the last two decades, the treaty has taken on quite a different significance. Progressive Maori leaders often use the rallying cry "Honor the Treaty!" as they seek to affirm the special rights of New Zealand's indigenous population within the nation's larger political and economic framework.

Compared to the population of New Zealand as a whole, the Maori—especially young males—suffer from staggering rates of poverty, disease, undereducation, and criminal activity. This has prompted Maori leaders to use the treaty to reestablish traditional cultural and social values and to lay claim to the resources that might improve their living conditions. In short, the treaty has become a centerpiece in contemporary New Zealand discussions about justice.

In this widely read and highly regarded book, political scientist Andrew Sharp provides a history of treaty claims and debates in recent years and analyzes the assumptions about fairness and rights implicit in these controversies. The author shows why the treaty remains a vital part of contemporary political culture in New Zealand. Readers interested in a historical study might consult *The Treaty of Waitangi* by Claudia Orange *(see main entry)*.

1716 Simms, Norman. *Silence and Invisibility: A Study of the Literatures of the Pacific, Australia, and New Zealand*. Illus. by Max-Karl Winkler. Three Continents 1986, $26.00 (0-89410-362-8); $14.00 (0-89410-363-6). 227pp. Nonfiction.

This collection of critical essays addresses in a single volume the central issues at stake for indigenous writing and writers in Australasia. Simms's essays consider the strategies indigenous authors use to point out their absence from mainstream culture and society; the authors offer alternative views, impressions, styles, and articulations (oral and written) that are particular to their culture or interest. Simms argues that the new literatures of the Pacific have a character very different from traditional Western literature. Consequently, the non-Pacific reader needs to develop a new orientation prior to judging these works as texts, events, and social constructs.

The volume consists of two parts: a collection of essays and a useful selection of background and bibliographical sources; the latter section alone is a valuable tool for further study.

1717 Spoonley, Paul. *The Politics of Nostalgia: Racism and the Extreme Right in New Zealand*. Dunmore 1987. o.p. Nonfiction.

New Zealand has long prided itself on a history of racial tolerance and harmony, an image it certainly projects to the outside world. The reality is somewhat different, however. Beyond the structural racism that keeps New Zealand's minorities (especially Maori and Pacific Islanders) in poverty and social exclusion, there are a number of right-wing, white-supremacist groups whose public profile and numbers have grown as the country's economic woes have deepened during the past two decades.

This volume by a leading authority on racism and race relations in contemporary New Zealand offers an overview of the various individuals and organizations involved in the racial conflict. While Spoonley notes that some of these racist movements draw strength from resentment at the claims to rights made by indigenous groups, he points out that their ideological roots can be traced to the more traditional soil of European fascism and anti-Semitism.

1718 Stanley, David. *The South Pacific Handbook.* 5th ed. Moon Publications 1993, $19.95 (0-918373-99-9). 778pp. Nonfiction.

David Stanley is one of the consummate travel guide writers in the English language, an inveterate traveler who to this day (after several decades) carries his home "on his back." His series of handbooks for Moon Publications, a specialist publisher in the field, covers the many island nations of the South Pacific. *The South Pacific Handbook* is an omnibus edition of several of his more specialized guides.

The book contains all of the usual information necessary for a successful holiday or other journey. What distinguishes it—and what prompted its recommendation on this list—is the author's acute awareness of the social, cultural, and historical features of island society and his sensitivity to the peoples and ecology of the region. In particular, his introductory overview is an indispensable primer for readers entirely unfamiliar with the political and social issues in contemporary Pacific life—issues that have generated what Stanley terms "trouble in paradise."

1719 Sutter, Frederic K. *The Samoans: A Global Family.* Illus. Univ. of Hawaii Pr. 1989, $34.95 (0-8248-1238-7). 221pp. Nonfiction.

This unique book, the final installment in a trilogy of photo essays about the indigenous inhabitants of Western and American Samoa, is a collective meditation on the contemporary Samoan condition. Containing 285 beautiful full-color photographic plates, the volume traces the lives and careers of Samoans, both in their homeland and throughout the world. Accompanying the photographs are appropriate comments translated from more than thirty languages—the languages used in the countries to which Samoans have immigrated.

The book documents a kind of worldwide Samoan diaspora. Many of its subjects (each of whom has contributed a brief autobiography) were not even born in the islands and are clearly struggling to retain elements of their cultural distinctiveness in the face of pressures from their present homes. Others, having made successful careers outside Samoa (such as former major league baseball player Tony Solaita), have chosen to return and contribute to their people. Although the photographs graphically demonstrate how the "global family" of Samoans has flourished, the autobiographies testify to the costs and sacrifices individuals have made, especially in relation to their Samoan cultural and social identities.

Suzuki, David, and Peter Knudtson. *Wisdom of the Elders: Honoring Sacred Native Visions of Nature.*
See entry 532.

1720 Tampke, Jürgen, and Colin Doxford. ***Australia, Willkommen: A History of the Germans in Australia***. Illus. New South Wales Univ. Pr. 1990, $34.95 (0-86840-307-5). 281pp. Nonfiction.

781
_____
AUSTRALIA, NEW
ZEALAND, AND
THE PACIFIC

The role of German immigrants to Australia has not received much attention from students of multiculturalism. Germans are not prominent among the most recent wave of Australian immigration, which has tended to come from the periphery of Europe as well as from Asia. But it is seldom recognized that, after the Aborigines and the Anglo-Irish, Germans were the earliest group to settle Australia in significant numbers. In particular, two Australian states, Queensland and South Australia, attracted heavy German immigration as early as the mid-nineteenth century.

In this book the authors set out to rectify ignorance about the contributions Australia's German settlers have made to the country's economic, social, political, and cultural development. They ascribe much of this ignorance to the lingering anti-German sentiment produced by two world wars. Their book explains the sources of German immigration to Australia, describes the living conditions and activities of immigrants over the course of the past two centuries, and closes with a summary of German social and cultural life in contemporary Australia.

1721 Terrill, Ross. ***The Australians***. Simon & Schuster 1988. o.p. Nonfiction.

After decades of living in the United States and writing about China, Australian-born Terrill returned to his land of origin to evaluate its character and the changes that have occurred there. As this book reveals, he found much that is new. Immigrants from Southern Europe, China, and Southeast Asia have moved into traditionally white neighborhoods, established small businesses, and become involved in the political system. Terrill's region-by-region exploration includes interviews with Australians of all backgrounds and political stripes; in addition to chapters on immigrants, he discusses the Aborigines, politicians, and cultural figures. Racism is explored in some detail as he presents, in frank language, the opinions of those who resist the emergence of an increasingly multicultural society. In Terrill's view, Australia's ability to adapt to a more diverse society and to the economic developments of the Pacific Basin will determine whether it becomes an economic backwater or one of the great powers of the twenty-first century. This readable account provides a solid overview of a nation in transition. LML

1722 Thompson, Liz, ed. ***Aboriginal Voices: Contemporary Aboriginal Artists, Writers and Performers***. 2nd ed. Illus. North Atlantic 1992, $18.95 (1-55643-131-7). 176pp. Essays.

According to the text of this intriguing book, "Aboriginal culture is what Aboriginal people today are, with all our collective experiences." In this book, Aboriginal writers, painters, playwrights, dancers, and designers from throughout Australia discuss their oppression, pain, despair, anger, and loss of identity. They often also speak of their hope for a brighter future, which they greet with optimism and humor while searching for truth and expressing pride in calling themselves Aboriginal.

The opinions and anecdotes of the contributors are varied. In some cases, the theme of their art is a plea to be understood by white Australians. Others completely reject assimilation and argue that Aboriginal culture is the only true culture in Australia. In all cases, these voices allow readers to increase their awareness of the issues surrounding the contemporary situation of the Aborigines.

The book includes a map of Australia that locates the artists according to the region in which they live. Each personal statement includes a sample of the artist's work, such as a writing excerpt or an illustration, and candid photos of the artist.

1723 Thompson, R. C. *Australian Imperialism in the Pacific.* Melbourne Univ. Pr. $34.95 (0-522-84207-0). 289pp. Nonfiction.

It might be supposed that the relationship between Australia and Britain was primarily that of colony to home country, a relationship in which the direction of imperial policy flowed from center to periphery. But this book demonstrates that Australia itself during the nineteenth and early twentieth centuries took an active role in promoting the expansion of the British Empire in the South Pacific region.

A dozen years in the making, Thompson's study is a meticulous reconstruction of Australian agitation for the British annexation of Melanesia and sections of Polynesia. He demonstrates that the interests and desires of the Australian elites and populace were often perceived to be in conflict with those of Britain. Thompson offers a compelling account of the history of Australian adventurism in relation to its island neighbors, a history that continues to bear bitter fruit today.

1724 Viviani, Nancy. *The Long Journey: Vietnamese Migration and Settlement in Australia.* Illus. Melbourne Univ. Pr. 1984, $39.95 (0-522-84274-7). 316pp. Nonfiction.

According to a survey by a major Sydney daily newspaper, Vietnamese immigrants to Australia have roughly the same low status in "mainstream" Australian society as Italian and Greek immigrants had in an earlier generation. This study of the influx of Vietnamese refugees into Australia helps to make sense of this fact. According to the author, the Vietnamese are saddled with a double burden. On one hand, they are the first immigrant group that has challenged *en masse* the long-standing "White Australia" policy. On the other hand, they have entered Australia at a time of economic decline and unemployment. Consequently, the Vietnamese have been the object of widespread resentment out of proportion to their actual social and economic impact. They have borne the brunt of a public backlash against the multicultural and multiracial image of Australia promoted by political and cultural leaders.

Viviani explains the context for the admission of large numbers of Vietnamese refugees into Australia after 1975, and she documents the real costs and contributions of these people to the nation. She concludes that it is by no means certain that conditions of the late twentieth century will afford to the Vietnamese the same opportunities afforded to earlier immigrants to Australia.

1725 Withey, Lynne. *Voyages of Discovery: Captain Cook and the Exploration of the Pacific.* Illus. Univ. of California Pr. 1989, $15.00 (0-520-06564-6). 512pp. Nonfiction.

One of the direct consequences of the worldwide movement by indigenous people to assert their cultural identities has been a reevaluation of the process of interaction between the European explorers and the original inhabitants of the regions they explored. Many writers are attempting a more balanced view of the mutual influence of Europeans and indigenous peoples in the early days of contact.

Withey adopts this general approach in her analysis of the voyages of Captain James Cook, the most famous European explorer of the South Pacific. Her purpose is not simply to recount the well-known events of Cook's three journeys. Rather, her clearly written narrative sets Cook's contacts with Pacific islanders within the context of the indigenous peoples' own experiences and dilemmas. Even readers familiar with the Cook expeditions will find many new insights as a result of Withey's framework. The book is amply illustrated with plates of contemporary paintings, maps, and drawings.

1726 York, Barry. *Empire and Race: The Maltese in Australia, 1881–1949.* New South Wales Univ. Pr. 1990, $24.95 (0-86840-092-0). 229pp. Nonfiction.

One of the least widely recognized of the immigrant groups to settle Australia was the Maltese. Technically members of the British Empire (and later the Commonwealth), the people of Malta, with their close ties to Mediterranean culture, were not so readily assimilated into Australian society. Nonetheless, the doubling of the population of the island of Malta between the end of the nineteenth century and the middle of the twentieth placed pressures on its inhabitants to emigrate to locales with greater economic opportunity. The official policy of Britain supported such newcomers to Australia (particularly as settlers in the sparsely populated northern regions of the continent). This sometimes led to conflicts between Australian wishes and British programs.

In this book York presents a thoughtful account of the Maltese place in the development of a multicultural Australia. He focuses on the period of heaviest immigration from Malta and incorporates a great deal of material derived from personal interviews with immigrants. The result is a comprehensive picture of the Maltese contribution to the building of Australia.

BIOGRAPHY

1727 Ashton-Warner, Sylvia. *Teacher.* Illus. Simon & Schuster 1986, $9.95 (0-671-61768-0). 234pp. Autobiography.

New Zealand is considered to be among the world leaders in education, especially at the elementary level. Much of the credit for these pioneering learning strategies belongs to Sylvia Ashton-Warner. During the mid-twentieth century, she developed an organic approach to teaching while working with supposedly uneducatable Maori pupils. Today her fame is so widespread that an acclaimed motion picture was produced about her life.

Teacher is an unconventional autobiography. It recounts many of her experiences (both frustrations and breakthroughs) as an educator of Maori children, mainly at Fernhill School. She is forthright in narrating her clashes with the educational establishment in New Zealand as she fought to have her techniques accepted. She confronts directly the full range of issues posed by the education of Maori students, whose first language was often not English and whose cultural assumptions and values were decidedly different than those of the Pakeha (Europeans). The book is also meant as an introduction to and explanation of her curriculum. To that end, she includes many illustrations and pictures of student work and activities. General readers as well as educators are bound to be impressed and inspired by her contribution.

1728 Binney, Judith, and Gillian Chaplin. *Nga Morehu: The Survivors.* Oxford Univ. Pr. 1987, $34.50 (0-19-558135-0). 144pp. Collective biography.

This book is a collection of the stories of eight Maori women, speaking about their lives in their own words. These women, ranging in age from fifty-nine to ninety-three, were all brought up in small rural communities on the eastern part of the North Island of New Zealand. Also, they all practiced the Ringatu faith, a distinct Maori religious movement founded in the late nineteenth century by charismatic leader Te Kooti Arikirangi Te Turuki.

Although this is not a religious book, its origin does lie in the history of Te Kooti. It is a book about Maori women who share personal strength and an abiding sense of cultural identity. They narrate experiences of arranged marriages, the extended family, the movement of the young away from the tribal lands to the cities, and the near loss of their mother tongue. Their interviews are filled with personal gains and losses, such as the death of a child.

The followers of Te Kooti in the late 1860s called themselves *Nga Morehu*— The Survivors. This richly illustrated collection of narratives ensures the survival of Maori women's voices.

1729 Edwards, Mihi. *Mihipeka: Early Years.* Viking 1990. 168pp. Autobiography.

This book, the first part of a two-part autobiography of Mihi Edwards's life, narrates the experiences of a young Maori woman growing up in rural New Zealand before World War II. The second volume, *Mihipeka: Time of Turmoil* (Viking, 1992), takes up her story from the war to the present day.

The Depression created poverty and deprivation for both Maori and Pakeha (Europeans), yet at this time the Maori were also being deprived of their language and cultural identity. For example, Maori children were punished for speaking Maori in school. As a child struggling to make sense of conflicting values, Mihi suffered an identity crisis. She quickly learned that, in white society, to be Maori is to know deprivation and abuse, and so she decided that the only way to survive in the Pakeha world was to renounce her Maori heritage and become "white." Her pale complexion (Mihi's paternal grandfather was English) facilitated this deception, but she was still not accepted among the Pakeha. This book narrates Mihi's growing realization that she would be unable to achieve personal happiness by denying her Maoriness. So, after thirty years of living as a Pakeha, Mihi Edwards returned to her Maori roots. Since then she has devoted her life to teaching the Maori (and the Pakeha) the importance of maintaining the Maori cultural tradition.

1730 Frame, Janet. *An Autobiography: To the Is-Land; An Angel at My Table; Envoy from Mirror City.* Braziller 1991, $17.50 (0-8076-1259-6). 400pp. Autobiography.

The life story of New Zealand's most internationally renowned living author is a poetic and sensitive account both of her personal development and of her evolution as a writer. This single volume comprises three parts, originally published as separate volumes.

Janet Paterson Frame begins her story with "To the Is-land," which contains her impressions of school and home life from childhood to adolescence. Part Two, "An Angel at My Table," includes accounts of her lengthy spell as a voluntary inmate of a mental institution; the publication of her first work; her productive time spent living and writing at the home of Frank Sargeson, a fellow New Zealand author; and her travels abroad to England and Europe on a grant from the State Literary Fund. "The Envoy from Mirror City" describes her return to New Zealand as an established author after the death of her father.

The autobiographical trilogy was recently made into a successful feature film called *An Angel at My Table.* Frame's novels include *Living in the Maniototo* (Braziller, 1979), *State of Siege* (Braziller, 1981), *Faces in the Water* (Braziller, 1982), and *The Edge of the Alphabet* (Braziller, 1991). Set in New Zealand, these novels offer a view of the dominant white culture, although political issues and the themes of death and personal growth lie at the heart of her fiction.

1731 Hasluck, Paul. *Shades of Darkness: Aboriginal Affairs, 1925–1965.* Melbourne Univ. Pr. 1988, $29.95 (0-522-84362-X). 154pp. Autobiography.

During his twelve-year stint as Minister for the Territories during the 1950s and early 1960s, former Australian Governor-General Paul Hasluck was heavily involved in shaping the nation's policy of Aboriginal assimilation. This policy has been widely criticized by both Aborigines and whites in recent times as tantamount to cultural genocide, because the ideal of equality that it promotes requires that indigenous peoples live according to the standards of the dominant Western culture.

Shades of Darkness is both Hasluck's political memoir and his explanation and defense of the assimilationist program that he helped to formulate and apply. The first part of the book reviews the conditions of Aborigines prior to World War II, based in part on Hasluck's personal observations. He then turns to his own role in promoting assimilation and he closes with a vindication of that policy in relation to the issues that currently face Australian Aborigines. Hasluck's reflections permit the reader a direct insight into the thinking behind the policies toward Aborigines pursued by the white establishment earlier in the century.

1732 Houbein, Lolo. *Wrong Face in the Mirror: An Autobiography of Race and Identity.* Univ. of Queensland Pr. 1990, $14.95 (0-7022-2248-8). 274pp. Autobiography.

Houbein, a forceful advocate of multiculturalism, believes that strength through diversity is the best (and most realistic) hope for Australia's future. She formulated this view at an early age as a Dutch child growing up in war-torn Europe. One day she looked in the mirror and was surprised to see a white face; she felt black on the inside. Her life story narrates her efforts to meet, live with, and understand nonwhite peoples and to impart to others the value of learning about cultures other than their own. What became a consuming desire to be "other" caused her to leave the Netherlands in 1958 to emigrate with her family to South Australia.

The author tells her story in a lively and absorbing way. An immigrant herself, she concludes by discussing "The Future Australian Face." Given that there are about 140 different ethnic groups in Australia today, she argues that, with time, intermarriage, education, understanding, and respect of difference, Australia has the opportunity to lead the rest of the world in interracial and intercultural relations. She posits that the island continent's future strength is in its diversity.

1733 King, Michael. ***Whina: A Biography of Whina Cooper***. Illus. with photos. Viking 1991. o.p. Biography.

Dame Whina Cooper was one of the central figures in the rise of New Zealand Maori self-consciousness and self-assertion during the twentieth century. The daughter of a widely respected Maori chief, she was regarded as possessed of *ihi* (authority) from an early age. By the time she was eighteen, she had conducted a successful protest against the infringement of Maori land rights. She was the driving force behind and first president of the Maori Women's Welfare League, which exercised considerable influence on public policy throughout the middle of the century. And in 1975, at the age of eighty, she helped organize and lead the famous Maori Land March, which galvanized support for the claims of her people.

King's biography of this remarkable woman, drawn mainly from interviews conducted in the early 1980s, is testimony to her accomplishments as a spokesperson for her people. Although her contributions have been criticized by younger and more radical Maori leaders, she managed to retain prominence and influence among both the Pakeha (European) and the Maori communities. King's text is accompanied by many photographs from Dame Whina's life.

1734 Macdonald, Robert. ***The Fifth Wind: New Zealand and the Legacy of a Turbulent Past***. Illus. Trafalgar Sq. 1990, $39.95 (0-7475-0356-7). 356pp. Autobiography.

The life path of journalist and artist Robert Macdonald followed the predictable course of many other talented young New Zealanders. Macdonald received his early training there, but, feeling confined, he soon made his way to England, where he achieved success and acclaim. What makes Macdonald's story different, however, is that twenty-five years after his departure from New Zealand, he returned home to rediscover his roots. During that visit, he became involved in the political protests demanding the recognition of Maori rights under the Treaty of Waitangi.

The Fifth Wind is a remarkable synthesis of autobiography, historical analysis, and chronicle of contemporary events. Macdonald sets the story of his personal encounter with Maori culture and society against the background of the historical relations between Maori and Pakeha (Europeans) that have characterized the nation for more than 150 years. The book presents a profound and, when first published, controversial portrait of the complex New Zealand identity. Readers interested in knowing more about the pivotal Treaty of Waitangi can consult the study by Claudia Orange and *Justice and the Maori* by Andrew Sharp *(see main entries)*.

1735 McGinness, Joe. ***Son of Alyandabu***. Univ. of Queensland Pr. 1991, $16.95 (0-7022-2335-2). 121pp. Autobiography.

The author is one of the elder statesmen of modern Aboriginal politics, having helped to organize his people under the banner of the Federal Council for the Advancement of Aborigines, of which he served as president for a long time. Born to an Irish father and Aboriginal mother (to whom the title of this book refers), McGinness relates the brutal experiences at the hands of the Australian state and society that led him to discover and appreciate fully the consequences of his Aborigine heritage, especially following the death of his father. The book is partially an autobiography and partially a political testament to the Aboriginal rights movement.

Although McGinness acknowledges marked improvements in the treatment of Australian Aborigines, he is by no means sanguine about the future. He points to the forms of inequality, exploitation, and racism that have plagued Aboriginal peoples through the 1980s, and he argues that only continued vigilance and pressure on governments and elites will assure any lasting changes in Australia's social structure.

1736 Meredith, John. ***The Last Kooradgie***. Kangaroo 1989. o.p. Biography.

This slender volume represents a significant contribution to our knowledge of traditional Aboriginal culture. It is also a tribute by the author to Moyengully, a great *kooradgie* (medicine man) who flourished during the nineteenth century. Moyengully was by all accounts a charismatic and inspirational figure who exercised great influence in the tribal lands of the Gundungurra, a people who once occupied much of the Blue Mountains of New South Wales.

Meredith became familiar with Moyengully's life over a number of years as a result of his discovery of ceremonial carvings in the Blue Mountains, carvings that narrate the story of the kooradgie. The book, the product of several decades' research, weaves together contemporary settlers' accounts with bits of archaeological and oral evidence. What emerges is a portrait of a remarkable man living in the final days of his besieged people.

1737 Morgan, Sally. ***My Place: Vol. 1***. Little, Brown 1993, $12.95 (0-316-58289-1). 360pp. Autobiography.

This is a wonderful, moving, and often humorous autobiography that traces the author's frequently painful search for her Aboriginal origins. The life stories of the author's mother and grandmother are also central to this voyage of discovery.

Sally Morgan was born in Perth, Western Australia, in 1951. School playmates were curious about her "different" appearance, a difference the author herself had never considered. To answer the children's questions, Sally's mother told her and her siblings that they were Indian. It was not until she was in her teens that Sally Morgan discovered that she was, in fact, an Aborigine.

The lie had been told to protect the children. Sally Morgan's mother and grandmother had suffered all their lives for being of Aboriginal descent. Australian law declared that Aboriginal mothers were unfit to raise children with white blood. Morgan's mother and her grandmother both had been taken away from their families at a very young age because they had white fathers. Even in the 1960s, the mother held the not-unrealistic fear that, because the children's father was white, the authorities might remove them from her care.

What began as the author's personal search for identity grew to include the whole family, culminating when the author and her mother go on a pilgrimage to the tribal lands of their people. This book is the result of that quest.

AUTHOR INDEX

Authors are arranged alphabetically by last name. Authors' and joint authors' names are followed by book titles—also arranged alphabetically—and the text entry number.

Banville, John. *The Book of Evidence*, 796

Bar-On, Dan. *Legacy of Silence*, 912

Baraka, Amiri. *Dutchman*, 8

Baraka, Amiri, ed. *LeRoi Jones–Amiri Baraka Reader*, 9

Barakat, Halim. *The Arab World*, 1157

Baranczak, Stanislaw, ed. *Polish Poetry of the Last Two Decades of Communist Rule*, 990

Barlow, Cleve. *Tikanga Whakaaro*, 1670

Barlow, Tani. *Teaching China's Lost Generation*, 1506

Barme, Geremie. *New Ghosts, Old Dreams*, 1507

Barnes, Marian E., ed. *Talk That Talk*, 151

Barreiro, José. *The Indian Chronicles*, 366

Barrio, Raymond. *The Plum Plum Pickers*, 367

Barrios de Chungara, Domitila. *Let Me Speak!* 718

Barton, Rachel. *The Scarlet Thread*, 818

Basham, A. L. *The Wonder That Was India*, 1393

Bassani, Giorgio. *The Garden of the Finzi-Continis*, 877

Bassler, Gerhard P. *German Canadian Mosaic Today and Yesterday*, 614

Bataille, Gretchen M. *American Indian Women*, 542

Batt, Judy. *Economic Reform and Political Change in Eastern Europe*, 1044

Bauer, Walter. *A Different Sun*, 558

Beach, Hugh. *A Year in Lapland*, 913

Beall, Cynthia M. *Nomads of Western Tibet*, 1523

Bean, Frank D. *The Hispanic Population of the United States*, 423

Beauchemin, Yves. *The Alley Cat*, 559

Beckham, Barry. *Runner Mack*, 10

Bedini, Silvio A. *The Life of Benjamin Banneker*, 215

Behranqi, Samad. *The Little Black Fish and Other Modern Persian Short Stories*, 1115

Bell, Derrick. *And We Are Not Saved*, 124

Bell, Diane. *Daughters of the Dreaming*, 1671

Bell, J. Bowyer. *The Irish Troubles*, 819

Bellegarde-Smith, Patrick. *Haiti*, 719

Belleme, Jan. *Culinary Treasures of Japan*, 1508

Belleme, John. *Culinary Treasures of Japan*, 1508

Ben Jelloun, Tahar. *With Downcast Eyes*, 878

Ben-Jochannan, Yosef. *Black Man of the Nile and His Family*, 1279

Benedict, Ruth. *The Chrysanthemum and the Sword*, 1509

Bennett, Amanda. *The Man Who Stayed Behind*, 1587

Bennett, Scott. *Aborigines and Political Power*, 1672

Bennis, Phyllis, ed. *Beyond the Storm*, 1158

Bentley, Jerry H. *Old World Encounters*, 914

Berry, Mary Frances. *Military Necessity and Civil Rights Policy*, 125

Berry, Scott. *A Stranger in Tibet*, 1510

Berson, Misha, ed. *Between Worlds*, 256

Besher, Alexander. *Pacific Rim Almanac*, 1511

Betts, Katharine. *Ideology and Immigration*, 1673

Bhutto, Benazir. *Daughter of the East*, 1430

Bickerton, Ian J. *A Concise History of the Arab-Israeli Conflict*, 1159

Bierhorst, John. *The Mythology of North America*, 475

Biko, Steve. *I Write What I Like*, 1280

Billingsley, Andrew. *Climbing Jacob's Ladder*, 126

Bing Xin. *The Photograph*, 1446

Binney, Judith. *Nga Morehu*, 1728

Bissoondath, Neil. *On the Eve of Uncertain Tomorrows*, 560

Björgo, Tore, ed. *Racist Violence in Europe*, 915

Blackett, R. J. *Building an Antislavery Wall*, 820

Blainey, Geoffrey. *Triumph of the Nomads*, 1674

Blair, Lawrence. *Ring of Fire*, 1614

Blair, Lorne. *Ring of Fire*, 1614

Blais, Marie-Claire. *Mad Shadows*, 561

Blanke, Richard. *Orphans of Versailles*, 916

Blassingame, John W. *Black New Orleans, 1960–1880*, 127

The Slave Community, 128

Blumberg, Rhoda. *Commodore Perry in the Land of the Shogun*, 1512

Blunden, Caroline. *Cultural Atlas of China*, 1513

Blyden, Edward W. *Christianity, Islam, and the Negro Race*, 1281

Bo Yang. *Secrets*, 1447

The Ugly Chinaman and the Crisis of Chinese Culture, 1514

TITLE INDEX

<u>A</u>ll titles that are annotated within the text are listed here. All numbers refer to entry numbers, not page numbers.

SUBJECT INDEX

Subject heading are to nonfiction works unless designated with the word "Fiction." Numerals refer to entry numbers, not page numbers.

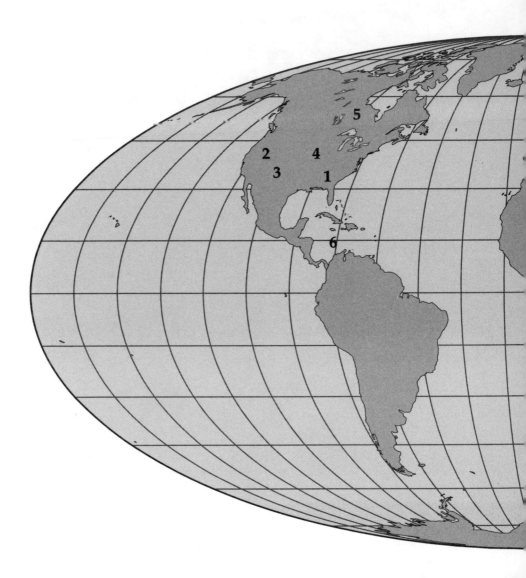

1. African Americans
2. Asian Pacific Americans
3. Latinos
4. Native Americans
5. Canada

6. Latin America and th
7. Britain and Ireland
8. Western Europe
9. Eastern Europe
10. The Middle East